Fodor's 99
California

D1086074

The complete guide, thoroughly up-to-date

Packed with details that will make your trip

The must-see sights, off and on the beaten path

What to see, what to skip

Mix-and-match vacation itineraries

City strolls, countryside adventures

Smart lodging and dining options

Essential local do's and taboos

Transportation tips, distances and directions

Key contacts, savvy travel tips

When to go, what to pack

Clear, accurate, easy-to-use maps

Books to read, videos to watch, background essays

Fodor's Travel Publications, Inc.
New York • Toronto • London • Sydney • Auckland
www.fodors.com

Fodor's California

EDITOR: Daniel Mangin

Editorial Contributors: Sasha Abramsky, Christopher Baty, David Brown, Deke Castleman, Arian Collins, Maureen Daly, Kate Deely, Stephen Dolainski, Jeanne Fay, Therese Iknoian, Edie Jarolim, Allison Joyce, Michelle Kaye, Christina Knight, Stacey Kulig, Kristina Malsberger, Amy McConnell, Andy Moore, Clark Norton, Marty Olmstead, Lisa Oppenheimer, Megan Pincus, Heidi Sarna, Helayne Schiff, M. T. Schwartzman (Gold Guide editor), Kathryn Shevelow, Sharon Silva, Wendy Smith, Bill Stern, Cynthia LaFavre Yorks, Bobbi Zane
Editorial Production: Linda K. Schmidt
Maps: David Lindroth, *cartographer*; Steven K. Amsterdam, *map editor*
Design: Fabrizio La Rocca, *creative director*; Guido Caroti, *associate art director*; Jolie Novak, *photo editor*
Production/Manufacturing: Robert B. Shields
Cover Photograph: Galen Rowell

Copyright

Special Sales

Fodor's Travel Publications are available at special discounts for bulk purchases for sales promotions or premiums. Special editions, including personalized covers, excerpts of existing guides, and corporate imprints, can be created in large quantities for special needs. For more information, contact your local bookseller or write to Special Markets, Fodor's Travel Publications, 201 East 50th Street, New York, NY 10022. Inquiries from Canada should be directed to your local Canadian bookseller or sent to Random House of Canada, Ltd., Marketing Department, 2775 Matheson Boulevard East, Mississauga, Ontario L4W 4P7. Inquiries from the United Kingdom should be sent to Fodor's Travel Publications, 20 Vauxhall Bridge Road, London SW1V 2SA, England.

PRINTED IN THE UNITED STATES OF AMERICA

10 9 8 7 6 5 4 3 2 1

CONTENTS

Maps

ON THE ROAD WITH FODOR'S

WHEN I PLAN A VACATION, the first thing I do is cast around among my friends and colleagues to find someone who's recently been where I'm going. That's because there's no substitute for a recommendation from a good friend who knows your tastes, your budget, and your circumstances, someone who's just been there. Unfortunately, such friends are few and far between. So it's nice to know that there's *Fodor's California '99.*

In the first place, this book won't stay home when you hit the road. It will accompany you every step of the way, steering you toward the highlights and away from dull or disastrous. It includes a full-color map from Rand McNally, the world's largest commercial mapmaker. Most important, it's written and assiduously updated by the kind of people you *would* hit up for travel tips if you knew them. They're as choosy as your pickiest friend, except they've probably seen a lot more of California. In these pages, they don't send you chasing down every town and sight in California but have instead selected the best ones, the ones that are worthy of your time and money. To make it easy for you to put it all together in the time you have, they've created short, medium, and long itineraries and, in cities, neighborhood walks that you can mix and match in a snap. Just tear out the map at the perforation, and join us on the road in California.

About Our Writers

Our success in helping to make your trip the best of all possible vacations is a credit to the hard work of our extraordinary contributors.

Sasha Abramsky, a freelance journalist who has written for *New York* magazine and other periodicals, had just returned from covering several regions of India for *Fodor's India* when he took on a less arduous assignment: chic Santa Barbara and the beautiful Central Coast. A frequent visitor to California whose relatives live in the southern part of the state, he enjoyed the chance to explore the coastal highlights and the inland backroads.

Deke Castleman, who updated the Lake Tahoe chapter, grew up in New York and Boston but fled the East Coast for the wide-open spaces of the American West. He discovered the region's many wonders while engaged in a variety of occupations—door-to-door vacuum-cleaner salesman in central California, tour guide at Alaska's Denali National Park, and locksmith on Lake Tahoe's north shore.

Andy Moore was born across the street from Disney Studios near beautiful downtown Burbank. His childhood included many family vacations throughout the Golden State, including gold-panning expeditions with his grandfather, memories he relived while updating the Sacramento and the Gold Country chapter. Andy also updated the San Joaquin Valley chapter.

Clark Norton, author of Fodor's *Where Do We Take the Kids? California,* wrote the San Joaquin Valley chapter, updated the Monterey Bay chapter, and expanded the coverage of the eastern Sierra region with new sections on Mono Lake and Mammoth Lakes. The recipient of several major travel-writing awards, Clark has written about traveling with children for *Parenting, Family Fun, California Travel Ideas, Baby Talk,* and the *San Francisco Examiner.*

Marty Olmstead, who updated the North Coast, Far North, and Wine Country chapters, is the former travel editor of *San Francisco Focus* magazine, for which she crisscrossed the state many times. Accounts of her voyages around the globe have appeared in *Travel and Leisure,* the *Los Angeles Times, Geo, Glamour,* and the *San Francisco Chronicle.* She is also the author of *Hidden Tennessee* and the forthcoming *Hidden Georgia.* Marty, who lives in Sonoma County, writes a column about the Wine Country for the *Marin Independent Journal.*

Bobbi Zane, who revised the Palm Springs chapter, has been visiting the state's southern desert region since her grandfather, a Hollywood producer, took her on weekend getaways to La Quinta Resort. She returns to the area yearly. She has contributed to *California's Best Bed & Breakfasts* and *San Diego '99* among many other Fodor's titles. With her husband, Gregg, she publishes *Yellow Brick Road,* a monthly newsletter about bed-and-breakfast inns.

Daniel Mangin, the editor of *California '99,* moved to New York to work as a senior editor at Fodor's after spending 20 years in the Golden State, most of them in San Francisco. He first traversed California as the stage manager and lighting director of two '70s punk rock bands, one of which, he reminisces, "hit just short of the big time. One year we stayed at low-budget motels, the next year it was four-star hotels with private butlers and antique furniture (we were well-behaved rockers). The experience taught me what travelers of all budgets need and expect."

Connections

We're pleased that the American Society of Travel Agents continues to endorse Fodor's as its guidebook of choice. ASTA is the world's largest and most influential travel trade association, operating in more than 170 countries, with 27,000 members pledged to adhere to a strict code of ethics reflecting the Society's motto, "Integrity in Travel." ASTA shares Fodor's devotion to providing smart, honest travel information and advice to travelers, and we've long recommended that our readers—even those who have guidebooks and traveling friends—consult ASTA member agents for the experience and professionalism they bring to your vacation planning.

On Fodor's Web site (www.fodors.com), check out the new Resource Center, an online companion to the Gold Guide chapter of this book, complete with useful hot links to related sites. In our forums, you can also get lively advice from other travelers and more great tips from Fodor's experts worldwide.

How to Use This Book

Organization

Up front is the **Gold Guide,** an easy-to-use section arranged alphabetically by topic. Under each listing you'll find tips and information. You'll also find addresses and telephone numbers of organizations and companies that offer destination-related services and detailed information and publications.

The first chapter in the guide, Destination: California, helps get you in the mood for your trip. New and Noteworthy cues you in on trends and happenings; What's Where gets you oriented; Pleasures and Pastimes describes the activities and sights that make California unique; Books and Videos includes suggestions for pretrip research; Fodor's Choice showcases our top picks; and Festivals and Seasonal Events alerts you to special events.

Chapters in *Fodor's California '99* are arranged geographically, from the northern part of the state to the south. Each regional chapter is divided by geographical area; within each area, towns are covered in logical geographical order, and attractive stretches of road and minor points of interest between towns are indicated by the designation *En Route.* And within town sections, all restaurants and lodgings are grouped together.

Each city chapter in *Fodor's California '99* begins with an Exploring section, which is subdivided by neighborhood; each subsection recommends a walking or driving tour and lists sights in alphabetical order. Dining, lodging, nightlife and the arts, outdoor activities and sports, and shopping sections follow the exploring tours.

To help you decide what to visit in the time you have, all chapters begin with our recommended itineraries. The A to Z sections at the end of each chapter cover getting to and getting around the destinations covered and provide contacts and resources.

Icons and Symbols

★ Our special recommendation
✕ Restaurant
🏠 Lodging establishment
✕🏠 Lodging establishment whose restaurant warrants a special trip
⚇ Campground
🐤 Good for kids (rubber duck)
☞ Sends you to another section of the guide for more information
✉ Address
☏ Telephone number
☉ Opening and closing times
💰 Admission prices (those we give apply to adults; substantially reduced fees are almost always available for children, students, and senior citizens)

Numbers in white and black circles ③ ❸ that appear on the maps, in the margins, and within the tours correspond to one another.

Hotel Facilities

Unless otherwise noted, assume that the rooms in the lodgings reviewed have private baths and that the rates include no meals. If a lodging serves breakfast, we specify whether it is full or Continental in the italicized service information at the end of the review; if more than breakfast is served, we specify whether the lodging operates on the **Modified American Plan** (MAP, with breakfast and dinner daily), or the **Full American Plan** (FAP, with all meals).

Restaurant Reservations and Dress Codes

Reservations are always a good idea; we mention them only when they're essential or are not accepted. Book as far ahead as you can, and reconfirm as soon as you arrive. Unless otherwise noted, the restaurants listed are open daily for lunch and dinner. We mention dress only when men are required to wear a jackct or a jacket and tie.

Credit Cards

The following abbreviations are used: **AE**, American Express; **D**, Discover; **DC**, Diners Club; **MC**, MasterCard; and **V**, Visa.

Don't Forget to Write

You can use this book in the confidence that all prices and opening times are based on information supplied to us at press time; Fodor's cannot accept responsibility for any errors. Time inevitably brings changes, so always confirm information when it matters—especially if you're making a detour to visit a specific place.

Were the restaurants we recommended as described? Did our hotel picks exceed your expectations? Did you find a museum we recommended a waste of time? Keeping a travel guide fresh and up-to-date is a big job, and we welcome your feedback, positive and negative. If you have complaints, we'll look into them and revise our entries when the facts warrant it. If you've discovered a special place that we haven't included, we'll pass the information along to our correspondents and have them check it out. So send us your thoughts via e-mail at editors@fodors.com (specifying the name of the book on the subject line) or on paper in care of the California editor at Fodor's, 201 East 50th Street, New York, New York 10022. In the meantime, have a wonderful trip!

Karen Cure
Editorial Director

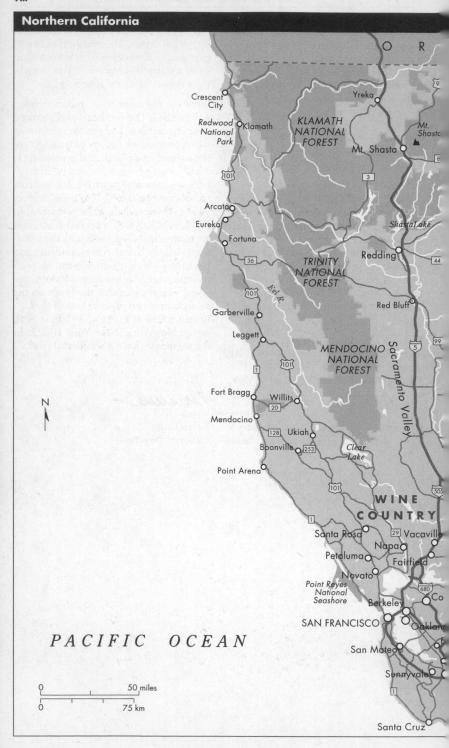

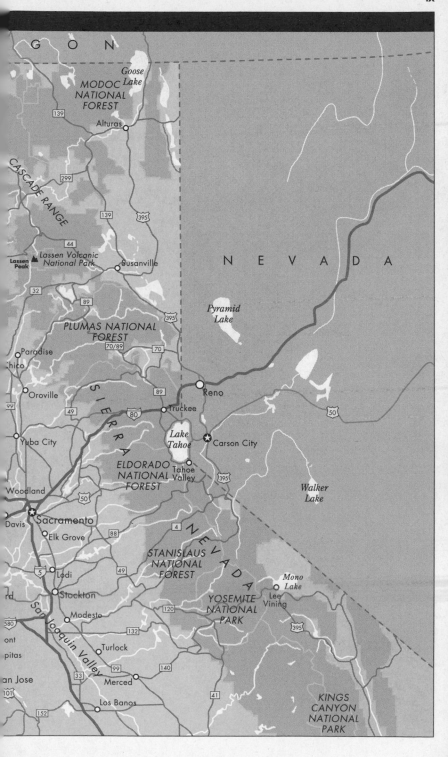

Southern California

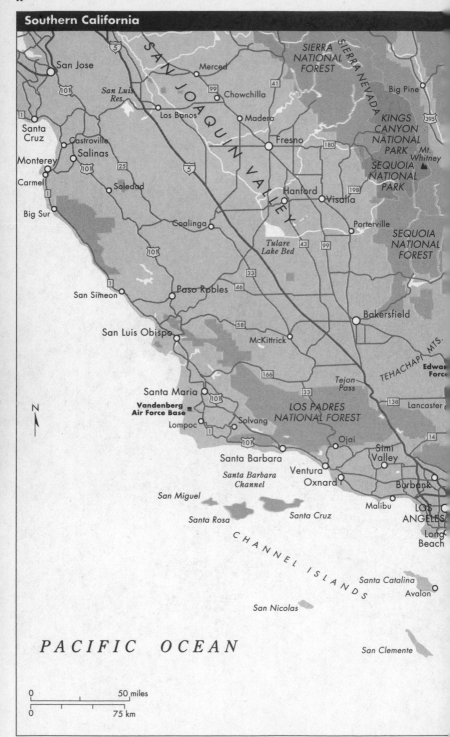

PACIFIC OCEAN

0 50 miles
0 75 km

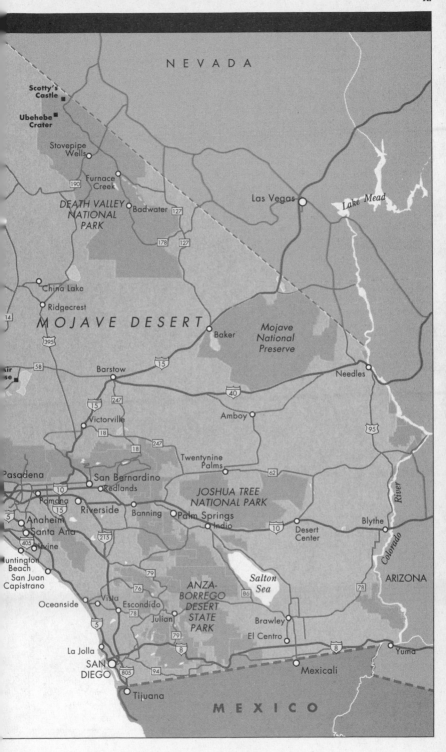

The United States

CANADA

SASKATCHEWAN

MANITOB

Vancouver
Victoria

BRITISH
COLUMBIA

Calgary

ALBERTA

Regina

Trans-Canada Hwy.

Winnipeg

Seattle
Olympia
WASHINGTON

Spokane

Columbia R.

Great Falls

Missouri R.

NORTH DAKOTA

Farg

Portland
Salem

MONTANA

Helena

Bismarck

OREGON

IDAHO

Billings

Snake R.

Boise

SOUTH DAKOTA

Pierre

WYOMING

Missouri R.

NEBRASKA

Carson City
Sacramento

NEVADA

Salt Lake
City

Cheyenne

Linco

San Francisco

UTAH

Denver

Fresno

Colorado Springs

COLORADO

KANSAS

Las
Vegas

Colorado R.

CALIFORNIA

Santa
Barbara
Los
Angeles

Flagstaff

Taos

OKLAHOMA

Santa Fe

Oklahoma City

San Diego

ARIZONA

Albuquerque

Amarillo

Phoenix

NEW MEXICO

Dalla

PACIFIC
OCEAN

Tucson

BAJA
CALIFORNIA

SONORA

El Paso

Rio Grande

TEXAS

Austin

CHIHUAHUA

San Antonio

RUSSIA

ARCTIC
OCEAN

MEXICO

Bering Strait

ALASKA

COAHUILA

Bering Sea

Nome

Fairbanks

CANADA

NUEVO
LEON

TAM-
AULIPA

ALEUTIAN ISLANDS

Anchorage

Juneau

Honolulu

Oahu

Maui

HAWAII

Hawaii

PACIFIC OCEAN

N

PACIFIC OCEAN

0   400 miles

0   400 km

N

| 0 | 500 miles |
| 0 | 800 km |

World Time Zones

Numbers below vertical bands relate each zone to Greenwich Mean Time (0 hrs.).
Local times frequently differ from these general indications,
as indicated by light-face numbers on map.

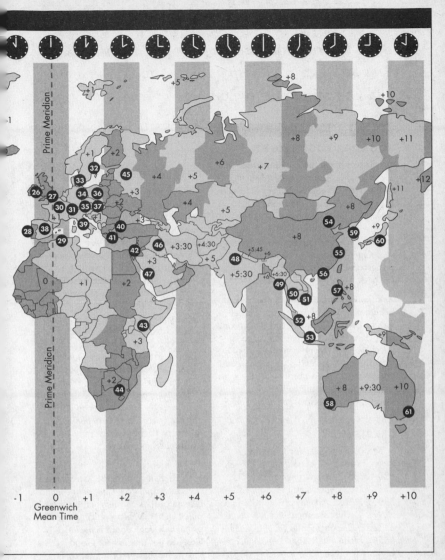

SMART TRAVEL TIPS A TO Z

Basic Information on Traveling in California, Savvy Tips to Make Your Trip a Breeze, and Companies and Organizations to Contact

AIR TRAVEL

BOOKING YOUR FLIGHT

When you book **look for nonstop flights** and **remember that "direct" flights stop at least once.** Try to **avoid connecting flights,** which require a change of plane. Two airlines may jointly operate a connecting flight, so ask if your airline operates every segment—you may find that your preferred carrier flies you only part of the way.

Ask your airline if it offers electronic ticketing, which eliminates all paperwork. There's no ticket to pick up or misplace. If you have no baggage to check, at most airports you can go directly to the gate and give the agent your confirmation number. There's no worry about waiting in line at the airport while precious minutes tick by.

CARRIERS

➤ MAJOR AIRLINES: **Air Canada** (☎ 800/776–3000). **Alaska** (☎ 800/426–0333). **America West** (☎ 800/235–9292). **American** (☎ 800/433–7300). **British Airways** (☎ 800/247–9297). **Cathay Pacific** (☎ 800/233–2742)**Continental** (☎ 800/231–0856). **Delta** (☎ 800/241–4141). **Japan Air Lines** (☎ 800/525–3663). **Northwest** (☎ 800/225–2525). **Qantas** (☎ 800/227–4500). **Southwest** (☎ 800/435–9792). **TWA** (☎ 800/892–4141). **United** (☎ 800/241–6522). **US Airways** (☎ 800/428–4322).

➤ SMALLER AIRLINES: **American Trans Air**(☎ 800/435–9282). **Midwest Express** (☎ 800/452–2022). **Mountain Air Express** (☎ 562/595–1011 or 800/788–4247). **Reno Air** (☎ 800/736–6247). **Skywest** (☎ 800/453–9417).

➤ FROM THE U.K.: **American** (☎ 0345/789–789). **British Airways** (☎ 0345/222–111). **Delta** (☎ 0800/414–767). **United** (☎ 0800/888–555). **Virgin Atlantic** (☎ 01293/747–747).

CUTTING COSTS

The least-expensive airfares to California are priced for round-trip travel and usually must be purchased in advance. It's smart to **call a number of airlines, and when you are quoted a good price, book it on the spot**—the same fare may not be available the next day. Airlines generally allow you to change your return date for a fee. If you don't use your ticket, you can apply the cost toward the purchase of a new ticket, again for a small charge. However, most low-fare tickets are nonrefundable. To get the lowest airfare, **check different routings.** Compare prices of flights to and from different airports if your destination or home city has more than one gateway. Also, price off-peak and midweek flights, which may be significantly less expensive.

Travel agents, especially those who specialize in finding the lowest fares (☞ Discounts & Deals, *below*), can be especially helpful when booking a plane ticket. When you're quoted a price, **ask your agent if the price is likely to get any lower.** Good agents know the seasonal fluctuations of airfares and can usually anticipate a sale or fare war. However, waiting can be risky: The fare could go *up* as seats become scarce, and you may wait so long that your preferred flight sells out. A wait-and-see strategy works best if your plans are flexible. If you must arrive and depart on certain dates, don't delay.

CHECK IN & BOARDING

Airlines routinely overbook planes, assuming that not everyone with a ticket will show up, but sometimes everyone does. When that happens, airlines ask for volunteers to give up their seats. In return these volunteers usually get a certificate for a free flight and are rebooked on the next flight out. If there are not enough volunteers, the airline must choose who will be denied boarding. The first to get bumped are passengers who checked in late and those flying on discounted tickets, so **get to the gate and check in as early as possible,** especially during peak periods.

Although the trend on international flights is to drop reconfirmation requirements, many airlines still ask you to reconfirm each leg of your international itinerary. Failure to do so may result in your reservation being canceled.

Always **bring a government-issued photo ID to the airport.** You may be asked to show it before you are allowed to check in.

FLYING TIMES

Flying time is roughly five hours from New York and four hours from Chicago. Flying between San Francisco and Los Angeles takes one hour.

HOW TO COMPLAIN

If your baggage goes astray or your flight goes awry, complain right away. Most carriers require that you **file a claim immediately.**

➤ AIRLINE COMPLAINTS: U.S. Department of Transportation **Aviation Consumer Protection Division** (✉ C-75, Room 4107, Washington, DC 20590, ☎ 202/366–2220). **Federal Aviation Administration Consumer Hotline** (☎ 800/322–7873).

AIRPORTS

Major gateways to California are **Los Angeles International Airport, San Francisco International Airport,** and **San Diego International Airport.**

➤ AIRPORT INFORMATION: **Los Angeles International Airport** (☎ 310/646–5252). **San Diego International Airport** (☎ 619/231–2100). **San Francisco International Airport** (☎ 650/761–0800).

BIKES IN FLIGHT

Most airlines will accommodate bikes as luggage, provided they are dismantled and put into a box. Call to see if your airline sells bike boxes (about $5; bike bags are at least $100)

although you can often pick them up free at bike shops. International travelers can sometimes substitute a bike for a piece of checked luggage for free; otherwise, it will cost about $100. Domestic and Canadian airlines charge a $25–$50 fee.

BUS TRAVEL

BUS LINES

Greyhound (☎ 800/231–2222).

CAMERAS & COMPUTERS

EQUIPMENT PRECAUTIONS

Always **keep your film, tape, or computer disks out of the sun.** Carry an extra supply of batteries, and **be prepared to turn on your camera, camcorder, or laptop** to prove to security personnel that the device is real. Always **ask for hand inspection of film,** which becomes clouded after successive exposure to airport X-ray machines, and **keep videotapes and computer disks away from metal detectors.**

ONLINE ON THE ROAD

Checking your e-mail or surfing the Web can sometimes be done in the business centers of major hotels, which usually charge an hourly rate. Web access is also available at many fax and copy centers, many of which are open 24 hours and on weekends. In major cities look for cyber cafés, where tabletop computers allow you to log on while sipping coffee or listening to live jazz. Whether you have e-mail at home or not, you can **arrange to have a free e-mail address** from several services, including one available at www.hotmail.com (the site explains how to apply for an address).

TRAVEL PHOTOGRAPHY

➤ PHOTO HELP: **Kodak Information Center** (☎ 800/242–2424). *Kodak Guide to Shooting Great Travel Pictures,* available in bookstores or from Fodor's Travel Publications (☎ 800/533–6478; $16.50 plus $4 shipping).

CAR RENTAL

Rates in Los Angeles begin at around $28 a day and $140 a week. This does not include tax on car rentals, which is 8¼%. In San Diego, rates for an economy car with unlimited mileage begin around $23 a day and $137 a week. This does not include tax on car rentals, which is 7¾%. In San Francisco, rates begin around $38 a day and $138 a week. This does not include tax on car rentals, which is 8¼%.

CUT COSTS

When pricing cars, **ask about the location of the rental lot.** Some off-airport locations offer lower rates, and their lots are only minutes from the terminal via complimentary shuttle.

➤ MAJOR AGENCIES: **Alamo** (☎ 800/327–9633, 0800/272–2000 in the U.K.). **Avis** (☎ 800/331–1212, 800/879–2847 in Canada, 008/225–533 in Australia). **Budget** (☎ 800/527–0700, 0800/181181 in the U.K.). **Dollar** (☎ 800/800–4000; 0990/565656 in the U.K., where it is known as Eurodollar). **Hertz** (☎ 800/654–3131, 800/263–0600 in Canada, 0345/555888 in the U.K., 03/9222–2523 in Australia, 03/358–6777 in New Zealand). **National InterRent** (☎ 800/227–7368; 0345/222525 in the U.K., where it is known as Europcar InterRent).

INSURANCE

When driving a rented car you are generally responsible for any damage to or loss of the vehicle. You also are liable for any property damage or personal injury that you may cause while driving. Before you rent, **see what coverage you already have** under the terms of your personal auto-insurance policy and credit cards.

For about $15 to $20 per day, rental companies sell protection, known as a collision- or loss-damage waiver (CDW or LDW), that eliminates your liability for damage to the car; it's always optional and should never be automatically added to your bill. Some states, including California, have capped the price of the CDW and LDW.

In most states you don't need a CDW if you have personal auto insurance or other liability insurance. However, **make sure you have enough coverage to pay for the car.** If you do not have

auto insurance or an umbrella policy that covers damage to third parties, purchasing liability insurance and a CDW or LDW is highly recommended.

REQUIREMENTS

In California you must be 21 to rent a car, and rates may be higher if you're under 25. You'll pay extra (about $3) for child seats, which are compulsory for children under five. Non-U.S. residents will need a reservation voucher, a passport, a driver's license, and a travel policy that covers each driver, in order to pick up a car.

SURCHARGES

Before you pick up a car in one city and leave it in another, **ask about drop-off charges or one-way service fees,** which can be substantial. Some rental agencies charge extra if you return the car before the time specified in your contract. To avoid a hefty refueling fee, **fill the tank right before you turn in the car.**

CAR TRAVEL

Three major highways—Interstate 5 (I–5), U.S. 101, and Highway 1—run north-south through the state. The main routes into the state from the east are I–15 and I–10 in southern California and I–80 in northern California.

AUTO CLUBS

➤ IN AUSTRALIA: **Australian Automobile Association** (☎ 06/247–7311).

➤ IN CANADA: **Canadian Automobile Association** (CAA, ☎ 613/247–0117).

➤ IN NEW ZEALAND: **New Zealand Automobile Association** (☎ 09/377–4660).

➤ IN THE U.K.: **Automobile Association** (AA, ☎ 0990/500–600), **Royal Automobile Club** (RAC, ☎ 0990/722–722 for membership, 0345/121–345 for insurance).

➤ IN THE U.S.: **American Automobile Association** (☎ 800/222–4357).

EMERGENCY SERVICES

Dial 911 to report accidents on the road and to reach police, the California Highway Patrol, or fire department.

GASOLINE

Prices vary widely depending on location, oil company, and whether you buy full-serve or self-serve gasoline. Prices on the West Coast also tend to be higher than in the Midwest. At press time, regular unleaded gasoline at self-serve stations cost about $1.25 a gallon.

ROAD CONDITIONS

Avoid major urban highways during rush hour. Some of the smaller routes over the mountain ranges are prone to flash flooding—drivers should check road conditions before heading into stormy weather. During snowy weather, tire chains are required in many mountain areas. When the rains are severe, coastal Highway 1 can quickly become a slippery nightmare, buffeted by strong winds and obstructed by falling debris from the cliffs above.

➤ ROAD CONDITIONS

Statewide hotline (☎ 800/427–7623). **Northern California updates** (☎ 916/445–7623). **Southern California updates** (☎ 213/628–7623).

ROAD MAPS

You can buy detailed maps in bookstores and gas stations and at some grocery and drug stores. The various California branches of the American Automobile Association (☞ *above*) have state and local maps that are free to members.

RULES OF THE ROAD

The speed limit on many rural highways is 70 mph. In the cities, freeway speed limits are between 55 and 65 mph. Many city routes have commuter lanes, but the operating rules vary from city to city: in San Francisco, for example, you need three people in a car to use these lanes, in Los Angeles only two.

Seat belts are required at all times. Tickets can be given for failing to comply. Small children must be in child safety seats. Unless otherwise indicated, right turns are allowed on red lights after you've come to a full stop, and left turns onto adjoining one-way streets are allowed on red lights after you've come to a full stop. Drivers stopped by the police who

have a blood-alcohol level higher than 0.08 are subject to arrest.

CHILDREN & TRAVEL

CHILDREN IN CALIFORNIA

In many ways California is made to order for traveling with children: Kids love Disneyland, the San Diego Zoo, the Monterey Aquarium, the San Francisco cable cars, the city-owned gold mine in Placerville, and the caverns at Lake Shasta.

Be sure to plan ahead and **involve your youngsters** as you outline your trip. When packing, include things to keep them busy en route. On sightseeing days try to schedule activities of special interest to your children. If you are renting a car, don't forget to **arrange for a car seat** when you reserve. Most hotels in California allow children under a certain age to stay in their parents' room at no extra charge, but others charge them as extra adults; be sure to **ask about the cutoff age for children's discounts.**

Local Information: CONSULT FODOR'S LIVELY BY-PARENTS, FOR-PARENTS WHERE SHOULD WE TAKE THE KIDS? CALIFORNIA (AVAILABLE IN BOOKSTORES, OR ☎ 800/533–6478); $17.

FLYING

As a general rule, infants under two not occupying a seat fly at greatly reduced fares or even for free. If your children are two or older, **ask about children's airfares.** In general, the adult baggage allowance applies to children paying half or more of the adult fare. Experts agree that it's a good idea to **use safety seats aloft** for children weighing less than 40 pounds. Airlines, however, can set their own policies: U.S. carriers allow FAA-approved models but usually require that you buy a ticket, even if your child would otherwise ride free, because the seats must be strapped into regular seats. Airline rules vary, so it's important to **check your airline's policy about using safety seats during takeoff and landing.** Safety seats cannot obstruct the movement of other passengers in the row, so get an appropriate seat assignment as early as possible.

When making your reservation, **request children's meals or a free-**

THE GOLD GUIDE / SMART TRAVEL TIPS

standing **bassinet** if you need them; the latter are available only to those seated at the bulkhead, where there's enough legroom. Remember, however, that bulkhead seats may not have their own overhead bins, and there's no storage space in front of you—a major inconvenience.

GROUP TRAVEL

When planning to take your kids on a tour, look for companies that specialize in family travel.

➤ FAMILY-FRIENDLY TOUR OPERATORS: **Families Welcome!** (✉ 92 N. Main St., Ashland, OR 97520, ☎ 541/482–6121 or 800/326–0724, ℻ 541/482–0660). **Rascals in Paradise** (✉ 650 5th St., Suite 505, San Francisco, CA 94107, ☎ 415/978–9800 or 800/872–7225, ℻ 415/442–0289).

CONSUMER PROTECTION

Whenever possible, **pay with a major credit card** so you can cancel payment or get reimbursed if there's a problem, provided that you can provide documentation. This is the best way to pay, whether you're buying travel arrangements before your trip or shopping at your destination.

If you're doing business with a particular company for the first time, **contact your local Better Business Bureau and the attorney general's office** in your state and the company's home state, as well. Have any complaints been filed?

Finally, if you're buying a package or tour, always **consider travel insurance** that includes default coverage (☞ Insurance, *below*).

➤ LOCAL BBBs: **Council of Better Business Bureaus** (✉ 4200 Wilson Blvd., Suite 800, Arlington, VA 22203, ☎ 703/276–0100, ℻ 703/525–8277).

CUSTOMS & DUTIES

When shopping, **keep receipts** for all of your purchases. Upon reentering the country, **be ready to show customs officials what you've bought.** If you feel a duty is incorrect, appeal the assessment. If you object to the way your clearance was handled, get the inspector's badge number. In either case, first ask to see a supervisor, then write to the appropriate authorities, beginning with the port director at your point of entry.

IN AUSTRALIA

Residents of Australia who are 18 or older may bring back $A400 worth of souvenirs and gifts (including jewelry), 250 cigarettes or 250 grams of tobacco, and 1,125 ml of alcohol (including wine, beer, and spirits). Residents under 18 may bring back $A200 worth of goods.

➤ INFORMATION: **Australian Customs Service** (Regional Director, ✉ Box 8, Sydney, NSW 2001, ☎ 02/9213–2000, ℻ 02/9213–4000).

IN CANADA

Canadian residents who have been out of Canada for at least seven days may bring in C$500 worth of goods duty-free. If you've been away less than seven days but more than 48 hours, the duty-free allowance drops to C$200; if your trip lasts 24–48 hours, the allowance is C$50. You may not pool allowances with family members. Goods claimed under the C$500 exemption may follow you by mail; those claimed under the lesser exemptions must accompany you. Alcohol and tobacco products may be included in the 7-day and 48-hour exemptions but not in the 24-hour exemption. If you meet the age requirements of the province or territory through which you reenter Canada, you may bring in, duty-free, 1.14 liters (40 imperial ounces) of wine or liquor *or* 24 12-ounce cans or bottles of beer or ale. If you are 16 or older, you may bring in, duty-free, 200 cigarettes and 50 cigars.

You may send an unlimited number of gifts worth up to C$60 each duty-free to Canada. Label the package UNSOLICITED GIFT—VALUE UNDER $60. Alcohol and tobacco are excluded.

➤ INFORMATION: **Revenue Canada** (✉ 2265 St. Laurent Blvd. S, Ottawa, Ontario K1G 4K3, ☎ 613/993–0534, 800/461–9999 in Canada).

IN NEW ZEALAND

Although greeted with a "Haere Mai" ("Welcome to New Zealand"), homeward-bound residents with goods to declare must present themselves for inspection. If you're 17 or older, you may bring back $700 worth of souvenirs and gifts. Your duty-free allowance also includes 4.5 liters of wine or beer; one 1,125-ml bottle of spirits; and either 200 cigarettes, 250 grams of tobacco, 50 cigars, or a combo of all three up to 250 grams.

➤ INFORMATION: **New Zealand Customs** (✉ Custom House, ✉ 50 Anzac Ave., Box 29, Auckland, New Zealand, ☎ 09/359–6655, ☎ 09/309–2978).

IN THE U.K.

From countries outside the EU, including the United States, you may import, duty-free, 200 cigarettes or 50 cigars; 1 liter of spirits or 2 liters of fortified or sparkling wine or liqueurs; 2 liters of still table wine; 60 milliliters of perfume; 250 milliliters of toilet water; plus £136 worth of other goods, including gifts and souvenirs.

➤ INFORMATION: **HM Customs and Excise** (✉ Dorset House, ✉ Stamford St., London SE1 9NG, ☎ 0171/202–4227).

IN THE U.S.

Non-U.S. residents ages 21 and older may import into the United States 200 cigarettes or 50 cigars or 2 kilograms of tobacco, 1 liter of alcohol, and gifts worth $100. Prohibited items include meat products, seeds, plants, and fruits.

➤ INFORMATION: **U.S. Customs Service** (Inquiries, ✉ Box 7407, Washington, DC 20044, ☎ 202/927–6724; complaints, Office of Regulations and Rulings, ✉ 1301 Constitution Ave. NW, Washington, DC 20229; registration of equipment, Resource Management, ✉ 1301 Constitution Ave. NW, Washington DC 20229, ☎ 202/927–0540).

DISABILITIES & ACCESSIBILITY

ACCESS IN CALIFORNIA

California is a national leader in making attractions and facilities accessible to people with disabilities. State laws provide special privileges, such as license plates allowing special parking spaces, unlimited parking in time-limited spaces, and free parking in metered spaces. Insignia from other states are honored.

MAKING RESERVATIONS

When discussing accessibility with an operator or reservations agent, **ask hard questions.** Are there any stairs, inside *or* out? Are there grab bars next to the toilet *and* in the shower/tub? How wide is the doorway to the room? To the bathroom? For the most extensive facilities meeting the latest legal specifications, **opt for newer accommodations,** which are more likely to have been designed with access in mind. Older buildings or ships may have more limited facilities. Be sure to **discuss your needs before booking.**

TRANSPORTATION

➤ COMPLAINTS: **Disability Rights Section** (✉ U.S. Department of Justice, Civil Rights Division, ✉ Box 66738, Washington, DC 20035–6738, ☎ 202/514–0301 or 800/514–0301, TTY 202/514–0383 or 800/514–0383, FAX 202/307–1198) for general complaints. **Aviation Consumer Protection Division** (☞ Air Travel, *above*) for airline-related problems. **Civil Rights Office** (✉ U.S. Department of Transportation, Departmental Office of Civil Rights, S-30, ✉ 400 7th St. SW, Room 10215, Washington, DC, 20590, ☎ 202/366–4648, FAX 202/366–9371) for problems with surface transportation.

TRAVEL AGENCIES & TOUR OPERATORS

As a whole, the travel industry has become more aware of the needs of travelers with disabilities. In the U.S., the Americans with Disabilities Act requires that travel firms serve the needs of all travelers. Note, though, that some agencies and operators specialize in making travel arrangements for individuals and groups with disabilities.

➤ TRAVELERS WITH MOBILITY PROBLEMS: **Access Adventures** (✉ 206 Chestnut Ridge Rd., Rochester, NY 14624, ☎ 716/889–9096), run by a former physical-rehabilitation counselor. **CareVacations** (✉ 5019 49th Ave., Suite 102, Leduc, Alberta T9E 6T5, ☎ 403/986–6404, 800/648–1116 in Canada) has group tours and is especially helpful with cruise vacations. **Flying Wheels Travel** (✉ 143 W. Bridge St., Box 382, Owatonna, MN 55060, ☎ 507/451–5005 or 800/535–6790, FAX 507/451–1685), a travel agency specializing in customized tours and itineraries worldwide. **Hinsdale Travel Service** (✉ 201 E. Ogden Ave., Suite 100, Hinsdale, IL 60521, ☎ 630/325–1335), a travel agency that benefits from the advice of wheelchair traveler Janice Perkins.

➤ TRAVELERS WITH DEVELOPMENTAL DISABILITIES: **New Directions** (✉ 5276 Hollister Ave., Suite 207, Santa Barbara, CA 93111, ☎ 805/967–2841 or 888/967–2841, FAX 805/964–7344). **Sprout** (✉ 893 Amsterdam Ave., New York, NY 10025, ☎ 212/222–9575 or 888/222–9575, FAX 212/222–9768).

DISCOUNTS & DEALS

CLUBS & COUPONS

Many companies sell discounts in the form of travel clubs and coupon books, but these cost money. You must use participating advertisers to get a deal, and only after you recoup the initial membership cost or book price do you begin to save. If you plan to use the club or coupons frequently, you may save considerably. Before signing up, find out what discounts you get for free.

➤ DISCOUNT CLUBS: **Entertainment Travel Editions** (✉ 2125 Butterfield Rd., Troy, MI 48084, ☎ 800/445–4137; $20–$51, depending on destination). **Great American Traveler** (✉ Box 27965, Salt Lake City, UT 84127, ☎ 801/974–3033 or 800/548–2812; $49.95 per year). **Moment's Notice Discount Travel Club** (✉ 7301 New Utrecht Ave., Brooklyn, NY 11204, ☎ 718/234–6295; $25 per year, single or family). **Privilege Card International** (✉ 237 E. Front St., Youngstown, OH 44503, ☎ 330/746–5211 or 800/236–9732; $74.95 per year). **Sears's Mature Outlook** (✉ Box 9390, Des Moines, IA 50306, ☎ 800/336–6330; $19.95 per year). **Travelers Advantage** (✉ CUC Travel Service, ✉ 3033 S. Parker Rd., Suite 1000, Aurora, CO 80014, ☎ 800/548–1116 or 800/648–4037; $59.95 per year, single or family). **Worldwide Discount Travel Club** (✉ 1674 Meridian Ave., Miami Beach, FL 33139, ☎ 305/534–2082; $50 per year family, $40 single).

CREDIT-CARD BENEFITS

When you use your credit card to make travel purchases you may get free travel-accident insurance, collision-damage insurance, and medical or legal assistance, depending on the card and the bank that issued it. American Express, MasterCard, and Visa provide one or more of these services, so **get a copy of your credit card's travel-benefits policy.** If you are a member of an auto club, always **ask hotel and car-rental reservations agents about auto-club discounts.** Some clubs offer additional discounts on tours, cruises, and admission to attractions.

DISCOUNT RESERVATIONS

To save money, **look into discount-reservations services,** which use their buying power to get a better price on hotels, airline tickets, even car rentals. When booking a room, always **call the hotel's local toll-free number** (if one is available) rather than the central reservations number—you'll often get a better price. Always ask about special packages or corporate rates.

➤ AIRLINE TICKETS: ☎ 800/FLY-4-LESS. ☎ 800/FLY-ASAP.

➤ HOTEL ROOMS: **Accommodations Express** (☎ 800/444–7666). **Central Reservation Service (CRS)** (☎ 800/548–3311). **Hotel Reservations Network** (☎ 800/964–6835). **Quickbook** (☎ 800/789–9887). **Room Finders USA** (☎ 800/473–7829). **RMC Travel** (☎ 800/245–5738). **Steigenberger Reservation Service** (☎ 800/223–5652).

PACKAGE DEALS

Packages and guided tours can save you money, but don't confuse the two. When you buy a package, your travel remains independent, as though you had planned and booked the trip yourself. Fly/drive packages, which combine airfare and car rental, are often a good deal.

ELECTRICITY

Many overseas visitors will need to bring adapters to convert their personal appliances to the U.S. standard: AC, 110 volts/60 cycles, with a plug of two flat pins set parallel to one another.

GAY & LESBIAN TRAVEL

San Francisco, Los Angeles, West Hollywood, San Diego, and Palm Springs are among the California cities with visible lesbian and gay communities.

LOCAL INFORMATION

Many California cities large and small have lesbian and gay publications available in sidewalk racks and at bars and other social spaces; most have extensive events and information listings.

➤ LOCAL PAPERS: **Bay Area Reporter** (⊠ 395 9th St., San Francisco 94103, ☎ 415/861–5019). **Bottom Line** (⊠ 1243 N. Gene Autry Trail, Suite 121, Palm Springs 92262, ☎ 760/323–0552). **Edge** (⊠ 6⊠ 434 Santa Monica Blvd., Los Angeles 90038, ☎ 323/962–6994). **Uptown Publications** (⊠ 3⊠ 911 Normal St., San Diego, 92103, ☎ 619/299–6397). **Mom Guess What Newspaper** (⊠ 1⊠ 725 L St., Sacramento 95814, ☎ 916/441–6397).

➤ SWITCHBOARDS AND HOT LINES: **Gay and Lesbian Community Services Center** (⊠ 1⊠ 625 N. Schrader Blvd., Los Angeles 90028, ☎ 323/993–7400). **Lambda Community Center** (⊠ 9⊠ 920 20th St., Sacramento 95814, ☎ 916/442–0185). **Lesbian and Gay Men's Community Center** (⊠ 3⊠ 916 Normal St., San Diego 92103, ☎ 619/692–4297). **Pacific Center Lesbian, Gay and Bisexual Switchboard** (☎ 510/841–6224).

➤ GAY- AND LESBIAN-FRIENDLY TOUR OPERATORS: **R.S.V.P. Travel Productions** (⊠ 2800 University Ave. SE, Minneapolis, MN 55414, ☎ 612/379–4697 or 800/328–7787, FAX 612/379–0484), for cruises and resort vacations for gays.

➤ GAY- AND LESBIAN-FRIENDLY TRAVEL AGENCIES: **Corniche Travel** (⊠ 8721 Sunset Blvd., Suite 200, West Hollywood, CA 90069, ☎ 310/854–6000 or 800/429–8747, FAX 310/659–7441). **Islanders Kennedy Travel** (⊠ 183 W. 10th St., New York, NY 10014, ☎ 212/242–3222 or 800/988–1181, FAX 212/929–8530). **Now Voyager** (⊠ 4406 18th St., San Francisco, CA 94114, ☎ 415/626–1169 or 800/255–6951, FAX 415/626–8626). **Yellowbrick Road** (⊠ 1500 W. Balmoral Ave., Chicago, IL 60640, ☎ 773/561–1800 or 800/642–2488, FAX 773/561–4497). **Skylink** (⊠ 3577 Moorland Ave., Santa Rosa, CA 95407, ☎ 707/585–8355 or 800/225–5759, FAX 707/584–5637), serving lesbian travelers.

HEALTH

MEDICAL PLANS

No one plans to get sick while traveling, but it happens, so **consider signing up with a medical-assistance company.** Members get doctor referrals, emergency evacuation or repatriation, 24-hour telephone hot lines for medical consultation, cash for emergencies, and other personal and legal assistance. Coverage varies by plan, so **review the benefits of each carefully.**

➤ MEDICAL-ASSISTANCE COMPANIES: **International SOS Assistance** (⊠ 8 Neshaminy Interplex, Suite 207, Trevose, PA 19053, ☎ 215/245–4707 or 800/523–6586, FAX 215/244–9617; ⊠ 12 Chemin Riant-bosson, 1217 Meyrin 1, Geneva, Switzerland, ☎ 4122/785–6464, FAX 4122/785–6424; ⊠ 10 Anson Rd., 14-07/08 International Plaza, Singapore, 079903, ☎ 65/226–3936, FAX 65/226–3937).

HOLIDAYS

Major national holidays include: New Year's Day (Jan. 1); Martin Luther King, Jr. Day (third Mon. in Jan.); President's Day (third Mon. in Feb.); Memorial Day (last Mon. in May); Independence Day (July 4); Labor Day (first Mon. in Sept.); Thanksgiving Day (fourth Thurs. in Nov.); Christmas Eve and Day (Dec. 24–25); and New Year's Eve (Dec. 31).

INSURANCE

Travel insurance is the best way to **protect yourself against financial loss.**

The most useful plan is a comprehensive policy that includes coverage for trip cancellation and interruption, default, trip delay, and medical expenses (with a waiver for preexisting conditions). Without insurance, you will lose all or most of your money if you cancel your trip, regardless of the reason. Default insurance covers you if your tour operator, airline, or cruise line goes out of business. Trip-delay covers unforeseen expenses that you may incur due to bad weather or mechanical delays. It's important to compare the fine print regarding trip-delay coverage when comparing policies.

Residents of the United Kingdom can buy an annual travel-insurance policy valid for most vacations taken during the year in which the coverage is purchased. If you are pregnant or have a preexisting condition, make sure you're covered. British citizens should buy extra medical coverage when traveling overseas, according to the Association of British Insurers. Australian travelers should buy travel insurance, including extra medical coverage, whenever they go abroad, according to the Insurance Council of Australia.

Always **buy travel insurance directly from the insurance company;** if you buy it from a cruise line, airline, or tour operator that goes out of business, you probably will not be covered for the agency or operator's default, a major risk. Before you make any purchase, **review your existing health and home-owner's policies** to find out whether they cover expenses incurred while traveling.

➤ Travel Insurers: In the U.S., **Access America** (✉ 6600 W. Broad St., Richmond, VA 23230, ☎ 804/285–3300 or 800/284–8300). **Travel Guard International** (✉ 1145 Clark St., Stevens Point, WI 54481, ☎ 715/345–0505 or 800/826–1300). In Canada, **Mutual of Omaha** (✉ Travel Division, ✉ 500 University Ave., Toronto, Ontario M5G 1V8, ☎ 416/598–4083, 800/268–8825 in Canada).

➤ Insurance Information: In the U.K., **Association of British Insurers** (✉ 51 Gresham St., London EC2V 7HQ, ☎ 0171/600–3333). In Australia, the **Insurance Council of Australia** (☎ 613/9614–1077, FAX 613/9614–7924).

LODGING

APARTMENT & VILLA RENTALS

If you want a home base that's roomy enough for a family and comes with cooking facilities, **consider a furnished rental.** These can save you money, especially if you're traveling with a large group of people. Home-exchange directories list rentals (often second homes owned by prospective house swappers), and some services search for a house or apartment for you and handle the paperwork. Some send an illustrated catalog; others send photographs only of specific properties, sometimes at a charge. Up-front registration fees may apply.

➤ Rental Agents: **Hometours International** (✉ Box 11503, Knoxville, TN 37939, ☎ 423/690–8484 or 800/367–4668). **Property Rentals International** (✉ 1008 Mansfield Crossing Rd., Richmond, VA 23236, ☎ 804/378–6054 or 800/220–3332, FAX 804/379–2073). **Rent-a-Home International** (✉ 7200 34th Ave. NW, Seattle, WA 98117, ☎ 206/789–9377 or 800/488–7368, FAX 206/789–9379). **Vacation Home Rentals Worldwide** (✉ 235 Kensington Ave., Norwood, NJ 07648, ☎ 201/767–9393 or 800/633–3284, FAX 201/767–5510). **Hideaways International** (✉ 767 Islington St., Portsmouth, NH 03801, ☎ 603/430–4433 or 800/843–4433, FAX 603/430–4444; membership $99) is a club for travelers who arrange rentals among themselves.

CAMPING

➤ Information: **California Travel Parks Association** (✉ Box 5648, Auburn, CA 95604, ☎ 530/823–1076, FAX 530/823–6331).

➤ Reservations: **National Parks** (☎ 800/365–2267). **State Parks** (☎ 800/444–7275).

HOME EXCHANGES

If you would like to exchange your home for someone else's, **join a home-exchange organization,** which will send you its updated listings of available exchanges for a year and will include your own listing in at least one of them. It's up to you to make specific arrangements.

➤ EXCHANGE CLUBS: **HomeLink International** (✉ Box 650, Key West, FL 33041, ☎ 305/294–7766 or 800/638–3841, FAX 305/294–1148; $83 per year).

HOSTELS

No matter what your age, you can **save on lodging costs by staying at hostels.** In some 5,000 locations in more than 70 countries around the world, Hostelling International (HI), the umbrella group for a number of national youth hostel associations, offers single-sex, dorm-style beds and, at many hostels, "couples" rooms and family accommodations. Membership in any HI national hostel association, open to travelers of all ages, allows you to stay in HI-affiliated hostels at member rates (one-year membership is about $25 for adults; hostels run about $10–$25 per night). Members also have priority if the hostel is full; they're eligible for discounts around the world, even on rail and bus travel in some countries.

➤ HOSTEL ORGANIZATIONS: **Hostelling International—American Youth Hostels** (✉ 733 15th St. NW, Suite 840, Washington, DC 20005, ☎ 202/783–6161, FAX 202/783–6171). **Hostelling International—Canada** (✉ 400-205 Catherine St., Ottawa, Ontario K2P 1C3, ☎ 613/237–7884, FAX 613/237–7868). **Youth Hostel Association of England and Wales** (✉ Trevelyan House, ✉ 8 St. Stephen's Hill, St. Albans, Hertfordshire AL1 2DY, ☎ 01727/855215 or 01727/845047, FAX 01727/844126); membership in the U.S. $25, in Canada C$26.75, in the U.K. £9.30).

HOTELS

When making your reservation, **ask all the necessary questions up front.** If you will be driving a car, ask if the hotel has a parking lot or covered garage and whether there is an extra fee for parking. If you like to eat your meals in, ask if the hotel has a restaurant or whether it has room service (most do, but not necessarily 24 hours a day—and be forewarned that

it can be expensive). Most hotels have in-room telephones, but double-check this at inexpensive properties and bed-and-breakfasts. Most hotels and motels have in-room TVs, often with cable movies (usually pay-per-view), but verify this if you like to watch TV. If you want an in-room crib for your child, there will probably be an additional charge. Most hotels will hold your reservation until 6 PM; **call ahead if you plan to arrive late.** Hotels will be more willing to hold a late reservation for you if you reserve with a credit-card.

Most major hotel chains are represented in California.

➤ TOLL-FREE NUMBERS: **Best Western** (☎ 800/528–1234). **Clarion** (☎ 800/252–7466). **Colony** (☎ 800/777–1700). **Comfort** (☎ 800/228–5150). **Days Inn** (☎ 800/325–2525). **Doubletree and Red Lion Hotels** (☎ 800/528–0444). **Embassy Suites** (☎ 800/362–2779). **Four Seasons** (☎ 800/332–3442). **Hilton** (☎ 800/445–8667). **Holiday Inn** (☎ 800/465–4329). **Howard Johnson** (☎ 800/654–4656). **Hyatt Hotels & Resorts** (☎ 800/233–1234). **Inter-Continental** (☎ 800/327–0200). **La Quinta** (☎ 800/531–5900). **Marriott** (☎ 800/228–9290). **Le Meridien** (☎ 800/543–4300). **Nikko Hotels International** (☎ 800/645–5687). **Omni** (☎ 800/843–6664). **Quality Inn** (☎ 800/228–5151). **Radisson** (☎ 800/333–3333). **Ramada** (☎ 800/228–2828). **Renaissance Hotels & Resorts** (☎ 800/468–3571). **Ritz-Carlton** (☎ 800/241–3333). **ITT Sheraton** (☎ 800/325–3535). **Sleep Inn** (☎ 800/221–2222). **Westin Hotels & Resorts** (☎ 800/228–3000). **Wyndham Hotels & Resorts** (☎ 800/822–4200).

MOTELS

➤ TOLL-FREE NUMBERS: **Econo Lodge** (☎ 800/553–2666). **Friendship Inns** (☎ 800/453–4511). **Motel 6** (☎ 800/466–8356). **Rodeway** (☎ 800/228–2000). **Super 8** (☎ 800/848–8888).

MONEY

COSTS

Los Angeles and San Francisco tend to be expensive cities to visit, and rates at coastal and desert resorts are nearly comparable. Hotel rates average from $150 to $200 a night (though you can find less expensive places), and three-course meals at even moderately trendy restaurants often cost from $30 to $50 per person. Costs in the Gold Country, the Far North, and the Mojave Desert/Death Valley region are considerably less—many fine Gold Country B&Bs charge around $100 a night, and some motels in the Far North and the Mojave charge from $50 to $70.

CREDIT & DEBIT CARDS

Should you use a credit card or a debit card when traveling? Both have benefits. A credit card allows you to delay payment and gives you certain rights as a consumer (☞ Consumer Protection, *above*). A debit card, also known as a check card, deducts funds directly from your checking account and helps you stay within your budget. When you want to rent a car, though, you may still need a credit card. Although you can always *pay* for your car with a debit card, some agencies will not allow you to *reserve* a car with a debit card.

Otherwise, the two types of plastic are virtually the same. Both will get you cash advances at ATMs worldwide if your card is properly programmed with your personal identification number (PIN).

➤ ATM LOCATIONS: **Cirrus** (☎ 800/424–7787). **Plus** (☎ 800/843–7587) for locations in the U.S. and Canada, or visit your local bank.

➤ REPORTING LOST CARDS: To report lost or stolen credit cards: **American Express** (☎ 800/327–2177); **Discover Card** (☎ 800/347–2683); **Diners Club** (☎ 800/234–6377); **MasterCard** (☎ 800/307–7309); and **Visa** (☎ 800/847–2911).

EXCHANGING MONEY

For the most favorable rates, **change money through banks.** Although fees charged for ATM transactions may be higher abroad than at home, Cirrus and Plus exchange rates are excellent, because they are based on wholesale rates offered only by major banks. You won't do as well at exchange booths in airports or rail and bus stations, in hotels, in restaurants, or in stores, although you may find their hours more convenient. To avoid lines at airport exchange booths, **obtain some currency of your destination country before you leave home.**

➤ EXCHANGE SERVICES: **Chase Currency To Go** (☎ 800/935–9935; 935–9935 in NY, NJ, and CT). **International Currency Express** (☎ 888/842–0880 on the East Coast, 888/278–6628 on the West Coast). **Thomas Cook Currency Services** (☎ 800/287–7362 for telephone orders and retail locations).

TRAVELER'S CHECKS

Do you need traveler's checks? It depends on where you're headed. If you're going to rural areas and small towns, go with cash; traveler's checks are best used in cities. Lost or stolen checks can usually be replaced within 24 hours.

NATIONAL & STATE PARKS

Look into discount passes to **save money on park entrance fees.** The Golden Eagle Pass ($50) gets you and your companions free admission to all parks for one year. (Camping and parking are extra). Both the Golden Age Passport ($10), for those 62 and older, and the Golden Access Passport (free), for travelers with disabilities, entitle holders to free entry to all national parks, plus 50% off fees for the use of many park facilities and services. You must show proof of age and of U.S. citizenship or permanent residency (such as a U.S. passport, driver's license, or birth certificate) and, if requesting Golden Access, proof of disability. All three passes are available at all national park entrances where entrance fees are charged. Golden Eagle and Golden Access passes are also available by mail.

➤ PASSES BY MAIL: **National Park Service** (✉ National Capitol Area Office, ✉ 1100 Ohio Dr. SW, Washington, DC 20242).

STATE PARKS

➤ INFORMATION: **California State Park System** (✉ Dept. of Parks and Recreation, Box 942896 Sacramento 94296, ☎ 916/653–6995).

OUTDOOR ACTIVITIES & SPORTS

FISHING

You'll need a license to fish in California. State residents pay $26.50 ($4.25 for senior citizens and those on limited income), but nonresidents are charged $71.95 for a one-year license, or $26.50 for a 10-day license. Both residents and nonresidents can purchase a one-day license for $9.45.

➤ INFORMATION: **Department of Fish and Game** (⊠ 3⊠ 211 S St., Sacramento 95816, ☎ 916/227–2244 or 916/227–2242).

PACKING

LUGGAGE

How many carry-on bags you can bring with you is up to the airline. Some airlines are beginning to allow only one per person, but some still allow two. Gate agents will take excess baggage—including bags they deem oversize—from you as you board and add it to checked luggage. To avoid this situation, make sure that everything you carry aboard will fit under your seat. If you are flying internationally, note that baggage allowances may be determined not by piece but by weight—generally 88 pounds (40 kilograms) in first class, 66 pounds (30 kilograms) in business class, and 44 pounds (20 kilograms) in economy.

Airline liability for baggage is limited to $1,250 per person on flights within the United States. On international flights it amounts to $9.07 per pound or $20 per kilogram for checked baggage (roughly $640 per 70-pound bag) and $400 per passenger for unchecked baggage. You can buy additional coverage at check-in for about $10 per $1,000 of coverage, but it excludes a rather extensive list of items, shown on your airline ticket.

Before departure, **itemize your bags' contents** and their worth, and label the bags with your name, address, and phone number. (If you use your home address, cover it so that potential thieves can't see it readily.) Inside each bag **pack a copy of your itinerary.** At check-in **make sure that each bag is correctly tagged** with the destination airport's three-letter code. If your bags arrive damaged or fail to arrive at all, file a written report with the airline before leaving the airport.

PACKING LIST

When packing for a California vacation, **prepare for changes in temperature.** Take along sweaters, jackets, and clothes for layering as your best insurance for coping with variations in temperature. Include shorts or cool cottons unless you are packing for a midwinter ski trip. Always tuck in a bathing suit; many lodgings have a pools, spas, and saunas. Casual dressing is a hallmark of the California lifestyle, but in the evening men will need a jacket and tie at some good restaurants, and women will be more comfortable in something dressier than sightseeing garb. Considerations of formality aside, bear in mind that **San Francisco and other coastal towns can be chilly** at any time of the year, especially in summer, when the fog is apt to descend and stay.

In your carry-on luggage **bring an extra pair of eyeglasses or contact lenses** and **enough of any medication you take** to last the entire trip. **Never put prescription drugs or valuables in luggage to be checked.**

PASSPORTS & VISAS

When traveling internationally, **carry a passport even if you don't need one** (it's always the best form of ID), and make **two photocopies of the data page** (one for someone at home and another for you, carried separately from your passport). If you lose your passport, promptly call the nearest embassy or consulate and the local police. The best time to apply for a passport or to renew is during the fall and winter. Before any trip, be sure to check your passport's expiration date and, if necessary, renew it as soon as possible. (Some countries won't allow you to enter on a passport that's due to expire in six months or less.)

Citizens of Australia, New Zealand, and the United Kingdom who plan to stay in the United States for fewer than 90 days **do not need entry visas.** A valid passport, a return-trip ticket, and proof of financial solvency are required; you'll be asked to fill out the Visa Waiver Form, 1-94W, upon entry. Travelers who plan to stay more than 90 days can apply for the appropriate visa at the United States embassy or consulates in their home country. Canadian citizens need **valid identification but neither a passport nor a visa** to enter the United States.

VISA OFFICES

➤ AUSTRALIAN CITIZENS: **U.S. Embassy** (⊠ Moonah Pl., Yaralumla, Canberra, ☎ 1–902–262–282).

➤ NEW ZEALAND CITIZENS: **U.S. Consulate General, Non-Immigrant Visa Section** (⊠ General Bldg., Shortland and O'Connell Sts., 4th Floor, Auckland 1, ☎ no phone inquiries).

➤ U.K. CITIZENS: **U.S. Embassy Visa Information Line** (☎ 01891/200–290; calls cost 49p per minute, 39p per minute cheap rate), for U.S. visa information. **U.S. Embassy Visa Branch** (⊠ 5 Upper Grosvenor St., London W1A 2JB), for U.S. visa information; send a self-addressed, stamped envelope. Write the **U.S. Consulate General** (⊠ Queen's House, ⊠ Queen St., Belfast BTI 6EO) if you live in Northern Ireland.

SENIOR-CITIZEN TRAVEL

To qualify for age-related discounts, **mention your senior-citizen status up front** when booking hotel reservations (not when checking out) and before you're seated in restaurants (not when paying the bill). Note that discounts may be limited to certain menus, days, or hours. When renting a car, **ask about promotional car-rental discounts,** which can be cheaper than senior-citizen rates.

STUDENT TRAVEL

➤ STUDENT IDS & SERVICES: **Council on International Educational Exchange** (⊠ CIEE, ⊠ 205 E. 42nd St., 14th floor, New York, NY 10017, ☎ 212/822–2600 or 888/268–6245, FAX 212/822–2699), for mail orders only, in the United States. **Travel Cuts** (⊠ 187 College St., Toronto, Ontario M5T 1P7, ☎ 416/979–2406 or 800/667–2887) in Canada.

➤ STUDENT TOURS: **Contiki Holidays** (⊠ 300 Plaza Alicante, Suite 900,

Garden Grove, CA 92840, ☎ 714/740–0808 or 800/266–8454, FAX 714/740–2034).

TELEPHONES

CREDIT-CARD CALLS

U.S. telephone credit cards are not like the magnetic cards used in some European countries, which pay for calls in advance; they simply represent an account that lets you charge a call to your home or business phone. On any phone, you can make a credit-card call by punching in your individual account number or by telling the operator that number. Certain specially marked pay phones (usually found in airports, hotel lobbies, and so on) can be used only for credit-card calls. To get a credit card, contact your long-distance telephone carrier, such as AT&T, MCI, or Sprint.

AREA CODES

The insatiable appetite of Californians for faxes, cellular phones, and other telephonic gadgets has led to numerous changes in area codes. Areas in both southern California and northern California where new area codes were added just a few years ago will be receiving still more area codes—the 619, 310, 415, and 408 codes will split again in 1999 or 2000. The 805 area code, which is used along the Central Coast and in inland central California, will be split in mid-February 1999, with the inland regions switching to a new area code (the number had not been announced at press time). Until mid-August both area codes will still work in the area covered by the change. After mid-August if you don't use the correct code, your call won't go through. All the area codes listed with telephone numbers in this book are the ones that were in effect on the date of publication (November 1998).

DIRECTORY & OPERATOR INFORMATION

For assistance from an operator, dial "0". To find out a telephone number within the same area code you're calling from, dial 411; in a few places it is necessary to dial 555–1212. These calls are free even from a pay phone. If you want to charge a long-distance call to the person you're calling, you can call collect by dialing "0" instead of "1" before the 10-digit number, and an operator will come on the line to assist you (the party you're calling, however, has the right to refuse the call).

INTERNATIONAL CALLS

International calls can be direct-dialed from most phones; dial 011, followed by the country code and then the local number (the front pages of many local telephone directories include a list of overseas country codes). To have an operator assist you, dial 0 and ask for the overseas operator. The country code for Australia is 61; New Zealand, 64; and the United Kingdom, 44. To reach Canada, dial 1 + area code + number.

LONG-DISTANCE CALLS

Competitive long-distance carriers make calling within the United States relatively convenient and let you avoid hotel surcharges. By dialing an 800 number, you can get connected to the long-distance company of your choice.

➤ LONG-DISTANCE CARRIERS: **AT&T** (☎ 800/225–5288). **MCI** (☎ 800/888–8000). **Sprint** (☎ 800/366–2255).

PUBLIC PHONES

Instructions for pay telephones should be posted on the phone, but generally you insert your coins—35¢ for most local calls—in a slot and wait for the steady hum of a dial tone before dialing the number you wish to reach. If you dial a long-distance number, the operator will come on the line and tell you how much more money you must insert for your call to go through.

TIPPING

At restaurants, a 15% tip is standard for waiters; up to 20% may be expected at more expensive establishments. The same goes for taxi drivers, bartenders, and hairdressers. Coat-check operators usually expect $1; bellhops and porters should get 50¢ to $1 per bag; hotel maids in upscale hotels should get about $1 per day of your stay. On package tours, conductors and drivers usually get $10 per day from the group as a whole; check whether this has already been figured into your cost. For local sightseeing tours, you may individually tip the driver-guide $1 if he or she has been helpful or informative. Ushers in theaters do not expect tips.

TOUR OPERATORS

Buying a prepackaged tour or independent vacation can make your trip to California less expensive and more hassle-free. Because everything is prearranged, you'll spend less time planning. Operators that handle several hundred thousand travelers per year can use their purchasing power to give you a good price. Their high volume may also indicate financial stability. But some small companies provide more personalized service; because they tend to specialize, they may also be more knowledgeable about a given area.

BOOKING WITH AN AGENT

Travel agents are excellent resources. In fact, large operators accept bookings made only through travel agents. But it's a good idea to **collect brochures from several agencies,** because some agents' suggestions may be influenced by relationships with tour and package firms that reward them for volume sales. If you have a special interest, **find an agent with expertise in that area;** ASTA (☞ Travel Agencies, *below*) has a database of specialists worldwide.

Make sure your travel agent knows the accommodations and other services. Ask about the hotel's location, room size, beds, and whether it has a pool, room service, or programs for children, if you care about these. Has your agent been there in person or sent others you can contact?

Do some homework on your own, too: Local tourism boards can provide information about lesser-known and small-niche operators, some of which may sell only direct.

BUYER BEWARE

Each year consumers are stranded or lose their money when tour operators—even very large ones with excellent reputations—go out of business. So **check out the operator.**

Find out how long the company has been in business, and ask several travel agents about its reputation. If the package or tour you are considering is priced lower than in your wildest dreams, **be skeptical.** Try to **book with a company that has a consumer-protection program.** If the operator has such a program, you'll find information about it in the company's brochure. If the operator you are considering does not offer some kind of consumer protection, then ask for references from satisfied customers.

In the U.S., members of the National Tour Association and United States Tour Operators Association are required to set aside funds to cover your payments and travel arrangements in case the company defaults. It's also a good idea to choose a company that participates in the American Society of Travel Agent's Tour Operator Program. This gives you a forum if there are any disputes between you and your tour operator; ASTA will act as mediator.

➤ TOUR-OPERATOR RECOMMENDATIONS: **American Society of Travel Agents** (☞ Travel Agencies, *below*). **National Tour Association** (✉ NTA, ✉ 546 E. Main St., Lexington, KY 40508, ☎ 606/226–4444 or 800/ 755–8687). **United States Tour Operators Association** (✉ USTOA, ✉ 342 Madison Ave., Suite 1522, New York, NY 10173, ☎ 212/599– 6599 or 800/468–7862, FAX 212/ 599–6744).

COSTS

The more your package or tour includes, the better you can predict the ultimate cost of your vacation. Make sure you know exactly what is covered, and **beware of hidden costs.** Are taxes, tips, and service charges included? Transfers and baggage handling? Entertainment and excursions? These can add up. Prices for packages and tours are usually quoted per person, based on two sharing a room. If traveling solo, you may be required to pay the full double-occupancy rate. Some operators eliminate this surcharge if you agree to be matched with a roommate of the same sex, even if one is not found by departure time.

GROUP TOURS

Among companies that sell tours to California, the following are nationally known, have a proven reputation, and offer plenty of options. The classifications used below represent different price categories, and you'll probably encounter these terms when talking to a travel agent or tour operator. The key difference is usually in accommodations, which run from budget to better, and better-yet to best.

➤ DELUXE: **Globus** (☎ 303/797– 2800 or 800/221–0090). **Maupintour** (☎ 913/843–1211 or 800/255– 4266). **Tauck Tours** ☎ 203/226– 6911 or 800/468–2825).

➤ FIRST CLASS: **Brendan Tours** (☎ 818/785–9696 or 800/421–8446). **Caravan Tours** (☎ 312/321–9800 or 800/227–2826). **Collette Tours** (☎ 401/728–3805 or 800/340–5158). **Gadabout Tours** (☎ 760/325–5556 or 800/952–5068). **Mayflower Tours** (☎ 708/960–3430 or 800/323– 7064). **Trafalgar Tours** (☎ 212/689– 8977 or 800/854–0103).

➤ BUDGET: **Cosmos** (☎ 303/797– 2800 or 800/221–0090).

PACKAGES

Like group tours, independent vacation packages are available from major tour operators and airlines. The companies listed below offer vacation packages in a broad price range.

➤ AIR/HOTEL: **American Airlines Vacations** (☎ 800/321–2121). **Continental Vacations** (☎ 800/634–5555). **Delta Vacations** (☎ 800/872–7786, FAX 954/357–4687). **United Vacations** (☎ 800/328–6877). **US Airways Vacations** (☎ 800/455–0123).

➤ CUSTOM PACKAGES: **Amtrak Vacations** (☎ 800/321–8684).

➤ FLY/DRIVE: **American Airlines Vacations** (☎ 800/321–2121). **Continental Vacations United Vacations** (☎ 800/328–6877).

➤ HOTEL ONLY: **SuperCities** (☎ 800/ 333–1234).

➤ FROM THE U.K.: **British Airways Holidays** (✉ Astral Towers, Betts Way, London Rd., Crawley, West Sussex RH10 2XA, ☎ 01293/723–121). **Jetsave** (✉ Sussex House, London Rd., East Grinstead, West Sussex RH19 1LD, ☎ 01342/327–711). **Key to America** (✉ 1–3 Station Rd., Ashford, Middlesex TW15 2UW, ☎ 01784/248–777). **Kuoni Travel Ltd.** (✉ Kuoni House, Dorking, Surrey RH5 4AZ, ☎ 01306/740–500). **Premier Holidays** (✉ Westbrook, Milton Rd., Cambridge CB4 1YG, ☎ 01223/516–516).

THEME TRIPS

➤ ADVENTURE: **Access to Adventure** (☎ 530/469–3322 or 800/552–6284). **American Wilderness Experience** (☎ 303/444–2622 or 800/444–0099). **Mountain Travel-Sobek** (☎ 510/527–8100 or 888/687–6235). **Tahoe Trips & Trails** (☎ 530/583–4506 or 800/581–4453).

➤ BICYCLING: **Backroads** (☎ 510/527–1555 or 800/462–2848). **Imagine Tours** (☎ 530/758–8782 or 888/592–8687).

➤ FISHING: **Anglers Travel** (☎ 702/324–0580 or 800/624–8429). **Fishing International** (☎ 707/539–3366 or 800/950–4242). **Rod & Reel Adventures** (☎ 209/785–0444).

➤ LEARNING: **Naturequest** (☎ 949/499–9561 or 800/369–3033). **Oceanic Society Expeditions** (☎ 415/441–1106 or 800/326–7491). **Smithsonian Study Tours and Seminars** (☎ 202/357–4700).

➤ RIVER RAFTING: **Access to Adventure** (☞ Adventure, *above*). **James Henry River Tours** (☎ 415/868–1836 or 800/786–1830). **OARS** (☎ 209/736–4677 or 800/346–6277). **Whitewater Voyages** (☎ 510/222–5994 or 800/488–7238).

➤ TENNIS: **Championship Tennis Tours** (☎ 602/990–8760 or 800/468–3664). ➤ TRAIL RUNNING: **Backroads** (☞ Bicycling, *above*).

➤ WALKING/HIKING: **American Wilderness Experience** (☞ Adventure, *above*). **Backroads** (☞ Bicycling, *above*).

➤ YACHT CHARTERS: **Five Star Charters** (☎ 415/332–7187 or 800/762–6287).

TRAIN TRAVEL

Amtrak's *California Zephyr* train from Chicago via Denver terminates in Oakland. The *Coast Starlight* train travels between southern California and the state of Washington. The *Sunset Limited* heads west from Florida through New Orleans and Texas to Los Angeles.

➤ INFORMATION: **Amtrak** (☎ 800/872–7245).

TRAVEL AGENCIES

A good travel agent puts your needs first. Look for an agency that has been in business at least five years, emphasizes customer service, and has someone on staff who specializes in your destination. In addition, **make sure the agency belongs to a professional trade organization,** such as ASTA in the United States. If your travel agency is also acting as your tour operator, *see* Buyer Beware in Tour Operators, *above*).

➤ LOCAL AGENT REFERRALS: **American Society of Travel Agents** (ASTA, ☎ 800/965–2782 24-hr hot line, FAX 703/684–8319). **Association of Canadian Travel Agents** (✉ Suite 201, 1729 Bank St., Ottawa, Ontario K1V 7Z5, ☎ 613/521–0474, FAX 613/521–0805). **Association of British Travel Agents** (✉ 55–57 Newman St., London W1P 4AH, ☎ 0171/637–2444, FAX 0171/637–0713). **Australian Federation of Travel Agents** (☎ 02/9264–3299). **Travel Agents' Association of New Zealand** (☎ 04/499–0104).

U.S. GOVERNMENT

Government agencies can be an excellent source of inexpensive travel information. When planning your trip, **find out what government materials are available.**

➤ PAMPHLETS: **Consumer Information Center** (✉ Consumer Information Catalog, Pueblo, CO 81009, ☎ 719/948–3334 or 888/878–3256) for a free catalog that includes travel titles.

VISITOR INFORMATION

TOURIST OFFICES

For general information about California, contact the state tourism office; for the numbers of regional and city visitors bureaus and chambers of commerce, see the A to Z sections at the end of Chapters 2 to 16.

➤ STATEWIDE INFORMATION: **California Division of Tourism** (✉ 801 K St., Suite 1600 , Sacramento, CA 95814, ☎ 916/322–2881 or 800/862–2543, FAX 916/322–3402 or 916/322–0501).

➤ IN THE U.K.: **California Tourist Office** (✉ ABC California, Box 35, Abingdon, Oxfordshire OX14 4TB, ☎ 0891/200–278, FAX 0171/242–2838). Calls cost 50p per minute peak rate or 45p per minute cheap rate. Brochures can be obtained by sending to the above address a cheque for £3 made to ABC California.

WEB SITES

Do **check out the World Wide Web** when you're planning. You'll find everything from up-to-date weather forecasts to virtual tours of famous cities. Fodor's Web site, www.fodors.com, is a great place to start your on-line travels. For more information specifically on California, visit the following sites.

GENERAL INFORMATION

The **California Division of Tourism web site** has travel tips, events calendars, and other resources, and the site will link you—via the Regions icon—to the web sites of city and regional tourism offices and attractions. http://gocalif.ca.gov/

THE GREAT OUTDOORS

The no-frills site of the **California Department of Fish and Game** provides information on fishing and hunting zones, licenses, and schedules. http://www.dfg.ca.gov/

The **California Parks Department** site has the lowdown on state-run parks and other recreational areas. http://cal-parks.ca.gov/

A must-visit for outdoors and adventure travel enthusiasts, the **Great Outdoor Recreation Page** is arranged into three easily navigated categories: attractions, activities, and locations. http://www.gorp.com/The **National Park Service site**, which lists national parks and other lands administered

by the park service, has extensive historical, cultural, and environmental information. http://www.nps.gov/

NEWSWEEKLIES

The state's newsweeklies are a great source of up-to-the-minute arts and entertainment information, from what shows are on the boards to who's playing the clubs.

L.A. Weekly maintains a hip site with lively features and and insiders' guides to dining, the arts, and nightlife in the L.A. metro area. http://www.laweekly.com/

The smart features on **MetroActive**, the online version of *San Jose Metro*, include guides to nightlife, the arts, dining, and entertainment in the San Francisco Bay Area, including Silicon Valley and Santa Cruz. http://www.sanjosemetro.com/

The site of the **San Diego Reader** isn't visually impressive, but it provides a thorough guide to what's happening in San Diego. http://www.sdreader.com/

The colorful and easy-to-navigate web site of **SF Weekly** has the lowdown on the San Francisco Bay Area. http://www.sfweekly.com/

WINERIES

The site of the **Wine Institute,** which is based in San Francisco, provides events listings and detailed information about the California wine industry and has links to the home pages of regional wine associations. http://www.wineinstitute.org/

WHEN TO GO

Any time of the year is the right time to go to California. There won't be skiable snow in the mountains between Easter and Thanksgiving; there will usually be rain in December, January, and February in the lowlands, if that bothers you; it will be much too hot to enjoy Palm Springs or Death Valley in the summer. But San Francisco, Los Angeles, and San Diego are delightful year-round; the Wine Country's seasonal variables are enticing; and the coastal areas are almost always cool.

The climate varies amazingly in California, not only over distances of several hundred miles but occasionally within an hour's drive. A foggy, cool August day in San Francisco makes you grateful for a sweater, tweed jacket, or light wool coat. Head north 50 mi to the Napa Valley to check out the Wine Country and you'll probably wear shirt sleeves and thin cottons.

Daytime and nighttime temperatures may also swing widely apart. Take Sacramento, a city that is at sea level but in California's Central Valley. In the summer, afternoons can be very warm, in the 90s and occasionally over 100°. But the nights cool down, often dropping 40°.

It's hard to generalize much about the weather in this varied state. Rain comes in the winter, with snow at higher elevations. Summers are dry everywhere. As a rule, compared to the coastal areas, which are cool year-round, inland regions are warmer in summer and cooler in winter. As you climb into the mountains, there are more distinct variations with the seasons: Winter brings snow, autumn is crisp, spring is variable, and summer is clear and warm.

CLIMATE

The following are average daily maximum and minimum temperatures for the major California cities.

➤ FORECASTS: **Weather Channel Connection** (☎ 900/932–8437), 95¢ per minute from a Touch-Tone phone.

Climate in California

LOS ANGELES

Jan.	64F	18C	May	72F	22C	Sept.	81F	27C
	44	7		53	12		60	16
Feb.	64F	18C	June	76F	24C	Oct.	76F	24C
	46	8		57	14		55	13
Mar.	66F	19C	July	81F	27C	Nov.	71F	22C
	48	9		60	16		48	9
Apr.	70F	21C	Aug.	82F	28C	Dec.	66F	19C
	51	11		62	17		46	8

SAN DIEGO

Jan.	62F	17C	May	66F	19C	Sept.	73F	23C
	46	8		55	13		62	17
Feb.	62F	17C	June	69F	21C	Oct.	71F	22C
	48	9		59	15		57	14
Mar.	64F	18C	July	73F	23C	Nov.	69F	21C
	50	10		62	17		51	11
Apr.	66F	19C	Aug.	73F	23C	Dec.	64F	18C
	53	12		64	18		48	9

SAN FRANCISCO

Jan.	55F	13C	May	66F	19C	Sept.	73F	23C
	41	5		48	9		51	11
Feb.	59F	15C	June	69F	21C	Oct.	69F	21C
	42	6		51	11		50	10
Mar.	60F	16C	July	69F	21C	Nov.	64F	18C
	44	7		51	11		44	7
Apr.	62F	17C	Aug.	69F	21C	Dec.	57F	14C
	46	8		53	12		42	6

THE GOLD GUIDE / SMART TRAVEL TIPS

1 Destination: California

RESTLESS NIRVANA

COASTAL CALIFORNIA began its migration from somewhere far to the south millions of years ago. It's still moving north along the San Andreas Fault, but you have plenty of time for a visit before Santa Monica hits the Arctic Circle. If you've heard predictions that some of the state may fall into the Pacific, take the long view and consider that much of California has been in and out of the ocean throughout its history. The forces that raised its mountains and formed the Central Valley are still at work.

Upheaval has always been a fact of life in California—below ground and above. Floods, earthquakes, racial strife, immigration woes, high unemployment, and Orange County's scandal-ridden bankruptcy are but a few of the high-profile traumas—not to mention the O. J. Simpson murder case—that have tarnished California's image in recent years. Things got so bad in the early 1990s that U-Haul declared a shortage of rental trucks because so many residents were moving out of the Golden State. This was fine with the many natives whose "Welcome to California: Now Go Home" bumper stickers had greeted new arrivals for several decades—few states have grown as rapidly as California, which had a population of about 7 million as World War II came to a close and now is home to 32 million people.

From the outside looking in, it may have seemed that, along with its AAA bond rating, California had lost its appeal as a travel destination. But even before its stunning mid-1990s economic turnaround, the Golden State had too many "positives" to be written off: dramatic coastline; rugged desert and mountain regions; Hollywood glitz and Palm Springs glamour; a potpourri of Pacific Rim, European, and Latin American influences; and a fabled history as a conduit for fame and fortune, hope and renewal.

California has always been a place where initiative—as opposed to class, family, or other connections—is honored above all else. The state has lured assertive types who

metaphorically or otherwise have come seeking "gold"—in the Sacramento foothills, in Hollywood, and, more recently, in the Silicon Valley. To be sure, not everyone achieves the mythical California dream, but neither is it totally an illusion. The sense of infinite possibility, as much a by-product of the state's varied and striking land forms as media hype, is what most tourists notice on their first trip. It's why so many return—sometimes forever.

More so than most of its residents are willing to admit, California is a land of contradictions, where "reality" is a matter of opinion—which is why the cinema, an enterprise based wholly on the manipulation of reality, is the perfect signature industry for the state. Take for instance two volumes in many local libraries about the historic chain of 21 California missions established by Spanish Catholic priests, most notably Father Junípero Serra. One book is titled *California's Missions: Their Romance and Beauty.* Its author details Serra's strategy "to convert and civilize the Indians" who resided in late–18th-century California. The other tome, *The Missions of California: A Legacy of Genocide,* disputes the contentions of "mission apologists" and illustrates how on levels physical and spiritual the mission system "was the first disaster for the Indian population of California" (the second being the gold rush of the mid-1800s).

The truth? It's likely somewhere in between, though recent scholarship has tended to show Serra and other missionaries in a less than favorable light. The treatment of other groups—from the Chinese who came to mine and build the railroads to Mexican farm workers—has been equally problematic through the years. The scapegoating of "foreigners"—often by first-generation Californians with no sense of the irony of their protestations—is a cyclical blot on the state's conscience.

California's move to the forefront of the controversy regarding affirmative action gave many people the impression that its residents wish only to roll back the clock. Undoubtedly, some do, but the circumstances here are more complex than they appear on the surface because the state has a more diverse population than most others in the Union. Many Asian Americans, for instance, supported the decision by the regents of the University of California to end the institution's affirmative-action program, arguing that it unfairly denied admittance to highly qualified Asian-American students. Parties on all sides of the affirmative-action issue were given pause, though, when statistics released in 1998 showed that minority enrollment had declined significantly at some key campuses—something the regents had asserted was not likely to happen. In any case, as with the "taxpayer revolts" of the 1970s and 1980s, the immigration debate, managed health care, and government by ballot initiative, the state's residents have forced discussion of an issue that citizens elsewhere have brooded over but not confronted.

C ALIFORNIA IS A RESTLESS nirvana. The sun shines and all is beautiful; then the earth shakes and all is shattered. It's time to rebuild. And the state bounces back—San Francisco from the 1906 and 1989 quakes, Los Angeles from ones in 1971 and 1994, much of the state from incredible flooding in 1997 and the El Niño–induced storms of 1998. Billions were made during the Cold War defense boom; then communism collapsed, bases closed, and unemployment skyrocketed. It was time to diversify. And the state did, making overtures to Asia and Latin America.

And to tourists, who find that although California isn't perfect—what place is?— it's a source of endless diversion, natural and man-made. "Wow!" is a word one hears often here—at Half Dome in Yosemite, during the simulated earthquake at Universal Studios, driving through the Mojave Desert, or walking among the redwoods of Humboldt County. If Texans like things "big" and New Yorkers like a little style, what delights Californians most is drama—indoors or out.

There is no way to take in this "show" in one trip, so don't try. Seventy-five percent of California's visitors return at least once, an impressive quotient of satisfied customers. As you travel through California's various regions you will get a sense of the great diversity of cultures, the ongoing pull between preservation and development, and the state's unique place in the landscapes of geography and the imagination.

NEW AND NOTEWORTHY

San Francisco

The renaissance of the South of Market Street (SoMa) area continues, as new galleries and museums join the area's flagship cultural institutions, the **San Francisco Museum of Modern Art,** and the **Yerba Buena Gardens** complex. The nearby **Moscone Convention Center** is slated for expansion during the next few years. The mix of public buildings and open space will include an an ice-skating rink, children's gardens, and a 1903 Charles I. D. Looff carousel—with 64 fanciful, hand-carved wooden animals—that once entertained visitors at Playland at the Beach, a San Francisco institution from 1913 until its closing in 1973.

Commuters had something to celebrate in 1998, with the opening of a **new Muni line** between the 4th Street Caltrain depot and Embarcadero station.

Plans are being finalized for the new **Chabot Observatory and Science Center,** an 81,000-square-foot complex in Oakland's Joaquin Miller Park. Scheduled to open in late 1999, the observatory and planetarium will feature NASA-designed mission control and space station simulators, plus children-friendly science exhibits.

Los Angeles

The major cultural event of the late-1990s has been the debut of the **Getty Center,** a billion-dollar facility that is drawing huge crowds and mostly rave reviews. Other museums are also creating waves. The **California Science Center,** formerly known as the Museum of Science and Industry, has reinvented itself with dazzling high-tech, interactive exhibits and a 3-D Imax theater. The **Los Angeles County Museum of Art** has undergone a major reorganization of its collection, and the **Norton Simon Museum of Art** in Pasadena now has a Frank Gehry–designed sculpture garden. Farther afield, the **Long Beach Aquarium of the Pacific** is the L.A. area's first major marine-themed attraction since Marineland closed years ago.

Disneyland heads into the millennium with its latest version of **Tomorrowland,** a fantasy future world where you can get shrunk, ride an Astro Orbiter, or tinker with the toys of tomorrow.

The major news on Rodeo Drive is the closing of Fred Hayman Beverly Hills, one-time kingpin of Oscar-night fashions (and also the birthplace of the Giorgio scent). In its place will be **Louis Vuitton.** Tommy Hilfiger's 25,000-square-foot flagship store in Beverly Hills brings the young designer's California-casual fashions closer to L.A.

San Diego

The long-awaited opening of **Legoland California** in Carlsbad adds a family destination that will spur additional development in the North County area. Upgrades at **San Diego International Airport** have eased congestion at the facility somewhat. New passenger-friendly terminals, roads, parking lots, and traffic control are in place. However, the airport remains too small to accommodate current and projected traffic—even a trivial problem can produce congestion and delays. Meanwhile, the debate continues about how, when, and where to further improve the airport.

You'll find it easier than ever to get around via the **San Diego Trolley,** a light-rail transit system that now can take you sightseeing in Old Town, shopping at the expanded **Fashion Valley Center** in Mission Valley, and to see the Chargers or Padres play at **Qualcomm Stadium.** You also have more options for traveling between San Diego, North Coast communities, and beyond via expanded **Amtrak** service and the **Coaster** commuter rail line. Or you can jet away from the North County area on United, American, and Delta airlines from newly enlarged **Palomar McClellan Airport** in Carlsbad.

Development continues in downtown San Diego. The next few years are expected to bring more waterfront hotels, a state-of-the-art library, and a Mission-style stadium for the San Diego Padres baseball team (one plan being floated includes an area where up to 4,000 people could picnic while taking in a ball game.

Around the State

The second year of the state's three-year **Sesquicentennial Celebration,** which acknowledges three 150th anniversaries—discovery of gold (1848), the gold rush (1849), and California's gaining of statehood (1850)—continues in 1999 with events that include a race of tall ships similar to the ones that brought gold-seekers to California.

The administrators of **Yosemite National Park** continue to develop long-range plans that will reduce congestion and preserve the park's natural resources. A new concessionaire began providing services in **Sequoia National Park** in 1998. The first building phase of Wuksachi Village, whose more ecologically sensitive dining, lodging, and other facilities will replace older ones a few miles away, is nearing completion. A new hotel at Grant Grove in **Kings Canyon National Park** is scheduled to be in operation by 1999.

Santa Barbara has always contained dozens of antiques shops, but many new ones have opened on State Street and nearby. Artists and art galleries continue to move into the thriving towns of **Los Olivos** and **Ojai.** Up the Central Coast in **San Simeon,** the theater at Hearst Castle shows a wide-screen film about the castle and the Pacific Ocean. A new exhibit at the **Monterey Bay Aquarium** will examine life in the deep sea.

WHAT'S WHERE

California's three most well-known cities—Los Angeles, San Diego, and San Francisco—are all on the coast. San Diego is 136 miles south of Los Angeles on Interstate 5. San Francisco is 380 miles north of Los Angeles (I–5 to I–580 east to I–80 east). Interstate 5 is the quickest route between Los Angeles and the San Francisco Bay Area, but many visitors travel the coastal route between Los Angeles and San Francisco, making stops at Santa Barbara, Hearst Castle, Big Sur, the Monterey Peninsula, and other points along the way. Keep in mind that stretches of this route, a combination of U.S. 101 and state Highway 1, are narrow and twisting (though often stunning) and that it takes a few hours longer to travel than I–5.

The Central Coast

The Central Coast encompasses the area from Santa Barbara to Monterey Bay (☞ *below*). Highway 1 between Big Sur and Santa Barbara is a spectacular stretch of terrain. The curving road demands an unhurried pace, but even if it didn't, you'd find yourself stopping often to take in the scenery. Hearst Castle in San Simeon is the region's biggest attraction.

The Far North

One of California's best-kept secrets is its far northeast corner. Away from the coast and north of Sacramento and the Gold Country on I–5, the Far North is a sports-lovers' paradise of soaring mountain peaks, wild rivers brimming with fish, and almost infinite recreational possibilities. Mount Shasta, Lake Shasta, and Lassen Volcanic National Park are among the draws. Chico and Redding are the area's two largest cities.

Lake Tahoe

The largest alpine lake in North America is famous for its clarity, deep blue water, and nearby snowcapped peaks. The lake, which is 198 miles east of San Francisco via I–80 or U.S. 50, possesses abundant natural beauty and accessible wilderness, though nearby towns are highly developed and the traffic is often congested. Summertime is generally cooler here than in the Sierra Nevada foothills, and the clean mountain air bracingly crisp.

Los Angeles

In certain lights Los Angeles, the hub of southern California and the state's largest city, displays its Spanish heritage. But much more evident is its participation in the Pacific Rim cultural and economic boom. Hollywood, the beaches, and Disneyland are all within an hour's drive. Also here are freeways (lots of them), important examples of 20th-century domestic architecture, and Beverly Hills, noted for its shops and mansions. The city is reached via I–5 from the north and south, U.S. 101 from the north, and I–10 and I–210 from the east.

The Mojave Desert and Death Valley

The glorious Mojave Desert begins north of the San Bernardino Mountains, along the northern edge of Los Angeles, and extends north 150 miles into the Eureka Valley and east 200 miles to the Colorado River. U.S. 395 travels north–south through the Western Mojave Desert; I–15 and I–40 head east through the Mojave toward Nevada. Death Valley National Park lies north and east of the Mojave. The easiest route to Death Valley from the Western Mojave is on Highway 190 heading east off U.S. 395; from I–15 in the Eastern Mojave, take Highway 127 north to Highway 178 west.

Monterey Bay

Monterey Bay forms a crescent that begins near Santa Cruz to the north and ends near Carmel to the south. Highway 1 follows this crescent; U.S. 101 travels inland a bit; and Highway 68 and Highway 156 connect U.S. 101 and Highway 1. The Monterey Bay area is steeped in history: Monterey was California's first capital, and the Carmel Mission was the headquarters for California's entire 18th-century mission system.

The North Coast

Migrating whales and other sea mammals swim past the dramatic bluffs that make the 400 miles of shoreline north of San Francisco to the Oregon state line among the most photographed landscapes in the country. Redwood-studded Highway 1 travels close to the coast; U.S. 101 parallels the highway inland a bit. The main attractions along the coast are Muir Woods National Monument and the Point Reyes National Seashore, both in Marin County; Bodega Bay and Fort Ross, along the Sonoma County coast; Mendocino and Fort Bragg, in Mendocino County; and the redwood country from Humboldt County north to Crescent City.

Palm Springs Desert Resorts

Palm Springs and its neighbors—Palm Desert, Rancho Mirage, Indian Wells—lure visitors and residents for the same reasons: striking scenery and the therapeutic benefits of a warm, arid climate. The drive to the region from Los Angeles takes about two hours via I–10 to Highway 111 east. From San Diego, I–15 connects with the Pomona Freeway (Highway 60), leading to I–10.

Sacramento and the Gold Country

California's capital, Sacramento, is 87 miles northeast of San Francisco on I–80, which continues into the northern part of the Gold Country—the site of the famed gold rush of 1849—in the Sierra Nevada foothills. Highway 49 travels north–south through the Gold Country, passing through old mining towns and several state parks, among them Marshall Gold Discovery State Historic Park, where John Marshall discovered the gold nugget that inspired thousands of people to head west.

San Diego

It's a straight shot 124 miles south on I–5 from Los Angeles to sunny, friendly San Diego, which is 18 miles north of Tijuana, Mexico, via I–5 or I–805. The first of California's 21 Spanish missions was established in San Diego in 1769, and the city's links to its Spanish past remain strong. With more than 1 million people living within the city limits, San Diego is California's second-largest city and the sixth-largest municipality in the United States. San Diego County, which encompasses the city, covers a vast area, extending from the coast to mile-high mountains east of I–15 off Highways 78 and 79 and to a point near sea level further east in the desert.

San Francisco

Interstate 80 ends its westward jaunt across the United States in the country's most popular tourist destination, San Francisco. The graceful Golden Gate Bridge (U.S. 101) provides access from the north, and U.S. 101 and I–280 enter the city from the south. A sophisticated city with world-class hotels and the greatest concentration of excellent restaurants in the state, San Francisco has an undeserved reputation as the kook capital of the United States. So why do people come here in such numbers? To use the vernacular, the vibe here is cool, from North Beach coffeehouses to Chinatown tea emporiums, Golden Gate Park, and Haight Street's head shops (yes, they're still around).

The San Joaquin Valley

The San Joaquin Valley, one of the world's most fertile agricultural zones, is California's heartland. Interstate 5 runs north-south through the region, but the more scenic route is Highway 99, which runs more or less parallel to the east. This sunbaked region, whose anchors are Stockton in the north and Bakersfield 226 miles to the south, contains a wealth of rivers, lakes, and waterways; the water, in turn, nurtures vineyards, dairy farms, orchards, fields, and pastures that stretch to the horizon.

The Sierra National Parks

The highlight for many California travelers is a visit to one of the national parks in the Sierra Nevada range. Yosemite Valley is 214 miles southeast of San Francisco on I–80 to I–580 to I–205 to Highway 120; it's 330 miles northeast of Los Angeles on I–5 to Highway 99 to Highway 41. Grant Grove in Kings Canyon National Park is about 150 miles south of Yosemite Valley on Highway 41 to Highway 180. In summer and early fall (or whenever snows aren't blocking the Tioga Pass) you can continue east from Yosemite National Park on Highway 120 to see the tufa towers of Mono Lake. The Mammoth Lakes area, with skiing in winter and many outdoor sports in summer, is south of Mono Lake on U.S. 395.

The Wine Country

The Wine Country north of San Francisco is one of California's most popular tourist regions. The Napa and Sonoma valleys, the two most well-known grape-growing areas, can be easily accessed from the city by heading across the Golden Gate Bridge on U.S. 101, east on Highway 37 and north on Highway 121. Highway 121 travels through the Carneros region, which straddles southern Sonoma and Napa counties. Highway 12 heads northwest from Highway 121 through the Sonoma Valley; Highway 29 heads northwest from Highway 121 through the Napa Valley.

PLEASURES AND PASTIMES

Beaches

With 1,264 miles of coastline, California is well supplied with beaches. You can walk, lie, and sun on them, watch seabirds and hunt for shells, dig clams, or spot seals and sea otters at play. From December through March you can witness the migrations of the gray whales. What you can't always do at these beaches is swim. From San Francisco northward the water is too cold for all but the hardiest souls. Even along the southern half of the coast some beaches are too dangerous for swimming because of the undertow. Look for signs and postings and take them seriously.

Access to beaches in California is generally excellent. The state park system includes many fine beaches, and ocean-side communities maintain public beaches. Through the work of the California Coastal Commission, many stretches of private property that would otherwise seal off a beach from outsiders have public-access paths.

Dining

California's name has come to signify a certain type of healthful, sophisticated cuisine made from local ingredients, creatively combined and served in often stunning presentations. San Francisco and Los Angeles contain top-notch restaurants—an expensive meal at one of these gourmet shrines is often the high point of a trip to California. The Wine Country north of San Francisco is also known for superb restaurants, as is the city of Santa Barbara. In coastal areas, most menus usually include some seafood, fresh off the boat. Don't neglect the state's many ethnic eateries—among them Mexican, Chinese, Japanese, Scandinavian, Italian, French, Belgian, Vietnamese, English, Thai, and German.

Fishing

California has abundant fishing options: deep-sea, surf, and freshwater. *See* Sports *in* the Gold Guide to learn how to obtain the necessary license.

Golf

Golf is a year-round sport in California. Pebble Beach and the Palm Springs desert resorts have the most famous links, but there are championship courses all over the state. *See* Outdoor Activities and Sports in each chapter for listings of area courses.

Hot-Air Ballooning

Large, colorful balloons drift across the valleys of the Wine Country, where the air drafts are particularly friendly to this pastime, as well as in San Diego, the Palm Springs area, and the Gold Country. Hot-air ballooning is not cheap, however: a ride costs in excess of $100. *See* Tour Operators *in* the Gold Guide and the Outdoor Activities and Sports sections of each

chapter for listings of companies that operate in the state.

Parks

NATIONAL PARKS➤ There are eight national parks in California: Death Valley, Joshua Tree, Lassen Volcanic, Redwood, Sequoia, Kings Canyon, Yosemite, and the Channel Islands. National monuments include Cabrillo, in San Diego, and Muir Woods, north of San Francisco.

California has three national recreation areas: Golden Gate, with 87,000 acres both north and south of the Golden Gate Bridge in San Francisco; the Santa Monica Mountains, with 150,000 acres from Griffith Park in Los Angeles to Point Mugu in Ventura County; and Whiskeytown-Shasta-Trinity, with 240,000 acres, including four major lakes, in the Far North. The Point Reyes National Seashore is on a peninsula north of San Francisco.

STATE PARKS➤ California's state park system includes more than 200 sites; many are recreational and scenic, others historic or scientific. Among the most popular are Angel Island in San Francisco Bay, reached by ferry from San Francisco or Tiburon; Anza-Borrego Desert, 600,000 acres northeast of San Diego; Humboldt Redwoods, with its tall trees; Empire Mine, one of the richest mines in the Mother Lode, in Grass Valley; Hearst Castle at San Simeon; and Leo Carrillo Beach, north of Malibu, with lively tidal pools and numerous secret coves. Most state parks are open year-round.

Skiing

Snow skiing in the Lake Tahoe area and elsewhere is generally limited to the period between Thanksgiving and late April, though in years of heavy snowfall skiers can hit some trails as late as July. Other ski options include Mount Shasta and Lassen Volcanic National Park in the Far North; Mammoth Lake and the San Bernardino Mountains in southern California; and Badger Pass in Yosemite National Park.

Water Sports

Swimming and surfing, scuba diving, and skin diving in the Pacific Ocean are year-round pleasures in the southern part of the state, although these become seasonal sports on the coast from San Francisco northward. Sailboats are available for rent in many places along the coast and inland. River rafting—white-water and otherwise—canoeing, and kayaking are popular, especially in the northern part of the state.

Wine Tasting

You can visit wineries in many parts of the state, not only in the Wine Country of the Sonoma and Napa valleys. Vintners associations in the Gold Country, Santa Barbara, Santa Cruz, and other wine-growing areas provide brochures (*see* individual chapters for details) with lists of wineries that have tastings. Wineries and good wine stores will package your purchases for safe travel or shipping.

FODOR'S CHOICE

No two people will agree on what makes a perfect vacation, but it can be helpful to know what others think. Below is a list of Fodor's Choices. We hope you'll have a chance to experience some of them yourself while visiting California. We have tried to include something for everyone and from every price category. For more detailed information about each entry, refer to the appropriate chapters within this guidebook.

Breathtaking Sights

★ **El Capitan and Half Dome, Yosemite National Park.** Yosemite's two most famous peaks are also its most photographed.

★ **View from Emerald Bay Lookout, Lake Tahoe.** This aquatic cul-de-sac is famed for its jewel-like shape and colors.

★ **Golden Gate Bridge Vista Point and Marin Headlands, Marin County.** On a clear day, San Francisco glistens from this vantage point at the bridge's north end.

★ **Huntington Library, Art Gallery, and Gardens, Pasadena.** The botanical splendors here include the 12-acre Desert Garden and 1,500 varieties of camellias.

★ **La Jolla Cove at sunset.** It's beautiful any time of day, but as the sun goes down over the cove and its towering palms, the view is a postcard come to life.

Historic Buildings

★ **Coit Tower, San Francisco.** The 1930s murals at this monument to its city's vol-unteer firefighters are as striking as the view.

★ **Lachryma Montis (General Vallejo's Home), Sonoma.** The last Mexican governor of California built this large Victorian Gothic house with a white marble fireplace in every room.

★ **Griffith Park Observatory and Planetarium, Los Angeles.** One of the largest telescopes in the world is open to the public for free viewing every clear night. In the planetarium—immortalized in *Rebel Without a Cause*—dazzling daily shows duplicate the starry sky.

★ **Hearst Castle, San Simeon.** The renowned attraction, formerly a playground for the rich and famous, sits in solitary splendor on the 127 acres that were the heart of newspaper magnate William Randolph Hearst's 250,000-acre ranch.

★ **Hotel Del Coronado, San Diego.** Coronado's most prominent landmark was the world's first electrically lighted hotel.

★ **Mann's Chinese Theater, Hollywood.** The architecture of the former "Grauman's Chinese" is a fantasy of pagodas and temples. Its courtyard is open for browsing of celebrity hand- and footprints in the cement.

★ **Mission Santa Barbara.** The "queen" of the chain of 21 Spanish missions established in California is still active as a Catholic church.

★ **State Capitol, Sacramento.** The lacy plasterwork of the rotunda of this 1869 structure has all the complexity and color of a Fabergé egg. Outside, the 40-acre Capitol Park is one of the oldest gardens in the state.

Scenic Drives

★ **17-Mile Drive, Carmel.** The wonders are both man-made and natural as this road winds its way through Carmel and Pebble Beach.

★ **Highway 1 from Big Sur to San Simeon.** The twisting section of coastal highway affords some breathtaking ocean vistas before arriving at Hearst Castle.

★ **Highway 49, the Gold Country.** California's pioneer past comes to life in the many towns along this 325-mile highway at the base of the Sierra foothills.

★ **Kings Canyon Highway.** During the summer the stretch of Highway 180 in

Kings Canyon National Park from Grant Grove to Cedar Grove is spectacular.

★ **Mulholland Drive, Los Angeles.** One of the most famous thoroughfares in Los Angeles winds through the Hollywood Hills and across the spine of the Santa Monica Mountains, stopping just short of the Pacific Ocean.

Restaurants with Fabulous Atmosphere

★ **Jardiniere, San Francisco.** One of the city's most talked-about restaurants since its opening in 1997 has become a serious pre-performance event for symphony, opera, and theatergoers. $$$

★ **George's at the Cove, La Jolla.** A wall-length window in the elegant main dining room, renowned for its fresh seafood specials, overlooks the cove. $$–$$$

★ **Granita, Malibu.** Wolfgang Puck's coastal outpost has striking interior details and a menu that favors seafood, along with the chef's signature California-inspired dishes. $$–$$$

★ **Greens at Fort Mason, San Francisco.** The expansive bay views alone would be worth a visit to this airy restaurant. The bonus: a wide, eclectic, and creative spectrum of meatless cooking. $$–$$$

★ **Café Beaujolais, Mendocino.** All the rustic charm of peaceful, backwoods Mendocino is here, with great country cooking to boot. $$

★ **Montrio, Monterey.** If you like hearty cooking and clean, strong flavors, this European-inspired American bistro, a montage of brick, rawhide, and wrought iron, is the place to go. $$

★ **Samoa Cookhouse, Samoa (near Eureka).** Get a feel for dining during the heyday of the North Coast logging industry at this lumberman's hangout, which dates back to the late 19th century. $

Lodging

★ **Château du Sureau, Oakhurst.** The romantic château is a fairy-tale castle. With Erna's Elderberry House restaurant, one of California's best, right on the premises, you may find it hard to tear yourself away to visit nearby Yosemite National Park. $$$$

★ **Hotel Bel-Air, Los Angeles.** This secluded celebrity mecca's exotic gardens and creek (complete with swans) make for a resortlike ambience right in the city. $$$$

★ **Post Ranch Inn, Big Sur.** This luxurious retreat is the ultimate in environmentally conscious architecture. Each unit has its own hot tub, stereo, private deck, and massage table. $$$$

★ **Ritz-Carton Hotel, Laguna Niguel.** The classiest hotel along the coast, the Ritz draws guests from around the world with its antiques, gleaming marble, and ocean views. $$$$

★ **Sherman House, San Francisco.** The words "crème de la crème" best describe this French-Italianate mansion in Pacific Heights with a sumptuous Old World feel. $$$$

★ **Hotel Monaco, San Francisco.** With an impish postmodern design, the Monaco has snappy-looking public areas and comfortable rooms. $$$

★ **The Lodge at Torrey Pines, La Jolla.** This inn commands a view of miles of coastline. It's adjacent to a public golf course, a state beach, and a nature reserve. $$

BOOKS AND VIDEOS

San Francisco

BOOKS> Many novels are set in San Francisco, but none come better than *The Maltese Falcon,* by Dashiell Hammett, the founder of the hard-boiled school of detective fiction. *The Barbary Coast: An Informal History of the San Francisco Underworld,* published in 1933 and still in print, is Herbert Asbury's searing look at life in what really was a wicked city before the turn of the century. Another standout is Vikram Seth's *Golden Gate,* a novel in verse about life in San Francisco and Marin County in the early '80s. Others are John Gregory Dunne's *The Red White and Blue* and Alice Adams's *Rich Rewards.*

Two books that are filled with interesting background information on the city are Richard H. Dillon's *San Francisco: Adventurers and Visionaries* and *San Francisco: As It Is, As It Was,* by Paul C. Johnson and Richard Reinhardt.

Armistead Maupin's soap-opera-style *Tales of the City* stories are set in San Francisco; they were made into a successful 1993 PBS series; a sequel screened on Showtime in 1998.

VIDEOS➤ *San Francisco,* starring Clark Gable and Jeanette MacDonald, re-creates the 1906 earthquake with outstanding special effects. In *Escape from Alcatraz,* Clint Eastwood plays the prisoner who allegedly escaped from the famous jail on a rock in the San Francisco Bay. *The Times of Harvey Milk,* about San Francisco's first openly gay elected official, won the Academy Award for best documentary feature in 1984. Alfred Hitchcock immortalized Mission Dolores and the Golden Gate Bridge in *Vertigo,* the eerie story of a detective with a fear of heights, starring Jimmy Stewart and Kim Novak. A few other noteworthy films shot in San Francisco are *Dark Passage,* with Humphrey Bogart; the 1978 remake of *Invasion of the Body Snatchers;* and the 1993 comedy *Mrs. Doubtfire,* starring Robin Williams.

Los Angeles

BOOKS➤ *Los Angeles: The Enormous Village, 1781–1981,* by John D. Weaver, and *Los Angeles: Biography of a City,* by John and LaRee Caughey, will give you a fine background in how Los Angeles came to be the city it is today. The unique social and cultural life of the whole southern California area is explored in *Southern California: An Island on the Land,* by Carey McWilliams.

One of the most outstanding features of Los Angeles is its architecture. *Los Angeles: The Architecture of Four Ecologies,* by Reyner Banham, relates the physical environment to the architecture. *Architecture in Los Angeles: A Compleat Guide,* by David Gebhard and Robert Winter, is exactly what the title promises and is very useful.

Many novels have been written with Los Angeles as the setting. One of the very best, Nathanael West's *Day of the Locust,* was first published in 1939 but still rings true. Budd Schulberg's *What Makes Sammy Run?,* Evelyn Waugh's *The Loved One,* and Joan Didion's *Play It As It Lays* are unforgettable. Other novels that give a sense of contemporary life in Los Angeles are *Sex and Rage,* by Eve Babitz, and *Less Than*

Zero, by Bret Easton Ellis. Raymond Chandler and Ross Macdonald have written many suspense novels with a Los Angeles background.

VIDEOS AND TV➤ *Day of the Locust* and *Play It As It Lays* were made into two of the grimmer cinematic looks at life in Los Angeles. Billy Wilder's *Sunset Boulevard* is a classic portrait of a faded star and her attempt to recapture past glory. Roman Polanski's *Chinatown,* arguably one of the best American films ever made, is a fictional account of the wheeling and dealing that helped make L.A. what it is today. Southern California's varied urban and rural landscapes are used to great effect (as is an all-star cast that includes Ethel Merman and Spencer Tracy) in Stanley Kramer's manic *It's a Mad, Mad, Mad, Mad World.*

San Diego

BOOKS➤ There is no better way to establish the mood for your visit to Old Town San Diego than by reading Helen Hunt Jackson's 19th-century romantic novel, *Ramona,* a steady seller for decades and still in print. The Casa de Estudillo in Old Town has been known for many years as Ramona's Marriage Place because of its close resemblance to the house described in the novel. Richard Henry Dana Jr.'s *Two Years Before the Mast* (1869), based on the author's experiences as a merchant sailor, provides a masculine perspective on early San Diego history.

Other novels with a San Diego setting include Raymond Chandler's mystery about the waterfront, *Playback;* Wade Miller's mystery, *On Easy Street;* Eric Higgs's gothic thriller, *A Happy Man;* Tom Wolfe's satire of the La Jolla surfing scene, *The Pump House Gang;* and David Zielinski's modern-day story, *A Genuine Monster.*

VIDEOS AND TV➤ Filmmakers have taken advantage of San Diego's diverse and amiable climate since the dawn of cinema. Westerns, comedy-westerns, and tales of the sea were early staples: *Cupid in Chaps, The Sagebrush Phrenologist* (how's that for a title?), the 1914 version of *The Virginian,* and Lon Chaney's *Tell It to the Marines* were among the silent films shot in the area. Easy-to-capture outdoor locales have lured many productions south from Hollywood over the years, including the following military-oriented talkies, all or part of which were shot in San Diego: James Cagney's *Here Comes the Navy* (1934), Errol Flynn's *Dive Bomber* (1941), John Wayne's *The Sands of Iwo Jima* (1949), Ronald Reagan's *Hellcats of the Navy* (1956, costarring Nancy Davis, the future First Lady), Rock Hudson's *Ice Station Zebra* (1967), Tom Cruise's *Top Gun* (1986), Sean Connery's *Hunt for Red October,* Charlie Sheen's *Navy Seals* (1990), and Danny Glover's *Flight of the Intruder* (1991). Rob Lowe did not make his infamous home videos here, but he did shoot some of *Desert Shield* (1991).

In a lighter military vein, the famous talking mule hit the high seas in *Francis Joins the Navy* (1955), in which a very young Clint Eastwood has a bit part. The Tom Hanks—Darryl Hannah hit *Splash* (1984), *Spaceballs* (1987), *Hot Shots* (1991), *Wayne's World II* (1993), and Ellen Degeneres's *Mr. Wrong* (1996) are more recent comedies with scenes filmed here. One of the best comedies ever made, director Billy Wilder's *Some Like It Hot*—starring Marilyn Monroe, Jack Lemmon, and Tony Curtis—takes place at the Hotel Del Coronado (standing in for a Miami resort).

The amusingly low-budget *Attack of the Killer Tomatoes* (1976) makes good use of local scenery. The producers must have liked what they found in town as they returned for three sequels: *Return of the Killer Tomatoes* (1988), *Killer Tomatoes Strike Back* (1990), and—proving just how versatile the region is as a film location—*Killer Tomatoes Go to France* (1991). Unlike many films in which San Diego itself doesn't figure in the plot, the screen version of Helen Hunt Jackson's novel *Ramona* (1936), starring Loretta Young as the title character, incorporated historical settings or replicas.

Television producers zip south for series and made-for-TV movies all the time. The alteration of San Diego's skyline in the 1980s was partially documented on the hit show *Simon & Simon.* San Diego is virtually awash in syndicated productions: *Silk Stalkings, Baywatch, High Tide,* and *Renegade* are among the shows that have been shot here. Reality and cop shows love the area, too: *Unsolved Mysteries, Rescue 911, America's Missing Children, Totally Hidden Video, America's Most Wanted,* and *America's Funniest People* have all taped in San Diego, making it one of the most-seen—yet often uncredited—locales in movie and videoland.

Around the State

BOOKS➤ John Steinbeck immortalized the Monterey-Salinas area in numerous books, including *Cannery Row* and *East of Eden.* Joan Didion captured the heat—solar, political, and otherwise—of the Sacramento Delta area in *Run River.* Mark Twain's *Roughing It* and Bret Harte's *The Luck of Roaring Camp* evoke life during the gold rush. For a window on the past and present of the Central Valley, see *Highway 99: A Literary Journey Through California's Great Central Valley,* edited by Stan Yogi.

VIDEOS AND TV➤ Steinbeck's *East of Eden* was a hit film starring James Dean and later a television movie. Buster Keaton's masterpiece *Steamboat Bill, Jr.* was shot in Sacramento. The cult favorite *Harold and Maude* takes place in the San Francisco Bay Area. The exteriors in Alfred Hitchcock's *Shadow of a Doubt* were shot in Santa Rosa, and his ultracreepy *The Birds* was shot in Bodega Bay, along the North Coast. *Shack Out on 101* is a loopy 1950s beware-the-Commies caper also set on the California coast.

Erich von Stroheim used a number of northern California locations for his films: *Greed* takes place in San Francisco but includes excursions to Oakland and other points in the East Bay. Carmel is one of the locations for his *Foolish Wives.* The various Star Trek movies and Michelangelo Antonioni's *Zabriskie Point* are among the features that have made use of the eastern desert region. Initial footage of Sam Peckinpah's western *Ride the High Country* was shot in the Sierra Nevada mountains before his studio yanked him back to southern California, where he blended the original shots with ones of the Santa Monica Mountains and the Hollywood Hills.

FESTIVALS AND SEASONAL EVENTS

WINTER

➤ JANUARY: Palo Alto's annual **East-West Shrine All-Star Football Classic** (☎ 415/661–0291) is America's oldest all-star sports event. In Pasadena, the annual **Tournament of Roses Parade and Football Game** (☎ 626/449–7673) takes place on New Year's Day, with lavish flower-decked floats, marching bands, and equestrian teams, followed by the Rose Bowl game.

➤ FEBRUARY: The legendary **AT&T Pebble Beach National Pro-Am** golf tournament (☎ 831/649–1533) begins in late January and ends in early February. San Francisco's Chinatown is the scene of parades and noisy fireworks, all part of a several-day **Chinese New Year Celebration** (☎ 415/982–3000). Los Angeles also has a **Chinese New Year Parade** (☎ 213/617–0396). Indio's **Riverside County Fair and National Date Festival** (☎ 800/811–3247) is an exotic event with an Arabian Nights theme; camel and ostrich races, date exhibits, and tastings are among the draws.

SPRING

➤ MARCH: **Snowfest** in North Lake Tahoe (☎ 530/583–7625) is the largest winter carnival in the West, with skiing, food, fireworks, parades, and live music. The finest female golfers in the world compete for the richest purse on the LPGA circuit at the **Nabisco Dinah Shore Golf Tournament** in Rancho Mirage (☎ 760/324–4546). The **Mendocino/Fort Bragg Whale Festival** (☎ 800/726–2780) includes whale-watching excursions, marine art exhibits, wine and beer tastings, crafts displays, and a chowder contest.

➤ APRIL: The **Cherry Blossom Festival** (☎ 415/563–2313), an elaborate presentation of Japanese culture and customs, winds up with a colorful parade through San Francisco's Japantown. The **Toyota Grand Prix** (☎ 562/436–9953) in Long Beach, the largest street race in North America, draws top competitors from all over the world.➤ MAY: Thousands sign up to run the **San Francisco Examiner Bay to Breakers Race** (☎ 415/777–7770), a 7½-mile route from bay side to ocean side that's a hallowed San Francisco tradition. Inspired by Mark Twain's story "The Notorious Jumping Frog of Calaveras County," the **Jumping Frog Jubilee** in Angels Camp (☎ 209/736–2561) is for frogs and trainers who take their competition seriously. Sacramento hosts the four-day **Sacramento Jazz Jubilee** (☎ 916/372–5277); the late-May event is the world's largest Dixieland festival, with 125 bands from around the world. In Monterey, the squirmy squid is the main attraction for the Memorial Day weekend **Great Monterey Squid Festival** (☎ 831/649–6544). You'll see squid-cleaning and -cooking demonstrations, taste treats, and enjoy the usual festival fare: entertainment, arts and crafts, and educational exhibits.

SUMMER

➤ JUNE: Starting in late May and running into early June is a national ceramics competition and exhibition called **Feats of Clay** in the Gold Country (☎ 916/645–9713). The **Summer Solstice Ride & Arts Celebration** (☎ 209/223–5145) boosts spirits with bicycle rides, walks, and hands-on arts-and-crafts workshops for adults and children in Plymouth. During the first weekend in June, Pasadena City Hall Plaza hosts the **Chalk It Up Festival.** Artists use the pavement as their canvas to create masterpieces that wash away when festivities have come to a close. There are also musical performances and exotic dining kiosks. The proceeds benefit arts and homeless organizations of the Light-Bringer Project (☎ 626/449–3689). The **Napa Valley Wine Auction** in St. Helena features open houses, a wine tasting, and an auction. Preregistration by April 1 is required (☎ 707/942–9775).

➤ JULY: During the **Carmel Bach Festival,** the works of Johann Sebastian Bach and 18th-century contemporaries are performed for three weeks; events include concerts, recitals, and seminars (☎ 831/624–1521). During the last full weekend in July, Gilroy, the self-styled Garlic Capital of the World, celebrates its smelly but delicious product with the **Gilroy Garlic Festival** (☎ 408/842–1625), featuring such unusual concoctions as garlic ice cream.

➤ AUGUST: The **Cabrillo Music Festival** in Santa Cruz (☎ 831/426–6966), one of the longest-running contemporary orchestral festivals, brings in American and other composers for two weeks in early August. The **California State Fair** (☎ 916/263–3000) showcases the state's agricultural side, with high-tech exhibits, a rodeo, horse racing, a carnival, and big-name entertainment. It runs 18 days from August to Labor Day in Sacramento. Santa Barbara's **Old Spanish Days' Fiesta** (☎ 805/962–8101) is the nation's largest all-equestrian parade. The citywide celebration includes two parades, two Mexican

marketplaces, free variety shows with costumed dancers and singers, a carnival, and a rodeo.

AUTUMN

➤ SEPTEMBER: In Guerneville, jazz fans and musicians jam at Johnson's Beach for the **Russian River Jazz Festival** (☎ 707/869–3940). The **San Francisco Blues Festival** (☎ 415/826–6837) is held at Fort Mason in late September. The **Los Angeles County Fair** in Pomona (☎ 909/623–3111) is the largest county fair in the world. It hosts entertainment, exhibits, livestock, horse racing, food, and more.

➤ OCTOBER: The **Grand National Rodeo, Horse, and Stock Show** (☎ 415/469–6057) at San Francisco's Cow Palace is a 10-day, world-class competition. In Carmel, speakers and poets gather for readings on the beach, seminars, a banquet, and a book signing at the **Tor House Poetry Festival** (☎ 831/624–1813), which honors the late poet Robinson Jeffers, an area resident for many years.

➤ NOVEMBER: The **Death Valley '49er Encampment,** at Furnace Creek, commemorates the historic crossing of Death Valley in 1849, with a fiddlers' contest and an art show (☎ 760/786–2331). Pasadena's **Doo Dah Parade,** a fun-filled spoof of the annual Rose Parade, features the Lounge Lizards, who dress as reptiles and lip-synch to Frank Sinatra favorites, and West Hollywood cheerleaders in drag (☎ 626/449–3689).

➤ DECEMBER: For the **Newport Harbor Christmas Boat Parade** in Newport Beach (☎ 714/729–4400), more than 200 festooned boats glide through the harbor nightly December 17–23. In Columbia in early December, the **Miner's Christmas Celebration** features costumed carolers and children's piñatas. Related events include a Victorian Christmas feast at the City Hotel, lamplight tours, and **Las Posadas Nativity Procession** (☎ 209/536–1672). The internationally acclaimed **El Teatro Campesino** (☎ 831/623–2444) annually stages its nativity play *La Virgen Del Tepeyac* in the Mission San Juan Bautista.

2 The North Coast

*From Muir Beach
to Crescent City*

*Migrating whales and other sea
mammals swim past the dramatic
bluffs that make the 400 miles of
shoreline north of San Francisco to the
Oregon state line among the most
photographed landscapes in the
country. Along cypress- and redwood-
studded Highway 1 you will find many
small inns, uncrowded state beaches
and parks, art galleries, and restaurants
serving imaginative dishes that
showcase locally produced ingredients.*

BETWEEN SAN FRANCISCO BAY and the Oregon state line lies the aptly named Redwood Empire, where national, state, and local parks welcome visitors year-round. The shoreline's natural attributes are self-evident, but the area is also rich in human history, having been the successive domain of Native American Miwoks and Pomos, Russian fur traders, Hispanic settlers, and more contemporary fishing folk and loggers. All have left visible legacies. Only a handful of towns in this sparsely populated region have more than 1,000 inhabitants.

By Marty
Olmstead

Pleasures and Pastimes

Beaches

The waters of the Pacific Ocean along the North Coast are fine for seals, but most humans find the temperatures downright arctic. When it comes to spectacular cliffs and seascapes, though, the North Coast beaches are second to none. Explore tidal pools, watch for sea life, or dive for abalone. Don't worry about crowds: On many of these beaches you will have the sands largely to yourself.

Dining

Despite its small population, the North Coast lays claim to several well-regarded restaurants. Seafood is abundant, as are locally grown vegetables and herbs. In general, dining options are more varied near the coast than inland. Dress is usually informal, though dressy casual is the norm at some of the pricier establishments listed below.

CATEGORY	COST*
$$$$	over $50
$$$	$30–$50
$$	$20–$30
$	under $20

per person for a three-course meal, excluding drinks, service, and 7¼% tax

Fishing

Depending on the season, you can fish for rockfish, salmon, and steelhead in the rivers. Charters leave from Fort Bragg, Eureka, and elsewhere for ocean fishing. There's particularly good abalone diving around Jenner, Fort Ross, Point Arena, Westport, and Trinidad.

Lodging

Restored Victorians, rustic lodges, country inns, and chic new hotels are among the accommodations available along the North Coast. In several towns there are only one or two places to spend the night; some of these lodgings are destinations in themselves. Make summer and weekend B&B reservations as far ahead as possible—rooms at the best inns often sell out months in advance.

CATEGORY	COST*
$$$$	over $175
$$$	$120–$175
$$	$80–$120
$	under $80

All prices are for a standard double room, excluding 8%–10% tax.

Whale-Watching

From any number of excellent observation points along the coast, you can watch gray whales during their annual winter migration season or, in the summer and fall, blue or humpback whales. Another option is a whale-watching cruise (☞ Contacts and Resources *in* the North Coast A to Z, *below*).

Exploring the North Coast

Exploring the northern California coast is easiest by car. Highway 1 is a beautiful, if sometimes slow and nerve-racking, drive. You'll want to stop frequently to appreciate the views, and there are many portions of the highway along which you won't drive faster than 20–40 mph. You can still have a fine trip even if you don't have much time, but be realistic and don't plan to drive too far in one day. The itineraries below proceed north from San Francisco.

Numbers in the text correspond to numbers in the margin and on the North Coast maps.

Great Itineraries

IF YOU HAVE 3 DAYS

Some of the finest redwoods in California are found less than 20 mi north of San Francisco in **Muir Woods National Monument** ①. After walking through the woods, stop for an early lunch in **Inverness** (on Sir Francis Drake Boulevard, northwest from Highway 1) or continue on Highway 1 to **Fort Ross State Historic Park** ⑦, a reconstructed 19th-century Russian settlement. If you haven't eaten lunch, a deli-grocery store off Highway 1 sells picnic supplies. Catch the sunset and stay the night in ⊞ **Gualala.** On day two, drive to ⊞ **Mendocino** ⑨. Spend the next day and a half browsing the many galleries, shops, historic sites, and beaches and parks of this cliffside enclave. Return to San Francisco via Highway 1, or the quicker (3½ hours, versus up to 5) and less winding route of Highway 128 east (off Highway 1 at the Navarro River, 10 mi south of Mendocino) to U.S. 101 south.

IF YOU HAVE 7 DAYS

Early on your first day, walk through **Muir Woods** ①. Then visit **Stinson Beach** ② for a walk on the shore and lunch. In springtime and early summer head north on Highway 1 to Bolinas Lagoon, where you can see bird nestings at **Audubon Canyon Ranch** ③. At other times of the year (or after you've visited the ranch) continue north on Highway 1. One-third of a mile beyond **Olema,** look for a sign marking the turnoff for the **Bear Valley Visitor Center** ⑤, the gateway to the **Point Reyes National Seashore.** Tour the reconstructed Miwok Indian village that's near the visitor center. Spend the night in nearby ⊞ **Inverness** or one of the other coastal Marin towns. The next day, stop at **Goat Rock State Beach** and **Fort Ross State Historic Park** ⑦ on the way to ⊞ **Mendocino** ⑨. On your third morning, head to **Fort Bragg** for a visit to the **Mendocino Coast Botanical Gardens** and possibly a trip on the *Skunk Train.* If you're in the mood to splurge, drive inland on Highway 1 to U.S. 101 north and spend the night at the Benbow Inn in ⊞ **Garberville.** Otherwise, linger in the Mendocino area and drive inland the next morning. On day four continue north through parts of **Humboldt Redwoods State Park** ⑪, including the **Avenue of the Giants.** Stop for the night in the Victorian village of ⊞ **Ferndale** ⑫ and visit the cemetery and the **Ferndale Museum.** On day five drive to ⊞ **Eureka** ⑬. Have lunch in **Old Town,** visit the shops, and get a feel for local marine life on a Humboldt Bay cruise. Begin day six with breakfast at the **Samoa Cookhouse** before driving to **Patrick's Point State Park** ⑮. Have a late lunch overlooking the harbor in **Trinidad** before returning to Eureka for the night. Return to San Francisco on day seven. The drive back takes six hours on U.S. 101; it's nearly twice as long if you take Highway 1.

When to Tour the North Coast

The North Coast is a year-round destination, though when you go determines what you will see. The migration of the Pacific gray whales, for instance, is a wintertime phenomenon, roughly from mid-December to early April. In July and August, views are often obstructed by fog. The coastal climate is quite similar to San Francisco's, although winter nights are colder than in the city.

SOUTHERN COASTAL MARIN COUNTY
Muir Woods, Stinson Beach, and Bolinas

Much of the Marin County coastline is less than an hour away from San Francisco, but the pace is slower. Most of the sights in the southern coastal Marin area can easily be done as day trips from the city.

Muir Woods National Monument

★ ❶ *17 mi from San Francisco, north on U.S. 101 and west on Hwy. 1 (take Mill Valley/Stinson Beach exit off U.S. 101 and follow signs).*

The world's most popular grove of old-growth *Sequoia sempervirens* was one of the country's first national monuments. A number of easy hikes can be accomplished in an hour; there's even a short valley-floor trek, accessible to travelers with disabilities, that takes only 10 minutes to walk. The coast redwoods that grow here are mostly between 500 and 800 years old and as tall as 236 ft. Along Redwood Creek are other trees—live oak, madrone, and buckeye, as well as wildflowers (even in winter), ferns, and mushrooms. Parking is easier at Muir Woods before 10 AM and after 4 PM. ⊠ *Panoramic Hwy., off Hwy. 1,* ☎ *415/388–2595.* ☜ *$2.* ☉ *Daily 8 AM–sunset.*

OFF THE BEATEN PATH

MUIR BEACH – Small but scenic, this patch of shoreline 3 mi south of Muir Woods off Highway 1 is a good place to stretch your legs and gaze out at the Pacific.

Dining and Lodging

$$$–$$$$
★
✕⌂ **Pelican Inn.** This atmospheric Tudor-style B&B is a five-minute walk from Muir Beach. Rooms have Oriental rugs, English prints, velvet draperies, hanging tapestries, and half-tester beds. Even the bathrooms are special, with Victorian-style hardware and hand-painted tiles in the shower. Locals and tourists compete at darts in the ground-floor pub, which has a wide selection of brews, sherries, and ports. The Pelican's restaurant ($$–$$$; closed on Monday from January to March) serves sturdy English fare, from fish-and-chips to prime rib and Yorkshire pudding. ⊠ *10 Pacific Way, at Hwy. 1, 94965,* ☎ *415/383–6000,* ⅢΧ *415/383–3424. 7 rooms. Restaurant. Full breakfast. MC, V.*

Stinson Beach

❷ *8 mi from Muir Woods National Monument via Panoramic Hwy.; 25 mi from San Francisco, U.S. 101 to Hwy. 1.*

Stinson Beach has the most expansive sands in Marin County; it's as close (when the fog hasn't rolled in) as you'll get to the stereotypical feel of a southern California beach. On any hot summer weekend every road to Stinson Beach is jam-packed, so factor this into your plans.

Dining and Lodging

$–$$
✕ **Sand Dollar.** This pleasant pub serves hamburgers and other sandwiches for lunch and decent seafood for dinner; there's an outdoor dining deck. ⊠ *Hwy. 1,* ☎ *415/868–0434. AE, D, MC, V.*

$–$$
✕ **Stinson Beach Grill.** A great selection of beer and wine, art on the walls, and outdoor seating on a heated deck are among the draws here, but the food is memorable, too. Seafood, including several types of oys-

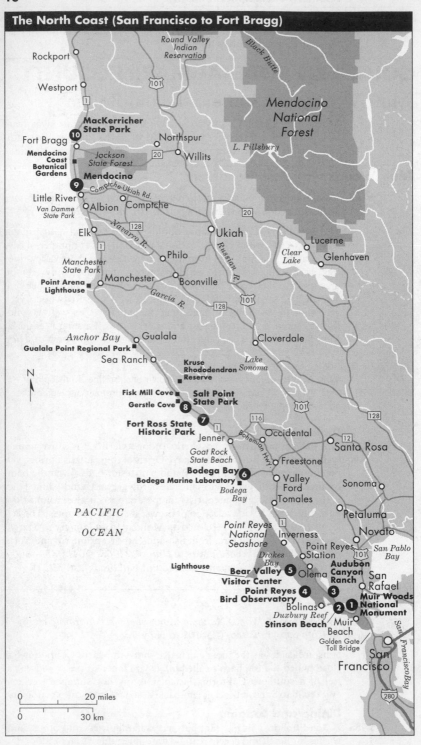

The North Coast (San Francisco to Fort Bragg)

Rockport

Westport

MacKerricher State Park

Fort Bragg ⑩

Mendocino Coast Botanical Gardens

Northspur

Jackson State Forest

Willits

Mendocino ⑨

Comptche-Ukiah Rd.

Little River

Albion   Comptche

Van Damme State Park

Elk

Navarro R.

Philo

Ukiah

Lucerne

Clear Lake

Glenhaven

Manchester State Park

Manchester   Boonville

Point Arena Lighthouse

Garcia R.

Round Valley Indian Reservation

Black Butte

Mendocino National Forest

L. Pillsbury

Russian R.

Cloverdale

Anchor Bay   Gualala

Gualala Point Regional Park

Sea Ranch

Kruse Rhododendron Reserve

Lake Sonoma

Fisk Mill Cove   **Salt Point State Park**

Gerstle Cove ⑧

Fort Ross State Historic Park ⑦

Jenner   Occidental

Goat Rock State Beach

Bohemian Hwy.

Freestone

Santa Rosa

Bodega Bay ⑥

Bodega Marine Laboratory

Bodega Bay

Valley Ford   Sonoma

Tomales

Petaluma

N

PACIFIC OCEAN

Point Reyes National Seashore

Inverness

Novato

Drakes Bay

Point Reyes Station

San Pablo Bay

Lighthouse

Bear Valley Visitor Center ⑤

Olema

Audubon Canyon Ranch

Point Reyes Bird Observatory ④

③

San Rafael

Bolinas   ②   ①

Muir Woods National Monument

Duxbury Reef

Stinson Beach

Muir Beach

Golden Gate Toll Bridge

San Francisco

San Francisco Bay

0   20 miles

0   30 km

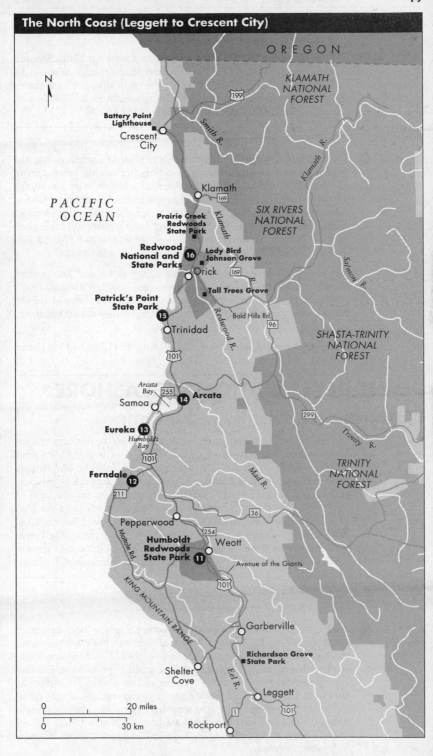

OREGON

KLAMATH NATIONAL FOREST

199

Smith R.

Klamath R.

Battery Point Lighthouse

Crescent City

PACIFIC OCEAN

Klamath
169

SIX RIVERS NATIONAL FOREST

Salmon R.

Prairie Creek Redwoods State Park

Redwood National and State Parks 16

Lady Bird Johnson Grove

Orick
169

Klamath R.

Tall Trees Grove

Patrick's Point State Park 15

Bald Hills Rd.
96

SHASTA-TRINITY NATIONAL FOREST

Trinidad

Redwood R.

101

Arcata Bay
255

14 **Arcata**

299

Trinity R.

Samoa

Eureka 13

Humboldt Bay

101

Mad R.

TRINITY NATIONAL FOREST

Ferndale 12
211

Pepperwood

Mattole Rd.

36

254

Weott

Humboldt Redwoods State Park 11

Avenue of the Giants

101

KING MOUNTAIN RANGE

Garberville

Richardson Grove State Park

Shelter Cove

Eel R.

Leggett

0   20 miles

0   30 km

Rockport
1
101

ters, is served at lunch and dinner; pasta, lamb, chicken, and south-western specialties are on the evening menu. ⊠ *3465 Hwy. 1,* ☎ *415/ 868–2002. AE, MC, V.*

$$$–$$$$ 🏨 **Casa del Mar.** One of the few places to hang your hat in Stinson, this Mediterranean-style inn has extensive landscaping and works by local artists. Accommodations are on the small side, but light colors and the many windows create a feeling of spaciousness. ⊠ *37 Belvedere Ave., 94970,* ☎ *415/868–2124. 5 rooms. AE, MC, V.*

Bolinas

❸   The **Audubon Canyon Ranch,** a 1,000-acre wildlife sanctuary along the Bolinas Lagoon, is open during courting and mating season, from mid-March to mid-July. Great blue herons and egrets are among the 60 species here. The egrets nest in the redwood trees in Schwarz Grove. Telescopes and bird-hide observation posts allow for easier viewing. A small museum surveys the geology and natural history of the region. ⊠ *4900 Hwy. 1, along Bolinas Lagoon,* ☎ *415/868–9244.* 🏷 *Donation requested.* ☉ *Mid-Mar.–mid-July, weekends 10–4.*

An unmarked road running west from Highway 1 about 2 mi beyond Audubon Canyon Ranch leads to the sleepy town of **Bolinas.** Don't expect a warm welcome: Some residents of Bolinas are so wary of tourism that whenever the state tries to post road signs, they take them down.

Nightlife
Smiley's Schooner Saloon (⊠ 41 Wharf Rd., ☎ 415/868–1311) hosts live music on Friday and Saturday.

POINT REYES NATIONAL SEASHORE
Duxbury Reef, Olema, and Inverness

The Point Reyes National Seashore, which borders the northern reaches of the Golden Gate National Recreation Area (☞ Chapter 5), is a great place for hiking to secluded beaches, viewing wildlife, and driving through rugged, rolling grasslands. Highlights include the ½-mi Earthquake Trail, which passes by what is believed to be the epicenter of the 1906 quake that destroyed much of San Francisco, and the late-19th-century Point Reyes Lighthouse, a good spot to watch for whales. Horses and mountain bikes are permitted on some trails. The towns of Olema, Point Reyes Station, and Inverness, all in or near the national seashore area, have dining, lodging, and recreational facilities.

Duxbury Reef Area
2 mi northwest of Bolinas off Mesa Rd.

❹   Birders love the **Point Reyes Bird Observatory,** a sanctuary and research center within the Point Reyes National Seashore but more easily accessible from Bolinas. The area harbors nearly 225 bird species; banding (for identification purposes) occurs, weather permitting, Tuesday through Sunday from May to November and on Wednesday and weekends from December to April. As you hike the trails, you're likely to see biologists banding the birds or measuring them. Trails pass waterfalls and a lake and lead to the national seashore. ⊠ *West on Mesa Rd. off Olema–Bolinas Rd.,* ☎ *415/868–0655.* 🏷 *Free.* ☉ *Visitor center daily sunrise–sunset.*

Mile-long **Duxbury Reef,** a nature preserve, is the largest shale intertidal reef in North America. Check a tide table if you plan to explore the reef, which is accessible only at low tide. Look for starfish, barnacles, sea anemones, purple urchins, limpets, sea mussels, and the occasional red and black abalone. ⊠ *From Bolinas, take Mesa Rd. off Olema–Bolinas Rd.; make left on Overlook Dr. and right on Elm Ave. to beach parking lot.*

Olema

9 mi from Bolinas on Hwy. 1.

★ ⑤ The Point Reyes National Seashore's **Bear Valley Visitor Center** has exhibits of park wildlife. The rangers here dispense advice about beaches, the Point Reyes Lighthouse, whale-watching, hiking trails, and camping. A reconstructed Miwok Indian village that is only a short walk from the visitor center provides insight into the daily lives of the region's first human inhabitants. ⊠ *Bear Valley Rd. west of Hwy. 1,* ☎ *415/663–1092.* 🎟 *Free.* ⊘ *Weekdays 9–5, weekends 8–5.*

Outdoor Activities and Sports

Many of the beaches in Point Reyes National Seashore are accessible off Bear Valley Road. **Limantour Beach** (⊠ End of Limantour Beach Rd.) is one of the most beautiful of Point Reyes sands; trails lead to other beaches north and south of here. **Trailhead Rentals** (⊠ 88 Bear Valley Rd., at Hwy. 1, ☎ 415/663–1958) supplies bicycles and binoculars. **Five Brooks Stables** (⊠ 8001 Hwy. 1, ☎ 415/663–1570) rents horses and equipment; from the stables, horseback trails wind through the Point Reyes woods and along the beaches.

Point Reyes Station

2 mi north of Olema on Hwy. 1.

The busiest place in Point Reyes Station, a stop on the North Pacific Coast Narrow-Gauge Railroad until 1933, is Toby's Feed Barn, which sells offbeat gifts (many festooned with cows) to tourists and locals and serious feed and grain to local farmers. There's a market on Main Street for picking up picnic supplies.

Lodging

$ 🏠 **Point Reyes Hostel.** These dorm-style lodgings in an old clapboard ranch house are a good deal for budget travelers. The family room is limited to families with children five and under and must be reserved well in advance. ⊠ *Off Limantour Rd., Box 247, 94956,* ☎ *415/663–8811. Shared kitchen. MC, V.*

Shopping

Gallery Route One (⊠ 11101 Hwy. 1, ☎ 415/663–1347), a nonprofit cooperative, shows the works of area artists in all media.

Inverness

4 mi from Point Reyes Station on Sir Francis Drake Blvd., northwest from Hwy. 1.

Inverness boomed after the 1906 earthquake when wealthy San Franciscans built summer homes in its hills. Today many of the structures serve as full-time residences or small B&B inns. A deli, a grocery store, restaurants, and shops are along Sir Francis Drake Boulevard.

The ★**Point Reyes Lighthouse Visitors Center** is a 45-minute drive from Inverness, across rolling hills that resemble Scottish heath. Parking near the lighthouse is difficult on weekends during summer. The view alone persuades most people to make the effort of walking down—and then back up—the hundreds of steps from the cliff-tops to the lighthouse below. ⊠ *Western end of Sir Francis Drake Blvd.,* ☎ *415/669–1534.* ☼ *Thurs.–Sun. 10–5 (steps close at 4:30).*

Dining and Lodging

$ ✕ **Grey Whale.** This casual place is a good stop for pizza, salad, pastries, and espresso. ⊠ *12781 Sir Francis Drake Blvd.,* ☎ *415/669–1244. MC, V.*

$$$ ✕⊡ **Manka's.** Three wood-panel dining rooms glowing with candlelight and piano music provide the setting for creative American cuisine. Specialties include line-caught fish, game such as caribou and pheasant that are grilled in the fireplace, and homemade desserts. Two of the four smallish guest rooms above the restaurant have private decks that look onto Tomales Bay. Rooms in the redwood annex and two cabins are also available. The restaurant, open for dinner only, is closed on Tuesday and Wednesday year-round and from Sunday to Thursday in January, February, and March. ⊠ *30 Calendar Way, 94937,* ☎ *415/669–1034. 14 rooms. Restaurant. Full breakfast. MC, V.*

$$$–$$$$ ⊡ **Blackthorne Inn.** A fantasy tree house, this imaginative structure is has as its centerpiece a 3,500-square-ft deck with stairways to higher decks. The solarium was made with timbers from San Francisco wharves; the outer walls are salvaged doors from a railway station. A glass-sheathed octagonal tower called the Eagle's Nest crowns the inn. ⊠ *266 Vallejo Ave., Box 712, Inverness Park 94937,* ☎ *415/663–8621. 5 rooms, 2 with shared bath. Hot tub. Full breakfast. MC, V.*

$$$–$$$$ ⊡ **Ten Inverness Way.** The living room of this low-key inn has a stone fireplace and a player piano. The cozy rooms contain homespun touches like patchwork quilts, lived in–looking antiques, and dormer ceilings with skylights. ⊠ *Inverness Way, Box 63, 94937,* ☎ *415/669–1648,* ℻ *415/669–7403. 5 rooms. Hot tub. Full breakfast. MC, V.*

Shopping

Shaker Shops West (⊠ 5 Inverness Way, ☎ 415/669–7256) carries fine reproduction Shaker furniture and gift items.

Valley Ford

23 mi north of Point Reyes Station on Hwy. 1.

Bird-watching is a favorite pastime in Valley Ford, where blue herons, egrets, hawks, and owls nest.

Lodging

$–$$ ⊡ **Inn at Valley Ford.** The rooms at this B&B, a Victorian farmhouse built in the late 1860s, are named after literary figures, characters, or periods. Books commemorating each chamber's theme grace the inn's bookshelves. The gourmet breakfast comes with old-fashioned cream scones. ⊠ *14395 Hwy. 1, Box 439, 94972,* ☎ *707/876–3182. 4 rooms with 2 shared baths, 1 cottage suite with private bath. Full breakfast. DC, MC, V.*

SONOMA AND MENDOCINO

Occidental and Bodega Bay to Fort Bragg

The gently rolling countryside of coastal Marin gives way to more dramatic scenery north of Bodega Bay. Cattle cling for their lives (or so it seems) to steep inclines alongside the increasingly curvy highway, now traveling right along the coast. Past Jenner, the road twists and turns; by the time it reaches Sea Ranch, hairpin curves and stunning vistas compete for drivers' attention.

Occidental

10 mi from Valley Ford, north on Hwy. 1, east on Hwy. 12 (Bodega Hwy.), and north on Bohemian Hwy.

A few miles south of the Russian River, surrounded by the redwood forests, orchards, and vineyards of western Sonoma County, Occidental is so small that you might drive right through the town and barely take notice. A 19th-century logging hub with a present-day bohemian feel, Occidental has a top-notch B&B, good eats, and a handful of art galleries and craft and clothing boutiques, all of which make the town an ideal base for day trips to Sonoma Coast beaches, Bodega Bay, Armstrong Redwoods Reserve, and Point Reyes National Seashore.

Dining and Lodging

$–$$ ✕ **Bohemian Cafe.** The name says it all: This is California free-to-be-you-and-me at its best. Colorful murals hang on the walls, and the crowd is mostly young and clad in tie-dyed togs. The main lunch and dinner staple is pizza with a decidedly unconventional twist: The Mediterranean has rock shrimp, spinach, roasted peppers, and apricots; the Bustelo is an even more outré combination of tomato, bell pepper, onion, chorizo, cumin, pineapple, hot sauce, honey, and Parmesan cheese. Rounding out the menu are unusual salads (one with strawberries, spinach, and walnuts), plus some more mainstream pastas and entrées. Breakfast is served daily. ⊠ *3688 Bohemian Hwy.,* ☎ *707/874–3931. Reservations not accepted. MC, V.*

$$–$$$$ 🛏 **The Inn at Occidental.** Innkeeper Jack Bullard is an insatiable col-
★ lector—every room showcases a collection of one sort or another. Antique English and Irish cut-glass jars, for instance, decorate the Cut Glass room, which has its own sunny garden and outdoor whirlpool tub. Antiques, quilts, and original artworks, including photographs taken by Jack, fill the rooms. A fireplace, fine Asian rugs, and antique clocks create a cozy but dignified mood in the ground-floor living room. Homemade granola and fresh-squeezed orange juice are served for breakfast, along with entrées like eggs Florentine or orange pancakes with Vermont maple syrup. ⊠ *3657 Church St., Box 857, 95465,* ☎ *707/ 874–1047 or 800/522–6324,* ℻ *707/874–1078. 5 rooms, 3 suites. AE, D, MC, V.*

OFF THE
BEATEN PATH

OSMOSIS ENZYME BATHS – The tiny town of Freestone, 3 mi south of Occidental and 7½ mi east of Bodega Bay off Highway 12 (Bodega Highway), has a few good shops, but the real reason to stop here is Osmosis Enzyme Baths. This spa, in a two-story clapboard house on extensive grounds, specializes in several treatments, including a detoxifying "dry" bath in a blend of enzymes and fragrant wood shavings. After 20 minutes in the tub, opt for a 75-minute massage in one of the freestanding Japanese-style pagodas near the creek that runs through the property. ⊠ *209 Bohemian Hwy., Freestone,* ☎ *707/823–8231.*

Bodega Bay

❻ *8 mi from Valley Ford on Hwy. 1; 65 mi north of San Francisco via U.S. 101 and Hwy. 1.*

Bodega Bay is one of the busiest harbors on the Sonoma County coast. Commercial boats pursue ocean fish as well as the famed Dungeness crabs. T-shirt shops and galleries line both sides of Highway 1; a short drive around the harbor leads to the Pacific. This is the last stop, townwise, before Gualala, and a good spot for stretching your legs and taking in the salt air. For a closer look, visit the **Bodega Marine Labo-**

ratory (☎ 707/875–2211 for directions), on a 326-acre reserve on nearby Bodega Head. The lab gives free one-hour tours and peeks at intertidal invertebrates, such as sea stars and sea anemones, on Friday from 2 to 3:45 PM.

Dining and Lodging

$$$$ ⊞ **Sonoma Coast Villa.** This secluded oasis in the coastal hills between Valley Ford and Bodega Bay is a most unusual inn. Founded as an Arabian horse ranch in 1976, the 60-acre property has a single-story row of accommodations beside a swimming pool. Red-tile roofs, a stucco exterior, Mediterranean-style landscaping, and two courtyards create a European ambience. Rooms are decorated individually, but all have slate floors, French doors, beamed ceilings, and wood-burning fireplaces. Massage treatments are available in a new spa building. The small restaurant ($$$) is open on weekends. ⊠ *16702 Hwy. 1, Bodega 94922,* ☎ *707/876–9818 or 888/404–2255,* ✆ *707/876–9856. 12 rooms. Restaurant, pool, hot tub. AE, MC, V.*

$$$–$$$$ ✕⊞ **Inn at the Tides.** The condominium-style buildings at this complex have spacious rooms with high ceilings and an uncluttered decor. All rooms have views of the harbor, and some have fireplaces. The inn's two restaurants ($$–$$$) serve both old-style and more adventurous seafood dishes; in season you can buy a slab of salmon or live or cooked crab at a seafood market on the premises. ⊠ *800 Hwy. 1, Box 640, 94923,* ☎ *707/875–2751 or 800/541–7788,* ✆ *707/875–2669. 86 rooms. 2 restaurants, bar, refrigerators, room service, pool, hot tub, sauna, coin laundry. Continental breakfast. AE, MC, V.*

Outdoor Activities and Sports

Bodega Bay Sportfishing (⊠ Bay Flat Rd., ☎ 707/875–3344) charters ocean-fishing boats and rents equipment. The operators of the 700-acre **Chanslor Guest Ranch** (⊠ 2660 Hwy. 1, ☎ 707/875–2721) lead guided horseback rides.

Shopping

The **Ren Brown Gallery** (⊠ 1781 Hwy. 1, ☎ 707/875–2922) in the north end of town is renowned for its selection of Asian arts, crafts, furnishings, and design books. This two-floor gallery also represents a number of local artists worth checking out.

Jenner

10 mi north of Bodega Bay on Hwy. 1.

The Russian River empties into the Pacific Ocean at Jenner. The town has a couple of good restaurants and some shops. South of the river is windy **Goat Rock State Beach,** where a colony of sea lions (walk north from the parking lot) resides most of the year. The beach is open daily from 8 AM to sunset; there's no day-use fee.

Dining

$$–$$$ ✕ **River's End.** At the right time of year, diners at this rustic restaurant
★   can view sea lions lazing on the beach below. The creative fare is eclectic/German—seafood, venison, and duck dishes. Brunch here is exceptional. ⊠ *Hwy. 1, north end of Jenner,* ☎ *707/865–2484. MC, V. Closed Jan.–mid-Feb. (hrs vary in the off season).*

Fort Ross State Historic Park

 ❼ *9 mi north of Jenner on Hwy. 1.*

Fort Ross, completed in 1821, became Russia's major fur-trading outpost in California. The Russians brought Aleut sea-otter hunters down from Alaska, but by 1841 the area was depleted of seals and otters, and the Russians sold their post to John Sutter, later of gold-rush fame. After a local Anglo rebellion against the Mexicans, the land fell under U.S. domain, becoming part of California in 1850. The state park service has reconstructed Fort Ross, including its Russian Orthodox chapel, a redwood stockade, the officers' barracks, and a blockhouse. The excellent museum here documents the history of the fort and some of the North Coast. ⊠ *Hwy. 1,* ☎ *707/847–3286.* ⊠ *$6 per vehicle (day use).* ⊘ *Daily 10–4:30. No dogs allowed past parking lot.*

Lodging

$$$$ 🏨 **Timberhill Ranch.** The winding country road south of Fort Ross that
★ leads east from Highway 1 to the Timberhill Ranch gives visitors enough time to ease into the restful pace of this secluded resort. Simple and serene, Timberhill has 15 cabins decorated with quilts and fresh flowers. Each cabin has a fireplace and a private patio where you can enjoy breakfast (it's delivered on a golf cart), perhaps sharing croissants with the resident ducks and geese. Timberhill's inspired six-course dinners (included, with breakfast, in the room rates) take place by candlelight. ⊠ *35755 Hauser Bridge Rd. (Timber Cove Post Office), 95421,* ☎ *707/847–3258,* ⅨX *707/847–3342. 15 cottages. Minibars, refrigerators, pool, outdoor hot tub, 2 tennis courts, hiking. MAP. AE, MC, V.*

$$–$$$$ 🏨 **Fort Ross Lodge.** The lodge, about 1½ mi north of the same-named fort, has a wind-bitten feel to it, but some of the rooms have views of the shoreline; others have private hot tubs. Six hill units have saunas, hot tubs, and fireplaces. ⊠ *20705 Hwy. 1, 95450,* ☎ *707/847–3333,* ⅨX *707/847–3330. 22 rooms. Refrigerators. AE, MC, V.*

Salt Point State Park

⑧ *11 mi north of Jenner on Hwy. 1.*

Salt Point State Park yields a glimpse of nature virtually untouched by humans. At the 6,000-acre park's **Gerstle Cove** you'll probably catch sight of seals sunning themselves on the beach's rocks and deer roaming in the meadowlands. The unusual formations in the sandstone are called tafoni and are the product of centuries of erosion. A very short drive leads to Fisk Mill Cove. A five-minute walk uphill brings you to a bench from which there is a dramatic overview of Sentinel Rock and the pounding surf below. ⊠ *Hwy. 1,* ☎ *707/847–3221; 800/444–7275 for camping information.* ⊠ *$5 per vehicle (day use). Camping $16. Fire rings, flush toilets, picnic areas, water.* ⊘ *Daily sunrise–sunset.*

Kruse Rhododendron Reserve, a peaceful, 317-acre forested park, has thousands of rhododendrons that bloom in light shade in the late spring. ⊠ *Hwy. 1, north of Fisk Mill Cove.* ⊠ *Free.*

Lodging

$ 🏨 **Stillwater Cove Ranch.** Seventeen miles north of Jenner, this former boys' school that overlooks Stillwater Cove has been transformed into a pleasant, if spartan, place to lodge. ⊠ *22555 Hwy. 1, 95450,* ☎ *707/ 847–3227. 6 rooms. No credit cards.*

Sea Ranch

18 mi from Fort Ross on Hwy. 1.

Sea Ranch is a development of stylish homes on 5,000 acres overlooking the Pacific. To appease critics the developers provided public beach-access trails off Highway 1 south of Gualala. Even some militant environmentalists deem the structures designed by architects William Turnbull and Charles Moore to be reasonably congruent with the surroundings; some folks find the weathered wood buildings beautiful.

Dining and Lodging

$$$–$$$$ ✕🖬 **Sea Ranch Lodge.** High on a bluff with ocean views, the lodge is close to beaches, trails, and golf. Some rooms have fireplaces, and some have hot tubs. Handcrafted wood furnishings and quilts create an earthy, contemporary look. The restaurant ($$–$$$), which overlooks the Pacific, serves good seafood and homemade desserts. ✉ *60 Sea Walk Dr., Box 44, 95497,* ☎ *707/785–2371 or 800/732–7262,* ℻ *707/785–2243. 20 rooms, 2 suites. Restaurant. AE, MC, V.*

$$–$$$$ 🖬 **Sea Ranch Escape.** The Sea Ranch houses, sparsely scattered on a grass meadow fronting a stretch of ocean, are a striking sight from Highway 1. Groups or families can rent fully furnished houses for two nights (minimum) or more. Linen, housekeeping, and catering services are available for a fee. You can dine at superb nearby restaurants or stock up on provisions from one of the markets in Gualala and make use of the full kitchens. All houses have TVs and VCRs; some have hot tubs; and some owners allow pets. The rates are most expensive for accommodations next to the surf; prices recede with distance from the beach. ✉ *60 Sea Walk Dr., Box 238, 95497,* ☎ *707/785–2426 or 800/732–7262,* ℻ *707/785–2124. 55 houses. In-room VCRs. MC, V.*

Gualala

11 mi north of Sea Ranch on Hwy. 1

This former lumber port remains a sleepy drive-through except for the several ocean-view motels that can serve as headquarters for visitors exploring the coast. The town lies north of the Gualala River (a good place for fishing), which serves as the county line for Mendocino. On the river's Sonoma side, **Gualala Point Regional Park** (✉ Hwy. 1, ☎ 707/785–2377), open daily from 8 AM until sunset, is an excellent whale-watching spot. The park has picnicking ($3 day-use fee) and camping ($15 per night). Campsites are available on a first-come, first-served basis and have fire rings, flush toilets, showers, and water but no hookups.

Dining and Lodging

$$–$$$$ ✕🖬 **St. Orres.** One of the North Coast's most eye-catching inns, St. Orres reflects the area's Russian influences. Crowned by two onion-dome towers, the main house is further accented by balconies, stained-glass windows, and wood-inlaid towers. Two rooms overlook the sea, and the other six are set over the garden or forest; all the rooms in the main house share baths. The tranquil woods behind the house hold 11 rustic cottages; eight have woodstoves or fireplaces. There's also a three-bedroom house. The inn's restaurant (closed on Wednesday in winter) serves dinner only, a fixed-price meal ($$$–$$$$) with a choice of five entrées (meat or fish) plus soup and salad. ✉ *Hwy. 1, 2 mi north of Gualala, Box 523, 95445,* ☎ *707/884–3303,* ℻ *707/884–3903. 8 rooms with shared baths, 11 cottages, 1 house. Restaurant, hot tub, sauna, beach. Full breakfast. MC, V.*

$$$–$$$$ 🖬 **Whale Watch Inn.** This fine inn lives up to its name—most rooms here have views (through cypress trees) down the coast, where whales often come close to shore on their northern migration in early spring. Year-round, the scent of pine and salt-sea air fills the rooms, all of which have fireplaces and small decks; some rooms have whirlpool baths or kitchens. A 132-step stairway leads down to a small, virtually private beach. Set amid 2½ acres, the Whale Watch maintains well-kept gardens that bloom even in winter. Breakfast is served in your room. ✉ *35100 Hwy. 1, 95445,* ☎ *707/884–3667 or 800/942–5342,* ℻ *707/884–4815. 13 rooms, 5 suites. Full breakfast. AE, MC, V.*

$$–$$$$ 🏨 **Old Milano Hotel.** Amid gardens and overlooking the coast north
★ of Gualala, the Old Milano, a 1905 mansion on the National Regis-
ter of Historic Places, is one of California's premier B&Bs. Exceptional
antiques decorate the rooms. Five of the upstairs rooms have ocean
views; all the upstairs rooms share bathrooms. The downstairs mas-
ter suite has a private sitting room and a picture window framing the
sea. Those in search of something different might consider the caboose
with a wood-burning stove or one of the new cottages that have fire-
places or whirlpool baths. Dinner, not included in the rates, is served
on weekends and most weeknights. ✉ *38300 Hwy. 1, 95445,* 🕿 *707/
884–3256. 13 rooms. Hot tub. MC, V. Full breakfast. No smoking.*

$ 🏨 **Gualala Hotel.** Gualala's oldest hotel, which once housed timber-
mill workers, has small, no-nonsense rooms furnished with well-worn
antiques. Most rooms share baths. Rooms in the front have ocean views
(and some street noise). The intensely atmospheric first-floor saloon
was an old Jack London haunt. ✉ *39301 Hwy. 1,* 🕿 *707/884–3441.
19 rooms, 5 with private bath. Restaurant, bar. AE, D, MC, V.*

En Route   For a dramatic view of the surf take the marked road off Highway 1
north of the fishing village of Point Arena to the **Point Arena Lighthouse**
(🕿 707/882–2777). First constructed in 1870, the lighthouse was de-
stroyed by the 1906 earthquake that also devastated San Francisco.
Rebuilt in 1907, it towers 115 ft from its base 50 ft above the sea. The
lighthouse is open for tours daily from 11 until 2:30, one hour later
in summer and on some holidays; admission is $2.50. As you continue
north on Highway 1 toward Mendocino there are several beaches, most
notably the one at **Manchester State Park,** 3 mi north of Point Arena.
If you're driving directly to Mendocino from points south and want
to grab a quick lunch or a good cup of coffee, visit the café at the **Green-
wood Pier Inn** (✉ 5928 Hwy. 1, 🕿 707/877–9997) in Elk.

Elk

39 mi north of Gualala on Hwy. 1.

Dining and Lodging

$$$$ ✗🏨 **Harbor House.** Constructed in 1916 by a timber company, this
redwood ranch-style house has a dining room with a view of the Pa-
cific. Five of the six rooms in the main house have fireplaces, and some
are furnished with antiques original to the house. There are also four
smallish cottages with fireplaces and decks. The room rates include break-
fast and dinner. The restaurant ($$; reservations essential), which
serves California cuisine, is highly recommended; there's limited seat-
ing for those not spending the night. ✉ *5600 S. Hwy. 1, 95432,* 🕿
707/877–3203. 10 rooms. Restaurant. MAP. No credit cards.

$$–$$$$ ✗🏨 **Elk Cove Inn.** The inn's private and very romantic rooms and suites
★ are perched on a bluff above the pounding surf. The plushest suites
are in a new stone and cedar shingle Arts and Crafts–style building;
furnishings are Stickley reproduction, and all units have wet bars, re-
frigerators, stereos, and fireplaces. The older accommodations range
from a viewless but smartly furnished small room to a huge ocean-view
suite with a stereo, a whirlpool tub, and a wet bar. All rooms have cof-
feemakers and hand-embroidered cloths; some rooms have wood-
burning stoves. The breakfast is a massive buffet. The dining room
($–$$), open from Monday to Wednesday, serves California cuisine
and bistro dishes like a salmon burger. The full bar is open daily. Ask
about off-season discount packages. ✉ *6300 S. Hwy. 1, Box 367, 95432,*
🕿 *707/877–3321,* FAX *707/877–1808. 11 rooms, 8 suites. Restaurant,
bar, beach. Full breakfast. AE, MC, V.*

Albion

4 mi north of Elk on Hwy. 1.

Dining and Lodging

$$$ ✕ **Ledford House.** The menu at this restaurant on a bluff is divided into hearty bistro dishes, mainly stews and pastas, and equally large-portioned examples of California cuisine—ahi tuna, grilled meats, and the like. ✉ *3000 N. Hwy. 1,* ☎ *707/937–0282. AE, MC, V. Closed Mon. in summer, Mon.–Tues. in winter. No lunch.*

$$$–$$$$ ✕🏠 **Albion River Inn.** Modern two-room cottages at this inn overlook the dramatic bridge and seascape where the Albion River empties into the Pacific. All but two have decks facing the ocean. Six have hot tubs for two, and eight have double bathtubs. The decor ranges from antique furnishings to wide-back willow chairs. In the glassed-in dining room ($–$$), which serves grilled dishes and fresh seafood, the views are as captivating as the food. ✉ *3790 N. Hwy. 1, Box 100, 95410,* ☎ *707/937–1919; 800/479–7944 from northern CA;* 📠 *707/937– 2604. 20 rooms. Restaurant. Full breakfast. AE, MC, V.*

Little River

3 mi north of Albion on Hwy. 1.

Van Damme State Park is one of the coast's best spots for abalone diving. The visitor center here has interesting displays on ocean life and Native American history. ✉ *Hwy. 1,* ☎ *707/937–5804 for park, 707/ 937–4016 for visitor center.*

The nearby **Pygmy Forest** contains wizened trees, some more than a century old, that stand only 3 to 4 ft tall. Highly acidic soil and poor drainage combine to stunt the trees. To reach the forest by car, turn east on Little River Airport Road, ½ mi south of Van Damme State Park, and continue 3½ mi to the clearly marked parking area.

Dining and Lodging

$$–$$$ ✕ **Little River Inn Restaurant.** There are fewer than a dozen entrées on the inn's menu, but they're varied—loin of lamb, petrale sole, grilled polenta with vegetables. Main courses come with soup or salad. Less expensive appetizers, salads, and sandwiches are served in the ocean-view Ole's Whale Watch Bar. ✉ *7551 N. Hwy. 1,* ☎ *707/937–5942. MC, V*

$$–$$$$ ✕🏠 **Heritage House.** The cottages at this resort have stunning ocean views. All the rooms contain plush furnishings and period antiques, and many have private decks, fireplaces, and whirlpool tubs. The dining room ($$$), also with a Pacific panorama, serves breakfast, brunch, and dinner. Salmon, quail, sirloin, and elegant desserts are the standouts on the evening menu. ✉ *Hwy. 1, 95456,* ☎ *707/937–5885,* 📠 *707/937–0318. 72 rooms. Restaurant. MC, V. Closed Jan.–mid-Feb. and most of December.*

$$–$$$$ 🏠 **Glendeven Inn.** The New England–style main house of this tran-
★ quil inn has five rooms, all with private baths, three with fireplaces. A converted barn holds an art gallery and a two-bedroom suite with a kitchen. The 1986 Stevenscroft building, whose four rooms have fireplaces, has a high gabled roof and weathered barnlike siding. All the inn's rooms contain antiques, contemporary art, and ceramics. ✉ *8221 N. Hwy. 1, 95456,* ☎ *707/937–0083,* 📠 *707/937–6108. 9 rooms, 1 suite. Full breakfast. AE, MC, V.*

Mendocino

★ ❾ *2 mi north of Little River on Hwy. 1; 153 mi from San Francisco, north on U.S. 101, west on Hwy. 128, and north on Hwy. 1.*

Logging created the first boom in the windswept town of Mendocino, which flourished for most of the second half of the 19th century. As the timber industry declined in the early 20th century many residents left, but the town's setting was too beautiful for it to remain neglected for long. Artists and craftspeople began flocking here in the 1950s, and in their wake came entrepreneurial types who opened restaurants, cafés, and inns. By the 1970s a full-scale revival was under way. A bit of the old town can be seen in dives like Dick's Place, a bar near the Mendocino Hotel, but the rest of the small downtown area is devoted almost exclusively to contemporary restaurants and shops.

Mendocino may look familiar to fans of *Murder, She Wrote;* the town played the role of Cabot Cove, Maine, in the long-running television show. The subterfuge worked because so many of the original settlers had come here from the Northeast and built houses in the New England style. The Blair House at 45110 Little Lake Street was the home of Jessica Fletcher (Angela Lansbury's character) in the series. Mendocino has also played the part of a California town, most notably in the Elia Kazan production of John Steinbeck's novel *East of Eden.* The building on Main Street (at Kasten Street) that houses the astronomy-oriented Out of This World store was the Bay City Bank in the 1955 film, which starred James Dean.

An 1861 structure holds the **Kelley House Museum,** whose artifacts include antique cameras, Victorian-era clothing, furniture, and historical photographs of Mendocino's logging days. ⊠ *45007 Albion St.,* ☎ *707/937–5791.* ▨ *$1.* ☉ *June–Sept., daily 1–4; Oct.–May, Fri.–Mon. 1–4.*

The **Mendocino Art Center** (⊠ 45200 Little Lake St., ☎ 707/937–5818), which hosts exhibits and art classes and contains a gallery and a theater, is the nexus of Mendocino's flourishing art scene. The tiny green and red **Temple of Kwan Tai** (⊠ Albion St., west of Kasten St., ☎ 707/937–5123), the oldest Chinese temple on the North Coast, dates from 1852. It's open only by appointment, but you can peer in the window and see everything there is to see.

The restored **Ford House,** built in 1854, serves as the visitor center for Mendocino Headlands State Park. The house has a scale model of Mendocino as it looked in 1890, when the town had 34 water towers and a 12-seat outhouse. History walks leave from Ford House on Saturday afternoon at 1. The park itself consists of the cliffs that border the town; access is free. ⊠ *Main St., west of Lansing St.,* ☎ *707/937–5397.* ▨ *Free.* ☉ *Daily 11–4, with possible midweek closings in winter.*

★ The **Mendocino Coast Botanical Gardens** were established as a private preserve in 1962, with acreage added through the years. Along 2 mi of coastal trails, with ocean views and observation points for whale-watching, is a splendid array of flowers; the rhododendrons are at their peak from April to June, and fuchsias, heather, and azaleas are resplendent. You can have lunch or dinner at the on-site Gardens Grill (☞ Dining and Lodging *in* Fort Bragg, *below*). ⊠ *18220 N. Hwy. 1, between Mendocino and Fort Bragg,* ☎ *707/964–4352.* ▨ *$5.* ☉ *Mar.–Oct., daily 9–5; Nov.–Feb., daily 9–4.*

Side Trip to the Anderson Valley

Mendocino's ocean breezes might seem too cool for grape growing, but summer days can be quite warm just over the hills in the Anderson Valley, where the cool nights permit a longer ripening period. Chardonnays and pinot noirs find the valley's climate particularly hospitable. Tasting here is a decidedly more laid-back affair than in the Napa and Sonoma valleys. Most tasting rooms are open from 11 to 5 daily and charge a nominal fee (usually deducted if you purchase any wines) to sample a few vintages. To get to the Anderson Valley from Mendocino take Highway 1 south to Highway 128 east.

Husch (✉ 4400 Hwy. 128, Philo, ☎ 707/895–3216), one of the valley's oldest wineries, sells award-winning chardonnays and a superb gewürztraminer. At the elegant tasting room at **Roederer Estate** (✉ 4501 Hwy. 128, Philo, ☎ 707/895–2288), you can taste (for $3, deductible from wine purchase) sparkling wines produced by the American affiliate of the famous French champagne maker. **Scharffenberger Cellars** (✉ 8501 Hwy. 128, Philo, ☎ 800/824–7754) was the first Anderson Valley winery to produce award-winning sparkling wines. If you're not up for a trip to the valley, **Fetzer Vineyards** (✉ Main St. between Lansing and Kasten Sts., Mendocino, ☎ 707/937–6191) has a tasting room next to the Mendocino Hotel.

Dining and Lodging

$$–$$$ ✕ **Cafe Beaujolais.** All the rustic charm of peaceful, backwoods Men-
★   docino is here, with great country cooking to boot. The ever-evolving dinner menu is cross-cultural and includes such delicacies as Yucatecan Thai crab cakes and a barbecued rock-shrimp-filled corn crepe with avocado and blood-orange pico de gallo. Owner Margaret Fox runs the mail-order Cafe Beaujolais bakery—be sure to take home a package or two of her irresistible *panforte*, a dense cake made with almonds, hazelnuts, or macadamia nuts. ✉ *961 Ukiah St.,* ☎ *707/937–5614. No credit cards.*

$$ ✕ **955 Ukiah.** The interior of this smart restaurant beside Cafe Beaujolais is woodsy and the California cuisine creative. Specialties include fresh fish, duck cannelloni, peppercorn New York steak, and pastas topped with the house sauce. ✉ *955 Ukiah St.,* ☎ *707/937–1955. MC, V. Closed Mon.–Tues. July–Nov., Mon.–Wed. Dec.–June. No lunch.*

$$$$ ✕🏨 **Stanford Inn by the Sea.** Set back from the highway, this two-story
★   lodge has stylish wood-panel rooms and suites with ocean-view decks, four-poster or sleigh beds, fireplaces or woodstoves, and paintings by local artists. The inn, the only one on the North Coast with an organic garden *and* resident llamas, has a huge reception lounge where you can read by the fire or enjoy the ocean view while having afternoon wine and hors d'oeuvres. The inn's dining room ($$–$$$) serves pizzas, salads, soups, pastas, and, for dinner only, gourmet vegetarian entrées. ✉ *South of Mendocino, east on Comptche–Ukiah Rd. (off Hwy. 1), Box 487, 95460,* ☎ *707/937–5615 or 800/331–8884,* 🖷 *707/937–0305. 23 rooms, 10 suites. Refrigerators, indoor pool, hot tub, sauna, bicycles. Full breakfast. AE, D, DC, MC, V.*

$$–$$$$ ✕🏨 **MacCallum House.** With the most meticulously restored Victorian exterior in Mendocino, this 1882 inn, complete with gingerbread trim, transports patrons back to another era. Comfortable furnishings and antiques enhance the period feel. In addition to the main house, there are individual cottages and barn suites around a garden with a gazebo. The menu at the redwood-panel restaurant ($$–$$$; reservations essential) changes quarterly. The focus is on local seafood and organic and free-range meats. ✉ *45020 Albion St., Box 206, 95460,* ☎ *707/ 937–0289 or 800/609–0492. 19 rooms. Restaurant, bar. MC, V.*

$$-$$$$ ✕⊞ **Mendocino Hotel.** From the outside, this hotel looks like something out of the Wild West, with a period facade and balcony that overhangs the raised sidewalk. Stained-glass lamps, Remington paintings, polished wood, and Persian carpets lend the hotel a swank 19th-century appeal. All but 14 of the rooms have private baths. Deluxe garden rooms have fireplaces and TVs. The wood-panel dining room ($$–$$$), fronted by a glassed-in solarium, serves fine fish entrées and the best deep-dish ollalieberry pies in California. ⊠ *45080 Main St., Box 587, 95460,* ☎ *707/937–0511 or 800/548–0513,* ℻ *707/937–0513. 51 rooms. Restaurant, bar, room service. AE, MC, V.*

$$$–$$$$ ⊞ **Whitegate Inn.** With a white picket fence, a latticework gazebo, and
★ a romantic garden, the Whitegate is a picturebook Victorian. High ceilings, floral fabrics, and pastel walls define the public spaces and the luxurious rooms, some of which have fireplaces. The overall tone is elegant, not fussy. Best of all, you can watch the ocean breakers from the deck out back. ⊠ *499 Howard St., 95460,* ☎ *707/937–4892 or 800/531–7282,* ℻ *707/937–1131. 7 rooms. Full breakfast. AE, D, DC, MC, V.*

$$–$$$$ ⊞ **Agate Cove Inn.** Facing the Mendocino Headlands across a rocky cove, this inn is ideally situated for watching whales migrating during the winter. Adirondack chairs are set on a small deck for just that purpose; guests may borrow the inn's binoculars for a closer look. Each blue-and-white cottage unit is individually decorated, mostly in quilts, floral wallpaper, and canopy or four-poster beds. There are four single and four duplex cottages; two more rooms are in the 1860s farmhouse, where country breakfasts are prepared on an antique woodstove in a kitchen with a full view of the Pacific. ⊠ *11201 N. Lansing St., 95460,* ☎ *707/937–0551. 10 rooms. MC, V.*

$$–$$$ ⊞ **Blackberry Inn.** Kids are bound to go wild for the Wild West theme of this hilltop complex. Each single-story unit has a false front, creating the image of a frontier town—there's a bank, a saloon, Belle's Place (of hospitality), and "offices" for doctors and sheriffs, as well as other themed accommodations. The owners were inspired to build this place in the late 1970s by the 1969 James Garner movie *Support Your Local Sheriff!* The rooms are cheery and spacious—most have wood-burning stoves or fireplaces and at least partial ocean views. The inn is a short drive east of town down a quiet side street. Two rooms have kitchenettes. ⊠ *44951 Larkin Rd., 95460,* ☎ *707/937–5281 or 800/950–7806. 16 rooms. Continental breakfast. MC, V.*

$$–$$$ ⊞ **Joshua Grindle Inn.** The original farmhouse of this B&B on a 2-acre hilltop has five guest rooms, a parlor, and a dining room. Two outbuildings, the Watertower (an upper room has windows on all four sides) and the Cottage, hold five additional rooms. Furnishings throughout are simple but comfortable American antiques: Salem rockers, wing chairs, steamer-trunk tables, painted pine beds. ⊠ *44800 Little Lake Rd., 95460,* ☎ *707/937–4143. 10 rooms. Full breakfast. MC, V.*

Nightlife and the Arts

Mendocino Theatre Company (⊠ Mendocino Art Center, 45200 Little Lake St., ☎ 707/937–4477) has been around for more than two decades. The community theater's repertoire ranges from classics like *Uncle Vanya* to more recent plays like *Other People's Money.*

Patterson's Pub (⊠ 10485 Lansing St., ☎ 707/937–4782), an Irish-style watering hole, is a friendly gathering place day or night, though it does become boisterous as the evening wears on. Bands entertain on Friday night.

Outdoor Activities and Sports

Catch-a-Canoe and Bicycles Too (✉ Stanford Inn by the Sea, Mendocino, ☎ 707/937–0273) rents regular and outrigger canoes and mountain and suspension bicycles.

Shopping

Many artists exhibit their wares in Mendocino, and the streets of this compact town are so easily walkable that you're sure to find a gallery with something that strikes your fancy. You might start at the **Mendocino Art Center** (☞ *above*). **Old Gold** (✉ 6 Albion St., ☎ 707/937–5005) is a good place to look for locally crafted jewelry.

Fort Bragg

10 mi north of Mendocino on Hwy. 1.

Fort Bragg has changed more than any other coastal town in the past few years. The decline in what was the top industry, timber, is being offset in part by a boom in charter-boat excursions and other tourist pursuits. The city is also attracting many artists, some lured from Mendocino, where the cost of living is higher. This basically blue-collar town is the commercial center of Mendocino County.

The **Skunk Train,** a remnant of the region's logging days, dates from 1885 and travels a route, through redwood forests inaccessible to automobiles, from Fort Bragg to the town of Willits, 40 mi inland. A fume-spewing self-propelled train car that shuttled passengers along the railroad got nicknamed the *Skunk Train,* and the entire line has been called that ever since. Excursions are now given on historic trains and replicas of the *Skunk Train* motorcar that smell less foul than the original. In summer you can go partway to Northspur, a three-hour round-trip, or make the full seven-hour journey to Willits and back. ✉ *Foot of Laurel St., Fort Bragg,* ☎ *707/964–6371.* ☉ *Fort Bragg–Willits: departs daily 9:20 AM.* ☒ *$35 for Fort Bragg–Willits, $25 for Fort Bragg–Northspur.* ☉ *Fort Bragg–Northspur: departs early June–late Sept., daily 9:20 AM and 1:40 PM; Fort Bragg–Willits: late Sept.–mid-June 10 AM and 2 PM.*

★ ⑩ **MacKerricher State Park** includes 10 mi of sandy beach and several square miles of dunes. Fishing (at two freshwater lakes, one stocked with trout), canoeing, hiking, jogging, bicycling, camping (☞ *below*), and harbor-seal watching at Laguna Point are among the popular activities, many of which are accessible to travelers with disabilities. Whales can often be spotted from December to mid-April from the nearby headland. Rangers lead nature hikes throughout the year. ✉ *Hwy. 1, 3 mi north of Fort Bragg,* ☎ *707/937–5804.* ☒ *Free.*

Dining, Lodging, and Camping

$$–$$$ ✕ **Gardens Grill.** The restaurant at the Mendocino Coast Botanical Gardens (☞ Mendocino, *above*) specializes in applewood-grilled steak, seafood, and vegetarian dishes. The view of the gardens from the outdoor deck is splendid. Brunch is served on Sunday. ✉ *18218 N. Hwy. 1, at the south end of Fort Bragg,* ☎ *707/964–7474. MC, V. No dinner Sun.–Wed.*

$$ ✕ **The Restaurant.** The name may be generic, but this place isn't. California cuisine is served in a dining room that doubles as an art gallery. A jazz brunch takes place on Sunday. ✉ *418 N. Main St.,* ☎ *707/964–9800. MC, V. Closed Wed. No lunch Mon., Tues., Sat.*

$ ✕ **Headlands Coffee House.** The coffeehouse acts as a cultural center and local gathering place. Musicians perform on most nights. ✉ *120 E. Laurel St.,* ☎ *707/964–1987. No credit cards.*

$–$$$ ⊞ **Surf and Sand Lodge.** You have to go north of Fort Bragg to find lodgings with unimpeded ocean views, and they're just what you'll get at this souped-up motel. As its name implies, it's practically on the beach—right out the door are pathways down to the rock-strewn shore. The six cheaper rooms don't have views, but all the bright and fresh accommodations come with enough amenities (including coffeemakers, hair dryers, and binoculars) to make you feel that you're staying somewhere grander than a motel. The fancier of the second-story rooms have hot tubs and fireplaces. ⊠ *1131 N. Main St., 95437,* ☎ *707/964–9383 or 800/964–0184,* ℻ *707/964–0314. 30 rooms. Refrigerators, in-room VCRs. AE, D, DC, MC, V.*

🏕 **MacKerricher State Park.** The campsites at MacKerricher (☞ *above*) are in woodsy settings ¼ mi or so from the ocean. Reservations on summer weekends should be made as early as possible, although each day 25 sites are available on a first-come, first-served basis. ⊠ *Hwy. 1, 3 mi north of Fort Bragg,* ☎ *707/937–5804 for park; 800/444–7275 for campsite reservations, taken Apr.–mid-Oct.* ☎ *$16. 143 sites. Disposal station, fire rings, flush toilets, hot showers, water.* ☉ *Year-round.*

Nightlife
North Coast Brewing Company (⊠ 444 N. Main St., ☎ 707/964–3400) hosts jazz musicians on Saturday night and serves home-brewed beer and pub grub from Tuesday to Saturday.

Outdoor Activities and Sports
Ricochet Ridge Ranch (⊠ 24201 N. Hwy. 1, ☎ 707/964–7669) conducts guided trail rides to the Mendocino–Fort Bragg beaches. **Matlick's Tally Ho II** (⊠ 11845 N. Main St., ☎ 707/964–2079) operates whale-watching trips between December and April, as well as fishing excursions.

En Route   North on Highway 1 from Fort Bragg past the mill town of Westport, the road cuts inland around the **King Range,** a stretch of mountain so rugged that it was impossible to build the intended major highway through it. Highway 1 joins U.S. 101 at the town of Leggett. **Richardson Grove State Park,** north of Leggett along U.S. 101, marks your first encounter with the truly giant redwoods, but there are even more magnificent stands farther north in Humboldt and Del Norte counties.

REDWOOD COUNTRY
Garberville to Crescent City

The majestic redwoods that grace California's coast become more plentiful as you head north. Their towering ancient presence defines the landscape.

Garberville

70 mi from Fort Bragg, north and east on Hwy. 1 and north on U.S. 101; 197 mi north of San Francisco on U.S. 101.

Although it's the largest town in the vicinity of Humboldt Redwoods State Park, Garberville hasn't changed a whole lot since timber was king. The town is a pleasant place to stop for lunch, pick up picnic provisions, or poke through arts-and-crafts stores. A few miles below Garberville is an elegant Tudor resort, the **Benbow Inn** (☞ *below*). Even if you are not staying at the Benbow, stop in for a drink or a meal and take a look at the architecture and gardens.

Dining and Lodging

$ ✕ **Woodrose Cafe.** This unpretentious eatery serves basic breakfast items and healthy lunches. Dishes include chicken, pasta, and vegetarian specials. ⊠ *911 Redwood Dr.,* ☎ *707/923–3191. No credit cards. No dinner.*

$$–$$$$ ✕🏠 **Benbow Inn.** South of Garberville alongside the Eel River, this three-★ story Tudor-style manor resort is the equal of any in the region. The most luxurious of the antiques-filled rooms are on the terrace, with fine views of the Eel River; some rooms have fireplaces, and 18 have TVs with VCRs. Guests have canoeing, tennis, golf, and pool privileges at an adjacent property. The wood-panel dining room ($$–$$$) serves American cuisine, with the focus on fresh salmon and trout dishes. ⊠ *445 Lake Benbow Dr., 95442,* ☎ *707/923–2124 or 800/355–3301. 55 rooms, 1 cottage. Restaurant, lobby lounge, refrigerators, lake. AE, D, MC, V. Closed early Jan.–mid-Mar.*

Humboldt Redwoods State Park

⑪ *15 mi north of Garberville on U.S. 101.*

The **Avenue of the Giants** (Highway 254) begins about 7 mi north of Garberville and winds north, more or less parallel to U.S. 101, toward Pepperwood. Some of the tallest trees on the planet tower over this stretch of two-lane blacktop. The Avenue of the Giants, which follows the south fork of the Eel River, cuts through part of the more than 53,000-acre Humboldt Redwoods State Park.

At the **Humboldt Redwoods State Park Visitor Center** you can pick up information about the redwoods, waterways, and recreational opportunities. Brochures are available for a self-guided auto tour of the park. Stops on the auto tour include short and long hikes into redwood groves. ⊠ *Avenue of the Giants, 2mi south of Weott,* ☎ *707/946–2409 for park; 707/946–2263 for visitor center.* 🎟 *Free; $5 day-use fee for parking and facilities in Williams Grove and Women's Federation Grove.* ☉ *Park 24 hrs year-round. Visitor center Mar.–Oct., daily 9–5; Nov.–Feb., Thurs.–Sun. 10–4.*

Four miles north of the visitor center on the Avenue of the Giants is **Founders Grove,** reached via a ½-mi trail. One of the most impressive trees here—the 362-ft-long **Dyerville Giant**—fell to the ground; its root base points skyward 35 ft. Six miles north of the Visitor Center on Mattole Road is **Rockefeller Forest.** The largest remaining coast redwood forest, it contains 40 of the 100 tallest trees in the world.

Ferndale

⑫ *30 mi from Weott, north on U.S. 101 to Hwy. 211 west.*

The residents of the stately town of Ferndale maintain some of the most sumptuous Victorian homes in California, many of them built by 19th-century Scandinavian, Swiss, and Portuguese dairy farmers who were drawn to the mild climate. The queen of them all is the **Gingerbread Mansion** (☞ Dining and Lodging, *below*). A beautiful sloped graveyard sits on Ocean Avenue west of Main Street. Many shops carry a map with self-guided tours of this lovingly preserved town.

The main building of the **Ferndale Museum** hosts changing exhibitions of Victoriana and has an old-style barbershop and a display of Wiyot Indian baskets. In the annex are a horse-drawn buggy, a re-created blacksmith's shop, and antique farming, fishing, and dairy equipment. ⊠ *515 Shaw Ave.,* ☎ *707/786–4466.* 🎟 *$1.* ☉ *June–Sept., Tues.–Sat.*

11–4 Sun. 1–4; Oct.–Nov. and Feb.–May, Wed.–Sat. 11–4 Sun. 1–4. Closed Jan.

Lodging

$$$–$$$$ 🏠 **Gingerbread Mansion.** The exterior of this classic Victorian B&B has the most playful paint job on the North Coast. The mansion's carved friezes set off its gables, and turrets dazzle the eye. The comfortable parlors and spacious bedrooms are laid out in flowery Victorian splendor. Some rooms have views of the mansion's English garden, and one has side-by-side bathtubs. Innkeeper Ken Tolbert transformed the top floor into a suite so deluxe it would be suitable for a top San Francisco hotel—a vision in marble, with black and gold accents, it holds a claw-foot tub and a shower that could fit six. Ask about off-season discounts. ⊠ *400 Berding St., off Brown St., Box 40, 95536,* ☎ *707/ 786–4000. 10 rooms. Full breakfast. AE, MC, V.*

Outdoor Activities and Sports

Eel River Delta Tours (⊠ 285 Morgan Slough Rd., ☎ 707/786–4187) conducts a two-hour boat trip that emphasizes the wildlife and history of the Eel River's estuary and salt marsh.

Shopping

Ferndale's shops are lined up along Main Street. **Golden Gait Mercantile** (⊠ 421 Main St., ☎ 707/786–4891) seems to be lost in a time warp, what with Burma Shave products and old-fashioned long johns as well as penny candy. For gifts, you can't do better than **Withywindle** (⊠ 358 Main St., ☎ 707/786–4763), which sells local stoneware, porcelain, jewelry, and wearable art. The shop also specializes in gift baskets crammed with gourmet products.

Eureka

⑬ *10 mi north of Ferndale and 269 mi north of San Francisco on U.S. 101.*

Eureka, population 28,500, is the North Coast's largest city. It has gone through cycles of boom and bust, first with mining and later with timber and fishing. There are nearly 100 Victorian buildings here, many of them well preserved. The most splendid is the **Carson Mansion** (⊠ M and 2nd Sts.), built in 1885 for timber baron William Carson. A private men's club occupies the house. Across the street is another extravaganza popularly known as the **Pink Lady.**

For proof that contemporary architects still have the skills to design lovely Victoriana, have a look at the **Carter House** (⊠ 3rd and L Sts.) B&B and keep in mind that it was built in the 1980s, not the 1880s.

At the **Chamber of Commerce** you can pick up maps with self-guided driving tours of Eureka's architecture, and find out about organized tours. ⊠ *2112 Broadway,* ☎ *707/442–3738 or 800/356–6381.* ⊙ *Weekdays 9–5.*

The **Clarke Memorial Museum** contains extraordinary northwestern California Native American basketry and artifacts of Eureka's Victorian, logging, and maritime eras. ⊠ *240 E St.,* ☎ *707/443–1947.* 🎫 *Donations accepted.* ⊙ *Feb.–Dec., Tues.–Sat. noon–4.*

The structure that gave **Fort Humboldt State Historic Park** its name once protected white settlers from the Indians. Ulysses S. Grant was posted here in 1854. The old fort is no longer around, but on its grounds are a museum, some ancient steam engines (operators rev them up on the third Saturday of the month), and a logger's cabin. The park is a good place for a picnic. ⊠ *3431 Fort Ave.,* ☎ *707/445–6567.* 🎫 *Free.* ⊙ *Daily 9–5.*

To explore the waters around Eureka, take a **Humboldt Bay Harbor Cruise.** You can observe some of the region's bird life while sailing past fishing boats, oyster beds, and decaying timber mills. ✉ *Pier at C St.,* ☎ *707/445–1910 or 707/444–9440.* ☞ *$9.50; cocktail-cruise fare $7.50.* ⊙ *Departs Mar.–Nov., daily 1, 2:30, and 4. Cocktail-cruise departs daily 5:30.*

Dining and Lodging

$$–$$$ ✕ **Restaurant 301.** Mark and Christi Carter, owners of Eureka's fanciest hotels, also run one of the town's best restaurants. Most of the vegetables and herbs used at the 301 are grown at the hotel's greenhouse and nearby ranch. Try the superbly presented sea scallops, roasted pork chop, spring lamb rack, or local petrale sole, and don't skip the appetizers—especially if the vegetable ragouts or gnocchi are on the menu. The wine list is one of the finest in northern California. ✉ *301 L St.,* ☎ *707/444–8062. AE, D, DC, MC, V. No lunch.*

$$ ✕ **Celestino's in Old Town.** Pastas and made-to-order pizzas dominate the menu of this large restaurant, which serves grilled meats and several vegetarian choices (as well as vegan dishes on request). The tasty appetizers include grilled eggplant rolls and fried calamari. ✉ *421 3rd St.,* ☎ *707/444–8995. AE, MC, V. No lunch Sat.*

$$ ✕ **Chemin de Fer.** The food here is fresh and elaborate: grilled duck, prawns with curry and pears, pork tenderloin, and nearly a dozen first courses. The dessert list is even longer. ✉ *518 F St.,* ☎ *707/441–9292. AE, MC, V. Closed Mon. No lunch weekends.*

$–$$ ✕ **Cafe Waterfront.** This small eatery across from the marina has a long bar with a TV. Sandwiches and affordable seafood dishes are the menu mainstays. ✉ *102 F St.,* ☎ *707/443–9190. MC, V.*

$ ✕ **Ramone's.** A casual bakery café, Ramone serves light sandwiches. It's been voted Eureka's best place to grab a cup of coffee. ✉ *2223 Harrison Ave.,* ☎ *707/442–6082. No credit cards. No dinner.*

$ ✕ **Samoa Cookhouse.** The recommendation here is more for atmosphere,
★ of which there is plenty: This is a longtime loggers' hangout. The Samoa's cooks serve three substantial set meals family style at long wooden tables. Meat dishes predominate. Save room (if possible) for dessert. ✉ *Cookhouse Rd. (from U.S. 101, cross Samoa Bridge, turn left onto Samoa Rd., then left 1 block later onto Cookhouse),* ☎ *707/442–1659. AE, D, MC, V.*

$$$–$$$$ ⌂ **Carter House, Hotel Carter, and Cottages.** The Carter family runs
★ four properties in downtown Eureka, including the one-bedroom Honeymoon Cottage, which opened in early 1998. The Carter House, built in 1982 following the floor plan of a San Francisco mansion, has an antiques-laden sitting area and gorgeous rooms with heirloom furniture. Two doors down, the Cottage, an original Victorian, contains three rooms and a big sitting area with contemporary southwestern decorations. The hotel, catercorner to the Carter House, has an elegant lobby and suites. Handsome brocaded spreads cover the beds; some rooms have fireplaces and whirlpool tubs. Breakfast is served in the hotel's sunny dining room. ✉ *301 L St., 95501,* ☎ *707/444–8062,* FAX *707/445–8067. 32 rooms. Full breakfast. AE, D, DC, MC, V.*

$$–$$$$ ⌂ **An Elegant Victorian Mansion.** This restored Eastlake mansion in a
★ residential neighborhood east of the Old Town lives up to its name. Each room is decked out in period furnishings and wall coverings, down to the carved-wood beds, fringed lamp shades, and pull-chain commodes. The innkeepers may even greet you in vintage clothing and surprise you with old-fashioned ice-cream sodas in the afternoon. They'll lure you further into their time warp with silent movies on tape, old records played on the windup Victrola, croquet on the rose-encircled lawn, and guided tours of local Victoriana in their antique automobile. The Vic-

torian flower garden holds more than 100 rosebushes. ⊠ *14th and C Sts.,
95501,* ☎ *707/444–3144,* FAX *707/442–5594. 4 rooms with 4 shared
baths. Sauna, croquet, bicycles, laundry service. Full breakfast. MC, V.*

Nightlife
Lost Coast Brewery & Cafe (⊠ 617 4th St., ☎ 707/445–4480), a
bustling microbrewery, is the best place in town to relax with a pint
of strong ale or porter. Soups, salads, and light meals are served for
lunch and dinner.

Outdoor Activities and Sports
Hum-Boats (⊠ 2 F St., ☎ 707/443–5157) provides sailing rides, sail-
boat rentals, guided kayak tours, and sea kayak rentals and lessons.
The company also runs a water-taxi service on Humboldt Bay.

Shopping
Eureka has several art galleries in the district running from C to I streets
between 2nd and 3rd streets. Specialty shops in Old Town include the
original **Restoration Hardware** (⊠ 417 2nd St., ☎ 707/443–3152), a
good place to find stylish yet functional home and garden accessories
and clever polishing and cleaning products. The **Irish Shop** (⊠ 334 2nd
St., ☎ 707/443–8343) carries imports from the Emerald Isle, mostly
fine woolens.

Arcata

⑭ *9 mi north of Eureka on U.S. 101.*

The home of Humboldt State University is one of the few California
burgs to retain a town square. A farmers' market takes place in the
square on Saturday morning from May to November. For a self-guided
tour of Arcata that includes some of its restored Victorian buildings,
pick up a map from the **Chamber of Commerce** (⊠ 1062 G St., ☎ 707/
822–3619), which is open weekdays from 10 to 4.

Dining and Lodging
$$ ✗ **Abruzzi.** Salads and hefty pasta dishes take up most of the menu at
this upscale Italian restaurant in the lower level of Jacoby's Storehouse,
off the town square. One specialty is linguine *pescara,* with a spicy
seafood-and-tomato sauce. ⊠ *H and 8th Sts.,* ☎ *707/826–2345. AE,
D, MC, V. No lunch.*

$ ✗ **Crosswinds.** This restaurant serves Continental cuisine in a sunny
Victorian setting, to the tune of live classical music. ⊠ *10th and I Sts.,*
☎ *707/826–2133. MC, V. Closed Mon. No dinner.*

$ ▣ **Hotel Arcata.** Flowered bedspreads and claw-foot bathtubs lend char-
acter to the rooms of this historic landmark overlooking the town square.
⊠ *708 9th St., 95521,* ☎ *707/826–0217 or 800/344–1221,* FAX *707/
826–1737. 32 rooms. Restaurant. Continental breakfast (weekdays
only). AE, D, DC, MC, V.*

Shopping
For its size, Arcata has an impressive selection of book, housewares,
clothing, fabric, and other shops, especially near its town square. **Plaza
Design** (⊠ 808 G St., ☎ 707/822–7732) specializes in gifts, papers,
and innovative furnishings.

Trinidad

14 mi north of Arcata on U.S. 101.

A Portuguese expedition visited Trinidad in 1595. The waters here are
now sailed by fishing boats trolling for salmon. Picturesque Trinidad
Bay's harbor cove and rock formations look both raw and tranquil.

Dining and Lodging

$–$$ ✕ **Larrupin' Cafe.** This restaurant has earned widespread fame for its
★   Cajun ribs and fresh fish dishes, served in a bright-yellow two-story
      house on a quiet country road 2 mi north of Trinidad. ⊠ *1658 Patrick's
      Point Dr.,* ☎ *707/677–0230. Reservations essential. No credit cards.
      Closed Mon.–Wed. in winter, Tues. in summer. No lunch.*

$–$$ ✕ **Merryman's Dinner House.** Fresh fish and a romantic oceanfront set-
      ting make this a perfect spot for hungry lovers. ⊠ *100 Moonstone Beach,*
      ☎ *707/677–3111. No credit cards. Closed weekdays Oct.–Mar. No
      lunch.*

$ ✕ **Seascape.** With its glassed-in main room and deck for alfresco din-
      ing, this is an ideal place to take in the splendor of Trinidad Bay. The
      breakfasts are great, the lunches are substantial, and the dinners show-
      case local seafood. ⊠ *At pier,* ☎ *707/677–3762. MC, V.*

$$$ 🖭 **Trinidad Bay Bed and Breakfast.** This Cape Cod–style shingle house
      has an unforgettable ocean view. The innkeepers provide a wealth of
      information about the nearby wilderness, beach, and fishing habitats.
      A crackling fire warms the living room in chilly weather. ⊠ *560 Ed-
      wards St., Box 849, 95570,* ☎ *707/677–0840. 2 rooms and 2 suites
      (1 with fireplace). Full breakfast. D, MC, V. Closed Dec.–Jan.*

$$–$$$ 🖭 **Turtle Rocks Inn.** Named for some of the enormous formations
      within view offshore, this B&B has a two-tier "Whale Watch" deck
      where you can sit on rocking chairs or chaise longues and take cat-
      naps or scan the horizon. Contemporary and antique furnishings dec-
      orate the rooms, all but one of which have decks. ⊠ *3392 Patrick's
      Point Dr., 95570,* ☎ *707/677–3707. 6 rooms. Full breakfast. MC, V.*

Patrick's Point State Park

⑮   *5 mi north of Trinidad and 25 mi north of Eureka on U.S. 101.*

Relatively few people know about Patrick's Point State Park, but those
who do return again and again. On a forested plateau almost 200 ft
above the surf, it has stunning views of the Pacific, great whale- and
sea-lion-watching in season, picnic areas, bike paths, and hiking trails
through old-growth forest. There are tidal pools at Agate Beach and
a small museum with natural-history exhibits. The park's campsites
have fire rings, flush toilets, showers, and water. ☎ *707/677–3570.
🖾 May–Sept. $6 per vehicle (day use), camping $16 per vehicle;
Oct.–Apr. $5 per vehicle (day use), camping $14 per vehicle.*

Redwood National and State Parks

⑯   *22 mi north (Orick entrance) of Trinidad on U.S. 101.*

After 115 years of intensive logging, this 106,000-acre parcel of tall
trees came under government protection in 1968, marking the Cali-
fornia environmentalists' greatest victory over the timber industry.
Redwood National and State Parks (☎ 707/464–6101, ext. 5064) en-
compasses three state parks (Prairie Creek Redwoods, Del Norte Coast
Redwoods, and Jedediah Smith Redwoods) and is more than 40 mi
long. There is no admission fee to the national or state parks, but the
state parks charge $5 to use facilities such as the beach or picnic areas.
⊠ *Park Headquarters, 1111 2nd St., Crescent City,* ☎ *707/464–
6101, ext. 5064.*

At the **Redwood Information Center** you can get brochures, advice, and
a free permit to drive up the steep, 17-mi road (the last 6 mi are gravel)
to reach the **Tall Trees Grove,** where a 3-mi round-trip hiking trail leads
to the world's first-, third-, and fifth-tallest redwoods. Whale-watchers
will find the deck of the visitor center an excellent observation point,

and birders will enjoy the nearby Freshwater Lagoon, a popular lay-over for migrating waterfowl. ⊠ *Off U.S. 101, Orick,* ☏ *707/464–6101, ext. 5265.*

Within **Lady Bird Johnson Grove,** off Bald Hills Road, is a short circular trail to resplendent redwoods. This section of the park was dedicated by, and named for, the former first lady. For additional views, take Davison Road to Fern Canyon. This gravel road winds through 4 mi of second-growth redwoods, then hugs a bluff 100 ft above the pounding Pacific surf for another 4 mi.

To reach the entrance to **Prairie Creek Redwoods State Park** (☏ 707/464–6101, ext. 5300) take the Prairie Parkway exit off the U.S. 101 bypass. Extra space has been paved alongside the parklands, providing fine vantage points from which to observe an imposing herd of Roosevelt elk grazing in the adjoining meadow. Revelation Trail in Prairie Creek is fully accessible to visitors with disabilities.

Lodging and Camping

$ ✕ **Hostelling International—Redwood National Park.** This century-old inn is a stone's throw from the ocean; hiking begins just beyond its doors. Lodging is dormitory style. ⊠ *14480 U.S. 101, at Wilson Creek Rd. (20 mi north of Orick), Klamath, 95548,* ☏ FAX *707/482–8265. No credit cards.*

⚠ **Freshwater Lagoon.** A strip of sand between the ocean and Freshwater Lagoon holds an unofficial, primitive campground with no water or hookups—but great views. ⊠ *West side of U.S. 101, 1½ mi south of Orick (¼ mi south of Redwood Information Center),* ☏ *707/464–6101, ext. 5265. Chemical toilets, fire rings, picnic tables .* 🏕 *$6.*

Crescent City

40 mi north of Orick on U.S. 101.

Del Norte County's largest town (population just under 5,000) is named for the shape of its harbor; during the 1800s this was an important steamship stop. At the bottom of B Street at **Popeye's Landing** you can rent a crab pot, buy some bait, and try your luck at crabbing. At low tide from April to September, you can walk from the pier across the ocean floor to the oldest lighthouse on the North Coast, **Battery Point Lighthouse** (☏ 707/464–3089). Tours ($2) of the 1856 structure are given from Wednesday to Sunday between 10 and 4 from May to October and by appointment the rest of the year.

Dining and Lodging

$–$$ ✕ **Harbor View Grotto.** This glassed-in dining hall overlooking the Pacific prides itself on its fresh fish entrées. The white two-story building is marked only by a neon sign that reads "Restaurant." ⊠ *155 Citizen's Dock Rd.,* ☏ *707/464–3815. MC, V.*

$ 🏨 **Curly Redwood Lodge.** A single redwood tree produced the 57,000 board feet of lumber used to build this lodge. The room decor makes the most of that tree, with paneling, platform beds, and dressers built into the walls. ⊠ *701 Redwood Hwy. S, 95531,* ☏ *707/464–2137,* FAX *707/464–1655. 36 rooms. AE, DC, MC, V.*

En Route Travelers continuing north to the Smith River near the Oregon state line will find fine trout and salmon fishing as well as a profusion of flowers. Ninety percent of America's lily bulbs are grown in this area.

THE NORTH COAST A TO Z

Arriving and Departing

By Bus
Greyhound buses (☎ 800/231–2222) travel along U.S. 101 from San Francisco to Seattle, with regular stops in Eureka and Crescent City. Bus drivers will stop in other towns along the route if you specify your destination when you board.

By Car
Highway 1 and U.S. 101 are the main north–south coastal routes. Highway 1 is often curvy and difficult all along the coast. Driving directly to Mendocino from San Francisco is quicker if instead of driving up the coast on Highway 1 you take U.S. 101 north to Highway 128 west (from Cloverdale) to Highway 1 north. Once it gets into Humboldt County, U.S. 101 itself becomes as twisting as Highway 1 as it continues on to the northernmost corner of the state. **Hertz** (☎ 800/654–3131) rents cars at the Arcata/Eureka Airport (☞ *below*).

By Plane
Arcata/Eureka Airport (✉ off U.S. 101, McKinleyville, ☎ 707/839–5401) receives United Express (☎ 800/241–6522) flights from San Francisco to Arcata/Eureka.

Getting Around

By Bus
Redwood Transit System (☎ 707/443–0826) connects Eureka, Arcata, Scotia, Fortuna, and Trinidad.

By Car
Although there are excellent services along Highway 1 and U.S. 101, the main routes through the North Coast, gas stations and mechanics are few and far between on the smaller roads. If you're running low on fuel and see a gas station, stop for a refill.

Contacts and Resources

Emergencies
Ambulance (☎ 911). **Fire** (☎ 911). **Police** (☎ 911).

Guided Tours
New Sea Angler and Jaws (✉ Bodega Bay, ☎ 707/875–3495) runs cruises and fishing charters on weekends from December to April. **Oceanic Society Expeditions** (☎ 415/474–3385) conducts whale-watching and other nature cruises north and west of San Francisco throughout much of the year.

Visitor Information
Eureka/Humboldt County Convention and Visitors Bureau (✉ 1034 2nd St., Eureka 95501, ☎ 800/346–3482; 800/809–5908). **Fort Bragg–Mendocino Coast Chamber of Commerce** (✉ Box 1141, Fort Bragg 95437, ☎ 800/726–2780). **Redwood Empire Association** (✉ Cannery, 2801 Leavenworth St., San Francisco 94133, ☎ 415/543–8334). **Sonoma County Visitors and Convention Bureau** (✉ 10 4th St., Santa Rosa 95401, ☎ 707/586–8100). **West Marin Chamber of Commerce** (✉ Box 1045, Point Reyes Station 94956, ☎ 415/663–9232).

3 The Far North

Including Mount Shasta, Lake Shasta, and Lassen Volcanic National Park

Soaring mountain peaks, wild rivers brimming with fish, and almost infinite recreational possibilities make the Far North a sports-lover's paradise. Hot nightspots and cultural enclaves do not abound, but you will find some of the best hiking, fishing, and hunting in the state. Some Bay Area families return to this region year after year. Many enjoy the outdoors from their own piece of paradise—a private houseboat.

THE FAR NORTH LANDSCAPE has been writ large by ancient volcanic activity. The scenery is best symbolized
by Mount Shasta, a 14,162-ft-high mountain that
can be seen for miles around. Less dramatic but more extensive is Lassen
Volcanic National Park at the southern end of the Cascade Range. The
10,457-ft Mount Lassen and 50 wilderness lakes are the park's cen-
terpieces.

By Marty
Olmstead

The Far North's natural and artificially created wonders include immense Shasta Dam and the sulfur vents and bubbling mud pots of Lassen
Volcanic National Park. Plentiful access to the wilderness, without crowding, is the Far North's hallmark. There are few towns and fewer cities.
Natural history dwarfs the footsteps of mankind in this grand gymnasium for body and soul.

Pleasures and Pastimes

Dining

Redding, the urban center of the Far North, has the greatest selection
of restaurants. In the smaller towns, cafés and simple restaurants are
the rule, though there is the occasional culinary surprise. Dress is always informal in the Far North.

CATEGORY	COST*
$$$$	over $50
$$$	$30–$50
$$	$20–$30
$	under $20

per person for a three-course meal, excluding drinks, service, and 7¼% tax

Lodging

Aside from the large chain hotels and motels in the Redding area, most
accommodations in the Far North blend rusticity, simplicity, and coziness. Many visitors to rural areas spend much of their time in the
outdoors and prefer informal campsites and motels. Wilderness resorts
close in fall and reopen after the snow season ends in May.

CATEGORY	COST*
$$$$	over $175
$$$	$120–$175
$$	$80–$120
$	under $80

All prices are for a standard double room, excluding 8% tax.

Outdoor Activities and Sports

Fishing, houseboating, and animal-pack trips are popular regional diversions. Cascading rivers, mammoth lakes, and bountiful streams
draw sportfishers. Hikers, backpackers, hunters, skiers, and other outdoor enthusiasts also flock to the Far North. Castle Crags State Park
and Lassen Volcanic National Park have abundant hiking and walking trails. In winter the challenging, uncrowded slopes of Mount Shasta
tempt skiers. For information about campgrounds, contact Lassen
Volcanic National Park or the Shasta Cascade Wonderland Association (☞ Contacts and Resources *in* The Far North A to Z, *below*).

Exploring the Far North

The Far North encompasses three vast counties—Tehama, Shasta, and
Trinity—and part of Butte County. The area stretches from the valleys
east of the Coast Range to the Nevada border and from the almond
and olive orchards north of Sacramento to the Oregon border.

Numbers in the text correspond to numbers in the margin and on the Far North map.

Great Itineraries

IF YOU HAVE 3 DAYS

From I–5 north of Redding, head northeast on Highways 299 and 89 to **McArthur-Burney Falls Memorial State Park** ⑥. To appreciate the falls, take the short stroll to an overlook or hike down for an even closer view. Continue north on Highway 89. Long before you arrive in the town of ⚏ **Mount Shasta** ⑦ you will spy the conical peak for which it is named. The central Mount Shasta exit east leads out of town along the **Everett Memorial Highway.** Take this scenic drive, which climbs to almost 8,000 ft. The views of the mountain and the valley below are extraordinary. Stay overnight in town. On the second day, head south on I–5 toward the **Lake Shasta Caverns** ⑧ and the **Shasta Dam** ⑨. **Lake Shasta** is visible on both sides of the highway as it crosses the water near the dam, which is on the west side of I–5. Spend the night either in ⚏ **Weaverville** ⑩, on Highway 299, or in ⚏ **Redding** ⑪, on I–5. Near Redding, Highway 299 leads west toward the **Whiskeytown-Shasta-Trinity National Recreation Area.** Wherever you stay, take in Weaverville—don't miss its **Joss House**—on your third day.

IF YOU HAVE 5 OR 6 DAYS

Get a glimpse of the Far North's heritage in **Red Bluff** ② before heading north on I–5 to the town of ⚏ **Mount Shasta.** On day two drop by the Forest Service Ranger Station to check on trail conditions on **Mount Shasta** ⑦ and pick up maps. Pack a picnic lunch before taking the **Everett Memorial Highway** up the mountain. After exploring the mountain, head south on I–5 and spend the night in ⚏ **Dunsmuir** at the **Railroad Car Resort,** where all the accommodations are old cabooses. On your third day, take an early morning hike in nearby **Castle Crags State Park.** Continue south on I–5 and tour **Shasta Dam** ⑨. Spend the night camping in the area or in ⚏ **Redding** ⑪. On your fourth morning, head west on Highway 299 and visit the town of **Shasta.** Continue west on 299 to ⚏ **Weaverville** ⑩ and stay the night there or back in Redding. If you will be leaving the area on your fifth day but have a little time, zip north and visit **Lake Shasta Caverns** ⑧. If you're remaining and it's between late May and early October, spend the next day and a half exploring **Lassen Volcanic National Park.** Highway 44 heads east from Redding into the park.

When to Tour the Far North

This region attracts the greatest number of tourists during the summer, which can be dry and scorching. The valley around Redding is mild in the winter, but cooler temperatures prevail at the higher elevations to the east and north. In winter Mount Shasta is a good downhill ski area. The remainder of the Far North is too cold for outdoor pleasures, and snow closes the roads to the region's most awesome sights, including much of Lassen Volcanic National Park, from October until late May. Many restaurants and museums here have limited hours and sometimes close for stretches of the off season.

FROM CHICO TO MOUNT SHASTA

The Far North's most spectacular scenery lies along the two-lane roads that crisscross the region, which is bisected by I–5. East of I–5 are dramatic mountain peaks. To the west you'll find heavily forested areas and interesting small towns.

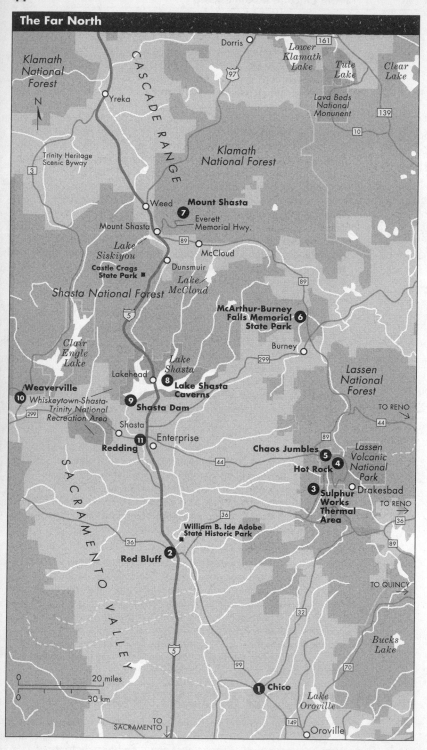

Chico

❶ *180 mi from San Francisco, east on I–80, north on I–505 to I–5, and east on Hwy. 32; 86 mi north of Sacramento on Hwy. 99.*

The presence of California State University at Chico lends this city of 40,000 a distinct flavor—actually, two flavors: beer (locally made Sierra Nevada pale ale, of course) and coffee (at least a dozen coffeehouses keep the students awake). Chico is also an agricultural center.

The 3,670-acre **Bidwell Park** (☎ 530/895–4972), which straddles Big Chico Creek, contains playgrounds, a golf course, and paved biking, hiking, and rollerblading trails. The city-run park starts as a sliver downtown and sprawls eastward toward the Sierra foothills.

Bidwell Mansion was built between 1865 and 1868 by General John Bidwell, who came west in 1841 with the first organized wagon train, worked in the gold mines, and then founded Chico. He and his wife settled into this 26-room mansion that was designed by Henry W. Cleaveland, architect of San Francisco's original Palace Hotel. The 45-minute tour takes in the dining room, parlor, library, and a half-dozen rooms, whose guests included President and Mrs. Rutherford B. Hayes, naturalist John Muir, and General William T. Sherman. ⊠ *Bidwell Mansion State Historic Park, 525 The Esplanade, ☎ 530/895–6144.* 🖼 *$3.* ☉ *Weekdays noon–5, weekends 10–5; last tour daily at 4.*

The award-winning **Sierra Nevada Brewing Company** is expanding rapidly, but still has a hands-on approach to beer-making that makes touring its sparkling brewery a pleasure. You can enjoy a hearty lunch or dinner in the brew pub, which serves sushi on some nights. ⊠ *1075 E. 20th St., ☎ 530/345–2739.* 🖼 *Free.* ☉ *Tours Tues.–Fri. at 2:30 and Sat. 12–3 on the ½-hr. Closed Mon.*

Dining

$–$$ ✕ **Kramore Inn.** Dinner crepes—from ham and avocado to crab cannelloni—are the inn's specialty. The menu also includes beef Stroganoff, Mexican dishes, several pastas, and, on Friday and Saturday, leg of lamb. ⊠ *1903 Park Ave., ☎ 530/343–3701. AE, D, MC, V. Closed Mon.*

$$$–$$$$ 🛏 **Johnson's Country Inn.** Two miles from downtown amid an almond orchard, this pink Victorian-style farmhouse complete with wraparound veranda is a welcome change from motel row. Johnson's was built in 1992, but the ambience is strictly 19th century. ⊠ *3935 Morehead Ave., 95928, ☎ FAX 530/345–7829. 4 rooms. Full breakfast. AE, MC, V.*

OFF THE
BEATEN PATH

QUINCY – A two-hour drive from Chico, south on Highways 99 and 149 and east on Highway 70, leads through the scenic Feather River Canyon, ending at elevation 3,500 ft in quaint and highly strollable Quincy. Traditional Maidu baskets, woven by members of the local Native American community, are among the items on exhibit at the **Plumas County Museum** (⊠ 500 Jackson St., ☎ 530/283–6320). The museum (admission $1) is open on weekdays year-round from 8 to 5 (and on weekends between May and September from 10 to 4). The cozy old **Feather Bed** (⊠ 542 Jackson St., ☎ 530/283–0102) B&B has large rooms and bikes for guests to use. The **Morning Thunder Cafe** (⊠ 557 Lawrence St., ☎ 530/283–1310), which serves breakfast until 2 PM, is always abuzz with espresso-heads. The most popular dinner spot is **Moon's** (⊠ 497 Lawrence St., ☎ 530/283–0765), where daily specials augment a mostly Italian menu. You can sit on the patio in good weather. Quincy is a good base for forays into the **Plumas National Forest** (⊠ Supervisor's Office, 159 Lawrence St., ☎ 530/283–2050), whose numerous waterfalls include the 640-ft-high Feather Falls. The supervisor's office has road and trail maps.

Red Bluff

❷ *179 mi north of San Francisco, I–80 to I–505 to I–5.*

Named for the color of its soil and its location above the Sacramento River, Red Bluff was established in the mid-19th century, before Victorian architecture became the style of choice in the Far North. Historic structures of two types remain: Restored Victorians line the streets west of Main Street; downtown looks like a stage set for a western movie.

The **Kelly-Griggs House Museum,** a restored 1880s home, holds an impressive collection of antique furniture, housewares, and clothing arranged as though a refined Victorian-era family were still in residence: An engraved silver tea server waits at the end table; a "Self Instructor in Penmanship" sits on a desk; and costumed mannequins seem frozen in conversation in the upstairs parlor. The museum's collection includes carved china cabinets and Native American basketry. *Persephone,* the painting over the fireplace, is by Sarah Brown, daughter of abolitionist John Brown, whose family settled in Red Bluff. ✉ *311 Washington St.,* ☎ *530/527–1129.* ▢ *Donation suggested.* ◷ *Thurs.–Sun. 1–4.*

The **William B. Ide Adobe State Historic Park** is a memorial to the first and only president of the short-lived California Republic of 1846. The Bear Flag Party proclaimed California a sovereign nation, no longer under the dominion of Mexico, and the republic existed for 25 days before it was occupied by the United States. The flag concocted for the republic has survived, with only minor refinements, as California's state flag. This adobe, thought to have been Ide's, was built in the 1850s. Furnishings and artifacts of that era are on display. ✉ *21659 Adobe Rd.,* ☎ *530/529–8599.* ▢ *$3 donation requested per vehicle.* ◷ *Park and picnic facilities 8 AM–sunset year-round; home 11–4 in summer (in winter, look for ranger to unlock house).*

Dining

$$ ✕ **Snack Box.** Unabashedly corny pictures and knickknacks, all rural and many depicting cattle and sheep, decorate the renovated Victorian cottage that holds the Snack Box. The food need make no apologies, however. Soups, omelets, country-fried steaks, and even simple items such as grilled-cheese sandwiches are perfectly crafted. ✉ *257 Main St., 1 block from Kelly-Griggs Museum,* ☎ *530/529–0227. MC, V. No dinner.*

Lassen Volcanic National Park

45 mi east of Redding on Hwy. 44; 48 mi east of Red Bluff on Hwy. 36.

Lassen Volcanic National Park provides a look at three sides of the world's largest plug volcano. Except for the Nordic ski area, the park is largely inaccessible from late October to late May because of heavy snow. The Lassen Park Road (the continuation of Highway 89 within the park) is closed to cars in winter but open to intrepid cross-country skiers, conditions permitting. Even in the best of weather, services are sparse. In the southwest corner of the park, a café and a gift shop are open during the summer. At the Manzanita Lake campground, another store, also open only in summer, sells gas and fast food. The *Lassen Park Guide,* available for a nominal fee at the visitor center and park entrance, details these and other facilities. ✉ *Headquarters and visitor center:* ✉ *38050 Hwy. 36 E, Mineral 96063,* ☎ *530/595–4444.* ▢ *$5 per vehicle in summer, free in winter; $8–$12 for campsites (reservations not accepted).* ◷ *Visitor center weekdays 8–4:30 year-round, summer weekends 8–4:30; hrs sometimes vary.*

In 1914 the 10,457-ft Mount Lassen began a series of 300 eruptions that continued for seven years. Molten rock overflowed the crater, and the mountain emitted clouds of smoke and hailstorms of rocks and volcanic cinders. Proof of the volcano's volatility becomes evident shortly

❸ after you enter the park at the **Sulphur Works Thermal Area.** Boardwalks take you over bubbling mud and hot springs and through the sulfur-emitting steam vents. ⊠ *Lassen Park Rd., south end of park.*

The **Lassen Peak Hike** winds 2.5 mi—a good workout if you're in shape; you'll be huffing and puffing if you're not—to the mountaintop. At the peak you can take a peek into the rim and view the entire park (and much of the Far North). Bring sunscreen and water. ⊠ *Off Lassen Park Rd. at Mile Marker 22.*

Along **Bumpass Hell Trail,** a 3-mi round-trip hike to the park's most interesting thermal-spring area, you can view hot and boiling springs, steam vents, and mud pots up close. The trail climbs and descends several hundred feet. Stay on trails and boardwalks near the thermal areas. What appears to be firm ground may be only a thin crust over scalding mud. ⊠ *Off Lassen Park Rd., 5 mi north of Sulphur Works Thermal Area.*

❹ **Hot Rock,** a 400-ton boulder, tumbled down from the summit during the volcano's active period and was still hot to the touch when locals found it. Although cool now, it's still an impressive sight. ⊠ *Lassen Park Rd., north end of park.*

❺ **Chaos Jumbles** was created 300 years ago when an avalanche from the Chaos Crags lava domes spread hundreds of thousands of rocks 2 to 3 ft in diameter over a couple of square miles. ⊠ *Lassen Park Rd., north end of park.*

Dining, Lodging, and Camping

$$$$ ✕🍴 **Drakesbad Guest Ranch.** This century-old guest ranch, at elevation 5,700 ft near Lassen Volcanic National Park's southern border, is isolated from most of the rest of the park, which is one reason it is so popular. Rooms in the lodge, bungalows, and cabins don't have electricity; they're lighted by kerosene lamps. But the spartan accommodations are clean and comfortable and have furnace heat and either a half or full bath. Breakfast and lunch are simple affairs, but evening meals are rather elegant. Reservations should be made well ahead (the waiting list can be up to two years long); all meals are included. ⊠ *Chester–Warner Valley Rd., north from Hwy. 36 (⊠ booking office:* ⊠ *2150 N. Main St., Suite 5, Red Bluff 96080),* ☎ *530/529–9820,* FAX *530/529–4511. 19 rooms. Dining room, pool, badminton, horseback riding, horseshoes, Ping-Pong, volleyball, fishing. FAP. MC, V. Closed early Oct.–early June.*

$ ✕🍴 **Lassen Mineral Lodge.** Reserve rooms at this motel-style property as far ahead as possible. You can rent cross-country skis at the lodge's ski shop; there's also a general store. ⊠ *Hwy. 36, Mineral 96063,* ☎ *530/595–4422. 20 rooms. Restaurant, bar, pool, tennis courts. MC, V.*

△ **Manzanita Lake Campground.** The largest of Lassen Volcanic National Park's seven campgrounds (reservations are not accepted at any of them) is near the northern entrance. A trail near the campground leads to Chaos Crags Lake. ⊠ *Off Lassen Park Rd. 2 mi east of junction of Hwys. 44 and 89,* ☎ *530/595–4444. 179 sites.* ▭ *$14. Fire rings, flush toilets, showers, water. Closed mid-Oct.–mid-May.*

McArthur-Burney Falls Memorial State Park

❻ *30 mi north of Lassen Volcanic National Park on Hwy. 89.*

Just inside the southern boundary of this state park, Burney Creek wells up from the ground and divides into two cascades that fall over a 129-ft cliff and into a pool below. The thundering water creates a mist at the base of the falls, often highlighted by a rainbow. Countless ribbonlike falls stream from hidden moss-covered crevices—an ethereal backdrop to the main cascades. Each day 100 million gallons of water rush over these falls; Theodore Roosevelt proclaimed them "the eighth wonder of the world." A self-guided nature trail descends to the foot of the falls. There is a lake and beach for swimming. A campground, picnic sites and other facilities are available. The camp store is open from Memorial Day to Labor Day. ⊠ *24898 Hwy. 89, Burney 96013, ☎ 530/335–2777; 800/444–7275 for campground reservations (necessary in summer). ⬛ $5 per vehicle (day use); $12–$14 (campsites).*

Mount Shasta

❼ *52 mi from McArthur-Burney Falls Memorial State Park on Hwy. 89; 61 mi north of Redding on I–5.*

Mount Shasta—the mountain and the town—made headlines in 1987 when participants in the worldwide Harmonic Convergence descended on the region, believing the mountain held special powers. They weren't the first: Legends of eerie phenomena and mythical animals have been part of the mountain's folklore for decades.

The crowning jewel of the 2.5 million-acre Shasta–Trinity National Forest, Mount Shasta is popular with day hikers, especially in spring, when flowers like the fragrant Shasta lily adorn the rocky slopes. But few people make it to the perennially ice-packed summit of this 16-million-year-old dormant volcano. An automobile road travels only as high as the timberline, and the final 6,000 ft are a tough climb of rubble, ice, and snow.

As for the town of Mount Shasta, it is not so much a destination as a place to eat and sleep. Even on the main thoroughfare there isn't much to do or see.

Dining and Lodging

$–$$ ✕ **Acacia Restaurant, Bar and Grill.** The menu at this upbeat eatery is a mélange of classic and trendy dishes—veal piccata, vegetable curry, prime rib, rack of lamb, and several seafood options. Acacia serves breakfast and brunch on Sunday. ⊠ *1136 S. Mt. Shasta Blvd., ☎ 530/926–0250. AE, D, MC, V.*

$–$$ ✕ **Lily's.** This restaurant in a white clapboard home—complete with picket fence—serves several fine pastas, including one with sun-dried tomatoes and artichoke hearts. Among the unusual salads are a spicy shrimp-and-chicken dish and the Jalisco—steak and greens with tomatoes. ⊠ *1013 S. Mt. Shasta Blvd., ☎ 530/926–3372. AE, D, MC, V.*

$–$$ ✕ **Michael's Restaurant.** Wood paneling, candlelight, and wildlife prints by local artists create an unpretentious setting for Italian specialties like stuffed calamari, filet mignon scallopini, and linguine pesto. ⊠ *313 N. Mt. Shasta Blvd., ☎ 530/926–5288. AE, D, MC, V. Closed Sun.–Mon.*

$–$$ ▥ **Best Western Tree House Motor Inn.** The clean, standard rooms at this motel less than a mile from downtown Mount Shasta are decorated with natural-wood furnishings. ⊠ *111 Morgan Way, at I–5 and Lake St., Box 236, 96067, ☎ 530/92626–3101 or 800/528–1234, FAX 530/926–3542. 95 rooms. Restaurant, lounge, refrigerators, indoor pool. AE, D, DC, MC, V.*

Outdoor Activities and Sports

HIKING

The **Forest Service Ranger Station** (☎ 530/926–4511) keep tabs on trail conditions. The **Fifth Season Mountaineering Shop** (☎ 530/926–3606) operates a recorded 24-hour climber-skier report (☎ 530/926–5555).

MOUNTAIN CLIMBING

Fifth Season Mountaineering Shop (✉ 300 N. Mt. Shasta Blvd., ☎ 530/926–3606) rents skiing and climbing equipment. **Shasta Mountain Guides** (☎ 530/926–3117) leads hiking, climbing, and ski-touring groups to the summit of Mount Shasta.

SKIING

Mt. Shasta Ski Park. On the southeast flank of Mount Shasta are three lifts on 300 skiable acres. The terrain is 20% beginner, 60% intermediate, 20% advanced. Its vertical drop is 1,100 ft, with a top elevation of 6,600 ft. The longest run is 1½ mi. You can ski until 10 PM from Wednesday to Saturday. A package for beginners, available through the ski school, includes a lift ticket, ski rental, and a lesson. The school also runs the Powder Pups program for children ages four to seven. Within the base lodge are food and beverage facilities, a ski shop, and a ski-rental shop. ✉ *Hwy. 89 exit east from I–5, south of Mt. Shasta,* ☎ *530/926–8610; 530/926–8686 for snow information.*

OFF THE BEATEN PATH

LAVA BEDS NATIONAL MONUMENT – Much of the beauty at this rugged monument, the product of volcanic eruptions, is underground in 300-plus lava tube caves, some of which can be explored. Wear hard-sole boots, and pick up the necessary equipment (lights, "bump" hats, etc.) at the Indian Well Visitor Center, at the park's south end. Guided walks and cave tours, which take place between Memorial Day and Labor Day, depart from the visitor center. ✉ *94 mi from the town of Mt. Shasta; head north on I–5, northeast on U.S. 97 at Weed, east on Hwy. 161 (3 mi north of Dorris), and south on Hwy. 139 (from town of Burney head east on Hwy. 299 and north on Hwy. 139),* ☎ *530/667–2282.* ✆ *$4 per vehicle; $2 per visitor on foot or bicycle.* ✆ *Park 24 hrs. Visitor center daily 8–5.*

Dunsmuir

10 mi south of Mt. Shasta on I–5.

Castle Crags State Park surrounds the town of Dunsmuir, which was named for a 19th-century coal baron. The town's other major attraction is the **Railroad Park Resort** (☞ *below*), where guests spend the night in restored railcars.

The 225 million-year-old granite crags at **Castle Crags State Park** tower over the Sacramento River at heights of up to 6,000 ft. There are excellent trails at lower altitudes in this 6,000-acre park, which also has picnic areas, rest rooms, showers, and plenty of campsites. ✉ *Off I–5, 6 mi south of Dunsmuir,* ☎ *530/235–2684.* ✆ *$5 per vehicle (day use); $12 (campsites). Disposal station, fire rings, flush toilets, hot showers, water.*

Lodging

$ 🏨 **Dunsmuir Inn Bed and Breakfast.** It's not fancy, but this homey inn—a good deal considering that room rates include a made-to-order breakfast—is comfortable and within easy walking distance of the historic downtown area. Rooms are decorated simply. ⊠ *5423 Dunsmuir Ave., 96025,* ☎ *530/235–4543. 5 rooms. Full breakfast. AE, D, DC, MC, V.*

$ 🖭 **Railroad Park Resort.** The antique cabooses here have been converted into cozy, wood-panel motel rooms in honor of Dunsmuir's railroad legacy. The resort has a vaguely *Orient Express*–style dining room and a lounge fashioned from vintage railcars. The landscaped grounds contain a huge logging steam engine and a restored water tower. ⊠ *100 Railroad Park Rd., 96025,* ☎ *530/235–4440 or 800/974–7245,* FAX *530/235–4470. 23 cabooses, 4 cabins. Restaurant (no lunch), pool, hot tub, camping. AE, D, MC, V.*

Lake Shasta Area

34 mi south of Mt. Shasta (to town of Lakehead) on I–5; 12 mi north of Redding on I–5.

The many Shastas—mountain, lake, river, town, dam, and forest—derive from the name of the Indians who inhabited parts of the region in the 19th century (variously, Shatasla and Sastise). The Indian pronunciation for the river was *tschasta.*

❽ Stalagmites, stalactites, odd flowstone deposits, and crystals entice visitors of all ages to the **Lake Shasta Caverns.** A two-hour tour includes a catamaran ride across the McCloud arm of Lake Shasta and a bus ride up Grey Rock Mountain to the cavern entrance. The caverns are 58°F year-round, making them an appealingly cool retreat on a hot summer day. The crowning jewel is the awe-inspiring cathedral room. The guides are friendly, enthusiastic, and knowledgeable. ⊠ *Shasta Caverns Rd. exit from I–5,* ☎ *530/238–2341 or 800/795–2283.* 🖼 *$14.* ☉ *Daily 9–4; tours May–Sept. on the hr, Oct.–Apr. at 10, noon, and 2.*

★ Twenty-one varieties of fish inhabit **Lake Shasta.** You can rent fishing boats, ski boats, sailboats, canoes, paddleboats, Jet Skis, and windsurfing boards at one of the many marinas and resorts along the 370-mi shoreline. Lake Shasta is known as the houseboat capital of the world. *See* Outdoor Activities and Sports, *below,* for information about rentals.

★ ❾ **Shasta Dam** is the second-largest and the fourth-tallest concrete dam in the United States. At twilight the sight is magical, with Mount Shasta gleaming above the not-quite-dark water and deer frolicking on the hillside beside the dam. The dam is lit after dark, but there is no access from 10 PM to 6 AM. The visitor center has fact sheets and photographic and historic displays. ⊠ *Shasta Dam Blvd.,* ☎ *530/275–4463.* ☉ *Dam 6 AM–10 PM; visitor center weekdays 8:30–5 (tours at 10, noon, 2 year-round, more often in summer), weekends 9–5 (tours 10, noon, 2 year-round, on the hr 9–4 in summer).*

Dining

$$ ✕ **Tail O' the Whale.** This restaurant overlooking Lake Shasta is distinguished by its nautical decor. Seafood, pasta, prime rib, poultry, and Cajun pepper shrimp are the specialties. ⊠ *10300 Bridge Bay Rd., Bridge Bay exit from I–5,* ☎ *530/275–3021. D, MC, V.*

Outdoor Activities and Sports

FISHING

The Fishin' Hole (⊠ 3844 Shasta Dam Blvd., Central Valley, ☎ 530/275–4123) carries supplies and provides information about conditions, licenses, and fishing packages.

HOUSEBOATING

Houseboats come in all sizes except small. As a rule these moving homes come with cooking utensils, dishes, and most of the equipment you'll need—you supply food and linens. Renters are given a short course in how to maneuver the boats before they set out on cruises; it's not difficult, as the houseboats are slow moving. You can fish, swim, sunbathe on the flat roof, or sit on the deck and watch the world go by. The shoreline of Lake Shasta is beautifully ragged, with countless inlets; it's not hard to find privacy. Expect to spend a minimum of $200 a day for a craft that sleeps six. There is usually a three-night minimum in peak season. **Shasta Cascade Wonderland Association** (☞ Contacts and Resources *in* the Far North A to Z, *below*) has more information.

Shasta

7 mi west of Redding on Hwy. 299.

The ruins of the once prosperous gold-mining town of Shasta are now the 13-acre **Shasta State Historic Park.** Poke around the few restored buildings on the self-guided tour, and you'll get a sense of the lives of 19th-century prospectors. The eclectic holdings of the park's museum include California paintings, memorabilia, and a *Prairie Traveler* guidebook with advice on encounters with Indians. In the basement of the building, formerly the town's courthouse, are iron-bar jail cells; murderers were hanged from the scaffold outside. ⊠ *Hwy. 299,* ☎ *530/ 243–8194.* ✑ *$2.* ☉ *Wed.–Sun. 10–5.*

Weaverville

❿ *40 mi west of Shasta on Hwy. 299 (called Main St. in town).*

This old mountain town with a population of 5,000 is one of the Far North's most charming. Although there are strips of car dealers and the like, the downtown blocks maintain their gold-rush ambience. Weaverville is a popular headquarters for family vacations and biking, hiking, fishing, hunting, and gold-panning excursions.

John Weaver was one of three men who built the first cabin, in 1850, in the town that would be named for him. By 1851 Weaverville was the Trinity County seat and included neighboring communities such as Frenchtown, Englishtown, Germantown, Irishtown, and a sizable Chinatown.

The most visible legacy of the Chinese presence is the **Weaverville Joss House,** a Taoist temple built in 1874. Called Won Lim Miao, the "Temple Amongst the Forest Beneath the Clouds," by Chinese miners, it attracts worshipers from around the world. With its golden altar, carved wooden canopies, and intriguing artifacts, the Joss House is a piece of California history that can best be appreciated in the company of a guide. The original temple building and many of its furnishings—some of which had come from China—were burned in 1873, but members of the local Chinese community soon rebuilt it. An ornate wooden gate leads to the porch of this bright-blue building. ⊠ *Oregon and Main Sts.,* ☎ *530/623–5284.* ✑ *Nominal charge for 40-min guided tours, on the hr 10–4.* ☉ *Summer daily 10–5, rest of yr Thurs.–Mon. 10–5.*

Fires destroyed many parts of Weaverville; surviving buildings are mostly brick. Since the upper floor of many old downtown buildings was often owned by a different person than the lower floor, outdoor spiral staircases were constructed to permit each owner a private entrance. Three such buildings remain visible in the downtown Historic District.

The **Trinity County Courthouse** (⊠ Court and Main Sts.), built in 1857 as a store, office building, and hotel, was converted to county use in 1865. The Apollo Saloon in the basement became the county jail.

Trinity County Historical Park is home to the Jake Jackson Memorial Museum, which has a blacksmith shop, a replica stamp mill, and the original jail cells of the Trinity County Courthouse. ⊠ *408 Main St.,* ☏ *530/623–5211.* ⊙ *May–Oct., daily 10–5; Nov.–Apr., Tues.–Sat. noon–4.*

Dining and Lodging

$–$$ ✕ **La Grange Cafe.** This eatery is one of the few places in Weaverville open for lunch and dinner six days a week. Stick to basics like chicken and pasta; the kitchen is not as dependable when it comes to dishes like trout. On the plus side, La Grange serves plenty of vegetables and sells beer and wine. ⊠ *315 N. Main St.,* ☏ *530/623–5325. AE, D, MC, V.*

$ ✕ **La Casita.** Here you'll find the standard regimen—all the quesadillas (including one with roasted chili peppers), tostadas, enchiladas, tacos, and tamales you could want, many of them available in a vegetarian version. This casual spot is open from late morning through early evening, so it's great for a mid-afternoon snack. ⊠ *254 Main St.,* ☏ *530/623–5797. No credit cards.*

$ ⌂ **Red Hill Motel.** Housekeeping cabins make this the best choice among Weaverville motels. A two-bedroom cabin with a full kitchen is popular with families. ⊠ *Red Hill Rd., Box 234, 96093,* ☏ *530/ 623–4331. 14 rooms, 10 of them cabins with carports. D, DC, MC, V.*

Outdoor Activities and Sports

Below the Lewiston Dam, east of Weaverville on Highway 299, is the **Fly Stretch** of the Trinity River, a world-class fly-fishing area. The **Pine Cove Boat Ramp** provides quality fishing access for visitors with disabilities—decks here are built over prime trout-fishing water. Contact the **Weaverville Ranger Station** (☏ 530/623–2121) for maps and information about hiking trails in the Trinity Alps Wilderness.

Shopping

Hays Bookstore (⊠ 106 Main St., ☏ 530/623–2516) carries books on the natural history, attractions, and sights of the Far North. Check out the **Western Shop** (⊠ 226 Main St., ☏ 530/623–6494) for outdoor gear, bolo ties, cowboy hats, and much more.

OFF THE   **TRINITY HERITAGE SCENIC BYWAY** – This road, shown on maps as High-
BEATEN PATH   way 3, runs north from Weaverville for 120 mi up to its intersection with I–5, south of Yreka. Natural attractions are visible all along this beautiful, forest-lined road, which is often closed during the winter months. A major portion of the route follows the path established by early miners and settlers as it climbs from 2,000 to 6,500 ft.

Redding

⑪   *218 mi from San Francisco on I–80 to I–505 to I–5 north; 12 mi south of Lake Shasta on I–5.*

With a population of 70,000, Redding is by far the largest city in the Far North. Though not of much interest, it serves as a useful headquarters for exploring the surrounding countryside.

Dining and Lodging

$$ ✕ **Hatch Cover.** This establishment's dark-wood paneling and views of the adjacent Sacramento River give diners a shipboard feel. The menu

emphasizes seafood, but you can also get steaks and combination plates. The appetizer menu is extensive, and there's an outside deck. ⊠ *202 Hemsted Dr. (from Cypress Ave. exit off I–5, turn left, then right on Bechelli La., and left on Hemsted Dr.)*, ☎ *530/223–5606. AE, D, MC, V. No lunch weekends.*

$ ✕ **Jack's Grill.** Although it looks like a dive from the outside, this steak house and bar is immensely popular areawide for its 16-ounce steaks. The place is usually jam-packed and noisy. ⊠ *1743 California St.,* ☎ *530/241–9705. AE, MC, V. Closed Sun. No lunch.*

$–$$ ✕⬚ **Doubletree Hotel.** Landscaped grounds and a large patio area with outdoor food service are the highlights here. Rooms are spacious and comfortable. Misty's, the lobby's fancy restaurant ($$–$$$), is popular among locals for its steak Diane. Pets are allowed with advance notice. ⊠ *1830 Hilltop Dr. (Hwy. 44/299 exit east from I–5), 96002,* ☎ *530/221–8700 or 800/222–8733,* ⑆ *530/221–0324. 193 rooms. Restaurant, bar, coffee shop, room service, pool, wading pool, hot tub, putting green. AE, D, DC, MC, V.*

$$$–$$$$ ⬚ **Brigadoon Castle Bed & Breakfast.** Fifteen winding miles from I–5 is a 83-acre estate crowned with an Elizabethan-style castle that opened as a B&B in 1996. Marble baths, antiques, and luxurious fabrics make the Brigadoon an elegant retreat. A separate cottage has a kitchen and a hot tub. From Friday to Sunday the rates include dinner. ⊠ *9036 Zogg Mine Rd., Igo 96047,* ☎ *530/396–2785 or 888/343–2836,* ⑆ *530/396–2784. 4 rooms, 1 cottage. Hot tub. Full breakfast. AE, D, MC, V.*

$ ⬚ **Howard Johnson Express.** Here's a budget option—doubles with queen-size beds go for around $65—off I–5's Cypress exit. ⊠ *2731 Bechelli La.,* ☎ *530/223–1935 or 800/354–5222,* ⑆ *530/223–1176. 75 rooms. Pool. AE, D, DC, MC, V.*

Outdoor Activities and Sports

The **Fly Shop** (⊠ 4140 Churn Creek Rd., ☎ 530/222–3555) sells fishing licenses and has information about guides, conditions, and fishing packages. **Park Marina Watersports** (⊠ 2515 Park Marina Dr., ☎ 530/246–8388) rents rafts and canoes from May to September.

THE FAR NORTH A TO Z

Arriving and Departing

By Bus

Greyhound Lines (☎ 800/231–2222) buses travel I–5, serving Chico, Red Bluff, Redding, Dunsmuir, and Mount Shasta.

By Car

Interstate 5, an excellent four-lane divided highway, runs up the center of California through Red Bluff and Redding and continues north to Oregon. Chico is east of I–5 on Highway 32. Lassen Park can be reached by Highway 36 from Red Bluff or (except in winter) Highway 44 from Redding. Highway 299 leads from Redding to McArthur-Burney Falls Memorial State Park. Highways 36 and 299 are good two-lane roads that are kept open year-round. If you are traveling through this area in winter, however, always carry snow chains in your car.

By Plane

Chico Municipal Airport (⊠ 150 Airpark Blvd., off Cohasset Rd., ☎ 530/898–2359) and **Redding Municipal Airport** (⊠ Airport Rd., ☎ 530/224–4320) are served by United Express (☎ 800/241–6522).

By Train

Amtrak (☎ 800/872–7245) has stations in Chico (✉ W. 5th and Orange Sts.), Redding (✉ 1620 Yuba St.) and Dunsmuir (✉ 5750 Sacramento Ave.).

Getting Around

By Bus

Butte County Transit (☎ 530/342–0221 or 800/822–8145) serves Chico, Oroville, and elsewhere. **Chico Area Transit System** (CATS; ☎ 530/342–0221) provides bus service within Chico. The vehicles of the **Redding Area Bus Authority** (☎ 530/241–2877) operate daily except Sunday. **STAGE** (☎ 530/842–8295) buses travel from Montague to Dunsmuir, stopping in Mount Shasta and other towns, and provide service in Scott Valley.

By Car

An automobile is virtually essential to tour the Far North unless you arrive by bus, plane, or train and intend to travel the region by foot or bicycle.

Contacts and Resources

Car Rental

Avis (✉ Redding Municipal Airport, ☎ 530/221–2855 or 800/331–1212). **Enterprise** (✉ 361 E. Cypress Ave., Redding, ☎ 530/223–0700 or 800/325–8007). **Enterprise** (✉ 570 Antelope Blvd., Red Bluff, ☎ 530/529–0177 or 800/325–8007). **Hertz** (✉ Redding Municipal Airport, ☎ 530/221–4620 or 800/654–3131).

Emergencies

Ambulance (☎ 911). **Fire** (☎ 911). **Police** (☎ 911).

Visitor Information

Chico Chamber of Commerce (✉ 500 Main St., ☎ 530/891–5556 or 800/852–8570). **Shasta Cascade Wonderland Association** (✉ 1699 Hwy. 273, Anderson 96007, ☎ 530/365–7500 or 800/326–6944).

4 The Wine Country

You don't have to be a wine enthusiast to appreciate the mellow beauty of Napa and Sonoma counties, whose rolling hills and verdant vineyards resemble those of Tuscany and Provence. Here, among state-of-the-art wineries, award-winning restaurants, and luxury hotels where mud baths and massage are daily rituals, you just might discover that life need have no nobler purpose than enjoying the fruits of the earth.

Updated by
Marty
Olmstead and
Sharon Silva

I**N 1862, AFTER AN EXTENSIVE TOUR** of the wine-producing areas of Europe, Count Agoston Haraszthy de Mokcsa reported a promising prognosis about his adopted California: "Of all the countries through which I passed, not one possessed the same advantages that are to be found in California. . . . California can produce as noble and generous a wine as any in Europe; more in quantity to the acre, and without repeated failures through frosts, summer rains, hailstorms, or other causes."

The "dormant resources" that the father of California's viticulture saw in the balmy days and cool nights of the temperate Napa and Sonoma valleys are in full fruition today. Although the wines produced here are praised and savored by connoisseurs throughout the world, the area continues to be a proving ground for the latest techniques of grape growing and wine making.

For many, wine making is a second career. Making wine is said to be a good way to turn a large fortune into a small one, but that hasn't deterred the doctors, former college professors, publishing tycoons, art dealers, and others who come here to try their hands at it. In 1975 the Napa Valley had about two dozen wineries; today there are more than 240. In Sonoma County, where the web of vineyards is looser, there are well more than 150 wineries, with much of the recent development in the relatively cool Carneros region, deemed ideal for growing the chardonnay grape.

In addition to great food and wine, you'll find a window into California history in the Wine Country. The town of Sonoma is filled with remnants of Mexican California and the solid, ivy-covered, brick wineries built by Haraszthy and his disciples. Calistoga is a virtual museum of Steamboat Gothic architecture, replete with the fretwork and clapboard beloved of gold-rush prospectors and 19th-century spa goers. St. Helena is home to a later architectural fantasy, the beautiful art nouveau mansion of the Beringer brothers.

The area's natural beauty draws a continuous flow of tourists—from the spring, when the vineyards bloom yellow with wild mustard, to the fall, when the grapes are ripe. Haraszthy was right: This is a chosen place.

Pleasures and Pastimes

Dining

Many star chefs from urban areas throughout the United States have migrated to the Wine Country, drawn by the area's produce and world-class wines—the products of fertile soil and near-perpetual sun. As a result of this marriage of imported talent and indigenous bounty, food now rivals wine as the principal attraction of the region—a reality underscored by the presence of the Culinary Institute of America's West Coast headquarters in St. Helena.

Higher quality has, of course, meant higher prices. However, those on a budget will also find appealing inexpensive eateries. Gourmet delis prepare superb picnic fare, and brunch is a cost-effective strategy at high-end restaurants.

With few exceptions (which are noted in individual restaurant listings), dress is informal. Where reservations are indicated as essential, you may need to reserve a week or more ahead; during the summer and early fall harvest seasons you may need to book several months ahead.

CATEGORY	COST*
$$$$	over $50
$$$	$30–$50
$$	$20–$30
$	under $20

per person for a three-course meal, excluding drinks, service, and 8.5% sales tax

Hot-Air Ballooning

Day after day, colorful balloons fill the morning sky high above the Wine Country's valleys. To aficionados, peering down at vineyards from the vantage point of the clouds is the ultimate California experience. Balloon flights take place soon after sunrise, when the calmest, coolest time of day offers maximum lift and soft landings. Prices depend on the duration of the flight, number of passengers, and services (some companies provide such extras as pickup at your lodging or champagne brunch after the flight). Expect to spend about $175 per person.

Lodging

In a region where first-class restaurants and wineries attract connoisseurs from afar, it's no surprise that elegant lodgings—inns, hotels, and spas—have sprung up to accommodate them. Many local bed-and-breakfasts have Victorian or Spanish architecture and serve a full country breakfast highlighting local produce and specialties. The newer hotels and spas are often state-of-the-art buildings offering comforts like massage treatments or spring water–fed pools; many house world-class restaurants or are just a walk or a short car ride away from gastronomic bliss.

Not surprisingly, a stay in the Wine Country is expensive. Santa Rosa ... center in the area; though it's not in the thick ... est selection of rooms, many at mod- ... le to find lodgings closer to the vine- ... Many B&Bs are fully booked well ... t some, small children are discouraged

	COST*
	over $200
	$120–$200
	$80–$120
	under $80

...ble room, excluding tax.

...and massage are rejuvenating local tradi- ...rldwide as the Hot Springs of the West, is ...g water–fed mineral tubs and mud baths ...na, St. Helena, and other towns also have

...e-tasting game, the Rob... winery and ... Cellars both give general... which ...'ll learn the basics of, respectively, wine and cham... what to look for when you taste. Unless oth... ies in this chapter are open daily year-round... mission, tours, or tastings.

Exploring the Wine Country

The Wine Country comprises two ma... Sonoma Valley. The Napa Valley, p...

northern part of the town of Napa and runs northwest to Calistoga.
The Sonoma Valley, in the southeasternmost portion of Sonoma County,
is due west of the Napa Valley. Five major paths cut through the Wine
Country: U.S. 101 and Highways 12 and 121 through Sonoma County,
and Highway 29 north from the town of Napa. The 25-mi Silverado
Trail, which runs parallel to Highway 29 north from Napa to Calistoga, is a more scenic, less crowded route.

*Numbers in the text correspond to numbers in the margin and on the
Wine Country map.*

Great Itineraries

IF YOU HAVE 2 DAYS

Start at the circa-1857 **Buena Vista Carneros Winery** ⑳. From there
take the Oakville Grade to historic ⊞ **St. Helena,** taking time to admire the views of Sonoma and Napa valleys from the Mayacamas Mountains. After lunch in St. Helena take the 30-minute tour of **Beringer
Vineyards** ⑬. The next day drive to **Calistoga** for an early morning balloon ride, an afternoon trip to the mud baths, and a visit to **Clos Pegase** ⑰ before heading back to St. Helena for dinner at Greystone—the
highly acclaimed restaurant of the Culinary Institute of America.

IF YOU HAVE 5 OR 6 DAYS

Begin in the town of **Sonoma.** Explore the town plaza and have lunch
there or pick up some fixings for a picnic at Jack London State Historic Park in ⊞ **Glen Ellen.** Explore the grounds at Jack London State
Historic Park, then take the tram tour at **Benziger Family Winery** ㉒.
The next morning visit **Kenwood Vineyards** ㉓ before heading north
on Highway 12 and U.S. 101 to **Healdsburg.** In this less trafficked haven
of northern Sonoma County, a host of "hidden" wineries—including
Dry Creek Vineyard ㉖ and **Quivira Vineyards** ㉗—lie nestled in the
woods. Spend the night in ⊞ **Healdsburg.** On the third day cross over
into Napa Valley—take Mark Springs Road east off U.S. 101's River
Road exit and follow the signs on Porter Creek Road to Petrified Forest Road to Highway 29. Spend the day, and the night, in ⊞ **Calistoga.**
Wake up early on the fourth day for a balloon ride. If you're feeling
energetic, take to the **Silverado Trail** for a bike ride with stops on the
north side of town at **Chateau Montelena** ⑱ and the south side of town
at **Clos Pegase** ⑰. On day five visit the galleries, shops, and eateries of
St. Helena before driving to **Yountville,** stopping for lunch at one of its
many acclaimed restaurants before heading up the hill to the **Hess Collection Winery and Vineyards** ③.

When to Tour the Wine Country

"Crush," the term used to indicate the season when grapes are picked
and crushed, usually takes place in September or October, depending
on the weather. From September to December the entire Wine Country celebrates with street fairs and festivals. Golf tournaments, wine
auctions, and art and food fairs dot the calendar throughout the fall.

In season (from April to October), the Napa Valley draws crowds of
tourists, and traffic along Highway 29 from St. Helena to Calistoga is
often backed up on weekends. The Sonoma Valley, Santa Rosa, and
especially Healdsburg are less crowded. In season and over holiday weekends it's best to book lodging, restaurant, and winery reservations well
ahead. Many wineries give tours at specified times and require appointments. To avoid crowds visit the Wine Country during the week
and get an early start in the morning (most wineries open around 10).

THE NAPA VALLEY

Famed for its unrivaled climate and neat rows of vineyards, the Napa Valley is made up of small, quirky towns with Victorian Gothic architecture. Calistoga feels like an Old West frontier town, posh St. Helena contains tony shops and elegant restaurants, and Yountville is redolent of American history but is an up-to-the-minute culinary hub.

Napa

47 mi from San Francisco, north on U.S. 101, west on Hwy. 37, north and east on Hwy. 121/12 to Hwy. 29; 46 mi from San Francisco, east and north on I–80 to Hwy. 37 west to Hwy. 29 north.

The town of Napa doesn't offer much in the way of attractions, but it is the largest town in the Carneros grape-growing region that straddles southern Napa and Sonoma counties. The Carneros area has a long, cool growing season tempered by maritime breezes and lingering fogs off the San Pablo Bay—optimum slow-growing conditions for pinot noir and chardonnay grapes.

Most destinations in the Napa and Sonoma valleys are easily accessible from Napa. For those seeking an affordable alternative to the hotels and B&Bs in the heart of the Wine Country, Napa's chain lodgings (most of the major companies are represented) are a good option—but stay on the north side of town near Yountville; some of the sections to the south are downright seedy.

❶ Domaine Carneros occupies a 138-acre estate dominated by a château inspired by Champagne Taittinger's Château de la Marquetterie in France. Carved into the hillside beneath the winery, Domaine Carneros's cellars produce sparkling wines reminiscent of the Taittinger style and using only Carneros grapes. At night the château is a glowing beacon rising above the dark vineyards. ⊠ *1240 Duhig Rd.,* ☎ *707/257–0101.* 🔲 *Tasting fees.* ☉ *Mon.–Thurs., 10:30–5, Fri.–Sun., 10:30–6. Tours Mon.–Thurs. at 11, 1, and 3, Fri.–Sun. hourly from 11–3.*

❷ Learn the history and folklore of the rare alambic brandy at the **Carneros Alambic Distillery.** Tours include an explanation of the double-distillation process, which eliminates all but the finest spirits for aging; a view of the French-built alambic pot stills that resemble Aladdin's lamp; a trip to the atmospheric oak barrel house, where taped chants create an otherworldly mood; and a sensory evaluation of vintage brandies (no tasting allowed, by law). ⊠ *1250 Cuttings Wharf Rd. (from Domaine Carneros, head 1 mi east on Carneros Hwy.),* ☎ *707/253–9055.* ☉ *Apr.–Oct., daily 10–5; Nov.–Mar., daily 10:30–4:30. Tours on the hr.*

★ ❸ The **Hess Collection Winery and Vineyards** is an unexpected discovery on a hilltop 9 mi northwest of Napa (don't give up; the road leading to the winery is long and winding). On display in the rustic limestone structure, built circa 1903, is Swiss owner Donald Hess's personal art collection, including works by contemporary artists like Robert Motherwell, Francis Bacon, and Frank Stella. Cabernet sauvignon is the winery's strong suit, though Hess also produces some fine chardonnays. Visitors are free to tour the property. ⊠ *4411 Redwood Rd., west off Hwy. 29,* ☎ *707/255–1144.* ☉ *Daily 10–4.*

❹ The winery at **Trefethen Vineyards** was built in 1886; today it's the only wooden, gravity-powered winery in Napa. Trefethen is known for its reserve cabernet as well as its 1993 merlot, available only on the premises. ⊠ *1160 Oak Knoll Ave., off Hwy. 29,* ☎ *707/255–7700.* ☉ *Daily 10–4:30. Tours by appointment.*

60

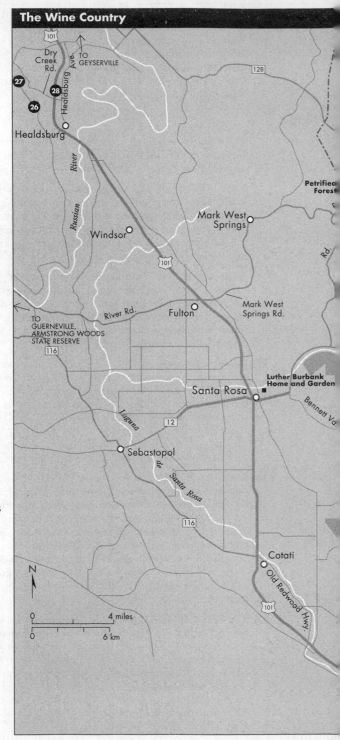

The Wine Country

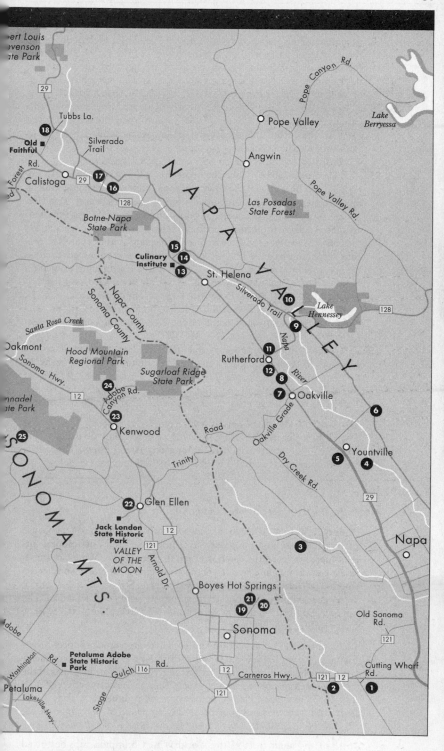

Robert Louis
Stevenson
State Park

29

Tubbs La.

18

Old
Faithful

Silverado
Trail

Rd.

Calistoga   29

17

16

128

Botne-Napa
State Park

15

Culinary
Institute   14

13   St. Helena

Napa County
Sonoma County

Santa Rosa Creek

Sonoma Creek

Hood Mountain
Regional Park

Oakmont

Sonoma Hwy.

12

Annadel
State Park

25

24   Adobe Canyon Rd.

23

Kenwood

Sugarloaf Ridge
State Park

Road

Trinity

22   Glen Ellen

Jack London
State Historic
Park

121

VALLEY OF THE
MOON

Arnold Dr.

12

Boyes Hot Springs

21

19   20

Sonoma

SONOMA   MTS.

Adobe

Washington   Rd.

Petaluma Adobe
State Historic
Park

Gulch   116   Rd.

Petaluma

Lakeville Hwy.

Stage

121

12   Carneros Hwy.

121   12

Pope Canyon   Rd.

Pope Valley

Angwin

Las Posadas
State Forest

Pope Valley Rd.

Lake
Berryessa

Silverado Trail

10   Lake
Hennessey

128

9

Rutherford   11

12

8

7   Oakville

Napa River

6

Oakville Grade

Dry Creek Rd.

5   Yountville

4

29

3   Napa

Old Sonoma
Rd.

121

Cutting Wharf
Rd.

2   1

N   A   P   A   V   A   L   L   E   Y

Dining and Lodging

$$ ✕ **Bistro Don Giovanni.** The ambience at this bistro is casual Mediterranean, with terra-cotta tile floors, and high ceilings; there's also a spacious outdoor patio with an expansive view of the valley. Don't miss the individual pizzas cooked in a wood-burning oven, the handmade pastas, or the focaccia sandwiches concealing grilled vegetables. ⊠ *4110 St. Helena Hwy. (Hwy. 29),* ☎ *707/224–3300. AE, D, MC, V.*

$–$$ ✕ **Brown Street Grill.** This downtown grill serves home-style fare in a casual setting. Simple salads and classic plates of roast chicken and grilled steak are masterfully handled, and the thick, tasty sandwiches, stuffed with valley-grown tomatoes, are trenchermen's treats at lunchtime. ⊠ *1300 Brown St.,* ☎ *707/255–6395. MC, V. Closed Sun.*

$$$–$$$$ ✕⊞ **Silverado Country Club.** The luxurious 1,200-acre Silverado Country Club, in hills east of the town of Napa, contains cottages, kitchen apartments, and one- to three-bedroom efficiencies, many with fireplaces. With two golf courses, nine pools, and 23 tennis courts, the country club is a place for serious sports enthusiasts and anyone who enjoys the conveniences of a full-scale resort. The elegant Vintner's Court restaurant serves dinner only (Pacific Rim cuisine; reservations essential)— there's a seafood buffet on Friday night and a champagne brunch on Sunday. The Royal Oak restaurant serves steak and seafood for dinner nightly. ⊠ *1600 Atlas Peak Rd. (6 mi east of Napa via Hwy. 121), 94558,* ☎ *707/257–0200 or 800/532–0500,* ☒ *707/257–2867. 277 condo units. 3 restaurants, bar, 9 pools, 2 18-hole golf courses, 23 tennis courts, bicycles. AE, D, DC, MC, V.*

$$ ⊞ **Chateau Hotel.** This country inn–style modern motel has facilities for travelers with disabilities and offers discounts to senior citizens. ⊠ *4195 Solano Ave. (west of Hwy. 29, exit at Trower Ave.), 94558,* ☎ *707/253–9300; 800/253–6272 in CA,* ☒ *707/253–0906. 115 rooms. Refrigerators, pool, hot tub. Continental breakfast. AE, D, DC, MC, V.*

Outdoor Activities and Sports

The 18-hole **Chardonnay Club** (⊠ 2555 Jameson Canyon Rd., ☎ 707/257–8950) course is a favorite among Bay Area golfers. The greens fee, $60 weekdays and $80 weekends, includes a cart.

Yountville

13 mi north of the town of Napa on Hwy. 29.

Yountville at first glance looks like a slightly backwater town because of its small size and bungalow-style houses. Despite its modest appearance, however, the town is home to three of the Wine Country's finest restaurants and two of its most esteemed wineries. Another attraction is **Vintage 1870** (⊠ 6525 Washington St., ☎ 707/944–2451), a 26-acre complex of boutiques, restaurants, and gourmet stores. The vine-covered brick buildings were built in 1870 and housed a winery, livery stable, and distillery.

5 Luggage-meister Louis Vuitton and French champagne producer Moet-Hennessey own **Domaine Chandon.** Tours of the sleek, modern facilities on the beautifully maintained property include sample flutes of the méthode champenoise sparkling wine. Champagne costs between $3.50 and $5.75 per glass. Hors d'oeuvres are complimentary, and an elegant restaurant beckons gourmets. ⊠ *California Dr., west of Hwy. 29,* ☎ *707/944–2280.* ☉ *Daily 11–6. Tours throughout the day.*

6 In 1993 and again in 1995 the World Wine Championships bestowed a platinum award on **Stag's Leap Wine Cellars** for its 1990 reserve chardonnay, designating it the highest-ranked premium chardonnay in the world. The winery's proprietary red table wine, Cask 23, consistently earns accolades as well. ⊠ *5766 Silverado Trail,* ☎ *707/944–2020.* ⊟ *$3 tasting fee.* ☉ *Daily 10–4. Tours by appointment.*

Dining and Lodging

$$$$ ✕ **Domaine Chandon.** The restaurant of the world-renowned winery serves French-inspired California cuisine. The cavernous dining room looks out over miles of vineyards and native oaks. When the weather is good, try for a seat on the tree-shaded terrace, an ideal spot for sipping a glass of the house vintage and admiring its source. ⊠ *California Dr. (take Yountville exit off Hwy. 29 toward Veterans' Home),* ☎ *707/944–2892. Reservations essential. AE, D, DC, MC, V. No dinner Mon.–Tues. Apr.–Oct.*

$$$$ ✕ **French Laundry.** Gardens, fresh flowers, and gentle lighting make
★ patrons of the French Laundry feel like well-tended country houseguests. The dinners of four or five courses always begin with two or three additional morsels to start, such as a tiny ice-cream cone filled with salmon tartare or a quail egg sandwiched between a crown of caviar and a base of brioche. Your meal thus launched, a full three hours will likely pass before you reach dessert. ⊠ *6640 Washington St.,* ☎ *707/944–2380. Reservations essential. AE, MC, V. Closed 1st 2 wks in Jan.; lunch hours and days vary with the season.*

$$ ✕ **Brix.** A spacious many-windowed dining room invites you to sit back and enjoy the East-West menu at Brix. Scallops are served with a Thai lime-butter sauce, and salmon is flavored with a light soy glaze. A wood-fired oven is used for cooking pizzas. Desserts receive Asian accents as well, with a ginger crème brûlée among the offerings. ⊠ *7377 St. Helena Hwy.,* ☎ *707/944–2749. AE, D, DC, MC, V.*

$$ ✕ **Mustards Grill.** Grilled fish, steaks, local fresh produce, and an im-
★ pressive wine list are the trademarks of this boisterous bistro with a black-and-white marble floor and upbeat artworks. The thin, crisp, golden onion rings are addictive. ⊠ *7399 St. Helena Hwy.,* ☎ *707/944–2424. Reservations essential. D, DC, MC, V.*

$–$$ ✕ **Ristorante Piatti.** The simpler regional Italian dishes—pasta tossed with greens, pizza topped with fresh tomatoes and creamy mozzarella—are the ones to try at this casual trattoria with an open kitchen. ⊠ *6480 Washington St.,* ☎ *707/944–2070. AE, MC, V.*

$ ✕ **The Diner.** A beloved Napa Valley stopover, this breakfast-centric eatery prepares local sausages and house potatoes that are not to be missed. Healthful versions of Mexican and American classics are served for dinner. ⊠ *6476 Washington St.,* ☎ *707/944–2626. No credit cards. Closed Mon.*

$$$–$$$$ ⊡ **La Residence.** Even though it's within feet of the St. Helena Highway, "La Res," as it's known, is secluded and romantic enough to make you feel as if you've flown to France, or at least New Orleans. The hotel buildings overlook a pool, a manicured garden, and towering oak trees that bathe the entire property in shade. The spacious rooms have period antiques, fireplaces, and double French doors opening onto verandas or patios. ⊠ *4066 St. Helena Hwy. (Hwy. 29), 4 mi south of Yountville,* ☎ *707/253–0337,* FAX *707/253–0382. 20 rooms. Dining room, pool, hot tub, business services. Full breakfast. AE, DC, MC, V.*

$$$–$$$$ ⊡ **Napa Valley Lodge.** Spacious rooms overlook the vineyards and the valley at this hacienda-style lodge; a tile roof, covered walkways, balconies, patios, and colorful gardens add to the Mediterranean mood. ⊠ *2230 Madison St., at Hwy. 29,* ☎ *707/944–2468 or 800/368–2468,* FAX *707/944–9362. 55 rooms. Refrigerators, pool, hot tub, sauna, exercise room. Continental breakfast. AE, DC, MC, V.*

$$$–$$$$ ⊡ **Vintage Inn.** All the rooms at this luxurious inn have fireplaces, whirlpool baths, refrigerators, private verandas or patios, hand-painted fabrics, window seats, and shuttered windows. Guests are treated to

a welcome bottle of wine, champagne with breakfast, and afternoon tea. ✉ *6541 Washington St., 94599,* ☎ *707/944–1112 or 800/351–1133,* FAX *707/944–1617. 80 rooms. Refrigerators, pool, hot tub, tennis court, bicycles. Continental breakfast. AE, D, DC, MC, V.*

$$$ 🖭 **Petit Logis.** In 1997, Jay and Judith Caldwell remodeled a row of shops into a charming motel-type inn. Wall murals and 11-ft ceilings lend the rooms a European elegance. Guests take breakfast at one of two nearby restaurants. ✉ *6527 Yount St., 94599,* ☎ *707/944–2332. 5 rooms. Full breakfast. MC, V.*

Hot-Air Ballooning

Balloons Above the Valley (☎ 707/253–2222; 800/464–6824 in CA) operates out of Napa. **Napa Valley Balloons** (☎ 707/944–0228; 800/253–2224 in CA) is based in Yountville.

Oakville

2 mi west of Yountville on Hwy. 29.

There are three reasons to visit the town of Oakville: its grocery store, its scenic mountain grade, and its magnificent, highly exclusive winery. The **Oakville Grocery** (✉ 7856 St. Helena Hwy.), built in the late 1880s to serve as a grocery store and Wells Fargo Pony Express stop, carries gourmet foods and difficult-to-find wines. Custom-packed picnic baskets are a specialty. In mid-1998, the store opened a café that serves fresh, light Cal-Mediterranean fare indoors and out.Along the mountain range that divides the Napa and Sonoma valleys, the **Oakville Grade** is a twisting half-hour route with breathtaking views of both valleys. Though the surface of the road is good, it can be difficult to negotiate at night, and trucks are advised not to attempt it at all.

❼ At **Robert Mondavi,** the winery that created fumé blanc, you're encouraged to take the 60-minute production tour with complimentary tasting, before trying the reserve reds (from $1 to $5 per glass). In-depth three- to four-hour tours and gourmet lunch tours are also popular. Afterward, visit the art gallery, or stick around for a summer concert. ✉ *7801 St. Helena Hwy.,* ☎ *707/259–9463.* ☉ *Daily 9–5. Tours by appointment.*

❽ **Opus One,** the combined venture of California wine maker Robert Mondavi and French baron Philippe Rothschild, is famed for its vast (1,000 barrels side by side on a single floor) semicircular barrel cellar modeled on the Château Mouton Rothschild winery in France. The futuristic building is the work of the same architects who built San Francisco's Transamerica Pyramid. The state-of-the-art facilities produce about 20,000 cases of ultrapremium Bordeaux-style red wine from grapes grown in the estate's own vineyards and in the surrounding Oakville appellation. ✉ *7900 St. Helena Hwy.,* ☎ *707/963–1979.* 🖭 *Tasting fee ($15).* ☉ *Daily 10–3:30. Tours by appointment.*

Rutherford

1 mi northwest of Oakville on Hwy. 29.

From a fast-moving car, Rutherford is a quick blur of dark forest, a rustic barn or two, and maybe a country store. Then it's gone. But don't speed by this tiny hamlet; with its singular microclimate and soil, this is an important viticultural center.

❾ The tour at **Mumm Napa Valley** is educational and entertaining. The winery, one of California's premier sparkling-wine producers, is best known for its Napa Brut Prestige and ultrapremium Vintage Reserve.

An art gallery contains a permanent exhibit of photographs by Ansel Adams that record the wine-making process. ⊠ *8445 Silverado Trail,* ☎ *707/942–3434.* ⊑ *Tasting fees vary.* ⊙ *May–Oct., 10:30–6; Nov.– Apr., 10:30–5. Tours 11–4.*

⑩ The wine at **Rutherford Hill Winery** is aged in French oak barrels stacked in more than 30,000 square ft of caves—one of the largest such facilities in the nation. Tours of the caves can be followed by a picnic in oak, olive, or madrone orchards. ⊠ *200 Rutherford Hill Rd., off the Silverado Trail,* ☎ *707/963–7194.* ⊑ *Tasting fees vary.* ⊙ *Daily 10–5. Tour times vary seasonally, call ahead.*

⑪ **Beaulieu Vineyard** utilizes the same wine-making process, from crush to bottle, as it did the day it opened at the turn of the last century. The winery's cabernet is a benchmark of the Napa Valley; the Georges du Latour Private Reserve remains a collector's favorite. ⊠ *1960 St. Helena Hwy. (Hwy. 29),* ☎ *707/963–2411.* ⊑ *Tasting fee in Reserve Room.* ⊙ *Daily 10–5. Tours daily 11–4.*

⑫ **Niebaum-Coppola Estate** has consistently received high ratings for its Rubicon and other wines. An extra bonus: the museum of memorabilia—including Don Corleone's desk and chair from *The Godfather* and costumes from *Dracula*—from films directed by the winery's owner, Francis Ford Coppola. ⊠ *1991 St. Helena Hwy. (Hwy. 29),* ☎ *707/963–9099.* ⊙ *Daily 10–5. Tours daily, times vary.*

Dining and Lodging

$$$$ ✕▦ **Auberge du Soleil.** Here you can sit on a wisteria-draped deck sip-
★ ping a late-afternoon glass of wine, with acres of terraced olive groves and rolling vineyards at your feet. Inside, Santa Fe accents create an atmosphere of irresistible indolence. The hotel's restaurant is a symphony of earth tones and wood beams, with a frequently changing menu that emphasizes local produce and also includes unusual specialties like roasted lobster sausage and rosemary-roasted rack of lamb. ⊠ *180 Rutherford Hill Rd. (off Silverado Trail just north of Rte. 128), 94573,* ☎ *707/963–1211 or 800/348–5406,* ﷼ *707/963–8764. 52 rooms. Restaurant, pool, hot tub, massage, steam room, 3 tennis courts, exercise room. AE, D, DC, MC, V.*

$$$–$$$$ ▦ **Rancho Caymus Inn.** California-Spanish in style, this inn has well-maintained gardens and large suites with kitchens and whirlpool baths. Well-chosen details include decorative handicrafts, beehive fireplaces, tile murals, stoneware basins, and llama-hair blankets. ⊠ *1140 Rutherford Rd. (junction of Hwys. 29 and 128), 94573,* ☎ *707/963–1777 or 800/845–1777,* ﷼ *707/963–5387. 26 rooms. DC, MC, V. 2-night minimum Apr.–Nov.*

St. Helena

2 mi northwest of Oakville on Hwy. 29.

By the time Charles Krug planted grapes in St. Helena around 1860, quite a few vineyards already existed. Today the town beckons visitors with its abundant selection of wineries—many of which lie along the route from Yountville to St. Helena—and restaurants, including Greystone, part of the Culinary Institute of America. Arching sycamore trees bow across Main Street (Highway 29) to create a shady drive.

⑬ Established in 1876, **Beringer Vineyards** is the oldest continuously operating winery in the Napa Valley. In 1883 the Beringer brothers, Frederick and Jacob, built the Rhine House Mansion, where tastings are now held among hand-carved oak and walnut furniture and stained-glass windows. Tours include a visit to underground wine tunnels, made of volcanic ash, that were dug by Chinese laborers during the 19th century. ✉ *2000 Main St.,* ☎ *707/963–4812.* ⊙ *Daily 9:30–4; summer hrs sometimes extend to 5. Tours daily every 30 mins.*

⑭ **Charles Krug Winery** opened in 1861 when Count Haraszthy loaned Krug a small cider press. The oldest winery in the Napa Valley, it is run by the Peter Mondavi family. The gift shop stocks everything from gourmet food baskets to books about the region and its wines. The joint tasting and tour fee is $3. ✉ *2800 N. Main St.,* ☎ *707/963–5057.* ⊙ *Daily 10:30–5:30. Tours 11:30, 1:30, and 3:30.*

⑮ **Freemark Abbey Winery,** originally called the Tychson Winery, was built in 1886 by Josephine Tychson, the first woman to establish a winery in California. Freemark is known for its cabernets, whose grapes come from the fertile Rutherford Bench; all other wines are estate grown, including a much-touted late-harvest Riesling. ✉ *3022 St. Helena Hwy. N,* ☎ *707/963–9694.* ⊙ *Daily 10–4:30. Tour daily at 2.*

Grapeseed mudwraps and Ayurvedic-inspired massages performed by two attendants are among the trademarks of the **Health Spa Napa Valley** (✉ 1030 Main St., ☎ 707/967–8800), which has a pool and a health club. Should your treatments leave you too limp to operate your car, you can walk to Tra Vigne and other St. Helena restaurants.

The **Silverado Museum,** inside a pristine Victorian, contains Robert Louis Stevenson memorabilia—more than 8,000 artifacts, including first editions, manuscripts, and photographs. ✉ *1490 Library La., at Adams St.,* ☎ *707/963–3757.* 🎟 *Free.* ⊙ *Tues.–Sun. noon–4.*

The **Culinary Institute of America,** the country's leading school for chefs, set up its West Coast headquarters in the century-old Greystone Winery, the former site of the Christian Brothers Winery and a national historic landmark. The CIA campus consists of 30 acres of herb and vegetable gardens, a 15-acre merlot vineyard, and a Mediterranean-inspired restaurant (☞ Wine Spectator Greystone Restaurant, *below*) that's open to the public. Also on the property are a well-stocked culinary store, a quirky corkscrew and winepress museum, and a culinary library. ✉ *2555 Main St.,* ☎ *800/333–9242.*

Dining and Lodging

$$$–$$$$ ✕ **Terra.** Hiro Stone and Lissa Doumani, the chef-owners of this unpretentious restaurant in a century-old stone foundry, honed their culinary skills at the side of chef Wolfgang Puck. Sone creates exquisite Mediterranean-inspired dishes, many with Asian touches. His sweetbreads ragout and osso buco are memorable, as are many of his fish dishes. Save room for Lissa's desserts. ✉ *1345 Railroad Ave.,* ☎ *707/963–8931. Reservations essential. MC, V. Closed Tues. No lunch.*

$$–$$$ ✕ **Showley's.** Garlic chicken and roasted monkfish with garlic mashed potatoes are among the recommended items on the changing menu here. Starters are equally well prepared, especially the chili *en nogada,* made with pork, pine nuts, and chutney and served with a walnut–crème fraîche sauce. ✉ *1327 Railroad Ave.,* ☎ *707/963–1200. AE, D, MC, V. Closed Mon.*

$$–$$$ ✕ **Wine Spectator Greystone Restaurant.** The restaurant of the Culinary Institute of America draws part of its staff from the institute, although professional chefs command the kitchen. The menu has a Mediterranean spirit and emphasizes small plates such as bruschetta topped with wild mushrooms and *muhammara,* a spread of roasted red peppers and walnuts. ✉ *2555 Main St.,* ☎ *707/967–1010. AE, DC, MC, V. Closed Tues.*

$$ ✕ **Brava Terrace.** Vegetables plucked straight from the restaurant's own garden are used to enliven chef Fred Halpert's trademark New Amer-

ican cuisine. With large stone fireplace, a romantic outdoor terrace overlooking a shady brook, and a heated deck with views of the valley floor and Howell Mountain, Brava has a comfortably casual ambience. ⊠ *3010 St. Helena Hwy. (Hwy. 29), ½ mi north of downtown St. Helena,* ☏ *707/963–9300. Reservations essential. AE, D, DC, MC, V. Closed Wed. Nov.–Apr. and last 2 wks of Jan.*

$$ ✕ **Tra Vigne.** This Napa Valley fieldstone building has been transformed
★ into a striking trattoria with a huge wood bar, high ceilings, and plush banquettes. Homemade mozzarella, olive oil, and vinegar and house-cured pancetta and prosciutto contribute to a one-of-a-kind tour of Tuscan cuisine. Getting a table without a reservation is sometimes difficult, but you can drop in and sit at the bar. The outdoor courtyard in summer is a sun-splashed Mediterranean vision of striped umbrellas and awnings, crowded café tables, and rustic pots overflowing with flowers. ⊠ *1050 Charter Oak Ave., off Hwy. 29,* ☏ *707/963–4444. Reservations essential in dining room. D, DC, MC, V.*

$$$$ ✕⬚ **Meadowood Resort.** Manicured croquet lawns, a golf course, and gorgeous hiking trails add to the glamour of this 256-acre resort with a rambling country lodge and 79 bungalow suites. For the prix-fixe weekend brunch (nonguests welcome), refined French cuisine receives a Californian twist. Dining is in a room with a cathedral ceiling, a fireplace, and greenery or outdoors on a terrace overlooking the golf course. Reservations are essential at the restaurants. ⊠ *900 Meadowood La., 94574,* ☏ *707/963–3646 or 800/458–8080,* ⬚ 707/963–5863. *40 rooms, 45 suites. 2 restaurants (reservations essential), bar, room service, 2 pools, hot tub, massage, sauna, steam room, 9-hole golf course, 7 tennis courts, croquet, health club. AE, D, DC, MC, V.*

$$$–$$$$ ⬚ **Harvest Inn.** This Tudor-style inn with 47 fireplaces overlooks a 14-acre vineyard and the hills beyond. Although the property is set close to a main highway, the lush landscaping and brick and stonework create an illusion of remoteness. Most rooms have wet bars, refrigerators, antique furnishings, and fireplaces. Pets are allowed in certain rooms for a $20 fee. ⊠ *1 Main St., 94574,* ☏ *707/963–9463 or 800/950–8466,* ⬚ 707/963–4402. *55 rooms. Refrigerators, 2 pools, hot tub. Continental breakfast. AE, D, DC, MC, V.*

$$$–$$$$ ⬚ **Wine Country Inn.** Surrounded by a pastoral landscape of vine-
★ yards and hills dotted with old barns and stone bridges, this is a peaceful New England–style retreat. Rural antiques fill all the rooms, most of which overlook the vineyards with either a balcony, patio, or deck. Most rooms have fireplaces, and some have private hot tubs. A hearty country breakfast is served buffet style in the sunny common room. ⊠ *1152 Lodi La. (off Hwy. 29), 94574,* ☏ *707/963–7077,* ⬚ *707/ 963–9018. 24 rooms. Pool, hot tubs. Full breakfast. MC, V.*

$–$$ ⬚ **El Bonita Motel.** A souped-up motel with window boxes and landscaped grounds, the conveniently located El Bonita inn contains accommodations with muted pastel walls and floral upholstery. ⊠ *195 Main St. (Hwy. 29), 94574,* ☏ *707/963–3216 or 800/541–3284,* ⬚ *707/963–5863. 41 rooms. Pool. AE, MC, V.*

Shopping

Handcrafted candles made on the premises are for sale at the **Hurd Beeswax Candle Factory** (⊠ 3020 St. Helena Hwy. N, ☏ 707/963–7211), next door to the Freemark Abbey Winery. Bargain hunters will delight in the many designer labels for sale at the **Village Outlet Sto**... complex on St. Helena Highway, across the street from Fre... Abbey Winery. **On the Vine** (⊠ 1234 Main St., ☏ 707/963–2... sents wearable art and unique jewelry inspired by fo... themes.

Calistoga

3 mi northwest of St. Helena on Hwy. 29.

In addition to its wineries, Calistoga is noted for its mineral water, hot mineral springs, mud baths, steam baths, and massages. The Calistoga Hot Springs Resort was founded in 1859 by maverick entrepreneur Sam Brannan, whose ambition was to found "the Saratoga of California." He tripped on the phrase at a formal banquet—it came out "Calistoga"— and the name stuck.

The **Sharpsteen Museum** has a magnificent diorama of the Calistoga Hot Springs Resort in its heyday. Other exhibits document Robert Louis Stevenson's time in the area and the career of museum founder Ben Sharpsteen, an animator at the Walt Disney studio. ⊠ *1311 Washington St.,* ☎ *707/942–5911.* 🖾 *Free.* ☉ *May–Oct., daily 10–4; Nov.– Apr., daily noon–4.*

At **Indian Springs,** $100 entitles enthusiasts to a mud bath, mineral-water shower, and mineral-water bath, plus time in the steam room, a blanket wrap, and a 25-minute massage. The cost without massage is $60. The spa has 16 cottages with studio or one-bedroom units. ⊠ *1712 Lincoln Ave.,* ☎ *707/942–4913.* ☉ *Daily 9–7. Reservations recommended for spa treatments.*

⑯ For the ultimate sybaritic splurge, treat yourself to a post-mud-bath glass of wine. A good place to start is **Sterling Vineyards,** which sits on a hilltop to the east of Calistoga, its pristine white Mediterranean-style buildings reached by an enclosed gondola from the valley floor. The view from the tasting room is superb. ⊠ *1111 Dunaweal La.,* ☎ *707/942–3300.* 🖾 *Tram $6.* ☉ *Daily 10:30–4:30.*

⑰ Designed by postmodern architect Michael Graves, **Clos Pegase** is a one-of-a-kind structure packed with unusual art objects from the collection of art book publisher and owner Jan Shrem. Works of art even appear in the underground wine tunnels. ⊠ *1060 Dunaweal La.,* ☎ *707/942–4981.* ☉ *Daily 10:30–5. Tours at 11 and 2.*

★ **⑱** **Château Montelena** is a vine-covered stone French château constructed circa 1882 and set amid Chinese-inspired gardens, complete with a man-made lake with gliding swans and islands crowned by Chinese pavilions. The pavilions are available for picnics on a first-come, first-served basis for wine purchasers. Château Montelena produces award-winning chardonnays and cabernet sauvignons. ⊠ *1429 Tubbs La.,* ☎ *707/942– 5105; 800/222–7288 outside the Bay Area.* ☉ *Daily 10–4. Tours by reservation at 11 and 2.*

🖑 **Old Faithful Geyser of California** blasts its 60-ft tower of steam and vapor about every 40 minutes (the pattern is disrupted if there's an earthquake in the offing). One of only three regularly erupting geysers in the world, it is fed by an underground river that heats to 350°F. The eruption lasts three minutes. ⊠ *1299 Tubbs La., 1 mi north of Calistoga,* ☎ *707/942–6463.* 🖾 *$6.* ☉ *During daylight savings time, daily ☉ . . . . ter, daily 9–5.*

. . . **ied Forest** contains the remains of the volcanic eruptions of
. . . Helena 3.4 million years ago. The force of the explosion
. . . he gigantic redwoods, covered them with volcanic ash, and
. . . he trees with silica and minerals, causing petrifaction. Ex-
. . . useum, then picnic on the grounds. ⊠ *4100 Petrified For-*
. . . *i west of Calistoga,* ☎ *707/942–6667.* 🖾 *$4.* ☉ *Daily*
. . . *6 in summer).*

🐝 **Robert Louis Stevenson State Park** encompasses the summit of 4,340-ft-high Mount St. Helena. It was here, in the summer of 1880, in an abandoned bunkhouse of the Silverado Mine, that Stevenson and his bride, Fanny Osbourne, spent their honeymoon. The stay inspired his short story "The Silverado Squatters." Spyglass Hill in his novel *Treasure Island* is thought to be a portrait of Mount St. Helena. ⊠ *Hwy. 29, 7 mi north of Calistoga,* ☎ *707/942–4575.* ◷ *8 AM–sunset.*

Dining and Lodging

$$–$$$ ✕ **All Seasons Café.** Bistro cuisine receives a Californian spin in this sun-filled setting with marble tables and a black-and-white checkerboard floor. The seasonal menu includes organic greens, wild mushrooms, local game birds, and house-smoked beef, chicken, and salmon. The breads, desserts, and ice cream are made on the premises. ⊠ *1400 Lincoln Ave.,* ☎ *707/942–9111. MC, V. Closed Wed.*

$$–$$$ ✕ **Catahoula Restaurant and Saloon.** Using a large wood-burning
★ oven, chef Jan Birnbaum churns out Cal-Cajun dishes such as spicy gumbo with andouille sausage and for dessert, wood-fire-cooked chocolate s'mores. Sit at the counter and watch the chef cook—it's the best entertainment in town. The barroom opposite the dining room has its own menu of small plates, which are ideal for sampling Birnbaum's kitchen wizardry. ⊠ *Mount View Hotel, 1457 Lincoln Ave.,* ☎ *707/942–2275. Reservations essential. MC, V. Closed Tues. and Jan.*

$$ ✕ **Calistoga Inn.** Grilled meat and fish for dinner and soups, salads, and sandwiches for lunch are prepared with flair at this microbrewery with a tree-shaded outdoor patio. ⊠ *1250 Lincoln Ave.,* ☎ *707/ 942–4101. AE, MC, V.*

$–$$ ✕ **Pacifico.** Technicolor ceramics and subtropical plants adorn this Mexican restaurant that serves Oaxacan and other fare. ⊠ *1237 Lincoln Ave.,* ☎ *707/942–4400. MC, V.*

$$$$ ⛺ **Cottage Grove Inn.** Moss-covered elm trees shade 16 cottages with various themes—botanical, nautical, musical, and floral among them. Rooms have skylights, pastel colors, and plush furnishings; fireplaces, CD players, VCRs, two-person hot tubs, and front porches with wicker rocking chairs add to the coziness. ⊠ *1711 Lincoln Ave., 94515,* ☎ *707/942–8400 or 800/799–2284,* ℻ *707/942–2653. 16 rooms. Breakfast room, refrigerators, in-room VCRs. Continental breakfast. AE, D, DC, MC, V.*

$$$–$$$$ ⛺ **Mount View Hotel.** The Mount View is one of the valley's most his-
★ toric resorts. A full-service European spa offers state-of-the-art pampering, and three cottages are each equipped with private redwood deck, Jacuzzi, and wet bar. Catahoula's saloon adds to the allure. ⊠ *1457 Lincoln Ave., 94515,* ☎ *707/942–6877,* ℻ *707/942–6904. 33 rooms. Restaurant, pool, spa. AE, MC, V.*

$$$ ⛺ **Brannan Cottage Inn.** This pristine Victorian cottage with lacy white fretwork, large windows, and a shady porch is the only one of Sam Brannan's 1860 resort cottages still standing on its original site. Rooms have private entrances, and elegant stenciled friezes of stylized wildflowers cover the walls. ⊠ *109 Wapoo Ave., 94515,* ☎ *707/942–4200. 6 rooms. Breakfast room. Full breakfast. MC, V.*

$$–$$$ ⛺ **Meadowlark Country House.** The ambience is decidedly laid-back (particularly for the Wine Country) at this inn surrounded by 20 hillside acres just north of downtown Calistoga. The main house, built in 1886, and a newer building down a gravel path hold unfussy but country-stylish rooms. ⊠ *601 Petrified Forest Rd.,* ☎ *707/942–5651 or 800/942–5651,* ℻ *707/942–5023. 7 rooms. Breakfast room, pool. Full breakfast. MC, V.*

$-$$ ⊡ **Calistoga Spa Hot Springs.** The spa's no-nonsense motel-style ac-
commodations have kitchenettes stocked with utensils and coffeemakers,
which makes the rooms popular with families and travelers on a budget (there's a supermarket a block away). Spa treatments include massage and mud and mineral baths. There's a two-night minimum on
weekends (three nights on holiday weekends). ⊠ *1006 Washington St.,
94515,* ☎ *707/942–6269. 57 rooms. Snack bar, kitchenettes, 2 pools,
wading pool, hot tub, health club, spa, meeting room. MC, V.*

Outdoor Activities and Sports

BIKING

Getaway Adventures and Bike Shop (⊠ 1117 Lincoln Ave., ☎ 707/
942–0332) rents bikes and conducts winery and other bike tours.

GLIDING, HOT-AIR BALLOONING

The **Calistoga Balloon Adventures** (☎ 707/942–2282 or 800/333–4359)
charters early morning flights (exact times vary) out of Calistoga or,
depending on weather conditions, St. Helena, Oakville, or Rutherford.
The company's deluxe balloon flight ($165 per person) includes a
catered brunch finale in Napa or Calistoga.

Calistoga Gliders (⊠ 1546 Lincoln Ave., ☎ 707/942–5000) operates
glider and biplane rides that yield a bird's-eye view of the entire valley. The flights cost from $80 to $179, depending on the number of
passengers (the maximum is two) and the length of the ride.

Shopping

For connoisseurs seeking extraordinary values, the **All Seasons Café
Wine Shop** (⊠ 1400 Lincoln Ave., ☎ 707/942–6828) is a true find.
A wine shop inside the **Calistoga Depot** (⊠ 1458 Lincoln Ave., ☎ 707/
942–5556), California's second-oldest existing train depot, carries
500 vintages.

SONOMA COUNTY

The word Sonoma is Miwok Indian for *many moons.* Sonoma County
stretches west from its border with Napa County to the Pacific Ocean.
The county's most famous winegrowing region is the Sonoma Valley,
which abuts the Napa Valley. Farther north, other Sonoma County valleys, such as Alexander, Dry Creek, and Russian River, are equally beautiful and just as prolific in their production of noteworthy wines. Here
tastings are usually free. The Sonoma countryside—from inland to coastal
valleys—also provides excellent opportunities for hiking, biking, camping, boating, and fishing.

Petaluma

32 mi north of San Francisco on U.S. 101.

Petaluma's claim to fame from the late 1800s into the 1950s was
chicken farming—so many chicks were hatched and raised here the town
had a pharmacy solely for its fowl. Banking, shipping (along the
Petaluma River), and the grain trade were other industries in this area
inhabited by Miwok, Wappo, and Pomo peoples prior to the arrival
of General Mariano G. Vallejo of Mexico in the 1830s. With factory
outlets and postmodern cuisine, Petaluma is thoroughly modern, but
in movies often stands in for small-town America—scenes from *American Graffiti* and *Peggy Sue Got Married* were shot here. (The darker
side of things pops up in *Basic Instinct* and *Shadow of a Doubt.*)

Petaluma bills itself as the gateway to the Wine Country, but it's a worthy stop in its own right, with a strollable historic downtown (look for a copy of the *Petaluma Visitor Guide,* which contains a self-guided tour of Victorian-era architecture) and some stellar restaurants. The navigable section of Petaluma River ends in downtown Petaluma. Shops and restaurants have sprung up around the **turning basin** (where boats turn around to head back down the river toward San Francisco).

A short drive from downtown is **Petaluma Adobe Historic State Park,** whose highlight is the two-story ranch headquarters General Vallejo built after receiving a 66,000-acre land grant as a reward for protecting Mexican interests in San Francisco. There's hardly ever a crowd at this smartly restored structure whose rooms include the tannery, granary, servants' quarters, and family quarters. ✉ *Adobe Rd. at Casa Grande Ave. (from downtown Petaluma, head east on Washington St. and south on Adobe Rd.),* ☎ *707/762–4871.* ▣ *$2.* ◷ *Daily 10–5.*

Dining

$$–$$$ ✗ **River House.** The kitchen within this 1888 Queen Anne–style home produces flavorful small plates that might include buttermilk fried calamari with sweet red-pepper-mango ketchup and robust entrées like fricassee of sea bass and slow-roast pork with clams in a fire-roasted tomato-chili broth. You can dine indoors or out. ✉ *222 Weller St.,* ☎ *707/769–0123. AE, D, MC, V.*

$–$$ ✗ **Dempsey's Restaurant/Brewery.** Chef Bernadette Burrell, formerly
★ of Mustards Grill in the Napa Valley, plies her innovative trade at this casually chic place beside the turning basin. Two menu mainstays are the pork chop marinated in hoisin sauce and the roasted half chicken in a mustard sauce. The ales are uniformly excellent. There's patio seating in fine weather. ✉ *50 E. Washington St.,* ☎ *707/765–9694. MC, V.*

Sonoma

14 mi west of Napa on Hwy. 12; 45 mi from San Francisco, north on U.S. 101, east on Hwy. 37, and north on Hwy. 121-12.

Sonoma is the oldest town in the Wine Country; its historic town plaza is the site of the last and the northernmost of the 21 missions established by the Franciscan order of Father Junípero Serra. The central plaza also includes the largest group of old adobes north of Monterey. The **Mission San Francisco Solano,** whose chapel and school were used to bring Christianity to the Native Americans, is now a museum with a fine collection of 19th-century watercolors. ✉ *114 Spain St. E,* ☎ *707/938–1519.* ▣ *$2, includes the Sonoma Barracks on the central plaza and General Vallejo's home, Lachryma Montis (☞ below)* ◷ *Daily 10–5.*

⑲ Planted by Franciscans of the Sonoma Mission in 1825, the **Sebastiani Vineyards** were bought by Samuele Sebastiani in 1904. Red wines are king here; to complement them, Sylvia Sebastiani has recorded her good Italian home cooking in a family recipe book, *Mangiamo.* ✉ *389 4th St. E,* ☎ *707/938–5532.* ◷ *Daily 10–5. Tours 10–4:30.*

⑳ **Buena Vista Carneros Winery** (follow signs from the plaza), set among trees and fountains, was where, in 1857, Count Agoston Haraszthy de Mokcsa laid the basis for modern California wine making, bucking the conventional wisdom that vines should be planted on well-watered ground by instead planting on well-drained hillsides. Chinese laborers dug tunnels 100 ft into the hillside, and the limestone they extracted was used to build the main house. The winery has a gourmet shop, an art gallery, and picnic areas. ✉ *18000 Old Winery Rd., off Napa Rd.,* ☎ *707/938–1266.* ◷ *Daily 10:30–4:30. Tour daily at 2.*

㉑ **Ravenswood** is literally dug into the mountains like a bunker and famous for its legendary zinfandel, although the merlot should be tasted as well. From late May to Labor Day the winery serves barbecued chicken and ribs in the vineyards to complement its hearty wines. ⊠ *18701 Gehricke Rd., off E. Spain St.,* ☎ *707/938–1960.* ⊙ *Daily 10–4:30. Tours by appointment at 10:30.*

A tree-lined approach leads to **Lachryma Montis,** which General Mariano G. Vallejo built for his large family in 1851; the state purchased the home in 1933. The Victorian Gothic house is secluded in the midst of beautiful gardens; opulent furnishings, including a white-marble fireplace in every room, are particularly noteworthy. ⊠ *W. Spain St., near 3rd St. E,* ☎ *707/938–1519.* ▣ *$2.* ⊙ *Daily 10–5. Tours by appointment.*

Dining and Lodging

$$–$$$ ✕ **Babette's.** Chef Daniel Patterson serves memorable five-course, prix-fixe dinners just three nights a week in the small back dining room of this downtown Sonoma wine bar, café, and restaurant. He offers three choices for each course, including tantalizing combinations like quail breast on a bed of watercress and quinoa, or raw scallops dressed simply with olive oil and lemon juice. Items off a café menu—cassoulet with house-made sausage and other rustic fare—are served daily in an adjoining room. The wine bar, which shares the same space, serves wonderful small bites with its vintages. The restaurant's hours vary from season to season, so call ahead. ⊠ *464 1st St.,* ☎ *707/939–8921. MC, V. Restaurant closed Sun.–Wed.*

$$–$$$ ✕ **Freestyle.** Steven and George Ann Levine, who both worked at top restaurants in New York, opened this highly urbane eatery in downtown Sonoma; their partners include Drew Nieporent of San Francisco's Rubicon, New York City's Nobu, and other hot spots. The "Freestyle appetizer taste of the day" showcases a single ingredient prepared three distinctive ways—prawns, for example, in gumbo, grilled and served with salsa, and deep-fried tempura-style. Main courses are often hearty—steak with grilled Portobello mushrooms, roasted chicken— as are the desserts. ⊠ *522 Broadway,* ☎ *707/996–9916. AE, DC, MC, V. Closed Tues. No lunch Mon.*

$$ ✕ **Ristorante Piatti.** Pizza from the wood-burning oven and northern Italian specials (spit-roasted chicken, ravioli with lemon cream) are prepared in Piatti's open kitchen. Dine in the mural-festooned drawing room or on the outdoor terrace. ⊠ *El Dorado Hotel, 405 1st St. W,* ☎ *707/996–2351. AE, MC, V.*

$ ✕ **La Casa.** Whitewashed stucco and red tiles adorn this restaurant just around the corner from Sonoma's plaza. There's bar seating, a patio out back, and an extensive menu of traditional Mexican food: chimichangas and snapper Veracruz for entrées, sangria to drink, and flan for dessert. The food is not the world's best, but locals appreciate the casual atmosphere. ⊠ *121 E. Spain St.,* ☎ *707/996–3406. AE, DC, MC, V.*

$$$–$$$$ ✕🏨 **Sonoma Mission Inn & Spa.** This 1920s resort blends Mediterranean and old-style California architecture for a look that's early Hollywood: Gloria Swanson would fit right in. Despite its unlikely location off the main street of tiny, down-home Boyes Hot Springs, guests come from afar to use the hotel's extensive spa facilities and treatments— including a pool that's heated by warm mineral water pumped from underground wells—and also for the classic spa food served at the Grille and at the less formal Café. Thirty suites in a secluded, tree-shaded area have verandas or patios, Jacuzzis, and fireplaces. ⊠ *18140 Hwy. 12 (2 mi north of Sonoma at Boyes Blvd.), Box 1447, 95476,* ☎ *707/938– 9000 or 800/358–9022; 800/862–4945 in CA;* FAX *707/996–5358. 198*

rooms, 30 suites. 2 restaurants, 2 bars, coffee shop, 2 pools, hot tub, spa, 2 tennis courts. AE, DC, MC, V.

$$$–$$$$ ⌸ **Thistle Dew Inn.** A half block from Sonoma Plaza, this turn-of-the-century Victorian home is filled with collector's-quality Arts and Crafts furnishings. Four of the six rooms have private entrances and decks, and all have queen-size beds with antique quilts, private baths, and air-conditioning. Some rooms have fireplaces; some have Jacuzzis. Welcome bonuses include a hot tub and free use of the inn's bicycles. ✉ *171 W. Spain St., 95476,* ☎ *707/938–2909; 800/382–7895 in CA. 6 rooms. Full breakfast. AE, MC, V.*

$$–$$$ ⌸ **El Dorado Hotel.** Rooms at this small hotel reflect Sonoma's Mis-
★ sion era, with Mexican-tile floors and white walls. The best rooms are Numbers 3 and 4, which have big balconies overlooking Sonoma Plaza. ✉ *405 1st St. W, 95476,* ☎ *707/996–3030 or 800/289–3031,* FAX *707/996–3148. 26 rooms. Restaurant, pool. Continental breakfast. AE, MC, V.*

$$ ⌸ **Vineyard Inn.** Built as a roadside motor court in 1941, this inn with red-tile roofs brings a touch of Mexican village charm to an otherwise lackluster location at the junction of two main highways. Set in the heart of Sonoma's Carneros region, across from two vineyards, it's the closest lodging to Sears Point Raceway. Rooms have queen-size beds. ✉ *23000 Arnold Dr. (junction of Hwys. 116 and 121), 95476,* ☎ *707/938–2350 or 800/359–4667,* FAX *707/938–2353. 9 rooms, 4 suites. Breakfast room. Continental breakfast. AE, MC, V.*

Shopping

Several shops in the four-block **Sonoma Plaza** attract gourmets from miles around. Serious picnickers stop at the **Sonoma French Bakery** (✉ Sonoma Plaza, 466 1st St. E, ☎ 707/996–2691), famous for its sourdough bread and cream puffs. The **Sonoma Cheese Factory** (✉ Sonoma Plaza, 2 Spain St., ☎ 707/996–1000) sells Sonoma Jack cheese and the tangy Sonoma Teleme.

Glen Ellen

7 mi north of Sonoma on Hwy. 12.

Jack London lived in the Sonoma Valley for many years; the craggy, quirky, and creek-bisected town of Glen Ellen commemorates him with place names and nostalgic establishments. **Jack London Village** (✉ 14301 Arnold Dr., ☎ 707/935–1240) has many interesting shops. The bookstore across the street from Jack London Village carries many of London's books. Century-old **Jack London Saloon** (✉ Arnold Dr., ☎ 707/996–3100) has a brooding, nostalgic appeal.

In the hills above Glen Ellen—known as the Valley of the Moon—lies **Jack London State Historic Park.** London's collection of South Seas and other artifacts can be seen at the House of Happy Walls, a museum of London's effects. The ruins of Wolf House, which London designed and which mysteriously burned down just before he was to move in, are close to the House of Happy Walls. London is buried on the property. ✉ *2400 London Ranch Rd.,* ☎ *707/938–5216.* ⌸ *Parking $6.* ☉ *Park, daily 9:30–5; museum, daily 10–5.*

Two million cases of wine are bottled annually in this area. As you drive along Highway 12, you'll see orchards and rows of vineyards flanked by oak-covered mountain ranges. One of the best-known local wineries is **Benziger Family Winery,** which specializes in premium estate and Sonoma County wines. Benizer's Imagery Series is a low-volume release of unusual red and white wines distributed in bottles with art labels by well-known artists from all over the world. Free tram tours through the vineyards depart several times a day, weather permitting. ⊠ *1883 London Ranch Rd.,* ☎ *707/935–3000.* ⌕ *Varying tasting fees (for premium estate wines only).* ☉ *Daily 10–4:30. Tours every ½ hr, Mar.–Sept., 9:30–5; Oct.–Feb., 9:30–4.*

Lodging

$$$–$$$$ ⌕ **Gaige House Inn.** Built in the 19th century as a personal residence, the Gaige House contains a mix of chic, contemporary rooms and older, more traditional accommodations. A large pool surrounded by a green lawn, striped awnings, white umbrellas, and magnolias conjures a manicured Hamptons-like glamour right in the middle of rustic Glen Ellen. The chef's first-rate gourmet country breakfast is served in a bright dining room downstairs or outside on the terrace. ⊠ *13540 Arnold Dr.95442,* ☎ *707/935–0237 or 800/935–0237,* ⒻⒶⓍ *707/935–6411. 13 rooms. Breakfast room, pool. Full breakfast. AE, D, MC, V.*

$$$ ⌕ **Beltane Ranch.** On a slope of the Mayacamas range on the eastern side of the Sonoma Valley lies this 100-year-old house built by a retired San Francisco madam. Beltane Ranch, surrounded by miles of trails through oak-studded hills, is part of a working cattle and grape-growing ranch—the nearby Kenwood Winery produces a chardonnay made from the ranch's grapes. The Wood family, who have lived on the premises for 50 years, have stocked the comfortable living room with dozens of books on the area. The rooms, all with private baths and antique furniture, open onto the building's wraparound porch. ⊠ *11775 Sonoma Hwy. (Hwy. 12), 95442,* ☎ *707/996–6501. 5 rooms. Tennis court, hiking, horseshoes. Full breakfast. No credit cards.*

$$–$$$ ⌕ **Glenelly Inn.** Just outside the hamlet of Glen Ellen, this sunny little establishment, built as an inn in 1916, offers all the comforts of home—including a hot tub in the garden. Innkeeper Kristi Hallamore serves breakfast in front of the common room's cobblestone fireplace and also provides local delicacies in the afternoon. On sunny mornings guests may eat outside under the shady oak trees. ⊠ *5131 Warm Springs Rd., 95442,* ☎ *707/996–6720,* ⒻⒶⓍ *707/996–5227. 8 rooms. Breakfast room, outdoor hot tub. Full breakfast. MC, V.*

Kenwood

3 mi north of Glen Ellen on Hwy. 12.

Kenwood has a historic train depot and several restaurants and shops that specialize in locally produced gourmet products. Its inns, restaurants, and winding roads nestle in soothing bucolic landscapes.

㉓ The rustic grounds at **Kenwood Vineyards** complement the attractive tasting room and artistic bottle labels. Kenwood produces all premium varietals, but is best known for its Jack London Vineyard reds—pinot noir, zinfandel, merlot, and a unique Artist Series cabernet. ⊠ *9592 Sonoma Hwy.,* ☎ *707/833–5891.* ☉ *Daily 10–4:30. No tours.*

㉔ The landscaping and design of **Landmark Vineyards** are as classical as its winemaking methods. Those methods include two fermentations in French oak barrels and the use of the yeasts present in the skins of the grapes to create the wine rather than the addition of manufactured yeasts. Landmark's Damaris Reserve and Overlook chardonnays have been particularly well received by wine critics, as has the winery's Grand Detour pinot noir. ⊠ *101 Adobe Canyon Rd., off Sonoma Hwy.,* ☎ *707/833–1144 or 800/452–6365.* ☉ *Daily 10–4:30. No tours.*

Dining

$$ ✕ **Kenwood Restaurant & Bar.** This is where Napa and Sonoma chefs eat on their nights off. Indulge in country cuisine in the sunny, South of France–style dining room or head through the French doors to the

patio for a memorable view of the vineyards. ⊠ *9900 Hwy. 12,* ☎ *707/ 833–6326. MC, V. Closed Mon.*

Santa Rosa

8 mi northwest of Kenwood on Hwy. 12; 58 mi north of San Francisco on U.S. 101.

Whole sections of Santa Rosa, the Wine Country's largest town, were bulldozed away in the 1960s and 1970s to make way for "progress," but charming enclaves remain here and there. The town's **visitors center** (⊠ 9 4th St., ☎ 707/577–8674 or 800/404–7673) is inside a restored railroad depot in Historic Railroad Square.

The **Luther Burbank Home and Gardens** commemorates the great botanist who lived and worked on these grounds for 50 years, single-handedly developing the modern techniques of hybridization. Arriving as a young man from New England, he wrote: "I firmly believe. . . that this is the chosen spot of all the earth, as far as nature is concerned." The Santa Rosa plum, Shasta daisy, and lily of the Nile agapanthus are among the 800 or so plants he developed or improved. ⊠ *Santa Rosa and Sonoma Aves.,* ☎ *707/524–5445.* 🎫 *Gardens free; guided tours of house and greenhouse $2.* ☉ *Gardens Nov.–Mar., daily 8– 5; Apr.–Oct., daily 8–7. Tours Apr.–Oct., Wed.–Sun. 10–4.*

★ ㉕ **Matanzas Creek Winery** specializes in three varietals—sauvignon blanc, merlot, and chardonnay; all three have won glowing reviews from various magazines. Huge windows in the visitor center overlook a field of 3,100 tiered and fragrant lavender plants. Acres and acres of gardens planted with unusual grasses and plants from all over the world have caught the attention of horticulturists. After you taste the wines, ask to see the self-guided garden tour book before taking a stroll. ⊠ *6097 Bennett Valley Rd.,* ☎ *707/528–6464.* ☉ *Daily 10–4:30. Tours by appointment.*

Dining and Lodging

$$$ ✗ **John Ash & Co.** The thoroughly regional cuisine served at John Ash relies on ingredients grown in Sonoma County and in the restaurant's organic garden. With patio seating outside and a cozy fireplace indoors, the slightly formal restaurant looks like a Spanish villa amid the vineyards. A café menu offers bites between meals. ⊠ *4330 Barnes Rd. (River Rd. exit west from U.S. 101),* ☎ *707/527–7687. Weekend reservations essential. AE, MC, V. No lunch Mon.*

$$–$$$ ✗ **Cafe Lolo.** This casual but sophisticated spot is the territory of chef and co-owner Michael Quigley. Fresh ingredients (including local produce whenever possible) and winning presentations are the hallmarks of his seafood, pasta, free-range chicken, and other dishes. Don't pass up the chocolate kiss, an individual cake with a wonderfully soft, rich center. ⊠ *620 5th St.,* ☎ *707/576–7822. AE, D, DC, MC, V. Closed Sun. No lunch Sat.*

$–$$ ✗ **Lisa Hemenway's.** A shopping center on the outskirts of town seems an unlikely location for a restaurant find, but chef Hemenway has created a light and airy eatery with soft colors and a garden view from the patio. She prepares a fresh fish special each day, often with Asian spices. The adjacent café, Tote Cuisine, sells tempting take-out selections for picnickers. ⊠ *714 Village Ct. Mall (east from U.S. 101 on Hwy. 12), at Farmer's La. and Sonoma Ave.,* ☎ *707/526–5111. AE, MC, V.*

$ ✗ **Mixx.** Great service and an eclectic mix of dishes define this small restaurant with large windows, booth and table seating, high ceilings, and Italian blown-glass chandeliers. Ravioli, grilled Cajun prawns, and lamb curry are among the favorites of the many regular customers. All the dishes are based on locally grown ingredients. ⊠ *135 4th St., at Davis (behind the mall on Railroad Sq.),* ☎ *707/573–1344. AE, MC, V. No lunch weekends.*

$$$–$$$$ 🏨 **Vintner's Inn.** Set on 50 acres of vineyards, this French provincial inn near John Ash & Co. restaurant (☞ *above*) has large rooms, many with wood-burning fireplaces, and a trellised sundeck. Guests are entitled to discount passes to an affiliated health club. ⊠ *4350 Barnes Rd. (River Rd. exit west from U.S. 101), 95403,* ☎ *707/575–7350 or 800/421–2584,* ☏ *707/575–1426. 44 rooms. Restaurant, hot tub. Continental breakfast. AE, DC, MC, V.*

$$$ 🏨 **Fountaingrove Inn.** A redwood sculpture and a wall of cascading
★ water distinguish the lobby at this comfortable inn. All rooms have work spaces with modem jacks. There's an elegant restaurant with a piano player and a stellar menu. Guests have access to a nearby 18-hole golf course, a tennis court, and a health club, all for an additional fee. ⊠ *101 Fountaingrove Pkwy. (near U.S. 101), 95403,* ☎ *707/578–6101 or 800/222–6101,* ☏ *707/544–3126. 126 rooms. Restaurant, in-room modem lines, room service, pool, hot tub, meeting rooms. Full breakfast. AE, D, DC, MC, V.*

$$ 🏨 **Los Robles Lodge.** This pleasant motel overlooks a pool that's set into a grassy landscape. Pets are allowed, except in executive rooms. Some rooms have whirlpools. ⊠ *1985 Cleveland Ave. (Steele La. exit west from U.S. 101), 95401,* ☎ *707/545–6330 or 800/255–6330,* ☏ *707/575–5826. 102 rooms. Restaurant, coffee shop, pool, outdoor hot tub, nightclub, coin laundry. AE, D, DC, MC, V.*

Nightlife and the Arts

The **Luther Burbank Performing Arts Center** (⊠ 50 Mark West Springs Rd., ☎ 707/546–3600) presents concerts, plays, and other performances by locally and internationally known artists. For symphony, ballet, and other live theater performances throughout the year, call the **Spreckels Performing Arts Center** (☎ 707/584–1700 or 707/586–0936) in Rohnert Park.

Outdoor Activities and Sports

The **Fountaingrove Country Club** (⊠ 1525 Fountaingrove Pkwy., ☎ 707/579–4653) has an 18-hole course. The greens fee, which includes a mandatory cart, runs between $35 and $70 depending on time of day and day of week. **Oakmont Golf Club** (⊠ west course: 7025 Oakmont Dr., ☎ 707/539–0415; ⊠ east course: 565 Oak Vista Ct., ☎ 707/538–2454) has two 18-hole courses. The greens fee runs between $17 and $35; an optional cart costs $20.

For views of the ocean coast, the Russian River, and San Francisco on a clear day, **Sonoma Thunder Wine Country Balloon Safaris** (☎ 707/538–7359 or 800/759–5638) operates out of Santa Rosa, though many flights originate outside Healdsburg. The cost is $175 per person, including a champagne brunch at a hilltop winery.

Healdsburg

17 mi north of Santa Rosa on U.S. 101.

The countryside around Dry Creek Valley and Healdsburg is a fantasy of pastoral bliss, beautifully overgrown and in constant repose. Alongside the untrafficked roads, country stores offer just-plucked fruits and vine-ripened tomatoes. Wineries here are barely visible, tucked behind groves of eucalyptus or hidden high on fog-shrouded hills.

Healdsburg itself is centered by a fragrant plaza surrounded by shade trees, appealing antiques shops, and restaurants. A whitewashed bandstand is the venue for free summer concerts, where the music ranges from jazz to bluegrass. For a free map of the area, contact the **Russian River Wine Road** (✉ Box 46, Healdsburg 95448, ☎ 707/433–6782).

㉖ **Dry Creek Vineyard** is well known for its fumé blanc. The winery's reds, especially zinfandels and cabernets, have also gained notice. Flowering magnolia and redwood trees provide an ideal setting for picnics. ✉ *3770 Lambert Bridge Rd.*, ☎ *707/433–1000.* ☉ *Daily 10:30–4:30. Tours by appointment.*

㉗ An unassuming winery in a wood and cinder-block barn, **Quivira Vineyards** produces some of the most interesting wines in the Dry Creek Valley. Though it is known for its exquisitely balanced and fruity zinfandel, it also makes a superb blend of red varietals called Dry Creek Cuvée. ✉ *4900 W. Dry Creek Rd.*, ☎ *707/431–8333.* ☉ *Daily 10–4:30. Tours by appointment.*

㉘ **Simi Winery.** Giuseppe and Pietro Simi, two brothers from Italy, began growing grapes in Sonoma in 1876. Though their winery's operations are strictly high-tech these days, its tree-studded entrance area and stone buildings recall a more genteel era. The tour highlights the winery's rich history. ✉ *16275 Healdsburg Ave. (take Dry Creek Rd. exit off U.S. 101)*, ☎ *707/433–6981.* ☉ *Daily 10–4:30. Tours at 11, 1, and 3.*

<table>
<tr><td>OFF THE
BEATEN PATH</td><td>**CLOS DU BOIS –** Ten mi north of Healdsburg on Highway 116, these vineyards produce the fine estate chardonnays of the Alexander and Dry Creek valleys that have been mistaken for great French wines. ✉ *19410 Geyserville Ave., Geyserville*, ☎ *707/857–3100 or 800/ 222–3189.* ☉ *Daily 10–4:30. No tours.*</td></tr>
</table>

Dining and Lodging

$–$$ ✕ **Bistro Ralph.** Ralph Tingle has created a culinary hit with his California home-style cuisine, serving up a small menu that changes weekly. The stark industrial setting includes a stunning wine rack of graceful curves fashioned in metal and wood. Take a seat at the bar and chat with the locals, who love this place just as much as out-of-towners do. ✉ *109 Plaza St., off Healdsburg Ave.*, ☎ *707/433–1380. Reservations essential. MC, V. No lunch weekends.*

$$$–$$$$ 🏨 **Healdsburg Inn on the Plaza.** This 1900 brick building on the town plaza has a bright solarium and a roof garden. The rooms, most with fireplaces, are spacious, with quilts and pillows piled high on antique beds. In the bathrooms claw-foot tubs are outfitted with rubber ducks. Afternoon coffee and cookies and early evening wine and popcorn are served. ✉ *110 Matheson St., Box 1196, 95448*, ☎ *707/433–6991. 10 rooms. Breakfast room. Full breakfast. MC, V.*

$$$–$$$$ 🏨 **Madrona Manor.** The 8 acres of wooded and landscaped grounds that surround this splendid 1881 Victorian mansion seem almost out of a storybook. You can stay in the carriage house or one of two separate cottages, but the mansion rooms are recommended: All nine have fireplaces, and five contain the antique furniture of the original owner. ✉ *1001 Westside Rd. (take central Healdsburg exit from U 101, turn left on Mill St.), Box 818, 95448*, ☎ *707/433–4231 or 258–4003*, ℻ *707/433–0703. 21 rooms. Restaurant, pool DC, MC, V.*

$$ 🏨 **Best Western Dry Creek Inn.** Comfortable and reasonab these parts), this three-story Spanish Mission–style extras like a complimentary bottle of wine, midwe direct bus service from San Francisco's airport. ✉ *95448*, ☎ *707/433–0300 or 800/528–1234;* ℻ *707/433–1129. 102 rooms. Pool, hot tub breakfast. AE, D, DC, MC, V.*

Shopping

Oakville Grocery (⊠ 124 Matheson St., ☎ 707/433–2200) has a bustling Healdsburg branch. Head to **Salami Tree** (⊠ 304 Center St., ☎ no phone) for picnic supplies. **Tip Top Liquor Warehouse** (⊠ 90 Dry Creek Rd., ☎ 707/431–0841) has a large selection of local wines, including hard-to-find labels.

Every Saturday morning beginning the first weekend in May, Healdsburg locals gather at the open-air **Farmers' Market** (⊠ North Plaza parking lot, North and Vine Sts., ☎ 707/431–1956) to pick up supplies from local producers of vegetables, fruits, flowers, cheeses, and olive oils.

OFF THE BEATEN PATH **KORBEL CHAMPAGNE CELLARS** – In order to be called champagne, a wine must be made in the French region of Champagne or technically it's just like any other bubbly—a sparkler. But despite the objections of the French, champagne has entered the lexicon of California wine makers, and many refer to their sparkling wines as champagne. Whatever you call it, Korbel produces a tasty, reasonably priced wine and now produces its own beer as well, which is available at the brew pub. The wine tour, one of the best in Sonoma County, clearly explains the process of making sparkling wine. The winery's 19th-century buildings and gorgeous rose gardens are a delight in their own right. ⊠ 13250 River Rd., Guerneville, ☎ 707/887–2294. ⦶ Oct.–Apr., daily 9–4:30; May–Sept., daily 9–5. Tours on the hr 10–3.

THE WINE COUNTRY A TO Z

Arriving and Departing

By Bus
Greyhound (☎ 800/231–2222) runs buses from the Transbay Terminal at 1st and Mission streets in San Francisco to Sonoma and Santa Rosa.

By Car
From San Francisco, cross the Golden Gate Bridge, go north on U.S. 101, east on Highway 37, and north and east on Highway 121. For Sonoma wineries, head north at Highway 12; for Napa's, turn left (to the northwest) when Highway 121 runs into Highway 29.

From Berkeley and other East Bay towns, take I–80 north to Highway 37 west to Highway 29 north. From points north of the Wine Country, take U.S. 101 south to Geyserville and follow Highway 128 southeast into the Napa Valley.

Getting Around

By Bus
Sonoma County Area Transit (☎ 707/585–7516) and **Napa Valley Tran-** ...631) provide transportation between towns in their ...untry counties.

...he two-lane country roads can be heavy, the best ... sprawling Wine Country is by private car. Rentals ...irports and in San Francisco, Oakland, Sonoma, ...pa.

...⊠ 484 Lake Park Ave., Suite 255, Oakland 94610, ...produces tapes about the history, landmarks, and ...oma and Napa valleys that you can play in your car (maps also provided). The tapes are available at some local Bay Area bookstores and can also be ordered directly from Rider's Guide for $12.95, plus $2.50 postage.

Contacts and Resources

B&B Reservation Agencies

Bed & Breakfast Exchange (✉ 1407 Main St., Suite 102, St. Helena, ☎ 707/942–5900). The **Bed & Breakfast Association of Sonoma** (✉ 3250 Trinity Rd., Glen Ellen, ☎ 800/969–4667). **The Wine Country Bed & Breakfast Inns of Sonoma County** (☎ 707/433–4667; 800/ 354–4743 for brochure). **Wine Country Reservations** (☎ 707/257– 7757).

Emergencies

Ambulance (☎ 911). **Fire** (☎ 911). **Police** (☎ 911).

Guided Tours

Full-day guided tours of the Wine Country usually include lunch and cost about $50. The guides, some of whom are winery owners themselves, know the area well and may show you some lesser-known cellars. Reservations are generally required.

Gray Line (✉ 350 8th St., San Francisco 94103, ☎ 415/558–9400) has bright red double-decker buses that tour the Wine Country. **Great Pacific Tour Co.** (✉ 518 Octavia St., San Francisco 94102, ☎ 415/626– 4499) operates full-day tours of Napa and Sonoma, including a summer picnic lunch and a winter restaurant lunch, in passenger vans that seat 14. **HMS Travel Group** (✉ 707 4th St., Santa Rosa 95404, ☎ 707/ 526–2922 or 800/367–5348) offers customized tours of the Wine Country for six or more people, by appointment only. The **Napa Valley Wine Train** (✉ 1275 McKinstry St., Napa 94559, ☎ 707/253–2111 or 800/ 427–4124) allows you to enjoy lunch, dinner, or weekend brunch on one of several restored 1915 Pullman railroad cars that run between Napa and St. Helena. Dinner costs between $70 and $82, lunch between $63 and $75, brunch $57; per-person prices include train fare, meals, tax, and service. On weekend brunch trips and weekday lunch trips you can ride a special "Deli" car for $25. Some weeks during the winter the train runs only from Thursday to Sunday; call ahead.

Visitor Information

Napa Valley Conference and Visitors Bureau (✉ 1310 Napa Town Center, Napa 94559, ☎ 707/226–7459). The **Redwood Empire Association** (✉ The Cannery, 2801 Leavenworth St., 2nd Floor, San Francisco 94133, ☎ 415/543–8334). **Sonoma County Convention and Visitors Bureau** (✉ 5000 Roberts Lake Rd., Rohnert Park 94928, ☎ 707/586– 8100 or 800/326–7666).

5 San Francisco

With Side Trips to Marin County, the East Bay, and the Peninsula

San Francisco is a sophisticated city with world-class hotels and the greatest concentration of excellent restaurants in the state. The town has an undeserved reputation as the kook capital of the United States, yet it's the country's number one tourist destination. Why? To use the vernacular, the vibe here is cool, from North Beach coffeehouses to Chinatown tea emporiums, Golden Gate Park, and Haight Street's head shops (yes, they're still around).

IN ITS FIRST LIFE, SAN FRANCISCO was little more than a small, well-situated settlement. Founded by Spaniards in 1776, it was prized for its natural harbor, so commodious that "all the navies of the world might fit inside it," as one visitor wrote. The 1848 discovery of gold at John Sutter's sawmill in the nearby Sierra foothills transformed the sleepy village into a city of 30,000 by the early 1850s. As millions of dollars' worth of gold was panned and blasted out of the hills, a "western Wall Street" sprang up. Just when gold production began to taper off, prospectors turned up a rich vein of silver in and around Virginia City, Nevada. San Francisco, the nearest financial center, prospered again. The city remains a financial hub, though nowadays its attentions are as much transoceanic as transcontinental. San Francisco prides itself on its role as a Pacific Rim capital, and overseas investment has become a vital part of its economic life. In terms of both geography and culture, San Francisco is about as close as you can get to Asia in the continental United States.

Loose, tolerant, and even licentious are words that are used to describe San Francisco; bohemian communities thrive here. As early as the 1860s, the "Barbary Coast"—a collection of taverns, whorehouses, and gambling joints on or near Pacific Avenue close to the waterfront— was famous, or infamous. North Beach, the city's Little Italy, became the home of the beat movement in the 1950s—the late *San Francisco Chronicle* columnist Herb Caen coined the term beatnik. The Haight-Ashbury district became synonymous with hippiedom, giving rise to legendary bands like the Jefferson Airplane, Big Brother and the Holding Company (fronted by Janis Joplin), and the Grateful Dead in the 1960s. And, as most of the world knows, lesbians and gay men have found the town hospitable.

Technically speaking, San Francisco is only California's fourth-largest city, behind Los Angeles, San Diego, and nearby San Jose. But that statistic is misleading: The Bay Area, which stretches from the bedroom communities north of Oakland and Berkeley south through Silicon Valley (the Peninsula and South Bay cities that have become the center of America's computer industry) and San Jose, is really one continuous megacity, with San Francisco as its heart.

EXPLORING SAN FRANCISCO

Updated by
Chris Baty

San Francisco is a relatively small city, with just over 750,000 residents nested on a 46½-square-mile tip of land between San Francisco Bay and the Pacific Ocean. San Franciscans cherish the city's colorful past, and many older buildings have been spared from demolition and nostalgically converted into modern offices and shops. Bernard Maybeck, Julia Morgan, Willis Polk, and Arthur Brown Jr. are among the noted architects whose designs still grace the city's downtown and neighborhoods.

San Francisco neighborhoods retain strong cultural, political, and ethnic identities. Locals know this pluralism is the real life of the city. Experiencing San Francisco means visiting the neighborhoods: the colorful Mission District, the gay Castro, countercultural Haight Street, serene Pacific Heights, bustling Chinatown, and still bohemian North Beach.

Exploring involves navigating a maze of one-way streets and restricted parking zones. Public parking garages or lots tend to be expensive, as are hotel parking spaces. The famed 40-plus hills can be a problem for drivers who are new to the terrain. Cable cars, buses, and trolleys can

Exploring San Francisco (*Boxes Refer to Detail Maps*)

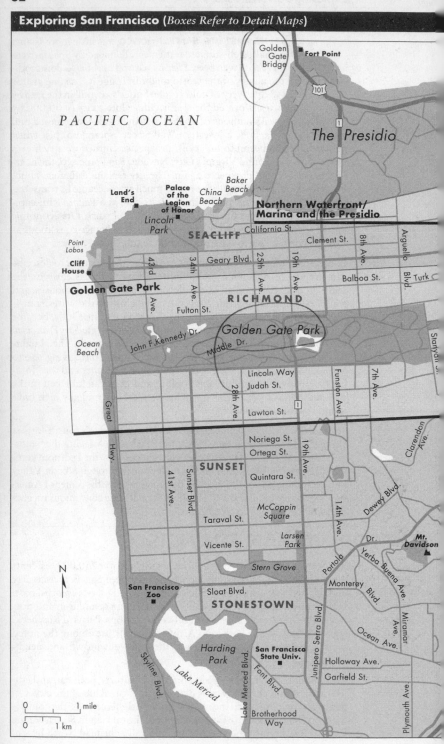

PACIFIC OCEAN

Golden Gate Bridge

Fort Point

101

The Presidio

Baker Beach

Land's End

Palace of the Legion of Honor

China Beach

Lincoln Park

Northern Waterfront/ Marina and the Presidio

Point Lobos

SEACLIFF

California St.

Clement St.

8th Ave.

Arguello Blvd.

Cliff House

43rd Ave.

34th Ave.

Geary Blvd.

25th Ave.

19th Ave.

Balboa St.

Turk

Golden Gate Park

Ave.

Fulton St.

RICHMOND

Starlyan

Ocean Beach

John F. Kennedy Dr.

Golden Gate Park

Middle Dr.

Lincoln Way

28th Ave.

Judah St.

Funston Ave.

7th Ave.

Great Hwy.

Lawton St.

1

Noriega St.

Ortega St.

19th Ave.

Clarendon Ave.

SUNSET

41st Ave.

Sunset Blvd.

Quintara St.

14th Ave.

Dewey Blvd.

Taraval St.

McCoppin Square

Vicente St.

Larsen Park

Dr.

Mt. Davidson

Stern Grove

Portola

Yerba Buena Ave.

Miramar Ave.

N

San Francisco Zoo

Sloat Blvd.

Monterey Blvd.

STONESTOWN

Junipero Serra Blvd.

Ocean Ave.

Harding Park

Skyline Blvd.

Lake Merced

Lake Merced Blvd.

San Francisco State Univ.

Font Blvd.

Holloway Ave.

Garfield St.

Plymouth Ave.

Brotherhood Way

0   1 mile

0   1 km

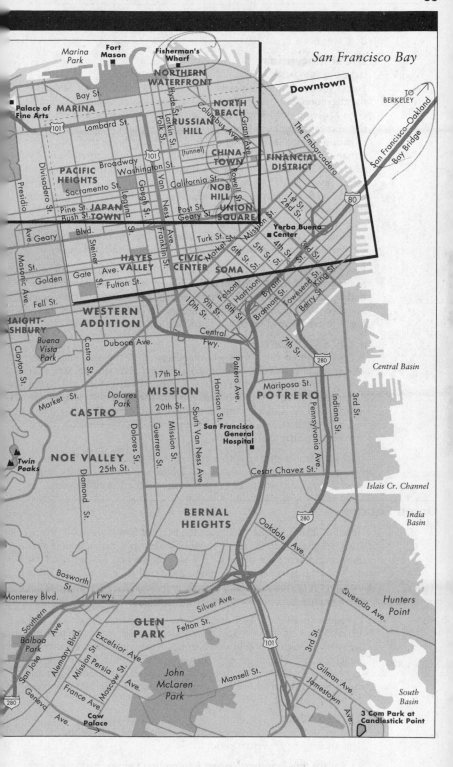

take you to or near many of the area's attractions. If you're staying downtown or at Fisherman's Wharf, you can get by for at least a few days without a car.

Great Itineraries

IF YOU HAVE 3 DAYS

Spend your first morning exploring Chinatown and North Beach. In the afternoon visit the South of Market area—don't miss the San Francisco Museum of Modern Art or Yerba Buena Gardens. Get up early the next morning for a boat ride to Alcatraz (make your reservations at least a week ahead during the summer; boats leave from the Fisherman's Wharf area). On your return, have lunch at any of Pier 39's many eateries. Check out the sea lions lounging on the docks (have your camera ready) or visit the Underwater World at Pier 39 aquarium. Stroll the Embarcadero Promenade toward the Ferry Building, ride up Market Street on one of the F-line antique trolleys to Powell Street, and walk north three blocks on Powell to Union Square. End your day on Nob Hill, where you can watch a tropical storm in dry comfort in the Polynesian-theme Tonga Room bar at the Fairmont Hotel.

Begin your third day in Golden Gate Park. In the late afternoon head to the famed corner of Haight and Ashbury, where you'll find hippies both vintage and newly minted crowding the sidewalks. In the evening, take in a performance of the long-running revue *Beach Blanket Babylon,* a hilarious send-up of San Francisco's idiosyncratic ways.

IF YOU HAVE 5 DAYS

Follow the three-day itinerary outlined above. Begin your fourth day along the Marina Green. Nearby is the rococo Palace of Fine Arts. Pass through the Presidio, exiting in the Richmond District for a visit to the California Palace of the Legion of Honor. The museum's stylish café has views of the Golden Gate—and good food, if you haven't yet had lunch. From the Legion, continue west to the Beach Chalet to catch the sunset (or the fog).

Start your fifth morning with a bracing walk across the Golden Gate Bridge. Continue on to Sausalito and Tiburon in Marin County, or get in your car and head south to Filoli estate on the Peninsula.

Union Square

Since 1850 Union Square has been the heart of San Francisco's downtown. Its name derives from a series of violent pro-union demonstrations staged here prior to the Civil War. This is where you will find the city's finest department stores and its most exclusive boutiques. There are about four dozen hotels within three blocks of the square, and the city's leading art galleries and downtown theater district are nearby.

The square itself is a 2.6-acre oasis planted with palms, boxwood, and seasonal flowers, and peopled with a kaleidoscope of characters: office workers sunning and brown-bagging, street musicians, a few vocal preachers, and a fair share of homeless people. Events throughout the year include fashion shows, free noontime concerts, ethnic celebrations, and noisy demonstrations. Auto and bus traffic is often gridlocked on the four bordering streets.

A Good Walk

Numbers in the text correspond to numbers in the margin and on the Downtown San Francisco map.

Start at the **San Francisco Visitors Information Center** ①, on the lower level of Hallidie Plaza at Powell and Market streets. Up the stairs from the center is the **cable car terminus** ②. If you don't hop right on a cable car, head three blocks north on Powell Street from the terminus to **Union Square** ③. The stately **Westin St. Francis Hotel** ④ dominates the corner of Geary and Powell streets. Directly across the square from the St. Francis is the **TIX Bay Area** ⑤ discount booth. Due east of the booth is boutique-lined **Maiden Lane** ⑥. At Kearny Street, turn right and walk to O'Farrell, then right again to return to Stockton Street. Union Square is something of a shopper's theme park, something you can experience vividly at either the **F.A.O. Schwarz** ⑦ toy store at Stockton and O'Farrell or two blocks north on Stockton (at Post) at the entertaining, if relentlessly commercial, **Niketown** athletic clothing and goods complex. A block north is Sutter Street; go right one block on Sutter to view the beaux arts–style **Hammersmith Building** ⑧ or left one block and check out the Art Deco building at **450 Sutter Street** ⑨. One and a half blocks east of the Hammersmith Building is the **Hallidie Building** ⑩, on the north side of Sutter; notice its graceful all-glass facade and Venetian detailing.

TIMING

Allow about two hours to roam the Union Square area. Stepping into the Macy's store on Union Square or browsing the other boutiques in the vicinity can eat up countless hours; if you're a shopper give yourself extra time here. The cable car ride from Powell and Market down to Fisherman's Wharf only takes about 20 minutes—but waiting in line can take twice as long.

Sights to See

② **Cable car terminus.** This is the starting point for two of the three cable-car lines. The Powell-Mason line climbs up Nob Hill, then winds through North Beach to Fisherman's Wharf. The Powell-Hyde car also crosses Nob Hill but then continues up Russian Hill and down Hyde Street to Victorian Park, across from the Buena Vista Cafe and near Ghirardelli Square. The cable-car system dates from 1873, when Andrew Hallidie demonstrated his first car on Clay Street; in 1964 the tramlike vehicles were designated national historic landmarks. In summertime there are often long lines to board any of the three systems; if possible, plan your ride for mid-morning or mid-afternoon during the week to avoid crowds. Buy your ticket ($2 one way) on board, at nearby hotels, or at the police/information booth near the turnaround. *See* Getting Around *in* San Francisco A to Z for more details about the system. ✉ *Powell and Market Sts.*

⑦ **F.A.O. Schwarz.** The prices are not Toys 'R' Us, but it's worth stopping by this three-floor playland to peek at the 6-ft-tall stuffed animals and elaborate fairy tale sculptures. Among the wares are a large Barbie section, an astounding supply of stuffed animals (the priciest is a whopping $15,000), and just about every other toy imaginable. ✉ *48 Stockton St.,* ☎ *415/394–8700.* ✆ *Mon.–Sat. 10–7, Sun. 11–6.*

⑨ **450 Sutter Street.** This 1928 terra-cotta skyscraper (now a medical and dental office) is an Art Deco masterpiece, with handsome Mayan-inspired designs covering both the exterior and interior surfaces. ✉ *Between Stockton and Powell Sts.*

⑩ **Hallidie Building.** Named for cable car inventor Andrew Hallidie, this building is best viewed from across the street. Willis Polk's revolutionary glass-curtain wall—believed to be the world's first such creation—hangs a foot beyond the reinforced concrete of the frame. With its reflecting glass, decorative exterior fire escapes that appear to be metal balconies, and Venetian Gothic cornice, the unusual building dominates the block. Also notice the horizontal ornamental bands of birds at feeders. ✉ *130 Sutter St., between Kearny and Montgomery Sts.*

Downtown San Francisco

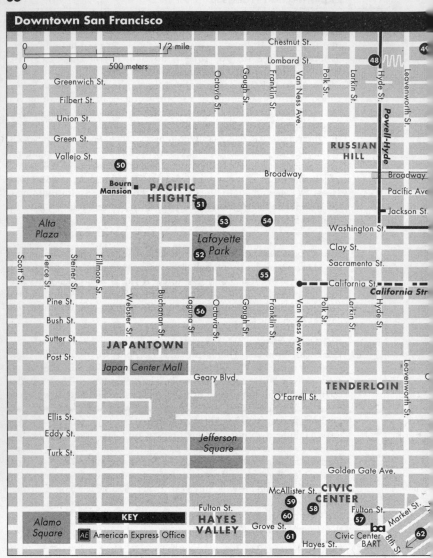

KEY

AE American Express Office

San Francisco Bay

TELEGRAPH HILL

NORTH BEACH

Powell-Mason

Chestnut St.

Lombard St.

Greenwich St.

Filbert St.

Union St.

Green St.

Vallejo St.

Mason St.

Columbus Ave.

Powell St.

Taylor St.

NOB HILL

CHINATOWN

FINANCIAL DISTRICT

Stockton St.

Grant Ave.

Kearny St.

Montgomery St.

Sansome St.

Battery St.

Front St.

Davis St.

Drumm St.

The Embarcadero

Stuart St.

Spear St.

Clay St.

Halleck St.

Bank of America

Embarcadero BART

Main St.

Beale St.

Fremont St.

Folsom St.

Harrison St.

UNION SQUARE

Bush St.

Post St.

Farrell St.

Ellis St.

Eddy St.

Turk St.

Market St.

Maiden Ln.

Montgomery BART

New Montgomery St.

California Historical Society

Mission St.

1st St.

2nd St.

Howard St.

Hawthorne St.

3rd St.

Powell BART

YERBA BUENA

4th St.

5th St.

6th St.

Folsom St.

Bryant St.

Brannan St.

Townsend St.

Howard St.

SOMA

Masonic Auditorium, **41**

Mission Dolores, **62**

Moscone Convention Center, **12**

Noteworthy Victorians, **56**

Old Chinese Telephone Exchange, **31**

Old St. Mary's Church, **28**

Pacific Stock Exchange, **22**

Pacific Union Club, **43**

Palace Hotel, **17**

Portsmouth Square, **30**

Rincon Center, **21**

Saints Peter and Paul, **35**

San Francisco Art Institute, **49**

San Francisco Brewing Company, **26**

San Francisco Museum of Modern Art, **11**

San Francisco Public Library, **57**

San Francisco Visitors Information Center, **1**

Spreckels Mansion, **53**

Telegraph Hill, **37**

Tien Hou Temple, **32**

TIX Bay Area, **5**

Transamerica Pyramid, **24**

Union Square, **3**

Veterans Building, **59**

War Memorial Opera House, **60**

Washington Square, **34**

Wells Fargo Bank History Museum, **23**

Westin St. Francis Hotel, **4**

Whittier Mansion, **51**

Yerba Buena Gardens, **13**

⑧ Hammersmith Building. Glass walls and a playful design distinguish this small, colorful beaux arts–style structure, built in 1907. The Foundation for Architectural Heritage once described the building as a "commercial jewel box"; appropriately, it was originally designed for use as a jewelry store. ⊠ *301 Sutter St.*

⑥ Maiden Lane. Known as Morton Street in the Barbary Coast era, this red-light district reported at least one murder a week. After the fires that followed the 1906 earthquake destroyed the brothels, the street emerged as Maiden Lane. It's now a daytime pedestrian mall, with a patchwork of umbrella-shaded tables, between Stockton and Kearny streets. Frank Lloyd Wright designed the brick structure at 140 Maiden Lane. The building, which has a circular interior ramp and skylights, is said to have been a model for the Guggenheim Museum in New York. Now at No. 140 are the Xanadu/Folk Art International galleries, showcases for Baltic, Latin American, and African folk art. ⊠ *Between Stockton and Kearny Sts.*

❶ San Francisco Visitors Information Center. Conveniently located below the cable car terminus, the center has a multilingual staff and maps, pamphlets, and events information. The center sells the **Citypass** ($29.95, good for discounted admission to several major attractions including museums, the zoo, and bay cruises), coupons, and hotel brochures. ⊠ *Hallidie Plaza, lower level, Powell and Market Sts.,* ☎ *415/391–2000.* ⊙ *Weekdays 9–5:30, Sat. 9–3, Sun. 10–2.*

❺ TIX Bay Area. This service provides half-price day-of-performance tickets (cash or traveler's checks only) to performing arts events, as well as regular full-price box office services. Telephone reservations are not accepted for half-price tickets. Also available are Explorer Passes, which provide entry to Golden Gate Park's museums at a discount rate, and Muni Passports, short-term tourist passes for all city buses and cable cars. ⊠ *Stockton St. at Union Square,* ☎ *415/433–7827.* ⊙ *Tues.–Thurs. 11–6, Fri.–Sat. 11–7.*

❸ Union Square. At center stage, the Victory Monument, by Robert Ingersoll Aitken, commemorates Commodore George Dewey's victory over the Spanish fleet at Manila in 1898. The 97-ft Corinthian column, topped by a bronze figure symbolizing naval conquest, was dedicated by Theodore Roosevelt in 1903 and withstood the 1906 earthquake. After the earthquake and fire of 1906, the square was dubbed "Little St. Francis" because of the temporary shelter erected for residents of the St. Francis Hotel. ⊠ *Between Powell, Stockton, Post, and Geary Sts.*

❹ Westin St. Francis Hotel. The second-oldest hotel in the city, originally built in 1904, was conceived by Charles Crocker and his associates as a hostelry for their millionaire friends. The hotel's Turkish baths once had ocean water piped in. After the 1906 fire gutted the hotel, a larger, more luxurious residence was opened in 1907. The hotel has had its share of notoriety. Silent-film comedian Fatty Arbuckle's career plummeted—faster than one of the St. Francis tower's glass-walled elevators—after a wild 1921 party in one of the suites in the older wing went awry. In 1975 Sara Jane Moore, standing among a crowd outside the hotel, attempted to shoot then-president Gerald Ford. As might be imagined, no plaques commemorate these events in the establishment's lobby. The ever-helpful staff will, however, gladly direct you to the traditional teatime ritual—or if you prefer, to champagne and caviar—in the dramatic Art Deco Compass Rose lounge. Elaborate Chinese screens, secluded seating alcoves, and soothing background music make this an ideal rest stop after frantic shopping or sightseeing. ⊠ *335 Powell St., at Geary St.,* ☎ *415/397–7000.*

South of Market (SoMa) and the Embarcadero

The vast tract of downtown land south of Market Street along the waterfront and west to the Mission District—also known by the acronym SoMa—is the center of a burgeoning arts scene.

Numbers in the text correspond to numbers in the margin and on the Downtown San Francisco map.

A Good Walk

The showpiece of the South of Market area is the **San Francisco Museum of Modern Art** ⑪, on 3rd Street between Howard and Mission streets. Across from the museum is the cluster of buildings known as Yerba Buena Center, between Folsom and Mission streets and 3rd and 4th streets. Within the Yerba Buena complex are the **Moscone Convention Center** ⑫ and **Yerba Buena Gardens** ⑬, which contains the **Center for the Arts** ⑭. Across 4th Street from Moscone Center is the **Ansel Adams Center for Photography** ⑮. From the Ansel Adams gallery, head north up 4th Street and cross Mission; walk a half block west to the **Cartoon Art Museum** ⑯.

Take 4th Street north to Market Street to where 3rd, Market, Kearny, and Geary streets converge. Walk east on Market Street past **Lotta's Fountain** to New Montgomery and the **Palace Hotel** ⑰. Continue east on Market Street, taking note of several "flatiron" buildings (including an older one at No. 540–548 and a newer one at No. 388) angling into the thoroughfare. Toward the end of Market is the **Embarcadero Center** ⑱, a five-block complex that holds retail stores, offices, and the Hyatt Regency Hotel. On the waterfront side of the hotel is outdoor **Justin Herman Plaza** ⑲.

Across the Embarcadero roadway from Justin Herman Plaza stands the **Ferry Building** ⑳. North of the Ferry Building at Pier 5 is a section of the 5-ft-wide, 2½-mi-long glass-and-concrete **Promenade Ribbon**, which the city says will be longest art form in the nation when it's completed, perhaps by 1999 (the project's going slower than expected). At Embarcadero and Mission, you can't miss the ornate **Audiffred Building,** built in 1889 by a homesick gentleman as a reminder of his native France, and now housing the Boulevard restaurant. Head west down Mission and turn south on Steuart Street; halfway down the block is the entrance to the **Rincon Center** ㉑, which houses some famous murals depicting California history. Across from the Rincon Center on Steuart is the **Jewish Museum,** housed in the Jewish Community Federation Building.

TIMING

This walk takes a couple of hours, not counting stops at the various museums. Plan on spending a couple of hours at SFMOMA. The Center for the Arts and the Ansel Adams Center each merit an hour or so.

Sights to See

⑮ **Ansel Adams Center for Photography.** Ansel Adams himself created this center in Carmel in 1967. In 1989 it moved to SoMa. The center presents historical and contemporary photography and changing exhibitions of Adams's work. ⊠ *250 4th St.,* ☎ *415/495–7000.* ▨ *$5.* ☉ *Tues.–Sun. 11–5, 1st Thurs. of month 11–8.*

California Historical Society. This vast repository of Californiana includes 500,000 photographs, 150,000 manuscripts, thousands of books, periodicals, prints, and paintings as well as gold-rush paraphernalia. The society's building is an airy, sky-lit space with a central gallery, two adjacent galleries, a research library (accessible by appointment only), and an excellent bookstore. ⊠ *678 Mission St.,* ☎ *415/357–1848.* 🎫 *$3.* ⊘ *Tues.–Sat. 11–5.*

⑯ Cartoon Art Museum. Krazy Kat, Zippy the Pinhead, Batman, and a crew of other colorful cartoon icons greet you at the entrance to the Cartoon Art Museum. Changing and permanent exhibits survey everything from the impact of underground comics and the "Peanuts" gang to the contributions of women and African-American cartoonists. ⊠ *814 Mission St., Suite 200,* ☎ *415/546–3922.* 🎫 *$4.* ⊘ *Wed.–Fri. 11–5, Sat. 10–5, Sun. 1–5.*

⑭ Center for the Arts. The center presents dance, music, performance, theater, visual arts, film, video, and installations—from the community-based to the international—with an emphasis on the cultural diversity of San Francisco. The complex includes a theater and a forum, three visual arts galleries, a film and video screening room, a gift shop, a café, and an outdoor performance stage where midday music is presented daily from April to October. ⊠ *701 Mission St.,* ☎ *415/978–2787.* 🎫 *Galleries $5; free 1st Thurs. of month 6–8 PM.* ⊘ *Galleries and box office Tues.–Sun. 11–6.*

⑱ Embarcadero Center. John Portman designed this complex of shops, restaurants, cinemas, hotels, and office space. Louise Nevelson's 54-ft-high black-steel sculpture, *Sky Tree,* stands guard over Building 3 and is among the 20-plus works of art throughout the center. The **Hyatt Regency Hotel** has a spectacular lobby with a 17-story hanging garden and glass elevators that are fun to ride (unless you suffer from vertigo). ⊠ *Clay St. between Battery St. and the Embarcadero.* ⊘ *Weekdays 10–7, Sat. 10–6, Sun. noon–5.*

⑳ Ferry Building. The beacon of the port area is the Embarcadero's quaint Ferry Building; its 230-ft clock tower was modeled after the campanile of Seville's cathedral. The building, which has held its post since 1896, is the headquarters of the Port Commission and the World Trade Center's office. A waterfront promenade that extends from the piers north of here to the San Francisco–Oakland Bay Bridge is great for jogging, in-line skating, watching sailboats on the bay, or enjoying a picnic. Ferries from behind the Ferry Building sail to Sausalito, Larkspur, Tiburon, and the East Bay. ⊠ *The Embarcadero, at the foot of Market St.*

The Jewish Museum. This small museum hosts exhibits on Jewish art, history, and culture. The curators here don't shy away from controversial programs, hosting exhibits such as *Art and the Rosenberg Era,* an in-depth look at freedom of expression, and *Bridges & Boundaries: African Americans and American Jews.* ⊠ *121 Steuart St.,* ☎ *415/543–8880.* 🎫 *$5; free 1st Mon. of month.* ⊘ *Mon.–Wed. noon–6, Thurs. noon–8, Sun. 11–6.*

⑲ Justin Herman Plaza. The plaza on the waterfront side of the Hyatt Regency plays host to arts-and-crafts shows, street musicians, and skateboarders almost daily during the summer and on many weekends year-round. On sunny days it's a good spot to enjoy a snack from one of Embarcadero Center's dozen or so take-out shops. During the winter holidays an ice rink is set up here. ⊠ *The Embarcadero north of Market St.*

Lotta's Fountain. This quirky monument, now largely unnoticed by local passersby, was a gift to the city from singer Lotta Crabtree, a Mae West prototype. The fountain itself is unspectacular, but Crabtree's history is interesting. Her "brash music-hall exploits" so enthralled San Francisco's early population of miners that they were known to shower her with gold nuggets and silver dollars after her performances. ⊠ *Intersection of 3rd, Market, Kearny, and Geary Sts.*

⑫ **Moscone Convention Center.** The site of the 1984 Democratic convention is distinguished by a contemporary glass-and-girder lobby at street level (all convention exhibit space is underground) and a monolithic, column-free interior. ⊠ *Howard St. between 3rd and 4th Sts.*

⑰ **Palace Hotel.** The Palace opened in 1875. The hotel has a storied past—President Warren Harding died here while still in office in 1923—some of which is recounted in the glass cases off the main lobby. Though it had a 28,000-gallon reservoir fed by four artesian wells, the original Palace was destroyed by fire following the 1906 earthquake. The current building dates from 1909; late-1980s renovations included the restoration of the glass-dome Garden Court restaurant and the installation of original mosaic-tile floors in Oriental-rug designs. Maxfield Parrish's wall-size painting, *The Pied Piper,* dominates the hotel's Pied Piper Bar. Ninety-minute guided tours of the hotel's grand interior are conducted on Tuesday and Saturday at 10:30 AM and on Thursday at 2 PM. ⊠ *2 New Montgomery St.,* ☎ *415/512–1111.*

㉑ **Rincon Center.** A five-story water column resembling a mini-rainstorm dominates the center's street-level mall area. In addition to the mall, there are two modern towers of offices and apartments. In front of all this is a former post office built in the Streamline Moderne style. In the post office's historic lobby is a series of murals by Anton Refregier that depict California life from the days when Native Americans were the state's sole inhabitants through World War I. A permanent exhibit below the murals contains interesting photographs and artifacts of life in the Rincon area in the 1800s. ⊠ *Between Steuart, Spear, Mission, and Howard Sts.*

★ ⑪ **San Francisco Museum of Modern Art.** SFMOMA has won acclaim for its adventurous programming, which includes traveling exhibits and multimedia installations. Works by Henri Matisse, Pablo Picasso, Georgia O'Keeffe, Frida Kahlo, Jackson Pollock, and Andy Warhol are among the highlights of the permanent collection. Post–World War II holdings in photography are particularly strong. The striking modernist structure, designed by Swiss architect Mario Botta, consists of a stepped-back, burnt-sienna brick facade and a central tower constructed of alternating bands of black and white stone. Inside, natural light from the tower floods the central atrium and some of the museum's galleries. SFMOMA's café, accessible from the street, is a comfortable spot with reasonably priced drinks and light meals. ⊠ *151 3rd St.,* ☎ *415/357–4000.* ▦ *$8; free 1st Tues. of each month.* ☉ *Mon.–Tues. and Fri.–Sun. 11–6, Thurs. 11–9 (½-price entry 6–9).*

★ ℭ ⑬ **Yerba Buena Gardens.** A large expanse of green is surrounded by a circular walkway lined with benches and sculptures. Powerful streams of water, part of a memorial to Martin Luther King Jr., surge over large, jagged stone columns, mirroring the enduring force of King's words, which are carved on the stone walls and on glass blocks behind the waterfall. Above the memorial are two restaurants and an overhead walkway to the Moscone Center's main entrance. Scheduled to open in late 1998 or early 1999 on the west side of Yerba Buena Gardens is a shopping and entertainment complex that will include a multiple-screen cinema. ⊠ *Between 3rd, 4th, Mission, and Howard Sts.* ☉ *Sunrise–10 PM.*

The Heart of the Barbary Coast

When San Francisco was a brawling, boozing, extravagant upstart of a town in the latter half of the 19th century, Jackson Square and the Financial District were at the heart of the action. The gold rush brought streams of people from across America and Europe, transforming the onetime frontier town into a cosmopolitan city almost overnight: The population of San Francisco jumped from a mere 800 in 1848 to more than 25,000 in 1850, and to nearly 150,000 in 1870. Along with the prospectors came many other fortune seekers: Saloon keepers, gamblers, and prostitutes all flocked to the so-called Barbary Coast (now Jackson Square and the Financial District). Underground dance halls, casinos, bordellos, and palatial homes sprung up. Along with the quick money came a wave of violence: In 1852 alone, the city suffered an average of two murders and one major fire each day.

By 1917 the excesses of the Barbary Coast had fallen victim to the Red-Light Abatement Act—the wild era was over, and the young city was forced to grow up. Jackson Square is now a sedate district of refurbished brick buildings housing high-end antiques shops and architecture firms. The Financial District has grown into a congested canyon of soaring skyscrapers, gridlocked traffic, and bustling pedestrians. Only one remnant of the gold-rush era remains: Along the former wharf-dominated streets below Montgomery between California and Broadway, and underlying many building foundations, lay at least 100 ships that were abandoned by frantic crews and passengers caught up in gold fever. Balance Alley, a short alley between Jackson and Gold streets, is said to have been named after the ship that's buried there.

Numbers in the text correspond to numbers in the margin and on the Downtown San Francisco map.

A Good Walk

Fifty sites are stops along a 3.8-mi-long Barbary Coast Trail. Marked with bronze sidewalk plaques on every street corner, the trail begins at the Old Mint, at 5th and Mission streets, and runs north through downtown, Chinatown, Portsmouth Square, Jackson Square, North Beach, and Fisherman's Wharf, ending at Aquatic Park. For information about the sites on the trail, pick up a brochure at the San Francisco Visitors Information Center (☞ Union Square, *above*). To catch its most interesting highlights, start at Montgomery and Market streets (Muni and BART both stop at the Montgomery station here), and walk two blocks east on Market (toward the Ferry Building clock tower) to Sansome Street. Go north two blocks to Pine Street to the **Pacific Stock Exchange** ㉒, built in 1915; around the corner on Sansome is the Art Deco–style Stock Exchange Tower. Head west on Pine Street to Montgomery and turn north to find the **Wells Fargo Bank History Museum** ㉓, between California and Sacramento streets; its collection provides a good introduction to gold-rush history.

Two blocks up from the Wells Fargo Museum is the landmark **Transamerica Pyramid** ㉔, on Montgomery Street between Clay and Washington streets. Walking through Transamerica's small park, on the east side of the building, you'll exit on Washington Street; to your left is Hotaling Place, a historic alley that leads to **Jackson Square** ㉕, the heart of the Barbary Coast. Of particular note is the former **A. P. Hotaling whisky distillery,** on the corner of Hotaling Place and Jackson Street. Head west to Montgomery and north up Columbus Avenue to take a swig of history at the **San Francisco Brewing Company** ㉖.

TIMING

Two hours should be enough time to see everything in this tour. The Wells Fargo Museum deserves a half hour. If you're interested in antiques, leave extra time for the shops in Jackson Square. Evenings and weekends are peaceful times to admire the distinctive architecture, though the antiques shops and the museums are closed at those times. If you want to see activity, go on a weekday around lunchtime.

Sights to See

Bank of America. This 52-story polished red granite-and-marble building dominates nearly an entire downtown block. Inside, small exhibits of impressive original art are displayed. A massive, abstract black-granite sculpture designed by the Japanese artist Masayuki commands the corner of the complex at Kearny and California streets; it's been dubbed the "Banker's Heart" by local wags. At the top of the complex is the **Carnelian Room** (☞ Skyline Bars *in* Nightlife and the Arts, *below*). ⊠ *Between California, Pine, Montgomery, and Kearny Sts.*

㉕ Jackson Square. Some of the city's earliest business buildings, survivors of the 1906 quake, still stand in Jackson Square between Montgomery and Sansome streets. The alley connecting Washington and Jackson streets is named for the head of the **A. P. Hotaling Company whiskey distillery,** which was at 451 Jackson. The distillery was the largest liquor repository on the West Coast. The alley is lined with restored 19th-century brick buildings. The old Hotaling building has been painted a dull green and reveals little of its infamous past, but a plaque on the side of the building repeats a famous query about its surviving the quake: IF, AS THEY SAY, GOD SPANKED THE TOWN FOR BEING OVER FRISKY, WHY DID HE BURN THE CHURCHES DOWN AND SAVE HOTALING'S WHISKY? The **Ghirardelli Chocolate Factory** was once housed at 415 Jackson, though nothing marks the spot as such; it's now an art gallery. ⊠ *Between Washington, Broadway, Montgomery, and Sansome Sts.*

㉒ Pacific Stock Exchange. Ralph Stackpole's 1930 granite sculptural groups, *Earth's Fruitfulness* and *Man's Inventive Genius,* flank this imposing structure, which dates from 1915. The Stock Exchange Tower, around the corner on Sansome Street, is a 1930 modern classic by architects Miller and Pfleuger, with an Art Deco gold ceiling and a black marble wall entry. ⊠ *301 Pine St. (tower at 155 Sansome St.).*

㉖ San Francisco Brewing Company. Built in 1907, this pub looks like a museum piece from the Barbary Coast days. An upright piano dating from the early 20th century sits in the corner under the original stained-glass windows. Take a seat at the beautiful old mahogany bar and look down at the white-tile spittoon. In an adjacent room look for the handmade copper brewing kettle, now used to produce a dozen beers—with names like Pony Express—using old-fashioned gravity-flow methods. ⊠ *155 Columbus Ave.,* ☎ *415/434–3344.*

㉔ Transamerica Pyramid. The city's most photographed high-rise is the 853-ft Transamerica Pyramid. Designed by William Pereira and Associates in 1972, the once controversial structure has become more acceptable to local purists over time. A fragrant redwood grove along the east side of the building, replete with benches and a cheerful fountain, is a nice place to unwind. ⊠ *600 Montgomery St.*

㉓ Wells Fargo Bank History Museum. There were no formal banks in San Francisco during the early years of the gold rush, and miners often entrusted their gold dust to saloon keepers. In 1852 Wells Fargo opened its first bank in the city, and the company established banking offices in the mining camps, using stagecoaches and pony express riders to service the burgeoning state. (California's population boomed from 15,000 to 200,000 between 1848 and 1852.) The museum displays samples of nuggets and gold dust from mines and has a mural-size map of the Mother Lode. The showpiece is the 140-year-old Concord stagecoach, the likes of which carried passengers from St. Joseph, Missouri, to San Francisco in three weeks. ⊠ *420 Montgomery St.,* ☎ *415/396–2619.* ▧ *Free.* ☉ *Weekdays 9–5.*

Chinatown

Chinatown, bordered roughly by Bush, Kearny, Powell, and Broadway, is home to one of the largest Chinese communities outside Asia. Immigrants from Southeast Asian countries also live in the neighborhood. The two main drags are Grant Avenue, where most of the tourist shops reside, and Stockton Street, where many locals do business.

Numbers in the text correspond to numbers in the margin and on the Downtown San Francisco map.

A Good Walk

Visitors usually enter Chinatown through the green-tiled **Chinatown Gate** ㉗, at Bush Street and Grant Avenue. A block and a half north at California is **Old St. Mary's Church** ㉘. From the church head east on California Street and take a left on Kearny Street. Two blocks north on the third floor of the Holiday Inn is the **Chinese Culture Center** ㉙. Take the suspended walkway over Kearny from the Holiday Inn to **Portsmouth Square** ㉚. West on Washington is the **Old Chinese Telephone Exchange** ㉛. Continue west past Grant Avenue to Waverly Place and the **Tien Hou Temple** ㉜. Head south a block and turn right on Clay Street; a half block up is the redbrick **Chinatown YWCA** ㉝. Return to Stockton and head south a half block to the **Kong Chow Temple.** Next door is the elaborate **Chinese Six Companies** building.

TIMING

Allow at least two hours to see Chinatown. The museums and temples deserve a half hour each.

Sights to See

㉗ **Chinatown Gate.** This pagoda-topped, green-tile gate, flanked on both sides of Grant Avenue by stone dragons, is an exotic introduction to one of San Francisco's most interesting and culturally cohesive neighborhoods. ✉ *Bush St. and Grant Ave.*

㉝ **Chinatown YWCA.** The handsome redbrick YWCA was originally established as a meeting place and residence for Chinese women in need of social services. A large Chinese lantern welcomes those who enter through the arched doorway. The lobby evokes early 20th-century Chinatown, with heavy, filigreed wood furniture and mirrors etched with delicate calligraphy. Julia Morgan, the architect of Hearst Castle (☞ Chapter 11), designed the building. The **Chinese Historical Society** (☎ 415/391–1188), whose exhibits survey the history of Chinese immigrants from the early 1800s to the present, is scheduled to relocate here in 1999. ✉ *965 Clay St.*

㉙ **Chinese Culture Center.** This community organization displays the work of Chinese and Chinese-American artists and presents traveling exhibits relating to Chinese culture. Weekend afternoon (2 PM) walking tours ($15) of historic points in Chinatown can be arranged through the center. ✉ *Holiday Inn, 750 Kearny St., 3rd floor,* ☎ *415/986–1822.* ▨ *Free.* ☉ *Tues.–Sun. 10–4.*

Chinese Six Companies. Many fine examples of Chinese architecture line Grant Avenue and Stockton Street, but this is perhaps the most noteworthy. With its curved roof tiles and elaborate cornices, the imposing structure's oversize pagoda cheerfully dominates the block. ✉ *843 Stockton St., between Sacramento and Clay Sts.*

Kong Chow Temple. Amid the statuary, flowers, orange offerings, and richly colored altars (red signifies "virility," green "longevity," and gold "majesty") are a couple of plaques announcing that MRS. HARRY S. TRUMAN CAME TO THIS TEMPLE IN JUNE 1948 FOR A PREDICTION ON THE OUT-

COME OF THE ELECTION. . . . THIS FORTUNE CAME TRUE. Place a dollar bill in the donation box as you enter. The air at Kong Chow Temple is often thick with incense, a bit ironic, what with the Chinese Community Smoke-Free Project two floors below. ⊠ *855 Stockton St., between Sacramento and Clay Sts.*

③ **Old Chinese Telephone Exchange.** The original Chinatown burned down after the 1906 earthquake, and this was the first building to set the style for the new Chinatown. The three-tier pagoda, now the Bank of Canton, was built in 1909. The exchange's operators were renowned for their "tenacious memories"—they knew all their callers by name rather than number. ⊠ *743 Washington St.*

NEED A BREAK?   Dim sum, a variety of pastries filled with meat, fish, and vegetables, is the Chinese version of a smorgasbord, delivered on stacked food-service carts from which customers make selections. At **New Asia** (⊠ 772 Pacific Ave., ☎ 415/391–6666), dim sum is served daily from 8:30 AM to 3 PM.

② **Old St. Mary's Church.** This brick and granite building dedicated in 1854 was the city's Catholic cathedral until 1891. (The current seat of the Catholic church in San Francisco, which replaced the successor to Old St. Mary's, is the ultramodern St. Mary's Cathedral, at 1111 Gough Street.) Old St. Mary's hosts a Noontime Concert series on Tuesday and Thursday at 12:30. Across California Street is **St. Mary's Park,** a tranquil setting for local sculptor Beniamino (Benny) Bufano's *Sun Yat-sen.* The 12-ft statue of the founder of the Republic of China was installed on the site of the leader's favorite reading spot during his years of exile in San Francisco during the early 20th century.

③ **Portsmouth Square.** This former potato patch is where Captain John B. Montgomery raised the American flag in 1846 to claim the territory for the United States. Note the bronze galleon atop a 9-ft granite shaft; designed by Bruce Porter, the sculpture was erected in 1919 in memory of Robert Louis Stevenson, who often visited the site when he lived in 1879 and 1880 on Russian Hill. Dotted with pagoda-shaped structures, the park is a favorite spot for morning t'ai chi. By noon, dozens of men play a Chinese version of chess, engaged in not always legal competition that the police occasionally interrupt. A sand-covered children's playground sits below the main level of the square. ⊠ *Kearny St. between Washington and Clay Sts.*

③ **Tien Hou Temple.** Day Ju, one of the first three Chinese to arrive in San Francisco, dedicated the temple to the Queen of the Heavens and the Goddess of the Seven Seas in 1852. Climb three flights of stairs past two mah-jongg parlors whose patrons hope the spirits above will favor them. In the entryway, elderly ladies can often be seen preparing "money" to be burned as offerings to various Buddhist gods. A (real) dollar placed in the donation box on their table will bring a smile (and is expected). Red-and-gold lanterns adorn the ceiling. Notice the wood carving suspended from the ceiling, depicting a number of gods at play. ⊠ *125 Waverly Pl.* ◎ *Daily 10–4.*

North Beach and Telegraph Hill

Novelist and resident Herbert Gold calls North Beach "the longest-running, most glorious American bohemian operetta outside Greenwich Village." Indeed, to anyone who's spent some time in its eccentric old bars and cafés or wandered its charming side streets and steep alleys, North Beach evokes everything from the wild Barbary Coast days to the no less sedate beatnik era. Family operettas are performed at Caffè Trieste, Italian bakeries appear frozen in time, and homages to Jack Kerouac, Allen Ginsberg, and other beat poets abound. Like neighboring Chinatown, this is a section of the city where eating is unavoidable: The streets are packed with Italian delicatessens, bakeries, Chinese markets, coffeehouses, and ethnic restaurants.

Numbers in the text correspond to numbers in the margin and on the Downtown San Francisco map.

A Good Walk

Washington Square ㉞ is at the intersection of Union Street and Columbus Avenue. North of the square is the cathedral of **Saints Peter and Paul** ㉟. Head south on the east side of Columbus Avenue past the **St. Francis of Assisi Church,** a Victorian-era structure. Continue south on Columbus and cross Broadway. On the west side of Columbus is a beat-era landmark, the **City Lights Bookstore** ㊱. Backtrack north on the east side of Columbus to **Grant Avenue,** which is filled with eclectic shops and old-time bars and cafés. When you reach Union Street, you're just a block and a half north of Washington Square.

Head up steep **Telegraph Hill** ㊲ to **Coit Tower** ㊳. Coit Tower can be reached by car (though parking is limited) or public transportation—board the No. 39-Coit at Columbus Avenue and Union Street. To walk up to the tower, head east up Filbert Street; turn north (left) at Grant, go one block to Greenwich, and ascend the steps on your right. Cross the street at the top of the first set of stairs and continue up the curving stone steps to Coit Tower.

Steps lead you down the east side of Telegraph Hill. At Montgomery Street, perched on the side of the hill, is **Julius' Castle** ㊴. Descend the Filbert Steps amid roses, fuchsias, irises, and trumpet flowers—courtesy of Grace Marchant, who labored for nearly 30 years to transform a dump into a treasure. The serene **Levi Strauss headquarters** ㊵ is at the foot of the hill.

TIMING

To wander North Beach, hike Telegraph Hill, and visit the sights mentioned here, set aside two to three hours. By its nature, though, North Beach is a place to linger—a visit here can easily fill an afternoon.

Sights to See

㊱ **City Lights Bookstore.** The hangout of beat-era writers—Allen Ginsberg, Gregory Corso, and longtime part owner Lawrence Ferlinghetti among them—remains a vital part of San Francisco's literary scene. The store's strengths include its poetry and Third World Literature sections. ⊠ *261 Columbus Ave.,* ☎ *415/362–8193.*

★ ㊳ **Coit Tower.** The 180-ft-tall Coit Tower stands as a monument to the city's volunteer firefighters. During the gold rush, Lillie Hitchcock Coit ("Miss Lil") was said to have deserted a wedding party and chased down the street after her favorite engine, the Knickerbocker Number 5, clad in her bridesmaid finery. She was soon made an honorary member of the Knickerbocker Company, and after that always signed herself "Lillie Coit 5" in honor of her favorite engine. When Lillie died in 1929, she left the city the $125,000 that was spent to build Coit Tower. Inside the tower are 19 Work Projects Administration–era murals depicting labor union workers. Ride the elevator to the top to enjoy sweeping views. ⊠ *On top of Telegraph Hill.* ☎ *$3.* ☉ *Daily 10–6.*

Grant Avenue. Originally called Calle de la Fundación, Grant Avenue is the oldest street in the city. In the section between Columbus Avenue and Filbert Street, you'll find atmospheric cafés, authentic Italian delis, odd curio shops and unusual import stores, and dusty bars—like

The Saloon and Grant & Green Blues Club. A Saturday afternoon must is **Caffè Trieste** (✉ 601 Vallejo St., at Grant Ave., ☎ 415/392–6739), where the Giotta family presents a weekly musical (patrons are encouraged to participate). Beginning at 1:30, the program ranges from Italian pop and folk music to operas. ✉ *Between Columbus Ave. and Filbert Sts.*

㊳ Julius' Castle. The dark-panel interior of this official historic landmark (founder Julius Roz had his craftsmen use materials left over from the 1915 Panama–Pacific International Exposition) is almost as dazzling as the view. Two restaurants, both open only for dinner, occupy the site. ✉ *1541 Montgomery St.,* ☎ *415/392–2222.*

㊵ Levi Strauss headquarters. This carefully landscaped complex appears so collegiate it is affectionately known as LSU (Levi Strauss University). Fountains and grassy knolls complement the redbrick buildings, providing a perfect environment for brown-bag and picnic lunches. Delis and other take-out shops are nearby. ✉ *Levi's Plaza, 1155 Battery St.*

St. Francis of Assisi Church. An 1860 Victorian Gothic building with a terra-cotta facade stands on the site of the frame parish church that served the gold-rush Catholic community. ✉ *610 Vallejo St.*

㊱ Saints Peter and Paul. The twin turrets of this Romanesque cathedral that was completed in 1924 are local landmarks. On the first Sunday of October a mass and a parade to Fisherman's Wharf are part of the annual Blessing of the Fleet. ✉ *666 Filbert St., at Washington Square Park.*

㊲ Telegraph Hill. Telegraph Hill residents command some of the best views in the city, as well as the most difficult ascents to their aeries (the flower-lined steps flanking the hill make the climb more than tolerable for them and visitors, though). The Hill is capped by Coit Tower (☞ *above*). ✉ *Between Lombard, Filbert, Kearny, and Sansome Sts.*

㊴ Washington Square. This may well be the daytime social heart of what was once considered "Little Italy"—though in the early morning the dominating sight is of a hundred or more elderly Asians engaged in t'ai chi. By mid-morning groups of conservatively dressed elderly Italian men arrive. Nearby, kids toss Frisbees, jugglers juggle, and Chinese matrons stare impassively at the passing parade. ✉ *Between Columbus Ave., Stockton, Filbert, and Union Sts.*

Nob Hill and Russian Hill

Once called the Hill of Golden Promise, the slope above Union Square was officially dubbed Nob Hill during the 1870s, when San Francisco's "the Big Four" financiers—Charles Crocker, Leland Stanford, Mark Hopkins, and Collis Huntington—built their hilltop estates. Nob Hill is still home to many of the city's elite, as well as several of San Francisco's finest hotels. During the 1890s, a group of bohemian artists and writers that included Charles Norris, George Sterling, and Maynard Dixon lived on Russian Hill.

Numbers in the text correspond to numbers in the margin and on the Downtown San Francisco map.

A Good Walk

Begin at California and Taylor streets at the **Masonic Auditorium** ㊶, an enormous high-columned structure—the lobby mural is the highlight of a visit. Across California Street is **Grace Cathedral** ㊷. East on California one block (toward Mason Street) is the stately **Pacific Union Club** ㊸. Across Mason from the club is the **Fairmont Hotel** ㊹, whose ornate lobby is worth a peek. Across California from the Fairmont is the **Mark Hopkins Inter-Continental Hotel** ㊺, famed for its Top of the Mark lounge. Head north three blocks on Mason Street to the **Cable Car Museum** ㊻, the "brain" of the cable-car network.

From the Cable Car Museum continue four blocks north on Mason Street to Vallejo Street. Steep stairs lead to the multilevel **Ina Coolbrith Park** ㊼. From here you can meander north on Mason Street to Union. Head west on Union and north on Hyde to the top of **Lombard Street** ㊽, a.k.a. the "crookedest street in the world." Take the steps down to Leavenworth Street. A block north and east (on Chestnut Street) is the **San Francisco Art Institute** ㊾.

TIMING

This tour covers a lot of ground, much of it steep. To do it all, including brief stops at Grace Cathedral and the Cable Car Museum, a person in reasonable shape will want to set aside about three hours.

Sights to See

★ ㊻ **Cable Car Museum.** On exhibit are photographs, old cable cars, signposts, ticketing machines, and other memorabilia dating from 1873. The four sets of massive powerhouse wheels that move the entire cable car system steal the show: The design is so simple it seems almost unreal. You can also go downstairs and check out the innards of the system. ⊠ *1201 Mason St., at Washington St.,* ☎ *415/474–1887.* ☒ *Free.* ☉ *Oct.–Mar., daily 10–5; Apr.–Sept., daily 10–6.*

㊹ **Fairmont Hotel.** The Fairmont's dazzling opening was delayed a year by the 1906 quake, but since then the marble palace has hosted presidents, royalty, movie stars (Valentino, Dietrich), and local nabobs. Things have changed since its early days: On the eve of World War I you could get a room for as low as $2.50 per night, meals included. Nowadays, prices run in the thousands—this being for a night in the eight-room penthouse suite. The lobby is a warm blend of flamboyant rose-floral carpeting, lush red-velvet chairs, gold faux-marble columns, and gilt ceilings. The hotel's kitschy **Tonga Room** (☞ Nightlife and the Arts, *below*), with its tiki huts, indoor tropical thunderstorms, and floating bandstand, is a must-see. ⊠ *950 Mason St.,* ☎ *415/772–5000.*

㊷ **Grace Cathedral.** This soaring Gothic structure erected on the site of Charles Crocker's mansion took 53 years to build. The gilded bronze doors at the east entrance were taken from casts of Ghiberti's Gates of Paradise on the baptistery in Florence. Perhaps the most unique feature of Grace, the local seat of the Episcopal church, is its 35-ft-wide meditation Labyrinth, a large, purplish rug that's a replica of the 13th-century stone labyrinth on the floor of the Chartres Cathedral. Outdoors is a terrazzo meditation labyrinth. Also noteworthy is an AIDS Interfaith Chapel with a sculpture by the late artist Keith Haring. ⊠ *1100 California St., at Taylor St.,* ☎ *415/749–6300.* ☉ *Daily 7–6.*

㊼ **Ina Coolbrith Park.** This attractive park is composed of a series of terraces on the side of a hill. An Oakland librarian and poet, Ina Coolbrith introduced both Jack London and Isadora Duncan to the world of books. In 1915 she was named poet laureate of California. The climb to the park is steep, so make use of the benches at various levels. ⊠ *Vallejo St. between Mason and Taylor Sts.*

★ ㊽ **Lombard Street.** San Francisco's "crookedest" street drops down the east face of Russian Hill in eight switchbacks. Few tourists with cars can resist the lure of the steep descent, but it's made less than scary by the very slow speed at which you must proceed. Pedestrians can make a quicker descent by taking the steps on either side of the street. ⊠ *Lombard St. between Hyde and Leavenworth Sts.*

⑤ Mark Hopkins Inter-Continental Hotel. A combination of French château and Spanish Renaissance architecture (with terra-cotta detailing), this hotel has hosted statesmen, royalty, and Hollywood celebrities. The **Top of the Mark** cocktail lounge is remembered fondly by thousands of World War II veterans who jammed the lounge before leaving for overseas duty; wives and sweethearts watching the ships depart gave the room's northwest nook its name—Weepers' Corner. ⊠ *1 Nob Hill, at California and Mason Sts.,* ☎ *415/392–3434.*

④ Masonic Auditorium. Formally called the California Masonic Memorial Temple, this building was erected by Freemasons in 1957. The impressive lobby mosaic depicts the Masonic fraternity's role in California history and industry. There's also an intricate model of King Solomon's Temple in the lobby. ⊠ *1111 California St.,* ☎ *415/776–4917.* ☉ *Lobby weekdays 8–5.*

④ Pacific Union Club. The quake and fire of 1906 knocked down all of Nob Hill's palatial mansions save one: the shell of James Flood's brownstone. This broad-beam structure was built by the Comstock silver baron in 1886. In 1909 the property was purchased by the Pacific Union Club, a bastion of the wealthy and powerful. Adjacent is a small park that hosts frequent art shows. ⊠ *1000 California St.*

④ San Francisco Art Institute. A Moorish-tile fountain in a tree-shaded courtyard greets you as you enter the institute. The Spanish colonial-style building was erected on Russian Hill in 1926. Don't miss the impressive seven-section fresco painted in 1931 by Mexican master Diego Rivera in the student gallery to the left of the institute's entrance: It's one of only three Bay Area murals painted by Rivera. ⊠ *800 Chestnut St.,* ☎ *415/771–7020.* ☒ *Gallery free.* ☉ *McBean Gallery Tues.– Sat. 10–5 (Thurs. until 8), Sun. noon–5; student gallery daily 9–9.*

Pacific Heights

Some of the city's most expensive and dramatic real estate—including mansions and town houses priced at $1 million and up—is in Pacific Heights. Grand old Victorians line the streets, and from almost any point in this neighborhood you get a magnificent view.

Numbers in the text correspond to numbers in the margin and on the Downtown San Francisco map.

A Good Walk

At Webster Street and Broadway are three notable **Broadway estates** ㊿. South on Webster Street is **Bourn Mansion.** Head east on Jackson Street to the red-sandstone **Whittier Mansion** ㊿, at the corner of Laguna Street. One block south on Laguna is **Lafayette Park** ㊿. Walking east on Washington along the edge of Lafayette Park, the most imposing residence is the formal French **Spreckels Mansion** ㊿ at the corner of Octavia Street. Continue east to Franklin Street and turn left (north). Halfway down the block is the **Haas-Lilienthal House** ㊿. Heading back south on Franklin, stop to see several **Franklin Street buildings** ㊿ and several more **noteworthy Victorians** ㊿ nearby.

TIMING

Set aside about two hours to see the sights mentioned here. Most of the attractions are walk-bys, but you'll be covering a good bit of pavement, some of it steep. Tours of the Haas-Lilienthal House, which is only open on Wednesday and Sunday afternoon, take about one hour. The guided tours of Pacific Heights from the house take two hours.

Sights to See

Bourn Mansion. This Georgian brick mansion was built in 1896 for William B. Bourn, who had inherited a Mother Lode gold mine. Architect Willis Polk, who designed this structure, also designed Bourn's palatial Peninsula estate, Filoli (☞ Side Trips from San Francisco, *below*). ✉ *2550 Webster St.*

(50) **Broadway estates.** Broadway uptown is home to several classic showplaces. The three-story Italian Renaissance palace at **2222 Broadway** (notice the intricately filigreed doorway) was built by Comstock mine heir James Flood and later donated to a religious order. The Convent of the Sacred Heart purchased the baroque brick Grant House at **2220 Broadway.** These two buildings, along with a Flood property at **2120 Broadway** are all used as school quarters. ✉ *Broadway between Fillmore and Buchanan Sts.*

(55) **Franklin Street buildings.** Don't be fooled by the neoclassical **Golden Gate Church** (✉ 1901 Franklin St.) building—what at first looks like a stone facade is actually redwood painted white. The stately brick Georgian at **1735 Franklin** was built in the early 1900s for a coffee merchant. On the northeast corner of Franklin and California streets is the tapestry brick **Christian Science church**; the Tuscan Revival building has noteworthy terra-cotta detailing. The **Coleman House** (✉ 1701 Franklin St.) is a twin-turreted Queen Anne mansion built for a gold-rush mining and lumber baron. Look for the large stained-glass window on the house's north side. ✉ *Franklin St. between Washington and California Sts.*

(54) **Haas-Lilienthal House.** This 1886 Queen Anne survived the 1906 earthquake and fire and is the only fully furnished Victorian open to the public. The carefully kept rooms provide an intriguing glimpse of late-Victorian taste and lifestyle. A small display of photographs on the bottom floor shows how modest this elaborate house was modest compared with some of the giants one block east on Van Ness Avenue that fell to the fire. Volunteers conduct tours two days a week and lead an informative two-hour tour of the eastern portion of Pacific Heights on Sunday afternoon. ✉ *2007 Franklin St., near Washington St.,* ☎ *415/441–3004.* 🎫 *$5.* ⏲ *Wed. noon–4 (last tour at 3), Sun. 11–5 (last tour at 4). Pacific Heights tours ($5) leave the house Sun. at 12:30.*

(52) **Lafayette Park.** Clusters of trees dot this oasis for sunbathers, dog-lovers, and Frisbee throwers. During the 1860s, a tenacious squatter, Sam Holladay, built himself a big wooden house in the center of the park. Holladay even instructed city gardeners as if the land were his own and defied all orders to leave. The house was finally torn down in 1936. ✉ *Between Laguna, Gough, Sacramento, and Washington Sts.*

(56) **Noteworthy Victorians.** Two stunning **Italianate Victorians** (✉ 1818 and 1834 California St.) stand out on the 1800 block of California. A block farther is the Victorian-era **Atherton House** (✉ 1990 California St.), which combines Queen Anne, Stick-Eastlake, and other architectural elements. The Victorians on the east side of the 1800 block of Laguna Street cost between $2,000 and $2,600 when they were built in the 1870s. ✉ *California St. between Franklin and Octavia Sts.; Laguna St. between Pine and Bush Sts.*

(53) **Spreckels Mansion.** This formal French estate was built for sugar magnate Adolph Spreckels and his wife, Alma. Mrs. Spreckels was so pleased with her house that she commissioned architect George Applegarth to design a similarly classical structure: the California Palace of the Legion of Honor in Lincoln Park. One of the city's great iconoclasts, Alma Spreckels is the model for the bronze figure atop the Victory Monument in Union Square. ✉ *2080 Washington St., at Octavia St.*

(51) **Whittier Mansion.** This red-sandstone structure was one of the most elegant 19th-century houses in the state. It has a Spanish-tiled roof and enormous scrolled bay windows on all four sides. The Whittier Mansion was built so solidly that only a chimney toppled over during the 1906 quake. ✉ *2090 Jackson St., at Laguna St.*

OFF THE BEATEN PATH

JAPANTOWN – Around 1860, a wave of Japanese-Americans arrived in San Francisco, which they named "Soko." After the 1906 fire destroyed wooden homes in other parts of the stricken city, many of these recent immigrants settled in the Western Addition. By the 1930s they had opened shops, markets, meeting halls, and restaurants and established Shinto and Buddhist temples. Japantown was virtually disbanded during World War II when many of its residents, including second- and third-generation Americans, were placed in detention camps. Japantown, or "Nihonmachi," is centered on the slopes of Pacific Heights, north of Geary Boulevard, between Fillmore and Laguna streets; the Nihonmachi Cherry Blossom Festival is celebrated on two weekends every April. The three-block-long Japan Center (✉ Post St. between Fillmore and Laguna Sts.) contains shops, restaurants, a cineplex, and the very fine Kabuki Hot Springs spa. Though Japantown is a relatively safe area, the adjoining Western Addition is less safe. It's best not to stray south of Geary after dark.

Civic Center and Mission Dolores

City Hall and the cluster of handsome adjoining cultural institutions that make up San Francisco's Civic Center stand as one of the country's great governmental building complexes—a seeming realization of the visions put forth by early 20th-century proponents of the City Beautiful. But illusion soon gives way to reality: On the streets and plazas of the Civic Center live many of the city's most destitute residents, and much of the area is undergoing seismic retrofitting in the wake of the 1989 Loma Prieta earthquake. Things will likely look better by the dawn of the 21st century. From the Civic Center, it's a quick ride on the underground or a manageable walk to historic Mission Dolores.

Numbers in the text correspond to numbers in the margin and on the Downtown San Francisco map.

A Good Tour

Start your walk at the **San Francisco Public Library** (57) at Fulton and Larkin streets. Across from the library to the west are Civic Center Plaza and **City Hall** (58). Across Van Ness Avenue from City Hall are—from north to south, each taking up most of a block—the **Veterans Building** (59), the **War Memorial Opera House** (60), and **Louise M. Davies Symphony Hall** (61). The Hayes Valley strip of galleries, shops, and restaurants is a block south of Grove on Hayes Street between Franklin and Laguna streets. After you've explored Hayes Valley, backtrack to Gough and head south to Market. To visit **Mission Dolores** (62), you have two options. The Van Ness Avenue Muni light-rail station is two blocks east; catch a J car, get off at 16th and Church streets, and walk one block east on 16th to Dolores Street. Or you can walk up Market Street to treelined Dolores Street (which runs into Market across from Safeway) and walk south to 16th Street. From the mission, you can easily proceed either to the **Mission District** or the **Castro.**

TIMING

Walking the Civic Center area takes about 45 minutes, not counting tours of the library or Davies Hall, or shopping in Hayes Valley. Add 20 to 30 minutes to walk or train up to Mission Dolores, which can be explored in a half hour.

Sights to See

⑤⑧ City Hall. This French Renaissance Revival masterpiece of granite and marble was modeled after the Capitol in Washington. City Hall's dome, which is even higher than the Washington version, dominates the area. The building is scheduled to reopen in 1999 after a seismic upgrade is completed. ⊠ *Between Van Ness Ave., Polk, Grove, and McAllister Sts.*

⑥① Louise M. Davies Symphony Hall. The 2,750-seat hall is the home of the San Francisco Symphony, which is led by Michael Tilson-Thomas. It took several years to sort out the modern structure's acoustical problems, the solutions to which are discussed on docent-led tours. ⊠ *201 Van Ness Ave.,* ☎ *415/552–8338.* 🎫 *Tours $3.* ☉ *Tours of Davies Hall Wed. and Sat. by appointment, tours of Davies and the Performing Arts Center Mon. hourly 10–2.*

Mission District. Home to Italian and Irish communities in the early 20th century—you'll still find Italian restaurants and Irish pubs here—the Mission District has been heavily Latino since the late 1960s, when immigrants from Mexico and Central America began arriving. More recently, Arabic and Southeast Asian immigrants have settled in the neighborhood. From Mission Dolores, you can head east on 16th Street to a "new bohemia" section of cafés and funky shops around 16th and Valencia streets, and then on into the commercial heart of the Mission District—Valencia and Mission streets between 16th and 24th streets. Since 1979, the **Women's Building** (⊠ 3543 18th St., ☎ 415/431–1180) has held workshops and conferences of particular interest to women. The building's striking two-sided exterior mural depicts women's peacekeeping efforts over the centuries. At 24th and Bryant Streets is the **Galería de la Raza/Studio 24** (⊠ 2857 24th St., ☎ 415/826–8009) complex, open from Tuesday to Saturday between noon and 6 PM. The gallery is an important showcase for local and international Latino artists. The nonprofit studio sells Mexican folk art and first-rate prints and paintings by Chicano artists. Once a year (in early November) the studio explodes with colorful skeleton figurines and art objects paying tribute to *Dia de los Muertos* (Day of the Dead).

⑥② Mission Dolores. The mission comprises two churches standing side by side. Completed in 1791, the small adobe building known as Mission San Francisco de Asis is the oldest standing structure in San Francisco and the sixth of the 21 California missions founded by Father Junípero Serra. Its ceiling depicts original Ohlone Indian basket designs, executed in vegetable dyes. Services are held in both the Mission San Francisco de Asis and next door in the handsome multidome Basilica. ⊠ *Dolores and 16th Sts.,* ☎ *415/621–8203.* 🎫 *$2.* ☉ *Daily 9–4.*

⑤⑦ San Francisco Public Library. The city's main library, which opened in April 1996, is a modernized version of the old Beaux Arts library that sits across Fulton Street (that building will house the Asian Art Museum within a few years). The new structure contains centers for the hearing and visually impaired, a gay-and-lesbian history center, African-American and Asian centers, and a rooftop garden and terrace. The San Francisco History Room and Archives displays a wealth of historic photographs, maps, and other memorabilia. At the library's center is a five-story atrium with a skylight, a grand staircase, and murals painted by local artists. Across Hyde Street behind the library is brick-lined United Nations Plaza. ⊠ *Larkin St. between Grove and Fulton Sts.,* ☎ *415/557–4440; 415/557–4567 for archives hrs.* ☉ *Mon. 10–6, Tues.–Thurs. 9–8, Fri. 11–5, Sat. 9–5, Sun. noon–5.*

⑤⑨ Veterans Building. The United Nations charter was signed in 1945 in the Herbst Theatre (☎ 115/392 4400) here. Herbst is a popular venue for lectures and readings, classical ensembles, and dance performances. The street-level **San Francisco Arts Commission Gallery** (☎ 415/554–6080) exhibits the work of local artists. The mayor's office and other city departments temporarily located here are scheduled to move back into City Hall in 1999. ⊠ *401 Van Ness Ave.*

⑥⓪ **War Memorial Opera House.** The opera house is modeled after its European counterparts, with a vaulted and coffered ceiling, a marble foyer, two balconies, and an unusual Art Deco chandelier that resembles a huge silver sunburst. The San Francisco Opera and Ballet companies perform here. ⊠ *301 Van Ness Ave.*, ☎ *415/621–6600.*

OFF THE
BEATEN PATH

THE CASTRO – In the 1970s a sleepy working-class neighborhood west of the Civic Center evolved into a mecca for lesbians and gay men. Especially on weekends, the streets fanning out from the intersection of Castro and Market streets teem with a wide assortment of folks out shopping, pushing political causes, heading to art films, and lingering in bars and cafés. Cutting-edge clothing stores and unique gift shops predominate, as do pairs of pretty young things of all genders and sexual persuasions (even heterosexual) holding hands. The 1,500-seat Castro Theatre (⊠ 429 Castro St.), which opened in 1922, is the neighborhood's landmark. The birthplace and workshop of the Names Project (⊠ 2362 Market St.), which manages the AIDS Memorial Quilt, is around the corner. Nurse a cappuccino at the Café Flore (⊠ 16th and Market Sts.) to overhear the latest Castro dish. To get to the Castro from the Civic Center, take the K, L, or M Muni light-rail cars, one of Market Street's aboveground antique trolleys, or Muni Bus 8.

The Northern Waterfront

For the sight, sound, and smell of the sea, hop the Powell-Hyde cable car from Union Square and take it to the end of the line. The views as you descend Hyde Street down to the bay are nothing short of breathtaking—tiny sailboats bob in the whitecaps, Alcatraz hovers ominously in the distance, and the Marin Headlands form a rugged backdrop to the often fog-shrouded Golden Gate Bridge. Be sure to bring good walking shoes and a jacket or sweater.

Many San Franciscans avoid this touristy—and in parts tacky—section of town, but it does contain stops of merit like the National Maritime Museum and the Hyde Street Pier. The Fisherman's Wharf area, where ferries depart for the deservedly popular Alcatraz Island, has many kids-oriented diversions.

Numbers in the text correspond to numbers in the margin and on the Northern Waterfront/Marina and the Presidio map.

A Good Walk

Begin at the **National Maritime Museum** ① and, two blocks east, the **Hyde Street Pier** ②. Across from the museum is redbrick **Ghirardelli Square** ③. A half block east of the Hyde Street Pier on Beach Street lies the three-story **Cannery** ④, another brick complex whose restaurants and shops overlook an open-air courtyard. North of the Cannery on Jefferson Street is **Fisherman's Wharf** ⑤. East a few more blocks is **Pier 39** ⑥, a playland and shopper's extravaganza. Backtrack a few hundred feet to Pier 41 to catch the boat to **Alcatraz Island.**

TIMING

For the entire Northern Waterfront circuit, set aside a half day, not including shopping or dining. Boat tours take from one to three hours.

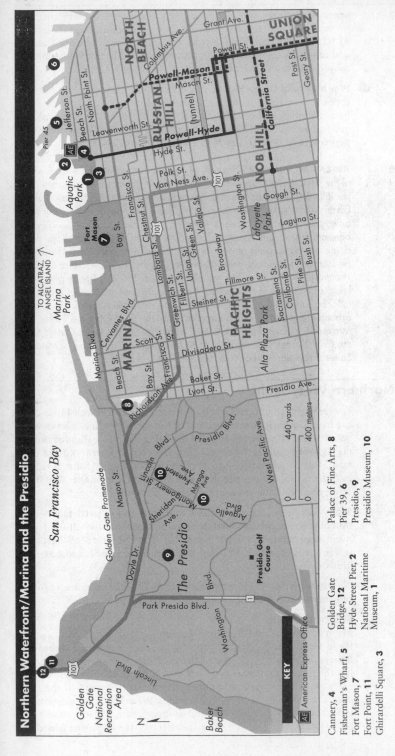

Northern Waterfront/Marina and the Presidio

San Francisco Bay

TO ALCATRAZ, ANGEL ISLAND

NORTH BEACH

UNION SQUARE

RUSSIAN HILL

NOB HILL

PACIFIC HEIGHTS

MARINA

The Presidio

Golden Gate National Recreation Area

Baker Beach

Marina Park

Presidio Golf Course

Grant Ave.
Columbus Ave.
Powell St.
Powell-Mason
Mason St.
(tunnel)
Powell-Hyde
Hyde St.
Post St.
Geary St.
California Street
Gough St.
Laguna St.
Pine St.
Bush St.
Sacramento St.
California St.
Lafayette Park
Washington St.
Broadway
Vallejo St.
Green St.
Union St.
Filbert St.
Greenwich St.
Lombard St.
Chestnut St.
Francisco St.
Bay St.
Polk St.
Van Ness Ave.
Jefferson St.
Beach St.
North Point St.
Leavenworth St.
Pier 45
Aquatic Park
Fort Mason
Fillmore St.
Steiner St.
Alta Plaza Park
Divisadero St.
Scott St.
Cervantes Blvd.
Marina Blvd.
Beach St.
Bay St.
Baker St.
Lyon St.
Richardson Ave.
Francisco St.
Presidio Ave.
West Pacific Ave.
Presidio Blvd.
Lincoln Blvd.
Funston Ave.
Moraga Ave.
Montgomery St.
Sheridan Ave.
Arguello Blvd.
Doyle Dr.
Mason St.
Golden Gate Promenade
Park Presido Blvd.
Washington
Blvd.
Lincoln Blvd.

440 yards
400 meters
0
0

Can;ery, 4
Fisherman's Wharf, 5
Fort Mason, 7
Fort Point, 11
Ghirardelli Square, 3

Golden Gate Bridge, 12
Hyde Street Pier, 2
National Maritime Museum, 1

Palace of Fine Arts, 8
Pier 39, 6
Presidio, 9
Presidio Museum, 10

KEY

AE American Express Office

Sights to See

★ **Alcatraz Island.** The boat ride to the island is brief (15 minutes) but affords beautiful views of the city, Marin County, and the East Bay. The audio tour, highly recommended, includes the observations of guards and prisoners about life in one of America's most notorious penal colonies. A ranger-led tour surveys the island's ecology. Plan to spend at least three hours for the visit and boat rides combined. Reservations, which can be made up to two weeks ahead, are strongly recommended, even in the off-season. ⊠ *Pier 41,* ☎ *415/705–5555.* ⌨ *$11 ($7.75 without audio); add $2 per ticket to charge by phone.* ☉ *Ferry departures Sept.–late May, daily 9:30–2:15; late May–Aug., daily 9:30–4:15.*

Angel Island. For an outdoorsy adventure, consider a day at Angel Island, northwest of Alcatraz. Discovered by Spaniards in 1775 and declared a U.S. military reserve 75 years later, the island was used from 1910 until 1940 as a screening ground for Asian immigrants, who were often held for months, even years, before being granted entry. In 1963 Angel Island was made a state park. A scenic path winds around the island's perimeter. ⊠ *Pier 41,* ☎ *415/435–1915 for park and ferry information; 415/773–1188 for San Francisco ferry tickets.* ⌨ *$10.* ☉ *Ferry departures weekdays at 10* AM, *weekends 10, noon, and 2.*

❹ **The Cannery.** This three-story repository of shops and restaurants was built in 1894 to house what became the Del Monte Fruit and Vegetable Cannery. The **Museum of the City of San Francisco** (☎ 415/928–0289) on the third floor merits a brief stop. ⊠ *2801 Leavenworth St.,* ☎ *415/ 771–3112.* ☉ *Mon.–Sat. 10–6, Sun. 11–6; until 8:30 Thurs.–Sat. in summer (restaurants open later).*

Ferries. Cruises are an exhilarating way to see the bay. Among the cruises offered by the **Blue and Gold Fleet** (⊠ Pier 41, ☎ 415/705–5555) are frequent one-hour swings under the Golden Gate Bridge and along the Northern Waterfront. More interesting—and just as scenic—are the tours to Sausalito, Angel Island, Alcatraz, Tiburon, Muir Woods, and the Napa Valley Wine Country. Blue and Gold also runs ferries to Oakland, Alameda, and Vallejo.

❺ **Fisherman's Wharf.** The chaotic streets of the wharf hold numerous seafood restaurants—including sidewalk crab pots and counters where take-out shrimp and crab cocktails are sold. T-shirts and sweats, gold chains galore, redwood furniture, and acres of artworks (some original) beckon visitors. The World War II submarine USS *Pampanito* (☎ 415/441–5819) at Pier 45 provides a fascinating (if claustrophobic) look at life down under during wartime. ⊠ *Jefferson St. between Leavenworth St. and Pier 39.*

❸ **Ghirardelli Square.** This complex of 19th-century redbrick factory buildings—once the home of the Ghirardelli Chocolate Company—has been transformed into a network of specialty shops, cafés, restaurants, and galleries. ⊠ *900 North Point,* ☎ *415/775–5500.* ☉ *Jan.–Mar., Sun.–Thurs. 10–6, Fri.–Sat. 10–9; Apr.–Dec., daily 10–9.*

❷ **Hyde Street Pier.** The pier, one of the wharf area's best bargains, always bustles with activity. The highlight is the collection of historic ships: the *Balclutha,* an 1886 full-rigged, three-mast sailing vessel that sailed around Cape Horn 17 times; the *Eureka,* a side-wheel ferry; the *C. A. Thayer,* a three-masted schooner; and the *Hercules,* a tugboat. ⊠ *Hyde St., north of Jefferson St.,* ☎ *415/561–6662.* ⌨ *$4.* ☉ *Fall–spring, daily 9:30–5; summer, daily 10–6.*

❶ **National Maritime Museum.** You'll feel as if you're out to sea when you step inside this sturdy, rounded structure. Part of the San Francisco Maritime National Historical Park, which includes the Hyde Street Pier, the museum exhibits ship models, photographs, maps, and other artifacts chronicling the development of San Francisco and the West Coast through maritime history. ⊠ *Aquatic Park at the foot of Polk St.,* ☎ *415/556–3002 or 415/929–0202.* ⊠ *Donation suggested.* ⊙ *Daily 10–5.*

❻ Pier 39. This shopping and entertainment complex is the most popular of San Francisco's waterfront attractions. Children enjoy the brilliantly colored double-decker **Venetian Carousel.** At **Underwater World** (☎ 415/623–5300), moving walkways transport visitors through a space surrounded on three sides by water filled with indigenous San Francisco Bay marine life. Above water, don't miss the sea lions that bask and play on the docks on the pier's northwest side. ⊠ *Pier 39 off Jefferson St.*

The Marina and the Presidio

The Marina district was a coveted place to live until the 1989 earthquake, when the area's homes suffered the worst damage in the city because the Marina is built on landfill. Though many homeowners and renters left in search of more solid ground, the Marina is still popular with young professionals. Especially on weekends, Chestnut Street, the neighborhood's main drag, is filled with a well-to-do crowd. Fort Mason is on the eastern edge of the Marina district, the Presidio on its western side.

Numbers in the text correspond to numbers in the margin and on the Northern Waterfront/Marina and the Presidio map.

A Good Tour

You can reach the Marina easily by public transportation. Muni Bus 38 from Union Square heads west on Geary Street to Fillmore Street (where you can transfer to Bus 22; Chestnut Street is one block north of Lombard Street and Fort Mason is three blocks east of the 22's terminus) and to Park Presidio Boulevard (transfer to Bus 28 to go through the Presidio). But this is the place to use your car if you have one; you might even consider renting one for a day to cover the area, as well as Lincoln Park, Golden Gate Park, and the western shoreline.

Begin with a visit to **Fort Mason** ⑦. To get to the **Palace of Fine Arts** ⑧ by car, take Lombard Street west and stay in the right lane as it curves toward Golden Gate Bridge (watch carefully for signs or you'll wind up on the bridge). Inside the Palace is the **Exploratorium,** a hands-on science museum. The least confusing way to get to the **Presidio** ⑨ from the Palace is to exit from the south end of the Lyon Street parking lot and head east (left) on Bay Street. Turn right (north) onto Baker Street, right on Francisco and take it across Richardson Avenue to Lyon Street. Make a left onto Lyon, a right at Lombard Street, and proceed through the main gate to Presidio Boulevard. Turn right onto Presidio, which becomes Lincoln Boulevard after a block or so. Turn left on Funston Avenue to reach the **Presidio Museum** ⑩, a 19th-century former hospital with exhibits on the history of the military in San Francisco. From here it's four blocks west on Lincoln to the Presidio Visitors Information Center, on Montgomery Street.

Just before the visitor center, a turnoff on the right leads to **Fort Point** ⑪, a collection of military buildings sitting in the shadow of the Golden Gate Bridge; the highlight is the redbrick fortress directly underneath the bridge. To get to Fort Point, follow Lincoln Boulevard for a couple of miles, curving past the large military cemetery. Before the bridge you'll see a parking lot marked FORT POINT on the right. Park and follow the signs leading to Fort Point, walking downhill through a lightly wooded area; to the right is the old mine depot and to the left is the Fort Point defense fortification, which is open for tours. To walk the short distance to the **Golden Gate Bridge** ⑫, follow the signs from the Fort Point parking lot; to drive across the bridge, continue past the parking lot and watch for the turnoff on the right. If you're going to walk across the bridge, park in the Fort Point lot.

TIMING

If you drive, plan to spend at least three hours, not including a walk across the Golden Gate Bridge or hikes along the shoreline—each of which will take a few hours. If you're coming with kids, you'll probably want to budget extra time for the Exploratorium.

Sights to See

★ ⓒ **Exploratorium.** The curious of all ages flock to this hands-on museum to enjoy and learn from some of the 600 exhibits. The touchy-feely Tactile Dome is immensely popular. Regular science demonstrations (lasers, dissection of a cow's eye, and the like) begin around 10:30. ⊠ *Baker and Beach Sts.,* ☎ *415/561–0360 for general information; 415/561–0362 for Tactile Dome reservations.* ▣ *$9; free 1st Wed. of month.* ☉ *Tues.–Sun. 10–5, Wed. until 9:30; legal holidays 10–5.*

❼ **Fort Mason.** Originally a depot for the shipment of supplies to the Pacific during World War II, Fort Mason was converted into a cultural center in 1977. Inside these warehouses are many worthwhile museums—including the Mexican, African-American, Craft and Folk Art, and the Museo Italo-Americano museums—as well as shops, galleries, performance spaces, and the vegetarian restaurant Greens (☞ Dining, *below*). The **SFMOMA Rental Gallery** (☎ 415/441–4777) rents and sells genre-bending art by up-and-coming artists. Most of the museums are closed on Monday and some also aren't open on Tuesday. ⊠ *Buchanan St. and Marina Blvd.,* ☎ *415/979–3010 for event information.*

⓫ **Fort Point.** Anticipating the Civil War, the U.S. Army constructed Fort Point between 1853 and 1861 to protect San Francisco from sea attack by Confederate forces. It was never used for that purpose but was a coastal defense fortification post during World War II. The national historic site is a museum filled with military memorabilia. The top floor affords a superb view of San Francisco Bay. National Park rangers lead group tours and conduct cannon drills. ⊠ *Marine Dr. off Lincoln Blvd.,* ☎ *415/556–1693.* ▣ *Free.* ☉ *Wed.–Sun. 10–5.*

★ ⑫ **Golden Gate Bridge.** San Francisco's connection to Marin County has long wowed sightseers with its rust-color beauty and simple but powerful Art Deco design. Nearly 2 mi across, it is one of the longest bridges in the world—and also one of the strongest, made to withstand winds of more than 100 mph. A vista point on the Marin side affords a spectacular view of the city. To get to the bridge from the Marina district, head north on Doyle Drive from Richardson Avenue or Marina Boulevard.

★ ❽ **Palace of Fine Arts.** San Francisco's rosy rococo Palace of Fine Arts is at the very end of the Marina. The palace is the sole survivor of the many tinted-plaster buildings, a temporary classical city of sorts, built for the 1915 Panama-Pacific International Exposition. Bernard Maybeck designed the classical beauty, which was reconstructed in concrete and reopened in 1967, thanks to the contributions of legions of sentimental citizens and a huge private donation. The massive columns, great rotunda (dedicated to the glory of Greek culture), and swan-filled lagoon have been used in countless fashion layouts and films. ⊠ *Baker and Beach Sts.,* ☎ *415/563–7337 for palace tours.*

⑨ Presidio. Part of the Golden Gate National Recreation Area, the Presidio was a military post for more than 200 years. Don Juan Bautista de Anza and a band of Spanish settlers first claimed the area in 1776. It became a Mexican garrison in 1822 when Mexico gained its independence from Spain, until U.S. troops forcibly occupied it in 1846. The U.S. Sixth Army was stationed here until October 1994. The more than 1,400 acres of rolling hills, majestic woods, and redbrick army barracks present an air of serenity in the middle of the city. There are two beaches, a golf course, and picnic sites, and the views of the bay, the Golden Gate Bridge, and Marin County are sublime. The **Presidio Visitors Information Center** (✉ Montgomery St. near Lincoln Blvd., ☎ 415/561–4323) has maps, brochures, and schedules for guided walking and bicycle tours. It's open daily from 9 to 5. ✉ *Between Marina and Lincoln Park.*

⑩ Presidio Museum. This museum in a former military hospital built in 1863 focuses on the role played by the military in San Francisco's development. Behind it are two cabins that housed refugees from the 1906 earthquake and fire. Photos on the wall of one cabin depict rows and rows of temporary shelters at the Presidio and in Golden Gate Park following the disaster. At press time, a proposal to move the museum to the Presidio Visitor Information Center (☞ *above*) had not been approved. ✉ *Lincoln Blvd. and Funston Ave.,* ☎ *415/561–4331.* 🎫 *Free.* ☉ *Wed.–Sun. noon–4.*

Golden Gate Park

In 1887 Scotsman John McLaren transformed this desolate brush- and sand-covered expanse in the central-western part of San Francisco into a rolling, beautifully landscaped 1,000-acre oasis that stretches more than 2 mi and ends dramatically at the ocean. On weekends you can park all day for $3 at the University of California at San Francisco garage (enter at Irving Street and 2nd Avenue); from there a shuttle leaves every 10 minutes for the park's museums. Muni (☞ A Good Tour, *below*) also serves the park . The No. 5 Fulton bus stops along its northern edge, and the N-Judah light-rail car stops one to two blocks south of the park. Much of the park east of Park Presidio Boulevard is closed to traffic on Sunday. The fog can sweep into the park with amazing speed; always bring a sweatshirt or jacket.

From May to October, free guided walking tours are offered every weekend by the **Friends of Recreation and Parks** (☎ 415/263–0991). If you plan to visit more than one attraction, consider purchasing a Golden Gate Explorer Pass ($12), which grants admission to the de Young and Asian Art museums, plus the California Academy of Sciences, and the Japanese Tea Garden. The passes are good for up to six months (the length depends on what time of year you buy the pass), so you can visit the attractions at your leisure. The passes can be purchased at any of the above sights or at TIX Bay Area in Union Square.

Numbers in the text correspond to numbers in the margin and on the Golden Gate Park map.

A Good Tour

If you're coming from downtown, take a westbound Bus 5-Fulton or Bus 21-Hayes to Arguello Boulevard and Fulton Street, then walk south about 500 ft into the park to John F. Kennedy Drive. You can also take the N-Judah streetcar (underground part of the way) to many stops parallel to the park; from any stop past Arguello, walk north a couple of blocks.

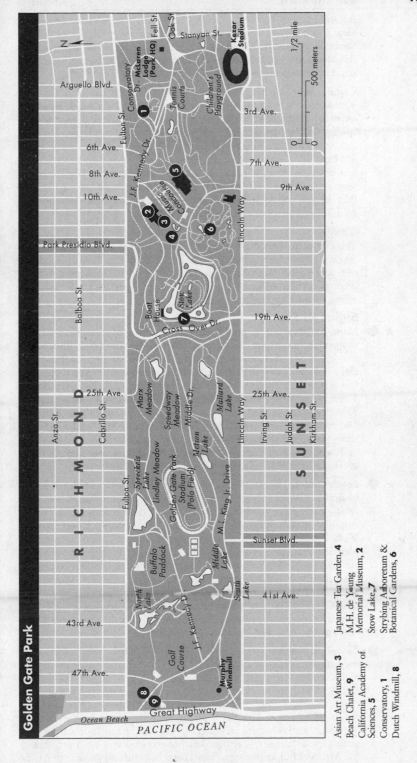

Golden Gate Park

Asian Art Museum, **3**
Beach Chalet, **9**
California Academy of Sciences, **5**
Conservatory, **1**
Dutch Windmill, **8**

Japanese Tea Garden, **4**
M.H. de Young Memorial Museum, **2**
Stow Lake, **7**
Strybing Arboretum & Botanical Gardens, **6**

A good place to start your Golden Gate Park tour is at the **Conservatory** ① and surrounding gardens, on Conservatory Drive near Fulton Street. Walk west on Conservatory Drive to the **M. H. de Young Memorial Museum** ② and the **Asian Art Museum** ③. Next to the Asian museum is the **Japanese Tea Garden** ④.

Coming out of the tea garden, cut across the Music Concourse, where outdoor concerts are sometimes held, to the **California Academy of Sciences** ⑤. To the west of the academy is a small but charming **Shakespeare Garden.** From here walk west to the main road, turn left, and follow its curves to **Strybing Arboretum & Botanical Gardens** ⑥. From Strybing walk west to peaceful **Stow Lake** ⑦. If you opt to walk the rest of the way to the ocean (a considerable distance), you'll pass by several meadows, a stadium, a buffalo paddock, and a few small lakes. Past the golf course and nearly at the ocean, are the **Dutch Windmill** ⑧, an adjoining garden, and the **Beach Chalet** ⑨.

TIMING

You can easily spend a whole day in Golden Gate Park, especially if you walk the whole distance. Set aside an hour each for the Academy of Sciences, the Asian Art Museum, and the de Young Museum. Even if you plan to explore only the eastern end of the park (up to Stow Lake), allot at least four hours.

Sights to See

★ ③ **Asian Art Museum.** A world-famous collection of more than 12,000 sculptures, paintings, and ceramics from 40 countries, illustrating major periods of Asian art, is housed here. On the first floor are special exhibitions as well as galleries dedicated to works from Korea and China. On the second floor are treasures from Iran, Turkey, Syria, India, Tibet, Nepal, Pakistan, India, Japan, Afghanistan, and Southeast Asia. There are daily guided tours. ✉ *Tea Garden Dr. off John F. Kennedy Dr., near 10th Ave. and Fulton St.,* ☎ *415/668–8921.* ✇ *$7 ($2 off with Muni transfer), good also for same-day admission to the M. H. de Young Museum and the Legion of Honor Museum in Lincoln Park.* ⊙ *Tues.–Sun. 9:30–5, 1st Wed. of month until 8:45.*

★ ⑨ **Beach Chalet.** This 1925 structure that overlooks Ocean Beach is one of architect Willis Polk's simpler designs, yet it still impresses. The chalet, which had been closed since the 1970s for renovations and lack of a suitable tenant, reopened to great fanfare in 1997. A wraparound Work Projects Administration mural on the ground-floor interior depicts San Francisco in the 1930s; the labels describing the various panels add up to a minihistory of Depression-era life in the city. A three-dimensional model of the park, artifacts from the 1894 Mid-Winter Exposition and other park events, and a visitor center are all here as well. On a clear day, the brew pub–restaurant upstairs (notice the carved bannister on the way up) has views of the Farallon Islands three dozen miles away. ✉ *Great Hwy. south of Fulton St.*

★ ✪ ⑤ **California Academy of Sciences.** One of the country's top natural history museums houses an aquarium and a planetarium, plus numerous exhibits. The **Steinhart Aquarium,** with its dramatic 100,000-gallon Fish Roundabout, contains 14,000 creatures, including a living coral reef with colorful fish, tropical sharks, and a rainbow of hard and soft corals. The "Touch Tide Pool" allows kids to cozy up to starfish, hermit crabs, and other sea creatures. Other exhibits include a floor that simulates various-level earthquakes, life-size elephant-seal models, and the **African Hall,** depicting animals (real but stuffed) specific to Africa in their native vegetation.

There is an additional charge (up to $2.50) for **Morrison Planetarium** shows (☎ 415/750–7141 for daily schedule). The Laserium presents evening laser light shows (☎ 415/750–7138 for schedule and fees) at Morrison Planetarium, accompanied by rock, classical, and other types of music; educational shows outline laser technology. At the southeast corner of the building is the **Shakespeare Garden,** with 200 flowers mentioned by the Bard, as well as engraved bronze panels with floral quotations. ⊠ *Music Concourse Dr. off South Dr. across from Asian Art and de Young museums,* ☎ *415/750–7145.* 🎫 *$8.50; $1 discount with Muni transfer; free 1st Wed. of month.* ⊙ *Memorial Day–Labor Day, daily 9–6; Labor Day–Memorial Day, daily 10–5.*

❶ **Conservatory.** The oldest building in the park (built in 1876) and the last remaining wood-frame Victorian conservatory in the country, the Conservatory is a copy of London's famous Kew Gardens. Because of damage from a 1995 storm, the Conservatory is closed indefinitely, but its outdoor gardens are still being maintained. ⊠ *Conservatory Dr. near Fulton St.,* ☎ *415/362–0808.*

❽ **Dutch Windmill.** At the very western end of the park is a restored 1902 windmill with a wood-shingled upper section and a heavy cement bottom. The windmill overlooks the curvy, photogenic **Queen Wilhelmina Tulip Garden,** which blooms in early spring and late summer. ⊠ *Off Fulton St. between 47th Ave. and the Great Hwy.*

❹ **Japanese Tea Garden.** This serene 4-acre landscape of small ponds, streams, waterfalls, stone bridges, Japanese sculptures, bonsai trees, miniature pagodas, and some nearly vertical wooden "humpback" bridges was created for the 1894 Mid-Winter Exposition. The Tea House is a popular spot for relaxing. Cherry blossoms bloom in spring. ⊠ *Tea Garden Dr. off John F. Kennedy Dr.,* ☎ *415/752–4227.* 🎫 *$2.50.* ⊙ *Daily 8:30–6:30 (closes earlier in winter).*

★ ❷ **M. H. de Young Memorial Museum.** The de Young contains a fine collection of American art—paintings, sculpture, textiles, and decorative arts from colonial times through the 20th century. The John D. Rockefeller III Collection of American Paintings is especially noteworthy, with more than 200 paintings of American masters such as John Singleton Copley, Thomas Eakins, George Caleb Bingham, and John Singer Sargent. The de Young also exhibits African, Native American, and Meso-American art, including sculpture, baskets, textiles, and ceramics. The **Café de Young** has outdoor seating in the Oakes Garden. ⊠ *Tea Garden Dr. off John F. Kennedy Dr. near 10th Ave. and Fulton St.,* ☎ *415/863–3330.* 🎫 *$7, ($2 off with Muni transfer) good also for same-day admission to the Asian Art Museum and the Legion of Honor Museum in Lincoln Park); free 1st Wed. of month until 5.* ⊙ *Tues.–Sun. 9:30–5, 1st Wed. of month until 8:45.*

❼ **Stow Lake.** This small body of water surrounds Strawberry Hill; a couple of bridges allow visitors to cross over and ascend the hill. A waterfall cascades down from the top of the hill; panoramic views make it worth the short hike up here. Down below, rent a boat or a bicycle (☎ 415/752–0347) or stroll around the perimeter. ⊠ *Off John F. Kennedy Dr. east of Crossover Dr.*

❻ **Strybing Arboretum & Botanical Gardens.** The 70-acre arboretum specializes in plants from areas with climates similar to that of the Bay Area, such as South Africa, the Mediterranean, and the west coast of Australia; more than 8,000 plants and tree varieties bloom in gardens throughout the grounds. Strybing regularly hosts classes, lectures, and plant sales. ⊠ *9th Ave. at Lincoln Way,* ☎ *415/661–1316.* 🎫 *Free.* ⊙ *Weekdays 8–4:30, weekends 10–5. Tours leave bookstore weekdays at 1:30, weekends at 10:30.*

OFF THE
BEATEN PATH

THE HAIGHT – East of Golden Gate Park is the neighborhood known as "the Haight." Despite the presence of a Gap store (on the legendary Haight-Ashbury corner, no less) and upscale galleries and shops, this is still home to anarchist book collectives and shops selling incense and tie-dye T-shirts. Even a few "smoke shops" remain from the area's 1960s flower-power heyday. The Haight's famous political spirit exists alongside some of the finest Victorian-lined streets in the city; more than 1,000 such houses occupy Golden Gate Park's "Panhandle" and Ashbury Heights. Haight Street itself is known for its vintage merchandise, including clothes, records, and books. The house at 710 Ashbury Street, near Waller Street, was the '60s crash pad of the late Jerry Garcia and his Grateful Dead bandmates.

Lincoln Park and the Western Shoreline

From Land's End in Lincoln Park you'll find some of the best views of the Golden Gate (the name given, long before the bridge was built, to the point at which San Francisco Bay opens out to the Pacific Ocean) and the Marin Headlands. From the historic Cliff House south to the sprawling San Francisco Zoo, the Great Highway and Ocean Beach run along the western edge of the city. The wind is often strong along the shoreline, summer fog can blanket the ocean beaches, and the water is cold and usually rough. Carry a jacket and binoculars.

Numbers in the text correspond to numbers in the margin and on the Lincoln Park and the Western Shoreline map.

A Good Drive

A car is very useful out here because the sights mentioned are far apart. Start at **Lincoln Park** ①. The park entrance is at 34th Avenue and Clement Street; those without a car can take Bus 38-Geary, which stops one block south of the entrance. Within Lincoln Park is the splendid **California Palace of the Legion of Honor** ② museum, at the end of 34th Avenue (also called Legion of Honor Drive). From the museum, head back out on Legion of Honor Drive to Clement Street and follow Clement west (turn right). The name of the road changes to Seal Rock Drive a couple of blocks before it ends at El Camino del Mar. Turn left on El Camino and right on Point Lobos. There's a parking area off Point Lobos just past 48th Avenue before the **Cliff House** ③. (If you're coming by bus from downtown, take the 38-Geary Limited—ask the driver of the first Bus 38 you see if the Limited is running at that time—to 48th Avenue and Point Lobos and walk down the hill; if you take the Bus 38-Geary marked OCEAN BEACH, you'll have to walk an extra 10 minutes to the Cliff House.) From the Cliff House it's a short jog downhill to windswept **Ocean Beach** ④. A couple of miles down, at the intersection of the Great Highway and Sloat Boulevard, is the **San Francisco Zoo** ⑤. If you're driving, follow the Great Highway and turn left on Sloat Boulevard, parking in one of the many spaces on the street across from the zoo entrance. If you're coming from downtown, you can take the L-Taraval Muni streetcar.

TIMING

Given the distances between sights and the sheer natural beauty you'll want to absorb, you'll need at least 3½ hours here—more if you don't have a car. An hour can easily be spent in the Palace of the Legion of Honor and 1½ hours at the zoo. Many linger at the Cliff House and Ocean Beach, soaking up the views.

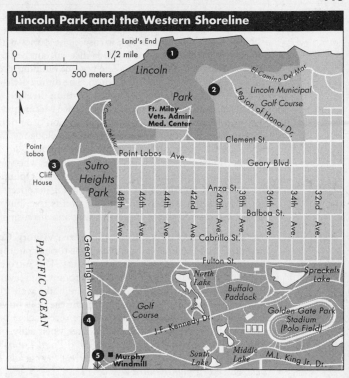

Lincoln Park and the Western Shoreline

Sights to See

2 **California Palace of the Legion of Honor.** Spectacularly situated on cliffs overlooking the ocean, the Golden Gate Bridge, and the Marin Headlands, this landmark structure came into being largely through the efforts of Alma Spreckels and her husband, sugar magnate Adolph Spreckels. The 20-plus galleries on the upper level are devoted to the permanent collection of European art (paintings, sculpture, decorative arts, tapestries) from the 14th to the 20th century. The Rodin collection is noteworthy—an original cast of Rodin's *The Thinker* welcomes you as you walk through the Legion's courtyard. The lower-level galleries exhibit prints and drawings, English and European porcelain, and ancient Assyrian, Greek, Roman, and Egyptian art; it also contains galleries for special exhibitions.

The Legion Café, on the lower level, has a garden terrace and a view of the Golden Gate Bridge. North of the museum (across El Camino del Mar) is George Segal's *The Holocaust,* a sobering sculpture that evokes life in European concentration camps during World War II. ⊠ *34th Ave. at Clement St.,* ☎ *415/863–3330 for 24-hr information.* 🖭 *$7 ($2 off with Muni transfer), good also for same-day admission to Asian Art and M. H. de Young museums, free 2nd Wed. of month (Golden Gate Park Explorer Pass; $12 includes 1-day admission to the de Young, Asian Art, and Legion of Honor museums, plus the Japanese Tea Garden and the California Academy of Sciences; available at any of the museums or at TIX Bay Area, in Union Square).* ⊘ *Tues.– Sun. 9:30–5.*

3 **Cliff House.** The original Cliff House, which dated from 1863, hosted several U.S. presidents and wealthy locals who would drive their carriages out to Ocean Beach; it was destroyed by fire on Christmas Day 1894. The second Cliff House, and the most beloved and resplendent of the three, was built in 1896; it rose eight stories with an observation tower 200 ft above sea level. It also succumbed to fire—a year after surviving the 1906 quake. The present building, erected in 1909, has restaurants, a pub, and a gift shop. The dining areas overlook Seal Rock (the barking marine mammals sunning themselves are actually sea lions). Below the Cliff House is the **Musée Mécanique** (☎ 415/386–1170, a time-warped arcade with a collection of antique mechanical contrivances, including peep shows and nickelodeons. Some of the favorites are the giant, rather creepy "Laughing Sal," an arm-wrestling machine, and mechanical fortune-telling figures who speak from their curtained boxes. Especially provocative is the "Opium-Den," a tiny diorama with Chinese figures clearly depicting the effects of heavy drug use. The museum is open daily; admission is free, but a little pocket change will bring some of these amusing anachronisms to life.

The **Golden Gate National Recreation Area Visitors' Center** (☎ 415/556–8642) here contains fascinating historical photographs of the Cliff House and the glass-roof **Sutro Baths.** The Sutro complex comprised six enormous baths, 500 dressing rooms, and several restaurants on 3 acres north of the Cliff House. The baths were closed in 1952 and burned down in 1966. You can explore the ruins on your own (they now look a bit like scenic water-storage receptacles) or take ranger-led walks on weekends. The visitor center, open daily, provides information on these and other trails. ⊠ *1090 Point Lobos Ave.,* ☎ *415/386–3330.* ☼ *Weekdays 8 AM–10:30 PM, weekends 8 AM–11 PM; cocktails served nightly until 2 AM.*

❶ Lincoln Park. At one time all the city's cemeteries were here, segregated by nationality. In 1900, the Board of Supervisors voted to ban cemeteries within city limits (the two exceptions are the cemetery at Mission Dolores and the one in the Presidio). Large and well-formed Monterey cypresses line the fairways at Lincoln Park's 18-hole golf course. There are scenic walks throughout the 275-acre park, with postcard-perfect views from many spots, especially **Land's End** (the trail starts outside the Palace of the Legion of Honor, at the end of El Camino del Mar). The trails out to Land's End, however, are for skilled hikers only: Landslides are frequent, and danger lurks along the steep cliffs. ⊠ *Entrance at 34th Ave. at Clement St.*

☺ ❺ San Francisco Zoo. Established in 1889 in Golden Gate Park, the zoo is home to more than 1,000 species of birds and animals, more than a hundred of which are designated as endangered. Among the protected are the snow leopard, the Sumatran tiger, the jaguar, and the Asian elephant. A favorite attraction is the greater one-horned rhinoceros, next to the African elephants. **Gorilla World** is one of the largest and most natural gorilla habitats of any zoo in the world. The **Primate Discovery Center** houses 14 endangered species in atriumlike enclosures. The **Feline Conservation Center,** a large naturalistic setting for rare cats, is designed to encourage breeding among endangered felines. Don't miss the big cat feeding—they love their horse meat—from Tuesday to Sunday at 2. The 7-acre **South American Gateway** exhibit re-creates habitats replete with howler monkeys, tapirs, and a cloud forest. The children's zoo has a minipopulation of about 300 mammals, birds, and reptiles, plus an insect zoo, a baby-animal nursery, and a beautifully restored 1921 Dentzel Carousel. A ride astride one of the 52 hand-carved animals costs $1. ⊠ *Sloat Blvd. and the Great Hwy.,* ☎ *415/753–7083.* ▣ *$7; free 1st Wed. of month; children's zoo $1.* ☼ *Daily 10–5; children's zoo weekdays 11–4, weekends 10:30–4:30.*

DINING

By Sharon
Silva

Practically every ethnic cuisine is represented in San Francisco. Most upper-end establishments offer valet parking—worth considering in crowded neighborhoods like North Beach, Union Square, Nob Hill, and the Civic Center. There is often a nominal charge and a time-length restriction on validated parking.

CATEGORY	COST*
$$$$	over $50
$$$	$30–$50
$$	$20–$30
$	under $20

per person for a three-course meal, excluding drinks, service, and 8½% sales tax

American

Castro

$$ ✕ **2223.** Dishes at John Cunin's restaurant include thin-crust pizzas, earthy seasonal soups, chicken with garlic mashed potatoes, pork loin with wilted escarole, and duck-confit salad. For Sunday brunch there might be French toast or eggs Benedict on a tasty herb scone. ⊠ *2223 Market St.,* ☎ *415/431–0692. MC, V. No lunch Sat.*

Civic Center

$$$ ✕ **Jardinière.** One of the city's most talked-about restaurants is one
★ of *the* places to dine before a performance at the nearby Opera House and Davies Symphony Hall. The chef-owner is Traci Des Jardins, late of Rubicon; the sophisticated interior, with its eye-catching oval atrium and curving staircase, is the work of designer Pat Kuleto. First courses of rabbit rillettes, duck confit, and foie gras are pricey but memorable ways to launch any repast. Alas, not all the main courses reach the same culinary heights, but the finely honed service helps you to forget the few shortcomings. ⊠ *300 Grove St.,* ☎ *415/861–5555. Reservations essential. AE, DC, MC, V. No lunch.*

$$$ ✕ **Stars.** Jeremiah Tower's dining room has a clublike ambience, and
★ the food ranges from grills to ragouts to sautés—some daringly creative and some more traditional. Dinners here are pricey, but those on a budget can order a stylish hamburger or chicken tacos at the counter or slowly enjoy a flute of champagne at the mile-long bar. ⊠ *150 Redwood Alley, at Van Ness Ave.,* ☎ *415/861–7827. Reservations essential. AE, DC, MC, V. No lunch weekends.*

Cow Hollow/Marina

$$ ✕ **Perry's.** The button-down singles set comes to this watering hole and meeting place for good, honest saloon food—London broil, corned-beef hash, seafood dishes, one of the best hamburgers in town, and a great breakfast. Brunch is served on weekends. ⊠ *1944 Union St.,* ☎ *415/922–9022. AE, MC, V.*

$ ✕ **World Wrapps.** This hip eatery serves burritos with fillings that range from Peking duck to Thai chicken, from roasted vegetables to couscous and cucumber. Healthful smoothies—papaya, blackberry, and the like—match up surprisingly well with the hearty wrapps. ⊠ *2257 Chestnut St.,* ☎ *415/563–9727; ⊠ 2227 Polk St.,* ☎ *415/931–9727. No credit cards.*

Embarcadero North

$$ ✕ **Fog City Diner.** The narrow dining room at Fog City emulates a luxurious railroad car. The innovative menu, drawing its inspiration from regional cooking throughout the United States, is both classic and

116

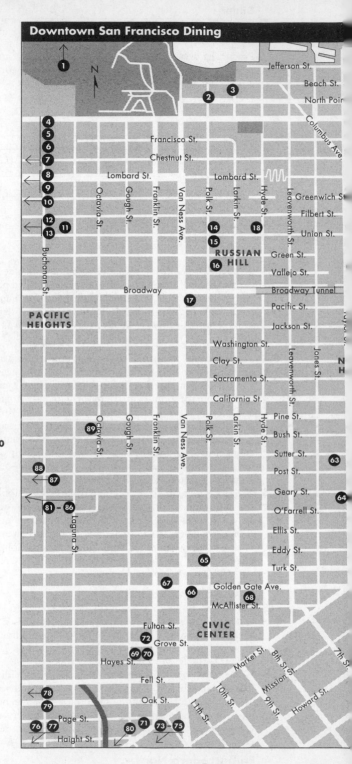

Downtown San Francisco Dining

contemporary, from burgers and fries and hot fudge sundaes to goat cheese–stuffed pasilla chilies, crab cakes, and salads of baby lettuce punctuated with candied walnuts. The shareable "small plates" are a fun way to go. ⊠ *1300 Battery St.,* ☎ *415/982–2000. D, DC, MC, V.*

$$ ✕ **MacArthur Park.** Year after year San Franciscans pronounce this handsomely renovated pre-earthquake warehouse their favorite spot for ribs, but the oak-wood smoker and mesquite grill also turn out other all-American fare, from steaks and hamburgers to seafood. ⊠ *607 Front St.,* ☎ *415/398–5700. AE, DC, MC, V. No lunch weekends.*

Embarcadero South

$$–$$$ ✕ **Boulevard.** Nationally acclaimed chef Nancy Oakes's menu is seasonally in flux, but you will always find her signature juxtaposition of aristocratic fare—foie gras is a favorite—with homey dishes like maple-cured pork loin. The weekday afternoon bistro service is less formal and expensive than regular dining. ⊠ *1 Mission St.,* ☎ *415/543–6084. Reservations essential. AE, D, DC, MC, V. No lunch weekends.*

$$–$$$ ✕ **One Market.** The bustling brasserie of Bradley Ogden, Michael Dellar, and George Morrone seats 170, and a large bar-café serves snacks from noon on. Seafood is the chefs' forte, so don't pass up the delicate cured salmon tartare or the boned whole trout swaddled in potato threads and then deep-fried. ⊠ *1 Market St.,* ☎ *415/777–5577. Reservations essential. AE, DC, MC, V. Closed Sun. No lunch Sat.*

Financial District

$$$ ✕ **Cypress Club.** Owner John Cunin calls this place a "San Francisco brasserie." This categorizes the contemporary American cooking somewhat, but the decor defies description. With stone mosaic floors, hammered copper arches, and overstuffed velvet upholstery, the look of Cypress could be interpreted as anything from a parody of an ancient temple to a futuristic space bar. ⊠ *500 Jackson St.,* ☎ *415/296–8555. AE, DC, MC, V. No lunch.*

$$$ ✕ **Globe.** This smart spot with brick walls and terra-cotta floors seats less than four dozen diners, so book ahead. The sophisticated fare, which delivers a Californian punch with a thick Mediterranean accent, includes the *frisée aux lardons* (salad of curly greens with bacon cubes, topped with a poached egg), fresh grilled sardines, and a lavish T-bone steak with all the trimmings. ⊠ *290 Pacific Ave.,* ☎ *415/391–4132. AE, DC, MC, V. No lunch Sat. Closed Sun.*

$$$ ✕ **Rubicon.** Sophisticated renditions of seafood and poultry—sautéed skatewing, duck confit, grilled quail—is served on two floors to Hollywood big shots (the investor list includes Robin Williams, Robert De Niro, and Francis Ford Coppola) and San Francisco's glamorous set. ⊠ *558 Sacramento St.,* ☎ *415/434–4100. AE, DC, MC, V. Closed Sun. No lunch Sat.*

The Haight

$$ ✕ **Eos Restaurant & Wine Bar.** Chef Arnold Wong has created an impressive East-West table at this popular spot. Grilled skirt steak is marinated in a Thai red curry and served with mashed potatoes and bok choy; rock shrimp cakes arrive with a gingery mayonnaise; and pork loin is flavored with ginger and soy and paired with Southeast Asian sticky rice. ⊠ *901 Cole St.,* ☎ *415/566–3063. Reservations essential. AE, MC, V. No lunch.*

Lower Pacific Heights

$$ ✕ **The Meetinghouse.** A regularly changing menu of modernized American dishes is served in this appealing dining room of creamy yellow walls, broad plank floors, and Shaker furniture. Johnnycakes filled with rock shrimp and accompanied by a colorful pepper relish are among the most popular first courses; hominy-crusted catfish and roast chicken

on warm frisée salad are satisfying entrées. ⊠ *1701 Octavia St.,* ☎ *415/922–6733. AE, MC, V. Closed Mon.–Tues. No lunch.*

The Mission District

$$ ✕ **42 Degrees.** Next door to the Esprit outlet store, this sleek industrial-style space with a curving metal staircase and a seductive view of the bay is a magnet for young San Franciscans with a few bucks to spend. The name refers to the latitude of Provence. The highlights of the Cal-Mediterranean menu include creamy bone marrow on toast, duck breast with fiddlehead ferns, and poussin (small chickens) with a hard-cider sauce. ⊠ *235 16th St.,* ☎ *415/777–5558. MC, V. Closed Sun. No dinner Mon. and Tues.*

North Beach

$$ ✕ **Bix.** This old-fashioned supper club is reminiscent of a theater, with a bustling bar and dining tables downstairs and banquettes on the balcony. The fare is contemporary renditions of American dishes like pan-fried rock-cod served with potato-mushroom hash and caviar butter. A pianist plays in the evening. ⊠ *56 Gold St.,* ☎ *415/433–6300. AE, D, DC, MC, V. No lunch weekends.*

South of Market

$$$ ✕ **Hawthorne Lane.** The high-ceiling bar at this popular SoMa eatery serves a selection of irresistible small plates—Thai-style squid, tempura-battered green beans with mustard sauce, stylish pizzas. Patrons in the light-flooded dining room engage in more serious eating, from perfectly seared foie gras to grilled quail on scalloped potatoes to roast chicken with spoon bread, all with Mediterranean and Asian touches. ⊠ *22 Hawthorne St.,* ☎ *415/777–9779. Reservations essential. D, DC, MC, V. No lunch weekends.*

$$ ✕ **Infusion Bar and Restaurant.** "Infusion" refers to the bevy of glass decanters lined up like foot soldiers behind the sleek wood bar of this up-to-the-minute SoMa destination. They hold flavored vodkas—mango, chili, anise, coconut. Many folks sip one of the enhanced spirits while sampling tasty appetizers like roasted mussels or batter-fried calamari. Steaks and pastas are among the entrées. The live music starts up at 9, so eat early if you are looking for a tranquil repast. ⊠ *555 2nd St.,* ☎ *415/543–2282. AE, DC, MC, V. No lunch weekends.*

Sunset District

$$ ✕ **Beach Chalet.** In a historic colonnaded building with handsome murals depicting San Francisco in the mid-1930s, this is *the* place to watch the sun set over the Pacific while indulging in fine microbrewery beers and eclectic American fare—steamed mussels and pizzette, house-made chorizo and seafood gumbo, and the like. ⊠ *1000 Great Hwy.,* ☎ *415/386–8439. MC, V.*

Union Square/Downtown

$$$–$$$$ ✕ **Postrio.** Palm trees and museum-quality contemporary paintings provide the accents in the three-level bar and dining area of this Wolfgang Puck enterprise. Attire is formal; food is Puckish Californian with Mediterranean and Asian overtones, emphasizing pastas, grilled seafood, and house-baked breads. Substantial breakfast and bar menus (the latter includes great pizzas) are served as well. ⊠ *545 Post St.,* ☎ *415/776–7825. Reservations essential. AE, D, DC, MC, V.*

$$$ ✕ **Campton Place.** Todd Humphries embellishes traditional American dishes with ethnic flavors. For a sampling of the chef's cuisine, order the six-course tasting menu, on which you'll find everything from caviar to squab. His delightfully crumbly cornbread can be addictive. Breakfast and brunch are major events. On the bar menu are some appetizers plus a caviar extravaganza. ⊠ *340 Stockton St.,* ☎ *415/955–5555. Reservations essential. AE, D, DC, MC, V.*

$$ ✕ **Grand Café.** This beaux arts–style establishment draws crowds from early morning until late at night. The dramatic dining room, formerly a hotel ballroom, is decorated with cabaret-style murals, striking chandeliers, and large booths. Dozens of pen-and-ink cartoon sketches lend the bar a more casual feel. The café's menu is French-Californian, with an emphasis on seasonal local ingredients. ✉ *Hotel Monaco, 501 Geary St.,* ☎ *415/292–0101. AE, D, DC, MC, V.*

$$ ✕ **Perry's.** The downtown branch of the Union Street singles hangout (☞ *above*) serves similar saloon-style fare. ✉ *185 Sutter St.,* ☎ *415/ 989–6895. AE, MC, V.*

Chinese

Chinatown

$–$$ ✕ **Great Eastern.** Large tanks in the busy Great Eastern dining room contain Dungeness crabs, black bass, abalone, catfish, shrimp, rock cod, and other creatures of the sea; a wall-hung menu in Chinese and English specifies their cost. Sea conch stir-fried with yellow chives, crab with vermicelli in a clay pot, and steamed fresh scallops with garlic sauce are among the many specialties. In the wee hours night owls often drop in for a plate of noodles or a bowl of *congee* (rice gruel). ✉ *649 Jackson St.,* ☎ *415/986–2550. AE, MC, V.*

$–$$ ✕ **R&G Lounge.** Downstairs (entrance on Kearny Street) is a no-tablecloth dining room; the classier upstairs space (entrance on Commercial Street) serves exceptional Cantonese banquet fare. A menu with photographs helps diners decide among the many exotic dishes, among them dried scallops with seasonal vegetables, steamed clams with eggs, and deep-fried salt-and-pepper Dungeness crab. ✉ *631 Kearny St.,* ☎ *415/982–7877 or 415/982–3811. AE, DC, MC, V.*

Embarcadero North

$$ ✕ **Harbor Village.** Cantonese cooking, dim sum lunches, and fresh, cre-
★ atively prepared seafood from the restaurant's tanks are the hallmarks of this 400-seat branch of a Hong Kong establishment. The setting is opulent, with Chinese antiques and teak furnishings. There's validated parking at the Embarcadero Center garage. ✉ *4 Embarcadero Center,* ☎ *415/781–8833. AE, DC, MC, V.*

Financial District

$ ✕ **Yank Sing.** The city's oldest teahouse remains among the best purveyors of the bite-size Chinese specialties—fried dumplings, steamed shrimp in rice noodles, parchment chicken, and the like—known as dim sum. ✉ *427 Battery St.,* ☎ *415/362–1640;* ✉ *49 Stevenson St., at Market St.,* ☎ *415/541–4949. AE, DC, MC, V. Stevenson branch closed weekends. No dinner.*

Richmond District

$$ ✕ **Hong Kong Flower Lounge.** This outpost of a famous Asian restaurant is known for its seafood—crabs, shrimp, catfish, lobsters, scallops—which is plucked straight from tanks and prepared in various ways. Dim sum is served at midday. ✉ *5322 Geary Blvd.,* ☎ *415/668–8998. AE, D, DC, MC, V.*

$–$$ ✕ **Ton Kiang.** The regional Hakka, China, specialties served here include salt-baked chicken, braised stuffed bean curd, wine-flavored dishes, delicate fish and beef balls, and casseroles of meat and seafood cooked in clay pots. The dim sum is among the finest in the city; especially noteworthy are the dumplings stuffed with shark's fin. ✉ *5821 Geary Blvd.,* ☎ *415/387–8273. MC, V.*

$ ✕ **San Tung No. 2.** Modest looking and bright, San Tung provides a good introduction to the cuisine of Shandong, a province of China that has produced some of the best chefs at Beijing's imperial kitchens. Specialties include the steamed dumplings stuffed with vegetables, meat, or seafood and the hand-pulled noodles, either in soup or stir-fried. Typical accompaniments include a salad of jellyfish, seaweed, or cucumber and a plate of cold poached chicken marinated in Shaoxing wine. ⊠ *1031 Irving St.,* ☎ *415/242–0828. MC, V.*

Eclectic

Civic Center

$$ ✕ **Carta.** The defining idea here is a difficult one to carry off: a menu from a different country or region every month. The talented chefs, alums of some of the city's toniest spots, travel to an assortment of destinations: Oaxaca, Turkey, Dordogne, Morocco, and New England, to name a few, seeking new recipes and ingredients. There are usually about 10 small plates, three main courses, and perhaps three desserts. The dining room is small, imaginatively turned out, and comfortable. Sunday brunch is a highlight. ⊠ *1772 Market St.,* ☎ *415/863–3516. AE, DC, MC, V. Closed Mon. No lunch Sat.*

Hayes Valley

$$$ ✕ **Absinthe.** Despite the restaurant's name, the long-banned cloudy green liqueur is not served here. But a number of classy house created cocktails are, including Death in the Afternoon, a mixture of Pernod and champagne that was reputedly a favorite of author Ernest Hemingway. The plush banquettes at Absinthe draw the city's social set for cold seafood platters, pissaladiere, Madeira-doused sweetbreads, imported French cheeses, and other delicacies. Though the burgundy walls, yards of wood, and sophisticated ambience recall a French brasserie, the menu's Italian influences are readily apparent. ⊠ *398 Hayes St.,* ☎ *415/551–1590. AE, DC, MC, V. Closed Mon. No lunch.*

French

Civic Center

$$–$$$ ✕ **California Culinary Academy.** Patrons watch student chefs at work on a double-tier stage while dining on classic French cooking offered as a prix-fixe meal or a bountiful buffet. On the lower level is an informal à la carte grill. ⊠ *625 Polk St.,* ☎ *415/771–3500. Reservations essential for Fri.-night buffet. AE, DC, MC, V. Closed weekends; hrs vary slightly with school programs.*

Cow Hollow/Marina

$$ ✕ **Bistro Aix.** Named for the southern French town of Aix-en-Provence, this lively bistro with light wood banquettes, a heated patio, and friendly service attracts diners from the surrounding neighborhood and beyond. On weekdays a two-course prix-fixe dinner includes a choice of soup or salad followed by roast chicken, top sirloin, or seafood pasta—for not much more than the price of a movie ticket. The cracker-crust pizzas, steamed mussels, and house-baked breads are additional lures. ⊠ *3340 Steiner St.,* ☎ *415/202–0100. MC, V. No lunch.*

$–$$ ✕ **Cassis Bistro.** This sunny yellow operation recalls small bistros tucked away on side streets in French seaside towns. The food—onion tart, sautéed chicken breast, veal ragout, braised rabbit, tarte Tatin—is comfortingly home style and reasonably priced. ⊠ *2120 Greenwich St.,* ☎ *415/292–0770. No credit cards. Closed Sun.–Mon. No lunch.*

Embarcadero North

$$ ✕ **Pastis.** At lunchtime the sunny cement bar and sleek wooden banquettes of chef-owner Gerald Hirigoyen's restaurant are crowded with workers from surrounding offices who have come to fuel up on dishes

like steamed salmon with celery root, and grilled prawns marinated in *pastis* (anise-flavored French liqueur). The evening menu might include a dreamy seared foie gras with *verjuice* (sour grape juice), oxtails with *sauce ravigote* (an herbed vinaigrette with capers and chopped onion), lamb medallions on herbed white beans, or duck confit. ⊠ *1015 Battery St.,* ☎ *415/391–2555. AE, MC, V. Closed Sun. No lunch Sat.*

$$ ✕ **Plouf.** A sleek spot whose catchy name means "splash," Plouf serves mussels in seven generously portioned, reasonably priced preparations, among them *marinière* (garlic and parsley), apple cider, leeks and cream, and crayfish and tomato. Main courses run the gamut from steak *frites* (with matchstick fries) to steamed sea bass. French vintages are well represented on the carefully selected wine list. ⊠ *40 Belden Pl.,* ☎ *415/986–6491. MC, V. Closed Sun. No lunch Sat.*

$ ✕ **Café Claude.** With a zinc bar, old-fashioned banquettes, and cinema posters, this is one of the most atmospheric French cafés downtown. Order a salade Niçoise or simple daube from the French-speaking staff, and you might forget what country you're in. ⊠ *7 Claude La.,* ☎ *415/392–3505. AE, DC, MC, V. Closed Sun.*

Midtown

$$$ ✕ **La Folie.** This storefront café showcases the nouvelle cuisine of Roland
★   Passot. Much of the food is edible art—whimsical presentations in the form of savory terrines, *galettes* (flat, round cakes), and napoleons—or accompaniments such as bone-marrow flan. ⊠ *2316 Polk St.,* ☎ *415/776–5577. AE, D, DC, MC, V. Closed Sun. No lunch.*

Nob Hill

$$$–$$$$ ✕ **Ritz-Carlton Dining Room and Terrace.** There are two distinctly dif-
★   ferent places to eat in this neoclassical Nob Hill showplace. A harpist plays at the formal Dining Room, which serves three- to five-course dinners. The Terrace, a cheerful, informal spot with a large garden patio for outdoor dining, serves breakfast, lunch, dinner, and a Sunday jazz brunch, with piano music at lunchtime and a jazz trio at weekend dinners. In the Dining Room executive chef Sylvain Portay turns out an urbane French menu with Bay Area touches. ⊠ *600 Stockton St.,* ☎ *415/296–7465. AE, D, DC, MC, V. Closed Sun. No lunch.*

North Beach

$ ✕ **Des Alpes.** Basque dinners at rock-bottom prices are the big draw here: Soup, salad, *two* entrées—sweetbreads on puff pastry and rare roast beef are a typical pair—ice cream, and coffee are all included in the price. Service is family style. ⊠ *732 Broadway,* ☎ *415/788–9900. D, DC, MC, V. Closed Mon. No lunch.*

South of Market

$$ ✕ **Fringale.** The bright yellow paint on this dazzling bistro stands out
★   like a beacon on an otherwise bleak industrial street. Biarritz-born chef Gerald Hirigoyen serves French Basque–inspired creations; his *frisée aux lardons* (curly salad greens with crisp bacon cubes and a poached egg), steak frites, and flaky apple tart are superb. ⊠ *570 4th St.,* ☎ *415/543–0573. Reservations essential. AE, MC, V. Closed Sun. No lunch Sat.*

$$ ✕ **South Park Cafe.** This utterly Gallic bistro in SoMa looks as as though it has been whisked out of a Paris arrondissement. The occasional French-speaking waiter adds to the charm, and no place in the City of Light itself serves a more authentic steak frites. A notable first-course is the salad greens with baked goat cheese; for an entrée try the *boudin noir* (black sausage) with sautéed apples. ⊠ *108 South Park, off 2nd St. south of Bryant St.,* ☎ *415/495–7275. MC, V. Closed Sun. No lunch Sat.*

Union Square/Downtown

$$$$ ✕ **Fleur de Lys.** The menu changes constantly at this award-winning restaurant; seared foie gras, lobster bisque, Maryland crab cakes, and venison medallions with tender braised greens bear witness to chef-partner Hubert Keller's international scope. There are tasting menus for omnivores and vegetarians. ⊠ *777 Sutter St.,* ☎ *415/673–7779. Reservations essential. Jacket required. AE, DC, MC, V. Closed Sun. No lunch.*

$$$$ ✕ **Masa's.** Presentation is as important as the food itself in this flower-
★ filled dining spot in the Vintage Court Hotel. Decadent ingredients such as foie gras and black truffles are incorporated into chef Julian Serrano's recipes. Try the quail salad with artichokes and pine nuts or the warm lobster salad with potatoes, crispy leeks, and truffle vinaigrette. Order à la carte or from one of two extensive prix-fixe menus. ⊠ *648 Bush St.,* ☎ *415/989–7154. Reservations essential. Jacket and tie required. AE, D, DC, MC, V. Closed Sun.–Mon. and 1st 2 wks of Jan. No lunch.*

Greek and Middle Eastern

Financial District

$$ ✕ **Faz.** Creamy *baba ghanoush* (eggplant spread), beef-and-rice-filled dolmas, and a Persian-inspired platter of feta cheese, pungent olives, and garden-fresh herbs are all great appetizers here. Entrées include pizzas from the wood-fired oven, pastas tossed with seafood, kabobs, and the signature smoked-fish platter. ⊠ *161 Sutter St.,* ☎ *415/362–0404. AE, DC, MC, V. Closed Sat. and Sun.*

North Beach

$$ ✕ **Maykadeh.** Lamb dishes with rice are the specialties of this authentic Persian restaurant, whose setting is so elegant that the modest check comes as a great surprise. The kabobs and the *chelo* (Persian pilaf) are especially good; first courses include lamb tongue in a sour cream-and-lime sauce and grilled lamb brains with saffron. ⊠ *470 Green St.,* ☎ *415/362–8286. MC, V.*

$ ✕ **Helmand.** Authentic Afghani cooking, white napery and rich Afghan carpets, and amazingly low prices make Helmand worth a visit. Highlights include *aushak* (leek-filled ravioli served with yogurt and ground beef) and any of the lamb dishes, in particular the kabob strewn with yellow split peas and served on Afghani flat bread. There's free nighttime validated parking at Helmand Parking at 468 Broadway. ⊠ *430 Broadway,* ☎ *415/362–0641. AE, MC, V. No lunch weekends.*

Indian

The Haight

$$ ✕ **Indian Oven.** The tandoori chef at this storefront restaurant has mastered the intricacies of northern Indian clay-oven cooking. There's an excellent roasted eggplant dish; the chicken curries and crisp vegetable *pakoras* (fritters), served with a sprightly tamarind chutney, are another good bet. ⊠ *223 Fillmore St.,* ☎ *415/626–1628. AE, D, DC, MC, V. No lunch.*

Northern Waterfront and Embarcadero

$$ ✕ **Gaylord's.** Mildly spiced northern Indian food is served here, along with meats and breads from the tandoori ovens and several vegetarian dishes. Though the kitchen sometimes stumbles, the comfortable banquettes, elegant interior, and gleaming silver service go a long way in soothing disappointments. So do the prime bay views. Validated parking is offered at the Ghirardelli Square garage. ⊠ *Ghirardelli Sq. (Beach and Larkin Sts.),* ☎ *415/771–8822. AE, D, DC, MC, V.*

Italian

Civic Center

$$$ ✕ **Vivande Ristorante.** Owner-chef Carlo Middione's spacious restaurant celebrates the rustic flavors of southern Italy in dishes like the focaccia with grilled radicchio and fennel, the stuffed calamari, the grilled lamb chops, and the pasta tossed with a tangle of mushrooms. A late-supper menu attracts the Performing Arts Center crowd. ⊠ *670 Golden Gate Ave.,* ☎ *415/673–9245. AE, MC, V.*

Cow Hollow/Marina

$$ ✕ **Pane e Vino.** The Italian-born owner-chef of Pane e Vino concentrates on specialties from Tuscany and the north. Roasted whole sea ★   bass, creamy risotto, and thick veal chops are among the dishes regulars can't resist. ⊠ *3011 Steiner St.,* ☎ *415/346–2111. MC, V. No lunch Sun.*

$$ ✕ **Zinzino.** Thin pizzas at this animated restaurant are topped with prosciutto and arugula, eggplant and bread crumbs, or fennel sausage and caramelized onions. A mound of lump-free mashed potatoes imaginatively flavored with Chianti accompanies a thick beef tenderloin. A moist roast half chicken is paired with a salad of frisée, warm potatoes, and goat cheese. For dessert, try the roasted apple with vanilla-bean ice cream and caramel sauce. ⊠ *2355 Chestnut St.,* ☎ *415/346–6623. MC, V. No lunch.*Embarcadero North

$$ ✕ **Il Fornaio.** The draws at this handsome combination café, bakery, and upscale trattoria include outdoor seats and moderately priced Tuscan specialties, among them pizzas from a wood-burning oven, stellar pastas and gnocchi, and grilled poultry and seafood. ⊠ *Levi's Plaza, 1265 Battery St.,* ☎ *415/986–0100. AE, DC, MC, V.*

North Beach

$$ ✕ **Rose Pistola.** The food at chef-owner Reed Hearon's eatery celebrates ★   the neighborhood's Ligurian roots. The many small antipasti plates— roasted peppers, house-cured fish, fava beans and pecorino cheese— and pizzas from a wood-burning oven are favorites, as are the cioppino and the roasted rabbit with polenta. The large and inviting bar area opens onto the sidewalk. ⊠ *532 Columbus Ave.,* ☎ *415/399–0499. Reservations essential. AE, MC, V.*

$ ✕ **Capp's Corner.** Diners at this trattoria sit elbow to elbow at oilcloth-★   covered tables to feast on bountiful, well-prepared five-course dinners. For calorie counters or the budget-minded, a simpler option includes a bowl of minestrone, a salad, and pasta. ⊠ *1600 Powell St.,* ☎ *415/989–2589. AE, D, DC, MC, V. No lunch weekends.*

$ ✕ **L'Osteria del Forno.** The northern Italian proprietors of this unpretentious restaurant prepare small plates of simply cooked vegetables, a few robust pastas, a roast of the day, creamy polenta, and wonderful thin-crust pizzas. ⊠ *519 Columbus Ave.,* ☎ *415/982–1124. Reservations not accepted. No credit cards. Closed Tues.*

Russian Hill

$$ ✕ **Antica Trattoria.** The dining room is starkly Italian, with off-white walls, dark wood, a partial view of the kitchen, and a strong sense of restraint. The food is characterized by the same no-nonsense quality, from whole-wheat pasta tossed with bolognese sauce to venison medallions partnered with wilted greens to pork loin matched with polenta. ⊠ *2400 Polk St.,* ☎ *415/928–5797. MC, V. Closed Mon.*

Union Square/Downtown

$$ ✕ **Kuleto's.** The contemporary cooking of northern Italy, the atmosphere ★   of old San Francisco, and a terrific bar menu showcasing contemporary and traditional antipasti have made this spot off Union Square a hit. Grilled seafood dishes are among the specialties. Breakfast is served here. ⊠ *221 Powell St.,* ☎ *415/397–7720. AE, D, DC, MC, V.*

$$ ✕ **Scala's Bistro.** A large open kitchen stands at the rear of a fashionable dining room that serves breakfast, lunch, and dinner. Grilled Portobello mushrooms and a tower of fried calamari are among the favorite antipasti; the pastas and grilled meats satisfy most main-course appetites. ⊠ *432 Powell St.,* ☎ *415/395–8555. AE, D, DC, MC, V.*

Japanese

Financial District

$$–$$$ ✕ **Kyo-ya.** Tempuras, one-pot dishes, deep-fried and grilled meats, and ★ three dozen sushi selections are among the spectacular offerings at this authentic Japanese restaurant. The lunch menu is more limited than the dinner one, but does include a sampler of four dishes arranged in a handsome lacquered lunch box. ⊠ *Palace Hotel, 2 New Montgomery St., at Market St.,* ☎ *415/546–5000. AE, D, DC, MC, V. Closed Sun. No lunch Mon. and Sat.*

Japantown

$ ✕ **Mifune.** Thin brown *soba* (buckwheat) and thick white *udon* (wheat) noodles are the specialties at this North American outpost of an Osaka-based noodle empire that prepares traditional Japanese combinations like the fish cake–crowned udon and the *tenzaru* (cold noodles and hot tempura with a gingery dipping sauce). Validated parking is available at the Japan Center garage. ⊠ *Japan Center, Kintetsu Building, 1737 Post St.,* ☎ *415/922–0337. Reservations not accepted. AE, D, DC, MC, V.*

$ ✕ **Sanppo.** This small place has an enormous selection of almost every type of Japanese food: yakis, nabemono dishes, donburi, udon, and soba, not to mention feather-light tempura, interesting side dishes, and sushi. Validated parking is available at the Japan Center garage. ⊠ *1702 Post St.,* ☎ *415/346–3486. Reservations not accepted. MC, V. Closed Mon.*

Richmond District

$$ ✕ **Kabuto Sushi.** Behind a black-lacquer counter, master chef Sachio Kojima flashes his knives with the grace of a samurai warrior. In addition to exceptional sushi and sashimi, traditional Japanese dinners are served. ⊠ *5116 Geary Blvd.,* ☎ *415/752–5652. MC, V. Closed Sun.–Mon. No lunch.*

Mediterranean

Civic Center

$$–$$$ ✕ **Zuni Café & Grill.** A window-filled balcony dining area overlooks ★ Zuni's large bar, where shellfish (the oyster selection here is one of the best in town) and drinks are dispensed. A whole roast chicken and Tuscan bread salad for two is a popular order, as are the grilled meats and vegetables. ⊠ *1658 Market St.,* ☎ *415/552–2522. Reservations essential. AE, MC, V. Closed Mon.*

Cow Hollow/Marina

$$–$$$ ✕ **PlumpJack Café.** The regularly changing menu spans the Mediter-★ ranean, with the herbed chicken flanked by polenta and the crispy duck confit among the possibilities. The café is an offshoot a nearby wine shop of the same name, which stocks the racks that line the dining room with some of the best-price vintages in town. ⊠ *3127 Fillmore St.,* ☎ *415/463–4755. AE, MC, V. Closed Sun. No lunch Sat.*

Financial District

$$$ ✕ **Vertigo.** This three-level dining room in the Transamerica Pyramid has an inviting Mediterranean menu with nods to France and California. Among the first courses, a slab of foie gras is paired with pickled pears and sautéed scallops; the entrées include perfectly cooked skatewing with chive-laced mashed potatoes and beef tenderloin atop a bed of white beans. ✉ *600 Montgomery St.,* ☎ *415/433–7250. AE, D, DC, MC, V. Closed Sun. No lunch Sat.*

The Mission District

$$ ✕ **Bruno's.** The menu at this smart retro-'50s eatery changes regularly but often includes a satisfying warm quail salad, steamed mussels in orange-saffron broth, and fork-tender braised lamb shanks. Two adjoining rooms book some of the hottest music entertainment in town. ✉ *2389 Mission St.,* ☎ *415/550–7455. Reservations essential. MC, V. Closed Mon. No lunch.*

North Beach

$$ ✕ **Moose's.** National luminaries head for Moose's when they're in town. Among the innovative creations are the warm shiitake and buffalo mozzarella salad, risotto with wild mushrooms, and guinea fowl on whipped parsnips with black olive sauce. The surroundings are comfortable, with views of Washington Square and Russian Hill from a front café area; the counter seats have a view of the open kitchen. Musicians perform in the evening, and there's a fine Sunday brunch. ✉ *1652 Stockton St.,* ☎ *415/989–7800. Reservations essential. AE, DC, MC, V.*

South of Market

$$–$$$ ✕ **LuLu.** Under the high barrel-vaulted ceiling, beside a large open
★ kitchen, diners feast on sizzling mussels roasted in an iron skillet, plus pizzas, pastas, and wood-roasted poultry, meats, and shellfish. Sharing dishes is the custom here. A smaller, quieter room off to one side makes conversation easier. The café on the opposite side serves food from morning until late at night. ✉ *816 Folsom St.,* ☎ *415/495–5775. Reservations essential. AE, DC, MC, V.*

Mexican/Latin American/Spanish

Cow Hollow/Marina

$$ ✕ **Café Marimba.** Fanciful folk art adorns the walls of this colorful Mexican café, where an open kitchen turns out contemporary renditions of regional specialties: silken mole *negro* (sauce of chilies and chocolate) from Oaxaca, served in tamales and other dishes; shrimp prepared with roasted onions and tomatoes in the style of Zihuatanejo; and chicken with a marinade from Yucatán stuffed into an excellent taco. ✉ *2317 Chestnut St.,* ☎ *415/776–1506. AE, MC, V. No lunch Mon.*

Russian Hill

$$ ✕ **Zarzuela.** Small and crowded Zarzuela serves nearly 40 different hot and cold tapas plus a dozen main courses. Among the tapas of note are the poached octopus atop new potatoes and the slabs of Manchego cheese with paper-thin slices of ham. ✉ *2000 Hyde St.,* ☎ *415/346–0800. D, MC, V. Reservations not accepted. Closed Sun.*

South of Market

$$ ✕ **Thirstybear.** The cavernous interior of concrete floors, rustic brick walls, and shiny tanks holding homemade brews is cool and utilitarian, but the small plates of garlic-and-sherry-infused fish cheeks, steamed mussels, grilled garlic-studded shrimp, and white beans with sausage and aioli will warm you right up. ✉ *661 Howard St.,* ☎ *415/ 974–0905. MC, V. No lunch Sun.*

Russian

Richmond District

$–$$ ✕ **Katia's.** Come here for live Russian music (on most evenings) and lively Russian food. A dollop of sour cream tops the tasty borscht, a mélange of beets, cabbage, and other vegetables. Smoked salmon, blini, and meat- or vegetable-filled piroshki make great starters, and light chicken or potato cutlets or delicate *pelmeni* (small meat-filled dumplings in broth) are fine main courses. ⊠ *600 5th Ave.,* ☎ *415/ 668–9292. AE, DC, MC, V. Closed Mon.*

Seafood

Civic Center

$$–$$$ ✕ **Hayes Street Grill.** Up to 15 different kinds of seafood are listed on the blackboard each night at this extremely popular restaurant. The fish is grilled simply, and accompanied by sauces ranging from tomato salsa to a spicy Szechuan peanut concoction to beurre blanc. Fresh crab slaw and crab cakes are regular appetizers, and the crème brûlée is exquisite. ⊠ *320 Hayes St.,* ☎ *415/863–5545. Reservations essential. AE, D, DC, MC, V. No lunch weekends.*

Financial District

$$$–$$$$ ✕ **Aqua.** Talented chef-owner Michael Mina creates contemporary ver-
★   sions of French, Italian, and American classics at this ultrafashionable spot: Expect mussel, crab, or lobster soufflés; chunks of lobster alongside lobster-stuffed ravioli; and rare *ahi* tuna paired with foie gras. The desserts are works of art—try the warm chocolate tart—and the wine list is comprehensive. ⊠ *252 California St.,* ☎ *415/956–9662. Reservations essential. AE, DC, MC, V. Closed Sun. No lunch Sat.*

Northern Waterfront

$$ ✕ **McCormick & Kuleto's.** This spot has fabulous views of the bay, an Old San Francisco atmosphere, and myriad fish and shellfish preparations (tacos, pot stickers, fish cakes, grills, pastas, and stews). The food has its ups and downs—stick with simple dishes like grilled fish or oysters on the half shell—but even on foggy days you can count on the view. Validated parking is available in the Ghirardelli Square garage. ⊠ *Ghirardelli Sq. (Beach and Larkin Sts.),* ☎ *415/929–1730. AE, D, DC, MC, V.*

Union Square/Downtown

$$$ ✕ **Farallon.** Outfitted with sculpted purple-and-pink jellyfish lamps,
★   kelp-covered columns, sea-urchin chandeliers, and seashell covered walls, this swanky Pat Kuleto–designed restaurant is loaded with style. Chef Mark Franz, who made his name at Stars, cooks up showy concoctions like spot prawns, scallops, and lobster suspended in a pyramid of aspic. The desserts, including a very adult peppermint patty, are by former Stars alumnus Emily Luchetti. ⊠ *450 Post St.,* ☎ *415/956– 6969. AE, DC, MC, V.*

Southeast Asian

Cow Hollow

$–$$ ✕ **Betelnut.** Pan-Asian offerings and an adventurous drinks menu draw a steady stream of hipsters for cuisine that is not always successful (but don't pass up a plate of the stir-fried dried anchovies, chilies, peanuts, garlic, and green onions), yet always intriguing. ⊠ *2030 Union St.,* ☎ *415/929–8855. D, DC, MC, V.*

The Mission District

$-$$ ✕ **Slanted Door.** Behind the canted facade of this trendy north Mission spot, you'll taste what owner Charles Phan describes as "real Vietnamese home cooking." The fresh spring rolls are packed with rice noodles, pork, shrimp, and pungent mint leaves, and the fried vegetarian imperial rolls conceal bean thread noodles, cabbage, and taro. The five-spice chicken, the green papaya salad, and the steamed seabass fillet are among the best dishes. ⊠ *584 Valencia St.,* ☎ *415/861–8032. MC, V. Closed Mon.*

Richmond District

$-$$ ✕ **La Vie.** This small Vietnamese restaurant caters to a mostly neighborhood clientele with traditional dishes like *nep chien* (deep-fried balls of sticky rice stuffed with a mixture of finely cut pork, shrimp, and mushrooms). One fun-to-eat entrée consists of small cakes made from shrimp, rice flour, and yellow mung beans: You wrap up the cakes in crisp lettuce leaves and dip them in a spicy fish sauce. ⊠ *5380 Geary Blvd.,* ☎ *415/668–8080. AE, MC, V.*

$-$$ ✕ **Le Soleil.** The food of Vietnam is the specialty of this light-filled restaurant. Try the excellent raw-beef salad, the crisp and flavorful spring rolls, the simple stir-fry of chicken and aromatic fresh basil leaves, or the large prawns simmered in a clay pot. ⊠ *133 Clement St.,* ☎ *415/668–4848. MC, V.*

Steak Houses

Marina

$$ ✕ **Izzy's Steak & Chop House.** Terrific steaks, chops, and seafood plus all the trimmings—such as cheesy scalloped potatoes and creamed spinach—are served here. There's validated parking at the Lombard garage. ⊠ *3345 Steiner St.,* ☎ *415/563–0487. AE, DC, MC, V. No lunch.*

Midtown

$$$ ✕ **Harris'.** Ann Harris serves some of the best dry-aged steaks in town,
★   but don't overlook the starter of spinach salad or the entrée of calves' liver with onions and bacon. Be sure to include a side of the fine creamed spinach. ⊠ *2100 Van Ness Ave.,* ☎ *415/673–1888. AE, D, DC, MC, V. No lunch.*

Vegetarian

Civic Center

$$ ✕ **Millennium.** The "organic cuisine" label translates to a menu of low-fat, dairy-free offerings that look to the Mediterranean: Pastas and polenta are among the most successful. For true believers, there is seitan (a whole-wheat meat substitute) steak in marsala sauce, a chocolate mousse cake made from tofu, and organic wines and beers. ⊠ *246 McAllister St.,* ☎ *415/487–9800. MC, V.*

Marina

$$ ✕ **Greens.** Owned and operated by the Zen Buddhist Center of Marin
★   County, this beautiful spot with expansive bay views serves à la carte on weeknights, but only a five-course prix-fixe dinner is served on Saturday. Sunday brunch is a good time for sailboat-watching. There's public parking at Fort Mason Center. ⊠ *Bldg. A, Fort Mason (enter across Marina Blvd. from Safeway),* ☎ *415/771–6222. MC, V. No lunch Mon., no dinner Sun.*

LODGING

Updated by
Wendy Smith

The hotels listed below are on or close to public transportation lines. Some properties on Lombard Street and in the Civic Center area have free parking, but parking fees at downtown and Fisherman's Wharf lodgings range between $17 and $26 a day. Reservations for all accommodations are advised, especially from May to October. Rates for double rooms downtown and at the wharf start at about $100 (slightly less on weekdays and off-season), not including the city's hefty 14% transient occupancy tax. For those in search of true budget accommodations (under $50), try the **Adelaide Inn** (☞ Union Square/Downtown, *below*) or the **YMCA Central Branch** (✉ 220 Golden Gate Ave., ☎ 415/885–0460).

An alternative to hotels and motels is staying in private homes and apartments, available through **American Family Inn/Bed & Breakfast San Francisco** (✉ Box 420009, San Francisco 94142, ☎ 415/931–3083, FAX 415/921–2273), **Bed & Breakfast California** (✉ 205 Park Rd., Suite 209, Burlingame 94010, ☎ 650/696–1690 or 800/872–4500, FAX 650/696–1699), and **American Property Exchange** (✉ 2800 Lombard St., San Francisco 94109, ☎ 415/863–8484, FAX 415/440–1008).

CATEGORY	COST*
$$$$	over $175
$$$	$120–$175
$$	$80–$120
$	under $80

All prices are for a standard double room, excluding 14% tax.

Union Square/Downtown

$$$$
★ 🎬 **Campton Place.** Behind a simple brownstone facade, quiet reigns. Highly attentive personal service begins the moment doormen greet guests outside the marble-floor lobby. Rooms, though small, are smartly decorated with Asian touches in subtle earth tones. The Campton Place Restaurant is famed for its breakfasts. Wednesday martini nights (from 5:30 to 8:30) in the lounge, with specially priced martinis and live music, have become a favorite midweek cruising ground. ✉ *340 Stockton St., 94108,* ☎ *415/781–5555 or 800/235–4300,* FAX *415/955–5536. 117 rooms. Restaurant, bar, in-room safes, minibars, no-smoking rooms, room service, laundry service and dry cleaning, concierge, meeting rooms, parking (fee). AE, DC, MC, V.*

$$$$ 🎬 **The Clift.** This Ian Schrager property, one of the city's grand dames, is a study in elegance. Some rooms are rich with dark woods and burgundies, others are refreshingly pastel, and all have large writing desks. The Art Deco Redwood Room, with its chandeliers, tinkling piano music, and sweeping redwood bar, is a must see from another era. ✉ *495 Geary St., 94102,* ☎ *415/775–4700 or 800/652–5438,* FAX *415/441–4621. 326 rooms. Restaurant, bar, in-room modem lines, minibars, no-smoking floor, room service, exercise room, laundry service and dry cleaning, concierge, meeting rooms, parking (fee). AE, DC, MC, V.*

$$$$
★ 🎬 **Hotel Monaco.** With its fanciful beaux arts–style facade, the Monaco stands in stark contrast to its more stately neighbor, the Clift. The small rooms are comfortable and inviting, with Chinese-inspired armoires and high-back upholstered chairs, but the riot of stripes and colors— pistachio and persimmon in one scheme; cherry red, royal blue, and apple green in another—though tasteful, may strike some as a bit outré. ✉ *501 Geary St., 94102,* ☎ *415/292–0100 or 800/214–4220,* FAX *415/292–0111. 221 rooms. Restaurant, bar, in-room modem lines, no-smoking rooms, room service, spa, laundry service and dry cleaning, business services, parking (fee). AE, D, DC, MC, V.*

Downtown San Francisco Lodging

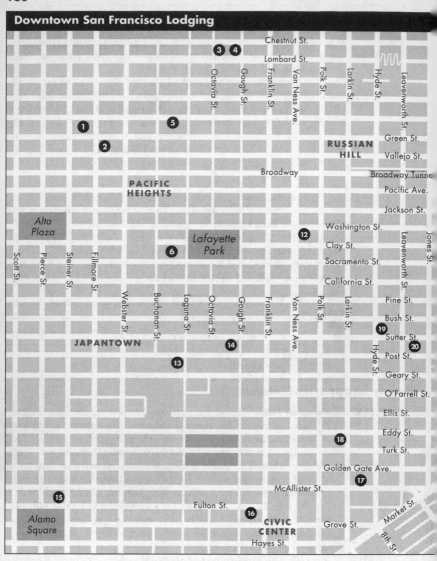

The Abigail, **17**
Adelaide Inn, **21**
The Andrews, **20**
The Archbishop's Mansion, **15**
Bed and Breakfast Inn, **5**
Bijou, **48**
Campton Place, **41**
Chancellor Hotel, **39**

The Clarion, **57**
The Clift, **34**
Commodore International, **22**
Embassy Suites San Francisco Airport—Burlingame, **53**
The Fairmont, **27**
Galleria Park, **44**
Harbor Court, **52**

Holiday Lodge and Garden Hotel, **12**
Hotel Bohème, **49**
Hotel Diva, **33**
Hotel Majestic, **14**
Hotel Monaco, **35**
Hotel Rex, **30**
Hotel Triton, **45**
The Huntington, **25**

Hyatt at Fisherman's Wharf, **8**
Hyatt Regency, **47**
Inn at the Opera, **16**
Inn at Union Square, **38**
King George, **37**
La Quinta Motor Inn, **54**
Mandarin Oriental, **50**

$$$$ 🏨 **Hotel Triton.** The Triton caters to fashion, entertainment, music, and film-industry types, who appreciate the iridescent pink-and-gold-painted rooms with S-curve dervish chairs, curly-neck lamps, and oddball light fixtures. Attached to the hotel is the trendy newsstand, coffeehouse, and dining room, the Café de la Presse, a gathering place for many foreign visitors. ✉ *342 Grant Ave., 94108,* ☎ *415/394–0500 or 800/433–6611,* 📠 *415/394–0555. 140 rooms. In-room modem lines, no-smoking floors, exercise room, laundry service, business services, meeting rooms, parking (fee). AE, D, MC, V.*

$$$$ 🏨 **Pan Pacific Hotel.** Exotic flower arrangements and Asian accents set this business hotel apart from others. A graceful sculpture, *Joie de Dance,* encircles the fountain in the lobby, where two fireplaces add to the refined atmosphere. Guest rooms contain amenities like fax machines and modem lines, not to mention bathrooms lined with terra-cotta Portuguese marble. The hotel's restaurant, Pacific, is well regarded for its California cuisine. ✉ *500 Post St., 94102,* ☎ *415/771–8600 or 800/327–8585,* 📠 *415/398–0267. 330 rooms. Restaurant, bar, lobby lounge, in-room modem lines, minibars, no-smoking floors, room service, exercise room, piano, laundry service and dry cleaning, concierge, business services, meeting rooms, parking (fee). AE, D, DC, MC, V.*

$$$$ 🏨 **Prescott Hotel.** The Prescott's rooms, which vary only in size and
★ shape, are traditional in style and decorated in a rich hunter green; bathrooms have marble-top sinks and gold fixtures. Complimentary coffee and tea service and evening wine and cheese receptions are held in the hunting-lodge-style living room, and guests can either dine in or order room service from Wolfgang Puck's famed Postrio, the hotel's on-site restaurant. ✉ *545 Post St., 94102,* ☎ *415/563–0303 or 800/283–7322,* 📠 *415/563–6831. 164 rooms. Restaurant, bar, lobby lounge, in-room modem lines, no-smoking floors, room service, concierge, business services, meeting rooms, parking (fee). AE, D, DC, MC, V.*

$$$$ 🏨 **Sir Francis Drake.** The Drake's opulent lobby has wrought-iron balustrades, chandeliers, and Italian marble, but the guest rooms have the flavor of a B&B, with Spanish colonial–style furnishings and floral-print fabrics. The decor appeals to pleasure travelers, but business travelers will appreciate the modem hookups and voice mail. ✉ *450 Powell St., 94102,* ☎ *415/392–7755 or 800/227–5480,* 📠 *415/395–8559. 417 rooms. 2 restaurants, in-room modem lines, no-smoking rooms, nightclub, concierge, meeting rooms, parking (fee). AE, D, DC, MC, V.*

$$$$ 🏨 **Westin St. Francis.** With an imposing facade, black marble lobby, and gold-top columns, this landmark property looks more like a great public building than a hotel. The effect is softened by the columns and exquisite woodwork of the Compass Rose bar and restaurant. Many rooms in the original building are small by modern standards, but all have Empire-style furnishings and retain their original Victorian-style molding. Rooms in the modern tower are larger, with Oriental-style lacquered furniture. For a spectacular view of the city, ask for a room above the 15th floor. ✉ *335 Powell St., 94102,* ☎ *415/397–7000 or 800/228–3000,* 📠 *415/774–0124. 1,189 rooms. 3 restaurants, 2 bars, in-room modem lines, in-room safes, no-smoking floors, room service, exercise room, nightclub, concierge, business services, meeting rooms, travel services, parking (fee). AE, D, DC, MC, V.*

$$$–$$$$ 🏨 **Hotel Rex.** The Rex celebrates literary and artistic creativity: Antiquarian books line the 1920s-style lobby, original artworks adorn the walls, and book readings and roundtable discussions are held in the common areas. Writing desks, lamps with hand-painted shades, and period furnishings evoke the spirit of 1920s salon society. ✉ *562 Sutter St., 94102,* ☎ *415/433–4434,* 📠 *415/433–3695. 94 rooms. Bar, lobby lounge, in-room modem lines, minibars, no-smoking rooms,* *laundry service and dry cleaning, concierge, parking (fee). AE, D, DC, MC, V.*

$$$–$$$$ ⊞ **Vintage Court.** This bit of the Napa Valley off Union Square has inviting rooms decorated with jade and rose floral fabrics. Complimentary wine is served nightly in front of the lobby fireplace. The lobby is home to Masa's, one of the city's finest French restaurants, and guests have access to a health club one block away. ⊠ *650 Bush St., 94108,* ☎ *415/392–4666 or 800/654–1100,* ℻ *415/433–4065. 107 rooms. Restaurant, bar, minibars, no-smoking floors, refrigerators, parking (fee). Continental breakfast. AE, D, DC, MC, V.*

$$$ ⊞ **Chancellor Hotel.** Though not as grand as some of its neighbors, this busy hotel more than lives up to its promise of comfort without extravagance—it's one of the best buys on Union Square. The moderate-size Edwardian-style rooms have high ceilings and peach and green color schemes. ⊠ *433 Powell St., 94102,* ☎ *415/362–2004 or 800/428– 4748,* ℻ *415/362–1403. 137 rooms. Restaurant, bar, no-smoking floors, room service, concierge, parking (fee). AE, D, DC, MC, V.*

$$$ ⊞ **Galleria Park.** A few blocks east of Union Square, this hotel with
★   a black marble facade is close to the Chinatown Gate and Crocker Galleria shopping arcade. The staff is remarkably pleasant and helpful. The comfortable rooms all have floral bedspreads, stylish striped wallpaper, and white furniture that includes a writing desk. A massive fireplace dominates the lobby, where complimentary coffee and tea are served in the mornings, wine in the evenings. ⊠ *191 Sutter St., 94104,* ☎ *415/ 781–3060 or 800/792–9639,* ℻ *415/433–4409. 177 rooms. 2 restaurants, in-room modem lines, minibars, no-smoking floors, room service, exercise room, jogging, concierge, business services, meeting rooms. AE, D, DC, MC, V.*

$$$ ⊞ **Hotel Diva.** The Diva's proximity to the Curran Theater attracts guests of an artistic bent, but the hotel is also popular with business travelers and tourists. The black-and-silver color scheme with touches of gray extends to the nightclub-esque lobby and to the rooms, which are comfortable but not fussy. ⊠ *440 Geary St., 94102,* ☎ *415/885–0200 or 800/553–1900,* ℻ *415/346–6613. 111 rooms. Restaurant, in-room modem lines, in-room safes, no-smoking floors, exercise room, business services, meeting room. AE, D, DC, MC, V.*

$$$ ⊞ **Inn at Union Square.** With its tiny but captivating lobby with trompe l'oeil bookshelves painted on the walls, this inn feels like someone's home. Comfortable Georgian-style rooms with sumptuous goosedown pillows promote indolence. Complimentary breakfast, afternoon tea, and evening wine and hors d'oeuvres are served in front of a fireplace in a sitting area on each floor. Tipping is not permitted. ⊠ *440 Post St., 94102,* ☎ *415/397–3510 or 800/288–4346,* ℻ *415/989– 0529. 30 rooms. No-smoking floors, parking (fee). Continental breakfast. AE, DC, MC, V.*

$$$ ⊞ **The Maxwell.** A simple but snappy-looking hotel a few blocks from Union Square, the Maxwell has a Victorian-style lobby with a green velvet sofa and boldly patterned chairs. Rooms have a clubby, retro feel and deep jewel tones. ⊠ *386 Geary St., 94102,* ☎ *415/986–2000 or 888/734–6299,* ℻ *415/397–2447. 153 rooms. Restaurant, bar, in-room modem lines, no-smoking floors, room service, laundry service, concierge, parking (fee). AE, D, DC, MC, V.*

$$$ ⊞ **Petite Auberge.** The dozens of teddy bears in the reception area may seem a bit precious, but the rooms in this re-creation of a French country inn never stray past the mark. They're small, but each has a teddy bear, bright flowered wallpaper, an old-fashioned writing desk, and a much-needed armoire—there's little or no closet space. Most rooms have working fireplaces; deluxe suites come equipped with Jacuzzi tubs. ⊠ *863 Bush St., 94108,* ☎ *415/928–6000 or 800/365–3004,* ℻ *415/*

775–5717. 26 rooms. Breakfast room, no-smoking floors, parking (fee). Full breakfast. AE, DC, MC, V.

$$$ ⊞ **White Swan Inn.** The White Swan has all the comforts of home—personal front-door keys, complimentary soft drinks, and free daily newspapers. Rooms are large, with dark wood furniture and an English country theme. Afternoon tea is served in the lounge, where comfortable chairs and sofas invite lingering. ⊠ *845 Bush St., 94108, ☎ 415/775–1755 or 800/999–9570, ℻ 415/775–5717. 26 rooms. Breakfast room, meeting rooms, parking (fee). Full breakfast. AE, MC, V.*

$$$ ⊞ **York Hotel.** Hitchcock fans may recognize the facade of this reasonably priced hotel; Kim Novak hid out here in *Vertigo*. The moderate-size rooms—done in terra-cotta, burgundy, and forest green—are a tasteful mix of Mediterranean styles, and all have huge closets. ⊠ *940 Sutter St., 94109, ☎ 415/885–6800 or 800/808–9675, ℻ 415/885–2115. 96 rooms. Bar, no-smoking floors, exercise room, nightclub, concierge, parking (fee). Continental breakfast. AE, D, DC, MC, V.*

$$–$$$ ⊞ **King George.** Behind the George's white-and-green Victorian facade, rooms are compact but nicely furnished in English style, with walnut furniture and a muted rose color scheme. British and Japanese tourists and suburban couples seeking a weekend getaway frequent this adult-oriented hotel. ⊠ *334 Mason St., 94102, ☎ 415/781–5050 or 800/288–6005, ℻ 415/391–6976. 143 rooms. Tea shop, no-smoking floors, meeting rooms, parking (fee). AE, D, DC, MC, V.*

$$ ⊞ **The Andrews.** Two blocks west of Union Square, this Queen Anne–style structure with a gray-and-white facade began its life as the Sultan Turkish Baths in 1905. Victorian antique reproductions, old-fashioned flower curtains with lace sheers, iron bedsteads, and large closets more than make up for the diminutive guest rooms and baths. ⊠ *624 Post St., 94109, ☎ 415/563–6877 or 800/926–3739, ℻ 415/928–6919. 48 rooms. Restaurant, no-smoking rooms, concierge, parking (fee). Continental breakfast. AE, MC, V.*

$$ ⊞ **Bijou.** With plush velvet upholstery and rich detailing, this hotel is decorated as a nostalgic tribute to 1930s cinema; the small, inexpensive rooms are decorated with black-and-white prints from the same classic films (many of which are San Francisco–themed) that are shown in the hotel's video room. The staff is friendly, but the service is definitely no-frills. ⊠ *111 Mason St., at Eddy St., 94102, ☎ 415/771–1200 or 800/771–1022, ℻ 415/346–3196. 65 rooms. No-smoking rooms, laundry service, parking (fee). AE, D, DC, MC, V.*

$$ ⊞ **Commodore International.** Entering the lobby is like stepping onto the deck of an ocean liner of yore: Neodeco chairs look like the backdrop for a film about transatlantic crossings, and steps away is the Titanic Cafe, where goldfish bowls and bathysphere-inspired lights add to the sea-cruise mood. The fairly large rooms with monster closets are painted in soft yellows and golds. ⊠ *825 Sutter St., 94109, ☎ 415/923–6800 or 800/338–6848, ℻ 415/923–6804. 113 rooms. Restaurant, no-smoking rooms, nightclub, laundry service and dry cleaning, parking (fee). AE, D, MC, V.*

$ ⊞ **Adelaide Inn.** The bedspreads at this quiet retreat may not match the drapes or carpets, and the floors may creak, but the rooms are sunny, clean, and remarkably cheap. Tucked away in an alley, the funky European-style pension hosts many guests from Germany, France, and Italy. ⊠ *5 Isadora Duncan Ct., at Taylor St. between Geary and Post Sts., 94102, ☎ 415/441–2474 or 415/441–2261, ℻ 415/441–0161. 18 rooms. Breakfast room, refrigerators. AE, MC, V.*

Financial District

$$$$ ⊞ **Hyatt Regency.** The drab, bunkerlike exterior of the Hyatt Regency gives no hint of the spectacular 17-story atrium lobby within. Rooms, some with bay-view balconies, have cherry-wood furniture and either black-and-brown or soft rose-and-plum color schemes. The Embarcadero Center's shops and restaurants are nearby. ⊠ *5 Embarcadero Center, 94111,* ☎ *415/788–1234 or 800/233–1234,* FAX *415/398–2567. 805 rooms. 2 restaurants, bar, lobby lounge, no-smoking floors, room service, exercise room, concierge, parking (fee). AE, D, DC, MC, V.*

$$$$ ⊞ **Mandarin Oriental.** The Mandarin comprises the top 11 floors (38
★   to 48) of San Francisco's third-tallest building (the First Interstate Center). All the rooms have vistas of the city and beyond. Rooms are decorated in creamy yellow with black accents; the Mandarin Rooms have bathtubs flanked by large windows. ⊠ *222 Sansome St., 94104,* ☎ *415/885–0999 or 800/622–0404,* FAX *415/433–0289. 158 rooms. Lobby lounge, in-room modem lines, minibars, no-smoking floors, room service, health club, laundry service and dry cleaning, concierge, business services, meeting rooms, parking (fee). AE, D, DC, MC, V.*

$$$$ ⊞ **Palace Hotel.** This landmark hotel—former guests include Woodrow Wilson and Amelia Earhart—has a business center, a health club, and an indoor lap pool. The rooms are not as lavish as the common areas, but modern amenities are carefully integrated into the decor, from the TV inside the mahogany armoire to the phone in the marble bathroom. ⊠ *2 New Montgomery St., 94105,* ☎ *415/521–1111 or 800/325–3535,* FAX *415/543–0671. 553 rooms. 3 restaurants, bar, room service, health club, laundry service, parking (fee). AE, D, DC, MC, V.*

$$$$ ⊞ **Park Hyatt.** Contemporary design meets Old World style at this well-managed hotel convenient to the waterfront, downtown, and the South of Market area. The spacious rooms have stylish furniture, fresh flowers, and amenities that include voice mail and top-quality toiletries. ⊠ *333 Battery St., 94111,* ☎ *415/392–1234 or 800/492–8822,* FAX *415/ 421–2433. 313 rooms, 47 suites. Restaurant, 2 bars, in-room modem lines, minibars, room service, laundry service, dry-cleaning, business services, conference center, valet parking (fee). AE, D, DC, MC, V.*

$$$–$$$$ ⊞ **Harbor Court.** This cozy former YMCA is noted for exemplary ser-
★   vice. The small rooms have either bay or garden views, and guests have free access to the adjacent YMCA (including a 150-ft heated indoor pool). Complimentary limousine service to the Financial District is provided. ⊠ *165 Steuart St., 94105,* ☎ *415/882–1300 or 800/346– 0555,* FAX *415/882–1313. 136 rooms. In-room modem lines, minibars, no-smoking floors, room service, business services, parking (fee). AE, D, DC, MC, V.*

Nob Hill

$$$$ ⊞ **The Fairmont.** A soaring vaulted ceiling, towering faux-marble
★   columns, gilt mirrors, red-velvet upholstered chairs, and a grand wraparound staircase are among the architectural elements of the Fairmont's awe-inspiring lobby. The tower rooms, which have city and bay views, reflect a more modern style than their smaller Victorian counterparts in the older building. ⊠ *950 Mason St., 94108,* ☎ *415/772– 5000 or 800/527–4727,* FAX *415/837–0587. 596 rooms. 4 restaurants, 5 bars, room service, barbershop, beauty salon, spa, health club, babysitting, laundry service and dry cleaning, concierge, business services, car rental. AE, D, DC, MC, V.*

$$$$ ⊞ **The Huntington.** Attentive personal service is the hallmark of this quiet hotel. Rooms and suites reflect the Huntington's traditional style, albeit with a '90s bent: Velvets and raw silks are combined in cocoa, gold, and burgundy color schemes. ⊠ *1075 California St., 94108,* ☎ *415/474–5400 or 800/227–4683; 800/652–1539 in CA;* FAX *415/ 474–6227. 137 rooms. Restaurant, bar, in-room modem lines, no-smoking rooms, room service, laundry service and dry cleaning, concierge, meeting rooms. AE, D, DC, MC, V.*

*$90 stay AV
Ramada Fisherman wharf
Plaza*

or

$$$$ 🏨 **Mark Hopkins Inter-Continental.** Rooms at this landmark have dramatic neoclassical furnishings of gray, silver, and khaki; Italian marble lines the bathrooms. Rooms on high floors have views of either the Golden Gate Bridge or the downtown cityscape. No visit would be complete without a trip to the panoramic Top of the Mark, *the* rooftop lounge in San Francisco since 1939. ⊠ *999 California St., 94108, ☎ 415/392–3434 or 800/662–4455, FAX 415/421–3302. 392 rooms. 2 restaurants, 2 lounges, room service, exercise room, laundry service and dry cleaning, concierge, business services, car rental. AE, D, DC, MC, V.*

$$$$ 🏨 **Nob Hill Lambourne.** This urban retreat, designed with the travel-
★ ing executive in mind, takes pride in pampering business travelers with personal computers, fax machines, and personalized voice mail; an on-site spa with massages, body scrubs, and manicures helps them relax. Rooms have queen-size beds with hand-sewn mattresses, silk-damask bedding, and contemporary furnishings in muted colors. ⊠ *725 Pine St., at Stockton St., 94108, ☎ 415/433–2287 or 800/274–8466, FAX 415/433–0975. 20 rooms. Lobby lounge, in-room modem lines, kitchenettes, no-smoking floors, in-room VCRs, spa, business services, parking (fee). Continental breakfast AE, D, DC, MC, V.*

$$$$ 🏨 **Ritz-Carlton, San Francisco.** Consistently rated one of the top ho-
★ tels in the world by *Condé Nast Traveler*, the Ritz-Carlton is a stunning tribute to beauty, splendor, and warm, sincere service. Crystal chandeliers and museum-quality 18th- and 19th-century oil paintings adorn an opulent lobby. Rooms are spacious, and their bathrooms have double sinks, hair dryers, and vanity tables. ⊠ *600 Stockton St., at California St., 94108, ☎ 415/296–7465 or 800/241–3333, FAX 415/296–8261. 336 rooms. 2 restaurants, bar, lobby lounge, laundry service and dry cleaning, concierge, business services, meeting rooms, parking (fee). AE, D, DC, MC, V.*

Fisherman's Wharf/North Beach

$$$–$$$$ 🏨 **Hyatt at Fisherman's Wharf.** Location is the key to this hotel's popularity with business travelers and families. The moderate-size guest rooms, a medley of greens and burgundies, have double-pane windows to keep out the often considerable street noise. Each floor has a laundry room. ⊠ *555 N. Point St., 94133, ☎ 415/563–1234 or 800/233–1234, FAX 415/563–2218. 313 rooms. Restaurant, sports bar, no-smoking floors, outdoor pool, outdoor hot tub, health club, coin laundry, meeting rooms, parking (fee). AE, D, DC, MC, V.*

$$$–$$$$ 🏨 **Marriott at Fisherman's Wharf.** Behind an unremarkable sand-color facade, the Marriott strikes a grand note in its lavish, low-ceiling lobby, with marble floors and English club–style furniture. Rooms, all with turquoise, blue, and white color schemes, have dark wood and either a king-size bed or two double beds. ⊠ *1250 Columbus Ave., 94133, ☎ 415/775–7555 or 800/228–9290, FAX 415/474–2099. 285 rooms. Restaurant, bar, no-smoking floors, health club, meeting rooms, parking (fee). AE, D, DC, MC, V.*

$$$ 🏨 **Tuscan Inn.** The condolike exterior of the inn—reddish brick with white concrete—gives little indication of the charm of the relatively small, Italian-influenced guest rooms, with their white-pine furniture and floral bedspreads and curtains. Room service is provided by Cafe Pescatore, the Italian seafood restaurant off the lobby. ⊠ *425 N. Point St., at Mason St., 94133, ☎ 415/561–1100 or 800/648–4626, FAX 415/561–1199. 208 rooms. Restaurant, room service, meeting rooms. AE, D, DC, MC, V.*

$$–$$$ 🏨 **Hotel Bohème.** In the middle of historic North Beach, this little bargain gives guests a taste of the past. The small rooms, decorated with

12.00

Cfm # 380442

2 Rooms

European armoires, bistro tables, and memorabilia from the '50s and '60s, recall the beat generation. ✉ *444 Columbus Ave., 94133,* ☎ *415/ 433–9111,* FAX *415/362–6292. 16 rooms. AE, D, MC, V.*

$$–$$$ 🏨 **Travelodge Hotel at Fisherman's Wharf.** Taking up an entire city block, the Travelodge is the only bay-front hotel at Fisherman's Wharf and is known for its reasonable rates (as low as $89 in the off season). Rooms are simply and brightly furnished with lacquered blond-wood furniture, leather chairs, and rose-color drapes and bedspreads. ✉ *250 Beach St., 94133,* ☎ *415/392–6700 or 800/578–7878,* FAX *415/986– 7853. 250 rooms. 3 restaurants, no-smoking rooms, outdoor pool, parking (fee). AE, D, DC, MC, V.*

Radisson

Std King

119.00

99.00

$–$$ 🏨 **San Remo.** This three-story blue-and-white Italianate Victorian has
★ a down-home ambience. The somewhat cramped rooms are crowded with furniture: vanities, rag rugs, pedestal sinks, ceiling fans, antique armoires, and brass, iron, or wooden beds. Guests share six shower rooms, one bathtub chamber, and six scrupulously clean toilets with brass pull chains and oak tanks. ✉ *2237 Mason St., 94133,* ☎ *415/ 776–8688 or 800/352–7366,* FAX *415/776–2811. 62 rooms. No-smoking rooms, parking (fee). AE, DC, MC, V.*

Pacific Heights, Cow Hollow, and the Marina

$$$$ 🏨 **Sherman House.** This landmark mansion on a low hill in residen-
★ tial Pacific Heights is San Francisco's most luxurious small hotel. Rooms are decorated with Biedermeier, English Jacobean, or French Second Empire antiques. Tapestry-like canopies over four-poster feath- erbeds, wood-burning fireplaces with marble mantels, and black-gran- ite bathrooms—some with whirlpool baths—complete the picture. ✉ *2160 Green St., 94123,* ☎ *415/563–3600 or 800/424–5777,* FAX *415/ 563–1882. 14 rooms. Dining room, room service, in-room VCRs, piano, concierge, airport shuttle. AE, DC, MC, V.*

$$$ 🏨 **Union Street Inn.** This ivy-draped Edwardian 1902 B&B affords a
★ cozy intimacy that has made it popular with honeymooners and other romantics. The private Carriage House, which has its own whirlpool tub, is separated from the main house by an English garden complete with lemon trees. Guests enjoy elaborate breakfasts served in the par- lor, the garden, or in their rooms. ✉ *2229 Union St., 94123,* ☎ *415/ 346–0424,* FAX *415/922–8046. 6 rooms. Breakfast room, no-smoking rooms, parking (fee). Full breakfast. AE, MC, V.*

$$ 🏨 **Holiday Lodge and Garden Hotel.** This three-story hotel with a red- wood-and-stone facade has a laid-back, West Coast mood. Rooms ei- ther overlook or open onto landscaped grounds with palm trees and a heated swimming pool. White beamed ceilings, beige wood panel- ing, and floral bedspreads give the rooms a vaguely '50s look. ✉ *1901 Van Ness Ave., 94109,* ☎ *415/776–4469 or 800/367–8504,* FAX *415/ 474–7046. 77 rooms. Kitchenettes, free parking. Continental break- fast. AE, D, DC, MC, V.*

$–$$$ 🏨 **Bed and Breakfast Inn.** Rooms at San Francisco's first B&B evoke the English countryside with antiques, plants, and floral paintings. The rooms with shared bath are quite small, but the Mayfair, a private apart- ment above the main house, and the Garden Suite, an even more deluxe apartment, are spacious alternatives for families or larger par- ties. ✉ *4 Charlton Ct., at Union St., 94123,* ☎ *415/921–9784. 9 rooms, 5 with bath, 2 apartments. Breakfast room, parking (fee). Continen- tal breakfast . No credit cards.*

$ 🏨 **Marina Inn.** This inn five blocks from the Marina offers B&B-style accommodations at motel prices. English country–style rooms are sparsely appointed, with queen-size two-poster beds, small pine-wood writing desks, nightstands, and armoires; the wallpaper and bedspreads are aggressively floral. ✉ *3110 Octavia St., at Lombard St., 94123,* ☎ *415/928–1000 or 800/274–1420,* FAX *415/928–5909. 40 rooms. Lobby lounge, no-smoking floor, barbershop, beauty salon. Continental breakfast. AE, MC, V.*

$ 📺 **Town House Motel.** What this recently renovated, family-oriented motel lacks in luxury and ambience, it makes up for in value: The simple rooms are nicely furnished with a southwestern pastel color scheme and lacquered-wood furnishings. ✉ *1650 Lombard St., 94123,* ☎ *415/ 885–5163 or 800/255–1516,* FAX *415/771–9889. 24 rooms. Airport shuttle, free parking. Continental breakfast . AE, D, DC, MC, V.*

Civic Center/Van Ness

$$$$ 📺 **Radisson Miyako Hotel.** Asian travelers and others with a taste for the East patronize this pagoda-style hotel in Japantown. Some rooms are in the tower building; others are in the garden wing, which has traditional seasonal gardens. Japanese-style rooms have futon beds with tatami mats; western rooms have traditional beds with mattresses. Japanese touches include shojis, and most accommodations have soaking rooms with a bucket, a stool, and a deep, Japanese-style tub. *1625 Post St., at Laguna St., 94115,* ☎ *415/922–3200 or 800/533–4567,* FAX *415/ 921–0417. 218 rooms. Restaurant, bar, exercise room, laundry service and dry cleaning, business services. AE, D, DC, MC, V.*

$$$–$$$$ 📺 **The Archbishop's Mansion.** This romantic hotel's 15 guest rooms,
★   each named for a famous opera, are decorated with intricately carved antiques; many have Jacuzzi tubs or fireplaces. The mansion isn't within easy walking distance of restaurants or tourist attractions, but its perch on the corner of Alamo Square near the Painted Ladies—San Francisco's famous Victorian homes—makes for a scenic, relaxed stay. ✉ *1000 Fulton St., 94117,* ☎ *415/563–7872 or 800/543–5820,* FAX *415/885–3193. 15 rooms. Breakfast room, lobby lounge, no-smoking rooms, in-room VCRs, piano, meeting room, free parking. Continental breakfast . AE, MC, V.*

$$$–$$$$ 📺 **Hotel Majestic.** One of San Francisco's original grand hotels, this five-story yellow-and-white Edwardian with gingerbread and scrollwork looks like a wedding cake. Most of the smallish rooms have fireplaces and either a hand-painted, four-poster canopied bed or two-poster bonnet twin beds, and most have a mix of French Empire and English antiques and custom furniture. ✉ *1500 Sutter St., 94109,* ☎ *415/441– 1100 or 800/869–8966,* FAX *415/673–7331. 57 rooms. Restaurant, bar, laundry service and dry cleaning, parking (fee). AE, DC, MC, V.*

$$$ 📺 **Inn at the Opera.** Behind the marble-floor lobby of this seven-story
★   hotel are rooms decorated with creamy pastels and dark wood furnishings. Even the smallest singles have queen-size beds. Sheet music lines the bureau drawers, and every room contains terry-cloth robes, a microwave, a minibar, fresh flowers, and a basket of apples. Those in the know say the back rooms are the quietest. ✉ *333 Fulton St., 94102,* ☎ *415/863–8400 or 800/325–2708; 800/423–9610 in CA;* FAX *415/861–0821. 48 rooms. Restaurant, lobby lounge, room service, concierge, parking (fee). Continental breakfast . AE, DC, MC, V.*

$$$ 📺 **The Mansions.** This twin-turreted 1887 Queen Anne is one of the most unusual hotels in the city. Rooms contain an odd collection of furnishings, varying in theme from the tiny Tom Thumb room to the opulent Josephine suite. Owner Bob Pritikin's pig painting and other "porkabilia"—the resident ghost, Claudia, has a penchant for pigs— are scattered throughout the hotel. ✉ *2220 Sacramento St., 94115,* ☎ *415/929–9444,* FAX *415/567–9391. 26 rooms. Breakfast room, dining room, billiards, laundry service, parking (fee). Full breakfast . AE, DC, MC, V.*

$$-$$$ 🏨 **The Abigail.** Faux-stone walls, a faux-marble front desk, and an old-fashioned telephone booth in the lobby typify the eclectic decor at this smallish hotel in a marginal neighborhood. Hissing steam radiators, down comforters, and antiques complete the mood. ✉ 246 McAllister St., 94102, ☎ 415/861–9728 or 800/243–6510, FAX 415/861–5848. 60 rooms. Restaurant, laundry service. AE, D, DC, MC, V.

$$ 🏨 **Phoenix Hotel.** This hideaway of the hip and famous on the edge of the scruffy Tenderloin district is a little bit south-of-the-equator and a little bit Gilligan's Island. The bungalow-style rooms, decorated with bamboo furniture and works of San Francisco artists, have white-beam ceilings, white wooden walls, and vivid tropical-print bedspreads. ✉ 601 Eddy St., 94109, ☎ 415/776–1380 or 800/248–9466, FAX 415/885–3109. 44 rooms. Restaurant, bar, room service, outdoor pool, massage, nightclub, laundry service, free parking. AE, D, DC, MC, V.

The Airport

Because they cater primarily to midweek business travelers, airport hotels often cut weekend prices drastically; be sure to inquire. Airport shuttle buses and a full complement of services are provided by all the following hotels.

$$$$ 🏨 **Embassy Suites San Francisco Airport–Burlingame** (✉ 150 Anza Blvd., Burlingame 94010, ☎ 650/342–4600 or 800/362–2779, FAX 650/343–8137). 🏨 **San Francisco Airport Hilton** (✉ San Francisco International Airport, Box 8355, 94128, ☎ 650/589–0770 or 800/445–8667, FAX 650/589–4696). 🏨 **The Westin** (✉ 1 Old Bayshore Hwy., Millbrae 94030, ☎ 650/692–3500 or 800/228–3000, FAX 650/872–8111).

$$–$$$ 🏨 **The Clarion** (✉ 401 E. Millbrae Ave., Millbrae 94030, ☎ 650/692–6363 or 800/223–7111, FAX 650/697–8556). 🏨 **La Quinta Motor Inn** (✉ 20 Airport Blvd., South San Francisco 94080, ☎ 650/583–2223 or 800/531–5900, FAX 650/589–6770).

$ 🏨 **Red Roof Inn.** (✉ 777 Airport Blvd., Burlingame 94010, ☎ 650/342–7772 or 800/843–7663, FAX 650/342–2635).

NIGHTLIFE AND THE ARTS

Updated by
Wendy Smith

A spirit of playfulness has pervaded San Francisco's arts, entertainment, and nightlife scenes ever since its days as a rowdy sailors' port. Perhaps nothing is more purely San Franciscan than *Beach Blanket Babylon,* a raucous cabaret act at Club Fugazi. The San Francisco Opera, the San Francisco Symphony, and the San Francisco Ballet are all nationally renowned, and dozens of alternative groups represent everything from performance art to family circus and mime.

Nightlife

Rock, Pop, Folk, and Blues

Bottom of the Hill (✉ 1233 17th St., at Texas St., ☎ 415/626–4455), in the Potrero Hill District, showcases some of the city's best local alternative rock and blues. **DNA Lounge** (✉ 375 11th St., near Harrison St., ☎ 415/626–1409), a two-floor SoMa haunt, hosts independent rock, funk, and rap on most weekends and DJ dancing on weeknights. **The Fillmore** (✉ 1805 Geary Blvd., at Fillmore St., ☎ 415/346–6000), one of the city's most famous rock music halls, also hosts national and local reggae, jazz, comedy, folk, and other acts. The **Freight and Salvage Coffee House** (✉ 1111 Addison St., Berkeley, ☎ 510/548–1761), one of the finest folk houses in the country, is worth a trip across the bay. Blues, Cajun, and bluegrass artists also perform in this smoke- and alcohol-free space.

The **Great American Music Hall** (✉ 859 O'Farrell St., at Polk St., ☎ 415/885–0750) hosts top-drawer entertainment—blues, folk, jazz, alternative rock, and occasionally comedy. The **Last Day Saloon** (✉ 406 Clement St., at 5th Ave., ☎ 415/387–6343) presents blues, Cajun, rock, and jazz. The **Red Devil Lounge** (✉ 1695 Polk St., at Clay St., ☎ 415/921–1695) is a trendy supper club that hosts jazz, funk, and rock acts, along with the occasional DJ dance night. **Slim's** (✉ 333 11th St., near Folsom St., ☎ 415/522–0333) specializes in what it labels "American roots music"—blues, jazz, and classic rock, and also presents alternative rock "spoken word" concerts.

Jazz

Bruno's (✉ 2389 Mission St., at 19th St., ☎ 415/550–7455) is a slice of retro heaven in the Mission District. Drink swanky cocktails while listening to jazz, swing, and other bands. **Cafe du Nord** (✉ 2170 Market St., at Sanchez St., ☎ 415/979–6545) hosts lively jam sessions in a "speakeasy hip" environment. The **Elbo Room** (✉ 647 Valencia St., between 17th and 18th Sts., ☎ 415/552–7788) is a convivial spot to hear up-and-coming jazz acts upstairs or relax in the hopping environs downstairs. **Enrico's** (✉ 504 Broadway, at Kearny St., ☎ 415/982–6223), a beat-era hangout, is hip once again—the indoor/outdoor café has a high-life ambience, a fine menu (tapas and Italian), and mellow nightly jazz combos. **Jazz at Pearl's** (✉ 256 Columbus Ave., near Broadway, ☎ 415/291–8255) is a good bet—there's rarely a cover and the talent level is remarkably high. **Kimball's East** (✉ 5800 Shellmound St., Emeryville, ☎ 510/658–2555), in a shopping complex off I–80 near Oakland, hosts such talents as El DeBarge, Jeffrey Osborne, and Mose Allison. With an elegant interior and fine food, it's one of the Bay Area's most luxurious supper clubs. The **Up and Down Club** (✉ 1151 Folsom St., ☎ 415/626–2388), a hip restaurant and club, books jazz artists downstairs and hosts dancing to a DJ upstairs, from Monday to Saturday. **Yoshi's** (✉ 510 Embarcadero St., near Jack London Sq., Oakland, ☎ 510/238–9200) books jazz greats like Betty Carter, local favorite Kenny Burrell, and Joshua Redman.

Cabarets

Club Fugazi (✉ 678 Green St., ☎ 415/421–4222) presents the long-running (two decades plus) *Beach Blanket Babylon,* a wacky musical send-up of San Francisco moods and mores. While the choreography is colorful, the singers brassy, and the songs witty, the real stars are the comically exotic costumes and famous ceiling-high "hats." Order tickets as far in advance as possible; the show has been sold out up to a month in advance. Those under 21 are admitted only to the Sunday matinee.

The **Coconut Grove** (✉ 1415 Van Ness Ave., ☎ 415/776–1616) has a '40s supper-club ambience, superb (if pricey) cocktails, and nouvelle cuisine. **Finocchio's** (✉ 506 Broadway, near Columbus Ave., ☎ 415/982–9388) hosts a drag revue that's decidedly retro—it's been running since 1936. **Josie's Cabaret and Juice Joint** (✉ 3583 16th St., at Market St., ☎ 415/861–7933), a small café and cabaret in the Castro district, books performers who reflect the countercultural feel of the neighborhood—from stand-up comedians to musicians to drag queens to monologuists. The **New Orleans Room** (✉ Fairmont Hotel, Mason and California Sts., ☎ 415/772–5259) has a somewhat tacky 1960s hotel-bar ambience, but the talent on display is first-rate.

Comedy Clubs

Cobb's Comedy Club (✉ The Cannery, ✉ 2801 Leavenworth St., at Beach St., ☎ 415/928 1320) books top stand-up comics. The **Punch**

Line (⊠ 444 Battery St., between Clay and Washington Sts., ☎ 415/ 397–7573) presents big-name comedians and up-and-comers. Buy tickets in advance at BASS outlets (☎ 510/762–2277) or from the club's charge line (☎ 415/397–4337).

Dance Clubs

El Rio (⊠ 3158 Mission St., ☎ 415/282–3325) is a casual Mission District spot with salsa dancing on Sunday (from 4 PM), '70s soul and funk on Wednesday, a global dance party on Friday, and live rock on Saturday and Sunday. The **Metronome Ballroom** (⊠ 1830 17th St., ☎ 415/252–9000) is at its most lively on weekend nights, when ballroom dancers come for lessons and revelry at this smoke- and alcohol-free spot.

Sol y Luna (⊠ 475 Sacramento St., near Battery St., ☎ 415/296–8191), a downtown Latin supper club, sizzles from Wednesday to Saturday.

Piano Bars

The **Plaza Lounge** (⊠ 345 Stockton St., at Sutter St., ☎ 415/398–1234), on the top floor of the Grand Hyatt, has views of North Beach and the bay. The **Redwood Room** (⊠ Clift Hotel, 495 Geary St., near Taylor St., ☎ 415/775–4700), a classy Art Deco lounge, has a low-key but sensuous ambience. Klimt reproductions cover the walls, and mellow sounds fill the air.

A pianist (occasionally accompanied by a vocalist) performs at the tastefully appointed lobby lounge at the **Ritz-Carlton Hotel** (⊠ 600 Stockton St., at Pine St., ☎ 415/296–7465) from the early evening until 11:30 on weeknights and 1:30 AM on weekends. The **Washington Square Bar and Grill** (⊠ 1707 Powell St., near Union St., ☎ 415/982–8123), affectionately known as the "Washbag," hosts pianists performing jazz and popular standards.

Skyline Bars

The **Carnelian Room** (⊠ 555 California St., at Kearny St., ☎ 415/433–7500), on the 52nd floor of the Bank of America Building, offers perhaps the loftiest view of San Francisco's magnificent skyline. Jackets are required, but ties are optional. The **Crown Room** (⊠ Fairmont Hotel, 650 Mason St., at California St., ☎ 415/772–5131) is one of the most luxurious of the city's skyline bars. Riding the glass-enclosed Skylift elevator is an experience in itself. **Harry Denton's Starlight Room** (⊠ Sir Francis Drake Hotel, 450 Powell St., ☎ 415/395–8595) has rose-velvet booths, romantic lighting, a small dance floor, and staff clad in tuxes or full-length gowns. When live combos aren't playing, taped Sinatra rules. The **Top of the Mark** (⊠ 999 California St., at Mason St., ☎ 415/392–3434) hosts musicians from Wednesday to Saturday and dancing to standards from the '20s, '30s, and '40s on Friday and Saturday. The view is superb seven nights a week.

Singles Bars

Well-dressed young professionals pack into **Harry Denton's** (⊠ 161 Steuart St., near the Embarcadero., ☎ 415/882–1333), one of San Francisco's liveliest saloons. **Holding Company** (⊠ 2 Embarcadero Center, at Front and Clay Sts., ☎ 415/986–0797), a popular weeknight Financial District watering hole, is where scores of office workers gather to enjoy friendly libations. The kitchen and bar are open on weekdays. **Johnny Love's** (⊠ 1500 Broadway, at Polk St., ☎ 415/931–8021) live-music offerings range from ska to swing to rockabilly to reggae. Late-night dancing to DJ-spun modern rock is also an option. **Perry's** (⊠ 1944 Union St., at Laguna St., ☎ 415/922–9022), the most famous of San Francisco's singles bars, is usually jam-packed.

Wine Bars

Eos Restaurant and Wine Bar (⊠ 901 Cole St., at Carl St., ☎ 415/566–3064) has hundreds of wines—many available by the glass. **Hayes and Vine** (⊠ 377 Hayes St., at Gough St., ☎ 415/626–5301) is dominated by a white-onyx bar. Patrons choose from 550 wines by the bottle or 40 by the glass. Cheeses, pâtés, and caviar are among the culinary offerings. **London Wine Bar** (⊠ 415 Sansome St., at Sacramento St., ☎ 415/788–4811), a warm Financial District spot (open on weekdays only), serves 40 wines by the glass from a cellar of 8,000 bottles.

Longtime Favorites

Bix (⊠ 56 Gold St., off Montgomery St., ☎ 415/433–6300), a supper club and North Beach institution, is yet another place credited with the invention of the martini. **Buena Vista** (⊠ 2765 Hyde St., ☎ 415/474–5044), the Fisherman's Wharf area's most popular bar, allegedly introduced Irish coffee to the New World. Tourists pile in for great views of the waterfront. **Cypress Club** (⊠ 500 Jackson St., at Columbus Ave., ☎ 415/296–8555) is an eccentric restaurant-bar where sensual, '20s-style opulence clashes with Fellini/Dalí frivolity.

The **Tonga Room** (⊠ 950 Mason St., at California St., ☎ 415/772–5278) is San Francisco's house of high kitsch. Fake palm trees and "grass huts," a "lake" (combos play pop standards on a floating barge), and sprinkler system "rain" (complete with simulated thunder and lightning) create a tropical atmosphere that only grows more surreal as you quaff the selection of very fruity and very potent novelty cocktails. **Vesuvio Cafe** (⊠ 255 Columbus Ave., between Broadway and Pacific Ave., ☎ 415/362–3370) is little altered since its heyday as a haven for the beat poets.

Gay and Lesbian Nightlife

GAY MALE BARS

Alta Plaza Restaurant & Bar (⊠ 2301 Fillmore St., at Clay St., ☎ 415/922–1444) is an upper Fillmore restaurant-bar that caters to nattily dressed guppies (gay yuppies) and their admirers. Jazz musicians play from Sunday to Thursday; a DJ takes over on weekends. The **Metro** (⊠ 3600 16th St., at Market St., ☎ 415/703–9750), more upscale than the nearby Detour, has a balcony that overlooks the intersection of Noe, 16th, and Market streets. The **Midnight Sun** (⊠ 4067 18th St., at Castro St., ☎ 415/861–4186) has riotously programmed video screens. **N Touch** (⊠ 1548 Polk St., at Sacramento St., ☎ 415/441–8413), a tiny dance bar, has long been popular with Asian–Pacific Islander gay men. In addition to videos, there's karaoke on Tuesday and Sunday night, and go-go boys sometimes perform.

The DJs at the **Stud** (⊠ Harrison and 9th Sts., ☎ 415/252–7883) mix up-to-the-minute music with new wave, funk, rock, and carefully chosen highlights from the heyday of gay disco.

LESBIAN BARS

Blondies' Bar and No Grill (⊠ 540 Valencia St., near 16th St., ☎ 415/864–2052), a mixed bar most of the week, plays host to "Red," an all-women's night every Sunday. **Club Q** (⊠ 177 Townsend St., at 3rd St., ☎ 415/647–8258), held on the first Friday of the month, is an always packed dance party. **CoCo Club** (⊠ 139 8th St., entrance on Minna St., ☎ 415/626–2337) presents theme nights, including a drag cabaret, a coed erotic cabaret, and a woman's speakeasy. Every other Friday is "In Bed with Fairy Butch," an all-women's dance night.

Girl Spot (⊠ 401 6th St., at Harrison St., ☎ 415/337–4962), nicknamed the G-Spot, takes place on Saturday night; several top San Francisco DJs spin a lively mix of Top 40, house, and R&B. The very fun **Lexington Club** (✉ 3464 19th St., at Lexington St., ☎ 415/863–2052) is popular with the young lesbian set. **Red Dora's Bearded Lady Café and Cabaret** (✉ 485 14th St., at Guerrero St., ☎ 415/626–2805), a neighborhood venue, serves a predominantly lesbian and gay clientele.

The Arts

Half-price, same-day tickets to many local and touring stage shows go on sale (cash only) at 11 AM, from Tuesday to Saturday, at the **TIX Bay Area** booth, on the Stockton Street side of Union Square between Geary and Post streets. TIX is also a full-service ticket agency for theater and music events around the Bay Area (open until 6 from Tuesday to Thursday and 7 on Friday and Saturday). For recorded information about TIX tickets, call 415/433–7827. The city's charge-by-phone ticket service is **BASS** (☎ 510/762–2277 or 415/776–1999). **City Box Office** (✉ 153 Kearny St., Suite 402, ☎ 415/392–4400) has a downtown charge-by-phone service.

Dance

The **San Francisco Ballet** (✉ 301 Van Ness Ave., ☎ 415/865–2000), under the direction of Helgi Tomasson, has a primary season of classic and contemporary works that runs from February to May. The company's annual December presentation of the *Nutcracker* is spectacular.

Music

The **San Francisco Symphony** (✉ Davies Symphony Hall, Van Ness Ave. at Grove St., ☎ 415/864–6000) performs from September to May under the direction of Michael Tilson Thomas. **Cal Performances** (✉ Zellerbach Hall, Bancroft and Telegraph Aves., Berkeley, ☎ 510/642–9988) presents acclaimed artists in all disciplines, from classical soloists to the latest jazz, world music, theatre, and dance ensembles. **Old First Concerts** (✉ Old First Presbyterian Church, Van Ness Ave. at Sacramento St., ☎ 415/474–1608) is a well-respected Friday evening and Sunday afternoon series that offers chamber music, vocal soloists, new music, and jazz.

Stern Grove (✉ Sloat Blvd. at 19th Ave., ☎ 415/252–6252) hosts the nation's oldest continual free summer music festival, 10 Sunday-afternoon performances of symphony, opera, jazz, pop music, and dance. The amphitheater is in a eucalyptus grove below street level; dress for cool weather.

Opera

The **San Francisco Opera** (✉ War Memorial Opera House, Van Ness Ave. at Grove St., ☎ 415/864–3330) performs a season of 10 operas from September to December and also schedules occasional summer festivals.

Theater

Three major commercial theaters, operated by the Shorenstein-Nederlander organization, are the **Curran** (✉ 445 Geary St., ☎ 415/551–2000), the **Golden Gate** (✉ Golden Gate Ave. at Taylor St., ☎ 415/551–2000), and the **Orpheum** (✉ 1192 Market St., near the Civic Center, ☎ 415/551–2000). **Marines Memorial Theatre** (✉ 609 Sutter St., at Mason St., ☎ 415/771–6900) presents touring shows plus some local productions. **Theatre on the Square** (✉ 450 Post St., ☎ 415/433–9500) is a popular smaller venue.

The city's major nonprofit theater company is the **American Conservatory Theater** (ACT), which presents plays, from classics to contemporary works, often in rotating repertory. ACT performs at the **Geary Theater** (✉ 415 Geary St., ☎ 415/749–2228).

The leading producer of new plays is the **Magic Theatre** (✉ Bldg. D, Fort Mason Center, Laguna St. at Marina Blvd., ☎ 415/441–8822), which presents works by Octavio Solis, Jon Robin Baitz, Claire Chafee, and others. The **San Francisco Shakespeare Festival** offers free performances on summer weekends in Golden Gate Park (☎ 415/422–2222). The major avant-garde presenting organization is **Theater Artaud** (✉ 450 Florida St., in the Mission District, ☎ 415/621–7797). Some contemporary theater events, in addition to dance and music, are scheduled at the theater in the **Center for the Arts at Yerba Buena Gardens** (✉ 3rd and Howard Sts., ☎ 415/978–2787).

The **Lorraine Hansberry Theatre** (✉ 620 Sutter St., ☎ 415/474–8800) specializes in plays by black writers. **Theatre Rhinoceros** (✉ 2926 16th St., ☎ 415/861–5079) showcases gay and lesbian performers. **BRAVA!** (✉ 2789 24th St., ☎ 415/826–5773) fosters work by women playwrights and directors.

Berkeley Repertory Theatre (☎ 510/845–4700) performs an adventurous mix of classics and new plays. **California Shakespeare Festival** (☎ 510/548–9666), the Bay Area's largest outdoor summer theater event, performs in an amphitheater east of Oakland on Gateway Boulevard, off state Highway 24.

OUTDOOR ACTIVITIES AND SPORTS

Beaches

Updated by
Wendy Smith

Baker Beach is a local favorite, with gorgeous views of the Golden Gate Bridge, the Marin Headlands, and the bay. Its strong waves make swimming a dangerous prospect, but the mile-long shoreline is ideal for fishing, building sand castles, or watching sea lions play in the surf. On warm days the entire beach is packed with bodies taking in the sun. The beach has picnic tables, grills, and trails that lead all the way to the Golden Gate Bridge. ✉ *In the Presidio, at the end of Gibson Rd., off Bowley St.*

Named for the poor Chinese fishermen who once camped here, **China Beach,** south of Baker Beach, has gentle waters from April to October. It's sometimes marked on maps as Phelan Beach. ✉ *In the Seacliff district; take 25th Ave. north to Scenic Way west to Seacliff Ave.*

South of the Cliff House, **Ocean Beach** stretches along the western (ocean) side of San Francisco. Though certainly not the city's cleanest beach, it's wide and sandy, and perfect for a long walk or jog. It's popular with surfers, but swimming is not recommended. ✉ *Great Hwy. south of Balboa St.*

Participant Sports

For information on participant sports, check the monthly issues of *City Sports* magazine, available free at sporting goods stores, tennis centers, and other recreational sites. The most important running event of the year is the ***Examiner* Bay-to-Breakers race** (☎ 415/512–5000, ext. 2222), held on the third Sunday in May.

The **San Francisco Marathon & 5K** (☎ 415/296–7111) is held on the second Sunday in July. The competition draws up to 7,000 runners.

Bicycling

With its legendary hills, San Francisco offers countless cycling challenges—but also plenty of level ground. A completely flat route, the

Embarcadero gives you a clear view of open waters and the Bay Bridge on the pier side, and sleek high-rises on the other. **Golden Gate Park** has paths throughout. Bike shops are strategically placed near favorite routes.

Boating and Sailing

A Day on the Bay (☎ 415/922–0227) is in San Francisco's small-craft marina, minutes from the Golden Gate Bridge and open waters. **Cass' Marina** (✉ 1702 Bridgeway, at Napa St., ☎ 415/332–6789), in Sausalito, has a variety of sailboats that can be rented as long as you have a qualified sailor in the group. **Stow Lake** (☎ 415/752–0347), in Golden Gate Park, has rowboat, pedal boat, and electric boat rentals. The lake is open daily for boating, but call for seasonal hours.

Fishing

Fishing boats leave from San Francisco, Sausalito, Berkeley, Emeryville, and Point San Pablo. They go for salmon and halibut outside the bay or striped bass and giant sturgeon within the bay (though heavy pollution in the bay may lower the quality of your catch). In San Francisco lines can be cast from San Francisco Municipal Pier, Fisherman's Wharf, Baker Beach, or Aquatic Park. Trout fishing is possible at Lake Merced; you can rent rods and boats and buy bait at the **Lake Merced Boating and Fishing Company** (✉ 1 Harding Rd., ☎ 415/753–1101). One-day licenses, good for ocean fishing only, are available for $5.75 on the charters; sporting-goods stores sell full-year state licenses. Most charters depart daily from Fisherman's Wharf during the salmon-fishing season.

Lovely Martha's Sportfishing (✉ Fisherman's Wharf, Berth 3, ☎ 415/871–1691) operates salmon-fishing excursions as well as bay tours. **Wacky Jacky** (✉ Fisherman's Wharf, Pier 45, ☎ 415/586–9800) will take you salmon fishing in a sleek, fast, and comfortable 50-ft boat.

Fitness

The drop-in fee is $15 at the various branches of the **24-Hour Fitness** center (✉ 1200 Van Ness St., ☎ 415/776–2200; ✉ 350 Bay St., ☎ 415/395–9595; ✉ 3742 Buchanan St., ☎ 415/563–3535; ✉ 100 California St., ☎ 415/434–5080; ✉ 2nd St. at Folsom St., ☎ 415/543–7808). The **Embarcadero YMCA** (✉ 169 Steuart St., ☎ 415/957–9622) has racquetball courts, a 25-meter swimming pool, and aerobics classes for $12. Those who prefer a women-only atmosphere can work out at the **Women's Training Center** (✉ 2164 Market St., ☎ 415/864–6835) for a $10 day fee, which includes use of the sauna.

Golf

Call the **golf information line** (☎ 415/750–4653) to get directions to the city's golf courses and reserve tee times. The **Presidio Golf Course** (✉ W. Pacific Ave. and Arguello Blvd., ☎ 415/561–4653), an 18-holer managed by Arnold Palmer's company, is by most accounts the city's best course. **Harding and Fleming parks** (✉ Harding Rd. and Skyline Blvd., ☎ 415/664–4690) have an 18-hole, par-72 course and a 9-hole executive course, respectively. **Lincoln Park** (✉ 34th and Clement Sts., ☎ 415/221–9911) is an 18-hole, par-68 course. **Golden Gate** (✉ 47th Ave. off Fulton St., ☎ 415/751–8987) is a 9-holer in Golden Gate Park.

Tennis

The San Francisco Recreation and Park Department maintains 132 public tennis courts throughout the city; all courts are free except those in Golden Gate Park. At **Mission Dolores Park** (✉ 18th and Dolores Sts.), six courts are available on a first-come, first-served basis. There are 16 public courts in **Golden Gate Park** (☎ 415/753–7101), the only facility that allows you to reserve a court.

Spectator Sports

Take along extra layers of clothing for any event held at windy and sometimes foggy **3Com Park at Candlestick Point** (✉ U.S. 101 at 3Com Park exit, 3 mi south of downtown, ☎ 415/467–8000 or 800/734–4268). City **shuttle buses** (☎ 415/673–6864) marked BALLPARK EXPRESS run from numerous bus stops to 3Com Park. To drive from San Francisco to the **Oakland Coliseum and Oakland Coliseum–Arena** (✉ Coliseum Way off I–880, ☎ 510/638–0500) take I–80 to I–580 to I–980 to I–880. Another (good) option is to take **BART** (☎ 800/817–1717); get off at the Coliseum stop.

Baseball

The **San Francisco Giants** (☎ 415/467–8000) play at 3Com Park. Games rarely sell out. The **Oakland A's** play at the Oakland Coliseum (☎ 510/638–0500). Game-day tickets are usually available.

Basketball

The **Golden State Warriors** play NBA basketball at the Oakland Coliseum Arena. Warriors tickets are available through **BASS** (☎ 510/762–2277).

Football

The **San Francisco 49ers** (☎ 415/468–2249) play at 3Com Park, but the games are almost always sold out far in advance. The brawling (on the field and off) **Oakland Raiders** (☎ 510/639–7700 or 510/762–2277) play at the Oakland Coliseum. Except for high-profile games, tickets are usually available.

Hockey

See San Jose Sharks *in* Side Trip to San Jose, *below.*

SHOPPING

From fringe fashions in the Haight to leather chaps in the Castro, San Francisco's distinctive neighborhoods offer consumers a bit of everything. There are ginseng health potions in Chinatown, fine antiques and art in Jackson Square, handmade kites and kimonos in Japantown, and bookstores specializing in everything from beat poetry to ecology throughout the city. For those who prefer the mainstream, there are high-end boutiques on Union Street and fine department stores in Union Square.

Major Shopping Districts

The Castro/Noe Valley

Updated by Wendy Smith

Often called the gay capital of the world, the Castro is filled with clothing boutiques, home accessory stores, and various specialty stores. **A Different Light Bookstore** (✉ 489 Castro St., ☎ 415/431–0891) doubles as an unofficial community center. **Under One Roof** (✉ 2362-B Market St., ☎ 415/252–9430) donates the profits from its home and garden items, gourmet foods, bath products, books, frames, and cards to northern California AIDS organizations.

Just south of Castro on 24th Street, the largely residential Noe Valley is an enclave of gourmet food stores, used record shops, clothing boutiques, and specialty gift stores. Parts of Armistead Maupin's *Tales of the City* were filmed in the villagelike neighborhood, whose small shops and relaxed street life evoke a '70s mood. At **Panetti's** (✉ 3927 24th St., ☎ 415/648–2414) you'll find whimsical picture frames, journals, costume jewelry, and more.

Chinatown

Racks of Chinese silks, toy trinkets, colorful pottery, baskets, and carved figurines are displayed in racks on the sidewalks, alongside herb stores that specialize in ginseng and roots. Dominating the neighborhood are the sights and smells of food: crates of bok choy, tanks of live crabs, and hanging whole chickens.

Embarcadero Center

Five modern towers of shops, restaurants, and offices plus the Hyatt Regency Hotel make up the Embarcadero Center, downtown at the end of Market Street. It's one of the few major shopping centers with an underground parking garage.

Fisherman's Wharf

Pier 39 is one of the world's most visited sites, though the shops at Ghirardelli Square and the Cannery are more interesting. All three also have restaurants plus musicians, mimes, magicians, and other entertainment.

The Haight

Haight Street is always an attraction for visitors, if only to see the sign at Haight and Ashbury streets. These days, in addition to tie-dyed shirts, you'll find high-quality vintage clothing, funky jewelry, art from around the world, and reproductions of art deco accessories.

Hayes Valley

Hayes Valley, just west of the Civic Center, is an up-and-coming shopping district. The area is packed with art galleries and unusual stores such as **Worldware** (⊠ 336 Hayes St., ☎ 415/487–9030), where everything from clothing to furniture to candles is made of organic materials.

Japantown

The three-block **Japan Center,** between Laguna and Fillmore streets and Geary Boulevard and Post Street, contains an 800-car public garage and three shop-filled buildings. Especially worthwhile are the Kintetsu and Kinokuniya buildings, where shops and showrooms sell cameras, tapes and records, new and old porcelains, pearls, antique kimonos, tansu chests (Japanese chests used mainly for storage), paintings, and more.

The Marina District

The hub of the Marina district is Chestnut Street, one block north of Lombard Street. The stretch of Chestnut from Fillmore Street to Broderick Street caters to the shopping whims of Marina residents with gift boutiques, pottery shops, galleries, and stores filled with gourmet food items. Cafés selling fancy coffee drinks abound—you'll never want for a pick-me-up cappuccino or latte.

The Mission

One of the city's sunniest neighborhoods, the Mission is one of its most ethnically diverse, with a large Latino population and a growing contingent of young artists, musicians, and new bohemians. In addition to those with a hunger for inexpensive Mexican food, the area draws bargain shoppers with its many used clothing, furniture, and alternative book stores. The main shopping streets are Mission and Valencia between 16th and 24th streets.

North Beach

Shopping here is clustered tightly around Washington Square and Columbus Avenue. Businesses include clothing boutiques and antiques and vintage wares shops. Once the center of the beat movement, North Beach still has a bohemian spirit that's especially apparent at **City Lights Bookstore,** (⊠ 261 Columbus Ave., ☎ 415/362–8193) where the beat poets live on.

Pacific Heights

Pacific Heights residents head for Fillmore Street between Post Street and Pacific Avenue, and Sacramento Street between Lyon and Maple streets, where private residences alternate with good bookstores, fine clothing and gift shops, thrift stores, and art galleries. A local favorite is the **Sue Fisher King Company,** (⊠ 3067 Sacramento St., ☎ 415/922–7276) whose quality home accessories fit right into this upscale neighborhood.

South of Market

Dozens of discount outlets, most open daily, have sprung up along the streets and alleyways bordered by 2nd, Townsend, Howard, and 10th streets. At the other end of the spectrum are the gift shops of the **Museum of Modern Art** (⊠ 151 3rd St.) and the **Center for the Arts at Yerba Buena Gardens** (⊠ 3rd and Mission Sts.); both sell handmade jewelry and various other great gift items.

Union Square

Serious shoppers head straight to Union Square, San Francisco's main shopping artery and the site of most department stores, including Macy's, Neiman Marcus, and Saks Fifth Avenue. Also here are the Disney Store, F.A.O. Schwarz, and the Virgin Megastore, along with the boutiques of Hermès of Paris, Gucci, Celine of Paris, Alfred Dunhill, Louis Vuitton, and Cartier. Across from the cable car turntable at Powell and Market streets is the **San Francisco Shopping Centre** (⊠ 865 Market St., ☎ 415/495–5656), with the Nordstrom department store, a Warner Bros. studio store, and three dozen other businesses.

Union Street

Out-of-towners sometimes confuse Union Street with Union Square. Nestled at the foot of a hill between Pacific Heights and the Marina district, the street is lined with contemporary fashion and custom jewelry shops, along with a few antiques shops and art galleries.

SIDE TRIPS FROM SAN FRANCISCO

Sausalito and Tiburon

Sausalito

Updated by
Chris Baty and
Sharon Silva

Like much of San Francisco, Sausalito had a raffish reputation before going upscale. Discovered in 1775 by Spanish explorers and named Saucelito (Little Willow) for the trees growing around its springs, the town served as a port for whaling ships during the 19th century. By the mid-1800s wealthy San Franciscans were making Sausalito their getaway across the bay; in the town's hills they built lavish Victorian summer homes, many of which still stand. Sausalito tilted bohemian in the '50s and '60s, but decades before that its many bordellos had attracted a more dissolute crowd—mainly sailors and dock workers out for a bawdy time. The town is friendly and casual, though summer traffic jams can fray nerves. If possible, visit on a weekday—and take the ferry.

Bridgeway is Sausalito's main thoroughfare and prime destination, with the bay, yacht harbor, and waterfront restaurants on one side, and more restaurants, shops, and hillside homes on the other. Stairs along the west side of Bridgeway climb the hill to Sausalito's wooded neighborhoods.

The **Village Fair** (⊠ 777 Bridgeway, ☎ 415/332–1902) is a four-story former warehouse that's been converted into a warren of clothing, crafts, and gift boutiques.

The Bay Area

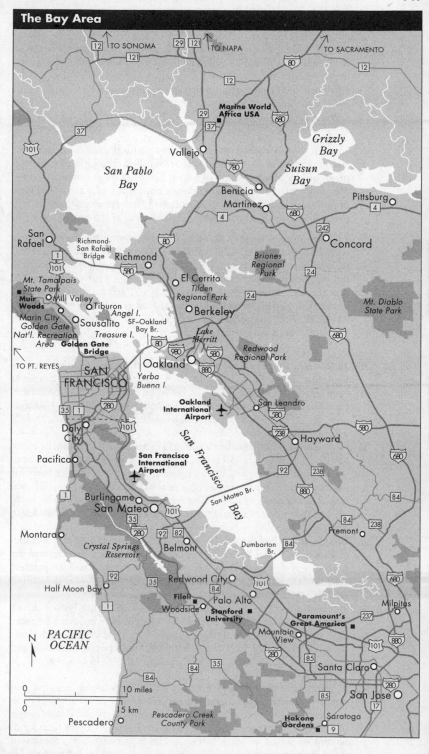

The U.S. Army Corps of Engineers uses the **Bay Model,** a 400-square-ft replica of the entire San Francisco Bay and the San Joaquin–Sacramento River delta, to reproduce the rise and fall of tides, the flow of currents, and the other physical forces at work on the bay. The model is housed in a former World War II shipyard building, along with a display on shipbuilding history. At the same site is the *Wapama,* a hulking World War I–era steam freighter being restored by volunteers. ⊠ *2100 Bridgeway, at Marinship Way,* ☎ *415/332–3871.* ⌑ *Free.* ☺ *Labor Day–Memorial Day, Tues.–Sat. 9–4; Memorial Day–Labor Day, Tues.–Fri. 9–4 and weekends 10–6.*

Some of the 400 **houseboats** that make up Sausalito's "floating homes community" line the shore of Richardson Bay. The sight of these colorful, quirky abodes is one of Marin County's most famous views—they range from rustic to eccentric to flamboyant. For a close-up view of the houseboats, head north on Bridgeway from downtown, turn right on Gate 6 Road, and park where it dead-ends at the public shore.

Ⓒ The **Bay Area Discovery Museum** fills five former military buildings with entertaining and enlightening hands-on exhibits. Youngsters and their families can fish from a boat at the indoor wharf, explore the skeleton of a house, and make multitrack recordings. From San Francisco take the Alexander Avenue exit from U.S. 101 and follow signs to East Fort Baker. ⊠ *557 McReynolds Rd., at East Fort Baker,* ☎ *415/487–4398.* ⌑ *$7.* ☺ *Summer, Tues.–Sun. 10–5; fall–spring, Tues.–Thurs. 9–4 and Fri.–Sun. 10–5.*

DINING AND LODGING

$$–$$$ ✗ **Mikayla at Casa Madrona.** Although the food at this longtime Sausalito hilltop dining room has been inconsistent, the view has never been less than superb. The menu, based on grilled fish and meats, emphasizes local ingredients. Sunday brunch is popular. ⊠ *801 Bridgeway,* ☎ *415/331–5888. Reservations essential weekends. AE, D, DC, MC, V. No lunch.*

$$ ✗ **Alta Mira.** This Sausalito landmark, in a Spanish-style hotel a block above Bridgeway, has spectacular views of the bay from a heated front terrace and a windowed dining room. It's a favored Bay location for Sunday brunch (try the famed eggs Benedict and Ramos Fizz), alfresco lunch, or cocktails at sunset. The American-Continental cuisine is so-so, but the view never fails. ⊠ *125 Bulkley Ave.,* ☎ *415/332–1350. AE, DC, MC, V.*

$$ ✗ **Spinnaker.** Bay views and straightforward pasta and seafood specialties are the attractions in this contemporary building beyond the harbor near the yacht club. You might spot a stately pelican perched on one of the pilings outside. ⊠ *100 Spinnaker Dr.,* ☎ *415/332–1500. AE, DC, MC, V.*

$–$$ ✗ **Christophe.** The early-bird dinners at this charming French dining room are a penny pincher's delight. A four-course meal costs no more than two admissions to a first-run movie, and the choices include irresistible plates like duck confit, lamb fillet with port-wine sauce, and chocolate profiteroles. ⊠ *1919 Bridgeway,* ☎ *415/332–9244. MC, V. Closed Mon. No lunch.*

$ ✗ **Lighthouse Café.** This inexpensive coffee shop serves breakfast and lunch—omelets, sandwiches, and burgers—every day from 6:30 (7 on weekends). Most find the down-to-earth atmosphere and simple fare—including Danish meatballs, herring, and salmon open-face sandwiches—a welcome break from Sausalito's more touristy eateries. ⊠ *1311 Bridgeway,* ☎ *415/331–3034. Reservations not accepted. No credit cards.*

$$$–$$$$ ⊡ **Hotel Sausalito.** Soft yellow, green, and orange tones and faux finishes create a warm, Mediterranean feel at this well-run inn decorated with handmade furniture and tasteful original art and reproductions. The rooms, some of which have harbor or park views, range from small ones that are good for budget-minded travelers to commodious suites. ⊠ *16 El Portal,* ☎ *415/332–0700 or 888/442–0700,* FAX *415/332–8788. 14 rooms, 2 suites. In-room modems, concierge. Continental breakfast. No smoking. No pets. 2-night minimum on weekends. AE, DC, MC, V.*

Tiburon

On a peninsula called Punta de Tiburon (Shark Point) by the Spanish explorers, this beautiful Marin County community maintains a villagelike atmosphere despite the encroachment of commercial establishments in the downtown area. The harbor faces Angel Island across Raccoon Strait. San Francisco is directly south, 6 mi across the bay, which makes the view from the decks of restaurants on the harbor a major attraction. More low-key than Sausalito, life in Tiburon has centered around the waterfront ever since the town's incarnation in 1884, when ferryboats from San Francisco connected here with a railroad to the town of San Rafael. Whenever the weather is pleasant, and particularly during the summer, the ferry is the most relaxing way to visit and avoid traffic and parking problems.

Tiburon's **Main Street** is lined on the bay side with restaurants with outdoor decks that jut out over the harbor, giving diners a bird's-eye view of San Francisco. On the other side of the narrow street are shops and galleries that sell casual clothing, gifts, jewelry, posters, and paintings.

At the end of the block, Main Street turns into **Ark Row,** a tree-shaded walk lined with antiques and specialty stores. Look closely, and you'll see that some of the buildings are actually old houseboats that once floated in Belvedere Cove before being beached and transformed into stores. **Windsor Vineyards** (⊠ 72 Main St., ☎ 415/435–3113) has free tastings in a converted 19th-century rooming house.

The stark-white **Old St. Hilary's Landmark and Wildflower Preserve,** an 1888 Carpenter Gothic church, stands like a puritanical matriarch overlooking the town from her hillside perch. Operated by the Landmarks Society as a historical and botanical museum, the church is surrounded by a wildflower preserve that is spectacular in May and June, when the rare black jewel flower is in bloom. ⊠ *Esperanza St. off Mar West St.,* ☎ *415/435–2567.* ⊞ *Suggested $2 donation.* ☉ *Apr.–Oct., Wed. and Sun. 1–4.*

In a wildlife sanctuary on the route into Tiburon is the 1876 **Lyford House,** a Victorian fantasy that serves as headquarters for the Richardson Bay Audubon Society. ⊠ *376 Greenwood Beach Rd., off Tiburon Blvd.,* ☎ *415/388–2524.* ⊞ *Free.* ☉ *Nov.–Apr., Sun. 1–4.*

$$ ✕ **Guaymas.** Come here for authentic Mexican dishes such as seviche, *carnitas ropa* (slowly roasted pork with salsa and black beans), mesquite-grilled fish, tamales, and *pollo en mole* (chicken with chocolate sauce, chilies, and countless spices). The heated terrace bar has views of the bay. Reservations are essential for Sunday brunch. ⊠ *5 Main St., at the ferry terminal,* ☎ *415/435–6300. DC, MC, V.*

$$ ✕ **Tutto Mare Ristorante.** A wood-burning oven here ensures crisp-crust pizzas, while upstairs an exhibition kitchen turns out pastas and grilled fish, meats, and fowl. The floor-to-ceiling windows on the second floor look out on a heated outdoor deck that is crowded with diners on mild days and evenings. ⊠ *9 Main St.,* ☎ *415/435–4747. AE, DC, MC, V.*

$ ✕ **Sam's Anchor Cafe.** Sam's is a major draw for tourists and old salts, who flock to its outside deck for bay views and beer. The informal restaurant has mahogany wainscoting and old photos on the walls. Crayons and a color-in menu cater to kids. The burgers, fresh seafood, sandwiches, soups, and salads receive standard preparations, but the food pales next to the atmosphere. ⊠ *27 Main St.,* ☎ *415/435–4527. AE, D, DC, MC, V.*

Sausalito and Tiburon Essentials

ARRIVING AND DEPARTING

By Bus: Golden Gate Transit (☎ 415/923–2000) serves Sausalito and Tiburon from 1st and Mission streets and other points in the city. The trip takes 45 minutes one-way.

By Car: To get to Sausalito from San Francisco, cross the Golden Gate Bridge and head north on U.S. 101 to the Sausalito exit. Go south on Bridgeway to the municipal parking lot (bring plenty of change for the meters) near the center of town. The trip takes from 20 to 45 minutes one-way. To get to Tiburon, take U.S. 101 past Sausalito to the Tiburon Boulevard exit.

By Ferry: The **Golden Gate Ferry** (☎ 415/923–2000) crosses the bay to Sausalito from the south wing of the Ferry Building (⊠ The Embarcadero at Market St.); the trip takes 30 minutes. **Blue and Gold Fleet** (☎ 415/705–5555) ferries depart daily for Sausalito and Tiburon from Pier 41 at Fisherman's Wharf. Ferries depart to Tiburon on weekdays only from the Ferry Building. Catamaran boats travel to Tiburon in 20 minutes, but the slower ferries can take up to an hour.

The East Bay

Oakland

Oakland's allure lies in its amazing diversity: Only here can you find a Nigerian clothing store, a beautifully renovated Italianate home, a Buddhist meditation center, and a salsa club, all in the same block. Oakland's multifaceted nature reflects its colorful and often tumultuous history. Once a cluster of Mediterranean-style homes and gardens that served as a bedroom community for San Francisco, the city became a hub of shipbuilding and industry almost overnight when the United States entered World War II. In the '60s and '70s, an intense community pride gave rise to militant groups like the Black Panther Party and the Symbionese Liberation Army, but the groups were no match for the economic hardships and racial tensions that plagued Oakland in the post-war era. In many neighborhoods the reality was widespread poverty and gang violence—subjects that have dominated the songs of myriad Oakland rappers during the past decade.

Oakland is a mosaic of its past: Affluent types have once again flocked to the city's hillside homes as a warmer and more spacious alternative to San Francisco, and a constant flow of new residents—many from Central America and Asia—ensures continued diversity, vitality, and growing pains. Many neighborhoods to the west and south of downtown remain run-down and unsafe, but a renovated downtown area and the thriving Jack London Square have injected new life into the city. Some areas, like Piedmont and Rockridge, are perfect places for browsing, eating, or relaxing between sightseeing trips to Oakland's architectural gems, rejuvenated waterfront, and numerous green spaces.

Numbers in the margin correspond to points of interest on the Oakland map.

❶ The **Oakland Museum of California** is housed in landscaped buildings that display the state's art, history, and natural science. The Gallery of

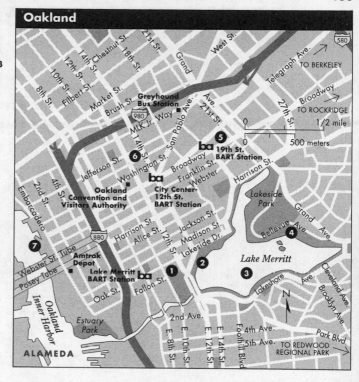

Natural Sciences surveys a typical stretch of California from the Pacific Ocean to the Nevada border, including plants and wildlife. A breathtaking film, *Fast Flight,* condenses the trip into five minutes. The museum's sprawling Cowell Hall of California History includes everything from Spanish-era artifacts to a gleaming fire engine that battled the flames in San Francisco during the 1906 earthquake. The museum's Gallery of California Art has an eclectic collection of modern works and early landscapes; of particular interest are paintings by Richard Diebenkorn, Joan Brown, Elmer Bischoff, and David Park, all members of the Bay Area Figurative School, which flourished here after World War II. ⊠ *1000 Oak St., at 10th St.,* ☎ *510/238–3401.* 🖭 *$5.* ⊘ *Wed.– Sat. 10–5, Sun. noon–7.*

2 A proud reminder of the days when Oakland was a wealthy bedroom community, the **Camron-Stanford House** exudes dignity from its foundation up to its ornate widow's walk. Built in 1876, the Italianate structure served as the home of the Oakland Museum from 1910 to 1967. Six painstakingly redecorated period rooms occupy the upper floor— a tribute to the craftsmanship and dedication that went into the 1978 restoration. ⊠ *1418 Lakeside Dr.,* ☎ *510/836–1976.* 🖭 *$4.* ⊘ *Wed. 11–4 and Sun. 1–5.*

3
4 **Lake Merritt** is a 155-acre oasis surrounded by parks, with several outdoor attractions on the north side. The **Rotary Nature Center and Waterfowl Refuge** (⊠ Perkins St., ☎ 510/238–3739, ⊘ Daily 10–5) is the nesting site of herons, egrets, geese, and ducks in the spring and summer. It's open daily from 10 to 5.

5 The **Paramount Theater** (⊠ 2025 Broadway, ☎ 510/465–6400), a venue for concerts and performances of all kinds, is the city's most striking

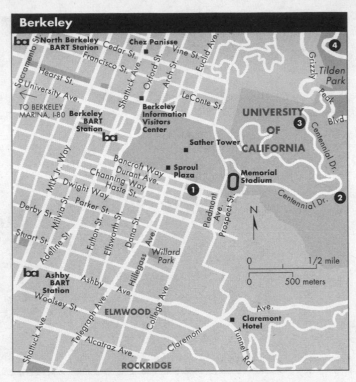

Art Deco–style structure. For $1 you can take a two-hour tour of the building at 10 AM on the first and third Saturday of each month.

6 **Preservation Park** is an idyllic little street lined with 14 restored Victorian homes and tidy, bright green lawns. Wooden benches surrounding a bubbling fountain provide an excellent place to enjoy the architecture and take a brief respite from the busy city center.

7 A former resident of Oakland, writer Jack London spent many a day boozing and brawling in the waterfront area now called **Jack London Square,** (✉ Embarcadero at Broadway, ☎ 510/814–6000) home to a collection of shops, restaurants, small museums, and historic sites. A bronze bust in the square commemorates London, author of *The Call of the Wild, The Sea Wolf, Martin Eden,* and *The Cruise of the Snark,* among others. **Heinold's First and Last Chance Saloon** (✉ 56 Jack London Sq., ☎ 510/839–6761) was one of London's old haunts.

The upscale neighborhood of **Rockridge,** northeast of downtown on Broadway, is one of Oakland's most desirable places to live. For a look at California bungalow architecture at its finest, explore the tree-lined streets that radiate out from College Avenue north and south of the BART station. **College Avenue** is the main shopping strip here. At **Market Hall** (✉ 5655 College Ave., ☎ 510/652–4680), an airy European-style marketplace, eight gourmet specialty shops carry everything from Napa Valley wines to garlic goat cheese to organic produce.

Berkeley

Although the University of California dominates Berkeley's heritage and contemporary life, the two are not synonymous: The city of 100,000 facing San Francisco across the bay has other interesting attributes. Surrounding the campus are several dozen cafés, without which the city might very well collapse. Students, faculty, and other

Berkeley residents spend hours nursing coffee concoctions of various persuasions while they read, discuss, and debate—or eavesdrop on others doing the same.

Numbers in the margin correspond to points of interest on the Berkeley map.

❶ The **U.C. Berkeley Art Museum** houses works spanning five centuries, though the emphasis is on contemporary art. Changing exhibits—line the spiral ramps and balcony galleries. Don't miss the vibrant paintings by the abstract expressionist Hans Hofmann. On the ground floor is the **Pacific Film Archive**, which programs historic and contemporary films. ⊠ *2626 Bancroft Way,* ☎ *510/642–0808 or 510/642–1124 for film-program information.* ▢ *$6.* ⊘ *Wed. and Fri.–Sun. 11–5, Thurs. 11–9.*

❷ Nurtured by Berkeley's temperate climate, more than 13,500 species of plants from all over the world flourish in the 34-acre **U.C. Botanical Garden.** Informative tours of the garden are conducted on weekends at 1:30. ⊠ *Centennial Dr.,* ☎ *510/642–3343.* ▢ *Free.* ⊘ *Daily 9–4:45.*

❸ The fortresslike **Lawrence Hall of Science** is a dazzling science-education center with hands-on displays for children. On weekends there are special lectures, demonstrations, and planetarium shows, and on clear Saturday nights from 8 to 11 the museum sets up telescopes on its outdoor plaza for the Saturday Night Stargazing sessions. ⊠ *Centennial Dr.,* ☎ *510/642–5132.* ▢ *$6.* ⊘ *Daily 10–5.*

❹ The 2,000-acre **Tilden Park** has a botanical garden, an 18-hole golf course, an environmental education center, and 2,000 acres crisscrossed by paths. Among the children's attractions are miniature steam trains, pony rides, and the vintage menagerie-style carousel. ⊠ *Off Grizzly Peak Blvd.,* ☎ *510/562–7275.*

DINING

$$–$$$$ **★** ✕ **Chez Panisse Café & Restaurant.** Alice Waters remains the mastermind behind this legendary eatery, though others do most of the cooking. In the downstairs restaurant, where formality and personal service create the ambience of a private club, the daily-changing menu is prix fixe and pricey. Upstairs in the café the atmosphere is informal, the prices lower, and both an à la carte and a fixed menu are offered. The food is simpler, too: penne with new potatoes, arugula, and sheep's milk cheese; butternut squash soup with herb croutons; and perhaps grilled tuna with savoy cabbage. ⊠ *1517 Shattuck Ave.,* ☎ *510/548–5525 for restaurant, 510/548–5049 for café. Reservations essential for restaurant. AE, D, DC, MC, V. Closed Sun.*

$$ ✕ **Café Rouge.** The short seasonal menu at this Mediterranean-style bistro runs the gamut from the sophisticated—salmon with fennel-and-olive compote—to the everyday—a hamburger topped with cheddar and flanked by a pile of fries. ⊠ *1782 4th St.,* ☎ *510/525–1440. MC, V. No dinner Mon.*

$ ✕ **Bette's Oceanview Diner.** Buttermilk pancakes that you'll never forget are among the specialties at this 1930s-inspired diner that's appointed with checkered floors and burgundy booths. *Huevos rancheros* (Mexican-style scrambled eggs) and lox and eggs are other breakfast options, and Bette's serves up kosher East Coast franks and a slew of sandwiches for lunch. ⊠ *1807 4th St.,* ☎ *510/644–3230. No credit cards. No dinner.*

$$$$ **★** ▢ **Claremont Hotel.** Straddling the Oakland–Berkeley border, the Claremont Hotel beckons like a gleaming white castle in the hills. Traveling executives come for the business amenities, including 40 new rooms outfitted with computer terminals, T-1 Internet connections, guest e-mail addresses, and oversize desks. The Claremont also shines for leisure travelers, attracting honeymooners and families alike with its luxurious suites, therapeutic massages, and personalized yoga work-outs at the on-site European spa. ✉ *41 Tunnel Rd., at Ashby and Domingo Aves., 94705,* ☎ *510/843–3000 or 800/551–7266,* FAX *510/848–6200. 282 rooms. 3 restaurants, 2 bars, in-room modem lines, no-smoking floors, in-room VCRs, 2 pools, spa, dry cleaning, concierge, meeting rooms, parking (fee). AE, D, DC, MC, V.*

$$$ 🏨 **Hotel Durant.** A mainstay of parents visiting their children at U.C. Berkeley, the Hotel Durant is a good option for those who want to be a short walk from campus and the restaurants and shops of Telegraph Avenue. Rooms, accented with dark woods and stately plaids, are small without feeling cramped. ✉ *2600 Durant Ave., 94704,* ☎ *510/845–8981,* FAX *510/486–8336. 140 rooms. Restaurant, bar, no-smoking rooms, room service, laundry service and dry cleaning, business ser-vices, meeting rooms, parking (fee). AE, D, DC, MC, V.*

East Bay Essentials

ARRIVING AND DEPARTING

By Car: To get to the East Bay from San Francisco take I–80 east across the Bay Bridge. To go to Oakland take I–580 off the Bay Bridge to the Grand Avenue exit for Lake Merritt. To reach downtown and the wa-terfront take I–980 from I–580 and exit at 12th Street. To get to Berke-ley, as you come off the Bay Bridge remain on I–80 (stay in the left two lanes); take the University Avenue exit to get to the U.C. Berke-ley campus. The drive to Berkeley or Oakland from San Francisco takes about 30 minutes, longer during rush hour.

By Light Rail: BART trains (☎ 650/992–2278) make stops in downtown Berkeley and in several parts of Oakland, including Rockridge. Use the Lake Merritt station for the Oakland Museum and southern Lake Merritt, the Oakland City Center–12th Street station for downtown, and the 19th Street station for the Paramount Theater and the north side of Lake Merritt. From the Berkeley station it's a five-minute walk on Center Street to the western edge of campus. Both trips take from 45 minutes to one hour one-way.

VISITOR INFORMATION

Oakland Convention and Visitors Authority (✉ 550 10th St., Suite 214, 94607, ☎ 510/839–9000).

Berkeley Convention and Visitors Bureau (✉ 2015 Center St., 94704, ☎ 510/549–8710).

The Peninsula

Depending on where you enter the peninsula area south of San Fran-cisco, you'll experience one of three faces. Along U.S. 101, on the east-ern side of the peninsula, you'll see office complex after shopping center after tower. A few miles west, I–280 takes you past lakes, reser-voirs, and rolling hills. Highway 1 travels along the coast.

Half Moon Bay

Updated by
Therese Iknoian

The San Mateo County coast is only a few miles from the inland peninsula and San Francisco, but its undeveloped hills, rugged coast-line, and small towns and inns are worlds away from urban sprawl, strip shopping centers, and traffic congestion. Set out from San Fran-cisco down scenic Highway 1, hugging the twists and turns of the coast, or drive down I–280 near San Mateo and get on Highway 92 head-ing west. Main Street in Half Moon Bay, the coast's most populated community (10,000 people) contains several blocks of small crafts shops, art galleries, and outdoor cafés, many housed in renovated 19th-century structures. Half Moon Bay comes to life on the third weekend in October, when 300,000 people gather for the **Half Moon Bay Art and Pumpkin Festival** (☎ 650/726–9652).

The 4-mi stretch of **Half Moon Bay State Beach** (⊠ Hwy. 1, west of Main St., ☎ 650/726–8819) is perfect for long walks, kite flying, and picnic lunches, though the 50°F water and dangerous currents prevent most visitors from swimming.

The **Bicyclery** (⊠ 101 Main St., ☎ 650/726–6000) rents bikes and has information about organized rides up and down the coast. If you prefer to go it alone, try the 3-mi bike trail that leads from Kelly Avenue in Half Moon Bay to Mirada Road in Miramar.

Built in 1928 after two horrible shipwrecks on the point, the **Point Montara Lighthouse** has its original light keeper's quarters from the late 1800s. Gray whales pass this point during their migration from November to April, so bring your binoculars. The lighthouse is a youth hostel known for its outdoor hot tub at ocean's edge. ⊠ 16th St. at Hwy. 1, Montara, ☎ 650/728–7177. ⊙ Call for hrs, tours, and lodging rates.

DINING AND LODGING

$–$$ ✗ **San Benito House.** On the ground floor of a historic inn in the heart of Half Moon Bay, this homey operation prepares memorable sandwiches with bread baked in the restaurant's oven. Fish and house-made pastas are the highlights of the candlelit dinners served here. ⊠ 356 Main St., ☎ 650/726–3425. MC, V. No lunch. No dinner Mon.–Wed.

$–$$ ✗ **Two Fools.** The kitchen tosses together big organic salads and packs contemporary burritos with a healthy mix of ingredients. A slice of old-fashioned American meat loaf topped with caramelized onions is sandwiched in a house-made bun at lunchtime. Locals stop here regularly for takeout at lunch and dinnertime. ⊠ 408 Main St., ☎ 650/712–1222. MC, V. No lunch weekends.

$$$$ 🏨 **Mill Rose Inn.** Perhaps the most decadent B&B in the entire Bay Area, the Mill Rose Inn pampers guests with in-room fireplaces, antique beds stacked high with down comforters, decanters of sherry and brandy on the tables, in-room coffee and cocoa, and baskets of fruit and candies. ⊠ 615 Mill St., 94019, ☎ 650/726–8750, 🅵🅰🆇 650/726–3031. 4 rooms, 2 suites. No-smoking rooms, refrigerators, in-room VCRs. Full breakfast. AE, D, DC, MC, V.

$$ 🏨 **Goose and Turrets.** Knickknacks from the international travels of innkeepers Raymond and Emily Hoche-Mong fill the shelves at the Goose and Turrets, and the common area with a wood-burning stove is like an art and history museum. ⊠ 835 George St., 94037, ☎ 650/728–5451. 5 rooms. Breakfast room, no-smoking rooms, boccie. Full breakfast. AE, D, DC, MC, V.

Palo Alto and Woodside

Palo Alto's main attraction is **Stanford University,** whose 8,200 acres of grass-covered hills were once part of Leland Stanford's farm. (Stanford, a railroad baron, was governor of California in the 1800s; the university is named for his son.) Surrounding the campus are residential neighborhoods lined with cafés, bookstores, and music shops.

The main campus entrance, **Palm Drive,** is an extension of University Avenue from Palo Alto. Lined with majestic palm trees and leading directly to the main quadrangle, this entrance will give you a full perspective of Stanford's unique California mission–Romanesque architecture and western Ivy League ambience. Free one-hour **walking tours** of Stanford University leave daily at 11 and 3:15 from the

Visitor Information Booth (☎ 650/723–2560 or 650/723–2053) at the front of the quadrangle.

The **Stanford Art Gallery** hosts visiting shows and exhibits some student works and a selection of the university's historical artifacts. ⊠ *Next to Hoover Tower,* ☎ *650/723–2842; 650/723–4177 for a recording of current exhibits.* 🎫 *Donation requested.* 🕓 *Tues.–Fri. 10–5, weekends 1–5. Guided gallery tours Thurs. at 12:15 and Sun. at 2.*

At the press time the long-delayed reopening of the **Stanford Museum of Art,** which suffered extensive damage during the 1989 Loma Prieta earthquake, was still set to occur in early 1999. The outdoor garden here contains an impressive collection of Rodin bronzes dating from 1840 to 1917, including awe-inspiring reproductions of the *Gates of Hell.* The museum's holdings include art from pre-Columbian times to the present. ⊠ *Lomita Dr. at Museum Way,* ☎ *650/723–4177 for recorded information.* 🕓 *Guided Rodin garden tours Wed. and weekends at 2.*

Tucked inconspicuously into a small, heavily treed plot of land, the **Papua New Guinea Sculpture Garden** is filled with tall, ornately carved wooden poles, drums, and carved stones—all created on location by 10 artists from Papua New Guinea who spent six months there in 1994. ⊠ *Santa Teresa St. and Lomita Dr.,* ☎ *650/723–3421.* 🎫 *Free.*

One of the few great country houses in California that remains intact in its original setting is **Filoli,** in Woodside. Built between 1915 and 1917 for wealthy San Franciscan William B. Bourn II, it was designed by Willis Polk in a Georgian Revival style, with redbrick walls and a tile roof. The name is not Italian but Bourn's acronym for "fight, love, live." As interesting to visitors as the house—whose exterior was shot as the Carrington mansion in the television series *Dynasty*—are the 16 acres of formal gardens. These were planned and developed over a period of more than 50 years and preserved for the public when the last private owner, Mrs. William P. Roth, deeded Filoli to the National Trust for Historic Preservation.

The gardens take advantage of the natural surroundings of the 700-acre estate and its vistas. In the middle of the gardens is a charming teahouse designed in the Italian Renaissance style. From May to early fall Filoli hosts a monthly series of Sunday afternoon jazz concerts: You bring a picnic or buy a box lunch; Filoli provides tables, sodas, wine, fruit, and popcorn. In December a crafts boutique, a Christmas brunch, and afternoon holiday teas take place in the festively decorated mansion. ⊠ *Cañada Rd. near Edgewood Rd.,* ☎ *650/364–2880.* 🎫 *$10.* 🕓 *Mid-Feb.–Oct. Tues.–Sat. for guided tours (reservations essential), Fri.–Sat. 10–2 for self-guided tours.*

DINING AND LODGING

$$$ ✕ **Spago.** Wolfgang Puck's splashy, dashing latest northern Califor-
★   nia hit opened on the site of Jeremiah Tower's failed Stars Palo Alto. The fare is inventive, the service flawless. Tasty breads will tide you over until the first course—perhaps Hudson Valley foie gras served with potato latkes dusted with pistachios—arrives. Dinner might include barbecued free-range squab in a pomegranate vinaigrette, tamarind-glazed rack of lamb, or any of several seafood dishes. The desserts are artistically presented. ⊠ *265 Lytton Ave.,* ☎ *650/833–1000. Reservations essential. AE, D, DC, MC, V. No lunch weekends.*

$$ ✕ **Evvia.** Oak floors, ceiling beams, a large fireplace, and hand-painted pottery create a stunning interior for this Greek restaurant that serves dishes with Californian influences. Start your meal with fried calamari and smelt or white beans baked with tomato sauce and topped with feta; follow with grilled striped bass with vinaigrette or lemony roast chicken. ⊠ *420 Emerson St., ☎ 650/326–0983. MC, V. No lunch weekends.*

$$ ✕ **Flea Street Café.** Sunday brunch at this intimate country inn is a local institution, with warm buttermilk biscuits, homemade jams, and seductive pancake, egg, and omelet creations as the star offerings. ⊠ *Alameda de las Pulgas (take Sand Hill Rd. west from the Stanford Shopping Center or east from I–280; turn right on Alameda), ☎ 650/854– 1226. MC, V. Closed Mon.*

$$ ✕ **Village Pub.** In this pleasant restaurant near Filoli, patrons elbow up to a carved oak bar to sample the ale or relax in the modern dining room to savor creative rustic fare. The menu includes farm greens, loin of lamb, roast venison, ravioli filled with buffalo ricotta, and ahi tuna with ginger shrimp dumplings. ⊠ *2967 Woodside Rd., ¾ mi from I–280W, ☎ 650/851–1294. AE, DC, MC, V. No lunch weekends.*

$ ✕ **Bok Choy.** This pan-Asian noodle house next to Bloomingdale's draws shoppers happy to sit down to a plate of reasonably priced fresh noodles tossed with seafood, meat, or poultry. Try the house-made ginger ale. ⊠ *2-A Stanford Shopping Center, ☎ 650/325–6588. MC, V.*

$$$ 🏠 **The Victorian on Lytton.** Only a block from downtown Palo Alto, this inn caters to business travelers who want comfort and amenities without teddy bears and lace. The spacious rooms have canopy beds. Breakfast is brought to your room in the morning. ⊠ *555 Lytton Ave., 94301, ☎ 650/322–8555, FAX 650/322–7141. 10 rooms. No-smoking rooms. Continental breakfast. AE, MC, V.*

The Peninsula Essentials

ARRIVING AND DEPARTING

By Car: The most pleasant direct route down the peninsula is I–280, the Junipero Serra Freeway, which passes by the Crystal Springs Reservoir. To get to Half Moon Bay, exit I–280 at Highway 92 and head west toward the coast. For Stanford University, exit at Sand Hill Road and drive east. Turn right on Arboretum, then right again on Palm Drive, which leads to the center of campus. U.S. 101, also known as the Bayshore Freeway, is more direct but also more congested; from there take Highway 92 to Half Moon Bay and University Avenue or Embarcadero Road west to Stanford. To get to Woodside take the Woodside Road exit off I–280 or U.S. 101 and drive west.

By Train: CalTrain (☎ 800/660–4287) runs from 4th and Townsend streets to Palo Alto ($3.75 each way). From the Palo Alto depot, take the free **Marguerite shuttle bus** (☎ 650/723–9362) to the Stanford campus and the Palo Alto area. Buses run about every 15 minutes from 6 AM to 8 PM and are timed to connect with trains and public transit buses.

VISITOR INFORMATION

Half Moon Bay Chamber of Commerce (⊠ 520 Kelly Ave., ☎ 650/ 726–8380). **Palo Alto Chamber of Commerce** (⊠ 325 Forest Ave., ☎ 650/324–3121).

THE SOUTH BAY

Revised by
Therese Iknoian

The South Bay contains old-fashioned neighborhoods, abundant green hills, and the prestigious corporate corridors of Silicon Valley—all within minutes of each other. To the surprise of many visitors, the world's high-tech capital is wonderfully multifaceted, with some of the Bay Area's finest restaurants and shops. No longer a nondescript suburb of San Francisco, San Jose and its environs have blossomed into a lively metropolis with a proud identity.

San Jose

In the last few years San Jose's downtown has become a major destination for entertainment, arts, nightlife, and sports; at the same time, Adobe Systems and other businesses have set up their headquarters here. Strikingly modern architecture coexists with restored 19th-century Victorians and mission-style buildings. Downtown can be easily explored by foot, with side trips by light-rail, but you'll need a car to get to outlying communities and sights like the Egyptian Museum and the Winchester Mystery House.

A Good Tour

Numbers in the text correspond to numbers in the margin and on the Downtown San Jose map.

Start on foot at the **Children's Discovery Museum** ① and be sure to wander around the outside of this outrageously purple building. Crossing through the surrounding park, take a stroll through the "herd" of larger-than-life animal sculptures facing San Carlos Street. The nearby steps lead down to Guadalupe Creek and a parallel walking path; a good detour leads north to the San Jose Arena and the **Guadalupe River Park** ②, with a carousel and children's playground.

Back at the sculpture park, continue east on San Carlos Street into the heart of downtown San Jose. Immediately on the left is the **Center for the Performing Arts.** San Jose's **McEnery Convention Center** and the Visitors Center are across the road. Continue down San Carlos Street and turn left on Market Street; ahead is Plaza de Cesar Chavez. On the square's northeast corner are the must-see **San Jose Museum of Art** ③ and the adjacent **Cathedral Basilica of St. Joseph** ④. On the square's western edge at Park Avenue is the splendid **Tech Museum of Innovation** ⑤.

Follow Market Street north from the plaza and turn left on Santa Clara Street. Walk one block, turn right on San Pedro Street, and continue two blocks—past the sidewalk cafés and restaurants—to St. John Street and turn left. The **Fallon House** ⑥ will be on your right, the **Peralta Adobe** ⑦ on your left. At this point, you can turn around and go east three blocks on St. John Street and board the light rail to return to downtown.

TIMING

The above downtown walk can be completed easily in about two hours. However, if you decide to spend time in the museums or at a café along San Pedro Street, give yourself at least four hours.

Sights to See

❹ **Cathedral Basilica of St. Joseph.** The multidome Renaissance-style cathedral, built in 1877, contains extraordinary stained-glass windows and murals. St. Joseph's occupies the site where a small adobe church served the first residents of the Pueblo of San Jose in 1803. ⊠ *90 S. Market St.,* ☎ *408/283–8100.*

🖑 ❶ **Children's Discovery Museum.** An angular purple building across the creek from the convention center at the rear of the Discovery Meadow park, the museum exhibits interactive installations about space, technology, the humanities, and the arts. Children can dress up in period costumes, create art from recycled materials, or play on a real fire truck. ⊠ *180 Woz Way, at Auzerais St.,* ☎ *408/298–5437.* ▭ *$6.* ☉ *Tues.– Sat. 10–5, Sun. noon–5.*

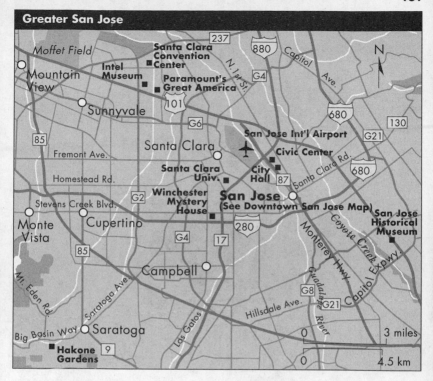

Greater San Jose

★ **Egyptian Museum and Planetarium.** Owned by the Rosecrucian Order, the museum exhibits the West Coast's largest collection of Egyptian and Babylonian antiquities, including mummies and an underground replica of a pharaoh's tomb. The 30-year-old museum's entrance is a reproduction of the Avenue of Ram Sphinxes from the Temple at Karnak in Egypt; the complex is surrounded by a garden filled with palms, papyrus, and other plants recalling ancient Egypt. The planetarium offers programs like the popular "Celestial Nile," which describes the significant role astrology played in ancient Egyptian myths and religions. ⊠ *1600 Park Ave., at Naglee Ave.,* ☎ *408/947–3636.* ⊠ *$6.75 museum, $4 planetarium.* ☼ *Daily 10–5, planetarium weekdays only.*

⑥ Fallon House. San Jose's seventh mayor, Thomas Fallon, built this Victorian mansion in 1855. The house's period-decorated rooms can be viewed on a 90-minute tour that includes the Peralto Adobe (☞ *below*) and the screening of a video about the two houses. Tickets are sold beside the Fallon House at the City Store gift shop, which carries books on local history. (If you're only interested in one of the houses, you can purchase a $3 ticket for a half-hour tour with no video.) ⊠ *175 W. St. John St.,* ☎ *408/993–8182.* ⊠ *$6 (includes admission to Peralta Adobe).* ☼ *Guided tours Tues.–Sun. 11–3:15.*

☾ ② Guadalupe River Park. Recent additions to this downtown park include the Arena Green, next to the sports arena, with a carousel, a children's playground, and artwork honoring five champion figure skaters from the area. By mid-1999, an interactive park is scheduled to open one block south on San Fernando Street. The design, which will encourage children to learn how rivers function, will contain hands-on displays plus swings, slides, a mist fountain, and water jets. ⊠ *W. Santa Clara St. and Woz Way,* ☎ *408/277–5904.*

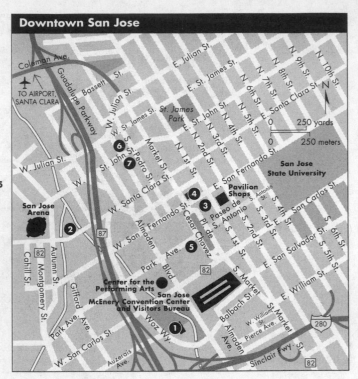

Downtown San Jose

⑦ Peralta Adobe. California pepper trees shade the circa-1797 last remaining structure from the pueblo that was once San Jose. The whitewashed two-room home has been furnished to interpret life in the first Spanish civil settlement in California and during the Mexican rancho era. ⊠ *184 W. St. John St.,* ☏ *408/993–8182.* ⊡ *$6 (includes admission to Fallon House).* ⊙ *Guided tours Tues.–Sun. 11–3:15.*

San Jose Historical Museum. On the outskirts of downtown San Jose, occupying 25 acres of Kelley Park, this outdoor "museum" recreates San Jose in the 1880s. Its reproduction of a dusty Main Street—with original Victorian homes and shops, a firehouse, and a trolley line—recalls small-town America without the brightly painted gloss of amusement-park reproductions. ⊠ *1600 Senter Rd., at Phelan Ave.,* ☏ *408/287–2290.* ⊡ *$4.* ⊙ *Weekdays 10–4:30, weekends noon–4:30.*

❸ San Jose Museum of Art. In a four-part collaboration with New York's Whitney Museum, the San Jose Museum of Art is exploring the development of 20th-century American art with exhibits of pieces from the permanent collections of both. The series will run through the year 2000, including works by American artists Willem de Kooning, Edward Hopper, and John Register. Housed in a former post office building, the museum has a wing with paintings, large-scale multimedia installations, photographs, and sculptures by local and nationally known artists. ⊠ *110 S. Market St.,* ☏ *408/294–2787.* ⊡ *$7, free 1st Thurs. of month.* ⊙ *Tues.–Wed. and Fri.–Sun. 10–5, Thurs. 10–8.*

★ ☺ **❺ Tech Museum of Innovation.** San Jose's nationally recognized museum of technology moved to a new building in 1998. The museum's high-tech and hands-on exhibits allow visitors to discover and demystify concepts and disciplines like multimedia, communications, biotechnology, robotics, and space exploration. ⊠ *201 S. Market St., at Park Ave.,* ☎ *408/279–7150.* ⊡ *$8 for museum or Imax, $12 for both.* ☉ *Daily 9–5 (to 6 PM June–Aug., to 8 PM the third Thurs. of each month).*

Winchester Mystery House. Firearms heiress Sarah Winchester became convinced that spirits would harm her if construction ever stopped on her house. So for 38 years, beginning in 1884, she kept hundreds of carpenters working around the clock, creating a bizarre 160-room Victorian labyrinth with stairs going nowhere and doors that open into walls. The brightly painted house, one of the goofier structures on the National Register of Historic Places, is a favorite family attraction, and though the grounds are no longer dark and overgrown, the place retains an air of mystery. ⊠ *525 S. Winchester Blvd., between Stevens Creek Blvd. and I–280,* ☎ *408/247–2101.* ⊡ *$13.95.* ☉ *Guided tours Nov.–Feb., daily 9:30–4; Mar.–Oct., hrs vary, call ahead.*

<table>
<tr><td>OFF THE
BEATEN PATH</td><td>**HAKONE GARDENS** – Designed in 1918 by a man who had been an imperial gardener in Japan, these carefully maintained gardens 10 mi west of San Jose contain koi (carp) ponds and sculptured shrubs. ⊠ *21000 Big Basin Way, Saratoga (from Hwy. 85 head west 2 mi on Saratoga Ave.),* ☎ *408/741–4994.* ⊡ *Free; parking $5, free first Tues. of month.* ☉ *Weekdays 10–5, weekends 11–5.*</td></tr>
</table>

Dining and Lodging

$$$ ✕ **Emile's.** Swiss chef and owner Emile Mooser's specialties include
★ house-cured gravlax, rack of lamb, and a Grand Marnier soufflé. The interior of his restaurant is distinguished by romantic lighting, stunning floral displays, and an unusual leaf sculpture on the ceiling. ⊠ *545 S. 2nd St.,* ☎ *408/289–1960. AE, D, DC, MC, V. Closed Sun.– Mon. No lunch Tues.–Thurs. and Sat.*

$$$ ✕ **Paolo's.** Rabbit stuffed with salsa verde and radicchio and delicate handmade pastas are among the appealing, up-to-the-moment offerings here. At lunchtime the dining room is a sea of suits, with bankers and brokers entertaining clients. At night well-dressed families and couples turn up. ⊠ *333 W. San Carlos St.,* ☎ *408/294–2558. AE, D, DC, MC, V. Closed Sun. No lunch Sat.*

$$ ✕ **Blake's Steakhouse and Bar.** Considered one of the finest spots for a steak in San Jose, Blake's fully satisfies the carnivore while managing not to neglect even diners who eschew red meat. Order any cut of beef you fancy, as well as roasted fowl and charbroiled fish. Uncluttered and tranquil, the restaurant has intimate high-back booths, some with a view of bustling San Pedro Square. ⊠ *17 N. San Pedro Sq.,* ☎ *408/298–9221. AE, D, DC, MC, V.*

$$ ✕ **Gordon Biersch Brewery Restaurant.** The scene at this brew pub is so busy on Friday night that the waitstaff hands out beepers to would-be diners so they can be signaled when their table is ready. Twenty- and thirtysomethings make up most of the crowd; they happily feast on glazed chicken wings, blue-cheese burgers, and garlic fries. ⊠ *33 E. San Fernando St.,* ☎ *408/294–6785. AE, MC, V.*

$ ✕ **Chez Sovan.** The original San Jose branch of this Cambodian restaurant, which serves only lunch, stands in a rather homely stretch of town, but the newer Campbell location offers a pleasant setting in addition to its satisfying fare. The spring rolls are delectable at both addresses, as are the noodle dishes, grilled meats, and flavorful curries. ⊠ *923 N. 13th St.,* ☎ *408/287–7619;* ⊠ *2425 S. Bascom Ave., Campbell,* ☎ *408/371–7711. AE, MC, V. Closed Sat. No lunch Sun. at San Jose location.*

$ ✕ **Arena Garden Restaurant.** Aficionados of the Vietnamese soup called *pho* will find this former drive-in fast-food joint a welcome way station. The soup—rice noodles and meats in a broth fragrant with star anise and other exotic spice arrives in oversize bowls, along with a plate of fresh mint and bean sprouts and a bottle of chili sauce. Diners receive free parking at the nearby sports arena when the bill comes to $10 or more, a great deal since arena parking costs at least $7. ⊠ *735 The Alameda,* ☎ *408/288–9900. D, MC, V.*

$$$$ 📼 **Fairmont Hotel.** Rooms at this affiliate of the same-named San Francisco hotel have every imaginable comfort, from down pillows and custom-designed comforters to oversize bath towels changed twice a day. ⊠ *170 S. Market St., at Fairmont Pl., 95113,* ☎ *408/998–1900 or 800/527–4727,* FAX *408/287–1648. 541 rooms. 2 restaurants, lobby lounge, no-smoking floors, room service, pool, health club, business services. AE, D, DC, MC, V.*

$$$ 📼 **Hotel De Anza.** Business travelers will appreciate the many amenities at this lushly appointed Art Deco hotel, including computers, cellular phones, and personal voice-mail services. ⊠ *233 W. Santa Clara St., 95113,* ☎ *408/286–1000 or 800/843–3700,* FAX *408/286–0500. 91 rooms, 9 suites. Restaurant, in-room modem lines, minibars, in-room VCRs, exercise room, nightclub. AE, D, DC, MC, V.*

$$ 📼 **Sundowner Inn.** Off U.S. 101 north of San Jose, this contemporary hotel offers full services for business travelers. A library stocks 500 complimentary videotapes; there's also a library full of best-sellers you can borrow. The breakfast buffet is served poolside. ⊠ *504 Ross Dr., Sunnyvale 94089,* ☎ *408/734–9900 or 800/223–9901,* FAX *408/747–0580. 93 rooms, 12 suites. Restaurant, no-smoking rooms, pool, sauna, exercise room, laundry service, meeting room. Continental breakfast. AE, D, DC, MC, V.*

Nightlife and the Arts

NIGHTLIFE

Big Lil's Barbary Coast Dinner Theater (⊠ 157 W. San Fernando St., ☎ 408/295–7469) delivers a fresh take on the Old West; it serves up comedy, melodrama, and ribs on Friday and Saturday evening. West of downtown, the **Garden City Lounge** (⊠ 360 S. Saratoga Ave., ☎ 408/244–3333) has free jazz nightly. **San Jose Live!** at the Pavillion (⊠ 150 S. 1st St., ☎ 408/294–5483) consists of five clubs and a restaurant, including a sports bar, a sing-a-long piano bar, a dance club, and a cigar bar. You can pick up a pool cue at trendy **South First Billiards** (⊠ 420 S. 1st St., ☎ 408/294–7800), in the SoFA (South of First Area) conglomeration of clubs.

Mirassou Vineyards (⊠ 3000 Aborn Rd., ☎ 408/274–4000) organizes elegant eight-course candlelight dinners, accenting food and wine pairings. Dinner ($85 per person) is served in spring and fall; call for a schedule.

THE ARTS

BASS (☎ 408/998–2277) sells tickets to many art events.

The **Center for Performing Arts** (⊠ 255 Almaden Blvd., ☎ 408/277–3900) is the city's main performance venue. **American Musical Theatre of San Jose** (☎ 408/453–7108), the **San Jose Symphony** (☎ 408/288–2828), and the **San Jose Cleveland Ballet** (☎ 408/288–2800) perform at the center.

The **San Jose Repertory Theatre** (⊠ 101 Paseo de San Antonio, ☎ 408/291–2255) occupies a contemporary four-story, 581-seat theater, dubbed "The Blue Box" because of its angular blue exterior. The season generally runs from September to June.

Sports

Home to the San Jose Sharks hockey team and known to area sports fans as the Shark Tank or, simply, the Tank, the 17,400-seat **San Jose Arena** (⊠ Santa Clara St. at Autumn St., ☎ 408/287–9200; 408/998–2277 for tickets) looks like a giant hothouse, with its glass entrance, shining metal armor, and skylight ceiling. Besides hockey, the arena also hosts tennis matches, basketball games, indoor soccer, national-name music concerts, ice-skating shows, and other events. The **San Jose Clash** (☎ 408/985–4625) play professional soccer at Spartan Stadium (⊠ 1257 S. 10th St.).

Santa Clara

Santa Clara University, founded in 1851 by Jesuits, was California's first college. The **de Saisset Art Gallery and Museum** on campus is named for Isabel de Saisset, the last member of a pioneer family, who bequeathed her estate to the university. California mission artifacts are among the permanent holdings; temporary exhibits include contemporary and historical works. ⊠ *500 El Camino Real,* ☎ *408/554–4528.* ⊑ *Free.* ☉ *Tues.–Sun. 11–4.*

In the center of Santa Clara University's campus is the **Mission Santa Clara de Asis,** the eighth of the 21 California missions founded under the direction of Father Junípero Serra and the first to honor a woman. A spectacular garden here has 4,500 roses, many classified as antiques. ⊠ *500 El Camino Real,* ☎ *408/554–4023.* ⊑ *Free.* ☉ *Weekdays 1–5, Sat. noon–3:30 for self-guided tours.*

☾ Popular attractions at **Paramount's Great America** include the Drop Zone Stunt Tower, billed as the tallest free-fall ride in the world; the Vortex, a stand-up roller coaster; a *Top Gun* movie–theme roller coaster; and Xtreme Skyflyer, which lifts you by harness more than 17 stories high and drops you back to earth at 60 mph. ⊠ *Great America Pkwy. between U.S. 101 and Hwy. 237 (6 mi north of San Jose),* ☎ *408/988–1776.* ⊑ *$30; parking $6.* ☉ *Mid-Mar.–May and Sept.–Oct., weekends; June–Aug., daily; opens 10 AM, closing times vary with season. AE, D, MC, V.*

Displays at the **Intel Museum** illustrate how computer chips are made and follow the development of Intel Corporation's microprocessor, memory, and systems product lines. You can make reservations for a guided tour. ⊠ *Robert Noyce Bldg., 2200 Mission College Blvd.,* ☎ *408/765–0503.* ⊑ *Free.* ☉ *Weekdays 8–5.*

Skylights cast natural light for viewing the exhibitions in the **Triton Museum of Art.** Sculpture by artists from the Bay Area is displayed in the garden, which you can see through a curved-glass wall at the rear of the building. Inside are rotating exhibits of contemporary works in various media and a permanent collection of 19th- and 20th-century American art, much of it created in California. ⊠ *1505 Warburton Ave.,* ☎ *408/247–3754.* ⊑ *$2 suggested donation.* ☉ *Tues. 10–9, Wed.–Sun. 10–5.*

Dining and Lodging

$$$ ✗ **Birk's.** Silicon Valley's businesspeople come to this sophisticated American grill to unwind after a hard day of paving the way to the future. The menu is traditional, strong on steaks and chops. Try the smoked prime rib, served with garlic mashed potatoes and creamed spinach, or rotisserie-grilled chicken or ribs. ⊠ *3955 Freedom Circle, at U.S. 101 and Great America Pkwy.,* ☎ *408/980–6400. Reservations essential on weekends. AE, D, DC, MC, V. No lunch weekends.*

$ ✕ **Su's Mongolian BBQ.** Come here not for the decor but for the food, which is cheap, tasty, and served in all-you-can-eat portions. Fill a bowl with your choice of thinly sliced, flash-frozen meats, then top it with a combination of vegetables and spices, oyster sauce, and hot chilies. A chef at the stand-up griddle turns out delicious stir-fry dishes. ⊠ *1111 El Camino Real,* ☎ *408/985–2958. No lunch Sun. MC, V.*

$$$–$$$$ 🏨 **Embassy Suites.** Silicon Valley business travelers and families bound for Great America like this hotel, where every room is equipped with a microwave and refrigerator. Guests receive complimentary cooked-to-order breakfasts and evening beverages. Also inquire about free tickets to the Winchester Mystery House in San Jose. ⊠ *2885 Lakeside Dr., 95054,* ☎ *408/496–6400 or 800/362–2779,* 🖷 *408/988–7529. 256 suites. Restaurant, lounge, room service, in-room modem lines, no-smoking rooms, pool, sauna, hot tub, exercise room, meeting rooms, airport shuttle, free parking. Full breakfast. AE, D, DC, MC, V.*

$$–$$$ 🏨 **Biltmore Hotel & Suites.** This hotel's central Silicon Valley location makes it popular with business travelers. There's a brew pub, an espresso bar, and 16 meeting rooms. If you stay in the suites, breakfast is complimentary. ⊠ *2151 Laurelwood Rd., 95054,* ☎ *408/988–8411 or 800/255–9925,* 🖷 *408/988–0225. 262 rooms. Restaurant, lounge, in-room modem lines, no-smoking rooms, pool, hot tub, health club, meeting rooms, airport shuttle, free parking. AE, D, DC, MC, V.*

$$ 🏨 **Madison Street Inn.** This refurbished Queen Anne Victorian has the feel of a private home. Afternoon refreshments are served on a brick garden patio with a bougainvillea-draped trellis. ⊠ *1390 Madison St., 95050,* ☎ *408/249–5541,* 🖷 *408/249–6676. 5 rooms, 3 with bath. No-smoking rooms, pool, hot tub, meeting rooms. Full breakfast. AE, D, DC, MC, V.*

South Bay Essentials

ARRIVING AND DEPARTING

By Car: The quickest route to downtown San Jose from San Francisco is I–280. In San Jose, take I–280's Guadalupe Parkway (also known as Highway 87) exit and head north; and exit the parkway on Santa Clara Street and head east. To reach Santa Clara from San Francisco take U.S. 101 and exit south on the San Tomas Expressway; turn left on El Camino Real (also known as Highway 82). To avoid the often heavy commuter traffic on U.S. 101, use I–280 during rush hour. Just before the San Jose exit, take I–880 north to the Alameda, which becomes El Camino Real; turn left off the exit ramp and follow the signs to Santa Clara.

By Plane: Many major airlines serve **San Jose International Airport** (⊠ Airport Blvd. off Hwy. 87, ☎ 408/277–4759). **South & East Bay Airport Shuttle** (☎ 408/559–9477) transports visitors ($15 to downtown) to and from the airport. A taxi to downtown costs about $12 plus tip. To drive to downtown San Jose from the airport, take Airport Boulevard east to Highway 87 (Guadalupe Parkway) south.

By Train and Bus: CalTrain (☎ 800/660–4287) runs from 4th and Townsend streets in San Francisco to the Railroad in Santa Clara and Franklin streets stop (near the university) and to San Jose's Rod Diridon station. The trip to Santa Clara takes approximately 1¼ hours; the trip to San Jose takes about 1½ hours. A **shuttle** (☎ 408/321–2300) links downtown San Jose to the CalTrain station, across from the San Jose Arena, every 20 minutes during morning and evening commute hours.

GETTING AROUND

By Light Rail and Trolley: In San Jose, light-rail trains serve most major attractions, shopping malls, historic sites, and downtown. Trains operate on weekdays every 10 to 15 minutes between 4:30 AM and 1:30 AM and on weekends every 15 to 30 minutes between 5:45 AM and 1:30 AM. Tickets are valid for two hours; they cost $1.10 one-way or $2.50 for a day pass. Historic trolleys operate in downtown San Jose from 11 to 7 during the summer and on some holidays throughout the year. Buy tickets for the light-rail and the trolleys at vending machines in any transit station. For information about passes call or visit the **Transit Information Center** (⊠ 4 N. 2nd St., San Jose, ☎ 408/321–2300).

VISITOR INFORMATION

Santa Clara Chamber of Commerce and Convention and Visitors Bureau (⊠ 1850 Warburton Ave., Santa Clara 95052, ☎ 408/244–8244). **San Jose Convention and Visitors Bureau** (⊠ 150 W. San Carlos St., 95110, ☎ 408/977–0900; ⊠ 333 W. San Carlos St., Suite 1000, San Jose 95110, ☎ 408/295–9600). **San Jose Tourist Bureau's FYI Hotline** (☎ 408/295–2265).

SAN FRANCISCO A TO Z

Arriving and Departing

By Bus

Greyhound (☎ 800/231–2222) serves San Francisco from the Transbay Terminal at 1st and Mission streets.

By Car

Interstate 80 finishes its westward journey from New York's George Washington Bridge at the San Francisco–Oakland Bay Bridge. U.S. 101, enters the city from the north at the Golden Gate Bridge and continues south down the peninsula, along the west side of the San Francisco Bay.

By Plane

San Francisco International Airport (⊠ U.S. 101, south of San Francisco, ☎ 650/761–0800) is the major gateway to San Francisco. **Oakland Airport** (⊠ 1 Airport Dr., off I–880, ☎ 510/577–4000) is across the bay. **San Jose International Airport** (☎ 408/277–4759) is 3 mi from downtown San Jose (☞ South Bay Essentials, *above*).

Carriers serving San Francisco include Alaska, America West, American, Continental, Delta, Midwest Express, Northwest, Reno Air, Southwest, TWA, United, and US Airways. Carriers flying into Oakland include America West, American, Delta, Southwest, and United. Carriers serving San Jose include Alaska, America West, American Continental, Delta, Northwest, TWA, and United. *See* Air Travel *in* the Gold Guide for airline phone numbers.

BETWEEN THE AIRPORT AND DOWNTOWN

From SFO: A taxi ride from SFO to downtown costs about $30. The **SFO Airporter** (☎ 415/495–8404) picks up passengers outside baggage claim (lower level) and stops at selected downtown hotels ($10). **SuperShuttle** (☎ 415/558–8500) stops at the upper-level traffic islands. The cost ranges from $10 to $28 depending on your destination within San Francisco. **Bayporter Express** (☎ 415/467–1800) shuttles to the East Bay (about $20) also depart from SFO's upper-level traffic islands. The cheapest way to get from the airport to San Francisco is via **SamTrans** (☎ 800/660–4287). Bus 7B (55 minutes; $2) and 7F (35 minutes; $2.50; only one small carry-on bag permitted) head to San Francisco; Bus 3X stops at the Colma BART station (☞ BART, Getting Around, *below*), where you can board a train headed downtown. Board the SamTrans buses on the upper (departures) level. If you have questions about the taxis, buses, and trains that serve the airport, you can talk to one of the staff members of the **Ground Transportation Hotline** (☎ 800/736–2008).

To drive to downtown San Francisco from the airport, take U.S. 101 north to the Civic Center (Ninth Street), Seventh Street, or Fourth Street exit. If you're headed to the Embarcadero or Fisherman's Wharf, take U.S. 101 north to just past 3Com Park and exit onto I–280 north, which you'll follow to the Fourth Street/King Street exit. King Street becomes the Embarcadero a few blocks east of the exit. The Embarcadero winds around the waterfront to Fisherman's Wharf.

From Oakland International: A taxi from Oakland's airport to downtown San Francisco costs between $30 and $35. **America's Shuttle** (☎ 515/841–0272 or 415/515–0273), Bayporter Express (☞ *above*), and other shuttles serve major hotels and provide door-to-door service to the East Bay and San Francisco; Bayporter Express also serves the Peninsula and the South Bay. The best way to get to San Francisco via public transit is to take the AIR BART bus ($2) to the Coliseum/Oakland International Airport BART station (BART fares vary depending on where you're going; the ride to San Francisco costs $2.75).

If you're driving to San Francisco from Oakland International Airport, take Hegenberger Road east to I–880 north and follow signs to I–80 west (eventually the San Francisco–Oakland Bay Bridge).

By Train
Amtrak (☎ 800/872–7245) trains—the *Zephyr,* from Chicago via Denver, and the *Coast Starlight,* traveling between Los Angeles and Seattle—stop in Emeryville (⊠ 5885 Landregan St.) and Oakland (⊠ 245 2nd St., in Jack London Sq.). Shuttle buses connect the Emeryville station and San Francisco's Ferry Building (⊠ 30 Embarcadero, at the foot of Market St.).

Getting Around

By Bus and Light Rail
San Francisco Municipal Railway System, or Muni (☎ 415/673–6864), includes buses, light-rail vehicles, and antique trolleys. There is 24-hour service, the fare is $1. The exact fare is always required; dollar bills or change are accepted. Transfers are issued free upon request at the time the fare is paid. They are valid for 90 minutes to two hours for two boardings of a bus or streetcar in any direction.

A $6 pass good for unlimited travel all day on all routes can be purchased from ticket machines at cable-car terminals and at the Visitor Information Center in Hallidie Plaza.

You can use **Bay Area Rapid Transit (BART)** (☎ 800/817–1717) trains to reach Oakland, Berkeley, Concord, Richmond, Fremont, Colma, and Martinez; extensions are expected to open southeast to Castro Valley and Dublin. Trains also travel south from San Francisco as far as Daly City. Fares run from $1.10 to $4.70, and a $3 excursion ticket buys a three-county tour.

By Cable Cars
Cable cars are popular, crowded, and an experience to ride: Move toward one quickly as it pauses, wedge yourself into any available space, and hold on! The sensation of moving up and down some of San Francisco's steepest hills in a small, open-air, clanging conveyance is not to be missed.

The fare (for one direction) is $2. Exact change is preferred, but operators will make change up to $20. There are self-service ticket machines (which do make change) at a few major stops and at all the terminals. The one exception is the busy cable car terminal at Powell and Market streets; purchase tickets at the kiosk there. Be wary of street people attempting to "help" you buy a ticket.

The Powell-Mason line (No. 59) and the Powell-Hyde line (No. 60) begin at Powell and Market streets near Union Square and terminate at Fisherman's Wharf. The California Street line (No. 61), often less crowded than the other two, runs east and west from Market Street near the Embarcadero to Van Ness Avenue.

By Car

Driving in San Francisco can be a challenge because of the hills, the one-way streets, and the traffic. Take it easy, remember to curb your wheels when parking on hills, and use public transportation whenever possible. This is a great city for walking and a so-so city for parking. On certain streets, parking is forbidden during rush hours. Look for the warning signs; illegally parked cars are towed.

The commercial parking lots downtown are often full and always expensive. The city-owned **Ellis-O'Farrell Garage** (✉ 123 O'Farrell St., at Stockton St., ☎ 415/986–4800), **5th and Mission Garage** (✉ 833 Mission St., at 5th St., ☎ 415/982–8522), and **Sutter-Stockton Garage** (✉ 330 Sutter St., at Stockton St., ☎ 415/982–7275) have the most reasonable rates in the downtown area. Even folks with good parking karma have trouble scaring up a spot in North Beach and Chinatown; if you're going to be visiting both these neighborhoods, try the **766 Vallejo Garage** (✉ 766 Vallejo St., at Powell St., ☎ 415/989–4490) in North Beach. A few blocks south in Chinatown is the convenient, if expensive, **Portsmouth Square Garage** (✉ 733 Kearny St., at Clay St., ☎ 415/982–6353). The **Pier 39 Garage** (✉ 2550 Powell St., at the Embarcadero, ☎ 415/705–5418) and the **Wharf Garage** (✉ Fisherman's Wharf, 350 Beach St., at Taylor St., ☎ 415/921–0226) are two large garages along the Northern Waterfront.

Contacts and Resources

Doctors

Two hospitals with 24-hour emergency rooms are **San Francisco General Hospital** (✉ 1001 Potrero Ave., ☎ 415/206–8000) and the **Medical Center at the University of California, San Francisco** (✉ 500 Parnassus Ave., ☎ 415/476–1000).

Physician Access Medical Center (✉ 26 California St., ☎ 415/397–2881) is a drop-in clinic in the Financial District, open weekdays 7:30 AM–5 PM. **Access Health Care** (☎ 415/565–6600) provides drop-in medical care at Davies Medical Center, Castro Street at Duboce Avenue, daily from 8 to 8.

Emergencies

Ambulance (☎ 911). **Fire** (☎ 911). **Police** (☎ 911).

Guided Tours

ORIENTATION TOURS

In addition to bus and van tours of the city, most tour companies run excursions to various Bay Area and northern California destinations such as Marin County and the Wine Country, as well as farther flung areas like Monterey and Yosemite. City tours generally last 3½ hours and cost between $25 and $30. It's wise to reserve space on tours at least a day ahead. Tour companies include **Golden Gate Tours** (☎ 415/788–5775), **Gray Line Tours** (☎ 415/558–9400), **Great Pacific Tour** (☎ 415/626–4499), and **Tower Tours** (☎ 415/434–8687).

WALKING TOURS

Trevor Hailey's 3¾-hour **Cruising the Castro** (☎ 415/550–8110) tour focuses on the history and development of the city's gay and lesbian community. The cost is $35, which includes brunch. Reservations are required. The **Chinatown with the "Wok Wiz"** (☎ 415/981–8989) tour by cookbook author Shirley Fong-Torres and her staff is a 3½-hour spin through Chinese markets, other businesses, and a fortune-cookie factory. The $37 fee includes lunch; the cost is $25 without lunch. Shorter group tours start at $15 per person. **Chinese Cultural Heritage Foundation** (☎ 415/986–1822) conducts two walking tours of Chinatown. The Heritage Walk leaves on Saturday at 2 PM and lasts about two hours; the cost is $15. The Culinary Walk, a three-hour stroll through the markets and food shops, plus a dim sum lunch, is is given from Tuesday to Friday at 10:30 AM; the fee is $30. **City Guides** (☎ 415/557–4266), a free service sponsored by the Friends of the Library, tours Chinatown, North Beach, Coit Tower, Pacific Heights mansions, Japantown, the Haight-Ashbury, historic Market Street, the Palace Hotel, and downtown roof gardens and atriums. Schedules are available at the San Francisco Visitors Center at Powell and Market streets and at library branches.

Late-Night Pharmacies

Several **Walgreen Drug Stores** have 24-hour pharmacies, including the locations at 135 Powell Street, near Market Street (☎ 415/391–7222) and 3201 Divisadero Street, at Lombard Street (☎ 415/931–6417).

Visitor Information

Redwood Empire Association Visitor Information Center (✉ The Cannery, 2801 Leavenworth St., 2nd Floor, 94133, ☎ 415/394–5991 or 888/678–8507). **San Francisco Convention and Visitors Bureau** (✉ 900 Market St., at Powell St., 94102, ☎ 415/391–2000).

6 Sacramento and the Gold Country

Including Highway 49 from Nevada City to Mariposa

The gold-mining region of the Sierra Nevada foothills is a less expensive, if less sophisticated, region of California but not without its pleasures, natural and man-made. Spring brings wildflowers, and in fall the hills are colored by bright-red berries and changing leaves. The hills are golden in the summer—and hot. The Gold Country has a mix of indoor and outdoor activities, one of the many reasons it's a great place to take the kids.

By Bobbi Zane

Updated by
Andy Moore

JAMES MARSHALL TURNED UP a gold nugget in the tailrace of a sawmill he was constructing along the American River and ushered in a whole new era for California. Before January 24, 1848, what would become the Golden State was a beautiful but sparsely populated land over which Mexico and the United States were still wrestling for ownership. With Marshall's discovery and its subsequent confirmation by President James Polk in his State of the Union speech on December 5, 1848, prospectors came to seek their fortunes in the Mother Lode.

As gold fever seized the nation, California's population of 15,000 swelled to 265,000 within three years—44,000 newcomers arrived by ship in San Francisco in the first 10 months alone, the majority of them men under 40, either unattached or with families back east. Most spent about two years in California before returning home, usually with empty pockets or having barely broken even. Historians have noted that the consequences of the gold rush were more than monetary: '49ers—the term used to describe those who arrived in search of gold— who remained in the state contributed to a freer culture that eschewed many of the constricting conventions and values of the eastern states.

Originally, the term Mother Lode denoted a gold-bearing quartz vein 120 mi long between Mariposa in the south and Auburn in the north. It ranged in width from 2 mi to only a few yards. By 1865 it had yielded more than $750 million in gold. As prospectors headed farther afield, the entire gold-rush region came to be known as the Mother Lode. Ironically, neither Marshall, nor John Sutter, on whose property Marshall discovered gold, got rich from the discovery.

The boom brought on by the gold rush lasted scarcely 20 years, but it changed California forever. It produced 546 mining towns, of which fewer than 250 remain. The hills were alive, not only with prospecting and mining but also with business, the arts, gambling, and a fair share of crime. Opera houses went up alongside brothels, and the California State Capitol in Sacramento was built with the gold dug out of the hills. Some of the nation's most treasured writers—Mark Twain and Bret Harte among them—began their careers writing about the mining camps. Gold-rush lore immortalized notorious bandits: When the law finally caught up with the debonair Black Bart, who targeted Wells Fargo stagecoaches and left behind poems (signed "Black Bart— PO-8") at his crime scenes, he turned out to be a well-known San Franciscan. Legend has it that Joaquin Murieta's crime spree—he robbed miners by day, then partied by night at local saloons—followed an assault on him and his family by Yankee prospectors.

Mexican miners weren't the only victims of the Yankee juggernaut. California's leaders in the mid-19th century engaged in a systematic plan to exterminate the local Indian population. Bounties were paid and private militias were hired to wipe out the Indians or sell them into slavery (this in a supposedly "free" state). The racist policies affected more than Native Americans. A law in force from 1850 to 1863 prohibited nonwhites from appearing as witnesses in civil cases—not surprisingly, verdicts and damage awards favored white plaintiffs and defendants.

The northern California cities of Sacramento, San Francisco, and Stockton grew quickly to meet the needs of the surrounding gold fields. Saloon keepers and canny merchants recognized that the real gold was to be made from the '49ers. Potatoes and onions sold for as much as $1 apiece, making entrepreneurs like storekeeper Samuel

Brannan millionaires. Much important history was made in Sacramento, the key center of commerce during this period. Pony Express riders ended their nearly 2,000-mi journeys in the city in the 1860s. The transcontinental railroad, conceived here by the Big Four (Leland Stanford, Mark Hopkins, Collis P. Huntington, and Charles Clocker), was completed in 1869.

By the 1960s the scars mining had inflicted on the Gold Country landscape had largely healed. To promote tourism, townspeople began restoring vintage structures, historians developed museums, and the state established parks and recreation areas to preserve this extraordinary episode in American history. Today visitors flock to Nevada City, Auburn, Coloma, Sutter Creek, and Columbia, not only to relive the past but also to explore museums and art galleries and to stay over at bed-and-breakfast inns.

Pleasures and Pastimes

Adventuring

Scenic and challenging Gold Country rivers, particularly the American and Tuolumne, lure white-water enthusiasts each spring and summer. Early-morning hot-air balloon excursions take aeronauts above treetops in deep canyons of the American River. Throughout the region weekend prospectors pan for gold, turning up nuggets frequently enough to inspire others to participate.

Dining

American, Italian, and Mexican fare are common in the Gold Country, but chefs also prepare ambitious Continental, French, and California cuisine. Away from Sacramento or the interstate highways, fast-food chains are few and far between. It's not difficult, though, to find the makings for a good picnic in most Gold Country towns.

CATEGORY	COST*
$$$$	over $50
$$$	$30–$50
$$	$20–$30
$	under $20

*per person for a three-course meal, excluding drinks, service, and 7¾% tax

Lodging

Full-service hotels, budget motels, small inns, and even a fine hostel can all be found in Sacramento. The main accommodations in the larger towns along Highway 49—among them Placerville, Nevada City, Auburn, and Mariposa—are chain motels and bed-and-breakfast inns. Many Gold Country B&Bs occupy former mansions, miners' cabins, and other historic buildings.

CATEGORY	COST*
$$$$	over $175
$$$	$120–$175
$$	$80–$120
$	under $80

*All prices are for a standard double room, excluding 7¼% tax (12% in Sacramento).

Shopping

Shoppers visit the Gold Country in search of antiques, collectibles, art, quilts, toys, tools, decorative items, and furnishings. Handmade quilts and crafts can be found in Sutter Creek, Jackson, and Amador City; Auburn and Nevada City support many gift boutiques.

Exploring Sacramento and the Gold Country

Visiting Old Sacramento's museums is a good way to steep yourself in gold-rush history, but the Gold Country's heart lies along Highway 49, which winds the 325-mi north–south length of the historic mining area. The highway, often a twisting, hilly, two-lane road, begs for a convertible with the top down.

Numbers in the text correspond to numbers in the margin and on the Gold Country and Sacramento maps.

Great Itineraries

IF YOU HAVE 1 DAY

Drive east from Sacramento on I–80 to **Auburn** ⑯ for a tour of the **Placer County Courthouse** and its museum. Travel south on Highway 49 to the **Marshall Gold Discovery State Historic Park** ⑰ at Coloma. Head back to Sacramento for a cocktail or a soda at the bar on the *Delta King* and an evening stroll and dinner along the waterfront in **Old Sacramento.** The historical attractions will be closed, but you'll still get a feel for life here during the last half of the 19th century.

IF YOU HAVE 3 DAYS

Begin your tour on Highway 49 north of I–80. Walk deep into the recesses of the **Empire Mine** ⑮ near **Grass Valley,** and then drive 4 mi north on Highway 49 for a visit to the **Miners Foundry** in **Nevada City** ⑭. After lunch, travel south to ⌖ **Auburn** ⑯, where you can take in the **Placer County Courthouse** and museum, have dinner, and spend the night. Early the next morning head south to tour **Marshall Gold Discovery State Historic Park** ⑰ in Coloma. Continue south to ⌖ **Sutter Creek** ⑲ and spend the afternoon exploring the boutiques and antiques stores. If exploring a good vintage is more your game, take a detour to the **Shenandoah Valley,** southeast of **Placerville,** and taste some wine before continuing on to Sutter Creek. Either way, spend the night in Sutter Creek. Return early the next day to **Sacramento** to visit the **California State Railroad Museum** ① and **Sutter's Fort** ⑫.

IF YOU HAVE 5 DAYS

Visit the **Empire Mine** ⑮, **Nevada City** ⑭, and ⌖ **Auburn** ⑯ on day one. See Coloma's **Marshall Gold Discovery State Historic Park** ⑰ on the second day, and then continue on to ⌖ **Sutter Creek** ⑲. On your third morning, visit the **Amador County Museum** in **Jackson** ⑳ before heading south on Highway 49 and east on Highway 4 for lunch in **Murphys** ㉒. Back on Highway 49 still southward is ⌖ **Columbia State Historic Park** ㉓. You can relive the 1800s by dining and spending the night at the City Hotel. If you've been itching to pan for gold, do that in the morning in the state park, and then head back to ⌖ **Sacramento** (Highway 49 north to Highway 16 west) for a riverboat cruise. Visit the **California State Railroad Museum** ① and **Sutter's Fort** ⑫ on day five.

When to Tour the Gold Country

The Gold Country is the most pleasant in the spring, when the wildflowers are in bloom, and in the fall. Summers are beautiful, too, but hot: Temperatures near or above 100°F are common all summer long. Sacramento winters tend to be cold and foggy. Throughout the year Gold Country towns stage community and ethnic celebrations. In December many towns deck themselves out for the Christmas holidays. Sacramento hosts the annual Jazz Jubilee in May and the California State Fair in August. Flowers bloom on Daffodil Hill in March.

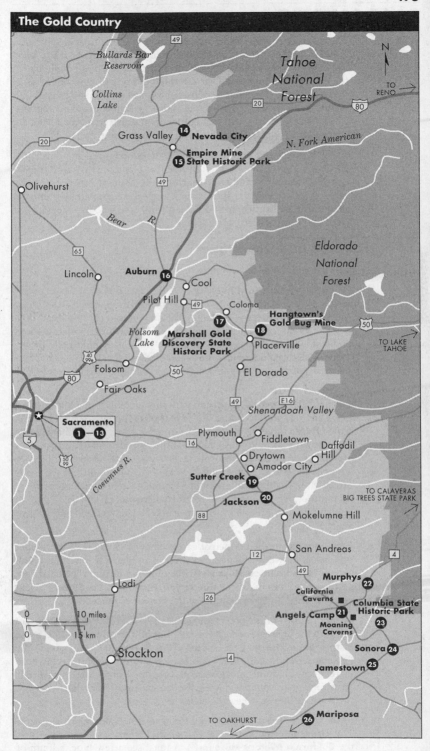

The Gold Country

- 49
- *Bullards Bar Reservoir*
- *Collins Lake*
- *Tahoe National Forest*
- 20
- 80
- TO RENO
- 20
- Grass Valley
- **14** **Nevada City**
- **15** **Empire Mine State Historic Park**
- *N. Fork American*
- 49
- Olivehurst
- *Bear R.*
- *Eldorado National Forest*
- 65
- Lincoln
- **Auburn** **16**
- Cool
- Pilot Hill
- 49
- Coloma
- **Hangtown's Gold Bug Mine**
- 50
- TO LAKE TAHOE
- **17**
- *Folsom Lake*
- **Marshall Gold Discovery State Historic Park**
- **18** Placerville
- 40 99e
- 80
- Folsom
- 50
- El Dorado
- Fair Oaks
- 49
- E16
- *Shenandoah Valley*
- ✪
- **Sacramento**
- **1** — **13**
- 5
- Plymouth
- Fiddletown
- Daffodil Hill
- 16
- Drytown
- Amador City
- **Sutter Creek** **19**
- 50 99
- *Cosumnes R.*
- **Jackson** **20**
- TO CALAVERAS BIG TREES STATE PARK
- 88
- Mokelumne Hill
- San Andreas
- 12
- 49
- 4
- **Murphys** **22**
- California Caverns
- **Columbia State Historic Park**
- Lodi
- 26
- **Angels Camp** **21**
- Moaning Caverns
- **23**
- **Sonora** **24**
- 0   10 miles
- 0   15 km
- Stockton
- 4
- **Jamestown** **25**
- TO OAKHURST
- **26** **Mariposa**

SACRAMENTO

The gateway to the Gold Country, the seat of California state government, and an agricultural hub, the city of Sacramento plays many important contemporary roles. One and a half million people live in the metropolitan area, and the continuing influx of newcomers seeking opportunity, sunshine, and lower housing costs than in coastal California have made it one of the nation's fastest-growing regions. Midtown's many new cafés and downtown's revived K Street Mall are testaments to Sacramento's growing sophistication.

Sacramento contains more than 2,000 acres of natural and developed parkland. This "city of a million trees" is planted with grand old evergreens, deciduous and fruit-bearing trees (some streets are virtually covered with oranges in springtime), and even giant palms, giving it a shady, lush quality. Genteel Victorian edifices sit side-by-side with Art Deco and postmodern skyscrapers.

Old Sacramento and Downtown

87 mi northeast of San Francisco, I–80 to Hwy. 99.

Wooden sidewalks and horse-drawn carriages on cobblestone streets lend a 19th-century feel to Old Sacramento, a 28-acre district along the Sacramento River waterfront. The museums at the north end hold artifacts of state and national significance. Historic buildings house shops and restaurants. River cruises and train rides bring gold-rush history to life. Call the **Old Sacramento Events Hotline** (☎ 916/558–3912) for information about living-history re-creations and merchant hours.

A Good Tour

Old Sacramento, the Capitol and park surrounding it, and Sutter's Fort lie on an east–west axis that begins at the Sacramento River. The walk from Old Sacramento to the State Capitol is easy, passing through the Downtown Plaza shopping mall and pedestrians-only K Street. This area takes on a festive atmosphere during an outdoor market held on Thursday evening. A free shuttle links the Convention Center, the K Street Mall, downtown, and Old Sacramento. The shuttle runs every 15 minutes, from Monday to Saturday between 11 and 7:30, and on Sunday between 11 and 6. Stops are marked by orange and purple "free shuttle" signs.

Park your car in the municipal garage under I–5 at 2nd Street (enter on I Street between 2nd and 3rd streets), and head to the superb **California State Railroad Museum** ①, then browse through the hardware and household items at the **Huntington, Hopkins & Co. Store** ②. Next door are the hands-on exhibits of the **Discovery Museum** ③.

To learn more about Sacramento's role in rail history walk a few paces south to the **Central Pacific Passenger Depot.** Across Front Street is the historic **Eagle Theater** ④. The **Central Pacific Freight Depot,** next to the Passenger Depot, houses a **Public Market** (closed on Monday), whose merchants sell food and gift items. The foot of K Street (at Front Street) is a great spot for viewing the Sacramento River wharf area and the restored sternwheeler the *Delta King.*

At the corner of 2nd and J streets is the historic **B. F. Hastings Building** ⑤. The **Visitor Information Center** ⑥ is on 2nd Street in the same block as the **California Military Museum** ⑦. A must-see a few blocks south of Old Sacramento is the **Crocker Art Museum** ⑧, the oldest art museum in the American West. From here walk south on Front Street to the **Towe Auto Museum** ⑨. If you'd rather skip the automotive museum, walk up 3rd Street to the Capitol Mall, which leads to the **Capitol** ⑩.

Sacramento

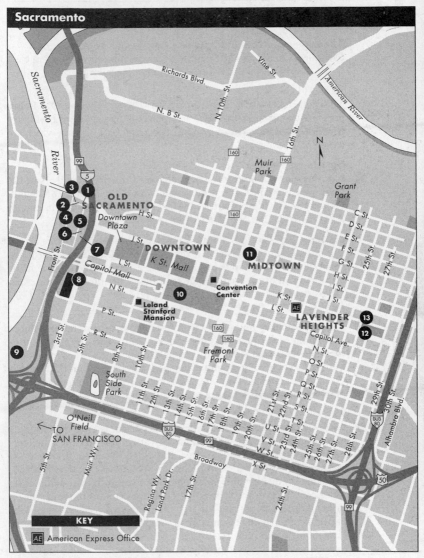

Sacramento River

Richards Blvd.

Vine St.

American River

N. 10th St.

N. B St.

16th St.

160

160

Muir Park

N

Grant Park

③ ①

OLD SACRAMENTO

② H St.

Downtown Plaza

C St.

D St.

E St.

F St.

④ ⑤

I St.

G St.

25th St.

27th St.

⑥

DOWNTOWN

H St.

⑦

K St. Mall

MIDTOWN

⑪

I St.

J St.

Capitol Mall

L St.

L St.

⑧

N St.

⑩

Convention Center

K St.

L St.

AE

LAVENDER HEIGHTS

⑬

Leland Stanford Mansion

P St.

⑫

Capitol Ave.

3rd St.

R St.

160

N St.

5th St.

160

O St.

South Side Park

8th St.

10th St.

Fremont Park

P St.

Q St.

R St.

29th St.

30th St.

Alhambra Blvd.

⑨

O'Neil Field

11th St.

12th St.

13th St.

14th St.

15th St.

16th St.

17th St.

18th St.

19th St.

20th St.

S St.

21st St.

22nd St.

T St.

23rd St.

24th St.

U St.

25th St.

26th St.

27th St.

28th St.

BUS 80

TO SAN FRANCISCO

BUS 80

V St.

W St.

99

X St.

50

5th St.

Muir Wy.

Regina Wy.

Land Park Dr.

17th St.

Broadway

24th St.

99

KEY

AE American Express Office

B.F. Hastings Building, **5**

California Military Museum, **7**

California State Railroad Museum, **1**

Capitol, **10**

Crocker Art Museum, **8**

Discovery Museum, **3**

Eagle Theater, **4**

Governor's Mansion, **11**

Huntington, Hopkins & Co. Store, **2**

State Indian Museum, **13**

Sutter's Fort, **12**

Towe Auto Museum, **9**

Visitor Information Center, **6**

If you're still going strong, walk up to H Street to **Governor's Mansion** ⑪. Otherwise, walk back to your car via J Street.

Though it requires a drive, **Sutter's Fort** ⑫ is not to be missed: It was Sacramento's earliest settlement; evocative exhibits bring that era back to life. North of the fort is the **State Indian Museum** ⑬.

TIMING

This tour makes for a leisurely day, less if you only visit Old Sacramento. Most of the attractions are open daily, except for the Military Museum, the Eagle Theater, and the Crocker Art Museum, which are closed on Monday.

Sights to See

❺ **B. F. Hastings Building.** A reconstruction of the first chambers of the California Supreme Court occupies the second floor of this 1853 building; on the first floor there's a Wells Fargo History Museum and an ATM. ✉ *1000 2nd St.,* ☎ *916/440–4263.* ☉ *Daily 10–5.*

Cal Expo. The California State Fair, a celebration of the state's agricultural and other industries, takes place at the Cal Expo fairgrounds between mid-August and early September. Livestock and other animals are always on display, competing for ribbons in untold categories. ✉ *Exposition Blvd. (north of downtown, take Cal Expo exit off I–80 Business Loop),* ☎ *916/263–3247.*

❼ **California Military Museum.** A storefront entrance leads to three floors containing more than 30,000 artifacts—uniforms, weapons, photographs, documents, medals, and flags of all kinds—that trace Californians' roles in military and militia activities throughout U.S. history. An interesting display outlines the African-American experience; another includes Civil War–era medical equipment. ✉ *1119 2nd St.,* ☎ *916/442–2883.* ☜ *$3.* ☉ *Tues.–Sun. 10–4.*

★ ☃ ❶ **California State Railroad Museum.** Near what was once the terminus of the transcontinental and Sacramento Valley railroads (the actual terminus was at Front and K streets), this 100,000-square-ft museum is the largest of its kind in North America, with 21 locomotives and railroad cars on display and 46 exhibits. You can walk through a post-office car and peer into cubbyholes and canvas bags of mail, enter a sleeping car that simulates the swaying on the roadbed and the flashing lights of a passing town at night, or glimpse the inside of the first-class dining car on the *Super Chief.* Allow at least a couple of hours to experience the museum fully. ✉ *125 I St.,* ☎ *916/445–6645.* ☜ *$6.* ☉ *Daily 10–5.*

❿ **Capitol.** The Golden State's Capitol was built in 1869. The lacy plasterwork of the 120-ft-high rotunda has the complexity and color of a Fabergé Easter egg. Underneath the gilded dome are marble floors, glittering chandeliers, monumental staircases, original artworks, replicas of 19th-century state offices, and legislative chambers decorated in the style of the 1890s. Hallway displays for each of California's counties reflect the state's diversity. Guides conduct tours of the building and the 40-acre Capitol Park, which contains a rose garden, an impressive display of camellias (Sacramento's city flower), and the California Vietnam Veterans Memorial. ✉ *Capitol Mall and 10th St.,* ☎ *916/324–0333.* ☜ *Free.* ☉ *Daily 9–4; tours hourly.*

☃ **Central Pacific Passenger Depot.** At this reconstructed 1876 station there's rolling stock to admire, a typical waiting room, and a little café. Rides on a steam-powered train depart from the freight depot, south of the passenger depot. The train makes a 40-minute loop along the Sacramento riverfront. ✉ *930 Front St.,* ☎ *916/445–6645.* ☜ *$6 (free with* *same-day ticket from California State Railroad Museum); train ride $5 additional.* ⊙ *Depot daily 10–5. Train operates every weekend Apr.– Sept., 1st weekend of month Oct.–Dec.*

★ ❽ **Crocker Art Museum.** The oldest art museum in the American West has a collection of art from Europe, Asia, and California, including *Sunday Morning in the Mines* (1872), a large canvas by Charles Christian Nahl depicting the mining industry of the 1850s, and the magnificent *The Great Canyon of the Sierra, Yosemite* (1871) by Thomas Hill. The museum's lobby and ballroom retain the original 1870s woodwork, plaster moldings, and imported English tiles. ⊠ *216 O St.,* ☎ *916/264–5423.* ⊡ *$4.50.* ⊙ *Tues.–Wed. and Fri.–Sun. 10–5, Thurs. 10–9.*

⬧ ❸ **Discovery Museum.** The building that holds this kids-oriented museum is a replica of the 1854 City Hall and Waterworks. The emphasis is on interactive exhibits that combine history, science, and technology. You can sift for gold, walk into an Indian thatched hut, or experience the goings-on in the print shop of the old *Sacramento Bee* newspaper. The Gold Gallery displays nuggets and veins. ⊠ *101 I St.,* ☎ *916/264– 7057.* ⊡ *$4.* ⊙ *Daily 10–5.*

❹ **Eagle Theater.** When the Eagle opened in 1849, audiences paid between $3 and $5 in gold coin or dust to sit on rough boards and watch professional actors. This replica was constructed with the tentlike canvas and ship's-timber walls of olden times, though now there's insulation and the bench seats are cushioned. The theater hosts programs that range from a 13-minute slide show to puppet, minstrel, and juggling acts. ⊠ *925 Front St.,* ☎ *916/323–6343.* ⊙ *Spring–summer, Tues.– Fri. 10–4; fall–winter, Tues.–Thur. 10–4.*

⓫ **Governor's Mansion.** This 15-room house was built in 1877 and used by the state's chief executives from the early 1900s until 1967, when Ronald Reagan vacated it in favor of a newly built home in the suburbs. Many of the Italianate mansion's interior decorative details were ordered from the Huntington Hopkins hardware store, one of whose partners, Albert Gallatin, was the original occupant. Each of the seven marble fireplaces has a petticoat mirror that ladies strolled past to see if their slips were showing. The mansion is said to have been one of the first homes in California to have an indoor bathroom. ⊠ *1526 H St.,* ☎ *916/323–3047.* ⊡ *$3.* ⊙ *Daily 10–4; tours hourly.*

❷ **Huntington, Hopkins & Co. Store.** This museum is a replica of the 1850 hardware store opened by Collis Huntington and Mark Hopkins, two of the Big Four businessmen who established the Central Pacific Railroad. Picks, shovels, gold pans, and other paraphernalia miners used during the gold rush are on display, along with household hardware and appliances used by later settlers. ⊠ *113 I St.,* ☎ *916/323–9280.* ⊙ *Hours vary.*

Leland Stanford Mansion. The home of Leland Stanford, a railroad baron, California governor, and U.S. senator, was built in 1856, with additions in 1862 and the early 1870s. Major restoration of this once-grand edifice will begin in 1999. Some of the floors of the mansion, which will operate as a museum and a site for official state receptions, may be open to the public by late 2000. ⊠ *802 N St.,* ☎ *916/ 324–0575.*

★ ⬧ ⓭ **State Indian Museum.** Among the interesting displays at this well-organized museum is one devoted to Ishi, the last Yahi Indian to emerge from the mountains, in 1911. Yahi provided scientists insight into the traditions and culture of this group of Native Americans. Arts-and-crafts exhibits, a demonstration village, and an evocative 10-minute video bring to life the multifaceted past and present of California's Indian peoples. ⊠ *2601 K St.,* ☎ *916/324–0971.* ⊠ *$3.* ☉ *Daily 10–5.*

★ ☾ ⑫ **Sutter's Fort.** Sacramento's earliest settlement was founded by German-born Swiss immigrant John Augustus Sutter in 1839. Visitors walk a self-guided tour; audio speakers at each stop explain exhibits that include a blacksmith's shop, a bakery, a prison, living quarters, and livestock areas. Costumed docents sometimes reenact fort life, demonstrating crafts, food preparation, and firearms maintenance. ⊠ *2701 L St.,* ☎ *916/445–4422.* ⊠ *$5 Memorial Day–Labor Day and on Living History Days; $3 rest of yr.* ☉ *Daily 10–5.*

☾ ⑨ **Towe Auto Museum.** The Internal Revenue Service seized many of the Ford automobiles of the former Towe Ford Museum of Automotive History in 1997, but with well over 100 cars it remains an interesting stop. Docents are usually available to provide information about specific models, including a 1931 Chrysler, a 1960 Lotus, and a bulletproof Cadillac limousine once used by the U.S. State Department. A 1920s roadside café and garage exhibit re-creates the early days of motoring. A gift shop sells vintage-car magazines, model kits, old license plates, and other car-related items. ⊠ *2200 Front St., one block off Broadway,* ☎ *916/442–6802.* ⊠ *$5.* ☉ *Daily 10–6.*

⑥ **Visitor Information Center.** This center is modeled on similarly helpful havens in Europe. You can obtain brochures about nearby attractions, arrange lodgings, check local restaurant menus, rent strollers or wheelchairs, send mail, and receive directions in five languages. ⊠ *1101 2nd St., at K St.,* ☎ *916/442–7644.* ☉ *Daily 9–5 (post office 9–4).*

Dining

CALIFORNIA

$$–$$$ ✕ **City Treasure.** A curved wall of windows shows off the interior of this "all world" restaurant to its fashionable midtown neighbors. Burnished copper tables and lamps, grapevine-pattern booths and banquets, and locally produced artworks create a delightful setting. The eclectic menu changes seasonally; grilled Asian chicken salad, Cajun fettuccine, grilled salmon, and braised beef and pork cannelloni are among the past offerings. From the wine list of more than 200 California wines, you can choose one of almost 50 by the glass, or have a trio—a sampler of three 3-ounce pours. ⊠ *1730 L St.,* ☎ *916/447–7380. AE, D, DC, MC, V. No lunch Sat.*

$$–$$$ ✕ **Restaurant 1201.** This dimly lit lobby restaurant and cocktail lounge, owned by the California Dental Association (no, there are no floss dispensers at the tables), overlooks the promenade at the east end of the K Street Mall. Dramatic presentations on the menu, which changes monthly, might include appetizers of Medusa crab cakes or an entrée of baked leg of rabbit in thyme mousseline. Among the desserts are the fresh berry tarts and the chocolate tulip cup with espresso ganache and caramel straws. ⊠ *1201 K St.,* ☎ *916/444–1015. AE, D, MC, V. No lunch weekends; no dinner Sun.–Mon.*

$$–$$$ ✕ **Rio City Café.** Eclectic lunch and dinner menus and huge floor-to-ceiling windows with views of an Old Sacramento wharf are the dual attractions of this bright restaurant. When the weather is good you can enjoy your meals at water's edge. Rio City serves light and hearty fare: calamari salad, duck enchiladas with tomatillo sauce, venison stew in pinot-noir sauce over spaetzle, fettuccine with sun-dried tomato pesto. ⊠ *1110 Front St.,* ☎ *916/442–8226. AE, D, DC, MC, V.*

$$-$$$ ✕ **Twenty Eight.** An intimate space with smoked mirrors, a rose-colored crushed satin ceiling, richly upholstered furniture, and artful lighting, Twenty Eight further charms with genteel and attentive service. The food—appetizers like wild-mushroom soup with cognac cream and main courses that include sesame-crusted ahi tuna with crispy noodles and grilled lamb loin with roasted artichokes—is as lush as the decor. ⊠ *2730 N St.,* ☎ *916/456–2800. AE, D, DC, MC, V. Closed Sun.; no lunch weekends.*

$-$$$ ✕ **Moxie.** Despite its simple decor and banklike schedule—the place
★ is closed on all holidays—Moxie has earned a reputation as one of the best restaurants in Sacramento. Start with the pork short ribs glazed with red wine and basil or grilled eggplant with feta and capers, and then move on to entrées like spicy jambalaya, roasted duck in espresso-red wine sauce, or prawns carbonara. ⊠ *2028 H St.,* ☎ *916/443–7585. AE, D, DC, MC, V. Closed Sun.–Mon. and Aug.*

$$ ✕ **Paragary's Bar and Oven.** Pastas and brick-oven pizzas are the specialties of this casual spot. You won't go hungry here— portions are enormous. A waterfall flows near the back patio, which holds hundreds of plants. ⊠ *1401 28th St.,* ☎ *916/457–5737. AE, D, DC, MC, V. No lunch weekends.*

CALIFORNIA–PACIFIC RIM

$$-$$$ ✕ **California Fats.** The menu at the better of two Old Sacramento restaurants carrying the Fats name combines intriguing flavors. Among the dishes are seared ahi tuna and glazed duck from a wood-fired oven, pastas with overtones of ginger and coriander, and venison in a cashew crust. ⊠ *1015 Front St.,* ☎ *916/441–7966. AE, MC, V.*

CHINESE

$$-$$$ ✕ **Frank Fat's.** A longtime favorite of lawmakers and lobbyists, Frank Fat's is renowned more for its watering-hole atmosphere than its so-so Chinese food. The menu emphasizes Cantonese cuisine, but there are items from other regions of China. Signature dishes include brandy-fried chicken, stir-fried clams in black-bean sauce, plus a couple of items from an American menu: New York steak and banana cream pie. ⊠ *806 L St.,* ☎ *916/442–7092. AE, MC, V. No lunch weekends.*

ITALIAN

$$$ ✕ **Biba.** Owner Biba Caggiano is an authority on Italian cuisine, au-
★ thor of several cookbooks, and the star of a national TV show on cooking. The Capitol crowd flocks here for delicate pasta dishes, baked spinach lasagna, and homemade tortelloni. Caggiano also offers a great osso buco, rabbit tenderloin, and grilled pork loin, as well as specialties from the Emilia-Romagna region of Italy. ⊠ *2801 Capitol Ave., ☎ 916/455–2422. AE, MC, V. Closed Sun. No lunch Sat.*

MEXICAN

$-$$ ✕ **Centro.** Its cuisine may not be as authentic as is claimed, but Centro deserves credit for conceiving dishes well outside the taco-burrito realm. Unusual items include adobo marinated pork and black-bean-chipotle chili tamales. ⊠ *2730 J St.,* ☎ *916/442–2552. AE, DC, MC, V. No lunch weekends.*

Lodging

$$$-$$$$ 🏠 **Amber House Bed & Breakfast Inn.** Three separate homes compose
★ this B&B near the Capitol. The original house, the Poet's Refuge, is a Craftsman-style home with five bedrooms named for famous poets. Next door the 1913 Mediterranean-style Artist's Retreat has a French Impressionist motif. The third, an 1897 Dutch Colonial Revival home named Musician's Manor, has gardens where weddings occasionally take place. All rooms have private baths tiled with Italian marble; several

rooms have fireplaces and bathrooms with two-person hot tubs and skylights. ⊠ *1315 22nd St., 95816,* ☎ *916/444–8085 or 800/755–6526,* ℻ *916/552–6529. 14 rooms. Air-conditioning, bicycles. Full breakfast. AE, D, DC, MC, V.*

$$$–$$$$ ⊞ **Hyatt Regency at Capitol Park.** With a marble-and-glass lobby and
★ luxurious rooms, this hotel across the street from the Capitol and adjacent to the convention center is arguably Sacramento's finest. The best rooms have Capitol Park views. The service is outstanding. ⊠ *1209 L St., 95814,* ☎ *916/443–1234 or 800/233–1234,* ℻ *916/321–6699. 500 rooms. 2 restaurants, bar, air-conditioning, pool, hot tub, exercise room, nightclub, meeting rooms, car rental. AE, D, DC, MC, V.*

$$–$$$ ⊞ **Abigail's Bed and Breakfast Inn.** Trees shade this 1912 Colonial Revival mansion near the Capitol, in the Boulevard Park neighborhood. The living room and parlor flank a grand staircase leading to guest rooms, some with four-poster or canopy feather beds. One room has a whirlpool tub. ⊠ *2120 G St., 95816,* ☎ *916/441–5007 or 800/858–1568,* ℻ *916/441–0621. 5 rooms. Air-conditioning, outdoor hot tub. Full breakfast. AE, D, DC, MC, V.*

$$–$$$ ⊞ **Delta King.** This grand old riverboat, now permanently moored on Old Sacramento's waterfront, once transported passengers between Sacramento and San Francisco. Among many design elements of note are its main staircase, mahogany paneling, and brass fittings. The best of the 44 staterooms are on the river side toward the back of the boat. ⊠ *1000 Front St., 95814,* ☎ *916/444–5464 or 800/825–5464,* ℻ *916/444–5314. 44 rooms. Restaurant, bar, air-conditioning, meeting rooms, parking (fee). Continental breakfast. AE, D, DC, MC, V.*

$$–$$$ ⊞ **Hartley House.** Innkeeper Randy Hartley's great-grandfather built
★ Hartley House in 1906. The quiet midtown inn has the feel of a small European hotel. All the antiques-filled rooms, which are named after British cities, have stereos and cable TV. Guests have access to a secluded courtyard hot tub. ⊠ *700 22nd St.,95816,* ☎ *916/447–7829 or 800/831–5806,* ℻ *916/447–1820. 5 rooms. Air-conditioning, inroom modem lines, hot tub. Full breakfast. D, DC, MC, V.*

$$–$$$ ⊞ **Holiday Inn Capitol Plaza.** Despite its decided lack of charm, this hotel has modern rooms and the best location for visiting Old Sacramento and the Downtown Plaza. The Holiday Inn is within walking distance of the Capitol. ⊠ *300 J St., 95814,* ☎ *916/446–0100 or 800/465–4329,* ℻ *916/446–0117. 364 rooms. Restaurant, bar, air-conditioning, pool, 2 saunas, convention center. AE, DC, MC, V.*

$–$$$ ⊞ **Radisson Hotel Sacramento.** Mediterranean-style two-story buildings clustered around a large artificial lake on an 18-acre landscaped site contain good-size rooms, with Art Deco appointments and furnishings. Many have patios or balconies. More of a resort than other Sacramento-area hotels, the Radisson presents summer jazz concerts in a lakeside amphitheater and holds barbecues on warm evenings. ⊠ *500 Leisure La., 95815,* ☎ *916/922–2020 or 800/333–3333,* ℻ *916/649–9463. 314 rooms. 2 restaurants, bar, air-conditioning, room service, pool, outdoor hot tub, exercise room, jogging trail, boating, bicycles, meeting rooms. AE, D, DC, MC, V.*

$$ ⊞ **Best Western Sutter House.** Many consider this family-owned property (formerly the Best Western Ponderosa) to be the best value downtown. Many rooms open onto a courtyard surrounding a pool. ⊠ *1100 H St., 95814,* ☎ *916/441–1314; 800/830–1314 in CA;* ℻ *916/441–5961. 98 rooms. Restaurant, lounge, air-conditioning, pool, laundry service, free parking, Continental breakfast. AE, D, DC, MC, V.*

$ ⊞ **Sacramento International Hostel.** This landmark 1885 Victorian mansion has a grand mahogany staircase, a stained-glass atrium, frescoed ceilings, and carved and tiled fireplaces. Dormitory rooms and bedrooms suitable for singles, couples, and families are available, as is a shared kitchen. ⊠ *900 H St., 95814,* ☎ *916/443–1691 or 800/909–4776, ext. 40,* ✉ *916/443–4763. 70 beds. MC, V.*

Nightlife and the Arts
Downtown Events Line (☎ 916/442–2500) has recorded information about seasonal events in the downtown area.

Busby Berkeley's (⊠ Hyatt Regency at Capitol Park, 1209 L St., ☎ 916/443–1234) has a view of the Capitol. DJs play Top-40 music from Tuesday to Saturday. The **Fox and Goose** (⊠ 1001 R St., ☎ 916/443–8825), a casual pub with live music (including open-mic Mondays), has been rated the "best breakfast spot" by the *Sacramento Bee*. Traditional pub food (fish and chips, Cornish pasties) is served on weekday evenings from 5:30 to 9:30. **Harlow's** (⊠ 2708 J St., ☎ 916/441–4693) draws a young crowd to its Art Deco bar–nightclub for DJ music after 9.

Sacramento Community Center Theater (⊠ 13th and L Sts., ☎ 916/264–5181) hosts concerts, opera, ballet, and Music Circus, which presents professional musical theater in summer. The **Sacramento Light Opera Association** (⊠ 1419 H St., ☎ 916/557–1999) presents Broadway shows at the Sacramento Community Center Theater and in the huge Music Circus tent during summer.

Outdoor Activities and Sports
The basement-level **California Family Health & Fitness** (⊠ 428 J St., at 5th St., ☎ 916/442–9090) has a workout area, weight machines, and a sauna. The drop-in fee for nonmembers is $10. **Jedediah Smith Memorial Bicycle Trail** runs for 23 mi from Old Sacramento to Beals Point in Folsom, mostly along the American River. The **Sacramento Kings** of the National Basketball Association play at the Arco Arena (⊠ 1 Sports Pkwy., ☎ 916/928–6900).

Shopping
Among the myriad T-shirt and yogurt emporiums in Old Sacramento are some interesting art galleries and bookstores. Top local artists and craftspeople exhibit their works at **Artists' Collaborative Gallery** (⊠ 1007 2nd St., ☎ 916/444–3764). **Bookmine** (⊠ 1015 2nd St., ☎ 916/441–4609) sells used and rare books. The **Elder Craftsman** (⊠ 130 J St., ☎ 916/264–7762) specializes in items made by local senior citizens.

Arden Fair Mall, northeast of downtown off I–80 in the North Area, is Sacramento's largest shopping center. **Downtown Plaza,** comprising the K Street Mall along with many neighboring shops and restaurants, has shopping and entertainment; there's a Thursday-night market, and in winter an outdoor ice-skating rink is set up. **Pavilions Mall** (⊠ Fair Oaks Blvd. and Howe Ave.) has many boutiques.

THE GOLD COUNTRY
Highway 49 from Nevada City to Mariposa

Highway 49 winds the length of the gold-mining area, linking the towns of Nevada City, Grass Valley, Auburn, Placerville, Sutter Creek, Sonora, and Mariposa. Most are gentrified versions of once rowdy mining camps, vestiges of which remain in roadside museums, old mining structures, and historic inns.

Nevada City

⑭ *62 mi north of Sacramento, I–80 to Hwy. 49.*

Nevada City, once known as the Queen City of the Northern Mines, is the most appealing of the northern Mother Lode towns. The iron-shuttered brick buildings that line the narrow downtown streets contain antiques shops, galleries, a winery, bookstores, boutiques, B&Bs, and many restaurants. Horse-drawn carriage tours add to the romance, as do gas-powered streetlights. At one point in the 1850s Nevada City had a population of nearly 10,000, enough to support much cultural activity. The **Nevada City Chamber of Commerce** (⊠ 132 Main St., ☎ 530/265–2692) has books about the area and a free walking-tour map.

With its gingerbread-trimmed bell tower, **Firehouse No. 1** is one of the Gold Country's most photographed buildings. A museum, it houses relics of the fateful Donner Party (victims of a severe Sierra Nevada snowstorm), gold-rush artifacts, and a Chinese joss house (temple). ⊠ *214 Main St., ☎ 530/265–5468. ⊙ Daily 11–4.*

The redbrick **Nevada Theatre,** constructed in 1865, is California's oldest theater building in continuous use. Mark Twain, Emma Nevada, and many other superstars of bygone times appeared on its stage. The Nevada, also the home of the **Foothill Theater Company** (☎ 530/265–8587 or 888/730–8587), screens films and hosts theatrical and musical events. ⊠ *401 Broad St., ☎ 530/265–6161.*

The **Miners Foundry,** erected in 1856, produced machines for gold mining and logging. The Pelton Water Wheel, a source of power for the mines (the wheel also jump-started the hydroelectric power industry), was invented here. A cavernous building, the foundry serves as a cultural center that presents plays, concerts, an antiques show, and other events. ⊠ *325 Spring St., ☎ 530/265–5040.*

You can watch while you sip at the **Nevada City Winery,** where the tasting room overlooks the production area. ⊠ *Miners Foundry Garage, 321 Spring St., ☎ 530/265–9463. ⊙ Tastings daily noon–5.*

Dining and Lodging

$$–$$$$ ✕ **Kirby's Creekside Restaurant & Bar.** Immaculate Kirby's perches over Deer Creek. You can dine on the large outdoor deck in warm weather or sit by the fireplace on cooler days. Among the inventive Continental preparations is the pork loin stuffed with roasted peppers. There are many pastas from which to choose. Or you can opt for the Chef's Culinary Adventure: The waitperson asks for your general food preferences and dietary restrictions, and the chef designs a meal (of three to six courses) for you. ⊠ *101 Broad St., ☎ 530/265–3445. AE, MC, V.*

$$–$$$ ✕ **Country Rose Café.** The lengthy country-French menu at this antiques-laden café includes seafood, beef, lamb, chicken, and ratatouille. In the summer there is outdoor service on a verdant patio. ⊠ *300 Commercial St., ☎ 530/265–6248. AE, DC, MC, V.*

$$–$$$ ✕ **Friar Tuck's.** A guitar player performs nightly at this vaguely 1960s-retro gathering spot that feels like a wine cellar; sometimes patrons sing along. Rack of lamb, roast duck, fondue, Iowa beef, Hawaiian fish specials, and Tuck's bouillabaisse are on the menu. There's an extensive wine and beer list as well as a full bar. ⊠ *111 N. Pine St., ☎ 530/265–9093. AE, MC, V. No lunch.*

$–$$ ✕ **Cirino's.** American-Italian dishes—seafood, pasta, and veal—are served at this informal bar and grill. The restaurant's handsome Brunswick bar is of gold-rush vintage. ⊠ *309 Broad St., ☎ 530/265–2246. AE, D, MC, V.*

$$–$$$ 🏨 **Deer Creek Inn.** The main veranda of this 1860 Queen Anne Victorian overlooks a huge lawn that rolls past a rose-covered arbor to the gurgling creek below. You can play croquet on the lawn or pan for gold from the creek. All rooms have king or queen beds; some rooms have unusual features like a two-person Roman tub. ⊠ *116 Nevada St, 95959,* ☎ *530/265–0363 or 800/655–0363,* 📠 *530/265–0980. 5 rooms. Full breakfast. MC, V.*

$$–$$$ 🏨 **Red Castle Inn.** A state landmark, this 1860 Gothic Revival man-
★ sion stands on a forested hillside overlooking Nevada City. Its brick exterior is trimmed with white icicle woodwork; a steep private pathway leads down through the terraced gardens into town. Handsome antique furnishings and Oriental rugs decorate the rooms. ⊠ *109 Prospect St., 95959,* ☎ *530/265–5135 or 800/761–4766. 7 rooms. Full breakfast. MC, V.*

$–$$$ 🏨 **Flume's End.** This homey and romantic inn was built at the end of a flume that once brought water into Nevada City's mines. Two rooms have hot tubs and most have creek views. The decor is eclectic Victorian, but with wall-to-wall carpeting. ⊠ *317 S. Pine St., 95959,* ☎ *530/ 265–9665 or 800/991–8118. 6 rooms. Full breakfast. MC, V.*

$–$$ 🏨 **Northern Queen Inn.** Most of the accommodations at this bright creek-side inn are typical motel units, but there are eight two-story chalets and eight rustic cottages with efficiency kitchens in a secluded, wooded area. ⊠ *400 Railroad Ave. (Sacramento St. exit off Hwy. 49), 95959,* ☎ *530/265–5824,* 📠 *530/265–3720. 86 rooms. Restaurant, refrigerators, pool, hot tub, convention center. AE, DC, MC, V.*

Grass Valley

4 mi south of Nevada City on Hwy. 49.

More than half of California's total gold production was extracted from mines around Grass Valley. Unlike in neighboring Nevada City, urban sprawl surrounds Grass Valley's historic downtown. The Empire Mine and the North Star Power House and Pelton Wheel Exhibit are among the Gold Country's most fascinating exhibits.

A great source of local information, the **Grass Valley/Nevada County Chamber of Commerce** is in a reproduction of the home on this site that was owned by the notorious dancer Lola Montez. Lola, who arrived in Grass Valley in the early 1850s, was no great talent—her popularity among miners derived from her suggestive spider dance—but her loves, who reportedly included composer Franz Liszt, were legendary. According to one account, she arrived in California after having been "permanently retired from her job as Bavarian king Ludwig's mistress," literary muse, and political adviser. She seems to have pushed too hard for democracy, which contributed to his overthrow and her banishment as a witch—or so the story went. The memory of licentious Lola lingers on in Grass Valley, as does her bathtub (in the front yard of the house). ⊠ *248 Mill St.,* ☎ *916/273–4667.*

The landmark **Holbrooke Hotel,** built in 1851, hosted Lola Montez, Mark Twain, Ulysses S. Grant, and a stream of other U.S. presidents. Its restaurant/saloon is one of the oldest still operating west of the Mississippi. ⊠ *212 W. Main St.,* ☎ *530/273–1353 or 800/933–7077.*

★ ⓯ The hard-rock gold mine at **Empire Mine State Historic Park** was one of California's richest—an estimated 5.8 million ounces were extracted from its 367 mi of underground passages between 1850 and 1956. On the 50-minute tours you can walk into a mine shaft, peer into the mine's deeper recesses, and view the owner's "cottage," whose woodwork is exquisite. The visitor center has mining exhibits, and a picnic area is nearby. ⊠ *10791 E. Empire St. (exit south from Hwy. 49),* ☎ *530/*

273–8522. ☎ $3. ⊙ June–Aug., daily 9–6; Sept.–Apr., daily 10–5; May, daily 9–6. Tours in summer on the hr 11–4; winter weekends only at 1 (cottage only) and 2 (mine yard only), weather permitting.

The **North Star Power House and Pelton Wheel Exhibit** stars a 32-ft-high Pelton enclosed waterwheel said to be the largest ever built. It was used to power mining operations and was a forerunner of the modern turbines that generate hydroelectricity. Hands-on displays are geared to children, and there's a picnic area. ⊠ *Empire and McCourtney Sts. (Empire St. exit north from Hwy. 49),* ☎ *530/273–4255.* ☎ *Donation requested.* ⊙ *May–Oct., daily 10–5.*

Lodging

$$–$$$ 🏨 **Murphy's Inn.** A gold baron built the main inn here as a wedding present for his bride. Both the 1866 inn, which revels in its Victorian opulence, and the historic Donation Day House across the street contain antiques, lace curtains, and floral print wallpaper; half the guest rooms have their own fireplaces. ⊠ *318 Neal St., 95945,* ☎ *530/273–6873 or 800/895–2488. 8 rooms. Full breakfast. AE, MC, V.*

Auburn

⑯ *24 mi south of Grass Valley on Hwy. 49; 34 mi northeast of Sacramento on I–80.*

Auburn is the Gold Country town most accessible to travelers on the interstate. An important transportation center during the gold rush, Auburn has a small old-town district with narrow climbing streets, cobblestone lanes, wooden sidewalks, and many original buildings. A $1 trolley operated by the **Placer County Visitor Information Center** (☎ 530/887–2111) loops through downtown and Old Town, with stops at some hotels and inns. Fresh produce, flowers, baked goods, and gifts are for sale at the farmers' market held each Saturday morning.

Auburn's standout structure is the **Placer County Courthouse.** The classic gold-dome building houses the Placer County Museum, which documents the area's history—Native American, railroad, agricultural, and mining—from the early 1700s to 1900. ⊠ *101 Maple St.,* ☎ *530/889–6500.* ☎ *Free.* ⊙ *Tues.–Sun. 10–4.*

The **Bernhard Museum Complex,** whose centerpiece is the former Traveler's Rest Hotel, was built in 1851. A residence and adjacent winery buildings reflect family life in the late Victorian era; in the carriage house are period conveyances. ⊠ *291 Auburn-Folsom Rd.,* ☎ *530/889–6500.* ☎ *$1 (includes entry to Gold Country Museum).* ⊙ *Tues.–Fri. 10:30–3, weekends noon–4.*

The **Gold Country Museum,** worth peeking into, surveys life in the mines. Exhibits include a walk-through mine tunnel, a gold-panning stream, and a replica saloon. ⊠ *1273 High St., off Auburn-Folsom Rd.,* ☎ *530/889–6500.* ☎ *$1 (includes entry to Bernhard Museum Complex).* ⊙ *Tues.–Fri. 10–3:30, weekends 11–4.*

Dining and Lodging

$–$$ ✕ **Latitudes.** An 1870 Victorian is the setting for delicious multicultural cuisine. The menu (with monthly specials from diverse geographical regions) includes seafood, chicken, and turkey entrées prepared with Mexican spices, curries, cheese, or teriyaki sauce. Sunday brunch is deservedly popular. ⊠ *130 Maple St.,* ☎ *530/885–9535. AE, MC, V. No lunch Sat., no dinner Mon.–Tues.*

$–$$ ✕ **Le Bilig French Café.** Simplicity and elegance of cuisine and decor are the goals of the chefs at this country-French café on the outskirts of Auburn. Escargots, coq au vin, and quiche are standard offerings;

specials might include salmon in parchment paper. ⊠ *11750 Atwood Rd., off Hwy. 49 near the Bel Air Mall,* ☎ *530/888–1491. MC, V. Closed Sun.–Tues. No lunch Wed.–Thurs. or Sat.*

$ ✗ **Awful Annie's.** Big patio umbrellas (and outdoor heaters when necessary) allow patrons to sit inside or outside and take in the view of old-town Auburn from this popular spot for breakfast—one specialty is an omelet with chili—or lunch. ⊠ *160 Sacramento St.,* ☎ *530/888–9857. AE, MC, V. No dinner.*

$$–$$$ ☷ **Powers Mansion Inn.** This inn hints at the lavish lifestyle enjoyed by the gold-rush gentry. Two light-filled parlors have gleaming oak floors, Asian antiques, and ornate Victorian chairs and settees. A second-floor maze of narrow corridors leads to the guest rooms, which have brass and pencil-post beds with handmade quilts. ⊠ *164 Cleveland Ave., 95603,* ☎ *530/885–1166,* ℻ *530/885–1386. 13 rooms. Full breakfast. AE, MC, V.*

$$ ☷ **Holiday Inn.** On a hill above the freeway across from Old Auburn, the hotel has an imposing columned entrance but a welcoming lobby. Rooms are chain-standard but attractively furnished; all have work areas and coffeemakers. Rooms nearest the parking lot can be noisy. ⊠ *120 Grass Valley Hwy., 95603,* ☎ *530/887–8787 or 800/814–8787,* ℻ *530/887–9824. 96 rooms, 8 suites. Restaurant, bar, in-room modem lines, room service, pool, spa, exercise room, business services, convention center. AE, D, DC, MC, V.*

$ ☷ **Auburn Inn.** The decor at this well-maintained property is contemporary, in teal and pastel colors. Though a short distance from the freeway, the inn is fairly quiet. ⊠ *1875 Auburn Ravine Rd. (Forest Hill exit north from I–80), 95603,* ☎ *530/885–1800 or 800/626–1900,* ℻ *530/888–6424. 81 rooms, 3 suites. No-smoking rooms, pool, spa, coin laundry. Continental breakfast. AE, D, DC, MC, V.*

Coloma

18 mi south of Auburn on Hwy. 49.

The California gold rush started in Coloma. "My eye was caught with the glimpse of something shining in the bottom of the ditch," James Marshall recalled. Marshall himself never found any more "color," as gold came to be called.

★ ⑰ Most of Coloma lies within **Marshall Gold Discovery State Historic Park.** Though crowded with tourists in summer, Coloma hardly resembles the mob scene it was in 1849, when 2,000 prospectors staked out claims along the streambed. The town's population grew to 4,000, supporting seven hotels, three banks, and many stores and businesses. But when reserves of the precious metal dwindled, prospectors left as quickly as they had come. A working replica of John Sutter's mill lies near the spot where John Marshall first saw gold; a trail leads to a monument marking Marshall's discovery. The museum is not as interesting as the outdoor exhibits. ⊠ *Hwy. 49,* ☎ *530/622–3470.* ☜ *$5 per vehicle (day use).* ◑ *Park daily 8 AM–sunset. Museum summer, daily 10–5; Labor Day–Memorial Day, daily 10–4:30.*

Lodging

$$–$$$ ☷ **Coloma Country Inn.** Five of the rooms at this B&B on 5 acres are inside a restored 1852 Victorian; two suites are in the carriage house. Appointments include antique double and queen-size beds, handmade quilts, stenciled friezes, and fresh flowers. Balloon and white-water rafting packages are available. ⊠ *345 High St., 95613,* ☎ *530/622–6919,* ℻ *530/622–1795. 5 rooms, 2 with shared bath; 5 suites. Full breakfast. No credit cards.*

Placerville

10 mi south of Coloma on Hwy. 49; 44 mi east of Sacramento on U.S. 50.

It's hard to imagine now, but in 1849 about 4,000 miners staked out every gully and hillside in Placerville, turning the town into a rip-roaring camp of log cabins, tents, and clapboard houses. The area was then known as Hangtown, a graphic allusion to the summary nature of frontier justice. It took on the name Placerville in 1854 and became an important supply center for the miners. Mark Hopkins, Philip Armour, and John Studebaker were among the industrialists who got their starts here.

★ ⑱ **Hangtown's Gold Bug Mine,** owned by the city of Placerville, has a fully lighted shaft and is open for self-guided touring. A shaded stream runs through the park, and there are picnic facilities. ⊠ *1 mi off U.S. 50, north on Bedford Ave.,* ☎ *530/642–5238.* 🎫 *$3.* ☉ *Mar.–mid-Apr., weekends 12–4; mid-Apr.–Oct., daily 10–4; Nov., weekends 12–4, weather permitting. Closed Dec.–Feb.*

OFF THE BEATEN PATH   **APPLE HILL** – Roadside stands sell fresh produce from more than 50 family farms in this area. During the fall harvest season (from September to December) members of the Apple Hill Growers Association (☎ 530/644-7692) open their orchards and vineyards for apple and berry picking, picnicking, and wine and cider tasting. Many sell baked items and picnic food. ⊠ *About 5 mi east of Hwy. 49; take Camino exit from U.S. 50.*

Dining and Lodging

$$–$$$ ★ ✕ **Zachary Jacques.** It's not easy to locate, but call for directions— finding this country-French restaurant is worth the effort. Appetizers on the seasonal menu might include escargots or mushrooms prepared in several ways, roasted garlic with olive oil served on toast, or spicy lamb sausage. Entrées such as roast rack of lamb, beef stew, and scallops and prawns in lime butter receive traditional preparation. ⊠ *1821 Pleasant Valley Rd. (3 mi east of Diamond Springs),* ☎ *530/626–8045. AE, MC, V. Closed Mon.–Tues. No lunch.*

$$ ✕ **Café Luna.** Tucked into the back of the Creekside Place shopping complex is a small restaurant with about 30 seats indoors, plus outdoor tables overlooking a creek. The healthful entrées include grilled chicken breast with blueberry and pasilla salsa. ⊠ *451 Main St.,* ☎ *530/642–8669. AE, D, MC, V. Closed Sun. No dinner Mon.–Tues.*

$–$$ ✕ **Lil' Mama D. Carlo's Italian Kitchen.** This comfortable Italian restaurant with a pleasant wait staff serves large portions of pasta, chicken, and some vegetarian dishes, heavy on the garlic, often in a red sauce. ⊠ *482 Main St.,* ☎ *530/626–1612. MC, V. No lunch.*

$$–$$$ 🏨 **Best Western Placerville Inn.** This motel's serviceable rooms are done in the chain's trademark pastels; the pool comes in handy during the hot summer months. ⊠ *6850 Greenleaf Dr., near U.S. 50's Missouri Flats exit, 95667,* ☎ *530/622–9100 or 800/854–9100,* 🖷 *530/622–9376. 105 rooms. Restaurant, pool, hot tub. AE, D, DC, MC, V.*

Shenandoah Valley

20 mi south of Placerville on Shenandoah Rd., east of Hwy. 49.

The most concentrated Gold Country wine-touring area lies in the rolling hills of the Shenandoah Valley, east of Plymouth. Robust zinfandel is the primary grape grown here, but vineyards also produce cabernet sauvignon, sauvignon blanc, and other varietals. Most wineries are open on weekend afternoons; several have shaded picnic areas, gift shops, and galleries or museums. Maps are available from the **Amador County Chamber of Commerce** (☞ Contacts and Resources *in* Sacramento and the Gold Country A to Z, *below*).

Sobon Estate (✉ 14430 Shenandoah Rd., ☎ 209/245–6554) operates the Shenandoah Valley Museum, illustrating pioneer life and wine making in the valley. It's open daily from 10 to 5. **Charles Spinetta Winery** (✉ 12557 Steiner Rd., ☎ 209/245–3384) is open daily except Monday between 10 and 5. The gallery at **Shenandoah Vineyards** (✉ 12300 Steiner Rd., ☎ 209/245–4455), open daily from 10 to 5, displays contemporary art.

Lodging

$$ 🏨 **Amador Harvest Inn.** This B&B adjacent to Deaver Vineyards occupies a bucolic lakeside spot in the Shenandoah Valley. A contemporary Cape Cod–style structure has homey guest rooms with private baths. Public areas include a living room with fireplace and a music room with a view of the lake. ✉ *12455 Steiner Rd., 95669, ☎ 209/245–5512. 4 rooms. Full breakfast. MC, V.*

Amador City

6 mi south of Plymouth on Hwy. 49.

The history of tiny Amador City mirrors the boom-to-bust-to-boom cycle of many Gold Country towns. With an output of $42 million in gold, its Keystone Mine was one of the most productive in the Mother Lode. After all the gold was extracted, the miners cleared out and the area suffered, but Amador City now derives its wealth from tourists, who come to browse through its antiques and specialty shops, many of them on or off Highway 49.

Dining and Lodging

$$–$$$ ✕🏨 **Imperial Hotel.** The whimsically decorated rooms at this 1879 hotel
★ mock Victorian excesses in a 20th-century way. Antique furnishings include iron and brass beds, gingerbread flourishes, and, in one room, Art Deco appointments. The two front rooms, which can be noisy, have balconies. The hotel's fine restaurant serves meals in a bright dining room and on the patio outdoors. The menu changes quarterly; the cuisine ranges from vegetarian to country-hearty to trendy. ✉ *Hwy. 49, 95601, ☎ 209/267–9172 or 800/242–5594, FAX 209/267–9249. 6 rooms. Restaurant, bar. Full breakfast. AE, D, DC, MC, V. 2-night minimum on weekends.*

Sutter Creek

★ ⑲ *2 mi south of Amador City on Hwy. 49.*

Sutter Creek is a charming conglomeration of balconied buildings, Victorian homes, and neo–New England structures. The stores along Highway 49 (called Main Street in the town proper) are worth visiting for works by the many local artists and craftspeople.

OFF THE   **DAFFODIL HILL –** Each spring a 4-acre hillside east of Sutter Creek erupts
BEATEN PATH   in a riot of yellow and gold as 300,000 daffodils burst into bloom. The garden is the work of members of the McLaughlin family, which has owned this site since 1887. Daffodil plantings began in the 1930s and continue each winter. The timing of the display depends upon weather but usually takes place between mid-March and mid-April. ✉ *From Main St. (Hwy. 49) in Sutter Creek take Shake Ridge Rd. east 13 mi, ☎ 209/223–0350. 🎟 Free. ☉ Daily in season 9–5.*

Dining and Lodging

$$–$$$ ✕ **Zinfandel's.** Black-bean chili in an edible bread terrine and smoked mussels and bay shrimp with roasted garlic cloves are among the appetizers at this casual restaurant with an adventurous menu. Entrées might include filet mignon soaked in a marinade of green onions and cumin or breast of chicken topped with caramelized onions, Gorgonzola cheese, and toasted walnuts. ⊠ *51 Hanford St.,* ☎ *209/267–5008. MC, V. Closed Mon.–Wed.*

$ ✕ **Somewhere in Time.** Sip tea, sample a sinful dessert, or lunch on sandwiches and salads before or after browsing through the antiques shops in this complex that's part Victorian boutique, part dining room. The building, erected in 1860, was originally a miners' saloon run by Chinese immigrants. ⊠ *34 Main St.,* ☎ *209/267–5789. D, MC, V. No dinner.*

$$–$$$ ⚏ **Foxes Bed & Breakfast.** The rooms in this white 1857 clapboard
★ house are handsome, with high ceilings, antique beds, and lofty armoires. All rooms have queen-size beds; four have wood-burning fireplaces or cable TV. Breakfast is cooked to order and delivered on a silver service to your room or the gazebo in the garden. ⊠ *77 Main St., 95685,* ☎ *209/267–5882 or 800/987–3344, *FAX* 209/267–0712. 7 rooms. Full breakfast. D, MC, V.*

$$–$$$ ⚏ **Grey Gables Inn.** Charming yet modern, this inn brings a touch of the English countryside to the Gold Country. Each room, named after a British literary figure, has a queen-size bed and a gas-log fireplace. Afternoon tea and evening refreshments are served in the parlor. Birds flit about the wisteria in the terraced garden. ⊠ *161 Hanford St., 95685,* ☎ *209/267–1039 or 800/473–9422, *FAX* 209/267–0998. 8 rooms. Air-conditioning. Full breakfast. MC, V.*

$–$$ ⚏ **Picture Rock Inn.** Original redwood paneling, wainscoting, beams, and cabinets lend the Picture Rock a cozy feel, as do leaded- and stained-glass windows. Eclectic furnishings span eras from Victorian to Art Deco—a 1920s carousel horse is suspended mid-leap in the front room. Most rooms have views and gas-log fireplaces. ⊠ *55 Eureka St., 95685,* ☎ *209/267–5500 or 800/399–2389. 5 rooms. Air-conditioning. Full breakfast. AE, D, MC, V.*

$ ⚏ **Aparicio's Hotel.** Budget-minded travelers will appreciate this clean hotel whose rooms contain two queen-size beds. ⊠ *271 Hanford St., 95685,* ☎ *209/267–9177, *FAX* 209/267–5303. 52 rooms. Bar. D, MC, V.*

Jackson

㉟ *8 mi south of Sutter Creek on Hwy. 49.*

Jackson once had the world's deepest and richest mines, the Kennedy and the Argonaut, which together produced $70 million in gold. These were deep-rock mines, tunnels for which extended as much as a mile underground. Most of the miners who worked the lode were of Serbian or Italian origin; they gave the town a European character that persists to this day. Jackson has aboveground pioneer cemeteries whose headstones tell the stories of local Serbian and Italian families. The terraced cemetery on the grounds of the handsome **St. Sava Serbian Orthodox Church** (⊠ 724 N. Main St.) is the most impressive.

Jackson wasn't the Gold Country's rowdiest town, but the party lasted longer here than most anywhere else: "Girls' dormitories" (brothels) and nickel slot machines flourished until the mid-1950s. The heart of Jackson's historic section is the **National Hotel** (⊠ 2 Water St.), which operates an old-time saloon in the lobby; the hotel is especially active on weekends, when people come from miles around to participate in the Saturday-night sing-alongs.

The **Amador County Museum,** built in the late 1850s as a private home, provides a colorful take on gold-rush life. Displays include a kitchen with a woodstove, the Amador County bicentennial quilt, and a classroom. A time line recounts the county's checkered past. The museum conducts hourly tours of large-scale working models of the nearby Kennedy Mine. ⊠ *225 Church St.,* ☎ *209/223–6386.* 🎫 *Museum free, building with mine $1.* 🕐 *Wed.–Sun. 10–4.*

Dining and Lodging

$$ ✕ **Upstairs Restaurant.** Chef Layne McCollum takes a creative approach to contemporary American cuisine—gourmet fowl, fresh seafood, and meat—in his 12-table restaurant. The baked-Brie and roast-garlic appetizer and homemade soups are specialties; local wines are reasonably priced. Downstairs there's a streetside bistro and wine bar. ⊠ *164 Main St.,* ☎ *209/223–3342. D, DC, MC, V. Closed Mon.*

$ ✕ **Rosebud's Classic Cafe.** Art Deco decor and music from the 1930s and 1940s set the mood at this homey café. Among the classic American dishes served are hot roast beef, turkey, and meat loaf with mashed potatoes smothered in gravy. Charbroiled burgers, freshly baked pies, and espresso or gourmet coffees round out the lunch menu. Omelets, hotcakes, and many other items are served for breakfast. ⊠ *26 Main St.,* ☎ *209/223–1035. MC, V. No dinner.*

$$–$$$ 🏨 **Court Street Inn.** This Victorian has tin ceilings and a redwood staircase. The cozy first-floor Angel Court room has a fireplace; the Crystal Court room has a large whirlpool and a Wedgewood stove. The Indian House, a two-bedroom cottage, has a large bathroom, a TV with VCR, and a stereo. ⊠ *215 Court St., 95642,* ☎ *209/223–0416 or 800/200–0416,* 🖷 *209/223–5429. 7 rooms. Air-conditioning, outdoor hot tub. Full breakfast. AE, D, MC, V.*

$ 🏨 **Best Western Amador Inn.** Convenience and price are the main attractions of this two-story motel right on the highway. Rooms are nicely decorated; many have fireplaces. ⊠ *200 S. Hwy. 49, 95642,* ☎ *209/223–0211 or 800/543–5221,* 🖷 *209/223–4836. 118 rooms. Restaurant, pool, laundry service. AE, D, DC, MC, V.*

Angels Camp

㉑ *20 mi south of Jackson on Hwy. 49.*

Angels Camp is famed chiefly for its May jumping-frog contest, based on Mark Twain's "The Jumping Frog of Calaveras County." The writer reputedly heard the story of the jumping frog from Ross Coon, proprietor of Angels Hotel, which has been operating since 1856.

Angels Camp Museum holds a granny's attic of gold-rush relics—photos, rocks, petrified wood, old mining equipment, and a horse-drawn hearse. The huge Pelton Water Wheel exhibit explains how the apparatus supplied water power to the mines. The carriage house out back holds 25 carriages and an impressive display of mineral specimens. ⊠ *753 S. Main St.,* ☎ *209/736–2963.* 🎫 *$1.* 🕐 *Jan.–Feb., weekends 10–3; Mar.–Nov., daily 10–3. Closed Dec.*

OFF THE
BEATEN PATH

THE CALIFORNIA CAVERNS AND MOANING CAVERN – A ½-mi subterranean trail at the California Caverns winds through large chambers and past underground streams and lakes. There aren't many steps to climb but it's a hefty walk, with some narrow passageways and steep spots. The caverns, at a constant 53°F, contain crystalline formations not found elsewhere; the 80-minute guided tour includes fascinating history and geology. A 235-step spiral staircase leads into the vast (big enough to hold the Statue of Liberty) Moaning Cavern. More adventurous sorts can rappel into the chamber—ropes and instruction are provided. Otherwise, the only way inside is via the 45-minute tour, during which you'll see giant (and still growing) stalactites and stalagmites and an archaeological site that holds some of the oldest human remains yet found in America (unlucky people have fallen into the cavern an average of once every 130 years starting 13,000 years ago). ✉ *California Caverns: 8 mi east of San Andreas, off Mountain Ranch Rd.,* ☎ *209/736–2708.* 🎫 *$8.* ☉ *Usually May–Oct., but call ahead.* ✉ *Moaning Cavern: Parrots Ferry Rd., 2 mi south of town of Vallecito, off Hwy. 4 east of Angels Camp,* ☎ *209/736–2708.* 🎫 *$7.75.* ☉ *May–Oct., daily 9–6; Nov.–Apr., daily 10–5.*

Murphys

㉒ *10 mi east of Angels Camp on Hwy. 4.*

Murphys is a well-preserved town of white picket fences, Victorian houses, and interesting shops. Horatio Alger and Ulysses S. Grant are among the guests who have signed the register at the **Murphys Historic Hotel and Lodge.** The men were among the 19th-century visitors to the giant sequoia groves in nearby Calaveras Big Trees State Park.

The **Kautz Ironstone Winery and Caverns** is worth a visit even if you don't drink wine; tours take visitors into underground tunnels cooled by a waterfall from a natural spring. The winery schedules concerts, art shows, and other events on weekends. On display near the gift area is a 44-pound specimen of crystalline gold. ✉ *1894 Six Mile Rd.,* ☎ *209/728–1251.* ☉ *Daily 11–5.*

Dining and Lodging

$–$$ ✕ **Grounds.** Light Italian entrées, grilled fresh vegetables, chicken, seafood, and steak are the specialties at this bistro and coffee shop. Sandwiches, salads, and homemade soups are served for lunch. The atmosphere is friendly and the service attentive. ✉ *402 Main St.,* ☎ *209/728–8663. MC, V. Closed Tues. No dinner Wed.*

$$$–$$$$ 🏠 **Dunbar House 1880.** The oversize rooms in this elaborate Italianate-style home have brass beds, down comforters, gas-burning stoves, and claw-foot tubs. Broad wraparound verandas encourage lounging, as do colorful gardens and shady elm trees. The Cedar Room's sunporch has a two-person whirlpool tub and a view of a white-flowering almond tree; in the Sequoia Room you can gaze at the garden while soaking in a bubble bath. Breakfast is an elegant affair. ✉ *271 Jones St., 95247,* ☎ *209/728–2897 or 800/692–6006, ext. 321,* 📠 *209/728–1451. 4 rooms. Refrigerators, in-room VCRs. Full breakfast. AE, MC, V.*

$$–$$$$ 🏠 **Redbud Inn.** Some rooms at this inn have double-sided fireplaces, cathedral ceilings, garden balconies, or Victorian claw-foot tubs. A room with brass beds and a tin ceiling replicates a miner's cabin. Wine and snacks are served in the parlor each evening. ✉ *402 Main St., 95247,* ☎ *209/728–8533 or 800/827–8533,* 📠 *209/728–9123. 13 rooms. Full breakfast. D, MC, V.*

$–$$ ✕🏠 **Murphys Historic Hotel and Lodge.** This 1855 stone hotel figured in Bret Harte's short story "A Night at Wingdam," and Mark Twain and the bandit Black Bart signed the register. Accommodations are in the hotel and a modern motel-style addition. The older rooms are furnished with antiques, many of them large and hand-carved. The hotel has a convivial old-time saloon, which can be noisy into the wee hours. ✉ *457 Main St., 95247,* ☎ *209/728–3444 or 800/532–7684,* 📠 *209/728–1590. 29 rooms (9 historic rooms share baths). Restaurant, bar, meeting rooms. Continental breakfast. AE, D, DC, MC, V.*

OFF THE
BEATEN PATH

CALAVERAS BIG TREES STATE PARK – This state park is home to 150 of the largest and rarest living things on the planet—magnificent giant sequoia redwood trees. Some are almost 3,000 years old, 90 ft around at the base, and about 250 ft tall. The park's self-guided trails range from a 200-yard trail to 1-mi and 5-mi loops through the groves. There are campgrounds and picnic areas; swimming, wading, and sunbathing on the Stanislaus River are popular in summer. ⊠ *Off Hwy. 4, 15 mi northeast of Murphys (4 mi northeast of Arnold),* ☎ *209/795-2334.* ⊠ *$5 per vehicle (day use); $16 for campsites. Disposal station, fire rings, flush toilets, hot showers, water.* ⊙ *Park 8 AM–sunset (day use). Visitor center May–Oct., daily 10–4; Nov.–Apr., weekends 11–3.*

Columbia State Historic Park

★ ㉓   *14 mi south of Angels Camp, Hwy. 49 to Parrots Ferry Rd.*

🖑   Columbia State Historic Park, known as the Gem of the Southern Mines, comes as close to a gold-rush town in its heyday as any site in the Gold Country. You can ride a stagecoach, pan for gold, or watch a blacksmith working at his anvil. Street musicians perform in summer. Restored or reconstructed buildings include a Wells Fargo Express office, a Masonic temple, stores, saloons, two hotels, a firehouse, churches, a school, and a newspaper office. All are staffed to simulate a working 1850s town. ☎ *209/532–4301.* ⊠ *Free.* ⊙ *Daily 8:30–5.*

Dining and Lodging

$$ ✕▦ **City Hotel.** The rooms in this restored 1856 hostelry are furnished with period antiques. Two have balconies overlooking Main Street, and six rooms open onto a second-floor parlor. All the accommodations have private half-baths with showers nearby; robes and slippers are provided. The restaurant ($$–$$$; closed on Monday), one of the Gold Country's best, serves French-accented California cuisine complemented by a huge selection of wines from California. The What Cheer Saloon is right out of a western movie. ⊠ *Main St., Columbia 95310,* ☎ *209/532–1479 or 800/532–1479,* ℻ *209/532–7027. 10 rooms. Restaurant, bar. Continental breakfast. AE, D, MC, V.*

$–$$ ▦ **Fallon Hotel.** The state of California restored this 1857 hotel. All rooms have antiques and a private half-bath; there are separate men's and women's showers. If you occupy one of the five balcony rooms, you can sit outside with your morning coffee and watch the town wake up. ⊠ *Washington St., Columbia 95310,* ☎ *209/532–1470,* ℻ *209/532–7027. 14 rooms. Continental breakfast. AE, D, MC, V.*

Nightlife and the Arts

Sierra Repertory Theater Company (☎ 209/532–4644), a local professional company, presents a full season of plays, comedies, and musicals at the Historic Fallon House Theater and another venue in East Sonora. The City Hotel (☞ *above*) offers combined lodging, dinner, and theater packages.

Sonora

㉔   *4 mi south of Columbia, Parrots Ferry Rd. to Hwy. 49.*

Miners from Mexico founded Sonora and made it the biggest town in the Mother Lode. Following a period of racial and ethnic strife, the Mexican settlers moved on; Yankees built the commercial city that is visible today. Sonora's downtown historic section sits atop the Big Bonanza Mine, one of the richest in the state. Another mine, on the site of nearby Sonora High School, yielded 990 pounds of gold in a single week in 1879. Reminders of the gold rush are everywhere in Sonora, in prim Victorian houses, typical Sierra-stone storefronts, and awning-shaded sidewalks. Reality intrudes beyond the town's historic heart with strip malls, shopping centers, and modern motels. If the countryside surrounding Sonora seems familiar, that's because much of it has appeared in western and other movies over the years. Scenes from *High Noon, For Whom the Bell Tolls, The Virginian, Back to the Future III,* and *Unforgiven* were filmed here.

The **Tuolumne County Museum and History Center** occupies a building that served as a jail until 1951. Restored to an earlier period, it houses a jail museum, vintage firearms and paraphernalia, a case with gold nuggets, and the libraries of a historical society and a genealogical society. ⊠ *158 W. Bradford St.,* ☎ *209/532–1317.* ⊡ *Free.* ☉ *Sun.– Mon. 9–4, Tues.–Fri. 10–4, Sat. 10–3:30.*

Dining and Lodging

$–$$ ✕ **Banny's Cafe.** Its pleasant environment and hearty yet refined dishes make Banny's a quiet alternative to Sonora's eateries with live music. Appetizers such as the wilted goat cheese with roasted whole garlic, herb croutons, and a sun-dried tomato vinaigrette can be followed by the grilled salmon fillet entrée with spinach–red pepper aioli or the egg-plant grilled with shiitake mushrooms, leeks, roasted-tomato pesto, and mozzarella. Salads include the spinach with smoked apple-wood bacon and a traditional Caesar. ⊠ *83 S. Stewart St.,* ☎ *209/533–4709. D, MC, V.*

$–$$ ✕ **Coyote Creek Cafe & Grill.** The fare at Coyote Creek is multinational: Lunch might include pasta Castroville (with artichoke-hearts marinara), a Zuni black-bean plate, and Szechuan chicken. Spanish tapas and grilled steak are among the possibilities for dinner. The low-key café heats up each night with live music and dancing that draw a youngish crowd. ⊠ *177 S. Washington St.,* ☎ *209/532–9115. Reservations not accepted. D, DC, MC, V.*

$–$$ ✕ **Josephine's California Trattoria.** This restaurant with indoor and out-door dining serves contemporary California and traditional Tuscan cuisine. Seared ahi tuna, roasted red peppers, duckling with polenta, Delta crayfish risotto, and angel-hair pasta with fresh seafood are among the dishes one might find on the seasonal menu. Single-portion pizzas are a staple. The reasonably priced wines showcase Sierra foothill and Italian vintages. Musicians perform on some nights, either in the bar or the dining room. ⊠ *Gunn House Hotel, 286 S. Washington St.,* ☎ *209/533–4111. Restaurant, bar. AE, D, MC, V. No lunch.*

$$–$$$ ⛻ **Ryan House 1855 Bed and Breakfast Inn.** Attentive innkeepers make this 1850s farmhouse a fine place to stay, and there's more privacy than might be expected at such a small inn. A suite in the attic has a large sitting area set into the gables, a pink and burgundy bath-room with a double soaking tub, and a brass-and-iron bed. Everyone has access to the three parlors and the sunny kitchen, where complimentary snacks and beverages are always available. In springtime the garden blooms with colorful flowers of all kinds, including some antique roses as old as the house itself. Lodging-and-theater packages are available. ⊠ *153 S. Shepherd St., 95370,* ☎ *209/533–3445 or 800/ 831–4897. 4 rooms. Air-conditioning. Full breakfast. AE, MC, V.*

$–$$$ ⛻ **Best Western Sonora Oaks Motor Hotel.** The standard motel-issue rooms at this East Sonora establishment are clean and roomy. The larger ones have outside sitting areas; four have fireplaces, whirlpool tubs, and tranquil hillside views. Because the motel is right off Highway 108, the front rooms can sometimes be noisy. ⊠ *19551 Hess Ave., 95370,* ☎ *209/533–4400 or 800/532–1944,* FAX *209/532–1964. 100 rooms. Restaurant, lounge, pool, meeting rooms. AE, D, DC, MC, V.*

Jamestown

㉕ *4 mi south of Sonora on Hwy. 49.*

Compact Jamestown supplies a touristy, superficial view of gold-rush-era life. Shops filling brightly colored buildings along Main Street sell antiques and gift items.

The California State Railroad Museum operates **Railtown 1897** at what were the headquarters and general shops of the Sierra Railway from 1897 to 1955. The railroad has appeared in more than 200 movies and television productions, including *Petticoat Junction, The Virginian, High Noon,* and *Unforgiven.* You can view the roundhouse, an air-operated 60-ft turntable, shop rooms, and old locomotives and coaches. Six-mile, 40-minute steam train rides through the country-side are operated on weekends during part of the year. ☒ *5th Ave. and Reservoir Rd., off Hwy. 49,* ☎ *209/984–1600.* ☜ *$2 roundhouse tour; $6 train ride.* ☉ *Railtown 1897 daily 9:30–4:30. Train rides Apr.–Oct., weekends 11–3; Nov., Sat. 11–3.*

Dining and Lodging

$$ ✕☜ **National Hotel.** The National has been in business since 1859. The decor is authentic—brass beds, patchwork quilts, and lace curtains—but not overly embellished. The saloon, which still has its original 19th-century redwood bar, is a great place to linger. The popular restaurant serves big lunches: hamburgers and fries, salads, and Italian entrées. More upscale Continental cuisine is prepared for dinner (reservations essential). Some rooms have no phone. ☒ *77 Main St., 95327,* ☎ *209/ 984–3446; 800/894–3446 in CA,* ℻ *209/984–5620. 9 rooms. Restaurant, air-conditioning. Continental breakfast. AE, D, DC, MC, V.*

Mariposa

㉖ *50 mi south of Jamestown on Hwy. 49.*

Mariposa marks the southern end of the Mother Lode. Much of the land in this area was part of a 44,000-acre land grant Colonel John C. Fremont acquired from Mexico before gold was discovered and California became a state.

At the **California State Mining and Mineral Museum** a glittering, 13-pound chunk of crystallized gold makes it clear what the gold rush was about. Displays include a replica of a typical tunnel dug by hard-rock miners, a miniature stamp mill, and a panning and sluicing exhibit. ☒ *Mariposa County Fairgrounds, Hwy. 49,* ☎ *209/742–7625.* ☜ *$3.50.* ☉ *May–Sept., Wed.–Mon. 10–6; Oct.–Apr., Wed.–Sun. 10–4.*

Dining and Lodging

$–$$ ✕ **Ocean Sierra Restaurant.** Deep in the woods about 14 mi southeast of Mariposa is this comfortable spot for seafood, meat, pasta, and veg-etarian dishes. The owner-chef grows many of her own fresh ingredients, including the delicate crystallized rose petals atop some of the desserts. ☒ *3292 E. Westfall Rd. (from Hwy. 49 take Triangle Rd. 2 mi northeast),* ☎ *209/742–7050. D, MC, V. Closed Mon. and Tues. No lunch.*

$ ✕ **Castillo's Mexican Food.** Tasty tacos, enchiladas, chili rellenos, and burrito combinations, plus chimichangas, fajitas, steak, and seafood, are served in a casual storefront setting. ☒ *4995 5th St.,* ☎ *209/742–4413. MC, V.*

$$ ☜ **Little Valley Inn.** Pine paneling, historical photos, and old mining tools recall Mariposa's heritage at this modern B&B with three rooms. A suite that sleeps five people includes a full kitchen. All rooms have private entrances and decks. The large grounds include a creek where guests can pan for gold (a helpful dog stirs the creekbed). ✉ *3483 Brooks Rd., off Hwy. 49, 95338,* ☎ *209/742–6204 or 800/889–5444,* 𝔽𝔸𝕏 *209/ 742–5099. 3 rooms. Air-conditioning, refrigerators, in-room VCRs, horseshoes. Full breakfast. AE, MC, V.*

$–$$ 🏨 **Comfort Inn of Mariposa.** This white three-story building with a broad veranda sits on a hill above Mariposa. Some of the comfortable rooms have sitting areas. ✉ *4994 Bouillon St., 95338,* ☎ *209/966–4344 or 800/321–5261,* 𝔽𝔸𝕏 *209/966–4655. 62 rooms. Air-conditioning, pool, outdoor hot tub. Continental breakfast. AE, D, DC, MC, V.*

SACRAMENTO AND THE GOLD COUNTRY A TO Z

Arriving and Departing

By Bus

Greyhound (☎ 800/231–2222) serves Sacramento, Auburn, and Placerville. It's a two-hour trip from San Francisco's Transbay Terminal at 1st and Mission streets to the Sacramento station at 7th and L streets.

By Car

Sacramento lies at the junction of I–5 and I–80, about 90 mi northeast of San Francisco. The 406-mi drive north on I–5 from Los Angeles takes seven to eight hours. Interstate 80 continues northeast through the Gold Country toward Reno, about 163 mi (three hours or so) from Sacramento.

By Plane

Sacramento International Airport (✉ 6900 Airport Blvd., 12 mi northwest of downtown off I–5, ☎ 916/874–0700) is served by Alaska, America West, American, Delta, Northwest, Southwest, and United airlines. *See* Air Travel *in* the Gold Guide for airline phone numbers.

By Train

Several trains operated by **Amtrak** (☎ 800/872–7245) stop in Sacramento. Trains making the 2½-hour trip from **Jack London Square** (✉ 245 2nd St., Oakland) stop in Emeryville, Richmond, Martinez, and Davis; some stop in Berkeley and Suisun-Fairfield as well. Shuttle buses connect the **Emeryville station** (✉ 5885 Landregan St.) , across the bay from San Francisco, and the city's **Ferry Building** (✉ 30 Embarcadero); other San Francisco pickup points are at the main entrance to Pier 39 and 835 Market Street at Powell Street, near Union Square.

Getting Around

By Bus

Sacramento Regional Transit (☎ 916/321–2877) buses and light-rail vehicles transport passengers in Sacramento. Most buses run from 6 AM to 10 PM, most trains from 5 AM to midnight. A free shuttle runs between Old Sacramento and the Sacramento Convention Center—between 13th and 14th and J and L streets—via the K Street Mall.

By Car

Traveling by car is the most convenient way to see the Gold Country. From Sacramento three highways fan out toward the east, all intersecting with Highway 49: Interstate 80 heads 30 mi northeast to Auburn; U.S. 50 goes east 40 mi to Placerville; and Highway 16 angles southeast 45 mi to Plymouth. Highway 49 is an excellent two-lane road that winds and climbs through the foothills and valleys, linking the principal Gold Country towns.

By Taxi and Water Taxi

A **water taxi** (☎ 916/448–4333) serves the Old Sacramento waterfront, stopping at points near restaurants and other sights. **Yellow Cab** (☎ 916/444–2208) serves all of Sacramento.

Contacts and Resources

Emergencies

Ambulance (☎ 911). **Fire** (☎ 911). **Police** (☎ 911).

Mercy Hospital of Sacramento Promptcare (✉ 4001 J St., ☎ 916/453–4424). **Sutter General Hospital** (✉ 2801 L St., ☎ 916/733–8900). **Sutter Memorial Hospital** (✉ 52nd and F Sts., ☎ 916/733–1000).

Guided Tours

Channel Star Excursions (✉ 110 L St., Sacramento 95814, ☎ 916/552–2933 or 800/433–0263) operates the *Spirit of Sacramento*, a paddlewheel riverboat, which takes passengers on happy-hour, dinner, luncheon, and champagne brunch cruises in addition to one-hour narrated river tours. The **Coloma Country Inn** (☎ 530/622–6919) offers rafting excursions on the American River and balloon rides as part of B&B packages. **Gold Prospecting Expeditions** (☎ 209/984–4653 or 800/596–0009), based in Jamestown, arranges gold-panning trips. **Gray Line/Frontier Tours** (✉ 2600 North Ave., Sacramento 95838, ☎ 916/927–2877 or 800/356–9838) operates city tours.

Visitor Information

Amador County Chamber of Commerce (✉ 125 Peek St., Jackson 95642, ☎ 209/223–0350). **El Dorado County Chamber of Commerce** (✉ 542 Main St., Placerville 95667, ☎ 530/621–5885 or 800/457–6279). **Grass Valley/Nevada County Chamber of Commerce** (✉ 248 Mill St., Grass Valley 95945, ☎ 530/273–4667 or 800/655–4667). **Mariposa County Visitors Bureau** (✉ 5158 Hwy. 140, Mariposa 95338, ☎ 209/966–2456 or 800/208–2434). **Placer County Tourism Authority** (✉ 13464 Lincoln Way, Auburn 95603, ☎ 530/887–2111 or 800/427–6463). **Sacramento Convention and Visitors Bureau** (✉ 1421 K St., Sacramento 95814, ☎ 916/264–7777). **Tuolumne County Visitors Bureau** (✉ Box 4020, 55 W. Stockton St., Sonora 95370, ☎ 209/533–4420 or 800/446–1333).

7 Lake Tahoe

*The California and
Nevada Shores*

*The largest alpine lake in North
America is famous for its clarity, deep
blue water, and snowcapped peaks.
Though Lake Tahoe possesses
abundant natural beauty and accessible
wilderness, nearby towns are highly
developed and roads around the lake
are often congested with traffic.
Summertime is generally cooler here
than in the Sierra Nevada foothills, and
the clean mountain air bracingly crisp.
When it gets hot, the plentiful beaches
and brisk water are only minutes away.*

Updated by
Deke
Castleman

LAKE TAHOE lies 6,225 ft above sea level in the Sierra Nevada range, straddling the state line between California and Nevada. The border gives this popular resort region a split personality. About half the visitors here arrive intent on low-key sightseeing, hiking, fishing, camping, and boating. The rest head directly for the Nevada side of the lake, where bargain dining, big-name entertainment, and the lure of a jackpot draw them into the glittering casinos. Tahoe is also a popular wedding and honeymoon destination: Couples can get married with no waiting period or blood tests at chapels all around the lake. On Valentine's Day the chapels become veritable assembly lines—four times as many ceremonies take place on that day than on any other. Incidentally, the legal marrying age in California and Nevada is 18 years, but one must be 21 to gamble or drink.

Summer's cool temperatures provide respite from the heat in the surrounding deserts and valleys. Swimming in Lake Tahoe is always brisk—68°F is about as warm as the water gets—but the lake's beaches are generally crowded at this time of year. Those who prefer solitude can escape to the many state parks, national forests, and protected tracts of wilderness that ring the 22-mi-long, 12-mi-wide lake. From mid-autumn to late spring, multitudes of skiers and winter-sports enthusiasts are attracted to Tahoe's downhill resorts and cross-country centers—North America's largest concentration of skiing facilities. Ski resorts try to open by Thanksgiving, if only with machine-made snow, and can operate through May or later. Most accommodations, restaurants, and even a handful of parks are open year-round.

The first white settler to find this spectacular region was Captain John C. Fremont in 1844, guided by famous scout Kit Carson. Not long afterward, silver was discovered in Nevada's Comstock Lode at Virginia City, and as the bonanza hit, the Tahoe Basin's forests were leveled to provide lumber for mine-tunnel supports. By the turn of the century wealthy Californians were building lakeside estates here, some of which still stand. Improved roads brought the less affluent in the 1920s and 1930s, when modest bungalows began to dot the landscape under second-growth forest. The first casinos opened in the 1940s. Ski resorts inspired another development boom and turned the lake into a year-round destination.

Lake Tahoe's water is 99.7% pure, cleaner than drinking water in most U.S. cities. The water is so clear that you can see as deep as 75 ft. During the past few decades, however, road construction and other building projects have washed soil and minerals into the lake, leading to a growth of algae that threatens its clarity. The efforts of environmentalists during the 1970s resulted in a moratorium on shoreline construction, and a master plan was instituted to control development; today Tahoe is one of the most strictly controlled environments in the country.

During some summer weekends it seems that absolutely every tourist—100,000 at peak periods—is in a car on the main road that circles the 72-mi shoreline. The crowds and congestion increase as the day wears on. But at a vantage point overlooking Emerald Bay early in the morning, on a trail in the national forests that ring the basin, or on a sunset cruise on the lake itself, one can forget the ubiquitous hordes and commercial development and absorb the grandeur.

Pleasures and Pastimes

Camping

Campgrounds abound in the Tahoe area, operated by the state's park department, the U.S. Forest Service, city utility districts, and private operators. Sites range from primitive and rustic to upscale and luxurious. Make reservations far ahead in summer, when sites are in high demand (☞ Contacts and Resources *in* Lake Tahoe A to Z, *below*).

Dining

On weekends and in high season expect a long wait in the more popular restaurants. During slower periods some places may close temporarily or limit their hours, so call ahead to make sure your choice is open.

Casinos use their restaurants to attract gaming customers. Marquees often tout "$5.99 prime rib dinners" or "$1.39 breakfast specials." Some of these meal deals, usually found in the coffee shops and buffets, may not be top quality. But the finer restaurants in casinos generally deliver good food, service, and atmosphere.

Unless otherwise noted, even the most expensive Tahoe restaurants welcome customers in casual clothes—not surprising in this year-round vacation mecca—but don't expect to be served in most places if you're barefoot, shirtless, or wearing a skimpy bathing suit.

CATEGORY	COST*
$$$$	over $50
$$$	$30–$50
$$	$20–$30
$	under $20

per person for a three-course meal, excluding drinks, service, and 7%–7¼% tax

Gambling

Nevada's major casinos are also full-service hotels and resorts. They offer discounted lodging packages throughout the year. The casinos share an atmosphere of garish neon and noise, but conditioned air and no-smoking areas have eliminated the hazy pall of the past. Six casinos are clustered on a strip of U.S. 50 in Stateline—Caesars, Harrah's, Harvey's, Horizon, and Lakeside, plus Bill's, a lower-stakes "junior" casino (no lodging) that appeals to frugal gamblers. Five other casinos operate on the north shore: the Hyatt Regency, Cal-Neva, Tahoe Biltmore, Crystal Bay Club, and Jim Kelley's Nugget. Open 24 hours a day, 365 days a year, these gambling parlors have table games (craps, blackjack, roulette, baccarat, poker, keno, pai gow poker, bingo, and big six), race and sports books, and thousands of slot and video poker machines—1,750, for instance, at Harrah's. There is no charge to enter and there is no dress code.

The hotels attract potential players into their high-profit casinos with shows, celebrity entertainers, and restaurants and lounges that are open around the clock. All gamblers are offered complimentary beverages; higher-stakes players can qualify for complimentary meals, rooms, room service, golf, even private yacht parties. Parking is plentiful in enclosed garages and open lots; valet parking is technically free, but a $1 or $2 tip is customary.

Golf

The Tahoe area is nearly as popular with golfers as it is with skiers. Half a dozen superb courses dot the mountains around the lake, with magnificent views, thick pines, fresh cool air, and lush fairways and greens. Encountering wildlife is not uncommon if you have to search for your ball out-of-bounds.

Hiking

There are five national forests in the Tahoe Basin and a half-dozen state parks. The main areas for hiking include the Tahoe Rim Trail, a 150-mi path along the ridgelines above the lake; Desolation Wilderness, a vast 63,473-acre preserve of granite peaks, glacial valleys, subalpine forests, the Rubicon River, and more than 50 lakes; and the trail systems near Lake Tahoe Visitor Center and D. L. Bliss, Emerald Bay, Sugar Pine Point, and Lake Tahoe–Nevada state parks.

Lodging

Quiet inns on the water, motels in the heart of the casino area, rooms at the casinos themselves, and lodges close to ski runs are among the Tahoe options. During summer and ski season the lake is crowded; reserve space as far ahead as possible. Spring and fall give you a little more leeway and lower—sometimes significantly lower—rates. Price categories listed below reflect high-season rates.

CATEGORY	COST*
$$$$	over $175
$$$	$120–$175
$$	$80–$120
$	under $80

All prices are for a standard double room, excluding 9%–10% tax.

Skiing

The Lake Tahoe area is a Nordic skier's paradise. You can even cross-country ski on fresh snow right on the lakeshore beaches. Skinny skiing (slang for cross-country) at the resorts can be costly, but you get the benefits of machine grooming and trail preparation. If it's bargain Nordic you're after, take advantage of thousands of acres of public forest and parkland trails.

The mountains around Lake Tahoe are bombarded by blizzards throughout the winter (and sometimes the fall and spring); 10- to 12-ft bases are not uncommon. The profusion of downhill resorts guarantees a nearly infinite variety of terrains, conditions, and challenges. To save money, look for packages offered by lodges and resorts; some include interchangeable lift tickets that allow you to try different slopes. Midweek packages are usually lower in price, and most resorts offer family discounts. Free shuttle-bus service is available between most ski resorts and lodgings.

Sno-Park Areas

There are five public Sno-Park areas, where you can park your car and then snowmobile, cross-country ski, or sled. All are maintained by the California State Department of Parks and Recreation (☞ Contacts and Resources *in* Lake Tahoe A to Z, *below*). To use them you need to obtain a permit in advance.

Exploring Lake Tahoe

The most common way to explore the Lake Tahoe area is to drive the 72-mi road that follows the shore through wooded flatlands and past beaches, climbing to vistas on the rugged west side of the lake and descending to the busiest commercial developments and casinos on its northeastern and southeastern edges. Undeveloped Lake Tahoe–Nevada State Park occupies more than half of the Nevada side of Lake Tahoe, stretching north from the glitzy border town of Stateline to the upscale master-planned community of Incline Village. The California side, particularly South Lake Tahoe, is more developed, though much wilderness remains.

Great Itineraries

Although, or perhaps because, the distance around Lake Tahoe is relatively short, the desire to experience the whole area can be overwhelming. It takes only one day "to see it"—drive around the lake, stretch your legs at a few overlooks, take a nature walk, and wander among the casinos at Stateline. If you have more time, you can laze on a beach and swim, venture onto the lake or into the mountains, and sample Tahoe's finer restaurants. If you have five days, you can write a guidebook. But be careful—you may become so attached to Tahoe that you begin visiting real-estate agents.

Numbers in the text correspond to numbers in the margin and on the Lake Tahoe map.

IF YOU HAVE 3 DAYS

On your first day, stop in **South Lake Tahoe** ① and pick up provisions for a picnic lunch. Start with some morning beach fun at the **Pope-Baldwin Recreation Area** ③ and check out the area's **Tallac Historic Site.** Head west on Highway 89, stopping at the **Lake Tahoe Visitor Center** ④ and the **Emerald Bay** ⑤ lookout. Have lunch at the lookout, or hike down be forewarned: The hike back up is steep—to **Vikingsholm,** a Viking castle replica. In the late afternoon explore the trails and mansions at **Sugar Pine Point State Park** ⑦, then backtrack on Highway 89 and U.S. 50 for dinner in South Lake Tahoe. On your second day, cruise on the *Hornblower's Tahoe Queen* glass-bottom sternwheeler out of South Lake Tahoe or the MS *Dixie II* sternwheeler out of **Zephyr Cove** ⑰ in the morning, and then ride the **Heavenly Tram** ② at Heavenly Ski Resort. Have lunch high above the lake and (except in snow season) take a walk on one of Heavenly's nature trails. If you're itching to try your luck at the casinos, **Stateline** ⑱ is only a few minutes' drive from the tram base; visit before having dinner in the area. Start your third day by heading north on U.S. 50, stopping at **Cave Rock** ⑯ and (after turning north on Highway 28) at **Sand Harbor Beach** ⑮. If *Bonanza* looms large in your memory, drop by **Ponderosa Ranch** ⑭, or continue on to **Crystal Bay** ⑫ to hike the Stateline Lookout Trail above Crystal Bay. If you have the time, drive to **Tahoe City** ⑧ to see its Gatekeeper's Log Cabin Museum.

IF YOU HAVE 5 DAYS

On your first day, have a picnic at **Pope-Baldwin Recreation Area** ③. Then head west to **Lake Tahoe Visitor Center** ④ and the **Emerald Bay** ⑤ lookout. Hike to **Vikingsholm** or, if that seems too strenuous, proceed directly to **Sugar Pine Point State Park** ⑦. Have dinner in **Tahoe City** ⑧ or **South Lake Tahoe** ①. On your second day, cruise on the *Hornblower's Tahoe Queen* or MS *Dixie II* in the morning, then ride the **Heavenly Tram** ② and have lunch and possibly a hike. Spend the late afternoon or early evening at one of the **Stateline** ⑱ casinos. On the third day, visit **Cave Rock** ⑯ and the **Ponderosa Ranch** ⑭, and hike the Stateline Lookout Trail above **Crystal Bay** ⑫. Have lunch in Crystal Bay and spend the afternoon at the nearby **Kings Beach State Recreation Area** ⑨. On the fourth day, hang out at **Sand Harbor Beach** ⑮ or, if it's winter, on the ski slopes. On day five, rent a bike and ride from **D. L. Bliss State Park** ⑥ to **Tahoe City** ⑧ and explore the Gatekeeper's Log Cabin Museum.

When to Tour Lake Tahoe

Except for ski bunnies, Tahoe is the most fun during the summer. The best strategy for avoiding crowds is to do as much as you can as early in the day as you can. The parking lots for the Lake Tahoe Visitor Center, Vikingsholm, and Gatekeeper's Log Cabin Museum can be jammed at any time. Weekends are the most congested, but weekdays are busy as well.

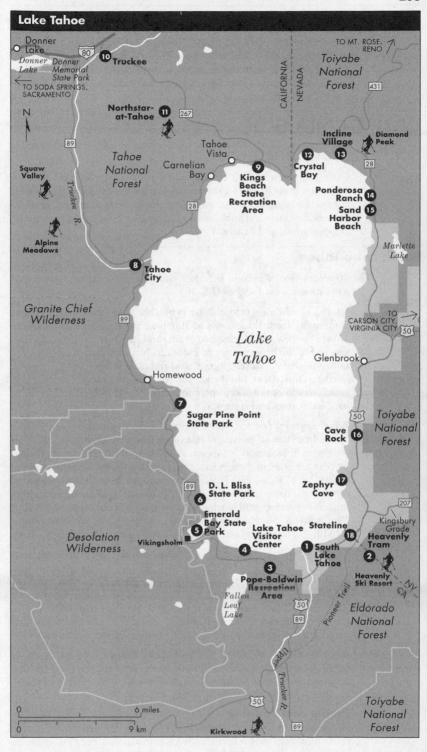

Lake Tahoe

If you can swing it, September and October, when the throngs have dispersed but the weather is still pleasant, are among the most satisfying months to visit Lake Tahoe. During the winter ski season Tahoe's population swells on the weekends—if you're able to come mid-week, you'll have the resorts and neighboring towns almost to yourself. Most of the visitor centers, mansions, state parks, and beaches are closed between November and May.

CALIFORNIA SIDE
South Lake Tahoe to Carnelian Bay

Lake Tahoe lends itself to a geopolitical division between the two states that share it. The California side is the more developed, both with commercial enterprises—restaurants, motels, lodges, resorts, residential subdivisions—and public-access facilities, such as historic sites, parks, campgrounds, and beaches.

South Lake Tahoe

❶ *50 mi south of Reno on U.S. 395 and U.S. 50; 198 mi northeast of San Francisco on I–80 to U.S. 50.*

South Lake Tahoe's raison d'être is tourism. The lake region's largest community feeds the casinos at Stateline; the ski slopes at Heavenly Valley; the beaches, docks, bike trails, and campgrounds of the south shore; and the backcountry of Eldorado National Forest and Desolation Wilderness. Motels, lodges, and restaurants line U.S. 50 heading northeast into town, but if you head to the northwest on Highway 89, which straddles the lakefront, commercial development gives way to national forests and state parks.

★ ☺ **❷** Whether you ski or not, you'll appreciate the impressive view of Lake Tahoe from the 50-passenger **Heavenly Tram,** which runs 2,000 ft up the slopes of Heavenly Ski Resort to 8,200 ft. When the weather's fine you can take one of three (successively more difficult) hikes around the mountaintop. Monument Peak Restaurant, open daily during tram hours, serves basic American food cafeteria style—lunch, dinner, and Sunday brunch in summer, and lunch only in winter. ⊠ *Head north on Ski Run Blvd. off U.S. 50 and follow signs to parking lot,* ☎ *702/586–7000.* ☞ *$12.* ☉ *Tram runs June–Oct., daily 9–9; Nov.–May, daily 9–3:30.*

The 500-passenger **Hornblower's Tahoe Queen** (⊠ Ski Run Marina, off U.S. 50, ☎ 530/541–3364 or 800/238–2463), a glass-bottom paddlewheeler, makes 1½-hour happy-hour cruises, 2¼-hour sightseeing cruises, and 3½-hour dinner-dance cruises year-round from South Lake Tahoe. Fares range from $16 to $40. In winter the boat becomes the only water-borne ski shuttle in the world: $75 covers hotel transfers, transportation across the lake to Squaw Valley, and a lift ticket.

A professional-size facility, the **South Lake Tahoe Ice Center** caters to ice skaters of all levels, from first-timers to figure skaters and hockey leaguers. ⊠ *1176 Rufus Allen Blvd.,* ☎ *530/542–4700.* ☞ *Prices vary.* ☉ *Mon.–Thurs. 10–8, Fri.–Sat. 10–10, Sun. 10–6.*

Dining and Lodging

$$–$$$ ✕ **Nepheles.** A chalet on the road to Heavenly Ski Resort houses this cozy restaurant that serves creative California cuisine. Entrées range from ahi tuna in a pineapple vinaigrette to broiled elk with a sauce made from black currants and merlot. Appetizers include escargots, swordfish egg rolls, and a taco filled with Thai-chicken and smoked ham. ⊠

1169 Ski Run Blvd., ☎ *530/544–8130. AE, D, DC, MC, V. No lunch.*

$$–$$$ ✕ **Swiss Chalet.** Swiss decor is carried out with great consistency at this Tahoe institution. The Continental menu includes schnitzel, sauerbraten, fondue, steaks, and homemade pastries. ⊠ *2544 U.S. 50,* ☎ *530/544–3304. AE, MC, V. Closed late Nov.–early Dec. No lunch.*

$–$$ ✕ **Scusa!** This intimate Italian restaurant on the road to the Heavenly Ski Resort has a smart, modern decor. Capellini, linguine, fettuccine, penne, ravioli, and lasagna are on the menu, along with hearty calzones, exotic pizzas, steak, chicken, and fresh fish entrées. The pan-fried calamari with red peppers and capers are a treat. Don't pass up the rosemary-flavored flat bread, baked fresh daily. ⊠ *1142 Ski Run Blvd.,* ☎ *530/542–0100. AE, MC, V. No lunch.*

$ ✕ **Red Hut Waffle Shop.** A vintage Tahoe diner, all chrome and red plastic, the Red Hut is a tiny place with a dozen counter stools and a dozen booths. It's a traditional breakfast spot for locals and visitors in the know, all of whom appreciate the huge omelets, the banana, pecan, and coconut waffles, and other tasty vittles. ⊠ *2749 U.S. 50,* ☎ *530/ 541–9024. Reservations not accepted. No credit cards. No dinner.*

$$–$$$ ✕🕅 **Christiania Inn.** An antiques-filled bed-and-breakfast across the street from the base of the Heavenly Tram, the Christiania is a local favorite. The American-Continental menu emphasizes fresh seafood, prime beef, and veal. Upstairs at the inn, two rooms and four suites come with king- or queen-size beds and private baths. Three of the suites are two-story affairs with wood-burning fireplaces and wet bars; two have saunas and one has a whirlpool tub. ⊠ *3819 Saddle Rd., 96151,* ☎ *530/544–7337 or 530/541–5210,* 𝔽𝔸𝕏 *530/541–5342. 6 rooms. Restaurant, bar. Continental breakfast. MC, V.*

$$$–$$$$ 🕅 **Embassy Suites.** In this opulent all-suites hotel, decorated Sierra-
★   lodge style, fountains and waterwheels splash in the nine-story atriums, where complimentary breakfasts and evening cocktails are served daily. Glass elevators rise to guest suites, each with a living room, dining area, and separate bedroom. ⊠ *4130 Lake Tahoe Blvd., 96150,* ☎ *530/544–5400 or 800/362–2779,* 𝔽𝔸𝕏 *530/544–4900. 400 suites. 3 restaurants, indoor pool, hot tub, sauna, exercise room, nightclub. Full breakfast. AE, D, DC, MC, V.*

$$$–$$$$ 🕅 **Tahoe Seasons Resort.** Most rooms at this resort, which is set among pine trees on a mountain across from the Heavenly Ski Resort, are outfitted with fireplaces. Every room has a whirlpool and a small kitchen. The decor is contemporary, heavy on the teal. ⊠ *3901 Saddle Rd., 96157,* ☎ *530/541–6700, 530/541–6010, or 800/540–4874,* 𝔽𝔸𝕏 *530/541– 0653. 183 suites. Restaurant, lounge, refrigerators, pool, hot tub, 2 tennis courts, volleyball, airport shuttle. AE, DC, MC, V.*

$$–$$$$ 🕅 **Inn by the Lake.** Across the road from a beach, this luxury motel
★   has spacious rooms furnished in contemporary style (blond oak and pale peach). All have balconies; some have lake views, wet bars, and in-room kitchens. The inn provides a free shuttle to the casinos. ⊠ *3300 Lake Tahoe Blvd., 96150,* ☎ *530/542–0330 or 800/877–1466,* 𝔽𝔸𝕏 *530/541–6596. 87 rooms, 12 suites. Pool, sauna, hot tub, bicycles, coin laundry. Continental breakfast. AE, D, DC, MC, V.*

$$–$$$$ 🕅 **Lakeland Village Beach and Ski Resort.** This complex with 1,000 ft of private beach has a range of accommodations: studios, suites, and town houses, all with kitchens, fireplaces, and private decks or balconies. Ask about ski packages. ⊠ *3535 Lake Tahoe Blvd., 96150,* ☎ *530/ 544–1685 or 800/822–5969,* 𝔽𝔸𝕏 *530/544–0193. 209 units. Kitchens, 2 pools, wading pool, hot tub, 2 saunas, 2 tennis courts, beach, boating, fishing, coin laundry. AE, D, MC, V.*

$$–$$$ 🕅 **Best Western Station House Inn.** This inn has won design awards
★   for its exterior and interior. The rooms have king- and queen-size beds

and double-vanity bathrooms. The location is good, near a private beach yet close to the casinos. An American breakfast is complimentary from October to May. ⊠ *901 Park Ave., 96150,* ☎ *530/542–1101 or 800/ 822–5953,* 𝔽𝔸𝕏 *530/542–1714. 100 rooms, 2 suites. Restaurant, lounge, pool, hot tub. AE, D, DC, MC, V.*

\$\$–\$\$\$ 🖬 **Forest Inn Suites.** The location is excellent—5½ acres bordering a forest, a half block from Harrah's and Harvey's, and adjacent to a supermarket, cinema, and shops. Rooms are modern and pleasant. Ski rentals are available, and free shuttles to Heavenly and Kirkwood ski areas stop here. ⊠ *1101 Park Ave., 96150,* ☎ *530/541–6655 or 800/ 822–5950,* 𝔽𝔸𝕏 *530/544–3135. 17 rooms, 101 suites. Kitchens, 2 pools, 2 hot tubs, sauna, putting green, health club, volleyball, bicycles, coin laundry. AE, D, DC, MC, V.*

\$\$ 🖬 **Travelodge.** There are two members of the national chain in South Lake Tahoe; both are convenient to casinos, shopping, and recreation and have some no-smoking rooms. Free local calls, cable TV, and in-room coffee add to the budget appeal. ⊠ *3489 U.S. 50 at Bijou Center, 96150,* ☎ *530/544–5266 or 800/982–1466,* 𝔽𝔸𝕏 *530/544–6985.* ⊠ *4003 U.S. 50, 96150,* ☎ *530/541–5000 or 800/982–2466,* 𝔽𝔸𝕏 *530/ 544–6910. 59 rooms at Bijou Center, 66 rooms at 4003 U.S. 50. Pool at each; Bijou Center has a restaurant. AE, D, DC, MC, V.*

\$–\$\$ 🖬 **Best Western Lake Tahoe Inn.** Near Harrah's on 6 acres, with gardens and the Heavenly Ski Resort directly behind, this large motel has modern rooms decorated in soothing colors. ⊠ *4110 Lake Tahoe Blv, 96150,* ☎ *530/541–2010 or 800/528–1234,* 𝔽𝔸𝕏 *530/542–1428. 392 rooms, 8 suites. Restaurant, lounge, 2 pools, hot tub. Full breakfast. AE, D, DC, MC, V.*

\$–\$\$ 🖬 **Royal Valhalla Motor Lodge.** Two- and three-bedroom suites with complete kitchens make this motel attractive to families. Some of the simple, modern rooms have private balconies. ⊠ *4104 Lakeshore Blvd., 96157,* ☎ *530/544–2233 or 800/999–4104,* 𝔽𝔸𝕏 *530/544– 1436. 80 suites. Pool, hot tub, coin laundry. Continental breakfast. AE, DC, MC, V.*

\$ 🖬 **Best Tahoe West Inn.** The Tahoe West is three blocks from the beach and casinos. The exterior is rustic, rooms are neatly furnished, and beds are queen-size. Twelve rooms have kitchenettes. The inn provides a free shuttle to the casinos and ski areas. ⊠ *4107 Pine Blvd., 96150,* ☎ *530/ 544–6455, 800/522–1021, or 800/700–8246,* 𝔽𝔸𝕏 *530/544–0508. 60 rooms. Pool, hot tub, sauna, beach. AE, D, DC, MC, V.*

Outdoor Activities and Sports

CROSS-COUNTRY SKIING

For the ultimate in groomed conditions head to America's largest cross-country ski resort, **Royal Gorge** (⊠ follow signs from Soda Springs–Norden exit off I–80, Box 1100, Soda Springs 95728, ☎ 530/ 426–3871), which has 197 mi of 18-ft-wide track for all abilities, 88 trails on 9,172 acres, two ski schools, and 10 warming huts. Four cafés, two hotels, and a hot tub and sauna are among the facilities. **Kirkwood Ski Resort** (☞ *below*) has 50 mi of groomed-track skiing, with skating lanes, instruction, and rentals.

DOWNHILL SKIING

Heavenly Ski Resort. When first seen from the California side, Heavenly's mogul-choked slopes look impossibly difficult. But this vast resort—comprised of nine peaks, two valleys, and three base-lodge areas—has something for every skier. Beginners can choose wide, well-groomed trails accessed via the Heavenly Tram, or short and gentle runs in the Enchanted Forest area. The Sky Express high-speed quad chair whisks intermediate and advanced skiers to the summit for wide cruisers or steep tree skiing. Mott and Killebrew canyons draw expert skiers to the Nevada side for the steep chutes and thick-timbered slopes. For snowboarders there's the Airport Park near the Olympic lift. The ski school, like everything else at Heavenly, is large and offers everything from learn-to-ski packages for novices to canyon adventure tours for advanced skiers. Skiing lessons and day care are available for children age 4 and up. ⊠ *Ski Run Blvd. off Hwy. 89/U.S. 50 (mailing address: Box 2180, Stateline, NV 89449),* ☎ *702/586–7000 or 800/243–2836; 530/541–7544 snow phone. 82 trails on 4,800 acres, rated 20% beginner, 45% intermediate, 35% expert. Longest run 5½ mi, base 6,540', summit 10,040'. Lifts: 26, including 1 aerial tram, 1 high-speed 6-passenger lift, and 3 high-speed quads.*

Kirkwood Ski Resort. Thirty-six miles south of Lake Tahoe in an alpine-village setting, Kirkwood is a destination resort with 120 condominiums, several shops and restaurants in the base village, overnight RV parking, and a shuttle bus to Lake Tahoe. Most of the runs off the top are rated expert-only, but intermediate and beginning skiers have their own vast bowl, where they can ski through trees or on wide, open trails. Snowboarding is permitted on all runs and in an exclusive terrain park. Skiing and snowboarding lessons and equipment rentals and sales are available. The children's ski school has programs for ages 4 to 12, and day care is available for children from age 2 to 6. Arrangements for younger children must be made in advance. For Nordic skiing, *see* Cross-Country Skiing, *above.* ⊠ *Hwy. 88 off Hwy. 89 (mailing address: Box 1, Kirkwood, CA 95646),* ☎ *209/258–6000; 209/258–7000 lodging information; 209/258–3000 snow phone. 65 trails on 2,300 acres, rated 15% beginner, 50% intermediate, 20% advanced, 15% expert. Longest run 2½ mi, base 7,800', summit 9,800'. Lifts: 12.*

Shopping

There's some good shopping south of town at the **Factory Outlet Stores** (⊠ *U.S. 50 at Hwy. 89).*

Pope-Baldwin Recreation Area

❸ *5 mi west of South Lake Tahoe on Hwy. 89.*

George S. Pope, who made his money in shipping and lumber, hosted the business and cultural elite of 1920s America at his home, the **Pope House.** The magnificently restored 1894 mansion and two other estates—those of entrepreneur "Lucky" Baldwin (which holds a museum of Baldwin memorabilia and Washoe Indian artifacts) and Walter Heller (the Valhalla, used for community events)—form the heart of the Pope-Baldwin Recreation Area's **Tallac Historic Site.** The lakeside site, a pleasant place to take a stroll or have a picnic, hosts cultural activities (including a Renaissance festival) throughout the summer. Docents conduct tours of the Pope House during summer. ☎ *530/541–5227.* 🎟 *Pope House tour $2.* ☉ *Tallac Historic Site grounds dawn–sunset; house and museum hrs vary.*

❹ The U.S. Forest Service operates the **Lake Tahoe Visitor Center** on Taylor Creek. You can visit the site of a Washoe Indian settlement; walk self-guided trails through meadow, marsh, and forest; and inspect the Stream Profile Chamber, an underground underwater display with windows that afford views right into Taylor Creek (in the fall you may see spawning salmon digging their nests). In summer Forest Service naturalists organize discovery walks and nighttime campfires, with singing and marshmallow roasts. ⊠ *Hwy. 89,* ☎ *530/573–2674 (in season only).* ☉ *June–Sept., daily 8–5:30; Oct., weekends 8–5:30.*

Emerald Bay State Park

★ **⑤** *4 mi west of Pope-Baldwin Recreation Area on Hwy. 9.*

Emerald Bay, a 3-mi-long and 1-mi-wide fjord-like bay, was carved by massive glaciers millions of years ago. Famed for its jewel-like shape and colors, it surrounds Fannette, Tahoe's only island. Highway 89 curves high above the lake through Emerald Bay State Park; from the Emerald Bay lookout, the centerpiece of the park, you can survey the whole scene.

A steep, 1-mi-long trail from the lookout leads down to **Vikingsholm,** a 38-room estate completed in 1929. The original owner, Lora Knight, had this precise replica of a 1,200-year-old Viking castle built out of materials native to the area. She furnished it with Scandinavian antiques and hired artisans to custom-build period reproductions. The sod roof sprouts wildflowers each spring. There are picnic tables nearby and a gray-sand beach for strolling. The hike back up is a major huff (especially if you're not yet acclimated to the elevation), but there are benches and stone culverts to rest on. At the 150-ft-high peak of Fannette Island are the remnants of a stone structure known as the Tea House, built in 1928 so that guests of Lora Knight could have a place to enjoy afternoon refreshments after a motorboat ride out to Fannette. The island is off-limits from February to June to protect nesting Canada geese; the rest of the year it's open for day use only. ☎ *530/525–7277.* 🎫 *$2.* ☼ *Memorial Day–Labor Day, daily 10–4.*

D. L. Bliss State Park

⑥ *3 mi north of Emerald Bay State Park on Hwy. 89.*

D. L. Bliss State Park takes its name from Duane LeRoy Bliss, a 19th-century lumber magnate. At one time Bliss owned nearly 75% of Tahoe's lakefront, along with local steamboats, railroads, and banks. The Bliss family donated these 1,200 acres to the state in the 1930s; the park now shares 6 mi of shoreline with Emerald Bay State Park. At the north end of Bliss is **Rubicon Point,** which overlooks one of the lake's deepest spots. Short trails lead to an old lighthouse and Balancing Rock, which weighs in at 250,000 pounds and balances on a fist of granite. Longer trails lead to remote beaches and all the way to Vikingsholm. ☎ *530/525–7277.* 🎫 *$5 per vehicle (day use).* ☼ *Memorial Day–Sept., daily sunrise–sunset.*

Camping

⛺ **D. L. Bliss State Park Campground.** A wooded, hilly, quiet setting makes for blissful family camping near the lake. Reserve sites as far in advance as possible. ✉ *Off Hwy. 89,* ☎ *800/444–7275. 168 sites.* 🎫 *$16–$20. Fire rings, flush toilets, disposal station, showers, water (no hookups).* ☼ *Memorial Day–Sept.*

Sugar Pine Point State Park

★ **⑦** *8 mi north of D. L. Bliss State Park on Hwy. 89.*

The main attraction at Sugar Pine Point State Park is **Ehrman Mansion,** a stone-and-shingle 1903 summer home, furnished in period style, that in its day was the height of modernity: It had a refrigerator, an elevator, and an electric stove. Also in the park are a trapper's log cabin from the mid-19th century, a nature preserve with wildlife exhibits, a lighthouse, the start of the 10-mi-long biking trail to Tahoe City, and an extensive system of hiking and cross-country trails. ☎ *530/525–7232 year-round; 530/525–7982 in season.* 🎫 *$5 per vehicle (day use).* ☼ *Memorial Day–Labor Day, daily 11–4.*

Camping

⚠ **General Creek Campground.** This homey campground on the mountain side of Highway 89 is one of the few public ones to remain open in winter, primarily for cross-country skiers. ✉ *Hwy. 89,* ☎ *800/444–7275. 175 sites.* 🚻 *$14. Fire rings, flush toilets, disposal station, showers, water (no hookups).* ☉ *Year-round.*

Tahoe City

❽ *10 mi north of Sugar Pine Point State Park on Hwy. 89; 14 mi south of Truckee on Hwy. 89.*

Tahoe City is home to many stores and restaurants within a compact area, and to the Outlet Gates, where water is spilled into the Truckee River to control the surface level of the lake. Giant trout, common before the severe drought of the late 1980s and early 1990s, have returned; look down and see them from Fanny Bridge, so called for the views of the backsides of visitors leaning over the railing. Here, Highway 89 turns north from the lake and leads to Squaw Valley, Donner Lake, and Truckee, and Highway 28 continues northeast around the lake toward Kings Beach and Nevada.

★ The **Gatekeeper's Log Cabin Museum** in Tahoe City preserves the area's past, displaying Washoe and Paiute artifacts as well as pioneer memorabilia. ✉ *130 W. Lake Blvd.,* ☎ *530/583–1762.* 🚻 *Free.* ☉ *May 15–Sept., daily 11–5.*

The **Watson Cabin Living Museum,** a 1909 log cabin built by Robert M. Watson and his son and filled with century-old furnishings, is in the middle of Tahoe City. Costumed docents act out the daily life of a typical pioneer family. ✉ *560 N. Lake Blvd.,* ☎ *530/583–8717 or 530/583–1762.* 🚻 *Free.* ☉ *June 15–Labor Day, daily noon–4.*

Dining and Lodging

$–$$$$ ✕ **Jake's on the Lake.** Handsome rooms of oak and glass provide a
★ suitably classy waterfront setting for Continental food. The seafood bar here is extensive; the varied dinner menu includes meat and poultry but emphasizes fresh fish. ✉ *Boatworks Mall, 780 N. Lake Blvd.,* ☎ *530/583–0188. AE, MC, V. No lunch weekdays in winter.*

$$–$$$ ✕ **Christy Hill.** Panoramic lake views and fireside dining distinguish this restaurant, which serves California cuisine—fresh seafood (such as Atlantic salmon with a ginger–pepper crust in a cabernet demi-glace) and game (including broiled New Zealand venison). ✉ *Lakehouse Mall, 115 Grove St.,* ☎ *530/583–8551. MC, V. Closed Mon. (spring and fall). No lunch.*

$$–$$$ ✕ **Grazie! Ristorante & Bar.** The smell of garlic warms you as soon as you enter this northern Italian restaurant, as does the fire in the wide, double-sided fireplace. Hearty pasta dishes and pizzas are on the menu, but the stars are the antipasti and pasta salads. Chicken is cooked on a wood-burning rotisserie and rack of lamb on the grill; both are served with homemade sauces. ✉ *Roundhouse Mall, 700 N. Lake Blvd.,* ☎ *530/583–0233. AE, D, DC, MC, V.*

$$–$$$ ✕ **Wolfdale's.** An intimate restaurant inside a 100-year-old house,
★ Wolfdale's serves cuisine with Japanese and Californian overtones. The menu, which changes weekly, showcases several imaginative entrées, such as grilled southwestern-style chicken with celery-root potatoes and brazed lamb shank with tomatoes, rosemary, and parsnip puree. ✉ *640 N. Lake Blvd.,* ☎ *530/583–5700. MC, V. No lunch.*

$$–$$$$ ✕🏨 **Sunnyside Restaurant and Lodge.** This impressive lodge has a ma-
★ rina and an expansive lakefront deck with steps down to a narrow gravel beach. Rooms are decorated in a crisp nautical style, with prints of boats hanging on the pinstripe wall coverings and sea chests as coffee tables.

Each room has its own deck with a lake or mountain view. Seafood is the specialty of the very fine American-Continental restaurant. Lunch is not served in the off season. ⊠ *1850 W. Lake Blvd., Box 5969, 96145,* ☎ *530/583–7200 or 800/822–2754,* ℻ *530/583–2551. 21 rooms, 2 suites. Restaurant, lounge, room service, beach. Continental breakfast. AE, MC, V.*

$$$–$$$$ 🏨 **Chinquapin Resort.** A deluxe development on 95 acres of forested
★ land 3 mi northeast of Tahoe City contains roomy one- to four-bedroom town houses and condos with great views of the lake and the mountains. Each unit has a fireplace, a fully equipped kitchen, and a washer and dryer. A one-week minimum stay is required in July and August. In winter the minimum is two nights. ⊠ *3600 N. Lake Blvd., 96145,* ☎ *530/583–6991 or 800/732–6721,* ℻ *530/583–0937. 172 town houses and condos. Pool, saunas, 7 tennis courts, hiking, horseshoes. MC, V.*

$$$–$$$$ 🏨 **Resort at Squaw Creek.** Nearly half the rooms are suites at this complex composed of a main lodge, an outdoor arcade of shops and boutiques, and a 405-room hotel. Some units have fireplaces and full kitchens, and all have original art, custom furnishings, and good views. Outside the hotel entrance is a triple chairlift to Squaw Valley's slopes. Dining options range from haute cuisine to pastries and coffee. ⊠ *400 Squaw Creek Rd., Olympic Valley 96146,* ☎ *530/583–6300 or 800/ 327–3353,* ℻ *530/581–6632. 235 rooms, 170 suites. 5 restaurants, bar, 3 pools, 4 hot tubs, sauna, spa, 18-hole golf course, 2 tennis courts, health club, ice-skating. AE, D, DC, MC, V.*

$–$$ 🏨 **Peppertree Inn.** This skinny seven-story tower is within easy walking distance of the beaches, marina, shops, and restaurants of Tahoe City. Rooms are clean and comfortable, if not luxurious, and have great lake views. ⊠ *645 N. Lake Blvd., 96145,* ☎ *530/583–3711 or 800/ 228–2000,* ℻ *530/583–6938. 46 rooms, 5 suites. Pool, hot tub. AE, D, DC, MC, V.*

Outdoor Activities and Sports

DOWNHILL SKIING

Alpine Meadows Ski Area. Alpine is an intermediate skier's paradise with two peaks. For snowboarders there's a terrain park with a half-pipe. The ski area has some of Tahoe's most reliable conditions; this is usually one of the first areas to open in November, and one of the last to close in May. There is a ski school for adults and children of all skill levels and for skiers with disabilities. There's also an area for overnight RV parking. ⊠ *6 mi northwest of Tahoe City off Hwy. 89, 13 mi south of I–80 (mailing address: Box 5279, 96145),* ☎ *530/583– 4232; 530/581–8374 snow phone; 800/441–4423 information. 100 trails on 2,000 acres, rated 25% easier, 40% more difficult, 35% most difficult. Longest run 2½ mi, base 6,835', summit 8,637'. Lifts: 12, including 1 high-speed 6-passenger lift and 1 high-speed quad.*

Squaw Valley USA. Home to some of the toughest skiing in the Tahoe area, Squaw was the site of the 1960 Olympics. Although the immense resort has changed significantly since then, the skiing is still world-class, with steep chutes and cornices on six Sierra peaks. Expert skiers often head directly to the untamed terrain of the infamous KT-22 face, which has bumps, cliffs, and gulp-and-go chutes. Plenty of wide, groomed trails start near the beginner-designated High Camp lift and around the more challenging Snow King Peak. Snowboarders have the run of two terrain parks. You can ski until 9 PM, and lift tickets for skiers under 12 are only $5. Nonskiing recreational opportunities—bungee jumping, rock climbing, and ice skating—abound. The Village Mall has shops, eateries, and accommodations. ⊠ *Hwy. 89, 5 mi northwest of Tahoe*

City (mailing address: Box 2007, Olympic Valley, 96146), ☎ 530/583–
6985; 800/545–4350 reservations; 530/583–6955 snow phone. 100
trails on 4,300 acres, rated 25% beginner, 45% intermediate, 30% advanced. Longest run 3 mi, base 6,200', summit 9,050'. Lifts: 29, including a gondola, a cable car, and 5 high-speed quads.

GOLF

Resort at Squaw Creek Golf Course (☒ 400 Squaw Creek Rd., Olympic
Valley, ☎ 530/583–6300), an 18-hole championship course, was designed by Robert Trent Jones Jr. The $110 greens fee includes the use
of a cart. Golfers use pull carts at the nine-hole **Tahoe City Golf Course**
(☒ Hwy. 28, Tahoe City, ☎ 530/583–1516). The greens fee is $25; a
power cart is $15 additional.

Carnelian Bay to Kings Beach

5 to 10 mi northeast of Tahoe City on Hwy. 28.

The small lakeside commercial districts of Carnelian Bay and Tahoe
Vista service the thousand or so locals who live in the area year-round
and the thousands more who have summer residences or launch their
boats here. Kings Beach, the last town heading east on Highway 28
before the Nevada border, is to Crystal Bay what South Lake Tahoe is
to Stateline: a bustling California village full of motels and rental condos, restaurants and shops, used by the hordes of hopefuls who pass
through on their way to the casinos.

🖐 **❾** The 28-acre **Kings Beach State Recreation Area,** one of the largest such
areas on the lake, is open year-round. Its long beach becomes crowded
with people swimming, sunbathing, jet skiing, riding in paddleboats,
and playing volleyball and Frisbee. There's a good playground here.
☒ *North Lake Blvd., Kings Beach,* ☎ *530/546–7248.* 🎟 *Free day use,
parking $5 in summer, free in winter.*

Dining

$$–$$$ ✕ **Captain Jon's.** The dining room at Captain Jon's is small and cozy,
with linen cloths and fresh flowers on the tables. On chilly evenings a
fireplace with a brick hearth warms diners. The lengthy dinner menu
is old-style country French, with two dozen daily specials; the emphasis
is on fish and hearty salads. The restaurant's lounge, which serves light
meals, is on the water in a separate building with a pier where guests
can tie up their boats. ☒ *7220 N. Lake Blvd., Tahoe Vista,* ☎ *530/
546–4819. AE, DC, MC, V. No lunch during ski season.*

$–$$$ ✕ **Gar Woods Grill and Pier.** This stylish but casual lakeside restau-
rant recalls the area's past with boating photographs and a river-rock
fireplace. Floor-to-ceiling picture windows overlook the lake. The
menu includes dishes like Thai chicken salad, grilled-salmon salad, a
seafood sauté, and pastas. There's an extensive wine list, and Sunday
brunch is served. ☒ *5000 N. Lake Blvd., Carnelian Bay,* ☎ *530/546–
3366. AE, MC, V.*

$ ✕ **Log Cabin Caffe.** Almost always hopping, this Kings Beach eatery
specializes in healthful, hearty breakfast and lunch entrées—pancakes,
waffles, freshly baked pastries, health-food sandwiches, and ice cream.
It's a good place on the north shore for an espresso or cappuccino. Get
here early on weekends; this is a popular spot for brunch. ☒ *8692 N.
Lake Blvd.,* ☎ *530/546–7109. MC, V.*

Outdoor Activities and Sports

SNOWMOBILING

Snowmobiling Unlimited (☒ Hwys. 267 and 28, Kings Beach, ☎ 530/
583–5858) conducts guided tours, rents equipment, and operates a track
to zoom around on.

SWIMMING

The **North Tahoe Beach Center** has a 26-ft hot tub and a beach with an enclosed swimming area and four sand volleyball courts. The complex includes a barbecue and picnic area, a fitness center, windsurfing and nonmotorized boat rentals, a snack bar, and a clubhouse with games. ⊠ *7860 N. Lake Blvd., Kings Beach,* ☎ *530/546–2566.* ⊒ *$7.*

Truckee

⑩ *13 mi northwest of Kings Beach on Hwy. 267; 14 mi north of Tahoe City on Hwy. 89.*

Old West facades line the main street of Truckee, a favorite stopover for people traveling from the Bay Area to the north shore of Lake Tahoe. Galleries and boutiques are plentiful, but you will also find low-key diners, discount skiwear, and an old-fashioned five-and-dime store. Stop by the **information booth** in the Amtrak depot (⊠ Railroad St. at Commercial Rd.) for a walking-tour map of historic Truckee.

Donner Memorial State Park commemorates the Donner Party, a group of 89 westward-bound pioneers who were trapped in the Sierra in the winter of 1846–47 in snow 22 ft deep. Only 47 survived, some by cannibalism and others by eating animal hides. The Immigrant Museum's hourly slide show details the Donner Party's plight. Other displays relate the history of other settlers and of railroad development through the Sierra. ⊠ *Off I–80, 2 mi west of Truckee,* ☎ *530/582–7892.* ⊒ *$2.* ☉ *Sept.–May, daily 9–4; June–Aug., daily 9–5.*

Northstar-at-Tahoe

⑪ *6 mi south of Truckee on Hwy. 267; 15 mi north of Tahoe City on Hwy. 28 to Hwy. 267.*

Dining and Lodging

$$$–$$$$　✕⊞ **Northstar-at-Tahoe Resort.** This is the area's most complete destination resort. The center of action is the Village Mall, a concentration of restaurants, shops, recreation facilities, and accommodations— hotel rooms, condos, and private houses. The many sports activities make the resort especially popular with families. Summer rates are lower than winter rates. ⊠ *Off Hwy. 267, Box 129, 96160,* ☎ *530/562– 1010 or 800/466–6784,* ⅻ *530/562–2215. 230 units. 4 restaurants, deli, 18-hole golf course, 10 tennis courts, horseback riding, bicycles, skiing, sleigh rides, snowmobiling, recreation room, baby-sitting. AE, D, MC, V.*

Outdoor Activities and Sports

CROSS-COUNTRY AND DOWNHILL SKIING

Northstar-at-Tahoe Resort. Two northeast-facing, wind-protected bowls provide some of the best powder skiing in the Lake Tahoe area, including steep chutes and long cruising runs. Top-to-bottom snowmaking and intense grooming assure good conditions for cross-country and downhill skiing. Northstar-at-Tahoe provides 40 mi of groomed, tracked trails, with a wide skating lane for Nordic skiers. For snowboarders there's a terrain park and trails with features like dragon tails and magic moguls, created especially for snowboarders. The ski school offers programs for skiers ages five and up, and day care is available for children older than two. ⊠ *Hwy. 267 between Truckee and Kings Beach (mailing address: Box 129, Truckee 96160),* ☎ *530/562–1010, 530/ 562–1330 snow phone,* ⅻ *530/562–2215. 63 trails on 1,800 acres, rated 25% beginner, 50% intermediate, 25% advanced. Longest run 2.9 mi, base 6,400′, summit 8,600′. Lifts: 12 lifts, including a gondola and 4 high-speed quads.*

NEVADA SIDE
From Crystal Bay to Stateline

You don't need a roadside marker to know when you've crossed from California into Nevada. The lake's water and the pine trees may be identical on the other side, but the flashing lights and elaborate marquees of casinos announce legal gambling in garish hues.

Crystal Bay

⑫ *1 mi east of Kings Beach on Hwy. 28; 30 mi north of South Lake Tahoe on U.S. 50 to Hwy. 28.*

Right at the Nevada border, Crystal Bay holds a cluster of casinos; one, the **Cal-Neva Lodge** (☞ Dining and Lodging, *below*), is bisected by the state line. This joint opened in 1927 and has weathered nearly as many scandals—the largest involving Frank Sinatra (he lost his gaming license in the 1960s for alleged mob connections)—as it has blizzards. The **Tahoe Biltmore** has a popular $1.39 breakfast special served 24 hours a day. **Jim Kelley's Nugget** closes during the winter months—the only casino in Nevada that ever closes.

Dining and Lodging

$$–$$$ ✕ **Soule Domain.** A romantic 1927 pine-log cabin with a stone fire-
★   place is the setting for some of Lake Tahoe's most creative and delicious dinners. Chef-owner Charles Edward Soule IV's specialties include the grilled tuna with papaya-mango salsa and the filet mignon with shiitake mushrooms, Gorgonzola, and brandy. ⊠ *Cove St. across from Tahoe Biltmore,* ☎ *530/546–7529. Reservations essential on weekends. AE, DC, MC, V. No lunch.*

$–$$$$ ⊡ **Cal-Neva Lodge.** All the rooms in this hotel-casino on Highway 28 at Crystal Bay have views of Lake Tahoe and the mountains. There is an arcade with video games for children, cabaret entertainment, and, in addition to rooms in the main hotel, seven two-bedroom chalets, and 12 cabins with living rooms. ⊠ *2 Stateline Rd., Box 368, 89402,* ☎ *702/832–4000 or 800/225–6382,* 📠 *702/831–9007. 261 rooms, 20 suites, 19 cabins. Restaurant, coffee shop, pool, hot tub, sauna, tennis courts, casino, 3 chapels. AE, D, DC, MC, V.*

Incline Village

⑬ *3 mi east of Crystal Bay on Hwy. 28.*

Incline Village, one of Nevada's few master-planned communities, dates back to the early 1960s; it's still privately owned. Check out **Lakeshore Drive** to see some of the most expensive real estate in Nevada. Incline is the only town on Lake Tahoe without a central commercial district, planned this way to prevent congestion and to preserve a natural feel. The town's **Recreation Center** (⊠ 980 Incline Way, ☎ 702/832–1300) has an eight-lane swimming pool, fitness area, a basketball court, a game room, and a snack bar.

OFF THE   **MOUNT ROSE –** If you want to ski some of the highest slopes in the Lake
BEATEN PATH   Tahoe region, Highway 431 leads north out of Incline Village to Mount Rose. Reno is another 30 mi farther. ☎ *702/849–0704.*

⑭ The 1960s television western *Bonanza* inspired the **Ponderosa Ranch** theme park. Attractions include the Cartwrights' ranch house, a western town, and a saloon. There's also a self-guided nature trail, free pony rides for children, and, if you're here from 8 to 9:30 in the morning, a breakfast hayride. During the winter you can tour the ranch house ($6.50) and visit the gift shop. ⊠ *Hwy. 28, 2 mi south of Incline Village,* ☎ *702/831–0691.* ⌑ *$8.50, hayride $2.* ☉ *Mid-Apr.–Oct., daily 9:30–5; Nov.–mid-Apr., 10–3:30.*

Dining and Lodging

$$–$$$ ✕ **Stanley's Restaurant and Lounge.** With its intimate bar and pleasant dining room, this local favorite is a good bet any time for straightforward American fare on the hearty side (barbecued pork ribs, beef Stroganoff). Lighter bites, such as seafood Cobb salad, are also available, along with ample breakfasts; try the eggs Benedict or a chili-cheese omelet. There's a deck for outdoor dining in summer. ⊠ *941 Tahoe Blvd.,* ☎ *702/831–9944. Reservations not accepted. AE, MC, V.*

$–$$ ✕ **Azzara's.** A typical Italian trattoria with light, inviting decor, Azzara's serves a dozen pasta dishes and many pizzas, as well as chicken, lamb, veal, shrimp, and beef. Dinners include soup or salad, a vegetable, a pasta, and garlic bread. ⊠ *Incline Center Mall, 930 Tahoe Blvd.,* ☎ *702/831–0346. MC, V. Closed Mon.*

$$–$$$$ ✕▥ **Hyatt Lake Tahoe Resort Hotel/Casino.** Some of the rooms in this luxurious hotel on the lake have fireplaces, but all the accommodations here are top-notch. The restaurants are the Lone Eagle Grille (fairly good Continental, with steak, seafood, pasta, and rotisserie dishes), the Ciao Mein Trattoria (Asian-Italian), and the Sierra Cafe (open 24 hours). ⊠ *Lakeshore and Country Club Drs., 89450,* ☎ *702/831–1111 or 800/233–1234,* ☒ *702/831–7508. 432 rooms, 28 suites. 3 restaurants, coffee shop, lounge, room service, pool, beach, 2 saunas, spa, 2 tennis courts, health club, bicycles, casino, children's programs, laundry service. AE, D, DC, MC, V.*

Outdoor Activities and Sports

BOAT CRUISE

The **Sierra Cloud** (☎ 702/831–1111), a trimaran with a big trampoline lounging surface, cruises the north-shore area mornings and afternoons from the Hyatt Regency Hotel in Incline Village from May to October. Fares run between $30 and $40.

CROSS-COUNTRY AND DOWNHILL SKIING

Diamond Peak. A fun, family atmosphere prevails at Diamond Peak, which has many special programs and affordable rates. Snowmaking covers 80% of the mountain, and runs are groomed nightly. The ride up the 1-mi Crystal chair rewards you with the best views of the lake from any ski area. Diamond Peak is less crowded than some of the larger areas, and provides free shuttles to lodging in nearby Incline Village. A first-timer's package, which includes rentals, a lesson, and a lift ticket, is $35; a parent-child ski package is $42, with each additional child's lift ticket $5. There is a half-pipe for snowboarders. **Diamond Peak Cross-Country** (⊠ off Hwy. 431, ☎ 702/832–1177) has 22 mi of groomed track with skating lanes. The trail system goes from 7,400 ft to 9,100 ft with endless wilderness to explore. ⊠ *1210 Ski Way, off Hwy. 28 to Country Club Dr., Incline Village, NV 89450,* ☎ *702/832– 1177 or 800/468–2463. 29 trails on 655 acres, rated 18% beginner, 46% intermediate, 36% advanced. Longest run 2½ mi, base 6,700', summit 8,540'. Lifts: 6, including 2 high-speed quads.*

GOLF

Incline Championship (⊠ 955 Fairway Blvd., ☎ 702/832–1144) is an 18-hole, par-72 course with a driving range. The greens fee of $90 to $115 includes an optional power cart. **Incline Mountain** (⊠ 690 Wilson Way, ☎ 702/832–1150) is an easy 18-holer; par is 58. The greens fee—from $40 to $50—includes an optional power cart.

OFF THE
BEATEN PATH **CARSON CITY AND VIRGINIA CITY** – Nevada's capital, Carson City, is a 30-minute drive from Stateline. At Spooner Junction, where Highway 28 meets U.S. 50, head east on U.S. 50, away from the lake. In 10 mi you reach U.S. 395, where you turn left and go 1 mi north to Carson City. Most of its historic buildings and other attractions are along U.S. 395, the main street through town. At the south end of town is the **Carson City Chamber of Commerce** (⊠ 1900 S. Carson St., ☎ 702/882–1565), which has visitor information. About a 30-minute drive northeast of Carson City, on Highway 342 off U.S. 50 East, is the fabled mining town of Virginia City, which has sights and activities of historical interest amid touristy diversions.

Sand Harbor Beach

★ ⑮ *4 mi south of Incline Village on Hwy. 28; 22 mi north of South Lake Tahoe on U.S. 50 to Hwy. 28.*

Sand Harbor Beach, within the Lake Tahoe–Nevada State Park, has a popular beach that is sometimes filled to capacity by 11 AM on summer weekends. A **pop-music festival** (☎ 702/832–1606 or 800/468–2463) is held here in July and a Shakespeare festival every August.

U.S. 50 from Spooner Junction to Zephyr Cove

13 mi south of Sand Harbor Beach (to Cave Rock), Hwy. 28 to U.S. 50.

★ ⑯ **Cave Rock,** 25 yards of solid stone at the southern end of Lake Tahoe–Nevada State Park, is the throat of an extinct volcano. This is the stuff of local lore: For the Washoe Indians this area is a sacred burial site. Tahoe Tessie, the lake's version of the Loch Ness monster, is reputed to live in a cavern below the impressive outcropping. Cave Rock towers over a parking lot, a lakefront picnic ground, and a boat launch; the rest area provides the best vantage point of this cliff. ⊠ *U.S. 50, 3 mi south of Glenbrook.*

⑰ The largest settlement between Incline Village and Stateline is **Zephyr Cove,** which is still only a tiny resort. It has a beach, a marina, a campground, a picnic area, a coffee shop in a historic log lodge, rustic cabins for rent, and nearby riding stables. The 550-passenger **MS Dixie II** (☎ 702/588–3508), a sternwheeler, sails year-round from Zephyr Cove Marina to Emerald Bay on lunch and dinner cruises. Fares range from $14 to $38. The **Woodwind** (☎ 702/588–3000), a glass-bottom trimaran, sails on regular and champagne cruises from April to October from Zephyr Cove Resort. Fares range from $18 to $28.

OFF THE
BEATEN PATH **KINGSBURY GRADE** – This road, also known as Route 207, is one of three roads that access Tahoe from the east. Originally a toll road used by wagon trains to get over the crest of the Sierra, it has sweeping views of the Carson Valley. Off Route 206, which intersects Route 207, is Genoa, the oldest settlement in Nevada. Along Main Street are small but interesting museums and the state's longest-standing saloon.

Stateline

⑱ *5 mi south of Zephyr Cove on U.S. 50.*

Stateline is a great border town in the Nevada tradition. Its four high-rise casinos are as vertical and contained as the commercial district of South Lake Tahoe on the California side is horizontal and sprawling. And Stateline is as relentlessly indoors-oriented as the rest of the lake

is focused on the outdoors. This strip is where you'll find the most concentrated action at Lake Tahoe: restaurants (including the typically
Nevadan buffets), showrooms with famous headliners and razzle-
dazzle revues, luxury rooms and suites, and 24-hour casino gambling.

Dining and Lodging

$$–$$$ ✕ **Chart House.** It's worth the drive up the steep grade to see the view
from here—try to arrive for sunset. The American menu of steak and
seafood is complemented by an abundant salad bar. The restaurant has
a children's menu. ✉ *329 Kingsbury Grade,* ☎ *702/588–6276. AE,
D, DC, MC, V. No lunch.*

$$–$$$ ✕ **Llewellyn's Restaurant.** Elegantly decorated in blond wood and
★ pastels, the restaurant atop Harvey's casino merits special mention. Almost every table has superb views of Lake Tahoe. Dinner entrées—
seafood, meat, and poultry—are served with unusual accompaniments,
such as sturgeon in potato crust with saffron sauce or veal with polenta, herbs, and pancetta. Lunches are reasonably priced, with gourmet
selections as well as hamburgers. ✉ *Harvey's Resort, U.S. 50,* ☎ *702/
588–2411 or 800/553–1022. AE, D, DC, MC, V.*

$$$–$$$$ ✕🏨 **Harrah's Tahoe Hotel/Casino.** Luxurious guest rooms here have
private bars and two full bathrooms, each with a television and tele-
phone. All rooms have views of the lake and the mountains, but the
least-obstructed vistas are from the higher floors. Top-name enter-
tainment is presented in the South Shore Room. Among the restaurants,
the romantic 16th-floor Summit is a standout. The menu changes
nightly and includes creatively presented salads; lamb, venison, or
seafood entrées with delicate sauces; and sensuous desserts. Other
restaurants serve Italian, deli, and traditional meat-and-potatoes cui-
sine. There's also a 24-hour café, a buffet with a view, and a candy
store. ✉ *U.S. 50, Box 8, 89449,* ☎ *702/588–6611 or 800/648–3773,*
FAX *702/788–3274. 472 rooms, 62 suites. 5 restaurants, café, room ser-
vice, indoor pool, barbershop, beauty salon, hot tubs, health club, casino,
video games, laundry service, kennel. AE, D, DC, MC, V.*

$$$–$$$$ ✕🏨 **Harvey's Resort Hotel/Casino.** Owner Harvey Gross played an im-
★ portant role in persuading the state to keep U.S. 50 open year-round,
making Tahoe accessible in winter. His namesake hotel, which started
as a cabin in 1944, is now the largest resort in Tahoe. Any description
of the place runs to superlatives, from the 40-ft-tall crystal chandelier
in the lobby to the 88,000-square-ft casino. Rooms have custom fur-
nishings, oversize marble baths, and minibars. Use of the health club,
spa, and pool is free to guests, a rarity for this area. ✉ *U.S. 50, Box
128, 89449,* ☎ *702/588–2411 or 800/648–3361,* FAX *702/782–4889.
705 rooms, 36 suites. 8 restaurants, pool, barbershop, beauty salon,
hot tub, spa, health club, casino, chapel. AE, D, DC, MC, V.*

$$–$$$$ 🏨 **Caesars Tahoe.** Most of the rooms and suites at this 16-story hotel-
casino have oversize Roman tubs, king-size beds, two telephones, and
a view of Lake Tahoe or the encircling mountains. The opulent casino
encompasses 40,000 square ft. Top-name entertainers perform in the
1,600-seat Circus Maximus. The local Planet Hollywood is here, plus
Chinese, Italian, and American restaurants, a 24-hour coffee shop, and
a frozen-yogurt emporium. ✉ *55 U.S. 50, Box 5800, 89449,* ☎ *702/
588–3515; 800/648–3353 reservations and show information,* FAX
*702/586–2068. 328 rooms, 112 suites. 5 restaurants, coffee shop, in-
door pool, hot tub, saunas, spa, 4 tennis courts, health club. AE, D,
DC, MC, V.*

$–$$$$ 🏨 **Horizon Casino Resort.** Many of the guest rooms at this hotel-casino
have lake views. The casino has a beaux arts decor, brightened by pale
molded wood and mirrors. The Grande Lake Theatre, Golden Cabaret,
and Aspen Lounge present shows, as well as up-and-coming and name

entertainers. Le Grande Buffet has a nightly prime-rib special. ✉ *U.S.*
50, Box C, 89449, ☎ *702/588–6211 or 800/322–7723,* FAX *702/588–*
1344. 516 rooms, 23 suites. 3 restaurants, pool, 3 hot tubs, exercise
room, casino, meeting rooms. AE, D, DC, MC, V.

$–$$ ⌘ **Lakeside Inn and Casino.** The smallest of the Stateline casinos, the
Lakeside has a rustic look. Guest rooms are in lodges, away from the
casino area. ✉ *U.S. 50 at Kingsbury Grade, Box 5640, 89449,* ☎ *702/*
588–7777 or 800/624–7980, FAX *702/588–4092. 115 rooms, 8 suites.*
Restaurant, pool, casino. AE, D, DC, MC, V.

Nightlife

The top entertainment venues are the Circus Maximus at Caesars
Tahoe, the Emerald Theater at Harvey's, the South Shore Room at Harrah's, and Horizon's Grand Lake Theatre. Each theater is as large as
a Broadway house. Typical headliners include Jay Leno, David Copper-
field, and Johnny Mathis. For Las Vegas–style production shows—fast-
paced dancing, singing, and novelty acts—try Harrah's or the Horizon.
The big showrooms occasionally present performances of musicals by
touring Broadway companies or casts assembled for the casino. Reservations are almost always required for superstar shows. Depending on
the act, cocktail shows usually cost from $12 to $40. Smaller casino
cabarets sometimes have a cover charge or drink minimum.

Bars around the lake present pop- and country-western singers and musicians, and in winter the ski resorts do the same. Summer alternatives
are outdoor music events, from chamber quartets to rock performers,
at Sand Harbor and the Lake Tahoe Visitors Center amphitheater.

Outdoor Activities and Sports

GOLF

Edgewood Tahoe (✉ U.S. 50 and Lake Pkwy., behind Horizon Casino,
Stateline, ☎ 702/588–3566) is an 18-hole, par-72 course with a driving range, and the only golf course with holes on the lakeshore. The
$150 greens fee includes a cart (though you can walk if you wish); the
course is open from 7 AM to 3 PM between May and October. The 18-
hole, par-70 **Lake Tahoe Golf Course** (✉ U.S. 50, between Lake Tahoe
Airport and Meyers, ☎ 530/577–0788) has a driving range. The
greens fee is $45; a cart (mandatory from Friday to Sunday) costs $18.

SCUBA DIVING

Sun Sports (✉ 1018 Herbert Ave., No. 4, South Lake Tahoe, ☎ 530/
541–6000) is a full-service PADI dive center with rentals and instruction.

LAKE TAHOE A TO Z

Arriving and Departing

By Bus

Greyhound Lines (☎ 800/231–2222) stops in Sacramento, Truckee,
and Reno, Nevada.

By Car

Lake Tahoe is 198 mi northeast of San Francisco, a drive of under four
hours when traffic and the weather cooperate. Try to avoid the heavy
traffic leaving the San Francisco area for Tahoe on Friday afternoon
and returning on Sunday afternoon. The major route is I–80, which
cuts through the Sierra Nevada about 14 mi north of the lake; from
there Highway 89 and Highway 267 reach the north shore. U.S. 50 is
the more direct highway to the south shore, taking about 2½ hours from
Sacramento. From Reno you can get to the north shore by heading west
on Highway 431 off U.S. 395, 8 mi south of town (a total of 35 mi).

For the south shore, continue south on U.S. 395 through Carson City, and then head west on U.S. 50 (55 mi total).

By Plane

Reno–Tahoe International Airport (⊠ U.S. 395, Exit 65B, Reno, NV, ☎ 702/328–6400), 35 mi northeast of the closest point on the lake, is served by airlines that include Alaska, American, America West, Continental, Delta, Northwest, Reno Air, Skywest, Southwest, and United. *See* Air Travel *in* the Gold Guide for airline phone numbers. **Tahoe Casino Express** (☎ 702/785–2424 or 800/446–6128) has daily scheduled transportation from Reno to South Lake Tahoe from 6:15 AM to 12:30 AM, $17 one-way and $30 round-trip.

Lake Tahoe Airport (☎ 530/542–6180) on U.S. 50 is 3 mi south of the lake's shore. No commercial carriers operate scheduled service to this airport; for charters or sightseeing, contact **Alpine Lake Aviation** (☎ 530/588–9748).

Getting Around

By Bus

South Tahoe Area Ground Express (STAGE, ☎ 530/573–2080) runs 24 hours along U.S. 50 and through the neighborhoods of South Lake Tahoe. **Tahoe Area Regional Transit** (TART, ☎ 530/581–6365 or 800/ 736–6365) operates buses along Lake Tahoe's northern and western shores between Tahoma (from Meeks Bay in summer) and Incline Village daily from 6:30 AM to 6:30 PM. Free shuttle buses run among the casinos, major ski resorts, and motels of South Lake Tahoe.

By Car

The scenic 72-mi highway around the lake is marked Highway 89 on the southwest and west, Highway 28 on the north and northeast shores, and U.S. 50 on the east and southeast. Sections of Highway 89 sometimes close during winter, making it impossible to complete the circular drive. Interstate 80, U.S. 50, and U.S. 395 are all-weather highways, but there may be delays as snow is cleared during major storms. Carry tire chains from October to May (car-rental agencies provide them with their vehicles). *See* Road Conditions, *below,* for hotline phone numbers.

By Taxi

Yellow Cab (☎ 530/588–1234) serves all of Tahoe Basin. **Sierra Taxi** (☎ 530/577–8888) serves Tahoe's south shore. On the north shore try **Tahoe-Truckee Taxi** (☎ 530/582–8294).

Contacts and Resources

Emergencies

Ambulance (☎ 911). **Fire** (☎ 911). **California Highway Patrol** (☎ 530/587–3510). **Nevada Highway Patrol** (☎ 702/687–5300). **Police** (☎ 911).

Guided Tours

BY BOAT

Hornblower's Tahoe Queen (☞ South Lake Tahoe *in* California Side, *above*), the **Sierra Cloud** (☞ Incline Village *in* Nevada Side, *above*), and **MS Dixie II and Woodwind** (☞ U.S. 50 from Spooner Junction to Zephyr Cove *in* Nevada Side, *above*) all operate guided boat tours.

BY BUS OR CAR

Gray Line (☎ 702/331–1147 or 800/822–6009) runs daily tours to South Lake Tahoe, Carson City, and Virginia City. **Tahoe Lake Lapper,** (☎ 530/542–5900) provides daily around-the-lake transportation in both directions: the Green Bus travels clockwise and the Blue Bus travels counter-clockwise. Buses leave South Lake Tahoe at 7, 10 and 11 AM and 1, 2, 4, and 5 PM; a late Blue Bus leaves at 8 PM on Friday and Saturday. The fare is $5.

Lake Tahoe Adventures (⌧ 2286 Utah Ave., South Lake Tahoe 96150, ☎ 530/541–5875) operates a trek skirting the Desolation Wilderness in four-wheel-drive all-terrain vehicles.

BY HOT-AIR BALLOON
Lake Tahoe Balloons (☎ 530/544–1221) conducts excursions year-round over the lake or over the Carson Valley for $99 a person for half-hour flights and $165 for hour-long flights (champagne brunch included).

BY PLANE
CalVada Seaplanes Inc. (☎ 530/546–3984) provides rides over the lake for $50 to $85 per person, depending on the length of the trip. **High Country Soaring** (☎ 702/782–4944) glider rides over the lake and valley depart from the Douglas County Airport, Gardnerville.

Reservations Agencies
Park.net (☎ 800/444–7275 for campgrounds in California state parks). **Lake Tahoe Visitors Authority** (☎ 800/288–2463 for south-shore lodging). **North Lake Tahoe Resort Association** (☎ 800/824–6348 for north-shore lodging).

Road Conditions
California roads in Tahoe area (☎ 530/445–7623). **California roads approaching Tahoe** (☎ 800/427–7623). **Nevada roads** (☎ 702/793–1313).

Visitor Information
California State Department of Parks and Recreation (☎ 916/324–4442). **Lake Tahoe Hotline** (☎ 530/542–4636 for south-shore events; 530/546–5253 for north-shore events; 702/831–6677 for Nevada events). **Lake Tahoe Visitors Authority** (⌧ 1156 Ski Run Blvd., South Lake Tahoe, CA 96150, ☎ 530/544–5050 or 800/288–2463). **North Lake Tahoe Resort Association** (⌧ Box 5578, Tahoe City, CA 96145, ☎ 530/583–3494 or 800/824–6348, FAX 530/581–4081). **Ski Report Hotline** (☎ 415/864–6440). **U.S. Forest Service** backcountry recording (☎ 530/587–2158).

8 The Sierra National Parks

With Mono Lake and Mammoth Lakes

The highlight for many California travelers is a visit to one of the national parks in the Sierra Nevada range. Yosemite is the state's most famous park and every bit as sublime as one expects. Its Yosemite-type or U-shape valleys were formed by the action of glaciers during the Ice Age. Other examples are found about 150 miles southeast in Kings Canyon and Sequoia national parks, which are adjacent to each other and usually visited together. All the Sierra National Parks contain tall groves of Sequoiadendron giganteum trees.

Y OSEMITE, KINGS CANYON, AND SEQUOIA national parks are famous throughout the world for their unique sights. Yosemite, especially, should be on your "don't miss" list. Unfortunately, it's on everyone else's as well (the park receives about 4 million visitors annually), so lodging reservations are essential. During a week's stay you can exit and reenter the parks as frequently as you wish by showing your pass.

Updated by
Michelle Kaye

Pleasures and Pastimes

Camping

One highlight of a camping trip to the Sierra national parks is opening your eyes in the morning to nearby meadows and streams and then suddenly seeing the unforgettable landscape of giant granite in the distance, as if for the first time. Another is looking up at an awe-inspiring number of constellations and spying a shooting star in the night sky. For reservations and other information *see* Contacts and Resources *in* Yosemite National Park A to Z *and* Kings Canyon and Sequoia National Parks A to Z, *below*).

Dining

Snack bars, coffee shops, and cafeterias in the parks are not expensive, but you may not want to waste precious time hunting for food, especially during the day; instead, stop at a grocery store and fill your ice chest with the makings of a picnic to enjoy under giant trees.

The three fanciest accommodations within Yosemite National Park are also the prime dining spots. Especially in the off-season it's easy to zip out of the park to dine at the restaurants in the border towns (☞ Outside Yosemite National Park, *below*). With few exceptions (all noted), dress is casual at the restaurants listed below.

CATEGORY	COST*
$$$$	over $50
$$$	$30–$50
$$	$20–$30
$	under $20

per person for a three-course meal, excluding drinks, service, and 10% tax

Hiking

Hiking is the primary outdoor sport in the Sierra national parks. Whether you walk the paved loops that pass by the major attractions or head well off the beaten path into the backcountry, a hike through groves, meadows, or alongside the numerous streams and waterfalls will allow you to see, smell, and feel nature up close. Many of the popular trails are described briefly in this chapter; stop by the visitor centers for maps and advice from park rangers.

Lodging

Most accommodations inside Yosemite, Kings Canyon, and Sequoia national parks can best be described as "no frills." Some have no electricity or indoor plumbing. Other than the Ahwahnee and Wawona hotels in Yosemite, lodgings tend to be basic motels or rustic cabins. Except during the off-peak season, from November to March, rates in Yosemite are pricey given the general quality of the lodging. Reserve well ahead, especially during summer. *See* Contacts and Resources *in* Yosemite National Park A to Z , *below,* for the phone of the park's reservations service.

Reservations are recommended for visits to Kings Canyon and Sequoia at any time of the year because it's a long way back to civilization if the lodgings there are full. All the park's lodges and cabins are open during the summer months, but in winter only some in Grant Grove remain open. Lodging rates are consistent throughout the year. The town of Three Rivers, on Highway 198 southwest of Sequoia, has some lodgings. Separate concessionaires operate the lodgings in Kings Canyon and Sequoia. *See* Contacts and Resources *in* Kings Canyon and Sequoia National Parks A to Z, *below,* for their phone numbers.

CATEGORY	COST*
$$$$	over $175
$$$	$120–$175
$$	$80–$120
$	under $80

All prices are for a standard double room, excluding 10% tax

Nature Lore

In Yosemite from early May to late September and during some holiday periods, actor Lee Stetson portrays naturalist John Muir, bringing to life Muir's wit, wisdom, and story-telling skill. Stetson's programs—"Conversation with a Tramp" and "The Spirit of John Muir"—are two well-loved shows. Locations and times are listed in the *Yosemite Guide,* the newspaper handed to visitors upon entering the park.

Exploring the Sierra National Parks

For the full Sierra experience, stay in the parks themselves instead of the "gateway cities" in the foothills or the Central Valley. Save your time and energy for exploring, not driving to and from the parks. Yosemite Valley is the primary destination for many visitors. Because the valley is only 7 mi long and averages less than 1 mi in width, you can visit its attractions in whatever order you choose and return to your favorites at different times of the day. Famous for their hiking trails and giant sequoias, Kings Canyon and Sequoia provide a true wilderness experience, less interrupted by civilization and crowds.

Separate A to Z information listings follow the Yosemite National Park, Outside Yosemite National Park, Mammoth Lakes, and Kings Canyon and Sequoia National Parks sections below.

Numbers in the text correspond to numbers in the margin and on the Yosemite and Kings Canyon and Sequoia national parks maps.

Great Itineraries

IF YOU HAVE 3 DAYS

If your time is limited, choose Yosemite National Park to explore. Enter the park via the Big Oak Flat Entrance, and head east on Big Oak Flat Road. As you enter the valley, traffic is diverted onto a one-way road. Continue east, following the signs to the **Valley Visitor Center** ①. Loop back west for a short hike near **Yosemite Falls** ②, the highest waterfall in North America. Continue west for a valley view of famous **El Capitan** ⑦ peak. This area is a good place for a picnic. Backtrack onto Southside Drive, stopping at misty **Bridalveil Fall** ③, then follow Highway 41/Wawona Road south 14 mi to the Chinquapin junction and make a left turn onto Glacier Point Road. From **Glacier Point** ⑨ you'll get a phenomenal bird's-eye view of the entire valley, including **Half Dome** ⑧, **Vernal Fall** ⑤, and **Nevada Fall** ⑥. If you want to avoid the busloads of tourists at Glacier Point, stop at **Sentinel Dome** ⑩ instead—after a mildly strenuous 1-mi hike you get a view similar to the one from the Glacier Point except for the peek into the valley. Continue south on Highway 41 to the Wawona Hotel, where you can have a relaxing drink on the veranda or in the cozy lobby bar.

On day two, visit the **Mariposa Grove of Big Trees** ⑫ and return to Wawona to tour the **Pioneer Yosemite History Center** ⑪. Head back to Yosemite Valley on Wawona Road for an early evening beverage at the Ahwahnee Hotel's bar (enjoy the patio view in good weather), and explore the hotel's lobby and other public areas. On the third day have breakfast near the Valley Visitor Center before hiking to **Vernal Fall** ⑤ or **Nevada Fall** ⑥.

IF YOU HAVE 5 DAYS

Spend your first day exploring the ⊡ **Yosemite Valley area** ①–⑩. On the second day, pack some food and drive to **Hetch Hetchy Reservoir** via Big Oak Flat Road and Highway 120. Then continue east on Tioga Road to **Tuolumne Meadows,** the largest subalpine meadow in the Sierra. Time permitting, head east to **Mono Lake** and **Bodie Ghost Town** ⑬. (Tioga Road closes for several months after the first snow; if the road isn't open, on day two you can instead take a hike to **Vernal Fall** ⑤ or **Nevada Fall** ⑥ in the morning and head south in the afternoon to Wawona's **Pioneer Yosemite History Center** ⑪.) Wake up early on day three and spend the morning wandering beneath the giant sequoias at Wawona's **Mariposa Grove of Big Trees** ⑫. Then head south to ⊡ **Kings Canyon National Park** (about a three- to four-hour drive), entering on Highway 180 at the Big Stump Entrance. Stop at **Grant Grove** ⑮. If you're camping, you'll need to get situated before sunset; if you're staying at one of the park's lodges, check in and then have dinner. On the fifth day, pass briefly through **Lodgepole** ⑳ in **Sequoia National Park** and pick up tickets to **Crystal Cave** ㉔. Visit the **Giant Forest** ㉒ before stopping at the cave.

When to Tour the Sierra National Parks

Summer is the most crowded season for all the parks, though things never get as hectic at Kings Canyon and Sequoia as they do at Yosemite. During extremely busy periods—when snow closes high-country roads in late spring or on crowded summer weekends—Yosemite Valley may be closed to all vehicles unless their drivers have overnight reservations. Avoid these restrictions by visiting from mid-April to Memorial Day and from Labor Day to mid-October, when the parks are less busy and the weather is usually hospitable.

The falls at Yosemite are at their most spectacular in May and June. By the end of summer, some will have dried up. They begin flowing again in late fall with the first storms, and during winter they may be hung with ice, a dramatic sight. Snow on the floor of Yosemite Valley is never deep, so you can camp there even in the winter (January highs are in the mid-40s, lows in the mid-20s). Tioga Road is usually closed from late October to May; you can't see Tuolumne Meadows then. The road to Glacier Point beyond the turnoff for Badger Pass is not cleared in winter, but it is groomed for cross-country skiing. In parts of Kings Canyon and Sequoia snow may remain on the ground into June; the flowers in the Giant Forest meadows hit their peak in July.

YOSEMITE NATIONAL PARK

Yosemite Valley, Wawona, the High Country

Yosemite, with 1,169 square mi of parkland, is 94½% undeveloped wilderness, most of it accessible only to backpackers and horseback riders. The western boundary dips as low as 2,000 ft in the chaparral-covered foothills; the eastern boundary rises to 13,000 ft at points along the Sierra crest.

Yosemite is so large that it functions as five parks. **Yosemite Valley** and **Wawona** are open all year. **Hetch Hetchy** closes after the first main snow and reopens in May or June. The high country, **Tuolumne Meadows,** is open for summer hiking. **Badger Pass Ski Area** is open in winter only. The fee to visit Yosemite National Park (good for seven days) is $20 per car, $10 per person if you don't arrive in a car.

Yosemite Valley Area

214 mi southeast of San Francisco, I–80 to I–580 to I–205 to Hwy. 120; 330 mi northeast of Los Angeles, I–5 to Hwy. 99 to Hwy. 41.

Such extravagant praise has been written of Yosemite Valley (John Muir described it as "a revelation in landscape affairs that enriches one's life forever") and so many beautiful photographs have been taken (by Ansel Adams and others) that you may wonder if the reality can possibly measure up. For almost everyone it does; Yosemite is a reminder of what "breathtaking" and "marvelous" really mean. The Miwok people, the last of several Native American tribes who inhabited the Yosemite area, called the valley "Ahwahnee," which is said to mean "the place of the gaping mouth." Members of the tribe, who were forced out of the area by gold miners in 1851, called themselves the Ahwahneechee.

❶ You can get your bearings, pick up maps, and obtain information from park rangers at the **Valley Visitor Center,** which has exhibits on the natural and human history of Yosemite Valley. The adjacent **Indian Cultural Museum** has displays about the Miwok and Pauite people who lived in the Yosemite region, and there's a re-created **Ahwahneechee village** nearby. The center is part of **Yosemite Village,** which contains restaurants, stores, a post office, a gas station, the Ahwahnee Hotel, Yosemite Lodge, a medical clinic, and other facilities. **A Changing Yosemite,** a 1-mi paved loop from the visitor center, traces the park's natural evolution. ✉ *Off Northside Dr.,* ☎ *209/372–0200.* ☼ *Daily 9–5; extended hrs in summer.*

The staff at the **Wilderness Center** provides trail-use reservations (recommended between May and September), permits ($3), maps, and advice to hikers heading into the backcountry. When the Wilderness Center is closed, you can make inquiries at the nearby Valley Visitor Center. *See* Hiking *in* Outdoor Activities and Sports, *below,* for more information about backcountry permits. ✉ *Yosemite Village between post office and Ansel Adams gallery (mailing address: Box 545, Yosemite 95389),* ☎ *209/372–0745 for information; 209/372–0740 for permit reservations.* ☼ *Apr.–Oct., daily 8–5.*

★ ❷   **Yosemite Falls** is the highest waterfall in North America and the fifth-highest in the world. The upper falls (1,430 ft), the middle cascades (675 ft), and the lower falls (320 ft) combine for a total of 2,425 ft and, when viewed from the valley, appear as a single waterfall. A ¼-mi trail leads from the parking lot to the base of the falls. The Yosemite Falls Trail is a strenuous 3½-mi climb rising 2,700 ft, taking you above the top of the falls. It starts at Sunnyside Campground.

★ ❸   **Bridalveil Fall,** a filmy fall of 620 ft that is often diverted as much as 20 ft one way or the other by the breeze, is the first view of Yosemite Valley for those who arrive via the Wawona Road. Native Americans called the fall Pohono ("spirit of the puffing wind"). A ¼-mi trail leads from the parking lot off Wawona Road to the base of the falls.

❹   At 1,612 ft, **Ribbon Fall** is the highest single fall in the valley but also the first one to dry up in the summer because the rainwater and melted snow that create the fall evaporate quickly at this height.

⑤ Fern-covered black rocks frame **Vernal Fall** (317 ft), and rainbows play in the spray at its base. The hike on a paved trail from the Happy Isles nature area to the bridge at the base of Vernal Fall is only moderately strenuous and less than 1 mi long. It's another steep ¾ mi along Yosemite's Mist Trail, which is open only in late spring, summer, and early fall, up to the top of Vernal Fall.

⑥ **Nevada Fall** (594 ft) is the first major fall as the Merced River comes out of the high country. A not-strenuous 2-mi section of the Mist Trail leads from Vernal Fall to the top of Nevada Fall.

Vernal and Nevada falls are on the Merced River at the east end of Yosemite Valley. The roads here are closed to private cars, but a free shuttle bus runs frequently from the village. Both falls can also be viewed from Glacier Point (☞ *below*). From about May to October the Happy Isles nature area, which contains ecology exhibits, is open daily between 9 and 5.

★ **⑦** **El Capitan,** rising 3,593 ft above the valley, is the largest exposed granite monolith in the world, almost twice the height of the Rock of Gibraltar.

★ **⑧** Astounding **Half Dome** rises 4,733 ft from the valley floor to a height 8,842 ft above sea level. The west side of the dome is fractured vertically and cut away to form a 2,000-ft cliff. The 16¾-mi, strenuous **John Muir Trail** leads from Yosemite Valley to the top of Half Dome.

★ **⑨** **Glacier Point** yields what may be the most spectacular view of the valley and the High Sierra—especially at sunset—that you can get without hiking. The Glacier Point Road leaves Wawona Road (Highway 41) about 23 mi southwest of the valley; then it's a 16-mi drive, with fine views into higher country. From the parking area walk a few hundred yards and you'll be able to see Nevada, Vernal, and Yosemite falls as well as Half Dome and other peaks. This road is closed beyond the turnoff for the Badger Pass Ski Area in winter.

⑩ The view from **Sentinel Dome** is almost the same as the one from Glacier Point, minus the peek into the floor of Yosemite Valley. A 1.1-mi path begins at a parking lot on Glacier Point Road a few miles below Glacier Point. The trail is long and strenuous enough to keep the crowds and tour buses away, but it's by no means rugged (though the last few hundred feet up the rock itself are a bit steep).

OFF THE **HETCH HETCHY RESERVOIR AND TUOLUMNE MEADOWS –** The Hetch
BEATEN PATH Hetchy Reservoir, which supplies water and hydroelectric power to San Francisco, is about 40 mi from Yosemite Valley via Big Oak Flat Road to Highway 120 to Evergreen Road to Hetch Hetchy Road. Some say John Muir died of heartbreak when this valley was dammed and buried beneath 300 ft of water in 1913. Tioga Road (Highway 120) stays open until the first big snow of the year, usually about mid-October. The road is the scenic route to Tuolumne Meadows, altitude 8,575 ft, which is 55 mi from Yosemite Valley. The largest subalpine meadow in the Sierra and the trailhead for many backpack trips into the High Sierra, the area contains campgrounds, a gas station, a store (with limited and expensive provisions), stables, a lodge, and a visitor center that is open from late June until Labor Day from 8 AM to 7:30 PM.

Dining, Lodging, and Camping

$$–$$$ ✕ **Mountain Room Restaurant.** The food becomes secondary when you see Yosemite Falls through this dining room's window-wall—almost every patron has a view of the falls. Gulf shrimp, sautéed blackened

Yosemite National Park

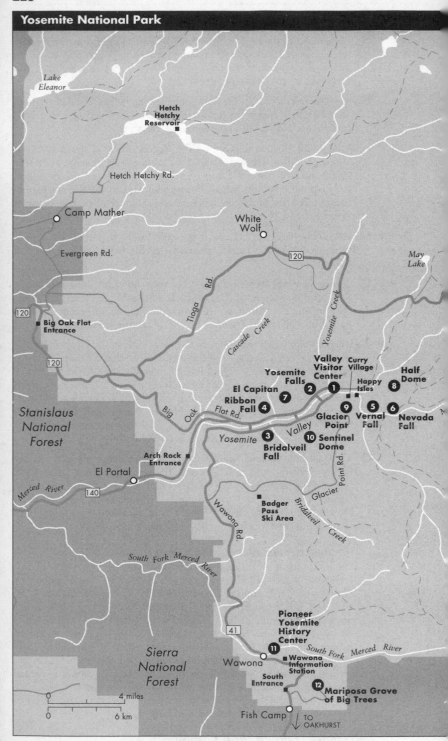

Lake Eleanor

Hetch Hetchy Reservoir

Hetch Hetchy Rd.

Camp Mather

White Wolf

120

May Lake

Evergreen Rd.

120

Big Oak Flat Entrance

120

Tioga Rd.

Cascade Creek

Yosemite Creek

Valley Visitor Center

Curry Village

Half Dome

Yosemite Falls

Happy Isles

El Capitan

Ribbon Fall

Stanislaus National Forest

Big Oak Flat Rd.

Yosemite

Valley

Glacier Point

Vernal Fall

Nevada Fall

Sentinel Dome

Bridalveil Fall

Arch Rock Entrance

El Portal

140

Merced River

Glacier Point Rd.

Badger Pass Ski Area

Glacier

Bridalveil Creek

Wawona Rd.

South Fork Merced River

Pioneer Yosemite History Center

South Fork Merced River

41

Wawona

Wawona Information Station

Sierra National Forest

South Entrance

Mariposa Grove of Big Trees

Fish Camp

TO OAKHURST

0   4 miles

0   6 km

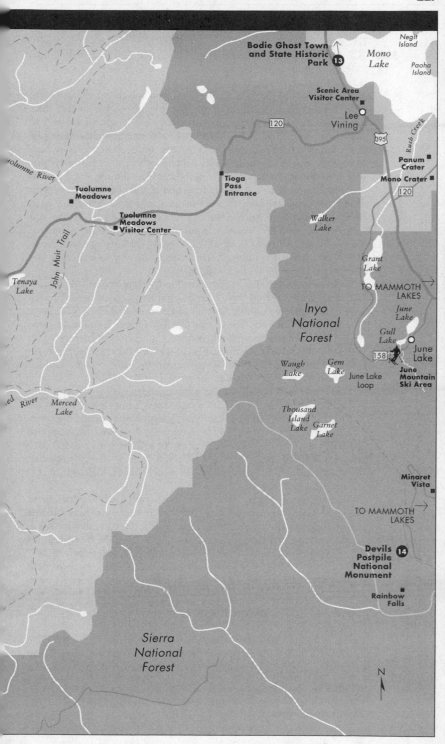

catfish with Cajun seasonings, and several children's dishes are on the menu. ⊠ *Yosemite Lodge, off Northside Dr.,* ☎ *209/372–1281. D, DC, MC, V. No lunch.*

$$$$ ✕🖻 **Ahwahnee Hotel & Restaurant.** This grand 1920s-style mountain
★ lodge is constructed of rocks and sugar-pine logs, with exposed timbers. The decorative style of the Great Lounge and Solarium is a tribute to the Miwok and Paiute Indians who inhabited the area; the motifs continue in the room decor. The Ahwahnee Restaurant ($$– $$$), with its 34-ft-tall trestle-beam ceiling, full-length windows, and twinkling chandeliers, is the most impressive and romantic eating establishment in the park. The classic American specialties include New York steak, broiled swordfish fillet, and prime rib, all competently prepared. Reservations lotteries are conducted for dinner on Christmas and New Years Eve; call for information about the lottery one year ahead. Also busy are January and February, when the Ahwahnee hosts its Chef's Holiday, which attracts leading cooks from all over the United States, who give lessons and put together banquets. ⊠ *Ahwahnee Rd. north of Northside Dr.,* ☎ *559/252–4848 for lodging reservations, 209/372–1489 for restaurant. 103 rooms, 24 cottages. Restaurant, lounge, pool, tennis. D, DC, MC, V.*

$–$$ ✕🖻 **Yosemite Lodge.** The rooms in this lodge near Yosemite Falls vary from ones with a shared bathroom down the hall to functional motel-style units with two double beds and bathroom included. None have TVs or air-conditioning. The nearby Garden Terrace Restaurant, open during the summer for dinner, prepares an all-you-can-eat, serve-yourself buffet of salads, soups, pastas, and hot meats. ⊠ *Off Northside Dr.,* ☎ *559/252–4848 for lodging reservations. 245 rooms. 2 restaurants, cafeteria, bar, outdoor pool. D, DC, MC, V.*

$–$$ 🖻 **Curry Village.** These are plain accommodations: cabins with bath and without, and tent cabins with rough wood frames and canvas walls and roofs. It's a step up from camping (linens, blankets, and maid service are provided), but food and cooking are not allowed. Showers and toilets are centrally located, as they would be in a campground. ⊠ *South side of Southside Dr.,* ☎ *209/372–8333; 559/252–4848 for reservations. 180 cabins, 427 tent cabins, 18 motel rooms. Cafeteria, pizzeria, pool. D, DC, MC, V.*

🛆 **Housekeeping Camp.** These rustic three-walled cabins with canvas roofs, set along the Merced River, may be rented up to seven nights but are difficult to get; reserving at least 366 days in advance is advised. You can cook here on gas stoves rented from the front desk. ⊠ *North side of Southside Dr. between Curry Village and chapel,* ☎ *209/ 372–8338; 559/252–4848 for reservations. 266 units, with no bath (maximum 4 per cabin). Toilet and shower in central shower house. D, DC, MC, V.*

Outdoor Activities and Sports

BICYCLING

Yosemite Lodge and Curry Village have bicycle rentals (☎ 209/372–1208) for $5.25 per hour or $20 per day, from April to October. You can also rent baby-jogger strollers and bikes with child trailers.

CAMPING

For information about campground reservations, *see* Yosemite National Park A to Z, *below.*

HIKING

The park's visitor centers have trail maps and information. Rangers will recommend easy trails to get you acclimated to the altitude. Overnight backpackers need wilderness permits, which can be obtained during the off-season at permit stations within the park. Reservations ($3 per person), which can be made through the **Wilderness Center** (⊠ Box 545, Yosemite, 95389, ☎ 209/372−0740), are strongly advised during summer.

ROCK CLIMBING
Yosemite Mountaineering (☎ 209/372−8344) conducts rock-climbing and backpacking classes.

WINTER SPORTS
Badger Pass Ski Area, off Yosemite National Park's Glacier Point Road, has nine downhill runs serviced by one triple and three double chairlifts, and two excellent ski schools. Its gentle slopes make **Yosemite Ski School** (☎ 209/372−8430) an ideal downhill beginners' area. Yosemite's **cross-country skiing center** has a groomed and tracked 21-mi loop from Badger Pass to Glacier Point. The **outdoor ice-skating rink** at Curry Village in Yosemite Valley is open from Thanksgiving Day to April.

Wawona

25 mi south of Yosemite Valley on Hwy. 41; 16 mi north of Fish Camp on Hwy. 41.

⑪ The historic buildings in **Pioneer Yosemite History Center** were moved to Wawona from their original sites in the park. From Wednesday to Sunday in summer, costumed park employees re-create life in 19th-century Yosemite in a blacksmith's shop, a Wells Fargo office, a jail, and other structures. Ranger-led walks leave from the covered bridge on Saturday at 10 AM in summer. Near the center are a post office, the Wawona General Store, and a gas station. ⊠ *On Hwy. 41.* ⊙ *Historic bldgs. open year-round (hrs vary).*

⑫ **Mariposa Grove of Big Trees,** a fine grove of naturally fire-resistant *Sequoiadendron giganteum,* can be visited on foot or, during the summer, on one-hour tram rides. The Grizzly Giant, the oldest tree here, with an estimated age of 2,700 years, has a base diameter of 30.7 ft, a circumference of 96½ ft, and a height of 210 ft. The road to the grove closes when Yosemite is crowded; park in Wawona and take the free shuttle, which picks up passengers near the Wawona gas station. ⊠ *Off Hwy. 41 near the Fish Camp entrance to Yosemite National Park.* ▧ *Grove: free; tram ride: $8.* ⊙ *Grove: 24 hrs; tram: May−Oct., daily 9−4; shuttle: Memorial Day−Labor Day, daily 9−5.*

Dining and Lodging

$−$$ ✕▦ **Wawona Hotel and Dining Room.** The Wawona Hotel, an 1879 National Historic Landmark, sits at the southern end of Yosemite National Park, near the Mariposa Grove of Big Trees. It's an old-fashioned Victorian estate of whitewashed buildings with wraparound verandas. The hotel has small but pleasant rooms, about half of which do not have private baths. You can watch deer graze on the meadow while dining in the Wawona's romantic, candlelit dining room ($$−$$$; reservations essential for dinner in summer), which dates from the late 1800s. The American-style cuisine favors California ingredients and flavors—trout is a menu staple. Sunday brunch is served. ⊠ *Hwy. 41, 95389, ☎ 209/375−6556 (front desk), 209/375−1425 (dining room). 78 rooms, 24 cottage rooms. Restaurant, lounge, outdoor pool, 9-hole golf course, tennis, horseback riding. D, DC, MC, V.*

Yosemite National Park A to Z

Arriving and Departing

BY BUS

Greyhound (☎ 800/231–2222) serve Fresno and Merced from many California cities. **Yosemite VIA** (✉ 710 W. 16th St., Merced, ☎ 800/ 369–7275) runs three daily buses from Merced to Yosemite Valley; buses also depart daily from Mariposa and Fresno. The 2½-hour trip costs $38 per person round-trip, which includes admission to the park.

BY CAR

Yosemite is a four- to five-hour drive from San Francisco (take I–80 to I–580 to I–205 to Highway 120) and a six-hour drive from Los Angeles (take I–5 north to Highway 99 to Fresno, and Highway 41 north to Yosemite). Highways 41, 120, and 140 all intersect with Highway 99, which runs north–south through the Central Valley. Try to fill up your gas tank in one of the gateway towns near the park; there's no longer a gas station in Yosemite Valley. Gas stations are in Crane Flat, Wawona, and, in summer only, Tuolumne Meadows.

Via Highway 41: If you're coming from the south, Highway 41, which passes through Fresno, is the most direct path to Yosemite. Highway 41 (called Wawona Road inside the park) provides the most stunning entrance, via the Wawona Tunnel, into Yosemite Valley. One hundred and five miles from Fresno (or 60 mi from Madera on Highway 145 to Highway 41), Highway 41 leaves the San Joaquin Valley floor to climb through oak-studded hills before descending to Oakhurst, the southern terminus of Highway 49, which links the Gold Country towns for 300-plus mi to the north. Highway 41 continues to the north past the Bass Lake turnoff into Fish Camp and on through the park's South Entrance.

Via Highway 140: Arch Rock Entrance is 75 mi northeast of Merced via Highway 140, the least mountainous route into the park. The highway is undergoing extensive widening and reconstruction that will continue into the 21st century. Construction-free periods will occur during summer months and holiday periods.

Via Highway 120: Highway 120 is the northernmost route—the one that travels farthest and slowest through the foothills. You'll arrive at the park's Big Oak Flat Entrance, 88 mi east of Manteca. If you are coming from the east, you could cross the Sierra from Lee Vining on Highway 120 (Tioga Road). This route takes you over the Sierra crest and past Tuolumne Meadows. It's scenic, but the mountain driving may be stressful for some, and it's open only in summer.

BY PLANE

Fresno Air Terminal (✉ 5175 Clinton Way, ☎ 559/498–4095), the nearest major airport, is served by Delta, American, United Express, US Airways, and several regional carriers. *See* Air Travel *in* the Gold Guide for airline phone numbers.

Getting Around

BY BUS

A free shuttle runs around the eastern end of Yosemite Valley (between 7 AM and 10 PM in the summer and early fall, from 9 AM to 10 PM the rest of the year). A free shuttle runs from Wawona to the Mariposa Grove of Big Trees in summer only from 9 AM to 4:30 PM. The last return shuttle from the grove departs at 5 PM.

BY CAR

Auto traffic in Yosemite National Park is sometimes restricted during peak periods. Check conditions before driving in. Large RVs and trailers are not allowed on some roads. Carry tire chains when you drive in the mountains from mid-October to April.

Contacts and Resources

CAMPING

Biospherics (☎ 800/436–7275) handles reservations for the campgrounds within Yosemite that accept them (☞ *below*). Beginning on the 15th of each month you can reserve a site up to three months in advance. **Yosemite Concession Services** (☎ 559/252–4848) handles reservations for the tent-cabin and other sites in Yosemite Valley at Curry Village and the camping shelters at Housekeeping Camp.

Campgrounds in Yosemite do not have water and electric hookups, but there are dump stations and shower facilities in Yosemite Valley year-round. The dump stations in Wawona and Tuolumne Meadows are open in summer only. Several of Yosemite's 15 campgrounds operate on a first-come, first-served basis. Reservations are strongly recommended for the campgrounds at Tuolumne Meadows, Hodgdon's Meadow, Lower Pines, North Pines, Upper Pines, Wawona, and Crane Flat. It is possible to get a campsite upon arrival by stopping at the Campground Reservations Office in Yosemite Valley, but this is a chancy strategy.

When you're at your site, use the metal food-storage boxes to prevent bears from pilfering your edibles. Move all food, coolers, and items with a scent (including toiletries and air fresheners) from your car to the metal storage box. (Canisters for backpackers can be rented for $3 a day in most park stores.) Keep an eye peeled for rattlesnakes, which live below 7,000 ft. Though rarely fatal, their bites require a doctor's attention. Marmots, small members of the squirrel family, enjoy getting under a vehicle and chewing on radiator hoses and car wiring. Always check under the hood before driving away. Don't drink water directly from streams and lakes, as intestinal disorders may result.

EMERGENCIES

Ambulance (☎ 911). **Fire** (☎ 911). **Police** (☎ 911).

GUIDED TOURS

California Parlor Car Tours (☎ 415/474–7500 or 800/227–4250) in San Francisco serves Yosemite. Lodging and some meals are included. **Yosemite Concession Services** (☎ 559/252–4848) operates daily guided bus tours of Glacier Point, the Yosemite Valley floor, and the Mariposa Grove of Big Trees. The company's Grand Tour ($44.50), which is given between June and November, covers the park's highlights.

LODGING RESERVATIONS

Yosemite Concession Services Corporation (✉ Central Reservations, 5410 E. Home, Fresno 93727, ☎ 559/252–4848).

ROAD CONDITIONS

Yosemite Area Road and Weather Conditions (☎ 209/372–0200).

VISITOR INFORMATION

Yosemite Concession Services Corporation (☎ 209/372–1000). **Yosemite National Park** (✉ National Park Service, Information Office, Box 577, Yosemite National Park 95389, ☎ 209/372–0200 or 209/372–0264).

OUTSIDE YOSEMITE NATIONAL PARK
Mono Lake, Bodie, and the Gateway Cities

The area to the north and east of Yosemite National Park includes some ruggedly handsome terrain, most notably around Mono Lake. Bodie

Ghost Town is north of the lake. Several gateway towns to the south and west of Yosemite National Park, most within an hour's drive of Yosemite Village, have food, lodging, and other services.

Mono Lake

★ *20 mi east of Tuolumne Meadows, Hwy. 120 to U.S. 395; 30 mi north of Mammoth Lakes on U.S. 395.*

Eerie tufa towers—calcium carbonate formations that often resemble castle turrets—rise from impressive Mono Lake. Since the 1940s the city of Los Angeles has been diverting water from streams that feed the lake, lowering its water level and exposing the tufa. Recent court victories by environmentalists have forced a reduction of the diversions, and the lake has risen almost 8 ft. Millions of migratory birds nest in and around Mono Lake.

The best place to view the tufa is at the south end of the lake along the mile-long **South Tufa Trail.** To reach it drive 5 mi south from Lee Vining on U.S. 395, then 5 mi east on Highway 120. The fee (well worth paying) is $2 to visit the trail and the **Scenic Area Visitor Center** (✉ U.S. 395, Lee Vining, ☎ 760/647–3044), open daily at 9 AM year-round (closing times vary, but it's always open until at least 4). You can swim (or float) in the highly salty water at nearby Navy Beach or take a kayak or canoe trip for close-up views of the tufa, though you can't row near Negit and Paoha islands between April and August, which is bird-nesting season. Rangers and naturalists lead walking tours of the tufa daily in summer and on weekends only (sometimes on cross-country skis) in winter.

Bodie Ghost Town and State Historic Park

23 mi from Lee Vining, north on U.S. 395, east on Hwy. 270 (last 3 mi are unpaved). Snow closes Hwy. 270 in winter and early spring, but park stays open.

★ ⑬ Old shacks and shops, abandoned mine shafts, a Methodist church, the mining village of Rattlesnake Gulch, and the remains of a small Chinatown are among the sights to be seen at the fascinating **Bodie Ghost Town,** elevation 8,200 ft. The town boomed from about 1878 to 1881 as gold prospectors, having worked the best of the western Sierra mines, headed to the high desert on the eastern slopes. Bodie had a nasty reputation—the booze flowed freely, shootings were commonplace, and licentiousness reined. The big strikes were made during the boom years, and though some mining continued into the 1930s, the town had long since begun its decline by then. By the late 1940s all the residents had departed. A state park, whose administrators' mandate was to preserve but not restore the town, was established in 1962. Evidence of Bodie's wild past survives at an excellent museum, and you can tour an old stamp mill (where ore was stamped into fine powder to extract gold and silver) and a ridge that contains many mine sites. Tours of the mines may begin in summer 1999. ✉ *Museum: Main and Green Sts.,* ☎ *760/647–6445.* 🎫 *Park: $2 per person, $1 per dog; museum: free.* ☉ *Park: Memorial Day–mid-Sept., daily 8–7; hrs vary rest of yr; Museum: May–Oct., daily 10–5; open sporadically rest of yr.*

Bass Lake

18 mi south of Yosemite National Park's South Entrance, Hwy. 41 to Bass Valley Rd.

Dining

$$–$$$ ✕ **Ducey's on the Lake.** With a lakeside view and elaborate chandeliers sculpted from antlers, the lodge-style restaurant at Ducey's attracts boaters, locals, and tourists with standard lamb, steak, lobster, and pasta dishes. Burgers, salads, soft tacos, and sandwiches are the fare at the upstairs Bar & Grill. Sunday brunch is served from 10 AM to 2 PM. ⊠ *54432 Rd. 432,* ☎ *559/642–3121. Reservations essential for brunch. AE, D, DC, MC, V.*

Outdoor Activities and Sports

Pines Marina (⊠ Bass Lake Reservoir, ☎ 559/642–3565), open from April to October and at other times as weather permits, rents ski boats, houseboats, fishing boats, and jet skis.

El Portal

14 mi west of Yosemite Valley on Hwy. 140.

Lodging

$$–$$$ ▥ **Yosemite View Lodge.** The back building at Yosemite View has rooms with balconies overlooking the boulder-strewn Merced River and majestic pines. Also in view is a picnic patio with hot tubs and heated pools. The pleasant facility is on the public bus route to Yosemite National Park and near fishing and river rafting. Many of the rooms have spa baths, fireplaces, and kitchenettes. The owners plan to add 136 rooms in 1999. ⊠ *11136 Hwy. 140, 95318,* ☎ *209/379–2681,* FAX *209/379–2704. 132 rooms. Restaurant, bar, 2 pools, 3 hot tubs, coin laundry, conference center. MC, V.*

$$ ▥ **Cedar Lodge.** The lobby of this complex in the pines is heavy on plaids and teddy bears. Rooms range from suites with kitchenettes to family units to romantic accommodations with spa tubs for two. ⊠ *9966 Hwy. 140, 95318,* ☎ *209/379–2612,* FAX *209/379–2712. 207 rooms, 9 suites. 2 restaurants, 2 pools, hot tubs. AE, MC, V.*

Fish Camp

37 mi south of Yosemite Valley floor on Hwy. 41; 4 mi south of Yosemite National Park's South Entrance on Hwy. 41.

In the small town of Fish Camp are a service station, a post office, a ⟲ general store, and the **Yosemite Mountain Sugar Pine Railroad,** a 4-mi steam-engine train ride through the forest. The Saturday-evening Moonlight Special excursion (reservations advised) includes dinner and old-fashioned entertainment. ⊠ *56001 Hwy. 41,* ☎ *559/683–7273.* ▤ *$10.50; $32.50 for Moonlight Special.* ☉ *Mar.– Oct., daily.*

Dining and Lodging

$$$$ ✕▥ **Tenaya Lodge.** One of the region's largest hotels is perfect for people who enjoy hiking in the wilderness but prefer coming home to luxury. A southwestern motif prevails in the ample regular rooms. The deluxe rooms have minibars and other extras, and the suites have balconies. Continental cuisine is prepared at the cozy Sierra Restaurant ($$–$$$); the fare at the lodge's casual grill includes burgers, salads and sandwiches. Off-season room rates at Tenaya run as low as $69. ⊠ *1122 Hwy. 41, Box 159, 93623,* ☎ *559/683–6555; 800/635– 5807 for lodging reservations and restaurant;* FAX *559/683–8684. 208 rooms, 36 suites. 2 restaurants, deli, bar, room service, indoor pool, outdoor pool, health club, mountain bikes, playground, laundry service, dry cleaning, meeting room. AE, D, DC, MC, V.*

$$ ✕▥ **Narrow Gauge Inn.** This motel-style property is comfortably furnished, with old-fashioned decor and railroad memorabilia. The inn's lodgelike restaurant, which serves cuisine inspired by the California

ranchero era of the late 1800s—is festooned with moose, bison, and other wildlife trophies. ⊠ *48571 Hwy. 41, 93623,* ☎ *559/683–7720,* FAX *559/683–2139. 24 rooms, 1 suite. Restaurant, bar, outdoor pool, hot tub. D, MC, V. Closed Nov.–Feb.*

Oakhurst

50 mi south of Yosemite Valley on Hwy.41; 23 mi south of Yosemite National Park's South Entrance on Hwy. 41.

Motels and restaurants line both sides of Highway 41 as it cuts through the formerly sleepy town of Oakhurst. A theater in the Oakhurst mall shows current movies, and you can stock up on major provisions at the grocery and general stores.

Dining and Lodging

$$$$ ✕ **Erna's Elderberry House.** The restaurant operated by Vienna-born
★ Erna Kubin, owner of Château du Sureau (☞ *below*), is another expression of her passion for beauty, charm, and impeccable service. White walls and dark beams accent the dining room's high ceilings, and arched windows reflect the glow of many candles. A six-course, prix-fixe dinner in rhythm with the seasons is elegantly paced and accompanied by superb wines. This is a dining experience to remember. Sunday brunch is also served. ⊠ *48688 Victoria La.,* ☎ *559/683–6800. AE, MC, V. Closed 1st 3 wks of Jan. No lunch Sat.–Tues.*

$$$$ ⌸ **Château du Sureau.** This romantic inn is a fairy tale. From the mo-
★ ment regal gates magically open and you step out of your car (think mice-driven coach), and a lady in waiting takes your coat and bags, you will not lift a finger. A winding staircase seems to carry you up to your room; you'll fall asleep in the glow of a crackling fire amid goose down pillows and a comforter that rivals Cloud Nine. Château du Sureau is enveloped in an alluring serenity that greets you when you raise the curtains the next morning and breathe in the fragrant gardens and cool air from the mist-shrouded pines. Eat a hearty European breakfast in the dining room downstairs and plan your Sierra stay in the piano room, which has an exquisite ceiling mural. ⊠ *48688 Victoria La., Box 577, 93644,* ☎ *559/683–6860,* FAX *559/683–0800. 9 rooms. Restaurant, outdoor pool. Full breakfast. AE, MC, V.*

$$–$$$ ⌸ **The Homestead.** Serenity is the order of the day at this secluded getaway in Ahwahnee, 6 mi west of Oakhurst. On 160 acres that once held a Miwok Indian village, the Homestead's cottages have fireplaces, living rooms, fully equipped kitchens, some antiques, and queen-size beds. Smoking and pets are not allowed on the premises. ⊠ *41110 Rd. 600, 2½ mi off Hwy. 49, Ahwahnee, 93601,* ☎ *559/683–0495,* FAX *559/ 683–8165. 4 cottages. AE, MC, V.*

$–$$$ ⌸ **Shilo Inn.** The Shilo's sunny, pine-furnished rooms come with wet bars and satellite TV. ⊠ *40644 Hwy. 41, 93644,* ☎ *559/683–3555,* FAX *559/683–3386. 80 rooms. Kitchenettes, pool, hot tub, sauna, steam room, exercise room, coin laundry. Continental breakfast. AE, D, DC, MC, V.*

Outside Yosemite National Park A to Z

Arriving and Departing
See Yosemite National Park A to Z, *above.*

Getting Around
The area surrounding Yosemite National Park is best visited by car. U.S. 395, the main north–south road on the eastern side of the Sierra Nevada, passes by the west edge of Mono Lake and west of Bodie Ghost Town. Highway 140 heads east from the San Joaquin Valley to El Por-

tal. Highway 41 heads north from Fresno to Oakhurst and Fish Camp; Bass Lake is off Highway 41.

Visitor Information

Bodie State Historic Park (✉ Box 515, Bridgeport 93517, ☏ 760/647–6445). **Mono Lake** (✉ U.S. 395, Lee Vining 93541, ☏ 760/647–3044). **Southern Yosemite Visitors Bureau** (✉ 49074 Civic Circle, Oakhurst 93644, ☏ 559/683–4636).

MAMMOTH LAKES

A jewel in the eastern Sierra Nevada, resting amid glistening mountain peaks and glacier-carved alpine lakes, Mammoth Lakes provides California's finest skiing and snowboarding south of Lake Tahoe. At 11,053-ft-high Mammoth Mountain, skiers hit the slopes as late as June or even July. As soon as snows melt, Mammoth transforms itself into a warm-weather playground—fishing, mountain biking, hiking, and horseback riding are among the options. Nine deep-blue lakes form the Mammoth Lakes Basin, and another 100 lakes dot the surrounding countryside. Crater-pocked Mammoth Mountain hasn't had a major eruption for 50,000 years, but the region is alive with hot springs, mud pots, fumaroles, and steam vents.

Mammoth Lakes

30 mi south of Mono Lake on U.S. 395.

Much of the architecture in the hub town of Mammoth Lakes, elevation 7,800 ft, is in the faux-alpine category. You'll find basic services here, plus dining and lodging options.

Even if you don't ski, it makes sense to start at the aptly named landmass in the middle of it all—Mammoth Mountain. Two **gondolas** serve skiers in winter and mountain bikers and sightseers in summer. By the beginning of the 1998–99 ski season, the installation of a high-speed 8-person gondola to the summit should be completed. Repairs to the lower gondola will take place during the 1999 summer season; at press time the Mammoth Mountain resort hadn't decided whether to cease operation of the upper gondola or use chairlifts to ferry passengers up to it. The boarding area for the lower gondola is at the main lodge of the ski area. ☏ 760/934–2571, ext. 3850. ⬚ $10. ☉ July 4–Oct., daily 9:30–5; Nov.–July 3, daily 8:30–3.

The sawtoothed, glacial-carved spires of the Minarets, the remains of an ancient lava flow, are best viewed from the **Minaret Vista,** off Highway 203 west of Mammoth Lakes.

The **lakes of the Mammoth Lakes Basin,** reached by Lake Mary Road southwest of town, are popular for fishing and boating in summer. First comes **Twin Lakes**, at the far end of which is Twin Falls, where water cascades 300 ft over a shelf of volcanic rock. **Lake Mary** is the largest lake in the basin. Others include **Lake Mamie** and **Lake George**. The only lake where you can swim is **Horseshoe Lake**.

🐾 ⑭   An easy 10-minute walk from the ranger station at **Devil's Postpile National Monument** takes you to the base of Devil's Postpile, a geologic formation of smooth, vertical basalt columns sculpted by volcanic and glacial forces. A short but steep trail winds to the top of the 60-ft-high rocky cliff for a bird's-eye view of the columns. A 2-mi hike past the Postpile leads to the monument's second scenic wonder, **Rainbow Falls,** where a branch of the San Joaquin River plunges more than 100 ft over a lava ledge. When the water hits the pool below, mists rise to form a rainbow of color; walk down a bit from the top of the falls for the best viewing. During the daytime in summer the national monument is accessible only via a shuttle bus ($7) that begins operation as soon as the road is cleared of snow—usually in June, but sometimes as late as July. The shuttle departs from Mammoth Mountain Inn (☞ *below*) every 20 minutes from 7:30 AM to 5:30 PM. The shuttle stops running after Labor Day, but you can drive to the falls until snows come again, usually around the beginning of November. Scenic picnic spots dot the bank of the San Joaquin River. ⊠ *Follow Minaret Rd. (Hwy. 203) 13 mi west from Mammoth Lakes.* ☎ *760/934–2289 (summer), 559/565–3341 (winter); 760/934–0606 for shuttle bus information.* 🎫 *Free.* ☉ *Late June–late Oct., daily, weather permitting.*

The **June Lake Loop** (⊠ Hwy. 158 west from U.S. 395), a wonderfully scenic 17-mi drive that follows an old glacial canyon past Grant, June, Gull, and other alpine lakes, is especially colorful in fall.

OFF THE
BEATEN PATH   **HOT CREEK GEOLOGIC SITE/HOT CREEK FISH HATCHERY** – Forged by an ancient volcanic eruption, the Hot Creek Geologic Site is a landscape of boiling hot springs, fumaroles, and occasional geysers about 10 mi southeast of the town of Mammoth Lakes. You can soak (at your own risk) in hot springs or walk along boardwalks through the canyon to view the steaming volcanic features. Fly-fishing for trout is popular upstream from the springs. En route to the geologic site is the Hot Creek Fish Hatchery, the breeding ponds for most of the 3 million to 5 million fish the state stocks annually in eastern Sierra lakes and rivers. ⊠ *Hot Creek Hatchery Rd., east off U.S. 395,* ☎ *760/924–5500 for site; 760/934–2664 for hatchery.* 🎫 *Free.* ☉ *Site: daily sunrise–sunset; hatchery: daily 8–4, weather permitting.*

Dining and Lodging

$$–$$$ ✕ **Nevados.** In a restaurant scene known mostly for meat, potatoes, and pizza, Nevados serves creative cuisine in a contemporary bistro setting. The menu changes frequently but always includes pasta dishes, fresh seafood, and grilled meats. Grilled eggplant lasagna, sesame-crusted ahi tuna, and orange-scented duckling are among the past entrées. ⊠ *Main St. and Minaret Rd.,* ☎ *760/934–4466. Reservations essential on weekends and holidays. AE, D, DC, MC, V. No lunch. Closed 1 wk. in early June and from late Oct.–early Nov.*

$–$$ ✕ **Berger's.** Don't even think about coming to this bustling pine-panel restaurant unless you're hungry. Berger's is known, appropriately enough, for burgers and other generously sized sandwiches—in fact, everything comes in big, even mountainous portions. For dinner try the beef ribs or the buffalo steak. ⊠ *Minaret Rd. near Canyon Blvd.,* ☎ *760/934–6622. MC, V. Closed 4–6 weeks in May and June and 4–6 weeks in Oct. and Nov. (call ahead).*

$–$$ ✕ **Giovanni's Pizza.** Kids enjoy this casual restaurant that serves good pizza and standard Italian dinners (best bet: stick to the pizza). Don't come here for quiet conversation—it's a high-decibel atmosphere. ⊠ *Minaret Village, Old Mammoth Rd. and Meridian St.,* ☎ *760/934–7563. AE, MC, V. No lunch Sun.*

$–$$ ✕ **The Mogul.** This steak house has a friendly, relaxed ambience. The charbroiled shrimp and the grilled beef or chicken come with a baked potato or rice pilaf and soup or salad. A children's menu is available. ⊠ *Mammoth Tavern Rd. off Old Mammoth Rd.,* ☎ *760/934–3039. AE, D, MC, V. No lunch.*

$ ✕ **Blondie's Kitchen and Waffle Shop.** A good place to stoke up before a morning on the slopes or trails, this comic-strip–theme diner serves up Belgian waffles, pancakes, omelets, and Dagwood "pig-out" plates. ⊠ *Main and Lupin Sts. ,* ☎ *760/934–4048. MC, V. No dinner.*

$$$–$$$$ 🏨 **Snowcreek Resort.** In a valley surrounded by mountain peaks, this 355-acre condominium community on the outskirts of Mammoth Lakes contains one- to four-bedroom units. All have kitchens, living and dining rooms, fireplaces, and TVs with VCRs. There's an on-premises nursery, and guests have free use of the well-supplied athletic club. The expansion of the golf course from nine holes to 18 was scheduled to be completed by 1999. ⊠ ⊠ *Old Mammoth Rd., Box 1647, 93546,* ☎ *760/934–3333 or 800/544–6007,* FAX *760/934–1619. 150 condo units. 2 pools, 5 hot tubs, sauna, 18-hole golf course , 9 tennis courts, racquetball, health club, nursery. AE, MC, V.*

$$–$$$$ 🏨 **Mammoth Mountain Inn.** If you want to be within walking distance of the Mammoth Mountain ski area, this is the place to stay. You can check your skis with the concierge after a day on the slopes and pick them up in the morning and head directly to the lifts, right across the way. At breakfast, inn personnel will keep you apprised of snow and weather conditions. The accommodations, some of which are cramped, include standard hotel rooms and condo units; the latter have kitchenettes and many have lofts. The inn has licensed on-site child care. ⊠ ⊠ *Minaret Rd. 4 mi west of Mammoth Lakes (Box 353), 93546,* ☎ *760/934–2581 or 800/228–4947,* FAX *760/934–0701. 124 rooms, 91 condo units. 2 restaurants, bar, 3 hot tubs, ski storage, video games, children's programs, nursery, playground. AE, MC, V.*

$–$$$$ 🏨 **Tamarack Lodge Resort.** Skiers (and, in summer, nature-lovers) favor this lodge that overlooks Twin Lakes, about 3 mi west of town. Lodge rooms and housekeeping cabins occupy a quiet, woodsy setting, and cross-country ski trails zip right past the cabins. In warm months, fishing, canoeing, hiking, and mountain biking are close by. The cozy cabins are modern, neat, and clean, with knotty-pine kitchens and private baths; some have fireplaces or wood-burning stoves. Alert the kids: There are no TVs. ⊠ *Lake Mary Rd. off Hwy. 203, 93546,* ☎ *760/ 934–2442 or 800/237–6879 in CA,* FAX *760/934–2281. 11 rooms, 25 cabins. Restaurant, cross-country ski trails. D, MC, V.*

$$–$$$ 🏨 **Sierra Lodge.** This motel on Main Street has spacious rooms. A covered parking garage with ski lockers is helpful in wintertime. Free shuttles take skiers to Mammoth Mountain. ⊠ *3540 Main St., 93546,* ☎ *760/934–8881; 800/356–5711 in southern CA,* FAX *760/934–7231. 35 rooms. Kitchenettes, microwaves, no-smoking rooms, refrigerators, hot tub, ski storage. MC, V.*

$–$$ 🏨 **Swiss Chalet.** One of the most reasonably priced motels in town, the Swiss Chalet has million-dollar views of the mountains. Among the amenities are an indoor sauna and whirlpool, a fish-cleaning area, and a freezer to keep your summer catch fresh. ⊠ *3776 Viewpoint Rd., Box 16, 93546,* ☎ *760/934–2403 or 800/937–9477,* FAX *760/934– 2403. 21 rooms. Hot tub, sauna. AE, D, MC, V.*

Nightlife and the Arts

The summertime jazz, country-western, rock, and reggae concerts of **Mammoth Mountain Music** (☎ 760/934–0606 or 800/228–4947) take place at Yodler Pavilion at the Mammoth Mountain ski area.

Goats Bar (⊠ Main St., ☎ 760/934–4629), a popular watering hole, has a pool table and a dart board. Rock, country, and blues acts perform at **La Sierra's** (⊠ Main St., ☎ 760/934–8083), which has Mammoth's largest dance floor. The bar at **Whiskey Creek** (⊠ Main St. and Minaret Rd., ☎ 760/934–2555) hosts bands or solo musicians on weekends year-round and on most nights in winter.

Outdoor Activities and Sports

BICYCLING

Mammoth Mountain Bike Park (☎ 760/934–0606), at the ski area, opens when the snows melt, usually by July, with 70-plus mi of single-track trails—from mellow to super-challenging. The **Mammoth Mountain Bike Center** (☎ 760/934–0706) next to the main lodge sells park passes and rents bikes.

DOG SLEDDING

Dog Sled Adventures (☎ 760/934–6270) operates 25-minute rides through the forest on 10-dog sleds.

FISHING

Crowley Lake is the top trout-fishing spot in the area; Convict Lake, June Lake, and the lakes of the Mammoth Basin are other prime spots. One of the best trout rivers is the San Joaquin near Devil's Postpile (☞ *above*). Hot Creek (☞ *above*), a designated Wild Trout Stream, is renowned for fly-fishing (catch and release only). The fishing season runs from the last Saturday in April until the end of October. **Kittredge Sports** (✉ Main St. and Forest Trail, ☎ 760/934–7566) rents rods and reels and conducts guided trips.

HIKING

Trails wind around the Lakes Basin and through pristine alpine scenery. Stop at the U.S. Forest Service ranger station (☞ Visitor Information, *below*) for a trail map and permits for backpacking in wilderness areas.

HORSEBACK RIDING

Stables are typically open from June to September. Outfitters include **Mammoth Lakes Pack Outfit** (✉ Lake Mary Rd., ☎ 760/934–2434); **McGee Creek Pack Station** (✉ Rte. 1, ☎ 760/935–4324 or 800/854–7407); and **Sierra Meadows Ranch** (✉ Sherwin Creek Rd., ☎ 760/934–6161).

HOT-AIR BALLOONING

The balloons of **Mammoth Ballooning** (☎ 760/934–7188 or 800/484–6936, ext. 1122) glide over the countryside in the morning from spring until fall, weather permitting.

SKIING AND SNOWBOARDING

June Mountain Ski Area. This low-key resort 20 mi north of Mammoth Mountain is a favorite of snowboarders, who have a halfpipe all to themselves. Seven lifts service the area, which has a 2,590-ft vertical drop; the skiing is from beginner to expert. A rental and repair shop, a ski school, and a sport shop are all on the premises, and there's child care. ✉ *Off June Lake Loop (Hwy. 158), June Lake 93529,* ☎ *760/648–7733.*

Mammoth Mountain Ski Area. With 29 lifts and more than 3,500 acres of skiable terrain, Mammoth is one of the West Coast's largest ski areas. The base elevation is 7,953 ft. On days when it's not too windy, you can ski off the top of the mountain (11,053 ft), for a 3,100-ft vertical drop. The terrain includes beginning-to-expert runs. Snowboarders are welcome on all slopes; the Unbound terrain park has a halfpipe and sculpted jumps for snowboarders. Mammoth's season begins in November and often lingers until June or beyond. Night skiing occurs on weekends and holidays, from Christmas to Easter. Lessons and rental equipment are available, and there's a kids' ski school. ✉ *Minaret Rd. west of Mammoth Lakes, Box 24, 93546,* ☎ *760/934–2571 or 888/462–6668.*

Trails at **Tamarack Cross Country Ski Center** (✉ Lake Mary Rd. off Hwy. 203, ☎ 760/934–2442), adjacent to Tamarack Lodge (☞ *above*) meander around several lakes. Rentals are available.

Sandy's Ski & Sport (✉ Main St. near Center St, ☎ 760/934–7518) rents and sells equipment.

Mammoth Snowmobile Adven-Tours (⊠ Main St., ☎ 760/934–9645) conducts guided and self-guided tours along wooded trails.

Mammoth Lakes A to Z

Arriving and Departing

BY CAR

In summer and early fall (or whenever snows aren't blocking Tioga Road) you can drive from San Francisco to Mammoth via Highway 120 (to U.S. 395 south) through the Yosemite high country, a distance of about 300 mi. The quickest route when Tioga Road is closed is I–80 to U.S. 50 in the Lake Tahoe area; from the lake's Nevada side take the Kingsbury Grade (Route 207) east to U.S. 395 south to Highway 203 west. This trip is a total of 320 mi. From the Los Angeles area, the route is the same all year: Highway 14 and U.S. 395 north to Highway 203 west, a distance of about 310 mi. If you're coming from Orange County, take I–15 north to U.S. 395 and follow that north to 203; this trip is about 320 mi.

BY PLANE

Mountain Air Express (☎ 562/595–1011 or 800/788–4247) operates flights to Mammoth Lakes from Long Beach, Fresno, and San Jose. Flights land at Mammoth Lakes Airport, about 6 mi south of town.

Getting Around

BY CAR

Highway 203 heads west from U.S. 395, becoming Main Street as it passes through the town of Mammoth Lakes and later Minaret Road as it continues west to the Mammoth Mountain ski area and Devil's Postpile National Monument.

BY SHUTTLE BUS

Mammoth Mountain runs four free **shuttle bus** (☎ 760/934–0687) routes around town to and from the ski area. Buses run from 7 AM to 5:30 PM daily in snow season, with limited night service from Christmas to Easter.

BY TAXI

Mammoth Shuttle (☎ 760/934–3030) provides airport and ski-lift transport.

Contacts and Resources

EMERGENCIES

Ambulance (☎ 911). **Fire** (☎ 911). **Police** (☎ 911).

VISITOR INFORMATION

Mammoth Lakes Visitors Bureau (⊠ Main St., Box 48, 93546, ☎ 760/934–2712 or 888/466–2666). **Snow Report** (☎ 760/934–6166 or 888/766–9778). **U.S. Forest Service ranger station** (⊠ Main St., 93546, ☎ 760/934–5500).

KINGS CANYON AND SEQUOIA NATIONAL PARKS

Grant Grove, Cedar Grove, and Lodgepole

General Grant and Sequoia national parks were established in 1890, along with Yosemite. Additions to General Grant National Park included the Redwood Canyon area and the drainages of the south and middle forks of the Kings River. The expanded region of General Grant Park was renamed Kings Canyon National Park in 1940. Though they're overshadowed by Yosemite, naturalist John Muir thought no less of these two parks—he declared that the beauty of Kings Canyon rivaled that of Yosemite and described the sequoia trees as "the most beautiful and majestic on Earth." *Sequoiadendron giganteum* trees are not as tall as the coast redwoods (*Sequoia sempervirens*), but they are older and more massive. Exhibits at the visitor centers explain the special relationship between these trees and fire (their thick, fibrous bark helps protect them from fire and insects) and their ability to live so long and grow so big.

A little more than 1.5 million people visit Kings Canyon and Sequoia annually, wandering trails through groves and meadows or tackling the rugged backcountry. The topography of the two parks runs the gamut from chaparral, at an elevation of 1,500 ft, to the giant sequoia belt, at 5,000 to 7,000 ft, to the towering peaks of the Great Western Divide and the Sierra Crest. Mount Whitney, the highest point in the contiguous United States at 14,494 ft, is the crown jewel of the eastern side.

Kings Canyon and Sequoia national parks share their administration and a main highway, called the Generals Highway, which connects Highway 180 in Kings Canyon to Highway 198 in Sequoia. The entrance fee to Kings Canyon and Sequoia (good for admission on seven consecutive days) is $10 per vehicle, $5 for those who don't arrive by car. The quarterly *Sequoia Bark,* which is given for free at the parks' entrances, has information and maps.

Grant Grove and Cedar Grove

100 mi southeast of Oakhurst, Hwy. 41 to Hwy. 180.

⓯ Grant Grove (✉ Kings Canyon Hwy./Hwy. 180, 1 mi from Big Stump Entrance), Kings Canyon's most highly developed area, is the original grove that was designated as General Grant National Park in 1890. A walk along the 1½-mi **Big Stump Trail,** which starts near the park entrance, graphically demonstrates the toll heavy logging takes on the wilderness. An alternate ⅓-mi trail is fairly accessible to travelers with disabilities. The **General Grant Tree Trail,** a paved ⅜-mi path through Grant Grove, winds past a sequoia, one of the world's largest, that's about 2,000 years old. The **Gamlin Cabin,** an 1867 structure listed on the National Register of Historic Places, is a pioneer cabin. Also within Grant Grove is the **Centennial Stump,** the remains of a large sequoia cut for display at the 1876 Philadelphia Centennial Exhibition.

Grant Grove Village has a visitor center, a grocery store, a gift shop, campgrounds, a coffee shop, overnight lodging, a horse-rental concession, and a post office. The visitor center has exhibits on the *Sequoiadendron giganteum* and the area.

⓰ Hume Lake (✉ Hwy. 180 northeast 8 mi from Grant Grove off Hume Lake Rd.), a reservoir built early this century by loggers, is now the site of many Christian camps, a gas station, and a public campground. This small lake outside Kings Canyon's borders has views of high mountains in the distance.

★ **⓱** The **Cedar Grove** area is a valley that snakes along the south fork of the Kings River. A spectacular drive along Kings Canyon Highway takes one hour from Grant Grove to the end of the road, where you can hike, camp, or turn right around for the ride back. Built by convict labor in the 1930s, the road (usually closed from mid-October to April) clings to some dramatic cliffs along the way: Watch out for falling rocks. The highway passes the scars where large groves of big trees were logged at the beginning of the 20th century. It runs along the south fork and

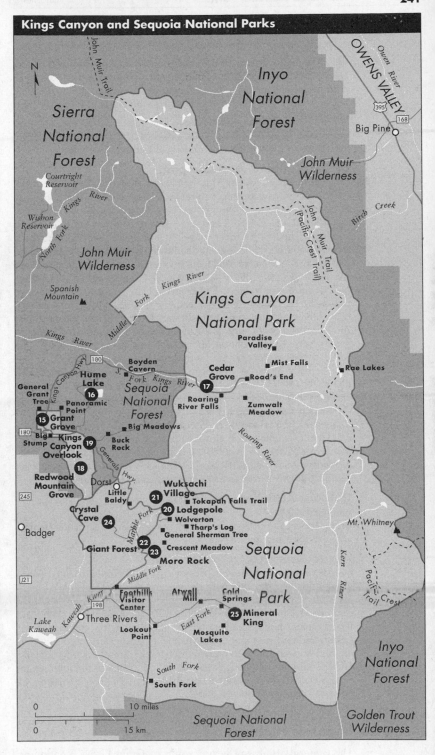

OWENS VALLEY

Owen River

395

168

Big Pine

Inyo
National
Forest

John Muir
Wilderness

Sierra
National
Forest

Courtright
Reservoir

Kings River

Wishon
Reservoir

North Fork

John Muir
Wilderness

Spanish
Mountain

Birch Creek

Kings River

Middle Fork

South Fork Kings River

Kings Canyon
National Park

Paradise
Valley

Mist Falls

Rae Lakes

John Muir Trail (Pacific Crest Trail)

Boyden
Cavern

Cedar
Grove

17

Road's End

Hume
Lake

16

Sequoia
National
Forest

Roaring
River Falls

Zumwalt
Meadow

General
Grant
Tree

180

Panoramic
Point

15 Grant
Grove

Big Meadows

Roaring River

180

Big
Stump

Kings
Canyon
Overlook

19

Buck
Rock

18

Redwood
Mountain
Grove

245

Dorst

Generals Hwy.

Wuksachi
Village

21

Tokopah Falls Trail

Little
Baldy

20 Lodgepole

Crystal
Cave

24

Wolverton

Tharp's Log

General Sherman Tree

Mt. Whitney

Badger

Marble Fork

22

23

Giant Forest

Crescent Meadow

Moro Rock

Sequoia

National

Kern River

Pacific Crest Trail

J21

Middle Fork

Foothills
Visitor
Center

Atwell
Mill

Cold
Springs

Park

198

Kaweah Hwy.

Three Rivers

East Fork

25 Mineral
King

Lake
Kaweah

Lookout
Point

Mosquito
Lakes

Inyo

National

Forest

South Fork

South Fork

Golden Trout
Wilderness

0   10 miles

0   15 km

Sequoia National
Forest

through dry foothills covered with yuccas that bloom in the summer. There are amazing views into the deepest gorge in the United States, at the confluence of the two forks, and up the canyons to the High Sierra.

Cedar Grove was named for the incense cedars that grow in the area. Horses can be rented here, a good way to continue your explorations; there are also campgrounds, lodgings, a small ranger station, a snack bar, a restaurant, a convenience market, a gift shop, and a gas station.

Short trails circle **Zumwalt Meadow.** The trails from the meadow lead to the base of **Roaring River Falls.** Hikers can self-register for wilderness permits at **Road's End,** 6 mi east of Cedar Grove Village.

Dining, Lodging, and Camping

$$ ✕⌂ **Cedar Grove Lodge.** Although accommodations are close to the road, Cedar Grove manages to retain a quiet atmosphere. Book way in advance—the motel-lodge has only 18 rooms. Each one is air-conditioned and carpeted and has a private shower and two queen-size beds. The fare for lunch and dinner at the self-serve restaurant is trout, hamburgers, hot dogs, and sandwiches. Breakfast is eggs, bacon, and toast. You can take food from the restaurant to picnic tables along the river's edge. ☎ *559/565–0100. MC, V. Closed mid-Oct.–mid-May.*

$ ✕⌂ **Grant Grove Village.** The carpeted cabins in this complex have private baths, propane wall heaters, and double beds. Simpler cabins, heated by woodstoves and lit by battery lamps, are near a central rest room and shower facility. The Kings Canyon concessionaire hopes to have a new 30-room hotel up and running by summer 1999. The Meadowview Room ($$–$$$) is the area's fine-dining option; a family-style coffee shop serves American standards for breakfast, lunch, and dinner. ☎ *559/335–5500,* ℻ *559/335–2498. 52 cabins. Coffee shop. MC, V.*

▲ **Azalea Campground.** One of three campgrounds in the Grant Grove area (the other two are Sunset and Crystal Springs), Azalea sits amid giant sequoias yet is close to restaurants, stores, and other facilities. Pay showers are available nearby. Sites are allocated on a first-come, first-served basis. ✉ ☎ *559/565–3341. Flush toilets, disposal station (summer only), fire rings, water.* ▭ *$12.* ☉ *Year-round.*

Outdoor Activities and Sports

WINTER SPORTS

Grant Grove (☎ 559/565–2314) has a cross-country ski center (rentals are available) and marked trails.

YEAR-ROUND SPORTS

Montecito-Sequoia Lodge provides year-round family-oriented recreation. Lodging rates vary with the season but always include a breakfast buffet and dinner. Visitors not staying at the lodge are welcome to drop in for meals. Winter activities include cross-country skiing and lessons, snowshoeing, and snowboarding. Among the summer activities offered in a six-night Club Med–like package are canoeing, sailing, and water-skiing on the resort's private lake, horseback riding, tennis, archery, and nature hikes. In spring and fall, some of the summer activities occur, but you can book shorter stays. ✉ *Generals Hwy., 11 mi south of Grant Grove,* ☎ *800/227–9900 for reservations, brochures and information. 38 rooms, 13 cabins. AE, D, MC, V.*

Along the Generals Highway

The **Generals Highway** begins south of Grant Grove, continuing through the lower portion of Kings Canyon National Park and through a grand section of the Sequoia National Forest before entering Sequoia National Park.

★ ⑱ The **Redwood Mountain Grove** is the largest grove of big trees in the world. As you exit Kings Canyon on the Generals Highway, there are several paved turnouts from which you can look out over the grove (and into the smog of the Central Valley). The grove itself is accessible only on foot or horseback.

⑲ **Kings Canyon Overlook,** a large turnout on the north side of the Generals Highway less than 2 mi from Redwood Mountain Grove, has views across the canyon of mountain peaks and the backcountry. If you drive east on Highway 180 to Cedar Grove along the south fork, you will see these canyons at much closer range.

Lodgepole

⑳ *26 mi south of Grant Grove on the Generals Hwy.*

Lodgepole sits in a canyon on the Marble Fork of the Kaweah River. Lodgepole pines, rather than sequoias, grow here because the U-shape canyon directs air down from the high country that is too cold for the big trees but is just right for lodgepoles. This developed area has a campground, a market and deli, a public laundry, a gift shop, and a post office. A pizza stand, an ice cream parlor, and showers are open in the summer only.

★ ⓒ The **Lodgepole Visitor Center** has the best exhibits in Sequoia or Kings Canyon, a small theater that shows films about the parks, and a first aid center. You can buy tickets for the Crystal Cave (☞ *below*), get advice from park rangers, purchase maps and books, and pick up wilderness permits (except during summer, when they're available from 7 AM to 4 PM at the permit office next door). ☎ *559/565–3782.* ⊙ *Mid-June–Labor Day, daily 8–6; Labor Day–mid-June, daily 9–6.*

The **Tokopah Falls Trail** is an easy and rewarding 1⅞₀-mi hike (each way) up the Marble Fork of the Kaweah River from the Lodgepole Campground. The walk to the 1,200-ft falls, which flow down granite cliffs, is the closest you can get to the high country without taking a long hike. Trail maps are available at the Lodgepole Visitor Center. Bring insect repellent during the summer, when the mosquitoes can be ferocious.

㉑ The project to complete **Wuksachi Village,** a key component in the master plan for Sequoia National Park, has proceeded in fits and starts during the past few years. Some dining and lodging facilities (☞ *below*), scheduled for completion by summer 1999, will enable the park to tear down antiquated ones in Giant Forest Village that were endangering the sequoias. For updated information, contact **Delaware North Park Services at Sequoia** (☎ 559/641–6354).

Lodging and Camping

$$–$$$ ⊞ **Wuksachi Village.** As we headed to press in fall 1998, construction was continuing on the modern-style rooms (with TVs and phones with modem hookups) at Wuksachi. The plans for the 15,000-square-ft main lodge include a sit-down restaurant where standard American cuisine will be served, a registration area, and meeting rooms. The facility is scheduled to open by summer 1999. ☎ *559/641–6354. 102 rooms. Restaurant, bar, in-room modems, hiking, meeting rooms. D, MC, V.*

⚠ **Lodgepole Campground.** The largest of the campgrounds in the Lodgepole area is also the noisiest, though even here things quiet down at night. Pay showers are nearby. Lodgepole and Dorst (a mile or so to the west) are the two campgrounds within Sequoia where reservations are accepted (up to five months in advance for stays between mid-

May and mid-October). ✉ *Off Generals Hwy.,* ☎ *559/565–3341, ext.*
2, for camping information; 800/365–2267 for reservations for stays
between mid-May–mid-Oct. Fire rings, flush toilets, disposal station
(summer only), water. 🖭 *$14.* ☉ *Year-round.*

Outdoor Activities and Sports
Wolverton (☎ 559/565–3435) has a cross-country ski center (rentals
are available) and marked trails.

Giant Forest

❷ *4 mi south of Lodgepole on the Generals Hwy.*

The Giant Forest is known for its trails through a series of sequoia groves.
You can get the best views of the big trees from the park's meadows,
where flowers are in full bloom by July. **Round Meadow,** which has a
⅓-mi, wheelchair-accessible "Trail for All People," is easiest to reach.
John Muir called **Crescent Meadow** the "gem of the Sierra"—brilliant
wildflowers bloom here in midsummer. A 2-mi trail that begins at Crescent Meadow leads to **Tharp's Log,** named for Hale Tharp, who built
a pioneer cabin (still standing) onto the end of a fallen sequoia.

The most famous tree in the area is the **General Sherman Tree,** off the
Generals Highway between Giant Forest and Lodgepole. In summer
there is usually a ranger nearby to answer questions, and there are
benches so you can sit and contemplate the tree's immensity: It is
274.9 ft tall and 102.6 ft around at its base. The first major branch is
130 ft above the ground.

The **Congress Trail** starts at the General Sherman Tree and travels past
large trees and younger sequoias. This is the most popular hike in the
area, and it also has the most detailed booklet, so it is a good way to
learn about the ecology of the groves. The booklet, which costs 75¢,
is available in summer at racks near the General Sherman Tree.

The **Moro Rock–Crescent Meadow Road** is a 3-mi spur road that begins at Giant Forest Village and explores the southwest portion of the
village's sequoia grove and intersects the trials to Crescent and Log meadows. The road passes through the Tunnel Log (there is a bypass for
RVs that are too tall—7 ft, 9 inches and more—to fit). Auto Log is a
fallen tree onto which you can drive your car for a photograph.

★ ❷ **Moro Rock,** a granite monolith, rises 6,725 ft from the edge of the Giant
Forest. Four hundred steps lead to the top; the trail often climbs along
narrow ledges over steep drops. The view from the top is striking. To
the southwest you look down the Kaweah River to Three Rivers, Lake
Kaweah, and—on clear days—the Central Valley and the Coast Range.
To the northeast you look up into the High Sierra. Below, you look
thousands of feet to the middle fork of the Kaweah River.

★ ❷ **Crystal Cave** is the best known of Sequoia's many caves. Its interior,
which was formed from limestone that metamorphosed into marble,
is decorated with stalactites and stalagmites of various shapes, sizes,
and colors. To visit the cave, you must first stop at the Lodgepole Visitor Center (☞ *above*) or the Foothills Visitor Center at Ash Mountain (on the Generals Highway, 1 mi inside Sequoia National Park) to
buy a ticket—they're not sold at the cave. Drive to the end of a narrow, twisting, 7-mi road off the Generals Highway, 2.2 mi south of
Giant Forest Village. From the parking area it is a 15-minute hike down
a steep path to the cave's entrance. It's cool inside—48°F—so bring a
sweater. ☎ *559/565–3759.* 🖭 *$5.* ☉ *Guided tours (45 min) mid-June–*
Labor Day, daily 11–4 on the half hr; mid-May–mid-June and Labor
Day–Sept., Fri.–Mon. 11–4 on the hr; closed rest of yr.

Mineral King

㉕ *52 mi south of Lodgepole on the Generals Hwy. and Mineral King Rd.*

The Mineral King area was incorporated into Sequoia National Park in 1978. It is accessible in summer only by a narrow, twisting, steep road (trailers and RVs are prohibited) off Highway 198 several miles outside the park entrance. This is a tough but exciting 25-mi drive (budget 90 minutes each way) to an alpine valley. There are two campgrounds and a ranger station here; facilities are limited, but some supplies are available. Many backpackers use this as a trailhead; fine day-hiking trails lead from here as well.

Kings Canyon and Sequoia National Parks A to Z

Arriving and Departing

BY BUS

Greyhound (☎ 800/231–2222) serves Fresno and Visalia.

BY CAR

Under average conditions, it takes about six hours to reach Kings Canyon and Sequoia national parks from San Francisco and about five hours from Los Angeles. Two major routes, Highways 180 and 198, intersect with Highway 99, which runs north–south through the San Joaquin Valley.

From the north, enter Kings Canyon via Highway 180, 53 mi east of Fresno. From the south, enter Sequoia via Highway 198, 36 mi from Visalia. If you are coming from Los Angeles, take Highway 65 north from Bakersfield to Highway 198 east of Visalia.

BY PLANE

Fresno Air Terminal (✉ 5175 Clinton Way, ☎ 559/498–4095) is the nearest major airport to Kings Canyon and Sequoia national parks. *See* Arriving and Departing *in* Yosemite National Park, *above,* for more information.

Getting Around

BY BUS

Delaware North Park Services at Sequoia (☎ 559/641–6354) runs a free shuttle bus between major points in the Giant Forest and Lodgepole.

BY CAR

Try to fill up your gas tank before you arrive. Buying gas in the parks is difficult, though there are stations 10 mi from Grant Grove at Hume Lake Christian Camp and 15 mi from the Grove at King's Canyon Lodge. Emergency gas is sold at the park markets.

Most people take Highway 180 to Kings Canyon–Sequoia, coming into Kings Canyon National Park at the Big Stump Entrance. Highways 180 and 198 are connected by the Generals Highway, a paved two-lane road that is open year-round, though portions between Lodgepole and Grant Grove may be closed for weeks at a time following heavy snowstorms (carry chains in winter). Drivers of RVs over 22 ft in length and those who are not comfortable driving on mountain roads should avoid the twisting, narrow, 16 mi southern stretch between the Potwisha Campground and Giant Forest Village. The rest of the Generals Highway is a well-graded two-lane road and a pleasure to drive.

Highway 180 (called Kings Canyon Highway inside the park) beyond Grant Grove to Cedar Grove is open only in summer, as is the road to Mineral King. Both roads may present a challenge to inexperienced drivers. Large vehicles are discouraged. Campers and RVs are not permitted on the Mineral King road. Trailers are not allowed in Mineral King campgrounds.

Contacts and Resources

CAMPING

Campgrounds near each of the major tourist centers in Kings Canyon and Sequoia parks are equipped with tables, fire grills, garbage cans, and either flush or pit toilets. All the sites have drinking water, but you may want to bring your own water, especially during off-season when taps can freeze. Except for Lodgepole and Dorst in Sequoia, all sites in the two parks are assigned on a first-come, first-served basis; on weekends in July and August they are often filled by Friday afternoon. *See* Reservations, *below,* for contact numbers.

RVs and trailers are permitted in most of the campgrounds, though space is scarce at some. The length limit is 40 ft for RVs and 35 ft for trailers, but the park service recommends that trailers be no longer than 22 ft. Disposal stations are available in most of the main camping areas. Lodgepole, Potwisha, and Azalea campsites stay open all year, but Lodgepole is not plowed and camping is limited to snow tenting or recreational vehicles in plowed parking lots. Other campgrounds are open from whenever the snow melts until late September or early October. Use the bear-proof food-storage containers that are provided.

EMERGENCIES

Ambulance (☎ 911). **Fire** (☎ 911). **Police** (☎ 911).

GUIDED TOURS

From mid-May to mid-October **Sequoia–Kings Canyon Park Services Company** (☎ 559/335–5500) conducts an all-day van tour (about $70) of Grant Grove, Cedar Grove, and other sights.

RESERVATIONS

Lodgepole/Dorst campgrounds: (☎ 800/365–2267). **Other campgrounds:** (☎ 559/565–3134).

Kings Canyon Lodging: (☎ 559/335–5500). **Sequoia Lodging:** (☎ 559/641–6354).

ROAD CONDITIONS

Sequoia–Kings Canyon Road and Weather Information (☎ 559/565–3351).

Northern California Road Conditions (☎ 800/427–7623).

VISITOR INFORMATION

National Park Service (✉ Fort Mason, Bldg. 201, San Francisco 94123, ☎ 415/556–0560). **Sequoia and Kings Canyon National Parks** (✉ Three Rivers 93271, ☎ 559/565–3134).

9 The San Joaquin Valley

From Stockton to Bakersfield

The San Joaquin Valley, one of the world's most fertile agricultural zones, is California's heartland. This sun-baked region contains a wealth of rivers, lakes, and waterways; the water, in turn, nurtures vineyards, dairy farms, orchards, fields, and pastures that stretch to the horizon. Cities, mountains, and national parks are just beyond the Valley, but you'll find that the area possesses attractions of its own, beginning with the warmth of its land and people.

By Clark
Norton

Updated by
Andy Moore

UNTIL THE MID-19TH CENTURY the San Joaquin Valley was a phenomenon waiting to happen. Millions of acres of flat, often parched land lay in wait for workers and water. When settlers and irrigation techniques did arrive, the region was transformed into a miracle of cultivation. Gold discoveries, starting in the 1850s, sparked the birth of some towns; the coming of the railroads in the next few decades spurred the development of others. During the past century and a half the Valley's open lands and untapped resources have attracted a polyglot of pioneers, adventurers, farmers, ranchers, developers, railroad tycoons, gold prospectors, oil riggers, dairymen, sheepherders, and war refugees—including immigrants from places as diverse as Oklahoma and Portugal, China and Mexico, Armenia and Laos.

The mix has produced sometimes volatile labor relations—most prominently in Cesar Chavez's United Farm Workers Union's controversial grape boycotts of the 1960s and '70s—and social strife: early battles between railroad men and farmers, long-standing discrimination against Chinese and other Asians. But the region's diversity has also created a vibrant social fabric that has been chronicled by some of the country's finest writers. Fresno native and Pulitzer Prize winner William Saroyan, Stockton native Maxine Hong Kingston, 19th-century novelist Frank Norris, and *Grapes of Wrath* author John Steinbeck have all contributed to the Valley's literary heritage.

Though the Valley's agricultural riches remain, potential changes whirl like dust devils in the fields. Modesto, Fresno, and Bakersfield are among the fastest growing cities in the country, as big-city dwellers arrive in search of cheaper real estate and more space. With development has come unsightly sprawl, traffic jams, air pollution, and pressure on crucial water supplies, all of which threatens to overwhelm the Valley's traditional charms.

For most travelers the Valley is primarily a place to pass through en route to Yosemite, Sequoia, and Kings Canyon national parks or while driving between San Francisco and Los Angeles. But if you spend a few hours or days here, you'll discover historic mansions, abundant outdoor recreation, and friendly people proud of their local treasures.

Pleasures and Pastimes

Dining
Fast-food places and chain restaurants dominate Valley highways and major intersections, but off the main drag the possibilities increase. Armenian, Basque, and Vietnamese restaurants—along with more common Mexican, Chinese, and Italian eateries—reflect the Valley's ethnic mix. A few cutting-edge bistros serve the type of California cuisine found in San Francisco and Los Angeles. And why not? The Valley produces many of those ingredients.

CATEGORY	COST*
$$$$	over $50
$$$	$30–$50
$$	$20–$30
$	under $20

per person for a three-course meal, excluding drinks, service, and 7¼% tax

Festivals, Tours, and Tastings
Anyone who likes to eat can enjoy an agricultural theme trip through the San Joaquin Valley. Apple ranches and almond, cheese, and choco-

late factories are among the many options. Watch for seasonal farmers' markets; some towns block off entire streets and turn the weekly markets into minifestivals. Official Valley festivals celebrate everything from the asparagus and raisin crops to residents' Chinese, Greek, Swedish, and Tahitian roots. If you know you'll be visiting a particular town, especially in the fall, call the local chamber of commerce (☞ Visitor Information *in* the San Joaquin Valley A to Z, *below*) for festival information.

Lodging

Chain motels and hotels are the norm in the San Joaquin Valley. Most are utilitarian but perfectly clean and comfortable, and prices tend to be considerably lower than those in more touristy destinations. A few Victorian-style bed-and-breakfasts, some of them great values, also operate here.

CATEGORY	COST*
$$$$	over $175
$$$	$120–$175
$$	$80–$120
$	under $80

All prices are for a standard double room, excluding 8% tax.

Outdoor Activities and Sports

Several cities and towns serve as convenient starting points for whitewater rafting trips on the Stanislaus, Merced, Kings, and Kern rivers. Fishing is another favored activity in the rivers and lakes; the lakes are also prime spots for boating and windsurfing. Stockton is a popular rental area for houseboating on the Sacramento Delta, and Bakersfield is a center for stock car racing. Wildlife refuges provide opportunities for watching birds and other animals.

Exploring the San Joaquin Valley

The 225-mi San Joaquin Valley cuts through San Joaquin, Stanislaus, Merced, Madera, Fresno, Kings, Tulare, and Kern counties, and is bounded by the mighty Sierra Nevada to the east and the smaller coastal ranges to the west. Besides the San Joaquin, other rivers include the Stanislaus, Tuolumne, Fresno, and Kern; an elaborate system of sloughs and canals also provides water to the countryside. Interstate 5 runs north–south through the Valley, as does Highway 99.

Numbers in the text correspond to numbers in the margin and on the San Joaquin Valley and Fresno Area maps.

Great Itineraries

IF YOU HAVE 1 DAY

Touring the Fresno area is a good strategy if you only have a day to spend in the Valley. Within the **Chaffee Zoological Gardens** in **Roeding Park** ⑦ is a striking tropical rain forest; **Playland** and **Storyland** are great stops if you have children. The **Forestiere Underground Gardens** ⑥ on Shaw Avenue is not to be missed if it's open. In springtime take the self-guided **Blossom Trail** driving tour through orchards, vineyards, and fields. Along the trail in **Reedley** is the **Mennonite Quilt Center.** Depending on your mood and the weather, you can spend part of the afternoon at **Wild Water Adventures** or visit the **Fresno Metropolitan Museum,** whose highlights include an exhibit about author William Saroyan.

IF YOU HAVE 3 DAYS

On your first morning, visit the ⬚ **Stockton** area. Start at the **Micke Grove Park** ①, 10 mi north of the city off Highway 99. The art-filled

The San Joaquin Valley

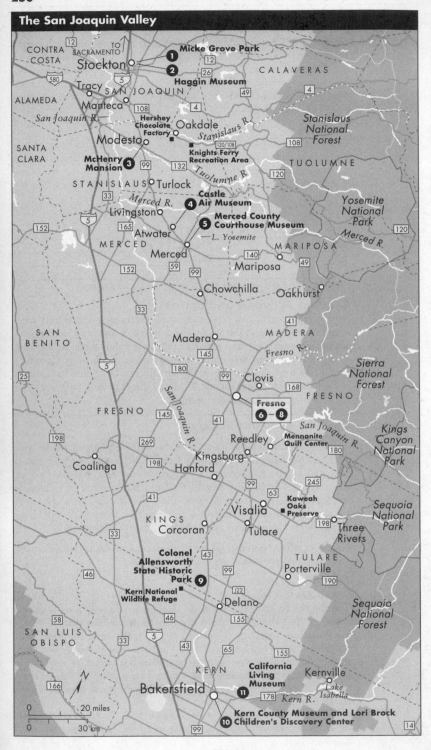

CONTRA COSTA

TO SACRAMENTO

Stockton

1 **Micke Grove Park**

2 **Haggin Museum**

CALAVERAS

Tracy

San Joaquin

ALAMEDA

Manteca

San Joaquin R.

Hershey Chocolate Factory

Oakdale

Stanislaus R.

Stanislaus National Forest

SANTA CLARA

Modesto

Knights Ferry Recreation Area

TUOLUMNE

McHenry Mansion **3**

STANISLAUS

Turlock

Tuolumne R.

Yosemite National Park

Merced R.

Livingston

Castle Air Museum **4**

5 **Merced County Courthouse Museum**

MARIPOSA

Merced R.

Atwater

L. Yosemite

MERCED

Merced

Mariposa

Chowchilla

Oakhurst

SAN BENITO

Madera

MADERA

Fresno R.

Sierra National Forest

Clovis

FRESNO

Fresno **6** – **8**

FRESNO

San Joaquin R.

Reedley

Mennonite Quilt Center

Kings Canyon National Park

Coalinga

Kingsburg

Hanford

KINGS

Corcoran

Visalia

Kaweah Oaks Preserve

Tulare

Three Rivers

Sequoia National Park

Colonel Allensworth State Historic Park **9**

Kern National Wildlife Refuge

TULARE

Porterville

Delano

Sequoia National Forest

SAN LUIS OBISPO

KERN

California Living Museum **11**

Bakersfield

Kernville

Lake Isabella

Kern R.

0   20 miles

0   30 km

10 **Kern County Museum and Lori Brock Children's Discovery Center**

Haggin Museum ② and the **World Wildlife Museum** are both in Stockton proper. The next morning, stop off at the **Castle Air Museum** ④ north of Merced in Atwater or proceed directly to ⊞ **Fresno** ⑥–⑧. In the evening take in a show at **Roger Rocka's** or the **Tower Theatre,** both in Fresno's Tower District. On the third morning, drive to **Hanford** via Highways 99 and 43 and stroll around **Courthouse Square** and **China Alley.** After lunch continue south on Highway 43 to **Colonel Allensworth State Historic Park** ⑨, which is on the site of a now deserted town founded by African Americans in 1908. Head south on Highway 43 and east on Highway 46 to return to Highway 99, which continues south to ⊞ **Bakersfield.** If you arrive before it closes, stop in for a quick visit to the **Kern County Museum** ⑩.

When to Visit the San Joaquin Valley

Spring, when wildflowers are in bloom and the scent of fruit blossoms is in the air, and fall, when leaves turn red and gold, are the prettiest times to visit. Many of the Valley's top festivals take place during these seasons. Summertime, when temperatures often top 100°F, can be oppressive. Wintertime can get cold and raw—with thick, ground-hugging tule fog a common driving hazard—and some attractions close.

NORTH SAN JOAQUIN VALLEY

The northern section of the Valley cuts through San Joaquin, Stanislaus, and Merced counties, from the edges of the Sacramento Delta and the fringes of the Gold Country south to the flat, almost featureless terrain between Modesto and Merced. If you're heading to Yosemite National Park from northern California, chances are you'll pass through (or very near) at least one of these gateway cities.

Stockton Area

80 mi from San Francisco, east on I–80 to I–580 to I–205 and north on I–5; 45 mi south of Sacramento on I–5 or Hwy. 99.

California's first inland port—connected since 1933 to San Francisco via a 60-mi-long deepwater channel—is wedged between I–5 and Highway 99, on the eastern end of the great Sacramento River Delta. Stockton, founded during the gold rush as a way station for miners traveling from San Francisco to the Mother Lode and now a city of 228,000, helps distribute the Valley's agricultural products to the world. Its best-known natives include author Maxine Hong Kingston and rock singer Chris Isaak. If you're here in late April, don't miss the **Stockton Asparagus Festival** (☎ 209/943–1987).

🐾 ❶ Among the attractions at oak-shaded **Micke Grove Park,** halfway between Stockton and Lodi, are a zoo (☞ *below*) and an agricultural museum. ⊠ *11793 N. Micke Grove Rd.; take Eight Mile Rd. off Hwy. 99, 8 mi north of Stockton, then go ½ mi west to Micke Grove Rd., Lodi,* ☎ *209/331–7400.* ⊡ *Park entry fee $2 weekdays, $4 weekends and holidays.* ⊙ *Park daily 8 AM–sunset.*

Ring-tailed lemurs and other endangered primates found only on the African island of Madagascar inhabit the An Island Lost in Time exhibit at the **Micke Grove Zoo.** Mountain lions have the run of Paseo Pantera, another highlight of this compact facility. ⊠ *Micke Grove Park,* ☎ *209/331–7270.* ⊡ *$1.50.* ⊙ *May–Aug., Mon.–Fri. 10–5, Sat.–Sun. 10–7; Sept.–Apr., daily 10–5.*

The rides and other diversions at **Funderwoods** (⊠ Micke Grove Park, ☎ 209/369–5437), a family-oriented amusement park (days and hours vary), are geared to children under 10. Ride tickets cost $1 (10 for $8).

★ ❷   The **Haggin Museum** in pretty Victory Park has one of the San Joaquin Valley's finest art collections. Late-19th-century American and French paintings—landscapes by Albert Bierstadt and Thomas Moran, a still life by Paul Gauguin—are among the highlights, supplemented by antiquities that include an Egyptian mummy. You can bone up on local history here, too. ⊠ *1201 N. Pershing Ave.,* ☎ *209/462–4116.* 🖙 *Free; suggested donation $2.* ۝ *Tues.–Sun. 1:30–5.*

🖰   The **World Wildlife Museum,** which claims to have the largest collection of mounted zoological specimens—more than 2,000—is aimed primarily at school groups but is open to the public. Two cavernous rooms are a testament to taxidermy: Displays include Alaska Yukon moose, Indian black bears, Russian wild boars, African bongos, and South American jaguars. At the Sheep Mountain Bighorns, you'll find ibexes, mountain goats, and rare argalis and golden takins. ⊠ *1245 W. Weber Ave.,* ☎ *209/465–2834.* 🖙 *$4.* ۝ *Wed.–Sun. 9–5.*

Dining and Lodging

$$$–$$$$ ✕ **Le Bistro.** The dishes at one of the Valley's most upscale restaurants are fairly standard Continental fare—lamb loin, filet of sole, sautéed prawns, soufflé Grand Marnier—but you can count on high-quality ingredients and presentation with a flourish. ⊠ *Marina Center Mall, 3121 W. Benjamin Holt Dr. (off I–5; behind Lyon's),* ☎ *209/951–0885. AE, D, DC, MC, V.*

$–$$ ✕ **On Lock Sam.** Run by the same family since 1898, this Stockton landmark is in a modern pagoda-style building, with framed Chinese prints on the walls, a garden outside one window, and a sparkling bar area. One touch of old-time Chinatown remains: A few booths have curtains that can be drawn for complete privacy. The Cantonese food would be ho-hum in San Francisco, but it's among the Valley's best. ⊠ *333 S. Sutter St.,* ☎ *209/466–4561. AE, D, MC, V.*

$$ 🏨 **Best Western Stockton Inn.** Four mi from downtown, this good-size motel has a convenient location off Highway 99. A big plus here on hot days is the large central courtyard with a pool and lounge chairs. Most rooms are spacious; free in-room movies are provided by satellite. ⊠ *4219 Waterloo Rd., 95215,* ☎ *209/931–3131,* FAX *209/931– 0423. 141 rooms. Restaurant, bar, no-smoking rooms, pool, wading pool, hot tub, laundry service, meeting rooms. AE, D, DC, MC, V.*

$ 🏨 **City Center Days Inn.** If you want to stay near Stockton's waterfront, this is a good budget choice. Rooms are decent size, and the rates include cable TV with free HBO. The motel is at a busy intersection; the smallish outdoor pool area can get noisy. ⊠ *33 N. Center St., 95202,* ☎ *209/948–6151,* FAX *209/948–1220. 95 rooms. No-smoking rooms, pool, meeting rooms. Continental breakfast. AE, D, MC, V.*

Outdoor Activities and Sports

Several companies rent houseboats (of various sizes, usually for three, four, or seven days) on the Delta waterways near Stockton. Call the **Delta Rental Houseboat Hotline** (☎ 209/477–1840), or try **Herman & Helen's** (⊠ Venice Island Ferry, ☎ 209/951–4634), **King Island Resort** (⊠ 11530 W. Eight Mile Rd., ☎ 209/951–2188), or **Paradise Point Marina** (⊠ 8095 Rio Blanco Rd., ☎ 209/952–1000).

En Route   Manteca, population 45,000, is the largest town between Stockton and Modesto. The top attraction is the **Manteca Waterslides at Oakwood Lake** (⊠ 874 E. Woodward Ave., between I–5 and Hwy. 99, ☎ 209/ 239–2500). The park has a children's area, and the attached resort has a lake, a campground (open all year), and picnic grounds. The water park is open from May to September (daily from Memorial Day to Labor Day, weekends the rest of May and September); call for hours.

Modesto

29 mi south of Stockton on Hwy. 99.

Modesto, a gateway to Yosemite and the southern reaches of the Gold Country, was founded in 1870 to serve the Central Pacific Railroad. The frontier town was originally named Ralston, after a railroad baron, but as the story goes he modestly declined—thus "Modesto." The Stanislaus County seat, a tree-lined city of 190,000, is perhaps best known as the site of the annual Modesto Invitational Track Meet and Relays and birthplace of film producer-director George Lucas, creator of *Star Wars* and *American Graffiti.* (Cruise 10th Street between G and K streets to relive the *Graffiti* days.)

The **Modesto Arch** (⊠ 9th and I Sts.), bears Modesto's motto: "Water, Wealth, Contentment, Health." Modesto holds a well-attended **International Festival** (☎ 209/521–3852) in early October that celebrates the cultures, crafts, and cuisines of many nationalities. The **Blue Diamond Growers Store** (⊠ 4800 Sisk Rd., ☎ 209/545–3222) shows a film about almond-growing and sells nuts in many flavors.

★ ❸ A wheat farmer and banker built the 1883 **McHenry Mansion,** the city's sole surviving original Victorian home. The Italianate-style mansion has been decorated to reflect Modesto life in the late 19th century. Oaks, elms, magnolias, redwoods, and palms shade the grounds. ⊠ *15th and I Sts.,* ☎ *209/577–5341.* ⊡ *Free.* ☺ *Jan.–mid-Nov. and Dec., Sun.–Thurs. 1–4, Fri. noon–3. Closed last 2 wks of Nov.*

The **McHenry Museum** is a jumbled repository of early Modesto and Stanislaus County memorabilia, including re-creations of an old-time barbershop, a doctor's office, a blacksmith's shop, and a general store—the latter stocked with goods from hair crimpers to corsets. ⊠ *1402 I St.,* ☎ *209/577–5366.* ⊡ *Free.* ☺ *Tues.–Sun. noon–4.*

Dining and Lodging

$–$$$ ✕ **Early Dawn Cattlemen's Steakhouse and Saloon.** The parking lots overflow at this local hangout, and so do the platters bearing barbecued steaks two pounds and even heavier. The whiskey-marinated saloon steak is a house specialty; chicken and seafood are among the lighter choices. ⊠ *1000 Kansas Ave.,* ☎ *209/577–5833. AE, D, MC, V. No lunch Sat.*

$–$$ ✕ **Hazel's Elegant Dining.** Hazel's is the special-occasion restaurant in Modesto. The seven-course dinners include Continental entrées served with soup, salad, pasta, dessert, and beverage. Members of the Gallo family, who own much vineyard land in the San Joaquin Valley, eat here often, perhaps because the wine cellar is so comprehensive. ⊠ *431 12th St.,* ☎ *209/578–3463. AE, D, DC, MC, V. Closed Sun.–Mon. No lunch Sat.*

$–$$ ✕ **Modesto Stanislaus Firehouse Pub & Grille.** Down the block from the McHenry Mansion, this casual restaurant serves up good soups, sandwiches, and salads, along with more hearty fare like baby back ribs and beef kabobs. The gutsy starters—garlic fries, buffalo wings, and onion rings—and other pub food go well with the 117 beers the bar serves. ⊠ *924 15th St.,* ☎ *209/575–3473. AE, MC, V. Closed Sun.*

$–$$ ⊞ **Best Western Mallard's Inn.** The duck decor is, thankfully, unobtrusive at this nicely landscaped motel off Highway 99. The comfortably furnished rooms are large and all have coffeemakers; some rooms have microwaves and refrigerators stocked with milk and cookies. ⊠ *1720 Sisk Rd., 95350,* ☎ *209/577–3825 or 800/294–4040,* ℻ *209/577–1717. 126 rooms and suites. Restaurant, no-smoking rooms, room service, pool, hot tub, laundry service, business services, meeting rooms. AE, D, DC, MC, V.*

$–$$ ▣ **Doubletree Hotel.** Modesto's largest lodging towers 15 stories over downtown; the convention center is adjacent, and a good brew pub, St. Stan's, is across the street. The rooms have coffeemakers, irons, desks, and three phones. ⊠ *1150 9th St., 95354,* ☎ *209/526–6000,* 𝖥𝖠𝖷 *209/ 526–6096. 258 rooms. Restaurant, café, bar, no-smoking rooms, room service, pool, hot tub, sauna, exercise room, nightclub, laundry service, meeting rooms, airport shuttle. AE, D, DC, MC, V.*

Oakdale

15 mi east of Modesto on Hwy. 108.

Oakdale, a bit off the beaten path from Modesto, has two year-round attractions of great interest to children. And if you're here in mid-May, check out the **Oakdale Chocolate Festival** (☎ 209/847–2244).

Ⅾ The only **Hershey Chocolate Factory** in the country that allows the public to tour its production facilities plays Willy Wonka to a host of chocolate lovers. After the half-hour guided walking tours—which cover the chocolate-making process from cocoa bean to candy bar—everyone gets a sample. ⊠ *120 S. Sierra Ave.,* ☎ *209/848–8126.* ▱ *Free.* ☉ *Weekday tours 8:30–3, visitor center weekdays 8:30–5.*

Ⅾ The featured attraction at the **Knights Ferry Recreation Area** is the 355-ft-long Knights Ferry covered bridge. Built in 1863, the bridge (closed to motor vehicles) crosses the Stanislaus River near the ruins of an old grist mill. The park has picnic and barbecue areas along the river banks. Fishing, hiking, rafting, and canoeing are among the activities here. ⊠ *Corps of Engineers Park, 18020 Sonora Rd., Knights Ferry; 12 mi east of Oakdale via Hwy. 108,* ☎ *209/881–3517.* ▱ *Free.* ☉ *Mon.–Fri. 8–noon and 1–4; Sat.–Sun. 10–2.*

You can sample the wares at **Oakdale Cheese & Specialties** (⊠ 10040 Hwy. 120, ☎ 209/848–3139), which has tastings and cheese-making tours. There's a picnic area next to a pond.

Merced and Atwater

38 mi south of Modesto (to Merced) on Hwy. 99; 53 mi from Oakdale, west and then south on Hwy. 108 and south on Hwy. 99.

Merced, population 56,000, is a common stopover en route to Yosemite National Park. The town of Atwater is 6 mi north of Merced on Highway 99.

Ⅾ ❹ At the outdoor **Castle Air Museum,** adjacent to the former Castle Air Force Base (now Castle Aviation, an industrial park) you can stroll among fighter planes and other historic military aircraft. The 44 restored vintage war birds include the B-25 Mitchell medium-range bomber (best known for the "Jimmy Doolittle raid" on Tokyo following the attack on Pearl Harbor) and the speedy SR-71 Blackbird, used for reconnaissance over Vietnam and Libya. ⊠ *Santa Fe Dr. and Buhach Rd. (take the Buhach Rd. exit off Hwy. 99 in Atwater and follow signs), Atwater,* ☎ *209/723–2178.* ▱ *$5.* ☉ *Memorial Day–Sept., daily 9– 5; Oct.–Memorial Day, daily 10–4.*

❺ Even if you don't go inside, be sure to swing by the **Merced County Courthouse Museum.** The three-story former courthouse, built in 1875, is a striking example of the Victorian Italianate style. The upper two floors are now a museum of early Merced history. Highlights include an 1870 Chinese temple with carved redwood altars, and an ornate restored courtroom. ⊠ *21st and N Sts., Merced,* ☎ *209/723–2401.* ▱ *Free.* ☉ *Wed.–Sun. 1–4.*

The **Merced Multicultural Arts Center** displays paintings, sculpture, and photography. Threads: A Tapestry of Cultures, a festival that celebrates the area's ethnic diversity, is held here on a mid-October weekend. ⊠ *645 W. Main St., Merced,* ☎ *209/388–1090.* 🎟 *Free.* ☉ *Weekdays 9–5, Sat. 10–2.*

Dining and Lodging

$$–$$$ ✕ **Sir James.** Merced's most earnestly upscale restaurant—low lighting, rose-colored linens, complimentary sorbet between courses—is still casual enough to attract a local jeans-and-flannel crowd. Prime rib, steak, and filet mignon are the staples here, but the seafood (including a fine mixed grill) is fresh and well prepared. ⊠ *1111 Motel Dr.,* ☎ *209/723–5551. AE, D, DC, MC, V. Closed Sun. No lunch.*

$ ✕ **Main Street Cafe.** This bright downtown café dishes up soups, salads, sandwiches, pastries, ice cream, and espresso. Sandwiches (try the chicken breast with pesto mayonnaise on Francesi bread) are served with tasty side salads. ⊠ *460 W. Main St.,* ☎ *209/725–1702. Closed Sun. No dinner. AE, MC, V.*

$ 🏨 **Days Inn.** The compact rooms here manage to pack in an impressive array of amenities: a writing table, a refrigerator, a microwave, an AM/FM radio, a coffeemaker, a bathroom phone, a safe, and a 27-inch TV with cable and a VCR (tapes are for rent in lobby). ⊠ *1199 Motel Dr., near the intersection of Hwys. 99 and 140, 95340,* ☎ *209/722–2726,* 𝖥𝖠𝖷 *209/722–7083. 24 rooms. No-smoking rooms, refrigerators, in-room VCRs, pool. AE, D, DC, MC, V.*

Outdoor Activities and Sports

At **Lake Yosemite Regional Park** (⊠ N. Lake Rd., off Yosemite Ave., 5 mi northeast of Merced, ☎ 209/385–7426), you can boat, swim, windsurf, waterski, and fish on a 387-acre reservoir. Boat rentals and picnic areas are available.

MID–SAN JOAQUIN VALLEY

Fresno, Hanford, and Visalia

The mid–San Joaquin Valley extends over three counties—Fresno, Kings, and Tulare. From Fresno, Highway 41 leads north 95 mi to Yosemite and Highway 180 snakes east 55 mi to Kings Canyon (Sequoia National Park is 30 mi farther). From Visalia, Highway 198 winds east 35 mi to the Generals Highway, which leads into Sequoia and Kings Canyon. Historic Hanford, about 16 mi west of Visalia along Highway 198, is a gem of a town.

Fresno

50 mi south of Merced on Hwy. 99; 110 mi north of Bakersfield on Hwy. 99.

Sprawling Fresno, with nearly 400,000 people, is the center of the richest agricultural county in America; grapes, cotton, oranges, and turkeys are among the major products. The city's most famous native, Pulitzer Prize–winning playwright and novelist William Saroyan (*The Time of Your Life, The Human Comedy*), was born here in 1908. The seemingly endless parade of strip malls and fast-food joints can be depressing, but local character does lurk beneath the commercialization. The city is home to 75 ethnic communities (from Armenian to Vietnamese), a burgeoning arts scene, and several public parks.

Woodward Park, 300 acres of jogging trails, picnic areas, and playgrounds in the northern reaches of the city, is especially pretty in the

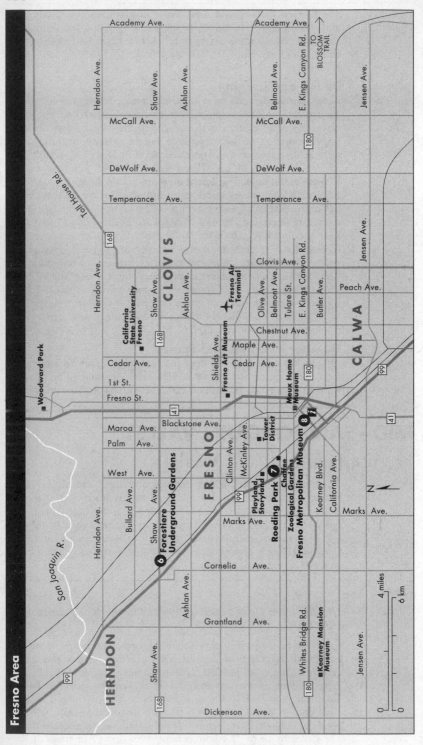

Fresno Area

spring—when plum and cherry trees, magnolias, and camellias bloom—
and the fall, when leaves burst into riots of color. Big-band concerts
take place in summer. Well worth a look is the **Shin Zen Japanese Friendship Garden**, which has a teahouse, a koi pond, arched bridges, a waterfall, and lakes. ⊠ *Audubon Dr. and Friant Rd.*, ☎ *559/498–1551.*
⊡ *Park $2 per car; garden $1 per person.* ⊙ *Mar.–Oct., daily 7 AM–
10 PM; Nov.–Dec., daily 7–5, Jan.–Feb., daily 7–7.*

★ ⓒ ➏ Sicilian immigrant Baldasare Forestiere spent four decades (1906–
1946) carving out the **Forestiere Underground Gardens,** a subter-
ranean realm of rooms, tunnels, grottoes, alcoves, and arched
passageways that extends for more than 10 acres beneath busy, mall-
pocked Shaw Avenue. Only a fraction of Forestiere's prodigious output is on view, but you can tour his underground living quarters,
including bedrooms (one with a fireplace), the kitchen, the living room,
the bath, a fish pond, and an aquarium. Skylights allow exotic, full-
grown fruit trees—including one that through grafting is able to bear
seven kinds of citrus—to flourish as far as 22 ft below ground. ⊠ *5021
W. Shaw Ave., 2 blocks east of Hwy. 99 , ☎ 559/271–0734. ⊡ $6.
Reservations essential.* ⊙ *Memorial Day–Labor Day, Wed.–Sun. 10–
4 (tours at 10, 12, 2, and 4); Easter–Memorial Day and Labor Day–
Thanksgiving (weather permitting; tour hrs vary), weekends noon–3.*

★ ⓒ ➐ Tree-shaded **Roeding Park,** Fresno's largest park, has picnic areas,
playgrounds, tennis courts, and a zoo (☞ *below*). ⊠ *Olive and Belmont Aves.,* ☎ *559/498–4239.* ⊡ *Parking $1 (Feb.–Oct.)* ⊙ *Mar.–
Oct., daily 7 AM–10 PM; Oct.–Mar., daily 7–7.*

The most striking exhibit at **Chaffee Zoological Gardens** is the tropical rain forest, where exotic birds often greet visitors along the paths
and bridges. Elsewhere you'll find tigers, grizzly bears, sea lions, tule
elk, camels, elephants, and hooting siamangs. Also here are a high-tech
reptile house and a petting zoo. ⊠ *Roeding Park,* ☎ *559/498–2671,*
⊡ *$4.50.* ⊙ *Mar.–Oct., daily 9–5; Nov.–Feb., daily 10–4.*

ⓒ A minitrain, a Ferris wheel, a small roller coaster, and a merry-go-round
are among the amusements at **Playland** (⊠ Roeding Park, ☎ 559/486–
2124), which is open (days and hours vary) between February and
November. Kids can explore attractions with fairy-tale themes and at-
ⓒ tend puppet shows at **Storyland** (⊠ Roeding Park, ☎ 559/264–2235).
Storyland is open between February and November. The admission fee
is $2.75.

The drive along palm-lined Kearney Boulevard is one of the best reasons to visit the **Kearney Mansion Museum,** which stands in shaded
225-acre **Kearney Park**, 7 mi west of town. Guided 45-minute tours
take you through the century-old home of M. Theo Kearney, Fresno's
onetime "Raisin King." ⊠ *7160 W. Kearney Blvd.,* ☎ *559/441–0862.*
⊡ *$4 (park entrance $3, waived for museum visitors).* ⊙ *Museum Fri.–
Sun., tours at 1, 2, and 3.*

ⓒ ➑ The **Fresno Metropolitan Museum** mounts art, history, and hands-on
science exhibits, many of them quite innovative. The William Saroyan
History Gallery presents a riveting introduction in words and pictures
to the author's life and times. ⊠ *1555 Van Ness Ave.,* ☎ *559/441–
1444.* ⊡ *$4.* ⊙ *Tues.–Sun. 11–5.*

The **Fresno Art Museum** exhibits American, Mexican, and French art;
highlights of the permanent collection include pre-Columbian works
and graphic art from the post-Impressionist period. The 152-seat Bon-
ner Auditorium hosts lectures, films and concerts. ⊠ *Radio Park,
2233 N. 1st St.,* ☎ *559/441–4220.* ⊡ *$2; free Tues.* ⊙ *Tues.–Fri. 10–
5, weekends noon–5. Closed last 2 wks of Aug.*

The **Meux Home Museum,** inside a restored 1888 Victorian, displays furnishings and decor typical of early Fresno. Guided tours lead from the front parlor to the backyard carriage house. ⊠ *Tulare and R Sts.,* ☎ *559/233–8007.* 🎟 *$3.* ☉ *Feb.–Dec., Fri.–Sun. noon–4.*

OFF THE
BEATEN PATH

BLOSSOM TRAIL – This 62-mi self-guided driving tour takes in Fresno-area orchards, citrus groves, and vineyards during spring blossom season. Almond, plum, apple, orange, lemon, apricot, and peach blossoms shower the landscape with shades of white, pink, and red. (The most colorful and aromatic time to go is from late February to mid-March.) The route passes through several small towns and past rivers, lakes, and canals. The Fresno Convention & Visitors Bureau (⊠ 808 M St., 559/233-0836 or 800/788-0836) has route maps; directional and crop identification signs also mark the trail. Allow at least two to three hours for the tour.

Dining and Lodging

$$–$$$ ✕ **Giulia's Italian Trattoria.** The look here is light and airy, but the Abruzzi cuisine (from southern Italy's Adriatic coast) is hearty and intensely flavored. Bruschetta, steamed mussels, and polenta with grilled sausage are top choices, but also look for seasonal specials. The adjoining b.b.'s Oyster Bar & Grill serves sandwiches and seafood appetizers; many patrons have cocktails at b.b.'s before dining at Giulia's. ⊠ *Winepress Shopping Center, 3050 W. Shaw Ave.,* ☎ *559/276–3573. AE, D, DC, MC, V. Closed Sun. No lunch weekends.*

$ ✕ **Armenian Cuisine.** Local Armenians flock to this small restaurant for tasty lamb, beef, and chicken kabobs, which come with pita bread, eggplant salad, and stuffed grape leaves. ⊠ *742 W. Bullard St.,* ☎ *559/435–4892. AE, DC, MC, V. Closed Sun.*

$ ✕ **Kim's Vietnamese Restaurant.** You'll find good food at bargain prices at Kim's: Specialties include hot beef salad, sizzling chicken, and sautéed seafood with ginger. Multicourse lunches or dinners—from soup to dessert and tea, with salad, entrée, and rice in between—cost as low as $10. ⊠ *5048 N. Maroa St.,* ☎ *559/225–0406. MC, V. Closed Sun.*

$$ ⊞ **Piccadilly Inn Shaw.** This two-story property is attractively landscaped, with a big central swimming pool and a restaurant with an outdoor patio. The sizable rooms have king- and queen-size beds and coffeemakers; some rooms have refrigerators, microwaves, and fireplaces. ⊠ *2305 W. Shaw Ave., 93711,* ☎ *559/226–3850,* ℻ *559/226–2448. 188 rooms, 6 suites. Restaurant, no-smoking rooms, pool, hot tub, exercise room, coin laundry, laundry service, business services, meeting rooms. AE, D, DC, MC, V.*

$ ⊞ **La Quinta Inn.** Rooms are good-size at this three-story motel near downtown. Some have king-size beds, microwaves, and refrigerators. ⊠ *2926 Tulare St., 93721,* ☎ *559/442–1110,* ℻ *559/237–0415. 130 rooms. No-smoking rooms, room service, pool. Continental breakfast. AE, D, DC, MC, V.*

Nightlife and the Arts

The **Tower Theatre for the Performing Arts** (⊠ 815 E. Olive Ave., ☎ 559/485–9050), a onetime movie house that has given its name to the trendy Tower District of theaters, clubs, restaurants, and cafés, presents theatrical, ballet, classical, jazz, and other cultural events from spring to fall. **Roger Rocka's Music Hall** (⊠ 1226 N. Wishon Ave., ☎ 559/266–9494 or 800/371–4747), a dinner theater in the Tower District, stages six Broadway-style musicals or comedies a year. The **Fresno Philharmonic Orchestra** (☎ 559/261–0600) performs classical concerts (sometimes pops) on weekends, usually at the William Saroyan Theatre (⊠ 700 M St.), from September to June.

Outdoor Activities and Sports

Wild Water Adventures (⊠ 11413 E. Shaw Ave., Clovis, ☎ 559/299–9453 or 800/564–9453), a 50-acre water theme park east of Fresno, is open from late May to early September.

Shopping

Old Town Clovis (⊠ 5th and Pollasky Sts., Clovis) is an area of restored brick buildings and brick sidewalks, with numerous antiques shops and art galleries (along with restaurants and saloons). Head east on Fresno's Shaw Avenue to get to Clovis.

OFF THE
BEATEN PATH

MENNONITE QUILT CENTER – The colorful handiwork of local Mennonite quilters is on display here. Try to visit on Monday (except holidays), when two dozen or so quilters come in to stitch, patch, and chat over coffee. Prime viewing time—with the largest number of quilts—is in February and March, right before the center holds its early-April auction. Ask a docent to take you to the locked upstairs room, where most of the quilts are hung; she'll explain the fine points of patterns such as the Log Cabin Romance, the Dahlia, and the Snowball-Star. ⊠ *1012 G St. (take Manning Ave. exit off Hwy. 99 and head east 12 mi), Reedley;* ☎ *559/638–3560.* 🎟 *Free.* ⊙ *Weekdays 9:30–4:30, Sat. 10–2.*

Hanford

★ *35 mi from Fresno, south on Hwy. 99 and Hwy. 43.*

Founded in 1877 as a Southern Pacific Railroad stop, Hanford had one of California's largest Chinatowns—the Chinese came to help build the railroads and stayed to farm and open restaurants. You can take a self-guided walking tour or sign up in advance for guided tours ($2.50 per adult) arranged by the **Hanford Visitor Agency** (☎ 559/582–5024). One tour explores the restored historic buildings of Courthouse Square. Another heads to narrow China Alley, with stops at the town's Taoist Temple and other sights.

The **Hanford Carnegie Museum,** inside the former Carnegie Library, a Romanesque building dating from 1905, displays fashions, furnishings, toys, and military artifacts. ⊠ *109 E. 8th St.,* ☎ *559/584–1367.* 🎟 *$1.* ⊙ *Tues.–Fri. noon–3, Sat. noon–4.*

In the 1893 **Taoist Temple** a first-floor museum displays photos, furnishings, and kitchenware from Hanford's once-bustling Chinatown. The second-floor temple, largely unchanged for a century, contains altars, carvings, and ceremonial staves. You can visit as part of a guided walking tour (☞ *above)* or by calling the temple directly and making an appointment two weeks in advance. ⊠ *12 China Alley,* ☎ *559/582–4508.* 🎟 *Free; donations welcome.* ⊙ *By appointment only.*

Dining and Lodging

$–$$$ ✕ **Imperial Dynasty.** Despite its name and elegant teak-and-porcelain Chinese decor, Imperial Dynasty serves primarily French cuisine. For a memorable meal, start with the garlicky escargots and continue with the veal sweetbreads or rack of lamb. Avoid the overcooked, over-sauced seafood. The extensive wine list contains many prized vintages. ⊠ *China Alley (corner of 7th and Green Sts.),* ☎ *559/582–0196. AE, MC, V. Closed Mon. No lunch.*

$ ✕ **Justo's.** With a late-1880s decor (it's in Hanford's former Opera House), a sometimes rowdy bar, and family-style Basque cuisine, Justo's is one of the liveliest restaurants in town. Entrées include calamari steak and a Basque variation on fried chicken. The side dishes—soup, salads, beef tongue, stew, rice and beans—could make an entire meal. ⊠ *129 W. 7th St.,* ☎ *559/583–7713. MC, V. No lunch Sun.*

$$ ⌂ **Irwin Street Inn.** This bed-and-breakfast inn is one of the few lodg-
ings in the Valley that warrants a detour. Four tree-shaded, restored
Victorian homes have been converted into spacious, comfortable rooms
and suites. Most have antique armoires, dark wood detailing, leaded-
glass windows, and four-poster beds; bathrooms come with old-
fashioned tubs, brass fixtures, and marble basins. The inn's restaurant
serves lunch daily and dinner every night except Sunday (from Thurs-
day to Saturday only in January). ✉ *522 N. Irwin St., 93230,* ☎ *559/
583–8000 or 888/583–8080,* 🖷 *559/583–8793. 30 rooms. Restau-
rant, pool. Continental breakfast. AE, MC, V.*

Nightlife and the Arts

The 1,000-seat, restored Moorish-Castillian–style **Hanford Fox The-
ater** (✉ 326 N. Irwin St., ☎ 559/584–7423), built as a movie palace
in 1929, now periodically hosts country-western bands and other live
performances.

Visalia

*16 mi from Hanford, east on Hwy. 198; 40 mi from Fresno, south on
Hwy. 99 and east on Hwy. 198.*

A native of Visalia, Kentucky, founded Visalia, the Tulare County seat,
in 1852. The center of one of the world's top milk-producing regions,
the town, population 93,000, is also major exporter of oranges, grapes,
plums, peaches, and cotton. On a clear day the views of the Sierra Nevada
peaks to the east are stunning. Visalia contains a number of historic
homes; ask at the **visitor center** (✉ 301 E. Acequia, 93921, ☎ 559/
738–3435 or 800/524–0303) for a free guide detailing them.

The **Chinese Cultural Center,** housed in a pagoda-style building, mounts
exhibits about Chinese art and culture. ✉ *500 Akers Rd., at Hwy. 198,*
☎ *559/625–4545.* ☜ *Free.* ☉ *Wed.–Sun. 11–6.*

☕ In oak-shaded **Mooney Grove Park** you can picnic alongside duck
ponds, rent a boat in a lagoon, and view a replica of the famous **End
of the Trail Statue** (the original, once here, is now in the Cowboy Hall
of Fame in Oklahoma). ✉ *27000 S. Mooney Blvd., 5 mi south of down-
town,* ☎ *559/733–6616.* ☜ *$3 per car.* ☉ *Daily 8 AM–sunset.*

The indoor-outdoor **Tulare County Museum** contains several re-created
environments from the pioneer era and displays Yokuts tribal artifacts
(basketry, arrowheads, clamshell-necklace currency). Also here are
saddles and guns, Victorian-era dolls, and quilts and gowns. ✉ *Mooney
Grove Park, 27000 S. Mooney Blvd., 5 mi south of downtown,* ☎ *559/
733–6616.* ☜ *$2.* ☉ *June–Aug., Mon. and Wed.–Fri. 10–4, week-
ends 12–6; Sept.–Oct., Thur.–Mon. 10–4; Nov.–Feb., Mon., Thur.,
Fri. 10–4, weekends 1–4; Mar.–May, Thur.–Mon. 10–4.*

Trails at the 300-acre **Kaweah Oaks Preserve,** a wildlife sanctuary off
the main road to Sequoia National Park and accessible only to hikers,
lead past oak, sycamore, cottonwood, and willow trees. Among the
125 bird species you might spot are hawks, hummingbirds, and great
blue herons. Lizards, coyotes, and cottontails also live here. ✉ *Follow
Hwy. 198 for 7 mi east of Visalia, turn north on Rd. 182, and proceed
½ mi to gate on left-hand side of road,* ☎ *559/738–0211.* ☜ *Free.* ☉
Daily sunrise–sunset.

Dining and Lodging

$$–$$$ ✕ **Michael's on Main.** With its open kitchen, wood-fired grill, ceiling
fans, and white floor tiles, Michael's adds contemporary sophistica-
tion to Visalia's downtown dining scene. Dishes are prepared with an
Italian accent, with pastas a mainstay. The exotic martinis will give you

a light head (but hopefully not a hangover). ⊠ *123 W. Main St.,* ☎ *559/635–2686. AE, D, DC, MC, V. Closed Sun.*

$ ✕ **Caliente.** This sparkling-clean taco and burrito place en route to Mooney Grove Park makes good use of char-broiled, fresh ingredients. Try the innovative gourmet wraps—wood-fired shrimp in a chipotle tortilla or grilled vegetables in a spinach tortilla. You'd have to be ravenous to spend $10 a person here. ⊠ *2250 S. Mooney Blvd.,* ☎ *559/733–8226. MC, V.*

$$ ▦ **The Spalding House.** Built in 1901, this restored Colonial-Revival B&B—decked out with antiques, Oriental rugs, hand-crafted woodwork, and glass doors—is one of several historic homes in the vicinity. The three guest suites have separate sitting rooms and private baths—but no phones or TVs. ⊠ *631 N. Encina St., 93291,* ☎ *559/ 739–7877,* ℻ *559/625–0902. 3 suites. No-smoking rooms. Full breakfast. MC, V.*

$–$$ ▦ **The Lamp Liter Inn.** Rooms here are decent-size, and some have refrigerators. Rates include free TV movies. A large partially tree-shaded pool beckons on hot days. ⊠ *3300 W. Mineral King Ave., off Hwy. 198, 93291,* ☎ *559/732–4511,* ℻ *559/732–1840. 100 rooms. Restaurant, coffee shop, lounge, pool, meeting rooms. AE, D, DC, MC, V.*

Colonel Allensworth State Historic Park

★ ◉   *40 mi from Visalia, south on Hwy. 99, west on J22 (at town of Earlimart) and south on Hwy. 43.*

An ex-slave who rose to become the country's highest-ranking black officer of his time founded Allensworth—the only California town settled, governed, and financed by African-Americans—in 1908. After enjoying early prosperity, **Allensworth** became a ghost town; its buildings have been rebuilt or restored to reflect the era when it thrived. Each October three days of festivities mark the town's rededication. ⊠ *4129 Palmer Ave.,* ☎ *805/849–3433.* ▦ *$3 per car.* ◷ *Daily 10–4:30.*

OFF THE   **KERN NATIONAL WILDLIFE REFUGE** – Ducks, snowy egrets, peregrine fal-
BEATEN PATH   cons, warblers, and other birds inhabit the marshes and wetlands here from November to April. Follow the 3½-mi radius tour route (pick up maps at the entrance), which has several good viewing spots. ⊠ *10811 Corcoran Rd., 19 mi west of Delano on Hwy. 155 (Garces Hwy.); from Allensworth take Hwy. 43 south to Hwy. 155 west,* ☎ *805/725-2767.* ▦ *Free.* ◷ *Daily sunrise–sunset.*

SOUTHERN SAN JOAQUIN VALLEY
Bakersfield and Kernville

When gold was discovered in Kern County in the 1860s, settlers flocked to the southern end of the San Joaquin Valley. Black gold—oil—is now the area's most valuable commodity, but Kern is also the country's third-largest agricultural-producing county. From the flat plains around Bakersfield, the landscape graduates to rolling hills and then mountains as it climbs east to Kernville, which lies in the Kern River Valley.

Bakersfield

80 mi from Visalia, west on Hwy. 198, south on Hwy. 99; 288 mi from San Francisco, east on I–80 and I–580, south on I–5; 112 mi north of Los Angeles, I–5 to Hwy. 99.

Bakersfield's founder, Colonel Thomas Baker, arrived with the discovery of gold in the nearby Kern River Valley in 1851. Now Kern County's largest city (population 212,000), Bakersfield probably is best known as "Nashville West," a country-music haven and hometown of performers Buck Owens and Merle Haggard. It's also home to a symphony orchestra and two good museums.

★ ☾ ❿ The **Kern County Museum and Lori Brock Children's Discovery Center** form one of the San Joaquin Valley's top museum complexes. The indoor–outdoor Kern County Museum—whose centerpiece is an open-air, walk-through historic village with more than 50 restored or re-created buildings—pays homage to the era of the 1860s to 1940s. The indoor part of the museum holds exhibits about Native Americans and the "Bakersfield Sound" in country music. The adjacent Children's Discovery Center has permanent and changing hands-on displays and activities. ✉ *3801 Chester Ave.,* ☎ *805/861–2132.* ☞ *$5.* ⊙ *Weekdays 8–5, Sat. 10–5, Sun. noon–5.*

★ ☾ ⓫ At the **California Living Museum** (CALM), a combination zoo, botanical garden, and natural-history museum—the emphasis is on zoo—all animal and plant species displayed are native to the state. Within CALM's reptile house lives every species of rattlesnake found in California. The landscaped grounds—nestled among the rolling hills about a 20-minute drive northeast of Bakersfield—also shelter bald eagles, tortoises, coyotes, mountain lions, and foxes. ✉ *14000 Alfred Harrell Hwy. (Hwy. 178 east, then 3½ mi northwest on Alfred Harrell Hwy.),* ☎ *805/872–2256.* ☞ *$3.50.* ⊙ *Tue.–Sun. 9–5.*

Dining and Lodging

$$ ✕ **Chalet Basque.** The trencherman-size dinners here include soup, pink beans, hors d'oeuvres, vegetables, and potatoes, all served family-style. Leave room for main courses like roast leg of lamb or beef bourguignonne, or Basque-style specials such as oxtail stew or lamb shanks. ✉ *200 Oak St.,* ☎ *805/327–2915. AE, MC, V. Closed Sun.–Mon.*

$–$$ ✕ **Uricchio's Trattoria.** This downtown restaurant draws everyone from office workers to oil barons—all attracted by the tasty food, trendy open kitchen, and indoor and outdoor seating. *Panini* (Italian sandwiches, served at lunch only), pasta, and Italian-style chicken dishes dominate the menu; the chicken piccata outsells all other offerings. ✉ *1400 17th St.,* ☎ *805/326–8870. AE, D, DC, MC, V. Closed Sun. No lunch Sat.*

$$ ⌂ **Doubletree Hotel.** The location is convenient, off Highways 99, 58, and 178. Some of the spacious rooms have refrigerators, and all of them have coffeemakers and balconies or patios. ✉ *3100 Camino Del Rio Ct., 93308,* ☎ *805/323–7111,* ☎ *805/323–0331. 246 rooms and 14 suites. Restaurant, bar, coffee shop, no-smoking rooms, room service, pool, hot tub, laundry service, business services, meeting rooms, free airport shuttle. AE, D, DC, MC, V.*

$ ⌂ **Quality Inn.** Near downtown in a relatively quiet location off Highway 99, this two-story motel offers good value. Most rooms have king- or queen-size beds, and all have free in-room movies. Some have refrigerators and a patio or a balcony looking out on the heated pool. Complimentary coffee and donuts are served. ✉ *1011 Oak St., 93304,* ☎ *805/325–0772,* ☎ *805/325–4646. 90 rooms. Pool, indoor hot tub, sauna, exercise room, coin laundry. AE, D, DC, MC, V.*

Nightlife and the Arts

The **Bakersfield Symphony Orchestra** (☎ 805/323–7928) performs classical music concerts at the Convention Center (✉ 1001 Truxton Ave.) on Sunday from October to May.

Buck Owens' Crystal Palace (✉ 2800 Pierce Rd., ☎ 805/328–7560) is a combination nightclub, restaurant, and showcase of country-music memorabilia. Country-western singers—owner Buck Owens among them—perform. A dance floor beckons customers who can still twirl after sampling the menu of steaks, burgers, nachos, and gooey desserts. Entertainment is free on most weeknights; Friday and Saturday nights bring a $5 cover charge, and some big-name acts require tickets.

Outdoor Activities and Sports

CAR RACING

At **Bakersfield Speedway** (✉ 304 Egret Ct., ☎ 805/393–3373), stock and sprint cars race around a ⅓-mi clay oval track. **Mesa Marin Raceway** (✉ 11000 Kern Canyon Rd., ☎ 805/366–5711) presents high-speed stock-car, super-truck, and NASCAR racing on a ½-mi paved oval course.

Shopping

Many antiques shops are on 18th and 19th streets between H and R streets, and H Street between Brundage Lane and California Avenue. **Goodies from the Past** (✉ 1610 19th St., ☎ 805/636–0368), **Central Park Antique Mall** (✉ 701 19th St., ☎ 805/633–1143), and the **Great American Antique Mall** (✉ 625 19th St., ☎ 805/322–1776) all have huge selections.

Kernville

50 mi from Bakersfield, northeast on Hwy. 178 and north on Hwy. 155.

The wild and scenic Kern River, which flows through Kernville en route from Mount Whitney to Bakersfield, delivers some of the most exciting white-water rafting in the state. Kernville (population 1,200) rests in a mountain valley on both banks of the river, and also at the northern tip of Lake Isabella (a dammed portion of the river used as a reservoir and for recreation). A center for rafting outfitters, Kernville has lodgings, eating places, and antiques shops. The main streets are lined with Old West–style buildings, reflecting Kernville's heritage as a rough-and-tumble gold-mining town known as Whiskey Flat (present-day Kernville dates from the 1950s, when it was moved upriver to make room for Lake Isabella). The scenic road from Bakersfield winds between the rushing river on one side and sheer granite cliffs on the other.

Dining and Lodging

$–$$$ ✕ **Ewing's on the Kern.** The views outshine the food at this restaurant, but there are few prettier spots to eat than high above the Kern, either at one of the outdoor tables—come early to get a seat for Sunday brunch—or at one of the indoor window tables. The menu is strictly old standards: prime rib, steaks, seafood, pastas, and chicken. ✉ *125 Buena Vista Dr.,* ☎ *760/376–2411. AE, D, DC, MC, V. No lunch.*

$ ✕ **Debbe Du's Diner.** This down-home diner ("Where Everyone Is Family") serves up some of the least expensive food in town—ask for the Strugglers Specials, all under $10—along with colorful talk from the locals, who drop in for biscuits and gravy, burgers, or meat loaf. ✉ *13423 Sierra Way,* ☎ *760/376–4663. No credit cards.*

$$–$$$ ▥ **Whispering Pines Lodge.** You can choose a cottage or a river-view bungalow here. Some accommodations have full kitchens, fireplaces, and whirlpool tubs; all have refrigerators, coffeemakers, and cable TV. ✉ *13745 Sierra Way, 93238,* ☎ *760/376–3733,* ⅿ *760/376–3735. 17 rooms. Pool. Full breakfast. AE, D, MC, V.*

$–$$ ▥ **River View Lodge.** This rustic motel has knotty-pine walls and compact but clean rooms, some with microwaves and VCRs. And yes, many units do have river views. Picnic and barbecue facilities are in the tree-shaded yard. ⊠ *2 Sirretta St., off Kernville Rd., 93238,* ☎ *760/376–6019,* FAX *760/376–4147. 10 rooms. No-smoking rooms, refrigerators. Continental breakfast. AE, DC, MC, V.*

Outdoor Activities and Sports

WHITE-WATER RAFTING

The three sections of the Kern River—known as the Lower Kern, Upper Kern, and the Forks—add up to nearly 50 mi of white water, ranging from Class I to Class V (easy to expert). The Lower and Upper Kern are the most popular and accessible sections. Organized trips can last from one hour (for as little as $15) to two days and more. Rafting season generally runs from late spring until the end of summer. Outfitters include **Chuck Richards Whitewater** (☎ 760/379–4444), **Kern River Tours** (☎ 760/379–4616), **Mountain & River Adventures** (☎ 760/376–6553 or 800/861–6553), and **Sierra South** (☎ 760/376–3745).

BOATING, FISHING, AND WINDSURFING

The Lower Kern River, which extends from Lake Isabella to Bakersfield and beyond, is open for fishing year-round. Catches include rainbow trout, catfish, smallmouth bass, crappie, and bluegill. Lake Isabella is popular with anglers, water skiers, sailors, and windsurfers. Its shoreline marinas—**French Gulch Marina** (☎ 760/379–8774), **Red's Kern Valley Marina** (☎ 760/379–1634 or 800/553–7337), and **Dean's North Fork Marina** (☎ 760/376–1812)—have boats for rent, bait and tackle, and moorings year-round.

THE SAN JOAQUIN VALLEY A TO Z

Arriving and Departing

By Bus

Greyhound Lines (☎ 800/231–2222) stops in Stockton, Modesto, Merced, Fresno, Visalia, and Bakersfield.

By Car

To drive to the San Joaquin Valley from San Francisco, take I–80 east to I–580, and I–580 east to I–5, which leads south into the Valley (several roads from I–5 head east to Highway 99); or continue east on I–580 to I–205, which leads to I–5 north to Stockton or (via Highway 120) east to Highway 99 at Manteca. To reach the Valley from Los Angeles, follow I–5 north; Highway 99 veers north about 15 mi after entering the Valley.

By Plane

Fresno Air Terminal (⊠ 5175 E. Clinton Ave., ☎ 559/498–4095) is serviced by America West Express, American and American Eagle, Delta, Skywest, United Express, and US Airways Express. **Kern County Airport at Meadows Field** (⊠ 1401 Skyway Dr., Bakersfield, ☎ 805/393–7990) is serviced by American and American Eagle, Skywest-Delta, and United Express. United Express flies from San Francisco to **Modesto City Airport** (⊠ 617 Airport Way, ☎ 209/577–5318) and **Visalia Municipal Airport** (⊠ 9500 Airport Dr., ☎ 559/738–3201). *See* Air Travel *in* the Gold Guide for airline phone numbers.

By Train

Amtrak's (☎ 800/872–7245) daily *San Joaquin* trains travel between San Jose, Oakland, and Bakersfield, stopping in Stockton, Riverbank (near Modesto), Merced, Fresno, and Hanford. Amtrak Thruway bus service connects Bakersfield with Los Angeles.

Getting Around

By Bus

Greyhound (☎ 800/231–2222) provides service between major Valley cities. **Orange Belt Stages** (☎ 800/266–7433) provides bus service, including Amtrak connections, to many Valley locations, including Stockton, Merced, Madera, Fresno, Hanford, and Bakersfield.

By Car

Highway 99 is the main route between the Valley's major cities and towns. Interstate 5 runs roughly parallel to it to the west, but misses the major population centers; its main use is for quick access from San Francisco or Los Angeles. Major roads that connect I–5 with Highway 99 are Highways 120 (to Manteca), 132 (to Modesto), 140 (to Merced), 152 (to Chowchilla, via Los Banos), 198 (to Hanford and Visalia), and 58 (to Bakersfield).

Contacts and Resources

Car Rentals

All the major car rental agencies except Alamo have outlets in the San Joaquin Valley. *See* Car Rental *in* the Gold Guide for company phone numbers.

Emergencies

Ambulance (☎ 911). **Fire** (☎ 911). **Police** (☎ 911).

Guided Tours

Central Valley Tours (✉ 1869 E. Everglade, Fresno 93720, ☎ 559/323–5552) provides general and customized tours of the Fresno area and the Valley. **Kings River Expeditions** (✉ 211 N. Van Ness, Fresno, ☎ 559/233–4881 or 800/846–3674) arranges white-water rafting trips on the Kings River. Contact **River Journey** (✉ 14842 Orange Blossom Rd., Oakdale, ☎ 209/847–4671 or 800/292–2938) and **Sunshine River Adventures** (✉ Box 1445, Oakdale 95361, ☎ 209/848–4800 or 800/829–7238) to raft the Stanislaus River.

Visitor Information

Fresno City & County Convention and Visitors Bureau (✉ 808 M St., 93721, ☎ 559/233–0836 or 800/788–0836). **Greater Bakersfield Convention & Visitors Bureau** (✉ 1325 P St., 93301, ☎ 805/325–5051 or 800/325–6001). **Hanford Visitor Agency** (✉ 200 Santa Fe Ave., Suite D, 93230, ☎ 559/582–5024). **Kern County Board of Trade** (✉ 2101 Oak St., Bakersfield 93302, ☎ 805/861–2367 or 800/500–5376). **Merced Conference and Visitors Bureau** (✉ 690 W. 16th St., 95340, ☎ 209/384–3333 or 800/446–5353). **Modesto Convention and Visitors Bureau** (✉ 1114 J St., 95353, ☎ 209/571–6480). **Stockton/San Joaquin Convention and Visitors Bureau** (✉ 46 W. Fremont St., Stockton 95202, ☎ 209/943–1987 or 800/350–1987). **Visalia Convention and Visitors Bureau** (✉ 301 E. Acequia, 93291, ☎ 559/738–3435 or 800/524–0303).

10 Monterey Bay

*From Santa Cruz to
Carmel Valley*

*The Monterey Peninsula is steeped in
history. The town of Monterey was
California's first capital, the Carmel
Mission headquarters for California's
mission system. The peninsula also has
a rich literary past. John Steinbeck's
novels immortalized the area, and
Robert Louis Stevenson strolled its
streets, gathering inspiration for
Treasure Island. The present is equally
illustrious. Blessed with a natural
splendor undiminished by time or
commerce, the peninsula is home to
high-tech marine habitats and
luxurious resorts.*

THE OHLONE INDIANS SETTLED IN THE MONTEREY AREA about 2,500 years ago, the first Native American people to build a community that centered on the region's maritime bounty. In 1542, Monterey Bay's white sand beaches, pine forests, and rugged coastline captivated explorer Juan Rodríguez Cabrillo, who claimed it for Spain. Spanish missionaries, Mexican rulers, and land developers would come and go, all of them, perhaps, instinctively knowing not to destroy the peninsula's natural assets or historical sites.

Revised and updated by Clark Norton

The region has never relied solely on its looks, however. You can't ignore its deep green forests of Monterey cypress—oddly gnarled trees that grow naturally nowhere else—its aquamarine waters, or the dance of cloud shadows upon its rolling emerald hills and winsome meadows. Yet there are industrial, and a bit messy, claims to fame—whaling for one, sardines for another. And the meticulously preserved adobe houses and missions, layers of a Spanish and Mexican past left remarkably undisturbed, create a terra-cotta skyline that testifies to the Monterey Peninsula's singular place in California history.

With the arrival of Father Junípero Serra and Commander Don Gaspar de Portola from Spain in 1770, Monterey became the military and ecclesiastical capital of Alta California (the Spanish-held territory north of present-day Baja California, in Mexico). Portola established the first of California's four Spanish presidios; Serra founded the second of 21 Franciscan missions, later moving it from Monterey to Carmel.

Century magazine, whose publisher was a major booster of California, published in the 1890s the reflections of Brigida Briones, a Monterey resident during the days of Spanish and Mexican rule. "The ladies of Monterey in 1827," she wrote, "were rarely seen in the street, except very early in the morning on their way to church. . . . The *rebozo* (shawl) and the petticoat being black, always of cheap stuff. . . . All classes wore the same; the padres told us that we must never forget that all ranks of men and women were equal in the presence of the Creator." Briones writes elsewhere in the magazine about the participants at a carnival ball held in 1829, "all on horseback and full of gaiety and youthfulness such as only a race that lives outdoors in such a climate as California, and without cares or troubles, can show."

Modern historians might argue that equality for all was more theory than practice for many in Briones's class, and though the ladies may have led a carefree life at this time, their husbands were caught up in the conflict between Mexico and the United States for control of California—with both nations casting a wary eye on England, which was thought to have designs on the state as well. Captain John Charles Fremont of the United States wrote later that "the men who understood the future of our country . . . regarded the California coast as the boundary fixed by nature to round off our national domain . . . it was naturally separated from Mexico, and events pointed to its sure and near political separation."

The Mexican government, which was formed in 1822 when Mexico revolted against Spain, disputed these notions about Alta California's natural and political separation from the rest of Mexico, but between the time of Mexican independence and the mid-1840s, Monterey had changed. It had grown into a lively seaport that drew many Yankee sea traders. By July 7, 1846, when Commodore John Sloat raised the

American flag over the Custom House and claimed California for the United States, many Monterey-area residents supported the U.S. cause.

Economics was a major factor: The majority of Monterey's business-people felt that being under the Yankee umbrella would be far more profitable than being aligned with Mexico. Their hunch proved correct, at least for them. For the Ohlone Indian population, however, the transition was disastrous: State and federal laws passed during the first half-century of U.S. rule divested them of rights and property granted under Spanish and Mexican rule.

California's Constitution was framed in Colton Hall, but Monterey was all but forgotten once gold was discovered at Sutter's Mill near Sacramento. After the gold rush, the state capital moved from Monterey and the town became a sleepy backwater, though the whaling industry boomed in the last half of the 19th century and thrived until the early 1900s.

As the 20th century dawned, the Monterey Peninsula had begun to draw tourists with the opening of the Del Monte Hotel, the most palatial resort the West Coast had ever seen. Writers and artists such as John Steinbeck, Henry Miller, Robinson Jeffers, Francis McComas, and Ansel Adams also discovered the peninsula, adding their legacy to the region while capturing its magic on canvas, paper, and film. In the 1920s and 1930s Cannery Row's sardine industry took off, but by the late 1940s and early 1950s the fish had disappeared. The cause is still in dispute, though overfishing, water contamination, and a change in ocean currents that lowered the area's water temperature are the likely culprits. Sardines were packed again in 1995 in nearby Salinas for the first time since the 1950s. Visitors can buy them on Cannery Row, where activity has returned in the form of renovated buildings that house shops, restaurants, hotels, and the Monterey Bay Aquarium.

All aspects of the peninsula's diverse cultural and maritime heritage can be felt today, from Monterey's 19th-century buildings to its busy harbor and wharf. Modern-day attractions include the Monterey Jazz Festival and the Monterey Bay National Marine Sanctuary—the nation's largest undersea canyon, bigger and deeper than the Grand Canyon. The sanctuary supports a rich brew of marine life, from fat, barking sea lions to tiny plantlike anemones. Annual events and festivities such as Pacific Grove's Butterfly Parade, the Carmel Shakespeare Festival, and Monterey's Christmas in the Adobes pay tribute to old traditions and link the past with the present.

Pleasures and Pastimes

Dining

Monterey is the richest area for dining along the coast between San Francisco and Los Angeles. The surrounding waters abound with fish, wild game roams the foothills, and the inland valleys are the vegetable basket of California; nearby Castroville dubs itself the Artichoke Capital of the World. Except at beachside stands and the inexpensive eateries listed below, casual but attractive resort wear is the norm. The few places where more formal attire is required are noted.

CATEGORY	COST*
$$$$	over $50
$$$	$30–$50
$$	$20–$30
$	under $20

*per person for a three-course meal, excluding drinks, service, and 7 ¼%–8¼% tax

Golf

Since the opening of the Del Monte Golf Course (now the Old Del Monte Golf Course) in 1897, golf has been an integral part of the Monterey Peninsula's social and recreational scene. Pebble Beach's championship courses host prestigious tournaments, and though the greens fees at these courses run well over $200, elsewhere on the peninsula you'll find less expensive—but still challenging and scenic—options. Many hotels will help with golf reservations or have golf packages; inquire when you make your room reservation.

Lodging

Monterey-area accommodations range from no-frills motels and historic hotels to upscale establishments that are a bit impersonal and clearly designed for conventions. Others pamper the individual traveler in grand style, especially some of the area's small inns and B&Bs, many of which provide full breakfasts and afternoon or early evening wine and hors d'oeuvres. Pacific Grove has quietly turned itself into the region's B&B capital. Carmel and Carmel Valley also have fine B&Bs. Even more luxurious are the resorts in exclusive Pebble Beach. The rates below are for two people in the high season, from April to October. Rates during winter, especially at the larger hotels, drop by as much as 50%, and B&Bs often offer midweek specials at this time of year. If you book lodgings through Monterey's 800/555–9283 number, request an informational brochure and discount coupons that are good at restaurants, attractions, and shops.

CATEGORY	COST*
$$$$	over $175
$$$	$120–$175
$$	$80–$120
$	under $80

*All prices are for a standard double room, excluding 10%–10½% tax.

Whale-Watching

On their annual migration between the Bering Sea and Baja California, 45-ft gray whales pass by not far off the Monterey coast. They are sometimes visible through binoculars from shore, but a whale-watching cruise is the best way to get a close look at these magnificent mammals. The migration south takes place between December and March—late January is prime viewing time. The migration north occurs between March and June. Two thousand blue whales and 600 humpbacks come pass the coast; they're easily spotted in late summer and early fall. Smaller numbers of minke whales, orcas, sperm whales, and fin whales have been sighted in mid-August. Even if no whales surface, bay cruises almost always encounter some unforgettable marine life.

Exploring Monterey Bay

The population centers here are towns, not cities, and their individual charms complement Monterey Bay's natural beauty. Santa Cruz sits at the northern tip of the crescent formed by Monterey Bay; the Monterey Peninsula, including Monterey, Pacific Grove, and Carmel, occupies the southern end. In between, Highway 1 cruises along the coastline, passing windswept beaches piled high with sand dunes. Along the route are artichoke fields and the towns of Watsonville and Castroville.

Numbers in the text correspond to numbers in the margin and on the Monterey Bay, Monterey and Pacific Grove, and Carmel and 17-Mile Drive maps.

Great Itineraries

Despite its compact size, the Monterey Peninsula is packed with diversions—it would take more than a weekend to get beyond the surface. If you have an interest in California history and historic preservation, the place to start is Monterey, with its adobe buildings along the downtown Path of History. Fans of Victorian architecture will want to explore the many fine examples in Pacific Grove. In Carmel you can shop till you drop, and when summer and weekend hordes overwhelm the town's clothing boutiques, art galleries, housewares outlets, and gift shops, you can slip off to enjoy the coast.

IF YOU HAVE 3 DAYS

Start at the far end of Cannery Row in **Monterey** ②–⑲ with a visit to the **Monterey Bay Aquarium** ⑲. Have lunch there or at one of the restaurants on Cannery Row. As you walk the Row, stop at **Steinbeck's Spirit of Monterey Wax Museum** ⑯ or the **Wing Chong Building** ⑰, then continue on foot via the oceanfront recreation trail to **Fisherman's Wharf** ⑬ to enjoy the sights and catch the sunset. If you're not up to the hubbub along the wharf, slip into the serene bar at the Monterey Plaza Hotel. On the following day, visit the **Larkin House** ⑥, **Cooper-Molera Adobe** ⑦, (Robert Louis) **Stevenson House** ⑧, and other historic Monterey buildings, stopping for lunch when the need hits. Then pick up some late-afternoon snacks and motor through **17-Mile Drive** ㉕–㉙. Catch the sunset along 17-Mile Drive or at nearby **Point Lobos State Reserve** ㉞. On the third day, drive south to **Carmel** ㉚–㉞. Visit the **Carmel Mission** ㉛ and have lunch while browsing through the **Ocean Avenue** shopping area before stopping (if open) at **Tor House** ㉜, the residence of the late poet Robinson Jeffers. No matter what time of year you're visiting Monterey Bay, stroll over to Scenic Road and spend time on Carmel Beach before leaving the area.

IF YOU HAVE 5 DAYS

On your first three days, visit **Monterey** ②–⑲, stopping at the **Custom House** ②, **Larkin House** ⑥, **Cooper-Molera Adobe** ⑦, **Stevenson House** ⑧, and **Colton Hall** ⑨ on day one. On your second morning, get a visceral feel for Monterey Bay marine life by boarding a **whale-watching or other cruise** vessel at **Fisherman's Wharf** ⑬. Have lunch upon your return to the wharf, and then visit Cannery Row for **Steinbeck's Spirit of Monterey Wax Museum** ⑯ and the **Wing Chong Building** ⑰. On day three, tour the **Monterey Bay Aquarium** ⑲, have lunch along Cannery Row, and then spend the rest of the afternoon either enjoying the Monterey waterfront or tasting wine at **Ventana Vineyards** on the Monterey–Salinas Highway. On your fourth day, visit **Carmel Mission** ㉛ and **Tor House** ㉜ (if open) and have lunch while exploring the shops along **Ocean Avenue** in Carmel. Pick up some late-afternoon snacks for a spin on **17-Mile Drive** ㉕–㉙. Catch the sunset along 17-Mile Drive or at nearby **Point Lobos State Reserve** ㉞. On day five, explore the shoreline and Victorian houses of **Pacific Grove** ⑳–㉔ in the morning and lunch there. If you have time, visit **San Juan Bautista** ㊲, a classic mission village 35 mi from Monterey (take Highway 1 to Highway 156).

When to Tour Monterey Bay

Summer is peak season, with crowds everywhere and generally mild weather. A sweater or windbreaker is nearly always necessary along the coast, where a cool breeze usually blows and fog is on the way in or out. Inland, temperatures in Salinas or Carmel Valley can be a good 15 or 20 degrees warmer than those in Carmel and Monterey. Off-season, from November to April, fewer people visit and the mood is more introspective. Rains fall heaviest in January and February. Most of the sights in Monterey are open daily.

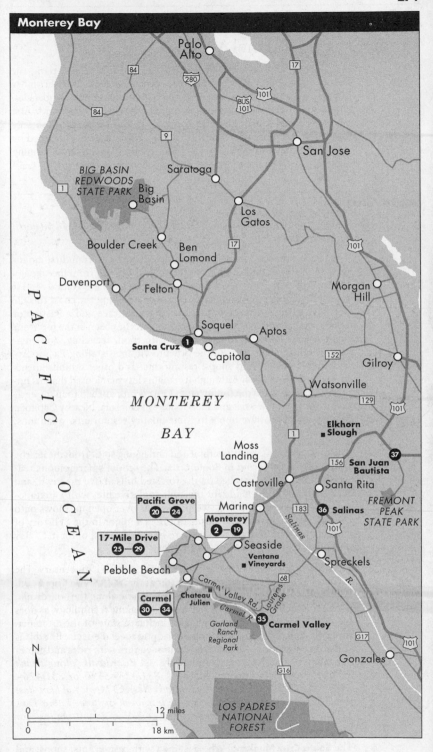

Monterey Bay

Palo Alto

84

280

84

101

BUS 101

17

9

San Jose

BIG BASIN REDWOODS STATE PARK

Saratoga

Big Basin

Boulder Creek

Ben Lomond

Los Gatos

17

P A C I F I C

Davenport

Felton

Soquel

Aptos

101

Morgan Hill

Santa Cruz 1

Capitola

152

Gilroy

MONTEREY

Watsonville

129

101

BAY

Moss Landing

Elkhorn Slough

37

Pacific Grove
20 — 24

Castroville

1

156

San Juan Bautista

Santa Rita

FREMONT PEAK STATE PARK

Monterey
2 — 19

Marina

183

36 **Salinas**

17-Mile Drive
25 — 29

O C E A N

Seaside

Ventana Vineyards

Salinas R.

101

Pebble Beach

Carmel
30 — 34

Chateau Julien

Carmel Valley Rd

68

Spreckels

Laureles Grade

35 **Carmel Valley**

Carmel R.

N

Garland Ranch Regional Park

G17

101

Gonzales

1

G16

0 ———— 12 miles

0 ———— 18 km

LOS PADRES NATIONAL FOREST

MONTEREY BAY
Santa Cruz to Carmel Valley

Set along 90 mi of arc-shaped coastline, like jewels in a tiara, the towns of Monterey Bay combine the somewhat funky, beachcomber aspects of California's culture with the state's more refined tendencies. Past and present merge gracefully here. As the city of Monterey's first mayor, Carmel Martin, described it early in this century: "Monterey Bay is the one place where people can live without being disturbed by manufacturing and big factories. I am certain that the day is coming when this will be the most desirable place in the whole state of California."

Santa Cruz

❶ *74 mi south of San Francisco, I–280 to Hwy. 17 to Hwy. 1; 48 mi north of Monterey on Hwy. 1.*

The beach town of Santa Cruz is sheltered by the surrounding mountains to the north and south from the coastal fog and from the smoggy skies of the San Francisco Bay Area. The climate here is mild, and it is usually warmer and sunnier than elsewhere along the coast this far north. A haven for those opting out of the rat race and a bastion of 1960s-style counterculture values, Santa Cruz has been at the forefront of such very Californian trends as health food, recycling, and environmentalism. The heart of the downtown area is along Pacific Avenue, where you'll find shops, restaurants, and other establishments in **Pacific Garden Mall.** Although it remains less manicured than its upmarket neighbors to the south, Santa Cruz is more urban than the agricultural towns between it and the Monterey Peninsula. Nearby Capitola, Soquel, and Aptos are home to some quality restaurants, small inns, and resorts.

The town gets some of its youthful and unflagging spirit from the nearby **University of California at Santa Cruz.** The school's harmonious redwood buildings are perched on the forested hills above the town, and the campus is tailor-made for the contemplative life, with a juxtaposition of sylvan settings and sweeping vistas over open meadows onto the bay. The humanities department offers a major in the "History of Consciousness," and this does seem to be the perfect spot for it. ✉ *Bay and High Sts.,* ☎ *831/459–0111.*

Santa Cruz has been a seaside resort since the mid-19th century. The carousel and Giant Dipper roller coaster at the ★☾ **Santa Cruz Beach Boardwalk** date from the early 1900s. Elsewhere along the boardwalk, the Casino Fun Center has its share of video-game technology, as does Neptune's Kingdom, whose highlights include a state-of-the-art miniature golf course with robotic and fiber-optic special effects. But this is still primarily a place for good old-fashioned fun, with rides and games appealing to toddlers, teens, and adults. ✉ *Boardwalk: along Beach St. west from San Lorenzo River,* ☎ *831/423–5590 or 831/426–7433.* ▣ *$18.95 (day pass for unlimited rides).* ◷ *Memorial Day–last week of June, 11 AM–midnight or so; last week of June–Labor Day, 11 AM–11 PM; rest of yr, weekends only, weather permitting (call for hours).*

The **Santa Cruz Municipal Wharf** is lined with restaurants, shops, and seafood takeout windows and is enlivened by the barking and baying of the sea lions that lounge in communal heaps under the wharf's pilings. Down the West Cliff Drive promontory at **Seal Rock,** pinnipeds hang out, sunbathe, and occasionally frolic.

The **Lighthouse,** which is south of the wharf, has a surfing museum with artifacts that include the remains of a board a shark munched on. ⊠ *W. Cliff Dr.,* ☎ *831/429–3429.* ⊑ *Free.* ☉ *Museum Wed.–Mon. noon–4.*

West of the lighthouse is secluded ☾ **Natural Bridges State Beach,** a stretch of soft sand with tidal pools and a natural rock bridge nearby. From late September to early March a colony of monarch butterflies resides here. ⊠ *2531 W. Cliff Dr.,* ☎ *831/423–4609.* ⊑ *$6 parking fee.* ☉ *Park 8* AM–*sunset. Visitor center Oct.–Feb., daily 10–4; Mar.– Sept., weekends 10–4.*

Dining and Lodging

$$–$$$ ✕ **Bittersweet Bistro.** An old tavern that was moved a few miles south
★ of Santa Cruz houses the popular eatery of chef-owner Thomas Vinolus. Start with a pizzetta or a mesclun salad; move on to a grilled vegetable platter, a seafood puttanesca (with fettuccine), or grilled lamb tenderloins; then finish with any of the chocolate desserts. ⊠ *787 Rio Del Mar Blvd., off Hwy. 1, Rio Del Mar,* ☎ *831/662–9799. AE, MC, V. Closed Mon. No lunch.*

$$–$$$ ✕ **Chez Renee.** The husband-and-wife team that owns this redwood-
★ shaded retreat serves French-inspired cuisine. Specialties include sweetbreads with two sauces (Madeira and mustard), duck with home-preserved brandied cherries, and sea scallops garnished with smoked salmon and dill. Save room for the excellent dessert soufflés. ⊠ *9051 Soquel Dr., Aptos,* ☎ *831/688–5566. MC, V. Closed Sun.– Mon. No lunch Tues. and Sat.*

$–$$$ ✕ **El Palomar.** The restaurant of the Palomar Hotel has vaulted ceilings, wood beams, and an atrium that opens up in warm weather. Among the best California-Mexican dishes are ceviche tostadas, chili verde, and fish tacos. The attractive taco bar, off to one side, is open all day. ⊠ *1336 Pacific Ave.,* ☎ *831/425–7575. Reservations not accepted for lunch or Fri.–Sat. dinner. AE, D, MC, V.*

$–$$ ✕ **Dolphin Restaurant.** Occupying a scenic site at the end of the Municipal Wharf, this casual restaurant serves filling breakfasts—hotcakes, French toast, omelets—plus seafood lunches and dinners. For a quick bowl of chowder or plate of fish and chips, visit the adjacent takeout window. ⊠ *At the end of Santa Cruz Municipal Wharf,* ☎ *831/426– 5830. MC, V.*

$–$$ ✕ **Gabriella Cafe.** In a small brown stucco building, the Gabriella is intimate without being stuffy. The seasonal Italian menu highlights local organic produce. Watch for dishes like steamed mussels, braised lamb shank, and grilled Portobello mushrooms. ⊠ *910 Cedar St.,* ☎ *831/ 457–1677. AE, D, DC, MC, V.*

$–$$ ✕ **India Joze.** Char-grilled meats and seafood with exotic marinades are the highlights at this eclectic downtown favorite. Good bets include the curries, chicken, or snapper in Javan pesto (fresh basil, ginger, and tamarind), and any of the grilled dishes with *panggang* (a ginger-lime marinade). ⊠ *1001 Center St.,* ☎ *831/427–3554. AE, DC, MC, V.*

$–$$ ✕ **Positively Front Street.** Cioppino, steamed clams, grilled prawns, and honey-glazed salmon are among the seafood entrées at this place near the wharf that caters to the beach-and-boardwalk crowd with burgers and pizza. The restaurant and several dishes (including the "It Ain't Meat, Babe" veggie burger) are named in honor of Bob Dylan songs. ⊠ *44 Front St.,* ☎ *831/426–1944. MC, V. No lunch Nov.–Mar., Mon.–Thurs.*

$ ✕ **Zachary's.** With its potted plants, rough wooden floors, and mostly young clientele, this noisy café defines the funky essence of Santa Cruz. It also dishes up great breakfasts: three-egg omelets, sourdough pancakes, artichoke frittatas, and Mike's Mess—eggs scrambled with bacon, mushrooms, and home fries, topped with sour cream, melted cheese, and fresh tomatoes. ⊠ *819 Pacific Ave.,* ☎ *831/427–0646. MC, V.*

$$$–$$$$ ⊡ **Inn at Depot Hill.** This inventively designed hotel in a former rail depot sees itself as a link to the era of train travel (you'll remain solidly put, however). Each double room or suite, complete with fireplace and feather beds, is inspired by a different destination—Portofino, Italy; the Côte d'Azur, France; Kyoto, Japan. One suite is decorated like a Pullman car for a railroad baron. Some accommodations have private patios with hot tubs. ⊠ *250 Monterey Ave., Capitola-by-the-Sea 95010,* ☎ *831/462–3376 or 800/572–2632,* ℻ *831/462–3697. 6 rooms, 6 suites. In-room modem lines, no-smoking rooms, in-room VCRs. Full breakfast. AE, MC, V.*

$$$–$$$$ ⊡ **Seascape Resort.** On a bluff overlooking Monterey Bay, with waves crashing on the beach below, Seascape is a place to unwind. Units here sleep from two to six people, and each has a kitchenette, a fireplace, a TV with VCR, and an ocean-view patio with a barbecue grill. The resort is about 9 mi south of Santa Cruz. ⊠ *1 Seascape Resort Dr., Aptos 95003,* ☎ *831/688–6800 or 800/929–7727,* ℻ *831/685– 2753. 284 suites. Restaurant, in-room modem lines, 2 pools, hot tub, spa, golf privileges, health club, beach, children's programs, laundry service, convention center, meeting rooms. AE, D, DC, MC, V.*

$$$–$$$$ ⊡ **WestCoast Santa Cruz Hotel.** Within a short stroll of the Beach Boardwalk and wharf, this resort opens right onto Cowell Beach. If it's too cold to swim in the ocean, you can head for the heated swimming pool and tub. Rooms have cable TV and oceanfront balconies or patios. Children under 12 stay free in their parents' room. ⊠ *175 W. Cliff Dr., 95060,* ☎ *831/426–4330 or 800/662–3838,* ℻ *831/427– 2025. 147 rooms, 16 suites. 2 restaurants, refrigerators, room service, pool, hot tub, sauna. AE, D, DC, MC, V.*

$$–$$$ ⊡ **Inn at Manresa Beach.** Ansel Adams once occupied the 1867 mansion that Brian Denny and Susan Van Horn moved to a country setting about 10 mi south of Santa Cruz. The rooms in their comfortable B&B, which have nature-theme decors, contain private baths and fireplaces. Children are welcome. ⊠ *1258 San Andreas Rd., La Selva Beach 95076,* ☎ *831/728–1000 or 888/523–2244,* ℻ *831/728–1000. 9 rooms. In-room VCRs, 2 tennis courts, volleyball. Full breakfast. AE, MC, V .*

$–$$$ ⊡ **Ocean Pacific Lodge.** By staying a few blocks from the beach, you can save money at this modern multistory motel that has a heated pool, a hot tub, and in-room microwaves. ⊠ *120 Washington St., 95060,* ☎ *831/457–1234 or 800/995–0289,* ℻ *831/457–0861. 44 rooms, 13 suites. Refrigerators, exercise room. Continental breakfast. AE, D, DC, MC, V.*

Nightlife and the Arts

Shakespeare Santa Cruz (⊠ Performing Arts Complex, University of California at Santa Cruz, ☎ 831/459–2121) stages a six-week Shakespeare festival in July and August that also may include one modern-day work. Most performances are outdoors in the striking Redwood Glen.

Outdoor Activities and Sports

BICYCLING
Bicycle Rental Center (⊠ 131 Center St., ☎ 831/426–8687).

BOATS AND CHARTERS
Original Stagnaro Fishing Trips (⊠ Center of Santa Cruz Municipal Wharf, ☎ 831/423–2010) operates salmon and rock-cod fishing ex-

peditions; the fees ($32–$42) include bait. The company also runs whale-watching cruises ($17–$20) between December and March.

SURFING

Manresa State Beach (✉ Manresa Dr., La Selva Beach, ☎ 831/761–1795), south of Santa Cruz, has premium surfing conditions, but the water is treacherous. The surf at **New Brighton State Beach** (✉ 1500 State Park Dr., Capitola) is challenging; campsites are available. Surfers gather for the spectacular waves and sunsets at **Pleasure Point** (✉ East Cliff and Pleasure Point Drs.) **Steamer's Lane,** between the boardwalk and the lighthouse, has a decent break. The area plays host to several competitions in the summer.

Cowell's Beach 'n' Bikini Surf Shop (✉ 109 Beach St., ☎ 831/427–2355) rents surfboards and wet suits.

Monterey

48 mi south of Santa Cruz on Hwy. 1; 122 mi south of San Francisco on I–280 to Hwy. 17 to Hwy. 1; 334 mi north of Los Angeles on U.S. 101 to Hwy. 68 west from Salinas.

★ ☺ Much of Monterey's early history can be gleaned from the well-preserved adobe buildings of **Monterey State Historic Park** (☎ 831/649–7118). Far from being a hermetic period museum, the park facilities are an integral part of the day-to-day business life of the town—within some of the buildings are a store, a theater, and government offices. The 2-mi Path of History, marked by round gold tiles set into the sidewalk, passes by several landmark buildings. A $5 all-day park ticket gains you entrance to Casa Soberanes, the Cooper-Molera Adobe, the Larkin House, and the Stevenson House (☞ *below*) and includes a guided walking tour.

❷ The **Custom House,** built by the Mexican government in 1827, was the first stop for sea traders whose goods were subject to duties. An upper story was later added to the adobe structure. At the beginning of the Mexican-American War in 1846, Commodore John Sloat raised the American flag over the building and claimed California for the United States. The house's lower floor displays typical cargo from a 19th-century trading ship. ✉ *1 Custom House Plaza, across from Fisherman's Wharf,* ☎ *831/649–2909.* 🎫 *Free.* ☉ *Daily 10–5.*

❸ The **Maritime Museum of Monterey** includes the private collection of maritime artifacts of a former Carmel mayor, Allen Knight. Among the exhibits of ship models, scrimshaw items, and nautical prints, the highlight is the enormous multifaceted Fresnel lens from the Point Sur Light Station. ✉ *5 Custom House Plaza,* ☎ *831/375–2553.* 🎫 *$5.* ☉ *Daily 10–5.*

❹ The **Pacific House,** a former hotel and saloon, is a park visitor center and museum that surveys life in early California with gold-rush relics, historical photographs of old Monterey, and a costume gallery of fashions from various periods. The upper floor displays Native American artifacts. ✉ *10 Custom House Plaza,* ☎ *831/649–7118.* 🎫 *Free.* ☉ *Daily 10–5.*

❺ **Casa Soberanes,** a low-ceiling classic adobe structure built in 1842, was once a Custom House guard's residence. Exhibits at the house survey life in Monterey from the era of Mexican rule to the present. There's a peaceful garden in back. ✉ *336 Pacific St.,* ☎ *831/649–7118.* 🎫 *House $5, garden free.* ☉ *Guided tours: daily noon, 2 PM. Garden: daily 8–5.*

Monterey and Pacific Grove

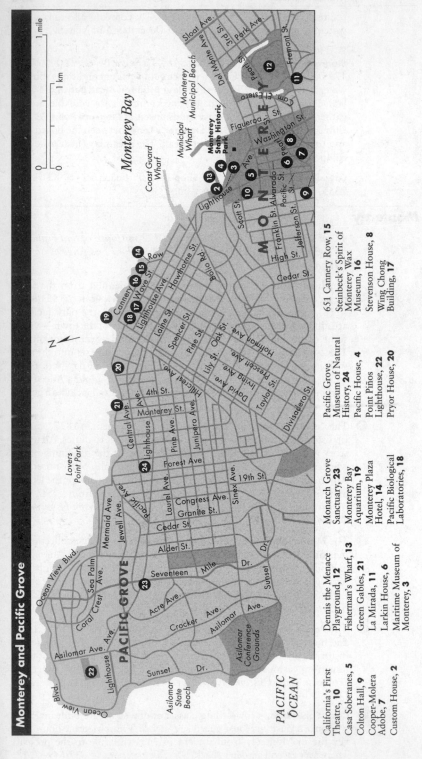

Monterey Bay

Coast Guard Wharf

Municipal Wharf

Monterey Municipal Beach

Monterey State Historic Park

M O N T E R E Y

PACIFIC GROVE

PACIFIC OCEAN

Lovers Point Park

Asilomar State Beach

Asilomar Conference Grounds

1 mile

1 km

California's First Theatre, **10**
Casa Soberanes, **5**
Colton Hall, **9**
Cooper-Molera Adobe, **7**
Custom House, **2**

Dennis the Menace Playground, **12**
Fisherman's Wharf, **13**
Green Gables, **21**
La Mirada, **11**
Larkin House, **6**
Maritime Museum of Monterey, **3**

Monarch Grove Sanctuary, **23**
Monterey Bay Aquarium, **24**
Monterey Plaza Hotel, **14**
Pacific Biological Laboratories, **18**

Pacific Grove Museum of Natural History, **24**
Pacific House, **4**
Point Piños Lighthouse, **22**
Pryor House, **20**

651 Cannery Row, **15**
Steinbeck's Spirit of Monterey Wax Museum, **16**
Stevenson House, **8**
Wing Chong Building, **17**

6 The **Larkin House** was built in 1835. A veranda encircles the second floor of this architecturally significant two-story adobe, whose design bears witness to the Mexican and New England influences on the Monterey style. The rooms are furnished with period antiques, many of them brought from New Hampshire to Monterey by the Larkin family. ⊠ *510 Calle Principal, between Jefferson and Pacific Sts.,* ☎ *831/649–7118.* 🎟 *$5.* ☉ *Guided tours daily 10 AM, 11 AM, and 3 PM.*

7 The restored **Cooper-Molera Adobe,** a 2-acre complex, includes a house dating from the 1820s, a visitor center, and a large garden enclosed by a high adobe wall. The mostly Victorian-era antiques and memorabilia that fill the tile-roof house provide a glimpse into the life of a prosperous pioneer family. ⊠ *Polk and Munras Sts.,* ☎ *831/649–7118.* 🎟 *$5.* ☉ *Guided tours daily 10 AM, 1 PM, and 4 PM.*

8 The **Stevenson House** was named in honor of author Robert Louis Stevenson, who boarded here briefly in a tiny upstairs room. Items from his family's estate furnish Stevenson's room; period-decorated chambers elsewhere in the house include a gallery of the author's memorabilia and a children's nursery stocked with Victorian toys and games. ⊠ *530 Houston St.,* ☎ *831/649–7118.* 🎟 *$5.* ☉ *Guided tours 11 AM, 1 PM, and 2 PM. Gardens daily 8–5.*

9 A convention of delegates met in 1849 to draft the first state constitution at **Colton Hall,** California's equivalent of Independence Hall. The white building, which has served as a school, a courthouse, and the county seat, is a museum furnished as it was during the constitutional convention. The extensive grounds outside the hall surround the Old Monterey Jail, where inmates languished behind thick granite walls. ⊠ *500 block of Pacific St., between Madison and Jefferson Sts.,* ☎ *831/646–5640.* 🎟 *Free.* ☉ *Mar.–Oct., daily 10–noon and 1–5; Nov.–Feb., daily 10–noon and 1–4.*

10 **California's First Theatre** was constructed in the 1840s by Jack Swan, an English sailor who settled in Monterey, as a saloon with adjoining apartments. Soldiers from the New York Volunteers who were on assignment in Monterey put on plays in the building. Melodramas and other theatrical performances are still staged here (☞ Nightlife and the Arts, *below*). ⊠ *Scott and Pacific Sts.,* ☎ *831/649–7118 or 831/375–4916 (box office).* 🎟 *Free.* ☉ *Wed.–Sat. 1–5.*

The **Monterey Peninsula Museum of Art** displays the works of photographers Ansel Adams and Edward Weston and other artists who have spent time on the peninsula. Another focus is international folk art; the colorful collection ranges from Kentucky hearth brooms to Tibetan prayer wheels. ⊠ *559 Pacific St., across the street from Colton Hall,* ☎ *831/372–7591.* 🎟 *$3.* ☉ *Wed.–Sat. 11–5, Sun. 1–4.*

11 At **La Mirada,** Asian and European antiques fill a 19th-century adobe house. A newer 10,000-square-ft gallery space, designed by Charles Moore, houses Asian and Californian regional art and a large netsuke collection. Outdoors are magnificent rose and rhododendron gardens. ⊠ *720 Via Mirada, at Fremont St.,* ☎ *831/372–3689.* 🎟 *$3.* ☉ *Thurs.–Sat. 11–5, Sun. 1–4.*

★ ☺ **12** **Dennis the Menace Playground** (⊠ Pearl St. and Camino El Estero), in Lake El Estero Park, is an imaginative play area designed by local resident and cartoonist Hank Ketcham. The equipment is on a grand scale and made for daredevils; there's a roller slide, a clanking suspension bridge, and a real Southern Pacific steam locomotive. You can rent a rowboat or a paddleboat to cruise about U-shape Lake El Estero, home to a varied assortment of ducks, mud hens, and geese.

Inevitably, visitors are drawn to Monterey's waterfront, lured in part by the mournful barking of sea lions. The whiskered marine mammals are best enjoyed while walking along **Fisherman's Wharf,** an aging pier across from Custom House Plaza that's lined with souvenir shops, fish markets, seafood restaurants, and popcorn stands. Although most commercial fishermen have moved to Wharf No. 2 down the way, Fisherman's Wharf, a lively and entertaining place to bring children, is still the departure point for fishing, diving, and whale-watching trips. The shallow waters of **Monterey Municipal Beach,** east of Wharf No. 2, are usually warm and calm enough for wading.

Cannery Row has undergone several transformations since it was immortalized in John Steinbeck's 1945 novel of the same name. The street that Steinbeck described was crowded with sardine canneries processing, at their peak, nearly 200,000 tons of the smelly silver fish a year. During the mid-1940s, however, the sardines disappeared from the bay, eventually causing the canneries to close. Through the years the old tin-roof canneries have been converted into restaurants, art galleries, and mini-malls with shops selling T-shirts, fudge, and plastic otters. Recent tourist development along the row has been more tasteful, however, including several stylish inns and hotels.

The **Monterey Plaza Hotel** (⊠ 400 Cannery Row), on the site of a historic estate, is a good place to relax over a drink and watch for otters. John Steinbeck would have trouble recognizing Cannery Row today, though wisps of its colorful past can be detected here and there. Check out **651 Cannery Row.** Its tiled Chinese dragon roof dates from 1929.

Characters from the novel *Cannery Row* are depicted in wax at **Steinbeck's Spirit of Monterey Wax Museum,** which presents an easy-to-digest 25-minute narration of 400 years of Monterey history, recorded by an actor playing John Steinbeck. ⊠ *700 Cannery Row,* ☎ *831/375–3770.* ☞ *$6.95.* ☉ *Memorial Day–Labor Day, daily 9–9; rest of yr, Mon.–Thurs. noon–6, Fri. and Sun. 10–8, Sat. 10–10.*

The **Wing Chong Building** (⊠ 835 Cannery Row) is the former Wing Chong Market that Steinbeck called Lee Chong's Heavenly Flower Grocery in *Cannery Row.* A weathered wooden building at 800 Cannery Row was the **Pacific Biological Laboratories** where Edward F. Ricketts, the inspiration for Doc in *Cannery Row,* did much of his marine research.

★ ☾ ⑲ The Outer Bay wing of the **Monterey Bay Aquarium** contains a million-gallon indoor ocean—observed through the largest window on Earth—that re-creates the sunlit blue water where Monterey Bay meets the open sea. In this habitat blue and soupfin sharks, barracuda, pelagic stingrays, ocean sunfish (which can weigh a ton or more), green sea turtles, and schools of fast-moving tuna swim together. The Outer Bay wing also houses a mesmerizing collection (the largest in the nation) of jellyfish. Expect long lines and sizable crowds at the aquarium on weekends, especially during the summer, but braving the masses is worth it. Don't miss the original wing's three-story Kelp Forest exhibit, the only one of its kind in the world, or the display of the sea creatures and vegetation found in Monterey Bay. Among other standouts are a bat-ray petting pool, where you can touch the flat velvetlike creatures as they swim by; a 55,000-gallon sea-otter tank; and an enormous outdoor artificial tidal pool that supports anemones, crabs, sea stars, and other colorful creatures. A special exhibit devoted to deep-sea life opens in March 1999. ⊠ *886 Cannery Row,* ☎ *831/648–4888; 800/756–3737 in CA for advance tickets.* ☞ *$14.75.* ☉ *Daily 10–6 (9:30–6 in summer); box office closes at 5:30.*

A short drive from downtown Monterey leads to **Ventana Vineyards,** known for chardonnays and Johannisberg Rieslings. Ventana's knowledgeable and hospitable owners, Doug and LuAnn Meador, invite guests to bring lunch to eat while tasting wines on a patio and deck. ✉ *2999 Monterey–Salinas Hwy. (Hwy. 68),* ☎ *831/372–7415.* ☉ *Daily 11–5.*

OFF THE
BEATEN PATH

ELKHORN SLOUGH – A few miles north of Monterey, east of the tiny harbor town of Moss Landing, is one of only two federal research reserves in California, the Elkhorn Slough at the National Estuarine Research Reserve. Its 1,400 acres of tidal flats and salt marshes form a complex environment that supports more than 200 species of birds. A walk along the meandering waterways and wetlands can reveal hawks, white-tailed kites, owls, herons, and egrets. Wander at your leisure or, on weekends, take a guided walk (10 AM and 1 PM) to the heron rookery. ✉ *1700 Elkhorn Rd., Watsonville,* ☎ *831/728–2822 for directions.* ✏ *$2.50; free with any California hunting or fishing license.* ☉ *Wed.–Sun. 9–5.*

Dining and Lodging

$$$–$$$$ ✕ **Fresh Cream.** The views of the bay are as superb as the imaginative French cuisine (with Californian accents) at this outstanding restaurant in Heritage Harbor. The menu, which changes weekly, might include rack of lamb Dijonnaise, roast boned duck in black-currant sauce, or blackened ahi tuna with pineapple rum-butter sauce. ✉ *99 Pacific St., Suite 100C,* ☎ *831/375–9798. AE, D, DC, MC, V. No lunch.*

$$$ ✕ **Duck Club.** The elegant and romantic dining room of the Monterey Plaza Hotel (☞ *below*) is built over the waterfront on Cannery Row, overlooking the bay. The seasonal dinner menu strongly emphasizes duck but also includes seafood, meat, and pasta. The Duck Club is open for breakfast. ✉ *400 Cannery Row,* ☎ *831/646–1706. AE, D, DC, MC, V. No lunch.*

$$–$$$ ✕ **Domenico's.** Italian seafood preparations, mesquite-grilled meats, and homemade pastas are the specialties at Domenico's. The blue-and-white nautical decor keeps the place comfortably casual; white drapery lends an air of elegance other wharf restaurants lack. ✉ *50 Fisherman's Wharf,* ☎ *831/372–3655. AE, D, DC, MC, V.*

$$–$$$ ✕ **Ferrante's.** Gorgeous views of the town and the bay complement the Italian cuisine at this restaurant atop the 10-story Monterey Marriott. The dishes, like the views, are meant to be shared: start with antipasti, then move on to risotto, pasta, or cioppino. ✉ *350 Calle Principal,* ☎ *831/647–4020. AE, D, DC, MC, V. No lunch.*

$$–$$$ ✕ **John Pisto's Whaling Station.** A pleasing mixture of rough-hewn wood
★ and sparkling white linen makes this restaurant above Cannery Row a festive yet comfortable place to enjoy seafood—try the sand dabs—and prime steaks. Chef-owner John Pisto (who appears on TV cooking shows) includes Monterey Bay sardines and anchovies on his menu. ✉ *763 Wave St.,* ☎ *831/373–3778. AE, D, DC, MC, V. No lunch.*

$$–$$$ ✕ **Monterey's Fish House.** Casual yet stylish and a real find away from the hubbub of the wharf, the always-packed Monterey Fish House attracts locals and frequent travelers to the city. If the dining room is full, you can wait at the bar and tide yourself over with deliciously plump oysters on the half shell. The bartenders and wait staff will gladly advise you on the perfect wine to go with your poached, blackened, or oakwood-grilled seafood. Steaks, chicken dishes, and pastas are also prepared. ✉ *2114 Del Monte Ave.,* ☎ *831/373–4647. Reservations essential for dinner. AE, D, DC, MC, V. No lunch weekends.*

$$–$$$ ✕ **Montrio.** If your appetite for hearty cooking and clean, strong fla-
★ vors has been stimulated by a day of bracing Monterey Bay breezes, this European-inspired American bistro, a montage of brick, rawhide,

and wrought iron inside Monterey's former firehouse, is the place to go. Grilled Portobello mushrooms with polenta—the most requested dish—and rotisserie chicken with garlic mashed potatoes are two of the menu highlights. ⊠ *414 Calle Principal,* ☎ *831/648–8880. Reservations essential on weekends. AE, D, MC, V.*

$$–$$$ ✕ **Stokes Adobe.** Chef Brandon Miller's sunny restaurant may be inside an 1833 adobe, but his cooking is strictly cutting edge. Miller specializes in the cuisines of Provence, northern Italy, and Catalan Spain, turning out imaginative pasta, seafood, and vegetarian dishes that change with the seasons. His past creations have included seared ahi tuna with lentil tomato salad, rustic pasta tubes with fennel sausage and Manila clams, and chicken under a brick with garlic mashed potatoes. ⊠ *500 Hartnell St.,* ☎ *831/373–1110. AE, DC, MC, V.*

$–$$$ ✕ **Abalonetti.** Squid reigns here: deep-fried, sautéed with wine and garlic, or baked with eggplant. Abalone is another specialty, and the fresh fish is broiled or blackened and served with beurre blanc or pesto. Next door, the Abalonetti Deli serves up antipasti and fried squid in casual surroundings. ⊠ *57 Fisherman's Wharf,* ☎ *831/373–1851. AE, D, DC, MC, V.*

$–$$$ ✕ **Cafe Fina.** Mesquite-grilled fish dishes and linguine in clam sauce with baby shrimp and tomatoes are among the highlights at this understated Italian restaurant on the wharf. The wine list is extensive. ⊠ *47 Fisherman's Wharf,* ☎ *831/372–5200. AE, D, DC, MC, V.*

$–$$$ ✕ **Paradiso Trattoria and Oyster Bar.** Follow the aroma of marinating olives, roasted garlic, and platters of focaccia to this bright Cannery Row establishment, under the same ownership as the Whaling Station, Domenico's, and Abalonetti. Cal-Mediterranean specialties and pizzas from a wood-burning oven are the luncheon fare. Seafood is a good choice for dinner, served in a dining room overlooking a lighted beachfront and lapping surf or at the gleaming oyster bar. ⊠ *654 Cannery Row,* ☎ *831/375–4155. AE, D, DC, MC, V.*

$–$$$ ✕ **Tarpy's Roadhouse.** Fun, dressed-down roadhouse lunch and dinner are served in this renovated farmhouse built in the early 1900s. The kitchen cooks everything Mom used to make, only better. Eat indoors by a fireplace or outdoors in the courtyard. ⊠ *2999 Monterey–Salinas Hwy. (Hwy. 68), at Canyon Del Rey Rd.,* ☎ *831/647–1444. AE, D, MC, V.*

$–$$ ✕ **Consuelo's.** Meals at this Mexican restaurant—housed somewhat incongruously in an 1886 Victorian—start with complimentary quesadillas, presented on a huge platter, then move on to fajitas, tostadas, enchiladas, marinated chicken, flautas, and other fare. If the weather's nice, you can sit outside in the shade of a huge Indian pine tree. ⊠ *361 Lighthouse Ave.,* ☎ *831/372–8111. AE, D, MC, V.*

$ ✕ **Old Monterey Cafe.** Breakfast here, which is served until closing time (2:30 PM), might include fresh-baked muffins and eggs Benedict. Soups, salads, and sandwiches appear on the lunch menu. This is also a good place to relax with a cappuccino or coffee made from freshly ground beans. ⊠ *489 Alvarado St.,* ☎ *831/646–1021. Reservations not accepted. D, V. No dinner.*

$$$$ ▥ **Hotel Pacific.** All the rooms at this modern adobe-style hotel are junior suites, handsomely appointed with featherbeds, hardwood floors, fireplaces, honor bars, and balconies or patios. The rates include parking. ⊠ *300 Pacific St., 93940,* ☎ *831/373–5700 or 800/554–5542 ,* FAX *831/373–6921. 105 suites. Refrigerators, 2 hot tubs, laundry service. Continental breakfast. AE, D, DC, MC, V.*

$$$$ ▥ **Hyatt Regency Monterey.** Although its rooms and atmosphere are less glamorous than those at some other resorts in the region, the facilities here are excellent. ⊠ *1 Old Golf Course Rd., 93940,* ☎ *831/*

372–1234; 800/824–2196 in CA, ⒻⒶⓍ *831/372–4277. 535 rooms, 40 suites. Restaurant, café, bar, 2 pools, 2 hot tubs, massage, 18-hole golf course, putting green, 6 tennis courts, exercise room, bicycles, children's programs. AE, D, DC, MC, V.*

$$$$ 🏨 **Monterey Bay Inn.** On Cannery Row and with breathtaking bay views from most rooms, this hotel takes full advantage of its location, even providing guests binoculars for viewing marine life. Rooms, decorated in peach and green tones, come with private balconies, TVs with VCRs, honor bars, and terry-cloth robes. ⊠ *242 Cannery Row, 93940,* ☎ *831/373–6242 or 800/424–6242,* ⒻⒶⓍ *831/373–7603. 47 rooms. Refrigerators, in-room VCRs, 2 hot tubs, sauna, exercise room. Continental breakfast. No smoking.. AE, D, DC, MC, V.*

$$$$
★ 🏨 **Monterey Plaza Hotel.** This sophisticated full-service hotel commands a waterfront location on Cannery Row, where frolicking sea otters can be observed from the wide outdoor patio and many room balconies. The architecture and decor blend early Californian and Mediterranean styles and retain elements of the old cannery design. ⊠ *400 Cannery Row, 93940,* ☎ *831/646–1700 or 800/631–1339; 800/334–3999 in CA,* ⒻⒶⓍ *831/646–0285. 285 rooms. 2 restaurants, exercise room, laundry service. AE, D, DC, MC, V.*

$$$$
★ 🏨 **Old Monterey Inn.** Perhaps no other inn conjures up the past and beauty of the Monterey Peninsula or provides such a complete escape so close to everything the area has to offer. The three-story English Tudor country manor was completed in 1929, replete with hand-carved window frames, balustrades, and Gothic archways. Loving restoration by proprietors Gene and Ann Swett included a rose garden now surrounded by giant holly trees, 100-year-old gnarled oaks, and majestic redwoods. The couple's thoroughness extends to their hospitality—a well-stocked medicine cabinet, sumptuous featherbeds with down comforters. ⊠ *500 Martin St., 93940,* ☎ *831/375–8284 or 800/350–2344,* ⒻⒶⓍ *831/375–6730. 10 rooms. Concierge. Full breakfast. MC, V.*

$$$$
★ 🏨 **Spindrift Inn.** This small hotel on Cannery Row, under the same management as the Hotel Pacific and the Monterey Bay Inn, has beach access and a rooftop garden that overlooks Monterey Bay. Spacious rooms with sitting areas, hardwood floors, fireplaces, and down comforters are among the indoor pleasures. ⊠ *652 Cannery Row, 93940,* ☎ *831/646–8900 or 800/841–1879,* ⒻⒶⓍ *831/646–5342. 42 rooms. Refrigerators. Continental breakfast. AE, D, DC, MC, V.*

$$$–$$$$ 🏨 **Embassy Suites.** As you drive into Monterey from the north on Highway 1, you can't miss the high-rise Embassy Suites, which towers over the town of Seaside just before the Monterey line. Two blocks from the beach, it overlooks Laguna Grande Lake and Monterey Bay. All accommodations here are smallish two-room suites with microwaves, refrigerators, and coffeemakers. ⊠ *1441 Canyon Del Rey, Seaside 93955,* ☎ *831/393–1115,* ⒻⒶⓍ *831/393–1113. 225 suites. Restaurant, bar, kitchenettes, refrigerators, indoor pool, hot tub, sauna, exercise room. Full breakfast. AE, D, DC, MC, V .*

$$$–$$$$ 🏨 **Cannery Row Inn.** Gas fireplaces are among the amenities at this small hotel on a street above Cannery Row. Some rooms have private balconies with bay views. ⊠ *200 Foam St., 93940,* ☎ *831/649–8580 or 800/876–8580,* ⒻⒶⓍ *831/649–2566. 32 rooms. Refrigerators, hot tub. Continental breakfast. AE, D, MC, V.*

$–$$$$ 🏨 **Best Western Monterey Beach Hotel.** The rooms here may be nondescript, but this hotel has a great waterfront location about 2 mi north of town, with views of the bay and the Monterey skyline. The grounds are pleasantly landscaped, and there's a large pool with a sunbathing area. ⊠ *2600 Sand Dunes Dr., 93940,* ☎ *831/394–3321 or 800/242–8627,* ⒻⒶⓍ *831/393–1912. 196 rooms. Restaurant, lounge, pool, hot tub, exercise room. AE, D, DC, MC, V.*

$$–$$$ ▣ **Monterey Bay Lodge.** Its location on the edge of Monterey's El Es-
★ tero Park gives this motel an edge over those along the busy Munras
Avenue motel row. Indoor plants and a secluded courtyard with a heated
pool are other pluses. ⊠ *55 Aguajito Rd., 93940,* ☎ *831/372–8057
or 800/558–1900,* 𝙵𝙰𝚇 *831/655–2933. 45 rooms. Restaurant, pool. AE,
D, DC, MC, V.*

$$–$$$ ▣ **Monterey Hotel.** Standard rooms in this restored Victorian are small
but contain well-chosen reproduction antique furniture; the master suites
have fireplaces and sunken baths. ⊠ *406 Alvarado St., 93940,* ☎ *831/
375–3184 or 800/727–0960,* 𝙵𝙰𝚇 *831/373–2899. 39 rooms, 6 suites.
No-smoking rooms, parking (fee). Continental breakfast. AE, D, DC,
MC, V.*

$–$$$ ▣ **Quality Inn.** This stylish motel has a friendly, country-inn atmosphere.
Breakfast is served in a pine-panel lobby; in-room coffee is also com-
plimentary. Rooms are light and airy, some with fireplaces and some
with accessibility for visitors with disabilities. ⊠ *1058 Munras Ave.,
93940,* ☎ *831/372–3381,* 𝙵𝙰𝚇 *831/372–4687. 55 rooms. Hot tub. Con-
tinental breakfast. AE, D, DC, MC, V.*

$–$$ ▣ **Del Monte Beach Inn.** The rooms at this small, reasonably priced
B&B are decorated the way rooms in your grandmother's or auntie's
home might have been. Check in or call before 8 PM, when the office
closes. ⊠ *1110 Del Monte Ave., 93940,* ☎ *831/649–4410,* 𝙵𝙰𝚇 *831/
378–3818. 16 rooms, 2 suites. Continental breakfast. AE, D, MC, V.*

Nightlife and the Arts

BARS, CLUBS

Doc's Nightclub (⊠ 95 Prescott St., ☎ 831/649–4241), one block above
Cannery Row, hosts bands—rock, blues, jazz, reggae, or folk—every
night but Sunday. **Planet Gemini** (⊠ 625 Cannery Row, ☎ 831/373–
1449) presents comedy shows on most nights, followed by dancing to
DJ or live music. **Sly McFlys** (⊠ 700-A Cannery Row, ☎ 831/649–
8050), a popular watering hole, has a pub-like atmosphere.

MUSIC FESTIVALS

Dixieland Monterey (⊠ 177 Webster St., Suite A-206, ☎ 831/443–
5260 or 888/349–6879), held on the first full weekend of March, presents Dixieland jazz bands in cabarets, restaurants, and hotel lounges
on the Monterey waterfront. The **Monterey Bay Blues Festival** (☎
831/394–2652 or 831/649–6544) draws blues fans to the Monterey
Fairgrounds in June. **Monterey Jazz Festival** (☎ 831/373–3366) attracts jazz and blues greats from around the world to the Monterey
Fairgrounds on the third full weekend of September.

THEATER

California's First Theatre (⊠ Scott and Pacific Sts., ☎ 831/375–4916)
is home to the Troupers of the Gold Coast, who perform 19th-century
melodramas year-round, mostly on weekends. **Monterey Bay The-
atrefest** (☎ 831/622–0700) presents free outdoor performances at Custom House Plaza on weekend afternoons and evenings from late June
to mid-July. The **Wharf Theater** (⊠ Fisherman's Wharf, ☎ 831/649–
2332) focuses on American musicals past and present.

Outdoor Activities and Sports

BICYCLING

For bicycle rentals try **Bay Sports** (⊠ 640 Wave St., ☎ 831/646–
9090) or **Adventures by the Sea Inc.** (⊠ 299 Cannery Row, ☎ 831/
372–1807).

CAR RACING

Five major races take place each year on the 2.2-mi, 11-turn **Laguna
Seca Raceway** (⊠ 1021 Monterey–Salinas Hwy., ☎ 831/648–5100).

FISHING

Half- and full-day fishing trips are conducted by **Monterey Sport Fishing** (✉ 96 Fisherman's Wharf, ☎ 831/372–2203 or 800/200–2203), **Randy's Fishing Trips** (✉ 66 Fisherman's Wharf, ☎ 831/372–7440), and **Sam's Fishing Fleet** (✉ 84 Fisherman's Wharf, ☎ 831/372–0577).

GOLF

The greens fee at the 18-hole **Old Del Monte Golf Course** (✉ 1300 Sylvan Rd., ☎ 831/373–2700) is $75, plus $18 for an optional cart. The $15 twilight special (plus $18 cart rental per person) begins two hours before sunset.

KAYAKING

Monterey Bay Kayaks (✉ 693 Del Monte Ave., ☎ 831/373–5357; 800/649–5357 in CA) rents equipment and conducts classes and natural-history tours.

ROLLERBLADING AND SKATING

Adventures by the Sea Inc. (✉ 299 Cannery Row, ☎ 408/372–1807) rents rollerblades. **Del Monte Gardens** (✉ 2020 Del Monte Ave., ☎ 831/375–3202) is an old-fashioned rink for skating and rollerblading.

SCUBA DIVING

The staff at **Aquarius Dive Shops** (✉ 2040 Del Monte Ave., ☎ 831/375–1933; ✉ 32 Cannery Row, ☎ 831/375–6605) gives diving lessons and tours and rents equipment. The **scuba-diving conditions information line** (☎ 831/657–1020) is updated regularly.

TENNIS

Monterey Tennis Center (☎ 831/372–0172) has details about area facilities.

WHALE-WATCHING

Monterey Sport Fishing (✉ 96 Fisherman's Wharf, ☎ 831/372–2203 or 800/200–2203), **Randy's Fishing Trips** (✉ 66 Fisherman's Wharf, ☎ 831/372–7440), and **Sam's Fishing Fleet** (✉ 84 Fisherman's Wharf, ☎ 831/372–0577) operate whale-watching expeditions.

Shopping

Alicia's Antiques (✉ 835 Cannery Row , ☎ 831/372–1423) occupies the back of the Wing Chong Building. Owner Alicia Harby-DeNoon, who knew John Steinbeck and Doc Ricketts, knows much about the old Cannery Row. **Old Monterey Book Co.** (✉ 136 Bonifacio Pl., off Alvarado St., ☎ 831/372–3111) specializes in rare old books and prints.

Pacific Grove

3 mi from Monterey south on Hwy. 1 and west on Hwy. 68; from Cannery Row, Wave St. heading west becomes Ocean View Blvd. at Monterey–Pacific Grove border.

If not for the dramatic strip of coastline in its backyard, Pacific Grove could easily pass for a typical small town in the Heartland. The town, which began as a summer retreat for church groups more than a century ago, recalls its prim and proper Victorian heritage in the host of tiny board-and-batten cottages and stately mansions lining its streets.

Even before the church groups flocked here, Pacific Grove had been receiving thousands of annual guests in the form of bright orange-and-black monarch butterflies. Known as Butterfly Town USA, Pacific Grove is the winter home of monarchs that migrate south from Canada and the Pacific Northwest to take residence in pine and eucalyptus groves between October and March. The sight of a mass of butterflies hanging from the branches like a long, fluttering veil is unforgettable.

A prime way to enjoy Pacific Grove is to walk or bicycle along its 3 mi of city-owned shoreline, a cliff-top area following Ocean View Boulevard that is landscaped with succulents and native plants and has benches on which to sit and gaze at the sea. You can spot marine life and birds here, including colonies of cormorants drawn to the massive rocks rising out of the surf.

⑳ Among the Victorians of note is the **Pryor House** (✉ 429 Ocean View Blvd.), a massive shingled structure with a leaded- and beveled-glass
㉑ doorway. **Green Gables** (✉ 5th St. and Ocean View Blvd.), a romantic Swiss Gothic–style mansion with steeply peaked gables and stained-glass windows, is a B&B.

Ⓒ The view of the coast is gorgeous from **Lovers Point Park,** on Ocean View Boulevard midway along the waterfront. The park's sheltered beach has a children's pool and picnic area. Glass-bottom boat rides, which provide views of the plant and sea life below, take place in summer.

★ Ⓒ **㉒** At **Point Piños Lighthouse,** the oldest continuously operating lighthouse on the West Coast—it's been at work since 1855—you can learn about the lighting and foghorn operations and wander through a small museum containing memorabilia from the U.S. Coast Guard. ✉ *Asilomar Ave. between Ocean View Blvd. and Lighthouse Ave.,* ☎ *831/648–3116.* ◪ *Free.* ☽ *Thurs.–Sun. 1–4.*

Monarchs sometimes vary their nesting sites from year to year, but the
㉓ **Monarch Grove Sanctuary** (✉ 1073 Lighthouse Ave., at Ridge Rd.) is a fairly reliable spot for viewing the butterflies.

If you are in Pacific Grove when the monarch butterflies aren't, an ap-
Ⓒ **㉔** proximation of this annual spectacle is on exhibit at the **Pacific Grove Museum of Natural History.** In addition to a well-crafted butterfly tree exhibit, the museum displays 400 mounted birds and has a Touch Gallery for kids. ✉ *165 Forest Ave.,* ☎ *831/648–3116.* ◪ *Free.* ☽ *Tues.– Sun. 10–5.*

A beautiful coastal area in Pacific Grove is ★**Asilomar State Beach,** on Sunset Drive between Point Piños and the Del Monte Forest. The 100 acres of dunes, tidal pools, and pocket-size beaches form one of the region's richest areas for marine life.

Dining and Lodging

$$$ ✕ **Melac's.** Complementing Pacific Grove's quiet charm, this country restaurant's owners are as friendly as their food is delicious. French-born Jacques Melac greets his guests personally and enjoys helping them pair wines with the creations of the chef, his wife, Janet. The menu changes monthly. If grilled quail with roasted garlic and Oregon chanterelles, seafood cassoulet, or roasted duckling with port and fresh figs are on the list when you visit, don't miss them. ✉ *663 Lighthouse Ave.,* ☎ *831/375–1743. AE, D, DC, MC, V. Closed Sun. No lunch Sat.*

$$$ ✕ **Old Bath House.** A romantic, nostalgic atmosphere permeates this
★ converted bathhouse overlooking the water at Lovers Point. The classic regional menu makes the most of local seafood and produce. When available, the salmon and Monterey Bay prawns are worth a taste. The restaurant has a less expensive menu for late-afternoon diners. ✉ *620 Ocean View Blvd.,* ☎ *831/375–5195. AE, D, DC, MC, V. No lunch.*

$$–$$$ ✕ **Fandango.** With its stone walls and country furniture, this restaurant has the earthy feel of a southern European farmhouse. Complementing the ambience are the robust flavors of the cuisine, which ranges from southern France, Italy, Spain, and Greece to North Africa, from paella and cannelloni to couscous. ✉ *223 17th St.,* ☎ *831/372– 3456. AE, D, DC, MC, V.*

$$–$$$ ✕ **Gernot's.** The ornate Victorian-era Hart Mansion is a delightful setting in which to dine on seafood and game served with light sauces. Austrian/Continental specialties include wild-boar bourguignonne, roast venison, and rack of lamb. ⊠ *649 Lighthouse Ave.,* ☎ *831/646–1477. AE, MC, V. Closed Mon. No lunch.*

$–$$$ ✕ **The Tinnery.** This family-oriented restaurant has a terrific location overlooking Lovers Point. The menu runs toward the tried-and-true: pancakes and omelets for breakfast, burgers and other sandwiches for lunch. Broiled salmon with fresh hollandaise sauce, mesquite-grilled meats, and English fish-and-chips are dinner-menu highlights. ⊠ *631 Ocean View Blvd.,* ☎ *831/646–1040. Reservations not accepted. AE, D, DC, MC, V.*

$–$$ ✕ **Crocodile Grill.** Wooden crocodiles, ant eaters, and toucans go hand in hand with the adventurous New American concoctions of the Crocodile. West Indies spiced ribs, the Mayan mixed grill, and pork posole (soup) are especially tasty. If you can't decide what to order, try the Caribbean platter, with a black-bean fritter, coconut prawns, sweet-potato fries, and more. ⊠ *701 Lighthouse Ave.,* ☎ *831/655–3311. AE, D, MC, V. Closed Tues. No lunch.*

$–$$ ✕ **Fishwife.** Fresh fish with a Mexican accent makes this the locals' choice for lunch or a casual dinner. ⊠ *1996½ Sunset Dr., at Asilomar Blvd.,* ☎ *831/375–7107. AE, D, MC, V. Closed Tues.*

$–$$ ✕ **Peppers Mexicali Cafe.** This cheerful white-walled restaurant serves fresh seafood and traditional dishes from Mexico and Latin America. The red and green salsas are excellent. ⊠ *170 Forest Ave.,* ☎ *831/373–6892. AE, D, DC, MC, V. Closed Tues. No lunch Sun.*

$–$$ ✕ **Toasties Cafe.** Three-egg omelets, burritos, pancakes, waffles, French toast, and other breakfast items are served at this crowded café until 3 PM. The lunch selections include burgers and other sandwiches. Toasties also serves dinner—fish and chips, seafood pasta—but it's best to stick to daytime meals. ⊠ *702 Lighthouse Ave.,* ☎ *831/373–7543. AE, MC, V.*

$$$–$$$$ ▦ **Martine Inn.** Most B&Bs in Pacific Grove are in Victorian houses; ★ this one is in a pink-stucco, Mediterranean-style villa overlooking the water. The many antiques include a mahogany suite exhibited at the 1893 Chicago World's Fair, movie costume designer Edith Head's bedroom suite, and an 1860 Chippendale Revival four-poster bed. The glassed-in parlor has a stunning ocean view. ⊠ *255 Ocean View Blvd., 93950,* ☎ *831/373–3388 or 800/852–5588,* ℻ *831/373–3896. 22 rooms, 1 suite. Full breakfast. AE, D, MC, V.*

$$$–$$$$ ▦ **Seven Gables Inn.** Four yellow-gabled clapboard buildings share a corner lot and a great view of the ocean. The main house was built in 1886, the other three between 1910 and 1940. European antiques of various periods—gold-leaf mirrors, crystal chandeliers, and marble statues—create a formal atmosphere. The gracious innkeeper, Susan Flatley, grew up in the house and shares her knowledge about it and the area. ⊠ *555 Ocean View Blvd., 93950,* ☎ *831/372–4341. 11 rooms, 3 cottages. Full breakfast. MC, V. No smoking indoors. 2-night minimum weekends, 3-night minimum holiday weekends.*

$$–$$$$ ▦ **Green Gables Inn.** Stained-glass windows framing an ornate fire- ★ place and other interior detail work compete with the spectacular bay views at this century-old Queen Anne–style mansion built by a sea captain for his mistress. Newly renovated rooms in a carriage house perched on a hill out back are larger, have ocean views and more modern amenities, and afford more privacy than rooms in the main house, which have more charm. ⊠ *104 5th St., 93950,* ☎ *831/375–2095 or 800/722–1774,* ℻ *831/375–5437. 10 rooms, 4 with shared bath; 1 suite. Full breakfast. AE, MC, V.*

$$-$$$$ ⊞ **Lighthouse Lodge and Suites.** On two sides of Lighthouse Avenue—
the lodge is on one side, the all-suites facility on the other—this com-
plex near the tip of the peninsula provides a woodsy alternative to
downtown Pacific Grove's B&B scene. The suites contain fireplaces,
in-room whirlpool tubs, and kitchenettes. Some of the standard rooms
could use remodeling, but they're decent in size yet much lower priced.
⊠ *1150 and 1249 Lighthouse Ave., 93950,* ☎ *831/655–2111 or 800/
858–1249,* 𝔽𝔸𝕏 *831/655–4922. 68 rooms, 31 suites. Pool, hot tub. Full
breakfast. AE, D, DC, MC, V.*

$$-$$$ ⊞ **The Centrella Inn.** A handsome century-old Victorian mansion two
   ★   blocks from Lovers Point Beach, the Centrella contains rooms with claw-
foot bathtubs, and wicker and brass furnishings. Five guest cottages
hold similar appointments. Depending on the time of day, a sideboard
in the mansion's large parlor is laden with breakfast treats, cookies and
fruit, sherry and wine, or hors d'oeuvres. ⊠ *612 Central Ave., 93950,*
☎ *831/372–3372 or 800/233–3372,* 𝔽𝔸𝕏 *831/372–2036. 19 rooms,
2 suites, 5 cottages. AE, D, MC, V.*

$$-$$$ ⊞ **Gosby House Inn.** Most rooms in this yellow Victorian B&B in the
town center have private baths, and some have fireplaces. The inn has
an informal, country air. Its knowledgeable innkeepers gladly provide
sightseeing or restaurant suggestions. ⊠ *643 Lighthouse Ave., 93950,*
☎ *831/375–1287 or 800/527–8828,* 𝔽𝔸𝕏 *831/655–9621. 22 rooms,
2 with shared bath. Full breakfast. AE, MC, V.*

$$ ⊞ **Asilomar Conference Center.** An atmosphere not unlike summer camp
prevails at this assortment of 28 rustic but comfortable lodges in the
middle of a woodsy 105-acre state park across from the beach. Rooms
are available when not they're not booked for conferences. ⊠ *800 Asilomar Blvd., Box 537, 93950,* ☎ *831/372–8016,* 𝔽𝔸𝕏 *831/372–7227. 314
rooms. Cafeteria, pool. Full breakfast . MC, V.*

Outdoor Activities and Sports

GOLF

The greens fee at the 18-hole **Pacific Grove Municipal Golf Links** (⊠ 77
Asilomar Blvd., ☎ 831/648–3177) runs between $25 and $30 (you
can play nine holes for between $15 and $18), with an 18-hole twilight rate of $14. Optional carts cost $25. The course has spectacular
ocean views on its back nine—and ice-plant-covered sand dunes that
make keeping the ball on the fairway a must. Tee times may be reserved
up to seven days in advance.

TENNIS

Pacific Grove Municipal Courts (☎ 831/648–3129) has information about
the town's public courts.

Shopping

American Tin Cannery Outlet Center (⊠ 125 Ocean View Blvd., ☎ 831/
372–3071) carries designer clothing, jewelry, accessories, and home
decorating items at discounts between 25% and 65%. **Wooden Nickel**
(⊠ Central and Fountain Aves., ☎ 831/646–8050) sells Victorian accent pieces for the home.

17-Mile Drive and Pebble Beach

Off Sunset Dr. in Pacific Grove or N. San Antonio Rd. in Carmel.

Primordial nature resides in quiet harmony with palatial estates along
★ **17-Mile Drive,** an 8,400-acre microcosm of the Monterey coastal landscape. Dotting the drive are rare Monterey cypress, trees so gnarled
and twisted that Robert Louis Stevenson once described them as
"ghosts fleeing before the wind." Some sightseers balk at the $7.25-
per-car fee collected at the gates, but most who do pay find the drive

In case you want to be welcomed there.

We're here to see that you're always welcomed at establishments everywhere. That's why millions of people carry the American Express® Card – for peace of mind, confidence, and security, around the world or just around the corner.

do more

Cards

In case you're running low.

We're here to help with more than 118,000 Express Cash locations around the world. In order to enroll, just call American Express before you start your vacation.

do more

Express Cash

And just in case.

We're here with American Express® Travelers Cheques and Cheques *for Two®*. They're the safest way to carry money on your vacation and the surest way to get a refund, practically anywhere, anytime.
Another way we help you...

do more

Travelers
Cheques

Carmel and 17-Mile Drive

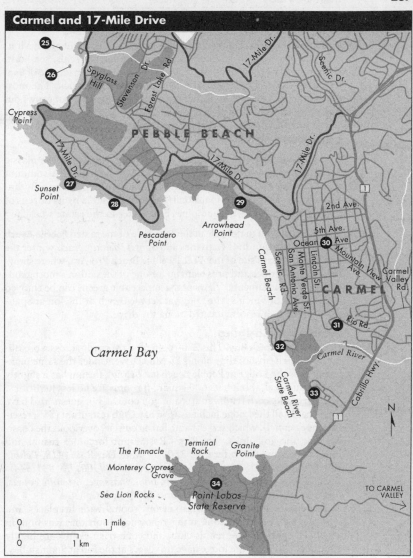

well worth the price. (If you really can't stand to pay, grab a bike—cyclists tour for free.)

㉕ **Bird Rock,** the largest of several islands at the southern end of the Monterey Country Club's golf course, teems with harbor seals, sea lions,

㉖ cormorants, and pelicans. Sea creatures and birds also make use of **Seal Rock,** the larger of a group of islands south of Bird Rock. The most

㉗ photographed tree is the weather-sculpted **Lone Cypress** that grows out of a precipitous outcropping above the waves. You can stop for a view of the Lone Cypress at a parking area, but you can't walk out to the tree.

Many of the stately homes along 17-Mile Drive reflect the classic Monterey or Spanish Mission style typical of the region. A standout

㉘ is the **Crocker Marble Palace,** a waterfront estate inspired by a Byzantine castle. This baroque mansion is easily identifiable by its dozens of marble arches. Underground pipes heat water in the estate's beach.

㉙ The ocean plays a major role in the 18th hole of the famed **Pebble Beach Golf Links** (☞ Outdoor Activities and Sports, *below*). Each winter the course is the main site of the AT&T Pebble Beach Pro-Am, where show-business celebrities and pros team up for one of the nation's most glamorous golf tournaments. Views of the impeccable greens can be enjoyed over a drink or lunch at the Lodge at Pebble Beach or the Inn at Spanish Bay, the two resorts located along the drive.

Dining and Lodging

$$$$ ✕▦ **Inn at Spanish Bay.** This 270-room resort sprawls across a breath-★ taking stretch of shoreline along 17-Mile Drive. Under the same management as the Lodge at Pebble Beach (☞ *below*), the inn has a slightly more casual feel, though its 600-square-ft rooms are no less luxurious. The inn has its own tennis courts and golf course, but guests also have privileges at all the Lodge facilities. The Bay Club restaurant ($$$; reservations essential), which serves haute Italian cuisine, overlooks the coastline and the golf links. Try Roy's Restaurant for more casual and innovative Euro-Asian fare. ⊠ *2700 17-Mile Dr., Box 1418, Pebble Beach 93953,* ☎ *831/647–7500 or 800/654–9300,* ㎊ *831/644–7960. 270 rooms. 3 restaurants, bar, pool, massage, 8 tennis courts, health club, hiking, horseback riding. AE, DC, MC, V.*

$$$$ ✕▦ **Lodge at Pebble Beach.** Luxurious rooms with fireplaces and ★ wonderful views set the tone at this renowned resort that was built in 1919. The golf course, tennis club, and equestrian center are highly regarded. Guests of the lodge have privileges at the Inn at Spanish Bay. Overlooking the 18th green, the very fine Club XIX restaurant is an intimate, café-style spot serving French cuisine prepared with a light touch. ⊠ *1700 17-Mile Dr., Box 1128, Pebble Beach 93953,* ☎ *831/624–3811 or 800/654–9300,* ㎊ *831/644–7960. 142 rooms, 19 suites. 3 restaurants, bar, coffee shop, pool, hot tub, massage, sauna, 18-hole golf course, 12 tennis courts, exercise room, health club, horseback riding, beach, bicycles. AE, DC, MC, V.*

Outdoor Activities and Sports

GOLF

The Links at Spanish Bay (⊠ 17-Mile Dr., north end, ☎ 831/624–3811), which hugs a choice stretch of shoreline, is designed in the rugged manner of a traditional Scottish course, with sand dunes and coastal marshes interspersed among the greens. The greens fee is $165, plus $25 cart rental ($150 for resort guests, including cart); reserve tee times as far ahead as possible.

Pebble Beach Golf Links (⊠ 17-Mile Dr., ☎ 831/625–8518) attracts golfers from around the world, despite a greens fee of $295, plus $25 for an optional cart ($245 with a complimentary cart for guests of the

Pebble Beach or Spanish Bay resorts). Nonguests can reserve a tee time only one day in advance on a space-available basis (up to a year for groups); resort guests can reserve up to 18 months in advance.

Peter Hay (✉ 17-Mile Dr., ☎ 831/625–8518), a nine-hole pitch-and-putt course, charges $10 per person, no reservations necessary.

Poppy Hills (✉ 17-Mile Dr., ☎ 831/625–2035), a splendid course designed in 1986 by Robert Trent Jones Jr., has a greens fee of $115 to $130; an optional cart costs $30. Individuals may reserve up to one month in advance, groups up to a year.

Spyglass Hill (✉ Spyglass Hill Rd., ☎ 831/624–3811) is among the most challenging Pebble Beach courses. With the first five holes bordering on the Pacific and the rest reaching deep into the Del Monte Forest, the views offer some consolation. The greens fee is $200; an optional cart costs $25 ($175 with complimentary cart for resort guests). Reservations are essential and may be made up to one month in advance (18 months for guests).

HORSEBACK RIDING

Riding a horse from the **Pebble Beach Equestrian Center** (✉ Portola Rd. and Alva La., ☎ 831/624–2756) is a great way to enjoy the Del Monte Forest, which has 26 mi of bridle trails.

Carmel

5 mi south of Monterey on Hwy. 1 (or via 17-Mile Drive's Carmel Gate).

Although the community has grown quickly through the years and its population quadruples with tourists on weekends and during the summer, Carmel retains its identity as a quaint village; buildings still have no street numbers, and live music is banned in the local watering holes. You can wander the side streets at your own pace, poking into hidden courtyards and stopping at Hansel-and-Gretel-like cafés for tea and crumpets.

Downtown Carmel's chief lure is shopping. Its main street, **Ocean Avenue,** is a mishmash of ersatz English Tudor, Mediterranean, and other styles. **Carmel Plaza,** in the east end of the village proper at Ocean and Junipero avenues, holds more than 50 shops, restaurants, and small branches of major department stores.

Before it became an art colony in the early 20th century and long before it became a shopping and browsing mecca, Carmel was an important religious center during the establishment of Spanish California. That heritage is preserved in the Mission San Carlos Borromeo del Rio Carmelo, more commonly known as the **Carmel Mission.** Founded in 1770, it served as headquarters for the mission system in California under Father Junípero Serra. Adjoining the stone church are a tranquil garden planted with California poppies. Museum rooms at the mission include an early kitchen, Serra's spartan sleeping quarters, and the oldest college library in California. ✉ *Rio Rd. and Lasuen Dr.,* ☎ *831/624–3600.* ⌐ *$2.* ☉ *Sept.–May, Mon.–Sat. 9:30–4:30, Sun. 10:30–4:30; June–Aug., Mon.–Sat. 9:30–7:30, Sun. 10:30–7:30.*

Scattered throughout the pines in Carmel are the houses and cottages that were built for writers, artists, and photographers who discovered the area decades ago. Among the most impressive dwellings is **Tor House,** a stone cottage built by the poet Robinson Jeffers in 1919 on a craggy knoll overlooking the sea. Portraits, books, and unusual art objects, including a white stone from the Great Pyramid in Egypt, fill the low-ceiling rooms. The highlight of the small estate is Hawk Tower, a detached edifice set with stones from the Carmel coastline as well as one from the Great Wall of China. Within the tower is the Gothic-style room that served as a retreat for the poet's wife, Una, an accomplished musician. The docents who lead tours (six persons maximum) are well informed about the poet's work and life. ✉ *26304 Ocean View Ave.,* ☎ *831/624–1813 or 831/624–1840.* ▣ *$7. No children under 12.* ☉ *Tours Fri. and Sat. 10–3; reservations essential.*

㉝ Carmel's greatest beauty is its rugged coastline, with pine and cypress forests and countless inlets. **Carmel River State Park** stretches for 106 acres along Carmel Bay. On sunny days the waters appear nearly as turquoise as those of the Caribbean. The park has a sugar-white beach and a nature preserve where you might spot pelicans, kingfishers, hawks, and sandpipers. ✉ *Off Scenic Rd., south of Carmel Beach,* ☎ *831/624–4909.* ☉ *Daily 9 AM–sunset.*

★ **㉞** **Point Lobos State Reserve,** a 350-acre headland harboring a wealth of marine life, lies a few miles south of Carmel. The best way to explore the reserve is to walk along one of its many trails. The Cypress Grove Trail leads through a forest of Monterey cypress (one of only two natural groves remaining), clinging to the rocks above an emerald-green cove. Sea Lion Point Trail is a good place to view sea lions. From those and other trails you can also spot otters, harbor seals, and (during winter and spring) migrating whales. An additional 750 acres of the reserve is an undersea marine park open to qualified scuba divers. No pets are allowed. ✉ *Hwy. 1,* ☎ *831/624–4909; 831/624–8413 for scuba-diving reservations.* ▣ *$7 per vehicle.* ☉ *May–Sept., daily 9–7; Oct.–Apr., daily 9–5.*

Dining and Lodging

$$$ ✕ **Kincaid's Bistro.** At chef-owner Robert Kincaid's country-French ★ bistro, dried sage and lavender hanging from exposed ceiling beams, rag-painted floors, and ochre-washed walls will make you feel as if you've stepped into an old farmhouse in Provence. Cassoulet made with white beans, duck confit, rabbit sausage, and garlic prawns is always on the stove and best enjoyed with a rustic red wine. Leave room for dessert, particularly the soufflé with lemon and orange zest or the chocolate bag with chocolate shake, a masterful invention. ✉ *Crossroads Center, 217 Crossroads Blvd.,* ☎ *831/624–9626. AE, D, MC, V. Closed Sun. No lunch Sat.*

$$–$$$ ✕ **Anton and Michel.** Expect superb European cuisine at this elegant restaurant in Carmel's shopping district. The tender lamb dishes are fantastic and well complemented by the wines poured. The ultimate treats, however, are the flaming desserts. You can dine in the outdoor courtyard in summer. ✉ *Mission St. and 7th Ave.,* ☎ *831/624–2406. AE, D, DC, MC, V.*

$$–$$$ ✕ **Casanova.** Southern French and northern Italian cuisine come together at Casanova, one of the most romantic restaurants in Carmel. A heated outdoor garden and the more than 1,000 domestic and imported wines enhance the dining experience. The menu changes weekly; highlights include house-made pasta and desserts. All entrées come with an antipasto plate and choice of appetizers. ✉ *5th Ave. between San Carlos and Mission Sts.,* ☎ *831/625–0501. MC, V.*

$$–$$$ ✕ **French Poodle.** Specialties on the traditional French menu at this intimate restaurant include the duck breast in port and the abalone; the floating island for dessert is delicious. ✉ *Junipero and 5th Aves.,* ☎ *831/624–8643. AE, DC, MC, V. Closed Sun. No lunch.*

$$–$$$ ✕ **Raffaello.** Sparkling Raffaello serves super pasta dishes, among them Monterey Bay prawns with garlic butter, local sole poached in champagne, and the specialty of the house, veal Piemontese. ✉ *Mission St. between Ocean and 7th Aves.,* ☎ *831/624–1541. AE, DC, MC, V. Closed Tues. and 1st 2 wks in Jan. No lunch.*

$$-$$$ ✕ **Simpson's.** Warm service and dependable if straightforward cuisine are the hallmarks of this family-run restaurant. An open dining room and tables with flowers and white tablecloths set the mood for grilled steak, fresh seafood, and roasted poultry; soups, breads, salad dressings, and desserts are all made in-house. ⊠ *San Carlos St. and 5th Ave.,* ☎ *831/624–5755. AE, MC, V. Closed Sun. No lunch.*

$–$$$ ✕ **Flaherty's Oyster Bar & Seafood Grill.** These bright and inviting side-by-side fish houses crank out steaming bowls of mussels, clams, cioppino, and crab chowder. Seafood pastas and daily fresh fish selections are also available. The Oyster Bar, with counter seating and a few tables, is the more casual and less expensive of the two restaurants. ⊠ *6th Ave. and San Carlos St.,* ☎ *831/624–0311 (Oyster Bar); 831/625–1500 (Seafood Grill). AE, MC, V.*

$–$$$ ✕ **Hog's Breath Inn.** Although resting a bit on its Hollywood laurels, this eatery co-owned by actor and former Carmel mayor Clint Eastwood has a pub-like atmosphere, with roaring fireplaces and rustic decor. The food is no-nonsense: meat and seafood entrées with sautéed vegetables. Several items—Dirty Harry Burger, Sudden Impact (Polish sausage) sandwich, and so on—are named after Eastwood movies. ⊠ *San Carlos St. and 5th Ave.,* ☎ *831/625–1044. Reservations not accepted for parties of 7 or fewer. AE, DC, MC, V.*

$–$$$ ✕ **Il Fornaio at the Pine Inn.** The Carmel branch of the upscale Il Fornaio chain serves up tasty antipasti, pastas, and steak Florentine. All the fresh-baked breads are winners. ⊠ *Ocean Ave. and Monte Verde St.,* ☎ *831/622–5100. AE, D, DC, MC, V.*

$–$$$ ✕ **Lugano Swiss Bistro.** Fondue is the centerpiece here. The house specialty is an original version made with Gruyère, Emmental, and Appenzeller—custom has it that if a lady loses her dipping cube in the fondue, she pays with a kiss; if a man loses one, he buys a bottle of wine. Rosemary chicken, plum-basted duck, and fennel pork loin rotate on the rotisserie. Call ahead for a table in the back room, which contains a hand-painted street scene of Lugano. ⊠ *The Barnyard, Hwy. 1 and Carmel Valley Rd.,* ☎ *831/626–3779. AE, MC, V.*

$–$$$ ✕ **Rio Grill.** Don't let its shopping center location fool you—the Rio
★ Grill is one of the Monterey Peninsula's most appealing restaurants. The best bets in this lively Santa Fe–style setting are the meat and seafood (such as fresh tuna or salmon) cooked over an oak-wood grill. The fire-roasted artichoke and the Monterey Bay squid are exceptional starters. ⊠ *Crossroads Center, 101 Crossroads Blvd., Hwy. 1 and Rio Rd.,* ☎ *831/625–5436. AE, MC, V.*

$$ ✕ **La Bohème.** The chefs at campy La Bohème prepare one entrée each night, accompanied by soup and salad. You may find yourself bumping elbows with your neighbor in the faux-European-village courtyard, but the predominantly French cuisine is delicious, and the atmosphere is convivial. ⊠ *Dolores St. and 7th Ave.,* ☎ *831/624–7500. Reservations not accepted. MC, V. No lunch.*

$–$$ ✕ **Cafe Gringo.** The zesty variations on Mexican cuisine at Gringo include the fresh tamales with spinach, zucchini, and mushrooms and the quesadilla with Monterey Jack and manchego cheeses, bacon, and roasted *pasilla* chilies, topped with mango salsa. The full bar serves margaritas, Mexican beers, and South American and local wines. Outdoor tables beckon in warm weather. ⊠ *Paseo San Carlos Courtyard, San Carlos St. between Ocean and 7th Aves.,* ☎ *831/626–8226. AE, MC, V.*

$–$$ ✕ **Caffé Napoli.** Redolent of garlic and olive oil, this small, atmospheric Italian restaurant is a favorite of locals, who come for the crisp-crusted pizzas, house-made pastas, and fresh seafood. Specialties include grilled artichokes, fresh salmon and grilled vegetable risotto, and fisherman's pasta. There's a good Italian wine list. ⊠ *Ocean Ave. and Lincoln St.,* ☎ *831/625–4033. Reservations essential on weekends. MC, V.*

$ ✕ **Friar Tuck's.** This busy wood-panel coffee shop serves huge omelets at breakfast and dishes up 16 different hamburgers at lunch. ⊠ *5th Ave. and Dolores St.,* ☎ *831/624–4274. Reservations not accepted. DC, MC, V. No dinner.*

$$$$ ✕🖾 **Highlands Inn.** An unparalleled location south of Carmel on high
★ cliffs above the Pacific gives the Highlands views that stand out even in a region famous for them. Accommodations are in plush spa suites and condominium-style units with wood-burning fireplaces and ocean-view decks; some rooms have full kitchens. The contemporary French menu at the inn's excellent Pacific's Edge restaurant ($$$–$$$$) includes roasted rack of lamb with goat-cheese potato gratin on a white-bean sauce; grilled Atlantic salmon wrapped in pancetta on saffron-infused couscous; and a brick-roasted half chicken with grilled Portobello mushrooms. ⊠ *Hwy. 1, Box 1700, 93921,* ☎ *831/624– 3801; 800/682–4811 in CA; 831/622–5445 restaurant;* ⅧⅩ *831/626– 1574. 102 suites, 40 rooms. 2 restaurants, lounge, refrigerators, pool, 3 hot tubs, bicycles, baby-sitting. AE, D, DC, MC, V.*

$$$$ 🖾 **Carriage House Inn.** This small inn with a wood-shingle exterior has spacious rooms with open-beam ceilings, fireplaces, down comforters, and sunken baths. ⊠ *Junipero Ave. between 7th and 8th Aves., Box 1900, 93921,* ☎ *831/625–2585 or 800/422–4732,* ⅧⅩ *831/624– 2967. 11 rooms, 2 suites. In-room safes, refrigerators. Continental breakfast. AE, D, DC, MC, V.*

$$$–$$$$ 🖾 **La Playa Hotel.** Norwegian artist Christopher Jorgensen built this structure in 1902 for his bride, a member of the Ghirardelli chocolate clan. The Terrace Grill and central garden, riotous with color, have vistas of Carmel's magnificent coastline. The rooms are done in pale terracotta with green and blue accents and contain hand-carved furniture. Some accommodations have ocean views. You can also opt for a cottage; all have full kitchens and a patio or a terrace, and some have wood-burning fireplaces. ⊠ *Camino Real at 8th Ave., Box 900, 93921,* ☎ *831/624–6476 or 800/582–8900,* ⅧⅩ *831/624–7966. 75 rooms, 5 cottages. Restaurant, bar, pool, laundry service. AE, DC, MC, V.*

$$$–$$$$ 🖾 **Tickle Pink Inn.** Atop a towering cliff, this inn has views of the Big
★ Sur coastline, which you can contemplate from your private balcony. Fall asleep to the sound of surf crashing below and wake up to Continental breakfast and the morning paper in bed. If you prefer the company of fellow travelers, breakfast is also served buffet-style in the lounge, as are complimentary wine and cheese in the afternoon. Many rooms have wood-burning fireplaces, and there are four luxurious spa suites. ⊠ *155 Highlands Dr., 93923,* ☎ *831/624–1244 or 800/635–4774,* ⅧⅩ *831/626–9516. 24 rooms, 11 suites. Refrigerators, outdoor hot tub . Continental breakfast. AE, MC, V.*

$$–$$$$ 🖾 **Best Western Carmel Mission Inn.** This modern inn on the edge of Carmel Valley has a lushly landscaped pool and hot tub area and is close to the Barnyard and Crossroads shopping centers. Rooms are large, some with spacious decks. ⊠ *3665 Rio Rd., at Hwy. 1, 93923,* ☎ *831/ 624–1841 or 800/348–9090,* ⅧⅩ *831/624–8684. 163 rooms, 2 suites. Restaurant, bar, refrigerators, pool, 2 hot tubs. Continental breakfast. AE, D, DC, MC, V.*

$$–$$$$ 🖾 **Cobblestone Inn.** Quilts and country antiques, stone fireplaces in
★ guest rooms and the sitting-room area, and a complimentary gourmet breakfast buffet and afternoon tea contribute to the homey feel at this English-style inn. ⊠ *8th and Junipero Aves., Box 3185, 93921,* ☎ *831/ 625–5222,* ⅧⅩ *831/625–0478. 22 rooms, 2 suites. No-smoking rooms, refrigerators. Full breakfast. Full breakfast. AE, DC, MC, V.*

$$–$$$$ ⊞ **Cypress Inn.** When Doris Day became part owner of this inn a decade ago, she added her own touches such as posters from her many movies and photo albums of her favorite canines. A generous breakfast is served in a sunny room, or you can enjoy your morning meal in a garden courtyard surrounded by bougainvillea. ⊠ *Lincoln St. and 7th Ave., 93921,* ☎ *831/624–3871 or 800/443–7443,* FAX *831/624–8216. 33 rooms, 1 suite. Refrigerators. AE, D, MC, V.*

$$–$$$$ ⊞ **Mission Ranch.** Sheep graze in the ocean-side pasture near the main 19th-century farmhouse at Mission Ranch. The six rooms in the main house are set around a Victorian parlor; other options include cottages, a hayloft, and a bunkhouse. Handmade quilts, princess-and-the-pea stuffed mattresses, and carved wooden beds lend all of the accommodations a country ambience. ⊠ *26270 Dolores St., 93923,* ☎ *831/624– 6436 or 800/538–8221,* FAX *831/626–4163. 31 rooms. Restaurant, piano bar, 6 tennis courts, exercise room, pro shop. MC, V.*

$$–$$$$ ⊞ **Tally Ho Inn.** This inn with an English garden courtyard is one of the few in Carmel's center with good views of the ocean. The penthouse units have fireplaces. ⊠ *Monte Verde St. and 6th Ave., Box 3726, 93921,* ☎ *831/624–2232 or 800/624–2290,* FAX *831/624–2661. 12 rooms, 2 suites. Continental breakfast. AE, D, DC, MC, V.*

$$–$$$ ⊞ **Lobos Lodge.** The white stucco units here are set amid cypress, oaks, and pines on the edge of the business district. All accommodations have fireplaces and some have private patios. ⊠ *Monte Verde St. and Ocean Ave., Box L-1, 93921,* ☎ *831/624–3874,* FAX *831/624–0135. 28 rooms, 2 suites. Refrigerators. Continental breakfast. AE, MC, V.*

$$–$$$ ⊞ **Pine Inn.** A favorite of generations of Carmel visitors, the Pine Inn
★   has Victorian-style decor, complete with grandfather clock, padded fabric wall panels, antique tapestries, and marble-topped furnishings. Only four blocks from the beach, the complex includes a brick courtyard of specialty shops and an Italian restaurant. ⊠ *Ocean Ave. and Lincoln St., Box 250, 93921,* ☎ *831/624–3851 or 800/228–3851,* FAX *831/624–3030. 43 rooms, 6 suites. Restaurant. AE, D, DC, MC, V.*

$–$$ ⊞ **Carmel River Inn.** Besides attracting those on a budget, this half-century-old inn appeals to travelers who enjoy a bit of distance from the madding crowd—downtown Carmel in July, for instance. Yet the area's beaches are only 1½ mi away. The blue and white motel at the front of the property contains units with cable TV, small refrigerators, and coffeemakers. Cabins out back sleep up to six; some have fireplaces and kitchens. Clean, safe, and across the street from a supermarket, the inn may be upscale Carmel's best lodging bargain. ⊠ *Hwy. 1 at Carmel River Bridge, Box 221609, 93922,* ☎ *831/624–1575 or 800/ 882–8142,* FAX *831/624–0290. 43 rooms. Pool. MC, V.*

Nightlife and the Arts

MUSIC

Carmel Bach Festival (☎ 831/624–2046) has presented the works of Johann Sebastian Bach and his contemporaries in concerts and recitals for more than several decades. The festival runs for 23 days, starting in mid-July. **Monterey County Symphony** (☎ 831/624–8511) performs concerts—from classical to pop—between September and May in Salinas and Carmel.

THEATER

Pacific Repertory Theater (☎ 831/622–0700) specializes in contemporary comedy and drama. **Sunset Community Cultural Center** (⊠ San Carlos St. between 8th and 10th Aves., ☎ 831/624–3996), which presents concerts, lectures, and headline performers, is the Monterey Bay area's top venue for the performing arts.

Shopping

ART GALLERIES

Carmel Art Association (⊠ Dolores St. between 5th and 6th Aves., ☎ 831/624–6176) exhibits the paintings, sculpture, and prints of local artists. **Cottage Gallery** (⊠ Mission St. and 6th Ave., ☎ 831/624–7888) focuses on traditional impressionism and classical realism. **Highlands Sculpture Gallery** (⊠ Dolores St. between 5th and 6th Aves., ☎ 831/624–0535) is devoted to indoor and outdoor sculpture, primarily works done in stone, bronze, wood, metal, and glass. **Masterpiece Gallery** (⊠ Dolores St. and 6th Ave., ☎ 831/624–2163) shows California Impressionist and Bay Area figurative art. **Photography West Gallery** (⊠ Ocean Ave. and Dolores St., ☎ 831/625–1587) exhibits photography by Ansel Adams and other 20th-century artists.

CHILDREN

Mischievous Rabbit (⊠ Lincoln St. between 7th and Ocean Aves., ☎ 831/624–6854) sells toys, nursery bedding, books, music boxes, party supplies, china, and hand-painted and handmade clothing embellished with characters from Beatrix Potter tales.

CLOTHING AND ACCESSORIES

Madrigal (⊠ Carmel Plaza and San Carlos Ave., ☎ 831/624–3477) carries sportswear, sweaters, and accessories for women and men. **Pat Areias** (⊠ Lincoln St., south of Ocean Ave., ☎ 831/626–8668) puts a respectfully modern spin on the Mexican tradition of silversmithing in its line of sterling silver buckles, belts, and jewelry.

GARDEN

Shop in the Garden (⊠ Lincoln St. between Ocean and 7th Aves., ☎ 831/624–6047) is an indoor-outdoor sculpture garden where you can buy fountains or garden accoutrements. You'll hear the babble of its outdoor fountains and tinkle of its wind chimes before you see the courtyard establishment.

MEMORABILIA

Golf Arts and Imports (⊠ Dolores St. and 6th Ave., ☎ 831/625–4488) carries antique golf prints and clubs, rare golf books, and other golfing memorabilia.

Carmel Valley

③⑤ *5 to 10 mi east of Carmel, Hwy. 1 to Carmel Valley Rd.*

Carmel Valley Road, which turns inland at Highway 1 south of Carmel, is the main thoroughfare through the town of Carmel Valley, a secluded enclave of horse ranchers and other well-heeled residents who prefer the area's sunny climate to the fog and wind on the coast. Tiny Carmel Valley village holds several crafts shops and art galleries. **Garland Ranch Regional Park** (⊠ Carmel Valley Rd., 9 mi east of Carmel, ☎ 831/659–4488) has hiking trails and picnic tables.

The beautiful **Château Julien** winery, recognized internationally for its chardonnays and merlots, gives tours on weekdays at 10:30 and 2:30 and weekends at 12:30 and 2:30, all by appointment. The tasting room is open daily. ⊠ *8940 Carmel Valley Rd., ☎ 831/624–2600. ☉ Weekdays 8:30–5, weekends 11–5.*

Dining and Lodging

$ ✕ **Wagon Wheel Coffee Shop.** Grab a seat at the counter or wait for
★ a table at this local hangout decorated with wood-beam ceilings, hanging wagon wheels, cowboy hats, and lassos. Then chow down on huge breakfasts of huevos rancheros, Italian sausage and eggs, or trout and

eggs; this is also the place to stoke up on biscuits and gravy. For lunch choose among a dozen types of burgers or other sandwiches. ⊠ *Valley Hill Center, Carmel Valley Rd. next to Quail Lodge,* ☎ *831/624–8878. No credit cards. No dinner.*

$$$$ ✕⚏ **Quail Lodge.** Guests at this resort on the grounds of a private coun-
★ try club have access to golf, tennis, and an 850-acre wildlife preserve frequented by deer and migratory fowl. Modern rooms with European decor are clustered in several low-rise buildings; each room has a private deck or patio overlooking the golf course, gardens, or a lake. The Covey at Quail Lodge ($$$; jacket required; no lunch) serves European cuisine in a romantic lakeside setting. The menu changes daily, but look for rack of lamb, mustard-crusted salmon, and mousseline of sole, all accompanied by fresh local produce. ⊠ *8205 Valley Greens Dr., 93923,* ☎ *831/624–1581 or 800/538–9516,* ℻ *831/624–3726. 86 rooms, 14 suites. 2 restaurants, 2 bars, room service, 2 pools, hot tub, sauna, 18-hole golf course, putting greens, 4 tennis courts, hiking, bicycles, concierge. AE, DC, MC, V.*

$$$$ ⚏ **Carmel Valley Ranch Resort.** This all-suites resort, well off Carmel
★ Valley Road on a hill overlooking the valley, is a stunning piece of contemporary California architecture. Down-home touches include handmade quilts, wood-burning fireplaces, and watercolors by local artists. Rooms have cathedral ceilings, oversize decks, and fully stocked wet bars. Guests have access to the resort's private 18-hole golf course; the $135 greens fee includes cart rental. ⊠ *1 Old Ranch Rd., 93923,* ☎ *831/625–9500 or 800/422–7635,* ℻ *831/624–2858. 100 suites. 2 restaurants, 2 pools, hot tubs, saunas, 18-hole golf course, 13 tennis courts. AE, DC, MC, V.*

$$$$ ⚏ **Stonepine Estate Resort.** The former estate of the Crocker banking family has been converted to an ultradeluxe inn nestled in 330 pastoral acres. The main house, richly paneled and furnished with antiques, holds eight individually decorated suites and a private dining room for guests only. The property's romantic cottages include one that is straight out of *Hansel and Gretel.* ⊠ *150 E. Carmel Valley Rd., Box 1543, 93924,* ☎ *831/659–2245,* ℻ *831/659–5160. 15 suites and cottages. Dining room, 2 pools, 2 tennis courts, archery, exercise room, horseback riding, mountain bikes. Full breakfast; MAP available. AE, MC, V.*

$$–$$$ ⚏ **Valley Lodge.** In this small inn there are rooms surrounding a garden patio and separate one- and two-bedroom cottages with fireplaces and full kitchens. ⊠ *8 Ford Rd., at Carmel Valley Rd., Box 93, 93924,* ☎ *831/659–2261 or 800/641–4646,* ℻ *831/659–4558. 23 rooms, 8 cottages. Pool, hot tub, sauna, exercise room. Continental breakfast. AE, MC, V.*

Outdoor Activities and Sports

GOLF

Golf Club at Quail Lodge (⊠ 8000 Valley Greens Dr., ☎ 831/624–2770) incorporates several lakes into its course. Although private, the course is open to guests at the adjoining Quail Lodge. The $95 greens fee ($125 for nonguests) includes cart rental. **Rancho Cañada Golf Club** (⊠ 4860 Carmel Valley Rd., 1 mi east of Hwy. 1, ☎ 831/624–0111) has 36 holes, some of them overlooking the Carmel River. Fees range from $30 to $70, plus $28 cart rental, depending on course and tee time selected.

TENNIS

Carmel Valley Inn Swim and Tennis Club (⊠ Carmel Valley Rd. and Laureles Grade, ☎ 831/659–3131) allows nonmembers to play on its courts for a small fee.

Salinas

36   *17 mi east of the Monterey Peninsula on Hwy. 68; from Carmel Valley Rd. take Laureles Grade north to Hwy. 68.*

Salinas is the population center of a rich agricultural valley where fertile soil, an ideal climate, and a good underground water supply produce optimum growing conditions for crops such as lettuce, broccoli, tomatoes, strawberries, flowers, and wine grapes. This unpretentious town may lack the sophistication and scenic splendors of the coast, but it will interest literary and architectural buffs. Turn-of-the-century buildings have been the focus of ongoing renovation, much of it centered on the original downtown area of South Main Street, with its handsome stone storefronts. The memory and literary legacy of Salinas native (and winner of the Pulitzer and Nobel prizes) John Steinbeck (1902–1968) are well honored here.

The **National Steinbeck Center,** which opened in June 1998, is a museum and archive dedicated to the life and works of John Steinbeck. Many exhibits are interactive, bringing to life Steinbeck worlds such as Cannery Row, Hooverville (from *The Grapes of Wrath*), and the Mexican Plaza (from *The Pearl*). The library and archives contain Steinbeck first editions, notebooks, photographs, and audio tapes. Access to the archives is by appointment only. The center has information about Salinas' annual Steinbeck Festival in August and about tours of area landmarks mentioned in his novels. ⊠ *1 Main St.,* ☎ *831/ 753–6411.* ☜ *$7.* ◷ *Daily 10–5.*

The **Harvey-Baker House,** a preserved redwood home built on another site in 1868 for Salinas's first mayor, a merchant, is one of the finest private residences built in the town during the 19th century. ⊠ *238 E. Romie La.,* ☎ *831/757–8085.* ☜ *Free (donation requested).* ◷ *1st Sun. of month 1–4, weekdays by appointment.*

The meadows above the Alisal Slough hold the **Jose Eusebio Boronda Adobe,** which contains furniture and artifacts of the early 19th century. ⊠ *333 Boronda Rd.,* ☎ *831/757–8085.* ☜ *Free (donation requested).* ◷ *Weekdays 10–2, Sun. 1–4, Sat. by appointment.*

Dining

$–$$ ✕ **Spado's.** One of several trendy restaurants in Salinas, gleaming Spado's brings Monterey-style culinary sophistication to the valley. For lunch, visit the antipasto bar for fresh salads and Mediterranean morsels; the panini are also excellent. For dinner, try the pizza with chicken and sun-dried-tomato pesto, the angel-hair pasta and prawns, or the risotto of the day. ⊠ *66 W. Alisal St.,* ☎ *831/424–4139. Closed Sun.*

$ ✕ **Steinbeck House.** John Steinbeck's birthplace, a Victorian frame house, has been converted into a lunch-only eatery run by the volunteer Valley Guild. The restaurant displays some Steinbeck memorabilia. The set menu incorporates locally grown produce. ⊠ *132 Central Ave.,* ☎ *831/424–2735.* ◷ *Weekdays for 2 sittings at 11:45 AM and 1:15 PM; Sat. 11:30 AM and 2 PM. Reservations essential.*

Outdoor Activities and Sports

The **California Rodeo** (☎ *831/757–2951*), one of the oldest and most famous rodeos in the West, takes place in mid-July.

San Juan Bautista

37   *18 mi north of Salinas on U.S. 101, then 2 mi east on Hwy. 156.*

Sleepy San Juan Bautista, protected from development since 1933, when
★   much of it became **San Juan Bautista State Historic Park,** is about as

close to early 19th-century California as you can get. On Living History Day, which takes place on the first Saturday of each month, costumed volunteers engage in quilting bees, tortilla making, butter churning, and other period activities. ⊠ *Hwy. 156,* ☎ *831/623–4881.* ᠊ᢑ *$2.* ⊙ *Daily 10–4:30.*

The centerpiece of San Juan Bautista is a wide, green plaza ringed by historic buildings: a restored blacksmith shop, a stable, a pioneer cabin, and a jailhouse. Running along one side of the square is **Mission San Juan Bautista,** a long, low, colonnaded structure founded by Father Fermin Lasuen in 1797. Adjoining it is Mission Cemetery, where more than 4,300 Native Americans who converted to Christianity are buried in unmarked graves. ⊠ *408 S. 2nd St.,* ☎ *831/623–2127.* ᠊ᢑ *$2.* ⊙ *Mon.–Sat. 9:30–5, Sun. 10–5.*

After the mission era, San Juan Bautista became an important crossroads for stagecoach travel. The principal stop in town was the **Plaza Hotel,** a collection of adobe buildings with furnishings from the 1860s. The **Castro-Breen Adobe,** furnished with Spanish colonial antiques, presents a view of domestic life in the village. It is next to the Plaza Hotel.

Shopping

Small antiques shops and art galleries line San Juan Bautista's side streets.

MONTEREY BAY A TO Z

Arriving and Departing

By Bus

Greyhound Lines (☎ 831/373–4735 or 800/231–2222) serves Monterey from San Francisco three times daily; the trip takes about 4½ hours.

By Car

The drive south from San Francisco to Monterey can be made comfortably in three hours or less. The most scenic way is to follow Highway 1 down the coast past flower, pumpkin, and artichoke fields and the seaside communities of Pacifica, Half Moon Bay, and Santa Cruz. Unless the drive is made on sunny weekends when locals are heading for the beach, the two-lane coast highway takes no longer than the freeway.

Of the freeways from San Francisco, a fast but enjoyable route is I–280 south to Highway 17, south of San Jose. Highway 17 crosses the redwood-filled Santa Cruz mountains between San Jose and Santa Cruz, where it intersects with Highway 1. Another option is to follow U.S. 101 south through San Jose to Salinas and then take Highway 68 west to Monterey.

From Los Angeles, the drive to Monterey can be made in less than a day by heading north on U.S. 101 to Salinas and then heading west on Highway 68. The spectacular but slow alternative is to take U.S. 101 to San Luis Obispo and then follow the hairpin turns of Highway 1 up the coast. Allow at least three extra hours if you take this route.

By Plane

Monterey Peninsula Airport (⊠ 200 Fred Kane Dr., ☎ 831/648–7000) is 3 mi east of downtown Monterey—on Highway 68 to Olmsted Road—and is served by American Eagle, Skywest-Delta, United, United Express, and US Airways Express. *See* Air Travel *in* the Gold Guide for airline phone numbers.

By Train
The **Amtrak** (☎ 800/872–7245) *Coast Starlight,* which runs between
Los Angeles, Oakland, and Seattle, stops in Salinas (✉ 11 Station Pl.).
Connecting Amtrak Thruway buses serve Monterey and Carmel.

Getting Around

By Bus
Monterey–Salinas Transit (☎ 831/424–7695) provides frequent service between the peninsula's towns and many major sightseeing spots
and shopping areas. The base fare is $1.50, with an additional $1.50
for each zone you travel into. A day pass costs from $3 to $6, depending
on how many zones you'll be traveling through. The transit company
runs the **WAVE shuttle,** which links major attractions on the Monterey
waterfront. The shuttle operates daily between Memorial Day and Labor
Day from 9 AM to 6:30 PM. The fare is $1 per day for unlimited rides.

By Car
Highway 1 runs north–south, linking the towns of Santa Cruz, Monterey, and Carmel. Highway 68 runs northeast from Pacific Grove toward
Salinas, which U.S. 101 bisects. North of Salinas, U.S. 101 links up
with Highway 156 to San Juan Bautista. Parking is especially difficult
in Carmel and in Monterey.

Contacts and Resources

Doctors
Community Hospital of Monterey Peninsula (✉ 23625 Holman Hwy.,
Monterey, ☎ 831/624–5311). **Monterey County Medical Society** (☎
831/655–1019).

Emergencies
Ambulance (☎ 911). **Fire** (☎ 911). **Police** (☎ 911).

Guided Tours
California Parlor Car Tours (☎ 415/474–7500 or 800/227–4250) operates motor-coach tours from San Francisco to Los Angeles that include the Monterey Peninsula. **Chardonnay Sailing Charters** (☎ 831/
423–1213) accommodates 49 passengers for year-round cruises on Monterey Bay aboard the *Chardonnay II,* leaving from the yacht harbor in
Santa Cruz. Reservations are essential. **Rider's Guide** (✉ 484 Lake Park
Ave., Suite 255, Oakland 94610, ☎ 510/653–2553) produces a self-
guided audiotape tour detailing the history, landmarks, and attractions
of the Monterey Peninsula and Big Sur for $12.95, or $15.95 in gift-
pack binder, plus $2.50 postage.

Pharmacy
The pharmacy at **Surf 'n' Sand** (✉ 6th and Junipero Aves., Carmel,
☎ 831/624–1543) is open on weekdays from 9 to 7, Saturday and holidays from 9 to 2.

Visitor Information
Monterey Peninsula Visitors and Convention Bureau (✉ 380 Alvarado
St., Monterey 93942, ☎ 831/649–1770). **Monterey County Vintners
and Growers Association** (☎ 831/375–9400). **Salinas Valley Cham-
ber of Commerce** (✉ 119 E. Alisal St., Salinas 93901, ☎ 831/424–
7611). **Santa Cruz County Conference and Visitors Council** (✉ 701 Front
St., Santa Cruz 95060, ☎ 831/425–1234 or 800/833–3494). **Santa
Cruz Mountain Winegrowers Association** (☎ 831/479–9463).

11 The Central Coast

From Big Sur to Santa Barbara

Highway 1 between Big Sur and Santa Barbara is a spectacular stretch of terrain. The curving road demands an unhurried pace, but even if it didn't, you'd find yourself stopping often to take in the scenery. Don't expect much in the way of dining, lodging, or even history until you arrive at Hearst Castle, publisher William Randolph Hearst's testament to his own fabulousness. Sunny, well-scrubbed Santa Barbara's Spanish-Mexican heritage is reflected in the architectural style of its courthouse and mission.

Updated by
Sasha
Abramsky

THE COASTLINE BETWEEN CARMEL and Santa Barbara, a distance of about 200 mi, is one of the most popular drives in California. Except for a few smallish cities—Ventura and Santa Barbara in the south and San Luis Obispo in the north—the area is sparsely populated. Grazing cattle dot the countryside, whose human inhabitants relish their isolation at the sharp edge of land and sea. Around Big Sur the Santa Lucia mountains drop down to the Pacific with dizzying grandeur, but as you move south, the shoreline gradually flattens into the long, sandy beaches of Santa Barbara and Ventura.

Artists create and sell their works in towns like Cambria and Ojai. The wineries of the Santa Ynez Valley are steadily building reputations for quality vintages. The Danish town of Solvang is an amusing stopover for hearty Scandinavian fare and an architectural change of pace. Santa Barbara, only 95 mi north of Los Angeles, is your introduction to the unhurried hospitality and easy living of southern California. Santa Barbara's setting, climate, and architecture combine to produce a Mediterranean feel and pace.

Pleasures and Pastimes

Dining

The Central Coast from Big Sur to Solvang is far enough off the interstate to ensure that nearly every restaurant or café has its own personality—from chic to down-home and funky. There aren't many restaurants between Big Sur and Hearst Castle. Cambria's cooks, true to the town's British-Welsh origins, craft English dishes complete with peas and Yorkshire pudding but also serve Continental and contemporary fare.

The dishes of Santa Barbara's chefs rival those of their counterparts in the state's larger centers. Fresh seafood is plentiful, prepared old-style American in longtime wharfside hangouts or with more trendy accents at newer eateries. If you're after good, cheap food with an international flavor, follow the locals to Milpas Avenue on the eastern edge of Santa Barbara's downtown. Dining attire on the Central Coast is generally casual, though slightly dressy casual wear is the custom at the expensive to very expensive restaurants listed below.

CATEGORY	COST*
$$$$	over $50
$$$	$30–$50
$$	$20–$30
$	under $20

*per person for a three-course meal, excluding drinks, service, and 7¼%–7¾% sales tax

Lodging

Big Sur has only a few lodgings, but even its budget accommodations have character. Many moderately priced hotels and motels—some nicer than others, but most of them basic places to hang your hat—can be found between San Simeon and San Luis Obispo. Wherever you stay, make reservations for the summer well ahead of time.

CATEGORY	COST*
$$$$	over $175
$$$	$120–$175
$$	$80–$120
$	under $80

*All prices are for a standard double room, excluding 9%–10% tax.

Missions

Three important California missions established by Franciscan friars are within the Central Coast region. La Purisima is the most fully restored, Mission Santa Barbara is perhaps the most beautiful of the state's 21 missions, and Mission San Luis Obispo de Tolosa has a fine museum with many Chumash Indian artifacts.

Wineries

Centered in the Solvang area and spreading north toward San Luis Obispo and south toward Santa Barbara is a wine-making region with much of the variety but none of the glitz or crowds of northern California's Napa Valley. The many wineries in the rolling hills of the Santa Maria and Santa Ynez valleys tend to be small, but most have tasting rooms (some have tours), and you'll often meet the wine makers themselves. There are maps and brochures at the visitor centers in Solvang, San Luis Obispo, and Santa Barbara, or you can contact the wine associations of Paso Robles and Santa Barbara (☞ Contacts and Resources *in* The Central Coast A to Z, *below*).

Exploring the Central Coast

Numbers in the text correspond to numbers in the margin and on the Central Coast and Santa Barbara maps.

Great Itineraries

Driving is the easiest way to experience the Central Coast. The three-day itinerary below is arranged as a loop from either San Francisco or Los Angeles. The seven-day trip is organized from north to south.

IF YOU HAVE 3 DAYS

Especially in the summertime, make reservations for a visit to Hearst Castle well before you depart for the coast. Maximize your time by taking U.S. 101 from San Francisco or Los Angeles directly to **San Luis Obispo** ⑩. North of town, poke your head into the kitschy **Madonna Inn.** Continue on to **Mission San Luis Obispo de Tolosa** and the nearby **County Historical Museum.** Drive west on Highway 46 and north on Highway 1 and stay overnight in ☷ **Cambria.** Take a morning tour of **Hearst Castle** ⑦, spend some time viewing the exhibits at the visitor center, and then head south on U.S. 101 to ☷ **Santa Barbara** ⑭–㉗. Spend the late afternoon exploring **Stearns Wharf** ⑮ and other waterfront sights. The next morning, tour the **Santa Barbara County Courthouse** ⑳ and **Mission Santa Barbara** ㉕. In the afternoon, stroll **State Street** if you like to shop, or catch some rays at **East Beach** ⑰.

IF YOU HAVE 7 DAYS

Make ☷ **Big Sur** your destination for the first day and most of the second. If you're in the area on a weekend, tour the **Point Sur Light Station** ②. Watch the waves break on **Pfeiffer Beach** ④, one of the few places where you can actually set foot on the shore. Observe the glories of **Los Padres National Forest** up close by hiking one of the many trails in the **Ventana Wilderness,** or stay along the shore and hunt for jade at **Jade Cove.** Plan to reach ☷ **Cambria** by the evening of day two. Have dinner and explore the town's shops.

On day three, have a beachfront breakfast at **Morro Bay,** tour **Hearst Castle** ⑦, have lunch, and take U.S. 101 south to Highway 246 west to get to **Mission La Purisima Concepción** ⑪. Loop back east on Highway 246 to U.S. 101 and head south to ☷ **Santa Barbara** ⑭–㉗. On day four, visit **Stearns Wharf** ⑮ and walk or bike to **East Beach** ⑰ and the **Andree Clark Bird Refuge** ⑱. Have dinner on **State Street** and check out the area's shops and clubs. On your fifth day, get a feel for the city's architecture, history, and vegetation at, respectively, the **Santa**

The Central Coast

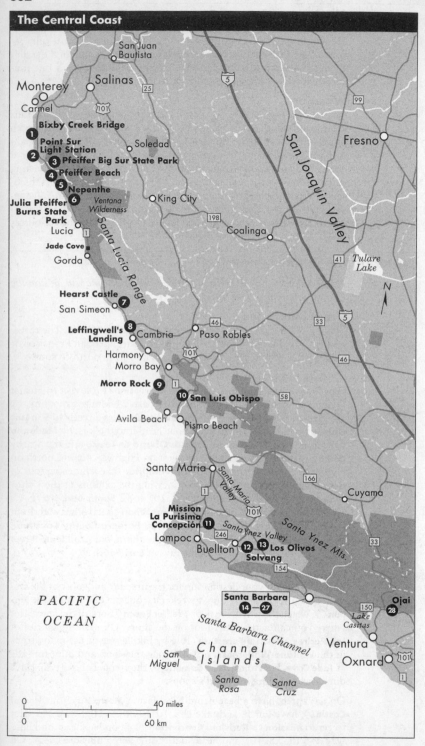

Bixby Creek Bridge 1
Point Sur Light Station 2
Pfeiffer Big Sur State Park 3
Pfeiffer Beach 4
Nepenthe 5
Julia Pfeiffer Burns State Park 6
Hearst Castle 7
Leffingwell's Landing 8
Morro Rock 9
San Luis Obispo 10
Mission La Purísima Concepción 11
Solvang 12
Los Olivos 13
Santa Barbara 14 — 27
Ojai 28

Monterey
Carmel
Salinas
San Juan Bautista
Soledad
King City
Coalinga
Fresno
San Joaquin Valley
Tulare Lake
Santa Lucia Range
Ventana Wilderness
Lucia
Jade Cove
Gorda
San Simeon
Cambria
Harmony
Morro Bay
Paso Robles
Avila Beach
Pismo Beach
Santa Maria
Santa Maria Valley
Cuyama
Santa Ynez Valley
Lompoc
Buellton
Santa Ynez Mts
Santa Barbara
Santa Barbara Channel
Lake Casitas
Ventura
Oxnard

PACIFIC OCEAN

Channel Islands
San Miguel
Santa Rosa
Santa Cruz

0   40 miles
0   60 km

N

Barbara County Courthouse ⑳, **Mission Santa Barbara** ㉕, and the **Santa Barbara Botanic Garden** ㉗. Have dinner in **Montecito** and explore the Coast Village Road shopping district. It's a short walk south from here to the shore to catch the sunset before or after you eat. On your sixth day, experience the area's marine life on a half-day cruise of the **Channel Islands.** On day seven, take U.S. 101 south to Highway 150 east to reach ⛔ **Ojai** ㉘.

When to Tour the Central Coast

The Central Coast is hospitable most of the year. Fog often rolls in north of Pismo Beach during the summer; you'll need a jacket, especially after sunset, close to the shore. The rains usually come between December and March. Santa Barbara is pleasant year-round. Hotel rooms fill up in the summer, but from April to early June and in the early fall the weather is almost as fine and it's less hectic.

HIGHWAY 1 TO SOLVANG

Big Sur, San Simeon, and San Luis Obispo

Big Sur

152 mi from San Francisco, south on I–280 and U.S. 101, west on Hwy. 68 and south on Hwy. 1; 27 mi south of Monterey on Hwy. 1.

Long a retreat of artists and writers, Big Sur contains ancient forests and a rugged coastline that residents have protected from overdevelopment. Much of the area lies within several state parks and the more than 165,000-acre **Ventana Wilderness,** itself part of the Los Padres National Forest. The counterculture spirit of Big Sur is evident today in tie-dyed clothing some locals wear and the presence of the Esalen Institute, a mecca of the human growth-potential movement. Established in 1910 as a haven with curative baths, Esalen exploded in the 1960s as a place to explore consciousness, environmental issues, and nude bathing.

❶ The graceful arc of **Bixby Creek Bridge** (⊠ Hwy. 1, 13 mi south of Carmel) is a photographer's dream. From the parking area on the north side you can take a photo or begin a walk across the 550-ft span.

★ ❷ **Point Sur Light Station,** a century-old beacon, stands watch from atop a sandstone cliff. Four lighthouse keepers lived here with their families. Their homes and working spaces are open to the public on 2½- to 3-hour, ranger-led tours. Considerable walking is involved. ⊠ *Point Sur State Historical Park, Hwy. 1, 19 mi south of Carmel,* ☎ *831/625–4419.* 🎟 *$5.* ☉ *Tours generally Sat. 10 AM and 2 PM, Sun. 10 AM, plus Apr.–Oct., Wed. 10 and 2; call ahead to confirm.*

❸ A short hiking trail at **Pfeiffer Big Sur State Park** leads up a redwood-filled valley to a waterfall. You can go back the same (easier) way or continue on the trail and take a loop that leads you along the valley wall, with views of the tops of the redwood trees you were just walking among. Stop in at the **Big Sur Station,** west of the park entrance, for information about the entire area. ⊠ *Hwy. 1, 8½ mi south of Point Sur Light Station,* ☎ *831/667–2315.* 🎟 *$6 per vehicle (day use).* ☉ *Daily sunrise–sunset.*

❹ Through a hole in one of the big rocks at secluded **Pfeiffer Beach** you can watch the waves break first on the sea side and then again on the beach side. ⊠ *Off Hwy. 1; the 2-mi road to beach is immediately past Big Sur Station.* 🎟 *$6 per vehicle (day use).*

❺ **Nepenthe** (⊠ Hwy. 1, 2½ mi south of Big Sur Station) overlooks lush meadows to the ocean below. The house was once owned by Orson Welles and Rita Hayworth, though one of his biographers writes that they spent little time here. Downstairs from the on-site restaurant and café is a crafts and gift shop displaying, among other items, the work of the acclaimed fabric designer Kaffe Fassett, who grew up at Nepenthe.

❻ **Julia Pfeiffer Burns State Park** has some fine hiking trails. The crowds in summertime lessen the appeal of the big attraction here, the coastal **MyWay Falls**, but you'll still get an idea why the park's namesake, a pioneer woman whose father was among the first white settlers in the Big Sur area, liked to sit near the falls to contemplate nature. A ½-mi path leads to a bluff with marvelous ocean views; the 6-mi Ewoldsen Trail loop, a fairly strenuous hike, winds through a cross-section of the region's plant life. ⊠ *Hwy. 1, 12 mi south of Big Sur Station,* ☎ *831/667–2315.* ☒ *$6.* ☉ *Daily sunrise–sunset.*

Dining, Lodging, and Camping

$$$–$$$$ ✕ **Nepenthe.** You'll not find a grander coastal view between San Francisco and Los Angeles than the one from here. The American fare—burgers, sandwiches, and salads at lunchtime—is overpriced, so it is the location that is the draw (don't bother coming after dark). Nepenthe serves dinner, too; the outdoor Café Kevah serves breakfast and lunch. ⊠ *Hwy. 1, south end of town,* ☎ *831/667–2345. AE, MC, V.*

$$–$$$ ✕ **Ragged Point Inn.** A good place to lunch on the way into or out of the area's parks, this restaurant perched over the southernmost end of Big Sur is not as fancy as the places farther north. But neither are the prices, and the food—sandwiches, salads, pastas, and fish and meat dishes—is downright tasty. ⊠ *Hwy. 1, 16 mi north of San Simeon,* ☎ *805/927–5708. AE, D, DC, MC, V.*

$$$$ ✕⊡ **Post Ranch Inn.** This luxurious retreat is the ultimate in environ-
★ mentally conscious architecture. The redwood guest houses, all with dizzyingly splendid views of the Pacific or the mountains, blend unobtrusively into a wooded cliff 1,200 ft above the ocean. Each unit, done in a spare, almost Japanese style, has its own spa tub, fireplace, stereo, private deck, massage table. A refrigerator holds free snacks. On-site activities include everything from guided hikes to tarot-card readings. The inn's restaurant, which serves cutting-edge American fare, is the best in the area. ⊠ *Hwy. 1, Box 219, 93920,* ☎ *831/667–2200 or 800/527–2200,* ℻ *831/667–2512. 30 units. Restaurant, bar, 2 pools, spa, exercise room, library. Continental breakfast. AE, MC, V.*

$$$$ ✕⊡ **Ventana Inn.** The activities at this quintessential California get-
★ away are purposely limited to sunning at poolside—there is a clothing-optional deck—and walks in the hills nearby. Buildings that are scattered in clusters on a hillside above the Pacific contain rooms with natural-wood walls and cool tile floors. The hotel's stone-and-wood Ventana Restaurant serves contemporary California cuisine with Continental influences. For a real event, come here for weekend brunch on the terrace, with spectacular views over golden hills down to the ocean. ⊠ *Hwy. 1, 93920,* ☎ *831/667–2331 or 800/628–6500,* ℻ *831/667–2419. 59 rooms, 3 houses. Restaurant, 2 pools, 2 Japanese baths, sauna, exercise room. Continental breakfast. AE, D, DC, MC, V. 2-night minimum stay on weekends and holidays.*

$–$$$$ ✕⊡ **Deetjen's Big Sur Inn.** This inn amid the redwoods has a certain rustic charm, especially if you're not too attached to creature comforts. The room doors lock only from the inside, half the rooms have only wood-burning stoves to supply heat, and your neighbor can often be heard through the walls. Still, Deetjen's is a special place. The restaurant (reservations essential) in the main house serves stylish fare that includes roasted half duck, rib-eye steak, and lamb sirloin for dinner and wonderfully light and flavorful pancakes for breakfast. Lunch is not served. ✉ *Hwy. 1, south end of town, 93920,* ☎ *831/667–2377 for inn; 831/667–2378 for restaurant.* FAX *831/667–0466. 20 rooms, 15 with bath. Restaurant. MC, V.*

$–$$$ ✕▢ **Big Sur River Inn.** The Big Sur River flows past the forested grounds of this old wooden structure—summertime guests often sip afternoon drinks on the river's banks. Some rooms are merely functional; others are quite nice. Ask for one of the upper-floor, gnarled-redwood–panel rooms. When there's a chill in the air, a fire roars in the stone fireplace in the inn's huge dining room ($$), which serves fresh fish entrées and specials like pasta Castroville (with artichokes and chicken in a pesto cream sauce). ✉ *Hwy 1. at Pheneger Creek., 93920,* ☎ *831/667–2700,* FAX *831/667–2743. 14 rooms, 6 suites. Restaurant, bar, general store. AE, D, MC, V.*

$–$$$ ▢ **Big Sur Lodge.** The motel-style cottages of this property in Pfeiffer Big Sur State Park make it a good choice for families. The lodging area sits in a meadow surrounded by redwood and oak trees. Some accommodations have fireplaces, some have kitchens; none have TVs or phones. ✉ *Hwy. 1, Box 190, 93920,* ☎ *831/667–3100 or 800/424–4787,* FAX *831/667–3110. 61 rooms. Restaurant, grocery, pool, shop. AE, MC, V.*

$$ ▢ **Glen Oaks Motel.** At this simple lodging in the heart of Big Sur you can choose between bland motel-style rooms and slightly more expensive log cabins in the woods. The cabins combine Laura Ashley flourishes with frontier style. ✉ *Hwy. 1, 93920,* ☎ *831/667–2105. 15 rooms, 2 cottages. No credit cards.*

△ **Pfeiffer Big Sur State Park.** Redwood trees tower over this large campground that is often crowded in summer (so reserve a site as far ahead as possible) but still a wonderful place to camp. ✉ *Hwy. 1, 8½ mi south of Point Sur Light Station,* ☎ *831/667–2315 for information; 800/444–7275 to reserve a site. 218 sites.* ▣ *$16–$23. Fire rings, flush toilets, showers, water.*

En Route Highway 1 snakes south along the coast from Big Sur toward San Simeon. Ten miles south of the town of Lucia is **Jade Cove,** a well-known jade-hunting spot. Rock hunting is allowed on the beach, but you may not remove anything from the walls of the cliffs.

San Simeon

57 mi south of Big Sur on Hwy. 1.

Whalers founded San Simeon in the 1850s but had virtually abandoned the town by the time Senator George Hearst reestablished it 20 years later. Hearst bought up most of the surrounding ranch land, built a 1,000-ft wharf, and turned San Simeon into a bustling port. His son, William Randolph, further developed the area during the construction of Hearst Castle. Today the town, which is 3 mi east of the road leading to the castle, is basically a row of gift shops, restaurants, and motels along Highway 1.

★ ❼ **Hearst Castle,** known officially as the Hearst San Simeon State Historical Monument, sits in solitary splendor atop La Cuesta Encantada (the Enchanted Hill). Its buildings and gardens are spread over the 127 acres that were the heart of newspaper magnate William Randolph Hearst's 250,000-acre ranch.

Buses from the visitor center at the bottom of the hill take visitors to the neoclassical extravaganza above. Hearst devoted nearly 30 years and about $10 million to building this elaborate estate. He commissioned renowned architect Julia Morgan—who was also responsible for buildings at the University of California at Berkeley—but was very much involved with the final product, a pastiche of Italian, Spanish, Moorish, and French styles. The art-filled main building and three guest "cottages" are connected by terraces and staircases and surrounded by pools, gardens, and statuary. In its heyday the castle was a playground for Hearst, Hollywood celebrities, and the rich and powerful from around the world.

Although construction began in 1919, the project was never officially completed. Work was halted in 1947 when Hearst had to leave San Simeon due to failing health. The Hearst family presented the property to the state of California in 1958.

Guides conduct four different daytime tours and (part of the year) one evening tour of various parts of the main house and grounds; if this is your first visit, Tour No. 1, the most basic, is recommended. Daytime tours take about two hours. Docents dress in period costume as Hearst's guests and staff for the slightly longer evening tour, which begins at sunset. All tours include a ½-mi walk and between 150 and 400 stairs. A 40-minute film shown at a giant-screen theater gives a sanitized version of Hearst's life and of the construction of the castle, but the shots of the scenery are dazzling. Reservations for the tours, which can be made up to eight weeks in advance, are a virtual necessity. ⊠ *San Simeon State Park, 750 Hearst Castle Rd.,* ☎ *805/927–2020 or 800/444–4445.* 🎫 *Day tour $14, evening tour (spring and fall) $25, film $6.* ☉ *Tours daily 8:20 AM–3:20 PM (later in summer); additional tours take place most Fri. and Sat. evenings Mar.–May and Sept.–Dec. MC, V.*

Dining and Lodging

$$ ✕ **Europa.** The menu here includes dishes from Germany, Hungary, and Italy—goulash with spätzle, stuffed pork roast with kielbasa, and homemade pasta. Steaks and fresh fish are also served. Crisp linen tablecloths brighten the small dining room. ⊠ *9240 Castillo Dr. (Hwy. 1),* ☎ *805/927–3087. MC, V. Closed Sun. No lunch.*

$$–$$$$ 🏨 **Best Western Cavalier.** Reasonable rates, an oceanfront location, and
★ well-equipped rooms—all with TVs with VCRs and some with woodburning fireplaces and private patios—make this motel a good choice. ⊠ *9415 Hearst Dr., 93452,* ☎ *805/927–4688 or 800/826–8168,* 🆁🅰🆇 *805/927–6472. 90 rooms. 2 restaurants, refrigerators, 2 outdoor pools, hot tub, exercise room, coin laundry. AE, D, DC, MC, V.*

Cambria

9 mi south of San Simeon on Hwy. 1.

Cambria, an artists' colony with many late-Victorian homes, is divided into the newer West Village and the original East Village. Each section has its own personality and B&Bs, restaurants, art galleries, and shops. You can still detect traces of the Welsh miners who settled in Cambria in the 1890s. Motels line Moonstone Beach Drive, which runs along the coast.

❽ **Leffingwell's Landing,** a state picnic ground, is a good place for examining tidal pools and watching otters as they frolic in the surf. Footpaths wind along the beach side of the the drive. ⊠ *Moonstone Beach Dr., northern end.*

Dining and Lodging

$$–$$$ 🏨 **Ian's.** The namesake chef no longer cooks here, but this is still one of the best restaurants in town. Simple pizzas and pastas and more elaborate dishes like the delicate salmon fillet receive careful preparation. ⊠ *2150 Center St.,* ☎ *805/927–8649. AE, MC, V.*

$$–$$$ ✕ **The Sea Chest.** By far the best seafood restaurant in town, this clifftop inn serves all kinds of fish, much of it locally caught. Oysters from the oyster bar are highly recommended. Come early to catch the sunset. ⊠ *6216 Moonstone Beach Dr.,* ☎ *805/927–4514. Reservations not accepted. No credit cards. No lunch.*

$–$$ ✕ **Hamlet at Moonstone Gardens.** In the middle of 3 acres of luxuri-
★ ant gardens, this restaurant has an enchanting patio that's perfect for lunch. The views from the upstairs dining room are of the Pacific or the gardens. The fish of the day comes poached in white wine; other entrées range from hamburgers to rack of lamb. The output of more than 50 wineries is represented downstairs at the Pacific Wine Works. ⊠ *Hwy. 1 at Moonstone Beach Dr.,* ☎ *805/927–3535. MC, V.*

$–$$ ✕ **Robin's.** "Multiethnic" only begins to describe the dining possibil-
ities at this antiques-filled restaurant amid Monterey pines. Tandoori prawns, quesadillas, a Thai red curry, an array of salads (more for lunch than dinner), numerous vegetarian entrées, hamburgers for the kids, and some truly fine desserts are all on Robin's menu. ⊠ *4095 Burton Dr.,* ☎ *805/927–5007. MC, V. No lunch Sun.*

$–$$ ✕ **The Greenwoods.** Ribs, filet mignon, and large New York steaks lure locals and tourists to the restaurant attached to the Cambria Pines Lodge. Bands in the lounge play light rock, jazz, and other music. ⊠ *2905 Burton Dr.,* ☎ *805/927–4200. AE, D, MC, V.*

$$–$$$$ ▦ **Blue Dolphin.** The luxurious beachfront rooms at the Blue Dolphin look like they've been transported straight out of a middle-class home in Surrey circa 1910. Heavy on frills and pinks and pastels, they have hair dryers, TVs with VCRs, and superb ocean views. Five rooms have whirlpool tubs. ⊠ *6470 Moonstone Beach Dr., 93428,* ☎ *805/927–3300. 18 rooms. Fireplaces, refrigerators. Continental breakfast. AE, D, DC, MC, V.*

$$–$$$$ ▦ **Fog Catcher Inn.** Its landscaped gardens and 10 thatched-roof buildings lend the Fog Catcher the feel of an English country village. Most rooms (among them 10 minisuites) have ocean views. All have fireplaces and are done in floral chintz with light wood furniture. ⊠ *6400 Moon-
stone Beach Dr., 93428,* ☎ *805/927–1400 or 800/425–4121,* ⅨX *805/
927–0204. 50 rooms, 10 suites. Pool, hot tub. Full breakfast. AE, D, DC, MC, V.*

$$–$$$ ▦ **Cypress Cove Inn.** Like many hotels on the beach, this recently built romantic getaway was designed in the Welsh style, with outside walls made of old stone and rooms on the upper floors crisscrossed by wood beams. Ask for a room facing the Pacific. ⊠ *6348 Moonstone Beach Dr., 93428,* ☎ *805/927–2600 or 800/568–8517. 21 rooms, 1 suite. No-smoking rooms, refrigerators, in-room VCRs, hot tub. AE, MC ,V.*

$$–$$$ ▦ **Squibb House.** Owner Bruce Black restored this 1877 Gothic Revival Italianate structure, and his craftsmen built many of the pine furnishings. The house radiates history, community, and pride of place. The rooms contain antiques but have modern conveniences like read-
ing lamps with ample light, and showers with sufficient water pres-
sure. ⊠ *4063 Burton Dr., 93428,* ☎ *805/927–9600,* ⅨX *805/927–9606. 5 rooms. No-smoking rooms. Continental breakfast. MC, V.*

$–$$$ ▦ **Best Western Fireside Inn.** This modern motel has spacious rooms with sofas, upholstered lounge chairs, refrigerators, and coffeemakers. Some rooms have whirlpools or ocean views, and all have fireplaces. The inn is across from the beach. ⊠ *6700 Moonstone Beach Dr., 93428,* ☎ *805/927–866 or 888/910–7100,* ⅨX *805/927–8584. 46 rooms. Pool, hot tub. Continental breakfast. AE, D, DC, MC, V.*

$–$$$ ▦ **Bluebird Motel.** Rooms at this garden motel near Cambria's East Village include simply furnished doubles and nicer creekside suites with patios, fireplaces, refrigerators, and TVs with VCRs. The Bluebird isn't the fanciest place, but if you don't require beachside accommodations, it's a decent bargain. ☒ *1880 Main St., 93428,* ☎ *805/927–4634 or 800/552–5434,* ☒ *805/927–5215. 37 rooms. D, DC, MC, V.*

$$ 🏨 **San Simeon Pines Resort.** Amid 9 acres of pines and cypress, this motel-style resort has its own golf course and is directly across from Leffingwell's Landing. The accommodations include cottages with landscaped backyards. Rooms in parts of the complex are for adults only; others are reserved for families. ☒ *7200 Moonstone Beach Dr. (mailing address: Box 117, San Simeon 93452,* ☎ *805/927–4648. 58 rooms. Pool, 9-hole golf course, croquet, shuffleboard, playground. AE, MC, V.*

Nightlife

Cambria doesn't have much of a nightlife, but if you're looking for a bar with music, cruise up Main Street until you hear some sounds that suit your fancy. A crowd of all ages hangs out at the pine-panel **Camozzi's Saloon** (☒ 2262 Main St., ☎ 805/927–8941), where the atmosphere is old-time cowboy but the music is rock and R&B.

En Route Seven miles south of Cambria on Highway 1 is the town of **Harmony,** population 18. The **Harmony Pottery Studio Gallery** (☒ Hwy. 1, ☎ 805/927–4293) shows some fine work.

Morro Bay

20 mi south of Cambria on Hwy. 1.

Fishermen in the town of Morro Bay slog around the harbor in galoshes, and old-style ships teeter in its protected waters. Chumash Indians were the area's main inhabitants when Portuguese explorer Juan Rodríguez Cabrillo dropped anchor in 1542. The Spanish claimed the region in 1587, but Morro Bay remained a relatively quiet place until the second half of the 19th century, when an enterprising farmer built the town's wharf. Fishing was the main industry in the early 20th century, and it remains a vital part of the economy.

★ ❾ Except for the highly visible smokestacks of an electric power plant (and a restaurant scene that's completely au courant), the town retains a retro feel. The other big landmark is 576-ft-high **Morro Rock.** A short walk to the base of the rock—one of nine such small volcanic peaks, or "morros," in the area—leads to a breakwater, with the harbor on one side and the crashing waves of the Pacific on the other. Morro Bay is a wildlife preserve where endangered falcons and other birds nest. You can't climb on Morro Rock, but even from its base you'll be able to divine that the peak is alive with birds.

The center of the action on land is the **Embarcadero,** which holds restaurants, lodgings, and a few attractions. The town's well-designed aquarium is here, as is the outdoor Giant Chessboard, made up of nearly life-size hand-carved pieces.

Dining and Lodging

$$–$$$$ ✗ **Hoppe's.** Morro Bay's most notable restaurant is the one place in town where you can get real caviar. On the second floor of a wooden seafront building, it is only open for dinner and Sunday brunch. The fish is always fresh and prepared with style. ☒ *699 Embarcadero, No. 7,* ☎ *805/772–9012. AE, D, MC, V.*

$$–$$$ ✗ **The Great American Fish Company.** Opposite Morro Rock, this is a great spot to come and watch the seagulls and look out for frolicking otters; the only drawback is the power plant looming behind the restaurant. Shark steaks, filet mignon with scampi, squid burgers, and other entrées come in generous portions. ☒ *1185 Embarcadero,* ☎ *805/ 772–4707. MC, V.*

$–$$ ✕ **Dorn's.** This seafood café that overlooks the harbor resembles a Cape Cod cottage. It's open for breakfast, lunch, and dinner. Excellent fish and native abalone are on the dinner menu. ✉ *801 Market Ave.,* ☎ *805/772–4415. AE, MC, V.*

$$–$$$$ ⌧ **The Inn at Morro Bay.** A bit away from town, inside Morro Bay State Park and across from a heron rookery, this upscale hotel complex has romantic country French–style rooms. Some have fireplaces, whirlpool tubs, and bay views; others look out at extensive gardens. There's a golf course across the road, and mountain bikes are free for guests. Even if you're a bird lover, it's best not to book a room near the rookery; the morning din can be overwhelming. ✉ *60 State Park Rd., 93442,* ☎ *805/772–5651 or 800/321–9566,* ☏ *805/772–4779. 96 rooms. Restaurant, bar, room service, pool. AE, D, DC, MC, V.*

$$–$$$ ⌧ **Embarcadero Inn.** A drab metallic exterior that seems influenced by social realism's bleakest tendencies hides a more welcoming interior of sparkling clean rooms, all of them with old maritime photographs on the walls and balconies that face the sea. ✉ *456 Embarcadero, 93442,* ☎ *805/772–2700 or 800/292–7625,* ☏ *805/772–1060. 26 rooms, 4 suites. Refrigerators, 2 hot tubs. AE, D, DC, MC, V.*

$–$$ ⌧ **Adventure Inn.** Nautical murals decorate this small motel on the harbor and facing Morro Rock. Rooms are plain but comfortable; amenities include coffeemakers and free HBO and local calls. ✉ *1150 Embarcadero, 93442,* ☎ *805/772–5607; 800/799–5607 in CA,* ☏ *805/772–8377. 16 rooms. Refrigerators, pool, hot tub. AE, MC, V.*

$–$$ ⌧ **Grays Inn and Gallery.** With only three rooms, you may have trouble getting a reservation at this tiny beachfront property. But make an effort, because the place is a hidden treasure whose cozy rooms have large glass walls facing the sea. ✉ *561 Embarcadero, 93442 ,* ☎ *805/ 772–3911. 3 rooms. Kitchenettes. AE, MC, V.*

Outdoor Activities and Sports

Kayaks of Morro Bay (✉ 699 Embarcadero, ☎ 805/772–1119) rents canoes and kayaks. **Sub-Sea Tours** (✉ 699 Embarcadero, ☎ 805/772–9463) operates fish-viewing boat rides in glass-bottom boats. **Virg's Sport Fishing** (✉ 1215 Embarcadero, ☎ 805/772–1222 or 800/762–5263) conducts deep-sea fishing trips.

San Luis Obispo

⑩   *14 mi south of Morro Bay on Hwy. 1; 230 mi south of San Francisco on I–280 to U.S. 101; 112 mi north of Santa Barbara on U.S. 101.*

About halfway between San Francisco and Los Angeles, San Luis Obispo is an appealing urban center set among rolling hills and extinct volcanos. It is home to two decidedly different institutions: California Polytechnic State University, known as Cal Poly, and the exuberantly garish Madonna Inn. The town has restored its old railroad depot as well as several Victorian-era homes; the Chamber of Commerce (☞ Contacts and Resources *in* the Central Coast A to Z, *below*) has a list of self-guided historic walks. On Thursday from 6 to 9 PM a 4-block-long farmers' market takes place on Higuera Street.

★   **Mission San Luis Obispo de Tolosa,** established in 1772, overlooks San Luis Obispo Creek. The mission's museum exhibits artifacts of the Chumash Indians and early Spanish settlers. ✉ *751 Palm St.,* ☎ *805/ 543–6850.* ✑ *$2 suggested donation.* ☉ *Memorial Day weekend–Dec., daily 9–5; Jan.–late May, daily 9–4.*

★   Inside an old redbrick building across from the mission, the **County Historical Museum** holds a captivating hodgepodge of exhibits—Native American arrows, tiles from the original mission roof, and an intriguing late–19th-century hand organ. ⊠ *696 Monterey St.,* ☎ *805/ 543–0638.* ☞ *$2.* ☉ *Daily 9–5.*

Dining and Lodging

$–$$ ✕ **Buona Tavola.** Homemade agnolotti (pasta) filled with scampi in a creamy saffron sauce and braised lamb shank with grilled polenta are among the northern Italian dishes served at this local favorite. In good weather you can dine outdoors on the flower-filled patio. ⊠ *1037 Monterey St.,* ☎ *805/545–8000. D, MC, V.*

$–$$ ✕ **Cafe Roma.** Authentic northern Italian cuisine is the specialty of this restaurant on Railroad Square. Under a large mural of sunny Tuscany, you can dine on squash-filled ravioli with sage and butter sauce or filet mignon glistening with port and Gorgonzola. ⊠ *1819 Osos St.,* ☎ *805/ 541–6800. AE, D, DC, MC, V. Closed Mon. No lunch weekends.*

$ ✕ **Big Sky Cafe.** The menu here roams the world—the Mediterranean,
★   the Sun Belt, North Africa, and the Southwest—but many of the ingredients are local: organic fruits and vegetables, hormone-free chicken, and pork and chicken sausages produced right in town. Big Sky is a hip gathering spot for breakfast, lunch, and dinner. ⊠ *1121 Broad St.,* ☎ *805/545–5401. MC, V.*

$$–$$$$ 🏨 **Apple Farm.** Decorated to the hilt with floral bedspreads and wall-
★   paper and watercolors by local artists, each room in this country-style hotel has a gas fireplace; some have canopy beds and cozy window seats. There's a working grist mill in the garden courtyard. ⊠ *2015 Monterey St., 93401,* ☎ *805/544–2040; 800/374–3705 in CA;* ℻ *805/ 546–9495. 103 rooms. Restaurant, pool, hot tub. AE, D, MC, V.*

$$–$$$$ 🏨 **Madonna Inn.** From its rococo bathrooms to its pink-on-pink, froufrou dining areas, the Madonna Inn is the ultimate in kitsch. Each room is unique, to say the least: Rock Bottom is all stone, even the bathroom; the Safari Room is decked out in animal skins. Humor value aside, the Madonna is pretty much a duded-up motel, so don't expect much in the way of luxury. ⊠ *100 Madonna Rd., 93405,* ☎ *805/543– 3000 or 800/543–9666,* ℻ *805/543–1800. 87 rooms, 22 suites. Bar, coffee shop, dining room, shops. MC, V.*

$$ 🏨 **La Cuesta Inn.** The room decor at this adobe-style motel on the northern edge of town is understated, almost to the point of being generic. If you can forgo elegance, this is a good bet. ⊠ *2074 Monterey St., 93401,* ☎ *805/543–2777 or 800/543–2777,* ℻ *805/544–0696. 72 rooms. Pool, hot tub. AE, D, DC, MC, V.*

$ 🏨 **Adobe Inn.** The friendly owners of this establishment of cheerful motel-style rooms serve excellent breakfasts. They'll help you plan your stay in the area, even if you don't choose to go on one of their reasonably priced winery, bicycle-tour, or other packages. ⊠ *1473 Monterey St., 93401,* ☎ *805/549–0321 or 800/676–1588,* ℻ *805/ 549–0383. 15 rooms. Kitchenettes. Full breakfast. AE, D, MC, V.*

Nightlife and the Arts

The **San Luis Obispo Mozart Festival** (☎ 805/781–3008) takes place in late July and early at settings that the Mission San Luis Obispo de Tolosa. Not all the music is Mozart; you'll hear Haydn and other composers. The Festival Fringe presents free concerts outdoors. The **Performing Arts Center** (⊠ Grand Ave., ☎ 805/756–7222) at Cal Poly hosts concerts and recitals.

The club scene in this college town is centered around Higuera Street off Monterey Street. **Linnaea's Cafe** (⊠ 110 Garden St., ☎ 805/541– 5888), a mellow java joint, sometimes hosts poetry readings, blues and alternative rock performances, and other diversions. Bands playing music from swing to blues to rock perform at **Mother's Tavern** (⊠ 725 Higuera St., ☎ 805/595–3764), which is something of a frat-party scene on the weekend.

En Route Highway 1 and U.S. 101 become one road for a short stretch south of San Luis Obispo. San Luis Bay Drive loops off the highway to Avila Beach, a usually quiet town that comes alive on weekends, when Cal Poly students take over. As you continue south, 20 mi of sandy, southern California–style shoreline begins at the town of Pismo Beach, where the action centers on the shops and arcades near the pier. From here there are **two routes to Solvang.** The direct route is U.S. 101, past Arroyo Grande, Santa Maria, and rural countryside that is becoming increasingly less rural. At Buellton, head east on Highway 246 to Solvang. The other option is to take Highway 1, which twists along the coast (and inland a bit at times) past Guadalupe, Vandenberg Air Force Base, and Lompoc. Along the roads near Lompoc, also known as the Flower-Seed Capital of the World, vast fields of brightly colored flowers bloom from May to August. At Lompoc, Highway 246 travels east from Highway 1, past Mission La Purisima Concepción through Buellton to Solvang. Highway 1 continues south and east until it rejoins U.S. 101 at Las Cruces, 9 mi below Buellton.

La Purisima Mission State Historic Park

58 mi south of San Luis Obispo, Hwy. 1 to Hwy. 246 east or U.S. 101 to Hwy. 246 west.

★ ⑪ **Mission La Purisima Concepción,** the most fully restored mission in the state, was founded in 1787. Its stark and still-remote setting powerfully evokes the lives of California's Spanish settlers. Displays illustrate the secular and religious activities at the mission, and once a month from March to September costumed docents demonstrate crafts. A corral near the parking area holds several farm animals, including sheep that are descendants of the original mission stock. ⊠ *2295 Purisima Rd., off Mission Gate Rd.,* ☎ *805/733–3713; 805/733–1303 to schedule a tour.* ▣ *$5 per vehicle.* ⊙ *Daily 9–5.*

Solvang

⑫ *23 mi east of Mission La Purisima Concepción on Hwy. 246; 3 mi east of U.S. 101 on Hwy. 246.*

You'll know when you've reached the Danish town of Solvang: The architecture suddenly turns to half-timbered buildings and windmills, with flags galore. Though the activities here are aimed squarely at tourists, the town has a genuine Danish heritage—more than two-thirds of the residents are of Danish descent. The 300 or so shops that sell Danish goods and knickknacks and specialty gift items are all within easy walking distance; many are along Copenhagen Drive and Alisal Road. Solvang Bakery, at 460 Alisal Road, is one of a half dozen aroma-filled bakeries. If Solvang seems too serene and orderly to be true, find a copy of William Castle's 1961 film *Homicidal,* which used the town as the backdrop for gender-bending murder and mayhem.

Dining and Lodging

$$–$$$ ✕ **The Hitching Post.** You'll find everything from grilled artichokes to ostrich at this casual eatery in Buellton, but most people come for what is said to be the best Santa Maria–style barbecue in the state. The oak used in the barbecue imparts a wonderfully smoky taste. ⊠ *406 E. Hwy. 246, Buellton,* ☎ *805/688–0676. AE, MC, V. No lunch.*

$–$$ ✕ **Bit O' Denmark.** Perhaps the most authentic Danish eatery in Solvang, this restaurant is in an old beamed building that was a church until 1929. The dishes have names like *Frikadeller* (heavy meatballs with pickled red cabbage, potatoes, and thick brown gravy) and *Medister-*

polse (Danish beef and pork sausage with cabbage). ✉ *473 Alisal Rd.,* ☎ *805/688–5426. AE, D, MC, V.*

$ ✕ **Restaurant Molle-Kroen.** Locals come to this cheerful upstairs dining room when they want a good Danish meal at a reasonable price. ✉ *435 Alisal Rd.,* ☎ *805/688–4555. AE, D, DC, MC, V.*

$$$$ ✕🏨 **Alisal Guest Ranch and Resort.** Sixteen hundred or so head of cattle graze the 10,000-acre grounds of Alisal Ranch, which opened to guests in 1946 and soon attracted the likes of Clark Gable and Doris Day. Rooms are plain, with appealing Western touches; all have refrigerators and wood-burning fireplaces. The land-based activities include golf, tennis, horseback riding, and nature-watching. Sailing, windsurfing, pedal boating, and fishing take place on the 90-acre lake. Hearty meals are served home-style in the rustic yet elegant Ranch Room if the weather isn't warm enough for an outdoor barbecue. Breakfast and dinner are included in the room rates, but many of the activities cost extra. ✉ *1054 Alisal Rd., 93463,* ☎ *805/688–6411 or 800/425–4725,* 🆉🆇 *805/688–2510. 36 rooms, 37 suites. Restaurant, bar, pool, 2 18-hole golf courses, 7 tennis courts, croquet, Ping-Pong, shuffleboard, volleyball, bike rentals, billiards. Full breakfast. AE, DC, MC, V.*

$$–$$$$ 🏨 **Petersen Village Inn.** As with most of the buildings in Solvang, this
  ★   property is heavy on the wood—the overall effect is along the lines of a hunting lodge. The four-poster beds here are plush, the bathrooms small but sparkling. The inn welcomes children over age seven. ✉ *1576 Mission Dr., 93463,* ☎ *805/688–3121 or 800/321–8985,* 🆉🆇 *805/688–5732. 39 rooms, 1 suite. Café, bar. Full breakfast. AE, MC, V.*

$–$$$ 🏨 **Story Book Inn.** Someone in Solvang had to do it: All the rooms at this B&B are named after Hans Christian Andersen stories. Some rooms are on the small side, but others are large and luxurious. The suites have large four-poster beds and roomy marble whirlpool tubs. ✉ *409 1st St., 93463,* ☎ *805/688–1703 or 800/786–7925,* 🆉🆇 *805/688–0953. 7 rooms, 2 suites. Full breakfast. AE, D, MC, V.*

$$ 🏨 **Chimney Sweep Inn.** The regular rooms at this inn with a landscaped garden are well maintained. The larger (and more expensive) cottages were inspired by the C. S. Lewis children's series, *The Chronicles of Narnia.* The six cottages have kitchens and fireplaces; five also have hot tubs. ✉ *1564 Copenhagen Dr., 93463,* ☎ *805/688–2111 or 800/824–6444,* 🆉🆇 *805/688–8824. 48 rooms, 8 suites. Hot tub. Continental breakfast. AE, D, MC, V.*

$–$$ 🏨 **Best Western Kronborg Inn.** Rooms at this comfortable motel three blocks from the center of town are spacious; most have balconies overlooking the pool. ✉ *1440 Mission Dr., 93463,* ☎ *805/688–2383,* 🆉🆇 *805/688–1821. 39 rooms. Pool, hot tub. Continental breakfast. AE, D, DC, MC, V.*

Nightlife and the Arts

Pacific Conservatory of the Performing Arts (☎ 805/922–8313; 800/549–7272 in CA) presents contemporary and classic plays, along with a few musicals, in different theaters in Solvang and Santa Maria. Summer events in Solvang are held in the open-air Festival Theatre, on 2nd Street off Copenhagen Drive.

Outdoor Activities and Sports

Cachuma Lake (✉ Hwy. 154, ☎ 805/688–4658), a jewel of an artificial lake 12 mi east of Solvang, has hiking, fishing, boating, and interpretive nature programs.

BICYCLING

Quadricycles, four-wheel carriages, and bicycles are available at **Breezy's Carriages** (✉ 414 1st St., ☎ 805/688–0091) and **Surrey Cycle Rental** (✉ 475 1st St., ☎ 805/688–0091).

GLIDER RIDES

The scenic rides operated by **Windhaven Glider** (⊠ Santa Ynez Airport, Hwy. 246 east of Solvang, ☎ 805/688–2517) cost between $65 and $135 and last up to 40 minutes.

Los Olivos

⑬ *1 mi north of Solvang on Alamo Pintado Rd.*

This pretty village in the Santa Ynez Valley was once on the Spanish-built El Camino Real and later on major stagecoach and rail routes. It's so sleepy today, though, that it was selected as the site for TV's *Return to Mayberry*. A row of art galleries, antiques stores, and country markets lines Grand Avenue. At **Los Olivos Tasting Room & Wine Shop** (⊠ 2905 Grand Ave., ☎ 805/688–7406) you can sample locally produced wines and pick up winery maps.

Dining and Lodging

$$$$ ✕🏠 **Los Olivos Grand Hotel.** The rooms at this luxury inn—the only place you can spend the night in Los Olivos—are in a lawn-fronted house and an equally attractive residence across the street with a pool and a hot tub. The spacious accommodations have fireplaces, seating areas, and wet bars; six also have hot tubs. At Remington's ($$–$$$), the hotel's dining room, well-selected local wines complement entrées like oven-roasted salmon and grilled lamb T-bone. ⊠ *2860 Grand Ave., 93441, ☎ 805/688–7788 or 800/446–2455, ℻ 805/688–1942. 20 rooms, 1 suite. Pool, hot tub. Full breakfast. AE, D, MC, V.*

OFF THE BEATEN PATH — **SAN MARCOS PASS** – Highway 154 winds its spectacular way south from Solvang (drive east on Highway 246 to 154) through the Los Padres National Forest. This former stagecoach route rejoins U.S. 101 north of Santa Barbara. The lively Cold Spring Tavern (☞ Santa Barbara Dining and Lodging, *below*) has been serving travelers since the stagecoach days.

SANTA BARBARA

45 mi south of Solvang on U.S. 101.

Santa Barbara has long been an oasis for Los Angeles residents in need of rest and recuperation, but combining as it does the best attributes of a resort town and a sophisticated city, it is hardly an outpost. The attractions in Santa Barbara begin with the ocean and end in the foothills of the Santa Ynez Mountains. In the few miles between the beaches and the hills are downtown, then the old mission, and, a little higher up, the botanic gardens. A few miles farther up the coast, but still very much a part of Santa Barbara, is the exclusive residential district of Hope Ranch. To the east is the district called Montecito, whose informal but classy Coast Village Road has shops and restaurants.

Santa Barbara is on a jog in the coastline, so the ocean is actually to the south. Directions can be confusing. "Up" the coast is west, "down" toward Los Angeles is actually east, and the mountains are north. A car is handy but not essential if you're planning to stay in town. The beaches and downtown are easily explored by bicycle or on foot, and the Santa Barbara Trolley (☞ Contacts and Resources in the Central Coast A to Z, *below*) takes visitors to most major hotels and sights, which can also be reached on the local buses.

The Waterfront

You'll hear locals refer to the waterfront as "the ocean," but by any name it's a beautiful area, with palm-studded promenades and plenty of sand.

A Good Tour

Start your tour at the **Santa Barbara Yacht Harbor** ⑭. Walk east on Cabrillo Boulevard, the main harborfront drag to **Stearns Wharf** ⑮, where the **Sea Center** ⑯ is a major attraction. Unless you're an inveterate walker, drive east along Cabrillo Boulevard to **East Beach** ⑰ and the nearby **Andree Clark Bird Refuge** ⑱. More creatures await at the **Santa Barbara Zoo** ⑲, which is adjacent to the refuge.

TIMING

You could make this an all-day excursion or devote only two or three hours to it if you drive and only stop briefly at the various attractions; a spin through the zoo takes about an hour.

Sights to See

⑱ **Andree Clark Bird Refuge.** This peaceful lagoon and gardens sits north of East Beach. Bike trails and footpaths, punctuated by signs identifying native and migratory birds, skirt the lagoon. ⊠ *1400 E. Cabrillo Blvd.* ☜ *Free.*

OFF THE BEATEN PATH

CHANNEL ISLANDS NATIONAL PARK AND NATIONAL MARINE SANCTUARY – The five Channel Islands often appear in a haze on the Santa Barbara horizon. The most popular is Anacapa Island, 11 mi off the coast. The islands' remoteness and unpredictable seas protected them from development and now provide a nature-enthusiast's paradise. On a good day you'll be able to view seals, sea lions, and much bird life. Migrating whales can be seen close up from December to March. Tidal pools are often accessible. Divers can view fish, giant squid, and coral. Frenchy's Cove, on the west end of the island, has a swimming beach and fine snorkeling. The waters of the channel are often rough and can make for a rugged boat ride out to the islands (*see* Boats and Charters *in* Outdoor Activities and Sports, *below,* for information about group outings).

⑰ **East Beach.** The wide swath of sand at the east end of Cabrillo Boulevard is a great spot for people-watching. Sand volleyball courts, summertime lifeguard and sports competitions, and arts-and-crafts shows on Sundays and holidays make for an often lively experience. Showers (no towels), lockers, and beach rentals—also a weight room—are provided at the **Cabrillo Pavilion Bathhouse** (⊠ 1118 Cabrillo Blvd., ☎ 805/965–0509). Next to the boathouse, there's an elaborate jungle-gym play area for children.

Moreton Bay Fig Tree. Planted in 1874 and transplanted to its present location in 1877, this tree is so huge it reputedly can provide shade for 10,000 people. ⊠ *Chapala St. at U.S. 101.*

⑭ **Santa Barbara Yacht Harbor.** A paved, man-made breakwater protects this harbor. You can take a ½-mi walk along the breakwater; check out the tackle and bait shops, or hire a boat. ⊠ *West end of Cabrillo Blvd.*

☾ ⑲ **Santa Barbara Zoo.** The natural settings of the zoo shelter elephants, gorillas, exotic birds, and big cats such as the rare amur leopard, a thick-furred, high-altitude dweller from Asia. For the kids there's a scenic railroad and barnyard petting zoo. ⊠ *500 Niños Dr.,* ☎ *805/962–6310.* ☜ *$5.* ☼ *Daily 10–5.*

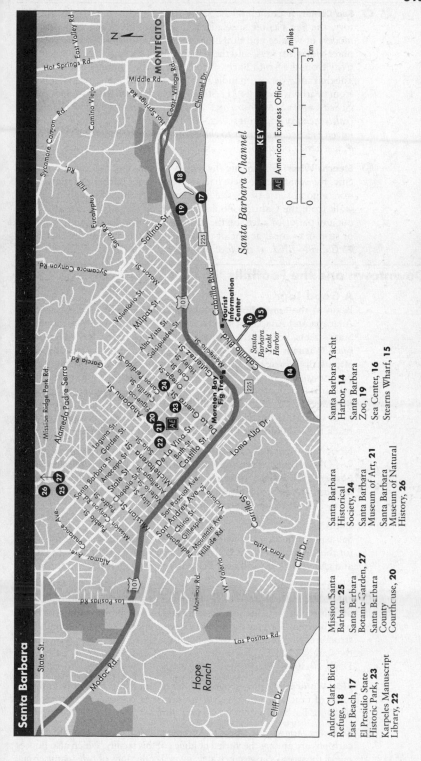

Santa Barbara

315

MONTECITO

Hot Springs Rd.

East Valley Rd.

Middle Rd.

Camino Viejo

Sycamore Canyon Rd.

Hill Rd.

Eucalyptus

Coast Village Rd.

Channel Dr.

Hot Springs Rd.

N

KEY

AE American Express Office

Santa Barbara Channel

2 miles

3 km

Salinas St.

Sycamore Canyon Rd

Mission Ridge Park Rd.

Voluntario St.

Milpas St.

Alta Vista St.

Salsipuedes St.

Mason St.

225

101

Cabrillo Blvd

Tourist
Information
Center

Santa
Barbara
Yacht
Harbor

17

18

19

16

15

14

225

Cabrillo Blvd

Quarantina St.

Garcia Rd.

Alameda Padre Serra

Canon Perdido St.

Carrillo St.

Ortega St.

Cota St.

Haley St.

Figueroa St.

Moreton Bay
Fig Tree

Anacapa St.

Laguna St.

Garden St.

Santa Barbara St.

Anacapa St.

State St.

Chapala St.

De La Vina St.

Bath St.

Castillo St.

24

23

20

21

22

AE

Loma Alta Dr.

Michieltorena
Sola St.

Valerio St.

Islay St.

Arrellaga St.

Mission St.

Padre St.

Pueblo St.

San Pascual Ave.

San Andres Ave.

Chino St.

Victoria St.

Mountain Rd.

Hillside Rd.

Gillespia

Pedregosa St.

Castillo St.

Flora Vista

Cliff Dr.

Mission Canyon Rd.

Alamar Ave.

Constance Ave.

26

25

27

101

Manitou Rd.

Las Positas Rd

W. Valerio St.

Las Positas Rd.

State St.

Modoc Rd.

Cliff Dr.

Hope
Ranch

☺ ⑯ **Sea Center.** A branch of the Santa Barbara Museum of Natural History, the Sea Center specializes in marine life. Aquariums, life-size models of whales and dolphins, undersea dioramas, interactive computer-video displays, and the remains of shipwrecks depict marine activity from the Santa Barbara coastline to the Channel Islands. At the Touch Tank you can handle invertebrates, fish, and plants collected from nearby waters. ⊠ *211 Stearns Wharf,* ☎ *805/962–0885.* ☜ *$3.* ☉ *Sea Center Sat.–Mon. and Wed. 10–5; Tues., Thurs., Fri. noon–5 (call weekday mornings Oct.–May to make sure school field trips haven't closed the center to the public). Touch Tank weekdays noon–4, weekends noon–5.*

⑮ **Stearns Wharf.** Extending the length of three city blocks into the Pacific, the wharf has a view back toward Santa Barbara that gives visitors a good sense of its size and general layout. Although it's a nice walk from the Cabrillo Boulevard parking areas, you can also drive out and park (for a fee) on the pier and then wander through the shops or stop for a meal at one of the wharf's restaurants or the snack bar. ⊠ *Cabrillo Blvd. at the foot of State St.,* ☎ *805/565–5526.*

Downtown and the Foothills

A Good Tour

Begin at the **Santa Barbara County Courthouse** ⑳, at the corner of Anacapa and Anapamu streets. A block or so away at Anapamu and State streets, beyond the Spanish-style public library, is the **Santa Barbara Museum of Art** ㉑; across State on Anapamu is the **Karpeles Manuscript Library** ㉒. Backtrack on Anapamu to the courthouse and head south on Anacapa. You'll soon pass **El Paseo,** a handsome shopping arcade built around an old adobe home. Make a right at East Cañon Perdido Street to reach **El Presidio State Historic Park** ㉓. From the park, head south one block to De La Guerra Street and turn left (east) to reach the museum of the **Santa Barbara Historical Society** ㉔.

Hop in your car and take State Street north (away from the water) to Los Olivos Street. Turn right (east) and you'll soon see **Mission Santa Barbara** ㉕. From the mission you can walk the block north to the **Santa Barbara Museum of Natural History** ㉖. You'll probably want to drive the 1½ mi north to the **Santa Barbara Botanic Garden** ㉗.

TIMING

Set aside an hour each for the art and natural-history museums and for the botanic gardens. Add more time if you're a shopper—the stores and galleries along and near State Street may sidetrack you for hours.

Sights to See

㉓ **El Presidio State Historic Park.** Founded in 1782, the Presidio was one of four military strongholds established by the Spanish along the coast of California. The guardhouse, El Cuartel, one of the two original adobe structures that remain of the complex, is the oldest building owned by the state. ⊠ *123 E. Cañon Perdido St.,* ☎ *805/966–9719.* ☜ *Free.* ☉ *Daily 10:30–4:30.*

☺ **Kids' World public playground.** Children and adults enjoy this complex maze of fantasy climbing structures, turrets, slides, and tunnels built by Santa Barbara parents. ⊠ *Santa Barbara St. near Micheltorena St.*

㉒ **Karpeles Manuscript Library.** Ancient political tracts and old Disney cartoons are among the varied holdings of this facility, which also houses one of the world's largest privately owned collections of rare manuscripts. Fifty cases contain a sampling of the archive's million-plus documents. ⊠ *21 W. Anapamu St.,* ☎ *805/962–5322.* ☜ *Free.* ☉ *Daily 10–4.*

OFF THE
BEATEN PATH

LOTUSLAND – Only a limited number of people are permitted to visit the 37-acre estate that once belonged to Polish opera singer Ganna Walska; the hours and time of year that Lotusland is open are limited, too, and one must take part in a 1½- to 2-hour guided group tour. That said, it's worth trying to get a reservation to see the celebrated gardens. Many of the exotic trees and other subtropical flora were planted in 1882 by horticulturist R. Kinton Stevens; Madame Walska, who purchased the estate in 1941, further developed the grounds. Among the highlights are an outdoor theater, a topiary garden, a horticultural clock, a huge collection of rare bromeliads, and a lotus pond. ⊠ *Ganna Walska Lotusland, 695 Ashley Rd., Montecito,* ☎ *805/969-9990.* 🖃 *$10.* ⊘ *Tours mid-Feb.–mid-Nov., Wed.–Sun. 10:30 AM and 1:30 PM.*

★ ㉕ **Mission Santa Barbara.** The architecture and layout of this mission, which was established in 1786, evolved from adobe-brick buildings with thatched roofs to more permanent edifices as its population burgeoned. An earthquake in 1812 destroyed the third church built on the site; its replacement, the present structure, is still a Catholic church, though during the post-Mission era it also served as a boys school and a seminary. Cacti, palms, and other succulents grow in the garden beside the mission. ⊠ *2201 Laguna St.,* ☎ *805/682–4713.* 🖃 *$3.* ⊘ *Daily 9 – 5.*

★ ㉗ **Santa Barbara Botanic Garden.** Five-plus miles of trails meander through the garden's 65 acres of native plants. The Mission Dam, built in 1806, stands just beyond the redwood grove and above the partially uncovered aqueduct that once carried water to Mission Santa Barbara. An ethnobotanical display contains replicas of the plants used by the Chumash Indians. ⊠ *1212 Mission Canyon Rd.,* ☎ *805/682–4713.* 🖃 *$3.* ⊘ *Mar.–Oct., weekdays 9–5, weekends 9–6; Nov.–Feb., weekdays 9–4, weekends 9–5. Guided tours Sun.–Tues. and Thurs.–Sat. at 2; additional tour at 10:30 AM Thurs., Sat., and Sun.*

★ ⑳ **Santa Barbara County Courthouse.** With its hand-painted tiles and spiral staircase, the courthouse has all the grandeur of a Moorish palace. This magnificent building was completed in 1929, part of a rebuilding process after a 1925 earthquake destroyed many downtown structures. At the time Santa Barbara was also in the midst of a cultural awakening, and the trend was toward an architecture appropriate to the area's climate and history. The result is the harmonious Mediterranean-Spanish look of much of the downtown area, especially municipal buildings. An elevator rises to an arched observation area in the courthouse tower that provides a panoramic view of the city. The murals in the supervisors' ceremonial chambers on the courthouse's second floor were painted by an artist who did backdrops for some of Cecil B. DeMille's silent films. ⊠ *1100 block of Anacapa St.,* ☎ *805/ 962–6464.* ⊘ *Weekdays 8:30–5, weekends 10–5. Free 1-hr guided tours Wed. and Fri. 10:30 AM, Tues.–Sat. 2 PM.*

㉔ **Santa Barbara Historical Society.** The society's museum exhibits decorative and fine arts, furniture, costumes, and documents from the town's past. Adjacent is the Gledhill Library, a collection of books, photographs, maps, and manuscripts about the area. ⊠ *136 E. De La Guerra St.,* ☎ *805/966–1601.* 🖃 *Museum $3 (suggested donation), library $2 per hr up to $5 for research work.* ⊘ *Museum Tues.–Sat. 10–5, Sun. noon–5; library Tues.–Fri. 10–4, 1st Sat. of month 10–1:30.*

㉑ **Santa Barbara Museum of Art.** The highlights of this museum's fine permanent collection include ancient sculpture, Asian art, French and Impressionist paintings, and American works in several media. ⊠ *1130 State St.,* ☎ *805/963–4364.* 🖃 *$4; free Thurs. and 1st Sun. of* *month.* ⊙ *Tues.−Sat. 11−5 (until 9 Thurs.), Sun. noon−5. Guided tours Tues.−Sun. 1* PM.

⊛ ㉖ **Santa Barbara Museum of Natural History.** A full-size skeleton of a blue whale at the entrance serves as a landmark for this museum complex. The major draws include the planetarium and E. L. Wiegand Space Lab. A room of dioramas illustrates Chumash Indian history and culture. Startlingly lifelike stuffed specimens, complete with nests and eggs, roost in the bird diversity room. Many of the exhibits have interactive components. ⊠ *2559 Puesta del Sol Rd.,* ☎ *805/682−4711.* ⊡ *$5.* ⊙ *Mon.−Sat. 9−5, Sun. 10−5.*

Dining and Lodging

$$$−$$$$ ✕ **The Stonehouse.** This atmospheric restaurant in a century-old granite farmhouse is part of the San Ysidro Ranch resort. The contemporary southern fare includes dry-aged New York steak with smoked tomato-horseradish sauce and clam hash, seared ahi tuna in an herb crust with sun-dried-tomato couscous, and excellent vegetarian options. Even better than the generally wonderful food is the pastoral setting. Have lunch—salads, pastas, and sandwiches—on the tree-house-like outdoor patio. At night the candlelit interior becomes seriously romantic. ⊠ *900 San Ysidro La., Montecito,* ☎ *805/969−4100. Reservations essential. AE, DC, MC, V.*

$$$ ✕ **Citronelle.** At this offspring of chef Michel Richard's Citrus in Los
★   Angeles, intriguing flavors animate dishes like the lamb loin with couscous and cumin sauce and the seared ahi tuna with an Anaheim-chili sauce. The desserts are stupendous. The dining room's picture windows yield splendid, sweeping views—try to arrive before sunset. ⊠ *901 E. Cabrillo Blvd.,* ☎ *805/963−0111. Reservations essential. AE, D, DC, MC, V.*

$$−$$$ ✕ **Andria's Harborside.** The seafood entrées are decent enough at this sprawling, nautical-style eatery, but most people come for the creamy clam chowder or the fresh oysters—and the harbor views. Nightly entertainment at the piano bar adds to the bustling atmosphere. ⊠ *336 W. Cabrillo Blvd.,* ☎ *805/966−3000. AE, D, DC, MC, V.*

$$−$$$ ✕ **Brophy Bros.** The outdoor tables at this casual restaurant have perfect views of the harbor and fishing vessels. A fine place to lunch, Brophy Bros. serves enormous, exceptionally fresh seafood plates—try the seafood salad. ⊠ *119 Harbor Way.,* ☎ *805/966−4418. . AE, MC, V.*

$$−$$$ ✕ **Harbor Restaurant.** This sparkling spot on the pier is where locals take out-of-town guests for great views and standard American food. The nautical-theme bar and grill upstairs serves sandwiches, large salads, and many appetizers; on a sunny day the outdoor terrace is a glorious spot for a sandwich or a beer. Downstairs you can dine on seafood, prime rib, and steaks. ⊠ *210 Stearns Wharf,* ☎ *805/963−3311. AE, MC, V.*

$$−$$$ ✕ **Palace Café.** The Palace has won acclaim for Cajun and Creole dishes like blackened redfish and jambalaya with dirty rice. Caribbean fare here includes delicious coconut shrimp. If the dishes aren't spicy enough for you, each table has a bottle of hot sauce. Be prepared to wait as long as 45 minutes on weekends. ⊠ *8 E. Cota St.,* ☎ *805/966−3133. AE, MC, V. No lunch.*

$$−$$$ ✕ **Trattoria Mollie's.** Ethiopian-born chef-owner Mollie Ahlstrand spent several years in Italy before ending up in California. Her seafood pasta and the plate of seafood and vegetables are among the many subtly flavored entrées. Lush potted plants surround the tables at this chic, popular trattoria. ⊠ *1250 Coast Village Rd.,* ☎ *805/563−9381. Reservations essential on weekends. AE, MC, V.*

BONUS MILES MAKE
GREAT SOUVENIRS.

MCI Calling Card

123 456 7891 2345
J.D. SMITH

WORLDPHONE®

Earn Miles With Your MCI Card.

Take the MCI Card along on this trip and start earning miles for the next one. You'll earn frequent flyer miles on all your calls and save with the low rates you've come to expect from MCI. Before you know it, you'll be on your way to some other international destination.

Sign up for MCI by calling 1-800-FLY-FREE

Is this a great time, or what? :-)

Earn Frequent Flyer Miles.

Delta Air Lines
SkyMiles®

MIDWEST EXPRESS AIRLINES

NORTHWEST AIRLINES
WORLDPERKS®

MILEAGE PLUS.
United Airlines

You've read the book. Now book the trip.

For all the best deals on flights, hotels, rental cars, and vacation packages, book them online at www.previewtravel.com. Then click on our Destination Guides featuring content from Fodor's and more. You'll find hotels, restaurants, attractions, and things to do around the globe. There are even interactive maps, videos, and weather forecasts. You'll have everything you need to make your vacation exactly what you want it to be. All it takes is a trip online.

Travel on Your Terms™
www.previewtravel.com
aol keyword: previewtravel

preview travel℠

$$–$$$ ✕ **Wine Cask.** Sautéed swordfish and Colorado lamb sirloin, each prepared with a wine-based sauce, are among the most popular entrées at this slick restaurant with a beautiful wood interior. In fine weather the outdoor patio is one of the most romantic dining spots in Santa Barbara. ✉ *813 Anacapa St.,* ☎ *805/966–9463. AE, MC, V.*

$–$$$ ✕ **Arigato Sushi.** Sushi fans will appreciate the fresh seafood served in this atmospheric Japanese restaurant and sushi bar. Innovation reigns, with creations such as sushi pizza on seaweed and Hawaiian sashimi salad. ✉ *11 W. Victoria St.,* ☎ *805/965–6074. Reservations not accepted. AE, MC, V. No lunch.*

$–$$$ ✕ **Brigitte's.** This lively State Street café serves California cuisine and local wines at relatively low prices. The individual pizzas are always worth trying, as are the pastas (such as basil fettuccine with prawns and roasted peppers in pesto), grilled fresh fish, and roast lamb. ✉ *1325– 1327 State St.,* ☎ *805/966–9676. AE, D, DC, MC, V. No lunch Sun.*

$$ ✕ **Emilio's.** Starters on the seasonal northern Italian menu at this harborside restaurant might include crispy roast duck on a risotto cake. The main courses of ravioli stuffed with butternut squash or potato gnocchi with rock shrimp are standouts. During the week a vegetarian tasting menu is available, as are two prix-fixe wine-tasting menus. ✉ *324 W. Cabrillo Blvd.,* ☎ *805/966–4426. AE, D, MC, V. No lunch.*

$$ ✕ **Pane & Vino.** This tiny trattoria with an equally small sidewalk dining terrace sits in a tree-shaded, flower-decked shopping center. The cold antipasto is very good, as are the salads, pastas, and grilled meats and fish. ✉ *1482 E. Valley Rd., Montecito,* ☎ *805/969–9274. Reservations essential. AE, MC, V. No lunch Sun.*

$–$$ ✕ **Café Buenos Aires.** Salads, sandwiches, pastas, and traditional Argentine empanadas (small turnovers filled with chicken, beef, or vegetables) are on the lunch menu at Buenos Aires. Dinner can be fashioned from potato omelets, Spanish red sausage in beer sauce, octopus stewed with tomato and onion, and other tapas. Pastas and Argentine specialties—larger empanadas or grilled rib-eye steak sautéed in sweet butter—are among the entrées. ✉ *1316 State St.,* ☎ *805/963–0242. Reservations essential for dinner Thurs.–Sun. AE, DC, MC, V.*

$–$$ ✕ **Cold Spring Tavern.** Well worth the drive out of town, this old roadhouse is on the former stagecoach route through the San Marcos Pass. It's part Harley-biker hangout and part romantic country hideaway, a mix that works surprisingly well. Game dishes—rabbit, venison, quail—are the specialty, along with American standards like ribs, steak, and a great chili. It's a one-of-a-kind spot. ✉ *5995 Stagecoach Rd., San Marcos Pass,* ☎ *805/967–0066. AE, MC, V.*

$–$$ ✕ **Montecito Café.** The ambience is upscale yet casual at this restaurant that serves contemporary cuisine—fresh fish, grilled chicken, steak, and pasta. The salads and lamb dishes are particularly inventive. ✉ *1295 Coast Village Rd.,* ☎ *805/969–3392. AE, MC, V.*

$ ✕ **D'Angelo.** The bread served by many of the town's best restaurants comes from the ovens of this bakery, which has a few indoor and outdoor tables. Come for breakfast—the brioches are awesome—or for a sandwich or pastry break. D'Angelo is open weekdays from 7 to 6 and weekends from 7 to 3. ✉ *25 W. Gutierrez St.,* ☎ *805/962–5466. MC, V. No dinner.*

$ ✕ **La Super-Rica.** Praised by Julia Child, this food stand with a patio
★ serves some of spiciest Mexican dishes between Los Angeles and San Francisco. Fans drive for miles to fill up on the soft tacos and incredible beans. ✉ *622 N. Milpas St., at Alphonse St.,* ☎ *805/963–4940. No credit cards.*

$ ✕ **Roy.** Owner-chef Leroy Gandy serves a $12.50 fixed-price dinner— a real bargain—that includes a small salad, fresh soup, and a tempting roster of Cal-Mediterranean main courses: shrimp ravioli, marinated leg of lamb with eggplant ratatouille, grilled salmon with pineapple-orange-mango chutney and a mint-butter sauce. Expect a wait at this downtown storefront on weekends. ⊠ *7 W. Carrillo St.,* ☎ *805/966–5636. AE, D, DC, MC, V.*

$ ✕ **Your Place.** Tasty seafood (try the sea scallops garnished with crispy basil), curries, and vegetarian dishes keep this small restaurant packed for lunch and dinner. Your Place has consistently been named as the best Thai restaurant by local periodicals. ⊠ *22 N. Milpas St.,* ☎ *805/ 966–5151. AE, MC, V. Closed Mon.*

$$$$ ✕🏠 **Four Seasons Biltmore Hotel.** Santa Barbara's grande dame has
★   long been the favored spot for the town's high society and the visiting rich and famous to indulge in quiet California-style luxury. Muted pastels and bleached woods give the cabanas behind the main building an airy feel without sacrificing the hotel's reputation for understated elegance. Surrounded by lush (but always perfectly manicured) gardens and palms, the Biltmore is a bit more formal than other properties in town. Dining is indoors and formal at the hotel's La Marina Restaurant—the California-Continental menu changes monthly—and outdoors and more casual at The Patio. ⊠ *1260 Channel Dr., Montecito 93108,* ☎ *805/969–2261 or 800/332–3442,* 𝖥𝖠𝖷 *805/969–5715. 200 rooms, 17 suites. 2 restaurants, bar, pool, hot tub, spa, putting green, 3 tennis courts, croquet, health club, shuffleboard. AE, DC, MC, V.*

$$$$ 🏠 **Montecito Inn.** Every room at this late-1920s marble palace is adorned with original posters from the films of Charlie Chaplin. The glass doors to the conference room are etched with the great man's image, and the video library contains his entire *oeuvre.* The rooms on the second floor lead onto a cloister-like arched colonnade. The bathrooms are fairly basic, although the newer suites have large marble whirlpool tubs. The suites also have vast Romanesque-style marble fireplaces. ⊠ *1295 Coast Village Rd., 93108,* ☎ *805/969–7854 or 800/843–2017,* 𝖥𝖠𝖷 *805/969–0623. 53 rooms, 7 suites. Restaurant, bar, refrigerators, in-room VCRs, pool, exercise room, bicycles. Continental breakfast. AE, D, MC, V.*

$$$$ 🏠 **San Ysidro Ranch.** At this luxury "ranch" you can feel at home in
★   jeans and cowboy boots, but be prepared to dress for dinner. A hangout for the Hollywood set, this romantic hideaway hosted John and Jackie Kennedy on their honeymoon. Guest cottages, all with down comforters and wood-burning stoves or fireplaces, are scattered among 14 acres of orange trees and flower beds; hiking trails crisscross 500 acres of open space surrounding the property. The Stonehouse Restaurant (☞ *above*) is a Santa Barbara institution. The hotel, which welcomes children and pets, provides personal beauty services and 24-hour room service. ⊠ *900 San Ysidro La., Montecito 93108,* ☎ *805/969–5046 or 800/368–6788,* 𝖥𝖠𝖷 *805/565–1995. 38 rooms. Restaurant, pool, massage, spa, tennis courts, boccie, exercise room, horseshoes. AE, MC, V. 2-day minimum stay on weekends, 3 days on holidays.*

$$$$ 🏠 **Simpson House Inn.** Traditional B&B fans will enjoy the beautifully
★   appointed Victorian main house of this inn on a quiet acre in the heart of town. Those seeking total privacy and sybaritic comfort should choose one of the exceptional cottages or century-old barn suites, each with a wood-burning fireplace, luxurious bedding, state-of-the-art electronics, and a whirlpool bath. In-room spa services such as massage and body wraps are available. ⊠ *121 E. Arrellaga St., 93101,* ☎ *805/ 963–7067 or 800/676–1280,* 𝖥𝖠𝖷 *805/564–4811. 7 rooms, 4 suites, 3 cottages. Full breakfast. AE, D, MC, V. 2-night minimum stay on weekends.*

$$$–$$$$ 🏠 **El Encanto Hotel.** Actress Hedy Lamarr and President Franklin D. Roosevelt are among the guests who have unwound at this woodsy property near Mission Santa Barbara. Mediterranean-style villas dot the lush

10-acre grounds, along with Craftsman cottages with pine beds and living rooms with old brick fireplaces. If gaudy is your thing, book one of the Fountain cottages, which have living rooms with large sofas. ⊠ *1900 Lasuen Rd., 93103,* ☎ *805/687–5000 or 800/346–7039,* FAX *805/ 687–3903. 84 rooms. Restaurant, bar, minibars, room service, pool, tennis court, conference rooms. AE, D, MC, V.*

$$$–$$$$ 🏨 **The Upham.** This restored Victorian hotel amid an acre of gardens in the historic downtown area was established in 1871. Period furnishings and antiques adorn the rooms and cottages, some of which have fireplaces and private patios. The rooms vary in size from small to quite spacious. ⊠ *1404 De La Vina St., 93101,* ☎ *805/962–0058 or 800/ 727–0876,* FAX *805/963–2825. 46 rooms, 4 suites. Restaurant. Continental breakfast. AE, D, DC, MC, V.*

$$–$$$$ 🏨 **Cheshire Cat Inn.** A five-minute walk from downtown, this B&B with
★ an *Alice in Wonderland* motif is accessible yet quiet. The largest rooms hold king-size beds and sunken whirlpool tubs. The smaller rooms, dominated by the beds, come with low-lying armchairs and have a twee, Edwardian look. ⊠ *36 W. Valerio St., 93101,* ☎ *805/569–1610,* FAX *805/682–1876. 13 rooms, 4 suites. Full breakfast. AE, D, MC, V.*

$$–$$$$ 🏨 **Glenborough Inn.** One of the best B&Bs in Santa Barbara County,
★ this inn is composed of four buildings constructed around the dawn of the 20th century. Several of the very private rooms retain an old, dark-wood feel. If you stay in the Craftsman Room, you'll nearly be swallowed up by the vast bed. As with several of the accommodations in this romantic abode, a 200-gallon private hot tub perches on the patio outside the room. ⊠ *1327 Bath St., 93101,* ☎ *805/966–0589 or 800/962–0589,* FAX *805/564–8610. 6 rooms, 8 suites. Full breakfast. AE, MC, V.*

$$–$$$$ 🏨 **Old Yacht Club Inn.** Built in 1912 as a private home in the California Craftsman style, this inn near the beach was one of Santa Barbara's first B&Bs. The rooms have century-old furnishings and Oriental rugs. The adjacent Hitchcock House holds five rooms with private entrances. ⊠ *431 Corona del Mar Dr., 93103,* ☎ *805/962–1277 or 800/ 676–1676; 800/549–1676 in CA;* FAX *805/962–3989. 10 rooms, 2 suites. Full breakfast. No smoking. AE, MC, V.*

$$–$$$$ 🏨 **Villa Rosa.** The rooms and intimate lobby of this Spanish-style stucco-and-wood hotel one block from the beach are decorated in an informal southwestern style. ⊠ *15 Chapala St., 93101,* ☎ *805/966– 0851,* FAX *805/962–7159. 18 rooms. Pool, hot tub. Continental breakfast. AE, MC, V. 3-night minimum during holiday periods.*

$$–$$$ 🏨 **Hotel Santa Barbara.** The central location of this hotel makes it one of the better bargains in town. You won't experience all the luxuries of Santa Barbara's pricier accommodations, but the rooms are clean and modern, if a tad charmless. The top-floor rooms have ocean views. Ask for a room in back, away from the noise of State Street. ⊠ *533 State St., 93101,* ☎ *888/259–7700. 72 rooms, 3 suites. Concierge. AE, D, MC, V.*

$ 🏨 **Motel 6.** The low price and location near the beach are the pluses of this no-frills place. Reserve well in advance at any time of the year. ⊠ *443 Corona del Mar Dr., 93103,* ☎ *805/564–1392,* FAX *805/963– 4687. 51 rooms. Pool. AE, D, DC, MC, V.*

Nightlife and the Arts

Most major hotels present entertainment nightly during the summer season and on weekends all year. State Street has a good jazz scene. Santa Barbara supports a professional symphony and a chamber orchestra. The proximity to the University of California at Santa Barbara assures an endless stream of visiting artists and performers. To see what's scheduled around town pick up a copy of the free weekly *Santa Barbara Independent* newspaper.

BARS AND CLUBS

Rich leather couches, a crackling fire in chilly weather, a cigar balcony, and pool tables draw a fancy Gen-X crowd to **Blue Agave** (✉ 20 E. Cota St., ☎ 805/899–4694) for good food and designer martinis. **The James Joyce** (✉ 513 State St., ☎ 805/962–2688), which sometimes hosts folk and rock performers, is a good place to while away an evening, beer in hand.

Old jazz photos and low lighting lend **Jazz Hall** (✉ 29 E. Victoria. St., ☎ 805/963–0404) an ambience that's about as close to the Greenwich Village experience as you're likely to get in these parts. Musicians perform on weekends. **Joe's Cafe** (✉ 536 State St., ☎ 805/966–4638), where steins of beer accompany hearty bar food, is a fun, if occasionally rowdy, collegiate scene.

The bartenders at **Left at Albuquerque** (✉ 803 State St., ☎ 805/564–5040) pour 141 tequilas, making the southwestern-style bar one of your less sedate nightspots. The determinedly pretentious **Martini Madness Lounge** (✉ ✉ 434 State St., ☎ 805/962–5516) hosts a chic crowd that sits on high stools and basks in fluorescent lighting (if you're not in the prime of youth, you'll look awwwwful). The **Plow & Angel** (✉ San Ysidro Ranch, 900 San Ysidro La., Montecito, ☎ 805/969–5046) books mellow jazz performers on Thursday and Friday; the bar is perfect for those seeking quiet conversation, perhaps even romance. **Soho** (✉ 1221 State St., ☎ 805/962–7776), a hip restaurant and bar, presents weeknight jazz music; on weekends the mood livens with good blues and rock.

PERFORMING ARTS

Arlington Theater (✉ 1317 State St., ☎ 805/963–4408), a Moorish-style movie palace, is home to the Santa Barbara Symphony. **Center Stage Theatre** (✉ Paseo Nuevo, 700 block of State St., 2nd floor, ☎ 805/963–0408) presents plays and readings. **Ensemble Theatre Company** (✉ 914 Santa Barbara St. , ☎ 805/962–8606) stages plays by authors ranging from Priestley to Mamet.

The **Granada Theatre** (✉ 1216 State St., ☎ 805/966–2324), a restored movie palace, is the headquarters of the Santa Barbara Civic Light Opera. The **Lobero Theatre** (✉ 33 E. Cañon Perdido St., ☎ 805/963–0761), a state landmark, hosts community theater groups and touring professionals. The **Music Academy of the West** (✉ 1070 Fairway Rd., Montecito, ☎ 805/687–7820), home to the area's chamber-orchestra players, showcases orchestral and operatic works.

Outdoor Activities and Sports

BEACHES

Santa Barbara's beaches don't have the big surf of the shoreline farther south, but they also don't have the crowds. Walk from the parking lot, and you'll usually find a solitary spot. Fog often hugs the coast until about noon in June and July.

The usually gentle surf at **Arroyo Burro County Beach** (✉ Cliff Dr. at Las Positas Rd.) makes it ideal for families with young children. **Goleta Beach Park** (✉ Ward Memorial Hwy.) is a favorite with college students from the nearby University of California campus. Successively west of Santa Barbara off U.S. 101 are **El Capitan, Refugio, and Gaviota state beaches,** each with campsites, picnic tables, and fire rings. East of the city is sheltered, sunny, often crowded **Carpinteria State Beach.**

BICYCLING

The level, two-lane, 3-mi Cabrillo Bike Lane passes the Santa Barbara Zoo, the Andree Clark Bird Refuge, beaches, and the harbor. There are restaurants along the way, or you can stop for a picnic along the palm-lined path looking out on the Pacific. **Beach Rentals** (⊠ 22 State St., ☎ 805/966–6733) has bikes, quadricycles, and skates. **Cycles 4 Rent** (⊠ Fess Parker's Doubletree Resort, 633 E. Cabrillo Blvd., ☎ 805/ 564–4333, ext. 444) has bikes and quadricycles.

BOATS AND CHARTERS

Island Packers (☎ 805/962–1127 for trips from Santa Barbara Harbor; 805/642–1393 for trips from Ventura Harbor) conducts day trips and camping excursions (reservations essential in summer) to the five Channel Islands. **Santa Barbara Sailing Association** (⊠ Santa Barbara Yacht Harbor launching ramp, ☎ 805/962–2826 or 800/350–9090) provides sailing instruction, rents and charters sailboats, and organizes dinner and sunset champagne cruises, island excursions, and whale-watching expeditions. **Sea Landing Sportfishing** (⊠ Cabrillo Blvd. at Bath St. and the breakwater, ☎ 805/963–3564) operates surface and deep-sea fishing charters year-round, plus dinner cruises and island and whale-watching excursions.

GOLF

Sandpiper Golf Course (⊠ 7925 Hollister Ave., Goleta, ☎ 805/968–1541) is a challenging 18-hole, par-72 course. The greens fee ranges from $70 to $110; an optional cart costs $24. **Santa Barbara Golf Club** (⊠ Las Positas Rd. and McCaw Ave., ☎ 805/687–7087) has an 18-hole, par-70 course. The greens fee is about $20; an optional cart costs $10.

HORSEBACK RIDING

The Circle Bar B Guest Ranch (⊠ 1800 Refugio Rd., Goleta, ☎ 805/ 968–3901) operates trail rides.

TENNIS

Many hotels in Santa Barbara have courts. Day permits ($3) can be purchased for these excellent public courts: **Las Positas Municipal Courts** (⊠ 1002 Las Positas Rd.), **Municipal Courts** (⊠ Near Salinas St. and U.S. 101), and **Pershing Park** (⊠ Castillo St. and Cabrillo Blvd.). For more information, call ☎ 805/564–5517.

Shopping

State Street, the commercial hub of Santa Barbara, is a joy to shop. Chic malls, quirky storefronts, antiques emporiums, elegant women's-wear boutiques, and funky thrift shops are on or near the street, and they're all accessible on foot or by taking the battery-powered trolley (25¢) that runs between the waterfront and the 1300 block. Swank boutiques line Montecito's **Coast Village Road,** where members of the landed gentry pick up truffle oil, picture frames, and designer sweats.

SHOPPING AREAS

Shops, art galleries, and studios share the courtyard and gardens of **El Paseo** (⊠ Cañon Perdido St. between State and Anacapa Sts.), an arcade rich in history. Lunch on the outdoor patio is a nice break during a downtown tour. Open-air **Paseo Nuevo** (⊠ 700 and 800 blocks of State St.), home to chains such as the Eddie Bauer Home Store, Macy's, and the California Pizza Kitchen, also contains cherished local institutions like Stampa Barbara (a rubber-stamp paradise) and the children's clothier This Little Piggy.

Antiques and gift shops are clustered in restored Victorian buildings on Brinkerhoff Avenue, two blocks west of State Street at West Cota Street. Some newer shops have opened along Anacapa Street. Serious antiques hunters head a few miles south of Santa Barbara to the beach town of Summerland, which is rife with shops and markets. For a map and guide to Santa Barbara antiques dealers, drop by 533 Brinkerhoff Avenue or call ☎ 805/962–4247 to have one mailed.

BOOKS

Barnes & Noble (⊠ 829 State St., ☎ 805/962–8509) and **Borders** (⊠ 900 State St., ☎ 805/899–3668) hold court on State Street. **Chaucer's Bookstore** (⊠ Loreta Plaza, 3321 State St., ☎ 805/682–6787) is a well-stocked independent. Rambling yet homey **Earthling Book Shop and Café** (⊠ 1137 State St., ☎ 805/965–0926) is arguably Santa Barbara's cultural and intellectual center. **Sullivan Goss** (⊠ 7 E. Anapamu St., ☎ 805/730–1460) stocks books on California history and art. **The Book Den** (⊠ 11 E. Anapamu St., ☎ 805/962–3321) has the town's largest selection of used books.

CLOTHING

The complete line of **Big Dog Sportswear** (⊠ 6 E. Yanonali St., ☎ 805/963–8728) is sold at the Santa Barbara–based company's flagship store. **Pacific Leisure** (⊠ 929 State St., ☎ 805/962–8828) stocks the latest in casual wear, shoes, and beach towels. **Territory Ahead** (⊠ 515 State St., ☎ 805/962–5558), a high-quality outdoorsy catalog company, sells fashionably rugged clothing for men and women. **Wendy Foster–Pierre LaFond** (⊠ 833 State St., ☎ 805/966–2276), an upscale local clothier, captures the fluid California style of women's wear. There are two even tonier branches in Montecito (⊠ 516 San Ysidro Rd., ☎ 805/565–1502; ⊠ 1221 Coast Village Rd., ☎ 805/565–1599). The store on Coast Village Road goes by the name Angel.

KITCHEN

Jordano's (⊠ 3025 De La Vina St., ☎ 805/965–3031) attracts cooks and kitchen junkies from Los Angeles and beyond. Part professional restaurant supply house, part gourmet store, and part cooking school, this sprawling shop stocks everything from seafood forks to espresso machines, flavored oils to herb pots.

OJAI

🕸 *40 mi southeast of Santa Barbara, U.S. 101 to Hwy. 150 to Hwy. 33.*

The acres of orange and avocado groves in and around rural Ojai look like the postcard images of agricultural southern California from decades ago. Recent years have seen an influx of artists, showbiz types, and others who have opted for a life out of the fast lane. The Ojai Valley, which director Frank Capra as a backdrop for his classic 1936 film *Lost Horizon,* sizzles in the summer, when temperatures routinely reach 90°F.

Compact Ojai can be easily explored on foot, or you can hop on **The Ojai Valley Trolley,** which takes riders on a one-hour loop (between 7:40 and 5:40 on weekdays, 9 and 5 on weekends). Tell the driver you're a visitor, and you'll get an informal guided tour.

The works of local artists can be seen in the Spanish-style shopping arcade along the main street. **The Art Center** (⊠ 113 S. Montgomery, ☎ 805/646–0117) exhibits artworks and presents theater and dance. **The Ojai Valley Museum** (⊠ 130 W. Ojai Ave., ☎ 805/640–1390) documents the valley's history and displays Native American artifacts.

Native oaks shelter the used titles at **Bart's Books** (⊠ 302 W. Matilija, ☎ 805/646–3755), an outdoor store. **Local Hero** (⊠ 254 E. Ojai Ave., ☎ 805/646–3165) sells books and hosts music, readings, and book signings on weekend evenings. There's also a café here.

Organic and specialty growers sell their produce on Sunday from 10 to 2 (9 to 1 in summer) at the **Farmers Market** behind the arcade. On Wednesday evening in summer the free all-American music played by the Ojai Band draws crowds to **Libbey Park** (⊠ Ojai Ave. in downtown Ojai).

The 9-mi **Ojai Valley Trail** is one of several paths in the hills surrounding town. **Ojai Valley Chamber of Commerce** (⊠ 150 W. Ojai Ave., ☎ 805/646–8126) publishes a regional trail map and runs a visitor center.

For more than five decades the **Ojai Festival** (☎ 805/646–2094) has attracted internationally known progressive and traditional musicians for outdoor concerts in Libbey Park on the weekend after Memorial Day.

Dining and Lodging

$$$ ✕ **The Ranch House.** The town's best eatery serves rich paté appetizers and main dishes like chicken soaked in vermouth and salmon poached in white wine. The verdant outdoor patio is a delight. ⊠ ⊠ *S. Lomita Ave.,* ☎ *805/646–2360. MC, V.*

$$–$$$ ✕ **Go Fish California Sushi & Grill.** Sushi mingles with American and Mexican seafood dishes on the menu of this fun place. Entertainers perform on the patio on weekend nights. ⊠ *469 E. Ojai Ave.,* ☎ *805/ 640–1057. MC, V.*

$$–$$$ ✕ **L'Auberge.** Tasty French–Belgian food is paired with a terrific country setting here. When the weather's fine, those in the know reserve an early table on the patio so they can accompany their rack of lamb with a glorious sunset. ⊠ *314 El Paseo Rd.,* ☎ *805/646–2288. AE, MC, V. No lunch weekdays.*

$$–$$$ ✕ **Suzanne's Cuisine.** Swordfish with ginger-lime sauce and salmon with sauerkraut in a dill beurre blanc are among the offerings at this European-style restaurant, where pastas and meat dishes dominate the dinner menu and salads and soups star at lunchtime. Most of the bread and all the desserts, including a warm chocolate tart with a white-coffee sauce, are made on the premises. ⊠ *502 W. Ojai Ave.,* ☎ *805/ 640–1961. MC, V. Closed Tues.; and 1st 2 wks in Jan.*

$$$$ ✕🏨 **Oaks at Ojai.** Comfortable but not luxurious, this spa has a fitness package that includes lodging, use of the spa facilities, 16 fitness classes, and three nutritionally balanced low-calorie meals. ⊠ *122 E. Ojai Ave., 93023,* ☎ *805/646–5573 or 800/753–6257,* ℻ *805/640– 1504. 46 rooms. Dining room, pool, beauty salon, massage, hot tub, sauna, spa, exercise room. D, MC, V. 2-day minimum stay.*

$$$$
★ 🏨 **Ojai Valley Inn & Spa.** This outdoorsy golf-oriented resort is set on landscaped grounds lush with flowers. The peaceful setting comes with hillside views in nearly all directions; nearby is the inn's 800-acre ranch, where you can hike, mountain bike, ride horses, and birdwatch. Some of the nicest rooms are in the original adobe building. Families make use of Camp Ojai, held in summer and on holidays for kids from age 4 to 12, and the remarkable collection of miniature animals in the petting farm. At the modern spa are massage and treatment rooms, a cardiovascular floor, a beauty salon, and quiet rooms. The two restaurants tout "Ojai regional cuisine" that incorporates locally grown produce and locally made foods. ⊠ *905 Country Club Rd., 93023,* ☎ *805/646–5511 or 800/422–6524,* ℻ *805/646–7969. 207 units. 2 restaurants, bar, 2 pools, spa, 18-hole golf course, 8 tennis courts, hiking, horseback riding, mountain bikes. AE, D, DC, MC, V.*

$$–$$$ 🏨 **The Blue Iguana Inn.** Local artists run this southwestern-style hotel west of downtown. Small and cozy, the inn is designed around a courtyard. The works of the artist-owners decorate the rooms (if you like a particular work, you can negotiate with the front desk to purchase it). ⊠ *11794 N. Ventura Ave. (Hwy. 33), 93023.,* ☎ *805/646–5277. 12 rooms. Pool, refrigerators. AE, D, MC, V.*

$$ ⊞ **Best Western Casa Ojai.** This modern hotel sits on Ojai's main drag, across from Soule Park Golf Course. Rooms are simple and clean. ⊠ *1302 E. Ojai Ave., 93023,* ☎ *805/646–8175 or 800/255– 8175,* FAX *805/640–8247. 45 rooms. In-room modem lines, pool, hot tub. Continental breakfast. AE, D, DC, MC, V.*

THE CENTRAL COAST A TO Z

Arriving and Departing

By Bus
Greyhound Lines (☎ 800/231–2222) provides service from San Francisco and Los Angeles to San Luis Obispo and Santa Barbara.

By Car
U.S. 101 and Highway 1 are the main routes into the Central Coast from Los Angeles and San Francisco. Interstate 280 to U.S. 101 to San Luis Obispo is the quickest route from San Francisco to the southern portion of the Central Coast, but it's not the scenic route. Highway 46 heads west from the Central Valley to Paso Robles, where it becomes narrower as it continues to the coast, intersecting Highway 1 a few miles south of Cambria. Highway 33 heads south from the Central Valley to Ojai; about 60 mi north of Ojai, Highway 166 leaves Highway 33, traveling due west through the Sierra Madre Mountains. Highway 166 intersects with U.S. 101 north of Santa Maria, and then continues west to Highway 1.

By Plane
America West Express, American/American Eagle, Skywest/Delta, United/United Express, and US Airways Express fly into **Santa Barbara Municipal Airport** (⊠ 500 Fowler Rd., ☎ 805/683–4011), 8 mi from downtown. *See* Air Travel *in* the Gold Guide for airline phone numbers.

Santa Barbara Airbus (☎ 805/964–7759 or 800/733–6354) shuttles travelers between Santa Barbara and Los Angeles for $35 one-way and $65 round-trip (slight discount with 24-hour notice). The **Santa Barbara Metropolitan Transit District** (☎ 805/683–3702) Bus 11 runs from the airport to the downtown transit center.

By Train
The **Amtrak** (☎ 800/872–7245) *Coast Starlight,* which runs between Los Angeles, Oakland, and Seattle, stops in Santa Barbara and San Luis Obispo. Several *San Diegan* trains operate daily between Santa Barbara, Los Angeles, and San Diego. Local numbers are, in Santa Barbara, ☎ 805/963–1015; in San Luis Obispo, ☎ 805/541–0505.

Getting Around

By Bus
From Monterey and Carmel, **Monterey–Salinas Transit** (☎ 831/899– 2555) operates buses to Big Sur between May and September. From San Luis Obispo, **Central Coast Transit** (☎ 805/541–2228) runs buses around the town and out to the coast. **Santa Barbara Metropolitan Transit District** (☎ 805/683–3702 or 805/963–3364) provides local service. The **State Street and Waterfront shuttles** cover their respective sections of Santa Barbara during the day.

By Car

The best way to see the most dramatic section of the Central Coast, the 70 mi between Big Sur and San Simeon, is by car. Heading south on Highway 1, you'll be on the ocean side of the road and will get the best views. Don't expect to make good time along here. The road is narrow and twisting with a single lane in each direction, making it difficult to pass the many lumbering RVs. In fog or rain the drive can be downright nerve-racking. Once you start south from Carmel, there is no route east from Highway 1 until Highway 46 heads inland from Cambria to connect with U.S. 101.

Highway 1 and U.S. 101 run north–south and more or less parallel, with Highway 1 hugging the coast and U.S. 101 remaining a few to a few-dozen miles inland. Along some stretches the two roads join and run together for a while. At Morro Bay, Highway 1 moves inland for 13 mi and connects with U.S. 101 at San Luis Obispo. From here south to Pismo Beach the two highways run concurrently. U.S. 101 is the quicker route to Santa Barbara; Highway 1 rejoins it north of town at Las Cruces.

Contacts and Resources

B&B Reservations Service

Bed and Breakfast Santa Barbara (☎ 805/687–7898 or 800/557–7898).

Doctors

Cottage Hospital (⊠ Pueblo St. at Bath St., Santa Barbara, ☎ 805/682–7111; 805/569–7210 for emergency).

Emergencies

Ambulance (☎ 911). **Fire** (☎ 911). **Police** (☎ 911).

Guided Tours

Eagle- and wildlife-watching excursions take place on the *Osprey,* a 48-ft cruiser that plies Cachuma Lake, a 20-minute drive from Solvang and a 40-minute one from Santa Barbara. For additional information, contact the **Cachuma Lake Recreation Area,** Santa Barbara County Park Department (⊠ Star Route, Santa Barbara 93105, ☎ 805/688–4658).

A motorized San Francisco–style cable car operated by **Santa Barbara Trolley Co.** (☎ 805/965–0353) makes 90-minute runs from 10 AM to 4 PM past major hotels, shopping areas, and attractions. Get off when you wish to, and pick up another trolley when you're ready to move on. The trolley departs from and returns to Stearns Wharf. The fare is $5.

Road Conditions

Caltrans (☎ 800/427–7623).

Visitor Information

Central Coast Tourism Council (⊠ Box 14011, San Luis Obispo, 93406, ☎ 805/544–0241). **Ojai Chamber of Commerce** (⊠ Box 1134, 150 W. Ojai Ave., 93024, ☎ 805/646–8126). **Paso Robles Vintners and Growers Association** (⊠ 1940 Spring St., Paso Robles 93446, ☎ 805/239–8463). **Santa Barbara Conference and Visitors Bureau** (⊠ 12 E. Carrillo St., 93101, ☎ 805/966–9222 or 800/927–4688). **Santa Barbara County Vintners' Association** (⊠ Box 1558, Santa Ynez 93460, ☎ 805/688–0881 or 800/218–0881).

12 Los Angeles

In certain lights Los Angeles displays its Spanish heritage, but even more evident is its vibrancy as a Pacific Rim cultural and economic center. Hollywood, the beaches, and the valleys are all within an hour's drive. Also here are important examples of 20th-century domestic architecture, miles of freeways, and glamorous enclaves like Beverly Hills. Everything about Los Angeles is grand—even overdone—which is part of the city's charm: It's all for show, but the show's usually a good one.

DON'T BELIEVE EVERYTHING YOU'VE HEARD about Los Angeles, because chances are it's an exaggeration, good or bad, and the truth is probably somewhere in between. Few places on this planet are as hard to categorize as L.A.—it's too large and diverse. The city of 3.5 million sprawls across 467 square mi of desert basin, mountain canyons, and coastal beaches. Outside the city limits, another 6 million people live in 80 incorporated cities within Los Angeles County. Another 5 million reside in the four surrounding counties.

The largest population of Pacific Islanders in the nation lives here, as well as the world's third-largest Hispanic population (after Mexico City and Guadalajara). People from 140 countries speaking 96 different languages call Los Angeles home. Signs in Spanish, Korean, Thai, Chinese, Japanese, Armenian, and Russian are as common in some areas of the city as English signs. What isn't so well known is that this diversity dates back to the city's beginnings: Indians, blacks, mestizos, and Spaniards were among the 44 settlers who first arrived from the Mexican provinces of Sonora and Sinaloa in September 1781.

Though its myriad cultures lend the city variety, life is not uniformly harmonious. There's ceaseless rankling about bilingual education in the schools, for instance, and bloody rioting has divided the city along racial lines more than once, most recently in 1992 when the acquittal of the police officers accused of beating motorist Rodney King provoked the nation's worst civil unrest ever. That experience left a scar of misunderstanding and mistrust that has yet to heal completely.

But communities throughout the region pulled together after the devastating 1994 Northridge earthquake and two years later, when wildfires raged in Malibu. The cooperation of Los Angelenos with each other in these times of crisis contradicts the mass media stereotype of a self-indulgent populace concerned only about going to the gym and buying expensive gadgets for themselves. And here's an interesting factoid: Research conducted in 1997 indicated that Los Angeles residents actually donate money to charity at a rate above the national average.

If there's a universal symbol of Los Angeles, it's the automobile. Cars and freeways have been a part of the L.A. image for so long that a driver's license is seen as something of a birthright. As for the freeways—well, they're really not so bad. They're well-signed and for travel at times other than rush hour the best route from one end of the city to the other. But here are a couple tips: Most freeways are known by a name and a number; for example, the Hollywood (U.S. 101). And depending on the time of day you're traveling, distance in miles doesn't mean much. The 10 mi between the San Fernando Valley and downtown Los Angeles, for instance, might take an hour to travel during rush hour but only 20 minutes at other times.

EXPLORING LOS ANGELES

Revised and Updated by Stephen Dolainski

Seeing Los Angeles requires covering a lot of territory, but contrary to popular myth that doesn't mean you have to spend all your time in a car. In fact, getting out of your car is the only way to really get to know the city. The nine walking and driving tours that follow, designed to cover the highlights, should give you a glimpse of what makes Los Angeles unique.

Downtown, where the city got its start, contains attractions that range from a restored funicular, Angels Flight, to museums and historic architecture.

Hollywood still reigns as the entertainment capital of the world after nearly a century; there's magic to be found amid what may to some visitors be shocking decay.

Museum Row and Farmers Market are full of entertaining novelties such as the fossil-filled La Brea Tar Pits and a museum of miniatures, but you'll also find high culture at the L.A. County Museum of Art. A cross-section of Angelenos patronizes the colorful Farmers Market.

Beverly Hills, one of the world's most glamorous addresses, is where you'll find some of the some of the most expensive shops and real estate in California.

Westside has become a hot destination with the arrival of the Getty Center. Also in the district are the Museum of Tolerance and the University of California, Los Angeles (UCLA).

Santa Monica, Venice, and Malibu are the coastal communities that give Los Angeles its sunny, surf-swept image.

The San Fernando Valley, home to Universal Studios, Warner Bros., and NBC, contains a mix of film and TV production studios and Hollywood-themed entertainment, as well as a historic mission.

Pasadena, famed for the annual Tournament of Roses parade, has a rich legacy of early–20th century architecture, as well as a top-notch museum, a botanical garden, a mission, and an old town with a lively street scene.

Long Beach, best known for its 1930s Art Deco luxury liner, the *Queen Mary,* also lures visitors with its high-tech aquarium.

Within the exploring sections, **Off the Beaten Path** entries call attention to sights outside the mapped areas but worth visiting.

Downtown Los Angeles

Many visitors to Los Angeles who aren't staying at one of the big convention hotels downtown never make it to this part of the city. After Beverly Hills, Disneyland, and Universal Studios, downtown is often an afterthought. Understandable, but a shame, because downtown is the heart of this great city, its financial core, as well as its historical and cultural soul.

A Good Tour
Numbers in the text correspond to numbers in the margin and on the Downtown Los Angeles map.

A convenient and inexpensive minibus service—DASH, or Downtown Area Short Hop—has several routes that travel past most of the sights on this tour, stopping every two blocks or so. Each ride costs 25¢, so you can hop on and off without spending a fortune. Special (limited) routes operate on weekends. Call DASH (☎ from all Los Angeles area codes, 808–2273) for routes and hours of operation.

Begin a downtown tour by heading north on **Broadway** ① from 8th or 9th street. At the southeast corner of Broadway and 3rd is the **Bradbury Building** ②, a Victorian beauty. Across the street is the **Grand Central Market** ③—once you've made your way through its tantalizing stalls you'll come out the opposite side on Hill Street.

Cross Hill Street and climb aboard **Angels Flight Railway** ④, a funicular that sweeps you up a steep incline to Watercourt, a courtyard surrounded by bubbling, cascading fountains. A half block north on Grand Avenue is the **Museum of Contemporary Art** ⑤, or MOCA, which is topped by a glass pyramidal skylight. Two blocks south on

Grand at 5th Street are two architectural treasures: the **Regal Biltmore Hotel** ⑥ and the **Central Library** ⑦. Behind the library are the tranquil MacGuire Gardens, and across 5th Street are the **Bunker Hill Steps** ⑧.

Hop in your car and drive north on Broadway to 1st Street. A right turn here will take you into **Little Tokyo** ⑨, where the **Japanese American National Museum** ⑩ is housed in a former Buddhist temple at 1st and Central Avenue. The **Geffen Contemporary** ⑪ art museum is a block north on Central. If your tours have left you frazzled, backtrack on Central to 2nd Street and head two blocks north to Los Angeles Street and restore your equilibrium at the rooftop **Japanese Garden** ⑫ at the New Otani Hotel.

From Little Tokyo, turn left (north) from 1st on Alameda Street. As you pass over the freeway, **Union Station** ⑬ will be on the right. Street parking is limited, so unless you're here on a weekend, your best bet is to park in the pay lot at Union Station (about $5). After a look inside this grand railway station, cross Alameda to **Olvera Street** ⑭, a re-created Mexican market street.

From Union Station, turn right on Alameda and then immediately left on Cesar Chavez Avenue for three blocks. At Broadway, turn right to reach **Chinatown** ⑮. If you have kids in tow, reverse your route on Broadway from Chinatown; cross back over the freeway, and at Temple Street make a left for the three-block drive to the **Los Angeles Children's Museum** ⑯ at the Los Angeles Mall. Look to the right as you drive down Temple to see the back of **Los Angeles City Hall** ⑰. A few blocks farther west at Grand Avenue is the **Music Center** ⑱.

TIMING

The weekend is the best time to explore downtown: There's less traffic, parking is easier to find on the streets (bring quarters for meters) and cheaper day rates prevail in the lots. Seeing everything mentioned on this tour would take at least a full day, if not two. Expect to spend at least an hour in Chinatown, on Olvera Street, and in Little Tokyo— longer if you stop to eat, watch a parade, or visit a museum. The **Los Angeles Conservancy** (☎ 213/623–2489) regularly conducts Saturday morning walking tours of downtown architectural landmarks and districts; call for reservations.

Sights to See

❹ **Angels Flight Railway.** The century-old funicular dubbed "the shortest in the world" began operating again in 1996 after having been closed for nearly 30 years. Two original orange-and-black wooden cable railway cars take riders on a 70-second ride up a 298-ft incline from Hill Street (between 3rd and 4th streets) to the fountain-filled Watercourt at California Plaza at a show-stopping 4 mph. ☎ *213/626–1901.* ✉ *25¢ one-way.* ⊙ *Daily 6:30 AM–10 PM.*

★ ❷ **Bradbury Building.** The classy Bradbury building is a marvelous specimen of Victorian-era commercial architecture. The 1893 structure's interior atrium courtyard, with its glass skylight and open balconies and elevator, has appeared in *Blade Runner* and countless other films. The building is open on weekdays from 9 to 6 and on weekends until 5; take a peek, but don't wander past the lobby. ✉ *304 S. Broadway,* ☎ *213/626–1893.*

❶ **Broadway.** From the late 19th century to the 1950s, Broadway was the main shopping and entertainment street downtown. About the only evidence of that period are the few movies palaces still in operation between 8th and 5th streets, among them the **Orpheum** (✉ 842 S. Broadway) and the **Million Dollar** (✉ 307 S. Broadway). Shops and businesses catering to a mostly Mexican and Central American immigrant

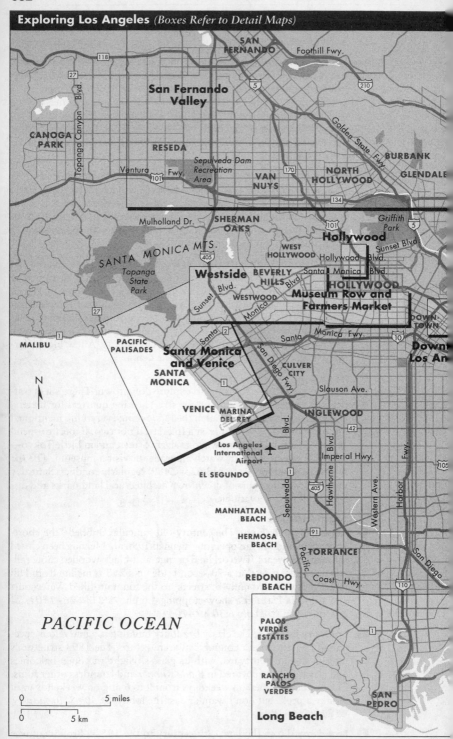

SAN
FERNANDO

Foothill Fwy.

118

27

**San Fernando
Valley**

5

210

**CANOGA
PARK**

Topanga Canyon Blvd.

RESEDA

*Sepulveda Dam
Recreation
Area*

Ventura

101

Fwy.

170

**VAN
NUYS**

**NORTH
HOLLYWOOD**

Golden State Fwy.

BURBANK

GLENDALE

134

Mulholland Dr.

**SHERMAN
OAKS**

SANTA   MONICA MTS.

405

*Topanga
State
Park*

**WEST
HOLLYWOOD**

Hollywood

Griffith
Park

5

Westside

Sunset   Blvd.

**BEVERLY
HILLS**

Hollywood   Blvd.

Santa Monica Blvd.

Sunset Blvd.

27

WESTWOOD

Monica

Blvd.

HOLLYWOOD

**Museum Row and
Farmers Market**

DOWN-
TOWN

1

MALIBU

**PACIFIC
PALISADES**

Santa

2

Santa

Monica Fwy.

10

**Down
Los An**

**Santa Monica
and Venice**

**SANTA
MONICA**

1

San Diego Fwy.

Santa

**CULVER
CITY**

Slauson Ave.

VENICE

**MARINA
DEL REY**

INGLEWOOD

42

Blvd.

N

*Los Angeles
International
Airport*

Imperial Hwy.

Hawthorne   Blvd.

Western Ave.

Harbor

Fwy.

105

EL SEGUNDO

Sepulveda

1

405

**MANHATTAN
BEACH**

**HERMOSA
BEACH**

91

TORRANCE

San Diego

**REDONDO
BEACH**

Pacific

Coast   Hwy.

110

PACIFIC OCEAN

**PALOS
VERDES
ESTATES**

**RANCHO
PALOS
VERDES**

1

0 ———— 5 miles

0 ———— 5 km

**SAN
PEDRO**

Long Beach

SAN GABRIEL MOUNTAINS

Angeles Crest Hwy. 2

LA CAÑADA
FLINTRIDGE

▲ Mt. Wilson

2

HIGHLAND
PARK

PASADENA

Foothill Fwy.
210

asadena Area

Pasadena Fwy.

SAN
MARINO

Dodger
Stadium

110

ALHAM-
BRA

SAN
GABRIEL

EL
MONTE

San Bernardino Fwy. 10

wn
les

MONTEREY
PARK

60

Pomona Fwy.

Santa Ana Fwy.

Rosemead Blvd.

WHITTIER

72

HUNTINGTON
ARK

710

River Fwy.

19

DOWNEY

42

San Gabriel River

39

5

OMPTON

Long Beach Fwy.

Riverside Fwy.
91

605

LAKEWOOD

ANAHEIM

710

19

Pacific Coast Hwy.

GARDEN
GROVE

San Diego Fwy.

39

LONG
BEACH

55

1

Downtown Los Angeles

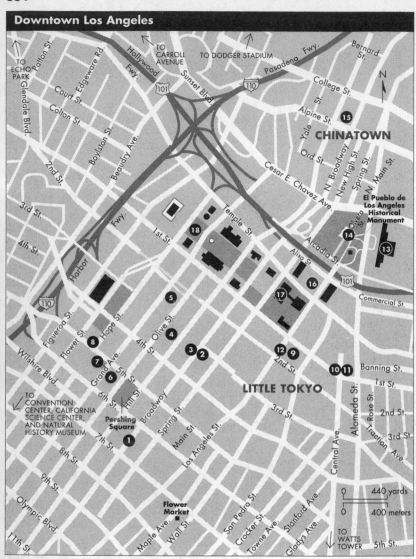

clientele have moved into some of the old movie palaces; between 1st and 9th streets you'll hear *mariachi* and *banda* music blaring from the speakers of electronics store and won't be able to miss the brightly colored fancy dresses for a young girl's *quinceanera* (15th birthday) hanging above store entrances.

⑧ Bunker Hill Steps. A "stream" flows down the center of this monumental staircase into a small pool at its base. The stream originates at the top of the stairs where Robert Graham's nude female sculpture *Source Figure* stands atop a cylindrical base that mimics the shape of the trunks of surrounding palm trees. The figure's hands are open, as if to offer water to the city. ⊠ *5th St. between Grand Ave. and Figueroa St.*

★ ♻ California Science Center. Exhibits at the center illustrate the relevance of science to everyday life. Tess, the animatronic star of "BodyWorks," demonstrates how the body's organs work together to maintain balance. In other exhibits, you can build a structure to see how it stands up to an earthquake, or ride a high-wire bicycle to learn first-hand about gravity. The Imax theater, with 3-D capabilities and a seven-story movie screen, shows science-related films. To get to the center, which is inside Exposition Park, pick up Los Angeles Street in downtown Los Angeles and head south; turn west on 11th Street and south on Figueroa Street. ⊠ *700 State Dr., Exposition Park,* ☎ *213/744–7400; Imax 213/744–2014.* ☒ *Free; Imax $7.25; parking $5.* ⊙ *Daily 10–5.*

★ ⑦ Central Library. Major fires in the 1980s closed the library for six years. Now twice its former size, it's the third-largest public library in the nation. The original building, designed by Bertram Goodhue, was completely restored to its 1926 condition. Take the elevator up to the second floor for a look at Dean Cornwell's murals depicting the history of California. The new Tom Bradley Wing has a soaring eight-story atrium. A 1½ acre outdoor garden within the library complex has a pricey, but good, restaurant. ⊠ *630 W. 5th St.,* ☎ *213/228–7000.* ☒ *Free.* ⊙ *Mon. and Thurs.–Sat. 10–5:30, Tues.–Wed. noon–8, Sun. 1–5; docent tours weekdays at 12:30, Sat. at 11 and 2, Sun. at 2.*

⑮ Chinatown. North Broadway is the heart of this district where you'll experience an authentic slice of Southeast Asian life. More than 15,000 Chinese and Southeast Asians actually live in the Chinatown area, but many thousands more regularly frequent markets stocked with dried squid, roots, shark's fin, and other exotic foods. Dim sum parlors are another big draw; **Empress Pavilion** (⊠ 988 N. Hill St., ☎ 213/617–9898) is one of the best. Call the **Chinatown Chamber of Commerce** (☎ 213/617–0396) for information about Chinese New Year and other events. ⊠ *Bordered by Yale, Bernard, Ord, and Alameda Sts.*

El Pueblo de Los Angeles Historical Monument. This site that commemorates Los Angeles's heritage encompasses many significant buildings, a park, and festive **Olvera Street** (☞ *below*). ⊠ *Olvera and Temple Sts.*

⑪ Geffen Contemporary at MOCA. In 1982, Los Angeles architect Frank Gehry transformed a warehouse in Little Tokyo into a temporary space while the permanent home for the Museum of Contemporary Art (☞ *below*) was being built a mile away. The Temporary Contemporary, now named for entertainment mogul David Geffen, was such a hit that it remains part of the museum facility. The Geffen houses part of MOCA's permanent collection, which spans the years from the 1940s to the present, and usually one or two temporary exhibits. "Elusive Paradise: Los Angeles Art from the Permanent Collection" will be on view through the end of 1999. ⊠ *152 N. Central Ave.,* ☎ *213/626–6222.* ☒ *$6, free with MOCA admission on same day; free Thurs. 5–8.* ⊙ *Tues.–Wed. and Fri.–Sun. 11–5, Thurs. 11–8.*

★ ❸ **Grand Central Market.** This block-long marketplace of colorful and exotic produce, herbs, and meat draws a faithful clientele from the Latino community, senior citizens on a budget, and the occasional Westside matron. The butcher shops display everything from lambs' heads to bulls' testicles and pigs' tails; the produce stalls are piled high with locally grown avocados and very ripe, very red tomatoes. Several taco stands provide tasty meals to go; you can even watch tortillas being flattened on a conveyor belt. ⊠ *317 S. Broadway,* ☎ *213/624–2378.* ▦ *Free.* ☉ *Mon.–Sat. 9–6; Sun. 10–5:30.*

★ ❿ **Japanese American National Museum.** How difficult was life for Japanese Americans interned in concentration camps during World War II? This and other questions are addressed by the changing exhibits at this Little Tokyo museum. Docents are on hand to share their own stories and experiences. The museum, inside a renovated 1925 Buddhist temple, will expand into an additional building across the street in early 1999. ⊠ *369 E. 1st St.,* ☎ *213/625–0414.* ▦ *$4.* ☉ *Tues.–Thurs. and Sat.–Sun. 10–5; Fri. 11–8; closed Mon..*

⓬ **Japanese Garden.** Landscape architect Sentaru Iwaki modeled this rooftop oasis at the New Otani Hotel and Garden after a 400-year-old garden in Tokyo. Like all Japanese gardens, this ½-acre plot of land represents the universe and its elements: a rock could symbolize a mountain or continent, and a plot of combed sand might represent an ocean. ⊠ *New Otani Hotel and Garden, 120 S. Los Angeles St.,* ☎ *213/629–1200.* ▦ *Free.*

❾ **Little Tokyo.** The original neighborhood of Los Angeles's Japanese community remains a cultural focal point. Nisei Week ("nisei" is the name for second-generation Japanese) is celebrated here every August with traditional drums, dancing, a carnival, and a huge parade. Little Tokyo has dozens of sushi bars, tempura restaurants, and trinket shops. **The Japanese American Cultural and Community Center** (⊠ 244 S. San Pedro St., ☎ 213/628–2725) presents Kabuki theater from Japan and other events. ⊠ *Bordered by 1st, San Pedro, 3rd, and Los Angeles Sts.*

🐚 ⓰ **Los Angeles Children's Museum.** Hands-on exhibits allow kids to record a song, make a TV show, learn about recycling, create arts and crafts, build a city out of pillows, and practice being a firefighter. ⊠ *310 N. Main St.,* ☎ *213/687–8800.* ▦ *$5.* ☉ *Sat.–Sun. 10–5 (during summer vacation, daily 10–5).*

⓱ **Los Angeles City Hall.** Erected in the late 1920s with a pointy spire at the top, the 28-story Art Deco treasure is closed for seismic renovations and won't be open again for touring until after the turn of the century. ⊠ *200 N. Spring St.*

★ ❺ **Museum of Contemporary Art at California Plaza.** The permanent collection of MOCA is split between Geffen Contemporary (☞ *above*) and the galleries at this site, a red sandstone building designed by Japanese architect Arata Isozaki. Mark Rothko, Franz Kline, Susan Rothenberg, Diane Arbus, and Robert Frank are among the artists represented at MOCA, whose temporary exhibits include the works of established and new artists in all media. **Patinette at MOCA** sells imaginative salads and sandwiches designed by the celebrated Los Angeles chef Joachim Splichal. ⊠ *250 S. Grand Ave.,* ☎ *213/626–6222.* ▦ *$6; free Thurs. 5–8.* ☉ *Tues.–Wed. and Fri.–Sun. 11–5, Thurs. 11–8.*

OFF THE
BEATEN PATH

MUSEUM OF NEON ART – Changing exhibits of neon, electric, and kinetic art light up this museum in the Renaissance Tower. In spring and summer, the facility schedules nighttime bus tours to historic and contemporary neon signs throughout the city. ⊠ *501 W. Olympic Blvd.; enter on Hope St.,* ☏ *213/489–9918.* ☞ *$5; free 2nd Thurs. of month (5–8 only).* ☉ *Wed.–Sat. 11–5, Sun. noon–5.*

⓲ **Music Center.** The major performing arts center in the city is the headquarters of the Los Angeles Philharmonic, the Los Angeles Opera, and the Center Theater Group. The Philharmonic and opera perform at the largest and grandest of the Music Center's three theaters, the **Dorothy Chandler Pavilion,** which alternates with the Shrine Auditorium as the site of the Academy Awards ceremony. The round building in the middle, the **Mark Taper Forum,** is a smaller theater showing mainly experimental works, many on a pre-Broadway run. The **Ahmanson,** at the north end, is the venue for big musicals. The vast complex's cement plaza contains a fountain and a Jacques Lipchitz sculpture. ⊠ *135 N. Grand Ave.,* ☏ *213/972–7211; 213/972–7483 tour information.* ☞ *Free.* ☉ *75-min tour Tues.–Fri. 10–1:30, Sat. 10–noon; no tours on Fri. Nov.–Apr..*

★ ⓒ **Natural History Museum of Los Angeles County.** The more than 3.5 million specimens at this superb museum in Exposition Park include a rich collection of prehistoric fossils; extensive bird, insect, and marine-life displays; an elaborate taxidermy exhibit; pre-Columbian artifacts; and crafts from the South Pacific. The Times-Mirror Hall of Native American Cultures surveys into the American Indian history of Los Angeles. The Ralph M. Parsons Discovery Center for children has hands-on science-oriented exhibits. For directions to Exposition Park from downtown, *see* the California Science Center, *above.* ⊠ *900 Exposition Blvd.,* ☏ *213/763–3466.* ☞ *$6; free 1st Tues. of month.* ☉ *Tues.– Sun. 10–5; 1-hr tours at 1.*

★ ⓒ ⓮ **Olvera Street.** Lively, one-block Olvera Street tantalizes with tile walkways, piñatas, mariachis, and authentic Mexican food. Restored as an open-air Mexican market in 1930, the street is the symbol of the city's beginnings when the original settlers built earthen and willow huts near the river. Vendors sell puppets, tooled leather goods, sandals, serapes, and other items from little stalls that line the center of the narrow street. On weekends, the restaurants are packed, and there is usually music in the plaza and along the street. Two Mexican holidays, Cinco de Mayo (May 5) and Independence Day (September 16), draw huge crowds. To see Olvera Street at its quietest and perhaps loveliest, visit late on a weekday afternoon, when long shadows heighten the romantic feeling of the passageway. For information, stop by the **Olvera Street Visitors Center** (⊠ Sepulveda House, 622 N. Main St., ☏ 213/628—1274), in an 1887 Victorian. The center is open from Monday to Saturday between 10 and 3.

Avila Adobe (⊠ E–10 Olvera St.), built in 1818, is said to be the oldest building in Los Angeles. This graceful, simple adobe with a traditional interior courtyard is furnished in the style of the 1840s. It is open daily from 9 to 5 (until 4 in winter).

The south wall of the **Italian Hall building** (⊠ 650 N. Main St.) bears a controversial mural. Mexican muralist David Alfaro Siqueiros shocked his patrons in the 1930s by depicting the oppressed workers of Latin America held in check by a menacing American eagle. The anti-imperialist mural was promptly whitewashed into oblivion. The whitewash has since been removed and work is underway to shelter the mural permanently and allow public viewing of it.

Olvera Street begins at **The Plaza,** a Mexican-style park shaded by a huge Moreton Bay fig tree. On weekends, mariachis and folkloric dance groups often perform. Two annual events particularly worth seeing are the Blessing of the Animals and Las Posadas. The blessing takes place on the Saturday before Easter. Residents bring their pets (not just dogs and cats but horses, pigs, cows, birds, hamsters) to be blessed by a priest. For Las Posadas (every night between December 16 and 24), merchants and visitors parade up and down the street, led by children dressed as angels, to commemorate the search by Mary and Joseph for shelter on Christmas Eve.

The Old Firehouse, an 1884 building on the south side of the Plaza, contains early fire-fighting equipment and old photographs. Free 50-minute walking tours of the area start from the docent office next door in the Hellman/Quon Building. On request, the docent will show you the tunnel passageways that were once used by Chinese immigrants to get from one building to another. Tours leave on the hour, from 10 to 1 daily except Monday.

NEED A BREAK?   Dining choices on Olvera Street range from fast-food stands to comfortable, sit-down restaurants. The most authentic Mexican food is at **La Luz del Dia** (✉ 107 Paseo de la Plaza, ☎ 213/628–7495)—*chiles rellenos* and pickled cactus, as well as handmade tortillas patted out in a practiced rhythm by the women behind the counter. **La Golondrina** (☎ 213/628–4349) and **El Paseo** (☎ 213/626–1361) restaurants, across from each other mid-block, have delightful patios and extensive menus.

⑥ Regal Biltmore Hotel. The Biltmore, a Beaux Arts structure, opened in 1923. The lobby has the feel of a Spanish palace, and the indoor pool looks like a Roman bath. Afternoon tea is served in the ornate Rendezvous Court. The Academy Awards ceremony took place here in the 1930s. ✉ *506 S. Grand Ave.*, ☎ *213/624–1011.*

★ **⑬ Union Station.** The Spanish-mission style of Union Station, which opened in 1939, subtly combines Streamline Moderne and Moorish design elements. The waiting room alone is worth a look, its majestic scale so evocative of movies past that you'll half expect to see Carole Lombard or Barbara Stanwyck step off a train and sashay through. The station's restaurant, Traxx (☞ Dining, *below*), is equally atmospheric. Union Station is the departure point for the Metro Rail Red Line of the Los Angeles subway system. ✉ *800 N. Alameda St.*

OFF THE BEATEN PATH   **WATTS TOWERS –** The jewel of rough South Central Los Angeles is the legacy of Simon Rodia, a tile setter who emigrated from Italy to California and erected one of the world's greatest folk-art structures. From 1921 until 1954, without any help, Rodia built the three main cement towers, using pipes, bed frames, and anything else he could find. He embellished them with bits of colored glass, broken pottery, and more than 70,000 seashells. The towers, now the centerpiece of a state park and cultural center. Daytime visits are best; the area can be dangerous at night. ✉ *Watts Towers Arts Center, 1727 E. 107th St. (take I–110 to I–105 east; exit north at S. Central Ave., turn right on 108th St., left on Graham Ave.).* ✇ *Free; weekend tours (scheduled to resume in summer 1999) $1.* ⏰ *Tues.–Sun. 9–5; closed Mon.*

Hollywood and Sunset Boulevard

For nine decades, Hollywood has enraptured the world with carefully manufactured images of glitz and glamour. Many visitors come to the city for a glimpse of that sexy sophistication, a chance to come close enough to be able to say, "I was there!" Reality check: The magic of Hollywood takes place on drafty sound stages, in nondescript film-processing labs, and at cramped editing bays. Go to Beverly Hills if you want glitz. As for glamour, well, Hollywood (along with the other centers of production around Los Angeles) is at heart a working town, where actors, directors, writers, composers, technicians may be among the highest paid workers in the world but commute daily to a factory—that is, a movie, television, or recording studio—and work long hours. Reality aside, though, Hollywood still fires our imaginations with glittering images of romance and adventure, and we must pay homage. The tour below will bring you close to some of that magic.

A Good Tour

Numbers in the text correspond to numbers in the margin and on the Hollywood map.

Start off by driving up into the Hollywood Hills on Beachwood Drive (off Franklin Avenue, east of Gower Street) for an up-close look at one of the world's most familiar icons: the **HOLLYWOOD sign** ①. Follow the small sign pointing the way to the Los Angeles Fire Department's Helispot. Turn left on Rodgerton Drive, which twists and turns higher into the hills. At Deronda Drive, turn right and drive to the end. The Hollywood sign looms off to the left. Turn around and retrace your route down the hill, back to Beachwood for the drive into Hollywood.

Turn west (to the right) at Franklin Avenue, and turn left at the next light at Gower Street. At Gower and Santa Monica Boulevard, look for the entrance to **Hollywood Memorial Park Cemetery** ②, half a block east on Santa Monica. If you visit the cemetery, retrace your route back to Gower Street, turn left and drive along the western edge of the cemetery. Abutting the cemetery's southern edge is **Paramount Pictures** ③. The famous gate Norma Desmond (Gloria Swanson in *Sunset Boulevard*) was driven through is no longer accessible to the public, but a replica marks the new entrance on Melrose Avenue: turn left from Gower Street to reach the gate.

Next, drive west (right off Gower) on Melrose for three blocks to Vine Street, turn right, and continue to Hollywood Boulevard. You've arrived at one of the world's most fabled intersections: **Hollywood and Vine** ④. Across the street is the cylindrical **Capitol Records Tower** ⑤. Look west to **Ivar Street** ⑥ for a glimpse of the former homes of literary giants William Faulkner and Nathanael West.

Drive west along Hollywood Boulevard for a look at the bronze stars that make up the **Hollywood Walk of Fame** ⑦. If you want to stop along the way to visit the Lingerie Museum at the purple **Frederick's of Hollywood** ⑧ or the **Hollywood Wax Museum** ⑨—both shrines to Hollywood camp—metered parking is fairly easy to find.

The elaborate pagoda-style movie palace **Mann's Chinese Theatre** ⑩ is a genuine, if kitschy, monument to Hollywood history. Across the street is the exuberant facade of the El Capitan theater. Stay on the north side of Hollywood Boulevard and continue west to the **Hollywood Entertainment Museum** ⑪. From the museum, cross Hollywood Boulevard and loop back east along the boulevard past the **Hollywood Roosevelt Hotel** ⑫. Continue east on Hollywood Boulevard; on Highland Avenue south of the boulevard is the **Hollywood History Museum** ⑬, inside the old Max Factor building.

Several blocks north of the Max Factor building on Highland Avenue is the **Hollywood Bowl** ⑭, where summertime concerts take place. The first feature-length film shot in Hollywood, Cecil B. DeMille's the *The Squaw Man,* was produced across from the Bowl in 1913 in the building at 2100 North Highland Avenue.

Hollywood

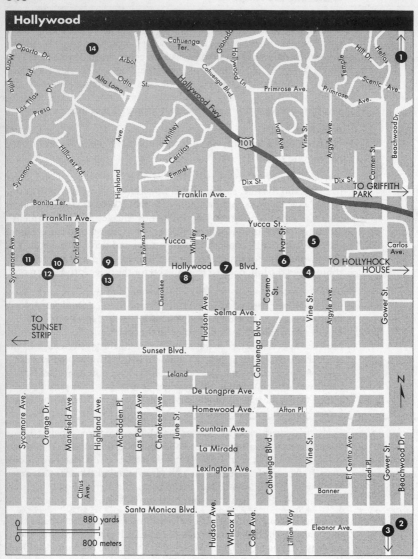

Capitol Records
Tower, **5**

Frederick's of
Hollywood, **8**

Hollywood and
Vine, **4**

Hollywood
Bowl, **14**

Hollywood
Entertainment
Museum, **11**

Hollywood History
Museum, **13**

Hollywood
Memorial Park
Cemetery, **2**

Hollywood
Roosevelt Hotel, **12**

Hollywood Sign, **1**

Hollywood Walk
of Fame, **7**

Hollywood Wax
Museum, **9**

Ivar Street, **6**

Mann's Chinese
Theatre, **10**

Paramount Pictures, **3**

Plan to spend the better part of a morning or afternoon taking in Hollywood and Sunset Boulevard. A walking tour of Paramount Studios will add at least two and half hours to your itinerary. Hollywood Boulevard attracts a sometimes-bizarre group of folks; your best bet for a safe walk down the boulevard is during the day.

Sights to See

★ ⑤ **Capitol Records Tower.** Architect Welton Beckett claimed he just wanted to design a structure that economized space, not resemble a stack of 45s. If you remember vinyl, though, you'll probably agree that this cylindrical office tower built in 1956 does. On its south wall, L.A. artist Richard Wyatt's mural *Hollywood Jazz, 1945–1972*, immortalizes musical greats Duke Ellington, Billie Holiday, Ella Fitzgerald, and Miles Davis. The blinking light at the top of the tower spells out "Hollywood" in Morse code. ✉ *1750 N. Vine St.*

⑧ **Frederick's of Hollywood.** Though you can stock up on risqué (and trashy) lingerie here, the real reason to visit Frederick's is to view the undergarments of some of Hollywood's legends: In the **Lingerie Museum**, Madonna's bustier shares space with Cher's kinky underwear and Marilyn Monroe's merry widow from *Let's Make Love*. (If you see an empty case, don't assume it represents Sharon Stone's interrogation outfit from *Basic Instinct*.) ✉ *6608 Hollywood Blvd.*, ☏ *323/ 466–8506.*

Griffith Park. Griffith Park is the Angeleno's great escape. Though most people come here simply to take in the tranquility of open space, several attractions are worthwhile in their own rights. The **Griffith Observatory and Planetarium** sits on a promontory overlooking Hollywood. On clear days, the Pacific Ocean can be seen 20 mi away, and at night the city below glitters as far as the eye can see. Inside the observatory, there's a viewing telescope and a domed planetarium theater with a Laserius light show. From April to October, it's an L.A. tradition to spend an evening at a concert at the 1,600-seat **Greek Theatre**, tucked into a sylvan canyon that forms a natural amphitheater. The **Los Angeles Zoo**, which is noted for its breeding of endangered species like the California condor, has unveiled the first phase of its Great Ape Forest, the Chimpanzees of Mahale Mountain. At the **Autry Museum of Western Heritage** memorabilia, art, and artifacts conjure up the American West—the movie and the real-life versions. Among the amusements for kids in Griffith Park are pony rides, a 1926 carousel, some vintage railroad and trolley engines and cars at **Travel Town**, and the miniature **Griffith Park & Southern Railroad**.

There are four main entrances to Griffith Park: from the west, enter at Western Canyon Road, off Los Feliz Boulevard and Western Avenue; from the south, at Los Feliz Boulevard and Vermont Avenue; from the east, at Crystal Springs Drive, near Los Feliz Boulevard and Riverside Drive; and from the north, at the Golden State Freeway (I–5) and Ventura Freeway (Highway 134). A free map of the park is available at the **rangers station** (✉ 4730 Crystal Springs Dr.). ✉ *Los Feliz Blvd. at Western Canyon Rd., Vermont Ave., Crystal Springs Dr., and Riverside Dr.*, ☏ *observatory and planetarium, 323/664–1191; laserium, 818/901–9405; zoo, 323/644–6400; museum, 323/667–2000; theater, 323/665–1927; Travel Town, 323/662–5874; railroad, 323/664– 6903; pony rides, 323/664–3266; carousel, 323/665–3051.* 🎟 *Observatory and Hall of Science free; planetarium $4; laserium $7–$8; zoo $8.25 (Safari Shuttle Tour $3); museum $7.50; Travel Town free, railroad $1.75; pony rides $1.50; carousel $1.* ☉ *Observatory and planetarium, daily 12:30–10 in summer (Tues.–Fri. 2–10, weekends*

*12:30–10 rest of yr); zoo, daily, 10–5 (animals removed from view
starting at 4:30); museum, Tues.–Sun. 10–5; theater performances Apr.–
Oct.; Travel Town weekdays 10–4, weekends and holidays 10–5;
railroad daily 10–5; carousel, weekends only (daily in summer); pony
rides, Tues.–Sun. 10–5, weather permitting.*

OFF THE
BEATEN PATH

HOLLYHOCK HOUSE – The first of several houses Frank Lloyd Wright designed in Los Angeles, this restored 1921 manse is a perfect example of
the pre-Columbian style of which Wright was so fond at that time. It contains original Wright-designed furniture. ⊠ *4800 Hollywood Blvd.,* ☎
323/913–4157. ⌨ *$2.* ☉ *Tours Wed.–Sun., noon, 1, 2, and 3.*

4 Hollywood and Vine. In the old days, this was the hub of the radio
and movie industry, and there was nothing unusual about film stars
like Gable and Garbo hurrying in or out of office buildings at the intersection of Hollywood Boulevard and Vine Street on their way to or
from their agents' offices. Hollywood and Vine is far from the action
these days, and foot traffic is rather pedestrian, so to speak. The Brown
Derby restaurant, which once stood a half-block south of the intersection
at 1628 North Vine, is no more, and the the Palace Theater (⊠ 1735
North Vine St.), where the 1950s TV show *This Is Your Life* was
recorded, is now a rental venue for rock shows. Within a block or two
of the intersection, however, you can see the Capitol Records Tower
(⊠ 1750 N. Vine St.) and the Pantages Theater (⊠ 6233 Hollywood
Blvd.), a former opulent movie palace that now hosts large-scale Broadway musicals on tour. The arrival of the Metro Rail Red Line subway
in 1999 may revive the intersection.

14 Hollywood Bowl. Summer evening concerts have been a tradition since
1922 at this amphitheater cradled in the Hollywood Hills. The Bowl
is the summer home of the Los Angeles Philharmonic, but the musical fare includes pop and jazz. The 17,000-plus seating capacity ranges
from boxes to concrete bleachers in the rear. Come early for a picnic
in the surrounding grounds. Before the concert, or during the day, visit
the **Hollywood Bowl Museum** (☎ 323/850–2058) for a capsule version of the Bowl's 75-year history. Listen on headphones to an 80-year-
old recording of soprano Amelita Galli-Curci, a superstar of her day,
singing "Caro Nome" from Verdi's *Rigoletto*—or Ella Fitzgerald or
Paul McCartney, all of whom performed at the Bowl. ⊠ *2301 N. Highland Ave.,* ☎ *323/850–2000.* ☉ *Museum, Tues.–Sat. 10–4; grounds
daily sunrise–sunset (call for performance schedule).*

11 Hollywood Entertainment Museum. A multimedia presentation in the
main rotunda and interactive exhibits track the evolution of Hollywood,
from the silent era to today's hyper-tech world of special effects. Highlights are the marvelously detailed miniature model of 1936 Hollywood,
and sets from television shows such as the bar from TV's *Cheers.* ⊠
7021 Hollywood Blvd., ☎ *323/465–7900.* ⌨ *$7.50 adults, $4.50 se-
niors and students, $4 children 5–12.* ☉ *Tues.–Sun. 11–6.*

13 Hollywood History Museum. The Max Factor building, the Art Deco–
style former domain of makeup czar Max Factor, reopened in the fall
of 1998 after a two-year restoration. The exhibits at the museum here
survey the movie business from the silent era to the present. Costumes,
artifacts, and props from famous and rare motion pictures are on display, as are posters, scripts, cameras, and other artifacts. Adjoining the
museum is Chasen's Hollywood Café, named after the legendary
restaurant where the stars used to gather for cocktails and conversation. ⊠ *1660 N. Highland Ave.,* ☎ *323/464–7776.* ⌨ *$8.* ☉ *Daily
9–9 (hrs subject to change, so call ahead).*

② **Hollywood Memorial Park Cemetery.** Rudolph Valentino, Tyrone Power, and Jayne Mansfield are among the stars buried here. Sadly, the cemetery has fallen into a state of neglect: Weeds have sprung up around many tombstones, and the place feels abandoned. You can pick up a map of the grounds in the office at the entrance. Inside the Cathedral Mausoleum is Rudolph Valentino's crypt (the mysterious Lady in Black, who for years visited on the anniversary of his death, comes no more). ⊠ *6000 Santa Monica Blvd.,* ☎ *323/469–1181.* ☉ *Daily 8–5.*

⑫ **Hollywood Roosevelt Hotel.** The first Academy Awards banquet was held here in 1927. A display of vintage Hollywood photographs and other historical memorabilia occupies the hotel's mezzanine level. In the hotel is Cinegrill, a cabaret steeped in Hollywood history. Have a look at the pool out back: David Hockney was commissioned to paint the "mural" at the bottom (actually nothing more than a series of blue blotches). ⊠ *7000 Hollywood Blvd.,* ☎ *323/466–7000.*

★ **①** **HOLLYWOOD Sign.** With letters 50 ft tall, Hollywood's trademark sign can be spotted from miles away. The sign, which originally spelled out "Hollywoodland," was erected in the Hollywood Hills in 1923 to promote a real-estate development. In 1949, the "land" portion of the sign was taken down. Over the years pranksters have altered it, albeit temporarily, to spell out "Hollyweed" (in the 1970s, to commemorate lenient marijuana laws), "Go Navy" (before a Rose Bowl game), and "Perotwood" (during the 1992 presidential election). In 1994, however, a fence and surveillance equipment were installed to deter intruders.

★ **⑦** **Hollywood Walk of Fame.** All along this mile-long stretch of Hollywood Boulevard sidewalk, the names of more than 2,000 entertainment legends are embossed in brass, each at the center of a pink star embedded in dark-gray terrazzo. The honor doesn't come cheap—upon selection by a special committee, the personality in question (or more likely his or her movie studio or record company) must pay $7,500 for the privilege. Celebrities are classified by one of five logos: a motion-picture camera, a radio microphone, a television set, a record, or a theatrical mask. Here's a miniguide to a few of the more famous celebs' stars: Marlon Brando at 1765 Vine, Charlie Chaplin at 6751 Hollywood, W. C. Fields at 7004 Hollywood, Clark Gable at 1608 Vine, Marilyn Monroe at 6774 Hollywood (in front of McDonald's), Rudolph Valentino at 6164 Hollywood, Michael Jackson at 6927 Hollywood, and John Wayne at 1541 Vine. Call the **Hollywood Chamber of Commerce** (☎ 323/469–8311) or the **Hollywood Visitor Information Center** (⊠ 6541 Hollywood Blvd., ☎ 323/236–2331) to find out where your favorite celebrity's star can be found. Ask when the next sidewalk star installation ceremony is scheduled to take place; in recent years stars have only been awarded when the honoree agrees to show up for the event.

⑨ **Hollywood Wax Museum.** Here you'll spot celebrities that real life can no longer provide (Mary Pickford, Elvis Presley, and Clark Gable) and a few that even real life never did (such as the *Star Trek* cast). Other living legends on display include actors Kevin Costner and Brad Pitt. A short film on Academy Award winners screens daily. ⊠ *6767 Hollywood Blvd.,* ☎ *323/462–8860.* ▣ *$8.95.* ☉ *Sun.–Thurs. 10 AM–midnight, Fri.–Sat. 10 AM–2 AM.*

NEED A BREAK?

Musso & Frank Grill (⊠ 6667 Hollywood Blvd., ☎ 323/467–5123), open since 1919, is the last remaining Old Hollywood watering hole. Wash down a plate of lamb chops, spinach, and sourdough bread with a martini, or just stop in for a Coke and soak up some atmosphere. Expect high prices and some attitude.

⑥ **Ivar Street.** William Faulkner wrote *Absalom, Absalom!* while he lived at the old Knickerbocker Hotel (⊠ 1714 N. Ivar St.), and Nathanael West wrote *The Day of the Locust* in his apartment at the Parva Sed-Apta (⊠ 1817 N. Ivar St.).

★ ⑩ **Mann's Chinese Theatre.** You have to buy a movie ticket to appreciate the interior trappings of the former "Grauman's Chinese," a fantasy of Chinese pagodas and temples, but the courtyard is open for browsing. Here you'll see those oh-so-famous cement hand- and footprints. This tradition is said to have begun at the theater's opening in 1927, with the premiere of Cecil B. DeMille's *King of Kings,* when actress Norma Talmadge accidentally stepped into the wet cement. Now more than 160 celebrities have contributed imprints of their appendages for posterity, along with a few other oddball imprints, like the one of Jimmy Durante's nose. ⊠ *6925 Hollywood Blvd.,* ☎ *323/464–8111.*

③ **Paramount Pictures.** The last major studio still in Hollywood is the best place to see what a movie studio looks like. Two-hour guided walking tours of the 85-year-old studio include historical narrative about Rudolph Valentino, Mae West, Mary Pickford, Lucille Ball, and other stars who worked on the lot. Movies and TV shows are still filmed here; if you're lucky you might see a show being produced. Tours are first come, first served and leave from the pedestrian walk-up gate on Melrose Street; park in the lot at Bronson and Melrose avenues. Children under 10 are not admitted. ⊠ *5555 Melrose Ave.,* ☎ *323/956–5575.* 🎟 *$15.* ☉ *2-hr tour weekdays on the hr, 9–2.*

Sunset Strip. For 60 years, the Hollywood nighttime crowd has headed for the 1⁷⁄₁₀-mi stretch of Sunset Boulevard between Crescent Heights Boulevard on the east and Doheny Drive on the west, known as the Sunset Strip. In the 1930s and '40s, stars like Tyrone Power, Errol Flynn, Norma Shearer, and Rita Hayworth got themselves gussied up in tuxedos and fancy gowns for wild evenings of dancing and drinking at nightclubs like Trocadero, Ciro's, and Mocambo. By the '60s and '70s, the Strip had become the center of rock 'n' roll: Johnny Rivers, the Byrds, the Doors, Elton John, and Bruce Springsteen gave legendary performances on stages at clubs like the **Whisky** (⊠ 8901 Sunset Blvd., ☎ 310/652–4202) and **Roxy** (⊠ 9009 Sunset Blvd., ☎ 310/276–2222). Nowadays it's the **Viper Room** (⊠ 8852 Sunset Blvd., ☎ 310/358–1880), the **House of Blues** (⊠ 8430 Sunset Blvd., ☎ 323/848–5100), and the **Key Club** (⊠ 9039 Sunset Blvd., ☎ 310/274–5800) that keep young Hollywood busy after dark. The Strip lies within the trendy city of West Hollywood.

Museum Row and Farmers Market

East of Fairfax Avenue in the Miracle Mile district is the three-block stretch of Wilshire Boulevard known as Museum Row, with five museums of widely varying themes and a prehistoric tar pit to boot. Only a few blocks away is the very-L.A. Farmers Market.

A Good Tour

Numbers in the text correspond to numbers in the margin and on the Museum Row and Farmers Market map.

Start the day with coffee and fresh-baked pastries at **Farmers Market** ①, a few blocks north of Wilshire Boulevard at 3rd Street and Fairfax Avenue. Drive south on Fairfax Avenue to the **Miracle Mile** ② district of Wilshire Boulevard. The black-and-gold Art Deco building on the northeast corner is a former department store that houses exhibition galleries shared by the Los Angeles County Museum of Art and the **Southwest Museum.** Turn left on Wilshire and proceed to Ogden Drive

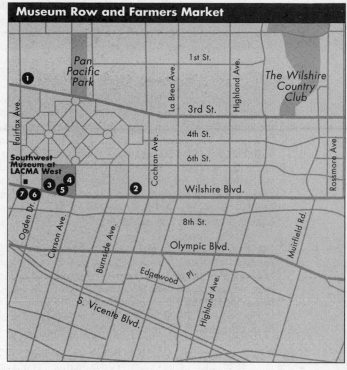

Museum Row and Farmers Market

or a block farther to Spaulding Avenue, where you can park the car and set out on foot to explore the museums.

The large complex of contemporary buildings surrounded by a park (on the corner of Wilshire and Ogden Drive) is **The Los Angeles County Museum of Art** ③, known as LACMA. Also occupying the park are the prehistoric **La Brea Tar Pits** ④, where many of the fossils displayed at the adjacent **George C. Page Museum of La Brea Discoveries** ⑤ were found. Across Wilshire are the **Carole & Barry Kaye Museum of Miniatures** ⑥ and, back at the corner of Wilshire and Fairfax, the **Petersen Automotive Museum** ⑦.

TIMING

The museums open between 10 and noon. LACMA is open on Monday but closed on Wednesday, and has extended hours into the evening, closing at 8 (9 on Friday). The other museums are closed on Monday. Weekends bring the largest crowds to Farmers Market and the museums. On the second Tuesday of the month, admission to all but ticketed exhibits at LACMA is free. Set aside a good portion of the day for this tour: an hour for the Farmers Market and from three to four hours for the museums.

Sights to See

⑥ **Carole & Barry Kaye Museum of Miniatures.** Besides scaled-down models of the Hollywood Bowl, the Vatican, and several famous European châteaux, the George Stuart Gallery of miniature historical figures is one of the highlights of this pint-size world. The tribute to America's First Ladies is a treat, and there's a soda fountain complete with a cherry as small as a fly's eye. ⊠ *5900 Wilshire Blvd.,* ☎ *323/937–6464.* ⊠ *$7.50.* ☉ *Tues.–Sat. 10–5, Sun. 11–5.*

★ ❶ **Farmers Market.** In July 1934, two entrepreneurs developed a European-style open-air market where farmers could sell their produce to local housewives. The idea was an instant success: Farmers paid the 50¢ daily parking fee; in exchange, they got to display their wares on the tailgates of their trucks. Blanche Magee, a local restaurateur, drove by one day and saw a crowd of customers buying buying produce and flowers from the backs of the trucks. The next day she returned with a hamper full of sandwiches and soft drinks, which she sold to the farmers and customers. Soon afterward Magee's Kitchen and Deli became the Farmers Market's first restaurant. (The restaurant is still here, run by Blanche's daughter-in-law, Phyllis.) The market has more than 110 stalls and more than 20 restaurants, many with alfresco dining under umbrellas. Because it's next door to CBS Television Studios, the market is a major hub for stars and stargazers, tourists and locals—it's one of the few community gathering points in the sprawling city of L.A. ⊠ *6333 W. 3rd St.,* ☎ *323/933–9211.* ⊙ *Mon.–Sat. 9–7, Sun. 10–6 (later in summer). Free parking.*

NEED A
BREAK?

Stop for a BLT on sourdough (rated one of L.A.'s favorite 100 dishes by *Los Angeles Magazine*), a chicken–chopped salad chock-full of veggies, or a slice of apple–ginger–buttermilk coffeecake and a mocha French-roast malt at **Kokomo Café,** (☎ 213/933–0773). At **Bob's Coffee & Donuts** (☎ 213/933–8929), Bob Tusquellas, a.k.a. "the Donut Man," churns out nearly 2,000 jelly-filled, cinnamon-rolled, and glazed creations each day.

---

❺ **George C. Page Museum of La Brea Discoveries.** At the La Brea Tar Pits, this member of the Natural History Museum family is set, bunker-like, half underground. A bas-relief around four sides depicts life in the Pleistocene era, and the museum has more than three million Ice Age fossils. Exhibits include reconstructed, life-size skeletons of mammoths, wolves, sloths, eagles, and condors. A permanent installation shows a robotic saber-toothed cat attacking a huge ground sloth. The glass-enclosed Paleontological Laboratory permits observation of the ongoing cleaning, identification, and cataloging of fossils excavated from the nearby asphalt deposits. ⊠ *5801 Wilshire Blvd.,* ☎ *323/936–2230.* ⊠ *$6; free 1st Tues. of month.* ⊙ *Tues.–Sun. 10–5.*

★ ❹ **La Brea Tar Pits.** About 40,000 years ago, deposits of oil rose to the Earth's surface, collected in shallow pools, and coagulated into sticky asphalt. In the early 20th century, geologists discovered that the sticky goo contained the largest collection of Pleistocene, or Ice Age, fossils ever found at one location: more than 600 species of birds, mammals, plants, reptiles, and insects. More than 100 tons of fossil bones have been removed in excavations over the last seven decades. Statues of a family of mammoths in the big pit near the corner of Wilshire and Curson depict how many of them were entombed: Edging down to a pond of water to drink, animals were caught in the tar and unable to extricate themselves.

❸ **Los Angeles County Museum of Art (LACMA).** LACMA's encyclopedic collection of more than 150,000 works from around the world is widely considered the most comprehensive in the western United States. Islamic, South and Southeast Asian, Far Eastern, and American works are especially well-represented. The museum's five buildings also house modern and contemporary art, costumes and textiles, decorative arts, European paintings and sculpture, photography, drawings, and prints.

The galleries of Islamic art are arranged chronologically, emphasizing visual connections and recurrent themes. Recent acquisitions at the South

Asian and Southeast Asian galleries include the *Hindu Saint Manikkava-cakar,* a 12th-century South Indian bronze statue, and *Buddha Calling the Earth to Witness,* a bronze image from 11th-century Tibet.

LACMA's collection of American art—paintings, sculpture, furniture, and decorative arts from the colonial era to the early 20th century—is one of the nation's finest. In addition to furniture, silver, glass, ceramics, paintings, and sculpture of these periods, there are landscape genre paintings from the Federal period, frontier art, works from the Ash Can School, and examples from regional developments such as California impressionism and surrealism. Among the masterworks are George Bellows's *Cliff Dwellers,* Mary Cassatt's *Mother About to Wash Her Sleepy Child,* and Winslow Homer's *The Cotton Pickers.*

Throughout the museum, wall panels introduce themes that provide a framework for viewing. A CD-ROM audio guide narrated by LACMA curators provides overviews and insights into the permanent collection. ⊠ *5905 Wilshire Blvd.,* ☎ *323/857–6000; 323/857–0098 TDD.* ⊠ *$6; free 2nd Tues. of month.* ⊙ *Mon, Tues., Thurs. noon–8, Fri. noon–9, weekends 11–8.*

NEED A BREAK? | From LACMA, walk one block east to the corner of Wilshire and Curson to **Callender's Wilshire** (⊠ 5773 Wilshire Blvd., ☎ 323/937-7952), where focaccia-bread sandwiches, grilled Portobello-mushroom burgers, and pastas are served on an inviting umbrella-shaded brick patio.

❷ Miracle Mile. The strip of Wilshire Boulevard between La Brea and Fairfax avenues was vacant land in the 1920s, when a developer bought the parcel to develop into a shopping and business district. The auto age was just emerging—the building designs incorporated wide store windows to attract attention from passing automobiles. The Miracle Mile area went into a decline in the '50s and '60s, but it's now enjoying a comeback as Los Angeles's Art Deco structures have come to be appreciated, preserved, and restored.

★ ❼ **Petersen Automotive Museum.** Highly entertaining but also informative, the Petersen contains lifelike dioramas and street scenes that establish a context for the history of the automobile and its influence. Rotating exhibits on the second floor might include the automobiles of celebrities, cars that have appeared in films, motorcycles, or commemorative displays. ⊠ *6060 Wilshire Blvd.,* ☎ *323/930–2277.* ⊠ *$7.* ⊙ *Tues.–Sun. 10–6.*

Southwest Museum at LACMA West. The oldest museum in Los Angeles expanded in 1998 from its main facility on Mt. Washington (☞ Pasadena Area, *below*) into this satellite location, an Art Deco structure that for years was the flagship of the May Co. department store chain. The additional exhibition space (which the museum shares with the Los Angeles County Museum of Art) affords the Southwest the opportunity to present even more of its fine collection of Native American art and artifacts dating from 1800 to the present. At press time admission prices and hours of operation had not been set. ⊠ *Wilshire Blvd. and Fairfax Ave. (northeast corner),* ☎ *323/221–2163.*

OFF THE BEATEN PATH | **WILTERN THEATRE–** This magnificent example of all-out Art Deco architecture is still used for major performances (☞ Nightlife and the Arts, *below*). The 1930s zigzag design was restored to its splendid turquoise hue in 1985. ⊠ *3790 Wilshire Blvd., at Western Ave..*

Beverly Hills

If you've got money to spend—lots of it—then come to Beverly Hills. Its main shopping street, Rodeo Drive, is the platinum vein of its commercial district (a.k.a. the Golden Triangle), where you'll find expensive retailers like Tiffany, Fendi, Gucci, and Cartier. Beverly Hills also means sky-high real estate prices, legendary hotels, high-powered restaurants, and—most of all—movie stars. Mary Pickford and Douglas Fairbanks Sr. led the way 80 years ago by setting up house here; Hollywood royalty followed suit, and pretty soon Beverly Hills, once a tract of bean patches known as Morocco Junction, was on its way to becoming a celebrity mecca. Entertainers still live in Beverly Hills, though nowadays, while their agents package multimillion dollar deals in offices on Wilshire Boulevard, the stars are as likely to be found hiding out on a ranch in Montana or Argentina as here. But the allure of Beverly Hills continues to draw armies of visitors on the lookout for a famous face and a glimpse of an opulent lifestyle.

A Good Tour

Numbers in the text correspond to numbers in the margin and on the Westside map.

Begin a tour of Beverly Hills with a drive into the hills above Sunset Boulevard. North of Sunset on Loma Vista Drive is the **Greystone Mansion** ①. Less than a mile west on Sunset is the landmark **Beverly Hills Hotel** ②. Behind the hotel, on Elden Way, is the **Virginia Robinson Gardens** ③, the oldest estate in Beverly Hills.

Across the street from the hotel is the pretty little triangular park named for the cowboy-philosopher Will Rogers, who was once honorary mayor of Beverly Hills. Turn south here on **Rodeo Drive** ④ (pronounced ro-*day*-o). You'll pass through a residential neighborhood before hitting the shopping stretch of Rodeo south of Santa Monica Boulevard. This is where you'll want to get out of the car and walk around. At Rodeo Drive and Dayton Way, the **Beverly Hills Trolley** ⑤ departs for 40-minute tours of the city (between May and December). Across Wilshire is the **Regent Beverly Wilshire Hotel** ⑥. The **Museum of Television & Radio** ⑦ stands a block east of Rodeo, on Beverly Drive at Little Santa Monica Boulevard. Adjacent to Beverly Hills on the west is the high-rise office-tower and shopping-center complex known as **Century City** ⑧.

TIMING

A drive through the hills of Beverly takes less than an hour unless you get out of your car to explore. As for Rodeo Drive (park the car in one of several municipal lots; the first one or two hours are free at most of them), you could easily spend a day here. There are many reasonably priced cafés and restaurants for lunch. The major routes in and out of Beverly Hills—Wilshire and Santa Monica boulevards—become congested during rush hour; it's best to tour the area at midday or on the weekend.

Sights to See

★ ❷ **Beverly Hills Hotel.** Even before Beverly Hills existed as a neighborhood, the "Pink Palace," which opened in 1912, was attracting Hollywood legends, among them Gloria Swanson and Rudolph Valentino. Clark Gable, Marlene Dietrich, Marilyn Monroe, and Elizabeth Taylor all bunked here, too. Greta Garbo, Howard Hughes, and other movie-industry guests kept low profiles when staying at this pastel landmark, but other film luminaries, notably Cecil B. DeMille, cut very visible deals in the Polo Lounge. ⊠ *9641 Sunset Blvd., 1 mi west of Doheny Dr.,* ☎ *310/276–2251.*

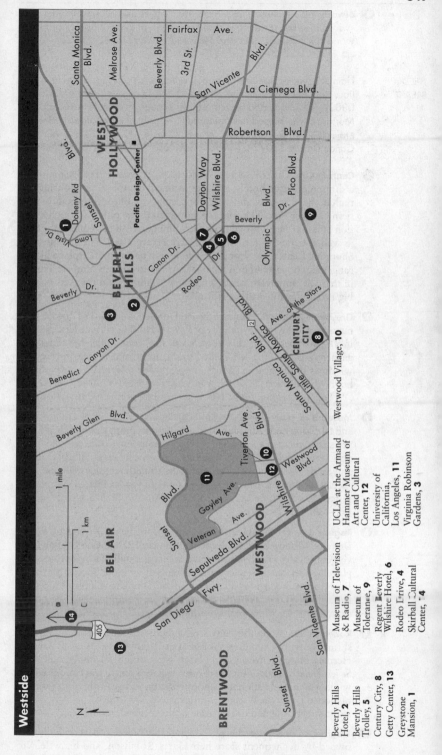

⑤ Beverly Hills Trolley. The 40-minute "Sights and Scenes" trolley tour swings into the residential area for a look at former homes of Hollywood celebrities. ⊠ *Dayton Way and Rodeo Dr.,* ☎ *310/285–2438.* ⬛ *$5.* ☉ *May–Dec., daily 11–5.*

NEED A   Ham sandwiches made with panini bread are enormous at the unpreten-
BREAK?   tious **Café Rodeo** (⊠ Summit Hotel, 360 N. Rodeo Dr., ☎ 310/273–
             0300). The salads and pizzas are big enough to split. Actress Cathy
             Moriarity, who starred in *Raging Bull,* owns the well-regarded **Mulberry
             Street** (⊠ 240 S. Beverly Dr., ☎ 310/247–8100; and ⊠ 347 N.
             Cañon Dr., ☎ 310/247–8998) pizzerias.

⑧ Century City. This 280-acre mixed-use development of office buildings, a shopping center, hotels, an entertainment complex, and housing was built in the '60s on what used to be the backlot of the film studio Twentieth Century Fox. The studio is not open to the public (though a portion of it may be glimpsed from Pico Boulevard and Avenue of the Stars as well as from the garden of the Park Hyatt hotel). The **Century City Shopping Center** (☞ Shopping, *below*) is a festive marketplace-like arrangement of eateries and cinemas. At the cavernous **Shubert Theater** in the ABC Entertainment Center (☞ Nightlife and the Arts *below*), big Broadway musicals perform.

① Greystone Mansion. Oilman Edward Doheny built this 1927 neo-Gothic mansion now owned by the city of Beverly Hills. Greystone has appeared in *The Witches of Eastwick, Indecent Proposal,* and other films. The gardens are open for self-guided tours, and you can peek through the windows of the house. Picnics are permitted in specified areas during hours of operation. ⊠ *905 Loma Vista Dr.,* ☎ *310/550–4796.* ⬛ *Free . ☉ Fall and winter, daily 10–5; spring and summer, daily 10–6.*

⑦ Museum of Television & Radio. Search for your favorite commercials and television and radio shows on easy-to-use computers, and then watch or listen to them in an adjacent room. The museum's collection of 90,000 programs spans 77 years. Screenings and listening series take place daily, and television and radio cast members sometimes give seminars. Past special exhibits have included television- and radio-related art and costumes. ⊠ *465 N. Beverly Dr.,* ☎ *310/786–1000.* ⬛ *$6.* ☉ *Wed. and Fri.–Sun. noon–5, Thurs. noon–9.*

⑥ Regent Beverly Wilshire Hotel. Anchoring the south end of Rodeo Drive at Wilshire Boulevard since opening in 1928, the hotel often hosts visiting royalty and celebrities; it's where the millionaire businessman played by Richard Gere ensconced himself with the hooker played by Julia Roberts in the movie *Pretty Woman.* Though the lobby is too small to explore, you might stop for a drink or meal in one of the hotel's restaurants. ⊠ *9500 Wilshire Blvd.,* ☎ *310/275–5200.*

★ **④ Rodeo Drive.** Along this tony stretch between Santa Monica and Wilshire boulevards, window shopping at Tiffany & Co., Gucci, Armani, Hermes, Harry Winston, and Lladro is about the only thing that's free. Several nearby restaurants have outside patios where you can sip a drink while watching fashionable shoppers saunter by. At the southern end of Rodeo Drive (at Wilshire Boulevard) is **Via Rodeo,** a curvy cobblestone street designed to resemble a European shopping *via.*

③ Virginia Robinson Gardens. The estate, the oldest in Beverly Hills, was owned by department store heir Harry Robinson, and his wife, Virginia, who bequeathed it to the County of Los Angeles. Nearly 6 acres of lush planted grounds surround the Mediterranean-style villa. The collection of King palms is reported to be the largest grove outside the tree's native Australia. Fountains and falls flow through a grove of citrus and camellias. Call in advance to schedule a tour. ⊠ *1008 Elden Way,* ☎ *310/276–5367.* ☉ *Tours by appointment.*

The Westside

An informal and unscientific survey of Westside districts like West Los Angeles, Westwood, Bel Air, Brentwood, and Pacific Palisades would probably reveal high concentrations of plastic surgeons and Land Rovers. This, after all, is the part of town where one health club, which costs thousands in annual membership dues, puts celebrity patrons in its magazine ads. The Westside, however, is rich cultural territory, and the rewards of visiting UCLA's Westwood campus, the Museum of Tolerance, and the Getty Center in Brentwood are great, even if you only work out at the Y or drive a rented Saturn.

A Good Tour
Numbers in the text correspond to numbers in the margin and on the Westside map.

The major Westside sights are spread out, so it's best to plan on visiting no more than two or three on any one day. A visit to the **Museum of Tolerance** ⑨ in the morning, for example, can be followed by lunch and shopping in Beverly Hills. Or you might drive through **Westwood Village** ⑩, home of the **UCLA** ⑪ campus and **UCLA at the Armand Hammer Museum of Art and Cultural Center** ⑫. The vast **Getty Center** ⑬, atop a hill in Brentwood, is currently the Westside's most high-profile attraction. About 2 mi north on Sepulveda Boulevard is the **Skirball Cultural Center** ⑭ and its gallery exhibition of Jewish life.

For a less destination-oriented tour of the posh Westside, simply follow Wilshire Boulevard west out of Beverly Hills. Once past the San Diego Freeway (I–405), detour to the right on San Vicente Boulevard and the urban-village center of **Brentwood.** At the Santa Monica city line, turn right on 26th Street and follow it as it turns into Allenford Avenue. The route will loop you around to Sunset Boulevard. A left turn here will take you to Pacific Palisades and the ocean. A right leads back toward Beverly Hills and West Hollywood, past the Getty Center and Bel Air mansions.

TIMING
You need to reserve ahead to visit the Museum of Tolerance, which is closed on Saturday, and the Getty Center, which is closed on Monday. You can easily spend a half day at each museum. In the evening and on weekends, Westwood Village and Brentwood's commercial district on San Vicente Boulevard come alive with a busy restaurant, café, and street scene. The afternoon rush hour is predictably congested along Wilshire and Sunset boulevards.

Sights to See
Brentwood. Ritzy Brentwood, the former home of Greta Garbo and other stars, has gotten more than its share of publicity in recent years, what with all the hubbub surrounding the O.J. Simpson murder trial and the travails of former resident Monica Lewinsky. The main stretch for dining and shopping is along San Vicente Boulevard.

★ ⑬ **Getty Center.** Architect Richard Meier designed the castlelike Getty Center to house what has instantly become one of the most popular attractions in Los Angeles; parking reservations, which are essential for guaranteed admission, are necessary months in advance.

J. Paul Getty, the billionaire oil magnate and art collector, began his museum at his Malibu estate in 1954. When he died in 1976, the museum received an endowment of $700 million that has grown to a reported $2.4 billion. The J. Paul Getty Museum, on the Malibu site, is closed until 2001, when it will reopen as the exhibition venue for the antiquities collection, a Getty strength. The Getty Center, atop a Brentwood hillside, contains the rest of the museum's collection and unites various research institutes and grant programs on one site.

Visitors park, or arrive by bus or cab, at the bottom of the hill and take a tram to the top. The principal destination for most visitors is the museum, a series of five pavilions built around a central courtyard and bridged by walkways that afford views from the San Gabriel Mountains to the Pacific Ocean. In a ravine separating the museum and one of the Getty research institutes, artist Robert Irwin created the **Central Garden,** whose focal point is an azalea maze in a pool. Inside the pavilions are the collections of European paintings, drawings, sculpture, illuminated manuscripts, and decorative arts, as well as American and European photographs. The Getty's collection of French furniture and decorative arts include a paneled Régence salon from 1710 and a neoclassical salon from 1788. In the paintings galleries, a computerized system of louvered skylights allows natural light to filter in, creating a closer approximation of the conditions in which the artists painted. Notable among the paintings are Rembrandt's *Portrait of Marten Looten* and *The Abduction of Europa,* Vincent van Gogh's *Irises,* Claude Monet's *Wheatstack, Snow Effects, Morning,* and James Ensor's *Christ's Entry Into Brussels.* A quick tour that takes in 15 highlights of the collection is outlined in a brochure available in the entrance hall. An instructive audio tour ($2) has commentaries by art historians. Art information rooms with multimedia computer stations contain more information about the collections. ⊠ *1200 Getty Center Dr.,* ☎ *310/ 440–7300.* ▧ *Free; $5 parking.* ☉ *Tues.–Wed. 11–7, Thurs.–Fri. 11– 9, weekends 10–6; call ahead for parking reservations.*

★ ⑨ **Museum of Tolerance.** Using state-of-the-art interactive technology, this museum challenges visitors to confront bigotry and racism. One of the most affecting sections covers the Holocaust, with actual film footage of deportation scenes and simulated sets of concentration camps. Upon arrival you're issued a "passport" bearing the name of a child whose life was dramatically changed by the German Nazi rule and by World War II; later, you learn the fate of that child. Anne Frank artifacts are part of the museum's permanent collection. Expect to spend at least three hours to see the whole museum. ⊠ *9786 W. Pico Blvd.,* ☎ *310/553–8403.* ▧ *$8.* ☉ *Sun. 10:30–5, Mon.–Thurs. 10–4, Fri. 10–1.*

⑭ **Skirball Cultural Center.** The core exhibition at the Skirball is "Visions and Values: Jewish Life from Antiquity to America," the story of the Jewish immigration experience. Highlights include a large collection of Judaica, a two-thirds-size replica of the torch of the Statue of Liberty, and a Hanukkah lamp with each of the eight branches fashioned after the Statue of Liberty. Children can participate in an outdoor simulated archaeological dig at the interactive Discovery Center. ⊠ *2701 N. Sepulveda Blvd.,* ☎ *310/440–4500.* ▧ *$8.* ☉ *Tues.–Sat. noon– 5, Sun. 11–5.*

⑫ **UCLA at the Armand Hammer Museum of Art and Cultural Center.** The eclectic permanent collection at this comparatively small museum includes thousands of works by Honoré Daumier, as well as a handful by Vincent van Gogh, Paul Gauguin, and Mary Cassatt. There's also an important collection of art by the Old Masters, including drawings by Michelangelo, Raphael, and Rembrandt. Free poetry readings take place on Thursday evening, art lectures and workshops are held on many weekdays, and on most Saturdays there are music and art events for children. ✉ *10899 Wilshire Blvd.,* ☎ *310/443–7000.* ✍ *$4.50, free Thurs. 6–9; parking $2.75.* ☉ *Tues.– Wed. and Fri.–Sat. 11–7, Thurs. 11–9, Sun. 11–5. Tours Sun. at 1.*

⑪ **University of California, Los Angeles.** The parklike UCLA campus is pleasant to stroll. Among the 70 works in the **Franklin Murphy Sculpture Garden,** in the heart of the north campus, are those of Henry Moore and Gaston Lachaise. Accessible from Tiverton Avenue in the southeast section of the campus is **Mildred Mathias Botanic Garden.** West of the main campus bookstore, the **Morgan Center Hall of Fame** displays the sports memorabilia and trophies of the university's athletic departments. Many visitors head straight to the **UCLA Fowler Museum of Cultural History** (☎ 310/825–4361), which presents changing exhibits about the art and culture of past and present peoples of Latin America, Oceania, Africa, and Asia.

Campus maps and information are available at drive-by kiosks at major entrances, and free 90-minute walking tours of the campus are given on weekdays at 10:30 and 2:30. The tour begins at the West Alumni Center, next to Pauley Pavilion; call 310/206–0616 for reservations, which are required at least one day ahead. The campus has several indoor and outdoor cafés, plus bookstores selling UCLA Bruins paraphernalia. The main entrance gate is on Westwood Boulevard. Campus parking costs $5. ✉ *Main entrance on Westwood Plaza; Le Conte, Hilgard, and Gayley Aves. and Sunset Blvd. border the campus.* ✍ *Campus free; Fowler Museum $5 (free Sun. and Thurs.)*

⑩ **Westwood Village.** Next to the UCLA campus, Westwood Village, with its first-run movie theaters, eateries, and a lively youth-oriented street scene, gets so busy on summer weekends that many streets are closed to car traffic and visitors must park at the Federal Building (✉ Wilshire Blvd. and Veteran Ave.) and shuttle over. Behind one of the behemoth office buildings on Wilshire Boulevard is **Westwood Village Memorial Park** (✉ 1218 Glendon Ave.), where Marilyn Monroe is buried in a simply marked crypt on the north wall. Also buried here are Truman Capote and Natalie Wood.

Santa Monica, Venice, and Malibu

In Los Angeles, all roads lead, eventually, to the beach and the coastal communities of Santa Monica, Venice, and Malibu. These communities hug the Santa Monica Bay, in an arc of diversity, from the rich-as-can-be Malibu to the bohemian-seedy mix of Venice. What they have in common, however, is cleaner coastal air and an emphasis on being out in the sunshine, always within sight of the Pacific.

A Good Drive

Numbers in the text correspond to numbers in the margin and on the Santa Monica, Venice, and Pacific Palisades map.

Look for the arched neon sign at the foot of Colorado Avenue marking the entrance to the **Santa Monica Pier** ①, the city's number-one landmark, built in 1906. Park on the pier and take a turn through **Pacific Park** ②, a 2-acre amusement park. The wide swath of sand on the north side of the pier is Santa Monica Beach, on hot summer weekends one of the most crowded beaches in southern California. From the pier, walk to Ocean Avenue, where **Palisades Park** ③, a strip of lawn and palms above the cliffs, provides panoramic ocean views. Three blocks inland is **Third Street Promenade** ④, an active outdoor mall with shopping, dining, and entertainment.

Retrieve the car and drive two blocks inland on Colorado to Main Street. Turn right and continue to Ocean Park Boulevard. Look for a colorful mural on the side of the building on the southeast corner. On the southwest corner you'll find the **California Heritage Museum** ⑤. The next several blocks south along Main Street are great for browsing.

Next stop: **Venice Boardwalk** ⑥. Walk up Main Street through the trendy shopping district until you hit Rose Avenue. Ahead on the left you'll spot an enormous pair of binoculars, the front of the Frank Gehry–designed Chiat-Day Mojo building. Turn right toward the sea and the boardwalk, where the classic California beach scene is in progress.

For the drive to Malibu, retrace your route along Main Street. At Pico Boulevard, turn west, toward the ocean, and then right on Ocean Avenue. When you pass the pier, prepare to turn left down the California Incline (the incline is at the end of Palisades Park at Wilshire Boulevard) to Pacific Coast Highway (Highway 1), also known as PCH. About 11 mi north, you'll enter Malibu proper. Malibu Pier is closed indefinitely due to storm damage, but you can park in the adjacent lot and take a walk on **Malibu Lagoon State Beach** ⑦, also known as Surfrider Beach. On the highway side of the beach is the Moorish-Spanish **Adamson House and Malibu Lagoon Museum** ⑧. From here, you can walk along the strand of beach that fronts the famed Malibu Colony, the exclusive residential enclave of film, television, and recording stars.

TIMING

If you've got the time, break your coastal visit into two excursions: Santa Monica and Venice in one, and Malibu in another. The best way to "do" Santa Monica and Venice is to park the car and walk, cycle, or skate along the 3-mi beachside bike path. Daytime is best, but only the Venice Boardwalk should be avoided at night, when the crowd becomes unsavory. You can park on the Santa Monica Pier and in small lots close to the beach in Venice (the smart thing to do, since break-ins are common in the area) and Malibu. Avoid driving to Malibu during rush hour, when traffic along Pacific Coast Highway moves at a snail's pace—but do try to be there before dusk to watch the sun dip into the mighty Pacific.

Sights to See

❽ **Adamson House and Malibu Lagoon Museum.** Magnificent tiles in rich blues, greens, yellows, and oranges cover this house originally occupied by the Rindge family, which owned much of the Malibu area in the early 20th century. Even an outside dog shower, near the servants' door, is a tiled delight. Docent-led tours provide insight into the history of Malibu and its real estate (you can't have one without the other). Signs posted around the grounds outside direct you on a self-guided tour. Park in the adjacent county lot, or in the lot at Pacific Coast Highway and Cross Creek Road. ⊠ *23200 Pacific Coast Hwy.,* ☎ *310/456–8432.* ⌑ *house tours, $2.* ⊙ *Wed.–Sat. 11–3.*

NEED A
BREAK?

Try **Windsail Malibu** (⊠ 22706 Pacific Coast Hwy., ☎ 310/456–0900), south of the Malibu Pier at the edge of the ocean, for sandwiches, vegetarian curry, salmon salad, or warm roast-lamb salad. A glass wall and open patio provide year-round ocean views.

Bergamot Station Art Center. This collection of old railroad cars behind the city recycling center houses more than 30 galleries and design studios. Also here is the Santa Monica Museum of Art, which presents performance and video art as well as exhibits of lesser-known painters and sculptors. On Friday evening free films, discussions, and readings take place. ⊠ *2525 Michigan Ave.,* ☎ *310/829–5854 Bergamot, 310/586–6488 museum.* ⌑ *Galleries free, Santa Monica Museum suggested donation $4.* ⊙ *Wed.–Sun. 11–6, Fri. 11–10.*

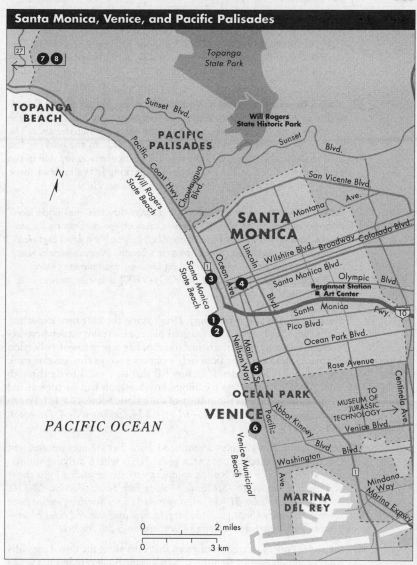

Santa Monica, Venice, and Pacific Palisades

Topanga State Park

Will Rogers State Historic Park

TOPANGA BEACH

Sunset Blvd.

PACIFIC PALISADES

Sunset Blvd.

Pacific Coast Hwy.

Chautauqua Blvd.

Will Rogers State Beach

San Vicente Blvd.

Ave.

N

SANTA MONICA

Montana

Lincoln

Wilshire Blvd.

Broadway

Colorado Blvd.

Santa Monica State Beach

Ocean Ave.

Santa Monica Blvd.

Olympic Blvd.

Bergamot Station Art Center

Santa Monica Fwy.

10

Pico Blvd.

Main St.

Neilson Way

Ocean Park Blvd.

Rose Avenue

Centinela Ave.

PACIFIC OCEAN

OCEAN PARK

VENICE

Abbot Kinney Blvd.

Pacific Blvd.

TO MUSEUM OF JURASSIC TECHNOLOGY →

Venice Blvd.

Venice Municipal Beach

Washington Ave.

MARINA DEL REY

Mindano Way

Marina Expwy.

0   2 miles

0   3 km

Adamson House and Malibu Lagoon Museum, **8**

California Heritage Museum, **5**

Malibu Lagoon State Beach, **7**

Pacific Park, **2**

Palisades Park, **3**

Santa Monica Pier, **1**

Third Street Promenade, **4**

Venice Boardwalk, **6**

❺ **California Heritage Museum.** Three rooms in this 1894 late-Victorian house have been fully restored: the dining room in the style of 1890–1910; the living room, 1910–1920; and the kitchen, 1920–1930. The second-floor galleries contain photography and historical exhibits as well as shows by contemporary artists from California. ✉ *2612 Main St.,* ☎ *310/392–8537.* 🎫 *$3.* ☉ *Wed.–Sat. 11–4, Sun. 10–4.*

❼ **Malibu Lagoon State Beach.** Visitors are asked to stay on the board-walks at this 5-acre haven for native and migratory birds so that the egrets, blue herons, avocets, and gulls can enjoy the marshy area. The signs listing opening and closing hours refer only to the parking lot; the lagoon itself is open 24 hours and is particularly enjoyable in the early morning and at sunset. Street-side parking is available at those times, but not at midday. ✉ *23200 Pacific Coast Hwy.*

OFF THE
BEATEN PATH

MARINA DEL REY – A brilliant sight on a sunny day, this man-made marina with moorings for 10,000 boats is south of Venice. Stop by Burton Chace Park (at the foot of Mindanao Way) to watch the wind carry colorful sailboats out to sea. Small "Mother's Beach" (Marina Beach) has calm, protected waters ideal for young children. Hornblower Dining Yachts (✉ 13755 Fiji Way, ☎ 310/301–9900) arranges marina and dining cruises.

Museum of Jurassic Technology. Don't bring the kids here expecting to see dinosaur bones. This unusual place, in a realm somewhere between a museum and an art installation, has a permanent collection of natural (and perhaps fictional) wonders such as the African stink ant and the "piercing devil" (a tiny bat that uses radar to fly through solid objects). Temporary exhibits cover a grab-bag of topics: old wives' tales or perhaps the culture of the mobile home. ✉ *9341 Venice Blvd., Culver City,* ☎ *310/836–6131.* 🎫 *$4.* ☉ *Thurs. 2–8, Fri.–Sun. noon–6.*

🐣 ❷ **Pacific Park.** The 12 rides at Santa Monica Pier's 2-acre amusement facility include a roller coaster, a giant Ferris wheel, a flying submarine, and the Rock and Roll, a spinning experience with a light show and rousing music. ✉ *380 Santa Monica Pier, Santa Monica,* ☎ *310/260–8747.* 🎫 *Rides $1–$4, all-day pass $15.* ☉ *Summer, entire park open 7 days May–Sept.; winter, Ferris wheel and selected rides Mon.–Thurs., entire park Fri. evening–Sun. evening; call for hrs.*

❸ **Palisades Park.** The ribbon of green that runs along the top of the cliffs from Colorado Avenue to north of San Vicente Boulevard has flat walkways where folks out strolling or jogging enjoy spectacular views of the Pacific.

★ 🐣 ❶ **Santa Monica Pier.** Eateries, souvenir shops, a psychic adviser, arcades, and the Pacific Park amusement facility are all part of this truncated pier at the foot of Colorado Boulevard below Palisades Park. The pier's trademark 46-horse carousel, built in 1922, has appeared in many films, including *The Sting.* ✉ *Colorado Ave. and the ocean,* ☎ *310/458–8900.* 🎫 *Rides 25¢ and 50¢.* ☉ *Carousel summer, daily 11–6; winter, weekends 10–5.*

❹ **Third Street Promenade.** Only foot traffic is allowed along a three-block stretch of 3rd Street lined with jacaranda trees and accented with ivy-topiary dinosaur fountains. Outdoor cafés, street vendors, several movie theaters, and a rich nightlife (the mix of folks down here is great, from elderly couples out for a bite to skateboarders and street musicians) make this one of Santa Monica's main gathering spots. ✉ *3rd St. between Wilshire Blvd. and Broadway.*

★ ⑥ **Venice Boardwalk.** "Boardwalk" may be something of a misnomer—Venice Boardwalk is really a paved walkway—but this L.A. must-see delivers year-round action: Bicyclists zip along and bikini-clad roller and in-line skaters attract crowds as they put on impromptu demonstrations, vying for attention with magicians, fortune tellers, a chainsaw juggler, and street artists. You can rent in-line skates, roller skates, and bicycles (some with baby seats) at the south end of the boardwalk (which is also known as Ocean Front Walk), along Washington Street, near the Venice Pier.

NEED A BREAK?	For a beach picnic you can buy food at one of the many fast-food stands that line the boardwalk. For a more relaxing meal, stand in line for a table at **Sidewalk Café** (✉ 1401 Ocean Front Walk, ☎ 310/399–5547). It's worth the wait for a patio table, where you can watch the free spirits on parade.

Will Rogers State Historic Park. The late cowboy-humorist Will Rogers lived on this site in the 1920s and 1930s. The house on his 187-acre estate is a folksy blend of Navajo rugs and Mission-style furniture, and includes a museum of Rogers memorabilia. Rogers was a polo enthusiast—in the 1930s, his front-yard polo field attracted friends like Douglas Fairbanks, Sr., for weekend games. The tradition continues, with free games scheduled when weather allows. The park's broad lawns are excellent for picnicking, and there's hiking on miles of eucalyptus-lined trails. From Pacific Coast Highway, turn inland at Sunset Boulevard. Follow Sunset for about 5 mi to the park entrance. ✉ *1501 Will Rogers State Park Rd., Pacific Palisades,* ☎ *310/454–8212.* ☜ *Free; parking $6.* ⊙ *Park, daily 8–sunset daily; house tours, daily 10:30–4:30.*

The San Fernando Valley

There are other valleys in the Los Angeles area, but this is the one that people refer to simply as the Valley. Large portions of the Valley are bedroom communities of neat bungalows and shopping centers, but most of the major film and television studios, among them Warner Bros. and NBC, are also here. Universal City is a one-industry town, and that industry is Universal Studios. The studio has been at this site since 1915, but things are bustling these days, what with the Universal Studios Hollywood theme park, the Universal Amphitheater, the CityWalk shopping and dining area, a movie theater complex, and two major hotels.

A Good Drive

Numbers in the text correspond to numbers in the margin and on the San Fernando Valley map.

On a clear day or evening, a drive along **Mulholland Drive** gives you a spectacular view of the sprawling San Fernando Valley below. Just over the hill from Hollywood via the Hollywood Freeway (U.S. 101 North) is **Universal Studios Hollywood** ①, on a large hill overlooking the Valley. Signs from Universal Studios point the way to Barham Boulevard. At Barham, turn left toward Burbank. After about a mile, the street curves around **Warner Bros. Studios** ②, whose outside wall is covered with billboards of current films and television shows. After the curve, you will be on West Olive Avenue. Keep to the right and look for the Gate No. 4 entrance at Hollywood Way.

Just a minute away at the second big intersection, West Olive and Alameda avenues, is the main entrance to **NBC Television Studios** ③. Continue east on Alameda; on the next block to your right is colorful

Disney Studios ④. Drive south on Buena Vista and then turn left on Riverside to get a good look at the whimsical architecture.

TIMING

The Valley is surrounded by mountains and the major routes to and from it go through mountain passes. During rush hour, traffic jams on the Hollywood Freeway (U.S. 101/Highway 170), San Diego Freeway (I–405), and Ventura Freeway (U.S. 101/Highway 134) can be brutal, so avoid trips to or from the Valley at those times. Expect to spend a full day at Universal Studios Hollywood and CityWalk; studio tours at NBC and Warner Bros. last about two hours.

Sights to See
Audiences Unlimited (⊠ 100 Universal City Plaza, Bldg. 153, ☎ 818/753–3483) is the best source for tickets to many television shows. For tickets and information about *The Tonight Show Starring Jay Leno*, contact **NBC** (☎ 818/840–3537). To commune with *Leeza*, call **Paramount Studios** (☎ 323/956–5575). Call **Sony Studios** (☎ 310/280–8856) for tickets to *Jeopardy* or to watch Vanna White turn those letters on *Wheel of Fortune* in person. Bob Barker still holds court at *The Price Is Right*; call **CBS** (☎ 323/852–2458) for tickets. Most shows have a minimum-age requirement for audience members.

OFF THE
BEATEN PATH

DESCANSO GARDENS – A forest of live oak trees at this 165-acre oasis furnishes a dramatic backdrop for thousands of camellias, azaleas, and a breathtaking 5-acre International Rosarium holding 1,700 varieties of antique and modern roses. The Tea House operates on weekends between February and November and, with its Zen garden, is a nice place spot to stop for refreshments and reflection. Tram tours traverse the grounds on a limited schedule. ⊠ *1418 Descanso Dr., at Foothill Blvd. (off I–210 or the Glendale Freeway), La Cañada/Flintridge,* ☎ *818/952–4400.* ⌲ *$5, $2.50 3rd Tues. of month.* ⊙ *Daily 9–4:30.*

❹ **Disney Studios.** Studio tours are not given at Disney, but a peek from Riverside Drive shows fanciful touches of architecture (note the little Mickey Mouse heads mounted on the surrounding fence). You can't miss this building—it looks like the hull of an ocean liner. ⊠ *500 S. Buena Vista.*

OFF THE
BEATEN PATH

MISSION SAN FERNDANDO REY ESPAÑA – An important member of a chain of 21 California missions established by Franciscan friars, Mission San Fernando was founded in 1797. Fifty-six Native Americans joined the mission and it flourished as a self-supporting community for many years. By the 1840s, however, it became unproductive and along with its properties (those being the entire San Fernando Valley), was sold for $14,000. During the next 40 years, the mission buildings were neglected; settlers stripped roof tiles, and the adobe walls were ravaged by the weather. Finally in 1923 a restoration program was initiated. As you walk through the mission, its arched corridors may seem familiar from an episode of *Gunsmoke* and *Dragnet* or the Steve Martin film *L.A. Story.* Inside the mission, Native American designs and artifacts of Spanish craftsmanship depict the mission's 18th-century culture. Look for the small museum and gift shop. ⊠ *15151 San Fernando Mission Blvd. (off I–405 or I–5),* ☎ *818/361–0186.* ⌲ *$4.* ⊙ *Daily 9–4:30.*

Mulholland Drive. Driving the length of the hilltop road that divides the San Fernando Valley and Los Angeles is slow and can be treacherous, but the rewards are sensational views of valley and city on each side and expensive homes along the way. From Hollywood, reach Mulholland via Outpost Drive off Franklin Avenue or Cahuenga Boulevard West via Highland Avenue north.

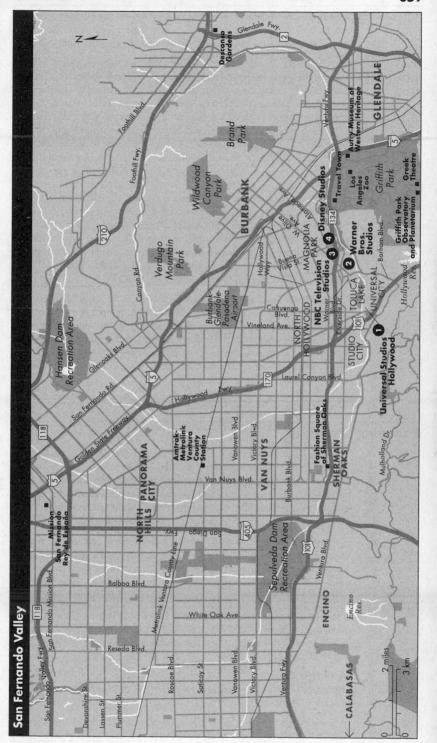

San Fernando Valley

N

Glendale Fwy.

Descanso Gardens

Foothill Blvd.

Foothill Fwy.

Brand Park

Wildwood Canyon Park

BURBANK

GLENDALE

Autry Museum of Western Heritage

Travel Town

Los Angeles Zoo

Griffith Park

Greek Theatre

210

Verdugo Mountain Park

Canyon Rd.

Disney Studios

MAGNOLIA PARK

Warner Bros. Studios

Griffith Park Observatory and Planetarium

Burbank Blvd.

Hansen Dam Recreation Area

Glenoaks Blvd.

Burbank-Glendale-Pasadena Airport

Cahuenga Blvd.

NBC Television Studios

TOLUCA LAKE

Hollywood Way

Buena Vista St.

UNIVERSAL CITY

Hollywood Blvd.

5

San Fernando Rd.

Vineland Ave.

NORTH HOLLYWOOD

Warner Blvd.

STUDIO CITY

101

Universal Studios Hollywood

Golden State Freeway

Hollywood Fwy.

170

Laurel Canyon Blvd.

Riverside Dr.

Mulholland Dr.

118

Amtrak-Metrolink Ventura County Station

Vanowen Blvd.

Victory Blvd.

VAN NUYS

Fashion Square of Sherman Oaks

SHERMAN OAKS

5

Van Nuys Blvd.

Burbank Blvd.

NORTH HILLS

PANORAMA CITY

Mission San Fernando Rey de España

405

Sepulveda Dam Recreation Area

San Diego Fwy.

101

Ventura Blvd.

Balboa Blvd.

ENCINO

Encino Res.

Metrolink Ventura County Line

White Oak Ave.

Reseda Blvd.

Roscoe Blvd.

Saticoy St.

Vanowen Blvd.

Victory Blvd.

Ventura Fwy.

CALABASAS

118

San Fernando Valley Fwy.

San Fernando Mission Blvd.

Devonshire St.

Lassen St.

Plummer St.

2 miles

3 km

0

0

Glendale Fwy.

2

5

Ventura Fwy.

134

W. Olive Ave.

Alameda Ave.

Hollywood Fwy.

Hollywood Rd.

1

2

3

4

❸ **NBC Television Studios.** Free tickets are made available for tapings of the various NBC shows, and 70-minute walking tours of the studio are given on weekdays. ⊠ *3000 W. Alameda Ave., Burbank,* ☎ *818/ 840–3537.* ✍ *$7.* ☉ *Tour weekdays 9–3.*

★ ℭ ❶ **Universal Studios Hollywood.** Though you probably won't see anything that actually has to do with making a real film, visiting the theme park is a sensational introduction to the principles of special effects. Seated aboard a comfortable tram (narrated, hour-long tours traverse the 420-acre complex all day long), you can experience the parting of the Red Sea, meet a 30-ft-tall version of King Kong, be attacked by the ravenous killer shark of *Jaws* fame, and endure a confrontation by aliens armed with death rays. A simulation of an 8.3 earthquake allows you to experience the perils of The Big One. If you missed Kevin Costner's epic film *Waterworld,* Universal delivers a facsimile in the form of a sea-war extravaganza. *Jurassic Park—The Ride* is a tour through a jungle full of dinosaurs with an 84-ft water drop. Long lines form at *Back to the Future,* a flight simulator disguised as a DeLorean car that shows off state-of-the-art special effects. Adjacent are the shops and restaurants of **CityWalk.** ⊠ *100 Universal City Pl.,* ☎ *818/508–9600.* ✍ *$36 adults, $26 children under 12.* ☉ *Daily 9–7.*

★ ❷ **Warner Bros. Studios.** The absorbing two-hour tours at Warners emphasize the actual workings of filmmaking more than the ones at Universal do. Tours vary from day to day to take advantage of goings-on at the lot. Most tours take in the back-lot sets, prop construction department, and sound complex. A museum chronicles the studio's film and animation history. It's recommended that you make reservations at least one week ahead; children under 10 are not admitted. Call for special needs. ⊠ *4000 Warner Blvd.,* ☎ *818/954–1744.* ✍ *$30.* ☉ *Tours weekdays 9–3 on the hour.*

Pasadena Area

Though it has long been fully absorbed into the general Los Angeles sprawl, Pasadena is a distinctly defined—and refined—city. Its varied residential architecture, augmented by lush landscaping, is among the most spectacular in southern California. Nearby Highland Park has two excellent museums, and San Marino is home to the famous Huntington Library, Art Collections, and Botanical Gardens.

To reach Pasadena from downtown Los Angeles, drive north on the Pasadena Freeway (Highway 110), which follows the curves of the arroyo (creek bed). The freeway, L.A.'s first, remains a pleasant drive in non–rush hour traffic, with old sycamores winding up the arroyo in a pleasant contrast to the more common 10-lane freeways of Los Angeles.

From Hollywood, take the Glendale Freeway (Highway 2) north, and from the San Fernando Valley, use the Ventura Freeway (Highway 134), which cuts east through Glendale, skirting the foothills, before arriving in Pasadena.

A Good Tour
Numbers in the text correspond to numbers in the margin and on the Pasadena Area map.

A good place to start a short driving tour of Pasadena is on Orange Grove Boulevard, a.k.a. Millionaire's Row, where wealthy Easterners built grand mansions at the turn of the century. One mansion that remains is the **Wrigley Mansion** ①. To get to the mansion, take the Orange Grove exit off the Ventura Freeway (Highway 134); turn right at Orange Grove and travel five blocks. From the Pasadena Freeway (Highway 110), stay on the freeway until it ends at Arroyo Parkway.

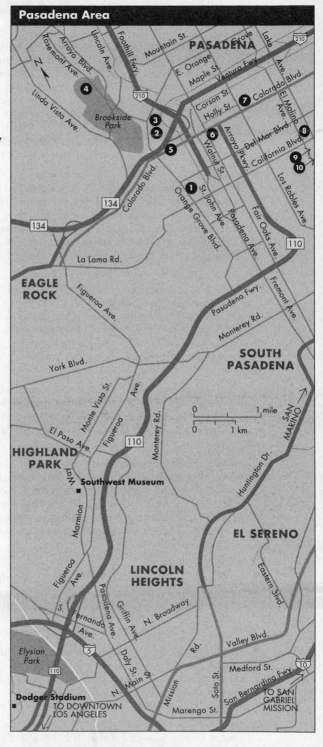

Pasadena Area

From Arroyo Parkway, turn left at California Boulevard and then right at Orange Grove.

From the Wrigley Mansion, travel north on Orange Grove to Walnut Street and the **Fenyes House** ②. Continue on Orange Grove to Arroyo Terrace, where a left turn will take you into an architectural wonderland. Greene and Greene, the renowned Pasadena architects, designed all of the houses on Arroyo Terrace. To view their Craftsman masterpiece, the three-story, shingled **Gamble House** ③, turn right on Westmoreland Place. Near here is the Frank Lloyd Wright–designed Millard House ("La Miniatura") on Prospect Crescent (from Westmoreland, turn left on Rosemont Avenue, right on Prospect Terrace, and right on Prospect Crescent to Number 645).

The famous **Rose Bowl** ④ is nestled in a gulley to the west off Arroyo Boulevard. Arroyo runs into Rosemont Avenue; take Rosemont south to Orange Grove Boulevard and turn right. Then, at Colorado Boulevard, turn left. Immediately on the left is the **Norton Simon Museum** ⑤. Continue east on Colorado Boulevard and enter **Old Town Pasadena** ⑥, where you can park and then walk this section of Pasadena, heading east.

For a look at domed Pasadena City Hall, turn left on Fair Oaks Avenue, then right on Holly Street. Garfield Avenue will bring you back to Colorado. The next intersection is Los Robles Avenue. One-half block north on Los Robles is the **Pacific Asia Museum** ⑦. Back on Colorado, head three blocks east to El Molino Avenue. Turn right past the Pasadena Playhouse and, if you have youngsters, continue along four blocks to **Kidspace** ⑧.

From this point, it's a short drive south on El Molino to California Boulevard, where a left turn will take you into San Marino and the **Huntington Library, Art Collections, and Botanical Gardens** ⑨ (follow the signs). Nearby is **El Molino Viejo** ⑩, an early 19th-century mill.

TIMING

Allow half a day for the entire driving tour. Get a late-morning or early afternoon start to see the important architectural sights, saving Old Pasadena for last. The latter has one of the best evening street scenes in southern California. Set aside at least two hours for the Norton Simon Museum and a half day for the Huntington Library, Art Collections, and Botanical Gardens—preferably a sunny day, when the gardens are most pleasant.

Sights to See

⑩ **El Molino Viejo.** Built in 1816 as a grist mill for the San Gabriel Mission, this is one of the last remaining examples in southern California of Spanish mission architecture. It's a restful place, with a flower-decked arbor and a tree-shaded garden. ⊠ *1120 Old Mill Rd., San Marino,* ☎ *626/449–5458.* 🎟 *Free.* ☉ *Tues.–Sun. 1–4.*

② **Fenyes House.** The 1905 mansion, now the **Pasadena Historical Museum**, has its original furniture and paintings on the main and second floors. Basement exhibits trace Pasadena's history. Well-landscaped gardens surround the house. ⊠ *470 W. Walnut St., Pasadena,* ☎ *626/577–1660.* 🎟 *$4.* ☉ *Thurs.–Sun. 1–4, 1-hr docent-led tour.*

★ ③ **Gamble House.** Architects Charles and Henry Greene built this spectacular 1908 Arts and Crafts–style bungalow. The term "bungalow" can be misleading—the Gamble House is a huge three-story home. To wealthy Easterners such as the Gambles (as in Procter & Gamble), this type of vacation home seemed informal compared with their accustomed mansions. Visitors swoon at the incredible amount of hand craftsmanship, including a teak staircase and cabinetry, Greene-designed furniture, and an Emil Lange glass door. To see more Greene and Greene homes in the neighborhood, buy a self-guided tour map in the bookstore. ⊠ *4 Westmoreland Pl., Pasadena,* ☎ *626/793–3334.* ☜ *$5.* ◷ *Thurs.–Sun. noon–3, 1-hr tour every 15–20 min.*

★ ❾ **Huntington Library, Art Collection and Botanical Gardens.** If you have time for only one stop in the Pasadena area, it should be San Marino, where railroad tycoon Henry E. Huntington built his hilltop home in the early 1900s. His estate is an extraordinary cultural complex. The library contains treasures like a Gutenberg Bible, the Ellesmere manuscript of Chaucer's *Canterbury Tales,* George Washington's genealogy in his own handwriting, and first editions by Ben Franklin and Shakespeare. The Huntington Gallery, housed in the original Georgian mansion Huntington built in 1911, holds a world-famous collection of British paintings, including the original *Blue Boy* by Gainsborough, *Pinkie,* by Thomas Lawrence, and the monumental *Sarah Siddons as the Tragic Muse* by Joshua Reynolds. American paintings (Mary Cassat, Frederic Remington, and more), and decorative arts are housed in the Virginia Steele Scott Gallery of American Art.

The awesome 150-acre Huntington Gardens include a 12-acre Desert Garden with the world's largest group of mature cacti and other succulents. The Japanese Garden contains traditional Japanese plants, stone ornaments, a drum bridge, a Japanese house, a bonsai court, and a Zen rock garden. Besides these gardens, there are collections of azaleas and 1,500 varieties of camellias. The 3-acre rose garden is displayed chronologically, so the development leading to today's strains of roses can be observed; also on the grounds is the **Rose Tea Garden Room,** where traditional high tea is served, and there are herb, palm, and jungle gardens. The Huntington Pavilion, a later addition to the property, has commanding views of the surrounding mountains and valleys. At the pavilion are displays, a bookstore, and information kiosks. A 1¼-hour guided tour of the gardens is led by docents at posted times, and inexpensive, self-guided tour leaflets are available in the entrance pavilion. ⊠ *1151 Oxford Rd., San Marino,* ☎ *626/405–2100.* ☜ *$8.50; free 1st Thurs. of month.* ◷ *Memorial Day–Labor Day, Tues.–Sun. 10:30–4:30; Labor Day–Memorial Day, Tues.–Fri. noon–4:30, weekends 10:30–4:30.*

☺ ❽ **Kidspace.** At this children's museum housed in the gymnasium of an elementary school, kids can direct a television or radio station; dress up in the real (and very heavy) uniforms of a firefighter, astronaut, or football player; or play in tunnels for exploring insect life first hand (don't worry, the bugs are fake). ⊠ *390 S. El Molino Ave., Pasadena,* ☎ *626/449–9143.* ☜ *$5.* ◷ *Sept.–July 1, Tues. 1:30–5, Wed.–Thurs. 1–5, Sat. 10–5, Sun. 1–5, hrs vary during school vacations.*

OFF THE
BEATEN PATH

MISSION SAN GABRIEL ARCHANGEL – In 1771 Father Junípero Serra dedicated this mission to the great archangel and messenger from God, St. Gabriel. As the founders approached the mission site, they were confronted by "savage" Native Americans. In the heat of battle, one of the padres revealed the canvas painting *Our Lady of Sorrows,* which so impressed the Indians that they laid down their bows and arrows. Within the next 50 years, the mission became the wealthiest of all California missions. Today, Mission San Gabriel Archangel's adobe walls preserve an era of history, and the magnificent cemetery stands witness to the many people who lived here. ⊠ *537 W. Mission Dr., San Gabriel,* ☎ *626/457–3048.* ☜ *$4.* ◷ *Daily 9:30–5.*

★ ❺ **Norton Simon Museum.** The Norton Simon is a tribute to the art acumen of an extremely wealthy businessman. In 1974, Simon reorganized the failing Pasadena Art Institute and assembled a respected collection that includes pivotal works by Rembrandt, Goya, Picasso, and most of all, Degas: This is one of the two U.S. institutions with a complete set of the artist's model bronzes (the other is the Metropolitan Museum of Art, in New York City). There are several Rodin sculptures throughout the museum. Rembrandt's development can be traced in three oils—*The Bearded Man in the Wide Brimmed Hat, Self Portrait,* and *Titus.* The most dramatic Goyas are two oils—*St. Jerome in Penitence* and the *Portrait of Dona Francisca Vicenta Chollet y Caballero.* Picasso's renowned *Woman with a Book* highlights a comprehensive collection of his paintings, drawings, and sculptures. The museum's collections of Impressionist work is extensive, and its Asian collection is one of the country's best. Early Renaissance, Baroque, and Rococo artwork includes church works by Raphael and Filippino Lippi, robust Rubens maidens and Dutch landscapes, and a magical Tiepolo ceiling. Frank Gehry designed a landscaped sculpture garden with a teahouse. ✉ *411 W. Colorado Blvd., Pasadena,* ☎ *626/449–6840.* ⌨ *$4.* ☾ *Thurs.–Sun. noon–6.*

❻ **Old Town Pasadena.** Once in decay, this area was revitalized in the 1990s. Brick buildings house bistros, restaurants, and boutiques. Old Town is bisected by Colorado Boulevard, which becomes thronged with people on New Year's Day to watch the Rose Parade.

NEED A
BREAK?

Walk down to Fair Oaks Avenue to seek out the **Market City Cafe** (✉ 33 S. Fair Oaks Ave., ☎ 626/568–0203), which you'll recognize by the life-size black-and-white cow in the window. Imaginative Italian fare, including food from the self-serve antipasto bar, brick-oven pizzas, and charbroiled fish, is served indoors and alfresco.

❼ **Pacific Asia Museum.** Designed in the style of a Chinese imperial palace, this elaborate building with a central garden is devoted to the arts and culture of Asia and the Pacific Islands. ✉ *46 N. Los Robles Ave.,* ☎ *626/449–2742.* ⌨ *$4; free 3rd Sat. of month.* ☾ *Wed.–Sun. 10–5.*

❹ **Rose Bowl.** This 100,000-seat stadium, host of many Super Bowls and the home field of the UCLA Bruins, is set at the bottom of a wide area of the arroyo in an older wealthy neighborhood. The stadium is closed except during games and special events such as the monthly Rose Bowl Swap Meet. Held on the second Sunday of the month, it is considered the granddaddy of West Coast flea markets. ✉ *Rosemont Ave., Pasadena,* ☎ *626/577–3100.* ☾ *Daily 9–5*

OFF THE
BEATEN PATH

SOUTHWEST MUSEUM – Readily spotted from the Pasadena Freeway (Highway 110), this huge Mission Revival building stands halfway up Mt. Washington. Inside is an extensive collection of Native American art and artifacts, with special emphasis on the people of the Plains, Northwest coast, Southwest coast, and California. The basket collection is outstanding. ✉ *234 Museum Dr., off Ave. 43 exit, Highland Park,* ☎ *323/221–2163.* ⌨ *$5.* ☾ *Tues.–Sun. 10–5*

❶ **Wrigley Mansion.** Chewing gum magnate William Wrigley Jr. purchased this white Italian Renaissance–style house in 1914. The headquarters for the Tournament of Roses Association, the house is open for tours on Thursday only. The gardens, with 1,500 varieties of roses, are open daily. ✉ *391 S. Orange Grove Blvd., Pasadena* ☎ *626/449–4100.* ☾ *House tours Feb.–Aug., Thurs. 2–4; gardens, daily sunrise–sunset.*

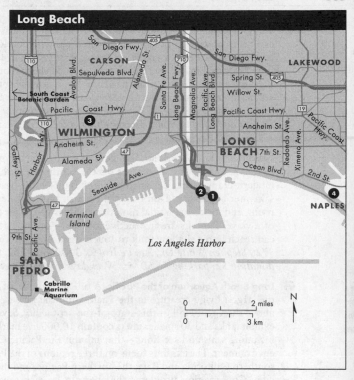

Long Beach

If you've planned a visit to the *Queen Mary* or an off-shore excursion to Catalina Island, you'll be headed to metropolitan Los Angeles's South Bay area and the port city of Long Beach. Wholly separate from the city of Los Angeles, Long Beach was a seaside resort in the 19th century. The city has tried to develop its waterfront with a convention center and most recently, the Long Beach Aquarium of the Pacific, which opened in 1998.

A Good Drive

Numbers in the text correspond to numbers in the margin and on the Long Beach map.

A Good Drive

From the Long Beach Freeway (I–710) or Pacific Coast Highway, follow signs leading to the **Queen Mary** ①. Then take the Queenaway Bridge back across the bay to the **Long Beach Aquarium of the Pacific** ②. Head back north up I–710 and west on Pacific Coast Highway to the **Banning Residence Museum and Park** ③. The scenic town of **Naples** ④ is east and south on Pacific Coast Highway.

TIMING

Guided tours of the *Queen Mary* last an hour, and the Long Beach Aquarium of the Pacific could occupy most of a morning or an afternoon. If you've planned well enough in advance, you could end the day with a sunset gondola cruise on the canals in Naples. Traffic in and out of Long Beach and the South Bay area during the rush hours keeps the Long Beach (710) and San Diego (405) freeways quite congested.

Sights to See

❸ Banning Residence Museum and Park. General Phineas Banning, an early entrepreneur in Los Angeles, is credited with developing the Los Angeles Harbor into a viable economic entity. Part of his estate has been preserved in a 20-acre park that's an excellent spot for a picnic. A 100-year-old wisteria, near the arbor, blooms in the spring. You can see the interior of the house on docent-led tours. ✉ *401 E. M St., Wilmington,* ☎ *310/548–7777.* ✑ *Suggested donation for house tours, $3.* ⊙ *Guided house tours Tues.–Thurs. 12:30, 1:30, 2:30, weekends 12:30–3:30 on the hr.*

Cabrillo Marine Aquarium. This gem of a small museum is dedicated to the marine life that flourishes off the southern California coast. A modern Frank-Gehry designed building right on the beach houses 35 saltwater aquariums. Don't miss the shark tank, whale and dolphin room, and see-through tidal tank that enables you to see the long view of a wave. Exhibits are instructive and fun—on the back patio, you can reach into a shallow tank to touch starfish and sea anemones. ✉ *3720 Stephen White Dr., San Pedro,* ☎ *310/548–7562.* ✑ *Suggested donation $2; parking $6.50 .* ⊙ *Weekdays noon–5, weekends 10–5.*

❷ Long Beach Aquarium of the Pacific. A full-scale model of a blue whale, the largest living creature in the Pacific and the planet, is suspended above the Great Hall of this state-of-the-art facility. Seventeen major exhibit tanks and 30 smaller tanks contain 10,000 live marine animals—including seals and sea lions—that inhabit the Pacific Ocean and its environment. The exhibits focus on three regions of the Pacific Ocean: southern California and Baja, the northern Pacific, and the tropical Pacific. Conservation problems that pertain to each area—pollution, over-harvesting, protecting coral reefs—are explained in detail. ✉ *100 Aquarium Dr.,* ☎ *562/590–3100.* ✑ *$13 adult, $6.50 children.* ⊙ *Daily 10–6.*

❹ Naples. In southern California's version of Venice, Italy, inaptly called Naples, the ancient art of gondola riding is all the rage. Actually three small islands in man-made Alamitos Bay, Naples is best experienced on foot. Park near Bay Shore Avenue and 2nd Street and walk across the bridge, where you can meander quaint streets with Italian names and eclectic architecture: vintage Victorians, Craftsman bungalows, and Mission Revivals. You may spy a real gondola or two on the canals. You can hire them for a ride, but not on the spur of the moment (reservations are best made a week ahead). **Gondola Getaway** offers one-hour rides, usually touted for romantic couples, though their gondolas can accommodate up to six people and serve bread, salami, and cheese—you bring the wine. ✉ *5437 E. Ocean Blvd.,* ☎ *562/433–9595.* ✑ *Rides $55 per couple, $10 each additional person.* ⊙ *Cruises 11 AM–midnight.*

★ ❶ Queen Mary. Be sure to get at least a glimpse of this huge passenger ship, now sitting snugly in Long Beach Harbor. The 80,000-ton *Queen Mary* was launched in 1934, a floating treasure of Art Deco splendor. It took a crew of 1,100 to tend to the needs of the ship's 1,900 passengers. The former first-class passenger quarters are now a hotel full of extensive wood paneling, gleaming nickel- and silver-plated handrails, and hand-cut glass. Stay late for fireworks on Saturday night in the summer. ✉ *Pier H,* ☎ *562/435–3511.* ✑ *$12, guided 1-hr tour $4 extra.* ⊙ *Tours daily 10–4:30, later in summer.*

OFF THE
BEATEN PATH

SOUTH COAST BOTANIC GARDEN– This Rancho Palos Verdes garden began life as a garbage dump-cum-landfill. With the intensive ministrations of the experts from the L.A. County Arboreta Department, the dump soon sprouted lush gardens, with all the plants eventually organized into color groups. Highlights on the self-guided walking tours include the Garden for the Senses, which is devoted to touching and smelling plants, and the Water-Wise garden, which showcases alternatives to grass lawns. The picnicking possibilities here are limited. ⊠ *26300 S. Crenshaw Blvd., south of Pacific Coast Hwy., Rancho Palos Verdes,* ☎ *310/544-6815.* ◻ *$5.* ⊙ *Daily 9-5.*

DINING

Revised and
Updated by
Bill Stern

Restaurants in Los Angeles reflect the city's reputation for culinary innovation and its ethnic diversity. Many of the country's star chefs are here—Wolfgang Puck, Joachim Splichal, Michel Richard—but so are many unheralded cooks who delight Angelenos daily with the cuisines of their native Shanghai, Oaxaca, Tuscany, and elsewhere. Whether you are looking for a traditionally elegant dinner, a culinary adventure, or just a really good burger, you can find them all here.

CATEGORY	COST*
$$$$	over $50
$$$	$30–$50
$$	$20–$30
$	under $20

*per person for a three-course meal, excluding drinks, service, and 8¼% tax

Beverly Hills, Hollywood and West Hollywood

Beverly Hills

AMERICAN

$$–$$$ ✕ **Grill on the Alley.** The simple American fare served at this fashionable spot for power lunching includes great steaks, fresh seafood, chicken potpies, and crab cakes. Repeat customers rave about the creamy Cobb salad and homemade rice pudding. ⊠ *9560 Dayton Way,* ☎ *310/276-0615. Reservations essential. AE, DC, MC, V. No lunch Sun. Valet parking evenings.*

CONTEMPORARY

$$–$$$$ ✕ **Dining Room.** Murals depicting 18th-century garden scenes cover
★ the paneled walls of this European-style salon whose menu includes loin of Colorado lamb accompanied by eggplant and sweet-pepper lasagna. Adjoining the Dining Room is a sophisticated cocktail lounge, with romantic lighting and a pianist playing show tunes. ⊠ *Regent Beverly Wilshire Hotel, 9500 Wilshire Blvd.,* ☎ *310/275-5200. Jacket and tie. AE, D, DC, MC, V. Valet parking.*

$$–$$$$ ✕ **Spago Beverly Hills.** Wolfgang Puck's Beverly Hills restaurant is more formal than the original Spago in West Hollywood. Selections change daily, but look for the warm crayfish salad with mustard potatoes and chino beets, a splendid appetizer. For something different, try a Puck childhood favorite such as *rindsgulasch mit spatzle,* Austrian beef stew made with sweet onions and served on a bed of Austrian pasta. Don't miss the sorbet soup for dessert. ⊠ *176 N. Canon Dr.,* ☎ *310/385-0880. Reservations essential. AE, D, DC, MC, V. No lunch Sun.*

$$–$$$ ✕ **Nouveau Café Blanc.** One of Beverly Hills' unexpected treats serves lunchtime entrées—such as the sautéed salmon with basil vinaigrette and the lobster ravioli with vin-blanc cream sauce—that cost as little as $10. Four- and five-course prix-fixe dinners, $33 and $43, have included saffron-marinated scallops, jasmine-tea–smoked squab, lobster risotto, and roasted lamb steak with ratatouille sauce. ⊠ *9777 Little Santa Monica Blvd.,* ☎ *310/888-0108. Reservations essential. AE, D, MC, V. Closed Sun., Mon.*

Beverly Hills, Hollywood, and West Hollywood Dining and Lodging

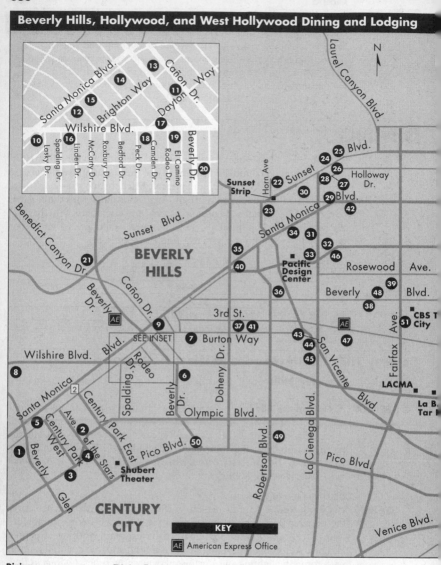

KEY

AE American Express Office

Dining

Arnie Morton's of Chicago, **44**
Authentic Cafe, **75**
Barney Greengrass, **18**
Bistro K, **20**
Boxer, **74**
Ca'Brea, **76**
Campanile, **77**
Canter's, **39**
Cava, **47**
Chan Dara, **69**
Citrus, **52**
Da Pasquale, **15**

Dining Room, **19**
Dive!, **5**
Drai's **32**
East India Grill, **73**
El Cholo, **67**
Fenix, **26**
Grill on the Alley, **17**
Gumbo Pot, **51**
Harry's Bar & American Grill, **2**
Hollywood Canteen, **66**
Hollywood Hills Coffee Shop, **57**

Ita-Cho, **60**
Jozu, **46**
La Cachette, **1**
Le Colonial, **36**
Le Dôme, **30**
Les Deux Cafés, **59**
Locanda Veneta, **41**
L'Orangerie, **31**
The Mandarin, **14**
Matsuhisa, **45**
Mimosa, **48**
Miss Gregory's American Kitchen, **42**
Nate 'n' Al's, **13**
Nouveau Café Blanc, **12**

The Palm, **35**
Patina, **68**
Pinot Hollywood, **61**
Restaurant Katsu, **64**
Roscoe's House of Chicken 'n' Waffles, **62**
Spago, **22**
Spago Beverly Hills, **11**
Swingers, **38**
Tavola Calda, **70**
Tommy Tang's, **71**
Trattoria Farfalla, **63**
Uzbekistan, **58**
Vida, **65**

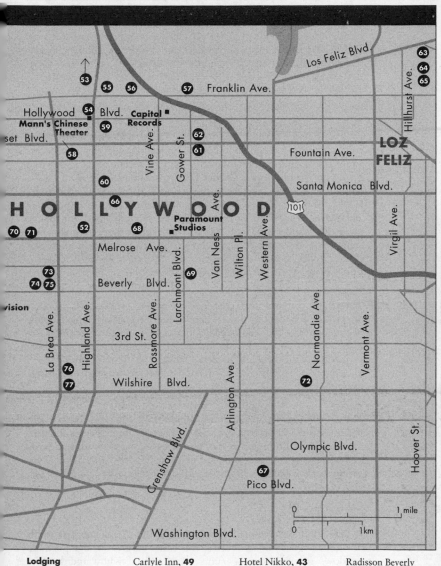

On the map: Los Feliz Blvd., Franklin Ave., Hollywood Blvd., Capital Records, Mann's Chinese Theater, Sunset Blvd., Vine Ave., Gower St., Fountain Ave., LOZ FELIZ, Santa Monica Blvd., HOLLYWOOD, Paramount Studios, Melrose Ave., Van Ness Ave., Wilton Pl., Western Ave., Virgil Ave., Beverly Blvd., Larchmont Blvd., Rossmore Ave., 3rd St., La Brea Ave., Highland Ave., Normandie Ave., Vermont Ave., Wilshire Blvd., Arlington Ave., Hoover St., Crenshaw Blvd., Olympic Blvd., Pico Blvd., Washington Blvd., Hillhurst Ave.

Scale: 0 – 1 mile; 0 – 1km

Lodging

The Argyle, **26**

Banana Bungalow
Hotel and International
Hostel, **53**

Beverly Hills
Hotel, **21**

Beverly Hills Inn, **16**

Beverly Hills Plaza
Hotel, **8**

Beverly Prescott
Hotel, **50**

Beverly Terrace
Hotel, **40**

Carlyle Inn, **49**

Century City
Courtyard by
Marriott, **3**

Chateau Marmont
Hotel, **25**

Crescent Hotel, **9**

Four Seasons Los
Angeles at Beverly
Hills, **37**

Highland Gardens
Hotel, **55**

Hollywood Holiday
Inn, **54**

Hotel Nikko, **43**

Hyatt West
Hollywood on Sunset
Boulevard, **24**

Le Parc Hotel, **33**

L'Ermitage, **7**

Magic Hotel, **56**

Mondrian, **28**

Park Hyatt, **4**

Park Sunset Hotel, **27**

Peninsula Beverly
Hills, **10**

Radisson Beverly
Pavilion Hotel, **6**

Radisson Wilshire
Plaza Hotel, **72**

Ramada West
Hollywood, **34**

Regent Beverly
Wilshire, **19**

Summerfield Suites
Hotel, **29**

Wyndham Bel Age
Hotel, **23**

CHINESE

$–$$ ✕ **The Mandarin.** The serene, traditional Mandarin serves Szechuan and Chinese country dishes. Minced chicken wrapped in lettuce leaves, Peking duck (order ahead of time), beggar's chicken, scallion pancakes, and several noodle dishes are among the specialties. ✉ *430 N. Camden Dr.,* ☎ *310/859–0926. Reservations essential. AE, DC, MC, V. No lunch weekends. Valet parking evenings.*

DELI

$$–$$$ ✕ **Barney Greengrass.** The delicious high-concept deli fare at the
★ eatery inside the Barneys department store includes Portobello mushrooms, roasted peppers, and arugula on sourdough. Expect flawless smoked salmon, sturgeon, and cod—with or without bagels, flown in fresh from the Big Apple. The deli keeps store hours, closing on Thursday at 8, Sunday at 6, and every other day at 7. ✉ *Barneys, 9570 Wilshire Blvd., ,* ☎ *310/777–5877. AE, MC, V. Valet parking.*

$ ✕ **Nate 'n' Al's.** A famous gathering place for Hollywood comedians, gag writers, and their agents, Nate 'n' Al's serves first-rate matzo-ball soup, lox and scrambled eggs, cheese blintzes, potato pancakes, and deli sandwiches. ✉ *414 N. Beverly Dr.,* ☎ *310/274–0101. Reservations not accepted. AE, MC, V. Free parking.*

FRENCH

$$–$$$ ✕ **Bistro K.** Brittany-born chef Lionel Deniaud produces flavors that are clear and uncomplicated: There's a simple but delectable triangle of tuna, pink grapefruit, green peppercorns, and broccoli rabe; a delicious seared swordfish with lemon, garlic, and spinach; and bistro favorites like roast beef in burgundy sauce with pommes frîtes. ✉ *267 S. Beverly Dr.,* ☎ *310/276–1558. AE, DC, MC, V. No lunch Sun. Meter parking.*

ITALIAN

$$ ✕ **Da Pasquale.** The pizza at affordable Da Pasquale is topped with ingredients like fresh tomato, garlic, and basil or three cheeses and prosciutto. The skillful kitchen staff also does a good job with standards such as antipasti, pastas, and roast chicken. ✉ *9749 Little Santa Monica Blvd.,* ☎ *310/859–3884. AE, MC, V. Closed Sun. No lunch Sat. Free parking.*

Century City

AMERICAN/CASUAL

$–$$ ✕ **Dive!** This Steven Spielberg creation is as much a theme park (with lines that can be long) as a restaurant. Water gurgles through porthole windows, fish swim by on giant screens, and every now and then the whole place makes a simulated submarine dive. In keeping with the theme, the kitchen's specialty is submarine sandwiches. Good ones include the Parisian chicken sub and the brick oven–baked Tuscan steak sub. The desserts are rich and delicious. ✉ *10250 Santa Monica Blvd.,* ☎ *310/788–3483. AE, D, DC, MC, V. Valet parking or free self-parking.*

FRENCH

$$–$$$ ✕ **La Cachette.** Owner-chef Jean-Francois Meteigner replaces butter-
★ rich French fare with lighter, more modern French cuisine. L.A.'s fortysomething crowd dresses up (by L.A. standards) to see and be seen at this flower-filled restaurant hidden on an undistinguished stretch of Little Santa Monica Boulevard. ✉ *10506 Little Santa Monica Blvd.,* ☎ *310/470–4992. Reservations essential. AE, MC, V. No lunch weekends. Valet parking.*

ITALIAN

$$–$$$ ✕ **Harry's Bar & American Grill.** The decor and selection of dishes—paper-thin carpaccio, grilled fish, and excellent pastas—are acknowledged copies of Harry's Bar in Venice, but the check will be far lower than it would be in Italy. ⊠ *2020 Ave. of the Stars,* ☎ *310/277–2333. Reservations essential. AE, DC, MC, V. No lunch weekends. Valet parking.*

Hollywood

AMERICAN

$–$$ ✕ **Miss Gregory's American Kitchen.** Country quilts set the mood at this aptly named restaurant that serves Rhode Island clam fritters, barbecued lamb steak, catfish with a lemon-walnut crust, and other American faves. A hit at Sunday brunch are the flannel cakes topped with caramelized apples or strawberries and cream. ⊠ *7986 Sunset Blvd.,* ☎ *323/822–9057. AE, MC, V. Closed Mon. No lunch Sat.*

AMERICAN/CASUAL

$$ ✕ **Hollywood Hills Coffee Shop.** The food at this modestly named eatery is surprisingly good. Among the breakfast items are corned-beef hash, huevos rancheros, and whole grilled salmon trout with eggs and red salsa. For dinner, there are vegetarian choices as well as fish and meat entrées. ⊠ *6145 Franklin Ave.,* ☎ *323/467–7678. Reservations not accepted. MC, V.*

$–$$ ✕ **Hollywood Canteen.** In the heart of working Hollywood, near soundstages, recording studios, and lighting companies, this handsome diner functions as a canteen for executives, actors, and technicians, who come here for simple but upscale grub: organic field-green salads, burgers, risotto with wild mushrooms, and various soups. ⊠ *1006 Seward St.,* ☎ *323/465–0961. AE, MC, V. Closed Sun. No lunch Sat. Valet parking.*

CAJUN/CREOLE

$ ✕ **Gumbo Pot.** Though not exactly down by the levee, this outdoor Cajun–Creole café in the Farmers Market serves a mean smoky and spicy gumbo rich in shrimp and chicken. It's also the place for *mufalatas* (hero sandwiches), corn-battered shrimp, jambalaya, and *beignets* (deep-fried pastry squares). ⊠ *Farmers Market, 6333 W. 3rd St.,* ☎ *323/933–0358. Reservations not accepted. MC, V.*

CONTEMPORARY

$$$$ ✕ **Patina.** The exterior of Joachim Splichal's flagship restaurant is so
★ understated that it's easy to miss, and the interior is a study in spare elegance. Among the mainstays are a corn blini filled with fennel-marinated salmon and crème fraîche, and scallops wrapped in potato slices with brown-butter vinaigrette. ⊠ *5955 Melrose Ave.,* ☎ *323/467–1108. Reservations essential. AE, D, DC, MC, V. No lunch Wed.–Mon. Valet parking.*

$$$–$$$$ ✕ **Citrus.** Lunch at chef Michel Richard's restaurant begins on the light
★ side, with starters such as an artichoke terrine or a shiitake-mushroom-and-garlic Napoleon, followed by sautéed Chilean sea bass or medium-rare *onglet* (hangar steak). The dinner menu has included crab cakes with tomato-mustard sauce, salmon with asparagus crust, and roast duck with apple fries and fig sauce. ⊠ *6703 Melrose Ave.,* ☎ *323/857–0034. Reservations essential. AE, MC, V. Closed Sun. Valet parking.*

$$–$$$ ✕ **Pinot Hollywood.** With an outdoor terrace, a martini bar, and a lounge in addition to the main dining room, this is a comfortable venue. Lunch entrées, which range in price from $13 to $16, include salad Niçoise with grilled ahi tuna and the grilled lamb sandwich with ratatouille and goat cheese. For dinner you might find a caramelized onion tart with marinated salmon or a breaded pork tenderloin with mustard greens and plum sauce. ⊠ *1448 N. Gower St.,* ☎ *323/461–8800. Reservations essential. AE, D, DC, MC, V. No lunch Sat. Closed Sun. Valet parking.*

FRENCH

$–$$$ ✕ **Les Deux Cafés.** The setting for Les Deux is a handsomely refitted 1904 house set, peculiarly enough, in a parking lot behind a barbed-wire-topped wall. Chef David Winn appeals to even the most jaded palates with lobster-and-tabbouleh salad, crayfish gratin, and a salad of beets, spinach, and horseradish; he also turns out splendid skate sautéed in brown butter and superb braised chicken in a bouillabaisse of fennel, onions, tomato, and saffron. ✉ *1683 Las Palmas Ave.,* ☎ *213/465–0509. Reservations essential. No lunch Sat., Sun. No dinner Sun. AE, MC, V. Valet parking.*

INDIAN

$ ✕ **East India Grill.** With a high-tech aesthetic, zesty food, and courteous service, this indoor-outdoor café is a winner. Traditional dishes such as green-coconut curries, *makhani tikka masalas* (tomato-based curries), and *sagwalas* (spinach dishes) are prepared as distinctively as the Californian-influenced novelties—tandoori chicken salad, mango ribs, and garlic-basil nan, to name a few. ✉ *345 N. La Brea Ave.,* ☎ *323/ 936–8844. AE, MC, V. Garage parking.*

JAPANESE

$$ ✕ **Ita-Cho.** Specializing in the delicate Japanese pub cuisine known as *koryori-ya,* this small dining room also serves flawless sashimi (but no sushi). Among the dishes are tender pork simmered for two days in sake and soy, lightly fried tofu cubes in soy-ginger-scallion sauce, and yellowtail braised with teriyaki. ✉ *6775 Santa Monica Blvd.,* ☎ *323/871–0236. Reservations essential. AE, MC, V. Closed Sun. Valet parking.*

MEXICAN

$–$$ ✕ **El Cholo.** The progenitor of a chain, this landmark south of Holly-
★ wood has been packing folks in since the '20s. First-rate L.A.-Mex standards are served here—chicken enchiladas, carnitas, and, from July to October, green-corn tamales. Friendly and fun, El Cholo churns out large portions for a reasonable number of pesos. ✉ *1121 S. Western Ave.,* ☎ *323/734–2773. AE, DC, MC, V. Valet and meter parking.*

RUSSIAN

$–$$ ✕ **Uzbekistan.** Brightly colored murals lend a fittingly folksy air to this restaurant, which serves a mix of Russian and Central Asian cuisine. Start with any of the meat dumplings, followed by a eggplant sautéed with tomatoes and garlic or any of the lamb dishes. ✉ *7077 Sunset Blvd.,* ☎ *323/464–3663. MC, V.*

SOUL

$ ✕ **Roscoe's House of Chicken 'n' Waffles.** The name of this casual eatery may not sound appetizing, but don't be fooled: This is *the* place for down-home, bargain-price southern cooking. ✉ *1514 N. Gower St.,* ☎ *323/466–9329. Reservations not accepted. AE, D, DC, MC, V.*

THAI

$–$$ ✕ **Chan Dara.** Try any of the noodle dishes, especially those with crab and shrimp, at this rambling restaurant that lures the rock-music and showbiz crowds. Also on the extensive menu are *satay* (appetizers on skewers), barbecued chicken, and catfish. ✉ *310 N. Larchmont Blvd.,* ☎ *323/467–1052. AE, D, DC, MC, V. No lunch weekends.*

Los Feliz

ECLECTIC

$–$$ ✕ **Vida.** Chef-owner Fred Eric's quirky cuisine is anything but predictable—and loaded with cute-as-a-cactus-button puns ("Okra Winfrey" gumbo; spicy Ty Cobb salad complete with duck confit cut into perfect squares). The hip-to-the-hilt dining room, heavy on bamboo, skylights, and shoji screens, is in a converted 1920s bungalow. ⊠ *1930 N. Hillhurst Ave.,* ☎ *323/660–4446. AE, DC, MC, V. No lunch. Valet parking.*

ITALIAN

$$ ✕ **Trattoria Farfalla.** The daily specials at this brick-walled trattoria are always good, but regulars tend to order the Caesar salad on a pizza-crust bed, the roasted free-range chicken, and the pasta alla Norma (studded with rich, smoky eggplant). ⊠ *1978 N. Hillhurst Ave.,* ☎ *323/ 661–7365. AE, DC, MC, V. No lunch weekends. Street parking.*

JAPANESE

$–$$$ ✕ **Restaurant Katsu.** Exquisitely presented, high-quality sushi is served
★ in this stark, peaceful sushi bar, in addition to other Japanese special-ties. At under $10, the tempura and teriyaki lunches are a good value. For dinner try the "dynamite" *yadokari* (a casserole made with scal-lops and white sauce), or grilled fish or beef. ⊠ *1972 N. Hillhurst Ave.,* ☎ *323/665–1891. Reservations essential. AE, DC, MC, V. Closed Sun. No lunch Sat. Valet parking.*

West Hollywood

AMERICAN/CASUAL

$ ✕ **Swingers.** Everyone from power lunchers to neopunk posers heads to this all-day, late-night coffee shop, so be prepared for a wait. Loud alternative music plays to the Gen-X crowd, and a casual menu—break-fast burritos, hamburgers, ostrich burgers, and chicken breast sand-wiches on fresh French bread—appeals to the pocketbook. ⊠ *8020 Beverly Blvd.,* ☎ *323/653–5858. AE, D, MC, V. Meter parking.*

CONTEMPORARY

$$$–$$$$ ✕ **Campanile.** Portofino meets Hollywood head-on in this stone-walled
★ restaurant that was once Charlie Chaplin's office complex. Distinguished appetizers include the celery-root soup with pesto and the grilled sar-dines with marinated fennel. Entrées include the bourride of snapper and Manila clams and the pork loin with sweet potatoes and turnip greens. The desserts are among the best in town. ⊠ *624 S. La Brea Ave.,* ☎ *323/938–1447. Reservations essential. AE, D, DC, MC, V. No dinner Sun. Valet parking.*

$$$–$$$$ ✕ **Fenix.** At Fenix you'll dine in Art Deco splendor on chef Ken Frank's renowned rösti potatoes with golden caviar; other signature dishes in-clude porcini-dusted scallops with a tomato-saffron sauce, and grilled Texas antelope with foie gras sauce. You may spot some Asian influ-ences, like the honey duck salad with mango and seared foie gras, on the Franco-Californian menu. Sunday dining is restricted to poolside. ⊠ *8358 Sunset Blvd.,* ☎ *323/848–6677. Reservations essential. AE, D, DC, MC, V. Valet parking.*

$$–$$$ ✕ **Boxer.** Chef Michael Plapp presents a seasonal menu with French influences. Start with a crab-and-prosciutto salad or a rich roasted veg-etable soup made without cream or butter, and follow with couscous and rock shrimp, striped bass in cardamom broth, or lamb shanks slow-cooked in red wine. The owners have no wine license, but you can buy your own bottle from the shop next door. ⊠ *7615 Beverly Blvd.,* ☎ *323/932–6178. AE, MC, V. Closed Sun. Valet parking.*

$$–$$$ ✕ **Jozu.** Executive chef Suzanne Tracht's Cal-Asian menu includes starters like the crisp Sonoma quail with tangerine glaze and the mus-sels with saffron-coconut broth. For an entrée, consider the grilled Maine scallops with Thai-rolled pasta or the grilled chicken marinated with a kefir-lime leaf on sticky rice. ⊠ *8360 Melrose Ave.,* ☎ *, 323/655–5600. AE, DC, MC, V. No lunch. Valet parking.*

$$-$$$ ✕ **Spago.** This is the restaurant that propelled chef-owner Wolfgang Puck into the international culinary spotlight. Among the standouts are the roasted cumin lamb on lentil salad with fresh coriander and yogurt chutney, the fresh oysters with green chili and black-pepper mignonette, and the grilled Alaskan baby salmon. ⊠ *1114 Horn Ave.,* ☎ *310/652–4025. Reservations essential. D, DC, MC, V. No lunch. Closed Mon. Valet parking.*

DELI

$ ✕ **Canter's.** The granddaddy of Los Angeles delicatessens (it opened in 1928) pickles its own corned-beef pastrami and has its own in-house bakery. ⊠ *419 N. Fairfax Ave.,* ☎ *323/651–2030. Reservations not accepted. MC, V. Parking in lot.*

FRENCH

$$$$ ✕ **L'Orangerie.** White flower arrangements and oils depicting Euro-
★ pean castles set an appropriately regal mood in this rococo dining room. The French Mediterranean specialties served here include coddled eggs served in the shell and topped with caviar, the duck with foie gras, and John Dory with roasted figs. A jug of double cream accompanies the rich apple tart. ⊠ *903 N. La Cienega Blvd.,* ☎ *310/652–9770. Reservations essential. AE, D, DC, MC, V. Closed Mon. No lunch. Valet parking.*

$$$–$$$$ ✕ **Drai's.** Rolls-Royce and Range Rover owners parade through Victor Drai's see-and-be-seen restaurant, where chef Claude Segal serves up Mediterranean-influenced French-bistro fare. Consider the leg of lamb, cooked for seven hours in its own juices, or standards like osso buco and beef bourguignonne. ⊠ *730 N. La Cienega Blvd.,* ☎ *310/ 358–8585. Closed Sun. No lunch. AE, DC, MC, V. Valet parking.*

$$$–$$$$ ✕ **Le Dôme.** This showbiz bistro dishes up French-country favorites and hearty American fare: escargots Burgundy style (served with garlic, shallots, and parsley), coq au vin, and steamed pig's knuckle appeal to Francophiles, and center-cut pork chops and grilled Sonoma lamb chops satisfy Yankees. ⊠ *8720 Sunset Blvd.,* ☎ *310/659–6919. Reservations essential. AE, MC, V. Closed Sun. No lunch Sat. Valet parking.*

$$–$$$ ✕ **Mimosa.** "No truffles, no caviar, no bizarre concoctions, simply our interpretation of French regional cuisine with a touch of Italy," says chef Jean-Pierre Bosc of his bistro's menu. The starters include the Lyonnaise salad, the pizzalike wood-fired onion tart, and the hearty chicken terrine with onion marmalade. Among the entrées of note are the bouillabaisse, the whole snapper à la Provençale, and the roasted pork with prunes and red cabbage. ⊠ *8009 Beverly Blvd.,* ☎ *213/655– 8895. No lunch Sat., Sun., no dinner Sun. AE, MC, V. Valet parking.*

ITALIAN

$$ ✕ **Ca'Brea.** Chef Antonio Tommasi turns out lamb chops with black-
★ truffle and mustard sauce, whole boneless chicken marinated and grilled with herbs, and a very popular osso buco. Starters make the meal—try baked goat cheese wrapped in pancetta and served atop a Popeye-size mound of spinach. ⊠ *346 S. La Brea Ave.,* ☎ *323/938– 2863. AE, D, DC, MC, V. Closed Sun. No lunch weekends.*

$$ ✕ **Locanda Veneta.** This up-market Italian trattoria has an open kitchen, terra-cotta walls, and stone floors. Specialties include flattened grilled chicken, veal chops, linguine with clams, lobster ravioli with saffron sauce, and an unusual apple tart with polenta crust and caramel sauce. ⊠ *8638 W. 3rd St.,* ☎ *310/274–1893. Reservations essential. AE, D, DC, MC, V. Closed Sun. No lunch Sat. Valet parking.*

$ ╳ **Tavola Calda.** With many entrées under $10, this low-tech Italian favorite draws budget-watchers. Best bets on the limited menu are the gourmet pizzas and the seafood and porcini risottos. ⊠ *7371 Melrose Ave.,* ☎ *323/658–6340. AE, DC, MC, V. Valet parking.*

JAPANESE

$$$–$$$$ ╳ **Matsuhisa.** Chef Nobu Matsuhisa creatively incorporates into his
★ signature dishes flavors he discovered while in Peru. Consider his caviar-capped tuna stuffed with black truffles or the sea urchin wrapped in a *shiso* leaf. The tempuras here are as light as can be, and the sushi is top-notch, fresh, and authentic. ⊠ *129 N. La Cienega Blvd.,* ☎ *310/ 659–9639. Reservations essential. AE, DC, MC, V. Valet parking.*

SOUTHWESTERN

$–$$ ╳ **Authentic Cafe.** The Gen-X crowd can't get enough of the Santa Fe salad, wood-grilled chicken with mole, chicken casserole with cornbread crust, and excellent vegetarian dishes served here: You'll have to wait at peak hours, but the reward is high-quality, sun-drenched cooking at reasonable prices. Breakfast is served on weekends. ⊠ *7605 Beverly Blvd.,* ☎ *323/939–4626. Reservations not accepted. MC, V.*

SPANISH

$$–$$$ ╳ **Cava.** At this trendy establishment you can graze on tapas like baked artichoke topped with bread crumbs and tomato or a fluffy potato omelet served with crème fraîche. Of the entrées the paella is a must, but you may also want to try *zarzuela* (lightly baked shrimp, scallops, clams, mussels, and fresh fish in a hearty tomato wine sauce) or *bistec flamenco* (aged New York steak with caramelized onions and a traditional Argentine steak sauce). ⊠ *8384 W. 3rd St.,* ☎ *323/658–8898. AE, D, DC, MC, V. Valet parking.*

STEAK

$$$–$$$$ ╳ **Arnie Morton's of Chicago.** In addition to a 24-ounce porterhouse, a New York strip, and a double-cut filet mignon, this place lays out giant veal and lamb chops, thick cuts of prime rib, swordfish steaks, and imported lobsters. ⊠ *435 S. La Cienega Blvd.,* ☎ *310/246–1501. AE, DC, MC, V. No lunch.*

$$$–$$$$ ╳ **The Palm.** At this West Coast replay of the famous Manhattan steak house you'll find huge lobsters, good steaks, prime rib, chops, French-fried onion rings, and paper-thin potato slices. ⊠ *9001 Santa Monica Blvd.,* ☎ *310/550–8811. AE, DC, MC, V. Reservations essential. No lunch weekends. Valet parking.*

THAI

$–$$ ╳ **Tommy Tang's.** A lot of people-watching goes on at this grazing ground for yuppies and celebs. Portions are on the small side but decidedly innovative. The kitchen turns out a crisp duck marinated in ginger and plum sauce, blackened sea scallops, and a low-calorie spinach salad tossed with grilled chicken. ⊠ *7313 Melrose Ave.,* ☎ *323/937–5733. AE, DC, MC, V. Valet parking.*

VIETNAMESE

$$–$$$ ╳ **Le Colonial.** Like the original Le Colonial in Manhattan, this is a bilevel restaurant with an opulent bar upstairs, and below, a seductive dining room serving dishes such as roasted chicken with lemongrass; fried spring rolls packed with pork, mushrooms, and shrimp; and shredded chicken and cabbage doused in lime juice. ⊠ *8783 Beverly Blvd.,* ☎ *310/289–0660. AE, DC, MC, V. No lunch weekends. Valet parking.*

Coastal and Western Los Angeles

Bel Air

CONTEMPORARY

\$\$\$–\$\$\$\$ ✕ **Hotel Bel-Air.** Chef Peter Roelant, a graduate of L'Orangerie, wows
★ diners with eclectic starters such as grilled asparagus with prosciutto,
figs, and chived sour cream. Among the entrées, the duck glazed with
sour cherries, the venison with port and poached pear, and the halibut
with a vodka-lime mousseline are exceptional. The Hotel Bel-Air hosts
one of the best high teas in town. ⊠ *701 Stone Canyon Rd.,* ☎ *310/
472–1211. Reservations essential. Jacket and tie. AE, DC, MC, V. Valet
parking.*

Brentwood

CONTEMPORARY

\$\$\$ ✕ **Vincenti.** Revolving on the mammoth rotisserie in this handsome
restaurant's open kitchen are the mouth-watering meats for which chef
Gino Angelini is known. You can order a platter of the day's meats
carved to order or whole spit-roasted fish served with sauces made with
beets, artichokes, and other unexpected ingredients. Fried calamari and
pastas like the pumpkin-squash lasagnette with asparagus-and-sage sauce
are among Angelini's creative takes on traditional Italian fare. ⊠
11930 San Vicente Blvd., ☎ *310/207–0127. Reservations essential.
No lunch Sat.–Thurs. No dinner Sun.*

Malibu

ITALIAN

\$\$–\$\$\$ ✕ **Tra di Noi.** Regular customers—film celebrities and nonshowbiz
folk alike—love the unpretentious atmosphere of this simple restaurant that's a great place to bring kids. Nothing fancy or *nuovo* on the
menu, just great lasagna, freshly made pasta, mushroom and veal
dishes, and crisp fresh salads. An Italian buffet is laid out for Sunday
brunch. ⊠ *3835 Cross Creek Rd.,* ☎ *310/456–0169. AE, MC, V.*

CONTEMPORARY

\$\$\$–\$\$\$\$ ✕ **Granita.** At Wolfgang Puck's beachside Granita, the menu favors
seafood items such as grilled Atlantic salmon in lemongrass broth
with seared carrots and wild mushrooms. But standard Puck favorites
are also available: peppered shrimp pizza with sun-dried tomatoes
and herb pesto, roasted Cantonese duck with dried-fruit chutney, and
sautéed foie gras with ginger–port-wine glaze. Brunch is served on weekends. ⊠ *23725 W. Malibu Rd.,* ☎ *310/456–0488. Reservations essential. D, DC, MC, V. No lunch weekdays.*

Pacific Palisades

AMERICAN/CASUAL

\$\$\$–\$\$\$\$ ✕ **Gladstone's 4 Fish.** The most popular restaurant along southern Cal-
ifornia's coast serves more than a million beachgoers every year. The
food is notable mostly for its Brobdingnagian portions: giant bowls of
crab chowder, mounds of steamed clams, three-egg omelets, heaps of
barbecued ribs, and the famous mile-high chocolate cake, which can
easily feed a small regiment. The real reason to visit Gladstone's is the
glorious vista of sea, sky, and beach. ⊠ *17300 Pacific Coast Hwy., at
Sunset Blvd.,* ☎ *310/454–3474. AE, D, DC, MC, V. Valet parking.*

Santa Monica

AMERICAN/CASUAL

\$–\$\$ ✕ **Broadway Deli.** This joint venture of Michel Richard and Bruce
★ Marder is a cross between a European brasserie and an upscale diner.
Whatever you feel like eating, you'll probably find it on the menu—
smoked fish, Caesar salad, shepherd's pie, carpaccio, or broiled salmon
with creamed spinach. ⊠ *1457 3rd St. Promenade,* ☎ *310/451–0616.*

Dining

Bombay Cafe, **9**
Border Grill, **15**
Broadway Deli, **19**
Chinois on Main, **27**
Drago, **7**
Gilliland's, **26**
Gladstone's 4 Fish, **2**
Granita, **1**
Hotel Bel-Air, **5**
JiRaffe, **12**
La Serenata
Gourmet, **30**
Lavande, **21**
Ocean Avenue
Seafood, **22**
Tra di Noi, **3**
U-Zen, **10**
Valentino, **23**
Vincenti, **6**

Lodging

Barnabey's Hotel, **34**
Best Western Ocean
View Hotel, **18**
Best Western Royal
Palace Inn &
Suites, **29**
Century Wilshire
Hotel, **13**
Continental Plaza Los
Angeles Aiport, **38**
Furama Hotel Los
Angeles, **36**
Holiday Inn LAX, **39**
Hotel Bel-Air, **5**
Hotel Carmel, **20**
Hotel del Capri, **11**
Hotel Oceana, **16**
Loews Santa Monica
Beach Hotel, **21**
Marina Beach
Marriott, **33**
Marina International
Hotel and
Bungalows, **32**
Marina Pacific Hotel
& Suites, **28**
Miramar Sheraton, **17**
Pacific Shore, **24**
Ritz-Carlton, Marina
del Rey, **31**
Shutters on
the Beach, **25**
Summerfield Suites, **35**
Summit Hotel
Bel Air, **4**
Westin LAX, **40**
Westwood Marquis
Hotel and Gardens, **12**
Wyndham Hotel at Los
Angeles Airport, **37**

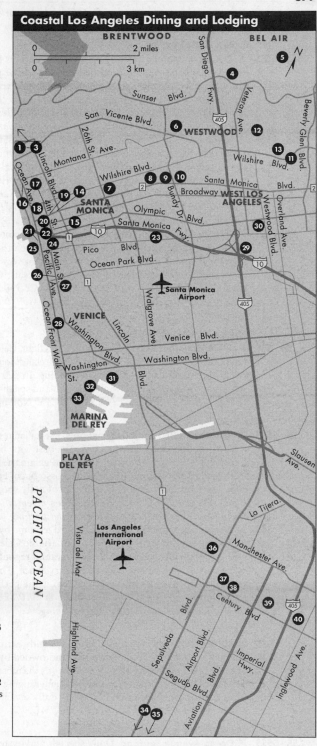

Coastal Los Angeles Dining and Lodging

Reservations not accepted. AE, MC, V. Valet parking weekends and evenings.

CONTEMPORARY

$$$–$$$$ ✕ **Chinois on Main.** The jazzy interior at Chinois is as loud as the clien-
★ tele, which feast on seasonal dishes such as the grilled Mongolian lamb chops with cilantro vinaigrette and wok-fried vegetables, the Shang-hai lobster with spicy ginger–curry sauce, and the rare duck with plum sauce. ✉ *2709 Main St.,* ☎ *310/392–9025. Reservations essential. AE, D, DC, MC, V. No lunch Sat.–Tues. Valet parking.*

$$$–$$$$ ✕ **Lavande.** Chef Alain Giraud, formerly of Citrus, prepares boldly fla-vored dishes like striped bass with fennel and Pernod sauce, fish soup Provençale with garlic croutons and rouille, and veal stew with red wine and green and black olives. For dessert, the vacherin with lavender ice cream and strawberries is a must. ✉ *Loews Santa Monica Beach Hotel, 1700 Ocean Ave.,* ☎ *310/576–3181. AE, D, DC, MC, V. No dinner Sun. Valet parking.*

$$–$$$ ✕ **JiRaffe.** The menu at this wood-panel restaurant is as tasteful as the decor. The pastas, such as butternut squash agnolotti with brown-butter sage sauce and squash chips, are an excellent way to kick off a meal of roasted Chilean sea bass with a ragout of salsify, chanterelles, and pearl onions. ✉ *502 Santa Monica Blvd.,* ☎ *310/917–6671. Reser-vations essential. AE, DC, MC, V. Closed Mon. No lunch weekends. Valet parking.*

IRISH

$$–$$$ ✕ **Gilliland's.** Chef Gerri Gilliland prepares light, Californian-influenced renditions of classics from her homeland, Ireland: soda bread, Irish stew, roast stuffed pork loin, and bread pudding. In deference to the beach setting, she also makes a few good salads and spa dishes. ✉ *2424 Main St.,* ☎ *310/392–3901. AE, D, DC, MC, V. No lunch Sat.*

ITALIAN

$$–$$$$ ✕ **Valentino.** Rated among the nation's best Italian restaurants, Valentino
★ is also generally considered to have the best wine list outside Western Europe. Try the superb prosciutto, fried calamari, lobster cannelloni, fresh broiled porcini mushrooms, and osso buco. For a true Valentino experience, order from the lengthy list of daily specials. ✉ *3115 Pico Blvd.,* ☎ *310/829–4313. Reservations essential. AE, DC, MC, V. Closed Sun. No lunch Sat.–Thurs. Valet parking.*

$$$ ✕ **Drago.** Authentic Sicilian fare is hard to come by in the City of An-
★ gels, but not at the culinary outpost of affable Celestino Drago. Sam-ple his *pappardelle* (wide noodles) with rabbit ragout; morel mushroom risotto; or ostrich breast with red-cherry sauce. The savory pumpkin soup accompanied by chestnut gnocchi is the perfect starter for any Drago meal. ✉ *2628 Wilshire Blvd.,* ☎ *310/828–1585. AE, DC, MC, V. No lunch weekends. Valet parking.*

MEXICAN

$$ ✕ **Border Grill.** Hipsters love this loud, trendy eating hall designed by
★ minimalist architect Josh Schweitzer and owned by the talented team of Mary Sue Milliken and Susan Feniger. It's the most progressive, eclec-tic Mexican restaurant in L.A., with a menu ranging from seafood tacos to vinegar-and-pepper-grilled turkey to daily seviche specials. ✉ *1445 4th St.,* ☎ *310/451–1655. AE, D, DC, MC, V.*

SEAFOOD

$$–$$$$ ✕ **Ocean Avenue Seafood.** Daily specials and oyster-bar offerings are always a good choice at this restaurant across the street from the Pa-cific Ocean—among the noteworthy dishes is the cioppino, a fish stew made with Dungeness crab, clams, mussels, and prawns. ✉ *1401 Ocean Ave.,* ☎ *310/394–5669. AE, DC, MC, V. Valet parking.*

West Los Angeles

INDIAN

$–$$ ✕ **Bombay Cafe.** Head to this lively minimall café for high-quality Indian street food. Regulars swear by the chili-laden lamb frankies (sausages), *sev puri* (little wafers topped with onions, potatoes, and chutneys), and other small dishes. ✉ *12113 Santa Monica Blvd.,* ☎ *310/820–2070. MC, V. Closed Mon. No lunch weekends.*

JAPANESE

$–$$ ✕ **U-Zen.** This highly regarded Japanese café serves fresh sushi and sashimi, a good selection of sakes, and pub food such as fried spicy tofu and salmon-skin salad. Prices are modest, unless you get carried away with the sushi and sashimi. ✉ *11951 Santa Monica Blvd.,* ☎ *310/477–1390. Reservations not accepted. MC, V. No lunch weekends. Self parking.*

MEXICAN

$–$$ ✕ **La Serenata Gourmet.** It lacks the grace and charm of its East L.A. parent, La Serenata de Garibaldi, but this Westsider earns points for its deeply flavorful Mexican cooking. Though the moles and pork dishes are delicious, the star here is seafood. ✉ *10924 W. Pico Blvd.,* ☎ *310/441–9667. Reservations not accepted. AE, D, MC, V. Valet parking.*

$–$$ ✕ **Monte Alban.** This family-owned café serves the subtle cooking of Oaxaca. Flavors here are intense without being overly spicy: Try any of the moles, the tender stewed goat with toasted avocado leaves, or the bright green chili peppers stuffed with chicken, raisins, and ground nuts. ✉ *11927 Santa Monica Blvd.,* ☎ *310/444–7736. MC, V.*

Downtown

AMERICAN/CASUAL

$$–$$$ ✕ **Water Grill.** As the name suggests, seafood is the be-all and end-all at this handsome, somewhat noisy brasserie. The oyster bar—stocked with every cold-water variety imaginable and all sorts of other cold shellfish—alone is worth a trip. Avoid the pastas and complicated dishes here and stick with fresh fish. ✉ *544 S. Grand Ave.,* ☎ *213/891–0900. Reservations essential. AE, DC, MC, V. No lunch weekends. Valet parking next door.*

$ ✕ **Philippe's the Original.** This downtown landmark near Union Sta-
★ tion and Chinatown has been serving its famous French dip sandwich (four kinds of meat on a freshly baked roll) since 1908. The home cooking includes potato salad, coleslaw, hearty breakfasts, and an enormous pie selection brought in fresh daily from a nearby bakery. The best bargain: a cup of java for only 10¢. ✉ *1001 N. Alameda St.,* ☎ *213/628–3781. Reservations not accepted. No credit cards.*

CONTEMPORARY

$$$–$$$$ ✕ **Checkers.** As serene as any luxury hotel dining room (and a lot less stuffy), this is a good place to talk business or romance. American standards like apple waffles and smoked salmon with bagels and cream cheese are served for breakfast. For lunch and dinner, French techniques are combined with robust Mediterranean flavors and Asian touches. Don't miss the crab cakes with pancetta and lentil coleslaw or the buttery pork tenderloin on a bed of white beans. ✉ *535 S. Grand Ave.,* ☎ *213/624–0000. Reservations essential. AE, DC, MC, V. Valet parking.*

$$–$$$ ✕ **Traxx.** Union Station is the setting for meals with Asian, Italian, and Californian influences. Past menus have included an ahi tuna Napoleon with crispy wontons and wasabi caviar and grilled lamb chops with Gorgonzola risotto. For dessert, the rosemary bread pudding is an unexpected delight. The smartly modern interior space vaguely resem-

Downtown Los Angeles Dining and Lodging

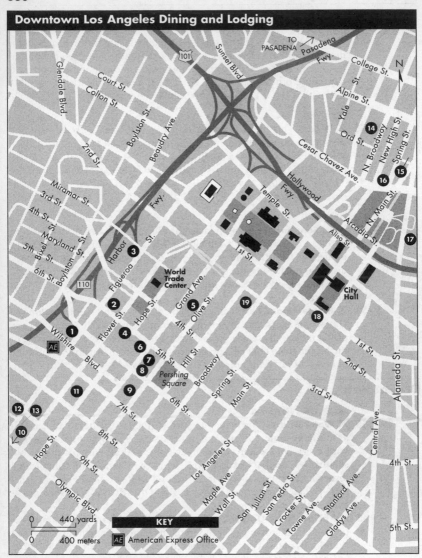

KEY

AE American Express Office

0   440 yards
0   400 meters

bles an old-fashioned dining car. You can also dine on the terrace, which extends out into the station's dramatic concourse, or a landscaped patio. ⊠ *Union Station, 800 N. Alameda St.,* ☎ *213/625–1999. AE, D, MC, V. No lunch Sat. Closed Sun. Valet parking or pay parking lot.*

CHINESE

$–$$$ ✕ **Yang Chow.** This longtime Chinatown favorite is known for its slippery shrimp (crisp, juicy, sweet, hot, and sour all at once), fiery Szechuan dumplings, and pan-fried dumplings. ⊠ *379 N. Broadway,* ☎ *213/625–0811. Reservations essential. AE, MC, V. Valet parking.*

$–$$ ✕ **Mon Kee Seafood Restaurant.** The name tells you what to expect but doesn't convey the morning-freshness of the fish or the lively flavors of dishes like garlic crab, steamed catfish, or shrimp in spicy salt. Mon Kee is often crowded; be prepared for a wait. ⊠ *679 N. Spring St.,* ☎ *213/628–6717. AE, DC, MC, V. Pay parking lot.*

ECLECTIC

$$–$$$ ✕ **Nicola.** Owner-chef Larry Nicola's cooking is mainly Mediterranean with Asian accents—vegetable spring rolls with tangerine sweet-and-sour sauce, lasagna made with rice noodles—but you'll also find fried calamari and seafood risotto on the wide-ranging menu. Nicola also operates a self-service kiosk at the Wilshire Boulevard end of the Sanwa building, serving breakfast and quick lunch snacks at reasonable prices (cash only). ⊠ *Sanwa Bank Bldg., 601 S. Figueroa St.,* ☎ *213/485–0927 or 213/485–0354 kiosk. AE, D, DC, MC, V. Closed weekends. No dinner weekdays. Valet parking.*

FRENCH

$$–$$$ ✕ **Café Pinot.** The warm and convivial restaurant of Joachim and ★ Christine Splichal, proprietors of Patina and the Pino bistros, is in a contemporary pavilion in the garden of the Los Angeles Central Library. If the weather's fine, you can eat outside on the terrace under one of the old olive trees. The menu is rooted in traditional French bistro standards—steak frites, roast chicken coated with three mustards, braised lamb shank—but it also includes some low-fat dishes, and fresh fish. ⊠ *700 W. 5th St.,* ☎ *213/239–6500. Reservations essential. DC, MC, V. No lunch weekends. Self and valet parking.*

ITALIAN

$$–$$$ ✕ **Cicada.** Cicada occupies the ground floor of a 1928 Art Deco architectural landmark, the Oviatt Building. Modern Italian best describes the menu: lobster salad with black olives, crab-meat risotto, goat-cheese ravioli, turbot with porcini mushrooms, and lamb chops with fresh basil. ⊠ *617 S. Olive St.,* ☎ *323/655–5559. Reservations essential. AE, DC, MC, V. Closed Sun. No lunch Sat.*

Pasadena

CONTEMPORARY

$$ ✕ **Shiro.** Hideo Yamashiro made quite a splash when he first began ★ serving sizzling whole catfish with a citrusy ponzu sauce. Not surprisingly, the dish started showing up on other menus, but Yamashiro's is still the best. The chef's other specialties include duck with orange sauce, lobster and scallops with saffron sauce, and herb-mustard chicken. ⊠ *1505 Mission St.,* ☎ *626/799–4774. Reservations essential. AE, DC, MC, V. Closed Mon. No lunch Tues.–Sun.*

$–$$$ ✕ **Twin Palms.** Chef Michael Roberts's Provençal cooking keeps spir- ★ its high. His garlic-rich, feel-good food—fish soup, a Portobello sandwich, succulent chicken cooked over a huge rotisserie—perfectly suits such a profoundly Californian setting. On warm evenings, there's an infectious air of bonhomie, influenced no doubt by two large bars and

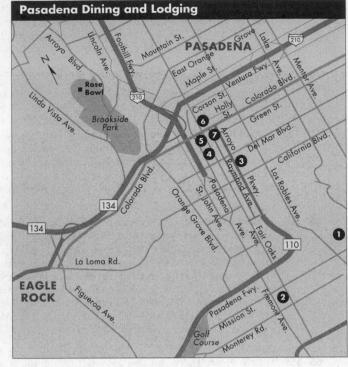

Pasadena Dining and Lodging

loud-and-swinging live music. ✉ *101 W. Green St.,* ☎ *626/577–2567.
AE, DC, MC, V. Valet parking.*

CHINESE

$$–$$$ ✕ **Yujean Kang's Gourmet Chinese Cuisine.** Mr. Kang is one of the finest
★ nouvelle Chinese chefs in the nation. Start with tender slices of veal
on a bed of enoki mushrooms topped with a tangle of quick-fried
shoestring yams, or sea bass with kumquats and passion-fruit sauce.
To finish, try the poached plums or the watermelon ice under a man-
tle of white chocolate. ✉ *67 N. Raymond Ave.,* ☎ *626/585–0855.
AE, D, DC, MC, V.*

ECLECTIC

$$–$$$ ✕ **Parkway Grill.** The always interesting dishes here draw from many
influences including Italian, Mexican, and Chinese. A typical Parkway
meal might start with a roasted *pasilla* chili stuffed with smoked
chicken, corn, and cilantro, progress to roasted Chinese crispy duck,
and then conclude with s'mores. ✉ *510 S. Arroyo Pkwy.,* ☎ *626/795–
1001. Reservations essential. AE, DC, MC, V. No lunch weekends. Valet
parking.*

INDIAN

$–$$ ✕ **All India Cafe.** The flavors produced by the chefs at this authentic
Indian restaurant are bold without depending on overpowering spici-
ness. Crisp rice wafers jazzed up with chutneys, lime, and cilantro are
a nice way to start a meal; follow this with the *bhel puri,* a savory puffed
rice-and-potatoes dish. In addition to meat curries and tikkas, there
are many vegetarian selections. A full lunch costs less than $6, and din-
ner isn't much more. ✉ *39 Fair Oaks Ave.,* ☎ *626/440–0309. AE,
MC, V. Reservations essential on weekends. City parking garage across
the street.*

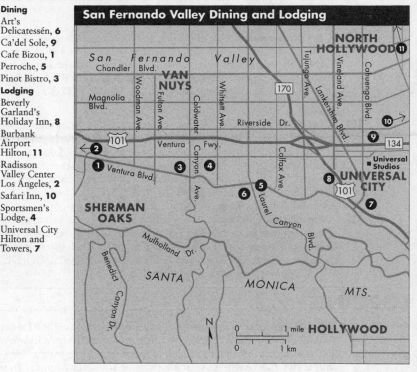

San Fernando Valley Dining and Lodging

$–$$ ✕ **Saladang.** Several blocks south of Old Pasadena, Saladang is off the beaten track. But since word got out about the spinach and duck salad, seafood soup, rice noodles with basil and bean sprouts, and beef panang, there's rarely been an empty seat in the house. ⊠ *363 S. Fair Oaks Ave.,* ☎ *626/793–8123. Reservations essential. AE, DC, MC, V. Free parking in lot.*

San Fernando Valley

North Hollywood
ITALIAN

$–$$ ✕ **Ca'del Sole.** The Italian specialties served at Ca'del Sole include sautéed
★ fresh rock shrimp in a spicy garlic–tomato sauce; citrus-marinated chicken wings braised with bacon, rosemary, and sage; and radicchio-and-arugula salad tossed in a creamy Venetian dressing. Finish up with a giant hunk of cheesecake covered with marinated strawberries. ⊠ *4100 Cahuenga Blvd.,* ☎ *818/985–4669. Reservations essential on weekends. AE, DC, MC, V. No lunch Sat. Valet parking.*

Sherman Oaks
CONTEMPORARY

$$ ✕ **Cafe Bizou.** This is the place for fine bistro fare at bargain prices.
★ The entrée sauces are textbook, the soups are rich (try the potato-leek), and the combinations are creative. If it's on the menu, consider the home-made ravioli appetizer, stuffed with lobster and salmon puree. If you bring your own bottle of wine, the corkage fee is a mere $2. ⊠ *14016 Ventura Blvd.,* ☎ *818/788–3536. Reservations essential. AE, MC, V. Valet parking.*

Studio City

DELI

$ ✕ **Art's Delicatessen.** One of the best Jewish-style delicatessens in the
★ city, this mecca serves mammoth corned beef and pastrami sandwiches.
Matzo-ball soup and sweet-and-sour cabbage soup are specialties, and
there is good chopped chicken liver. ✉ *12224 Ventura Blvd.,* ☎ *818/
762–1221. Reservations not accepted. AE, D, DC, MC, V.*

FRENCH

$$$ ✕ **Perroche.** Chef Grady Atkins's dishes, prepared from organic in-
gredients, are fresh and appealing. Two- and three-course lunches cost
$15 and $18 respectively—entrées include grilled pork loin, sautéed
halibut, and a cassoulet of vegetables. On the dinner menu you might
find sweetbreads with potato mousseline and sautéed bay scallops. ✉
1929 Ventura Blvd., ☎ *818/766–1179. AE, MC, V. Closed Sun. No
lunch Sat. Valet parking.*

$$–$$$ ✕ **Pinot Bistro.** Offerings at this Joachim Splichal bistro include fresh
oysters, country pâtés, bouillabaisse, braised tongue and spinach, pot-
au-feu, and steak with French fries. The pastry chef specializes in
chocolate desserts. ✉ *12969 Ventura Blvd.,* ☎ *818/990–0500. D, DC,
MC, V. No lunch weekends. Valet parking.*

LODGING

Revised by Lisa
Oppenheimer

Because Los Angeles is so spread out, you should select your hotel room
not only for its ambience, amenities, and price, but also for a location
that's convenient to where you plan to spend most of your time. Plan-
ning to hit the beach? Give some thought to Santa Monica. Into
nightlife? Try West Hollywood or head to more funky Hollywood, where
you'll find some bargains (though not everyone likes the neighborhood).
For upscale and posh, you can't do better than Beverly Hills. Some
tourists stay downtown, though the area is frequented mostly by con-
ventioneers and business travelers.

Prices for Los Angeles hotels run the gamut from budget-price to sky
high. Room taxes will add from 9% to 14% to your bill depending
on where in Los Angeles you stay. Because you will need a car no mat-
ter where you stay in Los Angeles, parking is another expense to con-
sider: Though a few hotels have free parking, most charge for the
privilege—and some resorts have valet parking only.

Hotels listed below are organized first by their location, then by price
category.

CATEGORY	COST*
$$$$	over $175
$$$	$120–$175
$$	$80–$120
$	under $80

*All prices are for a standard double room, excluding 9%–14% occupancy
tax.*

Beverly Hills, Hollywood, and West Hollywood

Beverly Hills and Vicinity

$$$$ 🏨 **Beverly Hills Hotel.** Celebrities favor the hotel's bungalows, which
★ have all of life's little necessities: wood-burning fireplaces, period furniture, and even (in some cases) grand pianos. Bungalow 5 even has
its own lap pool. Standard rooms are characteristically decadent, with
original artworks, butler-service buttons, walk-in closets, and huge marble bathrooms with double-vanity sinks and separate bath and shower.

All rooms have stereos with CD players, and personal fax machines. Twelve acres of landscaped (and carpeted) walkways make for prime strolling grounds. ☒ *9641 Sunset Blvd., 90210,* ☏ *310/276–2251 or 800/283–8885,* FAX *310/887–2887. 203 rooms, 21 bungalows. 4 restaurants, bar, in-room modem lines, in-room safes, kitchenettes, no-smoking rooms, room service, pool, barbershop, beauty salon, hot tub, massage, 2 tennis courts, exercise room, jogging, piano, baby-sitting, laundry service and dry cleaning, concierge, travel services, parking (fee). AE, DC, MC, V.*

$$$$ 🏨 **Beverly Prescott Hotel.** A partially enclosed patio and a tall atrium give this 12-story luxury hotel an airy feel. The stylish, spacious guest rooms are done in warm salmon and caramel tones; all have private balconies, fax machines, stereo/CD players, irons, hair dryers, and coffeemakers. Six suites are equipped with whirlpool tubs. ☒ *1224 S. Beverwil Dr., 90035,* ☏ *310/277–2800 or 800/421–3212,* FAX *310/203–9537. 137 rooms, 18 suites. Restaurant, bar, minibars, no-smoking rooms, room service, in-room VCRs, pool, massage, exercise room, baby-sitting, laundry service and dry cleaning, concierge, concierge floor, business services, meeting rooms, travel services, car rental, parking (fee). AE, D, DC, MC, V.*

$$$$ 🏨 **Four Seasons Hotel Los Angeles at Beverly Hills.** Extra touches at ★ the Four Seasons include everything from complimentary cellular phones to limo service every 15 minutes to Rodeo Drive shops. The ivory-hue guest rooms are eclectic, some done in pastels, others in black and beige. Suites have French doors and balconies. Lavish flower arrangements fill the public spaces, and tropical foliage gardens surround the hotel. An airline-ticketing machine and currency exchange are in the lobby. ☒ *300 S. Doheny Dr., 90048,* ☏ *310/273–2222 or 800/332–3442,* FAX *310/859–3824. 179 rooms, 106 suites. Restaurant, café, bar, in-room modem lines, minibars, no-smoking rooms, room service, pool, hot tub, exercise room, baby-sitting, laundry service and dry cleaning, concierge, business services, meeting rooms, car rental, free parking and parking (fee). AE, DC, MC, V.*

$$$$ 🏨 **Hotel Nikko.** Rooms and suites at this high-tech hotel have fax machines and bed-side gizmos that control in-room lighting, temperature, TVs, VCRs, and CD players. The luxurious bathrooms have deep Japanese soaking tubs. Weary travelers get to sit, rather than stand, through the check-in process, and unless you opt to use the valet, parking is free. Computers are available in the business center. ☒ *465 S. La Cienega Blvd., 90048,* ☏ *310/247–0400 or 800/645–5687,* FAX *310/247–0315. 297 rooms, 10 suites. Restaurant, bar, in-room modem lines, minibars, no-smoking floors, room service, pool, massage, sauna, exercise room, baby-sitting, laundry service and dry cleaning, concierge, business services, meeting rooms, travel services, car rental, free parking. AE, D, DC, MC, V.*

$$$$ 🏨 **L'Ermitage Beverly Hills.** After standing vacant for a few years, ★ L'Ermitage got a new lease on life with a $60 million face-lift. The smallish hotel off Rodeo Drive has uncluttered rooms with silk bedding, walk-in closets, and French doors that open to views of the city, the Getty Center, Beverly Hills, and the Hollywood Hills. Most rooms have balconies. For corporate travelers there are cellular phones with private numbers (extra charge for use) and contraptions that triple as fax machines, copiers, and printers. The rooftop pool has drop-dead views and classy poolside cabanas. ☒ *9291 Burton Way, 90210,* ☏ *310/278–3344 or 800/800–2113,* FAX *310/278–8247. 111 rooms, 13 suites. 2 restaurants, 2 bars, in-room modem lines, minibars, no-smoking floors, room service, pool, massage, steam room, exercise room, laundry service and dry cleaning, concierge, business services, meeting rooms, parking (fee). AE, D, DC, MC, V.*

$$$$ **Peninsula Beverly Hills.** The interior of this grand French Renais-
★   sance–style hotel feels a world removed from the bustle on Little Santa
Monica Boulevard. With fine antiques and marble floors, the rooms
resemble luxury apartments. Some suites in the two-story villas have
whirlpool tubs, terraces, fireplaces, and CD players. The fifth-floor pool,
looking out at the Hollywood Hills, is a gem of a place to relax. Other
frivolities include an on-site Bijan store and a courtesy Rolls-Royce for
Beverly Hills shopping. Afternoon tea, served in the living room by a
crackling fire, has become a popular venue for business meetings. ⊠
*9882 Little Santa Monica Blvd., 90212, ☎ 310/551–2888 or 800/462–
7899, FAX 310/788–2319. 196 rooms, 32 suites. 2 restaurants, bar, in-
room modem lines, in-room safes, minibars, no-smoking floors, room
service, in-room VCRs, lap pool, spa, health club, shops, baby-sitting,
concierge, business services, travel services, car rental, parking (fee).
AE, D, DC, MC, V.*

$$$$ **Radisson Beverly Pavilion Hotel.** This eight-floor boutique hotel is
in prime shopping territory, within blocks of Rodeo Drive. Guest
rooms and executive suites have private balconies; some also have refrigerators. The Radisson's frequent rate specials make it an econom-
ical alternative to some of the neighborhood's pricier establishments.
⊠ *9360 Wilshire Blvd., 90212, ☎ 310/273–1400 or 800/441–5050,
FAX 310/859–8551. 100 rooms, 10 suites. Restaurant, bar, no-smoking
rooms, room service, pool, laundry service and dry cleaning, concierge, business services, parking (fee). AE, D, DC, MC, V.*

$$$$ **Regent Beverly Wilshire.** Rooms in the older (1928) Wilshire wing
★   of this landmark Italian Renaissance–style hotel are especially large;
those in the Beverly wing (1971) have balconies overlooking the pool.
Personal services include fresh strawberries and cream and bottled water
delivered to your room upon arrival. Pets get the welcome treatment,
too, with amenities such as Evian water, biscuits served on a silver tray,
and a walk by the concierge. ⊠ *9500 Wilshire Blvd., 90212, ☎ 310/
275–5200, 800/421–4354 in the U.S., 800/427–4354 in CA; FAX 310/
274–2851. 275 rooms, 69 suites. 2 restaurants, bar, lobby lounge, in-
room modem lines, in-room safes, minibars, no-smoking floors, room
service, in-room VCRs, pool, beauty salon, spa, health club, piano, baby-
sitting, children's programs (ages 4–12), laundry service and dry cleaning, concierge, business services, travel services, car rental, parking (fee).
AE, D, DC, MC, V.*

$$$–$$$$ **Beverly Hills Plaza Hotel.** The overstuffed sofas and bevy of plants
★   in this hotel's lobby create a cozy atmosphere. The accommodations,
all suites, have white color schemes and with all the glass, plenty of
light. Bathrobes, hair dryers, in-room movies, and Nintendo are among
the amenities. ⊠ *10300 Wilshire Blvd., 90024, ☎ 310/275–5575, FAX
310/278–3325. 116 suites. Restaurant, bar, in-room modem lines, in-
room safes, kitchenettes, minibars, pool, massage, exercise room, video
games, laundry service and dry cleaning, concierge, business services,
parking (fee). AE, D, DC, MC, V.*

$$$ **Beverly Hills Inn.** Rooms at this inn surround a courtyard with
★   pool; some have French doors leading to an outdoor sitting area. Stay
here and you'll be steps from Wilshire Boulevard and within easy access of trendy shopping spots. The inn's convenient location, reasonable prices, and thoughtful service, have engendered a loyal
following—make reservations as far ahead as possible. ⊠ *125 S. Spald-
ing Dr., 90212, ☎ 310/278–0303, 800/463–4466; FAX 310/278–1728.
50 rooms, 4 suites. Bar, in-room modem lines, no-smoking floor, refrigerators, pool, sauna, exercise room, baby-sitting, laundry service
and dry cleaning, concierge, business services, free parking. Continental
breakfast. AE, DC, MC, V.*

$$ 🏨 **Beverly Terrace Hotel.** Rooms are basic (except for the leopard-print bedspreads) and the bathrooms have shower stalls instead of tubs, but the price is right at this hotel on the fringes of Beverly Hills, close to the Sunset Strip and the heart of West Hollywood. ⊠ *469 N. Doheny Dr., 90810,* ☎ *310/274–8141,* FAX *310/385–1998 39 rooms. Pool, free parking. Continental breakfast. AE, D, DC, MC, V.*

$$ 🏨 **Carlyle Inn.** Wine in the late afternoon and in-room extras such as bathrobes, hair dryers, and turndown service make this four-story inn a good choice. It's in a safe neighborhood close to Restaurant Row, Century City, and Beverly Hills; a complimentary shuttle runs within a 5-mi radius. A sun deck and hot tub are added bonuses. ⊠ *1119 S. Robertson Blvd., 90035,* ☎ *310/275–4445 or 800/322–7595,* FAX *310/859–0496. 32 rooms. Restaurant, in-room modem lines, minibars, no-smoking rooms, room service, in-room VCRs, hot tub, exercise room, laundry service and dry cleaning, business services, travel services, parking (fee). Full breakfast. AE, D, DC, MC, V.*

$$ 🏨 **Crescent Hotel.** The European-style Crescent has standard, some might say spartan, rooms but with unexpected touches like original paintings on the walls and clothes hangers that double as art. Upper-end suites are a bit expensive considering that their tubs and large-screen TVs are the only features that distinguish them from standard rooms. ⊠ *403 N. Crescent Dr., 90210,* ☎ *310/247–0505 or 800/451–1566,* FAX *310/247–9053. 39 rooms. No-smoking rooms, refrigerators, free parking. Continental breakfast. AE, D, DC, MC, V.*

Century City

$$$$ 🏨 **Park Hyatt.** Rooms at this luxury hotel are big and comfortable, with plants and upholstered furniture. Nice touches include high tea in the Garden Room and complimentary limousine service within Century City and Beverly Hills. ⊠ *2151 Ave. of the Stars, 90067,* ☎ *310/277–1234 or 800/233–1234,* FAX *310/785–9240. 367 rooms, 189 suites. Restaurant, 2 bars, in-room modem lines, minibars, no-smoking rooms, 24-hour room service, indoor and outdoor pools, hot tub, massage, sauna, steam room, spa, health club, piano, laundry service and dry cleaning, concierge, business services, convention center, meeting rooms, parking (fee). AE, D, DC, MC, V.*

$$$ 🏨 **Century City Courtyard by Marriott.** Near the Century City business complex, this hotel has reasonably priced rooms with hair dryers, coffeemakers, irons and boards, and Nintendo. A complimentary shuttle zips guests to businesses, shopping, dining, and entertainment within a 3-mi radius. ⊠ *10320 W. Olympic Blvd., 90064,* ☎ *310/556–2777 or 800/321–2211,* FAX *310/203–0563. 134 rooms. Restaurant, bar, minibars, no-smoking rooms, room service, hot tub, exercise room, babysitting, laundry service and dry cleaning, business services, car rental, free parking. AE, D, DC, MC, V.*

Hollywood and Vicinity

$$$$ 🏨 **Chateau Marmont Hotel.** Entertainment-industry types often stay in ★ the Marmont's opulent suites, cottages, bungalows, and penthouses. Though the hotel's 1920s feel is authentic, some may find the decor dated rather than antique. Rooms in the cottages have Frank Lloyd Wright–inspired fabrics; the 1956 bungalows are more contemporary. Not all rooms are air-conditioned, but those without A/C can be cooled with portable units available on request. An on-call beauty therapist, masseuse, private trainers, and airport meet-and-greeters are all at your beck and call. ⊠ *8221 Sunset Blvd., 90046,* ☎ *323/656–1010 or 800/242–8328,* FAX *323/655–5311. 10 rooms, 53 suites. Bar, dining room, in-room modem lines, in-room safes, minibars, no-smoking rooms, room service, in-room VCRs, pool, massage, exercise room,* *baby-sitting, laundry service and dry cleaning, concierge, business services, car rental, parking (fee). AE, DC, MC, V.*

$$$–$$$$ 🏨 **Radisson Wilshire Plaza Hotel.** One of the Mid-Wilshire business district's largest hotels has contemporary rooms with magnificent views of Hollywood or downtown through floor-to-ceiling windows. Rooms on the two business floors come with coffeemakers, bathrobes, and irons and boards. The hotel has a small exercise room, but guests also have use of a nearby health club. ✉ *3515 Wilshire Blvd., 90010,* ☎ *213/381–7411 or 800/333–3333,* FAX *213/386–7379. 380 rooms, 20 suites. Restaurant, bar, café, deli, in-room modem lines, minibars, no-smoking floor, room service, pool, barbershop, exercise room, laundry service and dry cleaning, concierge, business services, meeting rooms, travel services, parking (fee). AE, D, DC, MC, V.*

$$$ 🏨 **Hollywood Holiday Inn.** You can't miss the cylindrical tower of this 23-story hotel, one of Hollywood's tallest buildings. Though rooms are standard-issue Holiday Inn, there's a revolving rooftop restaurant-bar known for its Sunday brunch. You can walk to the Hollywood Walk of Fame and Mann's Chinese Theatre; the Hollywood Bowl and Universal Studios are a short drive away. ✉ *1755 N. Highland Ave., 90028,* ☎ *323/462–7181 or 800/465–4329,* FAX *323/466–9072. 470 rooms. Restaurant, bar, coffee shop, in-room modem lines, in-room safes, kitchenettes, no-smoking floors, pool, exercise room, baby-sitting, laundry service, business services, travel services, car rental, parking (fee). AE, D, DC, MC, V.*

$–$$ 🏨 **Magic Hotel.** Rooms here are spacious, there's a nice pool, and the parking is free. Some rooms overlook the pool; others face the street. Larger rooms have kitchens with eating areas. The hotel is close to the Hollywood Walk of Fame and other Hollywood Boulevard attractions. ✉ *7025 Franklin Ave., 90028,* ☎ *323/851–0800 or 800/741–4915,* FAX *323/851–4926. 10 rooms, 30 suites. No-smoking rooms, refrigerator, pool, coin laundry, free parking. AE, D, DC, MC, V.*

$ 🏨 **Banana Bungalow Hotel and International Hostel.** You'll get good value at this friendly hostel on 6.8 acres in the Hollywood Hills. Dorm rooms (only for travelers with international passports) have four bunk beds each and are equipped with lockers; there are also 18 private double-occupancy rooms. ✉ *2775 Cahuenga Blvd. W, 90068,* ☎ *323/851–1129 or 800/446–7835,* FAX *323/851–1569. 24 dorm rooms, 18 private rooms. Restaurant, fans, no-smoking rooms, pool, exercise room, billiards, recreation room, theater, coin laundry, travel services, airport shuttle, car rental, free parking. MC, V.*

$ 🏨 **Highland Gardens Hotel.** The studios and standard rooms here have kitchens with vinyl chairs and Formica tables that'll have children of the 1950s and 1960s waxing nostalgic. Basic but spacious sleeping areas have two queen-size beds and a desk and sitting area. The hotel is blocks from the Walk of Fame and a few minutes' drive from the Sunset Strip. ✉ *7047 Franklin Ave., 90028,* ☎ *323/850–0536 or 800/404–5472,* FAX *323/850–1712. 70 rooms, 48 suites. Kitchenettes, no-smoking rooms, refrigerators, free parking. AE, MC, V.*

West Hollywood

$$$$ 🏨 **The Argyle.** You can't miss the gunmetal-gray, pink, and burgundy
★   Art Deco facade of the Argyle. The rooms are also Deco; marble bathrooms have black-and-white fixtures. Though small, each accommodation has a separate living room with a fax machine, a two-line speakerphone, and many plants; the Frette linens and bathrobes are a nice touch. ✉ *8358 Sunset Blvd., 90069,* ☎ *323/654–7100 or 800/225–2637,* FAX *323/654–9287. 20 rooms, 44 suites. Restaurant, bar, in-room modem lines, in-room safes, minibars, no-smoking floors, room service, in-room VCRs, pool, sauna, exercise room, laundry ser-*

vice and dry cleaning, concierge, business services, meeting rooms, travel services, car rental, parking (fee). AE, DC, MC, V.

$$$$ 🏨 **Hyatt West Hollywood on Sunset Boulevard.** Its proximity to L.A.'s clubs of the moment (the Hyatt is across the street from the House of Blues) make this hotel popular with music-industry types. Rooms that face the boulevard have balconies; those facing the hills do not. Some rooms have aquariums, and all have a Deco feel. The view from the Rooftop pool is extraordinary—you can practically see inside some of the Hollywood Hills dwellings. ⊠ *8401 Sunset Blvd., 90069, ☎ 323/656–1234 or 800/233–1234, ℻ 323/650–7024. 262 rooms, 21 suites. Restaurant, sports bar, in-room modem lines, no-smoking floors, room service, pool, laundry service and dry cleaning, business services, parking (fee). AE, D, DC, MC, V.*

$$$$ 🏨 **Le Parc Hotel.** Suites in this modern low-rise have sunken living rooms with fireplaces and private balconies; other extras include microwaves, coffeemakers, stereos with CD players, and Nintendo. Cafe Le Parc serves excellent California-style cuisine to nonguests as well as guests. The hotel is on a residential street close to CBS Television City. ⊠ *733 N. W. Knoll Dr., 90069, ☎ 310/855–8888 or 800/578–4837, ℻ 310/659–7812. 154 suites. Restaurant, kitchenettes, minibars, no-smoking rooms, in-room VCRs, pool, hot tub, sauna, tennis court, basketball, health club, baby-sitting, coin laundry, concierge, business services, travel services, parking (fee). AE, DC, MC, V.*

$$$$ 🏨 **Mondrian.** The mod apartment-size accommodations at this hip prop-
★ erty have floor-to-ceiling windows, slip-covered sofas, and marble coffee tables; many have kitchens. The suave touches include scented candles, flowers, wool lap blankets, and vintage movie magazines in each room; a juice bar caters to L.A.'s well-known cult of the body. At 5 PM the lobby lights are dimmed, candles are lit, and a carpet of light creates visual magic. Be sure to meander over to the Sky Bar, where patrons (many of them celebrities) pay exorbitant prices for the right to drink cocktails out of plastic cups by a pool. ⊠ *8440 Sunset Blvd., 90069, ☎ 323/650–8999 or 800/525–8029, ℻ 323/650–5215. 53 rooms, 185 suites. Restaurant, 2 bars, outdoor café, in-room modem lines, kitchenettes, no-smoking rooms, refrigerators, room service, pool, massage, sauna, spa, steam room, health club, laundry service and dry cleaning, concierge, business services, meeting rooms, car rental, parking (fee). AE, D, DC, MC, V.*

$$$$ 🏨 **Summerfield Suites Hotel.** Suites here are basic, almost dormlike, but frequent specials make them a good value. Each suite has a private balcony, a sleeper sofa (in addition to beds), a gas fireplace, separate vanities, and a microwave; most have kitchens as well. On a residential side street, the hotel is steps from Santa Monica Boulevard, close to the Sunset Strip and La Cienega Boulevard's Restaurant Row. ⊠ *1000 Westmount Dr., 90069, ☎ 310/657–7400 or 800/833–4353, ℻ 310/854–6744. 109 suites. Breakfast room, in-room modem lines, no-smoking suites, refrigerators, in-room VCRs, pool, exercise room, coin laundry, laundry service and dry cleaning, meeting room, parking (fee). Continental breakfast. AE, D, DC, MC, V.*

$$$$ 🏨 **Wyndham Bel Age Hotel.** There's a residential feel to this all-suites
★ hotel near the Sunset Strip. South-facing rooms have private terraces that look out over the Los Angeles skyline as far as the Pacific. For some on-premise pampering, make an appointment at the Alex Roldan beauty salon, or enjoy a meal at the Diaghilev restaurant, where chef Tony Hodges creates Russian dishes with a French flair. ⊠ *1020 N. San Vicente Blvd., 90069, ☎ 310/854–1111 or 800/996–3426, ℻ 310/854–0926. 200 suites. 2 restaurants, bar, in-room modem lines, kitchenettes, no-smoking rooms, room service, pool, beauty salon, exercise*

room, laundry service and dry cleaning, concierge, travel services, parking (fee). AE, D, DC, MC, V.

$$$ ▦ **Ramada West Hollywood.** Though part of a chain, this hotel in the largely gay West Hollywood neighborhood has character. Flashy deco rooms have white leather furniture and ultracomfortable beds, and the bilevel loft suites with kitchenettes are an excellent value. Pizzeria Uno provides room service, and several restaurants are within walking distance. ⊠ *8585 Santa Monica Blvd., 90069,* ☎ *310/652–6400 or 800/ 845–8585,* FAX *310/652–4207. 135 rooms, 40 suites. Restaurant, bar, in-room modem lines, no-smoking floors, room service, refrigerators, pool, coin laundry, dry cleaning and laundry service, concierge, parking (fee). AE, D, DC, MC, V.*

$$ ▦ **Park Sunset Hotel.** The rooms are basic, but the location can't be beat. Clean and neat, the hotel has all the essentials, and puts you within walking distance of night spots such as the House of Blues (next door) as well as some tony shops. Suites have kitchenettes. ⊠ *8462 Sunset Blvd., 90069,* ☎ *323/654–6470 or 800/821–3660,* FAX *323/654– 2286. 66 rooms, 18 suites. Restaurant, no-smoking rooms, room service, pool, beauty salon, coin laundry, laundry services and dry cleaning, parking (fee). AE, D, DC, MC, V.*

Coastal and Western Los Angeles

Bel Air

$$$$ ▦ **Hotel Bel-Air.** Locals swear by this luxury treasure in a wooded canyon.
★   Bungalow-style Country French rooms feel like fine homes with extras such as a stereo with CD player, thick terry bathrobes, and slippers. Six of the suites have private whirlpool baths on the patio; some rooms have wood-burning fireplaces. For the quietest accommodations, ask for a room near the former stable area. ⊠ *701 Stone Canyon Rd., 90077,* ☎ *310/472–1211 or 800/648–4097,* FAX *310/476–5890. 59 rooms, 33 suites. Restaurant, bar, in-room modem lines, in-room safes, minibars, no-smoking rooms, room service, in-room VCRs, pool, beauty salon, hot tubs, massage, health club, baby-sitting, laundry service and dry cleaning, concierge, meeting rooms, travel services, parking (fee). AE, DC, MC, V.*

$$$$ ▦ **Summit Hotel Bel Air.** There's a southern Californian feel to this low-rise close to the Getty Museum in Brentwood, with patios and terraces overlooking 8 acres of gardens. The sleek, modern guest rooms are deco-inspired. Amenities include bathrobes, coffeemakers, and hair dryers. ⊠ *11461 Sunset Blvd., 90049,* ☎ *310/476–6571 or 800/468–3541,* FAX *310/476–1371. 161 rooms, 8 suites. Restaurant, bar, in-room modem lines, minibars, no-smoking rooms, room service, pool, massage, spa, 1 tennis court, exercise room, baby-sitting, laundry service and dry cleaning, concierge, business services, meeting rooms, travel services, car rental, parking (fee). AE, D, DC, MC, V.*

Los Angeles International Airport

$$$$ ▦ **Summerfield Suites.** This all-suites hotel is ideal for guests who
★   want to spread out. One- and two-bedroom suites are extra large, with kitchens and bedrooms as well as sleeper sofas in the living room. You can stock your kitchen at the little shop in the lobby; in-room meals are available through an outside service. ⊠ *810 S. Douglas Ave., El Segundo 90266,* ☎ *310/725–0100 or 800/833–4353,* FAX *310/725– 0900. 122 suites. Breakfast room, in-room modem lines, no-smoking rooms, pool, hot tub, exercise room, coin laundry, laundry service and dry cleaning, business services, meeting rooms, free parking. Continental breakfast. AE, D, DC, MC, V.*

$$$ ▦ **Holiday Inn LAX.** This 12-story international-style hotel appeals to families as well as businesspeople. The large rooms, done in earth tones,

have dataports and coffeemakers. Refrigerators can be rented. ⊠ *9901 La Cienega Blvd., Los Angeles 90045,* ☎ *310/649–5151 or 800/624–0025,* ℻ *310/670–3619. 401 rooms, 1 suite. Restaurant, bar, in-room modem lines, pool, exercise room, video games, coin laundry, airport shuttle, parking (fee). AE, D, DC, MC, V.*

$$$ 🏨 **Westin LAX.** This is a great place to stay if you want to be pampered
★ but also need to be close to the airport. Rooms and suites are spacious; many suites have private outdoor hot tubs. With 42 meeting rooms, a business center, currency exchange, and attentive service, the Westin has been recognized as a "Best of the West" meeting facility. ⊠ *5400 W. Century Blvd., Los Angeles 90045,* ☎ *310/216–5858 or 800/937–8461,* ℻ *310/670–1948. 720 rooms, 42 suites. Restaurant, bar, in-room modem lines, minibars, no-smoking rooms, refrigerators, pool, hot tub, sauna, exercise room, laundry service and dry cleaning, business services, meeting rooms, airport shuttle, car rental, parking (fee). AE, D, DC, MC, V.*

$$$ 🏨 **Wyndham Hotel at Los Angeles Airport.** You'll get to your plane in a hurry from this hotel that bills itself as the closest to LAX. Contemporary guest rooms are on the small side but have perks like fax machines, voice mail, direct-dial phones, and movies. ⊠ *6225 W. Century Blvd., Los Angeles 90045,* ☎ *310/670–9000 or 800/996–3426,* ℻ *310/670–8110. 591 rooms, 12 suites. 2 restaurants, bar, in-room modem lines, in-room safes, minibars, no-smoking floors, refrigerators, pool, hot tub, sauna, exercise room, baby-sitting, laundry service and dry cleaning, concierge, business services, meeting rooms, car rental, parking (fee). AE, D, DC, MC, V.*

$$ 🏨 **Continental Plaza Los Angeles Airport.** Low prices and friendly service make the Continental Plaza a good value. Rooms are well equipped, some with refrigerators, and guests have use of the health club next door. ⊠ *9750 Airport Blvd., Los Angeles 90045,* ☎ *310/645–4600 or 800/529–4683,* ℻ *310/216–7029. 570 rooms, 12 suites. Restaurant, coffee shop, bar, no-smoking floors, room service, pool, baby-sitting, coin laundry, laundry service and dry cleaning, concierge, business services, meeting rooms, travel services, airport shuttle, car rental, parking (fee). AE, D, DC, MC, V.*

$$ 🏨 **Furama Hotel Los Angeles.** Everything about this hotel has changed, including the name (it was the Airport Marina Resort Hotel) and the color (it's now green). In a quiet, residential area, the hotel is convenient to jogging paths, tennis, and golf. Rooms all have views of either the pool, ocean, or airport. A shuttle service goes to LAX, Marina del Rey, Venice Beach, and the Santa Monica Mall. ⊠ *8601 Lincoln Blvd., Los Angeles 90045,* ☎ *310/670–8111 or 800/225–8126,* ℻ *310/337–1883. 760 rooms, 6 suites. Restaurant, bar, no-smoking rooms, room service, pool, hot tub, 2 exercise rooms, laundry service and dry cleaning, business services, meeting rooms, airport shuttle, parking (fee). AE, D, DC, MC, V.*

Manhattan Beach

$$$ 🏨 **Barnabey's Hotel.** Modeled after a 19th-century English inn, Barn-
★ abey's has tidy rooms with lace curtains, antique furniture, flowered wallpaper, and vintage books. Added luxuries include a heated towel rack in the bathrooms, down comforters on the beds, and video games. ⊠ *3501 Sepulveda Blvd. (at Rosecrans), Manhattan Beach 90266,* ☎ *310/545–8466 or 800/552–5285,* ℻ *310/545–8621. 122 rooms, 1 suite. Restaurant, pub, in-room modem lines, no-smoking rooms, pool, hot tub, bicycles, nightclub, laundry service and dry cleaning, business services, meeting rooms, travel services, airport shuttle, car rental, parking (fee). Full breakfast. AE, D, DC, MC, V.*

Marina del Rey

$$$$ ⊞ **Marina Beach Marriott.** This Mediterranean-style, nine-story high-
★ rise has a high-tech design softened by pastel tones and accents of brass
and marble. There's a gazebo on the patio, and some rooms have
water views—ask for upper-floor rooms that face the marina. ⊠ *4100
Admiralty Way, 90292,* ☎ *310/301–3000 or 800/228–9290,* FAX *310/
448–4870. 375 rooms. Restaurant, bar, minibars, no-smoking rooms,
room service, pool, laundry service and dry cleaning, business services,
car rental, parking (fee). AE, D, DC, MC, V.*

$$$$ ⊞ **Ritz-Carlton, Marina del Rey.** The European-style Ritz occupies a patch
★ of prime real estate on the docks, affording panoramic views of the
Pacific. The traditionally styled rooms have French doors, marble
baths, honor bars, and many extras—from plush terry robes to maid
service twice a day and 24-hour room service (VCRs are available on
request). Bistro cuisine is served in the Terrace Restaurant, Mediterranean fare in the more formal Dining Room. ⊠ *4375 Admiralty
Way, 90292,* ☎ *310/823–1700 or 800/241–3333,* FAX *310/305–0019.
306 rooms, 12 suites. 2 restaurants, lobby lounge, in-room safes, minibars, no-smoking floors, room service, pool, hot tub, massage, spa, tennis court, exercise room, bicycles, baby-sitting, laundry service and dry
cleaning, concierge, business services, meeting rooms, travel services,
car rental, parking (fee). AE, D, DC, MC, V.*

$$$ ⊞ **Marina International Hotel & Bungalows.** The white shutters on each
window at the Marina and the private balconies overlooking its gar-
den or courtyard evoke Europe. The split-level bungalows, in a flower-
filled courtyard, are huge. Across from a sandy beach within the
marina, the hotel is a good choice for families with children; it's also
close to golf and tennis facilities. ⊠ *4200 Admiralty Way, 90292,* ☎
310/301–2000 or 800/529–2525, FAX *310/301–6687. 110 rooms, 25
bungalows. Restaurant, bar, in-room modem lines, minibars, room ser-
vice, pool, hot tub, health club, laundry service and dry cleaning, con-
cierge, business services, meeting rooms, travel services, airport shuttle,
free parking. AE, DC, MC, V.*

Santa Monica

$$$$ ⊞ **Hotel Oceana.** Thoughtful touches at this all-suites boutique hotel
across the street from the ocean include desks large enough for a com-
puter and refrigerators stocked with goodies like Wolfgang Puck frozen
dinners. For those who prefer the real thing, the hotel provides room
service via the nearby Wolfgang Puck Café. ⊠ *849 Ocean Ave., 90403,*
☎ *310/393–0486 or 800/777–0758,* FAX *310/458–1182. 63 suites. Bar,
in-room modem lines, kitchenettes, no-smoking rooms, refrigerators,
room service, pool, spa, exercise room, coin laundry, laundry service
and dry cleaning, concierge, business services, parking (fee). Continental
breakfast. AE, D, DC, MC, V.*

$$$$ ⊞ **Loews Santa Monica Beach Hotel.** The sand's right outside the door
at Loews. Most of the airy rooms have spectacular views of the Pa-
cific Ocean; some rooms have balconies. A shop on the beach rents bi-
cycles, skates, and rollerblades. Children under 18 stay free in their
parents' room or (summer only) at half price in an adjoining room. ⊠
1700 Ocean Ave., 90401, ☎ *310/458–6700 or 800/235–6397,* FAX *310/
458–6761. 350 rooms, 24 suites. 2 restaurants, café, bar, in-room modem
lines, minibars, no-smoking floors, room service, indoor-outdoor pool,
beauty salon, hot tub, massage, sauna, spa, steam room, health club,
beach, windsurfing, baby-sitting, children's programs (ages 5–12),
laundry service and dry cleaning, concierge, business services, meet-
ing rooms, travel services, car rental, parking (fee). AE, D, DC, MC, V.*

$$$$ ⊞ **Miramar Sheraton.** Centrally located for shopping and sunning, the
Miramar nevertheless feels like a secluded island resort. There's a bit
of Old Hollywood to this 1889 mansion (it was built as a private res-

idence), particularly in the lavish bungalows stocked with huge whirl-pool tubs, stereos with CDs, and bathroom speakers. Stay in a room in the 10-story tower and you'll be rewarded with spectacular ocean views. ✉ *101 Wilshire Blvd., 90401,* ☎ *310/576–7777 or 800/325–3535,* ℻ *310/458–7912. 213 rooms, 55 suites, 32 bungalows. 2 restaurants, bar, in-room modem lines, in-room safes, minibars, no-smoking floors, pool, beauty salon, health club, spa, piano, laundry service and dry cleaning, concierge, business services, meeting rooms, travel services, car rental, parking (fee). AE, D, DC, MC, V.*

$$$$ 🏨 **Shutters On The Beach.** You might forget you're only minutes from ★ the city if you stay in Los Angeles's only hotel directly on the sand. The luxurious rooms have sliding shutter doors (hence the hotel's name) that open onto tiny balconies, and deep whirlpool tubs. Suites have fireplaces, and all accommodations have luxurious beds with Frette linens. You'll pay a premium to face the ocean. ✉ *1 Pico Blvd., 90405,* ☎ *310/458–0030 or 800/334–9000,* ℻ *310/458–4589. 186 rooms, 12 suites. 2 restaurants, bar, lobby lounge, in-room modem lines, in-room safes, minibars, no-smoking floors, room service, in-room VCRs, pool, hot tub, sauna, spa, health club, beach, mountain bikes, baby-sitting, laundry service and dry cleaning, concierge, business services, meeting rooms, travel services, car rental, parking (fee). AE, D, DC, MC, V.*

$$$–$$$$ 🏨 **Pacific Shore.** This modern eight-story hotel is 200 steps from the beach and near restaurants. Some rooms have ocean views and small balconies. In-room extras include hair dryers, Nintendo, in-room movies; some also have wet bars and refrigerators. A complimentary shuttle runs to attractions within a 5-mi radius—perfect for seeing Santa Monica. ✉ *1819 Ocean Ave., 90401,* ☎ *310/451–8711 or 800/622–8711,* ℻ *310/394–6657. 168 rooms. Restaurant, bar, in-room modem lines, in-room safes, pool, hot tub, exercise room, baby-sitting, coin laundry, business services, meeting rooms, travel services, car rental, free parking. AE, D, DC, MC, V.*

$$–$$$$ 🏨 **Best Western Ocean View Hotel.** This relative newcomer (built in 1994) has attractive low-season rates considering its prime real estate across the street from the ocean. During the summer high season, however, the ocean-view room rate seems high, particularly for a hotel without a pool. The rooms are small but comfortable; ocean-view rooms have coffeemakers. ✉ *1447 Ocean Ave., 90401,* ☎ *310/458–4888 or 800/528–1234,* ℻ *310/458–0848. 72 rooms. In-room modem lines, no-smoking rooms, refrigerators, laundry service and dry cleaning, business services, parking (fee). AE, D, DC, MC, V.*

$$ 🏨 **Hotel Carmel.** Price and location are the calling cards of this hotel. Basic rooms are spacious; some have ocean views. The hotel doesn't have its own restaurant, but there are low- and high-price eateries within walking distance. The Third Street Promenade and the beach are a couple of blocks in either direction. Rooms often sell out in summer. ✉ *201 Broadway, 90401,* ☎ *310/451–2469 or 800/445–8695,* ℻ *310/393–4180 . 96 rooms, 8 suites. Laundry service and dry cleaning, parking (fee). Continental breakfast. AE, D, DC, MC, V.*

Venice

$ 🏨 **Marina Pacific Hotel & Suites.** The price is right at this hotel that faces the Pacific and one of the world's most vibrant boardwalks; it's nestled among Venice's art galleries, shops, and offbeat restaurants. The marina is a stroll away, giving guests easy access to ocean swimming and roller skating along the strand. Racquetball and tennis courts are also nearby. ✉ *1697 Pacific Ave. 90291,* ☎ *310/399–7770 or 800/421–8151,* ℻ *310/452–5479. 57 rooms, 35 suites. Restaurant, laundry service, meeting rooms, free parking. AE, D, DC, MC, V.*

West Los Angeles

$$–$$$ 🔁 **Century Wilshire Hotel.** This English-style hotel is a favorite among European travelers. Within walking distance of UCLA and Westwood Village, the homey hostelry has small but attractive rooms. ✉ *10776 Wilshire Blvd., 90024,* ☎ *310/474–4506 or 800/421–7223,* ℻ *310/ 474–2535. 87 rooms, 12 suites. Breakfast room, no-smoking rooms, pool, baby-sitting, laundry service and dry cleaning, concierge, travel services, car rental, free parking. Continental breakfast. AE, DC, MC, V.*

$ 🔁 **Best Western Royal Palace Inn & Suites.** Low prices and nice facilities make this Best Western a good deal. The rooms have microwaves and coffeemakers. ✉ *2528 S. Sepulveda Blvd. 90064,* ☎ *310/477– 9066 or 800/251–3888,* ℻ *310/478–4133. 23 rooms, 32 suites. Refrigerators, pool, hot tub, sauna, exercise room, billiards, coin laundry, laundry service, meeting room, free parking. AE, D, DC, MC, V.*

Westwood

$$$–$$$$ 🔁 **Westwood Marquis Hotel and Gardens.** This 15-story all-suites hotel near UCLA is a favorite of corporate and entertainment types. One-, two-, or three-bedroom suites have living rooms, dining areas, and views of either Bel Air, the Pacific Ocean, or Century City. Complimentary transportation runs to nearby areas. ✉ *930 Hilgard Ave., 90024,* ☎ *310/208–8765 or 800/421–2317,* ℻ *310/824–0355. 258 suites. 2 restaurants, bar, café, in-room modem lines, in-room safes, minibars, no-smoking floors, refrigerators, room service, 2 pools, hot tub, exercise room, laundry service and dry cleaning, concierge, business services, meeting rooms, parking (fee). AE, D, DC, MC, V.*

$$–$$$ 🔁 **Hotel Del Capri.** Despite the modest motel sign, you're as likely to see Jaguars in the parking lot as Jettas. Midway between Beverly Hills and Westwood, the small hotel has reasonably priced rooms, many with kitchenettes. Most rooms have whirlpool tubs (though some have showers only, so ask in advance if you care), and VCRs can be rented for a small fee. Ask about discounts for customers in the arts. ✉ *10587 Wilshire Blvd., 90024,* ☎ *310/474–3511 or 800/444–6835,* ℻ *310/470–9999. 34 rooms, 45 suites. No-smoking rooms, refrigerators, pool, coin laundry, laundry service and dry cleaning, meeting rooms, free parking. Continental breakfast. AE, D, DC, MC, V.*

Downtown

$$$$ 🔁 **Hotel Inter-Continental Los Angeles.** The Los Angeles version of the Inter-Continental might seem a little bland compared with some of its urban siblings around the country, but the service is still A-one. Rooms in the residential-style building are your basic business contemporary, though floor-to-ceiling windows add a dash of excitement; little extras include separate bath and shower stalls in some rooms. ✉ *251 S. Olive St., 90012,* ☎ *213/617–3300 or 800/442–5251,* ℻ *213/617– 3399. 433 rooms, 18 suites. Restaurant, bar, minibars, no-smoking floors, 24-hour room service, pool, exercise room, piano, laundry service and dry cleaning, concierge, concierge floor, business services, parking (fee). AE, D, DC, MC, V.*

$$$$ 🔁 **Hyatt Regency Los Angeles.** Windows with dramatic city views jazz up the mahogany- and cherry-wood–filled rooms at this hotel near the Music Center. If you're here to work, ask for the business plan, available on floors above the 18th—you'll have access to laptop computers and fax machines. ✉ *711 S. Hope St., 90017,* ☎ *213/683–1234 or 800/ 233–1234,* ℻ *213/629–3230. 485 rooms, 41 suites. 2 restaurants, 2 bars, in-room modem lines, no-smoking floors, room service, exercise room, laundry service and dry cleaning, concierge, concierge floor, business services, meeting rooms, parking (fee). AE, D, DC, MC, V.*

$$$$ ⚐ **Los Angeles Marriott Downtown.** The 14-story Marriott, near the
★ First Interstate World Trade Center and the Pacific Stock Exchange has
oversize rooms with dark-wood furniture, marble baths, and wall-to-
wall windows with city views. The extensive business center provides
secretarial services, and the seating area in the lobby is a comfortable
place to pull out your laptop between appointments. Guests have complimentary use of a fitness center one block away. Complimentary limo
service is provided within a 5-mi radius. ⊠ *333 S. Figueroa St., 90071,*
☎ *213/617–1133 or 800/260–0227,* FAX *213/613–0291. 469 rooms.
3 restaurants, 2 bars, in-room safes, minibars, no-smoking floors,
room service, pool, 4 cinemas, piano, laundry service and dry cleaning, concierge, business services, travel services, parking (fee). AE, D,
DC, MC, V.*

$$$$ ⚐ **New Otani Hotel and Garden.** "Japanese Experience" rooms at the
★ New Otani have tatami mats instead of beds, and extra-deep bathtubs
for up-to-your-chin soaks; you can also have tea and shiatsu massage
in the comfort of your own room. Shoji screens on windows lend an
Asian touch to the otherwise plain American-style rooms. The restaurants serve authentic Japanese cuisine along with American fare. ⊠ *120
S. Los Angeles St., 90012,* ☎ *213/629–1200, 800/421–8795 in CA,
800/421–8795 in the U.S. and Canada;* FAX *213/622–0989. 434 rooms,
20 suites. 3 restaurants, 3 bars, in-room safes, minibars, no-smoking
rooms, refrigerators, room service, sauna, health club, piano, baby-sitting,
laundry service and dry cleaning, concierge, business services, car
rental, parking (fee). AE, D, DC, MC, V.*

$$$$ ⚐ **Regal Biltmore Hotel.** This Spanish–Italian Renaissance landmark
property has rooms you can sink into (flowing draperies, French-style
armoires, and overstuffed chairs), making even one night feel like a great
escape. Afternoons and evenings, soak up some atmosphere in the beautifully restored Rendezvous Court (the original lobby). A complimentary shuttle travels within a 3-mi radius of the hotel. ⊠ *506 S. Grand
Ave., 90071,* ☎ *213/624–1011 or 800/245–8673,* FAX *213/612–1545.
627 rooms, 56 suites. 3 restaurants, 3 bars, 2 cafés, minibars, in-room
safes, no-smoking floors, refrigerators, room service, indoor pool, hot
tub, spa, health club, laundry service and dry cleaning, concierge, concierge floor, business services, travel services, car rental, parking (fee).
AE, D, DC, MC, V.*

$$$$ ⚐ **Westin Bonaventure Hotel & Suites.** You can't miss this hotel's
image on the downtown L.A. skyline: Its five cylindrical towers are tall
(35 stories) and mirrored. Rooms are fairly basic and on the small side,
but floor-to-ceiling glass windows provide terrific views. With fax machines and modem hookups, the ball-suites Green tower is geared
toward business travelers. ⊠ *404 S. Figueroa St., 90071,* ☎ *213/624–
1000 or 800/937–8461,* FAX *213/612–4800. 1,354 rooms, 135 suites.
17 restaurants, 5 bars, minibars, no-smoking floors, room service,
pool, beauty salon, 7 tennis courts, health club, baby-sitting, laundry
service and dry cleaning, concierge, business services, meeting rooms,
travel services, car rental, parking (fee). AE, D, DC, MC, V.*

$$$$ ⚐ **Wyndham Checkers Hotel.** This hotel, which opened as the Mayflower
★ in 1927, has more character than most downtown hotels, with a lobby
full of fine antique furniture and rooms with oversize beds and upholstered easy chairs. Checkers (☞ Dining, *above*), is one of downtown's best business restaurants. There's complimentary limo service
in the mornings and evenings within a 2-mi radius, but the financial
district is within walking distance. ⊠ *535 S. Grand Ave., 90071,* ☎
213/624–0000 or 800/996–3426, FAX *213/626–9906. 188 rooms, 15
suites. Restaurant, bar, minibars, no-smoking floors, room service,
pool, hot tub, spa, exercise room, library, baby-sitting, laundry service*

and dry cleaning, concierge, business services, travel services, car rental, parking (fee). AE, D, DC, MC, V.

$$$ ☷ **Inn at 657.** The apartment-size suites at this small B&B near the
★ University of Southern California have down comforters on the beds, Oriental silks on the walls, and huge dining tables that can also be used for spreading out work. Room rates include local phone calls. ⊠ 657 W. 23rd St., 90007, ☎ 213/741-2200 or 800/347-7512. 5 suites. In-room modem lines, kitchenettes, no-smoking suites, refrigerators, in-room VCRs, hot tub, laundry service, business services, free parking. Full breakfast. No credit cards.

$$ ☷ **Kawada Hotel.** This eclectic three-story redbrick hotel near the Music Center and local government buildings has European flair. The immaculate guest rooms are on the small side, but come with two phones and a wet bar. Added bonuses are a fine restaurant, a complimentary shuttle traversing downtown, and a discounted rate for airport transportation. ⊠ 200 S. Hill St., 90012, ☎ 213/621-4455 or 800/752-9232, FAX 213/687-4455. 116 rooms, 1 suite. Restaurant, bar, deli, kitchenettes, no-smoking rooms, refrigerators, room service, in-room VCRs, coin laundry, laundry service and dry cleaning, concierge, business services, meeting rooms, car rental, parking (fee). AE, DC, MC, V.

$-$$ ☷ **Figueroa Hotel and Convention Center.** The Spanish feel of this 12-story hotel built in 1926 is enhanced by terra-cotta-color rooms, hand-painted furniture, wrought-iron beds, and, in many rooms, ceiling fans. ⊠ 939 S. Figueroa St., 90015, ☎ 213/627-8971 or 800/421-9092, FAX 213/689-0305. 285 rooms, 2 suites. 2 restaurants, 2 bars, café, in-room modem lines, refrigerator, pool, hot tub, coin laundry, dry cleaning, concierge, travel services, car rental, free parking. AE, DC, MC, V.

$ ☷ **The InnTowne.** This modern three-story hotel 1½ blocks from the convention center has large rooms with beige-and-white or gray-and-white color schemes. Palm trees and a small garden surround the swimming pool. ⊠ 913 S. Figueroa St., 90015, ☎ 213/628-2222 or 800/457-8520, FAX 213/687-0566. 168 rooms, 2 suites. Bar, coffee shop, room service, pool, laundry service and dry cleaning, car rental, free parking. AE, D, DC, MC, V.

San Fernando Valley

Burbank

$$$ ☷ **Burbank Airport Hilton.** Across the street from the airport, this contemporary Hilton has room with coffeemakers, irons and boards, and hair dryers. Ask for a room with a mountain view. ⊠ 2500 Hollywood Way, 91505, ☎ 818/843-6000 or 800/468-3576, FAX 818/842-9720. 486 rooms, 77 suites. Restaurant, bar, in-room modem lines, no-smoking floors, room service, 2 pools, outdoor hot tub, sauna, 2 exercise rooms, coin laundry, laundry service and dry cleaning, concierge, convention center, travel services, airport shuttle, parking (fee). AE, D, DC, MC, V.

$ ☷ **Safari Inn.** Two miles from Warner Bros. and Universal Studios, the motel-like inn comprises two buildings. Common spaces are comfortable, colorful, and fun, with a jungle theme, but the rooms have a conservative elegant feel. All accommodations have coffeemakers, irons and boards, and in-room movies; some have refrigerators. ⊠ 1911 W. Olive Ave., 91506, ☎ 818/845-8586 or 800/782-4373, FAX 818/845-0054. 103 rooms, 15 suites. Restaurant, lobby lounge, no-smoking rooms, room service, in-room VCRs, pool, hot tub, laundry service and dry cleaning, business services, travel services, free parking. AE, DC, MC, V.

North Hollywood

$$$ ⊞ **Beverly Garland's Holiday Inn.** There's a country-club atmosphere to this lodgelike hotel in two separate buildings near Universal Studios. Rooms have distressed furniture and muted color schemes; private balconies and patios overlook the Sierra Madre and Santa Monica mountains. The hotel is next to the Hollywood Freeway, which can be noisy; ask for a room facing Vineland Avenue. ⊠ *4222 Vineland Ave., 91602,* ☎ *818/980–8000 or 800/238–3759,* FAX *818/766–5230. 258 rooms. Restaurant, bar, no-smoking rooms, room service, pool, wading pool, sauna, tennis, laundry service and dry cleaning, meeting rooms, airport shuttle, free parking. AE, D, DC, MC, V.*

Sherman Oaks

$$$ ⊞ **Radisson Valley Center Hotel Los Angeles.** Excellent service enhances the appeal of the standard accommodations at this hotel close to the Sherman Oaks Galleria shopping mall and excellent restaurants. ⊠ *15433 Ventura Blvd., at I–405 and U.S. 101, 91403,* ☎ *818/ 981–5400 or 800/333–3333,* FAX *818/981–3175. 188 rooms, 12 suites. Restaurant, bar, in-room modem lines, no-smoking floors, room service, pool, beauty salon, hot tub, massage, exercise room, laundry service and dry cleaning, concierge, business services, meeting rooms, car rental, parking (fee). Continental breakfast. AE, D, DC, MC, V.*

Studio City

$$$ ⊞ **Sportsmen's Lodge.** A low-slung, English country–style structure, this hotel is surrounded by waterfalls, a swan-filled lagoon, and a gazebo; the pool area and lush garden might make you forget you're near a city. The service may not be everything you've dreamed of, but the accommodations are comfortable. ⊠ *12825 Ventura Blvd., 91604,* ☎ *818/769–4700 or 800/821–8511,* FAX *323/877–3898. 191 rooms. 3 restaurants, bar, no-smoking floors, room service, pool, barbershop, beauty salon, hot tub, exercise room, baby-sitting, coin laundry, laundry service and dry cleaning, travel services, airport shuttle, car rental, free parking. AE, D, DC, MC, V.*

Universal City

$$$$ ⊞ **Universal City Hilton and Towers.** This ultramodern-looking tower has cozy rooms that feel surprisingly homey, with marble baths and nice views from floor-to-ceiling windows. The Sierra Café serves good contemporary cuisine; the daily buffet includes tasty Chinese dishes. A complimentary limo is on call, and the property is within walking distance of Universal Studios and CityWalk. ⊠ *555 Universal Terrace Pkwy., 91608,* ☎ *818/506–2500,* FAX *818/509–2058. 482 rooms, 8 suites. Restaurant, lobby lounge, in-room modem lines, in-room safes, minibars, no-smoking floors, room service, pool, hot tub, massage, exercise room, piano, baby-sitting, laundry service and dry cleaning, business services, convention center, meeting rooms, travel services, concierge floors, car rental, parking (fee). AE, D, DC, MC, V.*

San Gabriel Valley

Pasadena

$$$$ ⊞ **Ritz-Carlton Huntington Hotel.** The main building of this 1906 land-
★ mark is a Mediterranean-style structure that blends in seamlessly with the lavish houses of the surrounding San Marino neighborhood. Traditionally styled guest rooms are handsome, if a bit small for the price; bathrooms are marble. The Grill, the more formal of the two dining rooms, has been rated among the top 100 five-star restaurants in the world. ⊠ *1401 S. Oak Knoll Ave., 91106,* ☎ *626/568–3900 or 800/ 241–3333,* FAX *626/585–1842. 387 rooms, 31 suites. 2 restaurants, bar, in-room modem lines, in-room safes, minibars, no-smoking buildings,*

room service, in-room VCRs, pool, beauty salon, hot tub, mineral baths, spa, tennis court, health club, baby-sitting, laundry service and dry cleaning, concierge, business services, meeting rooms, travel services, car rental, parking (fee). AE, D, DC, MC, V.

NIGHTLIFE AND THE ARTS

Updated by
Mark Ehrman

Most bars, clubs, and bistros in this go-go-go city have a shelf life shorter than the vinyl skirts at Melrose boutiques. Hollywood, the locus of L.A. nightlife, is without question the place to start your search; you can't help but stumble into a happening joint if you cruise the streets long enough. Los Angeles is one of the best cities in the country to catch promising rock bands or check out jazz, blues, and classical acts. And culture vultures will find plenty going on, from ballet to film to theater.

For the most complete listing of weekly events, consult the current issue of *Los Angeles* magazine. The Calendar section of the *Los Angeles Times* also lists a wide survey of Los Angeles arts events, as do the more alternative publications, the *L.A. Weekly* and the *New Times Los Angeles* (both free). For a telephone report on current music, theater, dance, film, and special events, plus a discount ticket source, call 213/688–2787. Most tickets can be purchased by phone (with a credit card) from **Ticketmaster** (☎ 213/365–3500), **TeleCharge** (☎ 800/762–7666), **Good Time Tickets** (☎ 323/464–7383), **Tickets L.A.** (☎ 323/660–8587), or **Murray's Tickets** (☎ 323/234–0123). Half-price tickets to many shows are available at **Times Tix** (✉ Beverly Center, 8522 Beverly Blvd., 7th Floor, ☎ 310/659–3678). Tickets, cash only, must be purchased in person, and availability is never guaranteed.

Nightlife

Despite the high energy level of the L.A. nightlife crowd, don't expect to be partying until dawn—this is still an early-to-bed city. Liquor laws require that bars stop serving alcohol at 2 AM, and it's safe to say that by this time, with the exception of a few after-hours venues and coffeehouses, most clubs have closed for the night.

Nighttime diversions on the Sunset Strip run the gamut from comedy clubs and hard-rock clubs to cocktail lounges and restaurants with piano bars. There's a good mix of nightlife in the Mid-Wilshire area, which encompasses the area west of the Harbor Freeway (I–110), east of La Cienega Boulevard, south of Beverly Boulevard, and north of the Santa Monica (I–10) Freeway. Local beer bars abound in Westwood. Downtown Los Angeles has a small contingent of artsy performance spaces and galleries, and a handful of clubs and movie palaces. Some of Los Angeles's best jazz clubs, discos, and comedy clubs are scattered throughout the San Fernando and San Gabriel valleys. In West Hollywood, Santa Monica Boulevard is the heart of the gay-and-lesbian club and coffeehouse scene.

Bars

BEL AIR

There's serene musical entertainment every night (either a pianist or a vocalist) at the romantically secluded **Hotel Bel Air** (✉ 701 Stone Canyon Rd., ☎ 310/472–1211).

BEVERLY HILLS

A quaint bar with an immense wine selection, **La Scala** (✉ 410 N. Canon Dr., ☎ 310/275–0579) is filled with celebrities nightly. Behind the oak bar and brass rail at **R.J.'s** (✉ 252 N. Beverly Dr., ☎ 310/274–3474 or 310/274–7427) are 800 bottles stacked to the ceiling. Bend your elbow at the bar with a brace of new buddies during happy hour. Plush sofas and high tables set the mood at the piano bar of the **Regent Beverly Wilshire** (⊠ 9500 Wilshire Blvd., ☎ 310/275–5200).

BRENTWOOD

Neighborhood brat-packers and yuppies gather at **Q's** (⊠ 11835 Wilshire Blvd., ☎ 310/477–7550), an upscale pool hall with a dozen tables and a bar.

CENTURY CITY

Harper's Bar and Grill (⊠ 2040 Ave. of the Stars, ☎ 310/553–1855) is a central place to meet friends for cocktails before a show at the Shubert Theater. A reasonably authentic version of the famed Florentine bar and grill that Hemingway and other Lost Generation scribblers frequented, **Harry's Bar and American Grill** (⊠ ABC Entertainment Center, 2020 Ave. of the Stars, ☎ 310/277–2333) is unrivaled in L.A. for its potent cappuccinos.

DOWNTOWN

Downtown's loft-dwelling elite frequent **Boyd Street** (⊠ 410 Boyd St., ☎ 213/617–2491), a bar-restaurant with a streamlined '80s motif. In the Biltmore Hotel, the sleek **Grand Avenue Sports Bar** (⊠ 506 S. Grand Ave., ☎ 213/612–1595) serves pricey drinks late into the night. **Little Joe's** (⊠ 900 N. Broadway, ☎ 213/489–4900) is a must for sports buffs: Prices are low and the big-screen TV is always tuned to the hottest game. W. C. Fields frequented the bar in the '30s. Atop the 32-story Transamerica Building, **The Tower** (⊠ 1150 S. Olive St., ☎ 213/746–1554) is a snazzy cocktail bar and restaurant with an unbeatable view.

HOLLYWOOD

For a pick-me-up margarita, stop by the kitschy **El Coyote** (⊠ 7312 Beverly Blvd., ☎ 323/939–7766) restaurant and bar. A rowdy crowd plays billiards at the **Hollywood Athletic Club** (⊠ 6525 Sunset Blvd., ☎ 323/962–6600), which doubles as a dance club on Friday and Saturday. Adjacent to the venerable Canter's Restaurant, the **Kibitz Room** (⊠ 419 N. Fairfax Ave., ☎ 323/651–2030) is an of-the-moment gathering place with live music most nights. Don't be fooled by the seedy, minimall location of **Lava Lounge** (⊠ 1533 N. La Brea Ave., ☎ 323/876–6612): Inside you'll find groovy, neo-tiki decor and wall-to-wall scenesters. On weeknights there's live music. Occasionally there's a nominal cover.

Film-studio moguls and movie extras flock to longtime Hollywood hangout **Musso and Franks** (⊠ 6667 Hollywood Blvd., ☎ 323/467–5123), where the Rob Roys are as smooth as ever. The nondescript exterior of **3 Of Clubs** (⊠ 1123 N. Vine St., ☎ 323/462–1123) hardly prepares you for the plush environment within. This dressy bar is a prime location to scout out L.A.'s young and restless. An L.A. tradition is to meet at **Yamashiro's** (⊠ 1999 N. Sycamore Ave., ☎ 323/466–5125) for cocktails at sunset on the terrace, where a spectacular hilltop view spreads out before you.

LOS FELIZ

The **Dresden Room** (⊠ 1760 N. Vermont Ave., ☎ 323/665–4294) started the whole lounge revival. Gold lamé–clad patrons flock here to croon along with Marty and Elayne, who perform nightly (except Sunday) from 9 to 1:30. The Chinese motif (complete with paper lanterns) at the trendy **Good Luck Bar** (⊠ 1514 Hillhurst Ave., ☎ 323/666–3524) makes you feel as if you've stepped onto the set of a Hong Kong action movie. Be sure to check out the vintage jukebox.

MARINA DEL REY

Even locals often overlook the **Crystal Fountain Lounge** (✉ Marina International Hotel, 4200 Admiralty Way, ☎ 310/301–2000), where jukebox music blasts late into the night.

Ex-cinematographer Burt Hixon collected tropical-drink recipes on his South Seas forays. At his **Warehouse** (✉ 4499 Admiralty Way, ☎ 310/823–5451) he whips up one of the most sinfully rich piña coladas this side of Samoa.

MID-WILSHIRE AREA

Après-work business folks and Gen-Xers frequent **HMS Bounty** (✉ 3357 Wilshire Blvd., ☎ 213/385–7275), an old watering hole in the Gaylord apartment building. Brass plates above each booth bear the names of Hollywood heavies who once held court here. **Molly Malone's** (✉ 575 S. Fairfax Ave., ☎ 323/935–1577) is a small, cozy pub with Irish rock and traditional Gaelic music. Harp is the beer of choice. One of L.A.'s most frequented Irish pubs, **Tom Bergin's** (✉ 840 S. Fairfax Ave., ☎ 323/936–7151) is plastered with Day-Glo shamrocks bearing the names of regular patrons who have passed through its door.

PASADENA

Beckham Place (✉ 77 W. Walnut St., ☎ 626/796–3399), a fancy "Olde English" pub, is known for its huge drinks and free roast-beef sandwiches at happy hour. With two pool tables, a nautical motif, and reasonable prices, the **Colorado Bar** (✉ 2640 E. Colorado Blvd., ☎ 626/449–3485) is a divey refuge for art students, Gen-Xers, and aging barflies. Beer is the main attraction at the **Crown City Brewery** (✉ 300 S. Raymond Ave., ☎ 626/577–5548), but many technophiles are drawn to the video machines. **John Bull** (✉ 958 S. Fair Oaks Ave., ☎ 626/441–4353) looks as if it came straight from London, even though its Pasadena location draws a more American crowd. English types do come to play pool, though. In Pasadena's Old Town, **Market City Cafe** (✉ 33 S. Fair Oaks Ave., ☎ 626/568–0203) draws a crowd at lunchtime and in the early evening. A young collegiate crowd frequents **Q's** (✉ 99 E. Colorado Blvd., ☎ 626/405–9777), an upscale bar and pool hall in the middle of Old Town. With brass fixtures, an oversize fireplace, and a marble-top bar, the **Ritz-Carlton Huntington Hotel** (✉ 1401 S. Oak Knoll Ave., ☎ 626/568–3900) is a genteel setting for nighttime drinks.

SAN FERNANDO VALLEY

Residuals (✉ 11042 Ventura Blvd., Studio City, ☎ 818/761–8301) is so named because actors who present a residual check for less than a dollar can trade it for a free drink here. Naturally, the place is full of struggling thespians and wanna-bes—how very L.A. The lounge at **Sportsmen's Lodge** (✉ 12833 Ventura Blvd., Sherman Oaks, ☎ 818/984–0202) has a tranquil setting with brooks and swan-filled ponds. **Sagebrush Cantina** (✉ 23527 Calabasas Rd., Calabasas, ☎ 818/222–6062), an indoor-outdoor saloon next to a Mexican restaurant, is the Valley's version of the Via Veneto café scene. Motorcycle hippies mix comfortably with computer moguls and showbiz folk, including a platoon of stunt people. There's rock entertainment on weekends.

SANTA MONICA

Chez Jay (✉ 1657 Ocean Ave., ☎ 310/395–1741), a shack of a saloon near Santa Monica Pier, has endured for more than 30 years. Warren Beatty, Julie Christie, and former California governor Jerry Brown have all fueled up here. Named for its 360-degree bar, the **Circle** (✉ 2926 Main St., ☎ 310/392–4898) is the Santa Monica dive that survived Main Street's trendy makeover. **Gotham Hall** (✉ 1431 3rd St. Promenade, ☎ 310/394–8865) is designed like something off the set of *Batman*. The purple pool tables match the purple walls. Carved-wood tribal masks and other Indian and Southeast Asian deities decorate **Monsoon** (⊠ 1212 3rd St. Promenade, ☎ 310/576–9996), where the restaurant serves south Asian cuisine and there's usually live entertainment in the rear bar. There's a $10 minimum per person. From motorcycles to carriages, something old has been glued or nailed to every square inch of **Oar House** (⊠ 2941 Main St., ☎ 310/396–4725). Reeking of ale, **Ye Olde King's Head** (⊠ 116 Santa Monica Blvd., ☎ 310/451–1402) is a gathering place for Brits eager to hear or dispense news from home.

SILVER LAKE

Tiki Ti (⊠ 4427 W. Sunset Blvd., ☎ 323/669–9381), a small cocktail lounge, serves some of the city's best tropical rum drinks in a simulated Tahitian hut. Look out for singles on the make.

VENICE

Abstract art decorates the walls of **Hal's Bar & Grill** (⊠ Abbott Kinney Blvd., ☎ 310/396–3105), a regular haunt of local well-to-do professionals. There's a changing contemporary art show at **James Beach Cafe** (⊠ 60 N. Venice Blvd., ☎ 310/823–5396), a gathering place for Westside yuppies. The very upscale **Rebecca's** (⊠ 2025 Pacific Ave., ☎ 310/306–6266) is worth checking out for the outrageous and playful Frank Gehry interior and the opportunity to rub elbows with the Venice Beach elite.

WEST HOLLYWOOD

A mahogany bar and art nouveau mirrors make **Barefoot** (⊠ 8722 W. 3rd St., ☎ 310/276–6223) a swanky place to drink expertly mixed martinis. The old Hollywood restaurant and watering hole known as **Formosa** (⊠ 7156 Santa Monica Blvd., ☎ 323/850–9050), which was popped up in the Oscar-nominated film *L.A. Confidential,* is shaped like an old railroad car, with many booths. Pictures of nearly every celebrity who ever crossed the silver screen line the walls. A hetero bastion in an ultragay neighborhood, **J. Sloane's** (⊠ 8623 Melrose Ave., ☎ 310/659–0250) is a sawdust-on-the-floor, football-on-the-tube, frat-house kind of place with an ample dance floor. The circular bar at **Le Dôme** (⊠ 8720 W. Sunset Blvd., ☎ 310/659–6919) draws the likes of Rod Stewart and Richard Gere. The best time to visit is after 11 PM, when this upmarket hangout really starts to jump. Patrons (many of them celebrities) must either have a Mondrian room key, screen credit, or a model's body to enter **Sky Bar** (⊠ 8440 Sunset Blvd., ☎ 323/650–8999), the poolside city-view bar at the Hotel Mondrian. The bar at the **Sunset Marquis** (⊠ 1200 N. Alta Loma Rd., ☎ 310/657–1333) is a convenient watering hole for many visiting celebs.

WEST LOS ANGELES

You can't miss **Liquid Kitty,** (⊠ 11780 W. Pico Blvd., ☎ 310/473–3707), a cocktail lounge with a hip clientele and cool (occasionally live) music. Just look for the neon martini glass on the outside. Old prints adorn the walls and friendly bartenders listen to your troubles at the friendly **San Francisco Saloon** (⊠ 11501 W. Pico Blvd., ☎ 310/478–0152).

WESTWOOD

There's a good assortment of Mexican beers at **Acapulco** (⊠ 1109 Glendon Ave., ☎ 310/208–3884), a convivial Mexican restaurant and bar that's big with the college crowd.

Cabaret, Performance, and Variety

HOLLYWOOD

The Cinegrill (⊠ Clarion Hotel Hollywood Roosevelt, 7000 Hollywood Blvd., ☎ 323/466–7000) is well worth a visit, if not to hear top-tier jazz performers, then to admire the Hollywood artifacts lining the lobby of the landmark hotel that houses the club. The neighborhood's dicey though. **Gardenia Club** (⊠ 7066 Santa Monica Blvd., ☎ 323/467–7444) is an East Coast–style cabaret (closed on Sunday) with singers, comedy, and variety performances.

SAN FERNANDO VALLEY

At **Queen Mary** (⊠ 12449 Ventura Blvd., Studio City, ☎ 818/506–5619), female impersonators vamp it up as Diana Ross, Barbra Streisand, and Bette Midler.

SANTA MONICA

Westside bohemians come to **Highways** (⊠ 1651 18th St., ☎ 310/453–1755) to hear and see avant-garde spoken-word and performance artists. Reservations are recommended.

SILVER LAKE

Glaxa Studios (⊠ 3707 Sunset Blvd., ☎ 323/663–5295) is a bohemian café-arts venue presenting music, poetry, and performance with an emphasis on the literate, the avant-garde, and the offbeat. Hours and cover charges (for shows only) vary.

WEST HOLLYWOOD

Drag queens strut their stuff at **Luna Park** (⊠ 665 Robertson Blvd., ☎ 310/652–0611), a "club in progress" featuring an eclectic mix of music, with three stages and two bars.

Coffeehouses

DOWNTOWN

Amidst the murals and neon of downtown's artsy loft district, **Bloom's General Store** (⊠ 714 3rd St., ☎ 213/687–6571) sells cigars, candy, and videos and is also connected to a soul-food restaurant and art gallery.

HOLLYWOOD

Galaxy Gallery (⊠ 7224 Melrose Ave., ☎ 323/938–6500) is a head shop, café, art gallery, cigar bar, and smoke shop with occasional live music. With a trippy, sci-fi Tolkienesque motif, **Nova Express Cafe** (⊠ 426 N. Fairfax Ave., ☎ 323/658–7533) serves coffee, tea, and other snacks into the wee hours.

LOS FELIZ

Local bohemians idle away countless hours drinking lattes and cappuccinos at Formica tables at **Onyx/Sequel Coffeehouse/Gallery** (⊠ 1802 N. Vermont Ave., ☎ no phone.) It's open until 3 AM.

NORTH HOLLYWOOD

Valley poets, artists, and hipsters hang out at **Eagle's** (⊠ 5231 Lankershim Blvd., ☎ 818/760–4212), a laid-back café with occasional live music and spoken-word readings.

VENICE

At **Cyber Java** (⊠ 1029 Abbott Kinney Blvd., ☎ 310/581–1300) you can log onto the Internet while enjoying coffee and snacks. There's also a cozy patio with a tiny sculpture garden.

WEST LOS ANGELES

Half tiki, half sci-fi, with hand-painted tabletops, the tiny **Cacao** (⊠ 11609 Santa Monica Blvd., , ☎ 310/473–7283) is an aesthetic gem.

Comedy and Magic

PASADENA

From Wednesday to Sunday the **Ice House Comedy Club and Restaurant** (⊠ 24 N. Mentor Ave., ☎ 626/577–1894) presents three-act shows with comedians, celebrity impressionists, ventriloquists, and magicians from Las Vegas and TV.

Groundlings Theatre (✉ 7307 Melrose Ave., ☎ 323/934–9700) is considered a breeding ground for *Saturday Night Live* performers, with original skits, music, and improv. Shows take place from Thursday to Sunday.

WEST HOLLYWOOD
Los Angeles's premier comedy showcase, **Comedy Store** (✉ 8433 Sunset Blvd., ☎ 323/656–6225) has been going strong for more than a decade. Famous comedians occasionally make unannounced appearances. Liza Minnelli and Richard Pryor got their starts at the **Improvisation** (✉ 8162 Melrose Ave., ☎ 323/651–2583), a transplanted New York establishment showcasing comedians and some vocalists. Reservations are recommended for shows.

Country Music
GLENDALE
Learn the two-step or the West Coast swing at **In Cahoots** (✉ 223 N. Glendale Ave., ☎ 818/500–1665), a raucous dance hall à la Nashville. Dance lessons are given twice each night, and there's live music all week long.

Dance Clubs
BEVERLY HILLS
The **Coconut Club** (✉ Beverly Hilton, 9876 Wilshire Blvd., ☎ 310/274–7777), a throwback to the same-named club at the old Ambassador Hotel, has big-band music, on-the-air DJs, and a supper-club menu. The club takes over the Grand Ballroom of the Beverly Hilton Hotel on Friday and Saturday.

HOLLYWOOD
If you're nostalgic for the 1960s, stop by the happening **Crush Bar** (✉ 1743 Cahuenga Ave., ☎ 323/463–9017), open on Friday and Saturday. **Florentine Gardens** (✉ 5951 Hollywood Blvd., ☎ 323/464–0706) has one of Los Angeles's largest dance areas, with spectacular lighting and lots of Latin-fusion. It's open on Friday, Saturday, and Sunday. Every night of the week, a different promoter takes over **The World** (✉ 7070 Hollywood Blvd., ☎ 323/467–7070), a large, extremely popular dance venue on the ground floor of a Hollywood office building. You might hear anything from house and hip-hop to trance and techno, occasionally live. Cover charges vary.

SAN FERNANDO VALLEY
Big on the swing era, the high-energy **Moonlight Tango Cafe** (✉ 13730 Ventura Blvd., Sherman Oaks, ☎ 818/788–2000) gets moving in the wee hours, when a conga line inevitably takes shape on the dance floor.

Gay and Lesbian Clubs
HOLLYWOOD
An ethnically mixed gay and straight crowd flocks to **Circus Disco and Arena** (✉ 6655 Santa Monica Blvd, ☎ 323/462–1291), two huge side-by-side discos with techno and rock music, as well as a full bar.

MID-WILSHIRE
Jewel's Catch One (✉ 4067 W. Pico Blvd., ☎ 323/734–8849) attracts gays and straights of all races and backgrounds. Late hours—it's open until 3 AM on weeknights and 4 AM on weekends—and an underground vibe make it a prime destination for the serious dance fanatic. The neighborhood can be dicey.

SILVER LAKE
Gays and straights mingle easily at **Akbar** (✉ 4356 Sunset Blvd., ☎ 323/665–6810), a dark, cozy watering hole with one of the best juke-

boxes in town. Local Silver Lake bands get top billing. The **Cobalt Cantina** (✉ 4326 Sunset Blvd., ☎ 323/953–9991), a bar and trendy Tex-Mex restaurant, attracts a mix of daytime business and "biz" folk. At night the crowd is mostly gay. The signature drink is a blue margarita made with blue Curaçao.

WEST HOLLYWOOD

Axis (✉ 652 N. La Peer Dr., ☎ 310/659–0471) and **Love Lounge** (✉ 657 N. Robertson Blvd., ☎ 310/659–0472) share one site but have different entrances and schedule different events. Some nights are for lesbians and some are for gay men, and there are frequent theme parties. The music runs the gamut: new wave, hi-NRG, tribal, rock, and Latin house. Both clubs are open from Wednesday to Saturday; Love Lounge also opens its doors for Tuesday-night drag shows. With live music and drag shows, **Club 7969** (✉ 7969 Santa Monica Blvd., ☎ 323/654–0280) caters to gay, lesbian, and mixed crowds depending on the night. There's a large dance floor and a super sound system.

Lipstick lesbians show up for parties sponsored by **Girl Bar** (☎ 323/460–2531); call the information line for locations. In recent years, Girl Bar has been held on Friday at Axis and on Saturday at the Love Lounge (☞ *above*). Occasional parties are held at West Hollywood hotels such as the Mondrian. A friendly, publike lesbian bar with a pool table, **The Palms** (✉ 8572 Santa Monica Blvd., ☎ 310/652–6188) has DJ dancing six nights a week and live bands on Sunday. One-dollar drinks draw a crowd on Wednesday night, and Sunday's beer bust is a lively affair.

Rage (✉ 8911 Santa Monica Blvd., ☎ 310/652–7055), a longtime favorite of the gym-boy set, has a video lounge.

Jazz

CULVER CITY

Come to **Jazz Bakery** (✉ 3221 Hutchison, ☎ 310/271–9039), inside the former Helms Bakery, for coffee, desserts, and world-class jazz. The admission price (from $17 to $20; no credit cards) includes refreshments.

CRENSHAW DISTRICT

In the Crenshaw District's Leimert Park arts enclave, **Fifth Street Dick's Coffee Company** (✉ 3347½ W. 43rd Pl., ☎ 323/296–3970) is a great spot for coffee and traditional jazz. The upstairs performance space has hosted jazz legends like Billy Higgins and Ronald Muldrow. Owned by comedy star Marla Gibbs of *The Jeffersons* and *227*, **Marla's Memory Lane Supper Club** (✉ 2323 W. Martin Luther King Jr. Blvd., ☎ 323/294–8430) pops with blues, jazz, and easy listening. James Ingram plays here from time to time.

HOLLYWOOD

Big-name acts and innovators such as Latin-influenced saxophonist Paquito D. Rivera have played at **Catalina Bar and Grill** (✉ 1640 N. Cahuenga Blvd., ☎ 323/466–2210), a top Hollywood jazz spot.

MID-WILSHIRE

The eclectic entertainment at the **Atlas Bar & Grill** (✉ 3760 Wilshire Blvd., ☎ 213/380–8400) includes torch singers as well as a jazz band. The snazzy supper club is inside the Wiltern building.

NORTH HOLLYWOOD

Crowds squeeze in like sardines to hear powerhouse jazz and blues at the tiny **Baked Potato** (✉ 3787 Cahuenga Blvd. W, ☎ 818/980–1615). The featured item on the menu is the baked potato, jumbo and stuffed with everything from steak to vegetables.

You can hear exceptional jazz performers at **Club Brasserie** (✉ Wyndham Bel Age Hotel, 1020 N. San Vicente Blvd., ☎ 213/854–1111) from Thursday to Saturday. Impressionist paintings on the wall compete with the expansive city view. Best of all, there's no cover.

Rock, Blues, Reggae, and More

DOWNTOWN

One of L.A.'s oldest rock dives, **Al's Bar** (✉ 305 S. Hewitt St., ☎ 213/625–9703) is still going strong.

HOLLYWOOD

Dark, cozy, mysterious—everything a rock-and-roll dive should be—**Dragonfly** (✉ 6510 Santa Monica Blvd., ☎ 323/466–6111) plays an edgy mix of live and dance music. When you need to cool off, there's an outdoor patio. At the music-industry hangout the **Ghengis Cohen Cantina** (✉ 740 N. Fairfax Ave., ☎ 323/653–0640), you can hear up-and-coming talent in a refreshingly mellow format reminiscent of MTV's "Unplugged" performances. A plus is the restaurant's updated Chinese cuisine. **Jack's Sugar Shack** (✉ 1707 N. Vine St., ☎ 323/466–7005) books big-name alternative rock, surf, blues, rockabilly, Cajun, and country performers. You'll find an ample selection of umbrella drinks and on-tap microbrewery beers at this cartoony Polynesian-style place. The **Palace** (✉ 1735 N. Vine St., ☎ 323/462–3000) is a multilevel Art Deco venue with lively entertainment, a fabulous sound system, laser lights, two dance floors, four bars, a comfortable balcony, and a full bar and dining room on the top-level patio. Patrons here dress to kill. Friday nights are packed.

LOS FELIZ

You can put on the ritz at the **Derby** (✉ 4500 Los Feliz Blvd., ☎ 323/663–8979), a spacious club with a 360-degree brass-rail bar and plush-velvet curtained booths. There's live music nightly—swing, jazz, surf, and rock.

MID-WILSHIRE

The gloriously restored Art Deco **El Rey Theater** (✉ 5515 Wilshire Blvd., ☎ 323/936–4790) presents top-name performers such as Beck, Bob Dylan, and Willie Nelson. There are also occasional goth, hiphop, and swing dance nights and evenings dedicated to local bands. Vintage LPs hang from the ceiling at the **Mint** (✉ 6010 Pico Blvd., ☎ 323/954–9630), which hosts some of the best in blues, jazz, rockabilly and bluegrass.

NORTH HOLLYWOOD

Blue Saloon (✉ 4657 Lankershim Blvd., ☎ 818/766–4644) is the friendliest club around, with rock and roll, blues, country, and rockabilly.

SANTA MONICA

Alligator Lounge (✉ 3321 Pico Blvd., ☎ 310/449–1844) books musical acts and serves Cajun cuisine. It's open from Friday to Monday. Rap music and reggae are served up along with fine Jamaican food at **Kingston 12** (✉ 814 Broadway, ☎ 310/451–4423), open from Thursday to Sunday. **McCabe's Guitar Shop** (✉ 3101 Pico Blvd., ☎ 310/828–4497; 310/828–4403 concert information) is retro-central: Arlo Guthrie sings here on occasion. Folk, acoustic rock, bluegrass, and soul concerts (reservations essential) are presented on weekends, with coffee, herbal tea, apple juice, and homemade sweets served during intermission.

SILVER LAKE

Chandeliers and hubcaps decorate the **Garage** (✉ 4519 Santa Monica Blvd., ☎ 213/683–3447), a rock dive where some of the best local and alternative bands play. The hottest bands of tomorrow perform at **Spaceland** (⊠ 1717 Silver Lake Blvd., ☏ 213/413–4442), a tacky former disco that's ground zero of the burgeoning, ultratrendy Silver Lake scene.

WEST HOLLYWOOD

At **Coconut Teaszer** (⊠ 8117 Sunset Blvd., ☏ 323/654–4773) you can dance to raw rock at its best, dine on barbecued food, and sip killer drinks. One room, the Crooked Bar, is a low-key sanctuary usually reserved for acoustic acts. The pool tables are always crowded. Dan Aykroyd and Jim Belushi own the **House of Blues** (⊠ 8430 Sunset Blvd., ☏ 323/650–1451), home to jazz, rock, and blues performers. Past players have included Etta James, Lou Rawls, Joe Cocker, and the Commodores. Some shows are presented cabaret style, including dinner. Every Sunday there's a gospel brunch. The **Key Club** (⊠ 9039 Sunset Blvd., ☏ 310/786–1712) is a multitiered Sunset Strip rock club and restaurant that hosts bands before 11 PM and has dancing with guest DJs afterward.

The **Roxy** (⊠ 9009 Sunset Blvd., ☏ 310/276–2222), a Sunset Strip fixture, books local and touring alternative, country, blues, and rockabilly bands. The **Troubadour** (⊠ 9081 Santa Monica Blvd., ☏ 310/276–6168) opened as a folk-music club in the 1960s. Later a focal point for the now-moribund L.A. Heavy Metal scene, the old-timer has caught its third wind by booking alternative rock acts. Actor Johnny Depp is part-owner of the **Viper Room** (⊠ 8852 Sunset Blvd., ☏ 310/358–1880), a hangout for musicians and movie stars. There's a different theme going every night, from ballroom and swing to ultrahard rock. The basement is for gabbing and smoking. The **Whisky A Go Go** (⊠ 8901 Sunset Blvd., ☏ 310/652–4202) is the most famous rock-and-roll club on the Sunset Strip, with up-and-coming alternative, very hard rock, and punk bands. Monday gigs launch L.A.'s cutting-edge acts.

The Arts

The **Arts Line** (☏ 213/688–2787) has information about cultural events.

Concerts

MAJOR CONCERT HALLS

Part of the Los Angeles Music Center and—with the Hollywood Bowl—the center of L.A.'s classical music scene, the 3,200-seat **Dorothy Chandler Pavilion** (⊠ 135 N. Grand Ave., ☏ 213/972–7211) is the home of the Los Angeles Philharmonic. The L.A. Opera presents classics from September to June. In Griffith Park, the open-air auditorium known as the **Greek Theatre** (⊠ 2700 N. Vermont Ave., ☏ 323/665–1927) presents classical performances in its mainly pop-rock-jazz schedule from June to October.

Since it opened in 1920, in a park surrounded by mountains, trees, and gardens, the **Hollywood Bowl** (⊠ 2301 Highland Ave., ☏ 323/850–2000) has been one of the world's largest outdoor amphitheaters. Its season runs from early July to mid-September; the L.A. Philharmonic spends its summer season here. There are performances daily except Monday (and some Sundays); the program ranges from jazz to pop to classical. Concert goers usually arrive early, bringing or buying picnic suppers. There are picnic tables, and restaurant dining is available on the grounds (☏ 323/851–3588 to make reservations). Be sure to bring a sweater—it gets chilly here in the evening. You might also bring or rent a cushion—the seats are made of wood. Park-and-Ride buses service the venue from various locations around town; call the Bowl for information.

Baghdad and Beyond is an apt description of the **Shrine Auditorium** (✉ 665 W. Jefferson Blvd., ☎ 213/749–5123), which was built in 1926 by the Al Malaikah Temple. Touring companies from all over the world, along with assorted gospel and choral groups, appear in this one-of-a-kind, 6,200-seat theater, as do televised awards shows such as the American Music Awards and the Grammys. The Los Angeles Opera Theatre and a broad spectrum of other musical performers comes to the Spanish-style **Wilshire Ebell Theater** (✉ 4401 W. 8th St., ☎ 323/939–1128), erected in 1924. The **Wiltern Theater** (✉ 3790 Wilshire Blvd., ☎ 213/380–5005 or 213/388–1400), a green terracotta, Art Deco masterpiece built in 1930, is home to the Los Angeles Opera Theater and a venue for pop, rock, and dance performances.

Dance

Bella Lewitsky Dance Co. (☎ 213/580–6338), one of L.A.'s major resident companies, schedules modern dance performances at various locations. **Cal State L.A.'s Dance Department** (✉ 5151 State University Dr., ☎ 323/343–5124) presents several prominent dance events each year—including the Dance Fair in March and Dance Kaleidoscope in July—at Luckman Theater. **Shrine Auditorium** (✉ 665 W. Jefferson Blvd., ☎ 213/749–5123) hosts touring dance companies, such as the Kirov, the Bolshoi, and the American Ballet Theater. **UCLA Center for the Arts** (✉ 405 N. Hilgard Ave., ☎ 310/825–2101) welcomes visiting companies like Martha Graham and Paul Taylor.

Film

FESTIVALS, REPERTORY

The **American Cinematèque Independent Film Series** (✉ 6712 Hollywood Blvd., Hollywood, ☎ 323/466–3456) screens rare vintage and current independent films in the atmospheric Egyptian Theater. **Melnitz Hall** (✉ 405 Hilgard Ave., ☎ 310/825–2345) is UCLA's main film theater; here you'll find the old, the avant-garde, and the neglected. Film festivals, Hollywood classics, documentaries, and notable foreign films are the fare at the **New Beverly Cinema** (✉ 7165 Beverly Blvd., ☎ 323/938–4038), where there's always a double bill. **Nuart** (✉ 11272 Santa Monica Blvd., West L.A., ☎ 310/478–6379) is the best-kept of L.A.'s revival houses, with an excellent screen, good double bills, and special midnight shows. American independent and foreign films are screened at the **Royal Theatre** (✉ 11523 Santa Monica Blvd., Santa Monica, ☎ 310/478–1041). Rare 16mm film noir clips are screened from Thursday to Sunday at **Tales** (✉ 667 S. La Brea Ave., Mid-Wilshire, ☎ 323/933–2640), an espresso bar and bookstore that's a must for old-movie buffs.

MOVIE PALACES

Mann's Chinese Theater (✉ 6925 Hollywood Blvd., Hollywood, ☎ 323/464–8111) is perhaps the world's best-known theater, with three movie screens and many gala premieres. The geodesic **Pacific Cinerama Dome** (✉ 6360 Sunset Blvd., Hollywood, ☎ 323/466–3401) was the first theater designed specifically for Cinerama in the United States. The gigantic screen and multitrack sound system create an unparalleled cinematic experience. Across the street from Mann's Chinese Theater is the Art Deco **Pacific's El Capitan** (✉ 6838 Hollywood Blvd., Hollywood, ☎ 323/467–7674), where first-run features and Disney animation debut. At the intersection of Hollywood and Sunset boulevards, the 70-year-old **Vista Theater** (✉ 4473 Sunset Dr., Los Feliz, ☎ 323/660–6639) was once Bard's Hollywood Theater, where moving pictures and vaudeville played. A Spanish-style facade leads to an ornate Egyptian interior.

Television

Audiences Unlimited (✉ 100 Universal City Plaza, Bldg. 153, Universal City, 91608, ☎ 818/506–0043) helps fill seats for television programs (and sometimes theater events). There's no charge, but tickets are distributed on a first-come, first-served basis. Shows that may be taping or filming include *Suddenly Susan, Third Rock from the Sun,* and *The Drew Carey Show.* Tickets can be picked up at Fox Television Center (✉ 5746 Sunset Blvd., Van Ness Ave. entrance), which is open weekdays from 8:30 to 6. You must be 16 or older to attend a television taping. For a schedule, send a self-addressed, stamped envelope to Audiences Unlimited a few weeks prior to your visit.

Theater

MAJOR THEATERS

Geffen Playhouse (✉ 10886 Le Conte Ave., Westwood, ☎ 310/208–6500 or 310/208–5454), an acoustically superior, 498-seat theater, showcases new plays in the summer—primarily musicals and comedies. The 1,038-seat **James A. Doolittle Theatre** (✉ 1615 N. Vine St., Hollywood, ☎ 323/462–6666; 213/365–3500 Ticketmaster) presents plays, dramas, comedies, and musicals.

In addition to theater performances, lectures, and children's programs, free summer jazz, dance, and cabaret concerts take place at the **John Anson Ford Amphitheater** (✉ 2580 Cahuenga Blvd. E, Hollywood, ☎ 323/461–3673), a 1,300-seat outdoor venue in the Hollywood Hills.

There are three theaters in the big downtown complex known as **Music Center** (✉ 135 N. Grand Ave., ☎ 213/972–7211). The **Ahmanson Theatre** presents classics and new plays. The 3,200-seat **Dorothy Chandler Pavilion** (☞ *above*) occasionally presents plays in between performances of the L.A. Philharmonic, L.A. Master Chorale, and L.A. Opera. The 760-seat **Mark Taper Forum** (☎ 213/972–7353) presents new works that often go on to Broadway, as did *Angels in America* and *Master Class.*

The **Pantages** (✉ 6233 Hollywood Blvd., Hollywood, ☎ 323/468–1700; 213/365–3500 Ticketmaster) is a massive (2,600-seat) but splendid example of high-style Hollywood Art Deco, though the acoustics could use some updating. Large-scale Broadway musicals are usually presented here. The 1,900-seat, Art Deco **Wilshire Theater** (✉ 8440 Wilshire Blvd., Beverly Hills, ☎ 323/468–1716 or 323/468–1799; 213/365–3500 Ticketmaster) presents Broadway musicals.

SMALLER THEATERS

The founders of **Actor's Gang Theater** (✉ 6209 Santa Monica Blvd., Hollywood ☎ 213/465–0566) include film star Tim Robbins; the fare runs the gamut from Molière to Eric Bogosian to international works by traveling companies. At the **Bob Baker Marionette Theater** (✉ 1345 W. 1st St., at Glendale Blvd., downtown, ☎ 213/250–9995), kids sit on a carpeted floor and get a close-up view of the intricate marionettes. Ice cream and juice are served after the shows ($20; reservations essential), which take place from Tuesday to Friday at 10:30 AM, and weekends at 2:30. Musicals, revivals, and avant-garde improv pieces are performed at the **Cast Theater** (✉ 804 N. El Centro, Hollywood, ☎ 323/462–0265). Excellent original musicals and new dramas are the specialties at the 99-seat **Coast Playhouse** (✉ 8325 Santa Monica Blvd., West Hollywood, ☎ 323/650–8507). The **Fountain Theater** (✉ 5060 Fountain Ave., Hollywood, ☎ 323/663–1525) is an 80-seat venue for original American dramas and flamenco dance concerts.

The community-oriented **Japan America Theater** (✉ Japan Cultural Arts Center, 244 S. San Pedro St., downtown, ☎ 213/680–3700) hosts local theater groups, dance troupes, and the L.A. Chamber Orchestra, plus numerous children's theater groups; it has 880 seats.

The **Morgan-Wixon Theatre** (✉ 2627 Pico Blvd., Santa Monica, ☎ 310/828–7519) presents varied children's fare such as Imagination Station's fractured fairy tale, *Rumpelstiltskin*. Tickets generally cost between $5 and $7. The 99-seat **Santa Monica Playhouse** (✉ 1211 4th St., Santa Monica, ☎ 310/394–9779) presents high-quality comedies, dramas, and children's programs. Many highly inventive productions have been mounted in the 99-seat **Skylight Theater** (✉ 1816½ N. Vermont Ave., Los Feliz, ☎ 323/666–2202). Angelenos crowd into the 70-seat **Theatre/Theater** (✉ 1715 Cahuenga Blvd., Hollywood, ☎ 323/871–0210) to view original works by local authors and international playwrights.

OUTDOOR ACTIVITIES AND SPORTS

Updated by
Jeanne Fay

Transplants to Los Angeles know they've become acclimated when they go to a movie on a sunny day. For those who can't stay inside on a beautiful day—of which there are many—Los Angeles supports a range of activities for every level of athlete.

Beaches

From downtown, the easiest way to hit the coast is by taking the Santa Monica Freeway (I–10) due west. Once you reach the end of the freeway, I–10 runs into Highway 1, better known as Pacific Coast Highway, or PCH. Other routes west from downtown include Pico, Olympic, Santa Monica, Sunset, and Wilshire boulevards. The MTA bus line runs every 20 minutes to and from the beaches along each of these streets.

Los Angeles County beaches and state beaches operated by the county have lifeguards. Public parking is usually available, though fees can often be as high as $8; in some areas, it's possible to find free street parking. Generally, the northernmost beaches are best for surfing, hiking, and fishing, and the wider and sandier southern beaches are better for tanning and relaxing. Almost all are great for swimming, but beware: pollution in Santa Monica Bay sometimes approaches dangerous levels, particularly after storms. Call 310/457–9701 for beach conditions in Malibu, 310/578–0478 for Santa Monica, and 310/379–8471 for Manhattan and Redondo beaches.

The beaches below are listed in north–south order:

Leo Carrillo State Beach. On the edge of Ventura county, this narrow beach is better for exploring than swimming or sunning. On your own or with a ranger, venture down at low tide to examine the tide pools among the rocks. Sequit Point, a promontory dividing the east and west halves of the beach, has secret coves, sea tunnels, and boulders. The crowd, like that at many of the beaches in Malibu, is a mix of hippie canyon residents, semiprofessional surfers, and families. Picturesque campgrounds are set back from the beach. ✉ *35000 PCH, Malibu,* ☎ *818/880–0350; 800/444–7275 (camping reservations). Parking, lifeguard (summer), rest rooms, showers, fire pits.*

Robert H. Meyer Memorial State Beach. Perhaps Malibu's most beautiful coastal area, this state beach is made up of three separate minibeaches—El Pescador, La Piedra, and El Matador—all with the same spectacular view. Scramble down the steps to the rocky coves, where nude sunbathing appears unofficially to be sanctioned. The huge, craggy boulders that make this beach private and lovely also make it somewhat dangerous: Watch the tide and don't get trapped between the boulders when it comes in. ⊠ *32350, 32700, and 32900 PCH, Malibu,* ☎ *310/457–1324. Parking, rest rooms.*

Zuma Beach Park. Two miles of white sand usually littered with tanning teenagers, Zuma has all the fixin's: concessions, volleyball, and a playground. This is a great beach for swimming and socializing, and it's also a favorite of families with small children; beachgoers looking for maturity or privacy should head elsewhere. The surf is rough but inconsistent. ⊠ *30050 PCH, Malibu,* ☎ *310/457–9891. Parking, lifeguard (year-round), rest rooms, showers, food concessions, playground, volleyball.*

Malibu Lagoon State Beach/Surfrider Beach. Steady, 3- to 5-ft waves make this beach north of the dilapidated and currently closed Malibu Pier a popular surfing location. The International Surfing Contest is held here in September—the surf is best around that time. Water runoff from Malibu Canyon forms a natural lagoon that's a sanctuary for 250 species of birds. Unfortunately, the lagoon is often polluted and algae-filled, and the debris tends to spill over into the surf. If you're leery of the water, take a walk on one of the nature trails, perfect for romantic sunset strolls. ⊠ *23200 block of PCH, Malibu,* ☎ *818/880–0350. Parking, lifeguard (year-round), rest rooms, picnicking, visitor center.*

Topanga State Beach. The beginning of miles of solid public beach, Topanga has good surfing at the western end (at the mouth of the canyon); the water gets rockier and rougher as you go east. Close to a busy section of the PCH and rather narrow, Topanga is not as serene as other beaches, with hordes of teenagers zipping over Topanga Canyon Boulevard from the Valley. ⊠ *18700 block of PCH, Malibu,* ☎ *310/394–3266. Parking, lifeguard (year-round), rest rooms, food concessions.*

Will Rogers State Beach. A dozen volleyball nets, gymnastics equipment, and playground equipment for kids make this clean, sandy, 3-mi beach a favorite of families and young singles; it also has a sizeable gay and lesbian following. The waves are gentle, good for swimmers and novice surfers, but the beach has the dubious distinction of being one of the area's most polluted—beware after a storm. ⊠ *15100 PCH, 2 mi north of Santa Monica pier, Pacific Palisades,* ☎ *310/394–3266. Parking, lifeguard, rest rooms.*

Santa Monica State Beach. The first beach you'll hit when the Santa Monica Freeway (I–10) runs into PCH, this is one of L.A.'s best-known beaches. Be prepared for a mob scene on summer weekends, when parking becomes an expensive ordeal. The pier has an amusement park with a roller coaster, a Ferris wheel, an antique carousel, an arcade, and food stands; there are also bicycle paths, volleyball nets, and playgrounds. For a memorable view, climb up the stairway over PCH to Palisades Park, a grassy strip at the top of the bluffs. ⊠ *1642 Promenade, PCH at California Incline, Santa Monica,* ☎ *310/394–3266. Parking, lifeguard (year-round), rest rooms, showers.*

Venice City Beach. The surf and sands of Venice are fine, but the main attraction here is the boardwalk scene: a mile and a half of T-shirt shops, pizza stands, and tattoo parlors. Around 18th Avenue, look for Muscle Beach, a big cage where bodybuilders unabashedly pump iron—grab a seat on the bleachers and gape. For bike rentals try Venice Pier Bike Shop (⊠ 21 Washington Blvd., ☎ 310/301–4011) ; Skatey's (⊠ 102 Washington Blvd., ☎ 310/823–7971) is a good bet for skates. Whatever you do, hold on to your wallet. ⊠ *West of Pacific Ave., Venice,* ☎ *310/394–3266. Parking, rest rooms, showers, food concessions.*

Manhattan Beach. Rows of volleyball courts on a sandy strip make this the preferred destination of muscled, tanned young professionals. If you're into bikini watching, this is the place to come. ⊠ *West of Strand, Manhattan Beach,* ☎ *310/372–2166. Parking, lifeguard (year-round), rest rooms, showers, food concessions, volleyball.*

Redondo Beach. The Redondo Beach Pier marks the starting point of this busy beach, which continues south for about 2 mi along a heavily developed shoreline community. Restaurants and shops flourish along the pier; excursion boats and privately owned craft depart from launching ramps; and a reef formed by a sunken ship creates prime fishing and snorkeling conditions. Rock and jazz concerts take place at the pier every summer. ⊠ *Foot of Torrance Blvd., Redondo Beach,* ☎ *310/ 372–2166. Parking, lifeguard, rest rooms, showers, food concessions, volleyball.*

Parks and Playgrounds

Parks

In the **Angeles National Forest,** above Pasadena, you can drive to the top of Mount Wilson for spectacular views of Los Angeles. The Chilao Visitors Center, 13 mi north of Mount Wilson, has exhibits about the forest. The main park in the city of Los Angeles is the 4,000-acre **Griffith Park** (☞ Exploring Los Angeles, *above*); pick up a map at the visitors center. **Hancock Park,** near the L.A. County Museum of Art, is a wide grassy area most notable for the La Brea Tar Pits (☞ Exploring Los Angeles, *above*). Outdoorspeople cherish the canyons, waterfalls, lake, and more than 30 mi of trails at **Malibu Creek State Park,** at the summit of Malibu Canyon Road. **Will Rogers State Historic Park** (☞ Exploring Los Angeles, *above*) in Pacific Palisades is ideal for children, with broad lawns, walking trails, and even polo games on Saturday and Sunday in summer (☎ 310/454–8212 for polo information).

Playgrounds

Santa Monica's **Douglas Park** (⊠ 1155 Chelsea Ave.) has a busy playground, with street parking only a few feet away. An empty cement pond makes a great rink for young rollerbladers and trike riders. **Griffith Park** (☞ Exploring Los Angeles, *above*) has a small playground near the carousel; there's another one across from the Griffith Park Boulevard entrance, and one more past the golf course.

Participant Sports

For information about tennis courts, hiking and biking trails, and anything else sports-related, contact the **City of Los Angeles Department of Recreation and Parks** (☎ 213/485–5515). The **Los Angeles County Department of Parks and Recreation** (☎ 213/738–2961) also has information.

Bicycling

The most famous bike path in the city, and definitely the most beautiful, can be found on the **Pacific Ocean beach,** a 22-mi route from Temescal Canyon down to Redondo Beach. You can park at one of the many lots along Pacific Coast Highway (be prepared to pay a high parking fee). **Rental on the Beach** (⊠ 2100 Ocean Front Walk, ☎ 310/ 821–9338), which has several additional locations on the path in Venice, is among the many rental shops along the bike path. Rates are $5 an hour or $18 a day.

Griffith Park (⊠ Crystal Springs Dr. and Los Feliz Blvd.) has a tree-lined bike route with several options ranging from easy to hard. Stay on Crystal Springs Drive for an easier ride; turn left up Griffith Park

Drive for a tougher ride that rewards with great views. For Griffith Park rentals try **The Annex** (⊠ 3157 Los Feliz Blvd., ☎ 323/661–6665), which charges $15 per day. **Malibu Creek State Park,** at the summit of Malibu Canyon Road, has mountain-biking trails.

Bowling

Hollywood Star Lanes (⊠ 5227 Santa Monica Blvd., Hollywood, ☎ 323/665–4111) attracts everyone from quasi-professionals to twentysomething hipsters; it's open 24 hours.

Fishing

Shore fishing and surf casting are excellent on many of the beaches, and pier fishing is popular because no license is necessary at public piers. The **Santa Monica** and **Redondo Beach piers** all have nearby bait-and-tackle shops.

Marina del Rey Sport Fishing (⊠ Dock 52, Fiji Way, ☎ 310/822–3625) runs excursions for $20 per half day. **Redondo Sport Fishing Company** (⊠ 233 N. Harbor Dr., ☎ 310/372–2111) has half-day charters starting at $22 per person. Sea bass, halibut, bonita, yellowtail, or barracuda are the usual catch. Both companies run whale-watching excursions in winter.

Golf

The Parks and Recreation Department maintains seven public 18-hole courses in Los Angeles. **Rancho Park Golf Course** (⊠ 10460 W. Pico Blvd., ☎ 310/838–7373) is one of the most heavily played links in the country. It's a beautifully designed course, but the towering pines present an obstacle for those who slice or hook.

Several good public courses are in the San Fernando Valley. The **Balboa and Encino Golf courses** (⊠ 16821 Burbank Blvd., Encino, ☎ 818/995–1170) are next to each other. The **Woodley Lakes Golf Course** (⊠ 6331 Woodley Ave., Van Nuys, ☎ 818/780–6886) is as flat as a board and has hardly any trees. Summer in the Valley can be quite hot, so be sure to bring lots of sunscreen and water.

Griffith Park has two splendid 18-hole courses along with a challenging nine-hole course. **Harding Municipal Golf Course** and **Wilson Municipal Golf Course** (⊠ 4730 Crystal Springs Dr. for both, ☎ 323/663–2555) are about 1½ mi inside the park entrance at Riverside Drive and Los Feliz Boulevard. Bridle paths surround the outer fairways, and the San Gabriel Mountains make a scenic background. The 9-hole **Roosevelt Municipal Golf Course** (⊠ 2650 N. Vermont Ave., ☎ 323/665–2011) can be reached through the park's Vermont Avenue entrance.

Health Clubs

There are dozens of health-club chains in the city; some sell daily or weekly memberships. Two that do are **Bodies in Motion** (⊠ 1950 Century Park E, Century City, ☎ 310/836–8000), with a full range of aerobics classes including aerobic boxing and kick-boxing classes, and **24 Hour Fitness** (☎ 800/204–2400), with eight locations in the Los Angeles area. Both charge $10 per day.

Hiking

For information about hiking locations and scheduled outings in Los Angeles, contact the **Sierra Club** (⊠ 3345 Wilshire Blvd., Suite 508, Los Angeles, 90010, ☎ 213/387–4287).

Griffith Park is a great place to hike—pick up a map from the ranger station (⊠ 4730 Crystal Springs Dr.). Many of the paths in the park are not shaded and can be quite steep; a short hike from Canyon

Drive, at the southwest end of the park, takes you to **Bronson Caves,** where the Batman television show was filmed. Begin at the Observatory for a 3-mi round trip hike to the top of **Mount Hollywood.**

Head west for ocean views. At **Topanga State Park,** miles of trails wind high in the Santa Monica Mountains. **Will Rogers Historic State Park,** off Sunset Boulevard in Pacific Palisades, abuts Topanga and has a splendid nature trail. A 2-mi hike from Rogers's home takes you to a stunning ocean-to-downtown view atop Inspiration Point.

Horseback Riding

More than 50 mi of beautiful bridle trails are open to the public in the Griffith Park area. **Griffith Park Horse Rentals** (⌧ 480 Riverside Dr., Burbank, ☎ 818/840–8401) has a going rate of $15 per hour plus a $15 deposit. **Bar S Stables** (⌧ 1850 Riverside Dr., Glendale, ☎ 818/242–8443) rents horses for $13 an hour (plus a $10 deposit). **Sunset Ranch** (⌧ 3400 Beachwood Dr., Hollywood, ☎ 323/469–5450) also rents horses for $15 an hour, plus a $10 deposit; a Friday-evening package includes a trail ride over the hill into Burbank, where riders tie up their horses and dine at a Mexican restaurant. The package costs $35, not including the cost of dinner.

Ice-Skating

Rinks are all over the city, generally charging about $8 for admission and skate rental. In the Valley, there's the **Pickwick Ice Center** (⌧ 1001 Riverside Dr., Burbank, ☎ 818/846–0032). In Pasadena, try the **Ice Skating Center** (⌧ 310 E. Green St., ☎ 626/578–0800).

In-Line and Roller Skating

For rollerblades, **Boardwalk Skates** (⌧ 201½ Ocean Front Walk, Venice, ☎ 310/450–6634) charges $4 an hour or $12 for the day; **Skatey's** (⌧ 102 Washington St., Venice, ☎ 310/823–7971) charges $5 per hour or $10 per day.

For indoor skating, head to **Moonlight Rollerway** (⌧ 5110 San Fernando Rd., Glendale, ☎ 818/241–3630) or **Skateland** (⌧ 18140 Parthenia St., Northridge, ☎ 818/885–1491).

Jogging

San Vicente Boulevard in Santa Monica has a wide grassy median that splits the street for several picturesque miles. The reservoir at **Lake Hollywood,** east of Cahuenga Boulevard in the Hollywood Hills, is encircled by a 3.3-mi asphalt path with a view of the Hollywood sign. Within hilly **Griffith Park** are thousands of acres' worth of hilly paths and challenging terrain; **Crystal Springs Drive,** from the main entrance at Los Feliz to the zoo, is a relatively flat 5 mi. **Circle Drive,** around the perimeter of UCLA in Westwood, provides a 2½-mi run through academia.

Racquetball

The **Hollywood YMCA** (⌧ 1553 Schrader Blvd.; call ☎ 800/872–9622 for other locations) has racquetball courts ($12). In the San Fernando Valley at the **Racquet Center** (⌧ 10933 Ventura Blvd., Studio City, ☎ 818/760–2303), court time runs between $8 and $14 an hour, depending on when you play.

Tennis

Many public parks have courts that require an hourly fee. **Lincoln Park** (⌧ Lincoln and Wilshire Blvds., Santa Monica) and **Westwood Park** (⌧ 1375 Veteran Ave., West L.A.) have well-maintained courts with lights. **Griffith Park** has three sets of lighted courts: one at Riverside Drive south of Los Feliz Boulevard; another north of the Vermont Avenue entrance; and another at the intersection of Griffith Park and Crystal Springs drives. For a complete list of the public tennis courts in Los Angeles, contact the **L.A. Department of Recreation and Parks** (☎ 213/485–5515).

Water Sports

BOATING AND KAYAKING

Action Water Sports (✉ 4144 Lincoln Blvd., Marina del Rey, ☎ 310/306–9539) rents single kayaks for $35 and doubles for $45 per day.

SCUBA DIVING AND SNORKELING

Diving and snorkeling off Leo Carrillo State Beach, Catalina, and the Channel Islands is considered some of the best on the Pacific coast. Two dive shops are **New England Divers** (✉ 2936 Clark Ave., Long Beach, ☎ 562/421–8939) and **Dive 'n Surf** (✉ 504 N. Broadway, Redondo Beach, ☎ 310/372–8423).

SURFING

See Beaches, *above.*

WINDSURFING

Malibu Ocean Sports (✉ 22935 PCH, Malibu, ☎ 310/456–6302) gives lessons and rents boards.

Spectator Sports

The best source for tickets to all sporting events is **Ticketmaster** (☎ 714/740–2000). Among the major venues in the area are **Arrowhead Pond** (✉ 2695 E. Katella Ave., Anaheim, ☎ 714/704–2500), **Edison International Field** (✉ 2000 Gene Autry Way, Anaheim, ☎ 714/940–2000), the **Great Western Forum** (✉ 3900 W. Manchester Blvd., Inglewood, ☎ 310/419–3100), **L.A. Sports Arena** (✉ 3939 S. Figueroa St., downtown, next to Coliseum, ☎ 213/748–6136), **L.A. Memorial Coliseum** (✉ 3939 S. Figueroa St., downtown, ☎ 213/748–6131), and the **Rose Bowl** (✉ Rosemont Ave. off Arroyo Blvd., Pasadena, ☎ 626/577–3100).

Baseball

The **Los Angeles Dodgers** take on their National League rivals at Dodger Stadium (✉ 1000 Elysian Park Ave., exit off I–110, Pasadena Fwy., ☎ 323/224–1400 for ticket information). The **Anaheim Angels** (☞ Spectator Sports *in* Chapter 13) play at Edison International Field.

Basketball

COLLEGE

The **University of Southern California** (☎ 213/740–8480) plays at the L.A. Sports Arena, and the Bruins of the **University of California at Los Angeles** (☎ 310/825–8699 athletic department, 310/825–2101 tickets) play at Pauley Pavilion on the UCLA campus.

PROFESSIONAL

The **Los Angeles Lakers** (☎ 310/419–3182) of the National Basketball Association play at the Forum. L.A.'s "other" N.B.A. team, the much-maligned **Clippers** (☎ 213/748–8000) make their home at the L.A. Sports Arena; tickets are cheaper and easier to get than ones for Lakers' games. The **Los Angeles Sparks** (☎ 310/419–3193) of the Women's National Basketball Association play at the Forum; tickets are almost always available.

Football

The **Anaheim Piranhas** (☎ 714/475–0838) play arena football at the Arrowhead Pond in Anaheim. The **UCLA Bruins** (☎ 310/825–2101) play at the Rose Bowl. The home turf of the **USC Trojans'** (☎ 213/740–8480) is Memorial Coliseum.

Golf

The hot golf ticket each February is the PGA **Nissan Open** (☎ 800/752–6736), played in Pacific Palisades at the Riviera Country Club.

Hockey

The National Hockey League's **L.A. Kings** (☎ 310/673–6003) put their show on ice at the Forum. Disney's **Mighty Ducks** (☎ 714/704–2701) push the puck at the Pond in Anaheim.

Horse Racing

Santa Anita Race Track (✉ Huntington Dr. and Colorado Pl., Arcadia, ☎ 626/574–7223) is the dominant site for Thoroughbred racing. You can always expect the best racing in the world at this beautiful facility, from October to mid-November and late December to late April.

The track next to the Forum in Inglewood in **Hollywood Park** (✉ Century Blvd. and Prairie Ave., ☎ 310/419–1500) is another favorite racing venue. It's open from early November to late December and from late April to mid-July.

Polo

Will Rogers State Historic Park (✉ 1501 Will Rogers State Park Rd., Pacific Palisades, ☎ 310/454–8212 for polo information) has picnic grounds where you can enjoy an afternoon chukker of polo between May and September. Games are played on Saturday at 2 PM and Sunday at 10 AM, unless the grounds are muddy from rain. Parking costs $5 per car.

Soccer

The **Los Angeles Galaxy** (☎ 888/657–5425) professional soccer team plays from March to September at the Rose Bowl.

Tennis

The **Infiniti Open** (☎ 310/824–1010), held in summer at UCLA, attracts top-seeded pro players.

SHOPPING

Revised and Updated by Cynthia LaFavre Yorks

Most stores in Los Angeles are open from 10 to 6, but many stay open until 9 or later, particularly those on Melrose Avenue and in Santa Monica. Melrose shops, on the whole, don't get moving until 11 AM. In most areas, shops are open for at least a few hours on Sunday. Most stores accept credit cards; traveler's checks are often allowed with proper identification. Check the *Los Angeles Times* or *L.A. Weekly* for sales, and if you're curious about who's shopping where (after all, this is L.A.), take a peek at *In Style* magazine.

Beverly Hills Vicinity

Shopping in Beverly Hills centers mainly around the three-block stretch of **Rodeo Drive,** between Santa Monica and Wilshire boulevards and the streets surrounding it.

SHOPPING CENTERS AND MALLS

The **Beverly Center** (✉ La Cienega and Beverly Blvds., ☎ 310/854–0070) covers more than 7 acres and contains some 200 stores. The **Rodeo Collection** (✉ 421 N. Rodeo Dr., ☎ 310/276–9600), between Brighton Way and Santa Monica Boulevard, is one of several upscale European-style shopping enclaves in Beverly Hills. **Two Rodeo Drive** (✉ 2 Rodeo Dr., at Wilshire Blvd., ☎ 310/247–7040), a.k.a. Via Rodeo, is a collection of glossy retail shops housed on a private cobblestone street.

DEPARTMENT STORES

Barneys New York (✉ 9570 Wilshire Blvd., ☎ 310/276–4400), the West Coast branch of the Manhattan store, is a favorite among young hipsters. **Neiman-Marcus** (⊠ 9700 Wilshire Blvd., ☎ 310/550–5900) carries women's fashions and accessories, from the avant-garde to the traditional. **Robinsons-May** (⊠ 9900 Wilshire Blvd., ☎ 310/275–5464) has seen better days, but is still a reliable source for necessities like panty hose or lipstick. **Saks Fifth Avenue** (⊠ 9600 Wilshire Blvd., ☎ 310/275–4211) is one of the best accessory, shoe, and fragrance resources in town.

CHILDREN'S CLOTHING

Oilily (⊠ 9520 Brighton Way, ☎ 310/859–9145) sells whimsical, colorful Dutch clothing and gifts for children, infants, and even their moms. **Pixie Town** (⊠ 400 N. Beverly Dr., ☎ 213/323–6415) has impeccably designed clothing for infants and children up to size 14.

HOME ACCESSORIES AND GIFTS

Del Mano Gallery (⊠ 11981 San Vicente Blvd., Brentwood, ☎ 310/476–8508) carries wearable art and other creations by contemporary artists working in various media. Come to **Hammacher Schlemmer** (⊠ 309 N. Rodeo Dr., ☎ 310/859–7255) to buy presents for adults who never grew up. **Pratesi** (⊠ 9024 Burton Way, ☎ 310/274–7661) is a linen emporium. **Tesoro** (⊠ 401 N. Canon Dr., ☎ 310/273–9890) has everything from trendy Swid-Powell dishware to southwestern blankets, ceramics, and art furniture.

JEWELRY

Cartier (⊠ 370 N. Rodeo Dr., ☎ 310/275–4272; ⊠ 220 N. Rodeo Dr., ☎ 310/275–5155) carries all manner of luxury gifts and jewelry. **Harry Winston** (⊠ 371 N. Rodeo Dr., ☎ 310/271–8554) is the preferred destination for many celebrities looking for Oscar-night jewels. **Tiffany & Co.** (⊠ 210 N. Rodeo Dr., ☎ 310/273–8880), the famous name in fine jewelry, silver, and more, packages each purchase in a signature blue Tiffany box. **Van Cleef & Arpels** (⊠ 300 N. Rodeo Dr., ☎ 310/276–1161) sells extravagant baubles and fine jewelry.

MEN'S FASHIONS

Alfred Dunhill of London (⊠ 201 N. Rodeo Dr., ☎ 310/274–5351) caters to dapper gents in search of British-made suits, shirts, sweaters, and slacks. Pipes, tobacco, and cigars are this store's claim to fame. **Battaglia** (⊠ 306 N. Rodeo Dr., ☎ 310/276–7184) sells accessories, shoes, and Italian fashions—luxurious silks, woolens, cottons, and cashmeres. **Bernini** (⊠ 326 N. Rodeo Dr., ☎ 310/246–1121) specializes in contemporary Italian designer fashions. **Façonnable** (⊠ 9680 Wilshire Blvd., ☎ 310-754-1200) is the place to find tailored French sportswear with whimsical patterns.

MEN'S AND WOMEN'S FASHIONS

Emporio Armani Boutique (⊠ 9533 Brighton Way, ☎ 310/271–7790) houses three levels of this famous Italian designer's architecturally inspired sportswear, home and fashion accessories, and perfumes. **Gianfranco Ferre** (⊠ 2 Rodeo Dr., ☎ 310/273–6311) carries high-quality sportswear and dress apparel for men and women. **Gianni Versace** (⊠ 421 N. Rodeo Dr., ☎ 310/276–6799), part of the Rodeo Collection, carries the late designer's lines. **Polo/Ralph Lauren** (⊠ 444 N. Rodeo Dr., ☎ 310/281–7200) serves up a complete array of Lauren's all-encompassing lifestyle products. **Shauna Stein** (⊠ Beverly Center, 8500 Beverly Blvd., ☎ 310/652–5511) is a distinctive destination for female fans of Eurochic. The 25,000-square-ft antebellum-gone-Hollywood flagship store of **Tommy Hilfiger** (⊠ 425 N. Canon Dr., ☎ 310/888–0132) sells his athletic-inspired fashions for men, women, and children. **Traffic** (⊠ Beverly Center, 8500 Beverly Blvd., ☎ 310/659–4313), for men, and **Traffic Studio** (⊠ Beverly Center, 8500 Beverly Blvd. ☎ 310/

659–3438), for women, are adjoining boutiques with sportswear and dress apparel by the likes of Dolce & Gabanna, Hugo Boss, and Donna Karan.

WOMEN'S FASHIONS

BCBG Max Azria (✉ 201C N. Rodeo Dr., ☎ 310/278–3263) carries hip and affordable sportswear. **Chanel** (✉ 400 N. Rodeo Dr., ☎ 310/278–5500) houses two floors of fashions, cosmetics, and jewelry. **Harari** (✉ 9646 Brighton Way, ☎ 310/859–1131) is a favorite haunt of shoppers seeking forward-looking fashions and accessories that are less about labels than looks. **Mondi** (✉ 421 N. Rodeo Dr., ☎ 310/274–8380), another Rodeo Collection boutique, carries high-style German fashions in the Ralph Lauren mode. **Prada** (✉ 9521 Brighton Way, ☎ 310/276–8889) is a must for ladies who crave postmodern sportswear and the signature designer bags.

Century City Area

Century City is L.A.'s errand central, where entertainment executives and industry types do their serious shopping. More no-nonsense and affordable than Beverly Hills, the malls and speciality shops in this area appeal to a wider audience. **Century City Shopping Center & Marketplace** (✉ 10250 Santa Monica Blvd., ☎ 310/277–3898), set among gleaming, tall office buildings on what used to be the Twentieth Century–Fox film studio's back lot, is an open-air mall with an excellent roster of department stores (including Macy's and Bloomingdale's) and shops.

Downtown

FACTORY OUTLETS

The **Citadel Factory Stores** (✉ 5675 East Telegraph Rd., off I–5, Commerce, ☎ 323/888–1220), on the landmark site of the former Uniroyal Tire factory, carry the latest in off-price fashions from famous names like Benetton, Joan & David, Ann Taylor, FILA, and Betsey Johnson. There's an outdoor food court.

TOYS, GAMES, AND GIFTS

Since 1929 the artisans at **Gonzales Candle Shop** (Sepulveda House, ✉ W14 Olvera St., ☎ 213/625–8771) have supplied shoppers with everything from novelty candles to Gothic and religious candles. Look for art posters, books, tableware, children's toys, and jewelry by local and international artists at the **Museum of Contemporary Art Store** (✉ 250 S. Grand Ave., ☎ 213/621–1710). The museum and store are closed on Monday.

Melrose Avenue Vicinity

This trendy yet boho shopping street is a great place to pick up everything from inexpensive trinkets and used clothing to pricey Americana antiques. Most shops are concentrated within the 2-mi stretch of Melrose Avenue between La Brea Avenue and the blocks west of Crescent Heights Boulevard, but there are also some worthwhile stores east and west of this strip.

ANTIQUES

J. F. Chen Antiques (✉ 8414 Melrose Ave., ☎ 323/655–6310) specializes in ancient Asian pieces, among them Chinese bronzes and lacquered pieces. **Licorne** (✉ 8432 Melrose Pl., ☎ 323/852–4765), operated by French emigrants, sells fine 17th-century furnishings.

FURNITURE AND HOME ACCESSORIES

Freehand (✉ 8413 W. 3rd St., ☎ 323/655–2607) sells contemporary American crafts, clothing, and jewelry, mostly by artists from California. **Golyester** (✉ 136 S. La Brea Ave., ☎ 323/931–1339) sells funky used clothes and home furnishings. **Zipper** (✉ 8316 W. 3rd St., ☎ 323/951–

0620) focuses on design trends from the 1930s to the 1990s, with everything from furniture and books to candles and shaving kits.

MUSIC STORES

Aron's Records (⌖ 1150 N. Highland Ave., ☎ 323/469–4700) has an excellent selection of vinyl and the latest CD releases. **Virgin Megastore** (⌖ 8000 Sunset Blvd., ☎ 323/650–8666) is indeed huge, carrying even tiny indie releases; dozens of listening stations let you sample new and unusual tunes.

TOYS AND GAMES

Hollywood Magic Shop (⌖ 6614 Hollywood Blvd., ☎ 323/464–5610), a Tinseltown institution, sells costumes year-round and has tricks for beginners and experts. **Wound and Wound** (⌖ 7374 Melrose Ave., ☎ 323/653–6703) has a mind-boggling assortment of inexpensive windup toys, robots, music boxes, and rubber animals.

WOMEN'S AND MEN'S FASHIONS

Maxfield (⌖ 8825 Melrose Ave., ☎ 310/274–8800) is among the most elite clothing stores in L.A. Designers carried here include Azzedine Alaia, Comme des Garçons, Issey Miyake, Giorgio Armani, Missoni, and Yamamoto. **Swell Store** (⌖ 126 N. La Brea Ave., ☎ 323/937–2096) is an in-vogue place for shoes (especially Hush Puppies, in any shade including glow-in-the-dark), plus men's and women's clothing and accessories.

VINTAGE CLOTHING

Time After Time (⌖ 7425 Melrose Ave., ☎ 323/653–8463), decorated to resemble a Victorian garden, has time-honored garments from the late 1800s to the 1960s. **Wasteland** (⌖ 7428 Melrose Ave., ☎ 323/653–3028) carries the kind of retro clothing you might see on Winona Ryder and her celeb contemporaries. The store sells new clothing as well, at reasonable prices.

WOMEN'S FASHIONS

Betsey Johnson (⌖ 7311 Melrose Ave., ☎ 323/931–4490) epitomizes the neobizarro Melrose look with her whimsical, outlandish women's fashions. **Trashy Lingerie** (⌖ 402 N. La Cienega Blvd., ☎ 310/652–4543), despite its name, is actually a friendly, family-run establishment; the folks here will happily make you a custom bra or anything else you have in mind. There's a $2 annual membership fee, apparently to keep out the riffraff. **shu uemura** (⌖ 8606 Melrose Ave., ☎ 800/743–8205) is the emporium choice for celebrity makeup artists and their clients.

Todd Oldham (⌖ 7386 Beverly Blvd., ☎ 323/936–6045) is where you'll find the famous designer's brightly patterned women's clothes. **Tyler Trafficante** (⌖ 7290 Beverly Blvd., ☎ 323/931–9678) carries designer Richard Tyler's exquisitely tailored women's sportswear and evening wear.

Santa Monica

Less frenetic and status-conscious than Beverly Hills, Santa Monica is an ideal place for a leisurely shopping stroll; the cool ocean breezes felt along the boulevards may tempt you to stay for hours. On Wednesdays, some of the streets in Santa Monica are blocked off for the weekly farmers market, making it difficult to find a parking space.

SHOPPING CENTERS AND STREETS

Third Street Promenade is a pedestrian-only street lined with boutiques, movie theaters, clubs, pubs, and restaurants. It's as busy at night as it is in the day, with wacky street performers, missionaries, and protesters hawking their talents, causes, and wares. In addition to chain stores there are several interesting boutiques. Mainstream and funky boutiques line **Main Street,** which leads from Santa Monica to Venice. Quaint residential cottages and bungalows surround **Montana Avenue,** where the best shops are between 9th and 17th streets. **Santa Monica Place** (⊠ Colorado Ave. and 2nd St.) is a three-story enclosed mall with department stores and chains and a few uniquely L.A. emporiums.

Specialty Shops

GIFTS, TOYS, AND MEMORABILIA
Imagine (⊠ 1001 Montana Ave., ☎ 310/395–9553) carries custom-designed furniture and bedding as well as European wooden toys and gifts. **Star Wares on Main** (⊠ 2817 Main St., ☎ 310/399–0224) carries authentic and duplicate costumes from films and memorabilia from Loretta Swit, Liz Taylor, and other celebs.

HOME ACCESSORIES AND FURNITURE
Brenda Cain (⊠ 1211-A Montana Ave., ☎ 310/395–1559) sells antique jewelry and home accessories, but the hot ticket here is the amazing Arts and Crafts pottery. **Brenda Himmel Stationery** (⊠ 1126 Montana Ave., ☎ 310/395–2437) is known for its fine stationery, but antiques, frames, photo albums, and books are also for sale.

WOMEN'S AND MEN'S FASHIONS
ABS Clothing (⊠ 1533 Montana Ave., ☎ 310/393–8770) sells contemporary sportswear designed in L.A. **A/X Armani Exchange** (⊠ 2940 Main St., ☎ 310/396–8799) markets the coveted Giorgio Armani label to the masses.

WOMEN'S FASHIONS AND ACCESSORIES
Moondance Jewelry Gallery (⊠ 1530 Montana Ave., ☎ 310/395–5516) carries the unique jewelry of 70-odd artists. **Weathervane** (⊠ 1209 Montana Ave., ☎ 310/393–5344) has a friendly staff and fine European women's designer collections, including those of Paul Smith and Victor Victoria.

San Fernando and San Gabriel Valleys

Ventura Boulevard is the lifeblood of shopping in the Valley, which is more renowned for shopping malls than any other neighborhood in L.A.

SHOPPING MALLS
Glendale Galleria (⊠ 2148 Central Blvd., Glendale, ☎ 818/240–9481), the true star of *Fast Times at Ridgemont High,* has Nordstrom, Macy's, and assorted specialty stores. **Media City Center** (⊠ 201 E. Magnolia Blvd., Burbank, ☎ 818/566–8617) houses a beautiful Macy's as well as Mervyn's and Sears. **The Promenade** (⊠ 6100 Topanga Canyon Blvd., Woodland Hills, ☎ 818/884–7090), in Woodland Hills at the northern edge of the Valley, has a 24-hour hotline with the lowdown on daily bargains. Within the mall are Macy's and a separate Macy's Men's Store.

SIDE TRIPS FROM LOS ANGELES

Revised and Updated by Jeanne Fay

Big Bear and Lake Arrowhead, both about two to three hours away in the San Bernardino mountains, are rustic resorts with beautiful lakes, crisp air, and snowy winters. Catalina Island, an hour's boat ride off the coast, is the Greek isle of the West Coast, with crystal blue waters, a gentle climate, and a friendly, small-town feel. For approximate costs of dining and lodging establishments, *see* the charts in Dining and Lodging, *above.*

Lake Arrowhead and Big Bear Lake

Summer draws crowds to Lake Arrowhead, known for its cool mountain air, trail-threaded woods, and brilliant lake. Big Bear comes alive
in winter, when snowboarders and downhill and Nordic skiers head
here. The Rim of the World Scenic Byway, which connects with Lake
Arrowhead and Big Bear Lake, is a magnificent drive. During spring
and fall you can see some amazing views of the San Bernardino Valley from an elevation of 8,000 ft.

*Numbers in the margin correspond to points of interest on the Lake
Arrowhead and Big Bear Lake map.*

Lake Arrowhead

*90 mi from Los Angeles, I–10 east to I–215 north to Hwy. 30 east
(mountain resorts turnoff) to Hwy. 18 (Waterman Ave.), and then
Hwy. 138 north to Hwy. 173 (Lake Arrowhead turnoff); follow signs
from there.*

❶ **Lake Arrowhead Village** is an alpine community with offices, shops,
outlet stores, and eateries. You can take a scenic 45-minute cruise on
the **Arrowhead Queen** (☎ 909/336–6992) from the waterfront marina. Reservations are essential. The ☻ **Lake Arrowhead Children's Museum** (✉ Lower level of village, ☎ 909/336–1332) has plenty to
entertain pint-size explorers, including hands-on exhibits, a climbing
maze, and a puppet stage.

Past the town of Rim Forest, follow Bear Springs Road 2 mi north to
❷ the fire lookout tower at **Strawberry Peak.** Brave the steep stairway
to the tower, and you'll be treated to a magnificent view and a lesson
on fire spotting by the lookout staff.

❸ If you're up for a barbecue in a wooded setting, visit **Baylis Park Picnic Ground,** farther east on Highway 18.

❹ **Lake Gregory,** at the ridge of Crestline, was formed by a dam constructed
in 1938. Because the water temperature in summer is seldom extremely
cold—as it can be in the other lakes at this altitude—this is the best
swimming lake in the mountains. It's open in summer only, and there's
a nominal charge to swim. The lake has water slides, and you can rent
rowboats at Lake Gregory Village. Fishing is permitted on the lake.

Dining and Lodging

$$$ ✕ **Casual Elegance.** The menu changes weekly at this intimate house
a few miles outside Arrowhead Village, but the steaks and seafood re-
main first-rate. ✉ 26848 Hwy. 189, Agua Fria, ☎ 909/337–8932. AE,
D, DC, MC, V.

$$–$$$ ✕ **Royal Oak.** Dimly lit and publike, the Royal Oak serves dishes like
pepper steak with baked potato and creamed spinach and halibut fil-
let with hollandaise sauce. ✉ 27189 Hwy. 189, Blue Jay Village, ☎
909/337–6018. AE, MC, V. No lunch Sun.–Mon.

$$$–$$$$ ☷ **Lake Arrowhead Resort.** This lakeside lodge has an Old World feel
reminiscent of the Alps. Guests have access to the attached Village Bay
Club and Spa for a $5 daily fee. ✉ 27984 Hwy. 189, Lake Arrowhead
Village, 92352, ☎ 909/336–1511 or 800/800–6792, FAX 909/336–1378.
177 rooms, 4 suites. Restaurant, coffee shop, lobby lounge, pool,
health club, beach. AE, D, DC, MC, V.

$$–$$$ ☷ **Carriage House Bed & Breakfast.** Down comforters and lake views
add to the charm of this New England–style inn. ✉ 472 Emerald Dr.,
Lake Arrowhead Village 92352, ☎ 909/336–1400 or 800/526–5070,
FAX 909/336–6092. 3 rooms. AE, MC, V. Full breakfast.

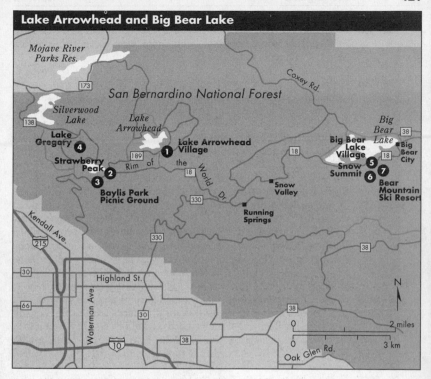

Lake Arrowhead and Big Bear Lake

Big Bear Lake

110 mi from Los Angeles, I–10 east to 215 north to Hwy. 30 east;
Hwy. 330 north to Hwy. 18 east; chains are sometimes needed in win-
ter.

⑤ You'll spot an occasional chaletlike building in **Big Bear Lake Village,**
an alpine- and Western-mountain-style town on Big Bear's south shore.
The paddle wheeler **Big Bear Queen** (☎ 909/866–3218) departs daily
from Big Bear Marina between May and October for 90-minute scenic
tours of the lake; the cost is $9.50. Fishing-boat and equipment rentals
are available from several lakeside marinas, including Pine Knot Landing (☎ 909/866–2628), adjacent to Big Bear Village. **Big Bear City,** at
the east end of the lake, has more restaurants, motels, and a small airport.

⑥ Southeast of Big Bear Village is **Snow Summit,** one of the area's top
ski resorts. It has an 8,200-ft peak and 31 trails, along with two high-
speed quads and nine other lifts. Summit has more advanced runs than
nearby ski resorts and usually has the best snow. Trails are open to mountain bikers in summer. ⊠ *880 Summit Blvd., off Big Bear Blvd.,* ☎
909/866–5766.

⑦ **Bear Mountain Ski Resort,** also southeast of Big Bear Lake Village, has
11 chairlifts and 35 trails. Bear Mountain is best for intermediate
skiers; Summit is more advanced. On busy winter weekends and holidays, it's best to reserve tickets before heading to the mountain. ⊠
43101 Goldmine Dr., off Moonridge Rd., ☎ *909/585–2519.*

Dining and Lodging

$$-$$$ ✕ **Madlon's.** Inside this gingerbread-style cottage, you'll be treated to sophisticated home cooking: lamb chops with Gorgonzola butter, cream of jalapeño soup, or perhaps a fillet with béarnaise sauce. ✉ *829 W. Big Bear Blvd., Big Bear City,* ☎ *909/585–3762. D, DC, MC, V.*

$$-$$$ ✕ **The Iron Squirrel.** Hearty French fare such as the veal scallopini sautéed with apples, calvados, and cream and the duck à l'orange (in a Grand Marnier sauce) are two specialties at this country French–style restaurant with seafood and grilled meats on its menu. ✉ *646 Pine Knot Blvd.,* ☎ *909/866–9121. AE, MC, V.*

$–$$ ✕ **Blue Ox Restaurant.** With a simple menu of steaks, ribs, burgers, and chicken, the Blue Ox is best known for its lively bar, where you can munch on peanuts and throw your shells on the floor. ✉ *441 W. Big Bear Blvd., Big Bear City,* ☎ *909/585–7886. AE, D, DC, MC, V.*

$$$–$$$$ ⊞ **Apples Bed & Breakfast Inn.** Despite its location on a busy road to
★ the ski lifts, the Apples Inn feels remote and peaceful, thanks to the surrounding pine trees. The colorful rooms have names like Golden Delicious, Royal Gala, and Sweet Bough; all have working fireplaces. A common room has a wood-burning stove, a baby grand piano, a game table, and a library loft. ✉ *42430 Moonridge Rd., 92315,* ☎ *909/866–0903. 12 rooms. Hot tub, piano. AE, D, MC, V. Full breakfast.*

$$$–$$$$ ⊞ **Gold Mountain Manor.** This restored log mansion dates from 1928. Each room has its own theme (ask for the Clark Gable room), and all have fireplaces and old-fashioned beds and quilts. ✉ *1117 Anita Ave., off North Shore Dr., Big Bear City 92314,* ☎ *909/585–6997 or 800/509–2604,* 𝔽𝔸𝕏 *909/585–0327. 4 rooms, 2 suites. AE, D, MC, V. Full breakfast.*

$$–$$$$ ⊞ **The Holiday Inn Big Bear Chateau.** Just two minutes from the lake, Big Bear's grandest hotel resembles a mountain château in the European tradition. Guest rooms have brass beds, antiques, and fireplaces. ✉ *42200 Moonridge Rd., 92315,* ☎ *909/866–6666 or 800/232–7466,* 𝔽𝔸𝕏 *909/866–8988. 76 rooms, 4 suites. Restaurant, lobby lounge, pool, exercise room. AE, MC, V.*

$$–$$$ ⊞ **Northwoods Resort.** Northwoods is a giant log cabin with all the amenities of a resort. The lobby resembles a 1930s hunting lodge, with canoes, antlers, fishing poles, and a grand stone fireplace. Rooms are large but cozy; some have fireplaces and whirlpool tubs. Ski packages are available. ✉ *40650 Village Dr., 92315,* ☎ *909/866–3121 or 800/866–3121,* 𝔽𝔸𝕏 *909/878–2122. 140 rooms, 8 suites. Restaurant, pool, outdoor hot tub, sauna, exercise room. AE, D, DC, MC, V.*

$–$$$ ⊞ **Robinhood Inn.** Across the street from the Pine Knot Marina, this family-oriented motel has affordable rooms, some with fireplaces or whirlpool tubs. All accommodations face a courtyard with an outdoor whirlpool spa. ✉ *40797 Lakeview Dr., 92315,* ☎ *909/866–4643 or 800/990–9956,* 𝔽𝔸𝕏 *909/866–4645. 17 rooms, 4 suites. Restaurant, outdoor hot tub. AE, MC, V.*

Lake Arrowhead and Big Bear Lake Essentials

LODGING RESERVATIONS

Most lodgings require two-night stays on weekends. **Lake Arrowhead Communities Chamber of Commerce** (☞ *below*) has information about camping and lodging. **Big Bear Lake Resort Association** (☎ 909/866–7000) will help you with lodging arrangements.

VISITOR INFORMATION

Lake Arrowhead Communities Chamber of Commerce (✉ 28200 Hwy. 189, Bldg. F, Suite 290, Box 219, Lake Arrowhead Village 92352, ☎ 909/337–3715). **Big Bear Chamber of Commerce** (✉ 630 Bartlett Rd., Box 2860, Big Bear Lake Village 92315, ☎ 909/866–4607).

Catalina Island

22 mi from the Los Angeles coastline.

In summer and on weekends and holidays, Catalina crawls with thousands boaters. White buildings dotting the semi-arid hillsides near the main town of Avalon lend it the ambience of a Greek Island. Avalon is an old-fashioned beach community, where palm trees shade the main street and yachts bob in the crescent-shape bay.

Cruise ships sail into Avalon twice a week and smaller boats shuttle between Avalon and Two Harbors, a small isthmus cove on the island's western end. You can also take bus excursions beyond Avalon. Roads are limited and nonresident vehicles are prohibited, so hiking (by permit only) is the only other means of exploring.

Catalina has long been a destination for filmmakers and movie stars. Even before Hollywood discovered the island it sheltered Russian trappers (seeking sea-otter skins), pirates, gold miners, and bootleggers. In 1919, William Wrigley Jr., the chewing gum magnate, purchased a controlling interest in the company developing the Catalina island, whose most famous landmark, the Casino, was built in 1929 under his orders. Wrigley was also responsible for making Catalina the site of spring training for the Chicago Cubs baseball team (before they moved in 1951).

In 1975 the Santa Catalina Island Conservancy, a nonprofit foundation, acquired about 86% of the island to preserve the area's natural resources. The conservancy is restoring the rugged interior country with plantings of native grasses and trees. Bus and van tours can bring you into the interior, where you may be lucky enough to see buffalo (descendants of ones brought to the island in the 1920s for the filming of *The Vanishing American*), plus goats, boar, and unusual species of sea life, including oddities like electric perch, saltwater goldfish, and flying fish.

Catalina can be seen in a day, but several inviting hotels make it worth extending your stay for one or more nights. A short itinerary might include breakfast along the boardwalk, a tour of the interior, a snorkeling excursion at Casino Point, and dinner in Avalon.

Avalon

1–2-hr ferry ride from Long Beach; 15-min helicopter ride from Long Beach or San Pedro

Avalon, Catalina's only real town, extends from the shore of its natural harbor to the surrounding hillsides. Most of the city's activity, however, is centered along the boardwalk of Crescent Avenue, and most sights are easily reached by foot. Though private autos are restricted and rental cars aren't allowed, taxis, trams, and shuttles can take you anywhere you need to go. Bicycles and golf carts can also be rented; look for rental shops along Crescent Avenue as you walk in from the dock. Permits for hiking the interior of the island are available free from the Catalina Conservancy (☞ Catalina Essentials, *below*).

A walk along **Crescent Avenue** is a nice way to begin a tour of the town. Vivid Art Deco tiles adorn the avenue's fountains and planters. Head to the **Green Pleasure Pier,** at the center of Crescent Avenue, for an overall vantage point of Avalon. From here, stand with your back to the harbor and you'll be in a good position to survey the sights. At the top of the hill on your left, you'll spot the Inn at Mt. Ada, now a B&B but once a getaway estate built by William Wrigley Jr. for his wife. On

Catalina Island

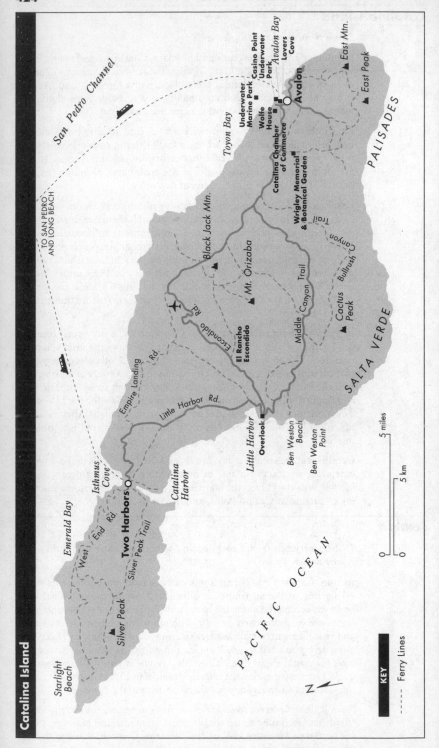

San Pedro Channel

TO SAN PEDRO AND LONG BEACH

Casino Point Underwater Park
Avalon Bay
Lovers Cove
East Mtn.
East Peak

Underwater Marine Park
Wolfe House
Avalon
Catalina Chamber of Commerce
PALISADES

Toyon Bay
Wrigley Memorial & Botanical Garden

Black Jack Mtn.
Trail
Bullrush Canyon

Mt. Orizaba
Cactus Peak
Middle Canyon Trail

Escondido Rd.
El Rancho Escondido

Empire Landing Rd.
Little Harbor Rd.
SALTA VERDE

Little Harbor Overlook
Ben Weston Beach
Ben Weston Point

Isthmus Cove
Catalina Harbor

Emerald Bay

West End Rd.
Two Harbors
Silver Peak Trail

Silver Peak

Starlight Beach

PACIFIC OCEAN

5 miles
5 km

N

KEY
----- Ferry Lines

the pier are the Catalina Island Visitor's Bureau, snack stands, the Harbor Patrol, and scads of squawking seagulls.

On the northwest point of Avalon Bay (looking to your right from Green Pleasure Pier), is the majestic landmark **Casino.** Built in 1929, this circular white structure is considered one of the finest examples of Art Deco architecture anywhere. Its Spanish-inspired floors and murals show off brilliant blue and green Catalina tiles. "Casino" is the Italian word for "gathering place," and has nothing to do with gambling here. Rather, Casino life revolves around the magnificent ballroom; the same big-band dances that made the Casino famous in the 1930s and '40s still take place on holiday weekends. Daytime tours (☎ 310/510–8687) of the establishment, lasting about 55 minutes, cost $8.50. You can also visit the **Catalina Island Museum,** in the lower level of the Casino, which surveys 7,000 years of island history; or stop in at the **Casino Art Gallery,** which displays the works of local artists. First-run movies are screened at the **Avalon Theatre,** noteworthy for its 1929 theater pipe organ. ⊠ *1 Casino Way,* ☎ *310/510–2414 for museum, 310/510–0808 for art gallery, 310/510–0179 for Avalon Theatre.* 🖃 *Museum $1.50, art gallery free.* ☉ *Museum daily 10:30–4, art gallery Fri.–Tues. 10:30–4.*

In front of the Casino, snorkelers and divers explore the clear waters of the **Casino Point Underwater Park,** where moray eels, bat rays, spiny lobsters, halibut, and other sea animals cruise around kelp forests and along the sandy bottom. The area is protected from boats and other watercraft. Snorkeling equipment can be rented on and near the pier. **Lover's Cove,** east of the boat landing, is also good for snorkeling.

Two miles south of the bay via Avalon Canyon Road is the **Wrigley Memorial and Botanical Garden,** where you'll find plants native to southern California. Several grow only on Catalina Island: Catalina ironwood, wild tomato, and the rare Catalina mahogany. The Wrigley family commissioned the garden as well as the monument, which has a grand staircase and a Spanish mausoleum inlaid with colorful Catalina tile. The mausoleum was never used by the Wrigleys, who are buried in Los Angeles. Tram service between the memorial and Avalon is available daily between 8 AM and 5 PM during summer, less regularly in winter. ⊠ *Avalon Canyon Rd.,* ☎ *310/510–2288.* 🖃 *$1.50.* ☉ *Daily 8–5.*

Walk through the residential hills of Avalon and you'll see interesting architecture like the **Wolfe House** on Chimes Tower Road, built in 1928 by noted architect Rudolf Schindler. Its terraced frame is carefully set into a steep site, affording extraordinary views. The house is a private residence, but you can get a good view of it from the path below and from the street. Across the street from the Wolf House, the **Zane Grey Estate** (☎ 310/510–0966 or 800/378–3256) has been transformed into a wonderful rustic hotel. ⊠ *124 Chimes Tower Rd.*

Dining and Lodging

$$–$$$ ✕ **Cafe Prego.** This Italian waterfront restaurant specializes in pasta, seafood, and steak. ⊠ *603 Crescent Ave.,* ☎ *310/510–1218. Reservations essential. AE, D, DC, MC, V.*

$$–$$$ ✕ **Channel House.** A longtime Avalon family owns this restaurant that
★ serves meals prepared with a Continental flair—Catalina swordfish, coq au vin, and pepper steak. An outdoor patio faces the harbor, and there's a comfortable dining room. ⊠ *205 Crescent Ave.,* ☎ *310/510–1617. AE, D, MC, V.*

$$–$$$ ✕ **Pirrone's.** On the second floor of the Hotel Vista del Mar, Pirrone's has a bird's-eye view of the bay. Specialties are local seafood, prime rib, steaks, and pasta; there's a prix-fixe brunch on Sundays. ⊠ *417 Crescent Ave.,* ☎ *310/510–0333. AE, D, DC, MC, V. No lunch.*

$$$$ ☎ **The Inn on Mt. Ada.** Occupying the onetime Wrigley family mansion, the island's most exclusive hotel has all the comforts of a millionaire's mansion—and at millionaire's prices, beginning at $350 a night during the summer season. The rates include all meals, beverages, and snacks and the use of a golf cart. The six traditionally styled bedrooms; some have canopy beds and overstuffed chairs. The hilltop view of the Pacific is spectacular, and service is discreet. ✉ *398 Wrigley Rd., 90704,* ☎ *310/510–2030 or 800/608–7669,* ℻ *310/510–2237. 6 rooms. FAP. MC, V.*

$$$–$$$$ ☎ **Pavilion Lodge.** Across the street from the beach, this popular motel has simple but spacious rooms. There's a large, grassy courtyard in the center of the complex. ✉ *513 Crescent Ave., 90704,* ☎ *800/851–0217. 73 rooms. AE, D, DC, MC, V. Continental breakfast.*

$$–$$$$ ☎ **Hotel Metropole and Market Place.** This romantic hotel could easily be in the heart of the French Quarter in New Orleans. Some guest rooms have balconies overlooking a flower-filled courtyard of restaurants and shops, others have ocean views ✉ *205 Crescent Ave., 90704,* ☎ *310/510–1884 or 800/541–8528. 42 rooms, 6 suites. AE, MC, V. Continental breakfast.*

$$–$$$ ☎ **Hotel Vista del Mar.** Rooms full of rattan furniture and greenery open onto a skylighted atrium. Some rooms have fireplaces, whirlpool tubs, and wet bars. Two suites have ocean views. ✉ *417 Crescent Ave., 90704,* ☎ *310/510–1452 or 800/601–3836,* ℻ *310/510–2917. 13 rooms, 2 suites. AE, D, MC, V. Continental breakfast.*

Nightlife

Warm summer afternoons bring loads of party goers to Catalina's many happy-hour bars, where festivities continue into the night. **El Galleon** (✉ 411 Crescent Ave., ☎ 310/510–1188) serves up microbrewery beers and karaoke. At **Luau Larry's** (✉ 509 Crescent Ave., ☎ 310/510–1919), cocktails are consumed with oyster shooters and calypso hats. The **Catalina Comedy Club** (✉ Glenmore Plaza Hotel, Sumner St., ☎ 310/510–0017) books comic acts all week in summer and on weekends in winter.

Two Harbors

45–60-min ferry ride (summer only) or 90-min bus ride from Avalon; 3-hr ferry ride (summer only) from Los Angeles.

This fairly primitive resort toward the western end of the island has long been a summer boating destination. The area is named for its two harbors, which are separated by a ½-mi-wide isthmus. Once inhabited by pirates and smugglers, Two Harbors recalls the days before tourism was the island's major industry. This side of the island is more untamed, with abundant wildlife. Activities here include swimming, diving, boating, hiking, mountain biking, beachcombing, kayaking, and sportfishing.

Lodging

Tiny Two Harbors has limited overnight accommodations, including a few campgrounds. All reservations are made through the **visitor services** office (✉ Box 5086, Two Harbors 90704, ☎ 310/510–7265), which you'll spot upon arriving.

Catalina Island Essentials

ARRIVING AND DEPARTING

By Boat: Catalina Cruises (☎ 800/228–2546) departs from Long Beach several times daily, taking an hour and 45 minutes to reach Avalon before continuing to Two Harbors. The fare to either destination is $25 round-trip. **Catalina Express** (☎ 310/519–1212 or 800/995–4386) makes an hour-long run from Long Beach or San Pedro to Avalon and Two Harbors; round-trip fare to either destination from Long Beach and San Pedro is $36. Reservations are advised in summer and on weekends.

Service from Newport Beach is available through **Catalina Passenger Service** (☎ 949/673–5245). Boats leave from Balboa Pavilion at 9 AM, take 75 minutes to reach the island, and cost $36 (reservations are advised). Return boats leave Catalina at 4:30 PM.

By Bus: Catalina Safari Shuttle Bus (☎ 310/510–7265) has regular bus service between Avalon and Two Harbors; the trip takes 90 minutes and costs $18 one-way.

By Helicopter: Island Express (☎ 310/510–2525) flies hourly from San Pedro and Long Beach. The trip takes about 15 minutes and costs $66 one-way, $121 round-trip.

GETTING AROUND

By Bicycle: Bike rentals are widely available in Avalon; the going rate is about $6 per hour. Look for rental stands on Crescent Avenue and Pebbly Beach Road. Try **Brown's Bikes** (⊠ Across from basketball court, ☎ 310/510–0986).

By Golf Cart: You can rent golf carts along Avalon's Crescent Avenue and Pebbly Beach Road for about $30 per hour. Try **Island Rentals** (⊠ 125 Pebbly Beach Rd., ☎ 310/510–1456).

On Foot: The requisite permits for hikes into the island's interior are available daily from 9 to 5 at the **Santa Catalina Island Conservancy** (⊠ 3rd and Claressa Sts., ☎ 310/510–2595) and at **visitor services** (☎ 310/510–7265) in Two Harbors. No permit is required for shorter hikes, such as the one from Avalon to the Botanical Garden. The Conservancy has maps of the island's east-end hikes, such as Hermit's Gulch trail. If you plan to backpack overnight, you'll need a separate camping permit. The interior is dry and desertlike; bring plenty of water.

GUIDED TOURS

Santa Catalina Island Company (☎ 310/510–8687 or 800/322–3434) and **Catalina Adventure Tours** (☎ 310/510–2888) conduct tours of the region.

VISITOR INFORMATION

The **Catalina Island Visitor's Bureau** (⊠ Green Pleasure Pier, Box 217, Avalon 90704, ☎ 310/510–1520).

LOS ANGELES A TO Z

Arriving and Departing

By Bus
Greyhound Lines (☎ 800/231–2222) serves Los Angeles from many U.S. cities. The terminal is at 1716 East 7th Street, at Alameda Street.

By Car
Los Angeles is at the western terminus of I–10, a major interstate highway that runs all the way east to Florida. I–15, angling southwest from Las Vegas, swings through the eastern communities around San Bernardino before heading on to San Diego. Interstate 5, which runs north–south through California, leads up to San Francisco and down to San Diego.

By Plane
The major gateway to Los Angeles is **Los Angeles International Airport** (☎ 310/646–5252), commonly called LAX; it is serviced by several dozen major airlines, including Alaska, America West, American, Con-

Los Angeles Freeways

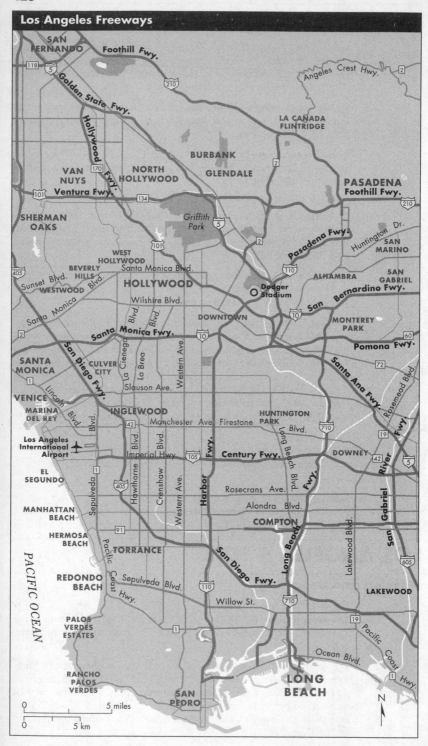

tinental, Delta, Northwest, Skywest, Southwest, TWA, United, and US Airways. *See* Air Travel *in* the Gold Guide for phone numbers.

Long Beach Airport (☎ 562/570–2600), at the southern tip of Los Angeles County, is served by America West, American, and Sunjet International.

Burbank/Glendale/Pasadena Airport (☎ 818/840–8847) serves the San Fernando Valley. Alaska, America West, American, Skywest, Southwest, and United are among the airlines that fly here.

Ontario International Airport (✉ Airport Dr., south from Vineyard Ave. exit of I–10, ☎ 909/937–2700) in Riverside County is served by Alaska, America West, American, Continental, Delta, Northwest, Skywest, Southwest, TWA, United, and US Air Express.

For information about **John Wayne Airport Orange County** (☎ 949/ 252–5006) *see* Orange County A to Z *in* Chapter 13.

BETWEEN THE AIRPORT AND DOWNTOWN
A taxi ride to downtown from LAX can take as little as 30 minutes, but substantially longer in traffic. Visitors should request the flat fee (about $30) to downtown or choose from the several ground transportation companies that offer set rates.

If you're **driving from LAX to downtown L.A.,** take the San Diego Freeway (I–405) north to the Santa Monica Freeway (I–10) east to the Harbor Freeway (I–110) north until you hit downtown. **To get to Beverly Hills,** take the San Diego Freeway north, exit at Santa Monica Boulevard, and turn right.

From Ontario Airport to downtown L.A., take the Harbor Freeway west to the San Diego Freeway north to the Harbor Freeway south; **to Beverly Hills,** take the Santa Monica Freeway west to the San Diego Freeway north, exit at Santa Monica Boulevard, and turn right.

From Long Beach Airport to downtown L.A., take the San Diego Freeway north to Highway 710 north to the Golden State Freeway (I–5) north. **To Beverly Hills,** take the San Diego Freeway north to the Santa Monica Freeway east, and exit at Century Park. **From the Burbank/Glendale/Pasadena Airport to dowtown L.A.,** take the Golden State Freeway to the Harbor Freeway south. From the Burbank airport **to Beverly Hills,** take the Golden State Freeway south to the Ventura Freeway (Highway 134) west to the Hollywood Freeway (U.S. 101) north to the San Diego Freeway south, and exit at Santa Monica Boulevard.

For directions to downtown and Beverly Hills from **John Wayne Airport,** *see* Orange County A to Z *in* Chapter 13.

SuperShuttle (☎ 310/782–6600 or 323/775–6600) offers direct service between the airport and hotels. The trip to or from downtown hotels costs about $12. The seven-passenger vans operate 24 hours a day. In the airport, call 310/782–6600 or use the SuperShuttle courtesy phone in the luggage area; the van should arrive within 15 minutes. **Shuttle One** (☎ 310/670–6666) provides door-to-door service and low rates ($10 per person from LAX to hotels in the Disneyland/Anaheim area). **Airport Coach** (☎ 714/938–8900 or 800/772–5299) provides regular service between LAX and the Pasadena and Anaheim areas.

From Ontario International, ground transportation possibilities include SuperShuttle as well as **Inland Express** (☎ 909/626–6599) and **Southern California Coach** (☎ 714/978–6415). At John Wayne, **Airport Coach** (☎ 800/772–5299) provides ground transportation.

Flyaway Service (☎ 818/994–5554) offers transportation between LAX and the central San Fernando Valley for $3.50. For the western San Fernando Valley and Ventura area, contact the **Great American Stage Lines** (☎ 800/287–8659). They charge from $11 to $21 one way.

The following limo companies charge a flat rate for airport service, ranging from $65 to $95: **A-1 West Coast Limousine** (☎ 213/756–5466), and **Dav-El Livery** (☎ 310/550–0070).

MTA (☎ 213/626–4455) has limited airport service to all areas of greater L.A.; bus lines depart from bus docks at the Transit Center attached to parking lot C. Prices vary from $1.35 to $3.10; some routes require transfers. The best line to take to downtown is Bus 42 ($1.35) or the express Bus 439 ($1.85). Both take about 70 minutes.

By Train

Los Angeles can be reached by **Amtrak** (☎ 800/872–7245). The *Coast Starlight,* offers service from Seattle to Portland and from Oakland to San Francisco through Los Angeles to San Diego. The *Sunset Limited* heads to Los Angeles from Florida via New Orleans and Texas. The *Southwest Chief* comes to the city from Chicago. Trains terminate at **Union Station** (✉ 800 N. Alameda St., ☎ 213/683–6979) in downtown Los Angeles.

Getting Around

By Bus

A ride on the **Metropolitan Transit Authority (MTA)** (☎ 213/626–4455) costs $1.35, with 25¢ for each transfer.

DASH (Downtown Area Short Hop) minibuses travel around the downtown area, stopping every two blocks or so. There are five different routes with pickups at five-minute intervals. You pay 25¢ every time you get on, no matter how far you go. Buses generally run on weekdays between 6 AM and 7 PM and on Saturday between 10 AM and 5 PM; a few downtown weekend routes run on Sunday as well.

By Car

In Los Angeles, it's not a question of whether wheels are a hindrance or a convenience: They're a necessity. If you plan to drive extensively, consider buying a *Thomas Guide,* which contains detailed maps of the entire county. Despite what you've heard, traffic is not always a major problem, especially if you avoid rush hour (between 7 and 9 AM and 3 and 7 PM). Seat belts must be worn by all passengers at all times. A right turn on red after stopping is permitted unless a sign indicating otherwise is posted. In California, pedestrians have the right of way.

If your car breaks down on an interstate highway, try to pull over onto the shoulder of the road and either wait for the state police to find you or, if you have other passengers who can wait in the car, walk to the nearest emergency roadside phone and call the state police. If you carry a cellular or car telephone, *55 is the emergency number to call. When calling for help, note your location according to the small green mileage markers posted along the highway. Other highways are also patrolled but may not have emergency phones or mileage markers.

More than 35 major companies and dozens of local rental companies serve a steady demand for cars at Los Angeles International Airport and various city locations. For a list of the major car-rental companies, *see* Car Rentals *in* the Gold Guide.

Parking rules are strictly enforced in Los Angeles; illegally parked cars are ticketed and towed very quickly. Parking is generally available in garages or parking lots; prices vary from 25¢ to $2 per half hour, or a few dollars to $25 per day. In the most heavily trafficked areas, garage rates may be as high as $20 an hour, though prices tend to drop on weekends. Metered parking is also widely available; meter rates vary from 25¢ for 15 minutes in the most heavily trafficked areas to 25¢ for one hour. In some areas, metered parking is free on weekends or on Sundays.

By Limousine

Limousines come equipped with everything from a full bar and telephone to a hot tub and a double bed. Reputable companies include **Dav-El Livery** (☎ 310/550–0070 or 800/826–5779), **First Class** (☎ 310/476–1960 or 800/400–9771), **Spectrum Limousine Service** (☎ 800/901–4546).

By Subway

The **Metro Red Line** (☎ 213/626–4455) runs 4½ mi through downtown, from Union Station to MacArthur Park, making five stops. The fare is $1.35.

By Taxi

You probably won't be able to hail a cab on the street. Instead, you should phone one of the many taxi companies. The rate is $1.90 to start and $1.60 per mile. Two reputable companies are **Independent Cab Co.** (☎ 213/385–8294) and **United Independent Taxi** (☎ 322/653–5050).

By Train

The **Metrorail Blue Line** (☎ 213/626–4455) runs daily between 5 AM and 10 PM from downtown Los Angeles (corner of Flower and 7th Streets) to Long Beach (corner of 1st Street and Long Beach Avenue), with 18 stops en route, most of them in Long Beach. The fare is $1.35 one-way.

Contacts and Resources

Emergencies

Ambulance (☎ 911). **Fire** (☎ 911). **Police** (☎ 911).

Most large hospitals in Los Angeles have 24-hour emergency rooms. Two are **Cedar-Sinai Medical Center** (⊠ 8700 Beverly Blvd., ☎ 310/855–5000) and **Queen of Angels Hollywood Presbyterian Medical Center** (⊠ 1300 N. Vermont Ave., ☎ 213/413–3000).

Guided Tours

Los Angeles is so spread out and has such a wealth of sightseeing possibilities that an orientation bus tour may prove useful. The cost is between $25 and $40. All tours are fully narrated by a driver-guide. Reservations must be made in advance. Many hotels can book them for you.

ORIENTATION TOURS

L.A. Tours and Sightseeing (☎ 323/937–3361 or 800/286–8752) has a $38 tour covering various parts of the city, including downtown, Hollywood, and Beverly Hills. The company also operates tours to Disneyland, Universal Studios, Magic Mountain, beaches, and stars' homes. **Starline Tours of Hollywood** (☎ 800/959–3131 or 323/463–3333) picks up passengers from area hotels as well as around the corner from Mann's Chinese Theater (⊠ 6925 Hollywood Blvd.). Universal Studios, Sea World, Knott's Berry Farm, stars' homes, Disneyland, and other attractions are on this company's agenda. Prices range from $26 to $68.

A more personalized look at the city can be had by planning a tour with **Casablanca Tours** (☎ 323/461–0156), which conducts a four-hour insider's look at Hollywood and Beverly Hills. Tours are in minibuses with a maximum of 14 people, and the prices are equivalent to the large bus tours—from $35 to $68.

PERSONAL GUIDES

Elegant Tours for the Discriminating (☎ 310/472–4090) is a personalized sightseeing and shopping service for the Beverly Hills area. Joan Mansfield shares her extensive knowledge of Rodeo Drive with one, two, or three people at a time. Lunch is included.

L.A. Nighthawks (☎ 310/392–1500) will arrange your nightlife for you. For a hefty price, you'll get a limousine, a guide, and immediate entry into L.A.'s hottest nightspots.

SPECIAL-INTEREST TOURS

Grave Line Tours (☎ 323/469–4149) is a clever off-the-beaten-track tour that digs up the dirt on notorious suicides and visits the scenes of various murders, scandals, and other crimes via a luxuriously renovated hearse. Tours, which begin daily at 9:30 AM and last 2½ hours (a 12:30 tour will be scheduled if the morning one is full, and sometimes a 3:30 PM tour leaves as well), are offered except Monday and cost $40 per person. **LA Today Custom Tours** (☎ 310/454–5730) has a wide selection of offbeat tours (costing from $6 to $85), some of which tie in with seasonal and cultural events, such as theater productions, museum exhibits, and the Rose Bowl game. The two-hour walking tour of downtown Los Angeles architecture costs $6.

Marlene Gordon of **The Next Stage** (☎ 626/577–7880) tours takes from 2 to 200 people by foot, buses, or vans in search of "the real L.A." Popular excursions include Victorian L.A., Notable Women in L.A., the Insomniac's Tour, and Secret Gardens. **Trolleywood Tours** (☎ 323/469–8184 or 800/782–7287) operates daily tours that takes you through downtown Hollywood and by the "Hollywood" sign, past star's homes and through historical parts of town. The cost is $16 to $37 per person, depending on the tour.

WALKING TOURS

The **Los Angeles Conservancy** (☎ 213/623–2489) offers low-cost walking tours of the downtown area. Each Saturday at 10 AM one of several tours leaves from the Olive Street entrance of the Regal Biltmore Hotel. The cost is $5 per person. Make a reservation, because group size is limited.

Late-Night Pharmacies

The **Kaiser Bellflower Pharmacy** (✉ 9400 E. Rosecrans Ave., Bellflower, ☎ 562/461–4213) is open around the clock. Many towns have a Thrifty or Sav-On pharmacy that stays open late.

Visitor Information

California Visitor Information Center (✉ 6✉ 85 S. Figueroa St., (☎ 213/689–8822). **Hollywood Visitor Information Center** (✉ 6✉ 541 Hollywood Blvd., ☎ 213/689–8822). **Los Angeles Convention and Visitors Bureau** (✉ 633 W. 5th St., Suite 6000, 90071, ☎ 213/624–7300 or 800/228–2452).

13 Orange County

No place in southern California evokes the stereotype of the California good life quite the way Orange County does: Million-dollar mansions dot the coast-line, golf courses meander through inland hills, and convertibles swarm Pacific Coast Highway. But though the coastal cities are all about relaxing under swaying palm trees, the inland cities are alive with convention activities, amusement parks, professional sports events, and dozens of hotels and restaurants, all within minutes of each other.

F EW OF THE CITRUS GROVES that gave Orange County
its name remain. This region south and east of Los
Angeles is now a high-tech business hub where tourism

Updated by
Megan Pincus
and Allison
Joyce

is the number-one industry. Anaheim's theme parks lure hordes of visitors; numerous festivals celebrate the county's culture and relatively
brief history; and the area supports fine dining, upscale shopping, and
several standout visual and performing arts facilities. With its tropical
flowers and palm trees, the stretch of coast between Seal Beach and
San Clemente is often called the "American Riviera." Exclusive Newport Beach, artsy Laguna, and the up-and-coming surf town of Huntington Beach are the stars, but lesser-known gems such as Corona del
Mar are also worth visiting.

Pleasures and Pastimes

Dining

Italian restaurants and burger joints abound in Orange County, but
you'll also find French, Chinese, Thai, Scandinavian, Cuban, and other
types of cuisine, in every type of setting—from the Dining Room at
the Ritz-Carlton, Laguna Niguel, to the ramshackle Ruby's, a diner
on the Newport Pier.

CATEGORY	COST*
$$$$	over $50
$$$	$30–$50
$$	$20–$30
$	under $20

per person for a three-course meal, excluding drinks, service, and 8¼% tax

Lodging

The prices listed in this chapter are based on summer rates. Prices are
often lower in winter, especially near Disneyland, unless there's a convention in Anaheim, and weekend rates are often rock-bottom at business hotels; it's worth calling around to find bargains.

CATEGORY	COST*
$$$$	over $175
$$$	$120–$175
$$	$80–$120
$	under $80

All prices are for a standard double room, excluding 14% occupancy tax.

Outdoor Activities and Sports

Bicycles and in-line skates are popular means of transportation along
the beaches. The county contains dozens of golf courses; we list a few
public ones in this chapter; for more information contact the Southern California Golf Association (☞ Visitor Information *in* Orange
County A to Z, *below*). Many hotels have tennis courts, and there are
public tennis facilities throughout the county, some of which are listed
below. Joggers enjoy the Santa Ana Riverbed Trail, which hugs the Santa
Ana River for 20½ mi between Pacific Coast Highway at Huntington
State Beach and Imperial Highway in Yorba Linda. Surfing is permitted at most beaches year-round—check local newspapers or talk to lifeguards to learn about conditions. The best waves are usually at San
Clemente, Newport Beach, and Huntington Beach. You'll find rental
stands at most beaches along the coast. Never go in the water when
flags with a black circle are flying, and avoid swimming near surfers.
Many beaches close at night.

Exploring Orange County

Like Los Angeles, Orange County stretches over a large area, lacks a focal point, and has limited public transportation. If you're headed to Disneyland, you'll probably want to stay in or near Anaheim, organize your activities around the inland-county attractions, and take excursions to the coast.

Numbers in the text correspond to numbers in the margin and on the Orange County map.

Great Itineraries

IF YOU HAVE 1 DAY

You're going to **Disneyland** ①!

IF YOU HAVE 3 DAYS

You're still going to **Disneyland** ① (stay overnight in 🏨 **Anaheim**), but on day two, head to the coast and explore **Newport Harbor** ⑰. Have lunch at Ruby's on the pier, and then take a 90-minute harbor cruise. Spend the night in 🏨 **Newport Beach.** On day three, visit **Laguna Beach** and, if there's time, **Dana Point** or **Huntington Beach,** then either hang out on the beach or head inland to **Costa Mesa,** where you can browse through **South Coast Plaza** ⑫, one of the world's largest retail, entertainment, and dining complexes.

When to Tour Orange County

The sun shines year-round in Orange County, but you can beat the crowds and the heat by visiting during spring and fall. Smart parents give kids their Disney fix during these periods (though you should still expect fairly long waits for many rides and shows). If you're traveling with children, you could easily devote several days to the theme parks—a day or two at the Magic Kingdom, a day at Knott's Berry Farm, and perhaps an additional day driving to some of the area's lesser-known diversions.

INLAND ORANGE COUNTY

About a 35-minute drive from downtown Los Angeles on I–5 (also known as the Golden State Freeway) is Anaheim, Orange County's tourist hub, which centers around the big D.

Anaheim

26 mi southeast of Los Angeles on I–5.

The snowcapped Matterhorn, the centerpiece of the Magic Kingdom, dominates Anaheim's skyline, an enduring reminder of the role Disneyland has played in the urbanization and growth of Orange County. Disneyland has attracted millions of visitors and thousands of workers, and Anaheim has been their host, becoming Orange County's most populous city and accounting for more than half the county's 40,000-plus hotel rooms. To understand the symbiotic relationship between Disneyland and Anaheim, one need only look at the $1 billion-plus being spent to expand the park and renovate run-down areas of the city. Anaheim's vast tourism complex also includes Edison International Field, home of the Anaheim Angels baseball team; the Arrowhead Pond, where the Mighty Ducks hockey team plays; and the enormous Anaheim Convention Center.

★ 🤚 ❶ One of the biggest misconceptions tourists have about **Disneyland** is that they've "been there, done that" if they've visited either the more mammoth Disney World or one of the two Disney parks overseas. But Disneyland, the only one of the four Kingdoms overseen by Walt him-

Balboa Pavilion, **18**

Bolsa Chica Ecological Reserve, **16**

Bowers Museum of Cultural Art, **8**

Children's Museum at La Habra, **5**

Crystal Cathedral, **7**

Disneyland, **1**

Entertainment Center at Irvine Spectrum, **10**

Huntington Pier, **14**

International Surfing Museum, **15**

Irvine Museum, **9**

Knott's Berry Farm, **2**

Laguna Art Museum, **21**

Mission San Juan Capistrano, **23**

Movieland Wax Museum, **3**

Newport Harbor, **17**

Old Towne Orange, **6**

Orange County Marine Institute, **22**

Orange County Museum of Art, **19**

Orange County Performing Arts Center, **13**

Richard Nixon Presidential Library and Birthplace, **4**

San Juan Capistrano Library, **24**

Sherman Library and Gardens, **20**

South Coast Plaza, **12**

Wild Rivers Water Park, **11**

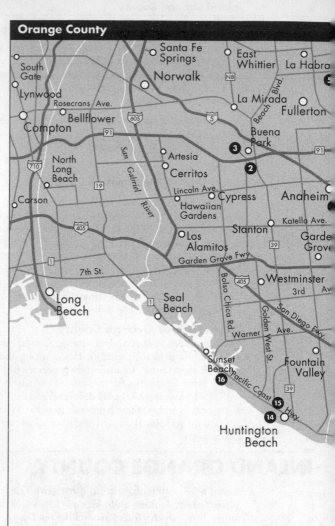

Orange County

PACIFIC OCEAN

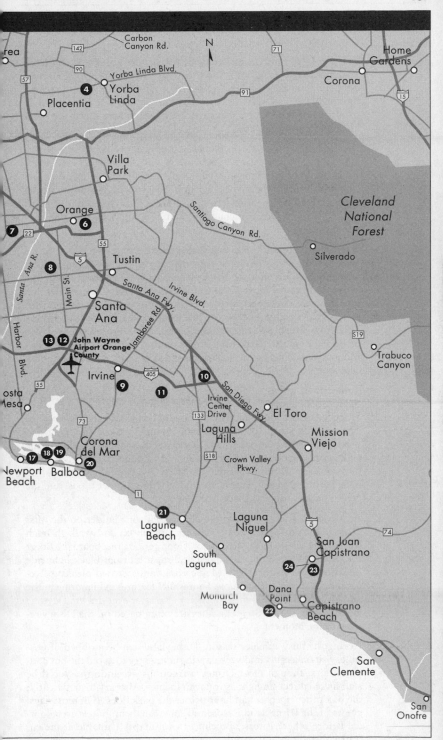

self, occupies a unique place in the Disney legend. His imprint, though perhaps not specifically quantifiable, can be felt in the park's genuinely historic feel.

You can start your Disneyland visit with a stroll along **Main Street,** a romanticized image of small-town America, circa 1900. Trollies, double-decker buses, and horse-drawn wagons travel up and down a thoroughfare lined with rows of interconnected shops selling everything from Disney products to magic tricks, crystal ware, sports memorabilia, and photo supplies.

Disneyland is divided into themed lands. **Fantasyland,** its entrance marked by Sleeping Beauty Castle, is where you can fly on Peter Pan's Flight, go down the rabbit hole with Alice in Wonderland, take an aerial spin with Dumbo the Flying Elephant, twirl around in giant cups at the Mad Tea Party, bobsled through the Matterhorn, or visit It's a Small World, where animatron children from 100 countries sing the well-known song.

In **Frontierland** you can take a cruise on the steamboat *Mark Twain* or the sailing ship *Columbia.* Kids of every age enjoy rafting to Tom Sawyer Island for an hour or so of climbing and exploring. Some visitors to **Adventureland** have taken the Jungle Cruise so many times that they know the operators' patter by heart. Special effects and decipherable hieroglyphics entertain guests on line for the Indiana Jones Adventure, a don't-miss thrill ride through the Temple of the Forbidden Eye. Also here are the animated bears of **Critter Country,** the steep and wet **Splash Mountain,** the Enchanted Tiki Room, and shops with African and South Seas wares.

Tomorrowland has a Buck Rogers–sci-fi feel. You can take a ride on the futuristic Astro Orbitor rocket, zip along on the Rocket Rods or Space Mountain, or tinker with the toys of tomorrow at Innoventions. The twisting streets of **New Orleans Square** are for shopping and browsing, to the tune of strolling Dixieland musicians. Also here is the ever-popular Pirates of the Caribbean ride, and the Haunted Mansion, populated by 999 holographic ghosts, is nearby. Theme shops sell hats, perfume, Mardi Gras merchandise, and gourmet foods, and the gallery carries original Disney art.

At **Mickey's Toontown** kids can climb up a rope ladder on the *Miss Daisy* (Donald Duck's boat), talk to a mailbox, and walk through Mickey's House to meet Mickey. For a loopy good time, board the Roger Rabbit Car Toon Spin, the largest and most unusual black-light ride in Disneyland history. The Magic Kingdom's crowd-pleasing live-action and special-effects show, **Fantasmic!** features exhilarating music and just about every animated Disney character ever drawn. Daytime and nighttime Main Street parades are often based on the Disney release of the moment.

During the busy summer season, Disneyland can be mobbed. If possible, visit on a rainy midweek day. In summer try to avoid the hot midday hours; though most Disney attractions are indoors, you'll be standing in direct sunlight as you wait in lines. Also, try to arrive early; the box office opens a half hour before the park does. (On most days, guests of the Disneyland Resort and some Anaheim hotels are admitted before other visitors.) Brochures with maps, available at the entrance, list show and parade times. You can move from one area of Disneyland to another via the Disneyland Railroad; in addition to touring all the "lands," the train travels through the Grand Canyon and a prehistoric jungle.

Characters appear for autographs and photos throughout the day, but you'll probably have to wait in line. Check with a Disneyland employee (or cast member, as they're called here) for information about designated character stops. You can also meet some of the animated icons at one of the character meals served at the Disneyland or Disneyland Pacific hotels (both open to the public).

Plan meals to avoid peak meal times. If you want to eat at the Blue Bayou restaurant in New Orleans Square, it's best to make reservations as soon as you get to the park. Fast-food spots abound, and healthy snacks such as fruit, pasta, and frozen yogurt are sold at various locations. For a quick lunch on the go, try the Blue Ribbon Bakery, which sells gourmet sandwiches.

You can store belongings and purchases in lockers just off Main Street; purchases can also be sent to the Package Pickup desk at the front of the park. If you're planning on staying for more than a day or two, ask about the Flex Pass, which gives you five-day admission to Disneyland for roughly the same price as a two-day passport (about $68 at press time). The passes are not sold at the park itself, but you can buy them through travel agents and at most area hotels. ⊠ *1313 Harbor Blvd.,* ☏ *714/781–4565.* ⊒ *$38.* ☉ *June–mid-Sept., Sun.–Fri. 9 AM–midnight, Sat. 9 AM–1 AM; mid-Sept.–May, weekdays 10–6, Sat. 9–midnight, Sun. 9–10.*

Dining and Lodging
Most Anaheim hotels have complimentary shuttle service to Disneyland, though many are within walking distance.

$–$$$$ ✕ **Yamabuki.** Part of the Disneyland Pacific Hotel complex, this stylish Japanese restaurant serves traditional dishes and has a full sushi bar. The plum-wine ice cream is a treat. ⊠ *Disneyland Pacific Hotel, 1717 S. West St.,* ☏ *714/956–6755. AE, DC, MC, V. No lunch weekends.*

$$–$$$ ✕ **The Catch/Hop City Blues and Brew.** Across from Edison International Field, this combination sports bar and House of Blues–style dinner-and-entertainment venue draws a crowd at night. The Catch serves hearty portions of steak, seafood, pasta, and salads. The adjacent Hop City steak house serves up live blues along with 14-ounce blackened rib eyes and 20-ounce T-bones. ⊠ *1929 and 1939 S. State College Blvd.,* ☏ *714/634–1829 (The Catch), 714/978–3700 (Hop City). AE, DC, MC, V.*

$$–$$$ ✕ **Mr. Stox.** Oriental rugs, intimate booths, and linen tablecloths create an elegant setting at this family-owned restaurant. Prime rib, mesquite-grilled rack of lamb, and fresh fish specials are excellent; the pasta, bread, and pastries are homemade; and the wine list wins awards. ⊠ *1105 E. Katella Ave.,* ☏ *714/634–2994. AE, D, DC, MC, V. No lunch weekends. Valet parking.*

$$–$$$ ✕ **Thee White House.** Crisp linens, candles, and flowers accent the small dining rooms within this 1909 mansion, where pastas, veal scallopini, and a large selection of fresh seafood dishes form the heart of the northern Italian menu. A three-course prix-fixe lunch, served on weekdays only, costs $16. ⊠ *887 S. Anaheim Blvd.,* ☏ *714/772–1381. AE, DC, MC, V. No lunch weekends.*

$–$$$ ✕ **Luigi's D'Italia.** Despite the simple surroundings—red vinyl booths and plastic checkered tablecloths—Luigi's serves outstanding Italian cuisine: spaghetti marinara, cioppino, and all the classics. Kids will feel right at home here; there's even a children's menu. ⊠ *801 S. State College Blvd.,* ☏ *714/490–0990. AE, MC, V.*

$$$$ ▦ **Anaheim Marriott.** With desks, two phones, and modem hookups, the rooms at this busy convention hotel are well equipped for business

440

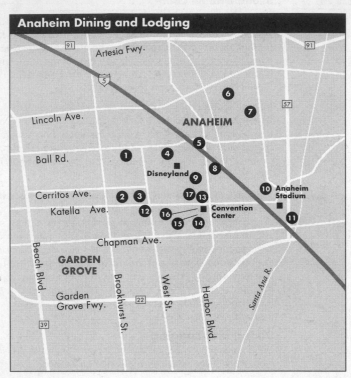

Anaheim Dining and Lodging

travelers. Some rooms have balconies. Accommodations on the north side have good views of Disneyland's summer fireworks shows. Discounted weekend and Disneyland packages are available. ✉ *700 W. Convention Way, 92802,* ☎ *714/750–8000 or 800/228–9290,* 𝖥𝖠𝖷 *714/750–9100. 1,033 rooms, 52 suites. 2 restaurants, 2 lounges, in-room modem lines, in-room safes, no-smoking rooms, room service, 2 pools, 2 hot tubs, health club, piano, coin laundry, laundry service and dry cleaning, concierge, concierge floor, meeting rooms, car rental, parking (fee). AE, D, DC, MC, V.*

$$$$ ★ 🏨 **Disneyland Hotel.** Disney products are for sale everywhere at this resort with a kitschy, retro-'50s charm. In Goofy's Kitchen, kids can dine with their favorite Disney characters. Rooms in the Bonita tower overlook the Fantasy Waters, a fountain that's illuminated at night. On most days, guests staying at the hotel are admitted to the park before the gates open to the general public. Room-and-ticket packages are available. ✉ *1150 W. Cerritos Ave., 92802,* ☎ *714/778–6600,* 𝖥𝖠𝖷 *714/956–6510. 1,074 rooms, 62 suites. 6 restaurants, 5 bars, in-room safes, minibars, refrigerators, room service, 3 pools, hot tub, health club, beach, boating, skating, baby-sitting, laundry service and dry cleaning, concierge, concierge floor, business services, rental car, travel services, airport shuttle, parking (fee). AE, D, DC, MC, V.*

$$$$ ★ 🏨 **Sheraton Anaheim Hotel.** If you're hoping to escape the commercial atmosphere of the hotels surrounding Disneyland, consider this sprawling replica of a Tudor-style castle. Fish swim in a pond in the lobby, which has a grand fireplace and is filled with flowers and plants. The sizable rooms open onto interior gardens. A Disneyland shuttle is available. ✉ *1015 W. Ball Rd., 92802,* ☎ *714/778–1700 or 800/325–*

3535, FAX 714/535–3889. *475 rooms, 16 suites. Restaurant, bar, deli, in-room modem lines, in-room safes, no-smoking rooms, room service, pool, outdoor hot tub, health club, baby-sitting, coin laundry, laundry service and dry cleaning, concierge, concierge floor, meeting rooms. AE, D, DC, MC, V.*

$$$ 🏨 **Anaheim Hilton and Towers.** Next to the Anaheim Convention Center, this busy Hilton is the largest hotel in southern California: It even has its own post office, as well as shops, restaurants, and cocktail lounges. A shuttle runs to Disneyland, or you can walk the few blocks. Special summer children's programs include a lending desk with games, toys, and books. The fee to use the health club is $10. ✉ *777 Convention Way, 92802,* ☎ *714/750–4321 or 800/445–8667,* FAX *714/740–4460. 1,574 rooms, 95 suites. 4 restaurants, 2 lounges, no-smoking floors, room service, pool, hot tub, health club, beauty salon, massage, sauna, piano, children's programs (under 12), baby-sitting, laundry service and dry cleaning, concierge, meeting rooms, business services, travel services, car rental, airport shuttle, parking (fee). AE, D, DC, MC, V.*

$$–$$$ 🏨 **Holiday Inn Anaheim at the Park.** Families frequent this Mediterranean-style hotel. Some rooms have separate sitting areas. A complimentary shuttle transports guests to nearby attractions, including Disneyland, Knott's Berry Farm, the Movieland Wax Museum, Medieval Times, and the Main Place and Anaheim Plaza shopping areas. ✉ *1221 S. Harbor Blvd., 92805,* ☎ *714/758–0900 or 800/545–7275,* FAX *714/533–1804. 252 rooms, 2 suites. Restaurant, bar, no-smoking rooms, room service, pool, outdoor hot tub, concierge, meeting rooms, travel services, free parking. AE, D, DC, MC, V.*

$$–$$$ 🏨 **Radisson Maingate.** The public areas at this friendly establishment have had a major overhaul, and the rooms in its two eight-story buildings have all-new furniture. Some rooms have have pull-out sofas in addition to beds. Shuttles zip hotel patrons to Disneyland or Knott's Berry Farm. ✉ *1850 S. Harbor Blvd., 92802,* ☎ *714/750–2801 or 800/333–3333,* FAX *714/971–4754. 487 rooms, 15 suites. Restaurant, bar, no-smoking rooms, room service, pool, coin laundry, laundry service and dry cleaning, concierge, meeting rooms, travel services, free parking. AE, D, DC, MC, V.*

$–$$$ 🏨 **Candy Cane Inn.** One of the Disneyland area's first hotels (deeds
★ were executed on Christmas Eve, hence the name) the Candy Cane has spacious standard rooms with no-nonsense decor; deluxe rooms have refrigerators and coffeemakers. A free Disneyland shuttle runs every half hour. ✉ *1747 S. Harbor Blvd., 92802,* ☎ *714/774–5284 or 800/345–7057,* FAX *714/772–5462 or 714/772–1305. 172 rooms. No-smoking rooms, refrigerators, pool, wading pool, outdoor hot tub, coin laundry, laundry service and dry cleaning, free parking. Continental breakfast. AE, D, DC, MC, V.*

$–$$$ 🏨 **Desert Palm Inn and Suites.** This hotel midway between Disneyland and the convention center is a great value, with $99 one-bedroom suites that can accommodate the whole family. All rooms, including the standard variety, have microwaves. Book well ahead of your visit. ✉ *631 W. Katella Ave., 92802,* ☎ *714/535–1133 or 800/635–5423,* FAX *714/491–7409. 50 rooms, 50 suites. In-room modem lines, no-smoking rooms, refrigerators, pool, outdoor hot tub, sauna, coin laundry, laundry service and dry cleaning, free parking. AE, D, DC, MC, V.*

$$ 🏨 **Best Western Stovall's Inn.** Nice touches at this well-maintained motel include a topiary garden, a free shuttle to Disneyland, and Nintendo and movie rentals. Ask about discounts if you're staying several nights. ✉ *1110 W. Katella Ave., 92802,* ☎ *714/778–1880 or 800/854–8175,* FAX *714/778–3805. 290 rooms. Bar, no-smoking rooms, room service, 2 pools, outdoor hot tub, coin laundry, laundry service and dry clean-*

ing, business services, meeting rooms, travel services, free parking. AE, D, DC, MC, V.

$$ ⊞ **Ramada Inn Conestoga at Disneyland.** Pint-size cowboys will love this Old West–style hotel with swinging saloon doors and a *Bonanza*-style lobby. The restaurants look like saloons, and there's a nice pool area for relaxing after a day in the saddle. The residential location makes for quiet evenings. A complimentary shuttle heads to Disneyland every hour. ⊠ *1240 S. Walnut Ave., 92802,* ☎ *714/535–0300 or 800/824–5459,* ₣ₐₓ *714/999–1727. 252 rooms. Restaurant, bar, no-smoking rooms, room service, pool, outdoor hot tub, laundry service and dry cleaning, airport shuttle, free parking. AE, D, DC, MC, V.*

$–$$ ⊞ **Anaheim Fairfield Inn by Marriott.** This hotel has a bit more character than the typical Fairfield, and the spacious rooms have sleeper sofas as well as beds. Across the street from Disneyland, the hotel runs a free shuttle service, and guests are admitted early to the park. A nearby restaurant provides room service, but kids usually prefer McDonald's Happy Meals, delivered right to your room. ⊠ *1460 S. Harbor Blvd., 92802,* ☎ *714/772–6777 or 800/854–3340,* ₣ₐₓ *714/999–1727. 467 rooms. Restaurant, no-smoking rooms, refrigerators, room service, pool, outdoor hot tub, concierge, travel services, meeting rooms, free parking. AE, D, DC, MC, V.*

$ ⊞ **Alpine Motel.** With a lobby that looks like a snow-covered lodge, this convenient motel is just steps from Disneyland and the convention center. Two-room suites are a great value, even during the busy summer season. ⊠ *715 W. Katella Ave., 92802,* ☎ *714/535–2186 or 800/772–4422,* ₣ₐₓ *714/535–3714. 41 rooms, 8 suites. No-smoking rooms, pool, coin laundry, laundry service and dry cleaning, free parking. AE, D, DC, MC, V. Continental breakfast.*

Nightlife

There's country music with line-dancing lessons on three dance floors from Tuesday to Saturday at **Cowboy Boogie Co.** (⊠ 1721 S. Manchester Ave., ☎ 714/956–1410). Sunday nights usually feature a different style of music; call ahead to see what's on. The club is closed on Monday.

Outdoor Activities and Sports

Pro baseball's **Anaheim Angels** play at Edison International Field (⊠ 2000 Gene Autry Way, ☎ 714/634–2000). The National Hockey League's **Mighty Ducks of Anaheim** play at Arrowhead Pond (⊠ 2695 E. Katella Ave., ☎ 714/740–2000). There are six public tennis courts at **Pearson Park** (⊠ 400 N. Harbor Blvd., at Sycamore St.); call the **Parks and Recreation Department** (☎ 949/765–5191) for details.

Buena Park

25 mi south of Los Angeles on I–5.

A humble farmer in Buena Park created the boysenberry by mixing red raspberries, blackberries, and loganberries; now on his land is Knott's Berry Farm, a major amusement park.

★ ☝ ❷ **Knott's Berry Farm** got its start in 1934, when Cordelia Knott began serving chicken dinners on her wedding china to supplement her family's income. Or so the story goes. The dinners and her boysenberry pies proved more profitable than husband Walter's berry farm, so the two moved first into the restaurant business and then into the entertainment business. Their park is now a 150-acre complex with 100-plus rides and attractions, 60 food concessions and restaurants, and 60 shops.

The first thing you'll encounter is **Ghost Town,** whose authentic old buildings have been relocated from their original mining-town sites.

You can stroll down the street, stop and chat with the blacksmith, pan for gold, crack open a geode, ride in an authentic 1880s passenger train, or take the Gold Mine ride and descend into a replica of a working gold mine. A real treasure here is the antique Dentzel carousel.

Camp Snoopy is a miniature High Sierra wonderland where Snoopy and his friends from the "Peanuts" comic strip hang out. Nearby is **Wild Water Wilderness,** where you can ride white water in an inner tube in Big Foot Rapids and commune with the native peoples of the Northwest coast in the spooky Mystery Lodge. For more water thrills, check out the dolphin and sea lion shows in the Pacific Pavilion at **The Boardwalk;** here you'll also find the 3-D Nu Wave Theater.

Thrill rides are placed throughout the park: Try the **Boomerang** roller coaster; **X-K-1,** a living version of a video game; **Kingdom of the Dinosaurs,** a *Jurassic Park*–like thrill ride; and **Montezooma's Revenge,** a roller coaster that goes from 0 to 55 mph in less than five seconds. **Jaguar!** simulates the motions of a cat stalking its prey, twisting, spiraling, and speeding up and slowing down as it takes guests on its stomach-dropping course. The park's newest ride, **Wind Jammer,** is the country's first outdoor dual-action roller coaster, with two cars racing simultaneously through twists and turns at top speed. Shows are scheduled in Ghost Town, the Bird Cage Theater, and the Good Time Theater throughout the day. ⊠ *8039 Beach Blvd., between La Palma Ave. and Crescent St.,* ☎ *714/220–5200.* ☎ *$36.* ☉ *June–mid-Sept., daily 9 AM–midnight; mid-Sept.–May, weekdays 10–6, Sat. 10–10, Sun. 10–7; closed during inclement weather.*

❸ More than 75 years of movie magic are immortalized at the **Movieland Wax Museum,** which holds several hundred wax sculptures, including ones of Michael Jackson, John Wayne, Marilyn Monroe, Geena Davis, George Burns, and Bruce and Brandon Lee. You can buy a combination ticket for $16.90 that also allows you admission to the so-so Ripley's Believe It or Not, across the street. ⊠ *7711 Beach Blvd., between La Palma and Orangethorpe Aves.,* ☎ *714/522–1155.* ☎ *$12.95.* ☉ *Daily 9–7.*

Dining and Lodging

$ ✕ **Mrs. Knott's Chicken Dinner Restaurant.** The restaurant at the entrance to Knott's Berry Farm, open for breakfast, lunch, and dinner, serves crispy fried chicken, along with tangy coleslaw and Cordelia Knott's signature chilled cherry-rhubarb compote. Expect long lines on weekends. ⊠ *Knott's Berry Farm, 8039 Beach Blvd.,* ☎ *714/220–5080. AE, D, DC, MC, V. No lunch Sun.*

$$ ⌂ **Buena Park Hotel and Convention Center.** Light-color oak furniture and earth-tone fabrics lend the rooms here a modern, muted feel. The hotel, within easy walking distance of Knott's Berry Farm, provides complimentary shuttle service to Disneyland. Ask about family vacation packages, which include admission to one of the parks. ⊠ *7675 Crescent Ave., 90620,* ☎ *714/995–1111 or 800/854–8792,* FAX *714/828–8590. 314 rooms, 36 suites. 2 restaurants, bar, pool, concierge floor. AE, D, DC, MC, V.*

Yorba Linda, La Habra, and Brea

7–12 mi north of Anaheim on Hwy. 57.

Clustered together north of Anaheim, the quiet suburban towns of Yorba Linda, La Habra, and Brea contain parks, shopping centers, and cinemas. Yorba Linda's main claim to fame is the **Richard Nixon Presidential Library and Birthplace,** the final resting place of the 37th U.S.

president and his wife, Pat. Exhibits illustrate the checkered career of Nixon, the only president forced to resign from office. Visitors can listen to the so-called smoking-gun tape from the Watergate days, among other recorded material. In contrast to some of the high-tech displays here are Pat Nixon's tranquil rose garden and the small farmhouse where Richard Nixon was born in 1913. ✉ *18001 Yorba Linda Blvd., at Imperial Hwy., Yorba Linda,* ☎ *714/993–3393.* ⌑ *$5.95.* ⊙ *Mon.–Sat. 10–5, Sun. 11–5.*

🖑 ❺　The **Children's Museum at La Habra** is housed in a 1923-vintage Union Pacific railroad depot, with old railroad cars resting nearby. Children can climb behind the wheel of Buster the Bus, a retired transit bus; "dig up" bones in the huge Dinosaur Dig sandbox; or pretend they're early settlers fishing, camping, and exploring caves. ✉ *301 S. Euclid St., at E. Lambert Rd., La Habra,* ☎ *562/905–9793.* ⌑ *$4.* ⊙ *Mon.–Sat. 10–5, Sun. 1–5.*

Dining

$$$–$$$$　✕ **La Vie en Rose.** It's worth the detour to Brea to sample the stylishly
★　　　presented traditional French cuisine served in this reproduction Norman farmhouse that's capped by a turret. There's seafood, lamb, veal, and for dessert, a silky crème brûlée and a Grand Marnier soufflé. ✉ *240 S. State College Blvd. (across from Brea mall),* ☎ *714/529–8333. AE, DC, MC, V. Closed Sun.*

Garden Grove and Orange

South of Anaheim, I–5 to Hwy. 22.

❻　Around the intersection of Glassell Street and Chapman Avenue is Orange Plaza (or Orange Circle, as locals call it), the heart of **Old Towne Orange.** One of the few historic towns in Orange County, this area contains many California Craftsman–style cottages.

❼　The main attraction in Garden Grove is the **Crystal Cathedral,** the domain of television evangelist Robert Schuller. Designed by architect Philip Johnson, the sparkling glass structure resembles a four-pointed star, with more than 10,000 panes of glass covering a weblike steel truss to form translucent walls. ✉ *12141 Lewis St. (take I–5 to Chapman Ave. W), Garden Grove,* ☎ *714/971–4013.* ⌑ *Donation requested.* ⊙ *Guided tours Mon.–Sat. 9–3:30; call for schedule.*

Dining and Lodging

$$–$$$$　✕ **La Brasserie.** Though this establishment doesn't look like a typical brasserie, the varied French cuisine befits the name over the door. The specialty here is veal chops. There's also an inviting bar-lounge. ✉ *202 S. Main St., Orange,* ☎ *714/978–6161. AE, DC, MC, V. Closed Sun. No lunch Sat.*

$$–$$$　✕ **P.J.'s Abbey.** Locals like to walk from their charming bungalow residences in historic Old Towne to this high-ceiling former abbey to enjoy American favorites such as pork tenderloin in cherry-walnut sauce with garlic mashed potatoes. ✉ *182 S. Orange St., Orange,* ☎ *714/771– 8556. AE, MC, V*

Santa Ana

12 mi south of Anaheim, I–5 to Hwy. 55.

🖑 ❽　Santa Ana, the county seat, is home to the **Bowers Museum of Cultural Art.** Permanent exhibits include sculpture, costumes, and artifacts from Oceania; sculpture from west and central Africa; Pacific Northwest wood carvings; dazzling beadwork of the Plains cultures; basketry from California ; and still-life paintings. The interactive exhibits at the **Bowers Kidseum,** adjacent to the main facility, are geared toward children between ages 6 and 12, in addition to classes, storytelling, and arts and crafts workshops. ✉ *2002 N. Main St., off I–5,* ☎ *714/567–3600.* ▦ *$6.* ⊙ *Tues.–Sun. 10–4, Thurs. 10–9.*

Dining

$$$–$$$$ ✕ **Gustaf Anders.** Grilled gravlax and a wonderful fillet of beef pre-
★ pared with Stilton cheese, a red-wine sauce, and creamed mushrooms are among the draws at this Scandinavian restaurant. Next door is the more casual, less expensive Gustaf Anders' Back Pocket, with equally excellent food—parsley salad, tasty flatbreads, and Swedish beef casserole. ✉ *South Coast Plaza Village, 1651 Sunflower Ave.,* ☎ *714/668– 1737. AE, DC, MC, V. No lunch Sun. at Back Pocket.*

$$$–$$$$ ✕ **Morton's of Chicago.** Luscious onion bread and huge portions of aged steaks make this wood-panel establishment the place to indulge carnivorous cravings. ✉ *South Coast Plaza Village, 1661 Sunflower Ave.,* ☎ *714/444–4834. AE, DC, MC, V. No lunch. Valet parking.*

$–$$ ✕ **National Sports Grill.** Here you can grab a burger, watch sports on TV, and play a round of pool. There's pasta, chicken, and more on the menu; the bartenders pour domestic and imported drafts. ✉ *101 Sand Pointe,* ☎ *714/979–0900. AE, D, DC, MC, V.*

Irvine

6 mi south of Santa Ana, Hwy. 55 to I–405; 12 mi south of Anaheim on I–5.

Irvine, with its tree-lined streets, manicured lawns, and child-filled parks, has been ranked in national surveys as America's safest city. Some visitors find this master-planned community a tad sterile, but it has well-regarded schools, dozens of shopping centers, and a network of well-lit walking and biking paths for the town's active residents.

❾ Some of the California impressionist paintings on display at the small **Irvine Museum** depict the California landscape in the days before freeways and housing developments. The paintings, which are displayed on the 12th floor of the circular, marble-and-glass Tower 17 building, were assembled by Joan Irvine Smith, granddaughter of James Irvine, who once owned one-quarter of what is now Orange County. ✉ *18881 Von Karman Ave., at Martin St.,* ☎ *949/476–2565.* ▦ *Free.* ⊙ *Tues.–Sat. 11–5.*

❿ The mind-boggling 32-acre **Entertainment Center at Irvine Spectrum** contains a huge, 21-theater cinema complex, lively restaurants and cafés, and an outdoor shopping arcade. Other highlights include Sega City's virtual-reality arcade and an Out Takes digital photo studio. ✉ *Exit Irvine Center Dr. at intersection of I–405, I–5, and Hwy. 133,* ☎ *949/ 450–4900 for film listings.*

⑪ **Wild Rivers Water Park** has more than 40 rides and attractions, including a wave pool, a few daring slides, a river inner-tube ride, and several cafés and shops. ✉ *8800 Irvine Center Dr., off I–405,* ☎ *949/768– 9453.* ▦ *$19.95.* ⊙ *Mid-May–Sept.; call for hrs.*

Dining and Lodging

$$$–$$$$ ✕ **Bistango.** A sleek, high-style, art-filled bistro, Bistango serves first-rate American cuisine with a European flair: salads, seafood pasta, pizzas, and grilled ahi tuna. Beautiful people come to savor the food, listen to live jazz, and mingle with their well-dressed peers. ✉ *19100 Von Karman Ave.,* ☎ *949/752–5222. Reservations essential. AE, D, DC, MC, V. Valet parking.*

$$–$$$　✕ **Prego.** Reminiscent of a Tuscan villa, this is a much larger version
　★　of the Beverly Hills Prego, with soft lighting, golden walls, and an out-
　　　door patio. Try the spit-roasted meats and chicken, charcoal-grilled fresh
　　　fish, or pizzas from the oak-burning oven. The wines are reasonably
　　　priced. ⊠ *18420 Von Karman Ave.,* ☎ *949/553–1333. AE, DC, MC,*
　　　V. No lunch weekends. Valet parking.

$–$$$　✕ **Sam Woo.** The service is graceful and the setting peaceful at this for-
　　　mal Chinese restaurant known for its seafood. Whole fish is presented
　　　tableside. ⊠ *15333 Culver Dr., Suite 720,* ☎ *949/262–0688. AE, MC, V.*

$–$$　✕ **Kitima Thai Cuisine.** Orange County's best Thai restaurant is a fa-
　　　vorite with the business-lunch crowd. The names may be gimmicky—
　　　"rock-and-roll shrimp salad," "Rambo chicken" (sautéed with green
　　　chilies and sweet basil), "Four Musketeers" (shrimp with asparagus,
　　　mushrooms, and spinach)—but fresh ingredients are used in every
　　　dish. ⊠ *2010 Main St., Suite 170,* ☎ *949/261–2929. AE, D, DC, MC,*
　　　V. Closed Sun.

$$$–$$$$　🏨 **Atrium Hotel.** Across the street from John Wayne Airport and near
　　　most area offices, this garden-style hotel caters to business travelers.
　　　Rooms have large work areas, coffeemakers, two phones, and private
　　　balconies overlooking either the pool or gardens. ⊠ *18700 MacArthur*
　　　Blvd., 92612, ☎ *949/833–2770 or 800/854–3012,* FAX *949/757–*
　　　1228. 211 rooms. Restaurant, bar, pool, health club, car rental. AE,
　　　D, DC, MC, V.

$$$–$$$$　🏨 **Irvine Marriott.** Towering over Koll Business Center, the Marriott
　　　is convenient for business travelers. Despite its size, the hotel has an
　　　intimate feel, due in part to the convivial lobby with love seats and
　　　evening entertainment (usually a jazz pianist). Weekend discounts and
　　　packages are usually available, and there's a courtesy van to the South
　　　Coast Plaza mall and the airport. ⊠ *18000 Von Karman Ave., 92715,*
　　　☎ *949/553–0100 or 800/228–9290,* FAX *949/261–7059. 484 rooms,*
　　　8 suites. 2 restaurants, sports bar, sushi bar, indoor-outdoor pool, hot
　　　tub, 4 tennis courts, health club, concierge floors, business services, air-
　　　port shuttle. AE, D, DC, MC, V.

$$$　🏨 **Hyatt Regency Irvine.** The modern rooms here have coffeemakers,
　　　irons, and hair dryers. Special golf packages at nearby Tustin Ranch
　　　and Pelican Hills are available, and a complimentary shuttle runs to
　　　local shopping centers. Rates are lower on weekends. ⊠ *17900 Jam-*
　　　boree Rd., 92714, ☎ *949/975–1234 or 800/233–1234,* FAX *949/852–*
　　　1574. 516 rooms, 20 suites. 2 restaurants, 2 bars, pool, 4 tennis courts,
　　　health club, bicycles, concierge, business services. AE, D, DC, MC, V.

Nightlife

The **Irvine Improv** (⊠ 4255 Campus Dr., ☎ 949/854–5455) comedy
club is open from Wednesday to Sunday. The **Irvine Meadows Amphitheater** (⊠ 8808 Irvine Center Dr., ☎ 949/855–4515 or 949/855–
6111), a 15,000-seat open-air venue, presents musical events from May
to October. **Metropolis** (⊠ 4255 Campus Dr., ☎ 949/725–0300) has
five pool tables, a sushi bar, a restaurant, entertainment, two large dance
floors, and theme nights throughout the week.

Costa Mesa

6 mi northeast of Irvine, I–405 to Bristol St.

★ ⑫ **South Coast Plaza,** Costa Mesa's most famous landmark, is an immense
retail, entertainment, and dining complex consisting of two enclosed
shopping areas—Jewel Court and Crystal Court—and an open-air
collection of boutiques at South Coast Village. The Plaza rivals Rodeo

Drive in its number of top international designers' shops—Gucci, Armani, Versace, and Prada, to name just a few—along with standard upscale shops. A free shuttle transports the Plaza's patrons between sections. ⊠ *3333 S. Bristol St., off I–405,* ☎ *714/435–2000.* ◷ *Weekdays 10–9, Sat. 10–7, Sun. 11–6:30.*

⓭ The **Orange County Performing Arts Center** (⊠ 600 Town Center Dr., east of Bristol St., ☎ 714/556–2787) contains a 3,000-seat facility for opera, ballet, symphony, and musicals. Richard Lippold's enormous "Firebird," a triangular-shape sculpture of polished metal surfaces that resembles a bird taking flight, extends outward from the glass-enclosed lobby. Free backstage tours are conducted on Monday, Wednesday, and Saturday at 10:30 AM. Within walking distance of the center is the **California Scenario** (⊠ 611 Anton Blvd.), a 1½-acre sculpture garden designed by Isamu Noguchi.

Dining and Lodging

$$–$$$ ★ ✕ **Diva.** If you're seeing a show at the South Coast Repertory Theater or the Performing Arts Center, Diva is a perfect place to stop for dinner. Entrées such as salmon with wilted greens and blackberry vinegar or grilled veal chops with hazelnut butter are good, as are the dessert soufflés. ⊠ *600 Anton Blvd.,* ☎ *714/754–0600. AE, D, DC, MC, V. No lunch weekends.*

$$–$$$ ✕ **Habana Restaurant and Bar.** With rustic candelabras and murals in a candlelit former industrial space, Habana blends an Old World flavor with a hip '90s flair. The Cuban and Caribbean specialties are as flavorful as the setting is cool: Try the *ropa vieja* (shredded beef) or the plantain-crusted chicken. ⊠ *2930 Bristol St.,* ☎ *714/556–0176. AE, D, DC, MC, V.*

$–$$$ ★ ✕ **Bangkok IV.** Despite its shopping-mall location—it occupies the third floor of the Crystal Court, an enclosed shopping area within the South Coast Plaza—Bangkok IV has a dramatic, white-and-black interior, with striking flower arrangements on every table. The *pla dung,* steamed catfish with a chili-garlic-lemongrass sauce, is exceptional. ⊠ *Across from South Coast Plaza, 3333 Bear St.,* ☎ *714/540–7661. AE, D, DC, MC, V.*

$–$$ ★ ✕ **Memphis Soul Café and Bar.** The gumbo prepared here is the best in the county, bar none. The turkey sandwich with pesto is addictive, and the pork chops are works of art. ⊠ *2920 Bristol St.,* ☎ *714/432–7685. AE, DC, MC, V.*

$$$–$$$$ ✇ **Westin South Coast Plaza.** This downtown high-rise adjoins the South Coast complex, making it convenient for shoppers and businesspeople. ⊠ *686 Anton Blvd., 92626,* ☎ *714/540–2500 or 800/228–3000,* FAX *714/662–6695. 373 rooms, 17 suites. Restaurant, lobby lounge, pool, 2 tennis courts, shuffleboard. AE, D, DC, MC, V.*

$$$–$$$$ ✇ **Country Side Inn and Suites.** The Queen Anne–style rooms here have a vaguely European feel. Complimentary cocktails and hors d'oeuvres are served each evening. ⊠ *325 Bristol St., 92626,* ☎ *714/549–0300 or 800/322–9992,* FAX *714/662–0828. 150 rooms, 150 suites. Restaurant, bar, 2 pools, 2 hot tubs, exercise room, business center. Full breakfast. AE, D, DC, MC, V.*

$$–$$$ ✇ **Doubletree Hotel.** Near John Wayne Airport, this modern, spacious hotel has an atrium lobby with glass elevators. ⊠ *3050 Bristol St., 92626,* ☎ *714/540–7000,* FAX *714/540–9176. 474 rooms, 10 suites. 2 restaurants, lounge, lobby lounge, pool, beauty salon, hot tub, health club. AE, D, DC, MC, V.*

Nightlife and the Arts

Orange County Performing Arts Center (⊠ 600 Town Center Dr., ☎ 714/556–2787) presents major touring companies, among them the

New York City Opera, the American Ballet Theater, and the Los Angeles Philharmonic Orchestra, along with musicals and theater productions. **South Coast Repertory Theater** (⊠ 655 Town Center Dr., ☎ 714/957–4033) is a Tony award–winning theater presenting new and traditional works on two stages.

THE COAST

Running along the Orange County coastline is the scenic Pacific Coast Highway (Highway 1, known locally as PCH); it's well worth the effort to take this route instead of the freeways. Wherever you pull over on PCH, a public beach is only steps away.

Huntington Beach

25 mi from Anaheim, south on Hwy. 57, west on Hwy. 22, and south on I–405.

Once a sleepy residential town with little more than a string of rugged surf shops, Huntington Beach has transformed itself into a shining resort area. The town's appeal arises from its broad white-sand beaches and often towering waves, as well as a pier, a large shopping pavilion on Main Street, and the luxurious Waterfront Hilton resort. The U.S. Open professional surf competition takes place here in August.

⑭ **Huntington Pier** stretches 1,800 ft out to sea, well past the powerful waves that made Huntington Beach America's "Surf City." At the end of the pier sits **Ruby's** (☎ 714/969–7829), part of a California chain of '40s-style eateries. The **Pierside Pavilion,** across Pacific Coast Highway from the pier, contains shops, restaurants, bars with live music, **⑮** and a theater complex. Just up Main Street, the **International Surfing Museum** (⊠ 411 Olive Ave., ☎ 714/960–3483), open from Wednesday to Sunday between noon and 5 (🎫 $2), pays tribute to the sport's greats in a Surfing Hall of Fame, with an impressive collection of surfboards and related memorabilia.

Huntington City Beach stretches for 3 mi from the pier area. The beach is most crowded around the pier; amateur and professional surfers brave the waves daily on its north side. Continuing north, **Huntington State Beach** (☎ 714/536–1454) parallels Pacific Coast Highway. On the state and city beaches there are changing rooms, concessions, lifeguards (except in winter), and ample parking; the state beach also has barbecue pits and RV campsites. In the northern section of the city, **Bolsa Chica State Beach** (☎ 714/846–3460) has barbecue pits and is usually less crowded than its southern neighbors.

★ ⑯ **Bolsa Chica Ecological Reserve** beckons wildlife-lovers and bird-watchers with an 880-acre salt marsh that is home to 315 species of birds, including great blue herons, snowy and great egrets, and common loons. Throughout the reserve are trails for hiking, bird-watching, and jogging. ⊠ *Entrance at Warner Ave. and PCH, opposite Bolsa Chica State Beach,* ☎ *714/897–7003.* 🎫 *Free parking.* ☉ *Daily sunrise–sunset.*

Dining and Lodging

$–$$$ ✕ **Baci.** Romantic or kitschy, depending on your style, Baci serves dependable Italian food. Among the best dishes are carpaccio with shrimp, tortellini soup, and cannoli for dessert. ⊠ *18748 Beach Blvd.,* ☎ *714/965–1194. AE, D, DC, MC, V.*

$–$$ ✕ **Louise's Trattoria.** The local branch of this Italian chain is just across the street from the Huntington Beach pier. The chicken marsala and fettuccine with sun-dried tomatoes in a chardonnay-cream sauce hit the spot, especially after a day at the beach. ⊠ *300 PCH,* ☎ *714/960–0996. AE, D, DC, MC, V.*

$ ✕ **Alice's Breakfast in the Park.** Consider starting your day at this brunch house tucked among the eucalyptus trees near Huntington Lake. There's seating on the outdoor patio, from which children can feed the ducks, and an indoor dining room with flowers and antiques. Be sure to try Alice's "outrageous cinnamon roll," freshly baked breads, and homemade muffins. ⊠ *Huntington Park, 6622 Lakeview, off Edwards St.,* ☎ *714/848–0690. No credit cards. No dinner.*

$ ✕ **Wahoo's Fish Taco.** Mahimahi- and wahoo-filled tacos are the specialty of this casual restaurant, part of a national chain that sells healthful fast food. ⊠ *120 Main St.,* ☎ *714/536–2050. MC, V.*

$$$–$$$$ ▥ **Waterfront Hilton.** Rising 12 stories above the surf, this Mediterranean-style resort occupies 8½ mi of white-sand beach. All rooms have private lanais, many with panoramic ocean views. ⊠ *21100 PCH, 92648,* ☎ *714/960–7873 or 800/822–7873,* ℻ *714/960–2642. 258 rooms, 32 suites. 2 restaurants, bar, pool, hot tub, 2 tennis courts, exercise room, children's programs (ages 5–12; summer only), concierge floor, meeting rooms. AE, DC, MC, V.*

Outdoor Activities and Sports

Team Bicycle Rentals (⊠ 8464 Indianapolis Ave., ☎ 714/969–5480) rents touring and other bicycles. **Edison Community Center** (⊠ 21377 Magnolia Ave., ☎ 714/960–8870) and the **Murdy Community Center** (⊠ 7000 Norma Dr., ☎ 714/960–8895) both have four courts available on a first-come, first-served basis in the daytime. Both accept reservations for play after 5 PM and charge $2 an hour.

Shopping

Jack's (⊠ 101 Main St., ☎ 714/536–4516) and **Huntington Beach Surf and Sport** (⊠ 300 PCH, at Main St., ☎ 714/841–4000) carry the latest styles in beachwear and surfing equipment. Or try the **Huntington Beach Mall** (⊠ Beach Blvd. off I–405, ☎ 714/897–2533).

Newport Beach

6 mi south of Huntington Beach on Hwy. 1.

Newport Beach has two distinct personalities. It's best known for its island-dotted yacht harbor and wealthy residents (Newport is said to have the highest number of Mercedes-Benzes per capita of any city in the world). And then there's inland Newport Beach, southwest of John Wayne Airport, a business and commercial hub with a shopping center and a clutch of high-rise office buildings and hotels.

★ ⑰ **Newport Harbor,** which shelters nearly 10,000 small boats, will seduce even those who don't own a yacht. Exploring the charming avenues and surrounding alleys can be great fun. To see Newport Harbor from the water, take a one-hour gondola cruise operated by the Gondola Company of Newport (⊠ 3400 Via Oporto, Suite 102B, ☎ 949/675–1212). It costs $60 for two.

Within Newport Harbor are eight small islands, including Balboa and Lido. The houses lining the shore may seem modest, but this is some of the most expensive real estate in the world. Several grassy areas on Lido Isle have views of Newport Harbor but, evidence of the upper-crust Orange County mind-set, each is marked "Private Community Park."

Newport Pier, which juts out into the ocean near 20th Street, is the heart of Newport's beach community. On the pier you can go fishing or grab a burger and shake at **Ruby's** (☎ 949/675–7829). Parking on the street is difficult here, so grab the first space you find and be prepared to walk. A stroll along West Ocean Front reveals much of the town's character. On weekday mornings head for the beach near the pier, where dory fishermen hawk their predawn catches as they've done for generations. On weekends the walk is alive with kids of all ages on rollerblades, skateboards, and bikes dodging pedestrians and whizzing past fast-food joints, swimsuit shops, and seedy bars.

⑱ Newport's best beaches are on **Balboa Peninsula,** whose many jetties create good swimming areas. The **Balboa Pavilion,** on the bay side of the Balboa Peninsula, was built in 1905 as a bathhouse and boathouse. Today it houses a restaurant and shops and is a departure point for harbor and whale-watching cruises. Look for it on Main Street, off Balboa Boulevard. Adjacent to the pavilion is the three-car ferry that connects the peninsula to Balboa Island.

⑲ The highlights at the **Orange County Museum of Art** include its Abstract Expressionist paintings and cutting-edge contemporary works by California artists. ⊠ *850 San Clemente Dr.,* ☎ *949/759–1122.* ☑ *$5.* ☉ *Tues.–Sun. 11–5.*

Dining and Lodging

$$$–$$$$ ✕ **Aubergine.** The husband-and-wife team who own this restaurant
★ (he runs the kitchen and she handles the dining room) serve a six-course prix fixe dinner that is surprisingly affordable; you can also order à la carte. Classic French dishes are prepared with a modern flair. ⊠ *508 29th St.,* ☎ *949/723–4150. Reservations essential. AE, MC, V. Closed Sun.–Mon. No lunch.*

$$$–$$$$ ✕ **Pascal.** You'll think you're in St-Tropez when you step inside this
★ bright and cheerful bistro in a shopping center. After one taste of Pascal Olhat's light Provençal cuisine, the best in Orange County, you'll *swear* you're in the south of France. Try the sea bass with thyme, rack of lamb, and lemon tart. ⊠ *1000 N. Bristol St.,* ☎ *949/752–0107. AE, DC, V. Closed Sun. No dinner Mon.*

$$$–$$$$ ✕ **The Ritz.** Indeed, this is one of the ritziest restaurants in southern California, complete with black leather booths, etched-glass mirrors, and polished brass trim. Don't pass up the "carousel" appetizer—a lavish spread of cured gravlax, prawns, Dungeness crab legs, Maine lobster tails, goose liver pâté, fillet of smoked trout, Parma prosciutto, filet mignon tartare, and marinated herring, all served on a lazy Susan. ⊠ *880 Newport Center Dr.,* ☎ *949/720–1800. Reservations essential. AE, DC, MC, V. No lunch weekends.*

$$–$$$$ ✕ **Twin Palms.** Pasta, chicken, pizza, fish specials, and salads are all on the creative menu at this intriguing, spacious, tentlike restaurant, a sister property to the original Twin Palms in Pasadena. ⊠ *630 Newport Center Dr.,* ☎ *949/721–8288. AE, DC, MC, V. Valet parking.*

$–$$ ✕ **Crab Cooker.** People line up at this shanty for fresh, mesquite-grilled fish served on paper plates at rock-bottom prices. The seafood skewers, clam chowder, crusty rounds of French bread, and coleslaw are all top-notch. ⊠ *2200 Newport Blvd.,* ☎ *949/673–0100. Reservations not accepted. No credit cards.*

$–$$ ✕ **El Torito Grill.** You'll find southwestern and south-of-the-border
★ specialties here: The just-baked tortillas with fresh salsa and the blackened chicken with pasta are good choices. The bar serves hand-shaken margaritas and 80 brands of tequila. ⊠ *Fashion Island, 951 Newport Center Dr.,* ☎ *949/640–2875. AE, D, DC, MC, V.*

$–$$ ✕ **P. F. Chang's China Bistro.** The tasty Cal-Chinese food at this trendy chain restaurant includes Mongolian spicy beef and Chang's chicken, stir-fried in a sweet-and-spicy Szechuan sauce. Almost every table has an ocean view. ⊠ *Newport Fashion Island, 1145 Newport Center Dr.,* ☎ *949/759–9007. Reservations not accepted. AE, MC, V.*

$$$$ ☷ **Four Seasons Hotel.** A stylish hotel in an ultrachic neighborhood,
★ the 20-story Four Seasons caters to seekers of luxury by offering weekend golf packages (in conjunction with the nearby Pelican Hill golf
course) and the use of extensive fitness facilities. Rooms have spectacular
views, private bars, and original artworks on the walls. Kids are given
special treatment: balloons, cookies and milk, game books, and more.
⊠ *690 Newport Center Dr., 92660,* ☎ *949/759–0808 or 800/332–*
3442, FAX *949/759–0568. 285 rooms. 2 restaurants, bar, pool, beauty*
salon, massage, sauna, steam room, 2 tennis courts, health club, moun-
tain bikes, concierge, business services. AE, D, DC, MC, V.

$$$$ ☷ **Sutton Place Hotel.** An eye-catching ziggurat design is the trademark
of this ultramodern hotel in Koll Center. Despite its modern exterior,
the inside remains traditional with beige and burgundy accents. Many
of the spacious rooms have canopy beds. ⊠ *4500 MacArthur Blvd.,*
92660, ☎ *949/476–2001 or 800/243–4141,* FAX *949/476–0153. 435*
rooms. 2 restaurants, 2 bars, in-room modem lines, minibars, refrig-
erators, pool, spa, 2 tennis courts, health club, basketball, bike rentals,
concierge, business services, airport shuttle. AE, D, DC, MC, V.

$$$–$$$$ ☷ **Newport Beach Marriott Hotel and Tennis Club.** A largely foreign
clientele patronizes this hotel overlooking Newport Harbor. A distinctive
fountain surrounded by a plant-filled atrium is the first thing you'll see
inside. Rooms are in one of two towers; all have balconies or patios
that look out onto lush gardens or the Pacific. ⊠ *900 Newport Cen-*
ter Dr., 92660, ☎ *949/640–4000 or 800/228–9290,* FAX *949/640–5055.*
570 rooms, 8 suites. Restaurant, bar, 2 pools, sauna, 8 tennis courts,
health club, concierge, business services. AE, D, DC, MC, V.

$$–$$$ ☷ **Sheraton Newport Beach.** Bamboo trees and palms in the lobby add
to the tropical feel of this hotel 5 mi from the beach. Vibrant teals,
mauves, and peaches make up the guest-room color scheme. The hotel
is convenient to John Wayne Airport. ⊠ *4545 MacArthur Blvd.,*
92660, ☎ *949/833–0570 or 800/325–3535,* FAX *949/833–3927. 329*
rooms, 4 suites. Restaurant, bar, pool, 2 tennis courts, exercise room.
AE, D, DC, MC, V.

Nightlife

The **Cannery** (⊠ 3010 Lafayette Ave., ☎ 949/675–5777) is a seaside
restaurant and bar with karaoke and live entertainment. The **Studio
Cafe** (⊠ 100 Main St., Balboa Peninsula, ☎ 949/675–7760), locally
famous for its blue drink concoctions, hosts blues and jazz musicians.

Outdoor Activities and Sports

BOAT RENTAL

You can rent sailboats ($25 an hour), small motorboats ($30 an hour),
and ocean boats ($65–$80 an hour) at **Balboa Boat Rentals** (⊠ 510
E. Edgewater Ave., ☎ 949/673–7200). You must have a driver's li-
cense, and some knowledge of boating is helpful. Rented boats are not
allowed out of the bay.

BOAT TOURS

A fun way to take in the scenery of Newport's harbor is on the two-
hour **Cannery Restaurant weekend brunch cruise** (⊠ 3010 Lafayette
Ave., ☎ 949/675–5777). Cruises, which cost $31, depart at 10 AM and
1:30 PM. **Catalina Passenger Service** (⊠ 400 Main St., ☎ 949/673–
5245) at the Balboa Pavilion operates sightseeing tours ($6 to $8), fish-
ing excursions ($33), and, during the winter, whale-watching cruises
($14). **Hornblower Dining Yachts** (⊠ 2431 W. Coast Hwy., ☎ 949/646–
0155) books 2½-hour Saturday dinner cruises with dancing for $56.95;
Sunday brunch cruises are $39.45. Reservations are required.

GOLF
Newport Beach Golf Course (⊠ 3100 Irvine Ave., ☎ 949/852–8681), an 18-hole, par-59 course, is lighted for nighttime play. The greens fee ranges from $14 to $17; hand carts rent for $2. Reservations are required one week in advance.

Pelican Hill Golf Club (⊠ 22651 Pelican Hill Rd. S, ☎ 949/640–0238) has two 18-hole courses (par 70 and 71). The greens fees range from $135 to $195 and include a mandatory cart.

SPORTFISHING

In addition to a complete tackle shop, **Davey's Locker** (⊠ Balboa Pavilion, 400 Main St., ☎ 949/673–1434) operates sportfishing trips starting at $25, as well as private charters and whale-watching trips.

SURFING

The River Jetties in northern Newport are good for beginners. The Wedge, farther south, is famous for its steep, punishing shore break.

TENNIS

Call the **recreation department** (☎ 949/644–3151) for information about use the city's 26 public courts, where play is free and first-come, first-served. You must reserve the courts at the **Newport Beach Marriott Hotel and Tennis Club** (⊠ 900 Newport Center Dr., ☎ 949/640–4000) for $25 per hour.

Shopping
The **Fashion Island** (⊠ Newport Center Dr. off PCH between Jamboree and MacArthur Blvds., ☎ 949/721–2022) complex contains upscale boutiques and major department stores, including Bloomingdale's, Neiman-Marcus, and Macy's.

Corona del Mar

2 mi south of Newport Beach on Hwy. 1.

A small jewel on the Pacific Coast, Corona del Mar has exceptional beaches that some say resemble those in northern California. **Corona del Mar Beach** (☎ 949/644–3044) is actually made up of two beaches, Little Corona and Big Corona, separated by a cliff. Facilities include fire pits, volleyball courts, food stands, rest rooms, and parking. Two colorful reefs (and the fact that it's off-limits to boats) make Corona del Mar great for snorkeling.

Midway between Corona del Mar and Laguna on the inland side of Pacific Coast Highway, **Crystal Cove State Park** (☎ 949/494–3539) is a hidden treasure: a 3½-mi stretch of unspoiled beach with some of the best tidepooling in southern California. Here you can see starfish, crabs, and other sea life on the rocks. The park's 2,400 acres of backcountry are ideal for hiking, horseback riding, and mountain biking. Docents lead nature walks on weekend mornings. Parking costs $6 per car.

The town of Corona del Mar stretches only a few blocks along Pacific Coast Highway, but some of the fanciest stores in the county line the route.

20 **Sherman Library and Gardens,** a botanical garden and library specializing in the history of the Pacific Southwest, provides a diversion from the beach. You can wander among cactus gardens, rose gardens, a wheelchair-height touch-and-smell garden, and a tropical conservatory. ⊠ 2647 PCH, ☎ 949/673–2261. ☞ $3; free Mon. ☉ Daily 10:30–4.

Dining

$$–$$$$ ✕ **The Bungalow.** Specializing in prime steaks and seafood, this restaurant in a Craftsman-style structure is known for its lobster with wild rice. The younger local moneyed set packs the place. ⊠ 2441 E. Coast Hwy., ☎ 949/673–6585. AE, MC, V. No lunch.

$–$$$ ✕ **Bandera.** Pork cutlets, barbecued salmon, and New Orleans–style jambalaya are a few of the American regional dishes served at this popular wood-panel eatery. ⊠ 3201 E. Coast Hwy., ☎ 949/673–3524. Reservations not accepted. AE, DC, MC, V. No lunch.

$ ✕ **Ruby's.** One of several branches of a home-grown chain of '40s-style diners serves Ruby's trademark burgers along with "frings" (a combination of onion rings and fries) and thick shakes. Vegetarian tacos on whole-wheat tortillas aim to satisfy health-conscious. ⊠ 2305 E. Coast Hwy., ☎ 949/673–7820. AE, D, DC, MC, V. No dinner.

Laguna Beach

★ 10 mi south of Newport Beach on Hwy. 1; 60 mi south of Los Angeles, I–5 to Hwy. 133 to Laguna Canyon Rd.

Traditionally a haven of conservative wealth, Laguna Beach attracted the beat, artistic, and far-out during the 1950s and '60s (among them what has grown to be Orange County's most visible gay community). The two camps coexist in relative harmony, with Art prevailing in the congested village, and Wealth entrenched in the surrounding canyons and hills. A 1993 fire, which destroyed more than 300 homes in the hillsides surrounding Laguna Beach, miraculously left the village untouched.

The town's main street, Pacific Coast Highway, is referred to as either South Coast or North Coast Highway, depending on the address. All along the highway and side streets such as Forest or Ocean avenues, you'll find dozens of eclectic fine-art and crafts galleries, clothing boutiques, and jewelry shops.

At the **Pageant of the Masters** (☎ 949/494–1145 or 800/487–3378), Laguna's most impressive event and part of the city's annual Festival of Arts, live models and carefully orchestrated backgrounds are arranged in striking mimicry of classical and contemporary paintings. The festival usually takes place in July and August.

㉑ The **Laguna Art Museum** displays American art, with an emphasis on artists and works from California. ⊠ 307 Cliff Dr., ☎ 949/494–6531. ⊠ $5. ☉ Tues.–Sun. 11–5.

Laguna Beach's **Main Beach Park,** at the end of Broadway at South Coast Highway, has sand volleyball, two half-basketball courts, children's play equipment, picnic areas, rest rooms, showers, and street parking. The colorful crowd ranges from authentic hippies to beach volleyball champs to celebrities such as Bette Midler, who has a home in Laguna.

Aliso Beach County Park (⊠ 31131 S. Coast Hwy., ☎ 949/661–7013) in south Laguna is a recreation area with a fishing pier, a playground, fire pits, parking, food stands, and rest rooms.

· **Woods Cove,** off South Coast Highway at Diamond Street, is especially quiet during the week. Big rock formations hide lurking crabs. As you climb the steps to leave, you can see an English-style mansion that was once the home of actress Bette Davis.

Dining and Lodging

$$$–$$$$ ✕ **Five Feet.** Others have mimicked this restaurant's innovative blend
★   of Chinese and French cooking styles, but Five Feet remains the leader
of the pack. Among the standout dishes: cheese wontons with rasp-
berry coulis, fish in a garlic black-bean sauce, and rabbit with foie gras
and wild mushrooms. The setting is pure Laguna: exposed ceiling, open
kitchen, high noise level, and brick walls hung with works by local artists.
⊠ *328 Glenneyre St.,* ☎ *949/497–4955. AE, D, DC, MC, V. No lunch.*

$$$ ✕ **Sorrento Grille.** High ceilings and two walls of floor-to-ceiling win-
dows create an illusion of space at this narrow restaurant on a quiet
side street downtown. Mesquite steaks, seafood, and pastas predominate on the contemporary menu. ⊠ *370 Glennerye St.,* ☎ *949/494–
8686. AE, DC, MC, V. No lunch.*

$$–$$$ ✕ **Ti Amo.** A romantic setting and creative Mediterranean cuisine have
earned Ti Amo acclaim. Try the seared tuna with a sesame-seed crust
or farfalle with smoked chicken and creamy bell-pepper sauce. All the
nooks and crannies are charming, candlelit, and private, but to maximize romance, request a table in the enclosed garden in back. ⊠
31727 S. Coast Hwy., ☎ *949/499–5350. AE, D, DC, MC, V. No lunch.*

$$–$$$ ✕ **Odessa.** Sweet-potato gnocchi with salmon, potato-crusted catfish,
and grilled lobster are on the Southern U.S.–influenced French menu.
In the romantically dim-lit space, you may not notice the celebrities at
the next table—or the stylish crowd heading upstairs to the nightclub.
⊠ *680 S. Coast Hwy.,* ☎ *949/376–8792. Reservations essential. AE,
D, DC, MC, V. No lunch. Valet parking.*

$–$$ ✕ **Tortilla Flats.** This hacienda-style restaurant with a fireplace has a
wide selection of Mexican tequilas and beers, and a quiet upstairs bar.
Sunday brunch is a lively affair. ⊠ *1740 S. Coast Hwy.,* ☎ *949/494–
6588. AE, MC, V.*

$ ✕ **Café Zinc.** Laguna Beach's health-conscious hipsters gather at the
tiny counter and plant–filled patio of this vegetarian breakfast-and-
lunch café. Oatmeal is sprinkled with berries, poached eggs are dusted
with herbs, and the orange juice is fresh-squeezed. For lunch, try a sam-
pler plate, with various salads like spicy Thai pasta, and asparagus salad
with orange peel and capers; or one of the gourmet pizzettes. ⊠ *350
Ocean Ave.,* ☎ *949/494–6302. No credit cards. No dinner.*

$$$$ ⊞ **Surf and Sand Hotel.** Laguna's largest hotel is right on the beach.
Rooms have an appropriately beachlike feel, with soft sand colors,
bleached-wood shutters, and private balconies. ⊠ *1555 S. Coast Hwy.,
92651,* ☎ *949/497–4477 or 800/524–8621,* 𝐅𝐀𝐗 *949/494–2897. 145
rooms, 19 suites. Restaurant, bar, health club, pool, beach, concierge.
AE, D, DC, MC, V.*

$$$$ ⊞ **Inn at Laguna Beach.** On a bluff overlooking the ocean, the inn has
★   a Mediterranean feel, with terra-cotta tiles and exotic flowers all over
the grounds. Most rooms have views; those on the coastal level border Laguna's oceanfront cliffs. The inn is close to Main Beach, yet far
enough away to feel secluded. ⊠ *211 N. Coast Hwy., 92651,* ☎ *949/
497–9722 or 800/544–4479,* 𝐅𝐀𝐗 *949/497–9972. 70 rooms. In-room
VCRs, minibars, refrigerators, pool. AE, D, DC, MC, V.*

$$–$$$$ ⊞ **Eiler's Inn.** A light-filled courtyard with a fountain is the focal point
★   of this European-style bed-and-breakfast. Every room is unique, but
all are full of antiques and travelers' journals for you to fill in. After-
noon wine and cheese is served in the courtyard or in the cozy read-
ing room, where you'll find the inn's only TV and phone. A sundeck
in back has an ocean view. ⊠ *741 S. Coast Hwy., 92651,* ☎ *949/494–
3004,* 𝐅𝐀𝐗 *949/497–2215. 12 rooms. Full breakfast. AE, D, MC, V.*

$$–$$$$ ⊞ **Hotel Laguna.** Manicured gardens, a private beach, and an ideal location downtown are among the assets of the oldest hotel in Laguna,

which opened in 1890. Four rooms have canopy beds and reproduction Victorian furnishings. Others have whitewashed furniture and pastel bedspreads and curtains (none has air-conditioning). ⊠ *425 S. Coast Hwy., 92651,* ☎ *949/494–1151 or 800/524–2927,* FAX *949/497–2163. 63 rooms. 2 restaurants, bar, beach. Continental breakfast. AE, D, DC, MC, V.*

$–$$$$ 🖭 **Coast Inn.** Gay men and some lesbians have been staying at the Coast Inn for more than three decades. Some rooms are standard motel-style; others are larger, with private decks and fireplaces. ⊠ *1401 S. Coast Hwy.,* ☎ *949/494–7588 or 800/653–2697,* FAX *949/494–1735. 23 rooms. Restaurant, bar. AE, D, DC, MC, V.*

Nightlife

The **Boom Boom Room** (⊠ Coast Inn, 1401 S. Coast Hwy., ☎ 949/494–7588) is Laguna Beach's most popular gay club. The **Sandpiper** (⊠ 1183 S. Coast Hwy., ☎ 949/494–4694), a hole-on-the-wall dancing joint, attracts an eclectic crowd. Laguna's **White House** (⊠ 340 S. Coast Hwy., ☎ 949/494–8088), a chic club on the main strip, has nightly entertainment and dancing.

Outdoor Activities and Sports

BICYCLING

Mountain bikes can be rented at **Rainbow Bicycles** (⊠ 485 N. Coast Hwy., ☎ 949/494–5806).

TENNIS

Six metered courts can be found at **Laguna Beach High School.** Two courts are available at the **Irvine Bowl.** Six courts are available at **Alta Laguna Park** on a first-come, first-served basis. **Moulton Meadows** has two lighted courts. For more information, call the **City of Laguna Beach Recreation Department** (☎ 949/497–0716).

WATER SPORTS

Because its entire beach area is a marine preserve, Laguna Beach has great snorkeling. Scuba divers head to the Marine Life Refuge area, which runs from Seal Rock to Diver's Cove. You can rent surfboards and bodyboards at **Hobie Sports** (⊠ 294 Forest Ave., ☎ 949/497–3304).

Shopping

Forest and Ocean avenues are full of art galleries and fine jewelry and clothing boutiques. The **Art Center Gallery** (⊠ 266 Forest Ave., ☎ 949/376–7596) exhibits the works of local artists. **Georgeo's Art Glass and Jewelry** (⊠ 269 Forest Ave., ☎ 949/497–0907) has a large selection of etched-glass bowls, vases, and fine jewelry.

Dana Point

10 mi south of Laguna Beach on Hwy. 1.

Dana Point's claim to fame is its small-boat marina set in a dramatic natural harbor and surrounded by high bluffs. Concerts, films, sports competitions, and a weekend street fair are among the festivities at the town's February whale festival. **Dana Point Harbor** was first described more than 100 years ago by its namesake, Richard Henry Dana, in his book *Two Years Before the Mast.* At the marina are docks for small boats, marine-oriented shops, and some restaurants.

Inside Dana Point Harbor, **Swim Beach** has a fishing pier, barbecues, food stands, parking, rest rooms, and showers. At the south end of Dana Point, **Doheny State Park** (☎ 949/496–6171) is one of southern California's top surfing destinations. The interpretive center here is devoted to the wildlife of the Doheny Marine Refuge. There are food stands and shops, picnic facilities, and a pier for fishing. Camping is permitted, though there are no hookups.

ᐸ ㉒ Two indoor tanks at the **Orange County Marine Institute** contain touchable sea creatures, as well as the complete skeleton of a gray whale. Anchored near the institute is *The Pilgrim*, a full-size replica of the square-rigged vessel on which Richard Henry Dana sailed. You can tour the boat on Sunday from 10 to 2:30. Weekend cruises are also available. You can arrange to go whale-watching from January to March, or to explore regional tide pools year-round. ⊠ *24200 Dana Point Harbor Dr.*, ☎ *949/496–2274.* ☷ *Donation requested.* ☉ *Daily 10–4:30.*

Dining and Lodging

$–$$$ ✕ **Luciana's.** This intimate Italian restaurant is a real find, especially for couples seeking a romantic evening. Try the linguine with clams, prawns, calamari, and green-lip mussels in a light tomato sauce; grilled cured pork chops in a fennel-herb marinade; or veal medallions with haricot verts and oven-dried tomatoes. ⊠ *24312 Del Prado Ave.*, ☎ *949/661–6500. AE, DC, MC, V. No lunch.*

$ ✕ **Proud Mary's.** On a terrace overlooking the fishing boats and pleasure craft in Dana Point Harbor, Proud Mary's serves the best burgers and sandwiches in southern Orange County. Steaks, chicken, and other American standards are served at dinnertime, and you can order breakfast all day. ⊠ *34689 Golden Lantern*, ☎ *949/493–5853. AE, D, MC, V. No dinner.*

$$$$ ✕🏨 **Ritz-Carlton, Laguna Niguel.** An unrivaled setting on the edge of
★ the Pacific combined with the hallmark Ritz-Carlton service have earned this grand hotel worldwide recognition. An imposing marble-columned entryway is surrounded by landscaped grounds; the overall impression is that of a Mediterranean country villa. Rooms have marble bathrooms and private balconies with ocean or pool views. Afternoon tea is served in the library. In the formal Dining Room (men must wear jackets), you can choose courses from chef Yvon Goetz's French-Mediterranean prix-fixe menu; the price depends on the number of courses. Foie gras with baby leeks in a truffle vinaigrette is one of the outstanding starters; for your main course consider the monkfish medallions with pearl onions or roasted duck breast. The Dining Room is open for dinner only; reservations are essential. ⊠ *1 Ritz-Carlton Dr., 92629*, ☎ *949/240–2000 or 800/241–3333*, FAX *949/240–0829. 332 rooms, 31 suites. 3 restaurants, lobby lounge, 2 pools, beauty salon, massage, 4 tennis courts, health club, concierge. AE, D, DC, MC, V.*

$$$–$$$$ 🏨 **Blue Lantern Inn.** Combining New England–style architecture with
★ a southern California setting, this white clapboard B&B rests on a bluff, overlooking the harbor and ocean. A fire warms the intimate living area, where guests are invited to enjoy complimentary afternoon snacks and play backgammon. The French country–style guest rooms also have fireplaces, as well as soda-filled refrigerators and whirlpool tubs. The top-floor tower suite has a 180° ocean view. ⊠ *34343 St. of the Blue Lantern, 92629*, ☎ *949/661–1304*, FAX *949/496–1483. 29 rooms. Exercise room, concierge. AE, DC, MC, V. Full breakfast.*

$$$–$$$$ 🏨 **Marriott's Laguna Cliffs Resort.** This whitewashed hillside hotel looks straight out of Cape Cod, except that its views are of the Pacific, not the Atlantic. On Sunday evening in summer, the Capistrano Valley Symphony performs on the resort's landscaped grounds. ⊠ *25135 Park Lantern, 92629*, ☎ *949/661–5000 or 800/533–9748*, FAX *949/ 661–5358. 332 rooms, 18 suites. Restaurant, bar, lobby lounge, 2 pools, 2 outdoor hot tubs, basketball, croquet, health club, volleyball. AE, D, DC, MC, V.*

Outdoor Activities and Sports

Rental stands for surfboards, Windsurfers, small powerboats, and sailboats can be found near most of the piers. **Embarcadero Marina** (✉ 34512 Embarcadero Pl., ☎ 949/496–6177) has powerboats and sailboats for rent near the launching ramp at Dana Point Harbor. **Hobie Sports** (✉ 24825 Del Prado, ☎ 949/496–2366) rents surfboards and Boogie boards. **Dana Wharf Sportfishing** (✉ 34675 Golden Lantern St., ☎ 949/496–5794) runs charters and weekend parasailing trips, and whale-watching excursions (from early December to late March).

San Juan Capistrano

5 mi north of Dana Point on Hwy. 74; 60 mi north of San Diego on I–5.

San Juan Capistrano is best known for its mission and for the swallows that migrate here each year from their winter haven in Argentina. The arrival of the birds on St. Joseph's Day, March 19, launches a week of festivities. After summering in the arches of the old stone church, the swallows head home on St. John's Day, October 23.

If you arrive by train, you will be dropped off across from the Mission at the San Juan Capistrano depot. With its appealing brick café and preserved Santa Fe cars, the depot retains much of the magic of early American railroads. If driving, park near Ortega and Camino Capistrano, the city's main streets, which are lined with colorful restaurants and boutiques.

★ ㉓ **Mission San Juan Capistrano,** founded in 1776 by Father Junípero Serra, was the major Roman Catholic outpost between Los Angeles and San Diego. Though the original Great Stone Church is permanently supported by scaffolding, many of the mission's adobe buildings have been preserved to illustrate mission life, with exhibits of an olive millstone, tallow ovens, tanning vats, metalworking furnaces, and padres' living quarters. The bougainvillea-covered Serra Chapel is believed to be the oldest building standing in California. Mass takes place at 7 AM daily. ✉ *Camino Capistrano and Ortega Hwy.,* ☎ *949/248–2049.* ▨ *$4.* ⊙ *Daily 8:30–5.*

㉔ Near Mission San Juan Capistrano is the **San Juan Capistrano Library,** a postmodern structure erected in 1983. Architect Michael Graves combined classical elements with the style of the mission to striking effect. ✉ *31495 El Camino Real,* ☎ *949/493–1752.* ⊙ *Mon.–Thurs. 10–9, Fri.–Sat. 10–5.*

Dining

$$–$$$ ★ ✕ **L'Hirondelle.** Roast duck, rabbit, and many Belgian dishes are on the menu at this French and Belgian restaurant. You can dine inside or out on the patio. ✉ *31631 Camino Capistrano,* ☎ *949/661–0425. AE, MC, DC, D, V. Closed Mon. No lunch Tues.*

$–$$$ ★ ✕ **Cedar Creek Inn.** Equally suitable for family meals and romantic dinners, the inn has a children's menu as well as a secluded outdoor patio with a roaring fireplace for couples. The contemporary American menu features crowd-pleasers like an ahi burger, rack of lamb, and herb-crusted halibut. ✉ *26860 Ortega Hwy.,* ☎ *949/240–2229. AE, DC, MC, V.*

$–$$ ✕ **El Adobe.** This historic early Mission–style eatery serves enormous portions of mildly seasoned Mexican food. Mariachi bands play on Friday and Saturday night and during Sunday brunch. ✉ *31891 Camino Capistrano,* ☎ *949/830–8620. AE, D, DC, MC, V.*

Nightlife

Coach House (✉ 33157 Camino Capistrano, ☎ 949/496–8930), a roomy club with long tables and a dark wood bar, draws crowds of varying ages for entertainment from hip new bands to mellow acoustic guitar to comedy acts.

OFF THE   **SAN CLEMENTE –** Ten miles south of Dana Point on Pacific Coast High-
BEATEN PATH   way, San Clemente has 20 sq mi of prime bicycling terrain. Camp
              Pendleton, the country's largest Marine Corps base, welcomes cyclists to
              use some of its roads—just don't be surprised to see a troop helicopter
              taking off right beside you. Surfers favor San Clemente State Beach,
              which has camping facilities, RV hookups, and fire rings. San Onofre
              State Beach, just south of San Clemente, is another surfing destination.
              Below the bluffs are 3½ mi of sandy beach, where you can swim, fish,
              and watch wildlife.

ORANGE COUNTY A TO Z

Arriving and Departing

By Bus

The **Los Angeles MTA** ☎ 213/626–4455 has limited service to Orange County. From downtown, Bus 460 goes to Knott's Berry Farm and Disneyland. **Greyhound** (☎ 714/999–1256) serves Anaheim and Santa Ana.

By Car

The San Diego Freeway (I–405) and the Santa Ana Freeway (I–5) run north and south through Orange County. South of Laguna I–405 merges into I–5 (which is called the San Diego Freeway south from this point). Avoid these freeways during rush hour (between 6 and 9 AM and 3:30 and 6 PM), when they can back up for miles.

By Plane

The county's main facility, **John Wayne Airport Orange County** (✉ MacArthur Blvd. at I–405, Santa Ana, ☎ 949/252–5252), is served by Alaska, America West, American, American Eagle, Continental, Delta, Northwest, Reno, Skywest, Southwest, TWA, United, United Express, US Airways, and several commuter airlines. ☞ Air Travel *in* the Gold Guide for airline phone numbers.

Los Angeles International Airport, known as LAX, is only 35 mi west of Anaheim. **Ontario International Airport** is northwest of Riverside, 30 mi north of Anaheim. **Long Beach Airport** is about 20 minutes by bus from Anaheim. *See* Air Travel *in* the Gold Guide for more information.

BETWEEN THE AIRPORTS AND HOTELS

If you're driving from John Wayne to downtown Anaheim, take Highway 55 north to the Golden State Freeway (I–5) north, and exit at Katella Avenue. To get to downtown L.A., take the San Diego Freeway (I–405) east to the Santa Monica Freeway (I–10) east to the Harbor Freeway (I–110) north; to get to Beverly Hills, take the San Diego Freeway north to Santa Monica Boulevard.

Airport Bus (☎ 800/772–5299), a shuttle service, carries passengers from John Wayne and LAX to Anaheim and Buena Park. The fare from John Wayne to Anaheim is $10, from LAX to Anaheim $14.

Prime Time Airport Shuttle (☎ 800/262–7433) provides door-to-door service from Orange County hotels to LAX and the San Pedro cruise terminal. The fare is $37 per person, plus $9 for each additional family member, from Anaheim hotels to LAX.

SuperShuttle (☎ 714/517–6600) provides 24-hour door-to-door service from all the airports to all points in Orange County. The fare to the Disneyland area is $10 per person from John Wayne, $34 from Ontario, $13 from LAX, and $33 from Long Beach Airport.

BY TRAIN

Amtrak (☎ 800/872–7245) makes several daily stops in Orange County: at Fullerton, Anaheim, Santa Ana, Irvine, San Juan Capistrano, and San Clemente. **Metrolink** (☎ 714/808–5465) is a weekday commuter train that runs to and from Los Angeles and Orange County, starting as far south as San Clemente and stopping in San Juan Capistrano, Irvine, Santa Ana, Orange, and Anaheim.

Getting Around

By Bus

The **Orange County Transportation Authority** (OCTA, ☎ 714/636–7433) will take you virtually anywhere in the county, but it will take time; OCTA buses go from Knott's Berry Farm and Disneyland to Huntington and Newport beaches. Bus 1 travels along the coast; there is also an express bus to Los Angeles.

By Car

Highways 55 and 91 head west to the ocean and east into the mountains: Take Highway 91 to Garden Grove and inland points (Buena Park, Anaheim). Highway 55 leads to Newport Beach. Pacific Coast Highway (Highway 1) allows easy access to beach communities and is the most scenic route.

Contacts and Resources

Emergencies
Ambulance (☎ 911). **Fire** (☎ 911). **Police** (☎ 911).

Anaheim Memorial Hospital (✉ 1111 W. La Palma Ave., ☎ 714/774–1450). **Western Medical Center** (✉ 1025 S. Anaheim Blvd., Anaheim, ☎ 714/533–6220). **Hoag Memorial Presbyterian Hospital** (✉ 301 Newport Blvd., Newport Beach, ☎ 949/645–8600). **South Coast Medical Center** (✉ 31872 PCH, Laguna Beach, ☎ 949/499–1311). **Children's Hospital of Orange County** (✉ 455 S. Main St., Orange, ☎ 714/997–3000).

Guided Tours
Pacific Coast Gray Line Tours (☎ 714/978–8855) provides guided tours from Orange County hotels to Disneyland, Knott's Berry Farm, Universal Studios Hollywood, Six Flags Magic Mountain, and the San Diego Zoo.

Visitor Information
Anaheim-Orange County Visitor and Convention Bureau (✉ Anaheim Convention Center, 800 W. Katella Ave., 92802, ☎ 714/999–8999). **Southern California Golf Association** (☎ 818/980–3630). **Southern California Public Links Golf Association** (☎ 714/994–4747).

14 San Diego

Exploring San Diego is an endless adventure. To visitors the city and county may seem like a conglomeration of theme parks: Old Town and the Gaslamp Quarter, historically oriented; the wharf area, a maritime playground; La Jolla, a throwback to southern California elegance; Balboa Park, a convergence of the town's cerebral and action-oriented personae. There are, of course, real theme parks—Sea World and the San Diego Zoo—but the great outdoors, in the form of forests, landscaped urban areas, and sandy beaches, is the biggest of them all.

SAN DIEGO IS A BIG CITY with a small-town feel. San Diego County covers a vast area, extending from the coast to mile-high mountains to a point near sea level in the desert, but central San Diego is delightfully urban and accessible.

San Diego is strongly defined by its relationship to the ocean—to some degree by default. During the latter half of the 19th century the town was banking on a rail link to the east. A building boom in the 1880s was largely based on the assumption that San Diego would become the western terminus of the Santa Fe Railway. The link was completed in 1885, but it proved unsuccessful for a variety of reasons, including the placement of the line through Temecula Canyon, where 30 mi of track were washed out repeatedly in winter rainstorms.

Instead, San Diego's future was sealed in 1908, when President Theodore Roosevelt's Great White Fleet stopped here on a world tour to demonstrate U.S. naval strength. The U.S. Navy, impressed during that visit by the city's excellent harbor and temperate climate, decided to build a destroyer base on San Diego Bay in the 1920s; the newly developing aircraft industry soon followed (Charles Lindbergh's plane *Spirit of St. Louis* was built here). Through the years San Diego's economy became largely dependent on the military and its attendant enterprises, which provided jobs as well as a demand for local goods and services by those stationed here.

The city conducts most of its financial business in a single neighborhood, the downtown district fronting San Diego Bay, in this way resembling New York more than Los Angeles. San Diego has set some of its most prestigious scientific facilities on the water—Scripps Institution of Oceanography, as well as the Salk Institute. Jonas Salk didn't need the Pacific marine environment for his research, but his regular morning runs along Torrey Pines State Beach no doubt cleared his head.

San Diego also has the ocean to thank for its near-perfect weather. An almost perpetual high-pressure system from the North Pacific is responsible for the city's sunshine and dry air; moderating breezes off the sea (caused by the water warming and cooling more slowly than the land) keep the summers relatively cool and the winters warm and help clear the air of pollution. In the late spring and early summer the difference between the earth and water temperatures generates coastal fogs.

EXPLORING SAN DIEGO

San Diego is more a chain of separate communities than a cohesive city. Many of the major attractions are separated by some distance from one another. The streets are fun for getting an up-close look at how San Diegans live, but true southern Californians use the freeways, which crisscross the county in a sensible fashion. If you are going to drive around San Diego, study your maps before you hit the road. If you stick with public transportation, plan on taking your time. The San Diego Trolley has expanded into Mission Valley; a commuter line called the Coaster runs from Oceanside into downtown; and the bus system covers almost all the county—but making the connections necessary to see the various sights is time-consuming.

Great Itineraries
IF YOU HAVE 3 DAYS
Head over to the San Diego Zoo in Balboa Park on the morning of your first day. It would be easy to spend your entire visit to the park here—and if you're traveling with kids, you may have little choice in

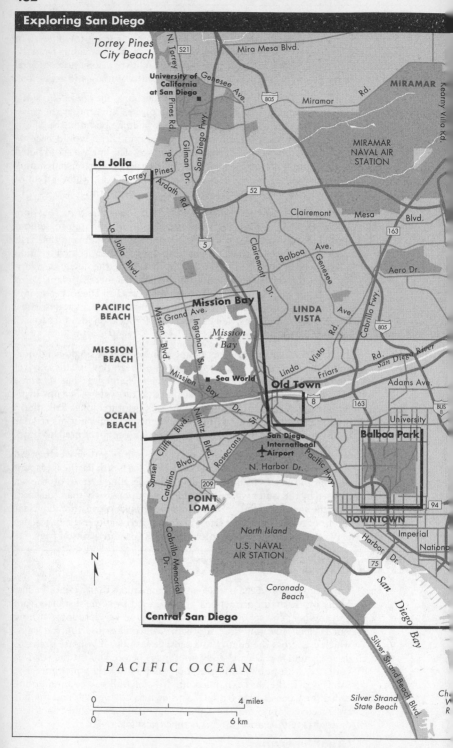

Torrey Pines
City Beach

S21

Mira Mesa Blvd.

N. Torrey

University of
California
at San Diego

Genesee Ave.

805

Miramar

Rd.

MIRAMAR

Kearny Villa Rd.

MIRAMAR
NAVAL AIR
STATION

La Jolla

Torrey

Pines Rd.

Gilman Dr.

San Diego Fwy.

Ardath Rd.

52

Clairemont

Mesa

Blvd.

163

La Jolla Blvd.

5

Clairemont Dr.

Balboa

Ave.

Genesee

Aero Dr.

Cabrillo Fwy.

805

PACIFIC
BEACH

MISSION
BEACH

OCEAN
BEACH

Mission Blvd.

Grand Ave.

Mission Bay

Ingraham St.

Mission
Bay

Mission

Bay

Dr.

Sea World

Nimitz Blvd.

LINDA
VISTA

Ave.

Vista

Rd.

San Diego River

Linda

Friars

Rd.

Adams Ave.

Old Town

8

163

University

BUS

Balboa Park

San Diego
International
Airport

N. Harbor Dr.

Pacific Hwy.

94

Sunset Cliffs Blvd.

Catalina Blvd.

Rosecrans Blvd.

209

POINT
LOMA

DOWNTOWN

Imperial

Cabrillo Memorial Dr.

North Island

U.S. NAVAL
AIR STATION

Harbor Dr.

Nationa

75

San

Diego

Bay

N

Coronado
Beach

Central San Diego

PACIFIC OCEAN

Silver Strand Beach Blvd.

Silver Strand
State Beach

Ch
V
R

0   4 miles

0   6 km

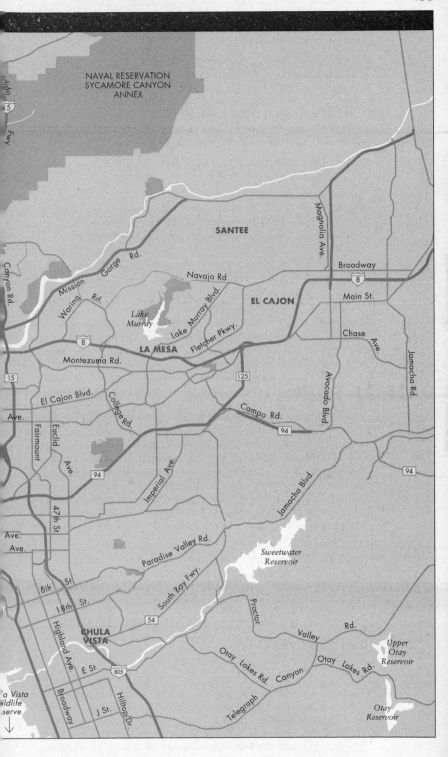

the matter—but it would be a shame to miss El Prado and its rows of architecturally interesting museums, a five-minute drive south of the zoo on Park Boulevard.

Start your second day downtown at Seaport Village; after browsing the shops catch a ferry from the Broadway Pier to Coronado. From Coronado's Ferry Landing Marketplace board a bus going down Orange Avenue to tour the town's Victorian extravaganza, the Hotel Del Coronado. Back in San Diego after lunch, stroll north on the Embarcadero to Ash Street; if you've gotten back early enough from Coronado, you can view the Maritime Museum.

On the third morning, visit La Jolla. Have lunch here before heading to the Gaslamp Quarter.

IF YOU HAVE 5 DAYS

Follow the three-day itinerary above, and begin your fourth day with a morning visit to Cabrillo National Monument. Have lunch at one of the seafood restaurants on Scott Street, and then head over to Old Town (take Rosecrans Street north to San Diego Avenue). If the daily schedule lists low tide for the afternoon, reverse the order to catch the tide pools at Cabrillo.

En route to North County on day five, stop off at Torrey Pines State Park. Then get on Interstate 5 (I–5) and head up to Del Mar for lunch, shopping, and sea views. Continue north on S21 to other coastal towns such as Encinitas and Carlsbad. A visit to Mission San Luis Rey, slightly inland from Oceanside on Highway 76, will infuse some history and culture into the tour.

BALBOA PARK

Overlooking downtown and the Pacific Ocean, 1,200-acre Balboa Park, the cultural center of the city, is home to most of San Diego's museums and the world-famous San Diego Zoo. Many of the park's Spanish-Moorish buildings were intended to be temporary structures, housing exhibits for the Panama–California International Exposition of 1915. The Spanish theme first instituted in the early 1900s was in part carried through in new buildings designed for the California Pacific International Exposition of 1935–36, but architectural details from the temples of the Maya and other indigenous peoples of the Americas were added.

The Laurel Street Bridge is the park's official gateway. Parking near Balboa Park's museums is no small accomplishment, especially on sunny summer days, when lots fill up quickly. If you're driving in via the Laurel Street Bridge, the first parking area you'll come to is off the Prado to the left, going toward Pan American Plaza. Free trams, which operate around the park, run about every 15 minutes from 9:30 to 4.

Two Good Walks

Numbers in the text correspond to numbers in the margin and on the Balboa Park map.

Enter via Cabrillo Bridge through the West Gate, which depicts the Panama Canal's linkage of the Atlantic and Pacific oceans. Park south of the **Alcazar Garden** ①. It's a short stretch north across El Prado to the landmark **California Building,** modeled on a cathedral in Mexico and now home to the **San Diego Museum of Man** ②. Look up to see busts and statues of heroes of the early days of the state. Next door is the **Simon Edison Centre for the Performing Arts** ③, which adjoins the sculpture garden of the **San Diego Museum of Art** ④, an ornate

Plateresque-style structure built to resemble the 17th-century University of Salamanca in Spain.

Continuing east you'll come to the **Timken Museum of Art** ⑤, the **Botanical Building** ⑥, and the Spanish colonial–style **Casa del Prado,** where the San Diego Floral Association has its offices and a gift shop. At the end of the row is the **San Diego Natural History Museum** ⑦; you'll have to detour a block north to visit the **Spanish Village Art Center** ⑧. If you were to continue north, you would come to the **carousel** ⑨, the **miniature railroad** ⑩, and, finally, the entrance to the **San Diego Zoo** ⑪.

Return to the history museum and cross Plaza de Balboa—its large central fountain is a popular meeting spot—to reach the **Reuben H. Fleet Space Theater and Science Center** ⑫. (Beyond the parking lot to the south lies the **Centro Cultural de la Raza** ⑬.) You're now on the opposite side of the Prado and heading west. You'll next pass **Casa de Balboa** ⑭, home to history, model-railroad, and photography museums. Next door in the newly restored **House of Hospitality** ⑮ is the **Balboa Park Visitors Center.** Across the Plaza de Panama, the **House of Charm** ⑯, a recently constructed Spanish-style building that blends well with older park architecture, is home to a folk art museum and a gallery for San Diego artists. Your starting point, the Alcazar Garden, is west of the House of Charm.

Another option is to walk south from the Plaza de Panama, which doubles as a parking lot. As most of the buildings along El Prado were created for the 1915 exposition, the majority of those along this route date to the 1935 fair, when the architecture of the Maya and native peoples of the Southwest was highlighted. The first building you'll pass is the **Japanese Friendship Garden** ⑰. Next comes the ornate, crownlike **Spreckels Organ Pavilion** ⑱. The round seating area forms the base, with the stage as its diadem. The road forks here; veer to the left to reach the **House of Pacific Relations** ⑲, a Spanish mission–style cluster of cottages and one of the few structures on this route built for the earlier exposition. Another is the Balboa Park Club, which you'll pass next. Now used for park receptions and banquets, the building resembles a mission church; you might want to step inside to see the huge mural. Continue on beyond the Palisades Building, which hosts the Marie Hitchcock Puppet Theater, to reach the **San Diego Automotive Museum** ⑳, appropriately housed in the building that served as the Palace of Transportation in the 1935–36 exposition.

The road loops back at the spaceship-like **San Diego Aerospace Museum and International Aerospace Hall of Fame** ㉑. As you head north again you'll notice the Starlight Bowl on your right. It sits in the flight path to San Diego International Airport; during the live musicals presented in the summer on its outdoor stage, actors freeze in their places when planes roar overhead. The Gymnasium Building—slated to become the home of the sports museum in a few years—follows. Next comes perhaps the most impressive structure on this tour, the **Federal Building,** slated to be the new home for the **San Diego Hall of Champions– Sports Museum** ㉒. Its main entrance was modeled after the Palace of Governors in the ancient Mayan city of Uxmal, Mexico. You'll be back at the Spreckels Organ Pavilion after this, having walked a total of a little less than a mile.

TIMING

You'll want to devote an entire day to the zoo. Though some of the park's museums are open on Monday, most are open from Tuesday to Sunday between 10–4; during the summer a number have extended hours. On Tuesday the museums have free admission on a rotating basis;

call the Balboa Park Visitors Center (☞ House of Hospitality, *below*) for a schedule. Free concerts take place Sunday afternoons and summer Monday evenings at the Spreckels Organ Pavilion, and the House of Pacific Relations hosts Sunday afternoon folk-dance performances.

Sights to See

1 **Alcazar Garden.** The gardens surrounding the Alcazar Castle in Seville, Spain, were the model for the landscaping here; you'll feel like royalty, resting on the benches by the tiled fountains. The flower beds are ever-changing horticultural exhibits, with bright orange and yellow poppies blooming in the spring and deep rust and crimson chrysanthemums appearing in the fall. The garden is off El Prado, next to the San Diego Art Institute and across from the Museum of Man.

6 **Botanical Building.** The graceful redwood-lathed structure built for the 1915 exposition houses more than 500 types of tropical and subtropical plants. Ceiling-high tree ferns shade fragile orchids and feathery bamboo. There are benches beside miniature waterfalls for resting in the shade. The lily pond, filled with giant koi fish and blooming water lilies, is popular with photographers. ⊠ *1550 El Prado,* ☎ *619/235–1114.* ☞ *Free.* ☉ *Fri.–Wed. 10–4.*

9 **Carousel.** Riders on this antique merry-go-round stretch from their seats to grab the brass rings suspended an arm's-length away and earn a free ride. Hand-carved in 1910, the bobbing animals include zebras, giraffes, and dragons; real horsehair was used for the tails. ⊠ *1889 Zoo Pl. (behind zoo parking lot).* ☞ *$1.25.* ☉ *Daily 11–5:30 during extended summer vacation; during school yr, only school holidays and weekends.*

14 **Casa de Balboa.** This building on El Prado's southeast corner houses three museums: the Museum of Photographic Arts, the Museum of San Diego History, and the San Diego Model Railroad Museum. *See* individual museum descriptions, *below.* ⊠ *1649 El Prado.*

13 **Centro Cultural de la Raza.** An old water tower was converted into this center for Mexican, Native American, and Chicano arts. Attractions include a gallery, a theater, and a permanent collection of mural art, a fine example of which may be seen on the tower's exterior. ⊠ *2004 Park Blvd.,* ☎ *619/235–6135.* ☞ *Free.* ☉ *Thurs.–Sun. noon–5.*

16 **House of Charm.** Two formerly far-flung museums found homes in this structure, built in Spanish style to fit in with the older El Prado structures: the Mingei International Museum of Folk Art and the San Diego Art Institute. (☞ Individual museum listings, *below.*)

15 **House of Hospitality.** At the reconstructed home of the **Balboa Park Visitors Center** you can pick up schedules and route maps for the free trams that operate around the park. You can also purchase the Passport to Balboa Park, which affords entry to 12 museums for $21; it's worthwhile if you want to visit more than a few and aren't entitled to the discounts that most give to children, senior citizens, and military personnel. The **Terrace on the Prado** (☎ 619/236–1935) restaurant's Spanish and early California menu includes recipes from the gold-rush days; there's also a tapas bar here. ⊠ *1549 El Prado,* ☎ *619/239–0512.* ☉ *Daily 9–4.*

19 **House of Pacific Relations.** The word "pacific" refers not to the ocean—most of the nations represented are European, not Asian—but to the goal of maintaining peace. The cottages, decorated with crafts and pictures, hold open houses on Sunday afternoon, during which you can chat with transplanted natives and try out different ethnic foods. ⊠ *2160 Pan American Rd. W,* ☎ *619/234–0739.* ☞ *Free.* ☉ *Sun. 12:30–4:30; hrs may vary with season.*

Balboa Park

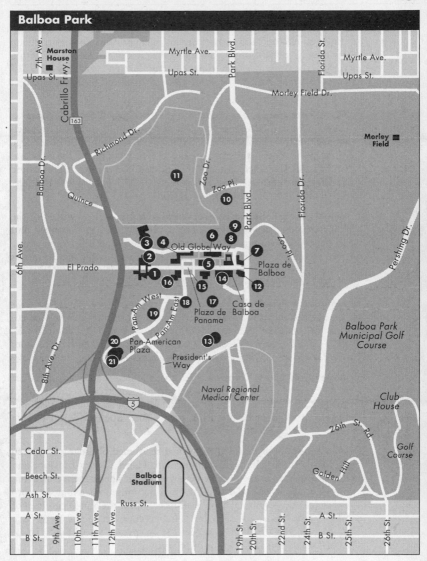

⑰ **Japanese Friendship Garden.** The rocks and trees in the park's Eastern-style garden are arranged to inspire contemplation. The complex includes an exhibit house where arts like origami and flower arranging are taught, a traditional sand-and-stone garden, a picnic area with a view of the canyon below, a snack bar, and a small gift shop. ⊠ *2215 Pan American Rd. E,* ☎ *619/232–2780.* ⊠ *$2.* ☼ *Fri.–Sun. and Tues. 10–4.*

The Marston House. The residence of businessman George W. Marston (1850–1946), a San Diego pioneer and philanthropist who financed the architectural landscaping of Balboa Park, sits at the northwest edge of the park. The 1905 structure is a classic example of the Arts and Crafts style. The 5-acre grounds are landscaped in the English Romantic tradition as interpreted in California. ⊠ *3525 7th Ave.,* ☎ *619/232–6203.* ⊠ *$3.* ☼ *Fri.–Sun. noon–4:30.*

★ ⑯ **Mingei International Museum of World Folk Art.** All ages will enjoy the colorful and creative exhibits of toys, pottery, textiles, costumes, and gadgets from around the globe at the Mingei. You'll find everything from antique American carousel horses to the latest in Japanese ceramics in this light-filled facility. ⊠ *1439 El Prado,* ☎ *619/239–0003.* ⊠ *$5.* ☼ *Tues.–Sun. 10–4.*

⑩ **Miniature railroad.** Adjacent to the zoo parking lot, a pint-size 48-passenger train runs a ½-mi loop through eucalyptus groves. The engine is a small-scale version of the General Motors F-3 locomotive. ⊠ *2885 Zoo Pl.,* ☎ *619/239–4748.* ⊠ *$1.25.* ☼ *Weekends and school holidays 11–4:30, daily during school summer break.*

Morley Field Sports Complex. The park's athletic center has a Frisbee Golf Course, a public pool, a velodrome, an archery range, playgrounds, and boccie, badminton, and tennis courts. The complex is at the far east end of Balboa Park, across Park Boulevard and Florida Canyon. ⊠ *2221 Morley Field Dr.,* ☎ *619/692–4919.*

⑭ **Museum of Photographic Arts.** World-renowned photographers such as Ansel Adams, Imogen Cunningham, Henri Cartier-Bresson, and Edward Weston are represented in the museum's permanent collection, more of which will be displayed when the museum's expansion into the space once occupied by next-door neighbor the San Diego Hall of Champions–Sports Museum (☞ *below*) is completed in 1999. ⊠ *Casa de Balboa, 1649 El Prado,* ☎ *619/239–5262.* ⊠ *$4.* ☼ *Daily 10–5; closed some holidays and for installations.*

⑭ **Museum of San Diego History.** The San Diego Historical Society maintains its research library in the Casa de Balboa's basement and organizes shows on the first floor. Permanent and rotating exhibits survey local urban history after 1850, when California became part of the United States. ⊠ *Casa de Balboa, 1649 El Prado,* ☎ *619/232–6203.* ⊠ *$4.* ☼ *Tues.–Sun. 10–4:30.*

★ ⑫ **Reuben H. Fleet Space Theater and Science Center.** Clever interactive exhibits at the Fleet Center illustrate scientific principles, and the Imax Dome Theater here screens exhilarating nature and science films shot to make viewers feel as though they're part of an expedition. A planetarium show takes over the theater on the first Wednesday of the month. A multimillion-dollar expansion program that doubled the facility's size also added a motion-based simulator, designed to take visitors on virtual voyages—stomach lurches and all. ⊠ *1875 El Prado,* ☎ *619/ 238–1233 or 619/232–6866 for advance tickets.* ⊠ *Science Center, $4; Science Center and Imax Theater or Science Center and Simulator, $8; Science Center, Imax Theater, and Simulator, $11; Planetar-*

ium show, $5. ⊙ *Mon.–Tues. 9:30–6, Wed.–Sun. 9:30–9 (hrs change seasonally; call ahead).*

㉑ **San Diego Aerospace Museum and International Aerospace Hall of Fame.** Every available inch of space in the rotunda is filled with exhibits about aviation and aerospace pioneers, including examples of enemy planes during the world wars. A collection of real and replicated aircraft fills the central courtyard. ⊠ *2001 Pan American Plaza,* ☎ *619/234–8291.* ⊞ *$6, active military personnel free.* ⊙ *Daily 10–4:30.*

⑯ **San Diego Art Institute.** Outside juries decide which works created by members of the Art Institute will be displayed in rotating shows, which change every five or six weeks. Painting, sculpture, watercolor, and other media are represented. ⊠ *House of Charm, 1439 El Prado,* ☎ *619/236–0011.* ⊞ *$3.* ⊙ *Tues.–Sat. 10–4, Sun. noon–4.*

⑳ **San Diego Automotive Museum.** The museum maintains a core collection of vintage motorcycles and cars, ranging from an 1886 Mercedes Benz to a De Lorean, as well as a series of rotating exhibits from collections around the world. ⊠ *2080 Pan American Plaza,* ☎ *619/231–2886.* ⊞ *$6.* ⊙ *Daily 10–4:30.*

㉒ **San Diego Hall of Champions–Sports Museum.** Scheduled to be closed from October 1998 through spring 1999, while its new, larger home is being made ready, this museum celebrates local jock heroes via a vast collection of memorabilia, uniforms, paintings, photographs, and computer and video displays. The bigger digs will include interactive exhibits. ⊠ *Federal Bldg., 2131 Pan American Rd.,* ☎ *619/234–2544.* ⊞ *$3.* ⊙ *Daily 10–4:30.*

⑭ **San Diego Model Railroad Museum.** When the six model-train exhibits are in operation, you'll hear the sounds of chugging engines, screeching brakes, and shrill whistles. On Tuesday and Friday evening between 7:30 and 11, there's no admission charge to watch the model-train layouts being created. ⊠ *Casa de Balboa, 1649 El Prado,* ☎ *619/696–0199.* ⊞ *$3.* ⊙ *Tues.–Fri. 11–4, weekends 11–5.*

★ ❹ **San Diego Museum of Art.** Known primarily for its Spanish Baroque and Renaissance paintings, including works by El Greco, Goya, Rubens, and van Ruisdael, San Diego's most comprehensive art museum also has strong holdings of Southeast Asian art, Indian miniatures, and contemporary California paintings. The Baldwin M. Baldwin wing displays more than 100 pieces by Toulouse-Lautrec. If traveling shows from other cities come to San Diego, you can expect to see them here. An outdoor Sculpture Garden exhibits both traditional and modern pieces in a striking natural setting. ⊠ *Casa de Balboa, 1450 El Prado,* ☎ *619/232–7931.* ⊞ *$7 Tues.–Thurs., $8 Fri.–Sun.* ⊙ *Tues.–Sun. 10–4:30.*

❷ **San Diego Museum of Man.** Exhibits at this highly respected anthropological museum focus on southwestern, Mexican, and South American cultures. Carved monuments from the Mayan city of Quirigua in Guatemala, cast from the originals in 1914, are particularly impressive. Among the museum's more recent additions is the Children's Discovery Center, which has interactive exhibits. ⊠ *California Bldg., 1350 El Prado,* ☎ *619/239–2001.* ⊞ *$4.* ⊙ *Daily 10–4:30.*

❼ **San Diego Natural History Museum.** The museum focuses on the plants and animals of southern California and Mexico; it frequently schedules free guided nature walks on the weekends, as well as films and lectures throughout the week. An $18 million expansion program began in 1998. ⊠ *1788 El Prado,* ☎ *619/232–3821.* ⊞ *$6.* ⊙ *Daily 9:30–4:30.*

★ ⓫ **San Diego Zoo.** Balboa Park's—and perhaps the city's—most famous attraction is its 100-acre zoo. Nearly 4,000 animals of some 800 diverse species roam in expertly crafted habitats that spread down into, around, and above the natural canyons. Exploring the zoo fully requires the stamina of a healthy hiker, but open-air trams that run throughout the day allow visitors to see 80% of the exhibits on the 3-mi tour. The Kangaroo bus tours include the same informed and amusing narrations as the others, but for a few dollars more you can get on and off as you like at eight different stops. The Skyfari ride, which soars 170 ft above the ground, gives a good overview of the zoo's layout and, on clear days, a panorama of the park, downtown San Diego, the bay, and the ocean, far past the Coronado Bridge.

Paths climb through the huge, enclosed **Scripps Aviary,** where brightly colored tropical birds swoop between branches just inches from your face. **Gorilla Tropics,** beside the aviary, is among the zoo's latest ventures into bioclimatic zone exhibits, where animals live in enclosed environments modeled on their native habitats. The zoo houses the largest number of koalas outside Australia as well as an impressive collection of hornbills.

The zoo's simulated Asian rain forest, **Tiger River,** has 10 exhibits with more than 35 species of animals. Here you'll see tigers, Malayan tapirs, and Argus pheasants among the $500,000 collection of exotic trees and plants. At the popular **Polar Bear Plunge,** where you can watch the featured animals take a chilly dive, Siberian reindeer, white foxes, and other Arctic creatures are separated from their predatory neighbors by a series of camouflaged moats. But these and other zoo locals are being overshadowed by the hoopla surrounding two glamorous overseas visitors: Shi Shi and Bai Yun, a pair of giant pandas on loan for 12 years from the People's Republic of China. Seeing them is certainly a not-to-be-missed experience, but because the pandas are here for conservation research purposes, there's also a chance that they won't be on display when you visit.

The zoo rents strollers, wheelchairs, and cameras; it also has a first-aid office, a lost and found, and an ATM. Behind-the-scenes tours, walking tours, tours in Spanish, and tours for people with hearing or vision impairments are available; inquire at the entrance. ⊠ *2920 Zoo Dr.,* ☎ *619/234–3153.* ☜ *$16 includes zoo, Children's Zoo, and animal shows; $22 includes above, plus 35-min guided bus tour and Skyfari ride; Kangaroo bus tour $9 additional; zoo free for children under 12 in Oct. and for all on Founder's Day (Oct. 3); $35.15 pass good for admission to zoo and San Diego Wild Animal Park (☞ Side Trip to Inland North County, below) within 5 days. AE, D, MC, V. ☉ Fall–spring, daily 9–4 (visitors may remain until 5); summer, daily 9–9 (visitors may remain until 10); Children's Zoo and Skyfari ride close earlier.*

❸ **Simon Edison Centre for the Performing Arts.** Even if you're not attending a play, the complex, comprising the Cassius Carter Centre Stage, the Lowell Davies Festival Theatre, and the Old Globe Theatre, is a pleasant place to relax between museum visits. The theaters, done in a California version of Tudor style, sit between the Sculpture Garden of the San Diego Museum of Art and the California Tower. ⊠ *1363 Old Globe Way,* ☎ *619/239–2255 or 619/234–5623.*

❽ **Spanish Village Art Center.** Glassblowers, enamel workers, woodcarvers, sculptors, painters, jewelers, photographers, and other artists rent space in the 35 little red tile–roof studio-galleries. The artists give demonstrations of their work on a rotating basis. ⊠ *1770 Village Pl.,* ☎ *619/232–3522.* ☜ *Free.* ☉ *Daily 10–4:30.*

⑱ **Spreckels Organ Pavilion.** The 2,000-seat pavilion, dedicated in 1915 by sugar magnates John D. and Adolph B. Spreckels, holds the 4,445-pipe Spreckels Organ, believed to be the largest outdoor pipe organ in the world. You can hear this impressive instrument at one of the year-round, 2 PM Sunday concerts. At Christmastime the park's Christmas tree and life-size Nativity display turn the pavilion into a seasonal wonderland. ✉ *2211 Pan American Rd. E,* ☎ *619/226–0819.*

⑤ **Timken Museum of Art.** This modern structure is made of travertine marble imported from Italy. The small museum houses a selection of minor works by major European and American artists as well as a superb collection of Russian icons. ✉ *1500 El Prado,* ☎ *619/239–5548.* 🎫 *Free.* ☉ *Oct.–Aug., Tues.–Sat. 10–4:30, Sun. 1:30–4:30.*

OFF THE
BEATEN PATH

UPTOWN DISTRICT AND HILLCREST – Northwest of Balboa Park, Hillcrest is San Diego's center for the gay community and artists of all types. University, 4th, and 5th avenues are filled with cafés, boutiques, and bookstores. The Guild Theater and the Ken, both on 5th Avenue, show first-run foreign films. The Uptown District, on University Avenue at 8th Avenue, is a self-contained residential-commercial center that was built to resemble an inner-city neighborhood.

DOWNTOWN

Thanks to a redevelopment effort started in the late 1970s, elegant hotels, upscale condominium complexes, and swank, trendy cafés now attract newcomers and natives to a newly developed city center that has retained an outdoor character. The Martin Luther King Jr. Promenade project, which will cost an estimated $25 million by the time it's completed, has put 12 acres of greenery along Harbor Drive from Seaport Village to the convention center. It includes a pedestrian walkway with benches, space for joggers and bicyclists, and assorted artwork. The San Diego Convention Center, which hosted its first events in 1990, is being expanded. A few blocks inland the hugely successful Horton Plaza shopping center led the way for hotels, restaurants, shopping centers, and housing developments.

There are reasonably priced (between $3 and $7 per day) parking lots along Harbor Drive, Pacific Highway, and lower Broadway and Market Street. The price of many downtown parking meters is $1 per hour, with a maximum stay of two hours; unless you know for sure that your stay in the area will be short, you're better off in a lot. If you're planning to tour the Embarcadero, the lot at the cruise ship terminal, which costs only $1 an hour with a maximum of $3 a day, is a bargain.

Two Good Walks

Numbers in the text correspond to numbers in the margin and on the Central San Diego map.

Two distinct areas of downtown can be easily explored on foot. If you want to stay near the water, begin at the **Embarcadero** ① at the foot of Ash Street on Harbor Drive, where the *Berkeley,* headquarters of the **Maritime Museum** ②, is moored. A cement pathway runs south from the *Star of India* along the waterfront to the pastel B Street Pier. Another two blocks south on Harbor Drive brings you to the foot of Broadway and the Broadway Pier, where you can catch the ferry to Coronado. Continue south past Tuna Harbor to **Seaport Village** ③. Six blocks north of Seaport Village on Kettner Boulevard is the **Transit Center** ④; you'll see the mosaic-domed Santa Fe Depot and the tracks for the Trolley to the Mexican border out front. Right next door is the downtown branch of the **Museum of Contemporary Art, San Diego** ⑤.

472

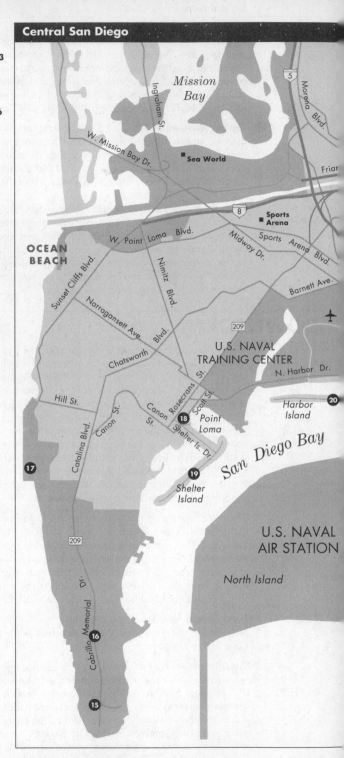

Central San Diego

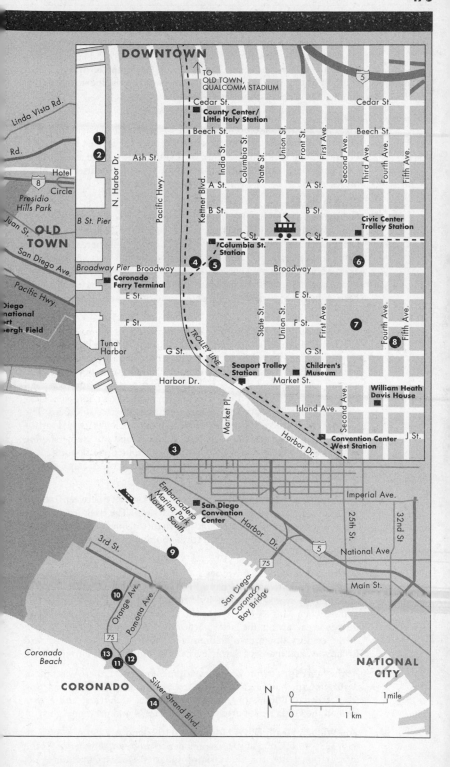

DOWNTOWN

TO
OLD TOWN,
QUALCOMM STADIUM

Linda Vista Rd.

Rd.

Hotel
Circle

8

Presidio
Hills Park

OLD
TOWN

San Diego Ave.

Juan St.

Pacific Hwy.

Diego
national
ort
ergh Field

Cedar St.

County Center/
Little Italy Station

Beech St.

N. Harbor Dr.

Ash St.

Pacific Hwy.

Ketner Blvd.

India St.

Columbia St.

State St.

Union St.

Front St.

First Ave.

Second Ave.

Third Ave.

Fourth Ave.

Fifth Ave.

Cedar St.

Beech St.

A St.

A St.

B St.

B St.

Civic Center
Trolley Station

B St. Pier

C St.

Columbia St.
Station

C St.

Broadway Pier

Broadway

Coronado
Ferry Terminal

E St.

F St.

Tuna
Harbor

G St.

Broadway

E St.

State St.

Union St.

F St.

First Ave.

Fourth Ave.

Fifth Ave.

G St.

G St.

TROLLEY LINE

Harbor Dr.

Seaport Trolley
Station

Market St.

Children's
Museum

William Heath
Davis House

Island Ave.

Second Ave.

Market Pl.

Harbor Dr.

Convention Center
West Station

J St.

Imperial Ave.

Embarcadero
Marina Park
North
South

San Diego
Convention
Center

Harbor Dr.

25th St.

32nd St

3rd St.

9

5

National Ave.

75

San Diego–
Coronado
Bay Bridge

Main St.

Orange Ave.

Pomona Ave.

10

75

Coronado
Beach

13

11

12

CORONADO

Silver Strand Blvd.

14

NATIONAL
CITY

N

0   1 mile

0   1 km

To explore the working heart of downtown, begin at the historic **U. S. Grant Hotel** ⑥ at Broadway between 2nd and 3rd avenues. Head south on 3rd Avenue to enter **Horton Plaza** ⑦, San Diego's favorite retail playland. Fourth Avenue, the eastern boundary of Horton Plaza, doubles as the western boundary of the 16-block **Gaslamp Quarter** ⑧. Head south to Island Avenue and the **William Heath Davis House,** where you can get a touring map of the district.

TIMING

The above walks take about an hour each, though there's enough to do in downtown San Diego to keep you busy for at least two days— or three if you really like to shop or if you decide to take a side trip to Coronado or Tijuana. Guided tours of the Gaslamp Quarter take place on Saturday.

Sights to See

❶ **Embarcadero.** The bustle along Harbor Drive's waterfront walkway comes less these days from the activities of tuna and other fishing folk, but it remains the nautical soul of San Diego. People here still make a living from the sea: fish houses and seafood restaurants line the piers, as do sea vessels of every variety—cruise ships, ferries, tour boats, houseboats, and naval destroyers. Many boats along the Embarcadero have been converted into floating gift shops, and others are awaiting restoration.

On the north end of the Embarcadero, at Ash Street, you'll find the Maritime Museum (☞ *below*). South of it, the **B Street Pier** is used by ships from major cruise lines as both a port of call and a departure point. The cavernous pier building has a cruise-information center and a small, cool bar and gift shop. Day-trippers getting ready to set sail gather at the **Broadway Pier,** also known as the excursion pier. Tickets for the harbor tours and whale-watching trips are sold here. The U.S. Navy has control of the next few waterfront blocks to the south— destroyers, submarines, and carriers cruise in and out, some staying for weeks at a time. On weekends you can tour these floating cities (☎ 619/532–3130 for information on hours and types of ships, or 619/ 545–2427 for the USS *Constellation*).

The **San Diego Convention Center,** on Harbor Drive between 1st and 5th avenues, was designed by Arthur Erickson. The backdrop of blue sky and sea complements the building's nautical lines. The center often holds trade shows that are open to the public, and tours of the building are available.

❽ **Gaslamp Quarter.** The 16-block national historic district centered between 4th and 5th avenues from Broadway to Market Street contains most of San Diego's Victorian-style commercial buildings from the late 1800s, when Market Street was the center of downtown. Businesses thrived in this area in the latter part of the 19th century, but at the turn of the century downtown's commercial district moved west toward Broadway, and many of San Diego's first buildings fell into disrepair.

As the move for downtown redevelopment emerged, there was talk of destroying the buildings in the quarter, bulldozing them and starting from scratch. But history buffs, developers, architects, and artists formed the Gaslamp Quarter Council in 1974 and prevented this.

The **William Heath Davis House** (✉ 410 Island Ave., at 4th Ave., ☎ 619/233–4692), one of the first residences in town, now serves as the information center for the Gaslamp Quarter. Docents give tours ($2) of the house during museum hours, which vary but are generally weekdays from 10 to 2, Saturday from 10 to 4, and Sunday from noon to

4. Two-hour walking tours of the historic district leave from the house on Saturday at 11; the cost for these or a self-guided audio tour (phone ahead to reserve a headset) is $5.

The Victorian **Horton Grand Hotel** (✉ 311 Island Ave.) was created in the mid-1980s by joining together two historic hotels, the Kahle Saddlery and the Grand Hotel, built in the boom days of the 1880s; Wyatt Earp stayed at the Kahle Saddlery—then called the Brooklyn Hotel—while he was in town speculating on real estate ventures and opening gambling halls. The two hotels were dismantled and reconstructed on a new site, about four blocks from their original locations. A small Chinese Museum serves as a tribute to the surrounding Chinatown district, a collection of modest structures that once housed Chinese laborers and their families.

The section of G Street between 6th and 9th avenues has become a haven for galleries; stop in one of them to pick up a map of the downtown arts district. For information about openings and other events in the district, call the **Gaslamp Quarter Association** (☎ 619/233–5227).

★ **7** **Horton Plaza.** Downtown's centerpiece is the shopping, dining, and entertainment mall that fronts Broadway and G Street from 1st to 4th avenues and covers more than six city blocks. Designed by Jon Jerde and completed in 1985, Horton Plaza is far from what one would imagine a shopping center—or city center—to be. The complex's architecture has strongly affected the rest of downtown's development—new apartment and condominium complexes along G and Market streets mimic its brightly colored towers and cupolas. Horton Plaza has a multilevel parking garage. The **International Visitor Information Center,** operated in the complex by the San Diego Convention and Visitors Bureau, is the best resource for information about the city.

2 **Maritime Museum.** With a collection of three restored ships that may be toured for one admission price, the museum affords a glimpse of San Diego during its heyday as a commercial seaport. Its headquarters are the *Berkeley,* an 1898 ferryboat moored at the foot of Ash Street. The steam-driven ship, which served the Southern Pacific Railroad at San Francisco Bay until 1958, played its most important role during the great earthquake of 1906, when it carried thousands of passengers across San Francisco Bay to Oakland. The most interesting of the ships is the *Star of India,* a windjammer built in 1863. The ship's high wooden masts and white sails flapping in the wind have been a harbor landmark since 1927. The *Star of India* made 21 trips around the world in the late 1800s, when it traveled the East Indian trade route, shuttled immigrants from England to New Zealand, and served the Alaskan salmon trade. ✉ 1306 N. Harbor Dr., ☎ 619/234–9153. ✍ $5. ☉ Daily 9–8.

5 **Museum of Contemporary Art, San Diego.** The downtown branch of the city's modern art museum, which opened in 1993 while the main facility in La Jolla was undergoing renovation, has taken on its own personality. The two-story building has four small galleries that host rotating shows. It's fronted by a sculpture plaza. ✉ 1001 Kettner Blvd., ☎ 619/454–3541 for exhibition information. ✍ $4; free 1st Tues. and Sun. of month. ☉ Tues.–Sat. 10–5, Sun. noon–5.

★ **3** **Seaport Village.** The village's three shopping plazas are designed to reflect the architectural styles of early California, especially New England clapboard and Spanish mission. A ¼-mi wooden boardwalk that runs along the bay and 4 mi of simulated dirt-road and cobblestone paths lead to specialty shops, snack bars, and restaurants—about 75 in all. You can browse through a kite store, a rubber-stamp emporium, and a shop devoted to left-handed people and nosh to your heart's delight on everything from fast Greek, Mexican, and Italian fare to seafood in nautical-style indoor restaurants. The **Broadway Flying Horses Carousel** and strolling clowns, mimes, musicians, and magicians entertain the kids. ☎ 619/235–4014 or 619/235–4013 for events hot line.

❹ **Transit Center.** A booth at the tile-domed **Santa Fe Depot,** which serves Amtrak and Coaster passengers, has bus schedules, maps, and tourist brochures. Formerly an easily spotted area landmark, it's now overshadowed by **1 America Plaza** across the street. At the base of this 34-story office tower is a center that links the train, trolley, and city bus systems. The building's signature crescent-shape, glass-and-steel canopy arches out over the trolley tracks. ✉ *Broadway and Kettner Blvd.*

❻ **U. S. Grant Hotel.** Far more formal than most other hotels in San Diego, the doyenne of downtown lodgings has a marble lobby, gleaming chandeliers, attentive doormen, and other touches that hark back to the more gracious era when it was built (1910). Funded in part by the son of the president for whom it was named, the hotel was extremely opulent; 350 rooms of 437 had private baths, highly unusual for that time. ✉ *326 Broadway.*

CORONADO

Although it's actually an isthmus, easily reached from the mainland if you head north from Imperial Beach, Coronado has always seemed like an island—and is often referred to as such. The streets of Coronado are wide, quiet, and friendly, with many neighborhood parks. Coronado is visible from downtown and Point Loma and accessible via the arching blue 2.2-mi-long San Diego–Coronado Bridge, a landmark just beyond downtown's skyline. There is a $1 toll for crossing the bridge into Coronado, but cars carrying two or more passengers may enter through the free carpool lane.

Until the bridge was completed in 1969, visitors and residents relied on the Coronado Ferry, which ran across the harbor from downtown. When the bridge was opened, the ferry closed down, much to the chagrin of those who were fond of traveling at a leisurely pace. In 1987 the ferry returned. You can board the ferry, operated by **San Diego Harbor Excursion** (☎ 619/234–4111; 800/442–7847 in CA), at downtown San Diego's Embarcadero from the Broadway Pier at Broadway and Harbor Drive; you'll arrive at the Ferry Landing Marketplace. Boats depart every hour on the hour from the Embarcadero and every hour on the half hour from Coronado, from Sunday to Thursday between 9 AM and 9:30 PM, Friday and Saturday between 9 AM and 10:30 PM; the fare is $2 each way, 50¢ extra for bicycles. San Diego Harbor Excursion operates **water-taxi service** (☎ 619/235–8294) from 10 AM to 10 PM between any two points in the San Diego Bay. The fare is $5.

A Good Tour

Numbers in the text correspond to numbers in the margin and on the Central San Diego map.

Hop on the ferry at the Embarcadero. When you get to Coronado, explore the shops at the **Ferry Landing Marketplace** ⑨ and from there catch the shuttle (50¢ fare) that runs down **Orange Avenue** ⑩. Get off near the tourist information office and pick up a map, or disembark at an appealing spot and keep strolling along the boutiques-filled promenade until you reach the **Hotel Del Coronado** ⑪ at the end of Orange Avenue. Right across the street from the Del is the **Glorietta**

Bay Inn ⑫. A bit northwest of the Del is the **Coronado Beach Historical Museum** ⑬. Orange Avenue turns into Silver Strand Boulevard on the way to **Silver Strand State Beach** ⑭.

TIMING

A leisurely stroll through Coronado takes an hour or so, more if you shop or walk along the beach. If you're a history buff, you might want to visit on Thursday or Saturday, when you can combine the tour of Coronado's historic homes that departs from the Glorietta Bay Inn at 11 AM with a visit to the Coronado Beach Historical Museum, open from Wednesday to Sunday in the afternoon.

Sights to See

⑬ **Coronado Beach Historical Museum.** An East Coast family built this Cape Cod–style cottage in 1898. The restored building now houses a museum that celebrates the island's history with photographs and displays of its formative events and major sites. ⊠ *1126 Loma Ave.,* ☎ *619/435–7242.* ⌕ *Free; donations accepted.* ☉ *Wed.–Sun. 10–4.*

⑨ **Ferry Landing Marketplace.** The aptly named point of disembarkation for the ferry, this collection of shops is actually a new development on an old site. Its buildings resemble the gingerbread domes of the Hotel Del Coronado, long the area's main attraction. ⊠ *1201 1st St. at B Ave.,* ☎ *619/435–8895.*

⑫ **Glorietta Bay Inn.** On Tuesday, Thursday, and Saturday morning at 11, this is the departure point for a fun and informative 1½-hour walking tour of a few of the area's 86 officially designated historical homes. Sponsored by the Coronado Historical Association, the tour focuses on the Glorietta Bay Inn and the Hotel Del Coronado across the street. ⊠ *1630 Glorietta Blvd.,* ☎ *619/435–5892 or 619/435–5444 for tour information.* ⌕ *$6 for historical tour.*

★ ⑪ **Hotel Del Coronado.** The island's most prominent landmark opened in 1888 as the first electrically lighted hotel in the United States. Broad steps lead up to the main lobby, with grand oak pillars and ceiling, which in turn opens out onto a central courtyard and gazebo. To the right is the cavernous **Crown Room,** whose arched ceiling of notched sugar pine was constructed without nails. The **Grand Ballroom** overlooks the ocean and a long white beach. The patio surrounding the sky-blue swimming pool is a great place for sitting back and imagining what the bathers looked like during the '20s, when the hotel rocked with the good times. More rooms have been added in high-rise towers beside the original 400-room building. ⊠ *1500 Orange Ave.,* ☎ *619/435–6611.* ⌕ *$10 for guided tour.* ☉ *1-hr guided tours (from lobby) Thurs.–Sat. at 10 and 11.*

⑩ **Orange Avenue.** It's easy to imagine you're on a street in Cape Cod when you stroll along this thoroughfare, Coronado's version of a downtown. But the East Coast illusion tends to dissipate as quickly as a winter fog when you catch sight of one of the avenue's many citrus trees—or realize it's February and the sun is warming your face. Off Orange Avenue is the **Coronado Visitors Bureau** (⊠ *1047 B Ave.,* ☎ *619/437–8788 or 800/622–8300).*

⑭ **Silver Strand State Beach.** The stretch of sand that runs along Silver Strand Boulevard from the Hotel Del Coronado to Imperial Beach dispels the illusion that Coronado is an island. The clean beach is a perfect family gathering spot, with rest rooms and lifeguards.

HARBOR ISLAND, POINT LOMA, AND SHELTER ISLAND

Point Loma curves around the San Diego Bay west of downtown and the airport, protecting the center city from the Pacific's tides and waves. Although military installations are based here and some main streets are cluttered with motels and fast-food shacks, Point Loma is an old and wealthy enclave of stately family homes. Its bay-side shores front huge estates, with sailboats and yachts packed tightly in private marinas. Nearby Harbor and Shelter islands have become tourist hubs, their high-rise hotels, seafood restaurants, and boat-rental centers looking as solid as those anywhere else in the city.

Numbers in the text correspond to numbers in the margin and on the Central San Diego map.

A Good Tour

Take Catalina Drive all the way south to the tip of Point Loma to reach **Cabrillo National Monument** ⑮; you'll be retracing the steps of the earliest European explorers if you use this as a jumping-off point for a tour. North of the monument, as you head back into the neighborhoods of Point Loma, you'll see the white headstones of **Fort Rosecrans National Cemetery** ⑯. Continue north on Catalina Boulevard to Hill Street and turn left to reach the **Sunset Cliffs** ⑰, at the western side of Point Loma near Ocean Beach. Return to Catalina Boulevard and backtrack south for a few blocks to find Canon Street, which leads toward the peninsula's eastern (bay) side. Almost at the shore you'll see **Scott Street** ⑱, the main commercial drag of Point Loma. Scott Street is bisected by Shelter Island Drive, which leads to **Shelter Island** ⑲, a most impressive product of landfill. For another example of what can be done with tons of material dredged from a bay, go back up Shelter Island Drive, turn right on Rosecrans Street, and make another right on North Harbor Drive to get to **Harbor Island** ⑳.

TIMING

If you're interested in seeing the tidal pools at Cabrillo National Monument, you'll need to call ahead to find out when low tide will occur. Scott Street, with its Point Loma Seafoods, is a good place to find yourself at lunchtime, and Sunset Cliffs Park is where you might want to be when the daylight starts to wane. This drive takes about an hour if you stop briefly at each sight, but you'll want to devote at least an hour to Cabrillo National Monument.

Sights to See

★ ⑮ **Cabrillo National Monument.** This 144-acre preserve marks the site of the first European visit to San Diego, made by Portuguese explorer Juan Rodríguez Cabrillo (circa 1498–1543)—his real name was João Rodrigues Cabrilho, but it was later Hispanicized. Cabrillo, who had earlier gone on voyages with Hernán Cortés, came to this spot, which he called San Miguel, in 1542. Government grounds were set aside to commemorate his discovery in 1913, and today the site, with its rugged cliffs and shores and outstanding overlooks, is one of the most frequently visited of all the national monuments. The **visitor center** presents films and lectures about Cabrillo's voyage, the sea-level tidal pools, and the gray whales migrating offshore. Rest rooms and water fountains are plentiful along the paths that climb to the monument's various viewing points, but, except for a few vending machines at the visitor center, there is no food. Exploring the grounds consumes time and calories; bring a picnic and rest on a bench overlooking the sailboats. A **statue of Cabrillo** overlooks downtown from the next windy promontory, where visitors gather to admire the stunning panorama over the bay, from the snowcapped San Bernardino Mountains, 130 mi north, to the hills surrounding Tijuana to the south.

The oil lamp of the **Old Point Loma Lighthouse** (☉ 9–5) was first lit in 1855. The light, sitting in a brass-and-iron housing above a white wooden house, shone through a state-of-the-art lens from France and was visible from the sea for 25 mi. The old lighthouse, recently refitted with furnishings more accurate to the era when it was erected, is open to visitors. The western and southern cliffs of Cabrillo National Monument are prime whale-watching territory. High-power telescopes help you focus on the whales' water spouts. The whales are visible on clear days in January and February, mostly in early morning. More accessible sea creatures can be seen in the **tidal pools** at the foot of the monument's western cliffs. Drive north from the visitor center to the first road on the left, which winds down to the coast guard station and the shore. When the tide is low you can walk on the rocks around saltwater pools filled with starfish, crabs, anemones, octopuses, and hundreds of other sea creatures and plants. ⊠ *1800 Cabrillo Memorial Dr.,* ☎ *619/557–5450.* ⌘ *$5 per car, $2 per person entering on foot or by bicycle; free for Golden Age, Golden Access, and Golden Eagle passport holders, and children under 17.* ☉ *Park daily 9–5:15.*

⑯ Fort Rosecrans National Cemetery. Many of those laid to rest at this place were killed in battles that predate California's statehood. Perhaps the most impressive structure in the cemetery is the 75-ft-tall granite obelisk called the Bennington Monument, which commemorates the 66 crew members who died in a boiler explosion and fire on board the USS *Bennington* in 1905. ☎ *619/553–2084.* ☉ *Weekdays 7–5, weekends 9–5.*

⑳ Harbor Island. In 1961 a 1½-mi-long peninsula was created adjacent to San Diego International Airport out of 12 million cubic yards of sand and mud dredged from San Diego Bay. Restaurants and high-rise hotels now line the inner shores of Harbor Island.

⑱ Scott Street. Deep-sea fishing charters and whale-watching boats depart from the piers along this street. It's a good spot from which to watch fisherfolk haul marlin, tuna, and puny mackerel off their boats.

⑲ Shelter Island. Actually a peninsula, this island is the center of San Diego's yacht-building industry. A long sidewalk runs from the landscaped lawns of the **San Diego Yacht Club** (tucked down Anchorage Street off Shelter Island Drive), past boat brokerages to the hotels and marinas, which line the inner shore, facing Point Loma. Within walking distance is the huge Friendship Bell, given to San Diegans by the people of Yokohama, Japan, in 1960.

⑰ Sunset Cliffs. As their name suggests, the 60-ft-high bluffs on the western side of Point Loma south of Ocean Beach are a perfect place to watch the sun descend over the sea. To view the tidal pools along the shore, you can descend a staircase off Sunset Cliffs Boulevard at the foot of Laredo Street.

LA JOLLA

La Jollans have long considered their village to be the Monte Carlo of California, and with good cause. Its coastline curves into natural coves backed by verdant hillsides and covered with homes worth millions. Though La Jolla is considered part of San Diego, it has its own postal zone and a coveted sense of class; it's become more plebeian these days, but the old-money set still mingles with visiting film stars and royalty who frequent established hotels and private clubs. Development and construction have radically altered the once serene and private character of the village, but it has gained a cosmopolitan air that makes it a popular vacation resort. Prospect Street and Girard Avenue, the village's main drags, are lined with expensive shops and office buildings.

Numbers in the text correspond to numbers in the margin and on the La Jolla map.

A Good Tour

At the intersection of La Jolla Boulevard and Nautilus Street, turn toward the sea to reach **Windansea Beach** ①, one of the best surfing spots in town. **Mount Soledad** ②, about 1½-mi east on Nautilus Street, is La Jolla's highest spot. In the village itself you'll find the town's cultural center, the **Museum of Contemporary Art, San Diego** ③, on the less trafficked southern end of Prospect. A bit farther north, at the intersection of Prospect and Girard Avenue, sits the pretty-in-pink **La Valencia Hotel** ④. The hotel looks out onto the village's great natural attraction, **La Jolla Cove** ⑤, which can be accessed from Coast Boulevard, one block to the west. Past the far northern point of the cove, a trail leads down to **La Jolla Caves** ⑥. The beaches along La Jolla Shores Drive north of the caves are some of the finest in the San Diego area, with long stretches allotted to surfers or swimmers. Nearby is the campus of the Scripps Institution of Oceanography. The institution's **Stephen Birch Aquarium-Museum** ⑦ is inland a bit.

TIMING

This tour makes for a leisurely day, though the drive can be completed in a couple of hours, including stops to take in the views and explore the village of La Jolla. The Museum of Contemporary Art is closed on Monday.

Sights to See

⑥ **La Jolla Caves.** It's a walk down 145 sometimes slippery steps to Sunny Jim Cave, the largest of the grottoes in La Jolla Cove. For many years, the caves were entered via the La Jolla Cave and Shell Shop, which closed in fall 1998; at press time, the caves were to remain accessible, though the hours for touring weren't available. ⊠ *1325 Coast Blvd..*

★ ⑤ **La Jolla Cove.** The wooded spread that looks out over a shimmering blue inlet is what first attracted everyone to La Jolla, from Native Americans to the glitterati; it is the village's enduring cachet. You'll find the cove—as locals always refer to it, as though it were the only one in San Diego—beyond where Girard Avenue dead-ends into Coast Boulevard, marked by towering palms along a promenade. Pathways lead down to the beaches. Keep an eye on the tide to keep from getting trapped once the waves come in. The **Children's Pool**, at the south end of the park, has a curving beach and shallow waters, protected by a seawall from strong currents and waves. Walk through **Ellen Browning Scripps Park**, past the groves of twisted junipers to the cliff's edge.

④ **La Valencia Hotel.** The Art Deco–style La Valencia, which has operated as a luxury hotel since 1928, has long been a gathering spot for Hollywood celebrities. The hotel's lobby has floor-to-ceiling windows overlooking La Jolla Cove. ⊠ *1132 Prospect St.,* ☎ *619/454–0771.*

② **Mount Soledad.** La Jolla's highest spot can be reached by taking Nautilus Street all the way east. Looking down from here you can see the coast from the county's northern border to the south far beyond downtown—barring smog and haze.

③ **Museum of Contemporary Art, San Diego.** The oldest section of San Diego's modern art museum was a residence designed by Irving Gill

La Jolla

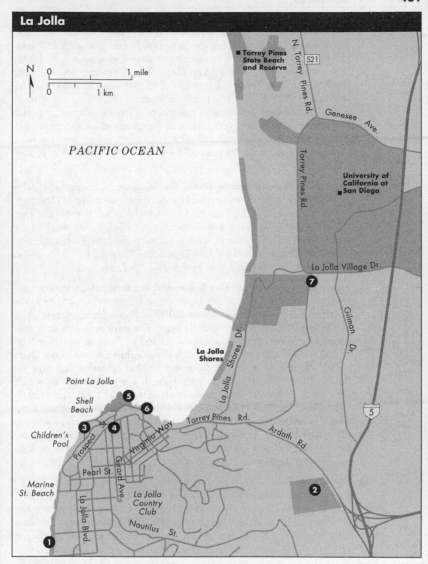

(1870–1936) for philanthropist Ellen Browning Scripps in 1916. Robert Venturi and his colleagues at Venturi Scott Brown and Associates updated and expanded the compound in the mid-1990s. The architects respected Gill's original geometric structure and clean, mission-style lines while adding their own distinctive touches. The result is a striking contemporary building that looks as though it's always occupied this site. The museum's permanent collection of post-1950s art includes the works of many artists from California, but also here are examples of every major art movement of the past half-century. ⊠ *700 Prospect St.,* ☎ *619/454–3541.* ☞ *$4; free 1st Tues. and Sun. of month.* ☉ *Tues. and Thurs.–Sat. 10–5, Wed. 10–8, Sun. noon–5.*

❼ Stephen Birch Aquarium-Museum. The largest oceanographic exhibit in the United States, a program of the Scripps Institution of Oceanography, has more than 30 huge tanks filled with colorful saltwater fish, and a 70,000-gallon tank simulates a La Jolla kelp forest. Besides the fish themselves, the most interesting attraction is the 12-minute simulated submarine ride. ⊠ *2300 Expedition Way,* ☎ *619/534–3474.* ☞ *$7.50, active military free, parking $3.* ☉ *Daily 9–5.*

Torrey Pines State Beach and Reserve. *Pinus torreyana,* the rarest native pine tree in the United States, enjoys a 1,750-acre sanctuary at the northern edge of La Jolla. About 6,000 of these unusual trees, some as tall as 60 ft, grow on the cliffs here. The park is one of only two places where the torrey pine grows naturally. The reserve has several hiking trails leading to the cliffs. **Los Penasquitos Lagoon** at the north end of the reserve is one of the many natural estuaries that flow inland between Del Mar and Oceanside. It's a good place to watch shorebirds. Volunteers lead guided nature walks at 11:30 and 1:30 on most weekends. ⊠ *N. Torrey Pines Rd. (also known as Old Hwy. 101). Exit I–5 onto Carmel Valley Rd. going west, then turn left (south) on Old Hwy. 101,* ☎ *619/755–2063.* ☞ *Parking $4 (two large parking lots on both sides of Los Penasquitos Lagoon; another up the hill by park visitor center).* ☉ *Daily 8–sunset.*

❶ Windansea Beach. Fans of pop satirist Tom Wolfe may recall *The Pump House Gang,* which pokes fun at the southern California surfing culture. Wolfe drew many of his barbs from observations he made at Windansea, the surfing beach west of La Jolla Boulevard near Nautilus Street. The wave action here is said to be as good as that in Hawaii.

MISSION BAY AND SEA WORLD

The 4,600-acre Mission Bay aquatic park is San Diego's monument to sports and fitness. Admission to its 27 mi of bay-shore beaches and 17 mi of ocean frontage is free.

Numbers in the text correspond to numbers in the margin and on the Mission Bay map.

A Good Tour

If you're coming from I–5, the **Visitor Information Center** ① is just about at the end of the Clairemont Drive–East Mission Bay Drive exit (you'll see the prominent sign). At the point where East Mission Bay Drive turns into Sea World Drive you can detour left to **Fiesta Island** ②, popular with jet skiers and speedboat racers. Continue around the curve to the west to reach **Sea World** ③, the area's best-known attraction. You'll next come to Ingraham Street, the central north–south drag through the bay. If you take it north, you'll shortly spot Vacation Road, which leads into the focal point of this part of the bay, the wa-

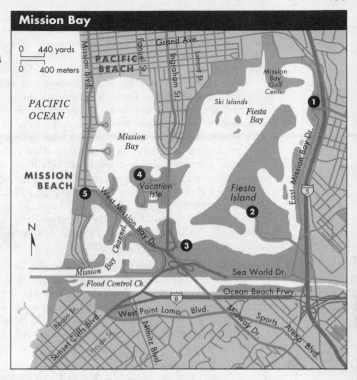

Mission Bay

terskiing mecca called **Vacation Isle** ④. At Ingraham, Sea World Drive
turns into Sunset Cliffs Boulevard and intersects with West Mission
Bay Drive. Almost immediately south of where West Mission Bay
Drive turns into Mission Boulevard is **Belmont Park** ⑤.

TIMING

It would take less than an hour to drive this tour. You may not find a
visit to Sea World fulfilling unless you spend at least a half day; a full
day is recommended. The park is open daily, but not all its attractions
are open year-round.

Sights to See

⑤ Belmont Park. Twinkling lights outline the star of Belmont Park, the
roller coaster, created as the Giant Dipper in 1925 and one of the few
old-time roller coasters left in the United States. Also at this dining,
shopping, and entertainment complex is **The Plunge**, an indoor swimming pool, also opened in 1925 as the largest saltwater pool in the world.
It's held fresh water since 1951. ⊠ *3146 Mission Blvd.,* ☎ *619/488-
0668 for park, 619/488-1549 for roller coaster, 619/488-3110 for
pool.*☼ *Park opens at 11 daily.*

② Fiesta Island. The most undeveloped area of Mission Bay Park is popular with bird-watchers (there's a large protected nesting site for the
California tern at the northern tip of the island) as well as with dog
owners—it's the only place in the park where their pets can run free.
Jet skiers and speedboat racers come here, too.

③ Sea World. One of the world's largest marine-life amusement parks is
spread over 100 tropically landscaped bay-front acres, where a cool

breeze always seems to rise from the water. The traditional favorite exhibit at Sea World is the **Shamu show,** with killer whales entertaining the crowds, but dolphins, sea lions, and otters at other shows also delight audiences. Other exhibits include the **Penguin Encounter,** the **Shark Encounter,** the **California Tide Pool,** and the **Forbidden Reef.** The newest attraction is **Wild Arctic,** which starts out with a simulated helicopter ride to a research post at the North Pole. Beluga whales, walruses, harbor seals, and polar bears can be viewed in areas designed to look like the wrecked hulls of two 19th-century sailing ships. Many hotels, especially those in the Mission Bay area, have Sea World specials. Some include price reductions, and others allow two days of entry for a single admission price—a good way to spread out what can otherwise be a very full day of activities. ⊠ *1720 South Shores Rd., near the west end of I–8,* ☎ *619/226–3815 or 619/226–3901 for recorded information.* 🖼 *$34.95; parking $5 cars, $2 motorcycles, $7 RVs and campers; 90-min behind-the-scenes walking tours $6 additional. D, MC, V. ☉ Daily 10–dusk; extended hrs during summer; call ahead for park hrs on day of your visit.*

❹ **Vacation Isle.** Ingraham Street bisects this Mission Bay island, which provides two distinct experiences for visitors. The west side is taken up by the San Diego Paradise Point Resort, but you don't have to be a guest to enjoy the hotel's lushly landscaped grounds and bay-front restaurants. The water-ski clubs congregate at **Ski Beach** on the east side of the island, where there's a parking lot as well as picnic areas and rest rooms.

❶ **Visitor Information Center.** The center, a gathering spot for runners, walkers, and exercisers, is the place to pick up a list of rules for playing in the water at Mission Bay Park or a self-guided tour map of the park's environmental resources. ⊠ *2688 E. Mission Bay Dr.,* ☎ *619/276–8200. ☉ Mon.–Sat. 9–5 (until 6 in summer), Sun. 9:30–4:30 (until 5:30 in summer).*

OLD TOWN

Old Town is often credited as being the first European settlement in southern California, but the true beginnings took place overlooking Old Town from atop Presidio Park, where Father Junípero Serra established the first of California's missions, San Diego de Alcalá, in 1769. In 1774 the hilltop was declared a Royal Presidio, or fortress, and the mission was moved 6 mi west to the San Diego River.

On San Diego Avenue, Old Town's main drag, art galleries and expensive gift shops are interspersed with tacky curios shops, restaurants, and open-air stands selling inexpensive Mexican pottery, jewelry, and blankets. The Old Town Esplanade between Harney and Conde streets is the best of several mall-like affairs constructed in mock Mexican-plaza style. Shops and restaurants also line Juan and Congress streets. You can take the Trolley here from downtown. If you drive, there are two large parking lots linked to the park by an underground pedestrian walkway.

Numbers in the text correspond to numbers in the margin and on the Old Town San Diego map.

A Good Tour

Visit the information center at Seeley Stable, off Old Town Plaza, to orient yourself to the various sights in **Old Town San Diego State Historic Park** ①. Cross north on the west side of the plaza to **Bazaar del Mundo** ②. Walk down San Diego Avenue, which flanks the south side of Old Town's historic plaza, east to Harney Street and the **Thomas**

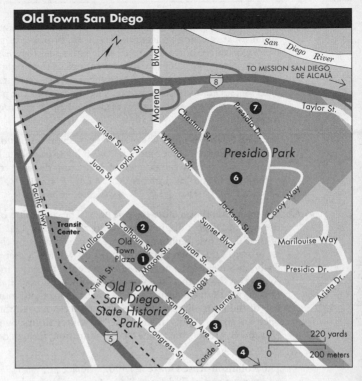

Old Town San Diego

Whaley Museum ③. Then continue east 2½ blocks on San Diego Avenue beyond Arista Street to the **El Campo Santo** ④ cemetery. **Heritage Park** ⑤ is on a hill above Juan Street, north of the museum and cemetery. Drive west on Juan Street and north on Taylor Street to Presidio Drive, which will lead you up the hill on which **Presidio Park** ⑥ and the **Junípero Serra Museum** ⑦ sit.

TIMING

Old Town can be toured in two to three hours. If you drive to Presidio Park, allot another hour to explore the grounds and museum. Finding a parking spot can be a challenge on weekends (this won't be a problem if you take the San Diego Trolley). Costumed volunteers conduct free tours of Old Town at 2 PM.

Sights to See

② Bazaar del Mundo. North of San Diego's Old Town Plaza lies the area's unofficial center, built to represent a colonial Mexican square. The central courtyard is always in bloom. Ballet Folklorico and flamenco dancers perform on weekend afternoons, and the bazaar frequently hosts arts-and-crafts exhibits and Mexican festivals. Colorful shops specializing in Latin American crafts and unusual gift items border the square. Although many of the shops here have high-quality wares, prices can be considerably higher than those at shops on the other side of Old Town Plaza. ⊠ *2754 Calhoun St.,* ☎ *619/296–3161.* ⊙ *Shops daily 10–9.*

④ El Campo Santo. This adobe-walled cemetery established in 1849 was the burial place for many members of Old Town's founding families, as well as for some gamblers and bandits who passed through San Diego until 1880. ⊠ *North side of San Diego Ave. S, between Arista and Ampudia Sts.*

⑤ Heritage Park. Among the most interesting of the six former residences here is the Sherman Gilbert House, which has a widow's walk and intricate carving on its decorative trim. Bronze plaques detail the history of all the houses, some of which may seem surprisingly colorful; they are in fact accurate representations of the bright tones of the era. The homes are now used for offices, shops, restaurants, and, in one case, a bed-and-breakfast inn. The climb up to the park is a little steep, but the view of the harbor is great. ⊠ *2455 Heritage Park Row (park office),* ☎ *619/694–3049.*

⑦ Junípero Serra Museum. The original Spanish presidio and California's first mission were perched atop the 160-ft hill overlooking Mission Valley; the park is now the domain of a museum devoted to the history of the Spanish and Mexican periods. ⊠ *2727 Presidio Dr.,* ☎ *619/297– 3258.* ⊠ *$3.* ⊙ *Tues.–Sat. 10–4:30, Sun. noon–4:30.*

★ **①** **Old Town San Diego State Historic Park.** The six square blocks on the site of San Diego's original pueblo are the heart of Old Town. Most of the 20 historic buildings preserved or re-created by the park cluster around **Old Town Plaza,** bounded by Wallace Street on the west, Calhoun Street on the north, Mason Street on the east, and San Diego Avenue on the south. The tour map available at Seeley Stable gives details about all of the historic houses on the plaza and in its vicinity; a few of the more interesting ones are noted below. All the houses are open to visitors daily from 10 to 5 (winter hours, which start in November, are shorter); none charge admission, though donations are appreciated.

The **Robinson-Rose House** (⊠ 4002 Wallace St., ☎ 619/220–5422), on the west end of Old Town Plaza, serves as the park administration office. This was the original commercial center of old San Diego, housing railroad offices, law offices, and the first newspaper press. One room has been restored and outfitted with period furnishings; park rangers distribute information from the living room. On San Diego Avenue and Twigg Street, **Dodson's Corner** is a modern retailer in a mid-19th-century setting; two of the shops in the complex, which sell everything from quilts and western clothing to pottery and jewelry, are reconstructions of the wood-frame homes that stood on the spot in the 1890s.

On Mason Street, at the corner of Calhoun Street, **La Casa de Bandini** is one of the prettiest haciendas in San Diego. Built in 1829 by a Peruvian, Juan Bandini, the house served as Old Town's social center during Mexican rule. Today the hacienda's colorful gardens and main-floor dining rooms house a popular Mexican restaurant. **Seeley Stable,** next door to La Casa de Bandini on Calhoun Street, became San Diego's stagecoach stop in 1867 and was the transportation hub of Old Town until near the turn of the century, when trains became the favored mode of travel. The stable now houses a collection of horse-drawn vehicles, some so elaborate that you can see where the term "carriage trade" came from. Also inside are western memorabilia, including an exhibit on the California *vaquero,* the original American cowboy, and an array of Native American artifacts.

⑥ **Presidio Park.** The rolling hillsides of the 40-acre green space overlooking Old Town from the north end of Taylor Street are popular with picnickers. The pleasant walk to the summit from Old Town takes people in good shape about a half hour. At the end of Mason Street, veer left on Jackson Street to reach the **Presidio Ruins,** where adobe walls and a bastion have been built above the foundations of the original fortress and chapel.

3 Thomas Whaley Museum. Thomas Whaley was a New York entrepreneur who came to California during the gold rush. His house, which served as the county courthouse and government seat during the 1870s, contains artifacts artifacts include one of the six life masks that exist of Abraham Lincoln. The house is perhaps most famed, however, for the ghosts that are said to inhabit it; this is one of the few places authenticated by the U.S. Department of Commerce as being haunted. ⊠ 2482 *San Diego Ave.,* ☎ *619/298–2482.* ⌨ *$4.* ☉ *Daily 10–5 in spring and summer; closed Tues. in fall and winter; shorter winter hrs (call ahead).*

OFF THE
BEATEN PATH

MISSION SAN DIEGO DE ALCALÁ – The first of a chain of 21 missions stretching northward along the California coast was established by Father Junípero Serra in 1769 on Presidio Hill and moved to its present location in 1774. The church here is the fifth to be built on this site; it was reconstructed in 1931 following the outlines of the 1813 church. A small museum documents the history of the mission. From the peaceful palm-bedecked gardens out back you can gaze at the 46-ft-high *campanario,* the mission's most distinctive feature; one of its five bells was cast in 1822. ⊠ *10818 San Diego Mission Rd. (from I-15, take Friars Rd. east and Rancho Mission Rd. south),* ☎ *619/281–8449.* ⌨ *$2.* ☉ *Daily 9–5.*

DINING

A stroll along 5th Avenue downtown will provide ample evidence of San Diego's love affair with Italian cuisine, but the cooking of Spain and France, as well as the various cuisines of Latin America, Asia, the Middle East—and even the United States—are well represented. San Diego is an informal city. The restaurants listed below are grouped first by type of cuisine, then by neighborhood; unless noted otherwise, casual attire is the norm.

CATEGORY	COST*
$$$$	over $50
$$$	$30–$50
$$	$20–$30
$	under $20

per person for a three-course meal, excluding drinks, service, and 7¼% sales tax

American

Downtown

$$–$$$$
★ ✕ **Rainwater's.** Classy Rainwater's is known both for the size of its portions and for the quality of its cuisine. The original Rainwater's, located on the second floor, offers chicken and fish dishes, but it is really the place to come if you crave a thick and tender prime steak. The seasonal contemporary menu at Downstairs at Rainwater's emphasizes seafood. ⊠ *1202 Kettner Blvd.,* ☎ *619/233–5757. AE, DC, MC, V. No lunch weekends.*

Uptown

$–$$ ✕ **Montanas American Grill.** One of Hillcrest's most popular restaurants serves hearty California-American food in a sleek, trendy setting. Stick with the least complicated dishes such as the barbecued meats, chicken, and salmon. The appetizer duck cakes are tasty and rich. Wash down your barbecue with one of the interesting microbrewery beers on tap. ⊠ *1421 University Ave.,* ☎ *619/297–0722. AE, DC, MC, V. No lunch weekends.*

San Diego Dining

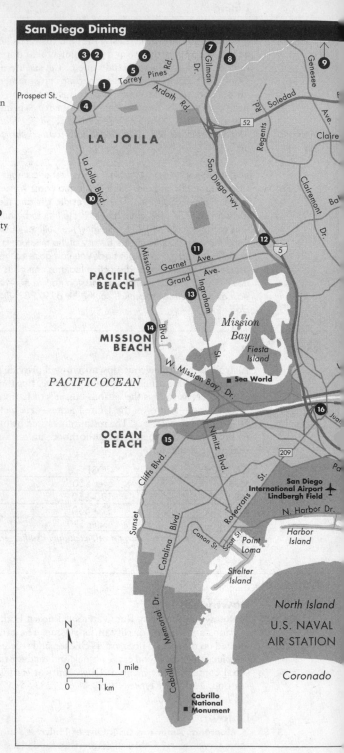

$ ✕ **Hob Nob Hill.** This restaurant is still under the same ownership and management as it was when it started in 1944. With its dark wood booths and patterned carpets, Hob Nob Hill seems suspended in the '50s, but you don't need to be a nostalgia buff to appreciate the bargain-priced American home cooking. Reservations are suggested for Sunday breakfast. ✉ 2271 1st Ave., ☎ 619/239–8176. AE, D, MC, V.

American/Casual

Beaches

$–$$ ✕ **Mission Cafe and Coffeehouse.** Comfy and laid-back, this Mission Beach café opens early for breakfast and stays open until the wee hours. All menu items can be made vegetarian. The café serves good beer on tap, specialty coffee drinks, and shakes and smoothies. ✉ 3795 Mission Blvd., ☎ 619/488–9060. AE, MC, V.

$–$$ ✕ **Tosca's.** At Tosca's you can opt for wheat or semolina crusts for your personal-sized pizzas or calzones; try the forest mushroom, pesto, or lamb sausage pizzas, or indulge in a rich pasta and wash it all down with a microbrewery beer. ✉ 3780 Ingraham St., Pacific Beach, ☎ 619/274–2408. AE, D, DC, MC, V. No lunch weekdays.

La Jolla

$–$$ ✕ **Mission Coffee Cup Cafe.** This popular condensed version of the Mission Cafe and Coffeehouse (☞ above) serves a similar menu of yummy "eclectic" cuisine; because it's a small place, you may have to wait for a table, especially for breakfast on weekends—but the French toast and roast beef hash are worth the wait. ✉ 1109 Wall St., ☎ 619/454–2819. AE, MC, V.

Uptown

$–$$ ✕ **Crest Cafe.** Often jammed with locals, this Hillcrest institution specializes in good renditions of basic American café food, from breakfast to late-night dinner. You can't go wrong with old favorites such as pancakes, burgers, onion rings, salads, and homemade desserts. ✉ 425 Robinson Ave., ☎ 619/295–2510. Reservations not accepted. AE, D, MC, V.

Belgian

Beaches

$$–$$$ ✕ **Belgian Lion.** Discerning diners come here for exquisite Belgian fare. One of the signature dishes is the cassoulet, a rich stew of white beans, sausage, and duck that makes you feel protected from the elements (even in San Diego, where there aren't that many elements). Seafood is well represented. An impressive selection of wines complements the food. ✉ 2265 Bacon St., Ocean Beach, ☎ 619/223–2700. Reservations essential. AE, D, DC, MC, V. Closed Sun.–Wed. No lunch.

Cajun and Creole

Downtown

$–$$ ✕ **Bayou Bar and Grill.** Ceiling fans, dark-green wainscoting, and light-pink walls help create a New Orleans atmosphere for dining on spicy Cajun and Creole specialties. The yummy seafood gumbo is a great starter. Rich Louisiana desserts include a praline cheesecake and an award-winning bread pudding. ✉ 329 Market St., ☎ 619/696–8747. AE, D, DC, MC, V.

Chinese

Downtown

$–$$$ ✕ **Panda Inn.** One of the better Chinese restaurants in town, this ele-
★ gant dining room in Horton Plaza serves subtly seasoned Mandarin

and Szechuan dishes. Try the Panda shrimp, the Peking duck, the spicy bean curd, and the twice-cooked pork. ⊠ *506 Horton Plaza,* ☎ *619/ 233–7800. AE, D, DC, MC, V.*

Contemporary

Downtown

\$\$–\$\$\$ ✕ **Dobson's.** Although the small, two-tier building that holds Dobson's
★ is suggestive of an earlier era, there's nothing outdated about the cuisine. The carefully prepared entrées change daily. Vintages from California predominate on the excellent wine list. ⊠ *956 Broadway Circle,* ☎ *619/231–6771. Reservations essential on weekends. AE, MC, V. Closed Sun. No lunch Sat.*

La Jolla

\$\$\$–\$\$\$\$ ✕ **Top O' the Cove.** Although glitzier newcomers now rival the Top O' the Cove, it still receives high marks from San Diego diners for its romantic ocean view and contemporary European cuisine. Inquire about the day's fresh salmon or swordfish creations. The restaurant has won awards for its comprehensive wine list. ⊠ *1216 Prospect St.,* ☎ *619/ 454–7779. AE, DC, MC, V.*

\$\$\$ ✕ **The Marine Room.** The menu has gotten a face-lift at this La Jolla Shores institution where diners can gaze at the ocean and, if they're lucky, watch the waves beat against the glass. Even if the ocean isn't producing any special effects, the Marine Room offers genteel beach-front dining-and-dancing and creative dishes like Alaskan halibut in a macadamia crust, served with tricolored orzo and saffron Sambuca tarragon sauce. Sunday brunch is lavish. ⊠ *2000 Spindrift Dr.,* ☎ *619/ 459–7222. AE, D, DC, MC, V.*

\$\$–\$\$\$ ✕ **Cafe Japengo.** One of the most stylish dining rooms in town, Cafe Japengo serves Asian-inspired cuisine with many North and South American touches. There's a selection of grilled, wood-roasted, and wok-fried entrées for dinner; try the 10-ingredient fried rice, the shrimp and scallops with rice noodles, or the lemongrass-marinated swordfish. You can also order very fresh sushi from your table or from a seat at the sushi bar. ⊠ *Aventine Center, 8960 University Center La.,* ☎ *619/450– 3355. AE, D, DC, MC, V. No lunch weekends.*

\$\$–\$\$\$ ✕ **St. James Bar and Restaurant.** In a handsome if slightly stiff setting, this establishment in the Golden Triangle area strives for variety. The contemporary menu, which changes seasonally, includes fresh fish and pan-seared meats; try the duck breast with cognac sauce. Don't miss the signature mussel bisque. The garden room is pleasant at lunch. ⊠ *Northern Trust Bldg., 4370 La Jolla Village Dr.,* ☎ *619/453–6650. AE, DC, MC, V. Closed Sun. No lunch Sat.*

¢ ¢¢¢ ✕ **Brockton Villa Restaurant.** This informal restaurant in a restored beach cottage overlooks La Jolla Cove and the ocean. Come for breakfast or lunch to take advantage of the daytime view, but don't overlook dinner. The extensive menu has something for everyone, and there's a good range of coffee drinks. Weekend brunches can be crowded. ⊠ *1235 Coast Blvd.,* ☎ *619/454–7393. AE, D, MC, V. No dinner Mon.*

Uptown

\$–\$\$\$ ✕ **California Cuisine.** The menu at this minimalist-chic dining room is
★ consistently innovative. The tasty warm chicken salad entrée is a regular feature. You can count on whatever you order to be carefully prepared and elegantly presented. The staff is knowledgeable and attentive, the wine list is good, and the desserts are mighty tempting. ⊠ *1027 University Ave.,* ☎ *619/543–0790. AE, D, DC, MC, V. Closed Mon. No lunch weekends.*

Deli

La Jolla

$–$$$ ✗ **SamSon's.** As close as you'll come to a real Jewish deli in San Diego, SamSon's serves enormous portions. For dinner try the Romanian skirt steak. ⊠ *8861 Villa La Jolla Dr.*, ☎ *619/455–1462. AE, D, DC, MC, V.*

French

Coronado

$$$–$$$$ ✗ **Marius.** The meals served here range from Parisian haute cuisine to Provençal country cooking. The food and presentation are top-notch, the service attentive and professional. The wine-tasting menu is particularly recommended. ⊠ *2000 2nd St.*, ☎ *619/435–3000. Reservations essential on weekends. AE, D, DC, MC, V. Closed Sun.–Mon. No lunch.*

La Jolla

$$–$$$ ✗ **Cindy Black's.** This quietly chic restaurant serves modern interpretations of French cuisine, offering subtle, stylishly presented dishes, often with a Mediterranean touch. The menu changes seasonally, but possibilities include chicken stew and a salad of hearts of palm and lobster. Prix-fixe meals are served on Sunday evening. ⊠ *5721 La Jolla Blvd.*, ☎ *619/456–6299. AE, D, DC, MC, V. No lunch.*

French and Mediterranean

Uptown

$$–$$$ ✗ **Laurel.** The menu changes daily at this restaurant that spotlights the
★   cooking of southern France and the Mediterranean. Among the entrées, the roasted fresh fish and the wild boar are always good. The wine list has been carefully assembled. ⊠ *505 Laurel St., at 5th Ave.*, ☎ *619/ 239–2222. AE, D, DC, MC, V. No lunch.*

Greek

Downtown

$–$$ ✗ **Athens Market.** This cheerful eatery bustles with downtown office workers and members of San Diego's small but active Greek community. Greek music and belly dancers add to the festive atmosphere on weekend evenings. ⊠ *109 W. F St.*, ☎ *619/234–1955. AE, D, DC, MC, V. No lunch weekends.*

Indian

Mission Valley

$ ✗ **KC's Tandoor.** KC's Tandoor, in an open-air shopping mall, defies expectations by serving genuine and tasty Indian food. The tandoori chicken is flavorful, the nan bread is rich and chewy, and the curries impress. Hearty appetites will find a bargain in the all-you-can-eat Sunday buffet brunch. ⊠ *Friars Mission Center, 5608 Mission Center Rd.*, ☎ *619/497–0751. MC, V.*

Uptown

$–$$ ✗ **Bombay Exotic Cuisine of India.** The dishes served at this elegant Indian restaurant are perhaps too Americanized for purists, who should firmly request greater spiciness, but no one can deny the lovely presentation. The chef's generous hand with raw and cooked vegetables gives each course a colorful freshness. ⊠ *Hillcrest Center, 3975 5th Ave., Suite 100*, ☎ *619/297–6969. AE, D, DC, MC, V.*

$–$$ ✗ **Maharajah.** Indian food lovers will find happy dining and great prices at this new Hillcrest restaurant that serves southern and northern Indian dishes. Sample the Madras specialities, such as the *dosas*, lentil

crepes stuffed with vegetables. Good tandoori dishes and aromatic curries are also on the menu. ⊠ *1220 Cleveland Ave., No. M113,* ☎ *619/
543–1163. AE, D, DC, MC, V. Closed Mon.*

Italian

Downtown

$$–$$$ ✕ **Fio's.** Contemporary variations on traditional northern Italian cui-
sine are served in a high-ceiling, brick-and-wood dining room overlooking the 5th Avenue street scene. The menu includes imaginative
pizzas (baked in a wood-fire oven), grilled salmon, and osso buco. ⊠
801 5th Ave., ☎ *619/234–3467. Reservations essential on weekends.
AE, D, DC, MC, V. No lunch weekends.*

$–$$$ ✕ **Bella Luna.** This small restaurant whose owner hails from the island
of Capri has developed a loyal following. The service is gracious and
attentive. The menu includes dishes from all over Italy. Linguine with
clams, fettuccine with salmon, and black squid-ink linguine served with
a spicy seafood sauce are among the many fine pastas. ⊠ *748 5th Ave.,*
☎ *619/239–3222. AE, MC, V. No lunch weekends.*

$–$$$ ✕ **Trattoria Mamma Anna.** The owners' native Sicilian cuisine shows
★ up on their menu, but the fare ventures into the rest of Italy as well.
Favorites are the spinach and ricotta ravioli with cream and mushroom
sauce and the deceptively simple fettuccine with garlic, tomatoes, and
wild mushrooms. ⊠ *644 5th Ave.,* ☎ *619/235–8144. AE, D, DC,
MC, V.*

La Jolla

$–$$$ ✕ **Piatti Ristorante.** A wood-burning oven turns out flavorful pizzas;
★ pastas include the *pappardelle fantasia* (wide saffron noodles with
shrimp, fresh tomatoes, and arugula) and a garlicky spaghetti *con
vongole verace* (served with clams in the shell). Brunch is served week-
ends. A fountain splashes softly on the tree-shaded patio, where heat
lamps allow diners to sit out even on chilly evenings. ⊠ *2182 Avenida
de la Playa,* ☎ *619/454–1589. AE, DC, MC, V.*

Japanese

Beaches

$–$$ ✕ **Sushi Ota.** One of San Diego's best sushi bars serves delicacies like
sea urchin and surf clams. For the cautious, Sushi Ota offers the cooked
as well as the raw. Choose between the sushi bar and the small dining
room. ⊠ *4529 Mission Bay Dr.,* ☎ *619/270–5670. Reservations essential. AE, D, MC, V. No lunch Sat.–Mon.*

Latin American

Old Town

$–$$ ✕ **Berta's Latin American Restaurant.** A San Diego rarity, Berta's serves
wonderful Latin American dishes. The wines are largely Chilean, and
the food manages to be tasty and healthful. ⊠ *3928 Twiggs St.,* ☎ *619/
295–2343. AE, MC, V.*

Mexican

Beaches

$–$$$ ✕ **Palenque.** A welcome alternative to the standard Sonoran-style
café, this restaurant in Pacific Beach serves regional Mexican dishes.
Seating is in comfortable round-back leather chairs; in warm weather
you can dine on a small deck in front. ⊠ *1653 Garnet Ave., Pacific
Beach,* ☎ *619/272–7816. AE, D, DC, MC, V. No lunch Mon.*

Mission Valley

$–$$ ✕ **El Tecolote.** The long-established El Tecolote (The Owl) does a good job with the usual taco-burrito fare, but come here also to sample Mexican specialties—the enchiladas in mole, the chicken breast with poblano or ancho chili sauce, or the rich Aztec layered cake (tortillas stacked with cheese, chilies, enchilada sauce, guacamole, and sour cream). ⊠ *6110 Friars Rd. W,* ☎ *619/295–2087. AE, D, DC, MC, V. No lunch Sun.*

Uptown

$ ✕ **Chilango's Mexico City Grill.** Proof that good things come in small packages is this tiny but cheerful storefront restaurant. The burritos and *tortas* (sandwiches) are like no others in the city. This much-loved restaurant, which opens at 9 AM from Friday to Sunday, quickly fills to overflowing in the evening, so consider coming in off-hours or ordering takeout. ⊠ *142 University Ave.,* ☎ *619/294–8646. No credit cards.*

Seafood

Downtown

$$$–$$$$ ✕ **Anthony's Star of the Sea Room.** The flagship of Anthony's local
★   fleet of seafood restaurants ensconces its patrons in a formal dining room with a vaguely marine decor. The menu changes seasonally, but expect to find fresh seafood dishes like garlic frog legs with green risotto, sautéed halibut with spinach and sorrel, and rock salt–roasted prawns. ⊠ *1360 N. Harbor Dr.,* ☎ *619/232–7408. Jacket. AE, D, DC, MC, V. No lunch.*

$–$$$$ ✕ **The Fish Market.** Diners at this informal restaurant, part of a local chain, choose from a large variety of fresh mesquite-grilled fish. Also good are the steamed clams or mussels and the fresh sushi. The view is stunning: enormous plate-glass windows look directly out onto the harbor. This is one of those rare places where families with young children can feel comfortable without sacrificing their taste buds. A more formal restaurant upstairs, the Top of the Market, is expensive but worth the splurge. Or economize by visiting for lunch or Sunday brunch. ⊠ *750 N. Harbor Dr.,* ☎ *619/232–3474 for the Fish Market, 619/234–4867 for the Top of the Market. AE, D, DC, MC, V.*

$$–$$$ ✕ **Blue Point Coastal Cuisine.** High ceilings, gleaming woodwork, and expansive windows give this seafood establishment an urbane air. But Blue Point situates its cuisine firmly on the Pacific Rim, incorporating Asian accents and south-of-the-border flavors. Go for the appetizers and seafood entrées here—the pasta dishes are disappointing. The wine list is serious, the service is efficient and friendly. ⊠ *565 5th Ave.,* ☎ *619/233–6623. AE, D, DC, MC, V. No lunch.*

$$–$$$ ✕ **Sally's.** Seafood is the star at Sally's. Order the light, greaseless crab cakes, the best in town, and bite into chunks of fresh crab. Recommended entrées include seafood paella (studded with pieces of fish and shellfish) and swordfish with a potato crust and gazpacho sauce. At the Sunday jazz brunch, served between 11 and 3, you can enjoy an appetizer, an entrée, and unlimited champagne and orange juice at a bargain price. ⊠ *Hyatt Regency San Diego, 1 Market Pl.,* ☎ *619/687–6080. AE, D, DC, MC, V.*

La Jolla

$$$ ✕ **George's at the Cove.** The elegant main dining room at George's,
★   with a wall-length window overlooking La Jolla Cove, is renowned for its daily fresh seafood specials and its fine preparations of beef and lamb. For more informal dining try the Cafe ($–$$) on the second floor. The rooftop Ocean Terrace ($–$$) has a sweeping view of the coast. The

Terrace (like the Cafe) does not take reservations. ⊠ *1250 Prospect St.,* ☎ *619/454–4244. Reservations essential for main dining room on weekends. AE, D, DC, MC, V.*

Old Town

$$–$$$ ✕ **Cafe Pacifica.** The airy Cafe Pacifica serves eclectic contemporary
★   cuisine with an emphasis on seafood. Fresh fish is grilled with your choice of savory sauces. Other good bets include the griddled mustard catfish, bouillabaisse, and roasted chicken rubbed with a Moroccan marinade. The crème brûlée is worth blowing any diet for. Cafe Pacifica's wine list has received kudos from *Wine Spectator* magazine. ⊠ *2414 San Diego Ave.,* ☎ *619/291–6666. AE, D, DC, MC, V. No lunch.*

Thai

Uptown

$–$$ ✕ **Taste of Thai.** Usually packed with value-minded diners, this modest café seats you at close quarters but compensates by serving yummy Thai and vegetarian cuisine at reasonable prices. Try the spicy seafood noodles, one of the red or yellow curries, and the chicken or tofu with sweet-basil bean sauce. ⊠ *527 University Ave.,* ☎ *619/291–7525. AE, D, DC, MC, V.*

$ ✕ **Saffron.** The specialty at this take-out restaurant is chicken spit-roasted over a wood fire and served with a choice of sauces—try the peanut or chili. Among the accompanying side dishes, the Cambodian salad is fresh and crunchy. There's limited outdoor seating, but this is an ideal place to pick up a meal to take to Mission Bay or the beach. ⊠ *3731B India St. (from downtown, take I–5 to Washington St. exit),* ☎ *619/ 574–0177. Reservations not accepted. MC, V.*

LODGING

San Diego is spread out, so the first thing to consider when selecting lodging is location. If you choose one of the many hotels with a waterfront location and extensive outdoor sports facilities, you need never leave the premises. But if you plan to sightsee, take into account a hotel's proximity to the attractions you most want to visit. In general, price need not be a major factor in your decision. Even the most expensive areas have some reasonably priced rooms.

The **Bed & Breakfast Guild of San Diego** (☎ 619/523–1300) lists a number of high-quality member inns. The **Bed & Breakfast Directory for San Diego** (⊠ Box 3292, 92163, ☎ 619/297–3130 or 800/619–7666) covers San Diego County.

CATEGORY	COST*
$$$$	over $175
$$$	$120–$175
$$	$80–$120
$	under $80

for a double room in high (summer) season, excluding 10½% San Diego room tax

Coronado

$$$$ 🏨 **Coronado Island Marriott.** Flamingos greet you at the entrance to
★   this 16-acre landscaped resort, formerly Le Meridien. Large rooms and suites in low-slung buildings are done in a cheerful California-country French fashion, with colorful Impressionist prints; all rooms have separate showers and tubs and come with plush robes. The spa facilities are top-notch, as is the award-winning Marius restaurant (☞ *above*).

San Diego Lodging

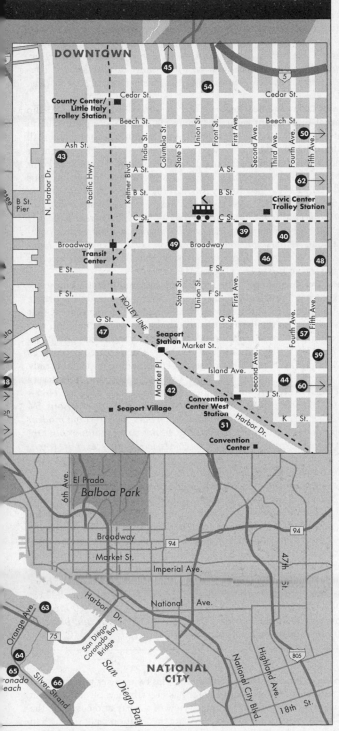

Lodge at Torrey Pines, **10**

Loews Coronado Bay Resort, **66**

Mission Bay Motel, **17**

Ocean Beach International Backpackers Hostel, **61**

Ocean Manor Apartment Hotel, **24**

Pacific Shores Inn, **15**

Pacific Terrace Inn, **13**

Prospect Park Inn, **5**

Radisson Hotel-Harbor View, **54**

Ramada Limited Point Loma, **29**

Ramada Plaza Hotel Old Town, **36**

Rodeway Inn, **50**

San Diego Hilton Beach and Tennis Resort, **12**

San Diego Marriott Hotel and Marina, **51**

San Diego Marriott Mission Valley, **55**

San Diego Marriott Suites, **62**

San Diego Mission Valley Hilton, **56**

San Diego Paradise Point Resort, **21**

Scripps Inn, **3**

Sea Lodge, **8**

Sheraton Grande Torrey Pines, **11**

Sheraton San Diego Hotel & Marina, **34**

Super 8 Bayview, **45**

Surfer Motor Lodge, **67**

Travelodge Point Loma, **31**

Travelodge Hotel-Harbor Island, **33**

U.S. Grant Hotel, **40**

Vacation Inn, **37**

Westgate Hotel, **39**

Westin Hotel San Diego–Horton Plaza, **46**

Wyndham Emerald Plaza Hotel, **42**

✉ *2000 2nd St., 92118,* ☎ *619/435–3000 or 800/543–4300 (central reservations),* 𝙵𝙰𝚇 *619/435–3032. 265 rooms, 7 suites, 28 villa units. 2 restaurants, bar, in-room modem lines, room service, 3 pools, barbershop, beauty salon, 2 outdoor hot tubs, massage, sauna, spa, 6 tennis courts, aerobics, health club, beach, snorkeling, windsurfing, bicycles, pro shop, shops, children's programs, laundry service, concierge, business services, convention center, meeting rooms, parking (fee). AE, D, DC, MC, V.*

$$$$ 🏨 **Loews Coronado Bay Resort.** You can park your boat at the 80-slip marina of this elegant resort set on a secluded 15-acre peninsula on the Silver Strand. Rooms are formally but tastefully decorated, and all have furnished balconies with views of water—either bay, ocean, or marina. The hotel lounge has nightly entertainment. The Azzura Point restaurant, which specializes in Pacific seafood, has won numerous awards. ✉ *4000 Coronado Bay Rd., 92118,* ☎ *619/424–4000 or 800/ 815–6397,* 𝙵𝙰𝚇 *619/424–4400. 403 rooms, 37 suites. 2 restaurants, bar, deli, in-room modem lines, room service, 3 pools, barbershop, beauty salon, 3 hot tubs, 5 tennis courts, health club, beach, windsurfing, boating, jet skiing, waterskiing, bicycles, pro shop, children's programs, laundry service, concierge, business services, convention center, meeting rooms, parking (fee). AE, D, DC, MC, V.*

$$$–$$$$ 🏨 **Hotel Del Coronado.** "The Del" is a social and historic landmark (☞ Exploring San Diego, *above*). The rooms and suites in the ornate 1888 building are charmingly quirky. Some have sleeping areas that seem smaller than the baths. Other rooms are downright palatial; two are even said to come with a resident ghost. A recent renovation has brightened up the grand public areas. More standardized room sizes are available in the newer high-rise. Air-conditioning is available only in the newer building. Robes, irons, ironing boards, and hair dryers are included in every room. ✉ *1500 Orange Ave., 92118,* ☎ *619/435– 6611 for hotel, 619/522–8000 or 800/468–3533 for reservations,* 𝙵𝙰𝚇 *619/522–8262. 692 rooms. 3 restaurants, 4 bars, deli, in-room modem lines, room service, 2 pools, barbershop, beauty salon, outdoor hot tub, massage, sauna, steam room, 6 tennis courts, lawn games, exercise room, beach, bicycles, shops, video games, concierge, business services, convention center, meeting rooms, parking (fee). AE, D, DC, MC, V.*

$$–$$$$ 🏨 **Glorietta Bay Inn.** The main building of this property—across the street from the Hotel Del, adjacent to the Coronado harbor, and near many restaurants and shops—was built in 1908 for sugar baron John D. Spreckels, who once owned much of downtown San Diego. Rooms in this Edwardian-style mansion and in the newer motel-style buildings are attractively furnished. The well-appointed inn is much smaller than the Hotel Del Coronado; its clients experience a quieter and less expensive stay. Tours ($6) of the island's historical buildings depart from the inn's lobby three mornings a week. ✉ *1630 Glorietta Blvd., 92118,* ☎ *619/435–3101 or 800/283–9383,* 𝙵𝙰𝚇 *619/435–6182. 100 rooms. In-room modem lines, refrigerators, pool, outdoor hot tub, bicycles, coin laundry, business services, free parking. AE, D, DC, MC, V.*

Downtown

$$$$ 🏨 **San Diego Marriott Hotel and Marina.** This twin-tower high-rise next to the San Diego Convention Center has everything a businessperson could want, not to mention a superb view of the bay and city from the upper floors. Vacationers will appreciate the location right on the San Diego Bay boardwalk. Be aware that standard rooms are smallish. The hallways can be noisy at night. ✉ *333 W. Harbor Dr., 92101,* ☎ *619/ 234–1500 or 800/228–9290 (central reservations),* 𝙵𝙰𝚇 *619/234–8678. 1,299 rooms, 56 suites. 3 restaurants, 3 bars, in-room modem lines, room service, 2 pools, barbershop, beauty salon, outdoor hot tub, sauna,*

6 tennis courts, aerobics, basketball, health club, jogging, shops, recreation room, coin laundry, concierge, business services, meeting rooms, car rental, parking (fee). AE, D, DC, MC, V.

$$$-$$$$ 🏨 **Embassy Suites San Diego Bay.** It's a short walk to the convention center, the Embarcadero, and Seaport Village from one of downtown's most popular hotels. The front door of each spacious suite opens out onto the 12-story atrium. A cooked-to-order breakfast and afternoon cocktails are complimentary, as are airport transfers. Room rates rise or fall depending on how full the hotel is. ✉ *601 Pacific Hwy., 92101,* ☎ *619/239–2400 or 800/362–2779 (central reservations),* FAX *619/239– 1520. 337 suites. Restaurant, bar, pool, barbershop, beauty salon, sauna, health club, bicycles, shops, coin laundry, business services, meeting rooms, airport shuttle, parking (fee). AE, D, DC, MC, V.*

$$$-$$$$ 🏨 **Hyatt Regency San Diego.** This high-rise adjacent to Seaport Vil-
★ lage successfully combines old-world opulence with California airiness. All British Regency–style guest rooms have views of the water. Sally's Restaurant (☞ *Dining, above*) serves inventive cuisine, and the 40th-floor lounge has 360-degree sunset views. ✉ *1 Market Pl., 92101,* ☎ *619/232–1234 or 800/233–1234 (central reservations),* FAX *619/233– 6464. 820 rooms, 55 suites and Regency Club rooms. 2 restaurants, 2 bars, in-room modem lines, room service, pool, outdoor hot tub, sauna, steam room, 4 tennis courts, health club, boating, bicycles, shops, laundry service, business services, meeting rooms, parking (fee). AE, D, DC, MC, V.*

$$$-$$$$ 🏨 **U. S. Grant Hotel.** Crystal chandeliers and polished marble floors in the lobby and Queen Anne–style mahogany furnishings in the stately and spacious rooms recall a more gracious era when dignitaries like President Franklin D. Roosevelt and Charles Lindbergh stayed here. ✉ *326 Broadway, 92101,* ☎ *619/232–3121 or 800/237–5029,* FAX *619/ 232–3626. 220 rooms, 60 suites. Restaurant, 2 bars, café, room service, exercise room, shops, concierge, business services, airport shuttle, parking (fee). AE, D, DC, MC, V.*

$$$-$$$$ 🏨 **Westgate Hotel.** A nondescript modern high-rise across from Hor-
★ ton Plaza hides one of the most opulent hotels in San Diego. The lobby, modeled after the anteroom at Versailles, has hand-cut Baccarat chandeliers; rooms are individually furnished with antiques, Italian marble counters, and bath fixtures with 24-karat-gold overlays. From the ninth floor up the views of the harbor and city are breathtaking. ✉ *1055 2nd Ave., 92101,* ☎ *619/238–1818 or 800/221–3802, 800/522– 1564 in CA,* FAX *619/557–3737. 223 rooms. 2 restaurants, bar, deli, in-room modem lines, room service, barbershop, exercise room, bicycles, concierge, business services, meeting rooms, airport shuttle, parking (fee). AE, D, DC, MC, V.*

$$$-$$$$ 🏨 **Wyndham Emerald Plaza Hotel.** The Wyndham's office and conference facilities draw many business travelers but the hotel is a fine choice for vacationers who want to be near downtown shopping and restaurants. Many of the upper-floor accommodations have panoramic views. The beige-dominated standard rooms are not overly large. The health club is quite good. ✉ *400 W. Broadway, 92101,* ☎ *619/239– 4500 or 800/996–3426,* FAX *619/239–4527. 416 rooms, 20 suites. Restaurant, bar, in-room modem lines, pool, outdoor hot tub, sauna, steam room, health club, shops, concierge, business services, meeting rooms, parking (fee). AE, D, DC, MC, V.*

$$-$$$$ 🏨 **Balboa Park Inn.** Directly across the street from Balboa Park, this all-suites B&B comprises four Spanish colonial–style 1915 residences connected by courtyards. Each of the romantic one- and two-bedroom suites has a different flavor, including contemporary versions of Italian, French, Spanish, or early Californian styles; some accommodations have fireplaces, wet bars, whirlpool tubs, patios, and kitchens with mi-

crowaves. ⊠ *3402 Park Blvd., 92103,* ☎ *619/298–0823 or 800/938–8181,* ⅎAX *619/294–8070. 26 suites. Continental breakfast. AE, D, DC, MC, V.*

$$–$$$$　🛉 **Horton Grand Hotel.** A Victorian confection in the heart of the historic Gaslamp Quarter, the Horton Grand comprises two 1880s hotels moved brick by brick from nearby locations and fit together. Its delightfully retro rooms are furnished with period antiques, ceiling fans, and gas-burning fireplaces. The choicest rooms overlook a garden courtyard that twinkles with miniature lights each night. The hotel is a charmer, but service can be erratic. ⊠ *311 Island Ave., 92101,* ☎ *619/544–1886 or 800/542–1886,* ⅎAX *619/239–3823. 105 rooms, 24 suites. Restaurant, bar, business services, meeting rooms, airport shuttle, parking (fee). AE, D, DC, MC, V.*

$$$　🛉 **Westin Hotel San Diego–Horton Plaza.** Although it is fronted by a startling lighted blue obelisk, this high-rise is all understated marble and brass. The spacious rooms are in pastels of blue and pale orange. With its prime downtown location, the hotel attracts many business travelers. The lobby lounge is packed every night with local financiers and weary shoppers from adjacent Horton Plaza. ⊠ *910 Broadway Circle, 92101,* ☎ *619/239–2200 or 800/528–0444 (central reservations),* ⅎAX *619/239–0509. 450 rooms, 14 suites. Restaurant, 2 bars, in-room modem lines, room service, pool, hot tub, 2 tennis courts, health club, basketball, business services, parking (fee). AE, D, DC, MC, V.*

$$–$$$　🛉 **Holiday Inn on the Bay.** On the Embarcadero and overlooking San Diego Bay, this high-rise hotel is convenient for vacationers and business travelers. Rooms lack character but are spacious and comfortable, and views from the balconies are hard to beat. ⊠ *1355 N. Harbor Dr., 92101,* ☎ *619/232–3861 or 800/877–8920 (central reservations),* ⅎAX *619/232–4924. 600 rooms, 17 suites. Restaurant, bar, in-room modem lines, pool, exercise room, shops, coin laundry, meeting rooms, airport shuttle, parking (fee). AE, D, DC, MC, V.*

$$–$$$　**San Diego Marriott Suites.** This 15-story hotel is near the financial district and Balboa Park. It's ideal for those in town on business. All rooms have modem connections, wet bars, coffeemakers, and cable TV. ⊠ *701 A St., 92101,* ☎ *619/696–9800 or 800/228–9290.* ⅎAX *619/696–1555. 264 suites. Restaurant, bar, indoor heated pool, sauna, hot tub, exercise room, meeting rooms, business services, airport shuttle, valet parking. AE, D, DC, MC, V.*

$–$$$　🛉 **Gaslamp Plaza Suites.** Listed on the National Register of Historic Places, this 11-story structure built in 1913 contains elegant public areas with old marble, brass, and mosaics. Book ahead if you're visiting in high season. ⊠ *520 E St., 92101,* ☎ *619/232–9500 or 800/874–8770,* ⅎAX *619/238–9945. 52 suites. Restaurant, bar, parking (fee). Continental breakfast. AE, D, DC, MC, V.*

$$　🛉 **Clarion Hotel Bay View.** Two blocks from the Gaslamp Quarter and close to the convention center, this is a good hotel for budget-minded conventioneers who want to be close to shopping, nightlife, and restaurants. All rooms have coffeemakers and safes. The two-room suites have wet bars. ⊠ *660 K St., 92101,* ☎ *619/696–0234, 800/252–7466,* ⅎAX *619/231–8199. 264 rooms, 48 suites. Restaurant, bar, in-room modem lines, hot tub, sauna, exercise room, video games, coin laundry, meeting rooms, airport shuttle, parking (fee). AE, D, DC, MC, V.*

$$　🛉 **Radisson Hotel–Harbor View.** The 16-story Radisson dwarfs most buildings in the area, so many rooms have great views of San Diego Bay and the downtown skyline. Although the hotel has its own restaurant, you should instead enjoy the eateries and coffeehouses of the Little Italy community that is within walking distance. ⊠ *1648 Front St., 92101,* ☎ *619/239–6800 or 800/333–3333 (central reservations),* ⅎAX *619/238–9461. 333 rooms. Restaurant, bar, pool, hot tub, sauna, ex-*

ercise room, business services, meeting rooms. AE, D, DC, MC, V.

$–$$ 🖭 **Rodeway Inn.** On one of the better and quieter streets downtown, this property is clean, comfortable, and nicely decorated. ✉ *833 Ash St., 92101,* ☎ *619/239–2285, 800/228–2000 for central reservations, 800/522–1528 in CA,* FAX *619/235–6951. 45 rooms. In-room modem lines, hot tub, sauna, coin laundry, business services, meeting rooms, free parking. Continental breakfast. AE, D, DC, MC, V.*

$ 🖭 **Super 8 Bayview.** This motel's location is less noisy than those of other low-cost establishments. The accommodations are nondescript but clean, and some have refrigerators. ✉ *1835 Columbia St., 92101,* ☎ *619/544–0164 or 800/537–9902,* FAX *619/237–9940. 101 rooms. Pool, coin laundry, airport shuttle, free parking. Continental breakfast. AE, DC, MC, V.*

Harbor Island, Shelter Island, and Point Loma

$$$–$$$$ 🖭 **Kona Kai Continental Plaza Resort and Marina.** Though the Kona Kai name may suggest a Polynesian theme, this 11-acre property is done in a mixture of Mexican and Mediterranean styles. The spacious and light-filled lobby opens onto a lush esplanade that overlooks the hotel's marina. The rooms are well-appointed, if a bit small, and most look out onto either the marina or San Diego Bay. ✉ *1551 Shelter Island Dr., 92106,* ☎ *619/221–8000 or 800/566–2524,* FAX *619/221–5953. 168 rooms, 38 suites. Restaurant, bar, room service, 2 pools, 2 hot tubs, 2 saunas, 2 tennis courts, jogging, health club, volleyball, beach, airport shuttle, free parking. AE, D, DC, MC, V.*

$$$–$$$$ 🖭 **Sheraton San Diego Hotel & Marina.** The smaller, more intimate West Tower has larger rooms with separate areas suitable for business entertaining. The East Tower has better sports facilities. Rooms throughout are California-style. Views from the upper floors of both sections are superb, but because the West Tower is closer to the water it has fine outlooks from the lower floors, too. ✉ *1380 Harbor Island Dr., 92101,* ☎ *619/291–2900 or 800/325–3535 (central reservations),* FAX *619/692–2337. 1,053 rooms. 2 restaurants, 2 bars, deli, patisserie, in-room modem lines, room service, 3 pools, wading pool, 2 outdoor hot tubs, massage, 4 tennis courts, health club, jogging, beach, boating, bicycles, pro shop, airport shuttle, parking (fee). AE, D, DC, MC, V.*

$$–$$$ 🖭 **Bay Club Hotel & Marina.** Rooms in this appealing low-rise Shelter Island property are large, light, and furnished with rattan tables and chairs and Polynesian tapestries; all have refrigerators and views of either the bay or the marina from outside terraces. A buffet breakfast and limo service to and from the airport or Amtrak station are included in the room rate. ✉ *2131 Shelter Island Dr., 92106,* ☎ *619/224–8888 or 800/672–0800,* FAX *619/225–1604. 95 rooms, 10 suites. Restaurant, bar, room service, pool, outdoor hot tub, exercise room, concierge, business services, meeting rooms, free parking. AE, D, DC, MC, V.*

$$–$$$ 🖭 **Best Western Island Palms Hotel & Marina.** This waterfront inn with an airy skylit lobby is a good choice if you have a boat to dock; the adjacent marina has guest slips. Both harbor- and marina-view rooms are available. Standard accommodations are fairly small; if you're traveling with family or more than one friend, the two-bedroom suites with kitchens are a good deal. ✉ *2051 Shelter Island Dr., 92106,* ☎ *619/222–0561 or 800/922–2336,* FAX *619/222–9760. 68 rooms, 29 suites. Restaurant, bar, in-room modem lines, pool, outdoor hot tub, business services, meeting rooms, free parking. AE, D, DC, MC, V.*

$$–$$$ 🖭 **Humphrey's Half Moon Inn.** This sprawling South Seas–style resort has grassy open areas with palm trees and tiki torches. Rooms, some with kitchens and some with harbor or marine views, have modern furnishings. Locals throng to Humphrey's, the on-premises seafood restaurant, and to the jazz lounge. The hotel hosts outdoor jazz and pop concerts between June and October. ✉ *2303 Shelter Island Dr., 92106,* ☎ *619/224–3411 or 800/345–9995,* 🅵🅰🅇 *619/224–3478. 128 rooms, 54 suites. Restaurant, bar, in-room modem lines, room service, pool, hot tub, putting green, croquet, Ping-Pong, boating, bicycles, coin laundry, business services, meeting rooms, airport shuttle, free parking. AE, D, DC, MC, V.*

$$–$$$ 🛏 **Travelodge Hotel–Harbor Island.** Lodgers here get the views and amenities of more expensive hotels for a lower rate. Those staying on the two executive floors also get a free buffet breakfast. The Waterfront Cafe & Club overlooks the marina. ✉ *1960 Harbor Island Dr., 92101,* ☎ *619/291–6700 or 800/578–7878 for central reservations,* 🅵🅰🅇 *619/293–0694. 201 rooms, 6 suites. Restaurant, bar, in-room modem lines, pool, outdoor hot tub, exercise room, jogging, shops, laundry service, meeting rooms, airport shuttle, free parking. AE, D, DC, MC, V.*

$$ 🛏 **Best Western Posada Inn.** Many rooms at this comfortable if plain inn have harbor views. Some rooms have microwaves, mini-refrigerators, and video players. Point Loma's seafood restaurants are within walking distance. Weekly rates, package plans, and senior discounts are available. ✉ *5005 N. Harbor Dr., 92106,* ☎ *619/224–3254 or 800/ 231–3811,* 🅵🅰🅇 *619/224–2186. 112 rooms. In-room modem lines, pool, outdoor hot tub, exercise room, laundry services, meeting rooms, airport shuttle, free parking. Continental breakfast. AE, D, DC, MC, V.*

$ 🛏 **Ramada Limited Point Loma.** One of the nicer motels near the Scott Street area, the Ramada has some rooms with bay views—quite a deal. The property is near a busy intersection, so ask for a room that's not right on the street. ✉ *1403 Rosecrans St., 92106,* ☎ *619/225– 9461 or 800/272–6232,* 🅵🅰🅇 *619/225–1163. 86 rooms. Bar, breakfast room, pool, meeting rooms, free parking, airport shuttle. Continental breakfast. AE, D, DC, MC, V.*

$ 🛏 **Travelodge Point Loma.** You'll get the same view here as at the higher-priced hotels—for far less money. Of course, there are fewer amenities and the neighborhood isn't as serene, but the rooms—all with coffeemakers—are adequate and clean. ✉ *5102 N. Harbor Dr., 92106,* ☎ *619/223–8171 or 800/578–7878 (central reservations),* 🅵🅰🅇 *619/222– 7330. 45 rooms. Pool, free parking. AE, D, DC, MC, V.*

Hotel Circle, Mission Valley, and Old Town

$$$–$$$$ 🛏 **San Diego Mission Valley Hilton.** This property has soundproof rooms decorated in a colorful contemporary style. The stylish public areas and lush greenery in the back will make you forget the hotel's proximity to the freeway. Although geared toward business travelers, children stay free in their parents' room, and small pets are accepted ($25). ✉ *901 Camino del Rio S, 92108,* ☎ *619/543–9000, 800/733– 2332, or 800/445–8667,* 🅵🅰🅇 *619/543–9358. 342 rooms, 8 suites. 2 restaurants, 2 bars, in-room modem lines, pool, outdoor hot tub, exercise room, free parking. AE, D, DC, MC, V.*

$$–$$$$ 🛏 **Heritage Park Bed & Breakfast Inn.** Rooms at this B&B range in
★ size from smallish to ample, and most are bright and cheery. A two-bedroom suite is decorated with period antiques, and there is also a mini-suite. There is a two-night minimum stay on weekends, and weekly and monthly rates are available. Some rooms share a bath. Transportation is available to area attractions and the Amtrak station. ✉ *2470 Heritage Park Row, 92110,* ☎ *619/299–6832 or 800/995– 2470,* 🅵🅰🅇 *619/299–9465. 10 rooms, 2 suites. In-room modem lines, airport shuttle. Full breakfast. AE, MC, V.*

$$–$$$ 🏨 **Best Western Hanalei Hotel.** The theme of this friendly Hotel Circle property is Hawaiian. Free transportation is provided to local malls and Old Town. The hotel is virtually surrounded by heavy traffic, which can make for a noisy stay. Many rooms and one of the restaurants were recently renovated. ⊠ *2270 Hotel Circle N, 92108,* ☎ *619/297–1101 or 800/882–0858,* FAX *619/297–6049. 416 rooms. 2 restaurants, bar, in-room modem lines, pool, hot tub, exercise room, meeting rooms. AE, D, DC, MC, V.*

$$–$$$ 🏨 **Doubletree Hotel San Diego Mission Valley.** The public areas at this property near a San Diego Trolley station are light-filled and comfortable, well suited to this hotel's large business clientele. Spacious rooms decorated in contemporary pastels have ample desk space; complimentary coffee, irons, and ironing boards are also provided. ⊠ *7450 Hazard Center Dr., 92108,* ☎ *619/297–5466 or 800/547–8010 for central reservations,* FAX *619/297–5499. 294 rooms, 6 suites. Restaurant, 2 bars, in-room modem lines, room service, 2 pools, outdoor hot tub, sauna, 2 tennis courts, shops, nightclub, business services, meeting rooms, airport shuttle, free parking. AE, D, DC, MC, V.*

$$–$$$ 🏨 **San Diego Marriott Mission Valley.** The Marriott is well equipped
★ for business travelers, but it caters to vacationers with comfortable rooms (with individual balconies), a friendly staff, and free transportation to the malls. ⊠ *8757 Rio San Diego Dr., 92108,* ☎ *619/692–3800 or 800/228–9290 (central reservations),* FAX *619/692–0769. 347 rooms, 6 suites. Restaurant, sports bar, in-room modem lines, room service, heated pool, outdoor hot tub, sauna, tennis court, exercise room, nightclub, coin laundry, business services, airport shuttle, free parking. AE, D, DC, MC, V.*

$$ 🏨 **Best Western Hacienda Hotel Old Town.** Pretty and white, with balconies and Spanish-tile roofs, the Hacienda is in a quiet part of Old Town, away from the freeway and the main retail bustle. The layout is somewhat confusing, and accommodations are not large enough to earn the "suite" label the hotel gives them, but they're decorated in tasteful southwestern style and equipped with microwaves, coffeemakers, and VCRs. ⊠ *4041 Harney St., 92110,* ☎ *619/298–4707 or 800/888–1991,* FAX *619/298–4771. 168 rooms. Restaurant, bar, refrigerators, pool, outdoor hot tub, exercise room, coin laundry, concierge, meeting rooms, airport shuttle, free parking. AE, D, DC, MC, V.*

$$ 🏨 **Ramada Plaza Hotel Old Town.** The hacienda-style Ramada has Spanish colonial–style fountains, courtyards, and painted tiles, and southwestern decor in the rooms. Breakfast, cocktail reception, and transfers to the airport, bus, and Amtrak are all complimentary. Business-class rooms have modem lines and other amenities. ⊠ *2435 Jefferson St., 92110,* ☎ *619/260–8500 or 800/272–6232,* FAX *619/297–2078. 182 rooms, 17 suites. Restaurant, pool, outdoor hot tub, exercise room, meeting rooms, airport shuttle, free parking. AE, D, DC, MC, V.*

$–$$ 🏨 **Days Inn–Hotel Circle.** Rooms in this large complex are par for a chain motel but have the bonus of Nintendo for the kids and irons and ironing boards; some units also have kitchenettes. Airport, Amtrak, zoo, and Sea World shuttles are provided. ⊠ *543 Hotel Circle S, 92108,* ☎ *619/297–8800, 800/227–4743 on weekdays 8–4:30, 800/325–2525 for central reservations,* FAX *619/298–6029. 280 rooms. Restaurant, refrigerators, pool, outdoor hot tub, barbershop, beauty salon, coin laundry, meeting rooms, airport shuttle, free parking. AE, D, DC, MC, V.*

$–$$ 🏨 **Vacation Inn.** This cheerful property throws in perks like garage park-
★ ing, afternoon snacks, coffeemakers, and microwave ovens. ⊠ *3900 Old Town Ave., 92110,* ☎ *619/299–7400 or 800/451–9846,* FAX *619/299–1619. 125 rooms. In-room modem lines, refrigerators, pool, out-*

door hot tub, coin laundry, business services, meeting rooms, airport shuttle, free parking. Continental breakfast. AE, D, DC, MC, V.

La Jolla

$$$$ 🖫 **La Jolla Cove Suites.** It may lack the charm of some of the older properties of this exclusive area, but this motel with studios and suites (some with spacious oceanfront balconies) gives its guests the same first-class views of La Jolla Cove at much lower rates. Snorkelers and divers can take advantage of lockers and outdoor showers. ⊠ *1155 S. Coast Blvd., 92037,* ☎ *619/459–2621 or 800/248–2683,* 𝖥𝖠𝖷 *619/454–3522. 96 rooms. Kitchenettes, pool, hot tub, putting green, coin laundry, business services, meeting rooms, free parking. Continental breakfast. AE, D, DC, MC, V.*

$$$$ 🖫 **La Valencia.** Many rooms at La Valencia have a genteel European
★   look, with antique pieces and rich-colored rugs. The personal attention provided by the staff, as well as in-room features such as plush robes and grand bathrooms, make the stay even more pleasurable. All rooms have wet bars, coffeemakers, safes, and video players. ⊠ *1132 Prospect St., 92037,* ☎ *619/454–0771 or 800/451–0772,* 𝖥𝖠𝖷 *619/456–3921. 107 rooms. 3 restaurants, bar, pool, outdoor hot tub, health club, shuffleboard, business services, meeting rooms, parking (fee). AE, D, DC, MC, V.*

$$$$ 🖫 **Sea Lodge.** Palms, fountains, red-tile roofs, and Mexican tile work lend a Spanish flavor to this low-lying compound on La Jolla Shores beach. Rooms, a few with kitchenettes, have rattan furniture and floral-print bedspreads; all have hair dryers, coffeemakers, irons, and wooden balconies that overlook lush landscaping and the sea. ⊠ *8110 Camino del Oro, 92037,* ☎ *619/459–8271 or 800/237–5211,* 𝖥𝖠𝖷 *619/456–9346. 128 rooms. Restaurant, bar, in-room modem lines, room service, pool, outdoor hot tub, sauna, 2 tennis courts, exercise room, Ping-Pong, beach, coin laundry, business services, meeting rooms, free parking. AE, D, DC, MC, V.*

$$$$ 🖫 **Sheraton Grande Torrey Pines.** The low-rise, high-class Sheraton
★   Grande blends discreetly into the Torrey Pines cliff-top. Amenities include complimentary butler service and free town-car service to La Jolla and Del Mar. The oversize accommodations are simple but elegant; most have balconies or terraces. In addition to easy access to the golf course, guests also have privileges ($7.50) next door at the fine health club–sports center at the Scripps Clinic. ⊠ *10950 N. Torrey Pines Rd., 92037,* ☎ *619/558–1500 or 800/325–3535 (central reservations),* 𝖥𝖠𝖷 *619/450–4584. 392 rooms, 17 suites. Restaurant, 2 bars, in-room modem lines, in-room safes, minibars, room service, pool, outdoor hot tub, sauna, putting green, 2 tennis courts, aerobics, croquet, exercise room, volleyball, bicycles, concierge, business services, meeting rooms, parking (fee). AE, D, DC, MC, V.*

$$$–$$$$ 🖫 **Colonial Inn.** A tastefully restored Victorian-era building, this is the oldest hotel in La Jolla. In keeping with the period, rooms are formal (some could use new carpets and furniture coverings). Ocean views cost more than village views. The inn is on one of La Jolla's main thoroughfares, near boutiques, restaurants, and La Jolla Cove. ⊠ *910 Prospect St., 92037,* ☎ *619/454–2181 or 800/832–5525, 800/826–1278 in CA,* 𝖥𝖠𝖷 *619/454–5679. 75 rooms. Restaurant, bar, pool, business services, meeting rooms, parking (fee). AE, DC, MC, V.*

$$$–$$$$ 🖫 **Hyatt Regency La Jolla.** The Hyatt is in the Golden Triangle area,
★   about 10 minutes from the beach and the village of La Jolla. Fluffy down comforters and cushy chairs and couches will make you feel right at home. Business travelers will appreciate the endless array of office and in-room services. The hotel's four trendy restaurants include Cafe

Japengo (☞ Dining *above*). Rates are lower here on weekends. ⊠ *Aventine Center, 3777 La Jolla Village Dr., 92122,* ☎ *619/552–1234 or 800/233–1234 for central reservations,* 𝔽𝔸𝕏 *619/552–6066. 400 rooms, 25 suites. 4 restaurants, bar, pool, outdoor hot tub, beauty salon, massage, 2 tennis courts, aerobics, basketball, health club, jogging, business services, meeting rooms, parking (fee). AE, D, DC, MC, V.*

$$–$$$$ 🏨 **Bed & Breakfast Inn at La Jolla.** This B&B in a quiet section of La Jolla is across the street from the Museum of Contemporary Art and one block from the beach. Nice touches include fresh fruit, sherry, and terry robes. The gardens in the back were designed by Kate Sessions, who was instrumental in landscaping Balboa Park. ⊠ *7753 Draper Ave., 92037,* ☎ *619/456–2066 or 800/582–2466,* 𝔽𝔸𝕏 *619/456–1510. 16 rooms, 15 with bath. Full breakfast. MC, V.*

$$–$$$$ 🏨 **Scripps Inn.** You'd be wise to make reservations well in advance for this small, quiet inn tucked away on Coast Boulevard; its popularity with repeat visitors ensures that it is booked year-round. Lower weekly and monthly rates (not available in summer) make it attractive to long-term guests. All accommodations have ocean views and in-room safes, and some have fireplaces, coffeemakers, microwaves, and refrigerators. ⊠ *555 S. Coast Blvd., 92037,* ☎ *619/454–3391,* 𝔽𝔸𝕏 *619/ 456–0389. 13 rooms. Continental breakfast. AE, D, MC, V.*

$$–$$$ 🏨 **Holiday Inn Express–La Jolla.** Many rooms at this modest property in southern La Jolla are large, with huge closets; some have kitchenettes, and three suites have separate eat-in kitchens. ⊠ *6705 La Jolla Blvd., 92037,* ☎ *619/454–7101 or 800/451–0358,* 𝔽𝔸𝕏 *619/454–6957. 51 rooms, 10 suites. Pool, outdoor hot tub, billiards, coin laundry, meeting rooms, free parking. AE, D, DC, MC, V.*

$$–$$$ 🏨 **Lodge at Torrey Pines.** On a bluff between La Jolla and Del Mar, ★ the lodge commands a view of miles and miles of coastline. The Torrey Pines Municipal Golf Course is adjacent, and scenic Torrey Pines State Beach and Reserve are close by. One drawback—the building is old; walls between units are thin, and the plumbing can be noisy. Still, the service is excellent and the lodge is a good value, especially for golfers. ⊠ *11480 N. Torrey Pines Rd., 92037,* ☎ *619/453–4420 or 800/ 995–4507,* 𝔽𝔸𝕏 *619/453–0691. 74 rooms. 2 restaurants, 2 bars, pool, golf privileges, free parking. AE, D, DC, MC, V.*

$$–$$$ 🏨 **Prospect Park Inn.** One block from the beach and near some of the ★ best shops and restaurants, this European-style inn with a delightful staff sits in a prime spot in La Jolla Village. Many rooms (some with kitchenettes) have sweeping ocean views. An upstairs sundeck has fantastic views. Smoking is not permitted at the inn. ⊠ *1110 Prospect St., 92037,* ☎ *619/454–0133 or 800/433–1609,* 𝔽𝔸𝕏 *619/454–2056. 20 rooms, 2 suites. In-room modem lines, business services, free parking. Continental breakfast. AE, D, DC, MC, V.*

Mission Bay and the Beaches

$$$$ 🏨 **Pacific Terrace Inn.** Even the smallest rooms at this terrific hotel are fairly large, and most of them have have great ocean views. All rooms have private balconies or patios, coffeemakers, and safes. Some rooms have spas, kitchenettes, and video players. The staff is friendly. ⊠ *610 Diamond St., 92109,* ☎ *619/581–3500 or 800/344–3370. 73 rooms, 8 suites. Refrigerators, pool, outdoor hot tub, coin laundry, meeting rooms, free parking. Continental breakfast. AE, D, DC, MC, V.*

$$$–$$$$ 🏨 **Bahia Resort Hotel.** This huge complex on a 14-acre peninsula in Mission Bay Park has furnished studios and suites with kitchens; many have wood-beam ceilings and tropical decor. The hotel's *Bahia Belle* cruises Mission Bay at sunset and also has a Blues Cruise on Saturday night and live entertainment on Friday night. Rates are reasonable for

a place so well located—within walking distance of the ocean—and with so many amenities, including use of the facilities at its sister hotel, the nearby Catamaran. ☒ *998 W. Mission Bay Dr., 92109,* ☎ *619/ 488–0551 or 800/288–0770, 800/233–8172 in Canada,* FAX *619/ 488–7055 or 619/488–1387 for reservations. 321 rooms. Restaurant, 2 bars, pool, outdoor hot tub, 2 tennis courts, bicycles, rollerblading, meeting rooms, free parking. AE, D, DC, MC, V.*

$$$–$$$$ ⊡ **Catamaran Resort Hotel.** Resident birds are often poised on a perch
★   in the lush lobby of this appealing hotel, set on Mission Bay in Pacific Beach. The room decor—dark wicker furniture and tropical prints— echoes the Polynesian theme. The popular Cannibal Bar hosts rock bands; a classical or jazz pianist tickles the ivories at the Moray Bar. ☒ *3999 Mission Blvd., 92109,* ☎ *619/488–1081 or 800/288–0770, 800/ 233–8172 in Canada,* FAX *619/488–1387 for reservations, 619/488– 1619 for front desk. 313 rooms. Restaurant, 2 bars, in-room modem lines, pool, outdoor hot tub, exercise room, boating, bicycles, night- club, meeting rooms, parking (fee). AE, D, DC, MC, V.*

$$$–$$$$ ⊡ **San Diego Hilton Beach & Tennis Resort.** Trees, Japanese bridges, and ponds surround the bungalow accommodations at this deluxe re- sort; rooms and suites in the high-rise building have views of Mission Bay Park. Most of the well-appointed rooms have wet bars, mini- refrigerators, coffeemakers, spacious bathrooms, and patios or terraces. There's complimentary day care for children over age five (daily dur- ing the summer, on weekends the rest of the year). ☒ *1775 E. Mission Bay Dr., 92109,* ☎ *619/276–4010 or 800/445–8667 for central reser- vations,* FAX *619/275–7991. 337 rooms, 20 suites. 2 restaurants, bar, in-room modem lines, pool, wading pool, 2 hot tubs, 4 putting greens, 5 tennis courts, exercise room, boating, bicycles, playground, meeting rooms, car rental, free parking. AE, D, DC, MC, V.*

$$$–$$$$ ⊡ **San Diego Paradise Point Resort.** This 44-acre resort, formerly the Princess, provides a wide range of recreational activities as well as ac- cess to a marina. Bright fabrics and plush carpets make for a cheery ambience; unfortunately, the walls here are motel-thin. All rooms pri- vate patios and coffeemakers, and some rooms have kitchens. ☒ *1404 W. Vacation Rd., 92109,* ☎ *619/274–4630 or 800/344–2626,* FAX *619/581–5929. 462 cottages. 3 restaurants, 2 bars, refrigerators, room service, 5 pools, outdoor hot tub, sauna, 18-hole putting golf course, 6 tennis courts, croquet, exercise room, jogging, volleyball, boating, bicycles, free parking. AE, D, DC, MC, V.*

$$–$$$$ ⊡ **Crystal Pier Motel.** A landmark since the 1930s, this place is no longer the bargain it once was, nor does it have the amenities of the other prop- erties in its price category. You're paying for character and proximity to the ocean—the blue-and-white cottages here are literally on the pier. The units sleep four but cost the same no matter what the occupancy. Call four to six weeks in advance for reservations. The minimum stay permitted is three nights from mid-June to mid-September, two nights the rest of the year. ☒ *4500 Ocean Blvd., 92109,* ☎ *619/483–6983 or 800/748–5894,* FAX *619/483–6811. 29 cottages. Kitchenettes, free parking. D, MC, V.*

$$–$$$$ ⊡ **Hyatt Islandia.** Its location in appealing Mission Bay Park is one of the many pluses of this property, which has rooms in several low-level lanai-style units, as well as marina suites and rooms in a high-rise build- ing. Many of the modern accommodations overlook the hotel's gar- dens and koi fish pond; others have dramatic views of the bay area. This hotel is famous for its lavish Sunday champagne brunch. In win- ter, whale-watching expeditions depart from the Islandia's marina. ☒ *1441 Quivira Rd., 92109,* ☎ *619/224–1234 or 800/233–1234 for cen- tral reservations,* FAX *619/224–0348. 346 rooms, 76 suites. 2 restau- rants, bar, in-room modem lines, pool, outdoor hot tub, exercise room,*

boating, fishing, laundry service, meeting rooms, free parking. AE, D, DC, MC, V.

$$$ 🏨 **Best Western Blue Sea Lodge.** Many of the rooms at this Pacific Beach low rise have balconies and ocean views; some have kitchenettes. A shopping center with restaurants and boutiques is nearby. ⊠ *707 Pacific Beach Dr., 92109,* ☎ *619/488–4700 or 800/258–3732,* FAX *619/488–7276. 100 rooms. In-room safes, pool, outdoor hot tub. Continental breakfast. AE, D, DC, MC, V.*

$–$$$ 🏨 **Dana Inn & Marina.** This hotel with an adjoining marina is a bargain. The rooms are done in bright pastels, and the lobby contains a fun aquarium. High ceilings in the second-floor rooms give a welcome sense of space, and some even have a view of the inn's marina. Many sports facilities are on the premises, and Sea World and the beach are within walking distance. ⊠ *1710 W. Mission Bay Dr., 92109,* ☎ *619/222–6440 or 800/445–3339,* FAX *619/222–5916. 196 rooms. Restaurant, bar, room service, pool, outdoor hot tub, 2 tennis courts, Ping-Pong, shuffleboard, boating, bicycles, coin laundry, business services, free parking. AE, D, DC, MC, V.*

$–$$ 🏨 **Pacific Shores Inn.** One of the better motels in the Mission Bay area, this property is less than a half-block from the beach. Rooms, some of them spacious, are decorated in a simple contemporary style. Kitchen units with multiple beds are available at reasonable rates; your pet (under 20 pounds) can stay for an extra $25. ⊠ *4802 Mission Blvd., 92109,* ☎ *619/483–6300 or 800/826–0715,* FAX *619/483–9276. 55 rooms. Refrigerators, pool, coin laundry, free parking. Continental breakfast. AE, D, DC, MC, V.*

$–$$ 🏨 **Surfer Motor Lodge.** This four-story building is right on the beach and directly behind a shopping center with restaurants and boutiques. Rooms are plain, but those on the upper floors have good views. ⊠ *711 Pacific Beach Dr., 92109,* ☎ *619/483–7070 or 800/787–3373,* FAX *619/274–1670. 52 rooms. Restaurant, pool, bicycles, free parking. AE, DC, MC, V.*

$ 🏨 **Mission Bay Motel.** A half-block from the beach and right on the local main street, this motel has modest units, some with kitchenettes. Great restaurants and nightlife are within walking distance, but you may find the area a bit noisy. ⊠ *4221 Mission Blvd., 92109,* ☎ *619/483–6440. 50 rooms. Pool, free parking. D, MC, V.*

$ 🏨 **Ocean Manor Apartment Hotel.** This Sunset Cliffs hotel rents units by the day (three-day minimum for ones with kitchens), week, or month in winter; you'll need to reserve well in advance. The comfortable studios and one- and two-bedroom suites are furnished plainly in the style of the 1950s, which is when the amiable owners took over the place. There is no maid service, but fresh towels are always provided. ⊠ *1370 Sunset Cliffs Blvd., 92107,* ☎ *619/222–7901 or 619/224–1379 for guest calls. 25 units. Pool, Ping-Pong, shuffleboard, free parking. MC, V.*

Hostels

$ 🏨 **Banana Bungalow San Diego.** All dorm rooms at this Pacific Beach hostel are coed. ⊠ *707 Reed Ave., 92109,* ☎ *619/273–3060 or 800/546–7835. Continental breakfast.*

$ 🏨 **Grand Pacific Hostel.** Bright, clean, and conveniently located, the ★ Grand Pacific has a friendly staff. There are 60 beds, and five private rooms. The facilities include recreation rooms, kitchen equipment, a TV room, a coin laundry, lockers, local shuttle service, and Internet access. ⊠ *726 5th Ave., 92101,* ☎ *619/232–3100 or 800/438–8622.*

$ 🏨 **HI–The Metropolitan Hostel–Downtown San Diego.** This new location ★ in the Gaslamp Quarter contains modern furnishings and facilities. There are 100 beds, a large common kitchen, a TV room, and a coin laundry. Most rooms are dorm-style with four bunks each. There are a few doubles, coed dorms, and group rooms (with 10 beds). A second floor with 50 more beds was scheduled to be completed by 1999. ✉ *521 Market St., 92101,* ☎ *619/525–1531 or 800/909–4776, code #43,* FAX *619/338–0129.*

$ ☷ **HI–Point Loma Hostel.** This hostel is different in that it's located in a large converted house, in a much quieter area. The kitchen is large, there's a coin laundry, and you can watch TV in a common room. ✉ *3790 Udall St., 92107,* ☎ *619/223–4778.*

$ ☷ **Ocean Beach International Backpacker Hostel.** This converted 1920s hotel is two blocks from the beach. There are 100 beds; private rooms with private baths are available. Dinner is free on Tuesday and Friday. The hostel, which is close to many Ocean Beach restaurants and night spots, has kitchen facilities, a coin laundry, a storage area, vending machines, a TV room, a recreation room, a patio, and Internet access. ✉ *4961 Newport Ave., 92107,* ☎ *619/223–7873 or 800/339–7263,* FAX *619/223–7881. Continental breakfast.*

NIGHTLIFE AND THE ARTS

Check the *Reader*, a free weekly, for band information or *San Diego* magazine's "Restaurant & Nightlife Guide" for the full slate of after-dark possibilities.

Nightlife

California law prohibits the sale of alcoholic beverages after 2 AM; last call is usually at about 1:40. You must be 21 to purchase and consume alcohol, and most places will insist on identification. Bars, nightclubs, and restaurants in California are smoke-free by law.

Bars and Nightclubs

BEACHES

The patrons of the **Cannibal Bar** (✉ 3999 Mission Blvd., Pacific Beach, ☎ 619/488–1081) come for oldies, contemporary jazz, blues, and swing performed by local bands. Darkly lit **Club Tremors** (✉ 860 Garnet Ave., Pacific Beach, ☎ 619/272–7278) entices a rocking crowd with live music on Thursday, Friday, and Saturday. **Daily Planet** (✉ 1200 Garnet Ave., Pacific Beach, ☎ 619/272–6066), painted in neon purple, yellow, and green, is sure to catch your eye. The crowd is fun-loving and unpretentious.

Hurricane's Bar and Grill (✉ 3105 Ocean Front Walk, Mission Beach, ☎ 619/488–1780) books talented rock bands that perform for a lively crowd. Fun music powers the dance floor at **Moose McGillycuddy's** (✉ 1165 Garnet Ave., Pacific Beach, ☎ 619/274–2323), a major pick-up palace. **Pacific Beach Bar & Grill** (✉ 860 Garnet Ave., Pacific Beach, ☎ 619/272–4745) is a popular nightspot with a huge outdoor patio on which you can enjoy star-filled skies as you party.

DOWNTOWN AND VICINITY

Aero Club (✉ 3365 India St., Middletown, ☎ 619/297–7211) has friendly bartenders and first-rate selection of beer. The **Bitter End** (✉ 770 5th Ave., ☎ 619/338–9300) contains a sophisticated martini bar, a hip dance club, and a private lounge. **Blue Tattoo** (✉ 835 5th Ave., ☎ 619/238–7191) enforces a strict dress code (no jeans, T-shirts, hats, sweatshirts, or tennis shoes) on Friday and Saturday nights. Entertainment varies nightly, and there is a nominal cover charge. **Club 66** (✉ 901 5th Ave., ☎ 619/234–4166), under the restaurant Dakota's, takes the old Route 66 as its inspiration, with stainless-steel decor and gas-station memorabilia. The dancing is to disco, high energy, and Top 40.

E Street Alley (⊠ 919 4th Ave., ☎ 619/231–9200) serves up live jazz on Thursday and blues the rest of the week. Club E is a smartly designed, spacious dance club with a DJ spinning Top 40 tunes.

Jimmy Love's (⊠ 672 5th Ave., ☎ 619/595–0123) combines a dance club, a sports bar, and a restaurant all into one venue. Rock and jazz bands perform. **Karl Strauss' Old Columbia Brewery & Grill** (⊠ 1157 Columbia St., ☎ 619/234–2739) draws an after-work downtown crowd and later fills with beer connoisseurs from all walks of life. The downtown edition of **Moose McGillycuddy's** (⊠ 535 5th Ave., ☎ 619/702–5595) is as lively as the Pacific Beach location.

OLD TOWN

O'Hungrys (⊠ 2547 San Diego Ave., Old Town, ☎ 619/298–0133) is famous for its yard-long beers and sing-alongs. The landmark saloon closes at midnight.

Coffeehouses
BEACHES

It's easy to lose track of time at **Café Crema** (⊠ 1001 Garnet Ave., Pacific Beach, ☎ 619/273–3558), a meeting spot for the pre- and post-bar crowd. **Zanzibar Coffee Bar and Gallery** (⊠ 976 Garnet Ave., Pacific Beach, ☎ 619/272–4762), a cozy, dimly lit spot along Pacific Beach's main strip, is a great place to mellow out.

DOWNTOWN AND VICINITY

Gelato Vero Caffe (⊠ 3753 India St., Middletown, ☎ 619/295–9269) is where a predominantly young crowd gathers for some fine desserts and a second-floor view of the downtown skyline.

HILLCREST AREA

Euphoria (⊠ 1045 University Ave., Hillcrest, ☎ 619/295–1769) has a Gen-X feel and is a great place to meet friends before dinner or barhopping. **Pannikin** (⊠ 523 University Ave., Hillcrest, ☎ 619/295–1600) is a bright coffeehouse with several other locations throughout the county. **The Study** (⊠ 401-A University Ave., Hillcrest, ☎ 619/296–4847) attracts those who value seclusion—private conversation or study is made easier with the cubicle-like seating areas. **Twiggs Tea and Coffee Co.** (⊠ 4590 Park Blvd., University Heights, ☎ 619/296–0616) has outdoor seating. The adjacent green room hosts poetry readings and, on occasion, music.

LA JOLLA

Brockton Villa Restaurant (⊠ 1235 Coast Blvd., ☎ 619/454–7393), a palatial café overlooking La Jolla Cove, has indoor and outdoor seating. It closes at 10.

Comedy and Cabaret
Comedy Store South (⊠ 916 Pearl St., La Jolla, ☎ 619/454–9176), like its sister establishment in Hollywood, hosts some of the best national touring and local talent. **Tidbits** (⊠ 3838 5th Ave., Hillcrest, ☎ 619/543–0300) showcases the best of southern California's female impersonators in hilarious nightly cabaret and comedy "tidbits," with charity benefit shows on Sunday.

Country-Western
In Cahoots (⊠ 5373 Mission Center Rd., Mission Valley, ☎ 619/291–8635), with its great sound system, large dance floor, and occasional big-name performers, is the destination of choice for cowgirls, cowboys, and city slickers alike. **Zoo Country** (⊠ 1340 Broadway, El Cajon, ☎ 619/442–9900) attracts herds of line-dancin', two-steppin' cowpersons. Bands perform from Friday to Sunday, and there's a DJ seven nights a week.

Dance Clubs

BEACHES

Club Emerald City (✉ 945 Garnet Ave., Pacific Beach, ☎ 619/483–9920) attracts an uninhibited clientele for loud alternative dance music.

DOWNTOWN/GASLAMP QUARTER

Green Circle Bar (✉ 827 F St., ☎ 619/232–8080) is frequented by a mostly under-30 Euro-type crowd that grooves to anything from acid jazz to blues and soul. Live bands perform on Wednesday and Thursday. **Johnny M's Crabhouse Courtyard Club** (✉ 801 4th St., ☎ 619/233–1131) patrons get down and boogie to '70s and '80s dance music at this huge disco. A blues room is open on Wednesday, Friday, and Saturday from 10 PM to 1:30 AM. **Olé Madrid** (✉ 751 5th Ave., ☎ 619/557–0146) is not for the meek or mild. Leave the squares at street level and head straight to the basement for deep house grooves and tribal rhythms spun by celebrated DJs. **Romperoom** (✉ 505 Market St., ☎ no phone), an alcohol-free, Saturday-night-only club, lets night owls dance until dawn to house grooves and techno. **Sevilla** (✉ 555 4th Ave., ☎ 619/233–5979) provides a little bit of Brazil in San Diego with a tapas bar and salsa dancing. **Supper Club A-Go-Go**, (✉ 322 5th Ave., ☎ 619/235–4646) offers a swinging good time and a 1940s motif.

LA JOLLA

Taxxi (✉ 1025 Prospect St., ☎ 619/551–5230) lures Hollywood club-types for dancing to disco, funk, and house music.

Gay and Lesbian Nightlife

GAY MALE BARS

Bourbon Street (✉ 4612 Park Blvd., University Heights, ☎ 619/291–0173) is a piano bar with live entertainment nightly. **Brass Rail** (✉ 3796 5th Ave., Hillcrest, ☎ 619/298–2233) hosts dancing nightly and go-go boys on weekends. **Flicks** (✉ 1017 University Ave., Hillcrest, ☎ 619/297–2056) plays music and comedy videos on four big screens. **Kickers** (✉ 308 University Ave., Hillcrest, ☎ 619/491–0400) rounds up country-music cowboys to do the latest line dance. If you're hungry after all that dancing, Hamburger Mary's on the premises serves until 11 on weekends. **Numbers** (✉ 3811 Park Blvd., North Park, ☎ 619/294–9005) has a giant-screen video, six pool tables, darts, and daily drink specials. **Rich's** (✉ 1051 University Ave., Hillcrest, ☎ 619/295–2195), a popular dance club, has nightly male revues. **Wolf's** (✉ 3404 30th St., North Park, ☎ 619/291–3730) is a Levi's-leather bar that's open late every night.

LESBIAN BARS

Club Bom Bay (✉ 3175 India St., Middletown, ☎ 619/296–6789) occasionally has live entertainment and always attracts a dancing crowd. It also hosts Sunday barbecues. **The Flame** (✉ 3780 Park Blvd., Hillcrest, ☎ 619/295–4163) is a friendly dance club that caters to lesbians on most nights.

Jazz

Croce's (✉ 802 5th Ave., Gaslamp Quarter, ☎ 619/233–4355) books superb acoustic-jazz musicians. Next door, Croce's Top Hat puts on live R&B nightly. **Elario's** (✉ 7955 La Jolla Shores Dr., La Jolla, ☎ 619/459–0541), on the top floor of the Summer House Inn, delivers an ocean view and a lineup of internationally acclaimed musicians. **Humphrey's by the Bay** (✉ 2241 Shelter Island Dr., Shelter Island, ☎ 619/523–1010) hosts the city's best outdoor jazz, folk, and light-rock concert series. The rest of the year the music moves indoors to Humphrey's Lounge for some first-rate jazz on most Sunday, Monday, and Tuesday nights, with piano-bar and other music on other nights.

Piano Bars/Mellow

Hotel Del Coronado (⊠ 1500 Orange Ave., Coronado, ☎ 619/435–6611) presents piano music in its Crown Room and Palm Court. Bands perform nightly at the Ocean Terrace Lounge from 9 to 1. Pianists play show tunes and standards from the '40s to the '80s at the **Top O' the Cove** (⊠ 1216 Prospect St., La Jolla, ☎ 619/454–7779. There's also piano music at the **Westgate Hotel** (⊠ 1055 2nd Ave., downtown, ☎ 619/238–1818) in the elegant Plaza Bar.

Rock, Pop, Folk, Reggae, and Blues

BEACHES

Belly Up Tavern (⊠ 143 S. Cedros Ave., Solana Beach, ☎ 760/481–9022), an eclectic live-concert venue in converted Quonset huts, hosts critically acclaimed artists who play everything from reggae, rock, new wave, Motown, and folk to—well, you name it. Bustling **Blind Melons** (⊠ 710 Garnet Ave., Pacific Beach, ☎ 619/483–7844) presents rock, blues, and reggae bands nightly. **Brick by Brick** (⊠ 1130 Buenos Ave., Bay Park, near Mission Bay, ☎ 619/275–5483) is always abuzz with the music of San Diego's top alternative and experimental rock groups.The **G Lounge** (⊠ 228 Bacon St., Ocean Beach, ☎ 619/222–8131) makes the sleepy coastal community go metropolitan and causes beach bums to turn into lounge lizards. **Winston's Beach Club** (⊠ 1921 Bacon St., Ocean Beach, ☎ 619/222–6822), a bowling alley turned rock club, hosts local bands, reggae groups, and occasionally '60s rockers bands. The crowd, mostly locals, can get rowdy.

DOWNTOWN AND VICINITY

Bodie's (⊠ 528 F St., Gaslamp Quarter, ☎ 619/236–8988) presents the best rock and blues bands in San Diego, as well as up-and-coming bands from out of town. **Casbah** (⊠ 2501 Kettner Blvd., near the airport, ☎ 619/232–4355), a small club, showcases rock, reggae, funk, and every other kind of band—except Top 40. **4th & B** (⊠ 345 B St., Gaslamp Quarter, ☎ 619/231–4343) presents bands almost every night. **Patrick's II** (⊠ 428 F St., ☎ 619/233–3077) serves up live New Orleans–style jazz, blues, and rock in an Irish setting. **Pourhouse** (⊠ 528 F St., ☎ 619/232–7687) is a two-floor hot spot that headlines mostly local talent.

Singles Bars

Dick's Last Resort (⊠ 345 4th Ave., downtown, ☎ 619/231–9100) is not for Emily Post adherents. The surly waitstaff and abrasive service are part of the gimmick. Dick's has live music and one of the most extensive beer lists in San Diego. **Jose's** (⊠ 1037 Prospect St., La Jolla, ☎ 619/454–7655) is a hit with yuppies from La Jolla and other neighboring beach communities. **Old Bonita Store & Bonita Beach Club** (⊠ 4014 Bonita Rd., Bonita, ☎ 619/479–3537), a South Bay hangout, has a DJ spinning retro house music. **U. S. Grant Hotel** (⊠ 326 Broadway, downtown, ☎ 619/232–3121) is the classiest spot in town for meeting fellow travelers. The best local Latin, jazz, and blues bands alternate appearances.

The Arts

Half-price tickets to theater, music, and dance events can be bought on the day of performance at **Times Arts Tix** (⊠ Horton Plaza, ☎ 619/497–5000). Only cash is accepted. Advance full-price tickets can also be purchased. Visa and MasterCard holders can buy tickets for many events through **Ticketmaster** (☎ 619/220–8497).

Dance

California Ballet Company (☎ 619/560–5676 or 619/560–6741) performs high-quality contemporary and traditional works, from story bal-

lets to Balanchine. The *Nutcracker* is staged annually at the Civic Theatre (⊠ 202 C St., downtown).

Film

Science, space-documentary, observation-of-motion, and sometimes
psychedelic films are shown on the Imax screen at the **Reuben H. Fleet
Space Theater and Science Center** (⊠ Balboa Park, 1875 El Prado, ☎
619/238–1233). **Sherwood Auditorium** (⊠ 700 Prospect St., La Jolla,
☎ 619/454–2594) regularly hosts foreign and classic film series and
special cinema events, including the wildly popular Festival of Animation,
from January to March.

Music

La Jolla Chamber Music Society (☎ 619/459–3724) presents internationally acclaimed chamber ensembles, orchestras, and soloists at Sherwood Auditorium (☞ *below*) and the Civic Theatre. **Open-Air Theatre**
(⊠ San Diego State University, ☎ 619/594–6947) presents top-name
rock, reggae, and popular artists in summer concerts under the stars.
San Diego Chamber Orchestra (☎ 760/753–6402), a 35-member ensemble, performs once a month, between October and April. **San
Diego Opera** (⊠ Civic Theatre, 202 C St., downtown, ☎ 619/232–
7636 or 619/236–6510) draws international artists. Its season of five
operas runs between January and April. **Sherwood Auditorium** (⊠ 700
Prospect St., La Jolla, ☎ 619/454–2594), a 550-seat venue in the Museum of Contemporary Art, hosts classical and jazz events. **Spreckels
Organ Pavilion** (⊠ Balboa Park, ☎ 619/702–8138) holds a giant outdoor pipe organ dedicated in 1915 by sugar magnate Adolph Spreckels. Robert Plimpton performs on most Sunday afternoons and on most
Monday evenings in summer. **Spreckels Theatre** (⊠ 121 Broadway, ☎
619/235–0494) hosts everything from mostly Mozart to small rock
concerts. Ballets and theatrical productions are also held here. Its good
acoustics and historical status make this an appealing site.

Theater

California Center for the Arts (⊠ 340 N. Escondido, ☎ 760/738–4100)
presents mainstream theatrical productions such as *Grease* and *The
Odd Couple*. **Coronado Playhouse** (⊠ 1775 Strand Way, Coronado,
☎ 619/435–4856), a cabaret-type theater near the Hotel Del Coronado, stages regular dramatic and musical performances. **Diversionary
Theatre** (⊠ 4545 Park Blvd., University Heights, ☎ 619/220–0097)
is San Diego's premier gay and lesbian company. **Gaslamp Quarter Theatre Company** (⊠ Hahn Cosmopolitan Theatre, 444 4th Ave., downtown, ☎ 619/234–9583) stages comedies, dramas, mysteries, and
musicals at a 250-seat venue.

La Jolla Playhouse (⊠ Mandell Weiss Center for the Performing Arts,
University of California at San Diego, 2910 La Jolla Village Dr., ☎
619/550–1010) crafts exciting and innovative productions, from May
to November, under the artistic direction of Michael Greif. Many
Broadway shows, such as *Tommy* and *How to Succeed in Business Without Really Trying,* have previewed here before heading for the East Coast.
La Jolla Stage Company (⊠ Parker Auditorium, 750 Nautilus St., La
Jolla, ☎ 619/459–7773) presents lavish productions of Broadway favorites and popular comedies year-round on the La Jolla High School
campus. **Old Globe Theatre** (⊠ Simon Edison Centre for the Performing Arts, Balboa Park, 1363 Old Globe Way, ☎ 619/239–2255) is the
oldest professional theater in California, performing classics, contemporary dramas, and experimental works. It produces the famous summer Shakespeare Festival at the Old Globe, the Cassius Carter Centre
Stage and the Lowell Davies Festival Theatre.

San Diego Comic Opera Company (⊠ Casa del Prado Theatre, Balboa Park, ☎ 619/231–5714) presents four different productions of Gilbert and Sullivan and similar works from October to July. **San Diego Repertory Theatre** (⊠ Lyceum, 79 Horton Plaza, ☎ 619/235–8025), San Diego's first resident acting company, performs contemporary works year-round. **Sledgehammer Theatre** (⊠ 1620 6th Ave., ☎ 619/544–1484), one of San Diego's cutting-edge theaters, stages avant-garde pieces in St. Cecilia's church. **Starlight Musical Theatre** (⊠ Starlight Bowl, Balboa Park, ☎ 619/544–7827 during season), a local summertime favorite, is a series of musicals performed in an outdoor amphitheater from mid-June through early September. Because of the theater's proximity to the airport, actors are often forced to freeze mid-scene while a plane flies over. The **Theatre in Old Town** (⊠ 4040 Twiggs St., Old Town, ☎ 619/688–2494) presents punchy revues and occasional classics. Shows like *Forbidden Broadway, Ruthless, Gilligan's Island,* and *Forbidden Hollywood* have made this a popular place. **Welk Resort Theatre** (⊠ 8860 Lawrence Welk Dr., Escondido, ☎ 760/749–3448 or 800/932–9355), a famed dinner theater about a 45-minute drive northeast of downtown, puts on polished Broadway-style productions.

OUTDOOR ACTIVITIES AND SPORTS

People in this outdoors-oriented community recreate more than spectate. It's hard not to, with the variety of choices available, from boccie and ballooning to golf, surfing, sailing, and volleyball, plus the constant sunshine.

Beaches

San Diego's beaches are among its greatest natural attractions. In some places the shorefront is wide and sandy; in others it's narrow and rocky or backed by impressive sandstone cliffs. The beaches below are listed from south to north.

Coronado
Silver Strand State Beach. This quiet Coronado beach is ideal for families. The water is relatively calm, lifeguards and rangers are on duty year-round, and there are places to rollerblade or ride bikes. Four parking lots provide room for more than 1,500 cars. Campsites (from $12 to $16 per night) at a facility for self-contained RVs are available on a first-come, first-served basis. ⊠ *From San Diego–Coronado Bay Bridge, turn left onto Orange Ave., which becomes Hwy. 75, and follow signs,* ☎ *619/435–5184.* ⌑ *Parking $4, but not always collected Labor Day–Feb.*

Coronado Beach. With the famous Hotel Del Coronado as a backdrop, this stretch of sandy beach is one of San Diego County's largest and most picturesque. It's perfect for sunbathing or games of Frisbee. Parking can be difficult on the busiest days, but there are plenty of rest rooms and service facilities, as well as fire rings. ⊠ *From the bridge turn left on Orange Ave. and follow signs.*

Point Loma
Sunset Cliffs. Beneath the jagged cliffs on the west side of the Point Loma peninsula is one of the more secluded beaches in the area. It's popular with surfers and locals. At the south end of the peninsula, near Cabrillo Point, tidal pools teeming with small sea creatures are revealed at low tide. Farther north the waves lure surfers and the lonely coves attract sunbathers. Stairs at the foot of Bermuda and Santa Cruz avenues provide beach access, as do some (treacherous at points) cliff trails. There are no facilities. A visit here is more enjoyable at low tide; check

the local newspaper for tide schedules. ⊠ *Take I–8 west to Sunset Cliffs Blvd. and head west.*

San Diego
Ocean Beach. This mile-long beach is a haven for volleyball players, sunbathers, and swimmers. The area around the municipal pier at the south end is a hangout for surfers and transients; the pier itself is open to the public for fishing and walking and has a restaurant at the middle. The beach is south of the channel entrance to Mission Bay. You'll find food vendors and fire rings; limited parking is available. Swimmers should beware of unusually vicious currents here. ⊠ *Take I–8 west to Sunset Cliffs Blvd. and head west. Turn right on Santa Monica Ave.*

Mission Beach. San Diego's most popular beach draws huge crowds on hot summer days. The 2-mi-long continuous stretch extends from the north entrance of Mission Bay to Pacific Beach. A narrow boardwalk paralleling the beach is popular with walkers, runners, roller skaters, bladers, and bicyclists. Surfers, swimmers, and volleyball players congregate at the south end. Toward the north end, near the Belmont Park roller coaster, the beach narrows and the water becomes rougher. ⊠ *Exit I–5 at Garnet Ave. and head west to Mission Blvd. Turn south and look for parking.*

Pacific Beach/North Pacific Beach. The boardwalk turns into a sidewalk here, but there are still bike paths and picnic tables along the beachfront. Pacific Beach runs from the north end of Mission Beach to Crystal Pier. North Pacific Beach extends from the pier north. The scene here is particularly lively on weekends. There are designated surfing areas, and fire rings are available. On-street parking is your best bet, or you can try the big lot at Belmont Park near the south end. ⊠ *Exit I–5 at Garnet Ave. and head west to Mission Blvd. Turn north and look for parking.*

La Jolla
The beaches of La Jolla combine unusual beauty with good fishing, scuba diving, and surfing. On the down side, they are crowded and have limited parking facilities. Don't think about bringing your pet; dogs aren't even allowed on the sidewalks above some beaches here.

Tourmaline Surfing Park. This is one of the area's most popular beaches for surfing and sailboarding year-round. There is a 175-space parking lot at the foot of Tourmaline Street, but it normally fills to capacity by midday. ⊠ *Take Mission Blvd. north (it turns into La Jolla Blvd.) and turn west on Tourmaline St.*

Windansea Beach. If the scenery here seems familiar, it's because Windansea and its habitués were the inspiration for Tom Wolfe's satirical novel *The Pump House Gang*, about a group of surfers who protect their surf-turf from outsiders. The beach's towering waves (caused by an underwater reef) are truly world-class. With its incredible views and secluded sunbathing spots set among sandstone rocks, Windansea is also one of the most romantic of West Coast beaches, especially at sunset. ⊠ *Take Mission Blvd. north (it turns into La Jolla Blvd.) and turn west on Nautilus St.*

Marine Street Beach. Wide and sandy, this strand of beach often teems with sunbathers, swimmers, walkers, and joggers. The water is good for surfing and bodysurfing, though you'll need to watch out for riptides. ⊠ *Accessible from Marine St., off La Jolla Blvd.*

Children's Pool. In addition to panoramic views of ocean and coastline, this shallow lagoon, protected by a seawall, has small waves and no riptide. The pool is popular with scuba divers who explore the off-shore reef when the surf is low. It's also a good place to watch marine mammals—seals and sea lions frequent the cove. ⊠ *Follow La Jolla Blvd. north. When it forks, take the left, then turn right onto Coast Blvd.*

Shell Beach. North of Children's Pool is a small cove, accessible by stairs, with a relatively secluded beach. The exposed rocks off the coast have been designated a protected habitat for sea lions; you can watch them sun themselves and frolic in the water. ⊠ *Continue along Coast Blvd. north from Children's Pool.*

La Jolla Cove. This is one of the prettiest spots in the world. A palm-lined park sits on top of cliffs formed by the incessant pounding of the waves. At low tide the tidal pools and cliff caves provide a destination for explorers. Divers and snorkelers can explore the underwater delights of the San Diego–La Jolla Underwater Ecological Reserve. The cove is also a favorite of rough-water swimmers for whom buoys mark distances. ⊠ *Follow Coast Blvd. north to signs, or take the La Jolla Village Dr. exit from I–5, head west to Torrey Pines Rd., turn left, and drive down hill to Girard Ave. Turn right and follow signs.*

La Jolla Shores. On summer holidays all access routes are usually closed to one of San Diego's most popular beaches. The lures here are a wide sandy beach and the most gentle wave action in San Diego. A concrete boardwalk parallels the beach. Arrive early to get a parking spot in the lot at the foot of Calle Frescota. ⊠ *From I–5 take La Jolla Village Dr. west and turn left onto La Jolla Shores Dr. Head west to Camino del Oro or Vallecitos St. Turn right.*

Black's Beach. The powerful waves at this beach, officially known as Torrey Pines City Park Beach, attract surfers, and its relative isolation appeals to nudist nature lovers (though by law nudity is prohibited). Access to parts of the shore coincides with low tides. There are no lifeguards on duty, and strong ebb tides are common—only experienced swimmers should take the plunge. Storms have weakened the cliffs in the past few years; they're dangerous to climb and should be avoided. ⊠ *Take Genesee Ave. west from I–5 and follow signs to Glider Port; easier access, via a paved path, available on La Jolla Farms Rd., but parking limited to 2 hrs.*

Del Mar

Del Mar Beach. Parking can be a problem on nice summer days, but access is relatively easy. The portions of Del Mar south of 15th Street are lined with cliffs and are rarely crowded. Leashed dogs are permitted on most sections of Del Mar Beach year-round; between October and May dogs may run free at Rivermouth, Del Mar's northernmost beach. ⊠ *Take the Via de la Valle exit from I–5 west to Old Hwy. 101 (also known as Camino del Mar in Del Mar) and turn left.*

Torrey Pines State Beach and Reserve. One of San Diego's best beaches contains 1,700 acres of bluffs, bird-filled marshes, and sandy shoreline. A network of trails leads through rare pine trees to the coast below. The large parking lot is rarely full. Lifeguards are on duty weekends (weather permitting) from Easter until Memorial Day, daily from then until Labor Day, and again on weekends through September. ⊠ *Take the Carmel Valley Rd. exit west from I–5,* ☎ *619/755–2063.* 🚗 *Parking $4.*

Solana Beach

Fletcher Cove. Most of the beaches in Solana Beach are nestled under cliffs, and access is limited to private stairways. However, at the west end of Lomas Santa Fe Drive (at an area known as Pill Box because of the bunkerlike structures on top of the cliffs), you'll find access to a small beach known locally as Fletcher Cove. Also here are rest rooms and a large parking lot. ⊠ *From I–5 take Lomas Santa Fe Dr. west.*

Cardiff-by-the-Sea

Cardiff State Beach. This beach begins at the parking lot immediately north of the cliffs at Solana Beach. A reef break draws surfers, though this area otherwise is not particularly appealing. ⊠ *From I–5 turn west on Lomas Santa Fe Dr. to S21 (Old Hwy. 101) and turn right.* ☎ *760/ 753–5091.* ⊞ *Parking $4.*

San Elijo State Beach. There are campsites atop a scenic bluff at this park, which also has a store and shower facilities plus beach access for swimmers and surfers. ⊠ *From I–5 turn west on Lomas Santa Fe Dr. to S21 (Old Hwy. 101) and turn right.* ☎ *760/753–5091; 800/444– 7275 for campsite reservations.* ⊞ *Parking $4; sites $17–$23.*

Encinitas

Sea Cliff Roadside Park. Palms and the golden domes of the nearby Self Realization Fellowship earned this picturesque beach its local nickname, Swami's. The beach is also a top surfing spot; the only access is by a long stairway leading down from the cliff-top park. ⊠ *Follow S21 (Old Hwy. 101) north from Cardiff, or exit I–5 at Encinitas Blvd., go west to S21, and turn left.*

Moonlight Beach. Large parking areas and full facilities make this beach, tucked into a break in the cliffs, a pleasant stop. ⊠ *Take the Encinitas Blvd. exit from I–5 and head west until you hit the Moonlight parking lot.*

Participant Sports

Ballooning

Enjoy the views of the Pacific Ocean, the mountains, and the coastline south to Mexico and north to San Clemente from a hot-air balloon at sunrise or sunset. Ballooning companies operating in the San Diego area include **California Dreamin'** (⊠ 162 S. Rancho Santa Fe Rd., Suite F10, Encinitas, ☎ 760/438–9550 or 800/373–3359), and **Skysurfer Balloon Company** (⊠ 1221 Camino del Mar, Del Mar, ☎ 619/ 481–6800 or 800/660–6809 in CA).

Bicycling

On any given summer day Highway S21 from La Jolla to Oceanside looks like a freeway for cyclists. Never straying more than a quarter-mile from the beach, it is easily the most popular and scenic bike route around. San Diego also has a velodrome (☎ 619/296–3345) in Balboa Park. Local bookstores and camping stores sell guides to some challenging mountain-bike trails in outer San Diego County. A free comprehensive map of all county bike paths is available from the local office of the **California Department of Transportation** (⊠ 2829 Juan St., San Diego 92110, ☎ 619/688–6699). **Bicycle Barn** in Pacific Beach (⊠ 746 Emerald St., ☎ 619/581–3665) and **Hamel's Action Sports Center** in Mission Beach (⊠ 704 Ventura Pl., ☎ 619/488–5050) are among the places that rent bikes.

Boating

Vessels of various sizes and shapes—from small paddleboats to sleek 12-meters—can be rented from the **Harbor Sailboats** (⊠ 2040 Harbor Island Dr., Suite 104, ☎ 619/291–9568), the **Mission Bay Sportscenter** (⊠ 1010 Santa Clara Pl., ☎ 619/488–1004), and **Seaforth Boat Rental** (⊠ 1641 Quivira Rd., ☎ 619/223–1681).

Sailboat and powerboat charters and cruises can be arranged through the **Charter Connection** (✉ 1715 Strand Way, Coronado, ☎ 619/437–8877); **Fraser Charters, Inc.** (✉ 2353 Shelter Island Dr., ☎ 800/228–6779); **Hornblower Dining Yachts** (✉ 2825 5th Ave., ☎ 619/686–8700), which operates sunset cocktail and dining cruises; and **Classic Sailing Adventures** (✉ Shelter Island Marina, ☎ 619/224–0800), which has champagne sunset cruises. For information, including tips on overnight anchoring, contact the **Harbor Police** (☎ 619/686–6200).

Diving

At La Jolla Cove you'll find the **San Diego–La Jolla Underwater Ecological Park.** Farther north, off the south end of Black's Beach, the rim of **Scripps Canyon** lies in about 60 ft of water. The canyon plummets to more than 900 ft in some sections. Another popular diving spot is **Sunset Cliffs** in Point Loma, where the sea life and flora are relatively close to shore. Strong rip currents make it an area best enjoyed by experienced divers. It is illegal to take any wildlife from the ecological preserves in La Jolla or near Cabrillo Point. Spearfishing requires a license (available at most dive stores), and it is illegal to take out-of-season lobster and game fish. Diving equipment and boat trips can be arranged through **San Diego Divers Supply** (✉ 4004 Sports Arena Blvd., ☎ 619/224–3439) and **Ocean Enterprises** (✉ 7710 Balboa Ave., ☎ 619/565–6054). For recorded diving information, contact the **San Diego City Lifeguards Office** (☎ 619/221–8884).

Fishing

No license is required to fish from a public pier, such as the Ocean Beach pier. A fishing license from the state **Department of Fish and Game** (✉ 4949 Viewridge Ave., San Diego 92123, ☎ 619/467–4201), available at most bait-and-tackle stores, is required for fishing from the shoreline. Children under 15 do not need a license.

Several companies conduct half-day, full-day, or multiday fishing expeditions in search of marlin, tuna, and other deep-water fish. **Fisherman's Landing** in Point Loma (✉ 2838 Garrison St., ☎ 619/221–8506); **H & M Sportfishing Landings** in Point Loma (✉ 2803 Emerson St., ☎ 619/222–1144); and **Seaforth Boat Rentals** in West Mission Bay (✉ 1641 Quivira Rd., ☎ 619/223–1681) are among the companies operating from San Diego.

Fitness

Most major hotels have full health clubs, with at least weight machines, stationary bicycles, and spas. Several hotels with elaborate spas offer one-day spa-and-fitness programs for nonguests. **Frog's Athletic & Racquet Club** (✉ 901 Hotel Circle S, ☎ 619/291–3500) has a weight room, saunas, and tennis and racquetball courts. The **24 Hour Fitness Centers** in the area (✉ 5885 Rancho Mission Rd., ☎ 619/281 5513, ✉ 3675 Midway Dr., ☎ 619/224–2902; ✉ 4405 La Jolla Village Dr., ☎ 619/457–3930) welcome nonmembers for a small fee.

Golf

Most public courses in the area provide a list of fees for all San Diego courses. The following is not intended to be a comprehensive list but provides suggestions for some of the best places to play in the area. The greens fee is included for each course; carts (in some cases mandatory), instruction, and other costs are additional.

COURSES

Coronado Municipal Golf Course (✉ 2000 Visalia Row, Coronado, ☎ 619/435–3121) has 18 holes, a driving range, equipment rentals, and a snack bar. Views of San Diego Bay and the Coronado Bridge from the back nine holes on this good walking course make it popular—but rather difficult to get on. Greens fee: $20–$30.

Torrey Pines Municipal Golf Course in La Jolla (⊠ 11480 N. Torrey Pines Rd., ☎ 619/452–3226) has 36 holes, a driving range, and equipment rentals. One of the best public golf courses in the United States, Torrey Pines has views of the Pacific from every hole and is sufficiently challenging to host the Buick Invitational in February. It's not easy to get a good tee time here; out-of-towners are better off booking the instructional Golf Playing Package, which includes cart, greens fee, and a golf-pro escort for the first three holes. Greens fee: $45–$50.

RESORTS

Aviara Golf Club (⊠ 7447 Batiquitos Dr., Carlsbad, ☎ 760/929–0077) has 18 holes (designed by Arnold Palmer), a driving range, equipment rentals, and views of the protected adjacent Batiquitos Lagoon and the Pacific Ocean. Greens fee: $105–$125.

La Costa Resort and Spa (⊠ Costa del Mar Rd., Carlsbad, ☎ 760/438–9111 or 800/854–5000) has two 18-hole PGA-rated courses, a driving range, a clubhouse, equipment rentals, a golf school, and a pro shop. One of the premier golf resorts in southern California, La Costa hosts the Mercedes Championships in January. All this doesn't come cheap, but then again, how many courses will send a limo to pick you up at the airport? Greens fee: $130–$170.

Rancho Bernardo Inn and Country Club (⊠ 17550 Bernardo Oaks Dr., Rancho Bernardo, ☎ 619/675–8470, ext. 1) has 45 holes on-site, a driving range, equipment rentals, and a restaurant. Guests can play three other golf courses at company-operated resorts: Mount Woodson, Temecula Creek, and Twin Oaks. Ken Blanchard's Golf University of San Diego, based here, is world famous. Rancho Bernardo Inn lays out one of the best Sunday brunches in the county. Greens fee: $65–$80.

Hiking and Nature Trails

Guided hikes are conducted regularly through Los Penasquitos Canyon Preserve and the Torrey Pines State Reserve (☞ La Jolla *in* Chapter 2), the **San Dieguito River Valley Regional Open Space** (⊠ 21 mi north of San Diego on I–5 to Lomas Santa Fe Dr., east 1 mi to Sun Valley Rd., north into park, ☎ 619/235–5440), and the **Tijuana Estuary** (☎ 619/575–3613). A list of scheduled walks appears in the Night and Day section of the Thursday *San Diego Union-Tribune* and in the *Reader* weekly.

Mission Trails Regional Parks (⊠ 1 Father Junípero Serra Tr. 92119, ☎ 619/668–3275), which encompasses nearly 6,000 acres of mountains, wooded hillsides, lakes, and riparian streams, is only 8 mi northeast of downtown. Trails range from easy to difficult; they include one with a superb city view from Cowles Mountain and another along a historic missionary path.

Jet Skiing

Waveless Mission Bay and the small Snug Harbor Marina (☎ 760/434–3089), east of the intersection of Tamarack Avenue and I–5 in Carlsbad, are favorite spots. Jet skis can be launched from most beaches, although they need to be ridden beyond surf lines, and some beaches have special regulations governing their use. **California Water Sports** (☎ 760/434–3089) has information about equipment rentals and purchases. **Seaforth Boat Rentals** (☎ 619/223–1681) rents jet skis for use in the South Bay Marina in Coronado, and they are also available at Snug Harbor in Carlsbad.

Jogging

From downtown, the most popular run is along the Embarcadero, which stretches around the bay. There are uncongested sidewalks all through the area. The alternative for downtown visitors is to head east to Balboa Park, where trails snake through the canyons. Mission Bay is renowned among joggers for its wide sidewalks and basically flat landscape. Trails head west around Fiesta Island from Mission Bay, providing distance as well as a scenic route. Don't run in bike lanes, and check the local newspaper's tide charts before heading to the beach.

Surfing

If you're a beginner, consider paddling in the waves off Mission Beach, Pacific Beach, Tourmaline, La Jolla Shores, Del Mar, or Oceanside. More experienced surfers usually head for Sunset Cliffs, the La Jolla reef breaks, Black's Beach, or Sea Cliff Roadside Park in Encinitas. *See* Beaches, *above,* for descriptions. **Kahuna Bob's Surf School** (☎ 760/721–7700) conducts two-hour lessons seven days a week; all equipment is supplied. Many local surf shops rent boards, including **Star Surfing Company** (☎ 619/273–7827) in Pacific Beach and **La Jolla Surf Systems** (☎ 619/456–2777) and **Hansen's** (☎ 760/753–6595) in Encinitas.

Swimming

The most spectacular pool in town is Belmont Park's 58-yard-long **Plunge** (⊠ 3115 Ocean Front Walk, ☎ 619/488–3110) in Mission Beach.

Tennis

Most of the more than 1,300 courts around the county are in private clubs, but a few are public. The **Balboa Tennis Club at Morley Field** (☎ 619/295–9278) in Balboa Park has 25 courts, 19 of which are lighted. Nonmembers can make reservations after paying a $4 fee. Heaviest usage is between 9 AM and 11 AM and after 5 PM; at other times you can usually arrive and begin playing. The **La Jolla Tennis Club** (⊠ 7632 Draper Ave., ☎ 619/454–9950) has nine free public courts near downtown La Jolla; five are lighted. The 12 lighted courts at the privately owned **Peninsula Tennis Club** (⊠ Robb Field, ☎ 619/226–3407) in Ocean Beach are available to the public for a $3 day-use fee.

Waterskiing

Mission Bay is one of the most popular waterskiing areas in southern California. It is best to get out early when the water is smooth and the crowds are thin. Boats and equipment can be rented from **Seaforth Boat Rentals** (⊠ 1641 Quivira Rd., near Mission Bay, ☎ 619/223–1681). The private **San Diego and Mission Bay Boat and Ski Club** (⊠ 2606 N. Mission Bay Dr., ☎ 619/270–0840) operates a slalom course and ski jump in Mission Bay's Hidden Anchorage. Permission from the club or the Mission Bay Harbor Patrol (☎ 619/221–8985) is required.

Windsurfing

Also known as sailboarding, windsurfing is a sport best practiced on smooth waters, such as Mission Bay or the Snug Harbor Marina at the intersection of I–5 and Tamarack Avenue in Carlsbad. Rentals and instruction are available at the **Bahia Resort Hotel** (⊠ 998 W. Mission Bay Dr., ☎ 619/488–0551); the **Catamaran Resort Hotel** (⊠ 3999 Mission Blvd., ☎ 619/488–1081); **Mission Bay Sportscenter** (⊠ 1010 Santa Clara Pl., ☎ 619/488–1004); and **Windsport** (⊠ 844 W. Mission Bay Dr., ☎ 619/488–4642), all in the Mission Bay area. **Snug Harbor Marina** (⊠ 4215 Harrison St., Carlsbad, ☎ 760/434–3089) rents equipment.

Spectator Sports

Qualcomm Stadium (⊠ 9449 Friars Rd., ☎ 619/525–8282), formerly San Diego Jack Murphy Stadium, is at the intersection of I–15 and I–8. To get to the **San Diego Sports Arena** (⊠ 3500 Sports Arena Blvd., ☎ 619/224–4171), take the Rosecrans exit off I–5 and turn right onto Sports Arena Boulevard.

Baseball

The **San Diego Padres** (☎ 619/283–4494) of the National League play at Qualcomm Stadium. Tickets are usually available on game day.

Football

The **San Diego Chargers** (☎ 619/280–2111) of the National Football League usually fill Qualcomm Stadium.

The **San Diego State University Aztecs** compete in the Western Athletic Conference. The biggest game of the year is always a showdown with Brigham Young University. The WAC champion plays in the **Holiday Bowl** (☎ 619/283–5808), around the end of December in Qualcomm Stadium. The Aztecs also play their home games at Qualcomm.

Golf

The La Costa Resort and Spa (☎ 760/438–9111) hosts the prestigious **Mercedes Championships** in January, featuring the winners of the previous year's tournaments. The **Buick Invitational** brings the pros to the Torrey Pines Municipal Golf Course in February (☎ 619/452–3226).

Horse Racing

The annual summer meeting of the **Del Mar Thoroughbred Club** (☎ 619/755–1141) on the Del Mar Fairgrounds attracts the best horses and jockeys in the country. Racing begins in July and continues through early September, every day except Tuesday. You can also bet on races at tracks throughout California, shown on TV via satellite (☎ 619/755–1167). Take I–5 north to the Via de la Valle exit.

Soccer

The **San Diego Sockers** (☎ 619/224–4625), part of the Continental Indoor Soccer League, play at the San Diego Sports Arena.

SHOPPING

Coronado

Orange Avenue, in the center of town, has six blocks of ritzy boutiques and galleries. The elegant **Hotel Del Coronado** (✉ 1500 Orange Ave.) houses 26 exclusive specialty shops on its Galleria level. **Ferry Landing Marketplace** (✉ 1201 1st St., at B Ave.) has many boutiques and shops. **Coronado Holidays** (✉ Ferry Landing Marketplace, ☎ 619/435–6097) is a year-round Christmas shop.

Downtown

Horton Plaza, bordered by Broadway, 1st Avenue, G Street, and 4th Avenue, has department stores, fast-food counters, classy restaurants, the Lyceum Theater, and cinemas.

Victorian buildings and renovated warehouses in the historic **Gaslamp Quarter** along 4th and 5th avenues house art galleries, antiques, and specialty shops. **International Gallery** (✉ 643 G St., ☎ 619/235–8255) sells contemporary crafts and folk, primitive, and native art from Africa and central Asia. **San Diego Hardware** (✉ 840 5th Ave., ☎ 619/232–7123) may have that piece of antique Victorian hardware you've been seeking. **Le Travel Store** (✉ 743 4th Ave., ☎ 619/544–0005) stocks luggage, totes, travel packs, luggage carts, and packable accessories. Adjacent to the Gaslamp Quarter, **Unicorn Company Arts & Antiques Mall** (✉ 704 J St., ☎ 619/232–1696), the largest antiques complex in San Diego, is home to 100 dealers who purvey toys, jewelry, tools, and other items.

Golden Triangle

University Towne Centre (✉ La Jolla Village Dr. between I–5 and I–805, ☎ 619/546–8858), a handy outdoor mall several miles east of coastal La Jolla, has 160 specialty shops, department stores, cinemas, and restaurants.

Inland Farm Trails

Despite its urbanization, much of San Diego County remains rural; inland valleys and mountains support boutique farms that supply gourmet ingredients to the nation's finest restaurants. Summer visitors to **Dowle's San Pasqual Valley Produce** (✉ 15665 San Pasqual Valley Rd., Escondido, ☎ 760/789–7201), near Wild Animal Park, pick vegetables directly from the fields. **The Farm Stand** (✉ San Pasqual Valley Rd., 2¾ mi west of Wild Animal Park, ☎ 760/432–8912) sells fresh produce daily. **Bates Nut Farm** (✉ 15954 Woods Valley Rd., Valley Center, ☎ 760/749–3333) sells pecans, macadamia nuts, and almonds and has a petting zoo. Closer to the coast, the **Vegetable Shop** (✉ 6123 Calzada del Bosque, Rancho Santa Fe, ☎ 619/756–3184) grows premium fruits and vegetables for many of San Diego's upscale restaurants.

Kensington, Hillcrest, and North Park

More than 20 dealers in the **Adams Avenue** area of Kensington sell everything from postcards and kitchen utensils to cut glass and porcelain. The **Uptown District,** an open-air shopping center on University Avenue, includes several furniture, gift, and specialty shops.

Gay and funky **Hillcrest**, north of Balboa Park, is home to many gift, book, and music stores. **International Male** (✉ 3964 5th Ave., ☎ 619/294–8600) sells contemporary men's fashions at reasonable prices. Don't miss **Babette Schwartz,** a zany pop-culture store.

Retro rules in North Park. Nostalgia shops along **Park Boulevard** and **University Avenue at 30th Street** carry clothing, accessories, furnishings, wigs, and bric-a-brac of the 1920s–'60s. **Auntie Helen's** (✉ 4028 30th St., ☎ 619/584–8438), a nonprofit thrift emporium, sells heirlooms, collectibles, seasonal items, furniture, and brand-name clothing.

La Jolla

High-end and trendy boutiques line Girard Avenue and Prospect Street. Shopping hours vary widely in La Jolla, so it's wise to call specific stores in advance. The **Green Dragon Colony** (✉ Prospect St., near Ivanhoe St.), La Jolla's historic shopping area, dates back to 1895, when the first structure was built by Anna Held, who was governess for Ulysses S. Grant Jr. Perched on a bluff overlooking La Jolla Cove, the Green Dragon and adjacent **Coast Walk Plaza** contain 22 shops and three restaurants.

Mission Valley/Hotel Circle

The Mission Valley/Hotel Circle area, northeast of downtown near I–8 and Highway 163, has four major shopping centers. **Fashion Valley Center** (✉ 452 Fashion Valley), **Hazard Center** (✉ 7676 Hazard Center Dr.), **Mission Valley Center** (✉ 1640 Camino del Rio N), and **Rio Vista Shopping Center** (✉ Rio San Diego Dr., Stadium Way exit off I–8).

SIDE TRIP TO THE SAN DIEGO NORTH COAST

San Diego proper has more open space than most cities its size, but even its residents like to repair occasionally to the less-congested (though rapidly growing) North County. North County attractions continue to multiply, and the 1999 opening of the Legoland California theme park in Carlsbad will only increase tourism to the area.

Numbers in the margin correspond to points of interest on the San Diego North County map.

Del Mar

23 mi north of downtown San Diego on I–5, 9 mi north of La Jolla on S21.

Del Mar is best known for its racetrack, chic shopping strip, celebrity visitors, and wide beaches. Along with its collection of shops, **Del Mar Plaza** (⊠ 15th St., at S21—a.k.a. Camino del Mar) also contains outstanding restaurants and landscaped plazas and gardens with Pacific views. Del Mar has become headquarters for romantic hot-air-balloon excursions; the late afternoon is the best time to spot the colorful balloons as they float over the hills and coastline. *See* Ballooning *in* Chapter 7 for a list of operators.

Access to Del Mar's beaches is from the streets that run east–west off Coast Boulevard. Summer evening concerts take place at **Seagrove Park** (⊠ 15th St., west end), a small stretch of grass overlooking the ocean.

❶ The **Del Mar Fairgrounds** is home to the **Del Mar Thoroughbred Club** (⊠ 2260 Jimmy Durante Blvd., ☎ 619/755–1141). The racing season here (usually between July and September, from Wednesday to Monday, post time 2 PM) is one of the most fashionable in California. During the off-season, horse players can bet on races at other California tracks televised via satellite. Times vary, depending on which tracks in the state are operating. Del Mar Fairgrounds hosts more than 100 different events each year, including the San Diego County Fair. ⊠ *Head west at I–5's Via de la Valle Rd. exit,* ☎ *619/793–5555.*

☾ **Freeflight,** a small exotic-bird training aviary adjacent to the Del Mar Fairgrounds, is open to the public. Visitors are allowed to handle the birds—a guaranteed child pleaser. ⊠ *2132 Jimmy Durante Blvd.,* ☎ *619/481–3148.* ☜ *$1.* ☾ *Daily 10–4.*

Dining and Lodging

$$–$$$$
★ ✕ **Pacifica Del Mar.** The ocean view alone would lure crowds to this trendy restaurant, which emphasizes contemporary international cuisine. ⊠ *1555 Camino del Mar, Suite 321,* ☎ *619/792–0476. AE, D, DC, MC, V.*

$$–$$$ ✕ **Cilantros.** Seafood enchiladas, shark fajitas, and spit-roasted chicken with a mild chili sauce are among the subtly spiced southwestern-style dishes served at this Del Mar favorite. ⊠ *3702 Via de la Valle,* ☎ *619/259–8777. AE, DC, MC, V.*

$$–$$$ ✕ **Epazote.** The menu changes seasonally at this offspring of Cilantros, serving a similar menu of good southwestern-style cuisine. There's an ocean view from the patio, which gets busy on weekend nights and during the Sunday champagne brunch. ⊠ *1555 Camino del Mar, Suite 322,* ☎ *619/259–9966. AE, DC, MC, V.*

$$–$$$ ✕ **The Fish Market.** There's no view at the North Coast outpost of this local chain, but it's popular nonetheless for its oyster bar and simple preparations of very fresh fish. The scene is lively, crowded, and noisy. Singles flock here but this is also a great place to bring the kids. ⊠ *640 Via De La Valle,* ☎ *619/755–2277. Reservations not accepted. AE, D, DC, MC, V.*

$–$$$ ✕ **Torrey Pines Cafe.** Locals flock to this reasonably priced sister of the Bird Rock Cafe in La Jolla to enjoy an eclectic menu of home-style cooking. The dishes are categorized according to size, inviting diners

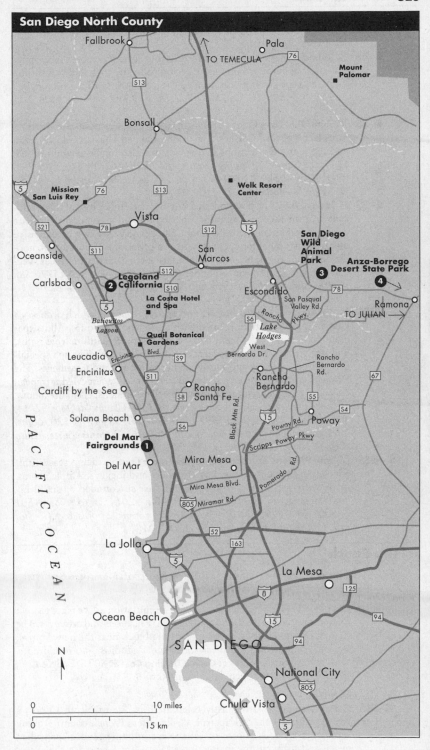

San Diego North County

Fallbrook

Pala

TO TEMECULA

S13

Mount
Palomar

Bonsall

Welk Resort
Center

Mission
San Luis Rey

76

S13

Vista

S12

15

San Diego
Wild
Animal
Park

Anza-Borrego
Desert State Park

S21

78

Oceanside

S11

San
Marcos

S12

3

78

4

Ramona

Carlsbad

2 Legoland
California

S10

Escondido

San Pasqual
Valley Rd.

TO JULIAN

5

La Costa Hotel
and Spa

S6

Rancho

Pkwy.

67

Batiquitos
Lagoon

Quail Botanical
Gardens

Lake
Hodges

Rancho
Bernardo
Rd.

Leucadia

Blvd.

S9

West
Bernardo Dr.

Encinitas

Encinitas

S11

Rancho
Santa Fe

Rancho
Bernardo

S5

Cardiff by the Sea

S8

Black Mtn Rd.

15

S4

Solana Beach

S6

Powny Rd.

Poway

**Del Mar
Fairgrounds** **1**

Scripps Poway Pkwy

Del Mar

Mira Mesa

Pomerado Rd.

Mira Mesa Blvd.

805

Miramar Rd.

52

La Jolla

163

5

La Mesa

125

PACIFIC OCEAN

Ocean Beach

8

15

94

SAN DIEGO

94

805

N

National City

805

0   10 miles

Chula Vista

5

0   15 km

to mix, match, and share. The menu changes seasonally. Brunch is served on Sunday. ⊠ *2334 Carmel Valley Rd.,* ☎ *619/259–5878. AE, D, DC, MC, V. No lunch Sat.*

$–$$ ✕ **Kitima.** This contemporary restaurant serves an elegant interpretation of Thai cuisine. Sample the spring rolls, the rock and roll shrimp salad, and the shrimp dish dubbed "the evil prince of a wild jungle." ⊠ *1555 Camino del Mar, Suite 201,* ☎ *619/792–7000. AE, D, DC, MC, V.*

$–$$ ✕ **Spices Thai Cafe.** One of the North County's most stylish ethnic restaurants serves beautiful dishes. The traditional pad Thai is a colorful feast, and the seafood selections and salads are also highly recommended. ⊠ *Piazza Carmel Shopping Center, 3810 Valley Centre Dr., Suite 903,* ☎ *619/259–0889;* ⊠ *16441 Bernardo Center Dr., Rancho Bernardo,* ☎ *619/674–4665. AE, D, DC, MC, V.*

$–$$ ✕ **Taste of Thai.** The postmodern decor and cheerful clamor of this restaurant near the racetrack make it a place to avoid if you desire intimate conversation and a leisurely dinner. But if you're seeking an extensive menu of tasty Thai food, come here and order one of the curries, noodle dishes, or vegetable-meat combinations in a variety of sauces. Vegetarians will find much to choose from on this menu. ⊠ *15770 San Andreas Rd. (at the east end of the Flower Hill Mall),* ☎ *619/793–9695. AE, D, DC, MC, V.*

$$$$ ✕🏠 **L'Auberge Del Mar Resort and Spa.** L'Auberge, which occupies a colorful garden setting, is filled with dark-wood antiques. All its spacious rooms have wet bars; many have fireplaces, full marble baths, and private balconies with garden and coastal views. The spa specializes in aromatherapy and European herbal wraps and treatments. The Dining Room at L'Auberge serves contemporary Pacific-Mediterranean cuisine in a casually elegant atmosphere. The dinner specials are among the best culinary bargains in San Diego. ⊠ *1540 Camino del Mar, 92014,* ☎ *619/259–1515 or 800/553–1336,* 𝔽𝔸𝕏 *619/755–4940. 120 rooms. 1 restaurant, bar, 2 pools, outdoor hot tub, spa, 2 tennis courts, health club, meeting rooms. AE, D, DC, MC, V.*

$$–$$$$ 🏠 **Best Western Stratford Inn of Del Mar.** During racing season this equestrian-theme inn hosts horse owners and jockeys. Ample rooms, many with ocean views or kitchenettes, are surrounded by six lushly landscaped acres. ⊠ *710 Camino del Mar, 92014,* ☎ *619/755–1501 or 800/446–7229,* 𝔽𝔸𝕏 *619/755–4704. 94 rooms. 2 pools, outdoor hot tub. Continental breakfast. AE, D, DC, MC, V.*

Solana Beach

1 mi north of Del Mar on S21, 25 mi north of downtown San Diego on I–5 to Lomas Santa Fe Dr. west.

Once-quiet Solana Beach is developing a reputation as *the* place to look for antiques, collectibles, and contemporary fashions and artworks. The Cedros Design District, occupying a long block near the new Amtrak station, contains shops, galleries, designers' studios, and restaurants. You can browse the stores at **Cedros Trading Co.** (⊠ 307 S. Cedros Ave., ☎ 619/794–9016), open daily from 10 to 6.

Dining

$$–$$$ ✕ **Pamplemousse Grill.** Justly celebrated as one of North County's
★   best restaurants, the "Grapefruit Grill" offers French country dining California-style. A choice of sauces accompanies succulent grilled meats and fish, and the main course salads are a feast for the eye as well as the palate. Other menu items include a seafood stew with lobster, and good crab cakes. Grapefruit sorbet clears the palate between courses. ⊠ *514 Via de la Valle,* ☎ *619/792–9090. AE, D, DC, MC, V. Closed Mon. No lunch Tues., weekends.*

$–$$$ ✕ **Parioli Italian Bistro.** This Italian bistro offers fine dining in a plain but appealing wrapper. In its simple dining room, Parioli serves Italian dishes graced with an occasional French note. ✉ *647 Hwy. 101,* ☎ *619/755–2525. AE, MC, V. Closed Mon. No lunch Sun.*

$–$$ ✕ **Fidel's.** One among a cluster of neighborhood Mexican restaurants in Solana Beach's "barrio Eden Gardens," Fidel's serves good renditions of traditional south-of-the-border dishes in a casual atmosphere. The restaurant's outdoor patio draws a lively crowd. There's also a Fidel's Norte up the coast in Carlsbad. ✉ *607 Valley Ave.,* ☎ *619/ 755–5292;* ✉ *3003 Carlsbad Blvd.,* ☎ *760/729–0903. MC, V.*

$ ✕ **Zinc Cafe.** Solana Beach's most popular sidewalk café lies at the head of trendy Cedros Avenue. Sit at one of the outdoor tables and enjoy the vegetarian breakfast and lunch selections or some truly decadent desserts. ✉ *132 S. Cedros Ave.,* ☎ *619/793–5436. No credit cards. No dinner.*

Rancho Santa Fe

4 mi east of Solana Beach on S8 (Lomas Santa Fe Dr.), 29 mi north of downtown San Diego on I–5 to S8 east.

Rancho Santa Fe, east of I–5 on Via de la Valle Road, is horse country. It's common to see entire families riding the many trails that crisscross the hillsides. The challenging Rancho Santa Fe Golf Course, the original site of the Bing Crosby Pro-Am and considered one of the best courses in southern California, is open only to members of the Rancho Santa Fe community and guests of the inn.

Dining and Lodging

$$$$ ✕ **Mille Fleurs.** The perennial winner of local and national fine dining
★ awards, this gem of a French auberge has a setting that is as romantic as its contemporary French cuisine is exquisite. The menu changes daily. Mille Fleurs is near Chino's, the county's most famous vegetable farm, where the chef shops daily. ✉ *6009 Paseo Delicias,* ☎ *619/756–3085. Reservations essential. AE, DC, MC, V. No lunch weekends.*

$$$$ ✕🏨 **Rancho Valencia Resort.** One of southern California's hidden
★ treasures has luxurious accommodations in Spanish-style casitas scattered among landscaped grounds. Gardens yield a year-round profusion of flowers. Spacious suites have corner fireplaces that can be seen from the bed, luxurious Berber carpeting, wet bars, and plantation-shuttered French doors leading to private patios shaded by market umbrellas. Rancho Valencia is adjacent to three well-designed golf courses and is one of the top tennis resorts in the nation. The inn's first-rate restaurant has earned raves for its California-Pacific cuisine. ✉ *5921 Valencia Circle, 92067,* ☎ *619/756–1123 or 800/548–3664,* 🅵🅰🆇 *619/ 756–0165. 43 suites. Restaurant, bar, 2 pools, 2 outdoor hot tubs, 18 tennis courts, croquet, health club, hiking, bicycles. AE, DC, MC, V.*

$$–$$$$ ✕🏨 **Inn at Rancho Santa Fe.** Understated elegance is the theme of this genteel old resort in the heart of the village. Most accommodations are in red-tile-roof cottages scattered about the property's parklike 20 acres. Some cottages have two bedrooms, private patios, fireplaces, and hot tubs. The inn also maintains a beach house at Del Mar for guest use and has membership at the exclusive Rancho Santa Fe Golf Club. ✉ *5951 Linea del Cielo, 92067,* ☎ *619/756–1131 or 800/843–4661,* 🅵🅰🆇 *619/759–1604. 90 rooms. Dining room, bar, room service, pool, golf privileges, 3 tennis courts, croquet, exercise room, meeting rooms. AE, DC, MC, V.*

OFF THE
BEATEN PATH

QUAIL BOTANICAL GARDENS– View more than 3,000 rare and exotic plants on 30 landscaped acres. There are 15 collections. Individual displays include Central American, Himalayan, Australian, and African tropical gardens; the largest collection of bamboo in North America; a California native plant display; an old-fashioned demonstration garden; and plantings of subtropical fruit. ⊠ *230 Quail Gardens Dr. (7 mi west of Rancho Santa Fe on S9, 28 mi north of downtown San Diego on I–5),* ☎ *760/436–3036.* ☜ *$5.* ⊙ *Daily 9–5.*

Carlsbad

6 mi from Encinitas on S21, 36 mi north of downtown San Diego on I–5.

During 1999 Carlsbad will receive international publicity when the long-awaited Legoland California opens. The city owes its name and Bavarian look to John Frazier, who lured people to the area a century ago with talk of the healing powers of mineral water bubbling from a coastal well. The water was found to have the same properties as water from the German mineral wells of Karlsbad—hence the name of the new community.Remnants from this era, including the original well and a monument to Frazier, are found at the **Alt Karlsbad Haus** (⊠ 2802A Carlsbad Blvd.).

🐚 ❷ With the March 1999 opening of **Legoland California,** Carlsbad will become an instant family destination. Legoland, the centerpiece of a development with golf courses, resort hotels, a winery, and a designer discount shopping mall, will offer a full day of entertainment for pint-size visitors and their parents. Kids will be able to climb on and over, operate, manipulate, and explore displays and attractions constructed out of plastic blocks. Included are a nature maze and power tower with an ocean view; a driving school with miniature cars and boats; a waterworks operated by joysticks; and a junior roller coaster. Stage shows and restaurants with kid-friendly buffets are also part of the mix. The admission fee for children between the age of 3 and 16 is $25; there's no charge for children two and under. At press time the park's hours were subject to change. ⊠ *1 Lego Dr. (take Cannon Rd. exit off I–5 and follow signs east ¼ mi),* ☎ *760/918–5346.* ☜ *$32.* ⊙ *Daily 10–6.*

Dining and Lodging

$–$$$ ✕ **The Armenian Cafe.** In a small cottage with an ocean-view patio, this casual family café serves breakfast, lunch, and dinner. The food is Middle Eastern and American. ⊠ *3126 Carlsbad Blvd.,* ☎ *760/720–2233. AE, D, DC, MC, V.*

$$$$ ✕🏨 **La Costa Hotel and Spa.** Don't expect glitz and glamour at this famous resort; it's surprisingly low-key, with low-slung buildings and vaguely southwestern contemporary–style rooms. Rooms are unusually large with opulent marble bathrooms; many have garden patios. The resort has one of the most comprehensive sports programs in the area. There are two PGA championship golf courses and a golf school, plus a large tennis center. The spa is world famous. The complex includes Pisces restaurant, long one of San Diego's top seafood venues. ⊠ *2100 Costa del Mar Rd., 92009,* ☎ *760/438–9111 or 800/854–5000,* ℻ *760/931–7569. 479 rooms. 5 restaurants, 2 lounges, in-room modem lines, room service, 5 pools, beauty salon, spa, 2 18-hole golf courses, 21 tennis courts, health club, hiking, jogging, conference center, car rental. AE, D, DC, MC, V.*

$$$$ 🏨 **Four Seasons Resort Aviara.** This new hilltop resort sitting on 30 acres overlooking Batiquitos Lagoon is the most luxurious in the San Diego area, featuring typical Four Seasons amenities: acres of gleaming marble corridors, original artwork on the walls, crystal chandeliers, and enormous flower arrangements in public areas. Rooms, somewhat smaller than those in nearby luxury resorts, boast every pos-

sible amenity: original artwork, plush carpeting, comfortable seating areas, oversize closets, private balconies or garden patios, and marble bathrooms with double vanities and deep soaking tubs. The resort is home to the Arnold Palmer–designed Aviara Golf Club and the Aviara Golf Academy. ⊠ *7100 Four Seasons Point, 92009,* ☎ *760/931– 6672 or 800/332–3442,* FAX *760/931–0390. 331 rooms. 4 restaurants, 3 lounges, pool, beauty salon, spa, 18-hole golf course, 6 tennis courts, health club, hiking, bicycles, meeting rooms, car rental. AE, DC, MC, V.*

$$$–$$$$ 🏨 **Carlsbad Inn.** Gabled roofs, half-timbered walls, and stone supports are among the architectural elements of note at this sprawling European-style inn and time-share condominium complex in the heart of Carlsbad. Rooms, which range from large to cramped, are furnished in old-world fashion, including pencil-post beds and wall sconces. Many have ocean views and kitchenettes; some also have fireplaces and hot tubs. Free underground parking is available. ⊠ *3075 Carlsbad Blvd., 92008,* ☎ *760/434–7020 or 800/235–3939,* FAX *760/729–4853. 60 rooms. Pool, outdoor hot tub, sauna, exercise room, coin laundry, meeting rooms. AE, D, DC, MC, V.*

OFF THE
BEATEN PATH

MISSION SAN LUIS REY– Built by Franciscan friars in 1798, the well-preserved San Luis Rey was the 18th and largest of the California missions. The *sala* (parlor), a friar's bedroom, a weaving room, the kitchen, and a collection of religious art convey much about early mission life. Retreats are still held here, but a picnic area, a gift shop, and a museum (which has the most extensive collection of old Spanish vestments in the United States) are also on the grounds. Self-guided tours are available. The mission is north of Carlsbad on Highway 76, which becomes Mission Avenue inland from S21 (from the ocean, continue east on Highway 76 about 4 mi, past the Mission Avenue business district and I-5). ⊠ *4050 Mission Ave. (37 mi north of downtown San Diego on I-5, east on Highway 76, which becomes Mission Avenue inland),* ☎ *760/757– 3651.* 💲 *$3.* ☉ *Mon.–Sat. 10–4:30, Sun. 11:30–4:30.*

San Diego North Coast Essentials

Arriving and Departing

BY BUS

The San Diego Transit District (☎ 619/233–3004) covers the city of San Diego up to Del Mar. The **North County Transit District** (☎ 760/743– 6283) serves San Diego County from Del Mar north.

BY CAR

Interstate 5 is the main freeway artery connecting San Diego to Los Angeles. To the west, running parallel to it, is S21 (known locally, but not signed, as Old Highway 101, and at points signed as Highway 101 or Coast Highway 101), which never strays too far from the ocean. Watch the signs, because the road has a different name as it passes through each community.

BY PLANE

McClellan Palomar Airport (⊠ 2198 Palomar Airport Rd., Carlsbad, ☎ 760/431–4646) is a general-aviation airport run by San Diego County and open to the public. American Eagle and United Airlines operate commuter service between Los Angeles and McClellan Palomar.

BY TRAIN

See Arriving and Departing *in* San Diego A to Z, *below.*

Visitor Information

San Diego North County Convention and Visitors Bureau (⊠ 720 N. Broadway, Escondido, 92025, ☎ 760/745–4741).

SIDE TRIP TO INLAND NORTH COUNTY

Even though the coast is only a short drive away, the beach communities seem far removed from the quiet lakes of Escondido, the avocado-growing country surrounding Fallbrook, or the vineyards of Temecula, which is just across the Orange County line. Home to missions, San Diego Wild Animal Park, the Welk Resort Center, and innumerable three-generation California families, the inland area of North County is the quiet rural sister to the rest of San Diego County.

Numbers in the margin correspond to points of interest on the San Diego North County map.

Rancho Bernardo

23 mi northeast of downtown San Diego on I–15.

Rancho Bernardo straddles a stretch of Interstate 15 between San Diego and Escondido. Primarily a suburban community, it is the location of the Rancho Bernardo Inn, one of San Diego's most delightful resorts. The town is also the home base of Ken Blanchard's Golf University of San Diego.

Lodging

$$$$ ✕🖬 **Rancho Bernardo Inn.** A gem of a resort, this adobe early
★ California–style inn feels as comfortable and cozy as a slipper. Public areas are a collection of small sitting rooms where Spanish mission–style sofas and chairs invite you to linger with a good book. There are fireplaces everywhere, overstuffed furnishings, and Oriental rugs on tiled floors. Bougainvillea-decked courtyards surround two-story red-roof buildings containing large guest rooms that are furnished simply and appointed with early California and Mexican art. The grounds comprise 265 oak-shaded acres including a championship golf course. The service here is exceptional. ⊠ *17550 Bernardo Oaks Dr., 92128,* ☎ *619/675–8500 or 800/542–6096,* ℻ *619/675–8501. 287 rooms. 2 restaurants, 2 bars, in-room modem lines, room service, 2 pools, 8 outdoor hot tubs, sauna, spa, steam room, driving range, 18-hole golf course, putting green, 12 tennis courts, health club, volleyball, bicycles, shops, children's programs, concierge, business services, meeting rooms. AE, D, DC, MC, V.*

Escondido

31 mi northeast of downtown San Diego on I–15.

Escondido is a thriving, rapidly expanding residential and commercial city of more than 80,000 people and the center of a variety of attractions.

The **California Center for the Arts,** an entertainment complex with two theaters, an art museum, and a conference center, presents operas, musicals, plays, dance performances, and symphony and chamber-music concerts. The museum's focus is 20th-century California art. ⊠ *340 N. Escondido Blvd.,* ☎ *760/738–4100.* 🎟 *Museum $4.* ۞ *Tues.–Sat. 10–5, Sun. noon–5.*

★ ☾ ❸ **San Diego Wild Animal Park** is an extension of the San Diego Zoo. The 2,200-acre preserve in the San Pasqual Valley is designed to protect endangered species of animals from around the world. Exhibit areas have been carved out of the dry, dusty canyons and mesas to represent the animals' natural habitats—North Africa, South Africa, East Africa, Heart of Africa, Australian Rain Forest, Asian Swamps, and Asian Plains. The best way to see these preserves is on the 50-minute, 5-mi Wgasa Bushline Monorail ride (included in the price of admission). As you pass in front of the large, naturally landscaped enclosures, you'll see animals bounding through prairies and mesas as they would in the wild. More than 3,000 animals of 450 species roam or fly above the expansive grounds. The trip is especially enjoyable in the early evening, when the heat has subsided and the animals are active and feeding. In summer the monorail travels through the park after dark, and sodium-vapor lamps highlight the active animals. ⊠ *Take I–15 north to Via Rancho Pkwy. and follow signs (6 mi),* ☎ *760/480–0100.* ☒ *$21.95, includes all shows and monorail tour; a combination pass ($35.15) grants entry, within 5 days of purchase, to both the San Diego Zoo and the San Diego Wild Animal Park; parking $3. V.* ☉ *Daily at 9; closing hrs vary with season (call ahead).*

San Pasqual Battlefield State Historic Park and Museum commemorates an important moment in the Mexican-American War. On December 6, 1846, a contingent of Americans, including famous frontier scout Kit Carson, was defeated by a group of Californios (Spanish-Mexican residents of California). ⊠ *15808 San Pasqual Valley Rd.,* ☎ *760/489– 0076.* ☒ *Free.* ☉ *Tues. 10–4, weekends 10–5.*

Dining and Lodging

$$–$$$ ✕ **150 Grand Cafe.** The seasonal menu of this pretty restaurant showcases contemporary California-style dishes prepared with a European flair. The café is within walking distance of the California Center for the Arts. ⊠ *150 W. Grand Ave.,* ☎ *760/738–6868. AE, DC, MC, V. Closed Sun., except certain performance nights (call for information).*

$–$$$ ✕ **Sirino's.** An excellent choice for dining before attending an event at the nearby California Center for the Arts. The simpler dishes are particularly recommended. The wine list is serious, as are the desserts. The service is friendly and attentive. ⊠ *113 W. Grand Ave.,* ☎ *760/745– 3835. Reservations essential. AE, D, DC, MC, V. Closed Sun.–Mon. No lunch Sat.*

$$–$$$$ 🏨 **Welk Resort Center.** This resort sprawls over 1,000 acres of rugged, oak-studded hillside. Built by band leader Lawrence Welk in the 1960s, the resort includes a hotel, time-share condominiums, and a recreation and entertainment complex. A museum displays Welk memorabilia, a theater presents Broadway-style musicals year-round, and there are many shops on the premises. Hotel rooms, decorated with a southwestern flair, have golf-course views. ⊠ *8860 Lawrence Welk Dr., 92026,* ☎ *760/749–3000 or 800/932–9355,* ᴀ̆ⅹ *760/749–6182. 136 rooms. Restaurant, deli, 3 pools, 3 outdoor hot tubs, 2 18-hole golf courses, theater, children's programs, meeting rooms. AE, D, DC, MC, V.*

OFF THE BEATEN PATH   **TEMECULA–** Once a stop on the Butterfield Overland Stagecoach route, Temecula, 29 mi north of Escondido and 60 mi north of San Diego, is southern California's only developed wine region. Premium wineries, most of which allow tasting for a small fee, can be found along Rancho California Road as it snakes through oak-studded rolling hills. Temecula draws thousands of visitors to its Balloon and Wine Festival held in April or May. Hot-air-balloon excursions are a good choice year-round; Grape Escape Balloon Adventure (☎ 909/698–9772) has morning flights. Once a hangout for cowboys, Old Town Temecula still looks the part. Park on Front Street and walk along the six-block stretch past the large 19th-century wooden buildings that line the streets; several antiques shops here specialize in local and Wild West memorabilia. ✉ *60 mi from San Diego on I–15 north to Rancho California Rd. east.*

Inland North County Essentials

Arriving and Departing

BY BUS

North County Transit District (☎ 760/743–6283) routes crisscross the Escondido area.

BY CAR

Escondido sits at the intersection of Highway 78, which heads east from Oceanside, and I–15, the inland freeway connecting San Diego to Riverside, which is 30 minutes north of Escondido. Del Dios Highway winds from Rancho Santa Fe through the hills past Lake Hodges to Escondido. Highway 76, which connects with I–15 north of Escondido, veers east to Mount Palomar. Interstate 15 continues north to Fallbrook and Temecula.

Visitor Information

Escondido Chamber of Commerce (✉ 720 N. Broadway, 92025, ☎ 760/745–2125).

SIDE TRIP TO THE BACKCOUNTRY

The Cuyamaca and Laguna mountains to the east of Escondido—sometimes referred to as the backcountry by county residents—are favorite weekend destinations for hikers, nature lovers, and apple-pie fanatics. Most of the latter group head to Julian, a historic mining town that is now better-known for apples than for the gold that once was extracted from its hills. Nearby Cuyamaca Rancho State Park is full of well-maintained trails and picnic and camping areas.

The **Sunrise National Scenic Byway Highway** is the most dramatic approach to Julian—its turns and curves reveal amazing views of the desert from the Salton Sea all the way to Mexico. You can spend an entire day roaming these mountains; an early morning hike to the top of Garnet Peak (mile marker 27.8) is the best way to catch the view. Springtime wildflower displays are spectacular, particularly along Big Laguna Trail from Laguna Campground. There are picnic areas along the highway at Desert View and Pioneer Mail.

An alternate route into the mountains is through **Cuyamaca Rancho State Park** (✉ Hwy. 79, 9 mi east of I–8, ☎ 760/765–0755). The park spreads over 24,677 acres of open meadows, forested mountains, and oak woodlands. Several peaks rise above 6,000 ft. Oak and pine trees adorn the park's hills; small streams and meadows provide a quiet escape for nature lovers. There are 120 mi of hiking and nature trails, campgrounds, and a small museum, and along the road you may spot the remains of a now-closed gold mine.

Julian

62 mi from San Diego (to Julian), east on I–8 and north on Hwy. 79.

Gold was discovered in the Julian area in 1869 and gold-bearing quartz a year later. More than $15 million worth of gold was taken from local mines in the 1870s. Today this mountain town retains some historic false-front buildings from its mining days. When gold and quartz became scarce the locals turned to growing apples and pears. During the fall harvest season you can buy fruit, sip cider, eat apple pie, and shop for antiques and collectibles. But spring is equally enchanting (and less congested with visitors), as the hillsides explode with wildflowers, lilacs, and peonies. Artists and craftspeople have long maintained studios in the hillsides surrounding Julian; their work is frequently on display in local shops and galleries.

Dining and Lodging

$–$$$ ✕ **Julian Grille.** The menu at this casual restaurant inside a historic home appeals to a variety of tastes, including vegetarian. Chicken dishes are popular. ⊠ *2224 Main St.,* ☎ *760/765–0173. AE, MC, V. No dinner Mon.*

$–$$ ✕ **Bailey Barbecue.** The ribs, sausages, and chicken at this backwoods barbecue joint are slowly smoked over a live-oak fire and served with a tangy, not-too-sweet sauce. Everything on the menu is available for takeout. ⊠ *2307 Main St.,* ☎ *760/765–9957. MC, V.*

$$$–$$$$ 🏨 **Orchard Hill Country Inn.** On a hill above town, this inn with a sweep-
★ ing view of the surrounding countryside sets a new standard for lux-
ury among backcountry accommodations. All rooms are decorated with antiques and handcrafted quilts. ⊠ *Washington St., 92036,* ☎ *760/765–1700. 22 rooms. Meeting rooms. Full breakfast. AE, MC, V.*

$–$$ 🏨 **Julian Lodge.** This B&B near the center of town is a replica of a late 19th-century Julian hotel. The rooms and public spaces are furnished with antiques. ⊠ *4th and C Sts., 92036,* ☎ *760/765–1420 or 800/542–1420. 23 rooms. Full breakfast. AE, D, MC, V.*

The Backcountry Essentials

Arriving and Departing

BY BUS
See The Desert Essentials, *below.*

BY CAR
A loop drive beginning and ending in San Diego is a good way to explore this area. You can take the Sunrise National Scenic Byway Highway (sometimes icy in winter) from I–8 to Highway 79 and return through Cuyamaca. If you're only going to Julian, take either the Sunrise Highway or Highway 79, and return to San Diego via Highway 78 past Santa Ysabel to Ramona and Highway 67; from here I–8 heads west to downtown.

Visitor Information

Julian Chamber of Commerce (⊠ 2129 Main St., 92036, ☎ 760/765–1857).

SIDE TRIP TO THE DESERT

Every spring the stark desert landscape east of the Cuyamaca Mountains explodes with colorful wildflowers. The beauty of this spectacle, as well as the natural quiet and blazing climate, lures many tourists and natives each year to Anza-Borrego Desert State Park, less than a two-hour drive from central San Diego. The desert is best visited between October and May to avoid the extreme summer temperatures. Winter temperatures are comfortable, but nights (and sometimes days) are cold, so bring a warm jacket.

Numbers in the margin correspond to points of interest on the San Diego North County map.

Anza-Borrego Desert State Park

❹ *88 mi from downtown San Diego (to park border due west of Borrego Springs), east on I–8, north on Hwy. 67, east on S4 and Hwy. 78, north on Hwy. 79, and east on S2 and S22.*

Today more than 600,000 acres are included in the Anza-Borrego Desert State Park, making it the largest state park in the contiguous United States. It is also one of the few parks in the country where people can camp anywhere. No campsite is necessary; follow the trails and pitch a tent wherever you like. Rangers and displays at the underground **Visitor Information Center** (⊠ Palm Canyon Dr., Borrego Springs, ☎ 760/767–5311, wildflower hot line 760/767–4684) can get you headed in the right direction. The center is open from October to May daily between 9 and 5 and keeps the same hours on weekends and holidays only from June to September.

Five hundred miles of paved and dirt roads traverse the park, and visitors are required to stay on them so as not to disturb the ecological balance. However, 28,000 acres have been set aside in the eastern part of the desert near Ocotillo Wells for off-road enthusiasts. Many of the park's sites can be seen from paved roads, but some require driving on dirt roads. Rangers recommend using four-wheel-drive vehicles when traversing dirt roads. Carry the appropriate supplies: shovel and other tools, flares, blankets, and plenty of water. Canyons are susceptible to flash flooding; inquire about weather conditions before entering. ⊠ *Park headquarters: 200 Palm Canyon Dr., Borrego Springs 92004,* ☎ *760/767–5311.* ▨ *$5 for a permit to use unpaved roads.* ☉ *Park, year-round 24 hrs.*

Borrego Springs

31 mi from Julian, east on Hwy. 78 and north on S3.

If you're not interested in communing with the desert without a shower and pool nearby, Borrego Springs has several hotels and restaurants. There is little to do in this oasis besides lie or recreate in the sun.

Lodging

$–$$$$ ▣ **La Casa del Zorro.** Although the ambience is laid-back, this resort is luxurious in every way, with accommodations ranging from ample standard rooms to private four-bedroom casitas with their own pools and outdoor spas. Service is excellent. The elegant Continental restaurant puts on a good Sunday brunch. ⊠ *3845 Yaqui Pass Rd., 92004,* ☎ *760/767–5323 or 800/824–1884,* FAX *760/767–5963. 77 rooms, including 42 suites and 19 casitas. Restaurant, bar, 3 pools, outdoor hot tubs, beauty salon, putting green, 6 tennis courts, health club, bicycles, children's programs, meeting rooms. AE, D, MC, V.*

$–$$$ ▣ **Palm Canyon Resort.** One of the largest properties around Anza-Borrego Desert State Park includes a hotel (¼ mi from the visitor center), an RV park, a restaurant, and recreational facilities. More upscale rooms have wet bars, refrigerators, ceiling fans, and balconies or patios. ⊠ *221 Palm Canyon Dr., 92004,* ☎ *760/767–5341 or 800/242–0044,* FAX *760/767–4073. 60 rooms. Restaurant, 2 pools, 2 outdoor hot tubs, coin laundry, meeting rooms. AE, D, DC, MC, V.*

SAN DIEGO A TO Z

Arriving and Departing

By Bus
Greyhound (☎ 619/239–8082 or 800/231–2222) operates 26 buses a day between the downtown terminal at 120 West Broadway and Los Angeles, connecting with buses to all major U.S. cities. Many buses are express or nonstop; others make stops at coastal towns en route.

By Car

Interstate 5 stretches from Canada to the Mexican border and bisects San Diego. Interstate 8 provides access from Yuma, Arizona, and points east. Drivers coming from Nevada and the mountain regions beyond can reach San Diego on I–15.

By Plane

San Diego International Airport (☎ 619/231–2100), about a five-minute drive from downtown, is San Diego's main airport. Carriers serving the city include Aeromexico, Alaska, America West, American, American Eagle, British Airways, Continental, Delta, Northwest, Reno Air, Southwest, TWA, United, and US Airways. *See* Air Travel *in* the Gold Guide for airline phone numbers.

BETWEEN THE AIRPORT AND DOWNTOWN

San Diego Transit (☎ 619/233–3004) Route 2 buses leave daily from 5:30 AM to 1 AM. Buses depart from the front of East Terminal's US Airways section and travel along Broadway, downtown. The fare is $1.50 per person.

Cloud 9 Shuttle (☎ 619/278–8877; in San Diego, 800/974–8885) and **Public Shuttle** (☎ 619/990–8770) operate van shuttles that take you directly to your destination, often for less than a cab would cost.

If you have rented a car at the airport, you can take Harbor Drive, at the perimeter of the airport, to reach downtown, which is 3 mi east. Take Harbor Drive west to reach Shelter Island and Point Loma. Harbor Island is adjacent to the airport. To reach I– 5 or I–8, take Harbor Drive west to Nimitz Boulevard, then right on Rosecrans Street. You can reach La Jolla and North County via I–5 North. Interstate 8 East leads to Hotel Circle and Qualcomm Stadium. To reach Mission Bay, continue on Nimitz Boulevard, which intersects with Sunset Cliffs Boulevard. To reach Coronado, take Harbor Drive east through downtown to the San Diego-Coronado Bay Bridge. The taxi fare from the airport to downtown hotels costs from $7 to $9 plus tip.

By Train

Amtrak (☎ 800/872–7245) services downtown San Diego's **Santa Fe Depot** (⊠ 1050 Kettner Blvd., ☎ 619/239–9021) with daily trains to and from Los Angeles and Santa Barbara. Amtrak stops in San Diego North County at Solana Beach and Oceanside.

Coaster (☎ 800/COASTER) commuter trains, which run between Oceanside and San Diego, stop at stations in Del Mar, Solana Beach, Encinitas, and Carlsbad.

Getting Around

By Bus

The **San Diego Transit Information Line** (☎ 619/233–3004, TTY/TDD 619/234–5005; in operation from 5:30 AM to 8:30 PM) has details about all routes.

Regional bus companies that service areas outside the city include **ATC Van Co.** (☎ 619/427–5660), for Coronado, the Silver Strand, and Imperial Beach; **Chula Vista Transit** (☎ 619/233–3004), for Bonita and Chula Vista; **National City Transit** (☎ 619/474–7505), for National City; **North County Transit District** (☎ 760/722–6283), for the area bound by the ocean, east to Escondido, north to Camp Pendleton, and south to Del Mar; and **Northeast Rural Bus System** (☎ 760/767–4287) or **Southeast Rural Bus System** (☎ 619/478–5875), for access to rural county towns.

By Car

A car is essential for San Diego's sprawling freeway system. Avoid the freeways during rush hour when possible. All the major car-rental companies are represented in San Diego. For a list, *see* Car Rentals *in* the Gold Guide.

Limousine companies operate airport shuttles and customized tours. Rates vary and are per hour, per mile, or both, with some minimums established. Companies that provide service include **La Jolla Limousines** (☎ 619/459–5891), **Premier Ride** (☎ 619/234–7433), and **Presidential Limousine Service** (☎ 619/291–2820).

By Ferry

The **San Diego–Coronado Ferry** (☎ 619/234–4111) leaves from the Broadway Pier daily, every hour on the hour, from 9 AM to 9 PM between Sunday and Thursday, until 10 PM on Friday and Saturday. The fare is $2 each way and 50þ for each bicycle.

By Taxi

Taxis departing from the airport are subject to regulated fares—all companies charge the same rate (generally $1.80 for the first mile, $1.20 for each additional mile). Fares vary among companies on other routes, however, including the ride back to the airport. If you call ahead and ask for the flat rate ($7) you'll get it, otherwise you'll be charged by the mile (which works out to $9 or so).

Cab companies that serve most areas of the city are **Co-op Silver Cabs** (☎ 619/280–5555), **Coronado Cab** (☎ 619/435–6211), **La Jolla Cab** (☎ 619/453–4222), **Orange Cab** (☎ 619/291–3333), and **Yellow Cab** (☎ 619/234–6161).

Contacts and Resources

Emergencies

Ambulance (☎ 911). **Fire** (☎ 911). **Police** (☎ 911).

Major hospitals are **Mercy Hospital and Medical Center** (✉ 4077 5th Ave., ☎ 619/294–8111), **Scripps Memorial Hospital** (✉ 9888 Genesee Ave., La Jolla, ☎ 619/457–4123), **UCSD Medical Center** (✉ 200 W. Arbor Dr., Hillcrest, ☎ 619/543–6222), and **Veterans Administration Hospital** (✉ 3350 La Jolla Village Dr., La Jolla, ☎ 619/552–8585).

Hotel Doctors (☎ 619/275–2663) provides 24-hour medical service to guests at San Diego hotels. The **San Diego County Dental Society** (☎ 619/275–0244) can provide referrals Monday through Friday to those with dental emergencies.## Guided Tours

ORIENTATION TOURS

Gray Line Tours (☎ 619/491–0011; 800/331–5077 outside CA) and **San Diego Mini Tours** (☎ 619/477–8687) operate sightseeing excursions for about $25.

The **Old Town Trolley** (☎ 619/298–8687) travels to almost every attraction and shopping area on open-air trackless trolleys. Drivers double as tour guides. You can take the full two-hour, narrated city tour or get on and off as you please at any of the nine stops. An all-day pass costs $20. The trolley, which leaves every 30 minutes, operates daily 9 to 5 in summer, 9 to 4 in winter.

Free two-hour trolley tours of the downtown redevelopment area, including the Gaslamp Quarter, are hosted by **Centre City Development Corporation Downtown Information Center** (☎ 619/235–2222). Groups of 35 passengers leave from 225 Broadway, Suite 160, downtown, the first and third Saturday of each month at 10 AM. Reservations are necessary.

Two companies operate one- and two-hour harbor cruises. **San Diego Harbor Excursion** (☎ 619/234–4111) and **Hornblower Invader Cruises** (☎ 619/234–8687) boats depart from the Broadway Pier. No reservations are necessary for the voyages, which cost between $12 and $17. Both vessels have snack bars on board. **Classic Sailing Adventures** (☎ 619/224–0800) has morning and afternoon tours of the harbor and San Diego Bay and nighttime in summer cruises for $45 per person.

SPECIAL-INTEREST TOURS

The Gaslamp Quarter Historical Foundation (☎ 619/233–4692) leads two-hour historical tours ($5) of the restored downtown district on Saturday at 11 AM.

Six-passenger hot-air balloons lift off from San Diego's North Country. Most flights are at sunrise or sunset and are followed by a champagne celebration. Companies with daily service, weather permitting, are **Skysurfer** (☎ 619/481–6800; 800/660–6809 in CA) and **Sunset Balloon Flights** 619/481–9211). Balloon flights average $130 per person.

Civic Helicopters (☎ 619/438–8424 or 800/438–4354) has helicopter tours starting at $75 per person per half hour.

On weekends, the **California State Park System** (☎ 619/220–5422) gives free walking tours of Old Town. Groups leave from 4002 Wallace Street at 2 PM daily, weather permitting. **Walkabout** (☎ 619/231–7463) conducts several free walking tours throughout the city.

Gray whales migrate south to Mexico and back north from mid-December to mid-March. As many as 200 whales pass the San Diego coast each day, coming within yards of tour boats. During whale-watching season, **Classic Sailing Adventures** (☎ 619/224–0800) tailors whale-watching expeditions for up to six people. **H&M Landing** (☎ 619/222–1144) and **Seaforth Sportfishing** (☎ 619/224–3383) have daily whale-watching trips in large party boats.

Visitor Information

International Visitor Information Center (✉ 11 Horton Plaza, at 1st Ave. and F St., ☎ 619/236–1212). **San Diego Convention & Visitors Bureau** (✉ 401 B St., Suite 1400, 92101, ☎ 619/232–3101). **San Diego Visitor Information Center** (✉ 2688 E. Mission Bay Dr., 92109, ☎ 619/276–8200).

15 Palm Springs

The Desert Resorts and Joshua Tree

Palm Springs and its neighbors—Palm Desert, Rancho Mirage, Indian Wells— are among the fastest-growing and wealthiest communities in the nation. The desert lures visitors and residents for the same reasons: striking scenery and the therapeutic benefits of a warm, arid climate. Resort hotel complexes contain championship golf courses, tennis stadiums, and sparkling swimming pools—lushly landscaped oases, towering palms, natural waterfalls, and hot mineral springs round out the picture.

T

HE DESERT AROUND PALM SPRINGS hasn't always been filled with luxury resorts, but various settlers through the years have recognized the region's rich

By Bobbi Zane natural attributes. The Agua Caliente Band of Indians discovered the hot springs in the Coachella Valley—the valley in which the desert-resorts area lies—and made use of their healing properties. In the last half of the 19th century, farmers established a date-growing industry at the southern end of the valley. By 1900, word had spread about the manifold health benefits of the area's dry climate, inspiring the gentry of the northern United States to winter under the warm desert sun.

By the time of the Great Depression, Palm Springs had caught Hollywood's eye. It was an ideal hideaway: Celebrities could slip into town, play a few sets of tennis, lounge around the pool, attend a party or two, and, unless things got out of hand, remain safely beyond the reach of gossip columnists.

Growth hit the desert in the 1970s, as developers began to construct the world-class golf courses, country clubs, and residential communities that drew not only pop celebrities but tycoons and politicians. Privacy is still the watchword, however; many communities are walled and gate-guarded.

The downside to the region's growth has included urban sprawl and overbuilding (of sometimes less than stellar structures). The city of Palm Springs lost some of its luster as the wealthy moved on to newer, more glamorous communities—Palm Desert, Rancho Mirage, Indian Wells—during this period. But Palm Springs has reinvented itself. Formerly exclusive Palm Canyon Drive is a lively avenue with coffeehouses, a brew pub, outdoor cafés and bars, and frequent special events.

You'll still find celebrities in the desert, where streets are named for Bob Hope, Gerald Ford, Dinah Shore, and Frank Sinatra. Hollywood stars, sports personalities, politicians, and other high-profile folks can be spotted at charity events, in restaurants, or on the golf course. Sean Connery, Kevin Costner, Roseanne, Elizabeth Taylor, and Joe Pesci have all swept into town in recent years. The prospect of a brush with glamour, along with the desert's natural beauty, heightens the area's appeal for tourists.

Pleasures and Pastimes

Desert Wildlife

Visitors who want to learn about the natural history of the desert and see some spectacular scenery can explore the terrain at ground level at the Living Desert Wildlife and Botanical Park and Joshua Tree National Park or take in the full panorama at the top of the Palm Springs Aerial Tramway. Exhibits in the Palm Springs Desert Museum (☞ Exploring Palm Springs, *below*) explain it all.

Dining

Long a culinary wasteland, the desert now supports many trendy if not overly adventurous restaurants—Italian and surf-and-turf cuisine still dominates the scene. Many menus include heart-healthy items for those who are careful about fat and cholesterol. Dining is casual.

CATEGORY	COST*
$$$$	over $50
$$$	$30–$50
$$	$20–$30
$	under $20

per person for a three-course meal, excluding drinks, service, and 7¾% tax

Golf

The Palm Springs area has more than 90 golf courses, many of which are familiar to golfing fans as the sites of championship tournaments. You can tee off where the pros play at PGA West, Mission Hills North, and La Quinta, all of which have instructors ready to help you finesse your swing.

Lodging

You can stay in Palm Springs for as little as $40 per night or more than $1,000. Rates vary widely from summer (low) to winter (high) season. Budget lodgings are most easily found in Palm Springs proper; the city-operated **visitor center** (☎ 800/347–7746) represents 85 properties. Discounts are sometimes given for extended stays. **Palm Springs Desert Resorts** (☎ 800/417–3529) can also make accommodation reservations throughout the area. Condos, apartments, and individual houses may be rented by the day, week, month, or for longer periods. Some hotels, including Marriott's Desert Springs Resort and Spa, have villas for rent.

CATEGORY	COST*
$$$$	over $175
$$$	$120–$175
$$	$80–$120
$	under $80

All prices are for a standard double room, excluding 9%–11% tax.

Nightlife and the Arts

The Fabulous Palm Springs Follies—a vaudeville-style revue starring retired professional performers—is a must-see for most visitors. Arts festivals occur on a regular basis, especially during the winter and spring. Nightlife options include a good jazz bar (Peabody's), several dance clubs, and hotel entertainment. The "Desert Guide" from *Palm Springs Life* magazine, available at most hotels and visitor information centers, has nightlife listings, as does the "Weekender" pullout in the Friday edition of the daily *Palm Desert Sun* newspaper. The gay scene is covered in the *Bottom Line*.

Outdoor Sports and Activities

With almost 30,000 pools in the desert region, swimming (or at least hanging out poolside) is a daily ritual. Several hundred courts make playing or watching tennis a serious pursuit. More than 35 mi of bike trails crisscross the Palm Springs area; the terrain here is mostly flat. Indian Canyons, Mount San Jacinto State Park and Wilderness, Living Desert Wildlife and Botanical Park, Joshua Tree National Park, and Big Morongo Canyon Preserve have hiking trails. Avoid outdoor activities midday during the hot season. Take precautions against the sun, and wear a hat any time of the year. Always drink plenty of water to prevent dehydration.

Shopping

More than half the respondents to a recent visitor survey ranked shopping as the "recreation" they enjoyed most, which may be the reason the Palm Springs area has begun to look like one big mall. Boutiques, art galleries, and an ever-growing collection of consignment, estate-sale, and antiques shops make for diverse browsing. El Paseo in Palm Desert has upscale galleries and shops, and Cabazon holds many factory outlets.

Exploring Palm Springs

Some visitors' idea of "exploring" Palm Springs is to navigate the distance from their hotel room to the pool or spa—this has, after all, always been a place for indulging oneself. Most social, sports, shopping, and entertainment scenes revolve around Palm Springs and Palm Desert. Cathedral City and Rancho Mirage are west of Palm Desert (and east of Palm Springs) on Highway 111. Indian Wells, La Quinta, and Indio are all east of Palm Desert on the highway. North of Palm Springs is Desert Hot Springs. As for the region's natural wonders, Joshua Tree National Park and other outdoor attractions are easily visited as day trips from any of the resort towns.

Numbers in the text correspond to numbers in the margin and on the Palm Springs Desert Resorts map.

Great Itineraries

IF YOU HAVE 1 DAY

If you've just slipped into town for a quick look-see, focus your activities around Palm Springs. Get an early-morning scenic overview by taking the **Palm Springs Aerial Tramway** ① to the top of Mount San Jacinto. In the afternoon, head for **Palm Canyon Drive** ② in Palm Springs, have lunch alfresco at the Blue Coyote Grill, and drop by the **Showbiz Museum** at the Plaza Theater, where you can pick up tickets for an evening performance of the **Fabulous Palm Springs Follies** (better still, make reservations ahead of your visit). In the afternoon, visit **Palm Desert,** the trendiest of the desert cities, for a walk through the canyons and hillsides of the **Living Desert Wildlife and Botanical Park** ⑨ and a pre-show dinner on **El Paseo.**

IF YOU HAVE 3 DAYS

On your first day head to the **Palm Springs Aerial Tramway** ① in the morning and have lunch on **Palm Canyon Drive** ②. Spend the afternoon browsing the Palm Canyon shops, or (unless it's the height of the summer) hiking through the **Indian Canyons** ⑥. On day two take an early morning drive to **Joshua Tree National Park** ⑩, where you can explore the terrain, crawl through the entrance to Hidden Valley, and stop by the Oasis of Mara visitor center. Have lunch in the park or head back to **El Paseo** in Palm Desert for a midafternoon bite before exploring the chic shopping area. On the third morning take in the **Palm Springs Desert Museum** ④. In the afternoon pamper yourself by partaking of the regimen at either the Givenchy Hotel and Spa or the Spa Hotel and Casino (☞ Lodging, *below,* for both). Then, appropriately relaxed, take in a performance of the **Fabulous Palm Springs Follies.**

IF YOU HAVE 5 DAYS

Ride the **Palm Springs Aerial Tramway** ① and cruise **Palm Canyon Drive** ② on the first day. Explore the **Living Desert** ⑨ and have lunch and shop on **El Paseo** ⑧ or visit the **Indian Canyons** ⑥. On the third day, visit the **Palm Springs Desert Museum** ④, have lunch, and then spend the afternoon lounging poolside at your hotel or touring **Moorten Botanical Garden** ⑤. Spend the entire fourth day touring **Joshua Tree National Park** ⑩, starting at the West Entrance near Joshua Tree and exiting at the Cottonwood Visitor Center (come back via I–10 unless you want to poke through some of the desert towns along slower Highway 111). Following all this activity, you'll be ready for a fifth day of total relaxation—including a massage, aromatherapy, herbal wraps, and other regimens.

When to Tour Palm Springs

During the "season" (from January to April) the desert weather is at its best, with daytime temperatures ranging between 70° and 90°F. This is the time when you're most likely to see a colorful display of wildflowers and when most of the golf and tennis tournaments take place. Prices soar and accommodations can be difficult to secure at this time

Palm Springs Desert Resorts

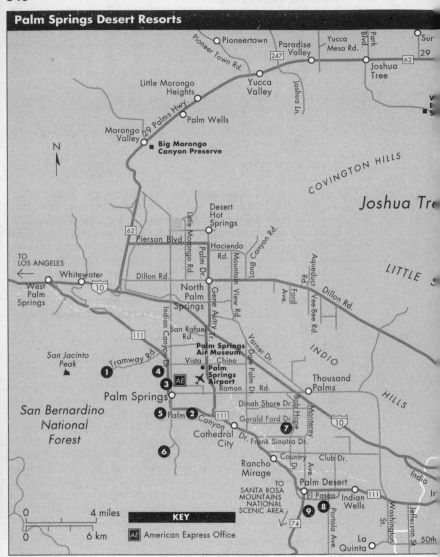

KEY

AE American Express Office

0 — 4 miles
0 — 6 km

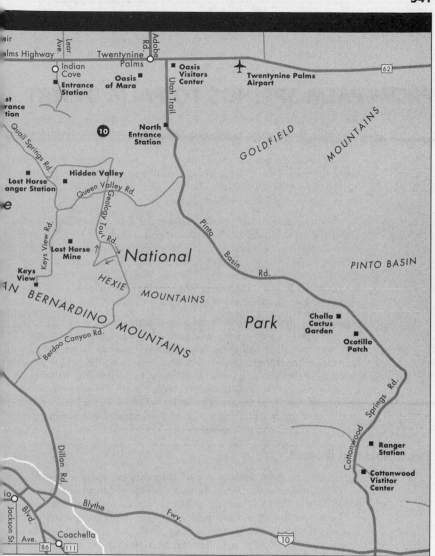

air
lms Highway

Lear Ave.

Twentynine Palms

Adobe Rd.

Indian Cove

Entrance Station

Oasis of Mara

Oasis Visitors Center

Utah Trail

Twentynine Palms Airport

62

st rance tion

Quail Springs Rd.

10

North Entrance Station

GOLDFIELD

MOUNTAINS

Hidden Valley

Lost Horse anger Station

Queen Valley Rd.

Geology Tour Rd.

National

Pinto Basin

Rd.

PINTO BASIN

Keys View Rd.

Lost Horse Mine

HEXIE

Keys View

MOUNTAINS

Park

Cholla Cactus Garden

Ocotillo Patch

AN BERNARDINO MOUNTAINS

Berdoo Canyon Rd.

Cottonwood Springs Rd.

Ranger Station

Cottonwood Vistitor Center

Dillon Rd.

io

Jackson St.

Blythe

Fwy.

10

Blvd.

Ave.

Coachella

86

111

without advance reservations. The fall months are nearly as lovely, less crowded, and less expensive. During the summer months daytime temperatures rise to 110°F or higher, though evenings cool to the mid-70s. Some attractions and restaurants close during this period. Hotel prices frequently average 50% less in summer than in winter and early spring.

FROM PALM SPRINGS TO PALM DESERT

The Agua Caliente Band of Cahuilla Indians settled in and around the Coachella Valley about 1,000 years ago. They considered the mineral springs to be sacred, with great curative and restorative powers. The springs became a tourist attraction in 1871 when the tribe built a bathhouse on the site to serve passengers on a pioneer stage route. The Agua Caliente still own about 32,000 acres of desert, 6,700 of which lie within the city limits of Palm Springs.

The desert became a Hollywood hideout in the 1920s, when La Quinta Hotel opened the Coachella Valley's first golf course. But it took a pair of tennis-playing celebrities to put Palm Springs on the map in the 1930s; actors Charlie Farrell and Ralph Bellamy bought 200 acres of land for $30 an acre and opened the Palm Springs Racquet Club, which soon listed Ginger Rogers, Humphrey Bogart, and Clark Gable among its members. Farrell served as the town's mayor in the '50s.

Joshua Tree, upgraded from "monument" status in the mid-1990s, is beginning to blossom as a national park. Major projects and facilities within the park are still in the future, but it will only be a matter of time before development in the communities around the park occurs. In the meantime, nature, particularly in the form of spring wildflowers, continues to bloom with spectacular regularity. The Cottonwood Springs area is one of the desert's best for wildflower viewing. Carpets of white, yellow, purple, and red flowers stretch as far as the eye can see on the hillsides east of the freeway.

Exploring the Desert

★ ☕ ❶ A trip on the **Palm Springs Aerial Tramway** provides a stunning overview of the desert. The 2½-mi ascent brings you to an elevation of 8,516 ft in less than 20 minutes. On clear days, which are common, the view stretches 75 mi from the peak of Mount San Gorgonio to the north to the Salton Sea in the southeast. At the top you'll find several diversions. The Mountain Station has an alpine cafeteria, a cocktail lounge, apparel and gift shops, a theater that screens a 22-minute film on the history of the tramway, and picnic facilities. The tram is a popular attraction; lines can be long. ⊠ *1 Tramway Rd.,* ☎ *760/325–1391.* ☞ *$17.65.* ⊙ *Tram cars depart at least every 30 mins from 10 AM weekdays and 8 AM weekends; last car up leaves at 8 PM, last one down 9:45 PM. Closed Aug. for maintenance.*

Mount San Jacinto Wilderness State Park, accessible only by hiking or taking the Palm Springs Aerial Tramway, has 54 mi of hiking trails, and camping and picnic areas; guided wilderness mule rides are available here during snow-free months. During winter the Nordic Ski Center has cross-country ski equipment for rent. ☎ *909/659–2607 for park information.* ☞ *Free; permits (also free) required for day or overnight wilderness hiking.*

OFF THE
BEATEN PATH
WINDMILLS – Four thousand windmills flutter mightily on the slopes surrounding Palm Springs, generating electricity used by southern California residents. Each windmill stands more than 150 ft high—the average one produces enough power to supply a household for a month. EV Ad-

ventures conducts 1½-hour tours among the turbines. ⊠ *20th Ave. north of I-10,* ☎ *760/251-1997.* ☜ *$20.* ☉ *Tours daily 9–3.*

② A stroll down **Palm Canyon Drive,** which is lined with shops, includes the **Palm Springs Starwalk,** with stars imbedded in the sidewalk (à la the Hollywood Walk of Fame). Some of the names you'll recognize; others are local celebs. The tiny but illuminating **Showbiz Museum** (⊠ 132 S. Palm Canyon Dr.) documents the area's roots in the entertainment industry. On Thursday night the ★**Village Fest** fills the section between Tahquitz Canyon Way and Baristo Road with street musicians, a farmers' market, and stalls with food, crafts, art, and antiques.

③ Three small museums at the **Village Green Heritage Center** (⊠ 221 S. Palm Canyon Dr., ☎ 760/323–8297) illustrate pioneer life in Palm Springs. There's a nominal fee for entrance to each. The adjacent **Agua Caliente Cultural Museum,** admission to which is free, is devoted to the culture and history of Cahuilla Indians.

④ The **Palm Springs Desert Museum** focuses on natural science, the visual arts, and the performing arts. The display on the natural history of the desert is itself worth a visit, and the grounds hold several striking sculpture courts. A modern-art gallery has works by artists such as Alberto Giacometti, Henry Moore, and Helen Frankenthaler. Of interest to movie fans are the exhibits of the late actor William Holden's art collection, and furniture designed and crafted by actor William Montgomery. The Annenberg Theater presents plays, concerts, lectures, operas, and other cultural events. ⊠ *101 Museum Dr.,* ☎ *760/325–0189.* ☜ *$7.50; free 1st Fri. of month.* ☉ *Tues.–Sat. 10–5, Sun. noon–5.*

The **Palm Springs Air Museum** showcases several dozen World War II aircraft including a B-17 Flying Fortress bomber, a P-51 Mustang, a Lockheed P-38, and a Grumman TBF Avenger. Guided tours are conducted on weekends at noon and 2 PM. ⊠ *745 N. Gene Autry Trail,* ☎ *760/778–6262.* ☜ *$7.50.* ☉ *Daily 10–5.*

⑤ Four-acre **Moorten Botanical Garden** nurtures more than 3,000 plant varieties in settings that simulate their original environments. Indian artifacts and rock, crystal, and wood forms are exhibited. ⊠ *1701 S. Palm Canyon Dr.,* ☎ *760/327–6555.* ☜ *$2.* ☉ *Mon.–Sat. 9–4:30, Sun. 10–4.*

⑥ The **Indian Canyons** are the ancestral home of the Agua Caliente Band of Cahuilla Indians, who selected them for their lush oases, abundant water, and wildlife. Visitors can see remnants of this life: rock art, house pits and foundations, irrigation ditches, bedrock mortars, pictographs, and stone houses and shelters built atop high cliff walls. Three canyons are open: Palm Canyon, noted for its stand of Washingtonia palms, Murray, home of Peninsula bighorn sheep and a herd of wild ponies; and Andreas, where a stand of fan palms contrasts with sharp rock formations. The trading post in Palm Canyon has hiking maps, refreshments, Indian art, jewelry, and weavings. ⊠ *38-500 S. Palm Canyon Dr.,* ☎ *760/325–5673.* ☜ *$5.* ☉ *Daily 8–5, summer 8–6.*

Much of the scenery in exclusive **Rancho Mirage** is behind the walls of gated communities and country clubs. The rich and famous live in celebrity estates or patronize the elegant resorts and fine-dining establishments, and the city's golf courses are the sight of world-class tournaments. The Betty Ford Center, for those recovering from alcohol or drug addiction, is also here.

☙ **⑦** The **Children's Discovery Museum of the Desert** contains instructive hands-on exhibits for kids—a miniature rock-climbing area, a magnetic sculpture wall, make-it-and-take-it-apart projects, a rope maze, a family center, and an area for toddlers. ✉ *71-701 Gerald Ford Dr., Rancho Mirage,* ☎ *760/321–0602,* ✍ *$5.* ☉ *Tues.–Sat. 10–5, Sun. noon–5.*

Some of the best desert people-watching, shopping, and dining can be **⑧** found along trendy **El Paseo,** west of Highway 111 in Palm Desert (☞ Shopping, *below*).

★ ☋ **⑨** Come eyeball to eyeball with coyotes, mountain lions, cheetahs, bighorn sheep, golden eagles, warthogs, and owls at the **Living Desert Wildlife and Botanical Park.** Easy to challenging trails traverse desert gardens populated with plants of the Mojave, Colorado, and Sonoran deserts. One exhibit depicts the path of the San Andreas earthquake fault across the valley. During the holidays the park presents Wildlights, an evening light show. Wildlife shows take place daily in Tennity Amphitheater. Shuttle service, strollers, and wheelchairs are available. The park is embarking on an expansion that will ultimately include re-creations of desert life on four continents. The initial exhibit, an authentic African village with an open-air marketplace, gardens, and animal exhibits, should debut in 1999. ✉ *47-900 Portola Ave. (follow signs west from Hwy. 111), Palm Desert,* ☎ *760/346–5694.* ✍ *$7.50.* ☉ *Oct.– mid-June, daily 9–5, mid-June–July and Sept., daily 8 AM–noon.*

The **Santa Rosa Mountains National Scenic Area Visitor Center,** operated by the Bureau of Land Management, contains exhibits illustrating the natural history of the desert and is staffed by knowledgeable volunteers. A landscaped garden displays native plants and frames a sweeping view. ✉ *51-500 Hwy. 74, Palm Desert,* ☎ *760/862–9984.* ☉ *Fri.–Mon. 9–4.*

Most major hotels in the desert that have spas and fitness facilities— the Givenchy and Spa hotels in Palm Springs and the Marriott Desert Springs resort in Palm Springs among them—offer day programs for nonguests as well as guests. **Desert Garden Salon and Day Spa** (✉ *72– 695 Hwy. 111, Palm Desert,* ☎ *760/773–0032*) specializes in beauty, with body wraps, massage, facials, and hair styling. The **Palms at Palm Springs** (✉ *572 N. Indian Canyon Dr., Palm Springs,* ☎ *760/ 325–1111,* ㏅ *760/327–0867*) has a one-day spa program that begins with a 6 AM walk. The package includes a choice of 14 classes, the use of exercise equipment, lectures, and low calorie meals. Massage, facials, and wraps are among the treatment options.

Dining

CATHEDRAL CITY

$$–$$$$ ✕ **The Wilde Goose.** Its name notwithstanding, the specialty of the house at the Wilde Goose is duck, served a number of ways. You'll also find steaks, poultry, fish dishes, and extravagant desserts at this restaurant that was voted the most romantic dining setting in a recent readers' poll in a local newspaper. ✉ *67-938 E. Palm Canyon Dr.,* ☎ *760/328– 5775. AE, D, DC, MC, V. No lunch.*

$$ ✕ **Oceans.** The many repeat customers at this small seafood restaurant tucked in the back of a shopping center testify to the creativity of its chefs and the hospitality of the waitstaff. Bouillabaisse and other Continental-style dishes are so fresh you might forget you're dining in the desert. ✉ *Canyon Plaza South, 67-555 E. Palm Canyon Dr.,* ☎ *760/324–1554. Reservations essential on weekends. AE, D, DC, MC, V. No lunch weekends.*

LA QUINTA

$$ ✕ **The Sandbar.** Sturdy steaks, hearty fresh-fish and pasta specials, and reasonable prices lure locals and tourists to this La Quinta take on a country-cowboy bar and restaurant. Musicians (not always country)

perform on most nights. ⊠ 78-120 Hwy. 111, ☎ 760/564–3660. AE, DC, MC, V. Closed some weekdays off-season. No lunch.

$–$$$ ✕ **La Quinta Cliffhouse.** Sweeping mountain views at sunset and the
★ early California ambience of a western movie set draw patrons to this restaurant perched halfway up a hillside. The eclectic menu roams the globe: Caesar salad with grilled chicken, ahi tuna Szechuan style, and for dessert Kimo's Hula Pie with house-made macadamia-nut ice cream. Sunday brunch (served in season) is always crowded. ⊠ 78-250 Hwy. 111, ☎ 760/360–5991. Reservations essential. AE, D, MC, V.

PALM DESERT

$$$–$$$$ ✕ **Augusta.** Artworks fill this showplace, one of the region's most talked-about eateries. The food in the main salon—French entrées like roasted veal cubes with garlic and mushrooms in a cream sauce—is pricey but worth it. ⊠ 73-951 El Paseo, ☎ 760/779–9200. Reservations essential in season. AE, DC, MC, V. Closed Aug. No lunch.

$$$–$$$$ ✕ **Cuistot.** Chef-owner Bernard Dervieux trained with French culi-
★ nary star Paul Bocuse, but he's taken a more worldly approach at his own restaurant, tucked into the back of an El Paseo courtyard. Signature dishes include grilled shrimp with spinach linguine, Chinese-style duck in a mango-Madeira-ginger sauce, and rack of lamb with rosemary. ⊠ 73-111 El Paseo, ☎ 760/340–1000. Reservations essential. AE, DC, MC, V. Closed Mon. No lunch Sun.

$$–$$$$ ✕ **Morton's of Chicago.** Palm Springs residents like their steaks served with style as well as sizzle, and posh, clublike Morton's delivers. A regular slab will cost you about $25 (à la carte), but if only a 48-ounce porterhouse will satisfy, the charge is $60. Ask for a smaller portion and the price will go down slightly. The bar is always busy—Sinatra (and only Sinatra) plays softly in the background. ⊠ 74-880 Country Club Dr., ☎ 760/340–6865. Jacket requested. AE, D, DC, MC, V. No lunch.

$$$ ✕ **Jillian's.** Husband-and-wife team June and Jay Trubee are the stars behind this fancy yet casual restaurant—he tends to the kitchen; she runs the business. Antiques and framed art decorate the three dining rooms, and the nighttime sky provides the ambience in the center courtyard. The distinctive dishes on the Continental-American menu include the fresh lobster ravioli and the fillet of farm-raised salmon baked in parchment. ⊠ 74-155 El Paseo, ☎ 760/776–8242. Reservations essential. Jacket preferred. AE, DC, MC, V. Closed 2nd week of June–Sept. No lunch.

$$–$$$ ✕ **Gila Steaks and Seafood.** Talented chef Fernando Valenzuela (no, not the pitcher) whips up fresh fish, Cajun shrimp, garlic-roasted chicken, certified Angus beef, and other fine dishes at this Palm Springs favorite. The ambience at Gila is casual sleek, and there's a patio for dining alfresco. ⊠ 71-950 Country Club Dr., ☎ 760/316–1152. Reservations essential in season. D, DC, MC, V.

$$–$$$ ✕ **Locanda Toscana.** Celebrities and celebrity-watchers patronize this Tuscan-style restaurant that's known for excellent service, myriad antipasti choices, and mighty-fine soups. Veal, chicken, and fish all receive snazzy preparation. ⊠ 72-695 Hwy. 111, next to Von's, ☎ 760/776–7500. Reservations essential weekends Nov.–May. AE, D, DC, MC, V. Closed July 4–Aug. No lunch Sun.

$$–$$$ ✕ **Omri and Boni.** Chef Omri Siklai showed the same flair decorating this establishment that he displays nightly in the kitchen. Caesar salads, great pastas, chicken and veal dishes—and even ostrich and kangaroo—are prepared with skill and imagination. The restaurant, which is managed by Omri's wife, Boni, is so popular the couple enlarged it three times in three years. ⊠ 73-675 Hwy. 111, ☎ 760/773–1735. Reservations essential. MC, V. Closed Sun. and July–Sept. No lunch.

$$–$$$ ✕ **Palomino Euro Bistro.** One of the desert's longtime favorites specializes in grilled and roasted entrées: spit-roasted garlic chicken, oak-fired thin-crust pizza, and oven-roasted prawns. Huge reproductions of famous French Impressionist paintings cover the walls of this active bistro. ⊠ *73-101 Hwy. 111,* ☎ *760/773–9091. Reservations essential. AE, D, MC, V. No lunch.*

$$–$$$ ✕ **Ristorante Mamma Gina.** The greatest hits of Florence and Tuscany appear on the menu at this festive, upscale restaurant. The appetizers and salads are superb, but save room for pasta dishes or smartly crafted chicken, veal, and fish dishes. The wine selection favors Italian and Californian vintages. ⊠ *73-705 El Paseo,* ☎ *760/568–9898. Reservations essential in season. AE, DC, MC, V. No lunch Sun. Summer hrs vary.*

$–$$$ ✕ **Doug Arango's.** Even the dish of liver and onions receives gourmet treatment at this bistro with colorful sidewalk umbrellas and tomato-red walls. The entrées include American standards and inventive Euro-tinged creations. ⊠ *73-520 El Paseo,* ☎ *760/341–4120. Reservations essential. AE, D, DC, MC, V. Closed Mon. year-round. Closed Sun., no lunch June–mid-Sept.*

$–$$ ✕ **Bananaz California Cantina.** The energy at this large, boisterous eatery is exceedingly convivial. The food is California cheap and catchy—husky sandwiches, entrée salads, roast chicken, and a dozen other options. The many TVs and frequent live entertainment will keep you amused while you dine. ⊠ *72-291 Hwy. 111,* ☎ *760/776–4333. AE, D, DC, MC, V.*

$–$$ ✕ **The Beer Hunter Bar and Grill.** You can choose from any of 100-plus beers at this ultramodern, ultra-American sports bar and restaurant. Multiple games on multiple TVs will keep you up-to-date on the world of sports while you chow down on pub favorites like pizza or fish and chips and filling salads and sandwiches. ⊠ *78-483 Hwy. 111,* ☎ *760/564–7442. AE, D, DC, MC, V.*

$–$$ ✕ **Café des Beaux Arts.** The café brings a little bit of Paris to the desert, with sidewalk dining, colorful flower boxes, and a bistro menu of French and Californian favorites like a hefty bouillabaisse and the broiled Portobello mushroom with grilled chicken and an artichoke heart, served with a sherry sauce. (Try to stop munching on those flavorful breads.) Leisurely dining is encouraged, which gives you more time to savor the well-chosen French and domestic wines. ⊠ *73-640 El Paseo,* ☎ *760/346–0669. AE, MC, V. Closed July–mid-Sept.*

$–$$ ✕ **Daily Grill.** A combination upscale coffee shop and bar, the Daily Grill serves good salads (the Niçoise is particularly scrumptious), a fine gazpacho, zesty pasta dishes, and various blue-plate specials. The sidewalk terrace invites people-watching. Sunday brunch is a regular party. ⊠ *73-061 El Paseo,* ☎ *760/779–9911. Reservations not accepted for parties of fewer than 5. AE, D, MC, V.*

$ ✕ **McGowan's Irish Inn.** Home-style comfort foods—meat loaf, chicken and dumplings, corned beef and cabbage, and beef stew—get the full Irish treatment at this family-owned restaurant with a full bar and sidewalk dining. The portions are beyond generous, and the service is good natured. ⊠ *73-340 Hwy. 111,* ☎ *760/346–6032. MC, V. Closed Sun. June–Sept.*

PALM SPRINGS

$$$–$$$$ ✕ **Le Vallauris.** In a tasteful old home with a beautiful garden, Le Vallauris serves Californian-accented French cuisine—dishes like the grilled veal chop with porcini ravioli and the grilled halibut with sun-dried–tomato crust and a lemon sauce. A pianist plays nightly. Sunday brunch is a hit with the locals. ⊠ *385 W. Tahquitz Canyon Way,* ☎ *760/325–5059. Reservations essential. AE, D, DC, MC, V. Closed Mon.–Tues. July–Aug. No lunch Wed.–Sat. July–Aug.*

$$–$$$$ ✕ **Otani Garden Restaurant.** Sushi, tempura, and teppan (grilled) specialties are served in a serene garden setting at Otani. An always fresh Sunday brunch buffet includes tempura, stir-fried entrées, salads, sushi, and desserts. ⊠ *266 Avenida Caballeros,* ☎ *760/327–6700. AE, DC, MC, V. No lunch Sat.*

$$–$$$ ✕ **Blue Coyote Grill.** Diners sit under blue umbrellas and munch on burritos, tacos, fajitas (or more unusual items, such as Yucatán lamb or orange chicken) at this casual restaurant that has several flower-decked patios in addition to inside dining rooms. Two busy cantinas serve up tasty margaritas to a youngish crowd. ⊠ *445 N. Palm Canyon Dr.,* ☎ *760/327–1196. AE, DC, MC, V.*

$$–$$$ ✕ **Palmie.** The humble location in the back of a shopping arcade and
★ the simple decor of Toulouse-Lautrec and other Gallic posters give nary a hint of the subtle creations prepared at this gem of a French restaurant. The two-cheese soufflé is one of several mouthwatering appetizers. Equally impressive are the duck confit and duck fillets dish served with pear slices in red wine, and Palmie's signature entrée, a perfectly crafted fish stew in a thin-yet-rich butter-cream broth. ⊠ *Galeria Henry Frank, 276 N. Palm Canyon Dr.,* ☎ *760/320–3375. AE, DC, MC, V. No lunch.*

$$–$$$ ✕ **St. James at the Vineyard.** A multihued interior, an outdoor terrace with street views, and a bubbling modern fountain set a playful mood at this hot spot for dining and sipping smart cocktails. Pastas, chicken dishes, and curries are the menu mainstays. The service can be mildly chaotic on weekend nights in-season. ⊠ *265 S. Palm Canyon Dr.,* ☎ *760/320–8041. Reservations essential. AE, D, DC, MC, V. Closed July–Aug. No lunch.*

$–$$ ✕ **Edgardo's Cafe Veracruz.** If you're hankering for Mexican dishes that eschew rice and beans and other staples of Sonoran cuisine, head to this high-spirited restaurant where the coastal Mexican fare includes treasured chicken, steak, and seafood recipes of the owner's family. The items for Sunday brunch are zestier than those at most places in the desert. ⊠ *494 N. Palm Canyon Dr.,* ☎ *760/320–3558. Reservations essential. AE, D, DC, MC, V. Closed Mon.*

$–$$ ✕ **Louise's Pantry.** A local landmark next to the Plaza Theater, this 1940s-style diner—bright yellow decor, with booths and a long counter—serves down-home cooking, such as chicken and dumplings and short ribs of beef. There's usually a line to get in. Breakfast is served all day. ⊠ *124 S. Palm Canyon Dr.,* ☎ *760/325–5124. DC, MC, V.*

RANCHO MIRAGE

$$$ ✕ **Basin Street West.** Alex Trebek of *Jeopardy* and Hal Linden of *Barney Miller* are among the owners of the valley's premier supper club. Frank Gorshin, Mort Sahl, Patti Page, and other performers put on polished shows (included in the cost of the prix fixe dinner) Meat, poultry, and fish prepared Continental style are on the menu. There's a full bar, and you can cut loose on the dance floor after the show. ⊠ *69-600 Hwy. 111,* ☎ *760/324–3369. Reservations essential. AE, D, DC, MC, V. Closed Mon. No lunch. Dinner seating at 6 PM; show at 8:30.*

$$–$$$ ✕ **Bangkok V.** Fresh flowers always adorn the tables at this attractively decorated Thai restaurant, where the food is prepared with sizzle (literally) and flair. Start with one of the spicy soups, followed by delicate wok-cooked catfish or any of the curries. Make your level of comfort with spices known, or you may find yourself on fire. ⊠ *69-930 Hwy. 111,* ☎ *760/770–9508. AE, D, DC, MC, V. Summer hrs vary. No lunch Sat.–Tues.*

$$–$$$ ✕ **Shame on the Moon.** Superior service and high-quality food at reasonable prices have made this restaurant a perennial desert favorite. The kitchen turns out consistently delicious Continental fare like roasted salmon with horseradish crust and calf's liver and onions with

a bourbon glaze, and the desserts are alluringly decadent. ⊠ *69-950 Frank Sinatra Dr.*, ☎ *760/324–5515. Reservations essential. AE, MC, V. No lunch.*

$–$$ ✕ **Las Casuelas Nuevas.** Hundreds of diverting artifacts from Guadalajara lend a festive charm to the dining room at this casual Mexican-style restaurant with a 100-seat garden patio. Tamales and shellfish dishes are among the specialties of the house. The margaritas will make you wish you'd brought your cha-cha heels. ⊠ *70-050 Hwy. 111*, ☎ *760/ 328–8844. AE, D, MC, V .*

Lodging

INDIAN WELLS

$$$$ 🏨 **Hyatt Grand Champions Resort.** This stark white resort on 34 acres of natural desert hosts the *Newsweek* Champions and State Farm Evert Cup professional tennis tournaments. Suite-style rooms have balconies or terraces, sunken sitting areas, and minibars. The villas here may be the most luxurious accommodations in the desert; resembling a private residence, each has a secluded garden courtyard with outdoor whirlpool tub, a living room with fireplace, a dining room, and a bedroom. A private butler awaits your commands. The pool area has been transformed into a garden waterpark surrounded by palms and private cabanas. ⊠ *44-600 Indian Wells La.*, *92210*, ☎ *760/341–1000 or 800/233–1234*, 🗚 *760/568–2236. 338 units. 2 restaurants, bar, 5 pools, beauty salon, 3 outdoor hot tubs, massage, sauna, spa, steam room, driving range, 2 golf courses, putting green, 12 tennis courts, aerobics, health club, bicycles, pro shop, children's programs, laundry service, business services, convention center, meeting rooms. AE, D, DC, MC, V.*

$$$$ 🏨 **Renaissance Esmeralda Resort.** The centerpiece of this luxurious Mediterranean-style resort is an eight-story atrium lobby with a fountain that flows through a rivulet in the floor, into cascading pools, and outside to lakes surrounding the property. Given its size, the hotel has a surprisingly intimate ambience. Spacious guest rooms are decorated in light wood with desert-color accents; they have sitting areas, balconies, refreshment centers, two TV sets, and travertine-marble vanities in the bathrooms. One pool has a sandy beach. Golf and tennis instruction are available. ⊠ *44-400 Indian Wells La.*, *92210*, ☎ *760/ 773–4444 or 800/408–3571*, 🗚 *760/773–9250. 560 rooms. 2 restaurants, lounge, minibars, 3 pools, wading pool, 2 outdoor hot tubs, massage, sauna, steam room, driving range, 2 golf courses, putting green, 7 tennis courts, basketball, health club, volleyball, bicycles, pro shop, children's programs, coin laundry, concierge, business services, meeting rooms. AE, D, DC, MC, V.*

LA QUINTA

$$$$ 🏨 **La Quinta Resort and Club.** The desert's oldest resort, which opened
★ in 1926, is a lush green oasis. Rooms are in adobe casitas separated by broad expanses of lawn and in newer two-story units surrounding individual swimming pools and brilliant gardens. Fireplaces, robes, stocked refrigerators, and fruit-laden orange trees contribute to a discreet and sparely luxurious atmosphere. A premium is placed on privacy, which accounts for La Quinta's continuing popularity with Hollywood celebrities. Frank Capra, for example, lived here for many years, and it's said that Greta Garbo roamed the grounds bumming cigarettes from guests. Managed jointly with PGA West, La Quinta arranges access to some of the desert's most celebrated golf courses. John Austin, brother of Tracy, directs the Tennis Center. ⊠ *49-499 Eisenhower Dr.*, *92253*, ☎ *760/564–4111 or 800/854–1271*, 🗚 *760/564– 7656. 640 rooms, including 27 suites. 5 restaurants, bar, lounge, 25 pools, beauty salon, 38 outdoor hot tubs, 4 golf courses, 30 tennis courts,*

health club, children's programs, concierge, business services. AE, D, DC, MC, V.

PALM DESERT

$$$$ ⊞ **Marriott's Desert Springs Resort and Spa.** This sprawling business-and convention-oriented hotel has a dramatic U-shape design. The building wraps around the desert's largest private lake, into which an indoor, stair-stepped waterfall flows. Rooms have lake or mountain views, balconies, and oversize bathrooms. There are long walks from the lobby to rooms; if driving, request one close to the parking lot. ⊠ *74-855 Country Club Dr., 92260,* ☎ *760/341–2211 or 800/331–3112,* FAX *760/341–1872. 884 rooms, 51 suites. 5 restaurants, 2 lounges, snack bar, minibars, 5 pools, barbershop, beauty salon, 3 outdoor hot tubs, spa, driving range, 2 golf courses, putting green, 20 tennis courts, badminton, basketball, croquet, health club, jogging, volleyball, shops, children's programs, laundry service, business services, convention center, car rental. AE, D, DC, MC, V.*

$$–$$$ ⊞ **Tres Palmas Bed and Breakfast.** Enormous windows, high open-beam ceilings, light wood, and textured peach tile floors lend this contemporary inn near El Paseo a bright and spacious feel. The southwestern decor in common areas and guest rooms (which are functional rather than luxurious) incorporates old Navajo rugs from the innkeepers' collection. ⊠ *73-135 Tumbleweed La.,* ☎ *760/773–9858. 4 rooms. Pool, outdoor hot tub. Continental breakfast. AE, MC, V.*

PALM SPRINGS

$$$$ ⊞ **Givenchy Hotel and Spa.** Indulgence is the word for this resort
★ modeled after the Givenchy spa in Versailles. The ambience is totally French, from the Empire-style decor to the perfectly manicured rose gardens. Most rooms are one- or two-bedroom suites, with separate salons, some with private patios and mountain or garden views. Personalized spa services include everything from facials to marine mud wraps to aromatherapy. Restaurant menus emulate those found in Paris; spa cuisine is also offered. ⊠ *4200 E. Palm Canyon Dr., 92264,* ☎ *760/770–5000 or 800/276–5000,* FAX *760/324–6104. 98 rooms. 2 restaurants, lounge, 2 pools, barbershop, beauty salon, spa, golf privileges, 6 tennis courts, health club, jogging, bicycles, shops, concierge, business services, meeting rooms. AE, D, DC, MC, V.*

$$$$ ⊞ **Hyatt Regency Suites.** This hotel's six-story asymmetrical atrium lobby holds an enormous metal sculpture suspended from the ceiling. One- and two-bedroom suites have private balconies and two TVs. The suites in the back have pool and mountain views. There's free underground parking, and guests have golf privileges at Rancho Mirage Country Club and six other area courses. ⊠ *285 N. Palm Canyon Dr., 92262,* ☎ *760/322–9000 or 800/233–1234,* FAX *760/325–1027. 192 suites. 3 restaurants, lounge, pool, beauty salon, outdoor whirlpool tub, golf privileges, exercise room, concierge, business services, meeting rooms, airport shuttle. AE, D, DC, MC, V.*

$$$$ ⊞ **Sundance Villas.** Two- and three-bedroom duplex homes in this complex are decorated in soft desert colors. All have full kitchens, bathrooms with huge sunken tubs, outdoor pools and hot tubs, and laundry facilities. The villas are away from most desert attractions in a secluded residential area at the north end of Palm Springs. Rates, though high, are for up to six people. ⊠ *303 W. Cabrillo Rd., 92262,* ☎ *760/325–3888 or 800/455–3888,* FAX *760/323–3029. 19 villas. Kitchenettes, in-room VCRs, pool, outdoor hot tub, golf privileges, tennis court, concierge, business services. AE, D, DC, MC, V.*

$$$–$$$$ ⊞ **Abbey West.** This property in a quiet residential neighborhood at the north end of town is a knockout, with deep-green and white decor in the Art Deco style of 1930s Hollywood. Large rooms have private entrances and patios, galley kitchens, and VCRs. There are several tree-shaded patios, a clothing-optional sunbathing area, and an outdoor exercise facility. Room rates at the gay-patronized Abbey include breakfast and lunch. ⊠ *772 Prescott Circle, 92262,* ☎ *760/416–2654 or 800/223–4073,* ℻ *760/322–8534. 16 rooms. Pool, outdoor hot tub. Full breakfast. AE, D, DC, MC, V.*

$$$–$$$$ ⌂ **Harlow Hotel.** A resort that caters to a gay clientele, this is ideal for those seeking secluded accommodations in a lush garden setting. Rooms are in hacienda-style buildings surrounding a pool; many have fireplaces, private patios, and unusually large bathrooms. Crimson bougainvillea cascades from the rooftops; date palms grow on the property, as do fruit-laden orange, tangerine, and grapefruit trees. There's a secluded clothing-optional sunbathing area. The room rates include breakfast and lunch. ⊠ *175 E. El Alameda, 92262,* ☎ *760/ 323–3977 or 800/223–4073,* ℻ *760/320–1218. 15 rooms. Pool, outdoor hot tub, exercise room. Full breakfast. AE, D, DC, MC, V.*

$$$–$$$$ ⌂ **Palm Springs Hilton Resort and Racquet Club.** The cool, white marble elegance of this plant-filled resort hotel off Palm Canyon Drive makes it a popular choice. Rooms have private balconies and refrigerators. ⊠ *400 E. Tahquitz Canyon Way, 92262,* ☎ *760/320–6868 or 800/ 522–6900,* ℻ *760/320–2126. 260 rooms. Restaurant, lounge, pool, barbershop, beauty salon, outdoor hot tub, sauna, golf privileges, 6 tennis courts, health club, pro shop, video games, children's programs, concierge, business services, convention center. AE, D, DC, MC, V.*

$$$–$$$$ ⌂ **Spa Hotel and Casino.** Rooms at this hotel built over the original Agua Caliente springs are decorated in soft desert pinks and blues and light wood furniture. Not trendy or splashy, the Spa, which is owned by the Agua Caliente tribe, appeals to an older crowd that appreciates its soothing waters and downtown location. The hotel's Spa Experience is a sampling of services—sink into a tub filled with naturally hot mineral water, rest in the cool white relaxation room, swim in the outdoor mineral pool, or let the sauna warm your spirits. ⊠ *100 N. Indian Canyon Dr., 92262,* ☎ *760/778–1507 or 800/854–1279,* ℻ *760/ 325–3344. 230 rooms. Restaurant, lounge, pool, barbershop, beauty salon, outdoor hot tub, spa, steam room, golf and tennis privileges, bicycles, shops, casino, concierge, business services, meeting rooms. AE, D, DC, MC, V.*

$$$–$$$$ ⌂ **Wyndham Palm Springs.** The main appeal of this hotel is its location adjacent to the Palm Springs Convention Center. The terra-cotta Spanish-colonial building surrounds the largest swimming pool in Palm Springs. Rooms are functional rather than glitzy. Because most of the Wyndham's customers are here on business, the atmosphere is more serious than at most desert establishments. ⊠ *888 Tahquitz Canyon Way, 92262,* ☎ *760/322–6000 or 800/996–3426,* ℻ *760/ 322–5551. 252 rooms, 158 suites. 2 restaurants, lounge, pool, wading pool, barbershop, beauty salon, 2 outdoor hot tubs, sauna, golf and tennis privileges, exercise room, bicycles, shops, recreation room, business services, convention center. AE, D, DC, MC, V.*

$$–$$$$ ⌂ **Ingleside Inn.** The hacienda-style Ingleside attracts its share of Hollywood personalities, who appreciate the attentive good service and relative seclusion. Many rooms have antiques, fireplaces, whirlpool tubs and steam showers, stocked refrigerators, and private patios. The accommodations in the main building are dark and cool, even in summer. The adjacent Melvyn's Restaurant, which serves Continental and American dishes, is locally popular. ⊠ *200 W. Ramon Rd., 92264,* ☎ *760/325–0046 or 800/772–6655,* ℻ *760/325–0710. 30 rooms. Restaurant, bar, outdoor pool, outdoor hot tub, concierge. Continental breakfast. AE, D, DC, MC, V.*

$$–$$$$ ⊞ **Korakia Pensione.** This Moorish-style villa, built in the 1920s by Scottish artist Gordon Coutts, has long been a haven for the creative set. Winston Churchill came here to paint; more recently photographer Annie Leibovitz has enjoyed the home's scenic mountain view. Inside, rooms are furnished with antiques, handmade furniture, and Oriental rugs; some have fireplaces, and most have kitchens. Innkeeper Doug Smith recently added to his complex a two-room house across the street. ⊠ *257 S. Patencio Rd., 92262,* ☎ *760/864–6411. 20 rooms. Pool, golf privileges. Continental breakfast. No credit cards. Closed mid-July–mid-Sept.*

$–$$$$ ⊞ **Casa Cody.** The service is personal and gracious at this Western-style B&B a few steps from the Palm Springs Desert Museum. Spacious studios and one- and two-bedroom suites are furnished simply. Some have fireplaces. ⊠ *175 S. Cahuilla Rd., 92262,* ☎ *760/320–9346 or 800/231–2639,* FAX *760/325–8610. 22 units. Kitchenettes, 2 pools, outdoor hot tub. Continental breakfast. AE, D, DC, MC, V.*

$–$$$$ ⊞ **Orchid Tree Inn.** Accommodations at this well-run property a block west of South Palm Canyon Drive vary from motel-style units and bungalows to a two-story town house and a detached house. Some rooms have kitchenettes, and all have contemporary furnishings. ⊠ *261 S. Belardo Rd.,* ☎ *760/325–2791 or 800/733–3435,* FAX *760/325–3855. 40 rooms. Breakfast room, 3 pools, 2 outdoor hot tubs. Continental breakfast. AE, D, MC, V.*

$–$$ ⊞ **Bee Charmer Inn.** This southwestern-style inn with a red-tile roof and terra-cotta tile floors caters exclusively to women. Spacious rooms surround a pool and tropical courtyard; comfortably but not lavishly decorated in soft pastel colors, they come with refrigerators and microwaves. Most rooms have wet bars, and one has a whirlpool bath. ⊠ *1600 E. Palm Canyon Dr., 92264,* ☎ *760/778–5883. 13 rooms. Pool. Continental breakfast. AE, D, MC, V.*

$–$$ ⊞ **Hampton Inn.** This chain motel at the north end of Palm Springs occupies landscaped grounds with views of Mount San Jacinto. Appointments are basic, but there are barbecues for guest use. ⊠ *200 N. Palm Canyon Dr., 92262,* ☎ *760/320–0555 or 800/732–7755,* FAX *760/320–2261. 96 rooms. Pool, outdoor hot tub, business services, meeting rooms. Continental breakfast. AE, D, DC, MC, V.*

$–$$ ⊞ **Howard Johnson Lodge.** This typical motel-style property is popular with tour groups. Ask about special discounts. ⊠ *701 E. Palm Canyon Dr., 92264,* ☎ *760/320–2700 or 800/854–4345,* FAX *760/320–1591. 205 rooms. Pool, wading pool, outdoor hot tub, coin laundry, business services. AE, D, DC, MC, V.*

$–$$ ⊞ **Vagabond Inn.** Rooms are smallish at this centrally located motel but are clean, comfortable, and a good value. ⊠ *1699 S. Palm Canyon Dr., 92264,* ☎ *760/325–7211 or 800/522–1555,* FAX *760/322–9269. 120 rooms. Coffee shop, pool, outdoor hot tub, 2 saunas. AE, D, DC, MC, V.*

$$$$ ⊞ **Marriott's Rancho Las Palmas.** The atmosphere is luxuriously laid-
★ back at this family-oriented resort on 240 landscaped acres. A Spanish theme prevails throughout the public areas and guest accommodations. Rooms in a series of two-story buildings are unusually large; all have sitting areas, private balconies or patios, and views of colorful gardens or well-manicured fairways and greens. A luxury spa is scheduled to open in early 1999. ⊠ *41-000 Bob Hope Dr., 92270,* ☎ *760/568–2727 or 800/458–8786,* FAX *760/568–5845. 450 rooms. 2 restaurants, bar, 2 snack bars, 2 pools, barbershop, beauty salon, 2 outdoor whirlpool tubs, 27-hole golf course, putting green, 25 tennis courts, health club, jogging, children's programs, playground, concierge, business services, convention center. AE, D, DC, MC, V.*

$$$$ 🏨 **Westin Mission Hills Resort.** A sprawling Moroccan-style resort on 360 acres, home to the Frank Sinatra Celebrity Golf Tournament, the Westin is surrounded by fairways and putting greens. Rooms, in two-story buildings that envelop patios and fountains, have soft desert colors, terra-cotta tile floors, and private patios or balconies. Paths and creeks meander through the complex, encircling a lagoon-style swimming pool with a several-story water slide. ✉ *71-333 Dinah Shore Dr., 92270,* ☎ *760/328–5955 or 800/937–8161,* FAX *760/770–2199. 512 rooms. 2 restaurants, 3 snack bars, 1 bar, 3 pools, beauty salon, 4 outdoor hot tubs, spa, steam room, 2 18-hole golf courses, 7 tennis courts, aerobics, croquet, health club, shuffleboard, volleyball, recreation room, children's programs. AE, D, DC, MC, V.*

$$–$$$$ 🏨 **Ritz-Carlton Rancho Mirage.** This hotel is tucked into a hillside in
★   the Santa Rosa Mountains with sweeping views of the valley below. The surroundings are elegant, with gleaming marble and brass, original artwork, plush carpeting, and remarkable comfort. All rooms are spacious and meticulously appointed with antiques, fabric wall coverings, marble bathrooms, and often two phones and two TVs. The service is impeccable. ✉ *68-900 Frank Sinatra Dr., 92270,* ☎ *760/321–8282 or 800/241–3333,* FAX *760/321–6928. 220 rooms, 19 suites. 3 restaurants, bar, pool, barbershop, beauty salon, outdoor hot tub, spa, golf privileges, putting green, 10 tennis courts, basketball, croquet, health club, hiking, volleyball, pro shop, shops, children's programs, business services, meeting rooms. AE, D, DC, MC, V.*

Nightlife and the Arts

BARS AND CLUBS

Bananaz Grill and Bar (✉ 72–291 Hwy. 111, Palm Desert, ☎ 760/776–4333) has dancing nightly, live music on Sunday, a billiards room, plus big screen TV. **C. C. Construction Company** (✉ Smoke Tree Shopping Center, Sunrise Way at E. Palm Canyon Dr., Palm Springs, ☎ 760/778–1234), a popular gay club, has a huge disco that is open from Friday to Sunday and a smaller dance floor open nightly. **Peabody's Jazz Studio and Coffee Bar** (✉ 134 S. Palm Canyon Dr., Palm Springs, ☎ 760/322–1877) attracts everyone from grannies to grungers for poetry readings and live jazz. **Touché Nightclub and Restaurant** (✉ 42-250 Bob Hope Dr., Rancho Mirage, ☎ 760/773–1111), which draws a thirty- to forty-something crowd ready to party, has live entertainment and dancing on weekends. **Zelda's** (✉ 169 N. Indian Canyon Dr., Palm Springs, ☎ 760/325–2375) has two rooms, one featuring techno jazz and another with Top-40 dance music and a male dance revue.

CASINOS

State law restricts Indian-run casinos from providing the type of action typically seen in Las Vegas, but they do have video slot machines that pay off with a printed chit redeemable for cash, and various versions of poker, bingo, and lottery-type games. **Casino Morongo** (✉ Cabazon off-ramp, I–10, west of Palm Springs, ☎ 800/252–4499). **Fantasy Springs Casino** (✉ Auto Center Dr. off I–10, Indio, ☎ 760/342–5000). **Spa Casino** (✉ 140 N. Indian Canyon Dr., Palm Springs, ☎ 760/323–5865). **Spotlight 29 Casino** (✉ 46-200 Harrison St., Coachella, ☎ 760/775–5566).

FESTIVALS

The mid-January **Nortel Palm Springs International Film Festival** (☎ 760/322–2930) brings stars and more than 150 feature films from 25 countries, plus panel discussions, short films, and documentaries, to Palm Desert's McCallum Theatre and other venues. The **La Quinta Arts Festival** (☎ 760/564–1244), normally held the third weekend in March, includes some fine work and has classy entertainment and food.

THEATER

Annenberg Theater (⊠ Palm Springs Desert Museum, 101 Museum Dr., ☎ 760/325–4490) hosts Broadway shows, opera, lectures, Sunday-afternoon chamber concerts, and other events. **Fabulous Palm Springs Follies** (⊠ Plaza Theater, 128 S. Palm Canyon Dr., ☎ 760/327–0225), the hottest ticket in the desert, presents 10 sellout performances each week from November to May. The vaudeville-style revue stars extravagantly costumed, retired (but very much in shape) showgirls, singers, and dancers. Tickets are priced from $27 to $65. **McCallum Theatre** (⊠ 73-000 Fred Waring Dr., Palm Desert, ☎ 760/340–2787), the principal cultural venue in the desert, presents film, classical and popular music, opera, ballet, and theater.

Outdoor Activities and Sports

BICYCLING

Big Horn Bicycles (⊠ 302 N. Palm Canyon, Palm Springs, ☎ 760/325–3367) operates tours to celebrity homes and Indian Canyons and rents bikes. **Mac's Bicycle Rental** (⊠ 70-053 Hwy. 111, Rancho Mirage, ☎ 760/321–9444) will deliver mountain, three-speed, and tandem bikes to area hotels. **Palm Springs Recreation Department** (⊠ 401 S. Pavilion Way, ☎ 760/323–8272) has maps of some city trails.

FAMILY FUN

Camelot Park (⊠ 67-700 E. Palm Canyon Dr., Cathedral City, ☎ 760/770–7522) has miniature golf, bumper boats, batting cages, an arcade, and video games. **Oasis Waterpark** (⊠ 1500 Gene Autry Trail, Palm Springs, ☎ 760/327–0499), open from mid-March through October (weekends only after Labor Day), has 13 water slides, a huge wave pool, an arcade, and other attractions.

FITNESS

Gold's Gym (⊠ 4070 Airport Center Dr., Palm Springs, ☎ 760/322–4653; ⊠ 39-605 Entrepreneur La., Palm Desert, ☎ 760/360–0565).

GOLF

The **Bob Hope Desert Classic** takes place in late January and early February. **Dinah Shore LPGA Championship** is a March or April event. Palm Springs hosts more than 100 golf tournaments annually. The Palm Springs Desert Resorts Convention and Visitors Bureau **Events Hotline** (☎ 760/770–1992) lists dates and locations.

Tahquitz Creek Palm Springs Golf Resort (⊠ 1885 Golf Club Dr., Palm Springs, ☎ 760/328–1005) has two 18-hole, par-72 courses and a 50-space driving range. The greens fee is $50 without cart (permitted from Monday to Thursday); it ranges from $60 to $90 with cart (mandatory from Friday to Sunday).

Tommy Jacobs' Bel-Aire Greens Country Club (⊠ 1001 S. El Cielo Rd., Palm Springs, ☎ 760/322–6062) is a nine-hole executive course. The greens fee is $19 ($12 for replay).

PGA West (⊠ 56-150 PGA Blvd., La Quinta, ☎ 760/564–7170) operates two 18-hole, par-72 championship courses and provides instruction and golf clinics. The greens fee ranges from $85 on weekdays in summer to $260 in February and March. The fee includes a mandatory cart.

Westin Mission Hills Resort Golf Club (⊠ 71-501 Dinah Shore Dr., Rancho Mirage, ☎ 760/328–3198), an 18-hole, par-70 course designed by Pete Dye, hosts major tournaments and well-known politicians and movie stars. The greens fee is $160 during peak season, including a mandatory cart; off-season promotional packages during the summer are sometimes as low as $35. Gary Player designed the Westin's other links, an 18-hole, par-72 course where the greens fee ranges from $35 to $175 depending on when you play.

POLO

The **Eldorado Polo Club** (⊠ 50-950 Madison St., Indio, ☎ 760/342–2223), known as the Winter Polo Capital of the West, is home to world-class polo events. You can pack a picnic and watch practice matches free during the week; there's a $6 per person charge on Sunday.

TENNIS

The *Newsweek* **Champions Cup** and **Evert Cup** professional tennis tournaments (☎ 760/340–3166) are held at the Hyatt Grand Champions Resort in Indian Wells for 10 days in March; they attract top-ranked players.

Demuth Park (⊠ 4375 Mesquite Ave., ☎ no phone) has four lighted courts. **Palm Springs Tennis Center** (⊠ 1300 E. Baristo Rd., ☎ 760/320–0020) has nine lighted courts—the fees run between $12 and $14. **Ruth Hardy Park** (⊠ Tamarisk and Caballeros, ☎ no phone) has eight lighted courts.

Shopping

SHOPPING DISTRICTS

Palm Desert's **El Paseo,** a long, Mediterranean-style avenue with fountains and courtyards, contains French and Italian fashion boutiques, shoe salons, jewelry stores, children's shops, restaurants, a Saks Fifth Avenue branch, and nearly 30 galleries. **Palm Desert Town Center** is the largest enclosed mall in the desert, with more than 140 specialty shops, major department stores, movie theaters, an ice-skating rink, and restaurants.

Palm Canyon Drive is the main shopping destination in the city of Palm Springs. Its commercial core extends from Alejo Road on the north to Ramon Road on the south. Anchoring the center of the drive is the Desert Fashion Plaza. The Village Fest, along Palm Canyon here on Thursday night, brings out craftspeople, antiques sellers, a farmers market, and entertainment.

ANTIQUES AND COLLECTIBLES

Some of the items for sale in the **Heritage Gallery and Antique District,** a collection of consignment and second-hand shops centered in the 700 and 800 blocks of North Palm Canyon Drive in Palm Springs, come from the homes of celebrities and other wealthy residents.

Classic Consignment Co. (⊠ 73-847 El Paseo, Palm Desert, ☎ 760/568–4948) shows full sets of Rosenthal china and Baccarat crystal, barely used contemporary glass and Lucite furnishings, accessories, fine art, and jewelry. Prices match the shop's trendy location.

Estate Sale Co. (⊠ 4185 E. Palm Canyon Dr., Palm Springs, ☎ 760/321–7628) is the biggest consignment store in the desert, with a warehouse of furniture, fine art, china and crystal, accessories, jewelry, movie memorabilia, and exercise equipment. Prices are set to keep merchandise moving out the door.

The Village Emporium (⊠ 849 N. Palm Canyon Dr., ☎ 760/320–6165) specializes in furniture and accessories from the 1960s and 1970s.

DRIED FRUIT

Hadley's Fruit Orchards (⊠ 48-190 Seminole Rd., Cabazon, ☎ 909/849–5255) sells dried fruit, nuts, date shakes, and wines.

Oasis Date Gardens (⊠ 59-111 Hwy. 111, Thermal, ☎ 760/399–5665) sells shakes and conducts twice-a-day tours that show how dates are pollinated, grown, sorted, stored, and packed for shipping.

Shields Date Gardens (⊠ 80-225 Hwy. 111, Indio, ☎ 760/347–0996) presents a continuous slide program on the history of the date and sells shakes.

FACTORY OUTLETS

Desert Hills Factory Stores (⊠ 48-650 Seminole Rd., Cabazon, ☎ 909/849–6641) is an outlet center with more than 150 brand-name discount fashion shops, among them Polo, Geoffrey Beene, Giorgio Armani, Nike, and Spa Gear.

VINTAGE CLOTHING

Patsy's Clothes Closet (⊠ 4121 E. Palm Canyon Dr., Palm Springs, ☎ 760/324–8825) specializes in high-fashion and designer clothing for women and men.

Side Trip to Joshua Tree National Park via Desert Hot Springs

Joshua Tree National Park in the Little San Bernardino Mountains preserves some of the desert's most interesting and beautiful scenery. For visitors it also provides a living example of the rigors of desert life. Highlights of rock formations, historic sites, and unusual plants can be seen in half a day. A more thorough expedition into the backcountry takes a day or more. There are campgrounds within the park, but no other accommodations (a few quaint lodgings can be found in the towns along the northern edge of the park). Desert Hot Springs, Joshua Tree, and Twentynine Palms are among the towns on the northern route to the park—Gene Autry Trail north from Palm Springs to Pierson Boulevard west in Desert Hot Springs to Highway 62. If you aren't going to visit Desert Hot Springs, you can take Interstate 10 northwest from Palm Springs to connect with Highway 62.

Desert Hot Springs

9 mi north of Palm Springs on Gene Autry Trail.

Known for its hot mineral springs, Desert Hot Springs is home to more than 40 spa resorts, ranging from tiny to large and offering a variety of exotic treatments.

LODGING

$$$$ 🏨 **Two Bunch Palms Resort and Spa.** This gate-guarded resort (you must call for advance reservations) is the most exclusive and romantic resort in the desert. According to legend, gangster Al Capone built the stone-fortress watchtower. Subsequently the resort has become the spa of choice for legions of celebrities who savor the 148° mineral waters, the laid-back atmosphere, and the privacy. Massage styles include Swedish, Japanese, and Native American. The landscaped grounds contain two rock-grotto mineral pools surrounded by palms, secluded picnic areas, meditation benches, and outdoor mud baths. Accommodations range from hotel-style rooms to luxury condos with living rooms, kitchens, private whirlpool tubs, and private patios. ⊠ 67–425 *Two Bunch Palms Trail, 92240,* ☎ *760/329–8791 or 800/472–4334,* FAX *760/329–1874. 44 rooms and suites. Restaurant, 2 pools, 2 tennis courts, health club, hiking. Continental breakfast. AE, MC, V.*

OFF THE BEATEN PATH

BIG MORONGO CANYON PRESERVE – Once an Indian village and later a cattle ranch, this serene natural oasis contains a year-round stream and waterfalls that support a variety of birds and animals. Cottonwoods and willows line a stream favored by great horned owls and many songbirds. A shaded meadow is a fine place for a picnic, and hiking options include several choice trails. No pets are permitted. ⊠ *East Dr., Morongo Valley,* ☎ *760/363–7190.* 🎫 *Free.* ☉ *Daily 7:30 AM–sunset.*

Joshua Tree

17 mi from Desert Hot Springs, north and east on Hwy. 62.

Primarily a gateway to the national park, the town of Joshua Tree has basic services, a few fast-food outlets, and one lodging of note.

LODGING

$$–$$$ ☷ **Joshua Tree Inn.** If these walls could talk: This 1950s-style B&B was a motel popular with rock stars in the 1970s and early 1980s. The building's cinderblock construction is still visible, but there's a nice garden and a pool. ⊠ *61259 29 Palms Hwy., 92252,* ☎ *760/366–1188,* ⅻ *760/366–3805. 10 rooms, 2 suites. In-room modem lines, pool. Full breakfast. AE, D, DC, MC, V.*

Twentynine Palms

11 mi east of Joshua Tree on Hwy. 62, 56 mi from Palm Springs, northwest on I–10 and north and east on Hwy. 62.

Colorful outdoor murals depicting local history are among the ways this onetime liberty town for U.S. Marines is trying to lure visitors headed to Joshua Tree National Park.

LODGING

$–$$$$ ☷ **29 Palms Inn.** The funky 29 Palms, on the Oasis of Mara (☞ Joshua Tree National Park, *below*), comprises a collection of adobe and wood-frame cottages scattered about 70 acres; the contemporary fare at the inn's popular restaurant is more sophisticated than its Western ambience. ⊠ *73950 Inn Ave., 92277,* ☎ *760/367–3505,* ⅻ *760/367–4425. 21 units. Restaurant, pool, hot tub. Continental breakfast. AE, D, DC, MC, V.*

$$–$$$ ☷ **Homestead Inn.** An authentic throwback to the old days in the desert, the Homestead is run by a salt-of-the-earth innkeeper who has a flock of roadrunners as pets. The rooms are comfortable, but not particularly stylish; a couple have their original tile work and fixtures and five have refrigerators, phones, and microwaves. *74153 Two Mile Rd., 92277,* ☎ *760/367–0030,* ⅻ *760/367–1108. 7 rooms. Full breakfast. No smoking. AE, D, MC, V. Closed early July–Sept.*

$$ ☷ **Roughley Manor.** No expense was spared by the wealthy pioneer who erected the stone mansion occupied by this B&B. A 50-ft-long planked maple floor is the centerpiece of the great room, the carpentry on the walls throughout is intricate, and huge stone fireplaces warm the house on the rare cold night. Original fixtures still gleam in the bathrooms, and the elegant bedrooms are furnished with pencil and canopied beds. An acre or so of gardens shaded by Washingtonia palms surrounds the house. ⊠ *74744 Joe Davis Dr., 92277,* ☎ *760/ 367–3238,* ⅻ *760/367–1690. 2 rooms with baths, 5 rooms share 2 baths. Hot tub. Full breakfast. No smoking indoors. AE, MC, V.*

$–$$ ☷ **Best Western Gardens Motel.** This bright complex has smartly furnished rooms, some of which have coffeemakers, refrigerators, and microwaves. ⊠ *71-487 Twentynine Palms Hwy., 92277,* ☎ *760/367–9141,* ⅻ *760/367–2584. 84 rooms. Pool, hot tub. Continental breakfast. AE, D, DC, MC, V.*

Joshua Tree National Park

★ ❿   *61 mi from Palm Springs, northwest on I–10, north and east on Hwy. 62 to the town of Joshua Tree; from here head southeast on Park Blvd. to the park's west entrance or continue east on Hwy. 62 to Twentynine Palms and follow signs to Utah Trail and the north entrance.*

The 794,000-acre Joshua Tree National Park contains complex, ruggedly beautiful scenery. Its mountains of jagged rock, natural cactus gardens, and lush oases shaded by tall fan palms mark the meeting place of the Mojave (high) and Colorado (low) deserts. This is prime hiking, rock-climbing and exploring country, where coyotes, desert pack rats, and exotic plants, such as the creamy white yucca, red-tipped ocotillo, and cholla cactus, reside. Extensive stands of Joshua trees give the park its name. The trees were named by early white settlers who felt their unusual forms resembled the biblical Joshua raising his arms toward heaven.

Portions of the park can be seen in a half-day excursion from desert-resort cities. A full day's driving tour would reveal highlights and allow time for a nature walk or two and stops at many of the 50 way-side exhibits, which provide insight into Joshua Tree's geology and rich vegetation. Some of the park is above 4,000 ft—it can be chilly in winter. There are no services within the park and little water; visitors are advised to carry a gallon of water per person per day.

Those planning a half-day visit to Joshua Tree National Park should enter through the West Entrance Station off Highway 62 at Joshua Tree and follow the Park Boulevard loop road to the North Entrance Station near Twentynine Palms, backtracking to the resort cities via Highway 62. The stands of Joshua trees along this route are particularly alluring in spring, when the upraised branches support creamy white blossoms. The many piles of rocks in this section are fun to explore and climb.

Those planning to spend a full day in the park can proceed through the west entrance, explore the northern loop, stop at the Oasis Visitor Center, and then take the stunning but winding desert drive southward toward the Cottonwood Springs area, which in springtime has one of the desert's best displays of wildflowers. The Cottonwood Visitor Center has a small museum, picnic tables, water, and a 1-mi interpretive trail to the **Cottonwood Spring Oasis**; it gets very crowded in spring.

The **Oasis Visitor Center** (⊠ Utah Trail, ½ mi south of Hwy. 62) has many free and inexpensive brochures, books, posters, and maps as well as several educational exhibits. Rangers are on hand to answer questions. **Oasis of Mara** (a ½-mi walk from the visitor center), inhabited first by Native Americans and later by prospectors and homesteaders, now provides a home for birds, small mammals, and other wildlife.

A crawl through the big boulders that block **Hidden Valley**, once a cattle rustlers' hideout, reveals a bit of the wild and woolly human history of Joshua Tree. The 1¹⁄₁₀-mi loop trail from Hidden Valley to **Barker Dam** goes past petroglyphs (painted over by a film crew) on the way to a dam built by early ranchers and miners; today the dam collects rainwater and is used by wildlife.

Keys View is the most dramatic overlook in Joshua Tree National Park. At elevation 5,185 ft, the view extends across the desert to Mount San Jacinto and on clear days as far south as the Salton Sea. Sunrise and sunset are magical times, when the light throws rocks and trees into high relief before (or after) bathing the hills in brilliant shades of red, orange, and gold.

Geology Tour Road, recommended for four-wheel-drive vehicles, is a self-guided 18-mi dirt road that winds through some of the park's most fascinating landscape.

At the **Cholla Cactus Gardens,** a huge stand of the legendary "jumping cactus," a short trail interprets the wildlife and plants typical of the Colorado Desert.

If you're entering the park from the south, you'll pass the Cottonwood Visitor Center a few miles after you exit Interstate 10 (head north) east of the town of Mecca. The center has a small museum, picnic tables, water, rest rooms, and a 1-mi interpretative trail to the **Cottonwood Spring Oasis.**

⊠ *Joshua Tree National Park, 74-485 National Park Dr., Twentynine Palms 92277,* ☎ *760/367–7511.* ☞ *$10 per car; $5 for those who arrive by other means.* ☉ *Visitor centers daily 8–4:30, park 24 hrs.*

PALM SPRINGS A TO Z

Arriving and Departing

By Bus
Greyhound (☎ 800/231–2222) provides service to the Palm Springs Depot (⊠ 311 N. Indian Canyon Dr., ☎ 760/325–2053).

By Car
Palm Springs is about a two-hour drive east of Los Angeles and a three-hour drive northeast of San Diego. Highway 111 brings you right onto Palm Canyon Drive, the main thoroughfare in Palm Springs and the connecting route to other desert communities. From Los Angeles take the San Bernardino Freeway (I–10) east to Highway 111. From San Diego, I–15 heading north connects with the Pomona Freeway (Highway 60), leading to the San Bernardino Freeway (I–10) east. An alternative, more scenic good-weather route from San Diego begins east on I–8. Then take Highways 67, 78, and 79 north to Aguanga, where Highway 371 heads east to Highway 74 (Palms to Pines Highway), which joins Highway 111 between Palm Desert and Indian Wells. Desert exits are clearly marked: Highway 111 for Palm Springs, Monterey for Palm Desert, Washington for La Quinta. If you're coming from the Riverside area, you can also take Highway 74 east.

By Plane
Major airlines serving **Palm Springs Regional Airport** (☎ 760/323–8161) include Alaska, American/American Eagle, America West/America West Express, Northwest, Skywest, United/United Express, and US Airways Express. *See* Air Travel *in* the Gold Guide for airline phone numbers. Most hotels provide service to and from the airport, which is about 2 mi from downtown Palm Springs.

By Train
The **Amtrak** (☎ 800/872–7245) *Sunset Limited,* which runs between Florida and Los Angeles, stops in Palm Springs and Indio.

Getting Around

By Bus
SunBus, operated by the Sunline Transit Agency (☎ 760/343–3451), serves the entire Coachella Valley from Desert Hot Springs to Mecca.

By Car
The desert-resort communities occupy a stretch of about 20 mi between Interstate 10 in the east and Palm Canyon Drive in the west. Although some areas such as Palm Canyon Drive in Palm Springs and El Paseo are walkable, having a car is the best way to get around.

By Taxi
Rainbow Cab (☎ 760/325–2868). **A Valley Cabousine** (☎ 760/340–5845).

Contacts and Resources

Car Rental

Most major car-rental companies are represented in the Palm Springs area (☞ Car Rental *in* the Gold Guide).

Emergencies

Ambulance (☎ 911). **Police** (☎ 911).

Desert Regional Medical Center (☎ 760/323–6511).

Guided Tours

AERIAL TOURS

Fantasy Balloon Flights (☎ 760/398–6322) organizes trips in the Coachella Valley. **Sunrise Balloons** (☎ 800/548–9912) has balloon excursions and helicopter tours.

CELEBRITY TOURS

Palm Springs Celebrity Tours (✉ 4751 E. Palm Canyon Dr., Palm Springs, ☎ 760/770–2700) has hour-long and 2½-hour tours that cover Palm Springs area history, points of interest, and celebrity homes. Prices range from $12 to $17.

DESERT TOURS

Covered Wagon Tours (☎ 760/347–2161) takes visitors on an old-time, two-hour exploration of the desert with a cookout at the end of the journey. **Desert Adventures** (☎ 760/864–6530) takes to the wilds with Jeep tours of Indian canyons, off-road in the Santa Rosa Mountains, and into a mystery canyon. **Desert Safari Guides** (✉ Box 194, Rancho Mirage, ☎ 760/776–6087 or 888/867–2327) leads tours of various lengths through Indian Canyons and conducts nighttime full-moon desert excursions.

Vacation Rentals

McLean Company Rentals (✉ 477 S. Palm Canyon Dr.,, Palm Springs 92262, ☎ 800/777–4606). **Rental Connection** (✉ 170 E. Palm Canyon Dr., Palm Springs 92263, ☎ 760/320–7336 or 800/462–7256). **Sunrise Co.** (✉ 76-300 Country Club Dr., Palm Desert 92211, ☎ 800/869–1130).

Visitor Information

Palm Springs Desert Resorts (✉ 69-930 Hwy. 111, Suite 201, Rancho Mirage 92270, ☎ 760/770–9000 or 800/967–3767; 760/770–1992 Activities Hotline). **Palm Springs Visitor Information Center** (✉ 2781 N. Palm Canyon Dr., Palm Springs 92262, ☎ 800/347–7746).

16 The Mojave Desert and Death Valley

When most people assemble their "must-see" list of California attractions, the desert isn't often among the top contenders. With its heat and vast, sparsely populated tracts of land, the desert is no Disneyland. But that's precisely why it deserves a closer look. The natural riches here are overwhelming: rolling waves of sand dunes, black cinder cones thrusting up hundreds of feet from a blistered desert floor, riotous sheets of wildflowers, bizarrely shaped Joshua trees basking in the orange glow of a sunset, and an abundant silence that is both dramatic and startling.

THE MOJAVE DESERT begins at the base of the San Bernardino Mountains, northeast of Los Angeles, and extends north 150 mi into the Eureka Valley and east 200 mi to the Colorado River. Death Valley lies north and east of the Mojave, jutting into Nevada near Beatty. The Mojave, with elevations ranging from 3,000 to 5,000 ft above sea level, is known as the High Desert; Death Valley, the Low Desert, drops to almost 300 ft below sea level and contains the lowest spot on land in the Western Hemisphere.

Updated by
Edie Jarolim

Because of the vast size of California's deserts, an area about as big as Ohio, and the frequently extreme weather, careful planning is essential. Conveniences, facilities, trails, gas stations, and supermarkets do not lurk around the corner from many desert sights. Be sure to fill your tank before entering Death Valley—fuel is cheaper on the interstates. Also, check your vehicle's fluids and tire pressure. Shut off your air-conditioning on steep grades to avoid engine overheating.

Believe everything you've ever heard about desert heat— it can be brutal. But during mornings and evenings, particularly in the spring and fall, the temperature ranges from cool and crisp to pleasantly warm and dry. Bring sunglasses, a hat, and sufficient clothing to block the sun's rays or the wind. Reliable maps are a must, as signage is limited and, in some places, nonexistent. Other important accessories include a compass, a cellular phone (though these don't always work in remote areas), extra food and water (three gallons per person per day is recommended, plus additional radiator water). A pair of binoculars can come in handy, and don't forget your camera: You're likely to see things you've never seen before.

Pleasures and Pastimes

Camping
Because vegetation in the desert is sparse, campers are truly one with the elements, including the hot sun: Bring equipment that can handle extreme temperatures. Campgrounds are inexpensive or free; most sites are primitive.

Dining
The restaurants in Death Valley range from a coffee shop to an upscale Continental restaurant. There are fast-food and chain establishments in Ridgecrest, Victorville, and Barstow, as well as some ethnic eateries. Experienced desert travelers carry an ice chest stocked with food and beverages. Replenish your food stash in the larger towns of Ridgecrest and Barstow, where you'll find a better selection and non-tourist prices.

CATEGORY	COST*
$$$$	over $50
$$$	$30–$50
$$	$20–$30
$	under $20

*per person for a three-course meal, excluding drinks, service, and tax

Hiking
Hiking trails are abundant throughout the desert and meander toward sights that would be missed from the road. Plan your walks for before or after the noonday sun, bring protective clothing, and be wary of tarantulas, snakes, and other potentially hazardous creatures (if you wear closed shoes and watch where you're walking, these shouldn't

be a problem). Paths through canyons are sometimes partially shielded from the sun and not as hot, so if your time is limited, save these for midday.

Lodging

Larger towns such as Barstow seem to have a motel on every corner, but there are only three places to sleep indoors in all of Death Valley, the cheapest being in Stovepipe Wells Village. Those preferring quiet nights and an unfettered view of the desert sky and Mosaic Canyon will enjoy Stovepipe. Families with children may prefer the Furnace Creek end of Death Valley, where there's easy access to the visitor center and various sights.

CATEGORY	COST*
$$$$	over $175
$$$	$120–$175
$$	$80–$120
$	under $80

All prices are for a standard double room, excluding tax.

Exploring the Desert

The Mojave Desert is a sprawling space, but many of its visitable attractions are conveniently situated on a north–south axis along U.S. 395 and Highway 178. The western Mojave region has Ridgecrest (on U.S. 395) as its major northern hub and Victorville (on I–15) as its southern one. If you plan to stop overnight en route to Death Valley, both Ridgecrest and Lone Pine have tourist services and accommodations, as do Barstow and Baker on I–15. The bulk of the eastern Mojave lies between the parallel routes of I–15 and I–40. Barstow, at the junction of the two interstates, is the region's western hub. Needles, at the intersection of I–40 and U.S. 95, has the most services on the eastern side. You may spot fossils at some of the archaeological sites in the desert. Leave any fossils you find where they are—it's against the law to remove them.

Numbers in the text correspond to numbers in the margin and on the Mojave Desert and Death Valley maps.

Great Itineraries

IF YOU HAVE 3 DAYS

Well-preserved Randsburg, part of the **Rand Mining District** ②, is a good starting point from either San Francisco or Los Angeles. Pack a picnic lunch and drive through colorful **Red Rock Canyon State Park** ③ and take a walk among the volcanic rock formations of **Fossil Falls** ④ before moving on to 🏨 **Ridgecrest** ⑤ for a stop at the Maturango Museum. Have dinner and spend the night in Ridgecrest. The following day, see the surreal **Trona Pinnacles** ⑥, and then continue on to the 🏨 **Furnace Creek** ⑪ visitor center before catching awe-inspiring perspectives of the Death Valley region from **Artists Palette** ⑭, **Zabriskie Point** ⑮, and **Dante's View** ⑯. Return home on the third day after stopping at the **Harmony Borax Works** ⑩, where the famed 20-mule teams once toiled, and hiking through **Golden Canyon** ⑫.

IF YOU HAVE 6 OR 7 DAYS

If you're already in southern California, head to the **Western Mojave Desert,** touring the **Rand Mining District** ②, **Red Rock Canyon** ③, and **Fossil Falls** ④ before stopping in 🏨 **Ridgecrest** ⑤ to dine and lodge. (If you're coming from northern California, visit Fossil Falls first and stop briefly at the Maturango Museum in Ridgecrest before driving to Red Rock Canyon and the Rand Mining District.) On your second day, visit the **Bureau of Land Management Regional Wild Horse and Burro Cor-**

rals on the way to the **Trona Pinnacles** ⑥ and Death Valley's 🖫 **Stovepipe Wells Village** ⑦. (If you're visiting on a spring or fall weekend, make advance arrangements at the Maturango Museum to tour the **Petroglyph Canyons** on day two.) On the third morning, stroll through **Mosaic Canyon** before driving north to spend a full day at **Scotty's Castle** ⑧ and **Ubehebe Crater** ⑨. Loop back toward 🖫 **Furnace Creek** ⑪ and stop in at the visitor center in the late afternoon. If you're in in the area on a performance day, zip down to Death Valley Junction to see the 7:45 PM show at **Marta Becket's Amargosa Opera House** ⑰. On day four, hike through **Golden Canyon** ⑫ and drive to **Badwater** ⑬ before returning via **Artists Palette** ⑭. Visit the lookout at **Zabriskie Point** ⑮ and walk along **Dante's View** ⑯ before driving south to 🖫 **Baker** ⑱. Use Baker as your fifth-day base. Drive along Kelbaker Road to the **Kelso Dunes** ⑲ and visit the **Mitchell Caverns** in **Providence Mountains State Recreation Area** ⑳. If time and road conditions permit, drive through **Afton Canyon** ㉑ before staying overnight in 🖫 **Barstow** ㉒. On day six, hike around the **Rainbow Basin National Natural Landmark** ㉓ and tour the **Calico Early Man Archeological Site** ㉕ (open from Wednesday to Sunday; the last tour starts at 3:30). On day seven, especially if you have kids, visit **Calico Ghost Town** ㉔ before leaving the desert.

When to Tour the Mojave Desert and Death Valley

Spring and fall are the best seasons to tour the desert. Winters are generally mild, but summers can be brutal (if you're on a budget, though, keep in mind that room rates drop as the temperatures rise). The early morning is the best time to visit sights and avoid crowds, but some museums and visitor centers don't open until 10. If you schedule your town arrivals for late afternoon, you can drop by the visitor centers just before closing hours to line up an itinerary for the next day. It's best to visit the Rand Mining District on the weekend or, if you must come during the week, in the afternoon, when some of the antiques shops open up. Plan indoor activities for midday during hot months. Because relatively few people visit the desert, many attractions have limited hours of access: Petroglyph Canyon tours are given on weekends only during fall and spring, the Calico Early Man Archeological Site does not offer tours Monday and Tuesday, and so on.

THE WESTERN MOJAVE

The prime western Mojave attractions are along or near U.S. 395 or Highways 14 and 178. The key sights after the San Andreas Fault are listed clockwise, heading north and west from Randsburg, looping around eastward to the Trona Pinnacles.

❶ The infamous **San Andreas Fault** traverses the desert near Cajon Pass, a few miles south of I–15's U.S. 395 exit. If you're driving from Los Angeles, it's an apocalyptic way to start a desert trip.

Rand Mining District

❷ *137 mi northeast of Los Angeles, I–10 to I–15 to U.S. 395; 360 mi southeast of San Francisco, I–80 to I–580 to I–5 to Hwy. 178 to Hwy. 14 to U.S. 395.*

The towns of Randsburg, Red Mountain, and Johannesburg make up the Rand Mining District. **Randsburg** first boomed with the discovery of gold in the Rand Mountains in 1895 and, along with the neighboring settlements, grew to support the successful Yellow Aster Mine. Rich tungsten ore, used in World War I to make steel alloy, was discovered in 1907, and silver was found in 1919. Randsburg is one of the few

Mojave Desert

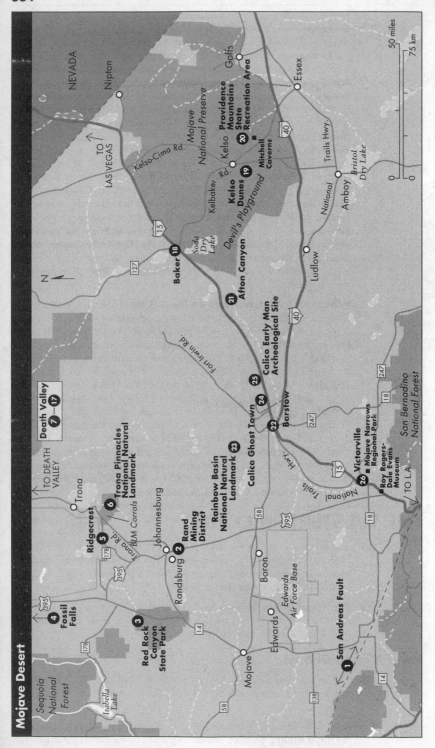

NEVADA

Nipton

TO LAS VEGAS

Mojave National Preserve

Kelso-Cima Rd.

Goffs

Providence Mountains State Recreation Area

Kelso 20

Mitchell Caverns

Kelbaker Rd.

Kelso Dunes 19

Devil's Playground

Essex

40

Trails Hwy.

Bristol Dry Lake

Amboy

National

Ludlow

Soda Dry Lake

Baker 18

15

122

N

Afton Canyon 21

40

Fort Irwin Rd.

Calico Early Man Archeological Site

Death Valley 7—17

TO DEATH VALLEY

Trona

Trona Pinnacles National Natural Landmark

Ridgecrest 5

Trona Rd.

6

BLM Corrals Rd.

Johannesburg

25

24

Barstow 22

Calico Ghost Town

247

18

San Bernadino National Forest

Rainbow Basin National Natural Landmark 23

Victorville

Mojave Narrows Regional Park

Roy Rogers-Dale Evans Museum

26

15

TO L.A.

Rand Mining District 2

Randsburg

58

395

National Trails Hwy.

Red Rock Canyon State Park 3

Fossil Falls 4

395

178

Sequoia National Forest

Isabella Lake

14

Mojave

Edwards

Boron

Edwards Air Force Base

58

395

18

San Andreas Fault 1

14

138

50 miles

75 km

gold-rush-era communities not to have become a ghost town; the former city jail is among the original buildings still standing. The small **Desert Museum** (✉ 161 Butte Ave., ☎ no phone) exhibits old mining paraphernalia. Staffed by volunteers, it's open only on weekends and holidays, usually from late morning until mid-afternoon. **The Randsburg General Store** (✉ 35 Butte Ave., ☎ 760/374–2418) serves as the town's informal visitor center, selling maps and rockhounding guides. It's open daily, unlike most of the town's dozen antiques shops, which tend to be shuttered during the week (though sometimes they open in the afternoon).

Lodging

$ 🏠 **The Cottage Hotel.** An unexpectedly civilized lodging in rough-and-tumble Randsburg, this B&B resulted from a painstaking makeover of the boom-time hotel for which it was named. You enter through an antiques shop to rooms done in Victorian style but with TVs and modern bathrooms; two rooms have balconies. A back garden and a cedar-lined room with a hot tub are bonuses. The housekeeping cottage next door has a kitchen; breakfast isn't included for its occupants as it is for the B&B guests. ✉ *130 Butte Ave., Randsburg, 93554,* ☎ *760/374–2285 or 888/268–4622,* 📠 *760/374–2132. 4 rooms, 1 cottage. Hot tub. Full breakfast. AE, D, MC, V.*

$ 🏠 **HI-Death Valley Hostel.** You don't need a reservation at this 12-bed ranch-style hostel. There are separate dorm-style quarters for men and women, a kitchen (fresh food is available for purchase), a dining area, and a common room. You can rent a bicycle, or sign up for one of many free tours of the region. ✉ *313 Broadway, Box 277, Johannesburg, 93528,* ☎ *760/374–2323. 2 dorm rooms, 1 private room, shared baths. No credit cards.*

Red Rock Canyon State Park

❸ *17 mi west of U.S. 395 via Red Rock–Randsburg Rd.*

A feast for the eyes with its layers of pink, white, red, rust, and brown rocks, **Red Rock Canyon State Park** is a region of fascinating biological diversity—the ecosystems of the Sierra Nevada, the Mojave Desert, and the Basin Range all converge here. Entering the park from the south, you'll pass through a steep-walled gorge and come to a wide bowl tinted pink by what was once hot volcanic ash. The human history of this area goes back 20,000 years to the canyon dwellers known as the Old People; Mojave Indians roamed the land for centuries. Gold-rush fever hit the region in the 1800s; remains of mining operations dot the countryside. In the 20th century, Hollywood invaded the canyon, which has been seen in westerns, TV shows, ads, and music videos. Its greatest claim to fame is as a backdrop in the Steven Spielberg film *Jurassic Park.* ✉ *Ranger station: Abbott Dr. off Hwy. 14,* ☎ *805/942–0662.* 💲 *$5 (day use).* ☉ *Year-round; visitor center weekends only.*

Camping

⚠ **Red Rock Canyon State Park.** The park's campground is in the colorful cliff region of the southern El Paso Mountains, which present many hiking opportunities. ✉ *Off Hwy. 14, 30 mi southwest of Ridgecrest,* ☎ *805/942–0662 for reservations. 50 sites. Fire pits, pit toilets, water.* 💲 *$10, $1 additional for dogs.* ☉ *Year-round.*

En Route Heading north from Red Rock Canyon on U.S. 395 toward Fossil Falls you'll pass **Little Lake,** a good place to view migrating waterfowl in the spring and fall—ducks, geese, perhaps even pelicans. The area north of the lake is often covered with wildflowers. As you pass the lake, a red cinder cone known as **Red Hill** comes into view. The hill, a small volcano that was last active about 10,000 years ago, is now being mined.

Fossil Falls

❹ *Off U.S. 395, 20 mi north of U.S. 395/Hwy. 14 junction.*

The stark, roughly hewn mostly black basalt rocks at **Fossil Falls** (✉ Cinder Cone Rd., ½ mi east of U.S. 395) are the result of volcanic eruptions in the western Mojave region about 20,000 years ago. The fossils at Fossil Falls are the falls themselves—their sources dried up centuries ago; the only time you'll see water is when it's raining. A study in shape and texture, the falls drop off an impressive distance along a channel cut by the Owens River through hardened lava flows. A brief hike leads to the bottom of the formation; Native Americans camped along the streams here. South of the falls, the Owens River cut the huge valley between the Sierra Nevada range to the west and the Coso Range to the east.

Ridgecrest

❺ *35 mi north of Randsburg, U.S. 395 to Hwy. 178.*

Ridgecrest, with stores and dining and lodging options, is a good base for exploring the northwestern Mojave.

The **Maturango Museum,** which also serves as a visitor information center, has pamphlets and books about the northern Mojave and Death Valley—the sights, history, flora, and fauna. Small but informative exhibits detail the natural and cultural history of the northern Mojave. ✉ 100 E. Las Flores Ave., at China Lake Blvd., 93555, ☎ 760/375–6900, ℻ 760/375–0479. ☞ $2. ☼ Daily 10–5.

On weekends in the spring and fall, the Maturango Museum arranges the only tours to the ★**Petroglyph Canyons,** among the desert's most amazing spectacles. (Call ahead; space is limited on these full-day excursions.) The two canyons, commonly called Big and Little Petroglyph, are in the Coso mountain range on the million-acre U.S. Naval Weapons Center at China Lake, which allows only limited access. Each of the canyons holds a superlative concentration of rock art, the largest of its kind in the Northern Hemisphere. Thousands of images of animals and humans are scratched or pecked into the shiny desert varnish—oxidized minerals—that coats the canyon's dark basaltic rocks. The age of these well-preserved glyphs remains a matter of debate. ☎ 760/375–6900. ☞ $20, children under 10 not admitted; $40 for less regular extended trips for photographers and others who want to see sunrise and sunset in the Little Petroglyph Canyon. ☼ Tours Mar.–June and Sept. or Oct.–1st weekend in Dec.

OFF THE BEATEN PATH   **BUREAU OF LAND MANAGEMENT REGIONAL WILD HORSE AND BURRO CORRALS** – Animals gathered from public lands throughout the Southwest are fed and prepared for adoption here. Unlike at urban zoos, it's OK to feed the animals, so bring along an apple or a carrot to share with the horses (the burros are usually too wild to approach). ✉ 3 mi east of Ridgecrest via Hwy. 178 (make a right turn as the road reaches the top of the rise), ☎ 760/446–6064 to arrange tours. ☞ Free. ☼ Weekdays 7:30–4.

❻ **Trona Pinnacles National Natural Landmark** is not easy to reach—the best road to the area can be impassable after a rainstorm. But it's worth the effort, especially to sci-fi buffs, who will recognize the pinnacles from the film *Star Trek V.* These fantastic looking formations of calcium carbonate, known as tufa, were formed underwater along fault lines in the bed of what is now Searles Dry Lake—first as hollow tubes, then as mounds, and finally as the spires visible today. A ½-mi trail winds around this surreal landscape of more than 500 spires, some of them rising as high as 140 ft. Wear sturdy shoes—tufa cuts like coral. ⊠ *From the Trona–Red Mountain Rd., take Hwy. 178 east for 8 mi. Or, from its junction with U.S. 395, take Hwy. 178 for 29 mi to dirt intersection; turn southeast and go ½ mi to a fork. Continue south via right fork, cross railroad tracks, and drive onward 5 mi.*

Dining and Lodging

$ ✕ **Santa Fe Grill.** The many Hollywood crews that film in the Ridge-
★ crest area might explain the presence of this unexpectedly hip and health-conscious New Mexican–style eatery in what is by and large a conservative military town. Hot tortillas, made on the premises, come to the table with a wonderful salsa, its distinctive smoky taste derived from fire-grilled chilies. Beans (not the refried kind) and a sweet corn cake accompany most of the entrées; specialties include seafood enchiladas and chicken fajitas. ⊠ *901 N. Heritage Dr.,* ☎ *760/446–5404. AE, D, MC, V.*

$–$$ ✕⊞ **Heritage Inn.** All the rooms here have refrigerators and microwaves. The well-appointed facility is geared toward commercial travelers, but the staff is equally attentive to tourists' concerns. A sister property nearby is an all-suites hotel. The inn's Farris Restaurant, with a Continental menu, is a favorite fine-dining spot of locals. ⊠ *1050 N. Norma St.,* ☎ *760/446–6543 or 800/843–0693,* ℻ *760/446–2884. 125 rooms. Restaurant, bar, refrigerators, pool, hot tub, coin laundry, business services, meeting rooms. AE, D, DC, MC, V.*

$ ⊞ **The BevLen Bed & Breakfast.** A central location, country-cute rooms, and outgoing hosts—the retired couple Bev and Len de Gues—make this B&B an appealing stop. The place is especially good for single guests, as the rates are low and only one of the three rooms is really large enough for two people. ⊠ *809 N. Sanders St., 93555,* ☎ *760/375–1988 or 800/375–1989,* ℻ *760/375–6871. 3 rooms. AE, D, MC, V.*

DEATH VALLEY

The topography of Death Valley is a lesson in geology. Two hundred million years ago seas covered the area, depositing layers of sediment and fossils. Between 35 million and 5 million years ago faults in the Earth's crust and volcanic activity pushed and folded the ground, causing mountain ranges to rise and the valley floor to drop. The valley was then filled periodically by lakes, which eroded the surrounding rocks into fantastic formations and deposited the salts that now cover the floor of the basin. The area has 14 square mi of sand dunes, 200 square mi of crusty salt flats, 11,000-ft mountains, hills, and canyons of many colors. There are more than 1,000 species of plants and trees—21 of which are unique to the valley, like the yellow Panamint daisy and the blue-flowered Death Valley sage.

With more than 3.3 million acres, **Death Valley National Park** is the largest national park outside Alaska—and certainly the most uncomfortable at times. But seeing nature at its most extreme is precisely what attracts many people, especially Europeans: There are more visitors to Death Valley in July and August than in December and January. Distances can be deceiving: Some sights appear in clusters, but others require extensive travel. The trip from Death Valley Junction to Scotty's Castle, for example, can take a half day. The entrance fee ($10 per vehicle), collected at the park's entrance stations and at the Visitor Center at Furnace Creek (☞ *below*), is valid for seven consecutive days.

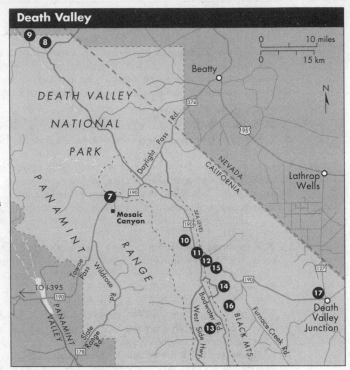

Stovepipe Wells Village

7 *102 mi northeast of Ridgecrest, Hwy. 178 to Hwy. 190.*

Stovepipe Wells Village was the first resort in Death Valley. The tiny town, which dates back to 1926, takes its name from the stovepipe that early prospectors left to indicate they'd found water. The area contains a motel, a restaurant, a grocery store, a landing strip, and campgrounds.

The polished, multicolored, partly marble walls of **Mosaic Canyon** are extremely narrow in spots. A reasonably easy ¾-mi hike yields the flavor of the area, but, if weather permits, it's rewarding to continue farther into the canyon for a few more miles. ⊠ *Off Hwy. 190, on 3 mi gravel road immediately southwest of Stovepipe Wells Village.*

Dining, Lodging, and Camping

$ ✕🏨 **Stovepipe Wells Village** An aircraft landing strip is an unusual touch for a motel, as is a heated mineral pool, but everything else here is pretty standard. Still, this is the best lodging bargain inside the park, with pleasant rooms at a reasonable rate. The Old West–style Toll Road restaurant ($$) serves up all-you-can-eat buffets in summer and à la carte American menus the rest of the year. The adjoining Badwater Saloon provides the park's only nightlife outside that in Furnace Creek. ⊠ *Hwy. 190, Death Valley National Park 92328,* ☎ *760/786–2387,* 𝖥𝖠𝖷 *760/786–2389. 83 rooms. Restaurant, bar, pool, coin laundry. AE, D, MC, V.*

⚠ **Mahogany Flat.** If you've got a four-wheel-drive vehicle and want to scale the park's highest mountain, you might want to sleep at one of the few shaded spots in Death Valley, located at a cool 8,133 ft. A 7-mi (one-way) trail leads from the campground to the summit of Telescope Peak (11,049 ft), but if you don't want to go the distance, many shorter strolls in this wooded high country area afford terrific valley views. ⊠ *Off Wildrose Rd., south of Charcoal Kilns. 10 sites. Pit toilets, no water.* ⊡ *Free.* ☉ *Mar.–Nov.*

En Route Visible from Highway 190 heading east past Stovepipe Wells are **sand dunes** that cover a 14-square-mi field. The sand that forms the hills is actually minute pieces of quartz and other rock.

Scotty's Castle Area

44 mi north of Stovepipe Wells Village; head east on Hwy. 190, then north at signs for castle.

⑧ Scotty's Castle is an odd apparition rising out of a canyon. This $2.5 million Moorish mansion, begun in 1924 and never completed, takes its name from Walter Scott, better known as Death Valley Scotty. An ex-cowboy, prospector, and performer in Buffalo Bill's Wild West Show, Scotty always told people the castle was his, financed by gold from a secret mine. That secret mine was, in fact, a Chicago millionaire named Albert Johnson, who was advised by doctors to spend time in a warm, dry climate. The house functioned for a while as a hotel—guests included Bette Davis and Norman Rockwell—and contains works of art, imported carpets, handmade European furniture, and a tremendous pipe organ. Costumed rangers re-create life at the castle circa 1939. Fifty-minute tours are conducted frequently, but waits of up to two hours are possible. Try to arrive for the first tour of the day, which will guarantee short lines following a traffic-free drive through desert country. ☎ 760/786–2392. ⊡ $8. ☉ *Daily 8–6; tours until 5.*

⑨ The impressive **Ubehebe Crater,** 500 ft deep and ½ mi across, is the result of violent underground steam and gas explosions about 3,000 years ago; its volcanic ash spreads out over most of the area, and the cinders are as thick as 150 ft near the crater's rim. You'll get some superb views of the valley from here, and you can take a fairly easy hike around the west side of the rim to Little Hebe Crater, one of a smaller cluster of craters to the south and west. It's always windy on this rise 8 mi northwest of Scotty's Castle, so hold on to your hat.

Camping

⚠ **Mesquite Springs.** There are tent and RV spaces here, some of them shaded. ⊠ *2 mi south of Scotty's Castle. 30 sites. Flush toilets, stoves or fireplaces, water.* ⊡ *$10.* ☉ *Year-round.*

En Route On Highway 190 south of its junction with Scotty's Castle Road and 14 mi north of the town of Furnace Creek is a 1-mi gravel road that leads to the ½-mi **Salt Creek Nature Trail.** The trail, a boardwalk circuit, loops through a spring-fed wash. The nearby hills are brown and gray, but the floor of the wash is alive with aquatic plants like pickerelweed and salt grass. The trail is the best place for bird-watching in Death Valley. You might see ravens, common snipes, killdeer, or great blue herons.

Furnace Creek Area

54 mi south of Scotty's Castle, 25 mi southeast of Stovepipe Wells Village on Hwy. 90.

⑩ The renowned mule teams hauled borax from the **Harmony Borax Works** to the railroad town of Mojave, 165 mi away. Those teams were a sight to behold: 20 mules hitched up to two massive wagons, each carrying a load of 10 tons of borax, through the burning desert. The teams plied the route between 1884 and 1907, when the railroad finally arrived in Zabriskie. The Borax Museum, 2 mi south of the borax works, houses original mining machinery and historical displays in a building that once served as a boardinghouse for miners; the adjacent structure is the original mule-team barn. ⊠ *Harmony Borax Works Rd., west off Hwy. 190.*

⑪ **Furnace Creek** is a center of activity amid the sprawling quiet of Death Valley. Covered with tropical landscaping, it has jogging and bicycle paths, golf, tennis, horseback riding, a general store, and, rare for these parts, dining options. The Furnace Creek Ranch (☞ Dining and Lodging, *below*) operates most of the above, plus guided carriage rides and hay rides for guests and nonguests. The rides traverse trails with views of the surrounding mountains, where multicolored volcanic rock and alluvial fans form a background for date palms and other vegetation.

Trail maps, brochures, and books and exhibits on the desert can be found at the **Visitor Center at Furnace Creek.** ⊠ *Hwy. 190,* ☎ *760/ 786–2331.* ⊙ *Daily 8–7 (6 in summer).*

⑫ **Golden Canyon** is named for the glowing color of its walls. A mild hike into this spacious landform affords some spectacular views of yellow and orange rock. Farther up the canyon, you'll encounter a colorful formation called Red Cathedral. ⊠ *Badwater Rd., 3 mi south from Furnace Creek; turn left into parking lot.*

⑬ Reaching **Badwater,** one sees a shallow pool, containing mostly sodium chloride, saltier than the sea, lying almost lifeless against an expanse of desolate salt flats—a sharp contrast to the expansive canyons and elevation not too far away. Here's the legend: One of the early surveyors saw that his mule wouldn't drink from the pool and noted "badwater" on his map. Badwater is the lowest spot on land in the Western Hemisphere—282 ft below sea level—and also one of the hottest. ⊠ *Badwater Rd., 19 mi south of Visitor Center at Furnace Creek.*

★ ⑭ The **Artists Palette,** named for the brilliant array of pigments created by volcanic deposits, is one of the most magnificent sights in Death Valley. Artists Drive, the approach to the area, is one-way heading north off Badwater Road, so if you're visiting Badwater it's more efficient to come here on the way back. The drive winds through foothills composed of colorful sedimentary and volcanic rocks. ⊠ *8 mi north of Badwater, Badwater Rd. to Artists Dr.; 10 mi south of Furnace Creek, Hwy. 190 to Badwater Rd. to Artists Dr.*

⑮ **Zabriskie Point** is one of Death Valley National Park's most scenic spots. Not particularly high—only about 710 ft—it overlooks a striking badlands panorama with wrinkled, multicolored hills. Film buffs of a certain vintage may recognize it—or at least its name—from the film *Zabriskie Point* by the Italian director Michelangelo Antonioni. ⊠ *Hwy. 190, 5 mi south of Furnace Creek.*

OFF THE **TWENTY MULE TEAM CANYON** – The thrills in this colorful canyon are
BEATEN PATH more than just natural. At times along the loop road off Highway 190 the soft rock walls reach high on both sides, making it seem like you're on an amusement-park ride. Remains of prospectors' tunnels are visible here, along with some brilliant rock formations. ⊠ *Twenty Mule Team Rd. off Hwy. 190, 1½ mi south of Zabriskie Point. Trailers not permitted.*

★ ⑯ **Dante's View** is more than 5,000 ft up in the Black Mountains. In the dry desert air you can see most of the 110 mi the valley stretches across. The oasis of Furnace Creek is a green spot to the north. The view up and down is equally astounding: The tiny blackish patch far below is Badwater, at 282 ft below sea level the lowest point on land in the Western Hemisphere; on the western horizon is Mt. Whitney, at 14,494 ft the highest spot in the contiguous United States. ⊠ *Dante's View Rd. off Hwy. 190, 21 mi south of Zabriskie Point.*

Dining, Lodging, and Camping

$$–$$$ ✕ **Inn Dining Room.** White stucco walls, lace tablecloths, two fireplaces, and windows with views of the Panamint Mountains make for a visual and culinary mirage at this restaurant. The upscale menu shows a new American influence: seared ahi tuna and fire-roasted corn chowder might be available as starters. Seasonally changing main courses might include sesame-crusted salmon or medallions of veal; a few vegetarian entrées are usually prepared as well. ⊠ *Furnace Creek Inn Resort, Hwy. 190,* ☎ *760/786–2345, ext. 150. AE, D, DC, MC, V.*

$$$–$$$$ ⊞ **Furnace Creek Inn Resort.** This historic stone structure is something of a desert oasis; the creek meanders through beautifully landscaped gardens, and the pool here is spring-fed. All the rooms have views; about half have balconies. Rates here drop considerably during the summer. ⊠ *Hwy. 190, Box 1, Death Valley National Park 92328,* ☎ *760/786–2361,* FAX *760/786–2423. Restaurant, bar, pool, 4 tennis courts, meeting rooms. AE, DC, MC, V.*

$$–$$$ ⊞ **Furnace Creek Ranch.** The ranch was originally crew headquarters for a borax company, the activities of which the on-site Borax Museum details. Four two-story buildings adjacent to the golf course have motel-type rooms that are good for families. The general store sells supplies and gifts. Death Valley tours operated by the Fred Harvey Company depart from here. ⊠ *Hwy. 190, Box 1, Death Valley National Park 92328,* ☎ *760/786–2345,* FAX *760/786–9945. 224 rooms. Restaurant, bar, coffee shop, pool, 18-hole golf course, 2 tennis courts, horseback riding, meeting rooms. AE, DC, MC, V.*

▲ **Furnace Creek.** This campground, 196 ft below sea level, has RV and tent sites (some shaded) and tables. Pay showers, a laundry, and a swimming pool are at nearby Furnace Creek Ranch (☞ *above*). Reservations are accepted for stays between mid-October and mid-April; at other times sites are available on a first-come, first-served basis. ⊠ *Adjacent to Visitor Center at Furnace Creek,* ☎ *760/786–2331; 800/365–2267 for reservations. 135 sites. Fireplaces, flush and pit toilets, disposal station, water.* ▭ *$16.* ☉ *Year-round.*

Death Valley Junction

30 mi south of Furnace Creek, 25 mi south of Zabriskie Point on Hwy. 190.

⑰ **Marta Becket's Amargosa Opera House** is an unexpected pleasure in an unlikely place. Marta Becket is an artist and dancer from New York who first saw the town of Amargosa while on tour in 1964. Three years later she came back and on impulse decided to buy a boarded-up theater amid a complex of run-down Spanish colonial buildings. The population is still in single digits (cats outnumber people here), but it swells when cars, motor homes, and buses roll in to catch her blend of classical ballet, mime, and 19th-century melodrama. To compensate for the sparse crowds in the early days, Becket painted herself an audience, turning the walls and ceiling of the theater into a trompe l'oeil masterpiece. Now she often performs to sell-out crowds (call ahead to reserve a seat). After the show you can meet her in the adjacent art gallery, where she sells her paintings and autographs her posters and books. An ice-cream parlor was added to the complex in 1997, and plans for a deli and pizza parlor are in the works. ⊠ *Hwy. 127,* ☎ *760/852–4441. Call ahead for reservations.* ▭ *$10.* ☉ *Performances Nov., Feb., Mar., and Apr., Sat. and Mon. 7:45 PM; Oct., Dec., Jan., and May (through Mother's Day weekend), Sat. only.*

THE EASTERN MOJAVE

The eastern Mojave is a sharp contrast to Death Valley, with welcome sights of vegetation and somewhat cooler temperatures. Much of this land is untended, so precautions are necessary when driving the many back roads, where towns and services are few and far between.

Baker

⑱ *84 mi south of Death Valley Junction on Hwy. 127.*

The small town of Baker lies between the east and west Mojave areas and Death Valley National Park. You can't miss the city's 134-ft thermometer, the height of which commemorates the corresponding U.S. temperature record, which was set in Death Valley on July 10, 1913.

The thermometer is also a landmark for the National Park Service's **Mojave Desert Information Center** (☎ 760/733–4040). Baker offers only minimal provisions. There are only a few restaurants, most of them fast-food outlets, one general store—as the site of the most Lotto jackpot winners in the state of California it tends to be popular—two motels, and several gas stations.

Dining and Lodging

$ ✕ **Bun Boy.** It doesn't have as much character inside as its 1926 facade promises, but Bun Boy does serve up primo diner food in a clean, comfortable setting. All the classics are represented—burgers, hot dogs, Reuben sandwiches, and more. The dessert specialty is strawberry pie. ✉ *I–15 at State Rd. 177,* ☎ *760/733–4363. AE, D, DC, MC, V.*

$ 🏨 **Wills Fargo Motel.** Both of Baker's motels are owned by the same person and they're just down the road from each other, so there's no difference in rates or location. This one, however, has rooms with more character, as well as a pool and a grassy lawn out front. ✉ *I–15 at State Rd. 177, Box 130, 92309,* ☎ *760/733–4477,* FAX *760/733–4680. 35 rooms. Pool. AE, D, DC, MC, V.*

Mojave National Preserve

The 1.4 million acres set aside in 1994 as the Mojave National Preserve don't conform to the standard image of the desert, encompassing as they do a surprising variety of plant and animal life at elevations up to nearly 8,000 ft. There's a good deal of evidence of human habitation, as well, including abandoned army posts and the vestiges of towns that grew up around the area's mines and ranches. The town of Cima still has a small functioning store. But as you enter the preserve from the north, passing beautiful red-black cinder cones, you'll encounter ⑲ stereotypical desert terrain in the **Kelso Dunes** (✉ Kelbaker Rd.; 42 mi south of Baker, 7 mi north of Kelso), perfect, pristine slopes of gold-white sand. They cover 70 square mi, often at heights of 500 to 600 ft, and can be reached in an easy ½-mi walk from where you leave your car. When you reach the top of one of the dunes, kick a little bit of sand down the lee side and find out why they say the sand "sings." In the town of Kelso a Mission Revival depot dating from 1925 is one of the few of its kind still standing.

⑳ The National Park Service administers most of the preserve, but **Providence Mountains State Recreation Area** is under the jurisdiction of the California Department of Parks. The visitor center, elevation 4,300 ft, has views of mountain peaks, dunes, buttes, crags, and desert valleys. The nearby **Mitchell Caverns Natural Preserve** provides the rare opportunity to see all three types of cave formations—dripstone, flowstone, and erratics—in one place. The year-round 65°F temperature provides a break from the heat. ✉ *Essex Rd., 16 mi north of I–40,* ☎ *760/928–2586.* 🎫 *$6.* ☉ *Guided tours of caves Sept.–June, weekdays 1:30, weekends 10, 1:30, and 3; July–Aug., weekends only. Tours depart from the visitor center.*

Camping

🏕 **Hole-in-the-Wall Campground.** At a cool 4,500 ft above sea level and backed by sculptured volcanic rock formations, this is a fine place to spend a quiet night and to begin a hike during the day. The area was named by Bob Hollimon, a member of the Butch Cassidy gang, because it reminded him of his former hideout in Wyoming. There's a visitor center nearby. ✉ *Black Canyon Rd. south of Kelso (for reservations write Mojave National Preserve, 222 E. Main St., Ste. 202, Barstow 92311),* ☎ *760/733–4040 or 760/255–8800 (Mon.–Fri.). 35 campsites for motor homes and trailers, 2 walk-in tent sites.* 🎫 *$10. Fire rings, pit toilets, disposal station, potable water (in limited supply). No credit cards.* ☉ *Year-round.*

Afton Canyon

㉑ *27 mi southwest of Baker, I–15 to Afton Canyon Rd.*

Because of its colorful, steep walls, **Afton Canyon** is often called the Grand Canyon of the Mojave. Afton was carved over many thousands of years by the rushing waters of the Mojave River, which makes one of its few aboveground appearances here. And where you find water in the desert you'll find trees, grasses, and wildlife. The canyon has been popular for a long time; Indians and later white settlers following the Mojave Trail from the Colorado River to the Pacific Ocean set up camp here, near the welcome presence of water. The dirt road that leads here is ungraded in spots, so this is best visited via all-terrain vehicle. Check with the Mojave Desert Information Center in Baker (☞ *above*) regarding road conditions before you head in. ✉ *Take Afton turnoff and follow dirt road about 3 mi southwest.*

Camping

🏕 **Afton Canyon Campground.** The camping here is at elevation 1,408 ft, in a wildlife area where the Mojave River surfaces. High-desert scenic cliffs and a mesquite thicket surround the campground. ✉ *Afton Canyon Rd. off I–15,* ☎ *760/252—6060. 22 sites. Fire rings, pit toilets.* 🎫 *$6 (reservations not accepted).* ☉ *Year-round.*

Barstow Area

㉒ *63 mi southwest of Baker on I–15.*

Barstow was established in 1886 when a subsidiary of the Atchison, Topeka, and Santa Fe Railway began construction of a depot and hotel here. Outlet stores and modern chain restaurants and motels abound, though old-time neon signs light up Barstow's main street, which is part of Historic Route 66. The **California Desert Information Center** (✉ 831 Barstow Rd., ☎ 760/252–6060) has exhibits about desert ecology, wildflowers, wildlife, and other features of the desert environment. Radio information for travelers is provided at 1610 AM.

★ **㉓** **Rainbow Basin National Natural Landmark** looks as if it could be on Mars, perhaps because so many science-fiction movies depicting the red planet have been filmed here. The sense of upheaval is palpable; huge slabs of red, orange, white, and green stone tilt at crazy angles like ships about to capsize. At points along the 6-mi drive, it is easy to imagine you are alone in the world, hidden among the colorful badlands that give the basin its name. Hike the many washes, and you'll likely see the fossilized remains of creatures that roamed the basin from

16 million to 12 million years ago: mastodons, large and small camels, rhinos, dog-bears, birds, and insects. ⊠ *8 mi north of Barstow (take Fort Irwin Rd. 5 mi north to Fossil Bed Rd., a graded dirt road, and head west 3 mi),* ☎ *760/252–6060.*

☺ ㉔ What's now **Calico Ghost Town** became a wild and wealthy mining town after a rich deposit of silver was found around 1881. In 1886, after more than $85 million worth of silver, gold, and other precious metals were harvested from the multicolored "calico" hills, the price of silver fell and the town slipped into decline. Frank "Borax" Smith helped revive Calico in 1889 when he started mining the unglamorous but profitable mineral borax, but that boom had gone bust by the dawn of the 20th century. Many of the buildings here are authentic, but it's a theme-park version of the 1880s you get strolling the wooden sidewalks of Main Street, browsing through western shops, roaming the tunnels of Maggie's Mine, and taking a ride on the Calico–Odessa Railroad. Festivals in March, May, October, and November promote Calico's Wild West theme. ⊠ *Ghost Town Rd., 3 mi north of I–15,* ☎ *760/254–2122.* ▦ *$6.* ☉ *Daily 8–sunset, shops 9–5.*

★ ㉕ If you're at all curious about life 200,000 years ago, the **Calico Early Man Archeological Site** is a must-see. Nearly 12,000 tools—scrapers, cutting tools, choppers, hand picks, stone saws, and the like—have been excavated from the site since 1964. Prior to the site's discovery, many archaeologists believed the first humans came to North America "only" 10,000 to 20,000 years ago. Dr. Louis Leakey, the noted archaeologist, was so impressed with the findings that he became the Calico Project director in 1963, serving until his death in 1972; his old camp is now a visitor center and museum. The earliest known Americans fashioned the artifacts buried in the walls and floors of the excavated pits. The only way in is by guided tour (call ahead; scheduled tours sometimes don't take place). ⊠ *15 mi northeast of Barstow, I–15 to Minneola Rd. north for 3 mi,* ☎ *760/252–6060.* ▦ *Small donation suggested.* ☉ *Guided tours of dig Wed.–Thurs. 1:30 and 3:30, Fri.–Sun. 9–4:30.*

Dining, Lodging, and Camping

$ ✕ **Carlos & Toto's.** If you've tired of chain restaurants and food from your cooler, head for this touch of Mexico. Locally famous for its fajitas, the restaurant is open seven days a week and lays out a Sunday buffet brunch from 9:30 to 2. ⊠ *901 W. Main St.,* ☎ *760/256–7513. AE, D, MC, V.*

$–$$ ▦ **Holiday Inn.** This large property has more facilities than the many other hotels that line Main Street, so it tends to attract business travelers. It's slightly more expensive than the others, but worth it if you want the highest level of comfort Barstow has to offer. ⊠ *1511 E. Main St.,* ☎ *760/256–5673,* ℻ *760/256–5917. 148 rooms. Restaurant, pool, hot tub, laundry service, meeting rooms. AE, D, DC, MC, V.*

⚠ **Calico Ghost Town Regional Park.** In addition to the campsites here there are cabins ($28) and bunkhouse accommodations ($5 per person). ⊠ *Ghost Town Rd., 3 mi north of I–15, east from Barstow,* ☎ *760/254–2122 or 800/862–2542 for reservations. 250 sites. Electric hookups, fire rings, flush toilets, showers, hot and cold water.* ▦ *$18 per night for tent camping, $22 for full RV hook-ups; 2-night minimum during festival weekends.* ☉ *Year-round.*

Victorville

㉖ *34 mi southwest of Barstow on I–15.*

At the southwest corner of the Mojave is the sprawling town of Victorville, home of the Roy Rogers–Dale Evans Museum.

Mojave Narrows Regional Park makes use of one of the few spots where the Mojave River flows aboveground. The park has 87 camping units, hot showers, secluded picnic areas, and two lakes, surrounded by cottonwoods and cattails. You'll find fishing, rowboat rentals, a bait shop, equestrian paths, and a trail for visitors with disabilities. ⊠ *18000 Yates Rd.,* ☎ *760/245–2226.* 🎫 *$5 per vehicle; dry camping $10, camping with utilities $15.* ⊙ *Daily 7:30–sunset.*

The **Roy Rogers–Dale Evans Museum** draws old-timers and cowboy kitsch fans, who come to see the personal and professional memorabilia of its namesake stars and their friends on the Western film circuit. Everything from glittering costumes and custom cars to cereal box promotions testifies to just how successful they all once were. Animal-rights activists will probably want to stay away: Exhibits include safari trophies—stuffed exotic cats and other animals shot by Roy and sometimes Dale. Even Trigger and Buttermilk have been preserved, though they apparently died of natural causes. ⊠ *15650 Seneca Rd. (take Roy Rogers Dr. exit off I–15),* ☎ *760/243–4547.* 🎫 *$7.* ⊙ *Daily 9–5.*

Lodging

$ 🏨 **Best Western Green Tree Inn.** This member of the chain sits off I–15, a few blocks from the Roy Rogers–Dale Evans Museum. Many of the rooms are suite-size and have refrigerators and microwaves, making the inn a good choice for families. The decor is no-nonsense but clean. Prime rib is a mainstay of the on-site restaurant, which prepares a weekday luncheon buffet. ⊠ *14173 Green Tree Blvd., 92392,* ☎ *760/245–3461 or 800/877–3644. 168 rooms. Restaurant, bar, coffee shop, pool, hot tub, shuffleboard, meeting rooms. AE, D, DC, MC, V.*

THE MOJAVE DESERT AND DEATH VALLEY A TO Z

Arriving and Departing

By Bus

Greyhound (☎ 800/231–2222) serves Baker, Barstow, Ridgecrest, and Victorville, but traveling by bus to the Mojave Desert is neither convenient nor inexpensive. There is no scheduled bus service to Death Valley National Park.

By Car

Much of the desert can be seen from the comfort of an air-conditioned car. Don't despair if you are without air-conditioning—just avoid the middle of the day and the middle of the summer, good advice for all desert travel.

The Mojave is shaped like a giant *L,* with one leg north and the other east. To travel north through the Mojave, take I–10 east out of Los Angeles to I–15 north and (just past Cajon Pass), pick up U.S. 395, which runs north through Victor Valley, Boron, the Rand Mining District, and China Lake. To travel east, continue on I–15 to Barstow. From Barstow you can take I–40, which passes through the mountainous areas of San Bernardino County, whisks by the Providence mountains, and enters Arizona at Needles. The more northerly option is I–15, which passes near Devil's Playground and the Kelso Sand Dunes, and then veers northeast toward Las Vegas.

To avoid Cajon Pass, elevation 4,250 ft, take I–210 north of Los Angeles and continue north on Highway 14. Head east 67 mi on Highway 58 to the town of Barstow and pick up I–15 there. Continue east on I–15 to Highway 127, a very scenic route north through the Mojave to Death Valley.

Death Valley can be entered from the southeast or the west. From the southeast, take Highway 127 north from I–15 and then link up with Highway 178, which travels west into the valley and then cuts north toward Badwater before meeting up with Highway 190 at Furnace Creek. To enter from the west, exit U.S. 395 at either Highway 190 or 178.

By Plane

Inyokern Airport (⊠ Inyokern Rd./Hwy. 178, 9 mi west of Ridgecrest, ☎ 760/377–5844) is served by United Express (☎ 800/241–6522) from Los Angeles. It takes about the same amount of time to drive from **McCarran International Airport** (☎ 702/261–5733) in Las Vegas (which is served by many more airlines) to Furnace Creek in Death Valley National Park as it does from Inyokern.

Getting Around

See Arriving and Departing, *above.*

Contacts and Resources

Camping

The Mojave Desert and Death Valley have about two dozen campgrounds in various desert settings. For further information the following booklets are useful. *High Desert Recreation Resource Guide,* from the Mojave Chamber of Commerce; *San Bernardino County Regional Parks,* from the Regional Parks Department; and *California Desert Camping,* from the Bureau of Land Management. *See* Visitor Information, *below,* for addresses and phone numbers.

Emergencies

Ambulance (☎ 911). **Fire** (☎ 911). **Police** (☎ 911).

BLM Rangers (☎ 760/255–8700). **Community Hospital** (⊠ Barstow, ☎ 760/256–1761). **San Bernardino County Sheriff** (☎ 760/256–1796 for Barstow, 760/733–4448 for Baker).

Guided Tours

Fred Harvey Tours (⊠ Furnace Creek Inn, Box 1, Death Valley National Park 92328 (☎ 760/786–2345, ext. 222). **Nature Conservancy** (⊠ Box 188, Thousand Palms, 92276, ☎ 760/343–1234). **Sierra Club** (⊠ 3345 Wilshire Blvd., Suite 508, Los Angeles 90010, ☎ 213/387–4287).

Visitor Information

Bureau of Land Management (⊠ California Desert District Office, 6221 Box Springs Blvd., Riverside 92507, ☎ 909/697–5200). **California Desert Information Center** (⊠ 831 Barstow Rd., Barstow 92311, ☎ 760/252–6060). **Mojave Chamber of Commerce** (⊠ 15836 Sierra Hwy., Mojave 93591, ☎ 805/824–2481). **National Park Service** (⊠ Visitor Center at Furnace Creek, 92328, ☎ 760/786–3211). **Ridgecrest Area Convention and Visitors Bureau** (⊠ 100 W. California Ave., Ridgecrest 93555, ☎ 760/375–8202 or 800/847–4830). **San Bernardino County Regional Parks Department** (⊠ 777 E. Rialto Ave., San Bernardino 92415, ☎ 909/387–2594).

WHALES & DOLPHINS

Humpback Whales and **Blue Whales** migrate to central California waters each year to feed during summer and fall. Monterey Bay is a prime feeding location for these whales. The whales often concentrate in a variety of locations within the Bay depending on movements and abundance of their primary prey - anchovies and krill. **Killer Whales, Minke Whales** and **Fin Whales** are occasionally sighted in the Bay as well. **Pacific White-Sided Dolphins, Risso's Dolphins, Northern Right Whale Dolphins, and Common Dolphins** occur in Monterey Bay year-round. These dolphins are frequently sighted in groups ranging from 100 to over 2000 animals. **Bottlenose Dolphins, Dall's Porpoise** and **Harbor Porpoise** are also present year-round.

Monterey Bay National Marine Sanctuary

Monterey's sanctuary is the largest in the U.S. which is a highly productive and nutrient rich region that supports a high diversity of marine animals. The Monterey Submarine Canyon is the largest and deepest in North America.

Monterey Bay and Boat Trips

Monterey Bay is the best place along the California coast to observe a variety of marine mammals and seabirds. Whales often shift feeding locations throughout the season, and 6 hr trips are needed to allow ample time to locate and observe them. On average, 3-7 species of whales/dolphins are sighted per trip. **We are unique in that we are the ONLY group that offers 6 hr trips led my marine biologists** who fully narrate and answer questions on trips. We offer quality trips compared to mass run shorter trips. Our marine biologists feel a 6 hr trip is needed to allow ample time to locate and observe whales and dolphins.

Trips subject to cancellation due to weather, undersubscription, or unforseen circumstances.

INDEX